P9-CQZ-023

SEEN THAT, NOW WHAT?

The Ultimate Guide to Finding the Video You Really Want to Watch

ANDREA SHAW

A Fireside Book
Published by Simon & Schuster
NEW YORK LONDON TORONTO SYDNEY TOKYO SINGAPORE

FIRESIDE
Rockefeller Center
1230 Avenue of the Americas
New York, NY 10020

Design concept and icons by Jean Goody.

Design adapted by Stanley S. Drate, Folio Graphics Co., Inc.

Manufactured in the United States of America

10 9 8 7 6 5 4 3 2 1

Library of Congress Cataloging-in-Publication Data
Shaw, Andrea.
Seen that, now what? : the ultimate guide to finding the video you really want to watch / Andrea Shaw.
p. cm.
"A Fireside book."
Includes index.
1. Motion pictures—Catalogs. 2. Video recordings—Catalogs.
I. Title.
PN1998.S488 1996
016.79143'75—dc20 95-47352
CIP

ISBN 0-684-80011-X

ACKNOWLEDGMENTS

Grateful acknowledgment is made to the following people who helped with all facets of the book's creation: Jennifer Robinson, David Dunton, Caroline Sutton, Peter Principle, Jeff McCloud; the folks at Kim's Video, Evergreen Video, Something Weird Video, and Sinister Video; Tara Terminiello, Dan Abramson, George Robinson, Chris Fitzpatrick, Jon and Emily, Monica, Elaine, Hank, Donna, James, Jean, Betsy, Eric, Loretta, and Carolina. But most of all to Alan.

CONTRIBUTORS

Chief Contributors:

- Ian Grey (Assistant Editor)
- Alan Grossman
- Chris Pangborn
- Megan Ratner
- James Terminiello

Other Contributors:

- Brian Camp
- Felicia Feaster
- Stephan Fortes
- David Licata
- Daniel Manu
- Mary Niebauer
- Michael Podwill
- Anthony Sacramone
- Drs. Donna and James Storey

CONTENTS

Contents

INTRODUCTION

"What do you want to rent tonight?"

For a lot of people that question is just the beginning of a frustrating and confusing quest for simple movie entertainment. Only a decade ago the VCR revolution gave people the freedom of choosing a film from their local video store that usually stocked a limited number of movies. It was fun browsing for an old favorite or picking a recent release you missed at the theater. Now choosing a movie is no longer a freedom, it's practically a job! Every week old and new films are released, packing video chainstore racks cheek-to-jowl with scores of low-budget action flicks, erotic thrillers, horror quickies, and other straight-to-video fodder. Browsing through several thousand titles at a video store is now so impractical and downright mind-numbing, many people just duck and run for cover in the New Releases section hoping to find a movie they recognize.

How do you figure out what movie you want to see? As in choosing a restaurant, personal taste and mood are the deciding factors. If you have a yen for Italian food or a quiet romantic spot, a Japanese sushi bar or a loud eatery just won't do it, even if they're both four-star restaurants. Likewise, if you're in the mood for a Schwarzenegger-style action film, watching a classic romantic tearjerker like *Magnificent Obsession* would be agony. And vice versa.

That's the reason for this book—to make choosing a video fun instead of an exercise in aggravation!

The format and approach of *Seen That, Now What?* is completely different from all other guides. Even better, it's simple and entertaining. Instead of an endless alphabetical listing of movies, *Seen That, Now What?* groups thousands of films according to similarities in look, tone, subject, and occasionally a director or star. Just as the *Yellow Pages* allows you to find a business by looking at the various categories, *Seen That, Now What?* allows you to browse through all the possible types of films and time periods so you can find (or figure out) the film you're in the mood to see. Films are generally grouped according to decade, although there is some "spillover" based on the look and tone of the movie. A romantic comedy released in 1962 may belong to the more coy 1950s-style romantic comedies instead of the 1960s "Swinging 60s" group. Occasionally films are grouped according to actor or director if those films are in the same genre and share a similar style (Danny Kaye's whimsical comedies, for example, or John Ford's westerns). In a few cases the groups that you see divided by decade in the film menu will be combined in the text of the book. (Shakespeare films are few, so all 30s, 40s, and 50s are described and grouped together.)

How to Use the Guide

The book is divided up into the standard categories drama, comedy, action, thrillers, musicals, westerns, horror, science fiction–fantasy, foreign films, kids, and documentaries. Each category has two parts, a Menu and the Film Groups.

Let's say you're in the mood for a comedy, but aren't sure what kind. All you need to do is follow two quick steps. First, turn to the Comedy Menu and you'll see the Comedy Film Groups with the classics and gold standards from that group in boldface. Here are a few you'll find under 1990s:

Sports (p. 133)
Bull Durham
Major League
Diggstown
A League of Their Own
The Mighty Ducks
White Men Can't Jump
The Air Up There
Cool Runnings
Little Big League
Major League II
Rookie of the Year

Romantic Comedy (p. 124)
True Love
Pretty Woman
Mr. Wonderful
Four Weddings and a Funeral
Speechless
Forget Paris
French Kiss
Miami Rhapsody

Generation X (p. 128)
Slackers
Singles
Three of Hearts
Floundering
Naked in New York
Reality Bites
Threesome
Before Sunrise

If you turned to 1940s comedies you'd see these groups:

Preston Sturges Satires (p. 67)
Christmas in July
The Great McGinty
Sullivans' Travels
Hail the Conquering Hero
The Miracle of Morgan's Creek
Sin of Harold Diddlebock (Mad Wednesday)
The Beautiful Blonde from Bashful Bend

Supernatural Romantic Comedies (p. 73)
Here Comes Mr. Jordan
I Married a Witch
Heaven Can Wait
The Bishop's Wife
The Ghost and Mrs. Muir
One Touch of Venus

Andy Hardy (p. 68)
Love Finds Andy Hardy
Andy Hardy Gets Spring Fever
Andy Hardy Meets a Debutante
Andy Hardy's Private Secretary
Life Begins for Andy Hardy
Andy Hardy's Double Life
Love Laughs at Andy Hardy

Hepburn and Tracy (p. 71)
Keeper of the Flame
Woman of the Year
Without Love
State of the Union
Adam's Rib
Pat and Mike
Desk Set

The menu allows you to see the different kinds of comedies as well as some you might overlook. Films are grouped in a logical manner; for example, by style, theme, genre, director, or performer—the idea being to offer select films that are clearly related to each other. The highlighted titles are movies generally considered the best of the batch or the most exemplary of that group of films. Once you've chosen a title or a film group from the menu, the second step is simply to turn to the page number where you will find the film groups that contain the reviews.

The film groups are an expanded version of the menus, with a description of the group followed by the film reviews. The group description may vary from a sentence to a paragraph depending on the films. Most viewers, for instance, know what they'll get from the 1990s Romantic Comedy group, whereas Japanese samurai films require a little more background. The film reviews look like this:

Four Weddings and a Funeral
(1994) 110m. **A-**

A lovely young American and a marriage-phobic Englishman carry on an almost-romance of fits and starts, as they meet each other at a series of weddings, one of which is hers. This simple format allows the viewer to enjoy a colorful cast of engaging uppercrust Brits and delight in the tease of McDowell and Grant's affection in this witty and verbal feast of a film.
D: Mike Newell. A: Hugh Grant, Andie MacDowell, Kristin Scott Thomas.

Suppose you'd like to see a film similar to a personal favorite. It's still an easy two-step process. Let's say you're looking for something like *Chinatown.* Simply find it in the film title index. When you turn to the *Chinatown* page, you'll see it listed under the New Gumshoes. This group will give you the reviews for these films:

The New Gumshoes

In the 1970s directors like Penn, Polanski, and Altman didn't just revive the detective and noir genres, they breathed new life into them. Some of these films are homages to noir, rich with art deco and women with padded shoulders and peek-a-boo eyes; others have updated the conventions with humor and a hip sensibility. But with few exceptions, these tales of corruption, dirty secrets, and the seamy side of life show an artistry and freshness that has not been dulled by 20 years.

They Might Be Giants
(1971) 88m. **B–**
Former New York City judge believes he's Sherlock Holmes and Dr. Mildred Watson, the psychiatrist who takes up his case, becomes involved in his all-consuming investigations. Witty performances and a collection of New York oddballs make up for the lame "are they saner than we" message.
D: Anthony Harvey. A: George C. Scott, Joanne Woodward, Jack Gilford.

Klute
(1971) 114m. **A**
A small-town detective follows the trail of a missing friend, which intersects with a high-priced call girl in New York City. A masterful mix of character study and thriller with a powerhouse performance from Fonda and a dark feel for the uncertainties and menace of modern urban life.
D: Alan J. Pakula. A: Jane Fonda, Donald Sutherland, Roy Scheider.

The Long Goodbye
(1973) 113m **B+**

This updated, shambling, private eye Marlowe seems to bumble through rather than investigate the puzzling chain of events in a sun-baked and sleazily affluent LA. The updated noir malaise and parade of oddball characters more than make up for a slightly muddled plot.
D: Robert Altman. A: Elliot Gould, Nina van Pallandt, Sterling Hayden.

Chinatown
(1974) 131m. **A+**

It's Los Angeles in the 1930s and a hard-bitten private eye finds himself on a trail that leads to land grabbing schemes, water rights, and the mysteries of a ruthless businessman's beautiful and neurotic daughter. A visual masterpiece, an acting tour de force, and a classic detective story that weaves its intricate story through a brooding LA landmined with corruption and nasty little secrets.
D: Roman Polanski. A: Jack Nicholson, Faye Dunaway, John Huston.

The Drowning Pool
(1975) 108m. **B–**

Laid-back PI Harper investigates a blackmail scheme in Louisiana that brings him together with a corrupt police chief, a sex-crazed client's daughter, big oil money, and a watery menace in an eerie deserted insane asylum. A muted cast runs through a cliché-heavy story that lacks any enthusiasm.
D: Stuart Rosenberg. A: Paul Newman, Joanne Woodward, Tony Franciosa.

Farewell My Lovely
(1975) 97m. **A–**

Mitchum is the classic gumshoe Marlowe, mixing cynicism, wit, and a romantic spirit in this workmanlike *noir* homage. The vivid 1940s details have a seedy smoky charm, and the complex plot oozing with snappy one-liners along with a rumpled Mitchum make this a well-balanced treat.
D: Dick Richards. A: Robert Mitchum, Charlotte Rampling, Sylvia Miles.

Night Moves
(1975) 99m. **A**

While trying to deal with his own sour private life, investigator Harry is hired by a fading Hollywood star to track down her reckless daughter, involving him in art smuggling, murder, and sex on Florida's Gulf Coast. This intricate detective story and incisive psychological drama manages to be both intelligent and entertaining.
D: Arthur Penn. A: Gene Hackman, Jennifer Warren, Susan Clark.

The Late Show
(1977) 93m. **B+**

A wheezing old private detective and a cat-loving new-age oddball make an unlikely team as they scour the seamy corners of LA, bickering all the way. The winning characters and messy mystery provide all the fun, marred only by the washed out cinematography that makes for a bleak LA.
D: Robert Benton. A: Art Carney, Lily Tomlin, Ruth Nelson.

The Big Fix
(1978) 108m. **B–**

A former 60s radical cum private investigator is hired by an old leftist buddy cum politician to find out who's trying to link him with crazed hippies from the old days. A solid detective thriller with the wisecracks, intrigue, and murder all served up with a dollop of 60s nostalgia.
D: Jeremy Paul Kagan. A: Richard Dreyfuss, Bonnie Bedelia, Susan Anspach.

The Big Sleep
(1978) 100m. **B–**

Marlowe is in present-day London to find out who's blackmailing two rich sisters, one who's had naughty pictures taken of her. The plot is cloudy, and though Mitchum is still his world-weary best, removing him from the 1940s and putting him in England takes away some of the charm.
D: Michael Winner. A: Robert Mitchum, Sarah Miles, Richard Boone.

There you have it! Nine movies in the same vein as *Chinatown.* Nine choices. No more wandering around aisles reading a jumble of titles.

So now it's up to you. If you have a hankering for one of those kitschy disco comedies from the 70s but can't recall a title, love *Sunset Boulevard* but aren't sure there's anything around to compare, or just want a good tearjerker, browse through these pages—and happy viewing!

A note about the films included in this guide. While there may be 20,000+ video titles somewhere in circulation, only a fraction of those can be found at any video store. Many can only be rented or purchased at specialized outlets or through the mail. To give you an idea of the rich variety of films available, the 5400 films chosen for this guide are the more commonly found selections, along with a few that are harder to find but worth seeking out.

The Rating System

Every film is rated from A+ to F.

Classic Renowned films of first rank, reference points in film mythology, or films that have become part of American cultural folklore. Examples are *Gone With the Wind, Grand Hotel, Casablanca, Psycho, Citizen Kane,* and *Bonnie and Clyde.*

Gold Standard Films that are the best and primary examples of a genre. If you see only one film in a genre, it's safe to go with a gold standard. If there are several archetypal films of uniformly high quality, they can all be gold standards. If a film is a classic it is also assumed to be a gold standard.

Examples are *Mrs. Miniver* (Wartime Women); On the Homefront/*Peyton Place, Imitation of Life* (50s Romantic Melodramas); *Dr. No, Goldfinger, Thunderball* (James Bond); and *Gold Diggers of 1933* (Busby Berkeley Backstagers).

Visual Treats Films that have photography, color, and composition that are remarkable. *Blow Up, 2001: A Space Odyssey, Raging Bull, Gates of Heaven, Bram Stoker's Dracula,* and *Edward Scissorhands* are some examples.

Camp Films Films that are so bad they're interesting, or films that are unintentionally (or intentionally) funny due to clichéd dialogue or overly dramatic acting. Examples are *Johnny Guitar, The Carpetbaggers, Valentino, The Blob,* and *Pink Flamingoes.*

Deserves Attention Films that are overlooked or not mainstream but worth considering because they've got something special. *American Hot Wax, Tremors, Specter of the Rose, Madam Satan, Skyscraper Souls, The Vanishing* (original version), and *The Rapture* are examples.

The general policy has been to rate films according to the merits of their group, so don't be surprised to see a lot more "A's" in the classic film noir group than in the slasher horror group. Of course the "A" given to a slasher is not the same sort of "A" given to a classic like Kubrick's *Paths of Glory.*

ACTION

Action Menu

ACTION MENU

ACTION FILM GROUPS

1930s

Gangsters

The key word to these gangland tales is *intensity*, as cars rip through dark studio streets spraying gunfire and lawless hoods live fast, talk faster, and die young. The earlier entries are raw, stagebound productions offering grainy images stained with shadows and Depression-era tattered sets, but by the mid-1930s crime films became more sophisticated action films. And even if the Production Code had by then put a stop to the portrayal of gangsters as glamorous anti-heroes, the stories still offered a good look at the lawless rags-to-riches underworld of criminals.

Little Caesar

(1931) 77m. B&W. **B** 🏛

Robinson is Rico, a petty crook sneering, snarling, and scraping his grubby way to the top of a Chicago racket. Pretty stagey, but thanks to Robinson's bulging-eyed criminal overachiever, the grim tone, and effectively distressed sets, this still feels like a classic.
D: Mervyn LeRoy. A: Edward G. Robinson; Douglas Fairbanks, Jr.; Glenda Farrell.

Public Enemy

(1931) 84m. B&W. **B** 🏛

Neither nature nor nurture can stop an Irish cop's son from becoming a notably rotten, fast-talking and -shooting hood. Any problems with pacing are amply compensated by Cagney's glinty-eyed, live-wire performance highlighted by the famous scene of him smashing a grapefruit in his gal's face because she annoyed him.
D: William Wellman. A: James Cagney, Edward Woods, Jean Harlow.

Scarface

(1932) 99m. B&W. **B+** 🏛

The most pungent, action-packed, and least-dated of the early gangster films follows an Italian immigrant's violent rise and fall in the bootlegging underworld of prohibition-era Chicago. A crackling story, colorful performances, and energetic pacing makes this fresh and entertaining.
D: Howard Hawks. A: Paul Muni, Ann Dvorak, George Raft.

Lady Killer

(1933) 74m. B&W. **B**

The crafty leader of a petty crime ring flees New York for Los Angeles where he becomes a movie star, only to be blackmailed by his old gang. A typically snappy Warner Bros. mix of comedy and gangster antics, making an excellent early showcase for the fast-talking charismatic amoral Cagney.
D: Roy Del Ruth. A: James Cagney, Mae Clarke, Margaret Lindsay.

G-Men

(1935) 85m. B&W. **A**

This fast-paced tale of New York City gangsters who embark on a Midwest crime spree employs all the classic gangster motifs, but from the point of view of the Feds. More hopeful and more violent than the previous pro-gangster films it was trying to counteract.
D: William Keighley. A: James Cagney, Robert Armstrong, Margaret Lindsay.

Bullets or Ballots

(1936) 81m. B&W. **A–**

A renowned police detective goes bad and joins the rackets in a daring bid to seek out their secret ring of bankers. A fast-paced immersion into New York City's underworld of swaggering tough guys, wisecracking dames, and conspiring businessmen.
D: William Keighley. A: Edward G. Robinson, Joan Blondell, Humphrey Bogart.

Angels with Dirty Faces

(1938) 97m. B&W. **A** 🏛

Two friends from the slums grow up; one becomes a priest trying to save the parish boys from a life of crime, the other a gangster who's the idol of those kids. This story of ghetto life still packs a wallop with its mix of cynicism and idealism, knife-sharp performances, and a gut-wrenching execution scene.
D: Michael Curtiz. A: James Cagney, Pat O'Brien, Humphrey Bogart, The Dead End Kids.

I Am the Law

(1938) 83m. B&W. **C+**

The setting is a college town instead of the city as a law professor - turned - special prosecutor uses students, rookie cops, and clever strategy instead of gunplay and violence to clean up the rackets. The fresh plot twists and lively characters make this entertaining, but the story gets increasingly far-fetched.
D: Alexander Hall. A: Edward G. Robinson, John Beal, Otto Kruger.

Smashing the Rackets

(1938) 80m. B&W. **B–**

A tough FBI agent-turned-special prosecutor takes on the big-city rackets in a slick thriller loosely based on the exploits of New York prosecutor Thomas E. Dewey. Lacks the grit and authenticity of many of the other entries but offers a more wide-ranging look at the underworld.
D: Lew Landers. A: Chester Morris, Frances Mercer, Bruce Cabot.

Each Dawn I Die

(1939) 92m. B&W. **C+**

Cagney is a reporter framed for murder by gangsters and sent to prison, where inmate gang boss Raft takes up his cause and works to clear his name. A standard and sharp Warner Bros. crime-and-prison film enlivened by the rare screen teaming of two great gangster stars.
D: William Keighley. A: James Cagney, George Raft, Jane Bryan.

The Roaring Twenties

(1939) 106m B&W. **A** 🏛

This hard-edged action-packed look at rivalry within the New York bootlegging rackets raised the crime film to a new level. Its historical sweep capturing the heady swirl of the Jazz Age and the crash landing of the Depression, along with the snappy

action scenes and street-smart interplay between the characters, helps make this a classic.
D: Raoul Walsh. A: James Cagney, Priscilla Lane, Humphrey Bogart.

High Sierra
(1941) 100m. B&W. **A**

Newly released convict Bogart agrees to lead a younger crew in one last heist and gets caught up with a cohort's moll and an innocent lame girl. A beautifully played drama about codes of honor, betrayal, and romance with Bogart playing the perfect sympathetic bad guy who has his last standoff in the Sierra mountains.
D: Raoul Walsh. A: Humphrey Bogart, Ida Lupino, Arthur Kennedy.

Dillinger
(1945) 70m. B&W. **C+**

Former bootleggers produced this noirish gangster film that sets the real-life bandit's Midwest exploits in urban settings. Slow and atmospheric with a grim deadpan Tierney as a memorable Dillinger.
D: Max Nosseck. A: Lawrence Tierney, Edmund Lowe, Anne Jeffreys.

Historical Swashbucklers

These are the rip-snorting adventures that focused on Europe's men of honor at odds with the royal powers during the empire-building eighteenth and nineteenth centuries. The action scenes—sea battles, castle duels, and romancing of damsels in distress—have an energetic, often humorous tone with lavish sets and costumes worthy of Hollywood's dashing action heroes like Errol Flynn and Douglas Fairbanks Jr.

The Count of Monte Cristo
(1934) 119m. B&W. **A**

A lively and lavish version of Dumas' oft-told tale of a ship's mate, wrongfully sent to an island prison, who escapes, digs up a treasure, and returns to Paris to take vengeance on the men who framed him. From dark dungeons to the spectacle of 1820s Paris, this focuses less on action and more on high drama of betrayal and retribution.
D: Rowland V. Lee. A: Robert Donat, Elissa Landi, Louis Calhern.

Captain Blood
(1935) 119m. B&W. **A**

A physician charged with treason is sold into slavery and goes on to lead a crew of pirates in the Caribbean. A model for swashbucklers, this is a perfect mix of swordfighting action, romance, hearty male hijinks, and historical atmosphere.
D: Michael Curtiz. A: Errol Flynn, Olivia de Havilland, Basil Rathbone.

Mutiny on the Bounty
(1935) 132m. B&W. **A**

First version of the famous tale of mutiny against the merciless Captain Bligh. A cornucopia of iconic acting styles, such as Laughton's imperious Bligh and Gable's noble Fletcher Christian, along with a lovely Tahitian idyll centerpiece, makes this a classically stirring sea fable.
D: Frank Lloyd. A: Charles Laughton, Clark Gable, Franchot Tone.

The Scarlet Pimpernel
(1935) 95m. B&W. **C**

That English fop is actually a master of disguise who rescues aristocrats from the guillotine during the French Revolution. The emphasis on the Pimpernel's marital troubles and the machinations of the French ambassador make for a dark, talky, and claustrophobic drama with little action.
D: Harold Young. A: Leslie Howard, Merle Oberon, Raymond Massey.

The Three Musketeers
(1935) 90m. B&W. **B**

The leanest, most straightforward version of the fun-loving seventeenth-century French court guards has an energetic mix of lighthearted swashbuckling and serious historical drama, but it still lacks star power.
D: Rowland V. Lee. A: Walter Abel, Paul Lukas, Heather Angel.

Anthony Adverse
(1936) 141m. B&W. **B–**

The illegitimate son of an Italian nobleman in the early 1800s amasses wealth in Cuba and Africa and then must battle for the right to the family fortune. A sweeping tale of romance, sex, greed, exotic adventure, and the Napoleonic Wars.
D: Mervyn LeRoy. A: Frederic March, Olivia de Havilland, Donald Woods.

Fire Over England
(1937) 89m. B&W. **B**

A young ship's officer is sent by Elizabeth I to spy on the court of Spain in this extremely talky blend of romance, espionage, court intrigue, and sea battles, all enhanced by the lavish production and florid star turns.
D: Alexander Korda. A: Laurence Olivier, Vivien Leigh, Flora Robson.

The Prisoner of Zenda
(1937) 101m. B&W. **B–**

Atmospheric castles and moody lighting help color this darker film about a Balkan king who's kidnapped and replaced by an English double. Relatively quiet with occasional bursts of action.
D: John Cromwell. A: Ronald Colman, Raymond Massey, Douglas Fairbanks, Jr.

The Adventures of Robin Hood
(1938) 102m. **A**

The medieval hero is now recast as a twelfth-century rebel who rallies the Saxons to oppose the conniving Prince John. Sweeping sumptuous Technicolor entertainment that contains all the classic scenes—archery contests, romancing Maid Marion, and the buddy scenes with Friar Tuck and the other merry bandits.
D: Michael Curtiz, William Keighley. A: Errol Flynn, Olivia de Havilland, Basil Rathbone.

Beau Geste
(1939) 114m. B&W. **B**

Family honor and legion honor are hashed out as three English upper-crust brothers join the foreign legion following the theft of a family heirloom. The harsh desert, the cruel sergeant, and the continual threat of death from natives are all featured in this classic foreign legion adventure.
D: William Wellman. A: Gary Cooper, Ray Milland, Robert Preston.

The Man in the Iron Mask
(1939) 110m. **B**

Tyrant Louis XIV has a good twin brother whom he exiles, imprisoned in an iron

mask. A gripping story with good historical flavor, but the three musketeers here are old and somewhat ill-used.
D: James Whale. A: Louis Hayward, Joan Bennett, Joseph Schildkraut.

Tarzan

Edgar Rice Burroughs' famous ape man became the hero of a long-running series of action-adventures pitting the white jungle man against wild animals, hostile natives, and greedy white hunters. The MGM series (1932–1942) remains the most memorable, mixing authentic looking sets, African footage of native ceremonies and wild animals, and of course the vine-swinging yodeling Tarzan with his pixieish mate Jane.

Tarzan, the Ape Man
(1932) 99m. B&W. **B+**

Tarzan abducts a proper English girl from a party of white hunters and impresses her so much with his raw physicality and natural ways that Jane decides to stay. Tarzan is a brutish primitive here, displaying a greater camaraderie with the animals, particularly the elephants and a jealous female gorilla.
D: W. S. Van Dyke. A: Johnny Weissmuller, Maureen O'Sullivan, C. Aubrey Smith.

Tarzan and His Mate
(1934) 93m. B&W. **A–**

There's nonstop action as Tarzan takes on hostile natives, wild animals, and white hunters, with time off for sexy pre-Code interludes with a scantily clad Jane. The peak in politically incorrect jungle adventures, replete with killing of "bad" animals and frequent violence done by and to African natives.
D: Cedric Gibbons. A: Johnny Weissmuller, Maureen O' Sullivan, Neil Hamilton.

Tarzan Escapes
(1936) 95m. B&W. **B+**

Tarzan and Jane, firmly ensconced in their jungle treehouse, are disrupted by a spectacularly greedy white hunter seeking to kidnap the ape man. There's more vine-swinging action, atmospheric sets, wild animals, African footage, and angry tribesmen in this last of the "wild" Tarzan films; the character gets more domesticated in future entries.
D: Richard Thorpe. A: Johnny Weissmuller, Maureen O'Sullivan, John Buckler.

Tarzan Finds a Son
(1939) 90m. B&W. **B**

Tarzan and Jane form a nuclear family when they adopt a baby rescued by Cheeta the chimp from a plane crash. The baby grows up to be Boy and the object of a search by heirs to the boy's family fortune. More wild animal footage in this entry.
D: Richard Thorpe. A: Johnny Weissmuller, Maureen O'Sullivan, Johnny Sheffield.

Tarzan's Secret Treasure
(1941) 81m. B&W. **C+**

Boy gets a native companion Tumbo while white hunters seek the gold waiting to be scooped out of Tarzan's river. Fun but by now formulaic jungle action is confined to imaginative studio sets, with a low-key Weissmuller merely part of an ensemble cast.
D: Richard Thorpe. A: Johnny Weissmuller, Maureen O'Sullivan, Johnny Sheffield.

Tarzan's New York Adventure
(1942) 72m. B&W. **B+**

This gives the much-needed boost of bringing Tarzan to the big city in pursuit of Boy, who's been kidnapped and sent to a circus. Lots of comic bits involving Tarzan's culture shock and great action high points, including a leap off the Brooklyn Bridge.
D: Richard Thorpe. A: Johnny Weissmuller, Maureen O'Sullivan, Johnny Sheffield.

Other Films:
Tarzan the Mighty (1928)
Tarzan the Fearless (1933)
New Adventures of Tarzan (1935)
Tarzan and the Green Goddess (1938)
Tarzan's Revenge (1938)

British Colonialism

While occasionally paying lip service to the contrary, these early action films offer an endorsement of imperialism, as beleaguered British or French soldiers hold down the fort against the hordes of dark-skinned natives. Thanks to the armies of stunt riders, lively stories, and colorful locales representing India or the Mideast, these films about "the white man's burden" make up in thrills what they lack in political correctness.

The Lives of a Bengal Lancer
(1935) 109m. B&W. **B**

Three young officers single-handedly try to stop a shipment of arms to a rebel movement in northwest India. Slower-paced more atmospheric version of the standard imperial adventure, but closes with a spectacular battle scene.
D: Henry Hathaway. A: Gary Cooper, Franchot Tone, Richard Cromwell.

Charge of the Light Brigade
(1936) 116m. B&W.
B+

This sweeping historical adventure of nineteenth-century British imperialism in India and romantic triangle may play hell with history, but its period trappings, dashing heroes, and vivid action remain vastly entertaining. The denouement depicting the famous charge of the 600 during the Crimean

War is truly spectacular.
D: Michael Curtiz. A: Errol Flynn, Olivia de Havilland, Nigel Bruce.

Elephant Boy
(1937) 81m. B&W. **B–**
A young native boy discovers the location of the mythical burial ground in India. Looking more like a flickering documentary travelogue than an adventure film, Sabu's debut is the main reason to watch, and you can see why he was forced to play the winsome native-boy role into old age.
D: Robert Flaherty, Zoltan Korda. A: Sabu, W. E. Holloway, Allan Jeayes.

King Solomon's Mines
(1937) 80m. B&W. **C+**
A group of whites seeking a legendary African diamond mine gets caught up in a battle over leadership of the tribe that controls it. A regal Robeson as the rightful ruler, the generous use of location footage, and emphasis on the native characters elevate this otherwise clichéd African adventure tale.
D: Robert Stevenson. A: Paul Robeson, Cedric Hardwick, Roland Young.

Drums
(1938) 99m. **C–**
A young Indian prince helps a Scottish regiment overcome a rebel conspiracy. A routine story distinguished only by Technicolor photography and Indian actor Sabu's engaging performance as the boy prince.
D: Zoltan Korda. A: Sabu, Raymond Massey, Roger Livesey.

The Four Feathers
(1939) 115m. **A**
A rousing saga of cowardice, bravery, and a crisis of conscience set against the 1898 British campaign to crush a native revolt in the Sudan. Grand-scale production shot in exotic North African locales teems with rebellious natives, blustery stiff-upper-lip heroics, and British pomp and circumstance.
D: Zoltan Korda. A: John Clements, Ralph Richardson, C. Aubrey Smtih.

Gunga Din
(1939) 117m. B&W. **B+**
This lighthearted story about an unlikely trio of brawling lusty sergeants who take on religious fanatics in India is more *Indiana Jones* than historical adventure. The far-fetched action scenes and rollicking performances almost make you forget the serious subject underneath it all.
D: George Stevens. A: Cary Grant; Douglas Fairbanks, Jr.; Victor McLaglen.

1940s
Historical Swashbucklers

The last great black-and-white swashbucklers were made in 1940. But even as the playful spirit and bombast of the 1930s entries became noticeably absent from the darker-toned, bloodier postwar swashbucklers, the genre shifted to Technicolor, allowing for costumes and settings that lent a storybook brilliance to the swordfights, sea battles, and hardy romances.

The Mark of Zorro
(1940) 93m. B&W. **A**
When nineteenth-century Los Angeles is oppressed by a corrupt governor who taxes the good citizens into starvation, self-styled fop Don Diego Vega becomes the masked rebel leader who attempts to overthrow him. Lighthearted and romantic with lots of broadly played action and humor.
D: Rouben Mamoulian. A: Tyrone Power, Basil Rathbone, Linda Darnell.

The Sea Hawk
(1940) 128m. B&W. **B**
Due to its World War II propaganda value, this tale of an Elizabethan English captain fighting the Spanish has none of the light tone and romantic hijinks of Flynn's earlier films, but still beautifully covers all the swashbuckling bases—court intrigues, sea battles, and a Panamanian jungle trek.
D: Michael Curtiz. A: Errol Flynn, Brenda Marshall, Claude Rains.

The Corsican Brothers
(1941) 111m. B&W. **C+**
When separated Siamese twins are reunited—one is a Parisian gentleman, the other a peasant bandit—they join forces to defeat the tyrannical Corsican baron. Modest budget, slow pacing, and a surprising paucity of action.
D: Gregory Ratoff. A: Douglas Fairbanks, Jr.; Ruth Warrick; Akim Tamiroff.

Captain Kidd
(1945) 83m. B&W. **C–**
Laughton hams it up in this low-budget version about the famous pirate captain whose attempt to go straight is undone by his own greed and the vengeance-seeking nobleman. Slow-paced and talky, and Scott seems out of place without a six-shooter.
D: Rowland V. Lee. A: Charles Laughton, Barbara Britton, Randolph Scott.

Sinbad the Sailor
(1947) 117m. **C–**
Douglas Fairbanks, Jr., tries to capture his father's jovial acrobatic style as he romances maidens and seeks out fabled treasures in a stylized pastel-colored Arabia. Overlong and given the Arabian Nights setting, short on the spectacle and fantasy elements.
D: Richard Wallace. A: Douglas Fairbanks, Jr.; Maureen O'Hara; Anthony Quinn.

The Adventures of Don Juan
(1948) 111m. **B+**
The famous sixteenth-century lover and swordsman leads his army of fencing students in the defense of the queen of Spain. Strong action is well balanced by romantic scenes.
D: Vincent Sherman. A: Errol Flynn, Viveca Lindfors, Robert Douglas.

The Three Musketeers
(1948) 127m. **B–**
The first half of MGM's all-star version of seventeenth-century royal shenanigans is colorful, witty, and chock-full of acrobatic swordplay à la Kelly with a second half that's more of a historical melodrama of court intrigue and treacherous love.
D: George Sidney. A: Gene Kelly, Lana Turner, Van Heflin, June Allyson.

World War II Action and Battles

These taut patriotic efforts portray a small band of melting-pot heroes that introduce us to the guy from Brooklyn, the guy from Billings, and the guy from Alabama, complete with a flashback or two to about the sweethearts or wives they left behind. But before too long, these low-budget morale boosters settle down to the unrelenting and noble business of fighting the good fight.

One of Our Aircraft Is Missing

(1941) 106m. B&W. **B**

An RAF bomber crashes into occupied Holland and the crew, aided by the Dutch resistance, evades Nazi patrols. A little musty but laced with riveting suspense, intelligent dialogue, and outstanding performances.

D: Michael Powell, Emeric Pressburger. A: Godfrey Tearle, Eric Portman, Peter Ustinov.

Air Force

(1943) 124m. B&W. **B**

This epic combat film follows the adventures of a single B-17 bomber crew from Pearl Harbor to the Philippines. A rousing blend of war action and male camaraderie, played to perfection by an offbeat cast.

D: Howard Hawks. A: John Garfield, Gig Young, Arthur Kennedy.

Bataan

(1943) 114m. B&W. **A**

A small squad of soldiers tries to hold overwhelming Japanese forces at bay in the Philippines. Gritty tough characters and graphic action—including outstanding hand-to-hand combat sequences—in a hopeless bleak atmosphere make this superlative on all counts.

D: Tay Garnett. A: Robert Taylor, Lloyd Nolan, Thomas Mitchell.

Guadalcanal Diary

(1943) 93m. B&W. **B**

Based on a newsman's on-the-spot reports, this detailed account of a major Marine invasion of a key Japanese fortress offers furious war action, a melting-pot Marine contingent, and a diabolical enemy.

D: Lewis Seller. A: Preston Foster, Lloyd Nolan, William Bendix.

Sahara

(1943) 97m. B&W. **A**

An American tank crew picks up assorted Allied stragglers in the North African desert before making a last stand at an abandoned watering hole against the pursuing Nazis. Tough gritty action and compelling characters make this a top and tough-as-nails entry.

D: Zoltan Korda. A: Humphrey Bogart, Lloyd Bridges, Bruce Bennett.

Wake Island

(1943) 87m. B&W. **A**

During the first weeks of war, a small marine post valiantly and vainly resists overwhelming Japanese forces. marine heroics, male bonding, and pining for lost loves are blended movingly with relentless aerial, naval, and infantry attacks. One of the best.

D: John Farrow. A: Brian Donlevy, Robert Preston, William Bendix.

We Dive at Dawn

(1943) 98m. B&W. **B+**

A British submarine on duty in the Baltic tries to sink a major German warship. This British war film focuses more on the human drama and less on action as the crew deals with the pressures of war and laments the life they left behind.

D: Anthony Asquith. A: John Mills, Eric Portman, Niall MacGinnis.

Thirty Seconds Over Tokyo

(1944) 138m. B&W. **A**

This sweeping account of the Doolittle raid, America's first air attack on Japan, has stupendous technical action and effects. Watch for the aircraft carrier takeoff, the thrilling bomb raid on Tokyo, and the stormy night crash on the China coast.

D: Mervyn LeRoy. A: Spencer Tracy, Van Johnson, Robert Walker.

Objective, Burma!

(1945) 142m. B&W. **B**

American paratroopers drop into Burma to destroy a vital Japanese radio transmitter. This one takes off the gloves as far as war action goes; it's closer to *Platoon* or *Apocalypse Now* in the way it brings you into the war, including the classic sequence of a nighttime defense on the hilltop.

D: Raoul Walsh. A: Errol Flynn, Henry Hull, George Tobias.

They Were Expendable

(1945) 135m. B&W. **A–**

The story of two officers' attempt to deploy PT boats in combat alternates combat action with telling scenes of the men's activities during the long waits between missions. Lacks the hysteria and violence of a war action film in order to focus on the relationships between people in wartime.

D: John Ford. A: John Wayne, Robert Montgomery, Donna Reed.

A Walk in the Sun

(1945) 117m. B&W. **A**

Made during the closing days of the war, this focuses entirely on the interactions of the American infantry who have landed in Italy as they march to their objective—a Nazi-held farmhouse in the Sicilian countryside. The foot soldiers' comaraderie, the flashes of battle, the growing tensions, and the final assault are all realistically portrayed in this sensitive and memorable tale.

D: Lewis Milestone. A: Dana Andrews, Richard Conte, Sterling Holloway.

Sands of Iwo Jima

(1949) 109m. B&W. **A**

This hard-hitting treatment of marine training, minus the propaganda, shows a relentless sergeant who makes men out of raw recruits and leads them into battle. The intense personality clashes at the beginning give way to a large-scale, harrowing recreation of Iwo Jima.

D: Allan Dwan. A: John Wayne, John Agar, Forrest Tucker.

Other Films:

Dangerous Moonlight (1941)
The Flying Tigers (1942)
Action in the North Atlantic (1943)
Bombardier (1943)
Gung Ho! (1943)
The North Star (1943)
The Fighting Seabees (1944)
A Wing and a Prayer (1944)
Back to Bataan (1945)

Bogart and Mitchum

These black-and-white action dramas showcase the deadpan cynic/veiled romantic Bogart and the laid-back tough and moral Mitchum. Like crime-oriented *Casablancas*, many of the stories take place in foreign lands where the lone rebel heroes come up against a motley crew of villains, adventurers, and women with dubious pasts.

They Drive by Night
(1940) 93m. B&W. **A**

When an independent trucker refuses the advances of the boss's wife, he gets implicated in her husband's murder. An exciting, if uneven, mix of working-class social drama and psychotic romance smoothed over by witty dialogue, an energetic cast, and a believable working man's milieu.
D: Raoul Walsh. A: George Raft, Humphrey Bogart, Ida Lupino.

To Have and Have Not
(1944) 100m. B&W. **A**

A cynical boat skipper on Vichy-occupied Martinique unwillingly gets involved with the intrigues of the French Resistance and a sultry footloose American girl. This snappy humor-injected little tale doesn't waste much time on wartime tensions; it's the sparks that fly between Bogie and Bacall that provide the real action.
D: Howard Hawks. A: Humphrey Bogart, Lauren Bacall, Walter Brennan.

Passage to Marseilles
(1944) 110m. B&W. **C+**

During World War II, escaped convicts are picked up by a steamer whose captain and passengers have diverging sympathies toward the Vichy regime and the Free French. Dramatic tension is dissipated by the awkward, sometimes confusing, flashback-laden construction.
D: Michael Curtiz. A: Humphrey Bogart, Claude Rains, Sydney Greenstreet.

Key Largo
(1948) 101m. B&W. **C+** 🏛

Gangsters hold hostage the occupants of a Florida Keys resort during the storm season. This moody, stagebound, and talky drama remains compelling for the powerhouse performances.
D: John Huston. A: Humphrey Bogart, Lauren Bacall, Edward G. Robinson.

The Treasure of the Sierra Madre
(1948) 124m. B&W. **A** 🏛

Three struggling prospectors mining for gold in the Mexican Sierra mountains discover a fortune, only to let their mistrust fester into violence and death. Classic tale of greed fueled by the rugged setting and spare dialogue, claustrophobic tone, and Bogart's unforgettable crazed and paranoid Fred C. Dobbs.
D: John Huston. A: Humphrey Bogart, Walter Huston, Tim Holt.

The Big Steal
(1949) 74m. B&W. **B**

This is one long chase through Mexico as wrongly accused Mitchum pursues a thief who stole from the army while the MPs pursue Mitchum. The breezy pace, light tone, and the Mexican locales make this an entertaining yarn with the right ratio of action and humor.
D: Don Siegel. A: Robert Mitchum, Jane Greer, William Bendix.

His Kind of Woman
(1951) 120m. B&W. **B**

Exiled crime boss Raymond Burr lures a sleepy-eyed drifter to a Caribbean resort for underhanded reasons, then has to contend with Mitchum's unlikely allies—a sultry songstress and a hammy movie star. An entertaining blend of crime drama and comic hijinks laced with witty dialogue.
D: John Farrow. A: Robert Mitchum, Jane Russell, Vincent Price.

Macao
(1952) 81m. B&W. **B−**

Three footloose Americans arrive in Macao: an ex-GI, a singer, and a NYC cop out to extradite the nightclub owner/gambling kingpin. Deception, betrayal, and mistaken identity are all part of this somewhat confusing, somewhat tongue-in-cheek melodrama with laid-back performances from Mitchum and Russell.
D: Josef von Sternberg. A: Robert Mitchum, Jane Russell, William Bendix.

Sirocco
(1951) 98m. B&W. **B**

Bogie is back in *Casablanca* territory as a cynical money-hungry American gunrunner who winds up aiding the French in their conflict with Syrian rebels. A studio-created Damascus is the moody backdrop for this trenchant, sometimes slow, noir-tinged adventure drama with a realistic downbeat ending.
D: Curtis Bernhardt. A: Humphrey Bogart, Lee J. Cobb, Marta Toren.

Thunder Road
(1958) 92m. B&W. **B** 🔍

This backwoods moonshine thriller follows an independent bootlegger who's up against both the Feds and the local syndicate. The prototype of the 70s good ole boys car-chase films, its sense of style and Mitchum as the cool modern outlaw in a black leather jacket make this a cult favorite.
D: Arthur Ripley. A: Robert Mitchum, Gene Barry, Jim Mitchum.

1950s
World War II Battles

1950s battle dramas weren't like the earlier fierce and sentimental little propaganda films about the "Japs" and "Krauts," but were wider-angled records of our boys' heroism. Blood and guts are still spilled here for a good cause, but the action dramas also hint at trouble within the ranks, showing dissension and the effects of battle stress.

Twelve O'Clock High
(1949) 132m. B&W. **A**
An air force general's rigid command of his war-weary but frightened bomber squadron nearly leads to mutiny. A cold anxiety hangs over this sober tale that shows the building tension between the "duty first" officer and battle-stressed all-American flyers.
D: Henry King. A: Gregory Peck, Dean Jagger, Gary Merrill.

Halls of Montezuma
(1950) 113m. B&W. **B+**
A battle-tough marine unit with two new recruits infiltrates Japanese lines to destroy the source of artillery attacks. The behind-enemy-lines tension along with the classic odd-lot mix of marines and jungle locales never surprises but moves at a brisk pace toward the big showdown.
D: Lewis Milestone. A: Richard Widmark, Jack Palance, Reginald Gardiner.

The Desert Fox
(1951) 88m. B&W. **B+**
This chronicles Germany's brilliant tank commander General Rommel's last years, from his military exploits to his aborted role in the attempt to assassinate Hitler. A sympathetic portrayal of an opponent in war is aided by a dignified and elegant Mason along with a documentary-like look and feel.
D: Henry Hathaway. A: James Mason, Jessica Tandy, Cedric Hardwicke.

The Desert Rats
(1953) 88m. B&W. **B+**
World War II and class war intersect when an English commander takes over a small group of stubborn Australians to ward off General Rommel's attack in North Africa. Contains sharp character sketches and an even sharper feel for just how dusty desert warfare is—everyone seems to be speaking with grit between his teeth.
D: Robert Wise. A: James Mason, Richard Burton, Robert Newton.

To Hell and Back
(1955) 106m. B&W. **B−**
The most decorated GI in World War II, Audie Murphy plays himself in this story of an "ordinary" infantryman in the European theater whose every heroic act seems natural and instinctive. A vivid look at personal courage with lots of bombs bursting and hand-to-hand combat, suffering only from Murphy's wooden impersonation of himself.
D: Jesse Hibbs. A: Audie Murphie, Marshall Thompson, David Janssen.

The Enemy Below
(1957) 98m. B&W. **B+**
An American destroyer in the Atlantic pursues a German submarine racing below to rendezvous with other warships. The tense maneuvering and cunning strategies, highlighted by shifting focus between pursued and pursuer, keep your gut clenched until the anticlimactic ending.
D: Dick Powell. A: Robert Mitchum, Curt Jurgens, Theodore Bikel.

Pursuit of the Graf Spee
(1957) 119m. B&W. **B**
Germany's major war vessel that had destroyed shipping and allied naval forces is tracked down and maneuvered into battle. A careful attention to naval details and plenty of officers with stiff upper lips and furrowed brows make England's first major naval victory in the war seem like a rousing slide show.
D: Michael Powell, Emeric Pressburger. A: Anthony Quayle, Ian Hunter, Peter Finch.

The Naked and the Dead
(1958) 131m. B&W. **C+**
Norman Mailer's novel makes it to the screen as a standard story about a platoon of soldiers who are battling the Japanese on the South Pacific beaches and jungles. The action sequences, like the turbulent beach landing, have a sweaty tension that fails to connect with the GIs who never stray from stereotype.
D: Raoul Walsh. A: Aldo Ray, Cliff Robertson, Raymond Massey.

Run Silent, Run Deep
(1958) 93m. B&W. **B**
The new captain of the submarine who's the sole survivor of a Japanese torpedo attack meets resistance from the crew suspicious of his obsessive preparation for revenge. A gray claustrophobic setting adds heightened anxiety to the skirmishes between Gable and Lancaster.
D: Robert Wise. A: Clark Gable, Burt Lancaster, Jack Warden.

Sink the Bismarck!
(1960) 97m. B&W. **A−**
British naval headquarters commences a plan to locate the elusive German war vessel Bismark. Despite naval battles that clearly use miniature models, the procedural part of the story has an earnest documentary feel that glorifies the military brass.
D: Lewis Gilbert. A: Kenneth More, Dana Wynter, Carl Mohner.

Hell Is for Heroes
(1962) 90m. B&W. **B+**
A determined, but decidedly angry and battle-weary group of GIs defends their tenuous position against the Germans. This battle story from a foxhole perspective has plenty of male camaraderie, the confusion of battle, and the brutality of hand-to-hand combat.
D: Don Siegel. A: Steve McQueen, Bobby Darin, Fess Parker.

Other Films:
The Flying Leathernecks (1951)
Battle Cry (1955)
The Sea Chase (1955)
The Sea Shall Not Have Them (1955)
Hellcats of the Navy (1957)
Never So Few (1959)

Historical Swashbucklers

Like other films in the 50s, swashbucklers got bigger, beefier, and more colorful. While these films cover much of the same territory as earlier historical actioners—knights-in-armor, Viking warfare, court intrigue, and piracy—most are now given the epic treatment.

The Flame and the Arrow

(1950) 88m. **A–**

A rousing lighthearted tale of rebels battling the evil German count who rules Lombardy in the twelfth century. Damsels in distress, oppressed villagers, and outlaws in their forest lairs are all pulled together by Lancaster's good-humored and acrobatic swashbuckling with his former circus partner Nick Cravat.
D: Jacques Tourneur. A: Burt Lancaster, Virginia Mayo, Nick Cravat.

Captain Horatio Hornblower

(1951) 117m. **B**

A grand sea adventure that awkwardly mixes plots ranging from a battle with Central American rebels in the Pacific to a shipboard romance to maneuvers against Napoleon's fleet. The bursts of action are lively, but often the supporting British cast has little to do.
D: Raoul Walsh. A: Gregory Peck, Virginia Mayo, Robert Beatty.

The Crimson Pirate

(1952) 104m. **A–**

Pirate captain Lancaster and his Harpo Marxlike mute sidekick Cravat are the acrobatic rebels fighting colonial rulers on an eighteenth-century Caribbean island. A cleverly staged climax involves makeshift forerunners of the flamethrower, tank, submarine, and, for good measure, a hot-air balloon.
D: Robert Siodmak. A: Burt Lancaster, Nick Cravat, Eva Bartok.

Ivanhoe

(1952) 106m **A**

A flavorful adaptation of Walter Scott's chivalric tale of a twelfth-century knight championing the cause of King Richard I. The Technicolor pageantry, the monumental scenes of jousts and castle sieges, and the colorful all-star cast of characters made this one of Hollywood's best knighthood epics.
D: Richard Thorpe. A: Robert Taylor, Joan Fontaine, Elizabeth Taylor.

The Prisoner of Zenda

(1952) 101m. **B**

A breezier brighter remake of the tale about a turn-of-the-century king of Ruritania who is kidnapped and replaced on the throne by an English double. A complicated plot of court intrigue is helped along by lively performances and the occasional bursts of swashbuckling action.
D: Richard Thorpe. A: Stewart Granger, Deborah Kerr, James Mason.

Scaramouche

(1952) 118m. **A–**

A traveling player in 1780s France wages war on the aristocrat who killed his radical friend in a duel. One of the most lavish swashbucklers, which offers a literate script, strong heroines, and a well-paced mix of action, humor, and romance.
D: George Sidney. A: Stewart Granger, Eleanor Parker, Janet Leigh.

Knights of the Round Table

(1953) 115m. **B**

This deluxe treatment of the King Arthur legend is long on pageantry, making good use of English locations, lavish sets, and a superb British supporting cast but is short on the excitement and plentiful action found in other historical adventures. Widescreen Cinemascope process loses a lot on TV.
D: Richard Thorpe. A: Robert Taylor, Ava Gardner, Mel Ferrer.

The Master of Ballantrae

(1953) 89m. **B+**

Errol Flynn's last decent swashbuckler is this tale of a Scottish clan leader who flees from the English to the Caribbean where he manages to get command of a pirate ship. A beautifully mounted production shot in Europe, with a darker, more serious Flynn.
D: William Keighley. A: Errol Flynn, Roger Livesey, Anthony Steel.

Prince Valiant

(1954) 100m. **C+**

An entertaining knights-in-armor romp with lots of swordfighting, castle sieges, boiling oil, rampaging Vikings, and beautiful maidens. Wagner is awful to the point of camp in this big-screen costume spectacle, but there's plenty of cartoon adventure to spice up the proceedings. Another widescreen entry that is partially lost on TV.
D: Henry Hathaway. A: Robert Wagner, James Mason, Janet Leigh.

Ulysses

(1955) 104m. **B**

One of the first Italian spectacles to focus on Greek mythology, this spare and athletic entry condenses *The Odyssey* into a standard mix of action, romance, and sea adventure, downplaying the fantastic elements in favor of the romantic encounters.
D: Mario Camerini. A: Kirk Douglas, Anthony Quinn, Silvana Mangano.

The Warriors

(1955) 85m. **C**

A hefty and dissipated Flynn can still give a good sword show in this tale set at the end of the Hundred Years War between England and France. Medium-budget production benefits from a strong supporting cast and an abundance of swordfighting shot at actual castles.
D: Henry Levin. A: Errol Flynn, Joanne Dru, Peter Finch.

The Buccaneer

(1958) 121m. **B**

Cecil B. DeMille's final production is this lively, colorful, and historically accurate retelling of how pirate Jean Lafitte came to General Andrew Jackson's aid in the Battle of New Orleans. Holds up well thanks to the all-star cast and energetic staging.
D: Anthony Quinn. A: Yul Brynner, Charlton Heston, Inger Stevens.

The Vikings

(1958) 114m. **A–**

This is part character drama and part bloody Viking actioner, where half-brothers in a deadly feud take time out to lay siege to an English castle. The engrossing story, intense performances, and rich historical flavor are enhanced by location shooting in Norway and France.
D: Richard Fleischer. A: Kirk Douglas, Tony Curtis, Janet Leigh.

Foreign Adventures

Unlike their dramatic counterparts, these big-scale action-dramas focus less on romance and more on the high drama and adventure of safari hunters, missionaries, and daredevils in tropical locales.

King Solomon's Mines
(1950) 102m. **B–**
A trio of whites—two men and a woman—trek through East Africa in search of a legendary treasure. Story and characters take a backseat to the location filming, native African performers, and animal stampedes in this fun but dramatically uninvolving tale.
D: Compton Bennett, Andrew Marton. A: Stewart Granger, Deborah Kerr, Richard Carlson.

The African Queen
(1951) 105m. **A**
An alcoholic boat captain and a spinster missionary find adventure and unlikely romance on an African river when they're thrust together on an improvised mission during World War I. This sparkling character study and rousing romantic adventure shot on location showcase the pros at their peak.
D: John Huston. A: Humphrey Bogart, Katharine Hepburn, Robert Morley.

The Devil at 4 O'Clock
(1961) 126m. **C+**
When a volcano erupts on a Pacific island, a priest and three convicts risk their lives to rescue children from a remote mountain hospital. Themes of faith and redemption are added to this standard disaster adventure that's enlivened by a craggy Tracy and a pleasantly subdued Sinatra.
D: Mervyn LeRoy. A: Spencer Tracy, Frank Sinatra, Jean-Pierre Aumont.

Hatari!
(1962) 159m. **B**
An international team of wildgame hunters set up camp in Africa to find large animals for zoos. This male adventure film takes time out from the chase for a romance between Wayne and photojournalist Martinelli, along with some comedic situations. If you're not concerned with animal rights, the scenes of pursuit are exhilarating.
D: Howard Hawks. A: John Wayne, Elsa Martinelli, Red Buttons.

The Naked Prey
(1966) 94m. **B–**
A safari guide whose party is slaughtered after offending a local chief is stripped naked and given an opportunity for freedom, provided he can outrun his pursuers. This rugged, purely visual adventure laced with raw violence is a *Tarzan*like adventure given a pretentious survival-of-the-fittest spin.
D: Cornel Wilde. A: Cornel Wilde, Gert Van Den Bergh, Ken Gampu.

1960s

All-Star World War II Battle Films

The wide-screen processes like Cinerama were perfect for war films, and with the casts of thousands and full-scale reenactments of famous battles, some of these entries look as if an actual war had been launched for just one movie. But despite the fact that most of these feature the top male stars of the day, the characters and the stories generally get buried under all the battle maneuvers.

The Longest Day
(1962) 180m. B&W. **B**
This epic recounts the events leading up to D Day, climaxing with a massive scale re-creation of the Allied invasion of Normandy. The all-star cast moves with military precision, if little emotion, in this war procedural that lavishes its attention on details at the expense of characters.
D: Ken Annakin, Andrew Marton, Bernhard Wicki. A: Robert Mitchum, Robert Ryan, John Wayne.

The Battle of the Bulge
(1965) 140m. **B**
This grand Cinerama spectacle offers a fanciful re-creation of the famous battle and glorifies combat as an elaborate, relatively hardship-free adventure. Plenty of action and very little insight in this showcase of solid dependable pros.
D: Ken Annakin. A: Henry Fonda, Robert Shaw, Charles Bronson.

In Harm's Way
(1965) 165m. B&W.
B+
This story of naval warfare in the early days of World War II begins with a reenactment of Pearl Harbor and moves into a smooth blend of war movie heroics and melodramatics among the officer class involving adultery, drunkenness, rape, and suicide. An assured, classy, and atypical war film.
D: Otto Preminger. A: John Wayne, Kirk Douglas, Patricia Neal.

Is Paris Burning?
(1966) 173m. B&W. **C–**
This multipart, multicharacter story covers the liberation of Paris in 1944 with the emphasis on the civilians of the city. Typically overblown with an international all-star cast, it contains some good vignettes but little dramatic focus and few action scenes for war buffs.
D: René Clement. A: Jean-Paul Belmondo, Charles Boyer, Leslie Caron.

Hell in the Pacific
(1968) 103m. **B**
An unusual two-character drama of enemy soldiers —an American and a Japanese—stranded on a desert island far from the action. It may not sound exciting, but the two rugged stars keep your interest as their attempts to survive and leave the island force enmity to give way to respect and partnership.
D: John Boorman. A: Lee Marvin, Toshiro Mifune.

Battle of Britain
(1969) 132m. **C**
A stiff-upper-lip rendition of how an outmanned, ill-equipped group of British fighter pilots valiantly defended England against Nazi bombers. Despite the expertly staged aerial combat scenes and vignettes depicting the English people's courage in a crisis, the overall effect remains sketchy and uninvolving.
D: Guy Hamilton. A: Christopher Plummer, Susannah York, Robert Shaw.

All-Star World War II Buddy Films

Male bonding is taken to a grand scale in these all-star adventures that throw a group of melting-pot characters together on a commando mission to knock out an impossible enemy target. The lengthy productions give you big-budget explosions and shoot-outs, along with the clowning, banter, and grudges that go into forging the esprit de corps of a killer team.

The Guns of Navarone

(1961) 157m. **B**

A team of hand-picked Allied soldiers, each a specialist, is assigned to take a Nazi-held Greek island. Originally a state-of-the-art action film with a clever plot, and superb special effects, it's now outclassed by the later entries.

D: J. Lee Thompson. A: Gregory Peck, Anthony Quinn, David Niven.

The Great Escape

(1963) 169m. **A**

In a German POW camp, officers direct a massive escape involving the digging of three tunnels and preparation of clothes and ID papers for hundreds of men. A large scale but intricately structured film with more suspense and teamwork than violence and explosions.

D: John Sturges. A: Steve McQueen, James Garner, Richard Attenborough.

Operation Crossbow

(1965) 116m. **B**

As the Nazis blitz London, three agents cross into Germany to infiltrate and sabotage a massive rocket plant. The suspense and sense of urgency never lets up in this large-scale, all-star thriller, complete with explosions, bombings, and a chaotic display of pyrotechnics.

D: Michael Anderson. A: George Peppard, Sophia Loren, Tom Courtney.

Von Ryan's Express

(1965) 117m. **B+**

An American major leads a British POW escape from an Italian prison camp, involving a train hijacking, betrayal, and dive bombers in pursuit. A smartly made and tense chase to the border, with the Yank rubbing the Brits the wrong way, but earning their respect in the end.

D: Mark Robson. A: Frank Sinatra, Trevor Howard, Edward Mulhare.

The Dirty Dozen

(1967) 149m. **A**

A maverick army major trains and leads 12 military prisoners on a suicide mission behind enemy lines. A raw, funny, and violent spectacle with an engaging band of misfits painfully and humorously developing an esprit de corps in time for the massive blowout at the end.

D: Robert Aldrich. A: Lee Marvin, Ernest Borgnine, Charles Bronson.

Where Eagles Dare

(1060) 155m. **A–**

A commando team is dropped behind enemy lines to rescue an American general from a Bavarian stronghold. This clever, elaborately staged action thriller has plenty of espionage, double crosses, chases, and suspense with a crafty Burton and dumbfounded second banana Eastwood.

D: Brian Hunt. A: Richard Burton, Clint Eastwood, Michael Hordern.

Kelly's Heroes

(1970) 145m. **B**

A platoon of U.S. infantrymen learn of a cache of gold hidden in a bank behind enemy lines and decide to break through to get it. A mix of creative staging, humorous camaraderie, and comic-book war violence with lots of shooting and explosions.

D: Brian Hutton. A: Clint Eastwood, Telly Savalas, Donald Sutherland.

World War II Spies and Suspense

In contrast to the large-scale World War II combat movies of the time, this group focused more on the quiet suspense, moral struggles, and cat-and-mouse conflicts behind the lines.

The Counterfeit Traitor

(1962) 140m. **A**

A fascinating and detailed true-life tale of espionage in Nazi Germany's upper echelons of industry by an American-born Swedish oilman. With an elegant, large-screen gloss and a sweeping use of major European locations, the only jarring note is Holden's Hollywood sheen clashing with his authentic European costars.

D: George Seaton. A: William Holden, Lilli Palmer, Hugh Griffith.

Moriluri

(1965) 123m. B&W. **B**

Two Germans become involved in a World War II cat-and-mouse game aboard a German cargo ship, which the British are determined to capture. A straightforward, intimate, and intriguing suspense/drama of double deception, carried by a compelling Brando and brooding Brynner.

D: Bernard Wicki. A: Marlon Brando, Yul Brynner, Trevor Howard.

The Train

(1965) 133m. B&W.
B+

A singleminded Nazi colonel tries to make off with a trainload of French art, but is opposed by an equally determined French railroad inspector. This is strong on ambiance with its cold overcast black-and-white look while offering a nonstop, spectacularly orchestrated barrage of assaults and countermeasures.

D: John Frankenheimer. A: Burt Lancaster, Paul Scofield, Jeanne Moreau.

Night of the Generals

(1967) 148m. **A–**

One of the more unusual World War II films, this follows a Nazi intelligence officer's dogged pursuit of a general accused of murdering prostitutes and the aftermath 20 years later. This stylish twisty suspense drama with a top-notch cast is a must for fans of the offbeat.

D: Anatole Litvak. A: Peter O'Toole, Omar Sharif, Tom Courtenay.

Historical Epics

These tales of real-life action heroes can practically overwhelm the viewer with historic detail, pageantry, and casts of thousands duking it out in spectacular battle scenes. But for all their bluster, unless the main character had something going for him—like believable heroic dimensions or some humanizing flaws—these military exercises would fall flat on the battlefield.

Damn the Defiant

(1962) 101m. **B**

A sadistic officer assumes command of a troubled ship during the Napoleonic Wars and mutiny follows. Within the rip-snorting formula lies a quiet British tale of father and son at sea.

D: Lewis Gilbert. A: Alec Guinness, Dirk Bogarde, David Robinson.

Lawrence of Arabia

(1962) 221m. **A**

An obscure but charismatic British officer becomes an international legend when he rallies Arab tribes to victory over a modern Turkish stronghold. A remarkably intimate epic that blends fascinating character study, breathtaking desert scenery, and rousing war story.

D: David Lean. A: Peter O'Toole, Omar Sharif, Alec Guinness.

Mutiny on the Bounty

(1962) 177m. **B**

When cruel Captain Bligh pushes his men too far, haughty second officer Christian leads a mutiny and then escapes to a tropical island. An overlong and lumbering version that features some still-enjoyable performances—including a foppish Brando, an expertly recreated eighteenth-century ship, and a gorgeously photographed tropical island.

D: Lewis Milestone. A: Marlon Brando, Trevor Howard, Richard Harris.

Taras Bulba

(1962) 122m. **C–**

While Bulba's army of Cossacks are fighting the Poles to reclaim their homeland, his son is falling in love with a Polish woman. Lots of hammy cavorting with hosts of big burly men in skins and furs, riding big horses and hacking away at each other.

D: J. Lee Thompson. A: Yul Brynner, Tony Curtis, Sam Wanamaker.

Sword of Lancelot

(1963) 115m. **B–**

Lancelot loves Guinevere and, when her husband King Arthur is murdered by his evil son, the love-hungry knight gets his chance. Brave men in armor clink about and maidens flutter in this fast-paced and occasionally witty throwback to 50s costume dramas.

D: Cornel Wilde. A: Cornel Wilde, Jean Wallace, Brian Aherne.

Zulu

(1964) 139m. **B**

A small group of British colonial soldiers display legendary gallantry as they defend a mission against 4000 Zulu warriors. It's cowboys and Indians in Africa with sterling performances and a surprising conclusion, but don't look for a balanced study of British/Zulu relations.

D: Cy Endfield. A: Stanley Baker, Jack Hawkins, Michael Caine.

The War Lord

(1965) 121m. **B–**

When a conquering commander invokes the *droit du seigneur* and takes a village girl on her wedding night, the villagers are up in arms. Tepid study of the brutality of feudalism along with the usual swordplay, battle sequences, and a good scene where boiling oil is poured from the castle walls.

D: Franklin Schaffner. A: Charlton Heston, Richard Boone, Maurice Evans.

Khartoum

(1966) 134m. **B**

Heroic British general tries to evacuate his people from Nile City besieged by Arab tribesmen led by a religious fanatic. Standard duel of wills, with battles deluxe and a diverting study of an eccentric British commander and an Ayatollah Khomeini-like leader played by Olivier.

D: Basil Dearden. A: Charlton Heston, Laurence Olivier, Richard Johnson.

Bikers

The sun glares and the highways blur as the gang of rough but noble outcasts burns rubber, hell-bent for the next beer, babe, or brawl. That's pretty much the sum total of these violent, sweaty, sometimes amateurish exploitation films that romanticize biker alienation. Like modern-day Vikings, these nonconformists ride in packs as they snub authority, trash the odd gas station, deal drugs, assault women, and head off into the next town. Hey, if it was good enough for Jack Nicholson . . .

The Wild Angels

(1966) 91m. **B**

This documentary-like look at the biker subculture follows one gang and offers the full menu: cemetery brawls, a drunken wake that erupts into violence and rape, drugs, chicks, leather jackets with swastikas, and society overreacting at every turn. *Easy Rider* was three years away.

D: Roger Corman. A: Peter Fonda, Nancy Sinatra, Bruce Dern.

Hell's Angels on Wheels

(1967) 95m. **B**

The classic biker flick has the soulful outsider accepted by the raucous but noble Hell's Angels, some snazzy desert and highway shots, battles over women, orgies, drugs, and brutality. This even has a biker wedding. Nicholson classes things up, along with some inventive camera work. As good as it gets.

D: Richard Rush. A: Adam Roarke, Jack Nicholson, Jana Taylor.

Rebel Rousers
(1967) 78m. **C–**
When a middle-aged architect's girlfriend is snatched by a biker gang, they have a drag race to see who gets her for the night. The spare plot and outlandish biker outfits are perfectly matched by the gory climax with pitchfork-wielding Mexicans.
D: Martin B. Cohen. A: Cameron Mitchell, Jack Nicholson, Bruce Dern.

Hell's Angels '69
(1969) 97m. **D+**
A strictly amateurish entry with real-life Angels mugging for the cameras, high-decibel levels of vrrrooom, and some ugly moments as two rich guys trying to hoodwink the Angels undergo painful brotherhood rituals. The contrast of tacky Vegas with the honest life of bikers gives pause.
D: Lee Madden. A: Tom Stern, Jeremy Slate, The Oakland Hell's Angels.

Angels Die Hard
(1970) 86m. **C**
It's the misunderstood Angels vs. the bigoted redneck townspeople when the gang members are falsely accused of beating the sheriff's daughter and are barely allowed to hold a funeral for a martyred member. Includes excellent stunt driving and some nasty fight scenes.
D: Richard Compton. A: Tom Baker, R. G. Armstrong, Carl Steppling.

Angels Hard as They Come
(1972) 90m. **C**
It's the good bikers (Hell's Angels) vs. the bad bikers (German-helmeted General and his boys), with the pacifist hippies caught in the middle in the desert town of Lost Cause. This one's strictly a turf war between subcultures with a bloodbath ending.
D: Joe Viola. A: Scott Glenn, Charles Dierkop, James Iglehart.

Bond, James Bond

In the 60s, audiences were introduced to a new kind of Cold War espionage hero: cool, sophisticated, ruthless, and irresistible to women. Agent 007 James Bond was equipped with high-tech gadgets, a license to kill for Her Majesty's Secret Service, and a taste for dry martinis, all making him the embodiment of Cold War, pre-sexual revolution male glamour.

Dr. No
(1962) 111m. **B+**
Bond investigates agent deaths in Jamaica and uncovers the nuclear blackmail plans of Dr. No. First of the series that established the guns/girls/gadgets/supervillain formula and may seem a little tame now—with its fading garish colors it's like leafing through an old thriller magazine—and just as much fun.
D: Terence Young. A: Sean Connery, Ursula Andress, Joseph Wiseman.

From Russia with Love
(1963) 125m. **A–**
The British and SPECTRE both want Russia's secret device, so it's a dash to the finish line between Bond and a hired homicidal assassin. Smooth and stylish caper with boat and helicopter chases, double-dealing women, exotic Turkish locales, and a dangerous ride on the Orient Express.
D: Terence Young. A: Sean Connery, Robert Shaw, Lotte Lenya.

Goldfinger
(1964) 117m. **A**
Industrialist Goldfinger plots with the Red Chinese to detonate a nuclear device in the gold vaults at Fort Knox. Bond at his best! A larger-than-life villain, a bowler-tossing henchman, dangerous blondes, great gadgets, a great car, and action syncopated to a brassy score.
D: Guy Hamilton. A: Sean Connery, Gert Frobe, Honor Blackman.

Thunderball
(1965) 125m. **B+**
Bond has to take care of the SPECTRE agent demanding ransom for the two nuclear warheads that he's stolen from NATO. The underwater scenes get slow but the cartoon violence with those pet sharks and piranhas, the Nassau setting, and deadly ladies are first rate.
D: Terence Young. A: Sean Connery, Adolfo Celi, Claudine Auger.

You Only Live Twice
(1967) 125m. **A**
U.S. and Soviet spacecrafts are being kidnapped, and Bond traces the plot to the Japanese lair of arch enemy Blofeld. Has the first of the really big villain sets, some wild gadgets, and the odd twist of Bond disguising himself as a Japanese and getting married.
D: Lewis Gilbert. A: Sean Connery, Akiko Wakabayashi, Tetsuro Tamba.

On Her Majesty's Secret Service
(1969) 144m. **C+**
Bond falls in love and marries a Spanish contessa while battling Blofeld's plans to brainwash young women. This entry is against the Bond grain and not just because Connery is missing. It's a less fantastic, more briskly told story, but you still get some of the usual Bond antics.
D: Peter R. Hunt. A: George Lazenby, Diana Rigg, Telly Savalas.

James Bond–like

These bubblegum-colored parodies attempt to cash in on the 60s Bond craze by making the heroes hipper, the plots zanier, the gadgets wilder, and the women dumber.

Our Man Flint
(1965) 107m. **B+**
Derek Flint is out to foil the villain's weather-controlling plans. He's a finely tuned killing machine, a Zen master, and a gourmet cook. His swinging bachelor pad boasts more gadgets than NASA, not to mention that harem. Entertaining fluff with amusing gags about Flint's ability to master any and all subjects.
D: Daniel Mann. A: James

Coburn, Lee J. Cobb, Gila Golan.

Murderer's Row
(1966) 108m. **D**

A super villain commands a death ray and Matt Helm must stop him. Little more than a chance for Martin to roll his eyes, ogle girls, hum a few notes from his hits, and punch out a bunch of bad guys.
D: Henry Levin. A: Dean Martin, Karl Malden, Ann-Margret.

In Like Flint
(1967) 114m. **B**

A group of man-hating women use the cover of a beauty cream empire to mask their plans for world domination. This sequel offers the same goofy escapades with a ridiculously hilarious male fantasy as a resolution to the war between the sexes.
D: Gordon Douglas. A: James Coburn, Lee J. Cobb, Jean Hale.

The Ambushers
(1968) 102m. **C**

A flying saucer belonging to the U.S. crashes in Mexico and Helm must find out where and why. Tongue-in-cheek and drink-in-hand Helm battles the usual collection of villains while keeping one eye out for the next hot female number.
D: Henry Levin. A: Dean Martin, Senta Berger, Janice Rule.

Russ Meyer

No director has so singlemindedly focused on a lone theme as Russ Meyer. Bluntly put, his brilliantly edited, campy, violent, and furiously paced films are paens to the limitless wonder of female breasts, the larger the better. Once deemed exploitation fare, his orb-obsessed oeuvre now offers an almost quaint charm and a deranged moral tone, and manages to be pretty much immune to any normal concept of criticism.

Faster Pussycat! Kill! Kill!
(1965) 83m. **C+**

They're fast living, they're stacked, and they can dish out a mean karate chop. Three go-go dancers rumble their way into a farm that's loaded with cash and tussle with the men of the house. The camera doesn't let you stop ogling for a minute while the dialogue whacks you on the head with hip and coy innuendo.
D: Russ Meyer. A: Tura Satana, Lori Williams, Haji.

Vixen
(1968) 70m. **C+**

A woman conducts her own personal sexual Olympics with every breathing male in sight. In terms of plot, this film could be identified as Meyer's minimalist period, but the upper contours of the female lead is consistent with the director's canon.
D: Russ Meyer. A: Erica Gavin, Garth Pillsbury, Harrison Page.

Cherry Harry and Raquel
(1969) 71m. **B−**

Despite confusing and constant inserts of a girl flouncing about wearing nothing but an Indian headdress, this tale of pot-smuggling in a border town still defines Meyer's vision of human behavior: namely that men beat the tar out of each other at the drop of a hat while voracious women sexually ravage the remains.
D: Russ Meyer. A: Ushi Digart, Charles Napier, Haji.

Beyond the Valley of the Dolls
(1970) 109m.
B+

An all-girl rock band hits the big time in the colorful sink of depravity called Hollywood. Drugs, swinging parties, murder, suicide, and groovy denizens virtually swimming in a sea of sex are played for camp or ham-handed moralizing. The brightest, funniest, and most sincere exploitation film you'll ever see.
D: Russ Meyer. A: Dolly Read, Cynthia Myers, Marcia McBroom.

Supervixens
(1975) 105m. **B**

This is a sort of cleavage noir as a young man framed for murder hits the road, is pursued by a maniacal impotent cop, and finds himself the object of every encountered female's ministrations. More violent in an overwrought cartoony way, but still offers a lively polka score.
D: Russ Meyer. A: Shari Ubanks, Charles Napier, Haji.

Nostalgic Gangsters

With the success of the TV show *The Untouchables*, prohibition gangsters returned with a vengeance via a host of studio-bound, low-budget films whose shoot-outs and rise-and-fall storylines echoed *Public Enemy* and *Little Caesar* minus the moralizing. But just when it seemed as if the films were becoming almost quaintly ritualistic, along came the high-toned, colorfully violent vision of *Bonnie and Clyde* to shake up the genre

Machine Gun Kelly
(1958) 80m. B&W. **B+**

The famous bank robber is portrayed as a weak-kneed, insecure failure, browbeaten by his moll and betrayed by his gang. A fascinating, intense, and low-budget Corman entry.
D: Roger Corman. A: Charles Bronson, Susan Cabot, Morey Amsterdam.

Al Capone
(1959) 105m. B&W. **B**

This version of the rise and fall of the prohibition-era Chicago gangster is done in the rapid-fire TV style that covers a lot of ground while playing fast and loose with the facts. Standard fare that's enlivened by Steiger's riveting and blatantly ethnic overacting.
D: Richard Wilson. A: Rod

Steiger, Fay Spain, James Gregory.

The Rise and Fall of Legs Diamond
(1960) 101m. B&W. **C**
This typical but energetic gangster tale, complete with the characters of Lucky Luciano, Arnold Rothstein, and Lepke Buchalter, offers several short, exciting shootouts, but is undermined by the miscast performers.
D: Budd Boetticher. A: Ray Danton, Karen Steele, Elaine Stewart.

King of the Roaring 20's
(1961) 106m. B&W. **C+**
The story of New York gambling kingpin Arnold Rothstein from youthful delinquency to downfall is strong on talk but weak on action. Mainly distinguished by Rooney's powerhouse performance as the partner Rothstein deserts when he becomes successful.
D: Joseph Newman. A: David Janssen, Dianne Foster, Mickey Rooney.

Bonnie and Clyde
(1967) 111m. **A**
One of the prime models for films about fun-loving, glamorous-looking lovers on a crime spree, this portrays the anti-heroic, bank-robbing couple as serious about each other and lighthearted about their crimes. A 60s style mix of humor, glamour, and violence with a final shoot-out that's a slow-motion ballet of bodies and bullets.
D: Arthur Penn. A: Warren Beatty, Faye Dunaway, Gene Hackman.

The St. Valentine's Day Massacre
(1967) 99m. **A**
Al Capone and Bugs Moran battle each other for control of bootlegging in Chicago in this colorful prohibition-era gangster epic. The episodic narration, complete with voiceover, charts the activities of the men who will die in the massacre, eliciting empathy for the seven victims to be.
D: Roger Corman. A: Jason Robards, Jr.; Ralph Meeker; Jean Hale.

International All-Stars

Men coping with life-or-death situations in exotic locales are at the center of these lavishly produced epics whose international all-star casts seem to need a full 2½ hours to wade through whatever desperate adventures are in store for them.

Flight of the Phoenix
(1965) 145m. **B**
A small plane is downed in the North African desert with a broken radio, little food and water, and quite a few tempers. Lots of shots of actors squinting in the sun and some good character moments blink through. Had they killed off a few stars earlier, this film might not have run so long.
D: Robert Aldrich. A: James Stewart, Richard Attenborough, Peter Finch.

Grand Prix
(1966) 170m. **C**
Wheels smoke, men grit their teeth, and road signs blur by in a series of stylishly shot, invigorating, but ultimately tedious racing events. The occasional soapy asides don't connect and despite the European locations, the action is strictly on the track. Multiple screen segments are lost on video.
D: John Frankenheimer. A: James Garner, Eva Marie Saint, Toshiro Mifune.

Ice Station Zebra
(1968) 152m. **B**
A submarine manned by a U.S./British team (and one a suspected spy) retrieves a crashed Russian satellite as Soviet paratroopers are on their way. Features lots of tech talk, some stunning underwater ice-breaking sequences, and a big polar research base for a climactic U.S./Soviet confrontation.
D: John Sturges. A: Rock Hudson, Patrick McGoohan, Ernest Borgnine.

The Red Tent
(1971) 121 m. **B+**
A fascinating, Italian-produced film about General Nobile's ill-fated 1928 dirigible expedition to the North Pole. The harrowing survival amid arctic conditions blends with the psychological study of a haunted leader forever questioning his actions when help arrived. Don't miss the terrific zeppelin crash.
D: Mikhail K. Kalatozov. A: Peter Finch, Massimo Girotti, Sean Connery.

1970s

All-Star World War II Battle Films

In defiance of the prevailing discomfort of the Vietnam War, these are the last of the old-fashioned gore-free war combat films; the soldiers are decisive, the war is an unquestioned necessity, and the enemy is a well-defined bad guy. Many of the films suffer from the 70s bloat with overlong productions and top-heavy all-star casts, but even when they are unwieldy messes, the climactic battles offer jaw-dropping spectacles of destruction.

Tora! Tora! Tora!
(1970) 143m. **A**
This American-Japanese production gives a gripping blow-by-blow account of the events leading up to the attack on Pearl Harbor from both countries' perspective, culminating in a surprisingly gut-wrenching re-creation of the attack itself. An unusual and rewarding approach for such a large-scale big-budget war film.
D: Richard Fleischer, Toshio Masuda, Kinji Fukasuku. A: Martin Balsam, So Yamamura, Jason Robards.

Murphy's War
(1971) 108m. **C+**
The sole survivor of a brutal German U-boat massacre seeks to avenge those deaths by launching attacks in a wrecked seaplane he has resurrected. A smaller-scale, unglamorous tale of revenge that draws its power from the energy of O'Toole going ballistic.
D: Peter Yates. A: Peter O'Toole, Sian Phillips, Philippe Noiret.

Midway
(1976) 132m. **C–**
A by-the-numbers re-creation of the pivotal sea and air battle in the Pacific mixing studio-created shots with actual color combat footage. Great for war buffs and star-watchers, but little to involve the rest aside from a romantic subplot involving a navy pilot and his Japanese girlfriend.
D: Jack Smight. A: Charlton Heston, Edward Albert, Henry Fonda.

A Bridge Too Far
(1977) 175m. **B–**
The Allies' attempt to secure a bridge behind German lines is foiled by miserable weather, poor planning, and bad luck. The cast lumbers through this overlong drama while spectacular scenes of advancing tank forces and errant parachuters get overwhelmed by details and character plot lines.
D: Richard Attenborough. A: Dirk Bogarde, Michael Caine, Sean Connery.

Cross of Iron
(1977) 119m. **C+**
An ambitious Nazi officer clashes with hardened, war-weary veteran troops on the Russian front. This story, told from a German's point of view, offers war as a stark grim bloody hell, but suffers from a confusing plot, a muddled message, and an inability to muster sympathy for any character despite the performances.
D: Sam Peckinpah. A: James Coburn, Maximilian Schell, James Mason.

The Eagle Has Landed
(1977) 123m. **B–**
This elaborate kidnap thriller follows a Nazi plan to kidnap Winston Churchill, which includes infiltrating an English country town. While offering a glossy portrait of small town life during the war, the film gets tangled in the intricate plot, which loses its suspense early on.
D: John Sturges. A: Michael Caine, Donald Sutherland, Robert Duvall.

The Big Red One
(1980) 113m. **B**
This entry offers much authentic war detail and well-staged re-creations of several key campaigns in North Africa and Europe, but suffers from the casting of four callow young actors as the main recruits. The episodic structure and bursts of action will appeal to war buffs.
D: Samuel Fuller. A: Lee Marvin, Mark Hamill, Robert Carradine.

Bond, James Bond

Unfortunately, by the 70s the Bond series got locked into the formula of gadgets/sexy women/megalomaniacal villains, and the only way to go was bigger and broader. What began as good-humored spy thrillers now turned into segmented action-adventures in travelogue settings, with Sean Connery's cool and dangerous Bond being replaced by Roger Moore's coy and arch one.

Diamonds Are Forever
(1971) 120m. **B**
Bond is still trying to stop Blofeld who's now creating a diamond-powered orbiting laser. Connery returns as an older Bond in this somewhat tired rehash of classic Bond tricks. Americans come off as boorish or stupid, and Vegas and other U.S. locations seem tacky.
D: Guy Hamilton. A: Sean Connery, Jill St. John, Charles Gray.

Live and Let Die
(1973) 131m. **B**
Bond messes around in island voodoo and Louisiana bayous as he searches for the network that is planning to flood the world market with free heroin to increase the number of addicts. More of a string of segmented action sequences with plenty of outrageous escapes.
D: Guy Hamilton. A: Roger Moore, Yaphet Kotto, Jane Seymour.

The Man with the Golden Gun
(1974) 134m. **C+**
Bond, now searching for the device that turns solar energy into electricity (remember the 70s energy crisis?), is stalked by the ultimate assassin. Lower-budget Bond with few thrills but lots of the usual coy dialogue. The tension of the two master killers at odds never materializes.
D: Guy Hamilton. A: Roger Moore, Christopher Lee, Britt Ekland.

The Spy Who Loved Me
(1977) 136m. **B+**
The spirit of détente teams Bond with a sexy Russian agent to foil their common arch villain. This one freely winks at the audience not to take things seriously. More of a travelogue with parades of sexy girls, ever more outrageous gadgets, and silly gags.
D: Lewis Gilbert. A: Roger Moore, Barbara Bach, Curt Jurgens.

Moonraker
(1979) 126m. **B**
An evil industrialist steals the space shuttle as part of his plan to destroy and repopulate the earth. Bond literally goes around and over the earth in this almost tongue-in-cheek imitation of a 007 film.
D: Lewis Gilbert. A: Roger Moore, Michael Lonsdale, Lois Chiles.

All-Star Disaster Films

Exploding zeppelins, burning skyscrapers, earthquakes, and capsized ocean liners give these films the appeal of watching something really huge get destroyed. Part adventure,

part soap opera, the plots are *Grand Hotel*–style interwoven stories of the various stock characters—the dedicated crew, the mad but poignant bomber, the dotty old lady, the sexy mistress—as they become united by a common peril.

Airport
(1970) 137m. **B**

Grand Hotel goes airborne as all the characters' Sturm und Drang takes precedence over the slight plane-in-peril subplot. This glossy melodrama with its nice mix of veteran actors and top stars of the day is not as silly as the later ones, but also not as much fun.
D: George Seaton. A: Burt Lancaster, Dean Martin, Jean Seberg.

The Poseidon Adventure
(1972) 117m. **A**

A luxury liner capsizes at sea, forcing a small group of survivors to work their way up through the bottom of the ship. The constant suspense, strong script, and a lively cast make this fresher and more gripping than many contemporary thrillers.
D: Ronald Neame. A: Gene Hackman, Ernest Borgnine, Shelley Winters.

Earthquake
(1974) 123m. **D+**

The earthquake scenes in Los Angeles are spectacular, but you may not be able to wade through the boring stories of the cardboard LA types for the final payoff. Even with the spectacle of LA being destroyed, this looks and feels like a TV movie.
D: Mark Robson. A: Charlton Heston, Genevieve Bujold, Ava Gardner.

Juggernaut
(1974) 109m. **B−**

A terrorist plants seven bombs somewhere on a luxury liner, and a special squad races the clock to discover and diffuse them. This taut thriller keeps its attention on the tough members of the bomb squad with fewer side stories about the passengers.
D: Richard Lester. A: Richard Harris, Omar Sharif, David Hemmings.

The Towering Inferno
(1974) 165m. **B+**

Fire ravages the tallest building in the world on the night of its gala opening, and the party guests either fight the fire or die in it. Notable for its escalating array of deaths by fire, explosion, and falls from great heights and the ease with which Newman and McQueen slip into this fun and mindless entertainment.
D: Irwin Allen. A: Paul Newman, Steve McQueen, Faye Dunaway.

Airport 1975
(1975) 106m. **B**

After a mid-air collision puts a 747 pilot out of commission, a stewardess takes the controls under radio direction. Some welcome humor, intentional and otherwise, and an unusual crop of old and new stars punch up this routine but well-paced entry.
A: Jack Smight. A: Charlton Heston, Karen Black, George Kennedy.

The Hindenburg
(1975) 125m. **B+**

During the famed dirigible's final trip, a soul-searching Nazi officer gets wind of a sabotage plot, but fails to stop it. The dramatics are blessedly mild-mannered for the stellar cast, and even the lack of real suspense can't dim the grandeur of the scenes of the skyscraper-size flying hydrogen bomb.
D: Robert Wise. A: George C. Scott, Anne Bancroft, William Atherton.

Airport 1977
(1977) 114m. **C**

The TV-style plot for this entry involves the hijacking of a 747 loaded with art treasures, its crash at sea, and a spectacular navy rescue sequence. Sometimes elegant, often silly, and always fun.
D: Jerry Jameson. A: Jack Lemmon, Lee Grant, James Stewart.

The Cassandra Crossing
(1977) 127m. **C+**

A luxury trans-European passenger train is diverted to an unsafe crossing to avert the spread of a lethal virus. Genuine suspense builds as the passengers discover the crisis and try to stop the train, but the plausible story gets undermined by a spectacular but unnecessarily catastrophic ending.
D: George P. Cosmatos. A: Richard Harris, Sophia Loren, Burt Lancaster.

Historical Adventures

These new-fashioned romantic adventures tended to be smaller-scaled than their epic antecedents with more attention spent on the characters and atmosphere of bygone times. Historical detail got to the point where even in these male-dominated films, heroes were lavishly outfitted and coiffed, creating a past where men were men but also terribly fashionable.

The Last Valley
(1970) 128m. **C+**

A peaceful Swiss valley in the seventeenth century has survived the ravages of the Thirty Years War until a band of marauding mercenaries arrive. A strange mix of philosophical treatise about the nature of war and man, and adventure yarn with graphic depictions of carnage and pillage.
D: James Clavell. A: Michael Caine, Omar Sharif, Nigel Davenport.

The Three Musketeers
(1973) 105m. **B**

Three daring and lusty soldiers and an inexperienced country lad combat the evil machinations of Cardinal Richelieu and handle some misbehaving ladies. Broadly played and slapsticky with occasional bouts of seriousness, this oft-told tale might be messy and too busy but it's still good earthy fun.
D: Richard Lester. A: Michael York, Oliver Reed, Richard Chamberlain.

The Four Musketeers
(1975) 108m. **B**

A less bumbling d'Artagnan and his band continue the struggle against Richelieu and his agents. The swords still flash; people still drop from hay lofts; bosoms heave; fruit, fowl, and flotsam are hurled in all directions; and you even get some

touching dramatic moments.
D: Richard Lester. A: Michael York, Oliver Reed, Richard Chamberlain.

The Man Who Would Be King
(1975) 129m. **A**

Two charming rogues, fresh from the British colonial army, seek to become kings of the primitive tribes of Kafiristan and succeed beyond their wildest dreams. Smooth and breezy buddy film with delightful characters and heavenly scenery.
D: John Huston. A: Michael Caine, Sean Connery, Christopher Plummer.

The Wind and the Lion
(1975) 120m. **B**

A rebel Arab leader kidnaps a straight-talking American widow and her family but gets more than he bargained for—including threats of war by a jingoistic Teddy Roosevelt. Sometimes amusing clash of culture tale with a dash of old-fashioned romance and adventure.
D: John Milius. A: Sean Connery, Candice Bergen, Brian Keith.

Robin and Marion
(1976) 106m. **C+**

A battle-weary, middle-aged Robin Hood returns from the Crusades to find things not well with Marion, England, and his old friends. Nice idea to follow up legends as their glory years become a depressing dismantling of everything that made them great. Solid cast labors with glum script.
D: Richard Lester. A: Sean Connery, Audrey Hepburn, Nicol Williamson.

Swashbuckler
(1976) 101m. **D**

A lusty pirate and a wronged lady who's good with a sword go after the corrupt colonial governor. Mix in all the clichés of old Errol Flynn films, add some sex, and you'll get . . . a tedious mess! Badly plotted with boisterous but hollow performances.
D: James Goldstone. A: Robert Shaw, James Earl Jones, Beau Bridges.

The Duellists
(1977) 101m. **C+**

A pair of puffed French officers in Napoleon's army engage in a personal feud that layers over many years. This atmospheric study of the vanity and pride of the officer class stars two dashing young men with stylish uniforms and American accents. You'll either soak up the exquisite moods of this subtle drama or wonder why you should care.
D: Ridley Scott. A: Keith Carradine, Harvey Keitel, Edward Fox.

The Prince and the Pauper
(1978) 113m. **B–**

The Mark Twain tale gets the all-star treatment as the grownups cavort around in costumes having a good time as British aristocrats. Dull in patches but enough swordplay, witty dialogue, and bosomy ladies to make it fun viewing.
D: Richard Fleischer. A: Oliver Reed, Mark Lester, Raquel Welch.

Zulu Dawn
(1979) 117m. **B**

Colonial stupidity leads to a titanic battle in which a British garrison is slaughtered by a wave of Zulu warriors. Offers some grand-scale battle scenes as generals and politicians ignore warnings by local folks that the natives are out for blood.
D: Douglas Hickox. A: Burt Lancaster, Peter O'Toole, Denholm Elliot.

Getaways and Heists

The bad guys were often the good guys in 70s crime films, demonstrated by these action thrillers. Like *Bonnie and Clyde*, the chase films are set in the wide-open spaces of the West and Southwest, with retribution and our felonious heroes' fate always in question. The two prison breakout films in this group display all the ingredients of that genre: desperation, claustrophia, and a painstaking attention to the details of the escape.

The Getaway
(1972) 123m. **A–**

A husband and wife team pull off a bank job and are chased across Texas by murderous associates and the alerted cops. A nasty series of double crosses, violent confrontations, and shoot 'em up getaways can't hide a weak plot and one-dimensional characters.
D: Sam Peckinpah. A: Steve McQueen, Ali McGraw, Ben Johnson.

Charley Varrick
(1973) 111m. **B**

A small-time bank robber and his partner unwittingly run afoul of the mob and are on the run through the small towns, back roads, and trailer parks of the Southwest. A low-keyed caper with Matthau's amiable, middle-aged, and wisecracking persona injecting a lighter tone to the film's grim brutality.
D: Don Siegel. A: Walter Matthau, Joe Don Baker, Felicia Farr.

Papillon
(1973) 150m. **B+**

This is a big-budget large-scale film based on the real life exploits of the man who made repeated attempts to escape from French penal colonies. The lush location photography, tropical adventures, and distinctly American name stars create an odd mixture of old and new Hollywood.
D: Frank Schaffner. A: Steve McQueen, Dustin Hoffman, Anthony Zerbe.

Thunderbolt and Lightfoot
(1974) 114m. **A–**

A lighthearted caper set in Montana follows a band of footloose petty criminals who decide to rob an armored car company. The leisure pace, beautiful visuals, and a rare all-star cast of 70s character actors add up to an entertaining and distinctly laid-back crime film.
D: Michael Cimino. A: Clint Eastwood, Jeff Bridges, George Kennedy.

The Gauntlet
(1977) 109m. **C+**

The shambling cop who's assigned to escort a witness from Las Vegas to Phoenix is galvanized into heroic action when he discovers that police in both states have been ordered to kill them on sight. Nonstop but unexciting shooting and destruction, including the complete leveling of a house by gunfire.
D: Clint Eastwood. A: Clint Eastwood, Sondra Locke, Pat Hingle.

Who'll Stop the Rain
(1978) 126m. **A–**

When Nolte is talked into smuggling drugs to the States by a journalist friend in Vietnam, the drop goes bad and he's on the run through California with the journalist's wife. Less a thriller than a relentlessly downbeat character-study drama about the effects of the Vietnam War on the American soul.
D: Karel Reisz. A: Nick Nolte, Tuesday Weld, Michael Moriarty.

Escape from Alcatraz
(1979) 112m. **B–**

A true story of the only successful escape from Alcatraz is turned into a star vehicle for the implacable Eastwood. A well-paced, methodical presentation of the breakout, from conception to execution, but it lacks suspense or any emotional involvement.
D: Don Siegel. A: Clint Eastwood, Patrick McGoohan, Roberts Blossom.

Revenge and Vigilantes

Films about populist heroes and the rage of Nixon's "silent majority" against crime and bureaucracy were pretty popular in the 70s. These are the action films that were supposed to make you stand up and cheer as the righteous underdog finally gets mad as hell and takes on the authority, whether it's criminal gangs, the Mafia, or the CIA.

Billy Jack
(1971) 115m. **C–**

A half-Indian ex-Green Beret becomes the protector of a commune of flower children but the righteous townsfolk aim to do something about those sick perverts. This badly acted, goofily sincere film preaches peace and love while building up steam so Billy Jack can stomp the hell out of the goons.
D: Tom Laughlin. A: Tom Laughlin, Delores Taylor, Clark Howat.

Sweet Sweetback's Badasssss Song
(1971) 97m. **C+**

A ghetto bordello entertainer kills the two cops who beat up a black revolutionary and takes off for Mexico. This low-budget entry by Melvin Van Peebles is filled with violence and racial stereotypes, but manages to surprise with allegorical and ironic touches.
D: Melvin Van Peebles. A: Melvin Van Peebles, Rhetta Hughes, John Amos.

The Mechanic
(1972) 100m. **B–**

Bronson plays a hit man who's in for some karmic payback; after completing his assignment to kill his mentor, he takes it upon himself to train the dead man's son. A taut game of one-upmanship right up to the end.
D: Michael Winner. A: Charles Bronson, Jan Michael Vincent, Keenan Wynn.

Walking Tall
(1973) 126m. **B**

Based on the exploits of real-life Tennessee sheriff Buford Pusser, this is like a classic western with its "one good man against a corrupt town" theme. Marred by loud, exploitation-style violence, the scene where the beaten-up Baker keeps going strong will have you cheering him on.
D: Phil Karlson. A: Joe Don Baker, Felton Perry, Elizabeth Hartman.

Death Wish
(1974) 93m. **B**

A peace-loving New Yorker's wife and daughter are raped and killed; he then discovers that bureaucratic red tape is his legal remedy and becomes a one-man cleanup campaign of urban scum. The first and the best of the modern vigilante films with Bronson as the homicidal Miss Manners who teaches the bad guys a lesson in civility by killing them off one by one.
D: Michael Winner. A: Charles Bronson, Vincent Gardenia, Hope Lange.

Mr. Majestyk
(1974) 93m. **C+**

Here's a plot you don't see too often: a watermelon farmer trying to fight off the Mafia, who have ruined all his neighbors' crops and now have him targeted. Bronson is the craggy farmer with courage and a mean punch. Don't take this too seriously, the filmmakers didn't.
D: Richard Fleischer. A: Charles Bronson, Al Lettieri, Paul Koslo.

The Killer Elite
(1975) 124m. **B–**

Headstrong government agent Caan is crippled by a colleague as a way of putting him out to pasture. When the colleague goes rogue, Caan is recalled to eliminate him. Director Peckinpah puts some raw power into this revenge tale, which also offers eerily dreamlike kung fu battles.
D: Sam Peckinpah. A: James Caan, Robert Duvall, Gig Young.

Rolling Thunder
(1977) 99m. **B+**

A Vietnam POW, home after seven years a prisoner, walks in on the brutal robbery of his family by a gang who also tortures and mutilates him. This story of revenge, swirling with bitter memories of Vietnam, keeps an edgy and frightening momentum thanks to the pre-*Rambo* attitudes of maniacal Devane and violent Jones.
D: John Flynn. A: William Devane, Tommy Lee Jones, Linda Haynes.

Cops and Detectives

These thrillers are the source of the modern, hyper-drive car chase, the maverick cop who plays by his own rules, and the appearance of big-name stars in action vehicles. Echoing

in look and tone the then current TV policiers (bright primary colors, "flat" images), these feature gritty locations, quirky streetwise characters, and graphically violent crimefighting.

Bullitt
(1968) 113m. **B+**

A police lieutenant faces ruin when a mob witness is killed on his watch, only to find he's been manipulated by an ambitious politician. Even with the contrived plot, this is a terse, hard-edged thriller that climaxes with the dazzling, often-imitated car chase up and over San Francisco's hills.
D: Peter Yates. A: Steve McQueen, Jacqueline Bisset, Robert Vaughn.

Coogan's Bluff
(1968) 94m. **B+**

Eastwood brings his western persona to the big city when he plays an Arizona deputy sheriff who comes to New York City to extradite a wanted criminal. Enjoyable scenes with cowboy Clint clashing with the Big Apple in the swinging 60s and a remarkable motorcycle chase outside the Cloisters.
D: Don Siegel. A: Clint Eastwood, Susan Clark, Lee J. Cobb.

The Detective
(1968) 114m. **C**

All the high-society types seem to be hiding a guilty secret in this daring (for the time) and unenlightened story of a homosexual murder and an ambitious detective's railroading of an innocent man to the electric chair.
D: Gordon Douglas. A: Frank Sinatra, Lee Remick, Jacqueline Bisset.

Madigan
(1968) 100m. **C+**

These parallel stories of two New York City cops tracking a thug who stole their guns and a police commissioner facing personal and professional crises open and close with decent action scenes but too often resemble a TV cop movie.
D: Don Siegel. A: Richard Widmark, Henry Fonda, Inger Stevens.

The French Connection
(1971) 104m. **A**

The brutist abusive narcotics detective, Popeye Doyle, and his partner doggedly pursue an international drug transaction through the streets, subways, and byways of the city. Even after *Speed*, this pioneering series of relentless, high-speed action scenes shot in New York City can still dazzle.
D: William Friedkin. A: Gene Hackman, Roy Scheider, Fernando Rey.

Fuzz
(1972) 92m. **C**

This slice of life at a Boston precinct shows inept plainclothes detectives coping with a variety of crimes including a series of bombings and extortion plots aimed at the city. A forced attempt at freewheeling satire in the vein of *M*A*S*H* is a waste of local Boston color and the lively cast.
D: Richard Colla. A: Burt Reynolds, Jack Weston, Raquel Welch.

Electra Glide in Blue
(1973) 113m. **C–**

Blake is the diminutive Arizona motorcycle cop with dreams of grandeur—his idol is Alan Ladd—but all he does is run up against crazy corrupt cops and bureaucratic indifference. An odd cop drama done from a vaguely counterculture point of view.
D: James William Guercio. A: Robert Blake, Billy Green Bush, Mitchell Ryan.

The Seven-Ups
(1973) 103m. **B**

A squad of New York City cops tracks down a gang kidnapping top mobsters, leading to shoot-outs and a harrowing extended car chase. Lacks a strong story or compelling characters, leaving you to enjoy all the off-the-beaten-track New York location shots.
D: Philip D'Antoni. A: Roy Scheider, Tony LoBianco, Larry G. Haines.

The Stone Killer
(1973) 95m. **B**

A New York cop travels to LA to break up a ring of Vietnam vets hired to slaughter mafiosi. Bronson comfortably strolls through the parade of wacked-out characters and changing scenery in this violent, fast-paced, and often incomprehensible thriller.
D: Michael Winner. A: Charles Bronson, Martin Balsam, Ralph Waite.

The Laughing Policeman
(1974) 111m. **B+**

A hunt for a mass murderer leads a detective team through San Francisco's world of gay bars, biker clubs, and drug underworld. An interesting drama that shows how the cops' search through darker subcultures exposes their own set of problems.
D: Stuart Rosenberg. A: Walter Matthau, Bruce Dern, Anthony Zerbe.

McQ
(1974) 116m. **C–**

In a late-in-life change-of-pace role, Wayne meets sex, cocaine, discos, radicals, and automatic weapons, but at 66 is hard put to keep up with all the action.
D: John Sturges. A: John Wayne, Eddie Albert, Diana Muldaur.

Brannigan
(1975) 111m. **C–**

A big gruff Chicago cop upsets genteel London while searching for a fugitive gangster. Wayne's paid trip to London results in a slow-going, badly acted thriller that exalts in sightseeing, but little else.
D: Douglas Kickox. A: John Wayne, Richard Attenborough, Judy Geeson.

Deadly Hero
(1976) 102m. **C+**

A disturbed cop harasses a burglary victim after she lodges a brutality complaint against him. Awkward scripting and a low-budget production hamper an otherwise daring twist on the 70s police thriller featuring good local New York color.
D: Ivan Nagy. A: Don Murray, Diahn Williams, James Earl Jones.

French Connection II
(1975) 118m. **B–**

Popeye Doyle is back, and he's tracking the drug dealer in Marseilles. Extensive location shots add color, but it's difficult to identify with either the boorish cop or the distant French characters in this dark noirish drama that's missing half of the zip and suspense of the first.
D: John Frankenheimer. A: Gene Hackman, Fernando Rey, Bernard Fresson.

Hustle
(1975) 120m. **B**

A love story between a cop and a beautiful French hooker alternates with a cynical and plodding police investigation into the murder of a girl involved in a mob-connected porno-film ring. A relatively thoughtful entry with less action and more soul-searching.
D: Robert Aldrich. A: Burt Reynolds, Catherine Deneuve, Paul Winfield.

The Yakuza
(1975) 112m. **A–**

Fascinating combination of culture-clash tale and gang-

ster film with definite noir sensibilities as an ex-GI returns to Japan to help a friend whose daughter has been abducted by the Yakuza—the Japanese version of the mob. Though colorwise a bit too TV movie-ish, this still has an eternally world-weary Mitchum, great action scenes, and a startlingly gruesome/touching finale.
D: Sydney Pollack. A: Robert Mitchum, Takakura Ken, Brian Keith.

Dirty Harry

Clint Eastwood grabbed audiences by the collar and shoved a magnum gun in their faces with these gritty, fast-paced cop thrillers that are part Mickey Spillane potboiler, part vigilante drama, and part reactionary rallying cry against "liberal" trends in the judicial system.

Dirty Harry
(1971) 102m. **A**
The original thriller that raised cries of "fascist!" depicts the cop-hero's extralegal methods of apprehending a psychotic killer terrorizing San Francisco. Still feels modern thanks to Eastwood's steely-eyed charisma and the story's mean-edged momentum.
D: Don Siegel. A: Clint Eastwood, Andy Robinson, John Vernon.

Magnum Force
(1973) 124m. **B+**
When vigilante highway cops assassinate freed criminals, even Dirty Harry is appalled and takes on the head of the ring. An intriguing follow-up that lacks the pace and suspenseful edge of the first.
D: Ted Post. A: Clint Eastwood, Hal Holbrook, Felton Perry.

The Enforcer
(1976) 96m. **B**
When a radical group kidnaps the mayor, Dirty Harry tries to track them down in spite of being saddled with an inexperienced female partner and the meddling police brass. An atmospheric climax shot at Alcatraz gives the routine proceedings some color and spark.
D: James Fargo. A: Clint Eastwood, Tyne Daly, Bradford Dillman.

Sudden Impact
(1983) 117m. **C+**
The spotlight is on Locke as an artist who commits a series of vigilante killings in retaliation against a gang of rapists. Harry's newfound feminism only means that he recognizes a kindred soul who gets rid of the bad guys as efficiently as he does.
D: Clint Eastwood. A: Clint Eastwood, Sondra Locke, Pat Hingle.

The Dead Pool
(1988) 91m. **C**
This entry, resembling a TV cop show episode, is strictly a whodunit as Harry discovers his name is on a list of celebrities to be murdered. Harry still looks good but by now the series has run out of juice.
D: Buddy Van Horn. A: Clint Eastwood, Patricia Clarkson, Liam Neeson.

Cars and Good Ole Boys

While the big city streets were ablaze with gunfire and car chases in the 1970s police thrillers, the backwoods and desert roads were awash with speeding drivers, moonshiners, lovers-on-the-run, rebel truckers with CB radios, and frustrated "smokeys." These small populist action-dramas are almost entirely devoted to high-speed chases over two-lane blacktops and dusty roads involving all manner of motor vehicles. Most are low-budget exploitation pictures, but you do get to see some efforts by directors like Ron Howard, Jonathan Demme, and Sam Peckinpah.

Vanishing Point
(1971) 107m. **B+**
A lone, pill-popping driver races a Dodge Challenger from Denver to California, leaving highway cops in the dust and encountering a host of eccentric characters. A counterculture favorite that's one long car chase broken up by dreamy flashbacks.
D: Richard Sarafian. A: Barry Newman, Cleavon Little, Dean Jagger.

White Lightning
(1973) 101m. **B–**
This tale of a moonshiner working undercover to get the goods on a corrupt sheriff is the first of Reynolds' redneck action films, and boasts a flavorful Deep South atmosphere, a darker tone, and more plausible action scenes than his later ones.
D: Joseph Sargent. A: Burt Reynolds, Jennifer Billingsley, Ned Beatty.

Dirty Mary, Crazy Larry
(1974) 93m. **B–**
There's nonstop car-chase action as the two bickering lovers race through Southern California eluding the highway patrol including Vic Morrow in a helicopter. A lighter, more entertaining chase thriller.
D: John Hough. A: Peter Fonda, Susan George, Adam Roarke.

Macon County Line
(1974) 87m. **C–**
In 1954 Georgia, an obsessive sheriff relentlessly pursues three innocent drifters he blames for the murder of his wife. "Jethro" from TV's *Beverly Hillbillies* wrote, produced, and overacted in this simpleminded backwoods melodrama.
D: Richard Compton. A: Max Baer, Alan Vint, Jesse Vint.

Return to Macon County
(1975) 90m. **B –**
Young Nolte and Johnson drive a souped-up Chevy en route to a California drag race, but the waitress they pick up starts trouble with some locals and the chase is on across state lines. Low-keyed, with the emphasis on character and some authentic flavor of rural America in 1958.
D: Richard Compton. A: Nick Nolte, Don Johnson, Robin Mattson.

White Line Fever
(1975) 89m. **C**
A dashing independent trucker, fresh out of the air force, stands up to corrupt bosses and strikes a blow for the honest worker. Earnest intentions are undermined by the predictable exploitation-style story and ordinary movie violence.
D: Jonathan Kaplan. A: Jan Michael Vincent, Kay Lenz, Slim Pickens.

Gator
(1976) 116m. **C –**
This sequel to *White Lightning* offers a lighter tone as Reynolds once again goes undercover—this time to get the goods on a corrupt political boss and old school friend. An awkward mix of comedy, wild chases, and harsh violence.
D: Burt Reynolds. A: Burt Reynolds, Lauren Hutton, Jerry Reed.

Jackson County Jail
(1976) 89m. **B**
A single woman fleeing the LA rat race gets caught up in a living nightmare of robbery, jail, rape, and a murder committed in self-defense. This sleeper hit is one deeply cynical, harsh, and menacing American trip.
D: Michael Miller. A: Yvette Mimieux, Tommy Lee Jones, Robert Carradine.

Convoy
(1978) 110m. **B –**
Peckinpah turned a popular song into a modern B-western about truckers in the Southwest banding together to protest unfair laws and police harassment. "Rubber Duck's" transformation into a media folk hero never rings true but the pageantry of the trucks and truckers have real flair.
D: Sam Peckinpah. A: Kris Kristofferson, Ali MacGraw, Ernest Borgnine.

The Great Smokey Roadblock
(1978) 84m. **C –**
Low-budget, rarely seen trucker film follows an old-timer on the lam from the finance company, who makes one last run—a truckload of prostitutes seeking a new home for their brothel. Mildly amusing but chiefly interesting for its cast.
D: John Leone. A: Henry Fonda, Eileen Brennan, Robert Englund.

Blaxploitation

Cashing in on the "inner city blues" of the black community in the 70s, Hollywood pumped out these action exploitation films featuring macho heroes who battled drug dealers, pimps, and hustlers of every stripe. While taking a formulaic approach to the guns-and-revenge theme, they still brought a sense of style to the genre with their outrageous fashions, colorful language, and irresistible soundtracks.

Shaft
(1971) 98m. **A –**
Private eye Shaft has the cool and bravado of 10 men as he looks for a kingpin's daughter kidnapped by the Mafia. This detective film in the Bogart mold serves up a Harlem underworld, colorful characters, and a relentless hero, all to an exhilarating Isaac Hayes score. Still fresh and the climactic rescue is a marvel of precision timing.
D: Gordon Parks, Jr. A: Richard Roundtree, Moses Gunn, Charles Cioffi.

Across 110th Street
(1972) 102m. **B**
A diamond in the rough, this highlights the symbiotic relationship between the cops and the mob during a manhunt for three losers who take off a Mafia-connected money drop. Features tough dialogue and a solid story from all sides, including the effects on innocent bystanders.
D: Barry Shear. A: Yaphet Kotto, Anthony Quinn, Paul Benjamin.

Shaft's Big Score!
(1972) 105m. **B –**
He's still tough-as-nails, but now Shaft is getting positively noble as he tries to play two rival mobsters off each other. The big car-boat-helicopter chase scene lacks the punch of the first film's rescue scene, the pace is slow, and Shaft is more fun when he's ruthless.
D: Gordon Parks, Jr. A: Richard Roundtree, Moses Gunn, Joseph Mascola.

Superfly
(1972) 96m. **A –**
O'Neal gives an edgy, about to explode performance as the drug dealer who wants out, but can only do it by pushing more drugs. A gritty story made somewhat glamorous with the help of Curtis Mayfield's seductive score, the extravagent fashions of wide-brimmed hats, full-length fur coats and suede suits, and a pre-"just say no" montage of New Yorkers doing cocaine.
D: Gordon Parks, Jr. A: Ron O'Neal, Carl Lee, Sheila Frazier.

Black Caesar
(1973) 94m. **C +**
This quirky and very low budget entry reworks *Little Caesar* as it traces the rise of a penniless shoeshine boy to Harlem kingpin. Don't miss the revenge scene where Caesar beats his main adversary to death with the shoeshine box that the man had used to cripple him as a boy.
D: Larry Cohen. A: Fred Williamson, Gloria Hendry, Julius W. Harris.

Cleopatra Jones
(1973) 89m. **B**
A smooth sophisticated international agent comes home to clean up her own neighborhood. This offers tongue-in-cheek action, clothes to rival *Superfly*'s, and Winters as the scenery-chewing villainess named Mommy.
D: Jack Starrett. A: Tamara Dobson, Bernie Casey, Shelley Winters.

Coffy
(1973) 91m. **C**
The nurse who's out to revenge her overdosed sister and murdered police friend infiltrates the drug lord's gang as a low-level hooker, and man by man works (and kills) her way to the top. A dark cautionary tale never to cross a woman with a sawed-off shotgun.
D: Jack Hill. A: Pam Grier,

Booker Bradshaw, Alan Arbus.

The Mack
(1973) 110m. **C**
This cult favorite shows how a small-time felon battles rivals and crooked cops to become the biggest and best pimp there is. Highlights include the Player's Ball (the Miss Universe of pimp contests), the always reliable Pryor, and some pimp costumes and cars that are not to be missed.
D: Michael Campus. A: Max Julien, Roger E. Mosley, Richard Pryor.

Foxy Brown
(1974) 92m. **B+**
A guilty pleasure among these films, this remake of *Coffy* lets the revenge plot take a backseat so that Grier can have the time of her life. Foxy is full of lusty sensuality, outrage, sisterhood and, yes, revenge; watch for the razor blade and pickle jar scenes.
D: Jack Hill. A: Pam Grier, Peter Brown, Terry Carter.

Truck Turner
(1974) 91m. **B**
Hayes isn't half bad as the skip tracer who's on the trail of a bail-jumping pimp. The dialogue is fun, the action is crisp, and *Star Trek*'s Lt. Uhura (Nichelle Nichols) camps it up as a Mae West-like madam in a leopard skin leotard.
D: Jonathan Kaplan. A: Isaac Hayes, Yaphet Kotto, Scatman Crothers.

Other Films:
The Final Comedown (1972)
Slaughter (1972)
Hell Up in Harlem (1973)
Hit! (1973)
Superfly T.N.T. (1973)
Black Belt Jones (1974)
The Black Gestapo (1974)
The Black Godfather (1974)
Three the Hard Way (1974)
Friday Foster (1975)
Bucktown (1975)
Sheba Baby (1975)

Bruce Lee

Lee was the world's reigning martial arts movie star when he died at 32, although he starred in only three Hong Kong films and one from the U.S. It's easy to fast-forward through much of these poorly dubbed, silly stories although they do have an exotic campy charm. Just don't miss any of Lee's scenes that showcase his wiry frame, rippling muscles, ferocious expression, and lightning-fast moves—often shot in slow motion for the viewer's benefit.

Fists of Fury (aka The Big Boss)
(1971) Dubbed. 103m. **C**
Lee's first starring vehicle is a sub-par crime story of a worker at an ice plant who uncovers the boss's heroin smuggling operation, which leads to a succession of fights with numerous thugs. Primarily for Lee completists.
D: Lo Wei. A: With Maria Yi, Tony Liu.

The Chinese Connection (aka Fist of Fury)
(1972) Dubbed. 107m.
A 🏆
In Japanese-occupied Shanghai, a kung fu student avenges the murder of his teacher, while contending with Japanese harassment. Formula kung fu tale of rival schools at war is enlivened by a steady succession of well-mounted fight scenes that showcase Lee's lightning movements.
D: Lo Wei. A: With Miao Ker Hsu, James Tien.

Enter the Dragon
(1973) 97m. **B**
Undercover agent Lee enters a martial arts tournament at an Asian crimelord's island stronghold. Lee's only Hollywood produced film (that's his real voice!) saddles him with two American martial arts costars and a hackneyed James Bond style story, but features some of his best fight scenes.
D: Robert Clouse. A: With John Saxon, Jim Kelly.

Return of the Dragon (aka Way of the Dragon)
(1973) 91m. **C+**
Lee is the naive country boy summoned to Rome to help a Chinese restaurant owner cope with the syndicate. Awkward script and direction (both by Lee) detract from the terrific action including a spectacular duel to the death with Norris in a studio re-creation of the Coliseum.
D: Bruce Lee. A: With Nora Miao, Chuck Norris.

Game of Death
(1978) 102m. **D–**
Enter the Dragon producers constructed a film around some fight scenes that Lee filmed before his death. An unconvincing double is used in this routine crime story while American actors pad out the action. Of interest for the match between Lee and seven-foot-tall Kareem Abdul Jabbar.
D: Robert Clouse. A: With Gig Young, Dean Jagger, Kareem Abdul-Jabbar.

Nostalgic Gangsters

The success of *Bonnie and Clyde* gave rise to these films about rural Depression-era bank robbers and lovers-on-the-run, and suddenly the gangster genre had a conscience, tongue-in-cheek humor, and irony between bloody shoot-outs. Despite or because these films have remained in the realm of low-budget and even exploitation films, most have aged well, losing none of their gritty immediacy or impact of raw-edged violence.

Bloody Mama
(1970) 90m. **B**
This stark, deglamorized, and often disturbing portrayal of the criminal life of Ma Barker and her four sons presents a depraved and dysfunctional family and its bloody trail of murder, rape, and robbery. The dark, ugly, and hopeless tone is relieved by a strong cast.
D: Roger Corman. A: Shelley Winters, Pat Hingle, Robert De Niro.

Boxcar Bertha
(1972) 92m. **B**
The true-life exploits of the gang of misfit train robbers, including orphan Bertha, an itinerant union organizer, and a con man/gambler. A dark doleful Depression atmosphere is enlivened by young director Scorsese's attempt to make an exploitation film more character- than action-driven.
D: Martin Scorsese. A: Barbara Hershey, David Carradine, Barry Primus.

Dillinger
(1973) 107m. **B+**
This action-packed and colorful version of a group of good ole boy career criminals on a Midwest crime spree is an energetic trip filled with humor, gunfire, and actors who seem to be
D: John Milius. A: Warren Oates, Ben Johnson, Michelle Phillips.

Big Bad Mama
(1974) 83m. **B**
A gutsy East Texan mother and her two dizzy young daughters embark on an interstate crime spree, picking up two male sidekicks along the way. Standard shoot-outs and chases are interspersed with comedy, sexual hijinks, and plenty of nude scenes of Angie, Shatner, and Skerritt. Sleazy and fun.
D: Steve Carver. A: Angie Dickinson, William Shatner, Tom Skerritt.

Lucky Luciano
(1974) 110m. **C**
The famed gangster is a shadowy ambiguous figure in this arty European production. Cold, stark, and very talky, it plays with time in an interesting way, almost like a thinking man's crime story.
D: Francesco Rosi. A: Gian Maria Volonte, Edmond O'Brien, Rod Steiger.

Crazy Mama
(1975) 82m. **C+**
Three generations of women go on a wild crime spree in 1950s middle America, with an added twang provided by Depression-era flashbacks. This has a comic approach tempered by a violent ending, but it still remains one of the best-looking, best-acted of the girls-with-guns films.
D: Jonathan Demme. A: Cloris Leachman, Ann Sothern, Linda Purl.

Lepke
(1975) 110m. **C**
Curtis makes an energetic Louis "Lepke" Buchalter, the notorious Jewish gangster of 1920s and 30s New York. The tawdry production compensates by packing a lot of lively episodes with characters like Dutch Schultz, Lucky Luciano, Walter Winchell, and Thomas E. Dewey.
D: Menahem Golan. A: Tony Curtis, Anjanette Comer, Warren Berlinger.

The Lady in Red
(1979) 93m. **C+**
The world of Chicago gangsters is seen from a woman's point of view as the title heroine goes from factory work to prison, prostitution, and waiting tables to romance with John Dillinger and a life of crime. This low-budget Corman production, written by John Sayles, makes up in energy and social conscience what it lacks in production values.
D: Lewis Teague. A: Pamela Sue Martin, Louise Fletcher, Robert Conrad.

Women Behind Bars

The plot: an innocent woman is thrown into a prison hellhole filled with hardened female criminals and leering guards with the lot of them lorded over by a sadistic warden. The only escape from a life sentence of showers and cat fights is over the wall. These earlier entries of the "Babes Behind Bars" genre boast chintzy production values worthy of the subject matter and an appeal that matches female mud-wrestling and wet T-shirt contests.

The Big Doll House
(1971) 93m. **C–**
On a remote banana republic island, a particularly cranky group of female convicts plans a breakout. Bug races, mud-bath cat fights, and not one, but two, sadistic wardenettes fill out this quick-paced lunacy.
D: Jack Hill. A: Pam Grier, Judy Brown, Roberta Collins.

The Big Bird Cage
(1972) 88m. **D+**
Revolutionary fervor and repressed passion seethe in a jungle jail, the title's bamboo hanging prison, filled with gay male guards. Washed-out Philippine location shooting adds to the low-class cachet.
D: Jack Hill. A: Pam Grier, Anitra Ford, Sid Haig.

The Big Bust Out
(1973) 75m. **D–**
Move the location of *The Big Bird Cage* to a Middle Eastern convent, replace Pam Grier with Vonetta McGee, and you have this tired rerun of the comparatively superior original.
D: Richard Jackson. A: Vonetta McGee, Linda Fox, Monica Taylor.

Caged Heat
(1974) 84m. **C–**
A variety of tough gals suffer and ultimately triumph over sadistic wheelchair warden Steele. Director Jonathan Demme's first feature is fast-paced, slipping bits of political and camp humor in between prison busts and obligatory shower scenes.
D: Jonathan Demme. A: Juanita Brown, Erica Gavion, Barbara Steele.

Fugitive Girls
(1975) 90m. **D**
Rag-tag femme cons go to jail, have sex, break out, join a commune, and take off their shirts as often as possible. The mind-twisting dialogue is courtesy of cowriter Ed Wood who also makes a cameo appearance.
D: A. C. Stephen. A: Renee Bond, Jackie Abercrombie, Edward D. Wood, Jr.

Survival

It's a jungle out there and innocent citizens hit all kinds of adversaries—whether urban gangs or rural rednecks—in the modern battle for survival.

Deliverance
(1972) 109m. **A**
A bloodcurdling account of a group of ordinary, middle-class joes white-water rafting their way into Southern, inbred horror. Nearly flawless on all accounts, with gorgeously shot backwoods locales, their filthy denizens, and an innocent river that turns into a spirit- and body-rending nightmare.
D: John Boorman. A: Jon Voight, Burt Reynolds, Ned Beatty.

Assault on Precinct 13
(1976) 90m. **A–**
The night turns into urban hell as the last occupants of a closing precinct station are suddenly under siege by a shadowy street gang. A low-budget, minimalist masterpiece with each scene a new terror-inducing turn-of-the-screw.
D: John Carpenter. A: Austin Stoker, Laurie Zimmer, Nancy Loomis.

The Warriors
(1979) 94m. **B**
New York becomes a surreal night world as opposing gangs fight their way from the Bronx to Brooklyn. With almost balletlike violence, this becomes a nonstop series of fever-pitched battles, with the characters' only goal to make it through the human-landmine strewn concrete jungle.
D: Walter Hill. A: Michael Beck, James Remar, Deborah Van Valkenburgh.

1980s–1990s

Kickboxing

Revenge and training for the Big Event are the leitmotifs of these low-budget actioners whose heroes overcome personal demons before winning a bloody and protracted kickboxing tournament. The most famous and probably the best of these star Belgian kickboxer Jean-Claude Van Damme, although his more recent films are emphasizing guns-and-bullets over flying-feet-and-fists.

Kickboxer 2: The Road Back
(1990) 90m. **B**
A pack of Asian gangsters menace a young American kickboxing competitor whose brother humiliated them in the past. The likable, fresh-faced hero adds some charm to his high-kicking abilities during the slow and bloody fight scenes.
D: Albert Pyun. A: Sasha Mitchell, Peter Boyle, Dennis Chan.

American Shaolin: King of the Kickboxers II
(1991) 103m. **B–**
After suffering a shattering defeat during a martial arts competition, a young American kickboxer travels to China to study Buddhism, only to be drawn back into the ring by his rivals. The typical karate battles and comeback storyline are helped by some creative plot twists.
D: Lucas Lowe. A: Reese Madigan, Daniel Dae Kim, Billy Chang.

Final Impact
(1991) 97m. **C+**
A fallen former kickboxing champion decides to help a novice fighter win the same competition he once lost. The ultraserious macho hero adds the only spark in this blatantly secondhand *Karate Kid*-style story.
D: Joseph Merhi, Stephen Smoke. A: Lorenzo Lamas, Mike Worth, Jeff Langton.

Other Films:
American Kickboxer (1991)
Breathing Fire (1991)
Desert Kickboxer (1992)
Kickboxer 3—Art of War (92)

Jean-Claude Van Damme

Bloodsport
(1987) 100m. **C+**
A young karate champion aims to be the first American winner of an infamously grueling Hong Kong martial arts competition. The intensity of the fighting sequences feels strangely muted in this predictable low-budget entry.
D: Newt Arnold. A: With Donald Gibb, Leah Ayres, Forest Whitaker.

Black Eagle
(1988) 93m. **B–**
After an American jet containing a secret tracking system goes down over the Mediterranean, a karate-chopping CIA agent must retrieve it before the Soviets do. Van Damme plays the villain in this weak blend of spy story with martial arts action.
D: Eric Carson. A: With Sho Kosugi, Vladimir Skomarovsky, Doran Clark.

Kickboxer
(1989) 97m. **C+**
After a kickboxing champion is crippled in the ring by a vicious rival, his younger brother vows to defeat him in retaliation. Standard revenge story is enlivened by some of the bone-crushing karate clashes.
D: Mark DeSalle, David Worth. A. With Denis Alexio, Dennis Chan, Tong Po.

Death Warrant
(1990) 89m. **C**
A Canadian Mountie goes undercover to solve a series of mysterious murders in prison, but his investigation is threatened by the arrival of a killer he once sent to jail. A suspenseful story punctuated by grueling fight scenes.
D: Deran Sarafian. A: With Robert Guillaume, Cynthia Gibb, George Dickerson.

Double Impact
(1991) 118m. **B+**
Separated after their parents are murdered by gangsters, twin baby boys grow up to become an aerobics instructor and a shady smuggler, eventually reuniting to catch their parents' killers. Van

Damme plays the twins in this fast-paced thriller containing unexpected humor and some romance.
D: Sheldon Lettich. A: With Geoffrey Lewis, Alan Scarge, Alonna Shaw.

Nowhere to Run
(1993) 95m. **B**

A lethal but good-natured escaped prisoner hides out at the home of a beautiful widow and her children, who are being harassed by land developers. The action is expertly staged, but the clichéd plot and awkward tender moments are major distractions.
D: Robert Harmon. A: With Rosanna Arquette, Kiernan Culkin, Ted Levine.

Hard Target
(1993) 92m. **B+**

A cartel of millionaires makes sport of hunting and killing human game until they target a homeless Vietnam vet with the lethal skills to fight back. Above-average entry features amazing stunts, gut-wrenching violence, and incredibly photographed karate and machine-gun confrontations.
D: John Woo. A: With Lance Henriksen, Wilford Brimley, Yancy Butler.

Martial Arts

The main difference between American kung fu films and the regular revenge action movies is that these martial arts heroes all have karate-chopping skills along with the usual arsenal of automatic weapons. The plots follow the maverick-loner against the gangster-villain routine, punctuated by glass smashing, bullets flying, and, of course, kicks and punches being thrown, often in slow motion.

Ninja III: The Domination
(1984) 95m. **C+**

A spirit of a ninja gangster killed by the police returns in the body of an American woman who must then battle his crimefighting rival. The best in the series features an unorthodox villain coupled with the usual swords and throwing stars action.
D: Sam Firstenberg. A: Lucinda Dicky, Jordan Bennett, Sho Kosugi.

No Retreat, No Surrender
(1985) 85m. **C**

Trained by the ghost of Bruce Lee, a wimpy Seattle teen becomes a karate fighter good enough to beat both street bullies and a fearsome Russian champion. The imaginative twist to the *Rocky/Karate Kid* formula makes up for the fake-looking fight scenes and shallow performances.
D: Corey Yuen. A: Kurt McKinney, Jean-Claude Van Damme, J. W. Fails.

American Ninja II
(1987) 96m. **B–**

Two karate-chopping American soldiers search for marines who vanished on a tropical island, and discover that the missing men are being trained by a heroin kingpin. The bland hero is assisted by a suspenseful story and some knockout fight sequences.
D: Sam Firstenberg. A: Michael Dudikoff, Steve James, Larry Poindexter.

No Retreat, No Surrender II
(1987) 92m. **C+**

An American karate ace travels to Vietnam where he battles the Communist soldiers who kidnapped his Asian girlfriend. Bearing no resemblance to the first in the series, this martial arts version of *Rambo* has a weak plot but almost nonstop action.
D: Corey Yuen. A: Loreen Avedon, Max Thayer, Keith Vitali.

Best of the Best
(1989) 95m. **B–**

A multiethnic team of American karate competitors must overcome personal demons while training to fight the undefeated Korean champions. The heroes actually have well-defined personalities, but there's more training scenes than combat, with the ever predictable conclusion.
D: Robert Radler. A: Eric Roberts, James Earl Jones, Chris Penn.

Blind Fury
(1990) 86m. **B+**

A blind Western samurai comes to the aid of a boy whose father, a fellow Vietnam vet, has been kidnapped by upscale drug lords. An appealing hero and relatively lighthearted atmosphere add a humorous edge to the sword-fighting and gangbusting.
D: Phillip Noyce. A: Rutger Hauer, Terry O'Quinn, Brandon Call.

Rage and Honor
(1992) 93m. **B**

A karate-kicking LA teacher pairs up with an Australian cop in order to stop a crack-peddling policeman led by her brother. A fiery heroine, her charming partner, and their blend of bullets and flying feet and fists help overcome the ridiculous plot.
D: Terence H. Winkless. A: Cynthia Rothrock, Richard Norton, Terri Treas.

Rapid Fire
(1992) 95m. **B+**

After witnessing a mob killing, a karate-trained college student and his girlfriend are hunted from California to China in this explosive combination of spectacular kung fu action and machine-gun shoot-outs.
D: Dwight Little. A: Brandon Lee, Powers Boothe, Nick Mancuso.

Bloodfist V: Human Target
(1993) 84m. **B–**

A federal agent must fight both crooks and his own colleagues after he loses his memory and they mistake him for a traitor. The authentic kickboxing skills of the hero are combined with the most original plot in the series.
D: Jeff Yonis. A: Don "The Dragon" Wilson, Denice Duff, Steve James.

Dragon: The Bruce Lee Story
(1993) 119m. **A–**

The life story of the international martial arts movie star is told as a love story, a kung fu epic, and a mystical fantasy. Jason Scott Lee is splendid, and the film's sincere corniness lets you relax and enjoy the dynamic kung fu battles that capture all the cartoonish exuberance of Hong Kong action films.
D: Rob Cohen. A: Jason Scott Lee, Laren Holly, Robert Wagner.

Other Films:
Enter the Ninja (1981)
Kill and Kill Again (1981)
Revenge of the Ninja (1983)
American Ninja (1985)
China O'Brien (1988)
China O'Brien (1989)
Bloodfist (1989)
Bloodfist 2 (1989)
Bloodfist III: Forced to Fight (1991)
Bloodfist IV: Die Trying (1992)
Bloodfist VI: Ground Zero (1994)
No Retreat, No Surrender III: Blood Brothers (1990)
My Samurai (1992)
Showdown in Little Tokyo (1991)
Rage and Honor II: Hostile Takeover (1993)
Only the Strong (1993)
Undefeatable (1993)

Swashbucklers

Would there have been a swashbuckler revival in the 80s without the wild success of *Raiders of the Lost Ark*? With rare exceptions these tongue-in-cheek tales center on a bestubbled adventurer and a spunky damsel as they romp through a series of near death escapes and battle a parade of cartoonish villains in search of one grail or another.

Raiders of the Lost Ark

(1981) 116m. **A+**

Rough and tumble archeologist Indiana Jones grapples with Nazis to secure a powerful religious artifact. Bursts with hilariously unbelievable escapes, chases, fights, and a dazzling conclusion that even includes the wrath of God.
D: Steven Spielberg. A: Harrison Ford, Karen Allen, Paul Freeman.

Indiana Jones and the Temple of Doom

(1984) 118m. **B+**

Indiana, accompanied by a lounge singer and a street-smart Chinese lad, battles Indian cult leaders and Thuggee killers while trying to recover a sacred stone. Includes juvenile romantic sparring, intense torture scenes, and some of the most invigorating and sustained chases ever filmed.
D: Steven Spielberg. A: Harrison Ford, Kate Capshaw, Ke Huy Kwan.

Romancing the Stone

(1984) 105m. **B+**

A romance novelist joins up with a gruff adventurer to search for her missing sister in a green and splashy South America. An attempt at a more mature *Lost Ark* with added romantic sparks. Offers lots of wild chases, feats of brinkmanship, and two comic greasy con men.
D: Robert Zemeckis. A: Michael Douglas, Kathleen Turner, Danny DeVito.

The Jewel of the Nile

(1985) 104m. **B–**

In this sequel to *Romancing the Stone*, the romance novelist accepts a writing job for a mysterious Arab, and gets neck deep in a jewel theft. Since we already know the characters, they cut straight to the action with more escapes and bigger explosions. There's heat under the Nile's bright sun, but the romance is over.
D: Lewis Teague. A: Michael Douglas, Kathleen Turner, Danny DeVito.

King Solomon's Mines

(1985) 100m. **C–**

Grizzled White Hunter Quatermain searches for a lost treasure in Africa with a tough-talking blonde in tow. Plenty of narrow escapes from wild beasts, comic villains, and cool 1930s trappings, but little chemistry between the leads.
D: J. Lee Thompson. A: Richard Chamberlain, Sharon Stone, Herbert Lom.

Remo Williams: The Adventure Begins

(1985) 121m. **C+**

Tough New York City cop is recruited to battle an arms merchant and rogue general but must first learn the mystic ways of a wise Korean taskmaster. It's *Indiana Jones* meets *Kung Fu* in this enjoyable East meets West that takes too long to get to the adventure.
D: Guy Hamilton. A: Fred Ward, Joel Grey, Wilford Brimley.

Big Trouble in Little China

(1986) 99m. **C**

Crusty truck driver and two guys from Chinatown battle an underworld figure who's kidnapped the green-eyed girl to enhance his magical powers. Now it's *Indiana Jones* meets *Kung Fu*, but with more mysticism thrown in. Cheeky humor and high action ratio moves it along.
D: John Carpenter. A: Kurt Russell, Kim Cattrall, Dennis Dun.

Allan Quatermain and the Lost City of Gold

(1987) 103m. **D**

Explorer Quatermain searches for his brother who was on the trail of a tribe of white men living in Africa. Incompetent, badly edited adventure that lacks the humor and thrills of this genre.
D: Gary Nelson. A: Richard Chamberlain, Sharon Stone, Henry Silva.

Indiana Jones and the Last Crusade

(1989) 127m. **A–**

Indiana's father disappears while searching for the Holy Grail and the chase is on with the Nazis in hot pursuit. The globe-trotting chases lack any sense of urgency, but father and son Jones bicker, spar, and bond winsomely.
D: Steven Spielberg. A: Harrison Ford, Sean Connery, Alison Doody.

Congo

(1995) 120m. **B–**

The diamond-filled city of Zinj and a home for a cyber-voiced gorilla are the goals for this very modern "safari" team headed for Africa. An entertaining homage to cheesy 50s B adventures complete with a mysterious, horrifying creature and a hilariously updated native menace.
D: Frank Marshall. A: Laura Linney, Dylan Walsh, Tim Curry.

Bond, James Bond

Bond may have started out as a debonair spy. Now he's becoming more of a tough action hero (and a rather hardy and cynical one as played by Timothy Dalton) as the 007 series continues to go the route of loud explosions, elaborate action sequences, and campily played sex scenes.

For Your Eyes Only
(1981) 136m. **B**

The British and Russians are back on opposite sides of the fence as they vie for a secret tracking device. A darker Bond kicks in with criminals and a vengeful daughter in a well-paced and exciting film that discards the gadgets and silliness.
D: John Glen. A: Roger Moore, Carole Bouquet, Topol.

Never Say Never Again
(1983) 134m. **B+**

The cool and sophisticated, not to mention older and wiser, Bond is back to duel with a SPECTRE baddie in Monte Carlo who has two cruise missiles and wants some cash. Updated *Thunderball* with a dynamic group of villains.
D: Irvin Kershner. A: Sean Connery, Klaus Maria Brandauer, Kim Basinger.

Octopussy
(1983) 140m. **B+**

Czarist treasures are being sold in a complex plot to plant a nuclear bomb in West Germany and begin a Russian invasion. A stunningly beautiful India is the background for this rousing blend of travelogue and Cold War drama with a hint of *Indiana Jones*.
D: John Glen. A: Roger Moore, Maud Adams, Louis Jourdan.

A View to a Kill
(1986) 131m. **C**

An evil industrialist plans to corner the microchip market by blowing up Silicon Valley. Tired-looking 007 saddled with a quirky but not very menacing villain, a totally ditzy female sidekick, and less than spectacular set action pieces.
D: John Glen. A: Roger Moore, Christopher Walken, Tanya Roberts.

The Living Daylights
(1987) 130m. **B**

Bond uncovers a Soviet double agent, protects his innocent girlfriend, and battles a ruthless arms dealer in a gritty and complex espionage tale. Dalton's Bond is still cool and still the best, but this Bond has to work hard and takes some blows along the way.
D: John Glen. A: Timothy Dalton, Maryam d'Abo, Jeroen Krabbé.

Licence to Kill
(1989) 133m. **C**

Bond gives up his 007 license to avenge the brutal maiming of his best friend by a South American drug kingpin. Jarringly un-Bondian tale of revenge featuring vicious fighting, gun-toting non-bimbo femme fatales, and a genuinely evil central villain.
D: John Glen. A: Timothy Dalton, Carey Lowell, Robert Davi.

Historical Epics and Swashbucklers

Hollywood action heroes aren't all muscle-bound urban vigilantes as witnessed by these tales that portray the bold exploits and violence that was the way of life for New World explorers and professional adventurers of times past.

Lion of the Desert
(1981) 160m. **B**

This history lesson from an Arab perspective presents the story of Omar Muktar, Islam scholar and tactical/spiritual leader of the Libyan resistance to Mussolini's invasion. Big entertaining adventure that pauses for moments of philosophy with an aim to being an inspiring epic, but finally settles for wartime action.
D: Moustapha Akkad. A: Anthony Quinn, Oliver Reed, Rod Steiger.

The Bounty
(1984) 132m. **B−**

A more evenhanded, less dramatic treatment of the classic tale in which rule-bound Captain Bligh is cast adrift by impetuous Christian and his mutineers. Features a beautifully built *Bounty,* a lush Pitcairn Island, enough fawning maidens to turn an old salt's head, and Hopkins who offers a quiet repressed dignity as Bligh.
D: Roger Donaldson. A: Mel Gibson, Anthony Hopkins, Daniel Day-Lewis.

Utu
(1984) 104m. **C+**

"Utu" means revenge for New Zealand Maori tribesmen, and that is what a former scout vows when the British troops who had employed him massacre his village. This offers little subtlety with vivid scenes of cruelty, bad dubbing, and a trial sequence that seems to have been edited down to nothingness.
D: Geoff Murphy. A: Anzac Wallace, Kelly Johnson, Tim Elliot.

The Sicilian
(1987) 115m. **C−**

A busy, bloody, and boring stew of Sicilian politics offers a postwar Sicily run by the Church, Mafia, and the local landowners. You need a scorecard to figure out who hates and kills who, since blood oaths and vendettas are the only social etiquette these characters seem to know.
D: Michael Cimino. A: Christopher Lambert, Terence Stamp, John Turturro.

The Deceivers
(1988) 112m. **C**

A British officer in Colonial India infiltrates the traveler-killing Thuggee cult and, with the help of drugs and culture immersion, begins to lose himself in their practices. An unfocused mix of white flannel costume drama with modern gore, drugs, and erotica.
D: Nicholas Meyer. A: Pierce Brosnan, Shashi Kapoor, Saeed Jaffrey.

Crusoe
(1989) 94m. **B−**

This politically correct retell-

ing casts Robinson Crusoe as a snobby Virginia slave-owner shipwrecked on an African island, whose life is saved any number of times by a noble black warrior. The Club Med island beauty and Quinn's expert performance help balance the obvious message that's served up a little too often.
D: Caleb Deschanel. A: Aidan Quinn, Ade Sapara, Jimmy Nail.

Return of the Musketeers
(1989) 101m. **C+**
The director and major cast members from the 70s *Musketeers* films have a brave go at reviving the bawdy slapstick and add a dash of melancholy for the old days. The genial spirit and deliciously earthy setting still may be there, but the exuberance in the action sequences isn't.
D: Richard Lester. A: Michael York, Oliver Reed, Richard Chamberlain.

Mountains of the Moon
(1990) 135m. **B+**
This true-life story of Victorian explorer Sir Richard Burton is both adventure yarn and study of the personalities and machinations involved in such exploits. The rousing action scenes of the perilous African expedition are marked by compelling ones in England as disputes about credit and funding split the Royal Geographic Society.
D: Bob Rafelson. A: Patrick Bergin, Iain Glen, Richard E. Grant.

Robin Hood: Prince of Thieves
(1991) 120m. **B–**
This updated tale has a Robin whose English accent waffles, a Marian with an attitude, and a Sheriff of Nottingham who is more psycho-sick than evilly plotting. Moody and slow-moving at first, it kicks in as Robin gathers his merry forces, and the arrowplay and action commence.
D: Kevin Reynolds. A: Kevin Costner, Morgan Freeman, Mary Elizabeth Mastrantonio.

Christopher Columbus: The Discovery
(1992) 120m. **D**
This account of Columbus' adventure misses nearly every chance for drama, even making Torquemada into a kind of nasty puppy dog. The voyage is a routine string of incidents (mutiny, sabotage), the brief visit to the New World involves some topless natives and a few skirmishes, and then it's back to Spain for some back-slapping.
D: John Glen. A: Georges Corraface, Rachel Ward, Marlon Brando.

1492: The Conquest of Paradise
(1992) 152m. **C–**
This Christopher Columbus entry nearly drowns itself in atmosphere from the ornate Spanish court to the ripe and greenish aura of the New World that is despoiled by the gold-hungry Christians. Edited scenes would make a beautiful documentary but as drama, it's as flat as the earth is round.
D: Ridley Scott. A: Gerard Depardieu, Armand Assante, Sigourney Weaver.

The Last of the Mohicans
(1992) 122m. **B+**
A white man raised by Indians falls in love with a young British woman during the French and Indian War. This lush version of Cooper's classic gives you a rousing history lesson, some romance, and a lot of scenes of longhaired, barechested Day-Lewis running through forests and mountain paths to save his lady love.
D: Michael Mann. A: Daniel Day-Lewis, Madeleine Stowe, Russell Means.

The Three Musketeers
(1994) 105m. **B–**
Generation X-keteers prance about in their dashing uniforms and cool goatees while Cardinal Richelieu is almost campily lascivious. The Dumas story gets pared down in favor of buddy quipping, hijinks, and MTV-style edited swordplay. Painless and fast, with no staying power.
D: Stephen Herek. A: Charlie Sheen, Kiefer Sutherland, Rebecca De Mornay.

Women Behind Bars

As the Women's Prison genre hacked its way into the 80s with its popularity—and lack of taste—undiminished, the films actually began to offer better photography, recognizable stars, and even an occasional glimmer of humor. But make no mistake; not one has tampered with the formula of violence, gratuitous nudity, and a sort of low-rent class-warfare plotline.

The Concrete Jungle
(1982) 99m. **D+**
A girl unjustly imprisoned for possession of coke goes head-to-head with the drug-dealing warden. Notably lacking in truly sleazy or overly ridiculous ingredients that fans of this genre admire.
D: Tom DeSimone. A: Tracy Bregman, Peter Brown, Jill St. John.

Chained Heat
(1983) 97m. **C–**
New inmate Blair is terrorized by fellow convicts and a scurrilous, Jacuzzi-lounging, cokehead male warden. Relatively well made, action-paced, and sure to be relished by aficionados.
D: Paul Nicolas. A: Linda Blair, Sybil Danning, Stella Stevens.

Caged Women
(1984) 97m. **F**
Trying to expose a prison's sadistic methods, a journalist poses as a prostitute to get inside the big house. Grungy looking and filled with repulsive scenes of torture.
D: Vincent Dawn. A: Laura Gemser, Gabriele Tinti.

The Naked Cage
(1986) 97m. **C**
This briskly directed entry nearly makes it as a "real" movie with its well-staged race war, antidrug stance, and almost serious treatment, but the obligatory nudity, MTV-style clothes, and pop music still trip it up.
D: Paul Nicholas. A: Shari Shattuck, Angel Tompkins, Lucinda Crosby.

Reform School Girls
(1986) 94m. **C+**
Part exploitation, part parody of the genre; still has copious nudity and more clichés than you can shake a guard's stick at, but is made almost interesting by leering punk rocker Williams and the Bible-quoting warden.
D: Tom DeSimone. A: Linda Carol, Wendy O. Williams, Sybil Danning.

Buddy Cops

Big city crime-busting is the excuse to pair up two mismatched guys in these loud, violent, and fast-paced crime thrillers that cross the joking camaraderie of *Butch Cassidy and the Sundance Kid* with the hard-boiled aesthetics of *Dirty Harry*. The shoot-outs, extended car chases, and exploding skyscrapers distract you from the formulaic plots, with the best of them providing some laughs as these odd couples squabble and battle the parade of bad guys.

48 Hrs.
(1982) 97m. **A–**
Grizzled detective Nolte "borrows" convicted thief Murphy for two days in order to catch the latter's ex-partner in crime. Even though the car chases and shoot-outs seem relatively tame, the edgy comic rapport between the burnt-out cop and the jive-talking hood make this fast and funny.
D: Walter Hill. A: Nick Nolte, Eddie Murphy, Annette O'Toole.

Running Scared
(1986) 106m. **B**
Two wisecracking cops vow to leave their dreary Chicago beats for the Caribbean, but first they have one last gangster to nail. The gag-a-minute banter makes for lighthearted fun in the Windy City, but the muddled plot and lack of notable action make this one for Crystal fans.
D: Peter Hyams. A: Billy Crystal, Gregory Hines, Stephen Bauer.

Lethal Weapon
(1987) 110m. **A**
By-the-book detective Glover is hilariously partnered with suicidal Gibson on the trail of a brutal LA drug cartel. The hard-edged characters, sharp jolts of violence, and sly sometimes rollicking comedy provide unrelenting thrills.
D: Richard Donner. A: Mel Gibson, Danny Glover, Gary Busey.

Red Heat
(1988) 106m. **C+**
Chasing a Russian dope dealer to Chicago, a starched Soviet policeman teams up with a sloppy local cop, and the usual cross-cultural jokes ensue, interrupted by action that's as ordinary as the story.
D: Walter Hill. A: Arnold Schwarzenegger, James Belushi, Laurence Fishburne.

Shoot to Kill
(1988) 110m. **B**
FBI agent Poitier must trek through the Pacific Northwest with the help of mountain man Berenger in order to catch an escaped killer who's hiding among a group of outdoorsmen. No loud and violent urban explosions here, just a rugged chase and athletic performances from the stars.
D: Roger Spottiswoode. A: Sidney Poitier, Tom Berenger, Kirstie Alley.

Lethal Weapon 2
(1989) 113m. **B+**
The cautious LA cop and his rule-breaking partner are hot on the trail of South African smugglers in this ultra-fast-paced sequel that features bigger and more expensive explosions, sharper wiseguy comedy, a little sex, and chatterbox Pesci to lighten things up.
D: Richard Donner. A: Mel Gibson, Danny Glover, Joe Pesci.

Tango and Cash
(1989) 98m. **C–**
Blow-dried, muscle-bound LA police rivals team up to trade barbs, drive armored vehicles, and wield ridiculously sophisticated machine guns in this dumb but harmless comic action film.
D: Andrei Konchalovsky. A: Kurt Russell, Sylvester Stallone, Jack Palance.

Air America
(1990) 112m. **C**
Rookie pilot Downey plays the idealistic straight man to Gibson's cynical smuggler in this true tale of a CIA-sponsored airline in Laos during the Vietnam War. Mildly funny at first, the film's shift to drama hasn't the substance or exciting action to sustain interest.
D: Roger Spottiswoode. A: Mel Gibson; Robert Downey, Jr.; Nancy Travis.

Another 48 Hrs.
(1990) 95m. **B**
Nolte gets convict Murphy to help him crack another case, this one involving a rampaging motorcycle gang. Has more explosive action sequences than the first one, but the leads act like they're in different movies, and Murphy seems stuck in overdrive.
D: Walter Hill. A: Nick Nolte, Eddie Murphy, Kevin Tighe.

The Rookie
(1990) 121m. **D**
A tough-as-nails veteran cop and a spoiled new guy are the odd couple chasing German villains in this mess of a movie. Limp comedy and by-the-numbers action are enlivened by the campy spectacle of Sonia Braga attempting to rape Clint.
D: Clint Eastwood. A: Clint Eastwood, Charlie Sheen, Raul Julia.

Lethal Weapon 3
(1992) 118m. **B+**
On the eve of retirement, family man Glover joins reckless Gibson to catch a crooked gun-dealing cop. Familiar mix of comedy and high-profile action with a bigger dash of romance, but the excitement is oozing away.
D: Richard Donner. A: Mel Gibson, Danny Glover, Joe Pesci.

Cops and Crime Thrillers

Every type of maverick cop disgusted with the system and big city crime turns up in these thrillers. Their adversaries are sleazy and sometimes charismatic but the snappiest lines and the sleekest handguns are left to the urban cowboy heroes, who shine brightest in these cop tales when paired with big budgets, clever plots, and full-throttle action sequences.

The Border
(1982) 107m. **B−**

Border cop Nicholson struggles with corruption in the ranks and his shrewish wife's material demands. This takes its time building to an explosive third reel, but a stellar cast, some nasty doings, evocatively arid locales, and a matching sleazy ambience make it worth the wait.
D: Tony Richardson. A: Jack Nicholson, Valerie Perrine, Harvey Keitel.

Blue Thunder
(1983) 108m. **C+**

An LA policeman avenges his partner's murder by "borrowing" a high-tech helicopter to battle a treacherous fellow cop and corrupt administrators. The sky high 'copter battle provides the action for an otherwise routine good cop vs. rogue cop story.
D: John Badham. A: Roy Scheider, Malcolm McDowell, Daniel Stern.

Beverly Hills Cop
(1984) 105m. **B+**

A street-smart Detroit cop tracks a killer to LA, where his brash style clashes with the uptight natives. Murphy's profane punch lines add much-needed hilarity to the flashy but predictable fish-out-of-water situations while a surprising level of violence provides the jolts.
D: Martin Brest. A: Eddie Murphy, Judge Reinhold, John Ashton.

Murphy's Law
(1986) 100m. **C−**

A dedicated detective must clear his name after being framed for murder by the crazy killer he captured years earlier. Bronson is totally unbelievable as a victim, even if it's of circumstances, and the climactic revenge sequence has the all too familiar *Death Wish*-style gunplay.
D: J. Lee Thompson. A: Charles Bronson, Carrie Snodgrass, Kathleen Wihoite.

Beverly Hills Cop II
(1987) 105m. **B−**

Detroit cop Murphy returns to Beverly Hills after his former captain is critically wounded and once again shakes up the town's high-society residents. The star's laugh is still infectious, but his sequel offers less comedy and more loud, big-budget action than the original.
D: Tony Scott. A: Eddie Murphy, Brigitte Nielsen, Judge Reinhold.

Fatal Beauty
(1987) 104m. **C−**

A scrappy undercover cop investigates the drug-related murder of a lowlife friend. This manages to be slow *and* violent, and for once Whoopi lacks charm.
D: Tom Holland. A: Whoopi Goldberg, Sam Elliot, Ruben Blades.

Action Jackson
(1988) 95m. **C**

This has all the ingredients: a dedicated rogue cop, a charismatic gangster, an evil seductress, shoot-outs and fisticuffs, with little sense of style or humor.
D: Craig Baxley. A: Carl Weathers, Craig T. Nelson, Sharon Stone.

Cop
(1988) 110m. **B+**

An unethical police detective breaks every rule in the book as he chases a vicious serial killer in New York City. Wood's own sadistic tendencies and complete disregard for morality make him the perfect "hero" for this hard-boiled thriller that blends unsettling violence with an obvious affection for classic pulp fiction
D: James B. Harris. A: James Woods, Lesley Ann Warren, Charles Durning.

Dead Bang
(1988) 103m. **C−**

A troubled cop leaves LA to hunt down a murderous white supremacist organization in the Southwest. Routine story isn't helped by the rule-bending hero and low-life villains singing the same note over and over.
D: John Frankenheimer. A: Don Johnson, Penelope Ann Miller, William Forsythe.

The Presidio
(1988) 97m. **B−**

While investigating a murder on a San Francisco army base, a cocky detective butts heads with his girlfriend's stubborn father, a military policeman on the same case. The action sequences of the Presidio may have a foggy feel, but the story's dull and the stars lack pizzazz.
D: Peter Hyams. A: Mark Harmon, Sean Connery, Meg Ryan.

Black Rain
(1989) 125m. **B+**

New York cops chase down an escaped mobster in Japan, aided by, and often clashing with, the Tokyo police. Visually stylish but both the chase and the story of gangster-style American cops vs. the traditional Japanese peters out a half-hour before the action finale.
D: Ridley Scott. A: Michael Douglas, Andy Garcia, Ken Takakura.

Harlem Nights
(1989) 118m. **D**

In 1930s Harlem, jive-talking nightclub owners spar with murderous vixens, crooked cops, and a gangster intent on putting them out of business. The talent here is amazingly wasted in this humorless period thriller, containing a confusing plot and plenty of unnecessary, unexciting violence.
D: Eddie Murphy. A: Eddie Murphy, Richard Pryor, Redd Foxx.

A Rage in Harlem
(1991) 98m. **B**

A beautiful con artist arrives in Harlem in the 1950s with contraband gold and proceeds to dupe a smitten innocent into keeping it from the local mobsters. Appealing characters, nice period flavor, and less violence make up for the slow pace in this con men/woman vs. con men tale.
D: Bill Duke. A: Forest Whitaker, Robin Givens, Gregory Hines.

Ricochet
(1991) 97m. **C+**

A hotshot cop collars a psychotic killer, but years later the wacko shows up to turn his life into hell. Every story element seems borrowed from better films, but this revenge fantasy's escalating level of sadistic violence —if that's your cup of tea—keeps it from growing dull.
D: Russell Mulcahy. A: Denzel Washington, John Lithgow, Lindsay Wagner.

Kuffs
(1992) 102m. **B–**
This attempt at a hipper approach to the genre—Slater addresses the camera with wry philosophical comments like a young George Burns—follows irresponsible George Kuffs who becomes a quasi-official San Francisco crime fighter. A relatively light and clean outing with more witticisms than gunfire.
D: Bruce Evans. A: Christian Slater, Tony Goldwyn, Milla Jovovich.

Boiling Point
(1993) 92m. **C+**
An FBI man is hot on the trail of the criminal sleazebag who killed his partner. Snipes and Hopper play this to the hilt, giving the little substance to the thin plot and action.
D: James B. Harris. A: Wesley Snipes, Dennis Hopper, Lolita Davidovich.

Burt Reynolds

After starring in his good ole boys car-crashing comedies in the 70s, Reynolds attempted the transition to action hero with this series of tough-minded, low-budget, and almost humorless crime thrillers.

Sharky's Machine
(1981) 119m. **B**
A tough maverick cop spies on, and eventually falls for, a beautiful call girl whose criminal employers are also police targets. A convincingly dark troubled hero combines with a raucous supporting cast of misfit lawmen and some brutal violence for a fairly exciting thriller.
D: Burt Reynolds. A: With Rachel Ward, Vittorio Gassman, Charles Durning.

Stick
(1985) 109m. **C+**
A master thief leaves prison and ingratiates himself with a Miami crime organization, planning to sabotage it from within. The subtle characters and fast dialogue from the Elmore Leonard novel are lost in this slow, cheap-looking thriller, which still possesses a spectacular climactic stunt.
D: Burt Reynolds. A: With Candice Bergen, Charles Durning, George Segal.

Heat
(1987) 101m. **C+**
While trying to locate a missing woman, a freelance mercenary tangles with the arrogant young Las Vegas gangster who brutalized his friend. A few scenes of inventive violence can't compensate for a flat story and a comatose star.
D: R. M. Richards. A: With Karen Young, Peter MacNicol, Howard Hesseman.

Rent-a-Cop
(1988) 96m. **C–**
A reckless police detective is in hot water over a series of brutal murders, and must find the killer with the help of a prostitute eyewitness. Burt is perkier here but the plot's not, and Minnelli is completely unconvincing as the hooker with the heart of gold.
D: Jerry London. A: With Liza Minnelli, James Remar, Dionne Warwick.

Teen Action

MTV video stylistics, Reagan-era jingoism, and whatever else was available for an exploitative thrill filled these quick-paced action films as Hollywood did its darnedest to cater to the youth of the go-go 80s.

Cloak and Dagger
(1984) 101m. **B+**
A lonely boy creates an imaginary super-spy pal named Jack Flack and gets mixed up in real-life espionage antics. Tight script, quick pace, and light but not moronic tone makes this the rare entry that can be responsibly called family fare.
D: Richard Franklin. A: Henry Thomas, Dabney Coleman, Michael Murphy.

The Goonies
(1985) 120m. **C–**
Oregon hardscrabble tots find a treasure map leading them to a world of whimsy, strange caverns, and riches. A mega-budget attempt at old-fashioned Saturday matinee-style adventure that's strictly aimed at the ten-year-old set.
D: Richard Donner. A: Sean Astin, Corey Feldman, Martha Plimpton.

Iron Eagle
(1986) 117m. **C–**
When a U.S. pilot is shot down by Arabs, his son goes in to rescue him with retired pilot Gossett and a couple of stolen planes. Another chest-thumping actioner, but with the pounding accompaniment of Twisted Sister's "We're Not Gonna Take It," this could be another Saturday at the arcade.
D: Sidney Furie. A: Lou Gossett, Jr.; Jason Gedrick; Tim Thomerson.

Gleaming the Cube
(1989) 105m. **C**
Barely postpubescent Slater is an ace skateboarder who hits the vengeance trail when his Vietnam vet brother is killed. Already dated in attitude and slang, with vertigo-inducing skateboard sequences for the faithful.
D: Graeme Clifford. A: Christian Slater, Steven Bauer, Ed Lauter.

Toy Soldiers
(1991) 104m. **C**
This could be called the *Dirty Half Dozen* as a group of hell-raising youths shows who's who to a bunch of terrorists taking over their military academy. A standard issue story with good performances by Astin and the über mentor of teens, Gossett.
D: Daniel Petrie, Jr. A: Sean Astin, Denholm Elliot, Lou Gossett, Jr.

Odd Couples on the Lam

These films offer a slight twist on the buddy road films: have a mismatched couple, like a cop and a criminal, chasing or being chased through America, and you've got a comic setup that's *The Odd Couple* meets the Roadrunner.

Midnight Run
(1988) 123m. **A**

A foul-mouthed bounty hunter has to escort his squirrely mob accountant prisoner across country, with both the FBI and the Mafia in pursuit. This pair's chemistry—Grodin nags De Niro about his cholesterol, De Niro barks back like a henpecked husband—is hilarious, and the fast-paced plot twists and action sequences won't let you catch your breath.
D: Martin Brest. A: Robert De Niro, Charles Grodin, Yaphet Kotto.

Pink Cadillac
(1989) 122m. **C+**

A chameleonlike bounty hunter tries to help his smooth-talking captive rescue her baby from her estranged husband and his ruthless friends. There's no spark in the story or between the characters, although Clint's amusingly awkward.
D: Buddy Van Horn. A: Clint Eastwood, Bernadette Peters, William Hickey.

Bird on a Wire
(1990) 111m. **B–**

A successful lawyer bumps into her ex-boyfriend who's hiding in the witness protection program, and the two go on the lam from his drug-dealing enemies. Gibson exudes his effortless charisma, Hawn is shrill, and the slapstick is lame.
D: John Badham. A: Mel Gibson, Goldie Hawn, David Carradine.

Flashback
(1990) 108m. **C+**

An uptight FBI agent is escorting a once-famous radical activist to prison when a case of mistaken identity occurs, and the captive becomes the captor. Hopper's manic self-parodying humor makes for a funny first half, but the film drags when it gets sentimental about the sixties.
D: Franco Amurri. A: Kiefer Sutherland, Dennis Hopper, Carol Kane.

Chuck Norris

After costarring with Bruce Lee, Norris established himself as a kung fu warrior in a series of interchangeable martial arts films in the late 70s, but soon switched from fists to machine guns, joining the ranks of the indestructible action heroes like Stallone and Schwarzenegger. These lower-budgeted films may have a lower quotient of explosions and gadgets, but make up for it with these intense *mano a mano* confrontations.

Good Guys Wear Black
(1979) 96m. **C–**

A karate champion and wronged Vietnam vet stumbles onto a political conspiracy while battling bureaucrats. The serious-minded plot is poorly matched with the karate-chopping action sequences, and Norris' fancy footwork only occasionally takes fire.
D: Ted Post. A: With Anne Archer, James Franciscus, Jim Backus.

Force of One
(1979) 90m. **C**

Norris is now entrusted with saving a small town from evil drug lords. Action is muted like in *Good Guys*, but at least has a foolproof good guy–bad guy story on which to hang the violence.
D: Paul Aaron. A: With Jennifer O'Neill, Clu Gulager, Ron O'Neal.

The Octagon
(1980) 103m. **C+**

A rich woman hires Norris as a bodyguard after she becomes the target of a gang of killer ninjas. One-dimensional throwback to vintage martial arts films, but boasts slightly better karate action and classic tough guy Van Cleef.
D: Eric Karson. A: With Karen Carlson, Lee Van Cleef, Art Hindle.

Lone Wolf McQuade
(1983) 107m. **A–**

Rule-bending Texas Ranger Norris spars with charismatic but homicidal arms dealer Carradine. A near-perfect combination of karate and machine-gun action, structured like a modern western, this features the most engaging Norris character to date along with a colorful supporting rogues' gallery.
D: Steve Carver. A: With David Carradine, Barbara Carrera, Robert Beltran.

Missing in Action
(1984) 101m. **C**

Vietnam vet Norris returns to Southeast Asia to rescue American POWs in this *Rambo* rip-off, with one-note villains, a politically misguided theme, and second-rate action sequences.
D: Joseph Zito. A: With M. Emmet Walsh, David Tress, Lenore Kasdorf.

Code of Silence
(1985) 102m. **B**

Maverick Chicago cop Norris pulls out the heavy artillery when he's caught in the middle of a feud between the Mafia and Hispanic drug dealers. A multilayered plot and plenty of car chases, shoot-outs, and fancy stunts make this an explosive entry.
D: Andrew Davis. A: With Molly Hagen, Nathan Davis, Mike Genovese.

Missing in Action 2: The Beginning
(1985) 96m. **C+**

Norris must resist grueling torture as he plots the escape of his platoon from a Vietnamese POW camp. Another *Rambo*-inspired postwar exploitation, this prequel is actually more pulse-racing due to the gory scenes of sadism inflicted on the good guys.
D: Lance Hool. A: With Steven Williams, Soon-Teck Oh, Bennett Ohta.

Invasion U.S.A.
(1985) 108m. **B+**

A Russian-led army wreaks havoc in Florida, and it's up to former spy Norris to put them out of commission. This is a *Red Dawn* on ste-

roids, with Norris decimating a flotilla of attack vehicles and an army of bad guys.
D: Joseph Zito. A: With Richard Lynch, Melissa Prophet, Alex Colon.

The Delta Force
(1986) 129m. **B**

Middle Eastern terrorists hijack a passenger plane and a special unit led by Norris is sent to stop them. Juxtaposing the hostages' plight with the heroes' progress creates genuine suspense, while a B-movie all-star cast and high-octane Norris action add plenty of mindless thrills.
D: Menahem Golan. A: With Lee Marvin, Martin Balsam, George Kennedy.

Delta Force 2: Operation Stranglehold
(1990) 110m. **C**

An evil kingpin of a South American drug cartel is the unlucky target of Norris and his specially trained squad of soldiers. The stale and cheap-looking military action with boring karate sequences make this a far cry from the original.
D: Aaron Norris. A: With John P. Ryan, Paul Perri, Richard Jaeckel.

Other Films:
Eye for an Eye (1981)
Forced Vengeance (1982)
Firewalker (1986)
Braddock: Missing in Action III (1988)
Hero and the Terror (1988)
The Hitman (1991)

Seagal

A dark man of mystery who breaks bones like others break twigs. A man whose films burst with violence while consistently showing an ecological bent. A man with a ponytail. In film after film, aikido black belt Steven Seagal battles mobsters, unsavory government agents, even nature-bashing oil magnates in actioners that started out as martial arts fests with the later ones taking the action-hero, guns-and-explosions route.

Above the Law
(1988) 97m. **B**

A karate-chopping Chicago cop/ex-CIA man goes after a dirty tricks Company operative. Excellently staged mindless violence, a fun turn by ex-blaxploitation star Grier as Seagal's tough-cookie partner and copious plot twists make this definitely *not* your usual action-fest.
D: Andrew Davis. A: With Pam Grier, Sharon Stone, Henry Silva.

Hard to Kill
(1990) 95m. **C+**

Corrupt cops gun down stand-up guy Seagal, starting a long-term plan for vengeance on the pony-tailed one's part. A slight stumble for Seagal, with near-campy macho-mysticism personified by *Rocky*-esque training/healing sequence, but gets back on mindless violence track by mid-film.
D: Bruce Malmuth. A: With Kelly LeBrock, Bill Sadler, Frederick Coffin.

Marked for Death
(1990) 93m. **C–**

A Jamaican druglord (appropriately named "Screwface") threatens the innocents of suburbia until Seagal steps in. Scattered direction, lack of a strong female lead, and generic plotting make this less than prime Seagal.
D: Dwight H. Little. A: With Joanna Pacula, Keith David, Basil Wallace.

Out for Justice
(1991) 90m. **B–**

A Brooklyn cop winds up taking on his best childhood pal who is now an obese, drug-dealing maniac. Seagal attempts a Brooklyn accent, beats up an entire bar full of colorfully disgusting baddies, and even metes out karate justice to some evil delicatessen owners: ridiculous mayhem at its finest.
D: John Flynn. A: With William Forsythe, Jerry Orbach, Jo Champa.

Under Siege
(1992) 103m. **B+**

Unaware that Seagal is on board, a group of lunatic terrorists tries to scuttle a nuke-heavy carrier and threaten the mainland with attack. Wonderfully brainless film wisely never takes itself seriously, and focuses on humor, nearly nonstop action, and a scene-stealing Jones as an amiably deranged top-dog terrorist.
D: Andrew Davis. A: With Tommy Lee Jones, Gary Busey, Erika Eleniak.

On Deadly Ground
(1994) 98m. **C–**

Seagal is an ordinary guy who singlehandedly takes on Caine and his evil minions before they can despoil Alaska with oil-mining operations. This combination action/environmental rights movie is an interesting hybrid in concept, but a filmic mess in execution, including embarrassing Eskimo shaman scenes and a well-meaning lecture-finale on endangered species.
D: Steven Seagal. A: With Michael Caine, Joan Chen, John C. McGinley.

Stallone

The *Rambo* trilogy about the revenge-seeking ex–Green Beret tapped into some Cold War frustrations with its savage, often cartoonish violence bracketed in political rhetoric. It also locked Sylvester Stallone into the successful formula of the action hero whose stoic attitude is provoked until he explodes with an apocalyptic fury, and then it's all you can do to keep track of the body count. The dialogue is inane, the plots could have been written by a six-year-old, but the action sequences where Stallone's granite athleticism is displayed keeps action fans cheering.

Nighthawks
(1981) 99m. **B**
Two New York City cops are transferred to a high-tech special unit to capture a ruthless terrorist. The action—including the climactic helicoptor rescue—is fast and inventive if somewhat tame by today's standards, and the special effects seem quaint.
D: Bruce Malmuth. A: With Billy Dee Williams, Rutger Hauer, Lindsay Wagner.

First Blood
(1982) 97m. **B+**
A bitter Vietnam veteran unleashes his killing skills in a Northwest small town when an abusive sheriff pushes him too far. Stallone seethes with righteous anger and heavy-handed politics in this furiously violent, sometimes stomach-churning revenge fantasy.
D: Ted Kotcheff. A: With Brian Dennehy, Richard Crenna, David Caruso.

Rambo: First Blood Part II
(1985) 95m. **B+**
Killing machine Stallone is sent back to Vietnam to free American MIAs, but ends up double crossed and trapped behind enemy lines. The hero's ridiculously naive ideology underscores the relentlessly brutal, though creative, series of action setups that easily outexplode the original.
D: George Pan Cosmatos. A: With Richard Crenna, Charles Napier, Julia Nickson.

Cobra
(1986) 87m. **C–**
Now Stallone's a rogue LA cop armed with the latest in laser-sighted weaponry, who aims to put generic criminal scum out of business permanently. A graceless vigilante thriller that's strictly for hard-core action junkies.
D: George Pan Cosmatos. A: With Brigitte Nielsen, Reni Santoni, Andrew Robinson.

Rambo III
(1988) 101m. **C+**
Terminally ticked-off Stallone is called back to duty again to rescue his Green Beret commander from Russians in Afghanistan. Plenty of helicopter explosions and flag-waving without the appealing hard edge of the first two.
D: Peter MacDonald. A: With Richard Crenna, Kurtwood Smith, Marc de Jonge.

Lock Up
(1989) 106m. **D–**
Soon-to-be released convict Stallone is unexpectedly transferred to a hellhole penitentiary run by a sadistic warden. Deliriously derivative prison flick that doesn't even have enough pulse-stirring action to keep viewers awake.
D: John Flynn. A: With Donald Sutherland, John Amos, Darlanne Fluegel.

Cliffhanger
(1993) **A–**
Mountain ranger Stallone must stop a criminal gang from grabbing stolen millions lost in the Rockies. There's a good ratio of breathtaking physical feats to violence in this fast-paced thriller, though the mountain-climbing sequences may trigger a vertigo attack.
D: Renny Harlin. A: With John Lithgow, Janine Turner, Michael Rooker.

The Specialist
(1994) 105m. **D+**
Two feuding ex-CIA explosives specialists get caught in a wily blonde's scheme for revenge. Strange, would-be erotic thriller/action film is almost torridly bad enough to achieve camp status, with a good supporting cast floundering amidst the explosions and dumb plot.
D. Luis Llosa A: With Sharon Stone and James Woods.

Schwarzenegger

Arnold has made a handful of comedies along with a few straightforward bullets-and-bodies action films, but his strength still seems to be in the action-fantasy film, which combines the big budget special effects and nifty ideas of a science fiction flick with bone crunching, action-hero violence. Both types of films boast economic dialogue ("Hasta la vista, baby," "I'll be back"), small but welcome doses of humor, and enough ammunition, ripped flesh, thermonuclear climaxes, and overall effects wizardry to launch a Third World country's revolution.

Action

Commando
(1985) 88m. **C+**
This could be a video for a soldier of fortune magazine: rocket launchers, machine guns, knives, boobytraps, and camouflaging gadgets are the real costars as Arnold does the *Rambo* routine in a South American jungle, leaving a twisted corpse trail behind him.
D: Mark Lester. A: With Vernon Wells, Rae Dawn Chong, Dan Hedaya.

Raw Deal
(1986) 97m. **C**
Looking awkward and out of place in a bulging gangster suit and slicked back hair, Arnold plays an ex-FBI agent who's gone undercover in the Chicago mob. Revenge leads to an orgy of bullets as Arnold wipes out the syndicate with periodic flashes of humor to interrupt the bloodshed.
D: John Irvin. A: With Kathryn Harrold, Sam Wanamaker, Darren McGavin.

True Lies
(1994) 141m. **B+**
Blend of a marriage-on-the-rocks comedy, James Bond adventure, and a shoot-em-up actioner finds Schwarzenegger and Curtis pulled into an Arab terrorist plan to nuke U.S. cities. Littered with amusing character moments and climaxes with a truly amazing sequence involving a Harrier jet.
D: James Cameron. A: With Jamie Lee Curtis, Tom Arnold, Bill Paxton.

Action-Fantasy

The Terminator
(1984) 108m. **B+**
A time-traveling cyborg assassin pursues the woman who will give birth to the man destined to threaten cyborg rule in the postnuclear future. A violent, vulgar-tongued, and breaknecked tale, climaxing with bombs being hurled at the mangled, dogged Terminator who, even as he melts down and splits in half, lunges for his prey.

D: James Cameron. A: With Linda Hamilton, Michael Biehn, Lance Henrickson.

Predator
(1987) 107m. **B–**
An American commando team in Central America first has to fight guerrillas, then deal with an invisible alien who's hunting humans. This starts out with muscular sweating men getting on each other's nerves, then turns into a heart-pounding, graphically violent test of metal and muscle of snarling alien vs. snarling man.
D: John McTiernan. A: With Carl Weathers, Bill Duke, Elpidia Carrillo.

The Running Man
(1987) 101m. **B–**
In a depressingly grungy future totalitarian state, a good cop is forced to participate in a government-sponsored bloodthirsty TV game show. Arnold starts to wise crack in this ultraviolent exercise that wheels out every type of sadistic fiend including a chainsaw killer and a psycho hockey player.
D: Paul Michael Glaser. A: With Yaphet Kotto, Maria Conchita Alonso, Richard Dawson.

Total Recall
(1990) 109m. **A–**
Twisty, mind-bending, special effects–heavy excursion finds Arnold taking the ultimate adventure vacation via a brain implant. Less hardcore violence and more pyrotechnics, morphing, and dazzling visuals to keep you watching and occasionally ducking. Includes great moments of character and plot disorientation.
D: Paul Verhoeven. A: With Sharon Stone, Rachel Ticotin, Ronnie Cox.

Terminator 2: Judgment Day
(1991) 135m. **A**
The now reformed cyborg T-800 returns to protect the future savior of the human race, with an evil cyborg killer in pursuit. This relentless sci-fi dazzler contains one titanic chase and battle scene after another, with the assassin morphing into any and every shape as he fights almost heart-of-gold Arnold.
D: James Cameron. A: With Linda Hamilton, Edward Furlong, Joe Morton.

Last Action Hero
(1993) 130m. **D+**
The saturation point for special effects and violent set pieces is surpassed in this oddly unpolished big budgeter. A few funny bits are jumbled together with massive explosions and a hail of bullets, but the old balance of danger, humor, and spectacle is missing.
D: John McTiernan. A: With Austin O'Brien, Charles Dance, Anthony Quinn.

Bruce Willis

Even without the puffed-up physique of Schwarzenegger or Stallone, Bruce Willis gives us an action hero who's handy with an automatic pistol, agile as a monkey, quick with the wisecracks, and an attitude to die for.

Die Hard
(1988) 131m. **A–**
A New York detective tries to reconcile with his estranged wife in LA only to become trapped in a high-rise that's become a battleground for international terrorists. Willis and his stylish villains play an explosive cat-and-mouse game that's a blend of muscle grease, sarcasm, and guns.
D: John McTiernan. A: With Alan Rickman, Bonnie Bedelia, Alexander Godunov.

Die Hard 2: Die Harder
(1990) 124m. **B+**
New York City cop Willis now has to thwart a terrorist group from sabotaging Dulles Airport on Christmas Eve. Faster-paced violence, with head-spinning chase scenes, airplane crashes, and crazy plot turns that leave Willis and the viewer breathless.
D: Renny Harlin. A: With Bonnie Bedelia, William Sadler, Dennis Franz.

Hudson Hawk
(1991) 95m. **B**
A former cat-burglar is forced to steal priceless art from the Vatican in this strange stew of satire, old-style serial adventure, and hip modern actioner. Willis' wisecracks and the cartoon villains provide the laughs while the weird plot and lighthearted action make this surprisingly watchable and goofy entertainment.
D: Michael Lehmann. A: With Danny Aiello, Andie McDowell, Sandra Bernhard.

The Last Boy Scout
(1991) 105m. **B**
Down-on-his-luck private detective Willis teams up with a drug-addicted, ex-football player to investigate corruption in the sport. With its truly shocking violence, dark humor, and two complete losers as its heroes, this film provides a gritty original twist to the buddy formula.
D: Tony Scott. A: With Damon Wayans, Noble Willingham, Taylor Negron.

Striking Distance
(1993) 105m. **C–**
Maverick cop Willis tracks down a serial killer in Pittsburgh with the help of his new partner and love interest. The clichés in this action-murder mystery may kill any suspense, although some of the continuity errors and hammy acting may puzzle you.
D: Rowdy Herrington. A: With Sarah Jessica Parker, Tom Sizemore, John Mahoney.

Die Hard: With a Vengeance
(1995) 135m. **D+**
Assorted Euro-trash scum invade New York to make wisecracking Gotham detective Willis' life miserable again. Features a cornucopia of action set pieces that you've seen before, confused editing, and Jackson as the only reason to sit through the film's elephantine running time.
D: John McTiernan. A: With Samuel Jackson, Jeremy Irons.

Other Action Heroes

Everyone from Eastwood to Swayze to Rourke has tried their hand at being an action hero. Relying more on the star power and acting ability of the lead, these films generally feature recycled Stallone/Schwarzenegger plots and lower budgets, which translate into fewer spectacular explosions and scenes of rampant destruction.

Firefox
(1982) 124m. **B**
An unstable veteran pilot is recruited by the CIA to steal a superfast new jet fighter from the Soviet Union. The impressive aerial combat and high-tech intrigue can't keep this adventure from losing altitude long before the finale.
D: Clint Eastwood. A: Clint Eastwood, Freddie Jones, David Huffman.

Extreme Prejudice
(1987) 104m. **B+**
Nolte is a Texas Ranger at odds with his former boyhood buddy, now a drug dealer who's horning in on his pal's territory and girlfriend. A tough and brawny reworking of the good friend–bad friend tale set in a hot border setting.
D: Walter Hill. A: Nick Nolte, Powers Booth, Maria Conchita Alonso.

Next of Kin
(1989) 108m. **C–**
Chicago policeman Swayze enlists his hillbilly relatives from Appalachia to exact revenge—backwoods style—for the death of his brother by a drug kingpin. Star-gazing among the supporting cast provides some interest in this strictly formulaic actioner and crime thriller.
D: John Irvin. A: Patrick Swayze, Liam Neeson, Adam Baldwin.

Road House
(1989) 107m. **C**
Swayze is a barroom bouncer with a Ph.D. in philosophy who fights the town extortionist by day and woos a local nurse by night. The plot, characters and acting are beyond belief, but the high-kicking action packs some power.
D: Rowdy Herrington. A: Patrick Swayze, Sam Elliott, Kelly Lynch.

Harley Davidson and the Marlboro Man
(1991) 99m. **C–**
Motorcycle-riding partners rob a bank and battle baddies in a fast-paced, window-smashing fashion. Bizarre semifuturistic setting and stereotypes-come-to-life characters ("Virginia Slims" is also featured) almost make up for the thin story and routine action.
D: Simon Wincer. A: Mickey Rourke, Don Johnson, Chelsea Field.

Point Break
(1991) 122m. **B+**
A young FBI agent goes undercover as a surfer in order to nail a gang of bank robbers. A mix of very cool surfing and skydiving sequences, California dharma bum philosophy and a few nasty shoot-outs will keep your interest throughout.
D: Kathryn Bigelow. A: Keanu Reeves, Patrick Swayze, Gary Busey.

Passenger 57
(1992) 84m. **B–**
Federal agent Snipes just happens to be on board a plane that is hijacked by a terrorist gang. This blatant, smaller-scale *Die Hard* homage has plenty of gripping, judo-tinged action and a cool-under-pressure Snipes to create pure mindless fun.
D: Kevin Hooks. A: Wesley Snipes, Bruce Payne, Tom Sizemore.

The Fugitive
(1993) 133m. **A–**
A U.S. marshal and most of Chicago's finest are after a doctor who has been unjustly accused of murdering his wife. From its astounding opening train wreck, this adrenalized revision of the TV series masterfully mixes eye-popping chase scenes, a suspenseful whodunit and the intriguing relationship between predator and prey.
D: Andrew Davis. A: Harrison Ford, Tommy Lee Jones, Jeroen Krabbe.

Blown Away
(1994) 120m. **D+**
In present-day Boston, an Irish-descended bomb expert becomes the object of a mad-IRA/part-time mass killer's wrath. Outside of frequent great explosions, a mediocre effort that suggests five other action plots were pasted together at random.
D: Stephen Hopkins A: Jeff Bridges, Tommy Lee Jones, Suzy Amis.

Drop Zone
(1994) 101m. **C**
Bad-ass U.S. Marshal Snipes is seeking revenge on some terrorists who killed his brother on board a 747. To do so he must become an expert parachutist (don't ask). Totally formulaic actioner plays like a politically correct episode of *The A Team* with too few spectacular parachuting scenes.
D: John Badham A: Wesley Snipes, Gary Busey, Yancy Butler.

Speed
(1994) 115m. **A**
Madman Hopper has wired an LA bus to blow up if it drops below 50 mph, which is pretty much the whole story of this nonstop paean to velocity, crashing vehicles, and general mayhem. Bulked-up Reeves adds his own special monosyllabic charm which never distracts you from one hell of a ride.
D: Jan De Bont. A: Keanu Reeves, Sandra Bullock, Dennis Hopper.

Terminal Velocity
(1995) 102m. **D+**
A rough 'n' ready parachutist becomes involved with a slinky Russian spy in this breathtakingly awful film, with spastic action scenes and pacing only a snail could admire. Sole reason to watch is climactic car-dropping-from-plane gag.
D: Deran Sarafian. A: Charlie Sheen, Nastassia Kinski, James Gandolfini.

Sports

"Because it's there" seems to be the main motivation of these modern machos as they take on everything from mountain climbing to bull riding. Along with the daredevil

action scenes, there's often romance and a *Rocky*-esque little-guy-conquers-all subtext for those who want a little drama with their thrills.

Days of Thunder
(1990) 108m. **C+**
Racing and romance mix it up at the Daytona 500. The on-track action is pretty amazing, with camera (and audience) often in the driver's seat while Duvall impresses as cranky pit-stop man, but otherwise, a Formula 1 formula melodrama.
D: Tony Scott. A: Tom Cruise, Nicole Kidman, Robert Duvall.

K2
(1992) 104m. **C**
Twenty-seven men have died trying to ascend mighty Savage Mountain ("K2"), so of course it's up to an attorney and physicist to give it another go. As a movie, not much, but as a sort of alpine "video aquarium," this might spice up the living room with its ravishing photography.
D: Franc Roddam. A: Michael Biehn, Matt Craven, Patricia Charbonneau.

Wind
(1992) 123m. **C**
A dreamy-eyed WASP and his matching girlfriend pursue the America's Cup yachting prize in this beautifully shot and quaintly romantic film. The sailing sequences are truly impressive but the drama on land makes you seasick.
D: Carroll Ballard. A: Matthew Modine, Rebecca Miller, Stellan Skarsgard.

8 Seconds
(1994) 97m. **B+**
This true story of bull-rider Lane Frost's short life from farm cowboy to stardom on the rodeo circuit is lower-keyed but more engaging than the other entries in this group. The awesome rodeo scenes, a sincere Perry, and a warm feel for simple family problems make this good down-home entertainment.
D: John G. Avildsen. A: Luke Perry, Cynthia Geary, Stephen Baldwin.

Survival

These cinematic versions of Outward Bound-type endurance tests let you watch average guys fight their way out of life-and-death predicaments without the benefit of Schwarzenegger's muscles, an arsenal of high-tech guns, or even the police to protect them.

Southern Comfort
(1981) 106m. **B**
Hapless National Guardsmen abuse the natives of the Louisiana bayou where they're training in the early 1970s, only to be savagely stalked and killed by revenge-seeking Cajuns. The stomach-clenching ambush seems almost a relief after the boorish behavior that is meant to mimic Vietnam.
D: Walter Hill. A: Keith Carradine, Powers Boothe, Fred Ward.

Red Dawn
(1984) 114m. **A**
Communist forces launch an invasion against the U.S. in Colorado but meet resistance from a band of teenage guerrilla fighters. From the opening scenes of Russian paratroopers overruning the high school, this revels in the bloody gunfights and the transformation of jocks to resistance fighters.
D: John Milius. A: Patrick Swayze, C. Thomas Howell, Powers Boothe.

Alive
(1993) 123m. **A–**
True-life tale of a rugby team that crashed in the Andes mountains and, among other things, resorted to cannibalism to survive. An all-around surprise, starting with one of the most terrifyingly realistic plane crash sequences, good ensemble acting, admirable restraint regarding the subject matter, and even some spiritual underpinnings.
D: Frank Marshall. A: Ethan Hawke, Vincent Spano, Josh Hamilton.

Judgment Night
(1993) 109m. **C–**
Witless white boys make a wrong turn in darkest Chitown and end up confronted with vicious inner-city gangs. A sort of young urban *Deliverance* minus the cleverness, but with lots of mud, paranoia, dark photography, and general grungy air.
D: Stephen Hopkins. A: Emilio Estevez; Cuba Gooding, Jr.; Denis Leary.

The River Wild
(1994) 112m. **B+**
While on a white-water rafting trip, a stressed couple and son are held hostage by a trio of criminals. Lucky for the family and film, Streep is pumped-up and the only accent here is on nonstop action as she kicks serious river butt: not brain-taxing, but has vertigo-inducing rafting scenes and a snarly Bacon.
D: Curtis Hanson. A: Meryl Streep, Kevin Bacon, David Strathairn.

Hybrid Action

Although full of the vehicular mayhem, gunfire, and carnage one expects from a decent modern action film, most of these add shotgun editing, inventive camerawork, prominent rock music soundtracks, and action heroes ranging from modern knights to firefighters.

Knightriders
(1981) 145m. **C+**
A traveling group of motorcyclists stage renaissance fairs with cycle-driven jousts, but their idyllic life is disrupted by internal strife, financial problems, and media intrusion. An interesting premise (imagine *Camelot* on Harleys), but over two hours of slow pacing spoil whatever points about society it's trying to make.
D: George Romero. A: Ed

Harris, Tom Savini, Amy Ingersoll.

Streets of Fire
(1984) 93m. **C+**
In a future that looks like the early 50s a beautiful rock star is kidnapped by vicious bikers, and her manager hires the ex-lover and his tomboy sidekick to rescue her. The retro-futuristic settings and throbbing music are what propels this tongue-in-cheek, cartoonish music-adventure.
D: Walter Hill. A: Michael Pare, Diane Lane, Rick Moranis.

Runaway Train
(1985) 112m. **A–**
A convict and his young pal bust out of Alaskan prison, starting an elaborate chase monitored by computer-wielding authorities. Performances, action, editing: the entire snow-drenched film seems buzzed with amphetamines, making it one of the best action for action's sake thrillers with philosophical bits thrown in.
D: Andrei Konchalovsky. A: Jon Voight, Eric Roberts, Rebecca DeMornay.

To Live and Die in L.A.
(1985) 116m. **B**
A rip-off gone wrong causes the unraveling of a government agent's plan to capture a counterfeiter. Everyone's a schemer in this bleak graphically violent adventure that features a shocking conclusion and one of the all-time great car chase scenes.
D: William Friedkin. A: William L. Petersen, Willem Dafoe, John Pankow.

Top Gun
(1986) 110m. **B–**
The star pilot at a navy flying school competes with his classmates, woos his instructor, and tries to uncover the truth of his dad's disappearance in Vietnam. On ground this turns to sludge; in the air, it shimmers with the head-spinning stunts featuring sleek jet fighters.
D: Tony Scott. A: Tom Cruise, Kelly McGillis, Val Kilmer.

Narrow Margin
(1990) 97m. **C+**
This remake of a 1952 noir semigem has a female witness hiding out on a train from various bad guys and a G-man determined to help her. Workmanlike effort, with nice action set pieces, location photography, and the usual fine Hackman performance, but short on logic and star chemistry.
D: Peter Hyams. A: Gene Hackman, Anne Archer, M. Emmet Walsh.

Backdraft
(1991) 136m. **C+**
A so-so tale of firemen, the women who love them, and a psycho arsonist who makes their lives difficult. With all this star firepower and the earnest attempt to portray some real heroes, all that really impresses are the digitally rendered flames.
D: Ron Howard. A: Kurt Russell, William Baldwin, Scott Glenn.

Freefall
(1994) 97m. **C+**
A photographer goes to Africa and gets mixed up in mistaken identity and international espionage. This entertainingly crafty thriller moves at such a quick canter that one doesn't notice that it makes only marginal sense.
D: John Irvin. A: Eric Roberts, Jeff Fahey, Pamela Girdley.

Female Action

Thelma and Louise
(1991) 128m. **A**
After murdering a man in self-defense two women hit the road and, even with the heat closing in, find a greater freedom than they had as law-abiding females. This gorgeously photographed, exuberant, hilarious, and tragic female buddy film uses well-drawn characters to get many themes across.
D: Ridley Scott. A: Susan Sarandon, Geena Davis, Harvey Keitel.

Point of No Return
(1993) 109m. **B–**
A cop-killing ex-druggie is reprogrammed as an assassin by a secret government agency in this remake of *La Femme Nikita*. Even with the fierce heroine and beautifully choreographed shootouts, this lacks the style and jangled nervousness of the original.
D: John Badham. A: Bridget Fonda, Gabriel Byrne, Dermot Mulroney.

The Real McCoy
(1993) 106m. **C+**
A bank-robbing Atlanta mother is released on parole, whereupon her son is kidnapped, forcing her to pull off the biggest heist of her career. Just when you think this is a duller version of *Straight Time,* Kim dolls up in her fashionable cat burglar outfit and masterminds a semi-enjoyable caper.
D: Russell Mulcahy. A: Kim Basinger, Val Kilmer, Terence Stamp.

Japanese Animation

If you think of animation as Bugs Bunny or Saturday morning cartoons, the sex and violence of Japanese *anime* (Japanimation) will knock your socks off. Usually aimed at teens and adults, its genres include occult/horror, crime thrillers, teen sex comedies, Sci-fi, and samurai adventures. This group offers good examples of the exquisitely rendered, highly detailed backgrounds that Japanese animators specialize in, while the characters are often of cruder design, as a preponderance of wide-eyed, western-looking youths are placed in the midst of shocking violence and apocalyptic destruction.

The Castle of Cagliostro
(1980) 100m. **B**
The high-living, international jewel thief Wolf intervenes to rescue a kidnapped princess from the castle of an evil Middle European count. A high comic adventure in the tradition of the 1960s spy and caper comedies with classical production design and fluid, fast-paced animation.
D: Hayao Miyazaki.

Warriors of the Wind
(1984) 85m. **B**
In a future polluted wasteland, a young girl with the power to communicate with the newly flourishing race of giant insects gets caught up in a war among the surviving kingdoms. An exquisitely animated adventure with an endearing heroine, a lyrical score, and an imaginative take on the world's ecological future.
D: Hayao Miyazaki.

Vampire Hunter D
(1985) 80m. **B**
A cloaked vampire hunter and a spunky young girl set out to overthrow a vampire ruler in a feudal village. Unique design and imaginative action scenes help viewers through a complicated plot, with gore that's very appropriate amidst the baroque angles and unearthly horrors.
D: Toyoo Ahida.

Fist of the North Star
(1986) 100m. **C**
Super-powerful warriors take on *Mad Max*–style barbarian clans amidst the post-apocalyptic ruins of the future. A good story and superbly rendered backgrounds of desert landscapes and crumbling skyscrapers are offset by stiff animation and extremely gory violence in which the heroes literally rip apart their opponents.
D: Toyoo Ahida.

Project A-KO
(1986) 86m. **C**
In the future, a rivalry erupts in a girls' school between the super-powered A-KO and the haughty B-KO over the affections of the daffy little C-KO, with interplanetary warfare thrown in for good measure. The broad comic tone and deliberately crude character design sharply contrast with violent battles and the wild alien invasion.
D: Katsuhiko Nishijima.

My Neighbor Totoro
(1988) 86m. **A**
When two young city girls move to the countryside in postwar Japan, they form a relationship with a group of furry forest sprites including the massive rabbitlike Totoro. Enchanting, lushly animated view of the natural world with a child's sense of wonder. A perennial favorite among buffs and suitable for young children.
D: Hayao Miyazaki.

Urotsukidoji: Legend of the Overfiend (aka The Wandering Kid)
(1989) 108m. **B**
An extremely bizarre apocalyptic tale of warring demons continuing an ancient battle by employing as "hosts" teens at an Osaka middle school. Awesome scenes of destruction mix with adults-only sex, violence, and semi-comic teen lust to create a mind-boggling experience for the strong of stomach only.
D: Hideki Takayama.

Dominion Tank Police, Part 2 (Acts III and IV)
(1989) 80m. **C**
The bumbling rookie officer from Crime Brigade is kidnapped by a cyborg gang leader, but winds up helping him retrace his roots to an abandoned secret government lab. Some poignant moments can't compensate for the crude design and the characters' shrill behavior.
D: Takaaki Ishiyama.

The Professional: Golgo 13
(1992) 95m. **B**
Golgo 13 is a trench-coated international hit man impervious to pain, emotion, or numerous attempts on his life by a trio of grotesque assassins. A sprawling crime thriller laced with liberal amounts of sex and graphic violence, marked by a stylized design, extreme camera angles, and unpredictable plot twists.
D: Osamu Dezaki.

Demon City Shinjuku
(1993) 82m. **B**
A teenage boy and girl enter the ravaged, demon-controlled Shinjuku district of Tokyo to stop a powerful evil force from achieving world domination. Expertly rendered creation of a truly nightmarish world of evil, grotesque monsters, and urban ruins is enhanced by well-designed characters and several moments of suspense.
D: Yoshiaki Kawajiri.

COMEDY

Comedy Menu

COMEDY MENU

COMEDY MENU

COMEDY MENU

COMEDY FILM GROUPS

1910s–1920s

Charlie Chaplin

Chaplin's early films are brisk and wild slapsticks, all exaggerated lighting, makeup, and set design, with little of the pathos that marked his later efforts. He began evolving his trademark character, the Tramp, that tragicomic figure deeply longing for romance but cursed to remain alone. Chaplin's films were soon feature-length, and the slapstick became more resourceful, the humor subtle, the plots elaborate, and the look a lighter-toned elegance. Chaplin's comedy remained primarily visual since he ''spoke'' with his face and physical stunts. When he finally introduced sound—aside from the sentimental scores that he composed himself—it was primarily used to give audiences a critical lecture on modern civilization.

Silent Films

Chaplin: The Early Years Vol. 1
(1916–1917) 61m. B&W. **A**
Includes:
The Immigrant Onboard ship to America, the Tramp romances a young woman, but the lovers become separated at the dock by immigration officials. Charlie then fights off loneliness and poverty by chiseling crooks and obnoxious waiters in the New World.

The Count A tailor's assistant stumbles into a party thrown by the beautiful Miss Moneybags, unaware that his former employer is there masquerading as a count. This minor effort still provides laughs, especially when Chaplin and Campbell make slobs of themselves at the dinner table.

Easy Street A derelict takes a job as a policeman, unaware that his beat will be the rough and tumble Easy Street. Charlie does his best to avoid mass hysteria while keeping peace in a gritty violent comedy that often looks noirish.
D: Charles Chaplin. A: With Edna Purviance, Eric Campbell.

Chaplin: The Early Years Vol. 3
(1916–1917) 63m. B&W. **A**
Includes:
The Cure A well-to-do fop checks into a sanitarium with a case full of liquor. He flirts with a beautiful young woman who tries to sober him up; to his delight, the healing waters taste just like booze.

The Floorwalker Charlie assumes the identity of a crooked look-alike floorwalker at a department store and is soon under the scrutiny of the store detective and the embezzling general manager in this cynical comedy filled with bizarre sight gags.

The Vagabond A poor violinist rescues a pretty girl from a band of cutthroat gypsies. He falls for her but she prefers a handsome artist. Early example of Chaplin's pathos eschewing the slapstick for heartbreak.
D: Charles Chaplin. A: With Edna Purviance, Eric Campbell.

The Chaplin Revue
(1918–1923) 115m. B&W. **A**
Includes:
A Dog's Life A charming template for *The Kid,* with the Tramp finding a best friend in the little mongrel he saved. Charlie falls for an unbearably shy singer, and the pooch digs up a wallet full of cash. Edna's weepy song and Charlie's two-hand pantomime with an unconscious thug are hilarious.

Shoulder Arms Life on the front is tough for Private Chaplin but his fortunes take a turn for the glorious when he single-handedly rounds up a regiment of Prussian soldiers.

The Pilgrim An escaped convict steals the clothes of a preacher and heads to Texas where he's expected to become the town's new minister. Low-key, folksy affair gets rolling the second half.
D: Charles Chaplin. A: With Edna Purviance, Sydney Chaplin, Mark Swain.

The Kid
(1921) 60m. B&W. **A** 🏛

Chaplin raises the tough but adorable waif who is later kidnapped when his wealthy mother wants him back. Contains a strange Victorian-looking dream sequence with the Tramp and the Kid flying in heaven.
D: Charles Chaplin. A: With Jackie Coogan, Carl Miller, Edna Purviance.

The Idle Class
(1921) 20m. B&W. **B**
Charlie has a dual role as the Tramp and the caddish drunken husband in this caustic commentary about the upper class.
D: Charles Chaplin. A: With Edna Purviance.

A Woman of Paris
(1923) 81m. B&W. **B–**
A French country girl becomes the mistress of a wealthy playboy in this sentimental cautionary tale. Chaplin makes only a cameo appearance, but as the director his flair for melodrama comes through.
D: Charles Chaplin. A: With Edna Purviance, Adolphe Menjou, Carl Miller.

The Gold Rush
(1925) 82m. B&W. **A** 🏛
The Tramp goes to Alaska in search of gold, is snowbound with a hungry partner, and falls in love with a dance hall girl. Exciting adventure containing classic comedy used in films today, including the scene in which he boils up his shoe to eat.
D: Charles Chaplin. A: With Georgia Hale, Mack Swain, Tom Murray.

City Lights
(1931) 86m. B&W. **A** 🏛
A blind flower girl mistakes

the Tramp for a wealthy man when he gives her money for an operation. The emotions that play across Chaplin's face during some of these scenes prove that dialogue was unnecessary for the master.
D: Charles Chaplin. A: With Virginia Cherrill, Harry Myers, Hank Mann.

Chaplin with Sound

Modern Times
(1936) 85m. B&W. **A** 🏛
Chaplin is the factory worker driven crazy by his repetitious job, who struggles to find other work and helps a rebellious orphan. Hilarious and biting satire of machine-age society. Chaplin finds his voice and sings a nonsensical song.
D: Charles Chaplin. A: With Paulette Goddard, Henry Bergman, Chester Conklin.

The Great Dictator
(1940) 126m. B&W. **B+** 🏛
Chaplin plays an innocent Jewish barber as well as the dictator of Tomania who's a dead ringer for Hitler. A funny but heavily messaged satire that gets ponderous toward the end.
D: Charles Chaplin. A: With Paulette Goddard, Jack Oakie, Reginald Gardiner.

Monsieur Verdoux
(1947) 123m. B&W. **B**
Chaplin is the debonair Frenchman who marries and kills elderly ladies for their money. Fine slapstick moments pepper this black comedy that lacks the charm of his earlier films.
D: Charles Chaplin. A: With Mady Correll, Martha Raye, Charles Evans.

Limelight
(1952) 145m. B&W. **B**
When a washed-up music hall comic rescues a suicidal ballerina, she gets him a job as a clown in the ballet. Slow, introspective, and very sentimental story with Chaplin pairing up with Keaton for a comic turn.
D: Charles Chaplin. A: With Claire Bloom, Nigel Bruce, Buster Keaton.

A King in New York
(1957) 105m. B&W. **B–**
After his country undergoes a revolution, a king relocates to New York City where he becomes a pawn for TV advertisers and a suspected communist. A heavy-handed and embittered satire with some awkward and downright uncomfortable scenes.
D: Charles Chaplin. A: With Dawn Addams, Michael Chaplin, Maxine Audley.

Other Films:
Rare Chaplin (1915)
Burlesque of Carmen (1916)
Charlie Chaplin Carnival (1916)
Charlie Chaplin Cavalcade (1916)
Charlie Chaplin . . . Our Hero (1914–1915)
Charlie Chaplin: The Early Years Vols. 2, 4 (1916–17)
The Circus/A Day's Pleasure (1928)

Buster Keaton

What the "Great Stoneface" lacked in emotional response he made up for with physical daring in films that contain some of the most clever, elaborate, and dangerous sight gags ever performed. The stories—usually about a logical loner's struggle against a world that rejects him—unfold at a steady deliberate pace, climaxing in a pull-out-the-stops, rip roarin', life-or-death chase scene.

Silent Films

The Blacksmith/Cops
(1922) 38m. B&W. **A**
The Blacksmith is pure slapstick with Keaton as the incompetent apprentice suddenly in charge of the blacksmith shop. In *Cops,* innocent Buster winds up chased by an entire city police force in a hilarious but grim look at the boys in blue, ending with Keaton's porkpie hat on a gravestone.
D: Buster Keaton. A: With Virginia Fox.

Our Hospitality
(1923) 75m. B&W. **A–**
Keaton accepts the Southern hospitality of a family before he finds out that they are the feuding clan that has wiped out his entire family. Brilliant comic sequences with Keaton trying to sneak away in disguise, and a breathtaking waterfall rescue sequence.
D: Buster Keaton, John Blystone. A: With Natalie Talmadge; Joe Keaton; Buster Keaton, Jr.

Sherlock Jr.
(1924) 45m. B&W. **A** 🎞
A projectionist enters the movie he is showing in order to solve a real-life crime. A clever spoof of film mechanics and conventions that's an old standby in every college Film 101 class.
D: Buster Keaton. A: With Kathryn McGuire, Ward Crane.

The General
(1927) 77m. B&W. **A–**
Loyal Southerner Keaton, who's a locomotive engineer, goes on a wild chase when the Yankees abduct his train and his girl. Good Matthew Brady-like photography as the backdrop for this Civil War slapstick.
D: Buster Keaton. A: With Marion Mack.

Steamboat Bill, Jr.
(1928) 80m. B&W. **A–** 🎞
Keaton comes home to his father, a riverboat captain who thinks his son is too citified to be of any use. The peaceful river locale is turned hellish when Keaton does battle in a spectacular cyclone sequence. Best stunt is the death-defying collapse of a building.
D: Charles Reisner. A: With Ernest Torrence.

Keaton with Sound

Free and Easy
(1930) 92m. B&W. **B–**
Keaton is a beauty queen's bumbling manager who tries to storm Hollywood in order to launch her film career. Unusual behind the scenes atmosphere of a film studio, with lots of cameo appearances in Keaton's first talkie.
D: Edward Sedgwick. A: With Anita Page, Robert Montgomery, Lionel Barrymore.

Speak Easily
(1932) 82m. B&W. **B**
A dull professor believes he's inherited a fortune and starts a new life by helping out a no-talent acting troupe. A fun romp with a slightly seedy feel, and though Durante's broad humor tends to overpower Keaton, Todd is always enjoyable as the girl who's been around the block more than once.
D: Edward Sedgwick. A: With Jimmy Durante, Thelma Todd, Sidney Toler.

Other Films:
Keaton Festival: Vols. 1–4 (1919–23)
The Balloonatic (1923)
The Three Ages (1923)
College (1927)
The Cameraman (1928)
Spite Marriage (1929)
Doughboys (1930)
Parlor, Bedroom and Bath (1932)
An Old Spanish Custom (1935)
Boom in the Moon (1946)

Harold Lloyd

After an apprenticeship with slapstick kings Hal Roach and Mack Sennett, Lloyd became the box-office king of all silent comedians in the 1920s, epitomizing the devil-may-care spirit and earnest sentimentality of the Jazz Age. While his impeccably crafted films may lack Keaton's sheer invention and Chaplin's emotional sweep, they're still comic masterpieces of slapstick, sight gags, car chases, and some truly death-defying stunts performed by Lloyd himself.

SILENT FILMS

Safety Last

(1923) 74m. B&W. **A–**

A struggling salesclerk sends a letter to his small town sweetheart claiming he's a department store executive. Then she arrives unexpectedly and a series of disasters forces Lloyd to crawl up the side of an office building in one of his most famous exhilarating scenes ever.
D: Fred Newmeyer, Sam Taylor. A: With Mildred David, Bill Strothers.

Girl Shy

(1924) 88m. B&W. **A–**

A shy author meets the girl of his dreams on a train traveling to the big city where he hopes to sell his book on lovemaking. The ridiculous tome is rejected and he alienates the girl by trying to cover up his failure in this charming comedy that ends with an extraordinary chase.
D: Fred Newmeyer, Sam Taylor. A: With Jobyna Ralston, Richard Daniels.

Hot Water

(1924) 60m. B&W. **B+**

Newlyweds Harold and his wife are burdened by her worthless family who anxiously await his paycheck and the delivery of his new car. A hilarious series of slapstick vignettes provides memorable scenes, but never really comes together as a feature.
D: Fred Newmeyer, Sam Taylor. A: With Jobyna Ralston, Josephine Crowell.

Kid Brother

(1927) 83m. B&W. **A**

The egghead son of a rugged mountain family masquerades as his sheriff father and wins the heart of a pretty medicine-show woman. Plenty of earthy humor and emotional power as gentle Harold fights off rednecks and a circus strongman in this neglected masterpiece.
D: Ted Wilde, J. A. Howe, Lewis Milestone. A: With Jobyna Ralston, Walter James.

Speedy

(1928) 71m. B&W. **A**

Lloyd drives a horse-drawn trolley and fights to keep the business going, which escalates into a grand—and bumpy—tour of old New York that includes a cameo of Babe Ruth.
D: Ted Wilde. A: With Ann Christy, Bert Woodruff, Brooks Benedict.

Lloyd with Sound

The Milky Way

(1936) 89m. B&W. **B+**

A mild-mannered milkman manages to knock out the middleweight champion and finds himself on the fast track to fame and riches in the crooked prizefight circuit. Lloyd seems long in the tooth to play a contender and ill at ease in this "talkie" madcap romp.
D: Leo McCarey. A: With Adolphe Menjou, Verree Teasdale, Helen Mack.

(See also *The Sin of Harold Diddlebock,* page 68.)

Fatty Arbuckle and Mabel Normand

Fatty and Mabel were two of the brightest stars of silent comedy. Fatty, a jovial 320-pound, pratfall-prone giant was always on the prowl for boyish mischief. As Fatty's usual love interest, raven-haired Normand seemed the prototype for future screwball comedy heroines: relaxed and enjoying her own silliness. Sadly, both were ruined by scandal, but the films they left us are fresh, often randy sight-gag feasts directed by slapstick genius Mack Sennett.

Keystone Comedies Vol. 1

(1915) 45m. B&W. **B+**

Includes:

Fatty's Faithful Fido Fatty enlists his spunky pooch to help him take on the rube who's been making a play for his girl.

Fatty's Tintype Tangle Fatty and his wife are living with her shrewish mother who makes life miserable for both of them. Fatty bolts and his wife rents the house to a jealous Alaskan who thinks Fatty's got eyes for his wife.

Fatty's New Role A mischievous prank leads the patrons of a bar to believe that a down-and-out bum is a mad bomber. The boozy Arbuckle takes over the joint in this strange cynical comedy.

Keystone Comedies Vol. 2

(1915) 43m. B&W. **B+**

Includes:

Fatty and Mabel at the San Diego Exposition The young couple has a rollicking good time at the Expo until Mabel catches Fatty flirting with another woman. The rides and sideshows are the story in this fun slice of Americana.

Fatty and Mabel's Simple Life Fatty wants to marry a cute neighbor but her father wants her to marry the rich and handsome village squire. Mabel flees with Fatty in a disastrous automobile leading to some crazy car antics.

Mabel and Fatty's Wash Day Fatty is henpecked and Mabel's hubby is an ogre. The unhappy duo flirt while doing the laundry and run off to have a drink together.

Keystone Comedies Vol. 3

(1915) 52m. B&W. **B+**

Includes:

Wished on Mabel Mabel and Mom take a walk in the park and meet up with Fatty. When a crook lifts Mom's watch, Fatty finds it and gives it to Mabel as a present.

Mabel, Fatty and the Law Fatty and Mabel pitch and woo but didn't see the "No Spooning" sign and are tossed in jail. The Keystone Kops make a brief appearance.

Fatty's Plucky Pup The dog catchers are after Fatty's pooch while kidnappers are trying to take his girl. Features a hilarious rear-projection chase sequence.

Other titles:

Keystone Comedies Vol. 4 (1915)

Keystone Comedies Vol. 5 (1915)

1930s

The Three Stooges

The godfathers of dumb and dumber cut their slapstick teeth on the vaudeville circuit before hitting their comic stride with bargain-basement jokes and cartoonish violence in a series of shorts at Columbia Studios (listed below). Despite awful casts and sub-par production, the boneheaded trio solidified the basic Stooge set-up: pugnacious top-dog Moe Howard, who terrorized his two mates with hair-pulling, sleight-of-hand tricks, and eye-poking tactics, straight man Larry Fine, sporting a shock of Brillo pad-like hair; and chrome-domed Brooklyn boy Curly Howard (eventually replaced by Shemp Howard and then Joe Besser).

The Three Stooges Comedy Capers

(1936–1947) 80m. B&W. **C+**

Includes:

Disorder in the Court (1936) A fan dancer is accused of shooting her shady lover and it's up to the boys to turn the trial upside down to get justice for the little lady.

Malice in the Palace (1940) The proud proprietors of the Orient's worst greasy spoon diner get involved in a plot to recover a diamond stolen from King Rutin–Tutin's tomb.

Sing a Song of Six Pants (1947) Faced with the prospects of their tailor shop going under, the Stooges plot to apprehend a notorious burglar so they can collect the reward and pay off the Skin & Flint Loan Company.

Higher Than a Kite

(1943–1944) 55m. B&W **B−**

Includes:

Higher Than a Kite (1943) Fearing disciplinary action after another screwup, the Stooges go AWOL and hide out in a sewer pipe. But as luck would have it, the pipe is actually a bomb headed for Nazi Germany.

The Yokes on Me (1944) Just because the boys are 4F doesn't mean they can't help their country; they become farmers and torment a band of escaped Japanese soldiers into giving up the cause.

No Dough Boys (1944) While wearing soldiers' garb for a photo layout, the Stooges are mistaken for Japanese soldiers by a band of Nazi spies who should know better.

3 Smart Saps and Other Yuks

(1944–1946) 55m. B&W **B−**

Includes:

Monkey Businessmen (1944) The Stooges decide they need a little peace and quiet, which is shattered when they end up in a sanitarium run by a crackpot doctor. Unfortunately getting out proves harder than getting in.

Beer Barrel Polecats (1946) The Stooges decide to make and sell their own beer but their business moxie only lands them in the hoosegow for selling suds to a cop.

3 Smart Saps (1946) The boys decide to take the plunge and marry three luscious dames, Stella, Mella, and Della. But when the girls' jail warden dad ends up in the slammer it looks like the happy day may never come.

Other Titles:

The Three Stooges, Vols. 1–19

The Three Stooges: Yes, We Have No Bonanza (1935)

The Three Stooges: Crash Goes the Hash (1940)

The Three Stooges: Idiots De Luxe (1943)

The Three Stooges: Cuckoo Cavaliers (1940)

The Three Stooges: Fuelin' Around (1948)

W. C. Fields

Whining, twitching, bulbous-nosed Fields perpetually had his patience tested by battle-ax wives, bratty kids, and polite society as he tried to get a little peace and quiet (usually so he could have a drink). These prosaic little films have wild plots that are simply a series of extended sight and sound gags, with Fields making sly, almost incomprehensible comments out of the side of his mouth.

International House

(1933) 70m. B&W. **B+**

A group of travelers in China is quarantined in a hotel where television is being demonstrated by a mad doctor. This compilation of skits and songs is charming, unique, and gives insight into the eccentric pop culture of the 1930s.
D: A. Edward Sutherland. A: With Peggy Hopkins Joyce, George Burns, and Gracie Allen.

It's a Gift

(1934) 73m. B&W. **A**

Grocery store owner Fields packs up his family and hits the road for California after buying an orange ranch. A classic battle of wits with wife, kids, neighbors, and ornery customers that never lets up.
D: Norman Z. McLeod. A: With Baby LeRoy, Kathleen Howard, Tommy Bupp.

You Can't Cheat an Honest Man

(1939) 76m. B&W. **B**

Fields is a circus owner who matches wits with ventriloquist dummy Charlie McCarthy. Vaudevillian episodic turns with good chemistry between W.C. and the dummy.
D: George Marshall. A: With Edgar Bergen and Charlie McCarthy, Constance Moore.

The Bank Dick

(1940) 73m. B&W. **A**

Incompetent and long-suffering bank detective Fields battles the customers and staff in a fast and steady series of comic bits.
D: Eddie Cline. A: With Cora Witherspoon, Una Merkel, Evelyn Del Rio.

My Little Chickadee

(1940) 91m. B&W. **B+**

Snake-oil salesman Fields marries Mae West who brings order to a Wild West town. Double entendres fill the air in this farcical but surprisingly tepid battle of the titans.
D: Eddie Cline. A: With Mae West, Joseph Calleia, Dick Foran.

Never Give a Sucker an Even Break

(1941) 70m. B&W. **B+**

Fields is the filmmaker who pitches his ideas for his next film to a producer. Pure farce with little plot and a huge chase scene.
D: Eddie Cline. A: With Gloria Jean, Franklin Pangborn, Leon Errol.

Marx Brothers

Groucho, Harpo, Chico, and, through 1933, Zeppo were Hollywood's funniest anarchists, creating an entirely new world of onscreen lunacy. Nonstop gags, verbal acrobatics, loopy songs, and a total lack of respect for any authority suffuse their films from the early, low-budget efforts to the glossy and sometimes formulaic MGM productions.

Cocoanuts

(1929) 96m. B&W. **C+**

This film version of a Marx Brothers stage comedy has assorted zanies and scam artists meeting up in Florida during the land boom. The stage-bound early talkie has poor sound and faded prints, but the boys' hilarious manic energy is still loud and clear.
D: Joseph Santley, Robert Florey. A: With Margaret Dumont, Kay Francis, Oscar Shaw.

Animal Crackers

(1930) 98m. B&W. **B+**

Another early entry that betrays its stage heritage with static direction and Groucho's frequent and hilarious asides. Harpo and Chico play a wild card game with society girls running in terror, Groucho's theme "Hooray for Captain Spaulding" is introduced along with classic bits like "One night I shot an elephant in my pajamas. . . ."
D: Victor Heerman. A: With Margaret Dumont, Lillian Roth, Louis Sorin.

Monkey Business

(1931) 77m. B&W. **A–**

The boys become bodyguards for rival gangsters on an ocean liner. Harpo chases girls, Chico overflows with bad puns, and even Zeppo gets to be a hero at fisticuffs. The gleeful anarchy and disregard for plot give this a fresh, almost improvised feel that's a true sign of polished comedy.
D: Norman Z. McLeod. A: With Thelma Tood, Ruth Hall, Harry Woods.

Horse Feathers

(1932) 69m. B&W. **A**

Academic anarchy reins when new college president Groucho deals with improvement suggestions by singing "I'm Against It" and proceeds to make a play for the late president's widow. With no breaks or gaps, this keeps the jokes coming, making it seem shorter than 69 minutes.
D: Norman Z. McLeod. A: With Thelma Todd, Robert Greig, David Landau.

Duck Soup

(1933) 70m. B&W. **A**

Rufus T. Firefly assumes power in Freedonia, offends everyone, hangs out with spies Chicolini and Pinky, and plunges the country into war over being called an upstart. Their zenith of absurd comedy blending political satire, terrible puns, pantomime, and the highest quotient of classic comic bits.
D: Leo McCarey. A: With Margaret Dumont, Louis Calhern, Edgar Kennedy.

A Night at the Opera

(1935) 92m. B&W. **A**

This is the Marx Brothers on a grand scale as they "help" an opera company on tour in America. The numerous musical interludes and sappy romantic subplot allow you to catch your breath in between some hi-

larious routines like the stateroom scene and Groucho's dissection of a legal contract.
D: Sam Wood. A: With Margaret Dumont, Kitty Carlisle, Allan Jones.

A Day at the Races
(1937) 111m. B&W. **B–**
Madness mixes with insanity when horse doctor Hackenbush takes over Standish Sanitarium. *A Night at the Opera* formula begins to take on a variety show look with a sappy love story and songs that dilute the comedy. Even chopped Marx makes the grade but be prepared for dull patches.
D: Sam Wood. A: With Margaret Dumont, Maureen O'Sullivan, Allan Jones.

Room Service
(1938) 78m. B&W. **B**
Groucho plays a shoestring producer holed up in a posh New York hotel trying to avoid the manager, keep his actors fed, and dupe the naive playwright from discovering that there's no backer. A zany theatrical comedy that was tailored for the Marxes with mixed results.
D: William Seiter. A: With Lucille Ball, Ann Miller, Donald McBride.

At the Circus
(1939) 87m. B&W. **B–**
Marxian madness is traded down for 30s style silly comedy in this pratfall-filled dip into the world of a near bankrupt circus. The setting seems apt for the brothers but they spend too much time in physical (and often stunt-doubled) action that has little to do with their brand of humor.
D: Edward Buzzell. A: With Margaret Dumont, Eve Arden, Nat Pendleton.

Go West
(1940) 81m. B&W. **C+**
The Marx Brothers begin their career descent from wreakers of discord and lunacy to softhearted but wacky do-gooders as they venture out west during the 1870s railroad boom. An inventive and exciting chase finale has the boys tearing apart an entire train to provide fuel for the speeding locomotive.
D: Edward Buzzell. A: With John Carroll, Walter Woolf King, Diana Lewis.

The Big Store
(1941) 80m. B&W. **C–**
This dull trifle reeks of un-Marxian 40s sappy humor as detective Wolf J. Flywheel tries to protect a store manager. Lots of chasing around the departments and lame jokes, all of which screech to a halt during Tony Martin's dreadful tribute to the melting pot with "The Tenement Symphony."
D: Charles F. Riesner. A: With Margaret Dumont, Tony Martin, Virginia Grey.

A Night in Casablanca
(1946) 85m. B&W. **C**
The Marxes rally some of their old charm in intrigue-filled post–World War II Casablanca where Groucho is the new hotel manager. ("I see. You expect the new manager NOT to steal. Good day, gentlemen!") The boys are pushing 60 and look a little old, but Groucho can still leer with the best of them.
D: Archie Mayo. A: With Lisette Verea, Charles Drake, Lois Collier.

Love Happy
(1949) 85m. B&W. **C–**
A woeful swan song film in which Groucho serves as the rarely seen narrator, recounting the story of Harpo and Chico on Broadway trying to put on the big show. The pair mix it up with mostly dead-on-arrival gags; most notable for a brief visit by Marilyn.
D: David Miller. A: With Vera-Ellen, Raymond Burr, Marilyn Monroe.

Laurel and Hardy

Laurel and Hardy made their mark in silent two-reelers, but an easy transition to sound helped cast their screen personas in gold: rotund and dignified Ollie trying to rise in the world, only to be unwittingly sabotaged by the blessedly simple, utterly hapless Stan. The short films of these babes in the woods are economic gems of heartfelt lunacy. The ensuing feature-length comedies followed suit, adding the occasional song and dance, and a romantic subplot that provided little more than a distraction.

Laurel and Hardy Classics Vols. 1–9
(1930) 75m.–100m. B&W.
A 🏛
Each volume contains four sound two-reelers that, given their wondrous comic pacing and delightful pervasive air of absurdity, are considered to be Laurel and Hardy's finest work. Outstanding are Volume I with the 1932 Oscar winner *The Music Box*, Volume 3 with *Their First Mistake*, Volume 6 with *Them Thar Hills*, and its sequel *Tit for Tat*.
D: James Horne. A: With Mae Busch, Charley Hall.

Pardon Us
(1931) 55m. B&W. **B**
A pair of bootleggers winds up in prison when they sell their wares to the law. Their first feature is an uneven but fascinating relic with wonderful bits, including a vaudeville-like school session and Ollie's sweet tenor rendition of "Lazy Moon."
D: James Parrott. A: With Wilfrid Lucas, Walter Long.

March of the Wooden Soldiers
(1934) 77m. B&W. **B+**
This rendition of Victor Herbert's operetta has Laurel and Hardy as some of the denizens of Toyland trying to save their village from an invasion of bogeymen. A charming musical spectacle and nice for the kiddies, but Stan and Ollie seem relegated to comic relief. Also released as *Babes in Toyland*.
D: Gus Meins. A: With Charlotte Henry, Henry Brandon.

Sons of the Desert
(1934) 68m. B&W. **A** 🎟
In order to go to Chicago for the big convention, the boys tell the wives they're off to Honolulu for health reasons. Rip-roaring, perfectly paced fun studded with zany characters, and it even has a hit song, "Honolulu Baby."
D: William Seiter. A: With Charley Chase, Mae Busch.

Bonnie Scotland
(1935) 80m. B&W. **B**
After chasing an inheritance, the boys wind up with a Scot-

tish regiment in India. Some excellent routines that get watered down with a lukewarm romantic subplot.
D: James Horne. A: With Jimmy Finlayson, Daphne Pollard.

The Bohemian Girl
(1936) 74m. B&W. **B**
A pair of hapless gypsies raise a young girl, not realizing that she's been kidnapped from a noble family. Some especially warm Laurel and Hardy fun, and Stan's lesson to Ollie on how to pick a pocket is hilarious. Unfortunately the operetta portion takes too much away from the boys.
D: James W. Horne.
A: With Mae Busch, Antonio Moreno.

Our Relations
(1936) 65m. B&W. **A**
Two sailors on the make get mixed up with their long lost identical twins, both happily married. Zips along with one wacky mix-up after another and contains a snazzy production number.
D: Harry Lachman. A: With Alan Hale, Sidney Toler.

Way Out West
(1937) 66m. B&W. **A**
In ornery Brushwood Gulch, the boys deliver a gold mine deed to the wrong person and go through raging rivers, saloon walls, and player pianos to get it back. The comedy bits are perfectly pitched and the boys do a soft-shoe dance to "The Trail of the Lonesome Pine."
D: James Horne. A: With Jimmy Finlayson, Rosina Lawrence.

Blockheads
(1938) 60m. B&W. **A**
Ollie rescues Stan from the Old Soldiers Home and makes the biggest mistake of his life: He brings Stan to his home. This one contains many of their classic routines stitched together seamlessly.
D: John G. Blystone. A: With Billy Gilbert, Patricia Ellis.

A Chump at Oxford
(1940) 63m. B&W. **B+**
In their last film with Hal Roach studios, the boys inadvertently stop a bank robbery and are treated to an Oxford education. After a slow and incongruous stateside start, Stan and Ollie hit their stride at college.
D: Alfred Goulding. A: With Jimmy Finlayson, Wilfrid Lucas.

Laurel and Hardy's Laughing 20's
(1965) 90m. B&W. **A**
This outstanding compilation of the finest moments from the silent years showcases Laurel and Hardy's physical comedy with epic pie-throwing events, monumental pants-ripping riots, and more.
D: Robert Youngson. A: With Jimmy Finlayson, Anita Garvin, Tiny Sanford.

Other Films:
Laurel and Hardy: On the Lam (1930–34)
Laurel and Hardy: At Work (1932–34)
Pack Up Your Troubles (1932)
Swiss Miss (1938)
Flying Deuces (1939)
Saps at Sea (1940)
Great Guns (1941)
Air Raid Wardens (1943)
Nothing but Trouble (1945)
The Bull Fighters (1945)
Atoll K (1950)

Pre-Code 30s Comedies

These gritty ribald comedies feature hard-boiled newspapermen, swindlers, and hot dames who thumb their nose at proprieties and crack wise in the most hilarious, licentious, and politically incorrect fashion imaginable.

Blonde Crazy
(1931) 79m. B&W. **A**
A silver-tongued ladies man who's a bellhop in a Midwestern hotel entices a blonde maid to combine her looks with his brains so they can be grifters in the big city. Cagney doesn't miss a beat, tossing out a gag or wisecrack for any occasion in this jubilantly risqué comedy.
D: Roy Del Ruth. A: James Cagney, Joan Blondell, Louis Calhern.

Blessed Event
(1932) 83m. B&W. **A**
You won't believe some of the dialogue in this hilarious tale of a hard-boiled gossip columnist who specializes in spreading news of pregnancies and extramarital affairs. Tracy's snide and witty motormouth is hilariously underscored by a plot and pacing that won't let you catch your breath.
D: Roy Del Ruth. A: Lee Tracy, Mary Brian, Dick Powell.

Employees Entrance
(1933) 75m. B&W. **B+**
The ruthless manager of a New York department store treats his employees like disposable products and will stop at nothing in the name of profit. As much a morality play about greed and Depression-era hardships with enough sordid runaway sexual situations to mark this as a pre-Code gem.
D: Roy Del Ruth. A: Warren William, Loretta Young, Wallace Ford.

She Done Him Wrong
(1933) 65m. B&W. **A–**
A Bowery beerhall-burlesque house in the Gay Nineties is the backdrop for the showgirl owner who can hold her own against the lowlife and still seduce a Salvation Army officer. West is her own hip-swaggering, one-woman burlesque show with bawdy double entendres, eyebrow-lifting come-ons, and not to be believed dirty songs.
D: Lowell Sherman. A: Mae West, Cary Grant, Owen Moore.

Jean Harlow

Harlow gave a distinctly salacious spin to these lightweight romantic comedies that showcased her persona as the smart-mouth, platinum vamp who often looked like she could eat her men for breakfast and spit them out again before lunch.

Platinum Blonde
(1931) 86m. B&W. **B+**
Harlow is the fancy-pants socialite bullying her reporter husband who's in love with girl reporter Young. The light and witty early comedy romp from Capra keeps the gags flying, taking special delight in the ribbing of Williams' cohorts about his status as a kept man.
D: Frank Capra. A: With Loretta Young, Robert Williams, Louise Hale.

Bombshell
(1933) 90m. B&W. **A–**
This frantically paced screwball follows the slightly dim sexpot who's dissatisfied with the flamboyant and exaggerated stories her studio's press agent is feeding the public. A funny, cleverly written spoof of Hollywood and behind-the-scenes working of the studio system with a wisecracking Harlow.
D: Victor Fleming. A: With Lee Tracy, Frank Morgan, Franchot Tone.

The Girl from Missouri
(1934) 75m. B&W. **B+**
A small town girl heads for New York, then Palm Beach as a would-be golddigger. Harlow's steamy image is given a perky, more wholesome makeover in this jaunty romp, though she can still match wits with a succession of smooth playboys.
D: Jack Conway. A: With Lionel Barrymore, Franchot Tone, Lewis Stone.

Suzy
(1936) 99m. B&W. **B+**
A British showgirl marries a wealthy duplicitous World War I aviator, then discovers her first husband is still alive. Crackling banter and some decent screen chemistry between Harlow and Grant distinguish this action-heavy romantic comedy.
D: George Fitzmaurice. A: With Franchot Tone, Cary Grant, Benita Hume.

Personal Property
(1937) 88m. B&W. **C+**
Harlow is a widow stranded in England by debt and saddled with overzealous watchdog Taylor who's been paid not to let her or her belongings out of his sight. A mildly engaging bedroom comedy that cooks up as many suggestive scenes as possible to capitalize on the two stars' sex appeal.
D: W. S. Van Dyke. A: With Robert Taylor, Reginald Owen, Una O'Connor.

Saratoga
(1937) 94m. B&W. **B+**
In her final film, Harlow plays the daughter of a horse breeder who attempts to recover the family farm from gambler Gable. Harlow glows in some of her best comic work next to Gable in this sharp and amusing behind-the-scenes look at thoroughbred racing.
D: Jack Conway. A: With Clark Gable, Lionel Barrymore, Walter Pidgeon.

Screwball Comedies

Take a bored rich heroine who sets her sights on an unlikely man, throw in a screwy family, some zany complications, and witty rapid-fire dialogue, and you've got the formula for these cynical, breathless, and hilarious roller coaster rides.

The Front Page
(1931) 100m. B&W. **B+** 🏛
An ace reporter agrees to postpone his wedding night to cover an execution, and then the condemned man escapes and practically falls in his lap. A snappy but stagy tale, but after some early verbal pyrotechnics, the roving camera and continually exploding dialogue get a little tiresome.
D: Lewis Milestone. A: Adolphe Menjou, Pat O'Brien, Mary Brian.

No Man of Her Own
(1932) 85m. B&W. **B–**
A gambler gets hitched to a good girl, and her loyalty and sweet ways begin to redeem hard-boiled hubby. Nice enough, but the thin story isn't helped by the fact that surprisingly few sparks fly between the two leads.
D: Wesley Ruggles. A: Clark Gable, Carole Lombard, Dorothy Mackaill.

Twentieth Century
(1934) 91m. B&W. **A–**
When the bombastic Broadway producer finds his prima donna star is flying the coop, he books a ride on the New York–Chicago train to beg, wheedle, and cajole her into returning. The two stars have a blast whining and howling like a couple of spoiled brats in this brassy but stagebound farce.
D: Howard Hawks. A: John Barrymore, Carole Lombard, Walter Connelly.

My Man Godfrey
(1936) 93m. B&W. **A** 🏛
An heiress hires an elegant down-and-outer to be the family butler, who then proceeds to redeem in one way or another the whole wacky crew. A loony sparkling comedy with Powell deftly dodging Lombard's amorous advances while keeping his past life and days off a secret.
D: Gregory LaCava. A: William Powell, Carole Lombard, Alice Brady.

The Awful Truth
(1937) 92m. B&W. **A** 🏛
A high-society couple divorces and then does everything in their means to sabotage each other's loveless engagement. The bubbly rhythm, the hilarious setups, and the graceful ease and erotic tension between Grant and Dunne make this a playful and seductive classic. Don't miss the Asta the dog clone.
D: Leo McCarey. A: Cary Grant, Irene Dunne, Ralph Bellamy.

Nothing Sacred
(1937) 75m. **B+**
When a Vermont girl is exposed to radium and thought to be dying, a sardonic beat reporter wines and dines her for a series of human interest stories. This cynical and biting entry about a Cinderella of the tabloids is lessened by some out-of place slapstick antics and a cop-out resolution.
D: William Wellman. A: Fredric March, Carole Lombard, Walter Connelly.

Topper
(1937) 97m. B&W. **B+** 🏛
When a high spirited society couple dies in a drunken car crash, they come back to give their stick-in-the-mud banker some lessons on how to cut loose and have fun. This film, along with its sequel *Topper Takes a Trip*, is a bright and zany screwball. The third, *Topper Returns*, goes gothic as Topper helps a young woman ghost solve the mystery of her own death.
D: Norman Z. MacLeod. A: Constance Bennett, Cary Grant, Roland Young.

Bringing Up Baby
(1938) 102m. B&W. **A** 🏛
A zany heiress shanghais a

bumbling zoologist on the eve of his wedding and the two of them try to deliver a pet leopard and find where her pooch hid a dinosaur bone. This daffiest of all screwballs is like an avalanche of sight gags and comic disasters with stars that don't miss a breathless beat.
D: Howard Hawks. A: Cary Grant, Katharine Hepburn, Charlie Ruggles.

Holiday

(1938) 93m. B&W. **B+**

When a socialite brings home her eccentric fiancé, daddy's not impressed, but her maverick younger sister thinks he's a pip. A sophisticated, slightly stagy chamber comedy with earnest trapped Kate yearning to capture her own moment of magic with the help of the most irregular Grant.
D: George Cukor. A: Katharine Hepburn, Cary Grant, Lew Ayres.

The Mad Miss Manton

(1938) 80m. B&W. **B–**

While walking her dog, a socialite stumbles over a body and, after being warned off by the police, quickly gets her bridge club to help track down some clues. There are plenty of madcap antics, but the story and romance never pick up much steam.
D: Leigh Jason. A: Barbara Stanwyck, Henry Fonda, Sam Levene.

Bachelor Mother

(1939) 81m. B&W. **B+**

A single working girl takes care of an abandoned baby, and her boss is convinced that it's hers—and his son's. Ginger's sexy naivete and some comic moments help this charming tale overcome its dated premise.
D: Garson Kanin. A: Ginger Rogers, David Niven, Charles Coburn.

Fifth Avenue Girl

(1939) 83m. B&W. **B**

A free-spirited girl charms an unhappy millionaire who promptly moves her into his mansion. Their friendship soon has his uncaring wife and kids eating out of his hands. This low-key "the rich could learn a thing or two from the poor" tale is pleasant but lacks any real comic invention.
D: Gregory LaCava. A: Ginger Rogers, Walter Connelly, Verree Teasdale.

Midnight

(1939) 94m. B&W. **A**

A broke young lovely in Paris has her sights set higher than a smitten cabby, especially when she gets paid to impersonate a Hungarian countess with French high society. A frothy and witty romantic comedy that continually surprises with a seemingly endless supply of comic situations.
D: Mitchell Leisen. A: Claudette Colbert, Don Ameche, John Barrymore.

His Girl Friday

(1940) 92m. B&W. **A**

A wily editor gets one last favor from his ex-wife, ace reporter: postponing her wedding to cover an execution. Everyone talks like a typewriter moving 140 words a minute in this sizzling, rapid-fire remake of *The Front Page*, as Grant and Russell scoop the rest of the city and rekindle old feelings.
D: Howard Hawks. A: Cary Grant, Rosalind Russell, Ralph Bellamy.

Ball of Fire

(1941) 111m. B&W. **A–**

When a group of musty professors needs a lesson in slang, they take in a fast-talking dame on the lam. She falls for a gawky handsome professor, and when the mob closes in, everyone takes to the road in this extremely silly but lovable romp.
D: Howard Hawks. A: Gary Cooper, Barbara Stanwyck, Oscar Homolka.

The Bride Came C.O.D.

(1941) 92m. B&W. **C+**

The father of a spoiled runaway bride hires a hard-boiled pilot to kidnap and bring her back. The scheme goes haywire when the pair ends up alone in the desert, with the pilot falling for the brat. The stars play it broad and brassy to make up for the script's lack of sparkle in this disappointing caper comedy.
D: William Keighley. A: James Cagney, Bette Davis, Jack Carson.

The Lady Eve

(1941) 97m. B&W. **A**

A father-daughter card shark team decides to take a gullible brewery heir to the cleaners, and then the daughter falls for the schnook. A drop-dead funny romantic comedy where the haughty upper class gets a kick in the pants from the naughty dame who gets sweet revenge on her proud dopey beloved.
D: Preston Sturges. A: Barbara Stanwyck, Henry Fonda, Charles Coburn.

The Palm Beach Story

(1942) 88m. B&W. **A**

Convinced that she can raise money for her inventor husband and live the high life she deserves, a beautiful wife heads for Florida to get a divorce and a rich new husband. A refreshingly shameless and sexy romp with a ludicrous and thoroughly appropriate finale that will leave you gaping in amazement.
D: Preston Sturges. A: Joel McCrea, Claudette Colbert, Rudy Vallee.

The Talk of the Town

(1942) 118m. B&W. **B+**

A man falsely accused of murder escapes and holes up in the country home of a Harvard law professor and his charming landlady. The dark urgent opening settles into a relaxed thinking man's comedy about law and the little people, with some subtle scene stealing by the charismatic leads.
D: George Stevens. A: Jean Arthur, Ronald Colman, Cary Grant.

Arsenic and Old Lace

(1944) 118m. B&W. **B+**

A drama critic fears he may have caught the family psychosis as he tries to cover up for his two sweet aunts who poison gentlemen callers with their elderberry wine. Wickedly funny black comedy is given a rather slick shrill treatment, with an ill-at-ease Grant.
D: Frank Capra. A: Cary Grant, Raymond Massey, Josephine Hull.

(See also *It Happened One Night*, page 67.)

Satires and Social Comedies

Like the screwball comedies, these antidotes to the Depression focused on romance and the peccadillos of the wealthy with lively pacing, razor sharp dialogue, and some of the most hilarious turns by Hollywood legends.

Dinner at Eight
(1933) 113m. B&W. **A–**
A down-at-the-heels matinee idol, a tart-tongued society matron, and a vulgar nouveau riche couple are among the Manhattan big shots invited to an elaborate dinner party. The bite is still here as the rich and famous scratch and claw one another in this savage, brilliantly cast satire.
D: George Cukor. A: John Barrymore, Marie Dressler, Jean Harlow

The Ruggles of Red Gap
(1935) 92m. B&W. **A–**
Thanks to a winning poker hand, a nouveau riche couple from the Wild West ends up with an English butler. He schools them in social graces while they give him lessons in social democracy. Laughton, Ruggles, and a raucous buddy getting drunk at a Paris cafe is one of many priceless scenes.
D: Leo McCarey. A: Charles Laughton, Mary Boland, Charles Ruggles.

Stage Door
(1937) 92m. B&W. **A–**
An upper-class aspiring actress moves into a theatrical boarding house and proceeds to drive everyone up the wall. The stunning cast is at top form as the women cope with poverty and sleazy producers while hustling for that big chance that will shoot them to stardom.
D: Gregory LaCava. A: Katharine Hepburn, Ginger Rogers, Lucille Ball.

The Women
(1939) 132m. B&W. **A**
A loving wife discovers her husband is straying, and who's her support group? Her catty snickering circle of society friends. You've never heard women talk as fast or as pointedly as in this funny wicked comedy that zooms along from gossip fest to female bonding to cat fights without missing a beat.
D: George Cukor. A: Norma Shearer, Rosalind Russell, Joan Crawford.

The Man Who Came to Dinner
(1941) 112m. B&W. **B**
It looks like it's going to be a long winter for a Midwestern family when a self-important columnist breaks his leg and ends up moving his base of operation to their house. Windbag Woolley is the voice that stirs the drink in this film version of a play that is stagy but a smorgasbord of verbal pyrotechnics.
D: William Keighley. A: Monty Woolley, Bette Davis, Ann Sheridan.

To Be or Not to Be
(1942) 99m. B&W. **A**
An uproarious Old World farce suddenly shifts gears into heart-thumping suspense as a Polish theater group, run by a vain matinee idol and his straying wife, try to track down a Nazi double agent. Benny and Lombard are hilarious and Benny's melancholic Hamlet is a howl not to be missed.
D: Ernst Lubitsch. A: Jack Benny, Carole Lombard, Robert Stack.

Romantic Comedies-Married

Romantic comedies seem to have more fun with the "boy meets girl, boy loses girl" formula when the couple is already married. Don't expect homey little domestic comedies here; many of these films have more pizzazz, romance, and heat than any of the will-they-or-won't-they tales. You already know they *do*, but with all the screwball complications of meddling in-laws, house dicks, and jealous schemings you just don't know when.

The Bride Walks Out
(1936) 81m. B&W. **C+**
A spoiled young model and a fledgling engineer tie the knot, but when she starts overspending he picks a fight and she flies the coop. Shrewd Stanwyck is miscast as the materialistic young thing who comes to her senses in this low-octane look at a marriage of opposites.
D: Leigh Jason. A: Barbara Stanwyck, Gene Raymond, Robert Young.

Vivacious Lady
(1938) 90m. B&W. **B+**
A college professor and a nightclub singer meet, court, and marry all in one night. He's reluctant to tell his folks and her impatience to consummate the marriage sets off a series of complications, which force Jimmy to win her all over again. A warmly funny, if dated, comedy.
D: George Stevens. A: James Stewart, Ginger Rogers, Charles Coburn.

Made for Each Other
(1939) 93m. B&W. **B+**
Money trouble, interfering in-laws, and other domestic problems threaten the perfect marriage between a lawyer and his wife. Things come to a head when their infant child becomes gravely ill, with the life-and-death struggle giving a soap operaish spin to this perceptive humane comedy.
D: John Cromwell. A: Carole Lombard, James Stewart, Charles Coburn.

The Philadelphia Story
(1940) 112m. B&W. **A–**
On the eve of her wedding, a young socialite meets up with her ex-husband who still carries a torch and a tabloid reporter who's out to expose some of the family dirt. A sparkling jaunt through high society with a delightful group of characters including lecherous Uncle Willie.
D: George Cukor. A: Katharine Hepburn, Cary Grant, James Stewart.

My Favorite Wife
(1940) 88m. B&W. **B+**
Just when he's about to remarry, Grant's dead wife shows up after spending seven years on a desert island with a beefcake scientist. Grant and Dunne, the dream team of adult comedy, begin the courtship all over again, turning the silly premise into a clever and engaging affair.
D: Garson Kanin. A: Cary Grant, Irene Dunne, Randolph Scott.

Love Crazy
(1941) 99m. B&W. **B**
As a wife gets ready to celebrate her anniversary, she discovers her husband is whooping it up with an old flame. Her mother tries to convince her to divorce, but instead the wife pretends to be insane. Powell and Loy are a delight, but this zany and strained effort goes too far in pulling out the stops.
D: Jack Conway. A: William Powell, Myrna Loy, Gail Patrick.

Mr. and Mrs. Smith
(1941) 95m. B&W. **B+**
When the marriage between a bickering young society couple is ruled invalid, it only takes one more fight and she's out the door. Soon

the pair is spending all their free time trying to make the other jealous. A funny trifle with the catty couple playing some wickedly funny games.
D: Alfred Hitchcock. A: Carole Lombard, Robert Montgomery, Gene Raymond.

Once Upon a Honeymoon
(1942) 117m. B&W. **C+**
A burlesque dancer, trapped in a marriage to a Nazi officer, looks to a radio commentator to smuggle her out of enemy territory. This truly bizarre film keeps a light tone while Cary and Ginger check in and out of a concentration camp and cross war-torn Europe.
D: Leo McCarey. A: Cary Grant, Ginger Rogers, Walter Slezak.

That Uncertain Feeling
(1942) 84m. B&W. **B+**
A listless wife with hiccups goes to her shrink and falls for another patient, an egotistical pianist who can only play in private. The zany setup and Meredith's berserk portrayal offers promise, but the surprising lack of sexual tension zaps some of the energy out of this.
D: Ernst Lubitsch. A: Merle Oberon, Melvyn Douglas, Burgess Meredith.

The Perfect Marriage
(1947) 87m. B&W. **B**
A couple celebrates their 10th anniversary by trying to question why they have it so good and before you know it, they decide that everything is rotten. What starts out as a smart look at marriage turns into a tiring talkfest, with the usual bickering in-laws and plots to make each other jealous.
D: Lewis Allen. A: Loretta Young, David Niven, Eddie Albert.

Romantic Comedies-Single

Though these lively tales of bickering lovers have much of the zip and irresponsible tone of screwball comedies, they still keep the action very firmly in the boy-meets-girl court.

Libeled Lady
(1936) 98m. B&W. **B**
When an heiress decides to sue a shady newspaper for slander, the editor sends out a muckraking reporter and his street-smart fiancée to dig some more dirt. A brassy and relentlessly one-note story keeps the wisecracking cast from being even funnier than they are.
D: Jack Conway. A: Jean Harlow, William Powell, Myrna Loy.

Double Wedding
(1937) 87m. B&W. **B**
A New York businesswoman is worried that a bohemian artist might endanger her younger sister's engagement. She agrees to pose for a portrait if he cuts little sis out of his life, and you can guess the rest. Including a bevy of lowlifes and kooks, this loony romp throws everything in but the kitchen sink.
D: Richard Thorpe A: William Powell, Myrna Loy, Florence Rice.

Rage of Paris
(1938) 75m. B&W. **B–**
A bubbly high-society romp about a beautiful and broke Parisian trying to make it in New York has all the ploys and mishaps involving mistaken identity, golddigging, and elusive millionaire rogues. Standard fare except for Darrieux.
D: Henry Koster. A: Douglas Fairbanks, Jr.; Danielle Darrieux; Mischa Auer.

The Divorce of Lady X
(1938) 91m. **B**
London is fogged in, forcing a society girl and a barrister to share a hotel room. He's smitten, but then believes that she's the femme fatale who's being divorced by his best friend. A charming and very British drawing room farce with game stars and vividly unnatural Technicolor.
D: Tim Whelan. A: Merle Oberon, Laurence Olivier, Binnie Barnes.

The Shop Around the Corner
(1940) 97m. B&W. **A** 🏛
In old Budapest, two bickering shop clerks are blissfully unaware that they are each other's romantic pen pal. The store becomes a battleground as the two feisty lonelyhearts curry favor with the boss, even as they're making plans to finally meet each other. A rich comedy that reaches for the sublime and makes it.
D: Ernst Lubitsch. A: Margaret Sullavan, James Stewart, Frank Morgan.

The Devil and Miss Jones
(1941) 92m. B&W. **C+**
A despotic tycoon poses as a salesman in his own store to weed out the malcontents. When he meets popular Miss Jones, his disposition goes from sour to sunny, and he starts fighting for employee's rights. Given the delightful stars, surprisingly flat and impersonal compared to similar fare from this period.
D: Sam Wood. A: Jean Arthur, Robert Cummings, Charles Coburn.

Tom, Dick and Harry
(1941) 86m. B&W. **C+**
A dimwitted small-town girl is wooed by three men, including a millionaire. Ginger's charm is completely missing in action here, but her weird fantasies of wedded bliss with each man, along with Meredith's hilarious turn, make it worth watching.
D: Garson Kanin. A: Ginger Rogers, George Murphy, Burgess Meredith.

Christmas in Connecticut
(1945) 101m. B&W. **B**
The New York career girl who pens a column for a housekeeping magazine has to convince her publisher that she's really a homebody with the requisite domestic skills. Then the boss brings along an attractive war hero to Christmas dinner at her "country house." A relaxed but lively Yuletide romp.
D: Peter Godfrey. A: Barbara Stanwyck, Sydney Greenstreet, Dennis Morgan.

Capra-Corn

Hollywood had no greater salesman for the American virtues of pluck, hard work, and small-town life than Frank Capra. Almost every film in this group of sentimental Depression-era fables is not only a classic, but still freshly entertaining with the decent little-man heroes, the broadsides at those in power, and the heartwarming and very dark-edged corn.

Lady for a Day

(1933) 96m. B&W. **A–**

When her daughter arrives in New York with a rich fiancé in tow, a sidewalk apple vendor is transformed into a wealthy woman with the help of a genial gangster and his thugs. A crackling hard-times farce served up with some sentiment that still doesn't leave a dry eye in the house.

D: Frank Capra. A: May Robson, Warren William, Guy Kibbee.

It Happened One Night

(1934) 105m. B&W. **A**

One of the quintessential screwball comedies about a street-smart reporter waylaid on a cross-country trip with his quarry, a society girl fleeing her fiancé. The sharp-witted dialogue is matched by the romantic sparks between the two mismatched lovers continually sniping at each other while being thrown together in close quarters.

D: Frank Capra. A: Clark Gable, Claudette Colbert, Walter Connelly.

Mr. Deeds Goes to Town

(1936) 115m. B&W. **A**

When an overnight millionaire moves to the big city, his competence is questioned after he decides to bequeath his fortune to the poor. Like other Capra fables, this manages to be warm and wholesome and slightly hysterical at the same time.

D: Frank Capra. A: Gary Cooper, Jean Arthur, George Bancroft.

You Can't Take It with You

(1938) 127m. B&W. **B**

Barrymore is the head of a quirky household oblivious to the financial worries that plague the nation. Then his secretary daughter falls for a rich family's son and teaches the swell a thing or two about true happiness. Entertaining, but lacks the incisive bite of better Capra fare.

D: Frank Capra. A: Lionel Barrymore, James Stewart, Jean Arthur.

Mr. Smith Goes to Washington

(1939) 129m. B&W. **A**

A Boy Scout leader becomes a senator and charms the pants off jaded Washington—and the viewer—before he discovers, struggles against, and finally rages against corrupt government. A razor-sharp look at politics with Stewart's classic filibuster scene a melodramatic, Washington-style David and Goliath battle.

D: Frank Capra. A: James Stewart, Jean Arthur, Claude Rains.

Meet John Doe

(1941) 123m. B&W. **A**

The most unsettling of Capra's fables about a reporter who cooks up an on-the-skids baseball player as a symbol of America's disenfranchised. From the cynical reporters and corrupt politicians to the adoring public who easily turns into a raging mob—everyone is manipulating or being manipulated in this dark, almost dreamlike tale.

D: Frank Capra. A: Gary Cooper, Barbara Stanwyck, Walter Brennan.

It's a Wonderful Life

(1946) 129m. B&W. **A**

Despite the endless TV broadcasts of this Christmas chestnut about a frustrated dreamer, it still remains the classic nostalgic vision of small-town life with a graceful winsome Stewart.

D: Frank Capra. A: James Stewart, Donna Reed, Lionel Barrymore.

(See also *State of the Union,* page 163.)

1940s

Preston Sturges Satires

These are among the most wicked satires to come out of Hollywood, populated by Sturges' galaxy of wide-eyed innocents, down on their luck romantics, and lovable rascals. As you listen to everyone rattle off subversive dialogue while diving headfirst into plots with a crazy convoluted dream logic, you'll occasionally wonder how some of these ever got past the Hollywood censors.

Christmas in July

(1940) 70m. B&W. **A–**

The clerk who's fired by one coffee company wins the jingle contest and $25,000 from their rival. The "brilliant" young man's rise and fall is told with spit and vinegar in this exhilarating, breathtakingly inventive comedy. A well-aimed jab at the fickleness of the trend-happy business world.

D: Preston Sturges. A: Dick Powell, Ellen Drew, Raymond Walburn.

The Great McGinty

(1940) 81m. B&W. **A–**

An American bartender in a south-of-the-border dive recalls his life as a puppet governor who turns the tables on his own corrupt machinery. While the exotic mood of the opening screams for a Dorothy Lamour sarong dance, the bristling, often savage political satire soon kicks in with plenty of barbed action.

D: Preston Sturges. A: Brian Donleavy, Akim Tamiroff, Muriel Angelus.

Sullivan's Travels

(1941) 90m. B&W. **A–** 🏛

A successful director of light comedies wants to do socially conscious message films and hits the road incognito to research the "little people." What begins as an engaging romantic comedy takes a harrowing turn when he winds up on a chain gang with no way out, in this potent mongrel of a film.
D: Preston Sturges. A: Joel McCrea, Veronica Lake, Robert Warwick.

Hail the Conquering Hero

(1944) 101m. B&W. **A** 🏛

A small white lie to his family gets out of control, and the 4F stooge is now his hometown's returning hero. Americana goes berserk in this hilarious and scary farce that rides along with the whims and passions of the frenzied masses who build up and tear down their returning hero.
D: Preston Sturges. A: Eddie Bracken, Ella Raines, William Demarest.

The Miracle of Morgan's Creek

(1944) 99m. B&W. **A** 🏛

When a good-time girl gets drunk at the ball, pregnant afterwards, and can't remember by whom, she's ready to marry the first lovesick nerd to come along. Just when this perverse whirlwind of a comedy is about to burst with giddy tomfoolery, the two leads begin an unlikely and sweet romance.
D: Preston Sturges. A: Betty Hutton, Eddie Bracken, Diana Lynn.

The Sin of Harold Diddlebock (Mad Wednesday)

(1947) 91m. B&W. **B–**

A middle-aged football hero gets fired from his comfortable job and, hoping to turn over an adventurous new leaf, puts down his life savings on a rag-tag circus. A loud slapstick sequel to *The Freshman,* that soon disintegrates into a sloppy series of disconnected gags.
D: Preston Sturges. A: Harold Lloyd, Frances Ramsden, Jimmy Conlin.

The Beautiful Blonde from Bashful Bend

(1949) 79m. **C+**

A gunslinging nightclub singer on the lam ducks into a small town posing as a schoolmarm. Soon her cover is blown by a handsome marshal and her shiftless boyfriend who's looking to collect the reward money in this colorful but surprisingly low-brow western spoof.
D: Preston Sturges. A: Betty Grable, Cesar Romero, Rudy Vallee.

(See also *Unfaithfully Yours, pg. 72*)

Andy Hardy

These films may be corny timepieces but they are the final word in optimistic, Depression-era, small-town Americana. This is the family that won a special Oscar certificate for its achievement in "representing an American way of life": wise Judge Hardy, understanding Mother dispensing a piece of cake, and the impetuous high-energy Andy, who's always in the midst of a puppy-love affair.

Love Finds Andy Hardy

(1938) 90m. B&W. **A–**

Andy annoys his steady date and breaks the heart of the girl next door when he escorts glamour-puss Lana Turner around town. Love's complications, intrigues, and misunderstandings keep things moving, with time-outs for Judy's singing.
D: George Seitz. A: Mickey Rooney, Lewis Stone, Judy Garland.

Andy Hardy Gets Spring Fever

(1939) 89m. B&W. **B**

When Andy develops a crush on his high school drama teacher, he writes and stages a play to impress her. Standard sentimentality with family and girlfriend on hand to nurse Andy through his heartache.
D: W. S. Van Dyke. A: Mickey Rooney, Lewis Stone, Ann Rutherford.

Andy Hardy Meets a Debutante

(1940) 89m. B&W. **A–**

The Judge and Andy go to New York City, where Rooney enlists the help of Garland to meet a glamorous deb. The big city setting and Judy's singing lends a little sophistication to the wholesome proceedings.
D: George Seitz. A: Mickey Rooney, Lewis Stone, Judy Garland.

Andy Hardy's Private Secretary

(1941) 101m. B&W. **B–**

Andy gets a second chance after he flunks his high school final and engages a secretary to manage his social engagements while he studies. Overly contrived situations make this less than sparkling.
D: George Seitz. A: Mickey Rooney, Lewis Stone, Kathryn Grayson.

Life Begins for Andy Hardy

(1941) 100m. B&W. **B+**

Before he starts college, Andy talks his parents into letting him strike out on his own in New York City. A comparatively mature and less bland entry with Andy learning how brutal life can be in the big city. Judy doesn't sing in this one.
D: George Seitz. A: Mickey Rooney, Lewis Stone, Judy Garland.

Andy Hardy's Double Life

(1942) 92m. B&W. **B**

Big man on campus Andy proposes to two coeds and they both accept. Typical romantic hijinks, and Andy gets involved with crazy money-making schemes.
D: George Seitz. A: Mickey Rooney, Ann Rutherford, Esther Williams.

Love Laughs at Andy Hardy

(1946) 94m. B&W. **C+**

Andy returns from World War II (apparently unaffected) and has his heart broken when he goes back to college. The story drags, the warmth is gone, and Andy, still his manic self, looks a little old.
D: Willis Goldbeck. A: Mickey Rooney, Lewis Stone, Bonita Granville.

Bob Hope

Armed with a quick wit and a desire to escape, Hope inevitably bumbles his way to the heart of every problem in these easygoing larks. His leading ladies usually have more guts, guile, and brains than he does, which makes it even easier for him to growl and leer at them with the lust of a ten-year-old. Whether they're the small black-and-white wartime comedies or the big Technicolor costume farces, Bob plays the same girl-hungry, incompetent wiseacre who's just brave enough to spout a one-liner before bolting from danger.

The Ghost Breakers

(1940) 82m. B&W. **B+**

A wisecracking radio performer is framed for murder and escapes to Cuba in the trunk of an heiress with a haunted castle laden with hidden treasures. Hope tosses off jokes while running from various spooks and zombies in this frenzied and somewhat complicated comedy.
D: George Marshall. A: With Paulette Goddard, Richard Carlson, Paul Lukas.

My Favorite Blonde

(1942) 78m. B&W. **B**

He's the talentless half of a vaudeville team that costars a penguin, but he's also the best hope for a curvy British agent who needs someone to elude the Nazis and transport plans across America. Plenty of warm-blooded growls for the blonde and zippy one-liners against the Axis powers.
D: Sidney Lanfield. A: With Gale Sondergaard, Madeleine Carroll, George Zucco.

They Got Me Covered

(1943) 95m. B&W. **B–**

Hope's the foreign correspondent who has blown the story of the century—the Nazi invasion of Russia—and now he's back in Washington to regain his reputation by tracking down Nazi saboteurs. Another simple and clean wartime comedy.
D: David Butler. A: With Dorothy Lamour, Lenore Aubert, Otto Preminger.

The Princess and the Pirate

(1944) 94m. **B+**

In this lavish South Seas pirate adventure, Hope is a fifth-rate performer helping a princess flee marriage and avoid the clutches of a snarling pirate and corrupt governor. A cheerful garish swashbuckling caper.
D: David Butler. A: With Virginia Mayo, Walter Slezak, Victor McLaglen.

Monsieur Beaucaire

(1946) 93m. **B–**

As Louis XV's barber sent to Spain disguised as a foppish courtier, Bob woos the princess, growls after a pert chambermaid, and blusters his way through court pomp and circumstance. Another bright Technicolor romp, but this one fusses too much over the frills, giving less time for Hope.
D: George Marshall. A: With Patric Knowles, Joan Caulfield, Marjorie Reynolds.

The Paleface

(1948) 91m. **B+**

An Easterner dentist is duped into marriage by sharpshooting Calamity Jane in a plan to help her rout some cowpokes selling guns to the Indians. Rollicking Wild West fun that doesn't avoid a single cliché of the genre.
D: Norman Z. McLeod. A: With Jane Russell, Robert Armstrong, Iris Adrian.

Son of Paleface

(1952) 95m. **B**

A wilder and breezier farce with Hope as the city boy son of the dentist from *Paleface*, who's playing at being a cowboy. Roy Rogers tries to keep the thin plot going as the straight arrow hero type tackling some gold thieves.
D: Frank Tashlin. A: With Jane Russell, Roy Rogers, Bill Williams.

The Seven Little Foys

(1955) 95m. **B–**

Vaudeville gagster Eddie Foy is left with a brood of seven children after the death of his wife. His solution—bring them into the act. A nostalgic, sometimes syrupy backstage comedy/drama with Hope toning down his barrage of quips for some dramatic moments.
D: Melville Shavelson. A: With Milly Vitale, George Tobias, James Cagney.

Other Films:

Louisiana Purchase (1941)
Caught in the Draft (1941)
My Favorite Brunette (1947)
Sorrowful Jones (1949)
The Great Lover (1949)
Here Come the Girls (1953)
Fancy Pants (1950)
The Lemon Drop Kid (1951)
Off Limits (1953)
Casanova's Big Night (1954)
Paris Holiday (1957)

Hope and Crosby Road Films

Smooth, mellow-voiced Bing Crosby and jumpy wisenheimer Bob Hope star in these light farces that offer easy quips, mellow music, light romance, and a dash of slapstick. The plot usually shows them as impoverished entertainers in an exotic locale looking to get the girl—Dorothy Lamour—and some means of making it to easy street. Cardboard villains, angry natives, and musical interludes provide diversions, but the real appeal here is the pair's easy rapport and the jokey glibness with which they deliver out-of-character ad libs about themselves, their contracts, and even the plots.

Road to Singapore

(1940) 84m. B&W. **B–**

The boys slip off to the South Seas to avoid marriage-hungry girls only to buck over the affections of a sarong-clad island girl with a nasty boyfriend. Not the best, but Bing and Bob's breezy rapport and the silky Lamour show how and why the series started.
D: Victor Schertzinger. A: With Dorothy Lamour, Charles Coburn, Anthony Quinn.

Road to Zanzibar

(1941) 92m. B&W. **B**

When American entertainers bomb with the African audiences, they kick in with two girls in search of lost diamonds. Hope and Crosby get to ham it up on safari and make with the jokes while cannibals debate flavoring for the captured pair.
D: Victor Schertzinger. A: With Dorothy Lamour, Una Merkel.

Road to Morocco

(1942) 83m. B&W. **B+**

The boys wash up in Morocco where Hope becomes the slave and pet of Princess Shalimar. Crosby wants in, and the sheik wants them dead. Nice and easy this time, with the boys trading quips on camelback and having strange visions as they wander the desert.
D: David Butler. A: With Dorothy Lamour, Anthony Quinn, Dona Drake.

Road to Utopia

(1945) 90m. B&W. **B+**

The frozen Klondike is the setting for this frantic farce as two crummy vaudevillians find a gold map and have every thug in the North following their treasure hunt. Silly narration and lots of quick escapes from bad guys in furry hats.
D: Hal Walker. A: With Dorothy Lamour, Hillary Brooke.

Road to Rio

(1947) 100m. B&W. **B–**

A Latin excursion for musicians Scat and Hot Lips brings them together with Lamour on a Rio-bound steamer. Latin rhythms and frequent musical interludes spice this entry, which offers more variety show entertainment and less breezy wordplay.
D: Norman Z. MacLeod. A: With Dorothy Lamour, Gale Sondergaard, The Andrews Sisters.

Road to Bali

(1952) 90m. **C+**

With the freshness gone, this recycled *Road to Singapore* (and the only entry in color) concentrates on broader gags including a bout with a giant squid and cameos such as Bogart and Hepburn appearing in their *African Queen* roles.
D: Hal Walker. A: With Dorothy Lamour, Peter Coe, various star cameos.

Road to Hong Kong

(1962) 91m. B&W. **C**

American drifters meet a sexy spy and battle a world domination-crazed group. This British made reunion film looks more like a cheap James Bond parody than a *Road* film, and the boys look a little long in the tooth for Joan Collins.
D: Norman Panama. A: With Joan Collins, Robert Morley, various star cameos.

Danny Kaye

With his hyperactive personality, incredible verbal virtuosity, and nimble physical skills, he was the clean-cut 1940s version of Robin Williams. In this series of films tailored to his humor and sweet-natured persona, Kaye demonstrated a charming, ever cheerful enthusiasm that captured audiences in the mood for lighthearted musical comedy.

Up in Arms

(1944) 106m. **B–**

One of the many "what swell fun we'd have in the army" flicks that rolled out during World War II stars Kaye as a fretful breathless hypochondriac draftee. Danny literally bounds around in all directions and demonstrates his remarkable verbal acuity in a machine-gun scat song.
D: Elliot Nugent. A: With Constance Dowling, Dana Andrews, Dinah Shore.

Wonder Man

(1945) 98m. **B+**

Danny in duel roles ricochets from the stylish showbiz type Buzzy, now a ghost from a gangland hit, to his twin brother, the timid Edwin, who must get the authorities to expose the gangsters. Of course there are two girls for one guy leading to complications. Songs include "Ortchi Chornya."
D: H. Bruce Humberstone. A: With Virginia Mayo, Donald Woods, Vera-Ellen.

The Kid from Brooklyn

(1946) 104m. **B+**

Milquetoast milkman Danny is thought to have decked a champion boxer in a nightclub shuffle and is set up with additional phony bouts leading to a champion fight. Amusing sequences include Kaye practicing his footwork to Viennese waltzes and some fine herky jerky moves in the ring.
D: Norman Z. McLeod. A: With Virginia Mayo, Walter Abel, Eve Arden.

The Secret Life of Walter Mitty

(1947) 105m. **B+**

Quiet Walter has an amazingly active imagination as he becomes a Luftwaffe bomber pilot, master surgeon, riverboat gambler, and other daredevils in his daydreams. The episodes are lively and Danny warbles through the nifty "Symphony for Unstrung Tongue."
D: Norman Z. McLeod. A: With Boris Karloff, Virginia Mayo, Fay Bainter.

A Song Is Born

(1948) 113m. **C+**

Shy and retiring professors—particularly Professor Frisbee—get hit with love when a nightclub singer on the lam shows up to help with their research on jazz music. As much a showcase for Big Band's greats as a small screwballish comedy caper of long hairs, hep cats, and gangsters.
D: Howard Hawks. A: With Virginia Mayo, Benny Goodman, Steve Cochran.

The Inspector General

(1949) 102m. **C+**

The assistant to a traveling medicine show in czarist Russia is mistaken for the royal Inspector General. The costumes and village are storybook cute, everyone gets to act Slavic-ethnic, and Danny's muggings go a little too far, though the "Gypsy Drinking Song" is lively.
D: Henry Koster. A: With Walter Slezak, Elsa Lanchester, Barbara Bates.

The Court Jester

(1956) 101m. **A**

Danny goes undercover as the King of Jesters and lands smack in the middle of court intrigue in merry olde England. A big colorful romp with flashy sword fights, jousts, songs, and a hilarious routine in which Danny must remember "The pellet with the poison's in the vessel with the pestle."
D: Norman Panama, Melvin Frank. A: With Glynis Johns, Basil Rathbone, Angela Lansbury.

Abbott and Costello

This vaudeville team became a hit with wartime movie audiences when they brought their high-spirited, middlebrow, schlubs-looking-for-an-angle stage routine to the screen. Smart, acid-voiced Bud Abbott was forever browbeating but never defeating pudgy, simple-minded Lou Costello, whose childishness was mixed with flashes of insight and street smarts. Their earlier, more successful efforts were slick, often military romps, with breaks for musical numbers while later adventures that saw them traveling west to fight off ghosts and monsters had bigger budgets and a little more plot.

Buck Privates

(1941) 84m. B&W. **B+**

The boys bumble their way into the army and hang out with a rich snob, his chauffeur, and the girl they both love. Innocent military hijinks with bouncy tunes (including "Boogie Woogie Bugle Boy of Company C") by the Andrews Sisters.
D: Arthur Lubin. A: With The Andrews Sisters, Alan Curtis.

Hold That Ghost

(1941) 86m. B&W. **B**

Bud and Lou and a bunch of strangers go fortune hunting in a haunted house while gangsters make some ghostly noises to scare them off. The fun here is watching Costello romp through one haunted house cliché after another while keeping the fear fresh and appealing. Has a spookhouse at the old amusement park feel.
D: Arthur Lubin. A: With Joan Davis, Mischa Auer, The Andrews Sisters.

In the Navy

(1941) 85m. B&W. **B+**

Sailors Bud and Lou try to protect a popular song-and-dance man who joined the Navy to escape his female fans. More military slapstick plus a stand-up-and-cheer musical number about the Navy.
D: Arthur Lubin. A: With Dick Powell, The Andrews Sisters, Dick Foran.

Keep 'Em Flying

(1941) 86m. B&W. **B**

An Army Air Corps instructor sets his sights on a USO girl while Bud and Lou get entangled with identical twins. The bland romance slows down the fun but Lou breaks everything you possibly can on a biplane and naturally gets stuck up in the air. Martha Raye makes sure things never get quiet.
D: Arthur Lubin. A: With Martha Raye, Dick Foran, Carol Bruce.

Ride 'Em Cowboy

(1942) 86m. B&W. **B**

Bud and Lou are hot dog slingers at a dude ranch that the bad guys will take over unless the singing cowboy visiting from Hollywood can save it. Briskly paced with some cute cowboy numbers and a wild, sometimes inventive final chase scene.
D: Arthur Lubin. A: With Anne Gwynne, Dick Foran, Ella Fitzgerald.

The Time of Their Lives

(1946) 82m. B&W. **B+**

Revolutionary War ghosts trapped by the curse of having been branded traitors haunt twentieth-century people in hopes of clearing their names. Unusual and occasionally touching entry in which Bud and Lou don't operate as a team. Not a laugh riot but it has much more of a story to follow.
D: Charles Barton. A: With John Shelton, Marjorie Reynolds, Gale Sondergaard.

Abbott and Costello Meet Frankenstein

(1948) 83m. B&W. **B+**

Bud and Lou get tangled up with a werewolf, and Dracula plans to revive the Frankenstein monster by using Lou's brain. Wildly funny as the monsters play it straight and Lou runs from one to the other in terror. The studio raided the archives for props from all the old monster films for this one, including a spooky castle and a mad lab.
D: Charles Barton. A: With Bela Lugosi; Lon Chaney, Jr.

Other films:
Rito Rita (1942)
Pardon My Sarong (1942)
Who Done It (1942)
Hit the Ice (1943)
Lost in a Harem (1944)
Abbott and Costello in Hollywood (1945)
The Naughty Nineties (1945)
Buck Privates Come Home (1947)
Wistful Widow of Wagon Gap (1947)
Mexican Hayride (1948)
The Noose Hangs High (1948)
Africa Screams (1949)
Abbott and Costello Meet the Killer, Boris Karloff (1949)
Abbott and Costello Meet the Invisible Man (1951)
Abbott and Costello Meet Dr. Jekyll and Mr. Hyde (1952)
Abbott and Costello Meet Captain Kidd (1952)

Hepburn and Tracy

Was it their offscreen romance or some magical film alchemy that made starchy Hepburn and stubborn Tracy such a compelling onscreen team? These sophisticated and comedic tales of professional couples are always smartened up by their battling bravado and easy camaraderie even if every effort isn't as scintillating as *Adam's Rib*; a few suffer from slow tempos and plodding stories that seem to rely a little too much on Kate and Spencer's chemistry to carry them home.

Keeper of the Flame
(1942) 100m. B&W. **B**
A war reporter draws an apparently mournful widow out of seclusion when he attempts to write the story of her dead husband. An unusual political drama without the usual Hepburn–Tracy romantic tension, this gives a spin to the gothic in which the reporter uncovers strange details about a dead hero.
D: George Cukor. A: With Richard Whorf, Margaret Wycherly, Donald Meek.

Woman of the Year
(1942) 112m. B&W. **A–**
Hepburn and Tracy's first team effort is a quick and lively tale of newspaper writers whose marriage is as racked with difficulties as their professional relationship. While some of the domestic squabbles seem a little dated, watching these two comrades spark and spar is still fresh and entertaining.
D: George Stevens. A: With Fay Bainter, Reginald Owen, William Bendix.

Without Love
(1945) 111m. B&W. **C+**
Widow Hepburn and inventor-scientist Tracy enter into a marriage of convenience to deal with the housing crunch in Washington, D.C. Terse witty dialogue and crack supporting work from Ball, but a slow, mediocre story.
D: Harold Bucquet. A: With Lucille Ball, Keenan Wynn, Carol Esmond.

State of the Union
(1948) 124m. B&W. **B+**
A presidential candidate needs the support of his estranged wife while she wants him to uphold the ideals he's now compromising to the special interest groups. A dark, almost somber Capra piece that's given spunk and dash by Hepburn and Tracy and a deliciously venal Lansbury.
D: Frank Capra. A: With Van Johnson, Angela Lansbury, Adolphe Menjou.

Adam's Rib
(1949) 102m. B&W. **A** 🏛
This urbane and sparkling battle-of-the-sexes tale has happily married lawyers testing the strength of their vows when they become opposing counsel in a crime of passion murder case. With screwball comedy pacing and witty dialogue, Hepburn and Tracy's hilarious attacks and counterattacks still feel modern.
D: George Cukor. A: With Judy Holliday, Tom Ewell, David Wayne.

Pat and Mike
(1952) 96m. B&W. **B**
Independent sportswoman Hepburn escapes her white-bread fiancé who's jinxing her career and teams up with gruff shady sports promoter Tracy. A breezy smart comedy featuring a slew of sports celebrity cameos and a daffy Ray as the lunkheaded boxer managed by Tracy.
D: George Cukor. A: With Aldo Ray, William Ching, Sammy White.

Desk Set
(1957) 103m. **B–**
She's in charge of the cozy little corner of the TV station's research department and he's the efficiency engineer who might install a computer that puts her out to pasture. A labored effort with pacing and timing that's so awkward you're not sure if this is a failed comedy or drama.
D: Walter Lang. A: With Gig Young, Joan Blondell, Dina Merrill.

Postwar Romantic Comedies

The films of the postwar years took a dramatic turn in style as noir, melodrama, and westerns were in, and sophisticated escapist fare began to decline. These films take a more common sensical approach to romance, eschewing the kooky, cute, and breakneck paces of the screwball films of the 30s and early 40s.

The Egg and I
(1947) 108m. B&W. **B**
A Boston lady thinks she's struck gold when she falls in love with a chicken farmer, but discovers being a farmer's wife is not exactly a rustic idyll. This leisurely comedy hangs its hat on the usually cool Claudette falling apart as her chicks run amok.
D: Charles Erskine. A: Claudette Colbert, Fred MacMurray, Marjorie Main.

The Farmer's Daughter
(1947) 97m. B&W. **B+**
A spirited Swedish servant is torn between duty and passion when she challenges her beloved boss for his seat in Congress. Then she captures the imagination of the little people and sits primed to take Washington by storm. Sweetly romantic with an intelligent cast helping to legitimize the story's fairy-tale flights of fancy.
D: H. C. Potter. A: Loretta Young, Joseph Cotten, Ethel Barrymore.

The Bachelor and the Bobby-Soxer
(1947) 95m. B&W. **B+**
A female judge "sentences" a womanizing painter to romance her smitten younger sister, in the hopes of disenchanting the lovesick sibling. Suave Grant endures the teenybopper's malt shop social agenda with an eye to reeling in Loy. Contains some hilarious bits, and Myrna almost outcools the master of sophisticated comedy.
D: Irving Reis. A: Cary Grant, Myrna Loy, Shirley Temple.

Every Girl Should Be Married
(1948) 85m. B&W. **B**
A young miss sets her cap on Grant, and after practically stalking him, embarrasses him into popping the question. Neither sex comes off looking so hot in this strange comedy whose dated attitude makes it veer between light and frothy and slightly frightening.
D: Don Hartman. A: Cary Grant, Franchot Tone, Betsy Drake.

Unfaithfully Yours
(1948) 105m. B&W. **B+**
A famous concert conductor believes his young wife is having an affair and, inspired by some blood and thunder classical scores, devises a grand scheme of revenge. The deliciously diabolical fantasy sequences are the showpieces of this often strained and slightly nasty look at a May–September romance.
D: Preston Sturges. A: Rex Harrison, Linda Darnell, Rudy Vallee.

I Was a Male War Bride
(1949) 105m. B&W. **A–**
Yankee ingenuity goes haywire in postwar Europe when a WAC tries to smuggle her French soldier husband past the bureaucratic red tape by having him impersonate a war bride. The bad wig and masculine gestures don't give Grant away in this low-key, sometimes slow, and often painfully funny comedy.
D: Howard Hawks. A: Cary Grant, Ann Sheridan, Marion Marshall.

Satires

Preston Sturges' giddy influence spreads itself over these broad and biting romps that lampoon greed, middle-class dreams, and of course, politics.

Brewster's Millions
(1945) 79m. B&W. **B+**
A returning GI inherits 8 million dollars from an eccentric uncle on the condition that he can spend a million in two months. The trouble is Brewster's insane investments are driving his friends up the wall and making him an unwanted mint in this funny, high-spirited farce.
D: Allan Dwan. A: Dennis O'Keefe, Helen Walker, Eddie "Rochester" Anderson.

Colonel Effington's Raid
(1945) 70m. B&W. **B**
A retired officer-turned-newspaper columnist stirs up a sleepy Georgia town when he pens a series of articles calling upon the populace to keep city hall from tearing down the historical courthouse. A daffy satire of political corruption in the Sturges tradition that loses steam in the second half.
D: Irving Pichel. A: Charles Coburn, Joan Bennett, William Eythe.

The Senator Was Indiscreet
(1947) 74m. B&W. **B–**
An addlebrained, lame-duck senator who is being groomed for the presidency keeps a racy diary about his adversaries that winds up in the hands of a reporter. Powell's perfectly charming, the script is witty, and the comedy strangely lackluster.
D: George Kaufman. A: William Powell, Ella Raines, Peter Lind Hayes.

Mr. Blandings Builds His Dream House
(1948) 94m. B&W. **A–**
A New York ad exec and his wife buy their dream house in the country, which plunges them into the world of architects, contractors, commuter train schedules, and every homeowning disaster imaginable. This prototype for suburban comedies is still hilarious with Grant and Loy adding their usual lighthearted sophistication.
D: H. C. Potter. A: Cary Grant, Myrna Loy, Melvyn Douglas.

Supernatural Romantic Comedies

Like *It's a Wonderful Life*, these films introduce a little supernatural help to get the characters in and out of crazy predicaments. While displaying the darkly sentimental and unabashedly corny tone of the war and postwar comedies, this group can be as refreshing as a sweet daydream.

Here Comes Mr. Jordan
(1941) 93m. B&W. **B+**
A young champion boxer shows up in heaven 40 years before his time, and when he's sent back to earth, he begins a desperate search for another body to inhabit. A glossy romantic fantasia with Rains adding ballast as Mr. Jordan the gatekeeper.
D: Alexander Hall. A: Robert Montgomery, Evelyn Keyes, Claude Rains.

I Married a Witch
(1942) 76m. B&W. **B+**
A father and daughter burned at the stake during the Salem witchhunt return to haunt the descendant of their Puritan nemesis. A sweet-tempered comedy with the daffy spooks having a blast driving their stodgy victim up the wall, until the young woman falls in love with the ghost father.
D: René Clair. A: Fredric March, Veronica Lake, Robert Benchley.

Heaven Can Wait
(1943) 112m. **A**
A recently deceased lothario recounts his "wicked" sexual history in this elegant masterwork that unfolds like an album of exquisite Victorian postcards. Shot in luscious Technicolor, the camera winks knowingly at us while the characters indulge the foolish lover who brought happiness to nearly every life he touched.
D: Ernst Lubitsch. A: Gene Tierney, Don Ameche, Charles Coburn.

The Bishop's Wife
(1947) 108m. B&W. **B+**
A strange triangle develops here with a well-meaning but overworked bishop, his neglected pretty wife, and a suave stranger who's really an angel. A charming if somewhat predictable Christmas tale that oozes Rockwellian Americana.
D: Henry Koster. A: Cary Grant, Loretta Young, David Niven.

The Ghost and Mrs. Muir
(1947) 104m. B&W. **A**
A young widow discovers that a cranky ghost of a naval captain also inhabits her English seaside cottage. They bicker, make friends, and have a falling out over her new romance, in what turns out to be a haunting story of sexual yearning. The end contains some classic tear-jerking scenes.
D: Joseph Mankiewicz. A: Gene Tierney, Rex Harrison, George Sanders.

One Touch of Venus
(1948) 81m. B&W. **C+**
A young decorator falls in

love with a store window statue of Venus de Milo who then comes alive and puts the moves on him. Even a classy and voluptuous Ava can't breathe more than a few moments of heat into this strangely flat romance.
D: William Seiter. A: Ava Gardner, Robert Walker, Dick Haymes.

1940s–1950s

Miscellaneous Comedies

These shaggy-dog stories, picaresque tales, and lowbrow satires are generally a comfortable lot, but show that the scintillating comedies of the 30s and 40s were pretty much gone with the war.

Spooks Run Wild
(1941) 69m. B&W. **B–**

The East Side Kids hole up in a spooky mansion owned by Lugosi in this slapstick mystery. An amusing jaunt for the street-smart, wisecracking loafers who manage to save the day time and time again in several dozen low-budget, lowbrow mystery quickies, first as The Dead End Kids, then The East Side Kids, and finally as The Bowery Boys.
D: Phil Rosen. A: Huntz Hall, Leo Gorcey, Bela Lugosi.

The Fuller Brush Man
(1948) 93m. B&W. **B**

An unassuming door-to-door salesman bumbles onto the scene of a murder and, spurred on by a pretty girl, tries to nail the killers. A high-spirited, lowbrow slapstick caper that bursts with comic invention while keeping Red's mugging to a minimum.
D: Frank Tashlin. A: Red Skelton, Janet Blair, Don McGuire.

A Connecticut Yankee in King Arthur's Court
(1949) 107m. **B**

A blacksmith travels back to the days of King Arthur and is declared a wizard when he wows merry old England with his slick contemporary smarts. Twain's folksy fairy tale is turned into a colorful musical comedy with Crosby smoothly crooning and winking his way through.
D: Tay Garnett. A: Bing Crosby, Rhonda Fleming, William Bendix.

Francis, the Talking Mule
(1949) 91m. B&W. **B**

A nerdy GI can't believe his ears when a talking mule begins to drop some hints on how to win the war. An uncommonly lowbrow and stupid affair that, depending on your mood for salty-tongued, four-hoofed stars, can still be quite a hoot. After several more *Francis* films, director Lubin expanded his horizons by creating TV's estimable *Mr. Ed.*
D: Arthur Lubin. A: Donald O'Connor, Patricia Medina, ZaSu Pitts.

Harvey
(1950) 104m. B&W **B**

Tippling neighborhood philosopher Stewart brings home his new pal, an invisible six-foot rabbit, to introduce to his sister who ships him off to the nuthouse. Then she learns that everybody there is beginning to see the big bunny too. Stewart slips into the sweet fuddy-duddy role with ease, but the cuteness is a little strained and dated.
D: Henry Koster. A: James Stewart, Josephine Hull, Peggy Dow.

The Quiet Man
(1952) 129m. **A** 🏛

A retired prizefighter returns to Ireland and woos a beautiful red-haired lass who has second thoughts when the New World man breaks with sacred custom. The sexual juices are bursting from Wayne and O'Hara in this rousing love story set in the midst of priests, drunks, and wily old coots of a Gaelic fairyland.
D: John Ford. A: John Wayne, Maureen O'Hara, Victor McLaglen.

Beat the Devil
(1954) 89m. B&W. **B+**

Five scoundrels blaze a trail to Africa in search of uranium ore, but their backstabbing ways and ramshackle barge ground them in strange territory. A truly odd and not completely successful dark screwballish comedy, with the self-parodying cast having a blast mugging their way through the perverse Truman Capote script.
D: John Huston. A: Humphrey Bogart, Jennifer Jones, Gina Lollabrigida.

We're No Angels
(1955) 106m. **B**

Three Devil's Island escapees take up with a shopkeeper who thinks they're parolees hired to fix his ceiling. After a promising start, Bogie and the boys settle into a predictable and not terribly funny rut as hardened criminals with hearts of gold.
D: Michael Curtiz. A: Humphrey Bogart, Peter Ustinov, Aldo Ray.

Auntie Mame
(1958) 143m. **A** 🏛

An eccentric and ebullient Manhattan socialite becomes the guardian of her little nephew and proceeds to teach him that "life is a feast and most poor suckers are starving to death." A bright bubbling film of bohemian high life with a cunning Roz maintaining things at a concert pitch.
D: Morton Da Costa. A: Rosalind Russell, Forrest Tucker, Fred Clark.

The Matchmaker
(1958) 101m. **B+**

The original non-musical version of *Hello Dolly* follows a matchmaker from 1880s Yonkers who, along with promoting love, is trying to snag the wealthy storeowner for herself. This sweet Americana comedy doesn't have any of the big brassiness of the musical, relying more on relaxed and hamish humor.
D: Joseph Anthony. A: Shirley Booth, Paul Ford, Anthony Perkins.

No Time for Sergeants
(1958) 111m. B&W. **B+**

A country yokel sets the U.S. Air Force on its ear and drives his sergeant up the wall with his homespun and innocent anarchic attitude. This model for *Gomer Pyle* may be the last word in folksy cornball humor, but who can fault a film that takes such relish in bits like the saluting toilet bowls?
D: Mervyn LeRoy. A: Andy Griffith, Myron McCormick, Nick Adams.

1950s

World War II

Humor and male bonding mix it up in these capers that use the War as an excuse to poke fun at authority and show a group of guys pitching in together when it counts and indulging in male hijinks when it doesn't.

Mr. Roberts
(1955) 123m. **A–**

Life aboard a Navy cargo ship that's not seeing any action is like a funny version of *Caine Mutiny* with a wacky crew squirming under the thumb of an SOB commander. Stagy and sentimental, with enough sly humor and robust camaraderie to keep the movie afloat.
D: John Ford, Mervyn Le Roy. A: Henry Fonda, James Cagney, Jack Lemmon.

Operation Petticoat
(1959) 124m. **B**

The misadventures of a submarine crew in the Pacific seem to mainly involve taking on, putting off, or dealing with inconvenient passengers like nurses who add their own frills to the warship. Grant and Curtis look like they're having a great time imitating each other.
D: Blake Edwards. A: Cary Grant, Tony Curtis, Dina Merrill.

The Teahouse of the August Moon
(1956) 123m. **B–**

American-occupied Okinawa doesn't become westernized, the occupying military just starts to lose its bearings. Brando is the wily native interpreter to a group of uprooted Americans who bumble their way to some kind of self-knowledge in this talky but sweet and sly stage play.
D: Daniel Mann. A: Marlon Brando, Glenn Ford, Eddie Albert.

The Wackiest Ship in the Army
(1960) 99m. **C+**

Another ship that's barely afloat and manned by a bungling crew is the center of this lame cookie-cutter entry that's a prototype of TV's *McHale's Navy.*
D: Richard Murphy. A: Jack Lemmon, Ricky Nelson, John Lund.

Ensign Pulver
(1964) 104m. **C+**

This sequel to *Mr. Roberts,* filled with more Navy shenanigans and all-American military characters, tries to recreate the charm of the original but seems bound by the nerdy main character and strained efforts at hijinks. Matthau lends some relaxed ballast to the proceedings.
D: Joshua Logan. A: Robert Walker, Jr.; Burl Ives; Walter Matthau.

Martin and Lewis

Suave, romantic Dean Martin and zany, infantile Jerry Lewis made one of the odder comedy teams to storm Hollywood, although their live performances were, by all accounts, screamingly, smuttily, and lawlessly funny. While the early films did record some of their comic bits, whatever magic the pair created finally dissolved in a series of pedestrian musical comedies enlivened by Lewis' manic slapstick and Dino's crooning.

Jumping Jacks
(1952) 96m. B&W. **C+**

Martin is a little rough, but Lewis effortlessly slips into his signature bumbling schtick in this quickie-style army comedy with musical numbers featuring GI chorus boys who are unintentionally funnier than some of the bits.
D: Norman Taurog. A: With Mona Freeman, Don DeFore, Robert Strauss.

The Caddy
(1953) 95m. B&W. **C**

Martin is a golfer who gets coached by caddie Lewis for the Pebble Beach tournament. An uninspired, thin vehicle that's more like a collection of small comic bits with cameo appearances by professional golfers and the boys singing "That's Amore."
D: Norman Taurog. A: With Donna Reed, Barbara Bates, Joseph Calleia.

Artists and Models
(1955) 109m. **B**

Martin illustrates in comic book form the dreams of number one fan Lewis and both are chased by crooks and the models who live in the next-door garret. As lush and frothy as any MGM musical, with Gabor and Lewis making a particularly weird pairing in some scenes.
D: Frank Tashlin. A: With Shirley MacLaine, Dorothy Malone, Eva Gabor.

Hollywood or Bust
(1956) 95m. **C**

Gambler Martin convinces movie fan Lewis to travel cross-country to Hollywood so Lewis can meet the girl of his dreams, Anita Ekberg. There's too much silly zaniness in this tiresome road picture that goes nowhere except the end of the line for the team's work together.
D: Frank Tashlin. A: With Anita Ekberg, Pat Crowley, Maxie Rosenbloom.

Jerry Lewis

Jerry Lewis' schtick as the perpetual juvenile with a full range of facial contortions, crazy vocal outbursts, and spastic slapstick is either your idea of the last word in physical humor or the first step in getting physically ill. Still, these films have the same bright candy-coated

look of an Elvis movie with even less plot, and are fueled by Jerry's inexhaustible manic energy.

The Delicate Delinquent
(1957) 100m. B&W. **B**

In this spoof of juvenile delinquent films, cowardly janitor Lewis is terrified of the neighborhood gangs but still manages to get busted in a street rumble and then reformed by a kindly cop. Jerry squeezes more pathos then slapstick into his quiet and serious first solo outing.
D: Don McGuire. A: With Darren McGavin, Martha Hyer, Robert Ivers.

The Sad Sack
(1957) 98m. B&W. **B–**

Hopelessly inept army private Jerry gets transferred to Morocco where a band of renegade Arabs hopes to use his photographic memory. Earnest, simplistic, and filled with typical Lewis humor, but it's depressing to see Lorre as Jerry's straight man.
D: George Marshall. A: With David Wayne, Phyllis Kirk, Peter Lorre.

The Bellboy
(1960) 72m. **B–**

Lewis plays a bellboy at the Fontainebleau hotel in a virtually plotless film that strings together unrelated sight gags and bumbling confusion. By the time you get annoyed with the lack of dialogue and cohesion in this unadulterated Lewis outing, the movie's over.
D: Jerry Lewis. A: With Alex Gerry, Bob Clayton, Sonny Sands.

The Ladies Man
(1961) 106m. **B**

Jerry is hoodwinked into becoming the houseboy at a Hollywood boarding school for aspiring actresses. The endless gags are mostly cute, Jerry acts a little less dopey, and there are two very weird cameo sequences—including a tango with George Raft—as the highlights.
D: Jerry Lewis. A: With Helen Traubel, Kathleen Freeman, Pat Stanley.

The Nutty Professor
(1963) 107m. **A–**

Nerdy chemistry professor Lewis discovers a formula that turns him into smooth, oily, and ultrahip lounge lizard Buddy Love. A fast-moving romantic comedy with a top-notch rendition of an obnoxious club performer by Jerry, with Stevens playing to perfection the dreamy blonde coed.
D: Jerry Lewis. A: With Stella Stevens, Del Moore, Kathleen Freeman.

The Patsy
(1964) 100m. **C+**

Lewis is a bellboy again but this time he's being groomed for superstardom by a team of show-biz managers. One of Jerry's more awkward mixes of slapstick-and-pathos with a few funny moments on *The Ed Sullivan Show* and some cameo appearances by Hollywood stars.
D: Jerry Lewis. A: With Ina Balin, Everett Sloane, Phil Harris, and others.

The Big Mouth
(1967) 107m. **B–**

Lewis is a bumbling fisherman who hunts for a sunken treasure while being pursued by gangsters. Standard mugging and slapstick with little plot to get in the way.
D: Jerry Lewis. A: With Harold J. Stone, Susan Dey, Buddy Lester, Del Morre.

Romantic Comedies

These comedies are colorful portraits of American middle-class life in the Eisenhower era, as well as updated reports on the war between the sexes. Bright, colorful, and blandly reassuring, they show the squabbles of lovers and married couples who may not be too sophisticated, but still enjoy a determined optimism about the good life in America.

Born Yesterday
(1950) 103m. B&W **B**

A junk dealer-turned-politician hires a tutor to teach his mistress culture and grammar. Judy makes the screechy, street-smart blonde appealing in this sharp, well-written comedy that still suffers from staginess.
D: George Cukor. A: Judy Holliday, William Holden, Broderick Crawford.

Father of the Bride
(1950) 93m. **A–**

A suburbanite family man is plunged into the whirlwind circus of his daughter's forthcoming wedding in this big glossy Hollywood production. Tracy is wryly humorous, and Liz is ever glamorous in this sunny look at a prosperous and conformist postwar America.
D: Vincente Minnelli. A: Spencer Tracy, Elizabeth Taylor, Joan Bennett.

Father's Little Dividend
(1950) 82m. **B+**

Father continues to offer droll observations on the excitement and turmoil caused by his daughter's "blessed event." Tracy is still wise and slightly befuddled, Taylor is still gorgeous in her designer clothes, and life is still a reassuring ritual of maintaining the status quo.
D: Vincente Minnelli. A: Spencer Tracy, Joan Bennett, Elizabeth Taylor.

Bedtime for Bonzo
(1951) 83m. B&W. **C+**

When psychology professor Reagan's future father-in-law disapproves of him because of dubious family background, Ron begins a "nurture over nature" experiment by raising a chimpanzee himself. The cute and tedious complications make this film serve only as a reminder of our ex-leader's background.
D: Fredrick De Cordova. A: Ronald Reagan, Diana Lynn, Walter Slezak.

People Will Talk
(1951) 110m. B&W. **B–**

An unorthodox physician-professor is a hero to his students and patients but a threat to his colleagues, thanks to a holistic approach to medicine. Then he marries a pregnant young woman who had tried to commit suicide. A truly bizarre hybrid of eccentric melodrama, romantic comedy, and polemics.
D: Joseph L. Mankiewicz. A: Cary Grant, Jeanne Crain, Finlay Currie.

Love Is Better Than Ever
(1952) 81m. **B–**

A dewy-eyed kids' dance instructor from New Haven

and a cynical New York talent agent spend a few days together. She thinks it's love, he thinks it's a fling. A strange, almost grim comedy, with Liz relentlessly out to snag Parks, who's such a selfish creep you wonder about that happy ending.
D: Stanley Donen. A: Elizabeth Taylor, Larry Parks, Josephine Hutchinson.

Monkey Business
(1952) 97m. **C+**

A scientist and his wife take a youth serum that turns him into a teenager ready to rumble with Monroe and the wife into an overgrown child. The tantrums and slapstick are mildly amusing, but wear thin pretty quickly. Like Disney's *The Absent Minded Professor* or *Son of Flubber* with a hint of sex.
D: Howard Hawks. A: Ginger Rogers, Cary Grant, Marilyn Monroe.

We're Not Married
(1952) 85m. B&W. **B**

An episodic look at five couples whose marriage licenses may be invalid due to the judge's error. Lightweight but amusing, especially Zsa Zsa as the wife who plans to sue her millionaire husband for divorce until she finds out she may not be married at all.
D: Edmund Goulding. A: Ginger Rogers, Marilyn Monroe, Zsa Zsa Gabor.

It Should Happen to You
(1954) 87m. B&W.
A–

A struggling model wants to be a celebrity and pays to put her name on a New York City billboard to do it. A small, sweet-natured satire and romantic comedy with an optimistic Holliday and surly Lemmon adding the zest.
D: George Cukor. A: Judy Holliday, Jack Lemmon, Peter Lawford.

The Long, Long Trailer
(1954) 103m. **B–**

Like an extended *I Love Lucy* episode, Lucy and Desi are the honeymooning couple traveling in their huge, state-of-the-art trailer home. The mishaps, slapstick, and romantic misunderstanding carry this lushly colored, widescreen comedy only so far, and then you're left stranded miles before the film's end.
D: Vincente Minnelli. A: Lucille Ball, Desi Arnaz, Marjorie Main.

The Girl Can't Help It
(1956) 99m. **B+**

This is actually a widescreen Technicolor sex comedy about a gangster who hires an agent to make his blonde bombshell fiancée a singing star, to which they've tacked on performances by the likes of Eddie Cochran, Little Richard, and Gene Vincent. The big, goofy, and funny exception to this group.
D: Frank Tashlin. A: Jayne Mansfield, Tom Ewell, Edmond O'Brien.

Designing Woman
(1957) 118m. **C+**

A fashion designer marries a sportswriter, and they spend the rest of the film in a string of odd couple episodes, wondering if their marriage can be saved. Everyone in this generic version of the Tracy–Hepburn comedies tries hard to make it fun and sparkling, but it just lays there.
D: Vincente Minnelli. A: Gregory Peck, Lauren Bacall, Dolores Gray.

Bell, Book and Candle
(1958) 103m. **B**

A lovely modern-day witch forgets her resolution to give up hocus-pocus and casts a love spell on her new neighbor. An appealing adult fairy tale with a downright strange atmosphere, sexual tension that comes off as hostility, and a hilarious Lemmon providing occasional comic relief.
D: Richard Quine. A: James Stewart, Kim Novak, Jack Lemmon.

Houseboat
(1958) 110m. **B**

Widowed Grant hires Loren to take care of his brood of kids aboard their houseboat. If you can believe that one, you may not mind that this sunny, occasionally sophisticated romp lacks energy despite the intense heat generated by the two stars.
D: Melville Shavelson. A: Cary Grant, Sophia Loren, Martha Hyer.

Indiscreet
(1958) 100m. **B+**

A famous stage actress and an American in London have a glorious love affair even though he's married. Then she discovers he's not. This elegant little comedy of love amongst the chic evokes more smiles than laughs, but Grant and Bergman's chemistry make it work.
D: Stanley Donen. A: Cary Grant, Ingrid Bergman, Cecil Parker.

Teacher's Pet
(1958) 120m. B&W. **B+**

Hard-boiled newspaperman Gable meets his match when he enrolls in a night school journalism class taught by sexy school marm Day. This black-and-white film has a grittier feel and Gable makes this less of a lighthearted romp than a rueful battle between the sexes. Mamie Van Doren's number is a nice curiosity piece.
D: George Seaton. A: Clark Gable, Doris Day, Gig Young.

Cash McCall
(1959) 116m. **B**

Garner is the smooth big-business operator negotiating a deal with Jagger whose daughter he's fallen for. One of those gorgeous 50s set design extravaganzas with all the usual petty complications looking more important because they take place in such grand settings.
D: Joseph Pevney. A: James Garner, Natalie Wood, Dean Jagger.

The Grass Is Greener
(1960) 105m. **B–**

The comfortable marriage of a British Lord is interrupted when his Lady falls for an American millionaire. A delightful and civilized drawing room comedy with clever dialogue, humorous plot twists, and a sophisticated cast.
D: Stanley Donen. A: Cary Grant, Deborah Kerr, Robert Mitchum.

Audrey Hepburn

These films tend to be more sophisticated and European in flavor than other romantic comedies from this era, with Hepburn playing her gamine role to leading men old enough to be her father.

Roman Holiday
(1953) 119m. B&W. **B+**
Hepburn is a princess who runs away to spend a carefree day incognito with reporter Peck. There's more charm than humor in this sparkling journey through the Roman locales, with a nonsyrupy romance that's unusual in Hollywood fare.
D: William Wyler. A: Audrey Hepburn, Gregory Peck, Eddie Albert.

Paris When It Sizzles
(1954) 110m. **C+**
A screenwriter has to finish a script in 48 hours, and acts out scenes from it with his newly hired secretary. The fantasy sequences in the Paris locales are nice, but this muddled talkative comedy relies too heavily on the stars' appeal and a few interesting cameos.
D: Richard Quine. A: Audrey Hepburn, William Holden, Noel Coward.

Sabrina
(1954) 113m. B&W. **A–**
The gangly young chauffeur's daughter finally gets her chance with the employer's playboy son after a few years at a Paris cooking school transforms her into a cosmopolitan swan. This glorious Cinderella story with a twist is anchored by the canny stars and the continental tone.
D: Billy Wilder. A: Audrey Hepburn, Humphrey Bogart, William Holden.

Love in the Afternoon
(1957) 130m. B&W. **B**
Hepburn is the Parisian private eye's daughter who has an affair with the playboy her father has been trailing. A très chic and slightly risqué comedy that takes its time in telling the story.
D: Billy Wilder. A: Audrey Hepburn, Gary Cooper, Maurice Chevalier.

Breakfast at Tiffany's
(1961) 114m. **A**
She's the ultrachic free spirit out to snag a millionaire in Manhattan, and he's a struggling writer living off the largesse of his wealthy married lover. The quintessential sophisticated tale about la vie bohème of the privileged poor with the leads saving it from glamorous blandness.
D: Blake Edwards. A: Audrey Hepburn, George Peppard, Patricia Neal.

Marilyn Monroe

Not all these films were strictly star vehicles for Marilyn, but she always managed to turn her dumb-blonde characters into vulnerable, vulgar, and hilariously inept vamps that knocked everyone else off center stage.

How to Marry a Millionaire
(1953) 95m. **A**
Three young women join forces to hunt for rich husbands with mixed and comic results. Every scene is horizontally composed to capitalize on the widescreen process, but even if this loses something on TV, the jewel-box settings and comic gifts of the stars still make this piece of fluff an absolute treat.
D: Jean Negulesco. A: Marilyn Monroe, Lauren Bacall, Betty Grable.

The Seven Year Itch
(1955) 105m. **A–**
When a happily married man becomes a summer bachelor, his fantasy life intersects with the sexy weather girl who lives upstairs. This sex farce may be stagy, but it contains some classic scenes—including the famous subway grate one—with a creamy and evanescent Marilyn lighting things up.
D: Melville Shavelson. A: Marilyn Monroe, Tom Ewell, Evelyn Keyes.

Bus Stop
(1956) 96m. **B–**
Marilyn is the sweet honkytonk entertainer who's been around the block, and Murray the naive cowboy who wants to take her away from it all. A wordy comedy-drama with a strong undertone of sadness, this lets you watch Marilyn successfully working to make her character resonate.
D: Joshua Logan. A: Marilyn Monroe, Don Murray, Arthur O'Connell.

The Prince and the Showgirl
(1957) 127m. **C+**
A ditzy American chorus girl resists the amorous attempts of the British regent in 1911. The remarkable lack of chemistry between the stars and an all talk and no action script makes this boring, and Marilyn looks like a stuffed sausage in her dress.
D: Laurence Olivier. A: Marilyn Monroe, Laurence Olivier, Sybil Thorndike.

(See also *Some Like It Hot,* page 83.)

Debbie Reynolds

Honest, confident Debbie was ideal wife-and-mother material who always hooked her man. These small comedies may lack a big budget, glamorous settings, and anything approaching a sophisticated tone, but they're still 100 percent all-American romantic corn.

The Tender Trap
(1955) 111m. **B+**
A swinging theatrical producer is the object of desire for a domestically minded actress in this backstage romp. The strong supporting cast keeps the dubious chemistry between Frank and Reynolds on course.
D: Charles Walters. A: Debbie Reynolds, Frank Sinatra, Celeste Holm.

Bundle of Joy
(1956) 98m. **A–**
When a salesgirl gets saddled with a foundling, the store owner's son believes it's hers and the store owner believes it's his son's. One of the goofier films thanks to Fisher's acting and a bizarre Cinderella scene where he opens the store at night to bestow on Debbie a complete evening outfit.

D: Norman Taurog. A: Debbie Reynolds, Eddie Fisher, Adolphe Menjou.

This Happy Feeling
(1958) 92m. **C+**
Pushy all-American Debbie causes romantic problems for a retired movie star-turned-horse breeder, before noticing the boy next door. The title says it all.
D: Blake Edwards. A: Debbie Reynolds, Curt Jurgens, John Saxon.

The Mating Game
(1959) 96m. **C+**
A nervous tax examiner falls for farm girl Debbie and assists her family to legally outsmart the government. Broader than Reynold's other comedies, this spends more time poking fun at city and country folk than on romance.
D: George Marshall. A: Debbie Reynolds, Tony Randall, Paul Douglas.

Alec Guinness

Alec Guinness' gallery of pasty-complexioned, bland-looking opportunists fit right into postwar England where everything seemed up for grabs. These lean-looking satires and black comedies are blessed with marvelously twisted plots, intelligent dialogue that shoots darts in all social and political directions, and a sharp feel for the manners of the old and newly emerging English lifestyles.

Kind Hearts and Coronets
(1949) 104m. B&W.
A–
The commoner who is ninth in line for a dukedom decides to kill off the other eight—ranging from a clergyman to a banker to a suffragette—all played by Guinness. Hitchcock meets Oscar Wilde in this Edwardian black comedy of manners.
D: Robert Hamer. A: With Dennis Price, Valerie Hobson.

The Lavender Hill Mob
(1951) 82m. B&W . **B+**
Guinness is the mousy bank clerk who proceeds to humbly pull off the bank heist of the century, only to flounder on the shoulders of his band of inept helpers. A droll and mild-mannered caper that shifts into high gear as the perfect crime unravels.
D: Charles Crichton. A: With Stanley Holloway, Sidney James.

The Man in the White Suit
(1952) 84m. B&W. **A–**
Guinness plays the guileless researcher who incites the wrath of both big business and the unions when he invents a dirt-resistant fabric. A biting satire delivered in the most amiable fashion.
D: Alexander Mackendrick. A: With Joan Greenwood, Cecil Parker.

The Promoter
(1952) 88m. B&W. **B**
Guinness, the son of a washerwoman, schemes and claws his way to the middle class while falling in love with a downwardly mobile rich girl. A cynical navigation through a postwar romance.
D: Ronald Neame. A: With Glynis Johns, Valerie Hobson.

The Captain's Paradise
(1953) 77m. B&W. **B**
The sedate wife and the sexy mistress never ask steamer captain Guinness what he does in the other port, and life is paradise until both women want to change the status quo. A dated marital comedy, but the stereotypical women switching roles provides genuine humor.
D: Anthony Kimmins. A: With Celia Johnson, Yvonne De Carlo.

The Ladykillers
(1955) 87m. **A–**
A gang headed by Guinness uses a little old lady's boarding house as headquarters for a robbery. When she discovers their secret they decide to kill her. But how can they, when the landlady functions as a constant banana peel upon which everyone tumbles? A richly colored, goofily charming tale with almost as much pathos as humor being provided by the misadventures.
D: Alexander Mackendrick. A: With Peter Sellers, Herbert Lom, Cecil Parker.

The Horse's Mouth
(1958) 93m. **B–**
A once successful painter just released from prison lies, cheats, and steals to get money to keep working—with a liberating effect on everyone around him. Feels more like unfocused mischief than a pointed assault.
D: Ronald Neame. A: With Kay Walsh, Renee Houston.

British Comedies

Like the Guinness and Sellers films from this period (see above and page 80), jaunty opportunists and bumbling criminals deliver pies in the face of staid and crumbling old England, usually via some completely inept crime caper. These may seem restrained by modern standards, but the dialogue is snappy, the actor-comedians engaging, and you even get glimpses of where Monty Python and company came from.

Doctor in the House
(1954) 92m. **B**
These medical students like to chase comely nurses, pull pranks, arch their eyebrows in amazement, toss witty phrases at one another, and move through their rounds with cheeky, but decidedly low-key delight.
D: Ralph Thomas. A: Dirk Bogarde, Muriel Pavlow, Kenneth More.

Genevieve
(1954) 86m. **B+**
Two couples race each other through the English countryside as they banter and spar. A light frothy romantic comedy that would have done Tracy and Hepburn justice.

D: Henry Cornelius. A: Kenneth More, Kay Kendall, John Gregson.

The Belles of St. Trinian's
(1955) 90m. B&W. **A**

The student body bottles gin, fixes horse races, and generally raises hell under the benign and corrupt headmistress of this wacky bankrupt girls boarding school. The crime caper in this is funny enough, but it's the dual role of Alastair Sim as headmistress and crooked gambler that keeps you holding your sides.
D: Frank Launder. A: Alastair Sim, Joyce Grenfell, Beryl Reid.

Lucky Jim
(1957) 95m. **B+**

A young lecturer toadies to everyone of importance in order to get ahead at a small British college. The mishaps and pratfalls seem tame, and the pace has the amiable feel of a drawing room farce, occasionally enlivened by some madcap scene like the completely haywire graduation ceremony.
D: John Boulting. A: Ian Carmichael, Terry-Thomas, Hugh Griffith.

The Naked Truth (aka Your Past Is Showing)
(1957) 92m. **C+**

A scandal-rag publisher on trial for blackmail is smuggled out of jail by his victims who intend to shut him up permanently. Looking like a series of Sid Caesar comedy skits, this light farce provides ample room for some crazy characters like Sellers as TV star "Wee Sonny MacGregor."
D: Mario Zampi. A: Terry-Thomas, Peter Sellers, Dennis Price.

1950s–1960s

Peter Sellers

Before starring in American comedies, Peter Sellers played in these small, wildly wicked satires of postwar Britain. Using his mobile face, spongy appearance, and deft mimicry of accents, Sellers tackled the new order's gallery of pompous and bureaucratic characters with a humor fueled by stinging verbal displays, a healthy dose of slapstick, and a solar system of Britain's best character actors.

I'm All Right Jack
(1959) 101m. B&W. **B+**

Greedy factory owners conspire while smug unionists protect their featherbedding in this satire of British labor and management. Union steward Sellers, wearing a Hitler mustache, is on hand to defend a perpetual state of union tea breaks.
D: John Boulting. A: With Terry-Thomas, Ian Carmichael.

The Mouse That Roared
(1959) 83m. **A–**

The world's tiniest nation declares war on the U.S. hoping to lose, but the duchy's mild-mannered general gets hold of a nuclear bomb. In this pre-*Dr. Strangelove* satire on the nuclear age's weird international relations, Sellers plays the blustery Prime Minister, busomy Grand Duchess, and inept General. A sweet and colorful fable that's told with a smirk and a smile.
D: Jack Arnold. A: With Jean Seberg, David Kossoff.

The Battle of the Sexes
(1960) 88m. B&W. **C+**

Sellers is the efficiency expert for a Scottish factory about to be bought by an American businesswoman. He decides that killing her is the only practical solution and his attempts make for a black comedy about big business. Clever wordplay but few laughs.
D: Charles Crichton. A: With Robert Morley, Constance Cummings.

Two-Way Stretch
(1961) 84m. **B**

Sellers and two fellow inmates break out of their low-security prison to commit a robbery and then return in order to establish the perfect alibi. Plenty of near fatal discoveries and ridiculous blunders keep this film securely in the banana peel department.
D: Robert Day. A: With Wilfrid Hyde-White, Lionel Jeffries.

Waltz of the Toreadors
(1962) 105m. **C+**

Retired army general Sellers, prisoner of a shrewish wife, is offered an opportunity to consummate an affair from his past, only to have his plan backfire. Creaky marital romp that feels less like a waltz than a slow walk.
D: John Guillermin. A: With Margaret Leighton.

The Wrong Arm of the Law
(1962) 94m. B&W **B+**

After an Australian gang impersonates London police in order to "confiscate" criminal loot, British gangsters join the police to nail them. Lots of action and madcap chases as Sellers plays the gang leader whose cover as a dress designer allows him to stage very unorthodox fashion shows.
D: Cliff Owen. A: With Lionel Jeffries, Bernard Cribbins.

Heaven's Above
(1963) 113m. B&W. **C+**

Sellers is the idealistic chaplain assigned to a wealthy and selfish congregation in this bumbling sedated comedy of manners.
D: John Boulting, Roy Boulting. A: With Cecil Parker, Isabel Jeans.

British Comedies

It's the swinging sixties and England seems like the center of the party. The Beatles' *A Hard Day's Night* opened a door and what followed were imitators whose cinematic style and frantic pacing kept up with all that youthful energy and sexual daring.

The Knack . . . And How to Get It
(1965) 85m. B&W. **B+**
A shy teacher will do anything to acquire "the knack" of getting girls. This jumps, twists, and skims along swinging London of the 60s with so many quick cut images that you feel like you've sat through a series of commercials.
D: Richard Lester. A: Michael Crawford, Rita Tushingham, Ray Brooks.

The Great St. Trinian's Train Robbery
(1966) 94m. **B–**
Gangsters make the fatal mistake of hiding their loot in the new school for those St. Trinian's girls. This is a pre-*Home Alone* world where kids get to drop, kick, and generally abuse and outwit dumb bad guys in a manner close to a series of vaudeville routines.
D: Frank Launder, Sidney Gilliat. A: Frankie Howerd, Reg Varney, Dora Bryan.

Bedazzled
(1967) 107m. **B+**
It's the Faust legend, with a devil who offers a meek and hopelessly in love nerd seven wishes and then frustrates each of them. This madcap film feels dated but it still motors along with enough humor to keep you watching.
D: Stanley Donen. A: Peter Cook, Dudley Moore, Raquel Welch.

The Bliss of Mrs. Blossom
(1968) 93m. **C–**
The discontented wife of a brassiere manufacturer secretly keeps a lover in the attic. This film version of a stage play feels like a dated but slightly risqué episode of *The Love Boat*.
D: Joe McGrath. A: Shirley MacLaine, Richard Attenborough, James Booth.

All-Star Journeys

Exotic locales, dozens of Hollywood stars, and a time-is-running-out momentum propel this group of farcical comedy-adventures in period costume. These globe-trotting extravaganzas often feel like one long chase film and can run a full hour longer than wiser heads would suggest, but they're also great for an evening of corny fun.

Around the World in 80 Days
(1956) 178m. **B+**
A colossal, lumbering, and splashy variety show of a film with no sense of pacing follows a Victorian gentleman as he travels the globe in every vehicle in creation. Every current star not yet in a coffin makes a brief appearance here so keep the fast-forward button ready.
D: Michael Anderson. A: David Niven, Shirley MacLaine, Cantinflas, and over 40 cameos.

Five Weeks in a Balloon
(1962) 101m. **B–**
A balloon crew in the 1860s must reach the Volta River in Africa and claim it for Britain before a pack of slavers get there. Cheerful, lower-budgeted, kid-level adventure with paunchy, middle-aged character actors all over the place.
D: Irwin Allen. A: Cedric Hardwicke, Red Buttons, Peter Lorre.

It's a Mad, Mad, Mad, Mad World
(1963) 192m. **B**
A frantic and sometimes boorish farce about human greed as a group of motorists go on a wild chase through California to claim a dead gangster's stash. Filled with a galaxy of comedians who spend as much time huffing and puffing as being funny.
D: Stanley Kramer. A: Spencer Tracy, Milton Berle, Sid Caesar.

The Great Race
(1965) 163m. **B+**
It's the first New York-to-Paris Auto Race and the leading contenders are a noble racer and a sniveling villain. Less of an all-star convention and more of a breezy parade of stunts, scenery, and actors at play.
D: Blake Edwards. A: Tony Curtis, Jack Lemmon, Natalie Wood.

Those Magnificent Men in Their Flying Machines
(1965) 133m. **B+**
Daredevil fliers gather for the first London-to-Paris race, and sabotage, romantic competition, and mechanical problems complicate the proceedings. High-spirited, mildly funny adventure features some remarkable aerial stunts and a spiffy collection of genuine pre-World War I aircraft.
D: Ken Annakin. A: Stuart Whitman, Sarah Miles, James Fox.

Those Daring Young Men in Their Jaunty Jalopies
(1969) 125m. **C–**
A slapstick car version of *Those Magnificent Men . . .* with a 1500-mile Monte Carlo rally providing the excuse for some glossy old cars and a few well-crafted auto stunts. Unsubtle, noisy, and unfunny. D: Ken Annakin. A: Tony Curtis, Susan Hampshire, Terry-Thomas.

Doris Day Sex Comedies

She's sunny, eager to please, well adjusted, and American sexy-clean. These colorful romantic comedies are some of the purest forms of sexual mythology from the prefeminist, presexual revolutionary 60s. The marvel is that Doris is such a good-humored comrade to her leading man, the stories are charming in more than just a dated way. The bedroom farces with Rock Hudson are delightfully goofy with an added fascination whether or not you're wearing your decoder ring for the campy humor.

Pillow Talk

(1959) 110m. **B+**

Doris is the virtuous interior decorator and Rock's a music composer lothario with whom she unwillingly shares a telephone line. When they meet in person, he pretends to be an inexperienced hayseed in order to seduce her. Light and goofy.
D: Michael Gordon. A: With Rock Hudson, Tony Randall, Thelma Ritter.

Please Don't Eat the Daisies

(1960) 111m. **A–**

He's the new drama critic of a major New York newspaper coping with the pitfalls of fame and power in the cynical world of theater, and she's his wife coping with their passel of kids in the city and later the suburbs. Less silly and more adult than the others.
D: Charles Walters. A: With David Niven, Janis Paige, Spring Byington.

Lover Come Back

(1961) 107m. **A**

Rock is Doris' cynical rival advertising exec here impersonating an inventor of a new product who's inexperienced with women, hoping to trump her professionally and romantically. Loopy fun includes a hilarious seduction scene.
D: Delbert Mann. A: With Rock Hudson, Tony Randall, Edie Adams.

That Touch of Mink

(1962) 99m. **A–**

Doris is an out-of-work secretary who's wooed by a rich debonaire businessman before they switch opinions on whether to go all the way. Beautiful and sometimes hilarious big-screen version of *That Cosmopolitan Girl*'s fantasy.
D: Delbert Mann. A: With Cary Grant, Gig Young, Audrey Meadows.

The Thrill of It All

(1963) 104m. **B+**

Doris is the happy suburbanite doctor's wife who unwittingly becomes a huge success as the slightly ditzy spokeswoman in soap commercials. More solid comedy and some funny satirical bits about TV.
D: Norman Jewison. A: With James Garner, Arlene Francis, Edward Andrews.

Send Me No Flowers

(1964) 100m. **B–**

Hypochondriac suburbanite Rock thinks he has a terminal illness and looks for a replacement spouse for his wife Doris. Runs out of steam but Rock's scenes with Randall are priceless.
D: Norman Jewison. A: With Rock Hudson, Tony Randall, Paul Lynde.

The Glass Bottom Boat

(1966) 110m. **C+**

Doris is the young breathless widow who gets involved with a rich scientist and some wacky spies. The romantic comedy portion soon gives way to some tedious slapstick and chases.
D: Frank Tashlin. A: With Rod Taylor, Arthur Godfrey, Paul Lynde.

Teen Romantic Comedies

Sandwiched between the Eisenhower years and the 60s Revolution, Hollywood made these youthful romances that have the charm of hoola hoops and Barbie dolls, populated with fresh-faced teens in perpetual motion either surfing, dancing, or hunting the opposite sex.

Where the Boys Are

(1960) 99m. **A**

Four coeds representing the spectrum of female types—brainy beauty, blonde romantic, gangly tall girl, and Connie Francis—head for Fort Lauderdale on spring break. This has everything a teen movie needs and more: 50s moralizing, tight swimsuits, good-girl and bad-girl romance, and Frank Gorshin playing jazz music.
D: Henry Levin. A: Dolores Hart, George Hamilton, Yvette Mimieux.

Palm Springs Weekend

(1963) 100m. **C+**

More spring break shenanigans as the cast cuts capers in Palm Springs searching for romance and kicks, personified by bronzed god Donohue. Lots of bikini abandon and Watusi dancing in this standard-issue entry.
D: Norman Taurog. A: Troy Donohue, Connie Stevens, Stefanie Powers.

A Swingin' Summer

(1965) 82m. **B–**

Three swingin' guys book The Righteous Brothers and Gary Lewis and the Playboys and soon the place is filled with frugging femmes. Kind of amazingly naive combination of squeaky-clean rock, leering males, female flesh, and let's-have-a-party cheeriness.
D: Robert Sparr. A: Raquel Welch, James Stacy, William Wellman.

The Trouble with Angels

(1966) 112m. **B**

A defiant girl from a broken home and her chum turn a Catholic boarding school upside down. Good clean Disney-like version of teen hijinks is given some weight by Russell doing her magisterial but generous routine as Mother Superior.
D: Ida Lupino. A: Rosalind Russell, Hayley Mills, June Harding.

Gidget

Gidget

(1959) 95m. **B–**

A saucy teenage girl is mad for heartthrob Moondogie and decides to catch his eye by flirting with an older-but-wiser beach bum. With characters named Stinky and Kahoona, lots of surf-induced wisdom from Robertson, and parents who know all, this looks like a relic from an alternate universe of cuteness.
D: Paul Wendkos. A: Sandra Dee, James Darren, Cliff Robertson.

Gidget Goes Hawaiian

(1961) 102m. **C+**

Despite come-ons from the local wave-mavens while in Hawaii, Gidget still finds herself all goofy over Moondogie. Walley makes a hypercute, fidgety Gidget, but otherwise, a watered-down clone of the first one.
D: Paul Wendkos. A: Deborah Walley, James Darren, Michael Callan.

Gidget Goes to Rome

(1963) 104m. **C+**

A slightly more cosmopolitan-looking Gidget hits the Eternal City with her gang of friends, and while Moondogie is checking out the local talent, Gidg is being wooed (or chaperoned) by a suave older Italian. Nice locales but Gidget is no Daisy Miller.
D: Paul Wendkos. A: Cindy

Carol, James Darren, Jeff Donnell.

Tammy

Tammy and the Bachelor
(1957) 89m. **B–**
A handsome young man crashes his plane and spunky backwoods girl Tammy and her warm-hearted kin come to the rescue. Reynolds is all pep and country wisdom as she nurses hunk Nielsen back to health and romance in this down-home, country corn fantasy.
D: Joseph Pevney. A: Debbie Reynolds, Leslie Nielsen, Walter Brennan.

Tammy and the Doctor
(1963) 88m. **C+**
Tammy goes to the big city to train to be a nurse in this outing that pairs hillbilly bedpan-and-bandages humor with hospital romance. Dee is nearly campy, overdrive-adorable, but Fonda is almost comatose as the object of her desire.
D: Harry Keller. A: Sandra Dee, Peter Fonda, Macdonald Carey.

1960s

Billy Wilder

Under the guise of 60s mainstream comedy, Billy Wilder managed to treat adult subjects such as transvestism, prostitution, and even American domination through soft drinks with an urbane wit and light cynicism rare in Hollywood. Amazingly, these films work beautifully on a strictly entertaining/comic level; they also have the added attraction of being intelligent and revealing a dark undercurrent to the American landscape.

Some Like It Hot
(1959) 119m. B&W. **A**
When two musicians witness the St. Valentine's Day Massacre, they dress like women and join an all-girl orchestra headed for Florida. This hilarious sex comedy belongs in equal parts to Lemmon and Curtis as the bickering buddies in drag and a vulnerable conniving Monroe as the unsuccessful golddigger.
D: Billy Wilder. A: Jack Lemmon, Tony Curtis, Marilyn Monroe.

The Apartment
(1960) 125m. B&W. **A**
A young clerk allows the boss to use his apartment for extramarital trysts and finds himself with a suicidal coworker (with whom he's smitten) on his hands. Brilliant juxtaposition of sweet romantics and heartless corporate types is visualized with stark photography and a great MacMurray as the ultimate cold fish company man.
D: Billy Wilder. A: Jack Lemmon, Shirley MacLaine, Fred MacMurray.

One, Two, Three
(1961) 110m. B&W. **B+**
The chief of a Coke bottling plant in West Germany is stuck with babysitting an executive's ditzy daughter who falls for a political insurrectionist. Cutting vintage dialogue on capitalism and politics is delivered by Cagney with perfect comic verve in this hilarious jab at Cold War politics and commerce.
D: Billy Wilder. A: James Cagney, Horst Buchholz, Arlene Francis.

Irma La Douce
(1963) 146m. **A–**
A French gendarme falls for one of the prostitutes on his beat, unwillingly becomes her pimp, and then goes to all kinds of trouble to be her only customer. Irresistible performances and the look and feel of a big Hollywood musical make this an adult giddy ride.
D: Billy Wilder. A: Shirley MacLaine, Jack Lemmon, Lou Jacobi.

The Fortune Cookie
(1966) 125m. B&W. **B+**
An injured cameraman becomes prey to the questionable tactics of his shyster brother-in-law who talks him into claiming total paralysis with hilarious consequences. With great shady characters (and Matthau nearly running off with the film), this gleefully gallops from funny to ridiculous.
D: Billy Wilder. A: Jack Lemmon, Walter Matthau, Judi West.

Families

These families have a lot in common with the classic sitcom clans: The parents are kind and understanding, the children are bothersome but respectful, and the teenagers act moony with regular abandon.

Mr. Hobbs Takes a Vacation
(1962) 116m. **B+**
An overworked banker takes his family to the seaside for summer vacation and discovers that the house is a wreck, his kids are running wild, and his neighbors are loony. A bright cheery excursion through standard family mishaps with a swoony teenage girl falling for hunk Fabian.
D: Henry Koster. A: James Stewart, Maureen O'Hara, Fabian.

Dear Brigitte
(1965) 100m. **B+**
A ten-year-old math prodigy with a gift for handicapping horses just wants to meet his idol Brigitte Bardot and manages to finagle it with the help of his benevolent professor father. A big boy's fantasy in larger-than-life color and sets, with a winning cameo by Bardot herself.
D: Henry Koster. A: James Stewart, Fabian, Billy Mumy, Glynis Johns.

With Six You Get Eggroll
(1968) 99m. **C+**
A chirpy widow with three kids marries a nice guy with one, and suddenly six people are trying to fit together as a family. A candy-colored story that's so corny you'll either go into sugar shock or

wistfully wonder why life can't be like this.
D: Howard Morris. A: Doris Day, Brian Keith, Barbara Hershey.

Yours, Mine and Ours
(1968) 111m. **C**
A widow with eight kids marries a widower with ten, in this standard "new family combo" adventure. Pesky plot requirements are solved by adding extra kids, but this may have you searching the tube for *The Brady Bunch* reruns.
D: Melville Shavelson. A: Lucille Ball, Henry Fonda, Van Johnson.

Romantic Comedies

These candy-colored big-screen productions cover the middle-class mating dance when the double standard prevailed and double beds were still exotic. Single or married, everyone lives in a bright bubble of urban or suburban sophistication of two martini lunches and wives who shop. The comedy tends to be broad and farcical and the persistently coy attitude toward sex can get silly, but these fluffy pieces that were once risqué now come across as sweet and reassuring as a *Leave It to Beaver* episode.

Boys' Night Out
(1962) 115m. **B+**
Four suburbanite buddies rent an apartment so they can have one swinging night out (three are married); a sociology student studying the American male poses as a high-class hooker and takes them for a ride. Less leers and also less laughs but the social satire is right on the mark.
D: Michael Gordon. A: Kim Novak, James Garner, Tony Randall.

Forty Pounds of Trouble
(1962) 106m. **B–**
Like an updated version of *Little Miss Marker*, a casino owner finds himself saddled with a cute little orphan while fighting off a marriage-minded girlfriend. Pretty goofy, with the finale a slapstick chase through Disneyland.
D: Norman Jewison. A: Tony Curtis, Phil Silvers, Suzanne Pleshette.

My Geisha
(1962) 120m. **B**
An actress impersonates a geisha so well with her director husband that he offers the starring role in his movie to that geisha. A thin story is made lush by the beautiful Japanese locales and big screen treatment.
D: Jack Cardiff. A: Shirley MacLaine, Yves Montand, Edward G. Robinson.

Period of Adjustment
(1962) B&W. 112m. **C+**
Newlyweds who start arguing the moment they get married arrive at a friend's house who's also having marital problems. Fonda affects an annoying whine of a Southern accent and the real question of why the couple ever got married at all is never answered.
D: George Roy Hill. A: Jane Fonda, Jim Hutton, Tony Franciosa.

A New Kind of Love
(1963) 110m. **B**
A butch-looking designer succumbs to the magic of Paris and winds up bewitching a womanizing reporter in her guise as a high-price hooker. Overlong but has an enjoyably corny 50s-style swinging attitude and a funny sequence showing the "old maids" of the Parisian fashion industry celebrating their holiday.
D: Melville Shavelson. A: Paul Newman, Joanne Woodward, Thelma Ritter.

The Courtship of Eddie's Father
(1963) 117m. **B+**
Eddie doesn't mind his dad dating but he still has final approval. Director Minnelli manages to make an essentially cozy, wholesome little romantic family comedy look as dazzling and colorful as a big musical.
D: Vincente Minnelli. A: Glenn Ford, Ronny Howard, Shirley Jones.

Man's Favorite Sport?
(1963) 120m. **B–**
Phony sports expert Hudson is forced into a fishing competition and undergoes a series of slapstick misadventures helped along by ditzy Prentiss who's trying to hook him. Howard Hawks' attempt to revive the screwball comedy doesn't quite come off, but Prentiss is adorable to watch.
D: Howard Hawks. A: Rock Hudson, Paula Prentiss, Maria Perschy.

The Wheeler Dealers
(1963) 106m. **B**
A Texas tycoon without money but plenty of persuasiveness gets a Wall Street firm to invest in what they think is worthless stock in his enterprise. A romantic comedy with Doris Day/Rock Hudson-style sparring, along with a twitting of the not-so-gentle art of money manipulation.
D: Arthur Hiller. A: James Garner, Lee Remick, Jim Backus.

Bedtime Story
(1964) 99m. **B+**
A continental roué competes with a vulgarian American GI to swindle rich women on the Riviera. Much funnier than *Dirty Rotten Scoundrels* with some hilarious scenes by Brando.
D: Ralph Levy. A: David Niven, Marlon Brando, Shirley Jones.

Father Goose
(1964) 115m. **B–**
A beachcomber in the South Seas keeps tabs on the Japanese during World War II while engaging in the battle of the sexes with plucky French schoolgirls. Bright and cheerful with kids on hand to provide ample doses of cuteness.
D: Ralph Nelson. A: Cary Grant, Leslie Caron, Trevor Howard.

Good Neighbor Sam
(1964) 130m. **B+**
An ad exec and his wife unchain a series of endless complications when he impersonates the husband of their sexy neighbor for the sake of a million dollars. A comedy of suburban manners and corporate life with screwball sequences showing the lengths to which people will go for money.
D: David Swift. A: Jack Lemmon, Dorothy Provine, Romy Schneider.

Sex and the Single Girl
(1964) 114m. **A**
Curtis is the ruthless trash magazine writer who's out to expose sex expert Wood, and beleaguered businessman Fonda is constantly bickering with jealous bored wife Bacall. The sex comedy

archetypes are hilariously rendered, with wonderful sparks flying between the sparring couples.
D: Richard Quine. A: Tony Curtis, Natalie Wood, Henry Fonda, Lauren Bacall.

How to Murder Your Wife
(1965) 118m. **B**

A Manhattan cartoonist enjoys a playboy lifestyle complete with butler, until one night in a blind drunk he marries an Italian sexpot. The war between the sexes get pretty degrading in a film that loses its fluffy tone when portraying marriage as a string of dank and bilious episodes.
D: Richard Quine. A: Jack Lemmon, Virna Lisi, Terry-Thomas.

Any Wednesday
(1966) 110m. **B–**

Fonda is the company president's good-girl mistress who's even more unhappy with her lot after a young exec accidentally discovers the corporate love nest. Standard and a little strident.
D: Robert Ellis Miller. A: Jane Fonda; Dean Jones; Jason Robards, Jr.

Walk, Don't Run
(1966) 114m. **B**

When a young woman is forced to share her Tokyo apartment with two strangers during the 1966 Olympics, proximity leads to confusion and sexual tension. A sluggish comedy, but Grant gives it some shine.
D: Charles Walters. A: Cary Grant, Samantha Eggar, Jim Hutton.

Barefoot in the Park
(1967) 106m. **A**

A buttoned-down attorney and his free-spirited wife are the newlywed couple ironing out different approaches to life in their quirky New York City apartment. This Neil Simon play adaptation features a stock Greenwich Village ethnic character, jokes about six-story walkups, and some hip clothes for Fonda.
D: Gene Saks. A: Robert Redford, Jane Fonda, Charles Boyer.

A Guide for the Married Man
(1967) 91m. **C+**

Supposedly sophisticated episodic comedy illustrating the pitfalls and joys of committing adultery. A not too funny, all-star film with a mean spirit running through it.
D: Gene Kelly. A: Walter Matthau, Robert Morse, Joey Bishop, and all-star others.

Buona Sera, Mrs. Campbell
(1968) 113m. **B**

An Italian woman must face the three American men who, for the past 20 years, have believed themselves to be her child's father. A lively and mature comedy with Gina and other Italian cast members providing a lot of shouting and emoting.
D: Melvin Frank. A: Gina Lollobrigida, Peter Lawford, Shelley Winters

The Impossible Years
(1968) 92m. **C+**

A psychiatrist has problems with his teenage daughter when she gets involved with the counterculture. Some leering sex jokes, cartoon hippies, silly predictable situations, and Ozzie Nelson as the neighbor place this firmly in the TV sitcom camp.
D: Michael Gordon. A: David Niven, Lola Albright, Chad Everett.

Where Were You When the Lights Went Out?
(1968) 94m. **C+**

The 1965 blackout creates confusion for the Broadway actress who can't remember if she slept with a white-collar thief on the lam. Her husband tries to convince her she did. Doris is outraged through most of the wink-wink, nudge-nudge comedy, but it's no surprise considering all her men are heels.
D: Hy Averback. A: Doris Day, Robert Morse, Terry-Thomas.

Old-Fashioned Eccentrics

Although made during the late 60s, these films are not the surreal tales of dreamy misfits that were popular then, but rather sweet-tempered portraits of more recognizable oddballs making their way through the everyday crazy world.

The World of Henry Orient
(1964) 106m. **B**

Two starstruck teens stalk a famous concert pianist they're in love with, who happens to be a dissolute, self-absorbed cad having an affair with a married woman. A funny quirky coming-of-age tale with nifty 60s Manhattan locales, and a darkly funny turn by Sellers as the egomaniac Casanova.
D: George Roy Hill. A: Peter Sellers, Paula Prentiss, Tom Bosley.

A Thousand Clowns
(1965) 118m. B&W. **A–**

A solid balance of laughs and pathos as a dropout TV writer and his precocious young nephew struggle to remain together as family. This acerbically witty ode to individualism has gritty New York City location black-and-white photography and finely tuned performances to ground it all in reality.
D: Fred Coe. A: Jason Robards, Jr.; Barry Gordon; Barbara Harris.

Enter Laughing
(1967) 112m. **B**

His mother wants him to be a pharmacist but David Kolowitz strikes off into the world of theater, even if it's a rundown one. A classic show-biz story that feels like a Neil Simon comedy, filled with colorful stereotypes and plenty of comedy schtick.
D: Carl Reiner. A: Reni Santoni, José Ferrer, Shelley Winters.

Up the Down Staircase
(1967) 124m. **C+**

An idealistic young teacher with dreams of teaching Keats and Thoreau to eager young minds gets a baptism of fire with her first job at a tough New York City high school. This tries to be *Blackboard Jungle* with humor, but ends up feeling like a winsome version of *Welcome Back Kotter*.
D: Robert Mulligan. A: Sandy Dennis, Eileen Heckart, Jean Stapleton.

The Night They Raided Minsky's
(1968) 99m. **B–**

A disarmingly silly piece about a nice Amish girl at the turn of the century who comes to New York and finds her way into the world of burlesque. Colorful, naive,

and sweet-toned throw-back to old-fashioned musical comedies that's given a 60s "with it" ending by Ms. Ekland flashing her breasts.
D: William Friedkin. A: Jason Robards, Jr.; Elliott Gould; Britt Ekland.

The Plot Against Harry
(1969) 81m. B&W. **B+**

A small-time Jewish gangster returns from prison to discover that his turf has been taken over and his family is suddenly demanding his attention. Priest is quietly hilarious as the long-suffering, hang-dog operator who tries to juggle family and business obligations in a jumpy, anxious, and greedy 60s New York City.
D: Michael Roemer. A: Martin Priest, Ben Lang, Maxine Woods.

The Prime of Miss Jean Brodie
(1969) 166m. **A**

Smith is a sheer delight as the highly singular girls' school teacher who's giving her girls lessons in politics, art, and character development, spicing up classes with her own sexual past. Richly photographed evocation of 1930s Edinburgh with a subtle ambiance that shifts from almost funny to wistfully melancholic.
D: Ronald Neame. A: Maggie Smith, Robert Stephens, Ceila Johnson.

1960s–1970s
Satires and Black Comedies

After years of dutiful nodding to the status quo, it almost became mandatory in the smart-alecky 60s to take potshots at any available icon, taboo, or representative of The Establishment. Whether it was war, bits of Americana, or even moviemaking itself, no cow was too sacred for these bitingly cynical films.

The Americanization of Emily
(1964) 117m. B&W. **A–**

A scheming naval attaché in World War II, whose skill is locating food and cigarettes, falls in love and is sent to the D-day landing for PR purposes. A cynical tale of manipulation sweetened by an old-fashioned romance.
D: Arthur Hiller. A: James Garner, Julie Andrews, James Coburn.

Dr. Strangelove or How I Learned to Stop Worrying and Love the Bomb
(1964) 93m. B&W. **A**

A lunatic general unleashes a nuclear attack on Moscow, setting in motion an absurdist apocalyptic comedy of errors. Sleek noir/pop-art sets, a constantly inventive script, and characters ranging from multiple brilliant turns by Sellers to Scott looning it up as a jingoistic madman combine to make this a hilariously pitch-black masterpiece.
D: Stanley Kubrick. A: Peter Sellers, George C. Scott, Sterling Hayden.

The Loved One
(1965) 116m. B&W
B+

A British poet visits his uncle in a Hollywood filled with drunken British expatriates, resident oddballs, and a singularly weird Mr. Joyboy, proprietor of a funeral home for pets and people. Darkly hilarious film is nearly festering with a seamy debauched air and an overlay of brittle, caustically homosexual innuendo.
D: Tony Richardson. A: Robert Morse, Robert Morley, Rod Steiger.

How I Won the War
(1967) 109m. **C+**

A vet's reminiscences about his wartime days, most of them impressively inaccurate. This war satire features a fun turn by Beatle Lennon and on-target spoofery of man's stupidest foible, but too often goes for obvious targets and has a certain know-it-all air.
D: Richard Lester. A: Michael Crawford, John Lennon, Michael Hordern.

The President's Analyst
(1967) 104m. **B+**

The Commander in Chief's clandestine therapist is neck deep in intrigue because of what everyone thinks he knows. A veritable time-capsule of 60s paranoia, political concerns, and lifestyles, with great op-art direction, tongue-in-cheek tone, and a remarkably nuts ending.
D: Theodore Flicker. A: James Coburn, Godfrey Cambridge.

I Love You Alice B. Toklas
(1968) 93m. **B+**

A good Jewish son/attorney drops out, turns on, and tunes into a new life as a carefree hippie. The years have treated this cultural fable surprisingly well, thanks to Sellers' hilarious performance, sharply satirical observations of the period's pretensions to hipness, and, of course, that scene where his folks eat the marijuana brownies.
D: Hy Averback. A: Peter Sellers, Leigh Taylor-Young, Jo Van Fleet.

The Party
(1968) 99m. **A–**

Sellers practically disappears into the role of an astonishingly clumsy Indian actor lost in a nearly film-long Hollywood party. A bright and razor sharp romp that succeeds in making the pratfall an art form, with satirical elements second always to the next hilarious physical calamity.
D: Blake Edwards. A: Peter Sellers, Claudine Longet, Gavin MacLeod.

Bob and Carol and Ted and Alice
(1969) 104m. **A**

Two affluent California couples: One has all the hang-ups of sexual stalemates and shrink sessions while the other explores the nascent swinging lifestyle with experimental Esalen-style touchy-feelie sessions, one-night stands, and pot-smoking. A big, generous, and wildly entertaining comedy of 60s manners.
D: Paul Mazursky. A: Natalie Wood, Robert Culp, Elliot Gould, Dyan Cannon.

The Magic Christian
(1969) 93m. **B**

The world's wealthiest man sets off with his adopted son to discover the extent to which people will do humiliating things for money. A brightly costumed landscape jammed with psychedelic images keeps you gazing as a series of sketches unfurl one irreverent misadventure after another.

D: Joseph McGrath. A: Peter Sellers, Ringo Starr, Raquel Welch.

Putney Swope

(1969) 88m. **B**

Madison Avenue loses it when a black man is appointed head of a major advertising firm. A low-budget, independent film that is visually inspired, with surreal commercials woven into the story and other strange asides while much of the humor is on-target despite the period specific problems.
D: Robert Downey. A: Arnold Johnson, Laura Green, Allen Garfield.

Alex in Wonderland

(1970) 110m. **B–**

A satirical Fellini-esque tale of a director's misadventures in Hollywood (so Fellini-esque that the famed Italian director makes a cameo). Good performances and scattered laughs at Tinseltown types are weighed down by excessive navel-gazing
D: Paul Mazursky. A: Donald Sutherland, Ellen Burstyn, Paul Mazursky.

Catch-22

(1970) 121m. **B**

This absurdist comedy of war madness follows a bombardier group struggling to save their sanity and skin in World War II. Though lacking the Heller novel's manic energy, this still has some grotesquely hilarious moments and a tone that veers wildly from slapstick to almost surreal gruesomeness.
D: Mike Nichols. A: Alan Arkin, Martin Balsam, Richard Benjamin.

M*A*S*H

(1970) 116m. **A**

Altman hit his stride with ensemble comedy and overlapping dialogue in this story of the screw-loose antics of iconoclastic surgeons and staff in a Korean War hospital unit. Nonchalantly harrowing and minus the TV show's feel-good attitude, this emerges as a hyperkinetic blend of antiwar, black, and slapstick comedy.
D: Robert Altman. A: Elliott Gould, Donald Sutherland, Sally Kellerman.

Myra Breckenridge

(1970) 94m. **C+**

A film critic gets his sex-change operation, turns into Raquel Welch, and heads for Hollywood looking to start her own sexual revolution. This leering patchwork of episodes, filled with notables and not-quite notables of the 60s, is a colorful, vulgar, and strangely static puzzle that should be a lot funnier than it is.
D: Michael Sarne. A: Raquel Welch, Mae West, John Huston.

Watermelon Man

(1970) 97m. **B**

An outrageously bigoted white salesman wakes up one day to discover that he has turned black. A classic role-reversal story that overcomes the one-note joke with inspiring comic performances.
D: Melvin Van Peebles. A: Godfrey Cambridge, Estelle Parsons, Howard Caine.

Cold Turkey

(1971) 99m. **C+**

An entire town stops smoking for a month when offered 25 million dollars. Looks and feels like an overlong TV sitcom, with a nicotine-deprived cast frenetically delivering a stream of very obvious jokes.
D: Norman Lear. A: Dick Van Dyke, Pippa Scott, Tom Poston.

The Hospital

(1971) 103m. **B+**

A chief doctor of a large New York City hospital is driven to the brink by mysterious deaths of two interns and a nurse, raging protests against expansion, and his new love for the daughter of a comatose patient. A wordy and relentlessly black satire of the red-tape world of hospital procedure.
D: Arthur Hiller. A: George C. Scott, Diana Rigg, Barnard Hughes.

Little Murders

(1971) 107m. **C+**

A random sniper's bullet throws a man and his family into a nightmare of violence, madness, and other things New York. Some clever bon mots here and there, but very dated and presented in a stagy fashion betraying its theatrical roots.
D: Alan Arkin. A: Elliott Gould, Marcia Rodd, Vincent Gardenia.

Slaughterhouse Five

(1972) 104m. **B**

A middle-aged optometrist time-trips between his past as a World War II POW in Dresden, his present drab life, and his future on an uncharted planet where he lives with a porn queen. Vonnegut's satiric fantasia is given a spirited rendering but you may want to keep a compass handy to handle all the frenetic crosscutting.
D: George Roy Hill. A: Michael Sacks, Ron Leibman, Valerie Perrine.

Shampoo

(1975) 109m. **A**

Armed with his trusty blow-dryer, hairdresser/lothario Beatty zips around town administering to women with bad hair days while juggling his current lover, a former lover, and the insatiable wife of the man he wants to invest in his salon. A wicked satire of the who's-bedding-who power structure of trendy LA.
D: Hal Ashby. A: Warren Beatty, Julie Christie, Goldie Hawn.

Smile

(1975) 113m. **B+**

A trenchant comedy about the most ridiculous of spectator sports shows the hilariously serious business and hoopla of staging a beauty contest in a small town in California. Ambition, trickery, lust, and those inimitable "talent contests" all get a good-natured lampooning in this underrated comedy.
D: Michael Ritchie. A: Bruce Dern, Barbara Feldon, Michael Kidd.

Hollywood Boulevard

(1976) 83m. **B–**

Using footage from their employer Roger Corman's various exploitation films, two directors fashioned this amusingly off-the-cuff tale of a loser film company's struggles to make exploitation films. A sleaze movie fan's delight.
D: Joe Dante, Allan Arkush. A: Candice Rialson, Mary Woronov, Rita George.

Network

(1976) 121m. **A**

When a newscaster breaks down on the air, announces his suicide, and harangues his audience for being TV boobs, the sky-high ratings get him his own show as a ranting madman/messiah. This biting extravagant satire of TV hasn't lost its edge with Dunaway a standout as a driven reptilian TV exec.
D: Sidney Lumet. A: William Holden, Faye Dunaway, Peter Finch.

Being There

(1979) 130m. **A**

A simpleminded gardener whose entire life has been tending plants and watching TV is suddenly turned out of his quarters. Sellers makes it all too believable how he becomes a political and moral philosopher who seduces a TV nation in this absurd, absorbing, and deadly funny satire.
D: Hal Ashby. A: Peter Sellers, Shirley MacLaine, Melvyn Douglas.

New-Fashioned Eccentrics

A certain zany energy runs through these small, alternative comedies featuring extremely eccentric characters. With young heroes who dress like a gorilla, want to fly like a bird, or have an affair with a septuagenarian, gritty realism is not in the forefront of these endearing portraits of odd people in even odder situations.

Morgan!
(1966) 97m. **B+**

A quirky tale of a gorilla-obsessed artist, his Marxist mom, and soon-to-be ex-wife. A Mod standard-bearer filled with the period's flip humor, Carnaby Street attire, and introduction of soon-to-be fashionable lunatic-as-hero gambit.
D: Karel Reisz. A: David Warner, Vanessa Redgrave, Robert Stephens.

You're a Big Boy Now
(1966) 96m. **C+**

This early Coppola offering portrays the adventures of a naive young fellow who's taught the ins and outs of life by a hip go-go dancer. Colorful, sometimes insightful, and with style-to-burn, but lack of plot development weighs down later reels.
D: Francis Ford Coppola. A: Peter Kastner, Elizabeth Hartman, Geraldine Page.

Brewster McCloud
(1970) 104m. **C+**

A mad fantasy of a film, tells of a young man's yearning to fly, even if it means jumping from the upper reaches of the Houston Astrodome. Propelled by a manic intensity that seems closer to Roadrunner than Greek myth, this surrealist saga sinks in its own whimsy.
D: Robert Altman. A: Bud Cort, Sally Kellerman, Michael Murphy.

Where's Poppa?
(1970) 82m. **B**

Oedipal problems rear their heads when a man's attempts at marriage are foiled by his overbearing mother's socially inappropriate behavior. Some big laughs, lots of bizarre activities by a game cast, and very much an artifact of the shocking sixties.
D: Carl Reiner. A: George Segal, Ruth Gordon, Trish Van Devere.

Harold and Maude
(1972) 90m. **B**

This is an ironic macabre delight when poor little rich boy Harold is staging a series of ludicrous suicide attempts. When he falls for septuagenarian and hardcore life-affirmer Maude, it either becomes a wonderfully whimsical look at true love or an intolerably cutesy, believability-straining fable.
D: Hal Ashby. A: Bud Cort, Ruth Gordon, Vivian Pickles.

The Ruling Class
(1972) 154m. **B**

O'Toole has a field day playing an heir to a royal fortune whose only problem is an utter belief that he is Christ incarnate. Like a more focused Ken Russell film, this amazing (if slightly dated) satire features macabre dance numbers, a Parliament full of corpses, and other unique visuals to complement its delightfully iconoclastic tale.
D: Peter Medak. A: Peter O'Toole, Alastair Sim, Coral Browne.

Woody Allen

He started the decade as the nebbish we love to feel superior to, obsessing over sex, death, and God while tripping over 30-foot bananas. Woody's primitive and wildly funny early films still look like a stand-up comic's intelligent spoof of literary and film works, be it a Russian epic or a sex manual. By the end of the 70s, these farces were replaced by slicker homages to films and more generally entertaining seriocomic meditations on the human condition.

Take the Money and Run
(1969) 85m. **B**

A mock-documentary on the fall and collapse of a neurotic petty criminal who can't get a break or even write a decent holdup note. ("I've got a gub.") Deadpan narration, interviews with his humiliated parents, and newsreel footage of his embarrassing origins and ultimate capture are uneven but hilarious.
D: Woody Allen. A: With Janet Margolin, Louise Lasser.

Bananas
(1971) 82m. **B**

The sight gags in the first part of this political satire come at you so fast and funny that you can barely catch your breath. Things bog down when products-tester Woody gets caught up in a Latin American revolution, but it remains a funny nerd-out-of-water tale.
D: Woody Allen. A: With Louise Lasser, Carlos Montalban.

Everything You Ever Wanted to Know About Sex but Were Afraid to Ask
(1972) 88m. **C+**

The perils of negotiating a medieval chastity belt and life of a sperm are some of the farcelets on sexual fantasies and apostasies. Sounds much funnier on paper than it is on film.
D: Woody Allen. A: With Louise Lasser, Lynn Redgrave.

Play It Again, Sam
(1972) 85m. **B+**

A lonesome loser obsessed with movies lives out his own version of *Casablanca* with the wife of his best friend, ably assisted by the ghost of Humphrey Bogart. Woody's first sweetly romantic comedy (written but not directed by Allen).
D: Herbert Ross. A: With Diane Keaton, Tony Roberts.

Sleeper
(1973) 88m. **B+**

Woody winds up in the twenty-first century, grap-

pling with a fascistic, high-tech society, and Keaton is one of the snooty and complacent citizens who becomes his comrade in arms. Like a comic New Yorker's version of *1984*.
D: Woody Allen. A: With Diane Keaton, John Beck.

Love and Death
(1975) 85m. **B+**
This spoof on Russian novels and costume dramas may leave some scratching their heads, but Allen is in high form rambling on about sex, death, and God, with the cossacks, orthodox priests, and loopy peasants.
D: Woody Allen. A: With Diane Keaton, Harold Gould.

Annie Hall
(1977) 93m. **A**
Woody's breakthrough Oscar winner as a stand-up comic walks us through his life, loves, and obsessions. Keaton steals the movie as the insecure would-be singer who he introduces to adult education and books on death. And then there's her clothes.
D: Woody Allen. A: With Diane Keaton, Tony Roberts.

Manhattan
(1979) 95m. B&W. **A**
Film becomes prophecy as a 40ish TV writer dating an insightful high school girl falls for the pretentious and insecure mistress of his married best friend. Allen is in full swing, poking fun at this museum-roaming class of New Yorkers in this beautiful black-and-white, Gershwin-cushioned elegy.
D: Woody Allen. A: With Diane Keaton, Mariel Hemingway.

Swinging 60s Romantic Comedies

Most of these films were considered pretty hip in their portrayal of young lovers coping with the freedom and anxiety of the sexual revolution. Now they may look like any conventional love story with some groovy period details, but you can still feel an exhilaration that comes from people who feel like they're taking a walk on the wild side.

What's New, Pussycat?
(1965) 108m. **A–**
A fashion magazine editor in Paris whom women find irresistible sees a psychiatrist to cure his wanton ways and remain true to his lady love. Problem is the shrink is even more out of control than he is. The comic heavy-hitters make this a consistently funny, raucous, and very engaging sex farce.
D: Clive Donner. A: Peter O'Toole, Peter Sellers, Woody Allen.

Alfie
(1966) 113m. **A–**
A cockney playboy swaggers from one conquest to another, occasionally taking breaks to address the camera with his arch observations on women and life. Caine makes the most of a thoroughly unlikable character in this tale that captures the era's sexual energy and stylishness.
D: Lewis Gilbert. A: Michael Caine, Shelley Winters, Millicent Martin.

Georgy Girl
(1966) 100m. B&W **B–**
An overweight and very self-conscious young woman is suddenly asked to be a mistress, a mother, and a lover. A winning portrayal by Redgrave, along with a charming story of self-discovery filled with heartwarming vignettes.
D: Silvio Narizzano. A: Lynn Redgrave, James Mason, Charlotte Rampling.

Two for the Road
(1967) 112m. **B+**
A married couple's tumultuous relationship is presented in a series of surprisingly adult bittersweet flashbacks. The lushly romantic European locales, air of well-worn sophistication, and the stars' tangible chemistry make this a love-story fan's perennial favorite.
D: Stanley Donen. A: Audrey Hepburn, Albert Finney, Jacqueline Bisset.

Petulia
(1968) 105m. **A**
A recently divorced doctor is plunged into a dizzying affair with a kooky beauty who has her own set of problems. The film's flashy fragmented style helps capture the era's cinematic style and the characters' disorientation in this funny and heartbreaking tale of emotional damage in the swinging 60s.
D: Richard Lester. A: George C. Scott, Julie Christie, Richard Chamberlain.

Three in the Attic
(1968) 91m. **C+**
Three comely females kidnap the campus Don Juan and hold him prisoner to better discuss sexual roles, wear flimsy 60s clothes, and wreak hormonal havoc. Would be a camp classic save for the tiresome repeating of the one-note plot.
D: Richard Wilson. A: Christopher Jones, Yvette Mimieux, Judy Pace.

Cactus Flower
(1969) 103m. **B**
A dentist proposes marriage to his effervescent and exasperatingly naive flower-child lover after she attempts suicide and has to get his nurse to impersonate a nonexistent estranged wife. The actors and the glossy 60s details in this lighthearted piece of fluff distract you from noticing the silliness.
D: Gene Saks. A: Walter Matthau, Goldie Hawn, Ingrid Bergman.

Goodbye, Columbus
(1969) 105m. **B+**
A Jewish boy from Trenton storms the ramparts of a Jewish American Princess and her upper-class suburban world in this film version of the classic Philip Roth story. The romance is tainted with *Love American Style* grooviness, but the film still contains some sharp and funny characterizations and episodes.
D: Larry Peerce. A: Richard Benjamin, Ali MacGraw, Jack Klugman.

1970s

Romantic Comedies

These lovers are educated, articulate, and more than a little prickly with each other: Some are dealing with the sexual revolution, some with middle age, and all with the complications of love. With all the sharp-tongued repartees and clash of souls at odds, these are warm, funny, and grownup portraits of people fumbling for warmth.

Lovers and Other Strangers

(1970) 106m. **B–**

When a young couple who has been living together decides to get married, their old-fashioned parents think the worries are over, but they've only just begun. Funny warm story of vivid family members who are trying to cope with the generation gap and the sexual revolution.

D: Cy Howard. A: Gig Young, Bea Arthur, Richard Castellano.

There's a Girl in My Soup

(1970) 95m. **C+**

The chemistry is engaging enough between the glib British food critic on the make who falls for a young, emotionally starved American girl, but otherwise this comic survey of late 60s mores has no juice.

D: Roy Boulting. A: Peter Sellers, Goldie Hawn, Tony Britton.

A New Leaf

(1971) 102m. **B**

A spoiled playboy is at the end of his trust fund and marries a rich, guileless, and homely botanist with plans of offing her. A loopy take on screwball comedies that mixes humor, pathos, and an unusual love story as May artlessly frustrates all of Matthau's murderous attempts.

D: Elaine May. A: Walter Matthau, Elaine May, Jack Weston.

The Heartbreak Kid

(1972) 104m. **A–**

A Jewish man meets his WASP fantasy girl while honeymooning with his very gawky bride. Depending on your point of view, watching Grodin's singleminded pursuit of his dream at all costs can be a smart and painfully funny viewing experience or just plain uncomfortable.

D: Elaine May. A: Charles Grodin, Cybill Shepherd, Jeannie Berlin.

A Touch of Class

(1972) 105m. **A–**

A married American man has a temperamental affair with an unflappable English clothing designer. Wonderful chemistry between these two, and Jackson is such a bracing antitype to the American male that this conventional love story remains interesting.

D: Melvin Frank. A: Glenda Jackson, George Segal, Paul Sorvino.

Blume in Love

(1973) 117m. **B+**

A divorced lawyer still loves his estranged wife, who's bedding down with a hunk, and resorts to any means to win her back. This neurotic and therapeutic comedy often hits the bull's eye in its satirization of the posthippie world of California kooks and the dark side of possessive love.

D: Paul Mazursky. A: George Segal, Susan Anspach, Kris Kristofferson.

Forty Carats

(1973) 110m. **C+**

A self-conscious 40ish female real estate agent has a brief affair with a handsome 20ish wanderer while on a Greek isle vacation. When he shows up later in New York City, her mother tries to fix him up with the agent's own daughter. Slow and dull adaptation of a French farce with Ullman uncomfortably out of place.

D: Milton Katselas. A: Liv Ullman, Edward Albert, Gene Kelly.

Same Time Next Year

(1977) 119m. **B–**

A happily married CPA from New Jersey and a California housewife have a one-night stand and continue to reunite once a year for the next 25 years. The actors are charming but this attempt to mirror the changes in American society and male/female relationships over time misses with the sitcom dialogue and superficial characters.

D: Robert Mulligan. A: Alan Alda, Ellen Burstyn.

House Calls

(1978) 98m. **B+**

A recently widowed surgeon-turned-lothario comes to the rescue of a patient with populist sentiments who ultimately beguiles him—and demands absolute loyalty. Entertaining mix of health-care hijinks, a la *The Hospital* and keen-witted romantic comedy.

D: Howard Zieff. A: Walter Matthau, Glenda Jackson, Richard Benjamin.

Lost and Found

(1979) 104m. **C+**

A recently widowed American and a recently divorced Brit collide in the Swiss Alps, fall in love, and start a new life together. Light and romantic story with a weak script that fails to do justice to the reteaming of Segal and Jackson.

D: Melvin Frank. A: George Segal, Glenda Jackson, Maureen Stapleton.

Starting Over

(1979) 106m. **B**

A Manhattan writer loses his flaky wife to a dubious showbiz career and another man and moves to Boston where he begins a romance with a dowdy schoolteacher. Burt tones it down with some earnest wooing of unsure Jill in this charming, low-key, character-driven comedy.

D: Alan J. Pakula. A: Burt Reynolds, Jill Clayburgh, Candice Bergen.

Streisand Modern Life

As with her other films, Barbra doesn't just star, she commandeers them. Her charisma and energy never fit in conventional roles, and the humor in these modern life tales rely on putting Streisand in wacky situations and then stepping back to see what happens.

The Owl and the Pussycat
(1970) 95m. **B+**

Streisand, the loud aggressive hooker who fancies herself an actress/model, invades the life of a nerdy book clerk who fancies himself the Great American Novelist. Segal is a formidable sparring partner for Streisand who can be shrill and silly when she's not being funny amidst the funky late-60s Manhattan locales.
D: Herbert Ross. A: With George Segal, Robert Klein.

Up the Sandbox
(1972) 98m. **C+**

Streisand is the urban housewife who escapes the emptiness of her existence in fantasies of alternate lives large with ideas and adventure. An updated, less charming version of *The Secret Life of Walter Mitty.*
D: Irvin Kershner. A: With David Selby, Conrad Bain.

For Pete's Sake
(1974) 90m. **C**

Streisand is the gutsy housewife who gets entangled in various money-making schemes—from prostitution (sort of) to playing a Mob bag man—for her unwitting hubby. Farcical fun but the high point is Molly Picon as the Jewish mother who's the madam of a call girl service.
D: Peter Yates. A: With Michael Sarrazin, Estelle Parsons.

The Main Event
(1979) 105m. **C+**

Streisand is the bankrupt perfume queen who learns her only hope of solvency is a halfhearted boxer whose contract she bought as a tax write-off. Rides the *Rocky* train, with a flat joke that Streisand is better fit for the ring than sensitive Ryan.
D: Howard Zieff. A: With Ryan O'Neal, Paul Sand.

Neil Simon

Like comfort food, Neil Simon provides people with New York comfort comedy. This is the world of the worried middle-class city dweller trying to cope with an often incomprehensible metropolis, the sexual revolution, marriage, and aging. Even when the action switches to California at the end of the 70s, the characters still sound like wisecracking Manhattanites.

The Odd Couple
(1968) 105m. **A**

An obsessive/compulsive photographer thrown out by his wife moves in with his best friend, a divorced, catastrophically casual sportswriter, and we quickly learn why their marriages failed. Sloppy Oscar and Fussy Felix have become archetypes, but this film is still fresh as paint and gorgeous to look at.
D: Gene Saks. A: Jack Lemmon, Walter Matthau, Herb Edelman.

The Out of Towners
(1970) 97m. **B−**

A middle-class couple from the Midwest flies to New York City for the job interview that could change both their lives; that is, if they can survive the city for one night. A bit obvious now and the relentless mishaps become more grating than funny.
D: Arthur Hiller. A: Jack Lemmon, Sandy Dennis.

Plaza Suite
(1971) 115m. **B**

A trilogy of one-acts about married couples, parents, and old lovers, each taking place in room 719 at the Plaza Hotel. Sad, pathetic, and farcical, you still wish you could argue like these characters do when things start getting rocky.
D: Arthur Hiller. A: Walter Matthau, Maureen Stapleton, Barbara Harris, Lee Grant.

Last of the Red Hot Lovers
(1972) 98m. **C+**

A responsible middle-aged family man encounters three eccentric women in his increasingly desperate pursuit of a memorable experience at the height of the sexual revolution. The women are cartoonish and Arkin goes from endearing to pathetic as his desperation escalates.
D: Gene Saks. A: Alan Arkin, Sally Kellerman, Paula Prentiss.

The Prisoner of Second Avenue
(1975) 105m. **B**

When an ad exec loses his job and wakes up to how crazy New York City is, it almost costs him his sanity. His wife barely holds on to hers while helping him beat back the urban jungle. Occasionally incoherent but offers crackling repartee.
D: Melvin Frank. A: Jack Lemmon, Anne Bancroft.

The Sunshine Boys
(1975) 111m. **D+**

A famous comedy team from 50 years ago is offered a TV special. Can they reteam one more time without dredging up ancient resentments and giving each other heart attacks? Benjamin is frantic and funny as the nephew/agent caught in between. Bittersweet, funny, and never maudlin.
D: Herbert Ross. A: George Burns, Walter Matthau, Richard Benjamin.

The Goodbye Girl
(1977) 110m. **B**

An insecure single mother and her wiseacre young daughter are maneuvered into sharing their apartment with an anarchic and dreamy actor on the verge of stardom. Familiarity breeds affection—but will it last? Charming, gentle-spirited romance.
D: Herbert Ross. A: Marsha Mason, Richard Dreyfus, Quinn Cummings.

California Suite
(1978) 103m. **C+**

The Beverly Hills Hotel is the backdrop for the four stories in this *Plaza Suite* goes west. Uneven, and Simon's New York edge seems dulled by laid-back California.
D: Herbert Ross. A: Maggie Smith, Michael Caine, Alan Alda.

Chapter Two
(1979) 124m. **B−**

A shy novelist grieving for his recently deceased wife gets swept up in a whirlwind romance with a recently divorced actress. Everyone talks, bickers, and makes up with endless abandon in this bittersweet story about grief that never gets lost in the shuffle of one-liners.
D: Robert Moore. A: James Caan, Marsha Mason, Valerie Harper.

Only When I Laugh
(1981) 121m. **C+**

There's a smaller hail of Simon wisecracks in this

story of a teenage girl and her alcoholic mother trying to work things out in New York. The pain and humor of a self-dramatizing parent come through in this restrained and serious effort.
D: Glenn Jordan. A: Marsha Mason, Kristy McNichol.

I Ought to Be in Pictures
(1982) 107m. **C–**

Young, would-be actress migrates to LA to begin her career and reunite with her screenwriter father whom she hasn't seen since childhood. Forced and cloying with little of Simon's verbal vitality.
D: Herbert Ross. A: Walter Matthau, Ann Margret, Dinah Manoff.

Homages

Nostalgia for old Hollywood was popular in the 70s and these homages paid a humorous and sometimes imaginative tribute to the classic genres like screwballs, noirs, World War II adventures, even Zorro movies. Some of these films are big-budget roundups of Hollywood stars, others are more modest nostalgic spoofs, and a few are delightful modern-day comedies that take their inspiration from the best that Hollywood once had to offer.

Casino Royale
(1967) 130m. **C+**

James Bond is pulled out of retirement to stop the evil machinations of SMERSH. This big-budget, psychedelic takeoff has several directors, a chaotic mind-boggling plot, endless cameos, and few laughs (usually provided by Bond's nephew Woody Allen).
D: John Huston, Ken Hughes, Robert Parrish, Joe McGrath, Val Guest. A: David Niven, Ursula Andress, Peter Sellers.

Schlock
(1971) 78m. **C+**

The Schlockthropus, a.k.a. The Missing Link, terrorizes a small town while the press covers it live. This low-budget spoof of monster movies would have worked better as an episode in *The Kentucky Fried Movie.* Funniest scene: The Monster goes to see *The Blob* and is annoyed when his view is obstructed.
D: John Landis. A: Eliza Garrett, Saul Kahan.

Gumshoe
(1972) 88m. **C+**

A latter-day vaudevillian transforms himself into a modern-day Sam Spade in an effort to advance his career. A listless tribute to Bogie and Raymond Chandler; one wishes the plot were as compelling as Finney's fast-talking would-be Bogie.
D: Stephen Frears. A: Albert Finney, Billie Whitelaw, Frank Finlay.

What's Up, Doc?
(1972) 94m. **A**

A nerdy musicologist collides—continually—with a wacky professional student while attending a convention with his imperious fiancée. This giddy and wildly charming latter-day screwball comedy has as many hilarious twists, mix-ups, and slapstick as *Bringing Up Baby.*
D: Peter Bogdanovich. A: Barbra Streisand, Ryan O'Neal, Madeline Kahn.

Paper Moon
(1973) 102m. B&W. **A–**

A Bible-selling con man traveling through Kansas during the Depression is overmatched by his precocious nine-year-old determined to win his love. Like a lugubrious and sharp-eyed Shirley Temple in a Damon Runyon tale, Tatum steals the show in this humorous black-and-white tribute to Depression-era tales and John Ford movies.
D: Peter Bogdanovich. A: Ryan O'Neal, Tatum O'Neal, Madeline Kahn.

Murder by Death
(1976) 95m. **A–**

The most brilliant detectives and crime novelists are assembled by a rich eccentric to solve the ultimate murder—his own. A cast of classy actors pay their own homage to movie detectives as Peter Falk's Bogie talks shop to Peter Sellers' Charlie Chan. Consistently funny and evocative of old murder mysteries.
D: Robert Moore. A: Peter Falk, Eileen Brennan, James Coco, and all-star others.

The Cheap Detective
(1978) 92m. **B+**

A Bogie-like private eye is accused of murdering his partner in order to run off with the partner's wife. This Neil Simon take-off on *Casablanca* and *The Maltese Falcon* is alternately silly (don't try to follow the plot) and funny, but the confluence of stars seems to be having a good time.
D: Robert Moore. A: Peter Falk, Eileen Brennan, Marsha Mason.

Movie Movie
(1978) 107m. **C+**

Two short movies, *Dynamite Hands,* a black-and-white boxing melodrama, and *Baxter's Beauties of 1933,* a lavishly staged color musical, make up this disappointing and dull tribute, which lacks the heart of the films they're evoking. Includes a mock-trailer of coming attractions.
D: Stanley Donen. A: George C. Scott, Red Buttons, Art Carney.

The Jerk
(1979) 94m. **B+**

A white guileless nitwit leaves his black sharecropper family to make his accidental fortune in the big city. Silly but very funny early Steve replete with cat juggling and inventive eyewear, this has the broad and sentimental tone of a Jerry Lewis film, only sweeter.
D: Carl Reiner. A: Steve Martin, Bernadette Peters, Jackie Mason.

Love at First Bite
(1979) 96m. **B+**

Dracula is pushed out of Rumania by Soviet bureaucrats, forcing him to emigrate to New York City where he meets a shallow model hungry for love. A surprisingly funny clash of the medieval legend and modern sensibilities, with a discoing Dracula hunted by a therapist brandishing a Star of David.
D: Stan Dragoti. A: George Hamilton, Susan Saint James, Richard Benjamin.

1941
(1979) 118m. **C–**

Southern California is on red alert after Pearl Harbor and Belushi and Co. prepare for the inevitable enemy attack. Watching this overblown overcrowded take-off on World War II flicks is like being on a merry-go-round that has spun out of control

in the middle of a Fourth of July celebration.
D: Steven Spielberg. A: John Belushi, Dan Aykroyd, John Candy.

Zorro, the Gay Blade
(1981) 93m. **D+**
Son of the legendary Zorro must assume his father's role and save his people from a tyrant, even as his fey twin brother arrives on the scene from England. Unlike *Love at First Bite,* this plays to the period instead of against it, resulting in dry dull costume stuff.
D: Peter Medak. A: George Hamilton, Lauren Hutton, Ron Leibman.

Spoofs

Before *Saturday Night Live* hit the airwaves and *Airplane!* and *Naked Gun* became blockbusters, these films took irreverent potshots at American pop culture icons like bad movies, cornball TV, and mindless commercials. Most are low-budget collections of sketches and skits that are cynical, politically incorrect, sometimes vulgar, and often very funny.

What's Up, Tiger Lily?
(1966) 90m. **B**
Allen took a bad Japanese spy flick and dubbed it with silly English-language non sequiturs. A stretched-out one-joke sketch that wears thin quickly. Music provided by the Loving Spoonful who appear briefly for no good reason, but it's still a forerunner of *MSFT 2000.*
D: Woody Allen. A: Woody Allen, Tatsuya Mihashi, Miya Hana.

What Do You Say to a Naked Lady?
(1970) 92m. **C**
Allen Funt focuses his *Candid Camera* on awestruck innocents as they encounter naked ladies in unexpected places. You may laugh in spite of yourself at some of the reactions of these poor pidgeons, but this abridged version of the X-rated original is an overlong practical joke, strictly for voyeurs, bachelor parties, and Howard Stern fans.
D: Allen Funt. A: Allen Funt, Richard Roundtree.

The Groove Tube
(1974) 75m. **B–**
A string of skits spoofing commercials, sitcoms, movie trailers, and news broadcasts, with tired gags that seem like the rejects from the better *Kentucky Fried Movie.*
D: Ken Shapiro. A: Chevy Chase, Ken Shapiro, Lane Sarasohn.

Tunnelvision
(1976) 70m. **B**
Set ten years in the future (1985), the creators of Tunnelvision are hauled before a Senate commission to defend their outrageous TV programs. As a spoof of TV shows and commercials it's made up of mostly cheap tasteless gags, but as prophecy it does anticipate raising murderers to the status of celebrities.
D: Neal Isreal, Brad Swirnoff. A: Howard Hesseman, Ron Silver, Joe Flaherty.

Kentucky Fried Movie
(1977) 85m. **A–**
A collection of sketches spoofing TV commercials, movie trailers, and industrial films, culminating in a hilarious take-off on *Enter the Dragon* and *The Wizard of Oz* (told as one story). Some tasteless duds in the mix, but more laugh-out-loud parodies like a pre-Court TV Wally and the Beav commenting on a lurid court trial being covered live.
D: John Landis. A: Evan Kim, Bill Bixby, Master Bong Soo Han.

Real Life
(1979) 99m. **B**
A slick, fast-talking filmmaker moves in with a middle-class family to capture their lives on film. In the process, the family, if not the film, falls apart. This parody of PBS-produced cinema verités is Brooks' first feature film, and it captures his wry sense of humor; but one wishes it were as consistently funny as it is telling.
D: Albert Brooks. A: Albert Brooks, Charles Grodin, Frances Lee McCain.

Mel Brooks and Company

Brooks began his career as a borscht-belt comic who got his laughs from the guests by, among other things, falling into hotel pools laden with luggage. He's remained loyal to this brand of slapstick humor in all of his movies, even the most expensively produced, historical set-laden ones. His parodies of movie genres—westerns, horrors, costume epics, and sci-fi flicks—are filled with sight gags, Groucho Marx leers, and an overall manic energy that has inspired other filmmakers like Gene Wilder and Marty Feldman (whose works are included here) to Zucker and Abrahams of *Airplane* and *Naked Gun* fame.

The Producers
(1968) 88m. **A**
A theatrical producer and a CPA stage the "worst play ever written" in order to scam investors, but unfortunately the audiences don't agree. Only Brooks could have gotten away with "Springtime for Hitler," a June Taylor-inspired tribute to der Führer.
D: Mel Brooks. A: Zero Mostel, Gene Wilder, Dick Shawn.

The Twelve Chairs
(1970) 94m. **B**
An unusual Brooks effort: A dispossessed Russian aristocrat and an angry con man search for 12 handcrafted chairs, one of which contains the aristocrat's family jewels. The poignant relationship between them—a combination of class hatred and desperate dependence—is paired uneasily with the farcical episodes involving DeLuise as a manic

greedy orthodox priest. Shot in Yugoslavia. Good for non-Brooks fans.
D: Mel Brooks. A: Frank Langella, Ron Roody, Dom DeLuise, Mel Brooks.

Blazing Saddles
(1973) 90m. **A–**

An evil land-snatcher plots to rid an old western town of its inhabitants by playing on everyone's bigotry and hiring a black sheriff. Bombastic, scatological, and surreal: You'll either be offended by or laugh yourself sick over this superior western parody.
D: Mel Brooks. A: Cleavon Little, Gene Wilder, Harvey Korman.

Young Frankenstein
(1974) 108m. B&W. **A**

Mad scientists, befuddled monsters, mobs of torch-hugging peasants, and Transylvania's only espresso machine—you get all these and more in this polished parody of 30s classic horror films. Brooks' wilder tendencies are restrained for once, and two of the characters even manage to spark a romance.
D: Mel Brooks. A: Gene Wilder, Marty Feldman, Cloris Leachman.

Silent Movie
(1976) 88m. **C+**

A silent movie about a director who hopes to revive his ailing career and save the studio from a corporate takeover by making a silent film rife with big stars. Typical gag: A giant plastic fly from the roof of an exterminator's truck falls into Henny Youngman's soup. If that's your bag, you're in for a lot of silly fun.
D: Mel Brooks. A: Mel Brooks, Dom DeLuise, Marty Feldman.

High Anxiety
(1977) 92m. **B–**

Parody of Hitchcock thrillers in which an agoraphobic psychiatrist at the Institute for the Very, Very Nervous uncovers a plot by its custodians to defraud rich patients. No real thrills, but plenty of visual yucks.
D: Mel Brooks. A: Mel Brooks, Harvey Korman, Cloris Leachman.

History of the World, Part One
(1981) 90m. **B–**

It's doubtful if there will ever be a Part Two. From the Stone Age to the Space Age, every era gets its comic comeuppance in the episodic romp through world history. A broad, scatological potpourri of sight gags that often fall flat against historically rich backgrounds.
D: Mel Brooks. A: Mel Brooks, Harvey Korman, Madeline Kahn.

To Be or Not to Be
(1983) 108m. **B–**

A theater troupe fights for its survival in Nazi-occupied Poland in this remake of the 1942 Lubitsch film. Brooks stars, not directs this so the characters are richer and more developed than in his usual fare, but the immediacy of the original is still missing.
D: Alan Johnson. A: Mel Brooks, Anne Bancroft, Charles Durning.

Spaceballs
(1987) 96m. **C+**

The unofficial fourth episode of the *Star Wars* saga. Can Lone Starr, his woolly companion Barf, Princess Vespa, and her robot chaperon Dot Matrix stop the evil Dark Helmet from cornering the galaxy's air supply before loan shark Pizza the Hut stops them? You get the picture.
D: Mel Brooks. A: Mel Brooks, Rick Moranis, Dick Van Patten.

Life Stinks
(1991) 95m. **C–**

A multimillionaire wages he can survive for 30 days on the streets of East LA—homeless and broke—in order to win some choice real estate. Brooks attempts to create a romance of homelessness, but his indigents are mere eccentrics subject to some tasteless gags.
D: Mel Brooks. A: Mel Brooks, Jeffrey Tambor, Leslie Ann Warren.

Robin Hood: Men in Tights
(1993) 105m. **C**

Occasionally funny throw away lines (mostly from Lewis as Prince John) dot this spoof, but Brooks' age is showing with languid gags that telegraph their punchlines (one character's name is Achoo, with every mention of his name resulting in Gesundheit), and anachronistic/self-referential jokes culled from earlier Brooks films.
D: Mel Brooks. A: Cary Elwes, Richard Lewis, Roger Rees.

And Company

Start the Revolution Without Me
(1970) 91m. **B**

Two sets of mispaired twins, one raised by a lower-class family, the other by aristocrats, cross paths and roles during the French Revolution. Wilder is engaging, the humor is broad, but the crossed swords and bad cockney accents become tiresome.
D: Bud Yorkin. A: Gene Wilder, Donald Sutherland, Hugh Griffith.

The Adventure of Sherlock Holmes' Smarter Brother
(1975) 91m. **B+**

A nineteenth-century London music-hall performer calls on Holmes' unappreciated and deeply resentful smarter brother, Sigerson. Wilder creates his ultimate comic persona: noble and silly, gallant and frantic while the other Brooksian characters are riotous.
D: Gene Wilder. A: Gene Wilder, Marty Feldman, Madeline Kahn.

The Last Remake of Beau Geste
(1977) 85m. **C–**

Twin brothers adopted by a war-mongering English Lord wind up in the French Foreign Legion, the last refuge of scoundrels, criminals, and the physically stunted. Strained buffoonish desecration of the genre's clichés.
D: Marty Feldman. A: Marty Feldman, Michael York, Peter Ustinov.

The World's Greatest Lover
(1977) 88m. **C**

A hapless husband is determined to win the "World's Greatest Lover" contest and win back his starstruck wife who's after Rudolf Valentino. A mix of silly sight gags and sloppy romance—in spots, reminiscent of Chaplin—fill this look at Hollywood of the 20s when silent Latin lovers, art deco, and mad movie moguls were all the rage.
D: Gene Wilder. A: Gene Wilder, Carol Kane, Dom DeLuise.

Haunted Honeymoon
(1986) 82m. **C–**

Wilder and Radner are a radio-acting team who specialize in thrillers, and where do they intend to spend their honeymoon? In a house haunted by, among other things, Dom DeLuise in drag. Abbott and Costello would have been funnier even with this silly material.
D: Gene Wilder. A: Gene Wilder, Gilda Radner, Dom DeLuise.

Early John Waters

Before going mainstream with such paeans to American kitsch as *Hairspray* and *Serial Mom*, Baltimore's bad boy cranked out these odes to bad taste set in a sleazy world of beehive beauty salons, grungy little shops, and run-down suburban wastelands, all populated by horrifically disgusting people and of course rotund, big-haired transvestite Divine.

Pink Flamingos

(1972) 95m. **B**

Divine is an obese trailer park matron who holds on to her title of The World's Filthiest Person with gusto. This assault on every concept of good taste features the Egg Lady (a 70ish human blimp attired in flesh-drooping outfits) and Divine's close encounter with a nervous poodle's body functions.
D: John Waters. A: Divine, Edith Massey, Mink Stole.

Female Trouble

(1973) 95m. **B–**

A 300-pound suburban princess has a nasty fight with her parents, turns to a life of crime, and becomes a media star. Divine is just that in two roles (in one inspired sequence she plays herself and a scuzzy slob with whom she has sex) while the rest of the film relies on disgusto displays, screechy humor, and a white-trashy wit.
D: John Waters. A: Divine, Edith Massey, Mink Stole.

Desperate Living

(1977) 90m. **B**

After a released mental patient pushes her 400-pound maid into murder, the two go on the lam, dally with a state trooper, and lay down roots in a land ruled by a debauched queen as her sex slaves. Like a depraved *Thelma and Louise* with rampant gender confusion and enough mental angst for six Joan Crawford movies.
D: John Waters. A: Mink Stole, Edith Massey, Liz Pency.

Polyester

(1981) 86m. **B**

When love-starved suburbanite Divine finds true love with porn-dealer Hunter, her perfectly constructed world of velvet couches and drip-dry pants suits seems to come crashing around her. Hunter in Divine's hefty embrace is worth the rental price alone in this wild and raunchy send up of 50s family melodramas. Originally shown in Odorama.
D: John Waters. A: Divine, Tab Hunter, Edith Massey.

Pink Panther

Peter Sellers' comic genius finally went mainstream with his portrayal of French inspector Jacques Clouseau, the earnest and naive bungler—half Sherlock Holmes, half Buster Keaton—whose strangulated diction became a hallmark in comic film history. These films offer slapstick and sight gags served up in sophisticated, mostly European settings as Clouseau searches for the stolen Pink Panther diamond. After Sellers' death in 1981, the character was revived (some would say exhumed) with less than sparkling results.

The Pink Panther

(1963) 113m. **B+**

Clouseau is on the trail of an international jewel thief, and the thief's nephew is on the trail of Clouseau's wife. The most sophisticated and deliberate of this group with solid characters, glossy European sites, and well-constructed gags.
D: Blake Edwards. A: Peter Sellers, David Niven, Robert Wagner, Capucine.

A Shot in the Dark

(1964) 101m. **A–**

Inspector Clouseau is back to save a beautiful woman from a murder charge. Similar in tone to the first, but funnier, with more slapstick and sight gags and Sellers as the center of the story.
D: Blake Edwards. A: Peter Sellers, Herbert Lom, Elke Sommer.

The Return of the Pink Panther

(1975) 113m. **B**

Farcically earnest Clouseau is out to catch a new thief of the Pink Panther diamond. Big sight gags, usually involving someone falling into or off something, provide some laughs, but Clouseau's unique diction remains the most memorable humor.
D: Blake Edwards. A: Peter Sellers, Herbert Lom, Christopher Plummer.

The Pink Panther Strikes Again

(1976) 103m. **B**

Chief Inspector Dreyfus, now totally bonkers, joins forces with a scientist to hold the world captive with a laser gun that has already destroyed the UN. Funny sequel to a sequel with a hilarious Clouseau dodging death and wooing Leslie Ann Down.
D: Blake Edwards. A: Peter Sellers, Herbert Lom, Colin Blakely.

The Revenge of the Pink Panther

(1978) 98m. **B–**

Is Clouseau dead? The Mob and Inspector Dreyfus think so, but master of disguises Clouseau knows better. Fewer zany villains as in the previous films, but Sellers' slapstick and accent still provide some laughs.
D: Blake Edwards. A: Peter Sellers, Dyan Cannon, Herbert Lom.

The Trail of the Pink Panther

(1982) 97m. **C+**

Clouseau disappears while tracking down the Pink Panther and a French journalist tries to discover the man behind the myth. Sellers died during the making of this, and the result is a disjointed series of sight-gaggy non sequiturs and some outtakes from previous films.
D: Blake Edwards. A: Peter Sellers, David Niven, Capucine.

The Curse of the Pink Panther

(1983) 110m. **C–**

Where is Clouseau? Detective Sleigh, introduced as Clouseau's successor, screams and falls down a lot, and some inflatable doll

jokes ripped right out of *Airplane!* are painful to watch.
D: Blake Edwards. A: Ted Wass, David Niven, Robert Wagner.

Son of the Pink Panther
(1993) 115m. **C**
Italian comic actor Begnini does a passable job imitating Sellers' verbal quirks and stumbling footsteps, but the humor is stale—i.e., mechanical hospital bed gone haywire, the mis-timed explosion, bodies falling out of windows—and the direction listless.
D: Blake Edwards. A: Roberto Begnini, Herbert Lom, Claudia Cardinale.

Buddy Capers

Recession frustration and the 70s trend of buddy films fueled these sprightly felonious tales of working people trying to beat the high cost of living via morally justifiable acts of thievery. Though not the most visually inspired group of films, all keep their plots in quick working order and feature plenty of stars acting like populist heroes as they pull off a heist or two.

Steelyard Blues
(1973) 93m. **B**
On his release from prison, a demolition derby driver resumes his affair with a hooker and takes up with a band of kooks who have a wild dream centering around rebuilding an old airplane. The dressed down stars and a quirky script inspire some humor if not believability in this aimless tale of small-town losers.
D: Alan Myerson. A: Jane Fonda, Donald Sutherland, Peter Boyle.

Uptown Saturday Night
(1974) 104m. **B–**
The search for a stolen lotto ticket becomes a comic nightmare when two Harlem pals lose it after a night of carousing. Basically a highly variable series of vignettes, the funniest one featuring Richard Pryor as a gumshoe and Belafonte doing a wicked turn as a soul Godfather.
D: Sidney Poitier. A: Bill Cosby, Sidney Poitier, Harry Belafonte.

Let's Do It Again
(1975) 113m. **B–**
Two dockworkers turn a trip to New Orleans with the wives into an opportunity to pull a scam to make money for their lodge, only to get embroiled with various Big Easy mobsters. Some funny bits along with a rapid tempo keep this second Poitier–Crosby caper amusing.
D: Sidney Poitier. A: Sidney Poitier, Bill Cosby, Jimmie Walker.

Silver Streak
(1976) 113m. **A–**
Hilariously frantic tale of a neurotic book editor who takes a cross-country train trip to relax and instead gets involved with romance, murder, and other nerve-wracking things. Expert pacing and the sparkling chemistry between Pryor and Wilder make this consistent fun.
D: Arthur Hiller. A: Gene Wilder, Richard Pryor, Jill Clayburgh.

Fun with Dick and Jane
(1977) 104m. **C**
When a middle-class fellow loses his job and experiences the resulting credit crunch, he and his plucky wife become robbers. Satire of corporate/keeping-up-with-the-Joneses mire has a good idea of its targets but misses them too often due to uneven tone, silly plot twist, and TV-show visuals.
D: Ted Kotcheff. A: George Segal, Jane Fonda, Ed McMahon.

A Piece of the Action
(1977) 135m. **B–**
Two big-time thieves are blackmailed by a clever detective into doing a good turn by using their street smarts to help local wayward teens. More lighthearted Poitier–Cosby crooked fun, if slightly naive by today's grim standards.
D: Sidney Poitier. A: Sidney Poitier, Bill Cosby, James Earl Jones.

Blue Collar
(1978) 114m. **B+**
Three auto assembly-line workers get the wild idea of robbing their union and find themselves in deep trouble with the Mob. A smart script, good feel for the tough environment, and great ensemble work help make this an unusual caper film as the consequences of the trio's heist suddenly make their lives grim and terribly exciting.
D: Paul Schrader. A: Richard Pryor, Harvey Keitel, Yaphet Kotto.

The Brinks Job
(1978) 103m. **B–**
Entertaining if somewhat uneven tale of real-life Brinks armored car robbery, set in 50s Boston and masterminded by a group of comedically inept thieves. Though more 70s than 50s in style, this has mucho energy and a great turn by Oates as a human time bomb.
D: William Friedkin. A: Peter Falk, Peter Boyle, Warren Oates.

The In-Laws
(1979) 103m. **B**
A mild-mannered suburban dentist is smooth-talked by his daughter's CIA-connected father-in-law into a crazy scheme to out a South American dictator. A quirky premise, rapid-fire comic banter, and hilarious characters combine for an all-out farce.
D: Arthur Hiller. A: Alan Arkin; Peter Falk; Ed Begley, Jr.

Teen Comedies

Academic anarchy, beer swilling, rock 'n' roll, and young love got their first posthippie airing in these films that are prototypes for all the modern teen films, from slob comedies to sensitive coming-of-age films to *Fast Times at Ridgemont High*.

American Graffiti
(1973) 111m. **A–**

A night in the hectic life of a bevy of California teens (and many future stars) cruising their way out of adolescence during the early 1960s. Time has shown this to be a bit less than the masterwork it was first hailed as, but still a funny poignant slice of Americana with a great oldies soundtrack.
D: George Lucas. A: Richard Dreyfuss, Ron Howard, Candy Clark.

Cooley High
(1975) 107m. **B**

American Graffiti goes to a Chicago high school in this spirited and nonexploitative teen comedy. Offers good performances and amazing 70s sartorial excesses, but some of the humor may sound quaint to audiences raised in a rougher world.
D: Michael Schultz. A: Glynn Turman, Garrett Morris, Lawrence Hilton-Jacobs.

Animal House
(1978) 109m. **A–**

This is the Kilimanjaro of slob comedy, complete with toga parties, food fights, lustful grapplings, and lots of trashy 60s hits. Still very funny in an evolutionary-backstep sort of way, with Belushi garnering chuckles even when the script doesn't call for them.
D: John Landis. A: John Belushi, Tim Matheson, Karen Allen.

Breaking Away
(1979) 100m. **A–**

Witty and well-observed character study of four "townie" teens living in a college town, one of whom is an Italy-obsessed, would-be bicycle champion. Filled with fully rounded characters, a wonderfully evoked small-town ambiance, and tone that shifts effortlessly from goofy comedy to straight drama, this is a near-flawless coming-of-age film.
D: Peter Yates. A: Dennis Christopher, Daniel Stern, Dennis Quaid.

Meatballs
(1979) 92m. **B–**

Goofball antics of a wisecracking counselor at a summer camp is the alpha and zeta in this cheap-looking film that would sink into its clichéd teen-joke depths without Murray's bemused and often hilarious presence.
D: Ivan Reitman. A: Bill Murray, Kate Lynch, Harvey Atkin.

Rock 'n' Roll High School
(1979) 93m. **B+**

A perky blonde dreams of bringing her ultimate rock 'n' roll fantasy heroes—those buzz-note punks The Ramones—to her high school. A totally ridiculous (and better for it) film that has lots of cool Ramones songs, goofy dream sequences, and every teen's fantasy of blowing up school.
D: Allan Arkush. A: P. J. Soles, Clint Howard, The Ramones.

Disco

Low on intellect but with kitschy style to burn are these prime examples of throwaway pop culture, which offer an abundance of goofy, garishly colorful, and musically driven fun.

Car Wash
(1976) 97m. **B–**

The wacky customers and hustling employees of the Dee Lux Car Wash share their dreams and woes during an average day, all to the beat of a disco soundtrack. A series of hits and many miss slice-of-life vignettes gets a needed jolt of hysteria when Pryor struts and shouts as a gaudy preacher.
D: Michael Schultz. A: Richard Pryor, George Carlin, Franklin Ajaye.

Saturday Night Fever
(1977) 118m. **A**

Tony lives with his family in Brooklyn, works at the paint store, and lives to boogie at the nightclub where he's the undisputed disco king. Most of this film is an entertaining if harsh tale of working-class youth, embroidered with some blow-out disco dance numbers that are corny but fun to watch.
D: John Badham. A: John Travolta, Karen Gorney, Donna Pescow.

FM
(1978) 104m. **C+**

Radio station owners inform the staff that they're dumping the cutting-edge format for a commercial playlist and the outraged DJs stage a takeover to plead their case to the listeners. A plodding comedy with the cool harbingers of taste spinning tunes from every major middle-of-the-road musical act.
D: John A. Alonzo. A: Michael Brandon, Martin Mull, Eileen Brennan.

Thank God It's Friday
(1978) 100m. **B**

The lives of people looking for action, a shot at stardom, or a partner for the dance contest converge on Friday night at California's hottest disco. Surprisingly fun mindless trash with a funny engaging ensemble of actors.
D: Robert Klane. A: Jeff Goldblum, Debra Winger, Donna Summer.

Can't Stop the Music
(1980) 120m. **C–**

An ex-model helps her roommate put together a musical group that includes a construction worker, a cop, a cowboy, and other Village People. This tries so hard to create instant camp with daffy production numbers, vapid characters, and tiresome screwball situations that you wish someone *could* stop the music.
D: Nancy Walker. A: Valerie Perrine, Bruce Jenner, The Village People.

Cars and Good Ole Boys

The redneck car-chase film from the 70s was played for laughs in this series of comedies featuring backwoods buffoonery, dim-witted sheriffs, and Ron Howard or Burt Reynolds. Whether a cross-country race or a lovers-on-the-run story, you can also count on these being

low-budget productions, since every cent seems to be spent on the army of stunt men and all those wrecked cars.

Cannonball

(1976) 93m. **B**

An eccentric action comedy that both satirizes and exploits car-chase films, this mix of humor, death, and destruction is jarring, but the wild cast includes appearances by Scorsese, Stallone, Joe Dante, and Paul Bartel.
D: Paul Bartel. A: David Carradine, Bill McKinney, Veronica Hamel.

Eat My Dust

(1976) 90m. **C+**

Ron Howard is still a sheriff's son, but now he steals a prize stock car to impress a girl, takes her on a wild ride fleeing the police, and wrecks 392 other cars in the process. Mindless and loud car-crash comedy.
D: Charles Griffith. A: Ron Howard, Christopher Norris, Warren Kemmerling.

Grand Theft Auto

(1977) 84m. **C+**

A couple elopes in dad's gold Rolls-Royce, launching an escalating chase from California to Las Vegas. Some very funny bits mixed in with the usual crashes as dozens of other drivers seek to get the reward offered for the return of the car.
D: Ron Howard. A: Ron Howard, Nancy Morgan, Marion Ross.

Smokey and the Bandit

(1977) 97m. **B+**

An even more cartoonish entry as Reynolds and his pal speed a cargo of beer past pursuing buffoonish "smokeys." Slightly glossier, bigger-budgeted version of these redneck exploitation films.
D: Hal Needham. A: Burt Reynolds, Sally Field, Jackie Gleason.

Thunder and Lightning

(1977) 95m. **B**

An independent moonshine driver runs afoul of a rotgut whisky kingpin in rural Florida, leading to a nonstop vehicular chase with good and bad moonshiners, mob hitmen, local police, and highway cops.
D: Corey Allen. A: David Carradine, Kate Jackson, Roger Carmel.

Cannonball Run

(1981) 95m. **D**

The overloaded star cast gets behind the wheels of a fleet of sporty vehicles for another illegal cross-country car race. Feeble humor, overlength, and a lack of thrills make you long for the shorter and sleeker *Cannonball*.
D: Hal Needham. A: Burt Reynolds, Roger Moore, Farrah Fawcett.

Sports

Before it was called "male bonding" there was the rough but friendly macho behavior, on ample display in these boisterous sports films. Filled with colorful locker-room talk and camaraderie, the best of these are often vulgar and enjoyable tales of guys who want to win, but are out to enjoy themselves as well.

The Bad News Bears

(1976) 102m. **B+**

An ex-minor league ballplayer winds up coaching a band of little league misfits. Old grump Matthau coddles and cajoles cussing tomboy Tatum and the rest of the runny-nosed gang in this best of the kids sports movies which thankfully eschews the sap that poisoned its sequels and imitators.
D: Michael Ritchie. A: Walter Matthau, Tatum O'Neal, Vic Morrow.

The Bingo Long Traveling All-Stars and Motor Kings

(1976) 110m. **A–**

Fed up with being underpaid by the owners of the Negro baseball league, a superstar pitcher recruits his own team and begins a wildly successful cross-country barnstorming tour. While showing the trials of racism and life on the road, this boisterously funny tale captures the spirit and character of baseball like few others.
D: John Badham. A: Billy Dee Williams, James Earl Jones, Richard Pryor.

Semi-Tough

(1977) 108m. **B+**

Two buddies on a Miami football team turn into friendly adversaries over the owner's daughter, but she wants to keep things platonic. The charismatic trio play it safe in this trendy, user-friendly ménage à trois littered with reminders from the 70s such as a show-stealing Convy as the self-help guru.
D: Michael Ritchie. A: Burt Reynolds, Kris Kristofferson, Jill Clayburgh.

Slapshot

(1977) 122m. **A–**

The aging coach of a losing minor league hockey team finally gets to enjoy a winning streak with the help of three myopic and brutal recruits, and pushes the team to cross-check, slash, and punch their way to a championship. A gloriously vulgar and howlingly funny story of greed and the bottom line of sports.
D: George Roy Hill. A: Paul Newman, Michael Ontkean, Lindsay Crouse.

Hooper

(1978) 100m. **C**

The aging king of stuntmen is ready to hang it up when a young rival challenges him to duel for a $50,000 jackpot. What follows is a grueling, body-abusing series of daredevil exploits in this rowdy aimless actioner which resembles an extended wacky sports highlight from the eleven o'clock news.
D: Hal Needham. A: Burt Reynolds, Jan-Michael Vincent, Sally Field.

1980s
British Comedies

The axiom that hard times breed better comedy is apparent in this group of films, most from the heyday of Thatcher's conservative policies. The British comedic staple of class differences still pops up in amusing guises while the biggest joy is how language can be wielded as deftly as a sight gag for serious belly laughs.

The Missionary
(1982) 86m. **B+**

A turn-of-the-century clergyman returns to London's East End and establishes a mission for fallen women, which soon begins to look and feel like a brothel. A funny romp even with the collegiate snickering about sex, thanks to Palin's turn as the increasingly randy clergyman whose path to salvation is off the beaten one.
D: Richard Loncraine. A: Michael Palin, Maggie Smith, Phoebe Nicholls.

Educating Rita
(1983) 110m. **B+**

Caine is a moribund alcoholic professor who tutors a Cockney hairdresser trying to find something better in life. Wonderful dialogue, discrete direction, a charming turn by Walters, and one of Caine's finest performances light up this small but winning film.
D: Lewis Gilbert. A: Michael Caine, Julie Walters, Michael Williams.

Letter to Brezhnev
(1985) 94m. **B–**

Things look up for a pair of bored Liverpudlian working-class girls when they pal around with two Russian sailors on shore leave despite language problems. It's all lighthearted until one of the couples actually falls for each other. Small in scope with some funny lines but finally feels like willfully naive fluff.
D: Chris Bernard. A: Alexandria Pigg, Alfred Molina, Peter Firth.

A Private Function
(1985) 93m. **B+**

Everyone is scrounging for food in strapped postwar England and a spineless podiatrist and his ambitious wife illegally come into possession of a pig. The humor is more often dark than goofy in this witty outing with a brilliant turn by Smith as the embittered, wannabee-snobbish, small-town wife.
D: Malcolm Mowbray. A: Maggie Smith, Michael Palin, Denholm Elliot.

Rita, Sue and Bob Too
(1986) 94m. **B–**

The man for whom two working-class girls are babysitting propositions them, and the girls, bored out of their brains, acquiesce at different times, leading to different results. Tawdry and rough little film that contains some genuinely funny moments.
D: Alan Clarke. A: George Costigan, Siobhan Finneran, Michelle Holmes.

Clockwise
(1987) 96m. **B**

A punctuality-crazed, control-freak professor travels to another town to give a lecture and gets tripped up by every mishap under the sun. Cleese, playing the upper-class twit, gives this plot-thin but slapstick-filled caper a loony, tight-jawed charm.
D: Christopher Morahan. A: John Cleese, Penelope Wilton, Alison Steadman.

Personal Services
(1987) 104m. **B**

A woman more or less falls into running a classy brothel catering to the kinky whims of its well-heeled clientele. Funny and fairly sophisticated romp with Walters making a delightfully down-to-earth and savvy small-town madam.
D: Terry Jones. A: Julie Walters, Terry Jones, Alec McCowen.

Sammy and Rosie Get Laid
(1987) 97m. **A**

This gritty, warm, and funny film about a couple of sexually and politically uninhibited London squatters along with their friends, lovers, and relatives works well on different levels: as an indictment of Thatcher's underprivileged-shunning policies and as an incisive character study of people making do in a crumbling society.
D: Stephen Frears. A: Shashi Kapoor, Frances Barber, Roland Gift.

Wish You Were Here
(1987) 92m. **B+**

In a small 1950s working-class town, a spirited young girl rails against her drunken father, judgmental aunt, lecherous men, and generally repressive community. Filled with amusingly terse dialogue and keen observations of conformity in Britain, this is still Lloyd's show, who is enraged, sexy, and always projecting a sense of seething intelligence.
D: David Leland. A: Emily Lloyd, Tom Bell, Jesse Birdsall.

Withnail and I
(1987) 108m. **B–**

Two drugged-out lads exit their dissolute 70s lifestyle for a holiday in a country home. While possessing a sure sense of the period and the absurdity of the characters, this is only intermittently funny as the leads come up against all the garden-variety disasters inflicted by nature and man.
D: Bruce Robinson. A: Paul McGann, Richard Grant, Richard Griffiths.

Consuming Passions
(1988) 98m. **C+**

An incompetent young chocolate company executive has a spot of good luck when three employees fall into a vat, and the corpse-spiced chocolate becomes a big seller. Like one of the more excessive Monty Python skits, this still suffers from a one-joke premise that doesn't sustain the film.
D: Giles Foster. A: Vanessa Redgrave, Jonathan Pryce, Tyler Butterworth.

A Fish Called Wanda
(1988) 108m. **A**

An unwitting barrister has his life up-ended when he unknowingly holds the key to some loot stashed by scheming thieves. This is a hilarious caper, an uproariously nasty satire of Brit and Yank stereotypes—including Kline as the particularly ugly American—and even a sweet romance.
D: Charles Crichton. A: John Cleese, Kevin Kline, Jamie Lee Curtis.

A Chorus of Disapproval
(1989) 99m. **B–**

Recently widowed and in a new town, a 30-something man joins the local theater

group and finds himself the object of two women's affection. Not quite as sparkly as it should be, but when this piece of ensemble acting works, it's a lively farce with witty lines.
D: Michael Winner. A: Jeremy Irons, Anthony Hopkins, Richard Briers.

Getting It Right
(1989) 101m. **B+**
Evoking classic 60s British comedies, this tells of a 31-year-old virgin heterosexual hairdresser who's still living at home and all his potential girlfriends. Filled with delightfully eccentric characters and a gently humane tone, this becomes a sweet and funny (late) coming-of-age tale.
D: Randal Kleiser. A: Jesse Birdsall, Jane Horrocks, Helena Bonham Carter.

How to Get Ahead in Advertising
(1989) 94m. **B+**
A high-strung ad exec gets stymied on the campaign for a pimple cream, and inspiration and chaos come when a growth on his neck becomes another head. As indicated, not your usual corporate satire, but a bizarre manic musing on media, greed, and anything else the filmmakers could get their lens on.
D: Bruce Robinson. A: Richard Grant, Rachel Ward, Richard Wilson.

The Rachel Papers
(1989) 92m. **C+**
A compulsive British lothario (he even keeps computer files on his conquests) is thrown for an amorous loop by a comely American female. This romantic comedy is heavy on the cute pedal and in the end feels like a high tea version of a John Hughes film.
D: Damian Harris. A: Dexter Fletcher, Ione Skye, James Spader.

Shirley Valentine
(1989) 109m. **B–**
Addressing the camera directly, a middle-aged housewife tells of her fears that life may have eluded her and of the solution for it: travel to Greece without her husband. A lively tale full of smart lines, funny characters—Collins' openness and sense of humor are infectious—and even some nice scenery.
D: Lewis Gilbert. A: Pauline Collins, Tom Conti, Julia McKenzie.

Nuns on the Run
(1990) 90m. **C+**
When they bungle their chance to go to Brazil, two burglars hide out in a convent in this caper that tries to be like *Some Like It Hot* in habits. The leads manage some laugh-out-loud scenes and the dialogue is often funny, though not enough to get things rollicking.
D: Jonathan Lynn. A: Eric Idle, Robbie Coltrane, Camille Coduri.

Hear My Song
(1991) 104m. **B**
A con-man nightclub owner pushes things too far when he bills an ex-patriot Irish tenor and then throws a fake at the crowd. Gentle small film has the feeling of a good shaggy dog story—the payoff is well worth the occasional lulls in the telling.
D: Peter Chelsom. A: Ned Beatty, Adrian Dunbar, Shirley Anne Field.

The Pope Must Diet
(1991) 90m. **C–**
A mistake in the Vatican leads to a good-natured country priest being elected as Pope. Film doesn't seem to be sure how far to go with the fish-out-of-water, one-note joke, especially with the Cardinals who covet the position for their own venal purposes. Originally titled *The Pope Must Die.*
D: Peter Richardson. A: Robbie Coltrane, Alex Rocco, Herbert Lom.

Blame It on the Bellboy
(1992) 79m. **B+**
Surprisingly amusing tale of a daffy bellboy at a Venice Grand Hotel who mixes up the guests' itinerary envelopes, setting off a series of misadventures. Pinchot steals the show as the manic Jim Carrey-esque bellboy while film supplies constant stream of pratfalls and belly laughs.
D: Mark Herman. A: Dudley Moore, Bronson Pinchot, Bryan Brown.

Bad Behavior
(1994) 103m. **C**
He's working for the city planning office and she's home supervising the remodeling of their bathroom. It's all very cozy middle-class London except that their marriage is falling apart. Despite the intimate moments and intelligent characters and script, only occasionally satisfying.
D: Les Blair. A: Stephen Rea, Sinead Cusack, Philip Jackson.

Leon the Pig Farmer
(1994) 98m. **B–**
A young Jewish Londoner learns that not only is he the product of artificial insemination, but that his biological father is a pig farmer. A somewhat amusing identity/culture confusion romp highlighted by Leon's new family welcoming him with Jewish food and Yiddish phrases.
D: Vadim Jean, Gary Sinyor. A: Mark Frankel, Maryam D'Abo, Janet Suzman.

Irish Comedies

There's an ambling, publike feel to these small and quirky films, with their tales of boisterous families, hardheaded dreamers, and strong-willed women.

The Commitments
(1991) 125m. **A**
A headstrong Dublin promoter tries to assemble, of all things, the ultimate Irish R&B band. Not a note rings untrue in this alternately boisterous, funny, and sometimes heartbreaking tale, with great characters, even better music, and beautifully seedy Irish locales.
D: Alan Parker. A: Robert Arkins, Maria Doyle, Angeline Ball.

The Playboys
(1992) 114m. **B+**
A young woman scandalizes her small town when she refuses to name the father of her child. The arrival of a troupe of performers only adds to the whimsical confusion in this charming and humorous tale of courtship rituals.
D: Gillies MacKennon. A: Albert Finney, Aidan Quinn, Robin Wright.

The Snapper
(1994) 95m. **A–**
A brightly directed look at the troubles an unexpected pregnancy brings to a working-class Dublin family when the daughter insists on keeping the baby but refuses to identify the father. A comic warm portrait of family life with lots of pub wit and irony.
D: Stephen Frears. A: Colm Meaney, Ruth McCabe, Tina Kellegher.

Monty Python

Pushing irreverence to hilarious and bizarre extremes, Monty Python's Flying Circus offers us inspired silliness featuring singing gay lumberjacks, knights fighting killer bunnies, even a skewed version of the Old Testament, in films that range from low-budget transfers from their British TV series to later slick features of the 80s.

And Now for Something Completely Different

(1972) 89m. **B+**

Primitive and grainy-looking transfer of the group's best BBC skits, but so what? With some of their uproarious classic bits like the Upper Class Twit of the Year sketch, the selling of a dead parrot, and lumberjacks singing about the joys of transvestism, this supplies more belly laughs than a year of network TV.
D: Ian McNaughton. A: Monty Python cast.

Monty Python and the Holy Grail

(1975) 90m. **A–**

The Hollywood image of King Arthur's roundtable and the crusaders will never be the same after this journey through a soiled murky era populated with foul-smelling toothless peasants, mad men, and psychotic knights. A strange mix of very clever verbal humor and surreal sight gags, including the throat-ripping bunny and God as a rude cartoon cut-out.
D: Terry Gilliam. A: Monty Python cast.

Jabberwocky

(1977) 100m. **C+**

A doltish medieval cooper gets mixed up in a heroic fight against a nasty creature called a Jabberwocky. A pair of Python members attempts to extend the grotty hijinks of *Holy Grail* with mixed results in this goo-and-grime-heavy film that makes you miss the rest of the Flying Circus.
D: Terry Gilliam. A: Michael Palin, Max Wall, Deborah Wallender.

Life of Brian

(1979) 92m. **A–**

Young Brian of Nazareth has the misfortune of being born at the same time as, and later mistaken for, his much more famous biblical neighbor. Wonderfully tasteless satire on religious films, this looks like the real item while offering an abduction-by-aliens sequence and final crucifixion sing-along that would make John Waters turn green with bad taste envy.
D: Terry Jones. A: Monty Python cast.

The Secret Policeman's Other Ball

(1982) 91m. **B**

Select Python members, some noted British comedy performers, and assorted rock musicians (Sting, Phil Collins, Eric Clapton) do a live charity gig for Amnesty International. Features a few good Python routines that only take up a small portion of the "Ball."
D: Julian Temple. A: Monty Python cast.

Monty Python's the Meaning of Life

(1983) 103m. **B+**

The Python cast sinks their satirical teeth into a series of vignettes dealing with birth, death, education, war, and other things related to the film's title. Perhaps the most concentrated Python bad-taste epic yet, with the funniest scenes unfit for family viewing or just so surreal you have to see it to believe it.
D: Terry Jones. A: Monty Python cast.

Bill Forsyth

Always on the side of the underdog, this Scottish filmmaker's work takes a small-scale, quirky approach to the eternal problems of love, happiness, and success.

Gregory's Girl

(1981) 91m. **B**

A Scottish teenage soccer player has just shot up five inches, leaving him a clumsy mess on the field, and then he's replaced on the team by a girl. Low-key, affecting, and refreshing subtle tale of teen fears and identity that, unlike American counterparts, never turns cute or mawkish.
D: Bill Forsyth. A: Gordon John Sinclair, Dee Hepburn, Jake D'Arcy.

Local Hero

(1983) 111m. **A**

An oil company executive goes off to buy an entire Scottish village—beach included—and finds his mission tested by the wily locals. The characters actually evolve at a natural pace, creating a delightful sense of real people stuck in an unusual situation, making this both funny and humane.
D: Bill Forsyth. A: Peter Riegert, Denis Lawson, Burt Lancaster.

Comfort and Joy

(1984) 93m. **B+**

When things go wrong for the DJ in this banana split of a film, they go absolutely wrong. His girlfriend leaves him, taking everything that's not nailed down, birds won't stop relieving themselves on his BMW, and he gets caught between two gangs feuding over control of ice cream production.
D: Bill Forsyth. A: Bill Paterson, Eleanor David, C. P. Grogan.

Woody Allen

Woody continues to film his small, character-driven comedy/dramas (and a few deadly serious Bergmanesque pieces) that celebrate a slice of New York life—albeit a sophisticated, upper-middle-class, college-educated one, with a humor, intelligence, and love for filmmaking that's rare in American cinema.

Stardust Memories
(1980) 91m. **B**

A semi-autobiographical tale of a filmmaker forced to confront childhood dreams, old troubled loves, and adoring fans with the same question: "Why don't you make those funny movies like you used to?" Self-pitying and contrived homage to Fellini's *8½*.
D: Woody Allen. A: Woody Allen, Charlotte Rampling, Jessica Harper.

A Midsummer Night's Sex Comedy
(1982) 88m. **B–**

Woody and Co. swap loves and ghost stories during a weekend outing in turn-of-the-century upstate New York. Offers shimmering photography and some funny moments but generally an aimless romance among the willows.
D: Woody Allen. A: Woody Allen, Mia Farrow, Tony Roberts.

Broadway Danny Rose
(1984) 88m. **B+**

A New York talent agent, loyal to a stable of acts that would break your heart, promotes a bloated Sinatra-wannabe and gets mixed up with the Mob and the crooner's screeching mistress. A sweet screwball comedy that revisits the earlier world of Woody's little people.
D: Woody Allen. A: Woody Allen, Mia Farrow, Nick Apollo Forte.

Zelig
(1984) 79m. B&W.
A–

Allen is the human chameleon who physically conforms to the temper of his times in this black-and-white, pseudo-documentary on the life of a human anomaly in the 1920s. The pre-*Forest Gump* special effects (that's Woody waving over Hitler's shoulder) never stifles this poignant seriocomedy of a man who would be us.
D: Woody Allen. A: Woody Allen, Mia Farrow, Saul Bellow.

The Purple Rose of Cairo
(1985) 84m. **B+**

An emotionally starved housewife in the 1930s seeks romance and adventure in the film exploits of a movie star who literally jumps off the screen and into her life. Beautiful contrast of somber dusty Depression-era colors with the lush 30s black-and-white films makes this film more fun to look at than to follow.
D: Woody Allen. A: Woody Allen, Mia Farrow, Jeff Daniels.

Hannah and Her Sisters
(1986) 103m. **A**

Three Manhattanite sisters are forced to come to terms with years of repressed aspirations and resentments as the loves of their lives slambang into each other. A delicious adult comedy and a feast for the eyes.
D: Woody Allen. A: Woody Allen, Mia Farrow, Michael Caine.

Radio Days
(1987) 96m. **A–**

Woody narrates the reminiscence of one boy's childhood in 1940s Queens, when radio was king, communism was a substitute religion, and the Mob still dumped bodies in Red Hook. Overflowing with funny colorful performances, this will make you nostalgic for this era of simple villains and silly diversions.
D: Woody Allen. A: Mia Farrow, Dianne Wiest, Julie Kavner.

September
(1987) 82m. **C–**

Six people reveal long-closeted skeletons and repressed feelings during a weekend in Vermont. Despite finely hued performances, this brooding, self-important drama feels like one long therapy session.
D: Woody Allen. A: Mia Farrow, Denholm Elliott, Dianne Wiest.

Another Woman
(1988) 81m. **B**

A well-organized, successful career woman is punched in the stomach by real life, which she had managed to keep at bay. One of Woody Allen's serious Bergmanesque set pieces, full of thoughtful analytical adult conversations.
D: Woody Allen. A: Gena Rowlands, Mia Farrow, Ian Holm.

Crimes and Misdemeanors
(1989) 104m. **A–**

A humanitarian eye doctor has his grasping mistress murdered; a high-minded filmmaker falls in love with another woman as he begins a documentary of his fatuous TV producer brother-in-law. Allen pulls off the right mix of comic and dramatic character studies along with his serious meditations, this time on the nature of guilt.
D: Woody Allen. A: Martin Landau, Anjelica Huston, Woody Allen.

Jim Jarmusch

From the depths of the 80s Manhattan too-hip-to-blink, downtown scene emerged director Jim Jarmusch. Filtered through a hyper self-aware, deadpan Gotham world view, these unique films (the first two filmed in grungy black-and-white, the latter two in grungy color) features amusing grouchy misfits and a sense of humor that ranges from annoyingly groovy to engagingly loopy.

Stranger Than Paradise
(1984) 90m. B&W. **A–**
A Hungarian émigré, his cousin, and a pal leave gloomy Cleveland and go on a largely accidental vacation to Florida. Combining a deadpan air with seedy hotel rooms, fast-food restaurants, and small-time weirdo characters, this purposefully random-looking film has a hard to describe but definitely absurd charm.
D: Jim Jarmusch. A: Richard Edson, John Lurie, Ester Balint.

Down by Law
(1986) 107m. B&W **B+**
Three very different losers break out of jail (mainly because they can't stand sharing a cell with each other) and seem stuck together as they journey through Louisiana bayou country. Bumbling and ever-cheerful Benigni, like a cross between Woody Allen in *Bananas* and Topo Gigio, practically steals the show in this lugubriously witty offering.
D: Jim Jarmusch. A: Tom Waits, John Lurie, Roberto Benigni.

Mystery Train
(1990) 110m. **B+**
Two Japanese hipsters, an Elvis fanatic and her Carl Perkins-adoring boyfriend, check into a seedy Memphis hotel on their way to visiting the shrines of the legendary rock 'n' rollers. Not much in the way of regular plot, but has the usual quirky characters, sleazy locales, and a sly, almost mythically weird take on low-culture Americana.
D: Jim Jarmusch. A: Elizabeth Bracco, Screamin' Jay Hawkins, Youki Kudoh.

Night on Earth
(1992) 128m. **B+**
Uneven but always interesting quintet of tales taking place in taxis late at night in five far-flung cities. With the outside world shown as a distant hazy place, the cab becomes a scaled-down world/psychiatrist's office as various characters—including hilariously oversexed Roman cabbie Benigni—tell their revealing and funny tales.
D: Jim Jarmusch. A: Gena Rowlands, Winona Ryder, Roberto Benigni.

Australian Comedies

As with the dramas, the exported comedies from Down Under consistently show an eccentric world view filled with skewed takes on culture and colorfully oddball characters.

Bliss
(1985) 112m. **B**
An ad executive survives a near-fatal heart attack, which succeeds in opening his eyes to, among other things, his cheating wife, his drug-dealing son, and a doped up communist daughter. Black comedy fable on greed and avarice occasionally stumbles, but has originality and a singular POV on its side.
D: Ray Lawrence. A: Barry Otto, Lynette Curran, Helen Jones.

The Coca-Cola Kid
(1985) 98m. **B+**
Subtly bizarre tale of an American marketing whiz trying to sell the famous soda down under, with all sorts of cultural and sexual confusion resulting. With its fascinating oddball characters, this sleeper is alternately funny, erotic, just plain weird, and definitely worth a look.
D: Dusan Makavejev. A: Eric Roberts, Greta Scacchi, Chris Haywood.

Young Einstein
(1989) 90m. **C+**
Fabled physicist/surfer Albert Einstein discovers that rock 'n' roll will save the world. Obviously not fact-based, this lunatic farce plays it broadly, to say the least, and gets some belly laughs despite already being musically dated and a mite Aussie-specific in its humor for U.S. viewers.
D: Yahoo Serious. A: Yahoo Serious, Odile Le Clezio, John Howard.

The Adventures of Priscilla, Queen of the Desert
(1994) 104m. **A**
Three drag queens mount a bus named Priscilla and cross the Aussie outback on their way to a gig. Stamp is a delight as a been-around-the-block older "woman" while the rest are a hoot in this delightful, generously spirited ode to individualism filled with great disco numbers, campy humor, and some touching scenes of self-discovery.
D: Stephan Elliott. A: Terence Stamp, Hugo Weaving, Guy Pearce.

Muriel's Wedding
(1994) 105m. **B+**
A dowdy young woman gets a complete makeover from a working-class friend and a new life in the big city; trouble starts when she's torn between helping her friend or accepting the marriage opportunity of a lifetime. With heavy ABBA soundtrack, a gaudy and ribald comedy that ventures into serious territory.
D: P. J. Hogan. A: Toni Collette, Rachel Griffiths, Bill Hunter.

Buddy Capers

These films feature a mismatched pair of guys who bumble, bluff, and clown their way out of dangerous or wacky situations with a little more humor and a lot less pyrotechnics than they do in action buddy-cop films. The best offer the kind of comedic camaraderie that made Laurel and Hardy or Abbott and Costello so popular; the worst get mired in lot of elaborate, unfunny, and very noisy situations.

Stir Crazy
(1980) 111m. **B**
Unemployed pals—a writer and an actor—end up in prison in a case of mistaken identities. The silly plot involving a prison rodeo competition is just a skeleton for the pair's hilarious jive-talking routines.
D: Sidney Poitier. A: Gene Wilder, Richard Pryor, JoBeth Williams.

Partners
(1982) 98m. **D**
A macho cop and his gay partner investigate a murder in LA's homosexual subculture. Tedious, offensive, and with unfunny routines involving O'Neal's homophobia and Hurt's limp-wristed caricature as old as the hills.
D: James Burrows. A: Ryan O'Neal, John Hurt, Kenneth McMillan.

Best Defense
(1984) 94m. **C−**
The ultimate army tank built by a government defense contractor goes haywire for a rule-bending tank commander in the Middle East. The multiple strands of this complicated unfunny story never connect while the broad jokes rely heavily on large-scale destruction.
D: Willard Huyck. A: Dudley Moore, Eddie Murphy, Kate Capshaw.

City Heat
(1984) 94m. **C**
This deadpan parody of 1930s detective films gives us private eye Reynolds and cop Eastwood trading barbs and dodging gangsters' bullets in an uneasy and often slow-paced mix of jokes and shoot-outs.
D: Richard Benjamin. A: Clint Eastwood, Burt Reynolds, Jane Alexander.

Johnny Dangerously
(1984) 90m. **C+**
This spoof of 1930s gangster films follows the rise of suave racketeer Keaton through the ranks of the underworld as the comically evil and cruel Piscopo attempts to dethrone him. Lots of lowbrow laughs, including some hilariously crude sexual gags.
D: Amy Heckerling. A: Michael Keaton, Joe Piscopo, Marilu Henner.

The Man with One Red Shoe
(1985) 93m. **C+**
A virtuoso violinist gets caught in the crossfire of competing spy outfits and falls for an undercover agent who's out to get him. A deadpan comedy of mistaken identity that's slow and predictable.
D: Stan Dragoti. A: Tom Hanks, Lori Singer, James Belushi.

Spies Like Us
(1985) 104m. **C−**
A scheming lech and an electronics whiz become decoy spies sent to tangle with Soviet agents in Afghanistan. All the sand, slapstick, and contrived plot make this resemble *Ishtar* meets *Saturday Night Live*.
D: John Landis. A: Dan Aykroyd, Chevy Chase, Donna Dixon.

Tough Guys
(1986) 104m. **D+**
A pair of legendary train robbers are finally released from prison and have trouble adjusting to 1980s customs. The old pros exude charm but the comedy is second-rate.
D: Jeff Kanew. A: Kirk Douglas, Burt Lancaster, Charles Durning.

Wise Guys
(1986) 92m. **B**
Two bumbling low-level mafiosi lose their boss's money and as punishment are secretly ordered to rub each other out. A funny idea and slapstick synergy between the stars generate abundant laughs in this unexpected black comedy.
D: Brian De Palma. A: Danny DeVito, Joe Piscopo, Harvey Keitel.

Dragnet
(1987) 107m. **B+**
When Joe Friday's straight-laced nephew and his crazy partner try to stop a religious cult, they're up to their badges in weird sacrifices, giant snakes, tanks, and hanky-panky. A glossy homage with broad jokes, bloodless violence, and a packaged feel.
D: Tom Mankiewicz. A: Dan Aykroyd, Tom Hanks, Christopher Plummer.

Happy New Year
(1987) 85m. **B−**
A couple of high-class thieves plan to rob a jewelry store in Palm Beach, but things go awry when one of them falls for the jeweler's comely neighbor. Part amiable romantic comedy and part fumbling buddy caper that has plenty of charm and no substance.
D: John Avildsen. A: Peter Falk, Charles Durning, Wendy Hughes.

Real Men
(1987) 96m. **C+**
A fast-talking CIA agent recruits an average suburbanite to act as his partner and courier of a top-secret device connected to aliens. The humor in this cartoonlike spy spoof is forced and flat while the plot gets so downright bizarre it is almost entertaining.
D: Dennis Feldman. A: John Ritter, James Belushi, Barbara Barrie.

Stakeout
(1987) 115m. **B**
Police partners spy on the young woman whose homicidal ex-lover has just busted out of jail, and comedic complications ensue when one of them falls for her. Frantic slapstick and the likable leads trapped together carry this while the tacked-on violence almost sinks it.
D: John Badham. A: Richard Dreyfuss, Emilio Estevez, Madeleine Stowe.

Throw Mama from the Train
(1987) 88m. **A−**
A novelist frustrated with his ex-wife and a sad sack tormented by his overbearing mother plot to murder each other's relatives. This Hitchcock-inspired, pitch-black comedy spiked with violent sight gags falters only when it turns sentimental.
D: Danny DeVito. A: Billy Crystal, Danny DeVito, Anne Ramsey.

Dirty Rotten Scoundrels
(1988) 110m. **B+**
A suave con artist on the French Riviera tutors a crude amateur and winds up his rival to defraud a wealthy young woman. The series of deliciously wicked scams combines pratfalls and black humor that climax with the perfect double cross. Fun, but stick with the original *Bedtime Story*.
D: Franz Oz. A: Michael Caine, Steve Martin, Glenne Headly.

The Experts
(1989) 94m. **C+**
A pair of cool New Yorkers is paid to start up a nightclub in a tiny Midwestern town that's really a secret training ground for Soviet spies. An overcomplicated story containing more plot than comedy that quickly sinks into a small-town sitcom.
D: Dave Thomas. A: John Travolta, Ayre Gross, Kelly Preston.

Sunset
(1988) 107m. **B**
Silent star Tom Mix and lawman Wyatt Earp buddy-buddy their way through a murder mystery involving a stew of sexual perversion in 20s Hollywood. Garner brings a reserved humanity

to Earp in this colorful and often witty film that strays too far into a complex mystery instead of keeping with the characters and the worlds they come from.
D: Blake Edwards. A: Bruce Willis, James Garner, Malcolm McDowell.

Things Change
(1988) 105m. **A–**
An old Italian shoemaker agrees to confess to a Mafia murder in exchange for a future fortune, and his bodyguard grants him one last night on the town. This is a slow and steady outing, with Mamet's poetic tough-guy dialogue and Ameche's quiet dignity making it a subtly poignant effort.
D: David Mamet. A: Don Ameche, Joe Mantegna, Robert Prosky.

Breaking In
(1989) 94m. **B–**
A veteran burglar takes a young rookie thief under his wing and teaches him lessons about larceny and life. This subtle gentle comedy will elicit appreciative chuckles rather than belly laughs, and Reynolds will surprise you.
D: Bill Forsyth. A: Burt Reynolds, Casey Siemaszko, Sheila Kelley.

Cookie
(1989) 93m. **C+**
Fluffy gangster/generation gap tale finds a wacky teen girl and her newly released mobster Pop involved in a plot to rub out a corrupt DA. With lots of frenetic banter between flying bullets, this shows the leads in fine fettle, even if the movie they're in is dopey.
D: Susan Seidelman. A: Peter Falk, Emily Lloyd, Dianne Wiest.

K-9
(1989) 105m. **D+**
A rule-straining San Diego cop gets saddled with a new partner: a police-trained German shepherd. Same old buddy action formula with canine complications.
D: Rod Daniel. A: James Belushi, Mel Harris, Kevin Tighe.

See No Evil, Hear No Evil
(1989) 103m. **C–**
Deaf Wilder and blind Pryor get caught in a murder plot involving a top-secret microchip. All the jokes are dispensed with upfront before this quickly settles into an uninspired madcap crime comedy.
D: Arthur Hiller. A: Gene Wilder, Richard Pryor, Joan Severance.

Three Fugitives
(1989) 93m. **B**
A young single father tries to rob a bank in order to support his daughter and ends up holding a tough ex-convict hostage. The genuinely sweet atmosphere and comic tension compensate for the same old situations and heartstring pulling.
D: Francis Veber. A: Nick Nolte, Martin Short, Sarah Rowland Droff.

Turner and Hooch
(1989) 97m. **C–**
An LA police detective is out to solve a murder whose only witness was the victim's lovable humongous dog. Hanks' wildly physical antics and the endless amount of doggy drool that passes for comedy will appeal to kids and Hanks' fans.
D: Roger Spottiswoode. A: Tom Hanks, Mare Winningham, Craig T. Nelson.

We're No Angels
(1989) 101m. **B–**
Two escaped convicts are mistaken for priests and hide out in the monastery of a sleepy Canadian town populated by eccentrics. Watching these two tough guys clown and mug provides some laughs in this offbeat but lumbering comedy.
D: Neil Jordan. A: Robert De Niro, Sean Penn, Demi Moore.

Kindergarten Cop
(1990) 111m. **B+**
An urban detective goes undercover as a school teacher in order to locate the son and wife of a fugitive drug dealer. The pumped-up hero's attempt to control small children makes for funny predictable sight gags while a romantic subplot and violent climax provide the action.
D: Ivan Reitman. A: Arnold Schwarzenegger, Pamela Reed, Penelope Ann Miller.

Loose Cannons
(1990) 94m. **C+**
A veteran cop and his brilliant but mentally disturbed rookie partner must solve a series of bizarre murders connected to neo-Nazis. Aykroyd's manic impersonations of television characters are occasionally funny, but the convoluted plot and dragged-out chase scenes are dull.
D: Bob Clark. A: Gene Hackman, Dan Aykroyd, Dom DeLuise.

Another You
(1991) 98m. **D–**
Wilder is now the mental patient and pathological liar who is released into the care of ex-convict Pryor, and the two plan a big-time swindle. No original gags and the duo's chemistry has lost its sparkle.
D: Maurice Phillips. A: Gene Wilder, Richard Pryor, Mercedes Ruehl.

The Hard Way
(1991) 111m. **B**
A pampered actor preparing for a cop movie tags along with a tough New York detective on the trail of a serial killer. The slick action sequences, profanely funny dialogue, and hilariously tense rapport between Fox and Woods make this better than most.
D: John Badham. A: Michael J. Fox, James Woods, Stephen Lang.

Another Stakeout
(1993) 109m. **C+**
This mischievous veteran detective, his young partner, and a brassy DA pose as a family in order to spy on a crook hiding in suburbia. The characters are more shrill than funny in this mix of unsatisfying action, slapstick, and insult humor.
D: John Badham. A: Richard Dreyfuss, Emilio Estevez, Rosie O'Donnell.

Cops and Robbersons
(1994) 95m. **C–**
A suburban family man thinks his dreams of becoming a policeman will come true when a crusty detective moves in to stake out a homicidal neighbor. The predictable conflict between the leads seems halfhearted, delivering sporadically amusing one-liners and pratfalls.
D: Michael Ritchie. A: Chevy Chase, Jack Palance, Dianne Wiest.

The Cowboy Way
(1994) 100m. **C+**
A squabbling pair of naive rodeo cowboys trace their missing friend to New York where they tangle with a gangster. A recycled *Crocodile Dundee* plot with some bawdy humor, formulaic chase scenes, and an unimaginative villain.
D: Gregg Champion. A: Woody Harrelson, Kiefer Sutherland, Dylan McDermott.

Jimmy Hollywood
(1994) 110m. **C–**
A struggling actor and his slow-witted pal finally gain widespread fame after they become urban vigilantes hunted by the police. The film's message about media manipulation is ho-hum while the unsympathetic hero's personality changes from optimistic to satirical to surprisingly violent.
D: Barry Levinson. A: Joe Pesci, Christian Slater, Victoria Abril.

Male Buddies

***B**utch Cassidy and the Sundance Kid* **proved how much fun—and profitable—Hollywood male bonding could be, and the modern buddy genre has been going strong ever since. Whether road films, ensemble pieces, or character studies of little people, these films tend to have more fleshed-out characters and a little less mindless action than buddy caper films.**

Oh, God!

(1977) 104m. **B**

God visits an assistant manager of a grocery store and prods him into passing on the good word, which he does, nearly losing his wife and job. The cigar-smoking Burns as God, who delivers one-liners, and the guileless Denver help produce the air of lunacy that turns some predictable material into a charming affair.
D: Carl Reiner. A: George Burns, John Denver, Teri Garr.

The Blues Brothers

(1980) 133m. **A**

A jailbird and his brother reunite their blues band, mixing it up with cops, ornery roadhouse patrons, and an array of rhythm and blues performers along the way. Great fun when it sticks to the music, including a knock-out scene with Aretha Franklin, but the final demolition derby-style car chase is tedious.
D: John Landis. A: John Belushi, Dan Aykroyd, Carrie Fisher.

Used Cars

(1980) 111m. **B+**

Two fiercely competitive brothers, both used-car salesmen, are out to top the other with customer-attracting gimmicks and oddball employees who include an aspiring politician and a sex fiend. Snappy writing, outlandish situations, and an ensemble of wacky characters make this winning.
D: Robert Zemeckis. A: Kurt Russell, Jack Warden, Gerrit Graham.

Diner

(1982) 110m. **A**

This episodic coming-of-age film in 1950s Baltimore follows a group of friends on the eve of their friend's wedding, with music, women trouble, gambling debts, and future careers all getting their innings. A lively cast and the unpredictable characters and situations make this shine.
D: Barry Levinson. A: Mickey Rourke, Kevin Bacon, Steve Guttenberg.

Night Shift

(1982) 105m. **B+**

A straight-laced drudge gets a night job at the morgue, where a cocky coworker decides to set up a prostitution service. Surprisingly funny with some solid gags and synergistic performances by an out-of-control Keaton and sincere Winkler.
D: Ron Howard. A: Henry Winkler, Michael Keaton, Shelley Long.

Last Night at the Alamo

(1983) 82m. **B**

A group of world-weary urban cowboys gather at their beloved run-down Texas bar to protest its imminent destruction. Despite a low-budget and no-name cast, this character study features a painfully realistic look at modern-day losers, filled with vulgar dialogue and a cynical edge.
D: Eagle Pennell. A: Sonny Davis, Lou Perry, Steve Mantilla.

Ishtar

(1987) 107m. **C+**

Hoffman is the sex symbol and Beatty the nerd in this tale of two loser singer-songwriters in North Africa who get involved with spies and Arab rebels. Despite the rampant self-indulgence in this megabucks faux Hope-Crosby road film, you'll actually find some painfully funny moments buried throughout.
D: Elaine May. A: Warren Beatty, Dustin Hoffman, Charles Grodin.

Planes, Trains and Automobiles

(1987) 93m. **A**

A businessman's trip home on Thanksgiving eve becomes a cross-country nightmare when a clumsy slob latches on to him. This screwball road film contains such well-timed slapstick, appealing characters, and every hilarious breakdown in the book that you won't even mind the sappy ending.
D: John Hughes. A: Steve Martin, John Candy, Kevin Bacon.

3 Men and a Baby

(1987) 102m. **C+**

Three womanizing roommates struggle to care for the baby left on their doorstep. This feels like three TV stars in search of a sitcom, with good-natured, saccharine jokes about baby formula and changing diapers, undercut by an unnecessary subplot involving a mysterious packet of drugs.
D: Leonard Nimoy. A: Tom Selleck, Ted Danson, Steve Guttenberg.

Tin Men

(1987) 112m. **B+**

It's Baltimore in the 1950s and two aluminum siding salesmen lock fenders, setting off a feud that unwinds with vitriol and humor. Very little plot but the delicious ruses revealed by the conniving salesmen along with Dreyfuss' strutting cockiness keep your attention from lagging.
D: Barry Levinson. A: Danny DeVito, Richard Dreyfuss, Barbara Hershey.

The Great Outdoors

(1988) 90m. **B−**

A devoted father's lakeside vacation with his family is spoiled by a surprise visit from his rich obnoxious in-laws. Lowbrow and contrived, the laughs are generated by the ultracompetitive dads, resulting in traded insults and exaggerated pratfalls.
D: Howard Deutch. A: John Candy, Dan Aykroyd, Annette Bening.

Twins

(1988) 107m. **B+**

When two genetically engineered twins separated at birth—a brawny brain and a small-time con man—are reunited, one of them comes across some top-secret stolen goods. A bright cheerful caper that doesn't waste a single comic opportunity availed by the Mutt and Jeff brothers.
D: Ivan Reitman. A: Arnold Schwarzenegger, Danny DeVito, Kelly Preston.

Rude Awakening

(1989) 100m. **C−**

Twenty years after blowing the country to start a commune in South America, a pair of 60s freaks returns to find that all their old counterculture pals have gone yuppie on them. Our ganja-addled heroes plug on in this time-warped and dreary, laugh-light reaffirmation on all things hairy and tie-died.
D: Aaron Russo. A: Cheech Marin, Eric Roberts, Julie Hagerty.

Female Crime Capers

These entertaining caper and buddy films offer some action-oriented humor with Whoopi, Bette, and Sarandon showing that women can bicker, commit crimes, and solve them every bit as well as men could.

Compromising Positions
(1985) 98m. **B**

A retired reporter, now a restless housewife, investigates the murder of a Long Island dentist / lothario and soon learns about the indiscretions of the townswomen. Sarandon and Julia sail through this clever whodunit that has fun with suburban life but turns maddeningly muddled in the second half.
D: Frank Perry. A: Susan Sarandon, Raul Julia, Judith Ivey.

Jumpin' Jack Flash
(1986) 100m. **B–**

A bank's computer programmer gets contacted on her terminal by a British agent behind the Iron Curtain and is drawn into some Cold War intrigue. A tepid spy thriller that's barely saved by Whoopi's charm and hijinks.
D: Penny Marshall. A: Whoopi Goldberg, Steven Collins, Carol Kane.

Ruthless People
(1986) 93m. **B+**

A couple kidnaps a rich housewife and then discovers her odious husband couldn't be happier with his wife gone. Danny and Bette make a perfectly trashy couple who grate on everyone, with Midler especially hilarious as the abducted woman chained in a basement watching TV.
D: Jim Abrahams, David Zucker, Jerry Zucker. A: Danny DeVito, Bette Midler, Judge Reinhold.

Burglar
(1987) 102m. **C+**

Ex-con Goldberg is set to pull off one last heist, witnesses a murder and becomes the number one suspect. Whoopi and her poodle-loving pal Bob scour the streets of San Francisco for the real killer in this occasionally amusing but mostly overwrought mystery/comedy.
D: Hugh Wilson. A: Whoopi Goldberg, Bob Goldthwait, Lesley Ann Warren.

Outrageous Fortune
(1987) 100m. **B**

It's hate at first sight between two actresses, and then they discover they've been dating the same dreamboat who's mysteriously disappeared. Their cross-country pursuit of the two-faced rascal becomes an exercise in who can drive the most men—especially hoodlums—absolutely crazy.
D: Arthur Hiller. A: Bette Midler, Shelley Long, Peter Coyote.

Big Business
(1988) 97m. **C+**

Two pairs of twins are separated at birth with one mixed pair living the simple life in West Virginia and the other running a high-powered corporation in Manhattan. How the two sets just barely miss meeting each other is supposed to supply some of the laughs in this uninspiring comedy of errors.
D: Jim Abrahams. A: Bette Midler, Lily Tomlin, Fred Ward.

Sister Act
(1992) 100m. **B+**

A small-time lounge singer witnesses her gangster boyfriend's murder and is forced to hide out in a convent disguised as a nun. A likable entry despite the predictable jokes and feel-good subplot—Whoopi turns the tone-deaf choir into a swinging musical act that saves the parish—thanks to charming performances.
D: Emile Ardolino. A: Whoopi Goldberg, Maggie Smith, Harvey Keitel.

Grass Roots Comedies

Here are warmly humorous slices of American life in which small-town, little-guy heroes reach for their dreams and eccentrics and beautiful losers find life outside the mainstream isn't always such a bad thing.

New West

Every Which Way but Loose
(1978) 115m. **B**

Truck-driving, brawling good ole boy and his pet orangutan hit the white-trash road, fighting, loving, and falling for a pixieish country singer. A vital entry in the dumb-is-good cinema with a constant stream of genial low comedy schtick packing the whoozy wallop of a six-pack of convenience-store beer.
D: James Fargo. A: Clint Eastwood, Sondra Locke, Beverly D'Angelo.

Any Which Way You Can
(1980) 116m. **B–**

Clint, his monkey, and his singing honey meet the Mob, who want to stage the street brawl to end all street brawls. So well made and amiable in tone, one feels like a grump pointing out how lame this all is.
D: Buddy Van Horn. A: Clint Eastwood, Sondra Locke, Ruth Gordon.

Bronco Billy
(1980) 117m. **B+**

A New Jersey clerk follows his dream and hits the road with his own Wild West Show. Filled with colorful losers and an almost childlike air, this shows the bittersweet delusions of various lost souls with warmth and uncloying humanity.
D: Clint Eastwood. A: Clint Eastwood, Sondra Locke, Geoffrey Lewis.

Hard Country
(1981) 101m. **C+**

A pretty Texas girl is torn between a California-bound country singer or resigning herself to small-town life by marrying her local beau. This very uneven, almost histrionic comedy-drama lays claim to scattered laughs and partial insights, but is mainly notable for presence of country great Tanya Tucker.
D: David Greene. A: Jan-Michel Vincent, Kim Basinger, Michael Parks.

Midwest

Citizen's Band
(1977) 96m. **B**
A hectic and slyly funny study of the lives, loves, and secret sides of an assortment of CB owners as the citizens of a small town reveal their "darker" sides via the radio. Low-budget early effort of Demme's still manages to charm.
D: Jonathan Demme. A: Paul Le Mat; Candy Clark; Ed Begley, Jr.

Melvin and Howard
(1980) 95m. **B+**
The life of a man who gave Howard Hughes a ride and was named to inherit $150 million is like a comic slightly skewed American dream: Good family man married three times, failing gas station owner and milkman, the guy who tried to write novelty songs and win game shows. Funny and warmhearted slice of "little guy" Americana.
D: Jonathan Demme. A: Paul Le Mat, Jason Robards, Mary Steenburgen.

Uforia
(1984) 92m. **B+**
A slightly loopy grocery-store cashier/trailer-park resident finds love with a rambling country-star wannabe and infects a small town with her obsessive belief that UFOs are the heaven-sent harbingers of judgment day. A sweet, low-budget, funny look at small-time dreamers, *National Enquirer*-reading Americana.
D: John Binder. A: Cindy Williams, Fred Ward, Harry Dean Stanton.

Slob Series

No sight gag is too crude and no pun too corny for these sequel-spawning comedies that are willing to go to any length, short of intelligence, for a laugh. There are more entries in the *National Lampoon* and *Police Academy* series than the ones listed here, but these include some of the brightest (if that's the word) of the bunch. If you and your friends have already cracked open that second keg of beer, you may not even need to see the best.

National Lampoon's Class Reunion
(1982) 84m. **C+**
A group of former classmates ranging from the prom queen to the class nerd gather for a reunion and become the target of a homicidal classmate. This spoof of teen slasher films has some funny ideas, but the cast rushes through their lines leaving you dazed and confused.
D: Michael Miller. A: Gerrit Graham, Stephen Furst, Michael Lerner.

National Lampoon's Vacation
(1983) 98m. **A−**
A bumbling, accident-prone father takes his family on a cross-country road trip that gets sidetracked by bad luck, annoying relatives, and a mysterious temptress. The colorful parade of character actors and comics, along with Chase's buffoonery, makes most of the detours hilarious.
D: Harold Ramis. A: Chevy Chase, Beverly D'Angelo, Christie Brinkley.

National Lampoon's European Vacation
(1985) 94m. **B**
The Griswald family has won a trip across Europe and cheerfully proceeds to offend foreigners and desecrate national monuments from country to country. It's the same bumbling and repetitive jokes in front of different locales.
D: Amy Heckerling. A: Chevy Chase, Beverly D'Angelo, Eric Idle.

National Lampoon's Christmas Vacation
(1989) 102m. **B**
Those luckless Griswalds stay at home for the holidays where they're plagued by overbearing visitors, malfunctioning ornaments, and financial woes. Everyone is straining to be funny, with one or two wild successes.
D: Jeremiah Chechik. A: Chevy Chase, Beverly D'Angelo, Randy Quaid.

National Lampoon's Loaded Weapon I
(1993) 83m. **C+**
Lethal Weapon takes a pounding as two rogue cops stop at nothing to prevent sleazy criminals from zapping people with drug-laced cookies. More a clone than a comedy, with many cameos and few laughs.
D: Gene Quintano. A: Emilio Estevez, Samuel L. Jackson, Tim Curry.

Police Academy
(1984) 97m. **C−**
In response to mounting crime, a police school lowers its entrance requirements, allowing in a band of wisecracking, trigger-happy goofballs. Like a cruder version of *Stripes,* this has the minimum of enough slapstick and sex jokes to produce lowbrow laughs.
D: Hugh Wilson. A: Steve Guttenberg, George Gaynes, Kim Cattrall.

Police Academy 2: Their First Assignment
(1985) 90m. **C+**
The misfit police rookies tear up the streets trying to stop a criminal gang terrorizing the city. More humorous violence, one-liners, and screw-ups, underscored by the screaming style of unstable Goldthwait. As mediocre as this is, it represents the pinnacle of the series, which still seems to be going strong.
D: Jerry Paris. A: Steve Guttenberg, Bobcat Goldthwait, David Graf.

Spoofs and Satires

Thanks to years of TV reruns and video movie rentals, the current crop of hybrid spoofs can layer parody upon parody within a single film featuring in-jokes and elements from dozens of movies. These films put a mustache on every Hollywood Mona Lisa, not to mention

First Ladies, queens, and Mideast dictators. The humor is topical and often juvenile, but so breakneck that you're assured of at least a few laughs.

Airplane!
(1980) 86m. **A**

This silly and often hilarious spoof of airline disaster films took well-known dramatic actors, placed them in absurd situations, and had them play it straight. Additional potshots at war films and a side-splitting disco sequence add to the madness.
D: Jim Abrahams, Jerry Zucker, David Zucker. A: Robert Hays, Robert Stack, Lloyd Bridges.

Airplane II: The Sequel
(1982) 85m. **C+**

Almost a clone of the deadpan first one, using the space shuttle instead of a 747. Markedly lower laugh count than the original, but still fun in spots.
D: Ken Finkelman. A: Robert Hays, Julie Hagerty, William Shatner.

Young Doctors in Love
(1982) 95m. **C–**

This spoof of hospital-bound soap operas features cameos of then-popular soap stars. It could be a long TV sketch, except for some raunchy sex humor, with the most obvious and clichéd pranks about lusty doctors, mistakes in the operating room, and paperwork blunders.
D: Garry Marshall. A: Michael McKean, Sean Young, Patrick Macnee.

Top Secret!
(1984) 90m. **C+**

Bizarre disjointed spoof on Elvis, 60s beach, French Resistance, and spy films. The too-clever blend gives you the uncomfortable feeling that you're flicking through five different films and heading nowhere really fast.
D: Jim Abrahams, David Zucker, Jerry Zucker. A: Val Kilmer, Lucy Gutteridge, Jeremy Kemp.

The Naked Gun: From the Files of Police Squad!
(1988) 85m. **B+**

Hard-boiled detective dramas get a going over with outrageous and relentless visual puns, an obtuse and clumsy detective that's hip-deep in romance, and a plot to assassinate Queen Elizabeth.
D: David Zucker. A: Leslie Nielsen, George Kennedy, Priscilla Presley, O.J. Simpson.

The Naked Gun 2½: The Smell of Fear
(1991) 85m. **B**

More wild slapsticky outrageousness with the bumbling detective who's trying to save the future of our environment and his relationship with an ex-girlfriend. Over-the top gags include Davy Crocket assisting a Swat Team and Nielsen accidentally pulverizing Barbara Bush.
D: David Zucker. A: Leslie Nielsen, Priscilla Presley, George Kennedy, O.J. Simpson.

Naked Gun 33⅓: The Final Insult
(1994) 82m. **B+**

He's married, retired, and getting on, but the thick-witted detective has one last go against an elusive terrorist. The visual puns are more predictable, and a bevy of low-glitter guest stars show up for the finale at the Academy Awards ceremony.
D: Peter Segal. A: Leslie Nielsen, Priscilla Presley, George Kennedy, O.J. Simpson.

Hot Shots!
(1991) 85m. **B+**

Top Gun gets a ribbing as an ace navy pilot overcomes an emotional crisis with the help of a sexy psychiatrist so he can bomb the hell out of the leader of Iraq. Other films get roasted including *The Fabulous Baker Boys* and *Dances with Wolves*.
D: Jim Abrahams. A: Charlie Sheen, Cary Elwes, Valeria Golino.

Hot Shots! Part Deux
(1993) 89m. **B**

Rambo and commando mission films get splattered with gags as an ace navy pilot leads a team against a bizarre, dainty, and psychotic Hussein. You might have fun counting the number of movies spoofed.
D: Jim Abrahams. A: Charlie Sheen, Lloyd Bridges, Valeria Golino.

Amazon Women on the Moon
(1987) 85m. B&W./Color **B**

Five directors who obviously watched too much TV as kids get their revenge in this lumpy goulash of spoofs. Some of the duds are compensated for by the 30s cautionary teen sex film, the delightfully tacky take on 50s space films, and a fundraising appeal for "Blacks Without Soul."
D: John Landis, Joe Dante, Carl Gottlieb, Peter Horton, Robert K. Weiss. A: Steve Forrest, Michelle Pfeiffer, Carrie Fisher.

UHF
(1989) 97m. **B**

When a Southern California schlub is given control of a nowhere UHF TV station, his bizarre mix of live shows attracts big ratings. Amiable silliness as "Weird Al" spoofs TV commercials and game shows, and has some Walter Mitty dreams as Rambo and Indiana Jones.
D: Jay Levey. A: "Weird Al" Yankovic, Kevin McCarthy, Michael Richards.

Homages

From a generation of directors raised on movies comes these largely affectionate send-ups of sci-fi, westerns, noir, and other classic Hollywood genres. In the better efforts, you don't need to be a fan of the spoofed genre to enjoy the comedy, though it adds to the fun when you do get to see a character, a scene, or a plot device from the films you watched as a kid.

The Incredible Shrinking Woman
(1981) 88m. **B–**

Part spoof on 50s mutating human sci-fi films and part satire on our consumer age follows the adventures of a suburban housewife who's ingested some product that's making her shrink. The story lacks a center, but Tomlin really ignites when she becomes a lunatic natural products advocate and does her standby Ernestine character.
D: Joel Schumacher. A: Lily Tomlin, Charles Grodin, Henry Gibson.

Dead Men Don't Wear Plaid

(1982) 89m. **B+**

On the trail of a missing scientist, ace detective Martin appears to talk and mingle with Bogie, Lana, Lancaster, and Company as footage from 40s noirs are seemlessly blended with the film's action. Stunning black-and-white achievement that's more "wow" than funny; slim on plot, but film buffs will drink it in.
D: Carl Reiner. A: Steve Martin, Rachel Ward, Carl Reiner.

The Man with Two Brains

(1983) 93m. **B**

A brain surgeon married to a hot-blooded but distant wife begins an affair with Anne, the loving but bodiless brain in a lab jar. Sometimes a spoof of 50s mad-scientist films and sometimes just plain odd (screw-top heads for quick brain removal?), Martin is at his lunatic best supported by a sexy Turner.
D: Carl Reiner. A: Steve Martin, Kathleen Turner, Paul Benedict.

This Is Spinal Tap

(1984) 82m. **A–**

This hilariously on-target spoof of the reverential behind-the-scenes documentaries of rock groups follows Spinal Tap, a debauched and declining British band on its disastrous U.S. tour. This covers it all—musical experiments gone wrong, naked girl album covers, drugs, creative bickering, and an astrologically moved concert booker.
D: Rob Reiner. A: Rob Reiner, Michael McKean, Harry Shearer.

Lust in the Dust

(1985) 85m. **D**

Rotund female impersonator Divine is the singer who cat fights with saloon keeper Kazan, winks at gunslinger Hunter, and wards off rape-minded Mexicans in this surprisingly leaden spoof on westerns. The characters are game, but the sweaty story tries too hard to be camp.
D: Paul Bartel. A: Divine, Tab Hunter, Lainie Kazan.

Morons from Outer Space

(1985) 87m. **B**

Aliens are here for a visit, but this time they're a bunch of dim-witted party blokes who become exploited as pop-culture icons and would-be rock singers. Forget the military conspiracy subplot and enjoy the sight gags as the aliens experiment with earth devices in this harmless space/slob comedy.
D: Mike Hodges. A: Griff Rhys Jones, Mel Smith, James B. Sikking.

Three Amigos

(1986) 105m. **B–**

Three career-sliding, silent western stars visit Mexico on a personal appearance tour only to find the local peasants expecting them to do battle with vicious bandits. This overblown one-joke take on *The Magnificent Seven* is almost carried off by energetic Steve Martin.
D: John Landis. A: Steve Martin, Chevy Chase, Martin Short.

I'm Gonna Git You Sucka!

(1989) 87m. **B+**

No cliché is barred from this mock tribute to blaxploitation films, with over-dressed pimps, kung fu fighting grandmas, ex-Black Panthers college teachers, and even middle-aged, leg weary Jim Brown and Isaac Hayes putting out one more time. The cast seems to have a good time and so will you.
D: Keenen Ivory Wayans. A: Keenen Ivory Wayans, Bernie Casey, Antonio Fargas.

Medusa: Dare to Be Truthful

(1992) 51m. B&W/color **B+**

It's difficult to satirize someone as exaggerated as Madonna, but Julie Brown does a dead-eyed impersonation of the rock diva on a world concert tour who flings emotions out in all directions while terrorizing all around her. The song parodies—"Get Vague" and "Expose Yourself" are so good, they blur with the real McCoy.
D: John Fortenberry. A: Julie Brown, Bobcat Goldthwait, Carol Leifer.

Fatal Instinct

(1994) 90m. **C+**

This spoof on the deadly ladies of *Fatal Attraction* and *Basic Instinct* contains a good half hour of on-target, often funny sexual wordplay and goofy situations. Unfortunately you have to wade through the rest of the flat jokes, embarrassing slapstick, and waste of a game cast to get to it.
D: Carl Reiner. A: Armand Assante, Sherilyn Fenn, Sean Young.

Cheech and Chong

Described as the first Chinese and Chicano dope humor stand-up (fall down?) comedians, Cheech and Chong became the Hope and Crosby of the reefer set in movies that followed their endless search for excellent pot and righteous babes in a laid-back, hedonistic LA. Cheech Marin went solo starting with *Born in East L.A.*, making the more garden-variety Hollywood-style dopey—not dope—films.

Up in Smoke

(1978) 87m. **B+**

This *Citizen Kane* of dope films has our intrepid cannabis consumers participate in a Battle of the Bands at Hollywood's venerable Whiskey a Go-Go. A van made out of marijuana, endless stoned-guy jokes, and a tumultuously ridiculous rock 'n' roll show are some of the attractions of this fun-silly film.
D: Lou Adler. A: Cheech Marin, Tommy Chong, Stacy Keach.

Cheech and Chong's Next Movie

(1980) 95m. **C+**

No real plot here, just a series of vignettes following our hop-head heroes through stoned adventures at a movie studio, a welfare office, massage parlor, and so on. Some funny bits, with a feel of naughty-boys-on-the-loose, but mainly for the converted.
D: Thomas Chong. A: Cheech Marin, Thomas Chong, Evelyn Guerrero.

Cheech and Chong's Nice Dreams

(1981) 88m. **D+**

The boys, looking a bit grizzled, are now peddling their herbs from an ice cream truck. A grainy-looking and rambling tale, with pot jokes wearing out their welcome.
D: Thomas Chong. A:

Cheech Marin, Thomas Chong, Evelyn Guerrero.

Born in East L.A.
(1987) 85m. **B**

Without Chong, this follows the tale of Hispanic Cheech who's caught without his I.D. in an immigration sweep and then struggles to get back home. Based on send-up video of similarly titled Springsteen song, it's full of satirical stereotyping and even includes a morally uplifting message.
D: Cheech Marin. A: Cheech Marin, Daniel Stern, Paul Rodriguez.

Shrimp on the Barbie
(1990) 87m. **C–**

Convoluted plot has Cheech living in Australia and having to give up his Mexican restaurant there because of a duplicitously vivacious female. A depressing sense of killing time colors this low-amusement offering.
D: Alan Smithee. A: Cheech Marin, Emma Samms, Vernon Wells.

Teen Comedies

While some of these are strictly prime examples of the current trend of teenage dumbness in movieland, many are actually witty tales of nerds, dunderheaded pizza boys, and girls trying to maneuver through hormonally landminded relationships. Besides these charms, it's also fun to see many current stars like Tom Hanks, Tom Cruise, and John Cusack cutting their teeth on these low-guilt pleasures.

Porky's
(1981) 94m. **C–**
Beer-swilling teens flock to redneck bar Porky's, which comes complete with a wall-hole through which the discerning may view unclad females. An *Ernest* movie crossed with soft-core comedy would give you some idea of the schtick involved.
D: Bob Clark. A: Mark Herrier, Wyann Knight, Kim Cattrall.

Fast Times at Ridgemont High
(1982) 92m. **A–**
This chronicles the life and controlled-substance times of a group of LA teens. Lust, teachers-from-Hell, partying, mall brats, and miserable first dates: The whole teen nine yards are here in a film that should be exploitative, but thanks to a smart hilarious script and good performances (and a priceless one from Penn) this ranks as a not-so-guilty pleasure.
D: Amy Heckerling. A: Sean Penn, Jennifer Jason Leigh, Phoebe Cates.

Risky Business
(1983) 96m. **A–**
All hell breaks loose when a suburban straight-arrow teen hires a comely call girl, who undoes all his best-laid plans to be good while his parents are away. Things continue to spiral crazily out of control in this lively teen screwball fantasy that established Cruise on the beefcake map.
D: Paul Brickman. A: Tom Cruise, Rebecca DeMornay, Curtis Armstrong.

Valley Girl
(1983) 95m. **B+**
Cultures clash, San Fernando Valley-style as a semi-brainy fox finds herself going ga-ga over a punk boy from the wrong side of the tracks. Though New Wave soundtrack dates this (or makes it a nostalgia piece), it's still a rare teen film that presents youths as thinking humans.
D: Martha Coolidge. A: Nicolas Cage, Deborah Foreman, Colleen Camp.

Bachelor Party
(1984) 100m. **B**
Slob comedy maintains a 1:4 ratio of hilariously stupid bits to just stupidly stupid bits, with Hanks managing to be snotty and sweetly innocent throughout.
D: Neal Israel. A: Tom Hanks, Tawny Kitaen, Adrian Zmed.

Revenge of the Nerds
(1984) 90m. **B+**
Ignore its sequels; this is a funny campus comedy about a fraternity of geeks who cope with jocks and their goddess girlfriends while trying to maintain dignity *and* get some action. Surprisingly sweet-natured despite some obvious sex jokes and only gets *Animal House*-formulaic in the last reel.
D: Jeff Kanew. A: Robert Carradine, Anthony Edwards, Curtis Armstrong.

Better Off Dead
(1985) 97m. **B**
When his girl leaves him for a no-brainer jock, our mopey hero takes on the film title's sentiments. One of the strangest of 80s teen comedies, with some quietly weird scenes and a general dream/nightmare tone. A bit slow, but worth it for some bizarrely wonderful moments.
D: Savage Steve Holland. A: John Cusack, David Ogden Stiers, Amanda Wyss.

Real Genius
(1985) 105m. **B+**
A group of campus megabrains realizes the physics experiments they're doing for their teacher are actually going to a pricey defense contract. Amusing outing with the first half playing like a witty campus comedy while the second part settles into a better than most comedy caper.
D: Martha Coolidge. A: Val Kilmer, William Atherton, Gabe Jarret.

The Sure Thing
(1985) 94m. **B+**
A smart but gawky guy blows it once with a brainy girl and finds himself sharing a cross-country ride with her, where love grudgingly blossoms. Despite contrived plot, the way it unravels makes the difference as the characters behave like full-fledged people rather than hormone-wracked movie teens.
D: Rob Reiner. A: John Cusack, Daphne Zuniga, Anthony Edwards.

Adventures in Babysitting
(1987) 100m. **B–**
While spending an evening babysitting three kids, a girl gets a frantic call from a pal needing to be rescued and the entire evening goes nuts. With Shue and kids tooling around a barren Chicago, this becomes a sort of diminutive *After Hours* that simply settles for garnering the once-every-ten-minutes teen chuckle.
D: Chris Columbus. A: Elizabeth Shue, Keith Coogan, Anthony Rapp.

Casual Sex?
(1988) 90m. **C+**
Two girls, one hot-to-trot, the other more repressed, hit the vacation trail in search of what people tend to be in search of: to their surprise,

they want something more than the title indicates. Pretty harmless teen fluff, with safe-sex angle a welcome plus.
D: Genevieve Robert. A: Lea Thompson, Victoria Jackson, Stephen Shellen.

Some Girls
(1988) 104m. **B+**

When a young man visits his college girlfriend in Montreal during Christmas vacation, he's swept into the adventures of her eccentric family that includes two very seductive sisters. Wonderfully offbeat take on young love, with humor and drama that comes from the quirky human moments of some colorful but very real characters.
D: Michael Hoffman. A: Patrick Dempsey, Andre Gregory, Lila Kedrova.

Tapeheads
(1988) 94m. **B**

Fired from their security job gigs, two ne'er-do-wells pursue their dream of becoming video producers, are promptly fired by Don Cornelius (of "Soul Train"), but carry on anyway. An odd case of a film being ahead of its time on release, but now dated, though the parade of music acts makes it worth a rental.
D: Bill Fishman. A: John Cusack, Tim Robbins, Mary Crosby.

Bill and Ted's Excellent Adventure
(1989) 90m. **A–**

The ultimate in Valley-speak opuses tells the tale of a brain-stunned duo's travels through time where they meet a staggering variety of historical figures willing to master air-guitar. Galloping pace, some nifty effects, and a plot as addled as our heroes make this a transcendent entry in the Dumb and Dumber comedy genre.
D: Stephen Herek. A: Keanu Reeves, Alex Winter, George Carlin.

Heathers
(1989) 110m. **A**

The dog-eat-dog world of modern high school is lampooned as an individualistic girl has the audacity to turn her back on the group of popular, socially dominating WASP monsters. Her alternative—a romantic rebel with homicidal tendencies—isn't much better in this hilarious clever pitch-black satire that transcends the teen film genre.
D: Michael Lehmann. A: Winona Ryder, Christian Slater, Kim Walker.

Pucker Up and Bark Like a Dog
(1989) 94m. **B–**

The mostly romantic adventures of a shy young artist who's looking for love in sunny LA. Looks like an early Generation-X romance with a good feel for the lifestyles of the young and aimless but eventually takes the traditional route despite some hip flourishes.
D: Paul Salvataore Paraco. A: Jonathan Gries, Lisa Zane, Sal Lopez.

Say Anything
(1989) 103m. **A**

Getting what seems like the smartest and most gorgeous girl in school to go out with him is just the beginning of the life problems faced by a sincere but rather shiftless young man. Much more than a teen comedy, this is a singularly well acted, quirky romantic comedy/drama about people who happen to be young.
D: Cameron Crowe. A: John Cusack, Ione Skye, John Mahoney.

Rodney Dangerfield

Looking highly uncomfortable inside his skin, this bug-eyed performer twitches, frets, throws off one-liners, and nervously eats up every scene in these slob comedies.

Caddyshack
(1980) 99m. **B–**

Rodney is the leisure-suited, fanny-pinching, newly rich slob doing his best to irritate the wealthy stuck-ups at the ritzy country club he wants to join. The teen romance in this is a snooze, but Dangerfield shines and Murray kicks in as a demented groundskeeper out to destroy an elusive woodchuck.
D: Harold Ramis. A: With Chevy Chase, Bill Murray, Ted Knight.

Easy Money
(1983) 95m. **B**

Poor Rodney. All he wants is to chuck it all and indulge in smoking, drinking, and gambling. Suddenly a huge inheritance can be his if he reforms—and doesn't smoke, drink, and gamble. A pleasant diversion with Rodney the perfect simple slob casting longing looks at every lost temptation.
D: James Signorelli. A: With Joe Pesci, Geraldine Fitzgerald, Candy Azzara.

Back to School
(1986) 96m. **B+**

Retail king Rodney wants to make sure his son succeeds in college even if he has to enroll in the school himself. The situations are funnier, the supporting cast is lively, and Rodney's one-liners are at their sharpest. Great gag: Kurt Vonnegut is hired to write Dangerfield's term paper.
D: Alan Metter. A: With Sally Kellerman; Burt Young; Robert Downey, Jr.

Ladybugs
(1992) 91m. **C–**

Rodney is the crusty super salesman who agrees to coach a girls soccer team in order to get his next promotion. With obvious sex-role jokes and strained crude humor that seems out of place with the kiddies, the few laughs come at a premium in this cheap TV movie-style entry.
D: Sidney Furie. A: With Jackee, Jonathan Brandis, Vinessa Shaw.

John Hughes Teens

For a few years in the 80s, writer-director John Hughes seemed to have reinvented the modern teen as a middle-class borderline misfit from Chicago suburbia who, alienated by media and pop-culture glut, wrestled with problems of identity, wrecking dad's car, and getting a date.

Sixteen Candles
(1984) 93m. **B**
The amiably rambling tale of a girl who, in one day, has her birthday forgotten, is pursued by a nerd while she has a crush on a hunky senior, and suffers through a sister's lame wedding. Though a virtual catalog of teen clichés, this is lifted by engaging performances and a witty script whose dialogue rings true.
D: John Hughes. A: Molly Ringwald, Anthony Michael Hall, Gedde Watanabe.

The Breakfast Club
(1985) 95m. **B+**
Five teens, screwed-up to varying degrees, chat away a Saturday of detention in the school library. The director uses this setting as a sort of group therapy and, despite inherent visual limitations, the film works because of script's on-target, often funny dialogue and well-etched characters who grow up during the course of the film.
D: John Hughes. A: Emilio Estevez, Anthony Michael Hall, Molly Ringwald.

Weird Science
(1985) 94m. **C–**
Via computer, centerfold pictures, and lightning, two nerds create the ultimate woman. Some nice effects, but otherwise as silly as it sounds, with the Ultimate Babe a moralizing tease in scant outfits teaching her creators valuable life-lessons.
D: John Hughes. A: Anthony Michael Hall, Kelly Le-Brock, Ilan Michael-Smith.

Ferris Bueller's Day Off
(1986) 103m. **B**
Broderick is a high-spirited lad who plays hooky to take a pal on a romp through better-known Chicago landmarks. More of a Huck Finn-guided travelogue with a few funny scenes (highlighted by Broderick's contagious rendition of "Twist and Shout" in mid-parade) and a lot of half-baked sentiments.
D: John Hughes. A: Matthew Broderick, Mia Sara, Alan Ruck.

Some Kind of Wonderful
(1987) 95m. **B**
An artsy proto-slacker pines for a date with a teen queen, assisted by his trusty tomboy pal. Masterson steals the show as the ever-suffering chum in this slow-paced saunter over familiar Hughes territory.
D: Howard Deutch. A: Eric Stoltz, Mary Stuart Masterson, Craig Sheffer.

Yuppies at Home and Abroad

Some of these capers of the young and (sort of) privileged are close to yuppie slob comedies, and most are formulaic time-passers while an occasional film actually sheds some light on this high-profile subspecies of the 80s.

Bad Medicine
(1985) 97m. **C–**
A small pack of med-school rejects goes to an absurdly sub-par one in a Latin American country. Aims for a zany feel but just ends up frenetic with Latinos portrayed as greasy opportunists and whites as cardboard dolts.
D: Harvey Miller. A: Steve Guttenberg, Alan Arkin, Julie Hagerty.

Volunteers
(1985) 107m. **C**
Suave and compulsive debtor Hanks (sporting a Cary Grant accent) flees 1962 U.S. to join the Peace Corps where he helps the Thais and finds true love and fiscal maturity. Strictly lightheaded formula fodder with exception of Candy as a gung-ho volunteer.
D: Nicholas Meyer. A: Tom Hanks, John Candy, Rita Wilson.

Club Paradise
(1986) 96m. **B**
Club Med-style resort owner has his hands full keeping the joint from falling apart, the customers happy, and a political revolution from breaking out. Surprisingly entertaining fluff thanks to the finely tuned supporting cast doing their bits, highlighted by Rick Moranis and Eugene Levy as nerds out to get some action.
D: Harold Ramis. A: Robin Williams, Peter O'Toole, Jimmy Cliff.

Water
(1986) 89m. **D+**
A Caribbean island owner has his paradise turned upside down when it's discovered a Perrier-like water gushes from the soil. Jaunty reggae soundtrack and a humorously flustered Caine don't make up for strained comedy in this greed parable.
D: Dick Clement. A: Michael Caine, Valerie Perrine, Brenda Vaccaro.

The Secret of My Success
(1987) 110m. **B–**
Kansas lad goes to Gotham with big dreams and ends up working in his uncle's mailroom; undeterred, he charms his way to the top. Surprisingly pleasant, cookie-cutter product with all of Fox's charms pressed into overtime in this you-can-have-it-all farce.
D: Herbert Ross. A: Michael J. Fox, Helen Slater, Richard Jordan.

Gross Anatomy
(1989) 109m. **B**
Pressures abound for the first-year medical students, especially for bright student-with-an-attitude-problem Modine. With an authentic but also cavalier tone, this film feels like a drama trapped in the body of a comedy or vice versa, with a little romance thrown in for good measure.
D: Thom Eberhardt. A: Matthew Modine, Daphne Zuniga, Christine Lahti.

Middle-Aged Sex Comedies

Beware middle-aged crisis! These modest contemporary farces feature 40-something men as they lurch for one last ride on the sexual express. Middle-class values and the suburban ideals usually win out in the end, after much fuss, occasional sexual heat, and no small degree of act-your-age embarrassment.

10

(1979) 121m. **A–**

A successful songwriter is in a creative and emotional slump until he spies Bo Derek on her wedding day, turning his life into one hectic, pratfall-filled journey to meet up with his erotic fantasy. A funny and adult comedy even if Bo's cornrow hairstyle and personally trained musculature are now any starlet's clichés.
D: Blake Edwards. A: Dudley Moore, Julie Andrews, Bo Derek.

A Change of Seasons

(1980) 102m. **C**

A college professor has a fling with a student and his wife retaliates by bedding down with the campus carpenter stud. This tired, middle - class - marriage - gone - stale plot is given a rigorous going over by the leads who are at their best when mulling over their mistakes.
D: Richard Lang. A: Shirley MacLaine, Anthony Hopkins, Bo Derek.

Just Tell Me What You Want

(1980) 112m. **B**

Pay a visit to the crass and surly side of New York affluence as a conniving business kingpin fights with his smart and ambitious longtime mistress who wants a career. She bolts, and he tries everything to get her back. King brings arm-waving gusto to this tale that foreshadows 80s greed.
D: Sidney Lumet. A: Alan King, Ali MacGraw, Keenan Wynn.

Loving Couples

(1980) 97m. **C–**

A middle-aged couple has parallel affairs with a younger couple and unintentionally meet on a getaway hotel weekend. Instead of carrying off this farce with broad humor and various states of undress, everyone smiles and squirms in discomfort as they try to act sophisticated.
D: Jack Smight. A: Shirley MacLaine, James Coburn, Susan Sarandon.

Middle-Age Crazy

(1980) 95m. **B**

Is it his affectionate and sexy wife or his dad's death that makes Bobby Lee feel his 40 years? Donning technicolor outfits and zipping around in a sports car, he finds himself coming on hard to a Dallas Cowboy cheerleader. Familiar territory is shaded with welcome pathos as Bobby Lee sees a fool in his clothes.
D: John Trent. A: Ann-Margaret, Bruce Dern, Eric Christmas.

The Man Who Loved Women

(1983) 110m. **B–**

A sculptor runs off at the mouth to his shrink about his overwhelming need to say yes to any woman he may encounter. This inverted male fantasy about a guy who gets "it" too much is occasionally touching and funny but often too chatty.
D: Blake Edwards. A: Burt Reynolds, Julie Andrews, Kim Basinger.

Blame it on Rio

(1984) 90m. **C+**

Rio is all bouncing nubile flesh in this smarmy sex farce about a flustered businessman trying to hide his fling with his best friend's ripe teenage daughter. Caine gamely throws himself into the corny slapstick situations for this crude, almost campily embarrassing comedy.
D: Stanley Donen. A: Michael Caine, Demi Moore, Michelle Johnson.

The Woman in Red

(1984) 87m. **B**

A perfect vehicle for Wilder's brand of repressed desire as he plays the bland executive bitten by the cheating bug. Frequently silly and often funny sequences as he tries every angle—fancy clothes, the athlete ploy, and planned accidental encounters—to meet the fantasy woman he's only caught glimpses of once.
D: Gene Wilder. A: Gene Wilder, Kelly Le Brock, Charles Grodin.

A New Life

(1988) 104m. **B–**

A married couple splits—agreeably—after 26 years, but find single life daunting and depressing at first. Aided by friends, both test the waters and find unlikely partners in unexpected places. An evenhanded and sometimes comic look at the 40ish dating scene with a sometimes cloyingly nice Alda.
D: Alan Alda. A: Alan Alda, Ann-Margret, Veronica Hamel.

Skin Deep

(1989) 102m. **C–**

Poor Zach wants to get back with his long-suffering wife, but the booze continues to lubricate his overactive libido and the women keep rolling in. In this pratfall-filled, bad happenstance comedy curdling in raunchy humor, they forgot to include a character to make you care about what goes down.
D: Blake Edwards. A: John Ritter, Julianne Phillips, Vincent Gardenia.

Quirky

These colorful flights of sometimes lunatic fancy are filled with twisted attitudes toward life, visuals ranging from totalitarian horror to circus goof, and a general sense of unchecked quirkiness not seen since the mid-1970s.

Repo Man

(1984) 92m. **A**

In a sun-soaked, grungy-looking Los Angeles populated by every manner of weird and disconnected soul, a punky teen learns a trade and the "repo man" philosophy from a master of car repossessing. Bizarre yet recognizable situations; a surly/surreal tone; and a dead-eyed, hilarious cast help make this unforgettable.
D: Alex Cox. A: Emilio Estevez, Harry Dean Stanton, Vonetta McGee.

Brazil

(1985) 131m. **A**

In some unspecified, Kafkaesque retro-future, a bored clerk dreams of an angelic girl while being harassed and finally tortured by various bureaucrats and terrorists. This breathlessly inventive satire is a visually stunning grab-bag of 1940s surrealist and mythic Japanese direction with black humor, dizzying plot, and alternately paranoid/whimsical tone.
D: Terry Gilliam. A: Jonathan Pryce, Bob Hoskins, Michael Palin.

Pee-Wee's Big Adventure

(1985) 90m. **A**

Helium-voiced Pee-Wee goes on an odyssey for his

beloved bicycle. Brightly shot and manic, this manages to be perfect family fare *and* a hilariously seditious romp through as many bits of American kitsch and movie/consumer-age lore as can fit into 90 minutes.
D: Tim Burton. A: Pee-Wee Herman (Paul Reubens), Elizabeth Daily, Mark Holton.

True Stories
(1986) 86m. **B**

This visit to fictional Virgil, Texas, takes us on a tour of the secret lives of the local rubes set to song and story. A sort of feature-length rock video, with Talking Heads' Byrne acting as our narrator/guide through the National Enquirer-type vignettes done for the downtown/art crowd.
D: David Byrne. A: David Byrne, John Goodman, Spaulding Gray.

Bagdad Cafe
(1988) 91m. **B+**

A Bavarian tourist of generous dimensions finds herself stranded in a peculiar tiny town in the Nevada desert, along with its even more peculiar occupants. A great performance by Palance as a slightly unhinged artist, fine ensemble work, and a humane whimsical tone get this low-key comedy past arid sketches.
D: Percy Adlon. A: Marianne Sagebrecht, C. C. H. Pounder, Jack Palance.

Beetlejuice
(1988) 93m. **A**

A newly dead couple hires "bio-exorcist" Beetlejuice to get rid of the chichi New Yorkers who bought their house. An afterlife envisioned as a blue Expressionist waiting room and modern art that comes alive are some of the visual riches in this unique and hilarious film, powered by Keaton's fright-wigged hyper-salacious con man.
D: Tim Burton. A: Michael Keaton, Alec Baldwin, Geena Davis.

Big Top Pee-Wee
(1988) 86m. **C+**

Pee-Wee and his trusty pet hog go to the circus where he falls in love with a sweet young thing. Unlike the first Pee-Wee film, this fails to maintain the level of inspired lunacy in celebrating everything goofy in pop culture.
D: Randal Kleiser. A: Pee-Wee Herman (Paul Reubens), Susan Tyrrell, Kris Kristofferson.

Who Framed Roger Rabbit?
(1988) 103m. **B+**

It's Los Angeles 1948 and a human gumshoe is investigating a murder in Toon Town where all the movie cartoons live. The plot is convoluted and some of the sequences remind you of how loud and irritating cartoon action can be, but it remains a high-spirited marvel of animation/live action with cameos of every legend in the cartoon pantheon.
D: Robert Zemeckis. A: Bob Hoskins, Christopher Lloyd, Joanna Cassidy.

Parents
(1989) 81m. **C+**

Cold creepy parents with a decidedly odd preference in dinner meats make the life of their son a living hell. Very stylized horror/comedy and satire of 50s suburban life that has a convincingly paranoid child's worldview and kitschy art direction but, after the first punch line, nowhere to go.
D: Bob Balaban. A: Randy Quaid, Mary Beth Hurt, Sandy Dennis.

Toys
(1992) 121m. **C+**

When a toy factory owner dies, his militaristic brother takes over with plans to make war toys while the owner's sweet and simple son thinks they're still in the whimsy business. With its surreally imaginative sets and light tone, this has a fun first hour before it lumbers toward an incredibly loud and long climactic battle between the toys.
D: Barry Levinson. A: Robin Williams, Michael Gambon, Robin Wright.

Serial Mom
(1993) 97m. **B+**

Mom (played with bright-eyed gusto by Turner) has had it up to here with bad table manners, improper dressing, and other heinous crimes, and goes on a murder spree to correct the foul offenders. This is what director Waters does best: disgusting, gruesome, hilariously warped looks at family values and other strange everyday things.
D: John Waters. A: Kathleen Turner, Sam Waterston, Ricki Lake.

Romantic Singles

These comic looks at modern romance follow the usual mating habits that range from sweet and fantastic—even mermaids and androids appear as possible dream dates—to the less-than-hearts-and-flowers skirmish in the war between the sexes.

Arthur
(1981) 97m. **B+**

A middle-aged souse/multi-millionaire who never grew up stands to lose his cognac money unless he marries a Long Island deb. Unfortunately, he falls for a ditzy working-class girl. This Peter Pan with a twist story is a surprisingly funny and charming throwback to classic 30s screwballs.
D: Steve Gordon. A: Dudley Moore, Liza Minnelli, John Gielgud.

Continental Divide
(1981) 103m. **B−**

A hard-boiled Chicago newsman gets an unwanted vacation in the Rockies, where he meets his match in the form of a reporter-loathing ornithologist. Belushi's fish-out-of-water story is funny while the romance is only so-so.
D: Michael Apted. A: John Belushi, Blair Brown, Allen Goorwitz.

Modern Romance
(1981) 93m. **B+**

A head-case film editor breaks up with his girlfriend while searching for real love, whatever *that* might be. A very funny examination of love, neurosis, and Hollywood, featuring a hilariously bad sci-fi film that Brooks is editing, an uproarious look at chemically induced dating, and many more uniquely mirthful bits.
D: Albert Brooks. A: Albert Brooks, Kathryn Harrold, Bruno Kirby.

Lovesick
(1983) 95m. **C**

A stressed-out psychoanalyst falls head over heels for a comely patient. Even with a guest appearance from an imaginary Freud, the film is still a contrived coy affair, with Moore's bewildered li'l-

boy-lost routine growing tiresome.
D: Marshall Brickman. A: Dudley Moore, Elizabeth McGovern, Alec Guinness.

Splash
(1984) 111m. **A**

A young Manhattanite falls in love with a lovely young woman who happens to be a mermaid. Literal fish-out-of-water romance is persistently amiable, with a great sequence involving the fine art of Gotham shopping and a fun turn by Candy as a loutish brother.
D: Ron Howard. A: Tom Hanks, Daryl Hannah, John Candy.

Making Mr. Right
(1987) 95m. **B**

A PR consultant falls for the android she's supposed to be palming off on an unsuspecting public. Perfect-man-as-Frankenstein-monster idea is intriguing, but outside of some hilarious swipes at Miami kitsch this stylish film drops a number of comedic balls.
D: Susan Seidelman. A: John Malkovich, Ann Magnuson, Glenne Headly.

Moonstruck
(1987) 102m. **A**

A warm and operatic tone fills this unabashedly romantic tale about a woman who gets swept off her feet by a fiery young future brother-in-law. Family, neighborhood, married love, and crazy love are all portrayed with a slightly wacky humor that helps make this hard to resist.
D: Norman Jewison. A: Cher, Nicolas Cage, Vincent Gardenia.

Roxanne
(1987) 107m. **A**

An incredible sweet-tempered update of the Cyrano legend tells of a Colorado small-town fireman, the beautiful astronomy student he falls in love with, and his really, *really* big nose that comes between them. One of Martin's most romantic bits of lunacy, highlighted by a breath-defying recitation of every big nose joke known to mankind.
D: Fred Schepisi. A: Steve Martin, Daryl Hannah, Rick Rossovich.

Surrender
(1987) 95m. **C–**

A flaky painter is torn between a penniless writer who offers undying love and a wealthy man who offers the kind of security she's always yearned for. Caine looks lost as the romantic who's been walked over by wives and lovers in this only occasionally amusing outing.
D: Jerry Belson. A: Sally Field, Michael Caine, Steve Guttenberg.

When Harry Met Sally
(1989) 95m. **A**

This *Annie Hall* homage attempts—and often succeeds—to portray the long-term, evolving relationship between two trendy, meant-for-each-other singles, with the wit, sophistication, Gotham locales, and urbane music of the original. Sweet performances and a sparkling funny script make this one of the best of the bunch.
D: Rob Reiner. A: Billy Crystal, Meg Ryan, Carrie Fisher.

Marriage and Families

Even with the light tone and guaranteed feel-good finales, these visions of family values still manage to reflect the changing homefront—single parents, domestic role reversals—while reasserting the status quo for a generation that wanted it all and got it.

Author, Author
(1982) 100m. **C+**

Just as a playwright gets funding for a new production, his wife up and leaves him stranded with four kids from three other marriages. Though watching a game, out-of-character Pacino deal with demanding tots has its humor value, this film is a somewhat TV-looking, sloppily constructed affair.
D: Arthur Hiller. A: Al Pacino, Tuesday Weld, Dyan Cannon.

Best Friends
(1982) 108m. **C+**

Reality, in-laws, and inferior screenplays plague two writers who, after five years, finally tie the knot. Nice chemistry between the stars but neither their disastrous honeymoon nor dreary wedded aftermath is particularly funny.
D: Norman Jewison. A: Burt Reynolds, Goldie Hawn, Ron Silver.

Mr. Mom
(1983) 92m. **B**

An executive gets fired, his wife becomes the breadwinner, and he's stuck with a house full of kids and chores. An engaging Keaton milks simple role reversal for every comic drop in this low-originality but fun caprice.
D: Stan Dragoti. A: Michael Keaton, Teri Garr, Martin Mull.

Micki and Maude
(1984) 118m. **B+**

With his wife unwilling to be with child, a TV reporter takes another wife without divorcing the first, and suddenly finds himself with two loving and beloved wives who are both pregnant. Moore makes a cuddly, self-pity-prone bigamist in this frenetic comedy complete with a hilarious climactic dual delivery scene.
D: Blake Edwards. A: Dudley Moore, Amy Irving, Ann Reinking.

Unfaithfully Yours
(1984) 96m. **C**

A world-class conductor becomes convinced that his lovely cellist wife is mucking about with a handsome violinist, and imagines all kinds of nasty retribution. Lackluster effort, with none of the charm of the Preston Sturges classic on which it's based.
D: Howard Zieff. A: Dudley Moore, Nastassia Kinski, Armand Assante.

Heartburn
(1986) 109m. **C+**

A Manhattan writer marries an acerbic and famously womanizing Washington columnist, and it's not long before it's lipstick-on-your-collar time. Despite the stars, a pedestrian (but intelligent) script and doddering pace make this dull as ditch water and unengaging.
D: Mike Nichols. A: Meryl Streep, Jack Nicholson, Jeff Daniels.

That's Life!
(1986) 102m. **B+**

A miserable daughter, a ne'er-do-well son, a pregnant daughter, a wife awaiting the results of hospital tests, and various LA-weird neighbors join a neurotic turning-60 architect for his birthday. Witty, flamboyant, and homey comedy of a messed-

up modern family with a madman at the helm.
D: Blake Edwards. A: Julie Andrews, Jack Lemmon, Sally Kellerman.

Overboard
(1987) 112m. **C**
After taking a spill from her yacht, a bratty and now amnesiac married heiress is saved by a single dad who takes her back to his homestead, telling her they're married. Part screwball, part sweet, slightly sappy family romance as Goldie learns how to be a mother and wife while her relatives are counting her dough.
D: Garry Marshall. A: Goldie Hawn, Kurt Russell, Edward Herrmann.

Far North
(1988) 90m. **C+**
When the patriarch of a Minnesota family is hospitalized, a headstrong daughter finds herself having to deal with an extremely dysfunctional family. Quirky and somewhat chaotic comedy/drama with some dark undertones: more interesting than laugh-out-loud funny.
D: Sam Shepard. A: Jessica Lange, Charles Durning, Tess Harper.

Cousins
(1989) 110m. **B**
During a series of seemingly endless family functions, two cousins-by-marriage, whose spouses are having an affair, strike up a friendship that turns into a full-blown romance. A colorful sloppy jumble that retains much of the breeziness of the original *Cousin, Cousine* without any of the sophistication.
D: Joel Schumacher. A: Ted Danson, Isabella Rossellini, Sean Young.

Look Who's Talking
(1989) 93m. **B**
Over-plotted and pretty dumb but still amusing tale of an accountant/newly single mother who would like to find a Daddy for her baby and a cabby who falls for the new tyke. The gimmick here is continuing smart-aleck, leering commentary from the baby, voiced by Bruce Willis (a plus or minus depending on viewer's taste).
D: Amy Heckerling. A: John Travolta, Kirstie Alley, Olympia Dukakis.

Nostalgic Coming of Age

In this past everything is still possible: family crises resolved and hearts' desires sated while your favorite songs fill the old Motorola again. Filmed with a certain golden-hued style standing in for cherished memory, these have a bittersweet to overly sweet tone signifying that however bad things were, these really were the good old days.

My Favorite Year
(1982) 90m. **B+**
An alcoholic swashbuckling film star is going to make his TV debut on a variety show and it's up to a young scriptwriter to keep him off the sauce and the ladies for a week. A funny colorful look at an endearingly primitive young TV industry with O'Toole's Errol Flynn-like hero an absolute delight.
D: Richard Benjamin. A: Peter O'Toole, Mark Linn-Baker, Jessica Harper.

The Flamingo Kid
(1984) 100m. **B+**
A college-bound, Brooklyn plumber's son gets a summer job—and the taste of the good life—at an exclusive beach club. Dillon brings real charm to the role of a kid who's dazzled by the successful car dealer/card sharp and the rich blonde coed in this bittersweet coming-of-age tale set in innocent 1963.
D: Garry Marshall. A: Matt Dillon, Richard Crenna, Janet Jones.

Brighton Beach Memoirs
(1986) 110m. **B–**
A baseball-loving 15-year-old has to cope with relatives, an overcrowded home, and first love. This adaptation of Neil Simon's autobiographical play weaves a rich tapestry of Depression-era characters and locales, but the coming-of-age tale soon gets stuck in neutral, taking a predictable route.
D: Gene Saks. A: Blythe Danner, Bob Dishy, Jonathan Silverman.

Peggy Sue Got Married
(1986) 104m. **A–**
Mother of two and on the verge of divorcing her high school sweetheart, Peggy Sue is magically allowed to re-experience—and perhaps undo—events in her senior year, armed with her knowledge of the future. An enjoyable romantic outing that almost demands a second viewing to appreciate its cleverness.
D: Francis Ford Coppola. A: Kathleen Turner, Nicolas Cage, Barry Miller.

In the Mood
(1987) 99m. **C+**
A 15-year-old elopes with a 21-year-old and becomes a sort of romantic folk hero for American women during the war years. Balsam and D'Angelo are charming as the loveless women who lead the young romantic astray, but Dempsey is a bit lightweight as "The Woo Woo Kid" in the true-life tale.
D: Phil Alden Robinson. A: Patrick Dempsey, Talia Balsam, Beverly D'Angelo.

Biloxi Blues
(1988) 106m. **B**
A young Brooklyn man is sent to a Mississippi boot camp where he becomes a whipping boy to the drill sergeant and hostile inductees. It's fun to see fish-out-of-water Matthew get some licks in on the good ole home boys, but his smug running commentary eventually grounds this coy Neil Simon reminiscence.
D: Mike Nichols. A: Matthew Broderick, Christopher Walken, Matt Mulhern.

Bloodhounds of Broadway
(1989) 93m. **C**
Gangsters, flappers, and socialites ring in 1928 at a swanky party in a Broadway speakeasy in this hodgepodge of Damon Runyon stories. Style oozes out of every frame, but the denizens of this underworld never look anything other than young Hollywood stars playing dress-up.
D: Howard Brookner. A: Matt Dillon, Madonna, Jennifer Grey.

Reincarnation and Hocus-Pocus

For reasons known only to a Higher Power, Hollywood in the late 80s produced a series of colorful supernatural romps featuring spirits, witches, aliens, and ghosts.

Date with an Angel
(1987) 114m. **D**

An everyday guy's wedding plans and advertising career are severely compromised when a foxy angel clips her wings on a satellite and falls into his pool. Combination ad-world satire/buddy film/domestic romantic comedy fails on all counts.
D: Tom McLoughlin. A: Michael E. Knight, Phoebe Cates, Emmanuelle Beart.

Maid to Order
(1987) 92m. **B–**

Cinderella-esque tale of a spoiled brat who is magically wiped out of her rich existence and is forced to work as a maid to a pair of show-biz types. Despite the moralizing, this takes some funny jabs at LA gilded youth and the nouveau riche before succumbing to its redemptive, feel-good intentions.
D: Amy Jones. A: Ally Sheedy, Michael Ontkean, Beverly D'Angelo.

Mannequin
(1987) 90m. **C–**

A young woman from ancient Egypt is reincarnated as a showroom dummy, and soon she and a smitten window dresser save the store from ruin via their inspired designs. Besides the brain-boggling premise, this comes equipped with lisping homosexual designers, sex-with-dummy jokes, and dissipated photography.
D: Michael Gottlieb. A: Andrew McCarthy, Kim Cattrall, James Spader.

High Spirits
(1988) 97m. **C**

To save his declining Irish castle, a soddenly charming old rake stages fake hauntings for some U.S. rubes, accidentally raising the shades of the real dead. This gets within an inch of succeeding as a weird mutation of sex farce, ghost story, and costume drama.
D: Neil Jordan. A: Daryl Hannah, Peter O'Toole, Steve Guttenberg.

My Stepmother Is an Alien
(1988) 108m. **C**

A widowed ET-hunter meets a swell gal in red at a party only to realize she's his alien dream date. Soon love blossoms as she eats batteries for nutrition and reads *Hustler* for sex advice. Not much plot-wise, but Basinger flirts with charm, and some of the rambling scenes are amusing.
D: Richard Benjamin. A: Dan Aykroyd, Kim Basinger, Jon Lovitz.

Chances Are
(1989) 108m. **B**

A woman still carrying the torch for her deceased husband meets her daughter's new boyfriend—who's also the reincarnated soul of her immortal beloved. Despite silly plot line, this is a generously toned, well-acted bit of comic and tear-jerking fluff, with moments of actual wit.
D: Emile Ardolino. A: Cybill Shepherd; Robert Downey, Jr.; Mary Stuart Masterson.

Ghost Dad
(1990) 90m. **D**

A neglectful Dad/executive is killed and heavenly sources inform him he has three days to become a good Dad or else. Painfully domestic comedy recycles Cosby's TV persona, placing him in predictable situations where he inexplicably does double takes with eyes bulging in amazement.
D: Sidney Poitier. A: Bill Cosby, Denise Nicholas, Christine Ebersole.

Drop Dead Fred
(1991) 97m. **C**

An imaginary childhood pal shows up to cause even more havoc when a young woman's life falls to pieces. Frustrating film has its funny moments—Cates at a shrink's office with others who claim to have invisible friends—but generally prefers the prosaic to the inspired.
D: Ate De Jong. A: Phoebe Cates, Rik Mayall, Tim Matheson.

Hocus Pocus
(1993) 95m. **C**

A lonely new kid in Salem, Massachusetts, conjures up three murderous witches who are only too pleased to cause some modern-day havoc. Scores on makeup, effects, and performances, but unsavory child-killing subplot and lack of laughs make this a macabrely attractive misfire.
D: Kenny Ortega. A: Bette Midler, Sarah Jessica Parker, Kathy Najimy.

Switching Roles

One of the stranger Hollywood trends in the 80s was the fantasy that people had a chance to switch bodies and identities with other people. The result is a very American version of role-playing, with grown movie stars getting to act out as women, children, or people of different age with the only side effect being an occasional moral lesson.

All of Me
(1984) 93m. **B**

Via a guru's ministrations, a rich, controlling, and sarcastic woman's mind is transferred on death into the body of a lawyer, with both of them battling over control of the overcrowded corpus. Martin shows serious slapstick chops while film gallops from crude to clever comedy, wisely never taking itself seriously.
D: Carl Reiner. A: Steve Martin, Lily Tomlin, Victoria Tennant.

Like Father, Like Son
(1987) 101m. **D+**

Moore pushes his man/boy charm to the limits in this tale of a surgeon who, via some Indian concoction, inhabits his son's body. See Dudley show off in class, hit homers on the baseball field, and show off at a rock concert. See viewers bypass tape at video store.
D: Rod Daniel. A: Kirk Cameron, Dudley Moore, Sean Astin.

18 Again!
(1988) 100m. **C**

A car crash flips an old patri-

arch's mind into his grandson's 18-year-old body. Though it's funny seeing the kid ape Burns' walk and cigar style, this is a pretty by-rote role-switch work, with only sporadic laughs.
D: Paul Flaherty. A: George Burns, Charlie Schlatter, Tony Roberts.

Vice Versa
(1988) 97m. **B–**

A smuggled Bangkok skull (!) exerts its strange powers on a boy who suddenly switches consciousness with his harried advertising executive Dad. Despite the usual Boy/Dad, Dad/Boy gambits, this is more entertaining due to comic performances and clever script.
D: Brian Gilbert. A: Judge Reinhold, Fred Savage, Swoosie Kurtz.

Heart Condition
(1990) 96m. **B–**

An LA cop receives a heart transplant from a chic black man whom the cop loathed when he was alive. When the black man's ghost starts talking to the cop, a variety of sartorial and emotional changes occur. Sex, bigotry, and men's fashion are all addressed in this fitfully entertaining lark.
D: James Parrott. A: Denzel Washington, Bob Hoskins, Chloe Webb.

War Between the Sexes

Immortal females, murderous spouses, men reborn in women's bodies—even the devil himself—make appearances in this markedly imaginative new wave of male-female attrition films. Colorful as all get-out and filled with big stars and budgets, even the special effects-laden efforts are often as intelligent and a lot more amusing than the more serious takes on inter-sex relationships.

Prizzi's Honor
(1985) 129m. **A**

A none too bright mob hit man finds true love in a beautiful blonde who happens to be a hired gun herself. Unfortunately the "family" isn't too happy, especially the don's jealous daughter. Turner and Nicholson make a deliciously sweet and daffy pair of lovers in this nimble-witted, completely unexpected fight-to-the-finish comedy.
D: John Huston. A: Jack Nicholson, Kathleen Turner, Anjelica Huston.

Me and Him
(1987) 94m. **B–**

A New York architect is awakened one morning by the voice of his penis talking to him; the little guy feels neglected and convinces him to dump the wife and seduce every woman in sight. Not quite as adolescent as it sounds, not quite as whimsically witty as it tries to be, but it's certainly an unusual premise in film.
D: Doris Dorrie. A: Griffin Dunne, Ellen Greene, Kelly Bishop.

The Witches of Eastwick
(1987) 118m. **A–**

Three unattached friends from a quaint New England town chew the fat about the "perfect man" and the very devil himself arrives to answer their prayers. Even without the sparkling stars, this is a wickedly funny and clever adult fable complete with magic and revenge.
D: George Miller. A: Jack Nicholson, Cher, Michelle Pfeiffer, Susan Sarandon.

She Devil
(1989) 99m. **C–**

A slatternly housewife decides to get even with her husband when he runs away with a pretentious romance novel writer. Meryl is a howl as the self-possessed monster who entraps dim-witted Begley and kids in her pink mansion, but the unusually taciturn Roseanne grounds this mean-spirited comedy to a halt.
D: Susan Seidelman. A: Meryl Streep; Roseanne Barr; Ed Begley, Jr.

The War of the Roses
(1989) 116m. **B+**

After 18 years of marriage, the Roses file for divorce but neither of them wants to relinquish their beautiful home. Pettiness and greed turn a civilized divorce into a devastatingly harrowing and funny battle as the stressed-out pair escalates their terrorist tactics in this unusual, sometimes unpleasant film.
D: Danny DeVito. A: Michael Douglas, Kathleen Turner, Danny DeVito.

I Love You to Death
(1990) 98m. **C+**

When a dowdy wife of a good-natured Italian-American pizza maker learns of his philandering ways she decides to kill him. Taking on a ragtag team of conspirators, she can't believe her bad luck when every attempt fails. A strange movie because everyone is funny (Hurt is a standout), but the film isn't.
D: Lawrence Kasdan. A: Kevin Kline, Tracey Ullman, William Hurt.

Scenes from a Mall
(1991) 86m. **C–**

A writer of self-help books and a sports attorney spend their anniversary on a shopping binge at the local mall but end up nitpicking each other to the brink of divorce. After a cute opening, this neurotic yuppie passion play runs out of steam and quickly becomes stifling with no help from the claustrophic setting.
D: Paul Mazursky. A: Bette Midler, Woody Allen, Bill Irwin.

Switch
(1991) 114m. **C+**

A murdered ladies man makes a deal that if he returns to Earth and finds one woman who truly loves him, he can go to heaven. Trouble is he has to return as the kind of voluptuous woman he used to enjoy seducing. This looks and feels like a 1950s sex comedy without any of the charm or camp appeal.
D: Blake Edwards. A: Ellen Barkin, Jimmy Smits, JoBeth Williams.

Death Becomes Her
(1992) 104m. **B–**

An aging actress is already distressed over her failing career when a fat old fiancée of her plastic surgeon husband shows up looking like a million bucks. A diabolical satire on romance and modern vanities—heavy on the special effects—that manages to be funny despite a sludgy meandering final reel.
D: Robert Zemeckis. A: Meryl Streep, Bruce Willis, Goldie Hawn.

Richard Pryor

These attempts to channel Pryor's outrageously funny and manic stand-up routines into more mainstream comedies have varying results: His roles as journalist, ball-player, and other nonthreatening characters may seem tame in comparison, but his comic genius always shows through.

Which Way Is Up?

(1977) 94m. **B+**

Loopy tale of a blue-collar worker mixed up with an assassination attempt by an Evil Company, a girl's pregnancy, and mistaken identities. Forget about the potboiler plot and just enjoy a manic Pryor in three roles: the put-upon worker, a sexually active Evangelical preacher, and a foul-mouthed grandfather.
D: Michael Schultz. A: With Lonette McKee, Margaret Avery, Dolph Sweet.

Bustin' Loose

(1981) 94m. **C+**

A parolee takes a job driving a busload of eight maladjusted kids cross-country along with their foxy teacher. Though filled with typical road-movie hijinks—flat tires, whining brats, accidents—the first half is hilarious with Pryor as the bad dude, but flounders when everyone learns to get along.
D: Oz Scott. A: With Cicely Tyson, Robert Christian, Janet Wong.

The Toy

(1982) 102m. **C–**

Working at a toy store, Pryor is an out-of-work journalist who is the unlucky object of a bratty boy's desires, who has his wealthy father "buy" him. Turgid, gaudy-looking, and bland, with attempts at social commentary glitzed over in favor of things warm and fuzzy.
D: Richard Donner. A: With Jackie Gleason, Scott Schwartz, Ned Beatty.

Brewster's Millions

(1985) 101m. **C+**

A minor league player can keep $300 million if he can spend 30 of it in one month. This remake gathers some juice with Pryor–Candy pair occasionally as funny as Pryor and Wilder and some maniacally funny scenes as Pryor shops his brains out, but it eventually peters out into moralizing mire.
D: Walter Hill. A: With John Candy, Lonette McKee, Stephen Collins.

Jo Jo Dancer, Your Life Is Calling

(1986) 97m. **B**

Directing himself in a semi-autobiography, Pryor gives us a toughly effective, sometimes stilted drama, with early childhood scenes rich with scuzzy characters and atmosphere, and the look of the film evolving from nostalgic glow to gritty reality as a grown artist stumbles to the clarion call of drugs and self-abuse.
D: Richard Pryor. A: With Debbie Allen, Art Evans, Fay Hauser.

Critical Condition

(1987) 99m. **C–**

A criminal hopes to avoid prison by faking insanity. Failed attempt at madcap comedy has a few good comedic riffs, but otherwise Pryor seems listless.
D: Michael Apted. A: With Rachel Ticotin, Ruben Blades, Joe Mantegna.

Entertainers

These colorful, high-spirited adult fairy tales of entertainers past and present all adopt the visual flair of old Hollywood musicals while still keeping some very modern concerns beneath their bubbly surface.

Under the Rainbow

(1981) 98m. **C**

A talent scout uncovers a trail of intrigue as midgets, Nazis, and Japanese agents invade a local hotel and the MGM soundstages during the filming of *Wizard of Oz.* A curiously tacky homage with bumbling Chevy playing the straight man in the tiresome string of spy incidents and backstage romances.
D: Steve Rash. A: Chevy Chase, Carrie Fisher, Eve Arden.

Victor/Victoria

(1982) 133m. **A–**

A flat-broke chanteuse becomes the toast of Paris when she performs in a nightclub as a man dressed up as a woman. Her secret's safe—only her gay roommate knows—until a handsome millionaire enters the picture. A bubbly romp that feels like one of the great comedies done in grand Hollywood style.
D: Blake Edwards. A: Julie Andrews, James Garner, Robert Preston.

Moon Over Parador

(1988) 105m. **B–**

A fascist dictator of a banana republic dies, and the powers-that-be recruit a struggling American actor to take his place. A big-budget and broad satire with funny performances, but seems to need some of the laid-back goofiness of a Hope–Crosby road movie.
D: Paul Mazursky. A: Richard Dreyfuss, Raul Julia, Sonia Braga.

Bert Rigby, You're a Fool

(1989) 94m. **B**

A British coal miner heads to Hollywood to pursue his dream of being a song-and-dance man just like in the old musicals that he dearly loves. Strange mixture of oddball comedy and little-guy-going-for-it tale, studded with musical numbers and satiric jabs at "The Business." Uneven but offbeat fun.
D: Carl Reiner. A: Robert Lindsay, Robbie Coltrane, Anne Bancroft.

Modern Life Social Comedies

With a broad spectrum of lively characters ranging from a professor-turned-jeans designer to some burned-out yuppies, these films all deal with the mazelike complications of modern-day life, with a snappy pace and style, brightly colored look, and good-naturedly kooky attitude.

Nine to Five
(1980) 110m. **B+**

Three overworked underpaid office workers go from slow burn to all-out revenge against their egocentric jerk boss. Though its barbs have softened with age, this is still an effective, brightly colored comedy with humor driven home by all three women.
D: Colin Higgins. A: Jane Fonda, Lily Tomlin, Dolly Parton.

Private Benjamin
(1980) 100m. **B+**

A Jewish American Princess becomes a widow on her wedding night, checks into the "new Army," and discovers that it's not the athletic version of Club Med that she imagined. An often hilarious film with Hawn's ditzy persona used to high comic effect.
D: Howard Zieff. A: Goldie Hawn, Eileen Brennan, Armand Assante.

Neighbors
(1981) 94m. **B−**

A happy middle-class couple have their lives systematically trashed when a couple in bizarre hyper-drive move in next door. Though filled with a surreally paranoid air, this remains distant, with laughs not so much falling flat, just frenetically flying out the window.
D: John Avildsen. A: John Belushi, Dan Aykroyd, Cathy Moriarty.

So Fine
(1981) 91m. **B**

The Mob, the garment industry, academia, and a dazzled professor who's dragged among all three fill this slightly frantic farce. A screwball pacing and the plot's centerpiece of jeans with the see-through plastic seats keeps your attention off Ryan's befuddled performance.
D: Andrew Bergman. A: Ryan O'Neal, Jack Warden, Mariangela Melato.

Stripes
(1981) 105m. **A−**

Guy loses girl, job, and car all in one day, so he and a buddy join the army in search of fun, adventure, and female pulchritude. Iron Curtain double dates, a platoon boot-strapping to the beat of "Do-Wah-Diddy," and Murray's own style of brattiness are the highlights of this gleefully trashy and funny film.
D: Ivan Reitman. A: Bill Murray, Harold Ramis, Warren Oates.

Take This Job and Shove It
(1981) 100m. **C+**

A young executive returns home to install a hardline policy at the local brewery but turns populist hero after getting the lowdown on management from his blue-collar buddies. A lively but predictable caper that climaxes with the stand-up-and-cheer confrontation between good labor and bad capitalists.
D: Gus Trikonis. A: Robert Hays, Art Carney, Barbara Hershey.

Trading Places
(1983) 117m. **A**

To settle a bet on the effects of nature vs. nurture, two eccentric millionaires secretly have a financier and a black con man switch jobs and social status. Murphy unleashes a torrent of jive-talking sass and antics on a white world of somber men's clubs in this funny and clever outing.
D: John Landis. A: With Dan Aykroyd, Eddie Murphy, Ralph Bellamy.

Gung Ho
(1985) 111m. **B−**

Japanese management takes over an ailing American auto factory, and one of the workers gets promoted to managerial and cultural liaison. An affable working stiff/culture-clash comedy livened by Keaton's usual manic presence.
D: Ron Howard. A: Michael Keaton, Gedde Watanabe, George Wendt.

Lost in America
(1985) **A−**

"It's *Easy Rider* with a nest egg!" boasts a hopeful aging yuppie to his wife as they sink all their money into a Winnebago and hit the road to start a new life. This being a Brooks film, everything imaginable goes wrong and does so with consistently mirthful results.
D: Albert Brooks. A: Albert Brooks, Julie Hagerty, Garry Marshall.

Down and Out in Beverly Hills
(1986) 102m. **B+**

A bum tries to drown himself in a rich couple's pool but is saved by the owners, who include a sexually dissatisfied wife, a Central Casting alienated teen, and a floundering patriarch. By-the-numbers comedy has a buoyant feel, bright look, and fun performances.
D: Paul Mazursky. A: Nick Nolte, Richard Dreyfuss, Bette Midler.

Broadcast News
(1987) 131m. **A**

Hurt is an empty-brained, hair-boy newscaster, Brooks a smart nerdy newswriter, and both are in love with the incredibly driven and self-righteous producer Hunter. A sparkling, funny, smart, behind-the-scenes tale of TV news, journalistic ethics, and romance, with the three leads a joy to watch.
D: James Brooks. A: William Hurt, Holly Hunter, Albert Brooks.

Parenthood
(1989) 124m. **A−**

Family values and the not-so-exact art of parenting are explored in the episodes of the various members of one extended, middle class clan. A warm and funny expedition that may have tidy, feel-good resolutions for treacherous areas, but gives you an entertaining ride anyway.
D: Ron Howard. A: Steve Martin, Mary Steenburgen, Dianne Wiest.

Scenes from a Class Struggle in Beverly Hills
(1989) 102m. **B+**

An ex-soap opera queen ends up dealing with assorted weekend visitors, amorous and opportunistic servants, even the ghost of her dead husband. Bright upper-class farce with lots of door slammings, sneaking around, couplings, and misunderstandings is more entertaining than amusing.
D: Paul Bartel. A: Jacqueline Bisset, Ray Sharkey, Mary Woronov.

New York Modern Life

Whether romantic comedies, social satires, or supernatural goofball capers, if filmmakers need comically exaggerated modern-life situations, it's always a safe bet to have them take place in the country's pressure-cooker metropolis.

Tootsie
(1982) 116m. **B+**

An actor desperate for work auditions in drag and wins a plum soap opera role in this smart and sweet-tempered romantic comedy. Hoffman's a joy to watch as the self-serious, persnickity actor who becomes a feminist role model, all the time he's trying to win the heart of the leading lady.
D: Sydney Pollack. A: Dustin Hoffman, Jessica Lange, Bill Murray.

Ghostbusters
(1984) 107m. **B+**

A quartet of questionable occult investigators become New York's first line of defense against a plague of ghosts, demons, and other things undead. H. P. Lovecraft meets frat-house comedy in this seamless blend of (then) state-of-the-art effects and hilarious script, with more jokes than can be enjoyed in one screening.
D: Ivan Reitman. A: Dan Aykroyd, Billy Murray, Sigourney Weaver.

The Lonely Guy
(1984) 90m. **B**

A sporadically hilarious account of a greeting card writer's attempt to end his lonely guy status. While there are static stretches, there's also side-splitting observations of a big-city isolation (including a nearly surreal, solo-dining restaurant scene) and a consistently amusing turn by Grodin as an eternally grumpy pal.
D: Arthur Hiller. A: Steve Martin, Charles Grodin, Judith Ivey.

Moscow on the Hudson
(1984) 115m. **B**

A Russian sax player ditches the KGB while shopping at Bloomie's, where he falls for a feisty Latina. Despite Williams being in his bearded cute, teddy-bear mode (a plus or minus depending on tastes), this remains a clear-headed and humanistic look at culture shock from both sides of the fence.
D: Paul Mazursky. A: Robin Williams, Maria Cochita Alonso, Alejandro Rey.

After Hours
(1985) 97m. **A–**

A near-classic absurdist comedy about a meek word processor who thinks he can find a nice girl in Manhattan without paying for it in blood: First he loses his money, meets a suicidal girl, and eventually gets involved in a series of increasingly insane and random events. A funny frightening urban nightmare that captures after-hours Manhattan.
D: Martin Scorsese. A: Griffin Dunne, Teri Garr, Rosanna Arquette.

Desperately Seeking Susan
(1985) 104m. **B+**

Bored New Jersey housewife Arquette, who dreams of romance, winds up taking over the downtown lifestyle of punked-out free spirit Madonna. Clever bright caper with satiric jabs at the excesses of both the new bohemians and the new suburbanites.
D: Susan Seidelman. A: Rosanna Arquette, Madonna, Aidan Quinn.

Crocodile Dundee
(1986) 98m. **A–**

A journalist travels down under to interview a legendary croc hunter and promptly almost falls in love. Everything clicks here: great Aussi and New York photography, a fun fish-out-of-water story when Dundee goes to New York, a light tone, sweet romance, and it's funny as well.
D: Peter Faiman. A: Paul Hogan, Linda Kozlowski, John Mellon.

The Money Pit
(1986) 91m. **C+**

Evicted from their city pad, a young couple buys their dream home on Long Island that starts resembling Hell House as it slowly self-destructs, taking their investment with it. A strained version of *Mr. Blandings Builds His Dream House* that has laughs, but suffers from its drawn-out, one-note tale.
D: Richard Benjamin. A: Tom Hanks, Shelley Long, Alexander Godunov.

Baby Boom
(1987) 103m. **B+**

A high-strung, high-power exec finds her life upended when she inherits a baby from a relative. An enjoyable fable/romantic comedy with some incisive satire of corporate life and a charming Keaton as a yuppie humanized by real-life problems, even if it does get a little cute when she and baby move to the country.
D: Charles Shyer. A: Diane Keaton, Harold Ramis, Sam Shepard.

Big
(1988) 102m. **B**

A mechanical genie turns a precocious boy into an instant adult who must suddenly cope with being "big" all by himself in the city. Hanks is fine as the boy-turned-successful toy designer but Loggia steals the show as a stressed-out exec in this amiable and whimsical adult fairy tale.
D: Penny Marshall. A: Tom Hanks, Elizabeth Perkins, Robert Loggia.

Married to the Mob
(1988) 103m. **B+**

When her hit man husband is knocked off by mob honchos, a young Long Island woman and her kid head to the Lower East Side to start life anew. This wacked-out, incredibly colorful comedy has an unerring eye for everything funny and kitschy, culminating in a hilarious showdown in Miami.
D: Jonathan Demme. A: Michelle Pfeiffer, Matthew Modine, Dean Stockwell.

Scrooged
(1988) 101m. **C+**

A severely disappointing spin on *A Christmas Carol* has Murray as a mean-spirited media executive who gets his comeuppance. Film goes from asking audience to revel in trademark Murray snottiness, then get all weepy for Christmas spirit near the end, draining both effects. Nice ghoul, though.
D: Richard Donner. A: Bill Murray, Karen Allen, David Johansen.

Working Girl
(1988) 113m. **B+**

Smart but frustrated Staten Island big-hair girl slips into her boss's clothes, does a *My Fair Lady* on herself, and soon acquires a handsome business beau as she begins her climb up the corporate ladder. The ultimate yuppie fantasy boasts charming performances with Weaver positively glowing in a gleeful turn as the Bitch-Goddess-from-Hell.

D: Mike Nichols. A: Melanie Griffith, Harrison Ford, Sigourney Weaver.

The Dream Team
(1989) 113m. **C+**
A well-meaning psychologist takes a group of his charges to a Yankee game and promptly loses them in Manhattan. Keaton is compulsively funny as usual—this time as a chronic liar—but a good cast is underused as the film's wildness grows tepid and the predictable redemption subplot kicks in.
D: Howard Zieff. A: Michael Keaton, Christopher Lloyd, Peter Boyle.

Ghostbusters II
(1989) 102m. **C**
Hobgoblins galore descend on Gotham, and who you gonna call? Not this tired uninspired sequel with its lax script, ho-hum effects, and cinematic proof that second time is definitely not the charm. A real letdown.
D: Ivan Reitman. A: Bill Murray, Sigourney Weaver, Harold Ramis.

New York Stories
(1989) 123m. **B–**
Three great directors and a bunch of good actors tackle the topic of Manhattan life and come up with a predictably stylish, but mostly listless troika of tales. Scorsese's slyly wicked portrait of sexual power-plays in the art world is the main reason to watch.
D: Woody Allen, Francis Ford Coppola, Martin Scorsese. A: Nick Nolte, Rosanna Arquette, Woody Allen.

Slaves of New York
(1989) 125m. **C–**
This strange departure for the Merchant/Ivory team follows a coterie of posturing downtown artists as they scramble for fame, cool clothes, and a place to live. An occasionally entertaining and truly interesting failure, with glimmers of humor and cleverness that may make this an 80s camp timepiece.
D: James Ivory. A: Bernadette Peters, Adam Coleman Howard, Chris Sarandon.

Weekend at Bernie's
(1989) 97m. **B**
Two shleps who discover an embezzlement plan are invited to their boss's Fire Island beach house only to find the boss dead. Amazingly, the joke that a dead man can be trotted through all the social activities of the moneyed beach crowd without notice remains funny in this amiably dopey comedy.
D: Ted Kotcheff. A: Andrew McCarthy, Jonathan Silverman, Catherine Mary Stewart.

1990s Teen Comedies

Most of these nerd-friendly, content-lite comedies are cinematic junk food for mall rats, with the occasional rough gem. Teen truths such as rebellion and hormonal overload are mixed with genre plots ranging from vampire tales to time-traveling Valley dudes, dressed up with special effects and blaring Top-40 soundtracks.

Coupe De Ville
(1990) 99m. **C+**
Three bickering brothers are corralled by their father into driving a 1954 Cadillac from Detroit to Miami in time for their mother's 50th birthday. Along the way they fight, bond, and see the country in this retread of teen/buddy/coming-of-age road films.
D: Joe Roth. A: Patrick Dempsey, Daniel Stern, Alan Arkin.

Welcome Home, Roxy Carmichael
(1990) 98m. **B–**
A Midwestern town goes into idol-worshipping contortions when a local-girl-turned-star is about to return home. Sullen teen Winona builds up her own set of expectations, convinced that the celebrity is her long lost mother. A slightly flat, small-town, coming-of-age tale that's still alternately wistful, funny, and satirical.
D: Jim Abrahams. A: Winona Ryder, Jeff Daniels, Laila Robins.

Bill and Ted's Bogus Journey
(1991) 88m. **B–**
Originally titled *Bill and Ted Go to Hell,* which about sums up the plot as the doltish duo, bummed that they might miss the battle of the bands, enlists Death to quell a coming apocalypse. Overreliance on impressive effects along with an hysterical spoof of *The Seventh Seal* help cover film's tediousness.
D: Pete Hewitt. A: Keanu Reeves, Alex Winter, William Sadler.

Don't Tell Mom the Babysitter's Dead
(1991) 105m. **B–**
Mom's on an extended trip, the ancient babysitter died, and the eldest daughter manages to pass herself off as a high-powered secretary, climbing the corporate ladder all in the span of a summer. Less of a teen comedy and more of a sweet but predictable business teen Cinderella fable.
D: Stephen Herek. A: Christina Applegate, Joanna Cassidy, John Getz.

Mystery Date
(1991) 99m. **C**
Shy boy sees dream girl and, when his older brother arranges a date, lending him car and clothes to look cool, spends an evening that turns into *Risky Business* meets *After Hours.* Frantic plot twists—corpses piling up, mob and police in pursuit—and black comedy half-measures sink this quickly.
D: Jonathan Wacks. A: Ethan Hawke, Teri Polo, Brian McNamara.

Big Girls Don't Cry . . . They Get Even
(1992) 96m. **C+**
A teen girl revolts against her various biological and stepparents and strikes out on her own. When all the families band together they're soon at each other's throats. An amusing idea grows sour with some really annoying characters and mostly low-octane gags.
D: Joan Micklin Silver. A: Hillary Wolf, David Strathairn, Margaret Whitton.

Buffy, the Vampire Slayer
(1992) 86m. **C**
The idea of a nubile Valley Girl suddenly becoming a small town's last hope against ravaging vampire hordes sounds amusing, but this film misses gag opportunities with numbing consistency. Paul Reubens (Pee-Wee Herman) as a cranky vamp is sole reason to see.
D: Fran Rubel Kuzui. A: Kristy Swanson, Luke Perry, Donald Sutherland.

Encino Man
(1992) 89m. **C+**
Wisecracking nerds find a

frozen prehistoric man in their backyard and, with the hopes of looking cool and cultivating babes, clean him up and pass him off as their new friend. A few scattered laughs for the MTV faithful, but already nostalgia fodder for its Big Hits soundtrack and ex-video jock Shore.
D: Les Mayfield. A: Sean Astin, Brendan Fraser, Pauly Shore.

Wayne's World
(1992) 95m. **B**

This is the tale of two aging Midwest dweebs, their cable-access show, their loves, their dreams, their fits of uncontrollable air-guitar. Expanded *Saturday Night Live* sketch performs the miracle of being consistently funny in a sex, drugs, and rock 'n' roll way with an amusing self-parodying performance by Lowe.
D: Penelope Spheeris. A: Mike Myers, Dana Carvey, Rob Lowe.

Calendar Girl
(1993) 90m. **C+**

Three buddies head to Hollywood in 1962 to have one last fling and meet Marilyn Monroe. Fudged 60s feel and look, bland leads, and basic moronic premise sink this from the get-go.
D: John Whitesell. A: Jason Priestly, Gabriel Olds, Jerry O'Connell.

PCU
(1993) 90m. **B**

An *Animal House*-style comedy with a twist: While looking for a suitable college, a young man spends a weekend at the title university, whose first two letters stand for Politically Correct. Topical jabs at the campus splinter groups such as antimale-style feminism and vegetarianism are funny, along with film's cheerful slob-comedy demeanor.
D: Hart Bochner. A: Jeremy Piven, Chris Young, David Spade.

Wayne's World 2
(1993) 94m. **B–**

The sequel doesn't stray too far from the formula of babelicious girls, kitschy rock antifavorites, and "party on" philosophy, with a funny desert meeting with Jim Morrison. Looks more like a real movie than the first, but still feels tired.
D: Stephen Surjik. A: Mike Myers, Dana Carvey, Christopher Walken.

Airheads
(1994) 81m. **D+**

A trio of desperately untalented musicians commandeer a radio station in order to get their tape played. This lamebrained combination of *Bill and Ted* and *Dog Day Afternoon* is a loud and aimless misfire.
D: Michael Lehmann. A: Brendan Fraser, Steve Buscemi, Adam Sandler.

The Inkwell
(1994) 112m. **B–**

A black teen whose only friend is a doll is less than thrilled about joining his folks on a summer trip to Martha's Vineyard. Once there he meets the ballerina of his dreams in this ambitious comedy/drama that deals with class problems and racism along with the usual coming-of-age trials.
D: Matty Rich. A: Larenz Tate, Joe Morton, Jada Pinkett.

Clueless
(1995) 97m. **A**

A gorgeous Beverly Hills teen discovers the joy of doing "make-overs" of other people's lives in this hilarious updated version of Jane Austen's *Emma*. Lively pacing, a buoyant tone, and a wickedly funny script studded with witty (instead of snide) barbs about material-girl consciousness and pop culture make this a unique comedy for both teens and adults.
D: Amy Heckerling. A: Alicia Silverstone, Stacey Dash, Brittany Murphy.

Romantic Comedies

Love comes in a variety of lighthearted affairs from Euro-style sophistication to fairy-tale fancy, so there's sure to be a film valentine for everybody's taste here.

True Love
(1989) 101m. **A–**

This documentary-style film follows a New York working-class couple as they prepare for an event of dubious success: their wedding. Low in budget, high in real human drama and humor, with entertaining scenes that are gritty-immediate of neighborhood, friends, and family of the young lovers who seem to be lurching toward a big mistake.
D: Nancy Savoca. A: Annabella Sciorra, Ron Eldard, Roger Rignack.

Funny About Love
(1990) 101m. **C–**

A middle-aged crazy cartoonist yearning for a baby leaves his wife for an attractive and more fertile young woman. The gender-switch idea of a male getting toddler-obsessed is fun, but Wilder's lovable-schmuck routine grows tiresome as film wallows in sentiment. Still, a good-natured and occasionally humorous film.
D: Leonard Nimoy. A: Gene Wilder, Christine Lahti, Mary Stuart Masterson.

Green Card
(1990) 107m. **C+**

Love blossoms from a marriage of convenience between a hunky Frenchman and a straight and narrow New York botanist. This love-by-accident tale breaks no new ground, but thanks to director Weir's sure hand and two charming leads, this is a tolerably saccharine slick piece of romantic fluff.
D: Peter Weir. A: Gerard Depardieu, Andie MacDowell, Bebe Neuwirth.

He Said, She Said
(1991) 115m. **B–**

Two diametrically opposed journalists turn their feuding columns into a hit TV show as well as an uneasy romance. Film gets bonus points for showing key scenes from each partner's point of view, with sporadically funny, but unfortunately even more sporadically insightful, results.
D: Ken Kwapis, Marisa Silver. A: Kevin Bacon, Elizabeth Perkins, Sharon Stone.

May Wine
(1990) 85m. **B–**

A French gynecologist is torn between a comely middle-aged lady and an alluring younger woman, and finds he has time and energy to pursue both. Film tries to go for Continental sophistication but ends up as a flat American imitation.
D: Carol Wiseman. A: Joanna Cassidy, Guy Marchand, Lara Flynn Boyle.

Pretty Woman
(1990) 89m. **B**

A dashing money-man falls for your everyday carefree, happy-go-lucky, squeaky-

clean streetwalker. Obviously, authenticity wasn't on the filmmakers' minds when they made this sparkling street-Cinderella/Pygmalion story. If the plot doesn't bother you, this is a breezy jaunt down love avenue with adorable Roberts as the smart and sweet hooker.
D: Garry Marshall. A: Julia Roberts, Richard Gere, Laura San Giacomo.

The Tall Guy
(1990) 92m. **B–**
A desperate (and quite tall) American in London takes a role in a ridiculous play, upstages the star, and wins both a nurse's affection and a lead role in a musical version of *The Elephant Man*. Thompson is winsome and Goldblum amusingly dazed and klutzy in this slightly quirky theatrical satire and smarter-than-average romantic outing.
D: Mel Smith. A: Jeff Goldblum, Emma Thompson, Rowan Atkinson.

L.A. Story
(1991) 98m. **B**
Feeling like an *Annie Hall* for The Big Orange, this romantic comedy of manners takes an ex-weatherman through the addled morass of LA's chic-freaks, spiritual loonies, and other usual ditzy suspects. Bright and witty film never quite sparkles, though romance between Brit journalist Tennant and Martin works nicely.
D: Mick Jackson. A: Steve Martin, Victoria Tennant, Richard E. Grant.

Once Around
(1991) 114m. **C+**
An Italian-American Princess takes up with a blustering businessman much to the horror of her family. Standard culture-clash romance rests heavily on Dreyfuss' hyper-exuberant charm while whimsical tone detracts from overall laugh quotient.
D: Lasse Hallstrom. A: Richard Dreyfuss, Holly Hunter, Laura San Giacomo.

Only the Lonely
(1991) 105m. **B+**
An amusing and sweet tale involving an unmarried cop, his smothering Irish Mom, and a comely morgue worker. Candy makes an unlikely and totally appealing romantic lead to Sheedy, who's prone to making up corpses' faces like old Hollywood stars, and O'Hara, who does a comically exaggerated reprise of her *Quiet Man* role.
D: Chris Columbus. A: John Candy, Maureen O'Hara, Ally Sheedy.

Housesitter
(1992) 102m. **B–**
A twisty screwball comedy of a man who builds a dream house for his paramour, only to have her turn him down. Then his on-the-rebound, one-night stand mercilessly weasels her way into his life. Hawn's brand of kookiness serves her well in this frequently hilarious throwback to when comedies had brains and hearts.
D: Frank Oz. A: Steve Martin, Goldie Hawn, Dana Delaney.

Man Trouble
(1992) 110m. **D**
Impressively bad film about a washed-up security man with mob connections and an opera singer who hires him to protect her. With muffed casting, lame dialogue, and a snail's pacing, this is a waste of talent on both sides of the camera.
D: Bob Rafelson. A: Ellen Barkin, Jack Nicholson, Harry Dean Stanton.

The Night We Never Met
(1993) 98m. **B**
Comedy of mistaken identity centers around an apartment that's rented out to various people on different days, including a sweet gourmet and an arty Queens girl who go through near-misses of meeting. Simple adorable comedy that has fresh performances and doesn't reach for anything besides the nice love story that it is.
D: Warren Leight. A: Matthew Broderick, Annabella Sciorra, Kevin Anderson.

Prelude to a Kiss
(1992) 106m. **B–**
After a whirlwind romance two people marry, but an old man's kiss at the altar brings mysterious changes for the bride. Ryan's squeaky clean image detracts from her character's enigmatic qualities, but otherwise this is a thoughtfully odd romantic fantasy brimming with a low-key, ambiguous air.
D: Norman René. A: Meg Ryan, Alec Baldwin, Kathy Bates.

A Fine Romance
(1993) 83m. **B+**
Two people in Paris whose spouses are having an affair meet, commiserate, and eventually spark each other. A sweet and, by Hollywood standards, sophisticated bit of romantic fluff made even better by the leads and a hilarious subplot involving a real estate developer son desperate to get mom Andrews out of her apartment.
D: Gene Saks. A: Julie Andrews, Marcello Mastroianni, Ian Fitzgibbon.

Made in America
(1993) 111m. **C+**
A proud black woman and her teen daughter discover to their combined horror that by an artificial insemination accident the daughter's father is a buffoonish white car dealer. Despite Whoopi's feisty charm and the funny exchanges between her and Danson, this frenetic farce comes off as test-marketed product.
D: Richard Benjamin. A: Whoopi Goldberg, Ted Danson, Nia Long.

Mr. Wonderful
(1993) 99m. **B**
A hardworking young man strapped by alimony payments simultaneously tries to find the right guy for his ex, rebuild his dream bowling alley, and initiate an affair with his childhood sweetheart. Brightly filmed, Brooklyn-set, Italian-American comedy/drama with a fine cast working overtime to make up for somewhat listless direction.
D: Anthony Minghella. A: Matt Dillon, Annabella Sciorra, Mary-Louise Parker.

Four Weddings and a Funeral
(1994) 110m. **A–**
A lovely young American and a marriage-phobic Englishman carry on an almost-romance of fits and starts as they meet each other at a series of weddings, one of which is hers. This simple format allows the viewer to enjoy a colorful cast of engaging upper-crust Brits and delight in the tease of MacDowell and Grant's affection in this witty verbal feast of a film.
D: Mike Newell. A: Hugh Grant, Andie MacDowell, Kristin Scott Thomas.

I.Q.
(1994) 95m. **C**
A winsome niece of Albert Einstein and a nice guy sci-fi fan/car mechanic fall in love, but she's already engaged, so the wily old scientist and his pals hatch a clever bit of role-playing for the young man to sweep her off her feet. A winning first hour, but thickening plot and thinning romance make the film unspool into tedium.
D: Fred Schepisi. A: Meg Ryan, Tim Robbins, Walter Matthau.

Only You
(1994) 108m. **B–**
Loopy tale of a young woman who, days before her wedding, believes she's

found her true love and follows him sight unseen to Italy. Sometimes fun travelogue romance (Venice, Rome, Positano) is a real loose cannon, shooting off plot twists like a demented offspring of *Moonstruck*.
D: Norman Jewison. A: Marisa Tomei; Robert Downey, Jr.; Bonnie Hunt.

Sirens
(1994) 94m. **C+**
Your basic repressed British couple visits a free-thinking Aussie painter, and the wife becomes more than casually interested in his sultry models. Artistically valid chance to see several famous models in various states of undress and sexual activity, with vacation brochure photography that often gives it the look of a Merchant-Ivory version of *Emmanuelle*.
D: John Duigan. A: Hugh Grant, Sam Neill, Tara Fitzgerald.

Speechless
(1994) 99m. **B**
Two speech writers for opposing candidates grudgingly fall for one another on the campaign trail. Really funny first half of film filled with witty repartee backslides into predictable love formula in the second, though Keaton and Davis make a sparkling couple throughout.
D: Ron Underwood. A: Michael Keaton, Geena Davis, Bonnie Bedelia.

Forget Paris
(1995) 111m. **C**
The continuing romantic crises of an NBA ref and an airline stewardess who fall in love in Paris. Fairly sophisticated comedy has plenty of atmosphere, but spends too much time chronicling the couple's breakup and looks rather weak next to the Hollywood classics it models itself on.
D: Billy Crystal. A: Billy Crystal, Debra Winger, Joe Mantegna.

French Kiss
(1995) 118m. **B+**
An American woman goes to Paris to win back her lover and instead falls prey to a charming French thief who would use her in his own nefarious schemes. Kline makes a good Gallic rake, but Ryan's whiny character makes things pretty grating as the two predictably fall in love.
D: Lawrence Kasdan. A: Meg Ryan, Kevin Kline, Timothy Hutton.

Miami Rhapsody
(1995) 95m. **A−**
A young woman on the verge of marriage thinks twice as she learns about the infidelities and conjugal vagaries of her family. Winning performances and literate witty dialogue help make this come off as a lighterhearted, less neurotic *Annie Hall*, Miami-style.
D: David Frankel. A: Sarah Jessica Parker, Mia Farrow, Antonio Banderas.

While You Were Sleeping
(1995) 103m. **B**
A woman saves a secretly adored man from death and later as he lies in a coma falls for his brother. Despite paper-thin premise, Bullock and the other game players charm this one away from pabulum into a surprisingly enjoyable romantic comedy.
D: Jon Turteltaub. A: Sandra Bullock, Bill Pullman, Peter Gallagher.

Eddie Murphy

Murphy plays his ultracool motormouth persona to profane perfection in these slick, fast-paced comedies. Like *Beverly Hills Cop*, these fish-out-of-water plots have Murphy using his street smarts to hustle authority figures, wealthy stuffed shirts, or people who just aren't as cool as he is.

The Golden Child
(1986) 96m. **B**
A specialist in locating lost children is hired to find a holy child kidnapped from Tibet by what turns out to be some of Satan's minions. This comedy swashbuckler, brimming with practically every cliché from *Perils of Pauline* to the *Raider* films, finds Murphy at his entertainingly jaundiced best dodging bullies and pursuing the beautiful babe.
D: Michael Ritchie. A: With Charlotte Lewis, Charles Dance.

Coming to America
(1988) 116m. **A**
A pampered African prince comes to the New World and gets a job in a New York City fast-food burger joint while he looks for the perfect wife. After you get past the lavish opening scenes in Africa, this settles into such a genial satire you may not mind the simple plot.
D: John Landis. A: With Arsenio Hall, John Amos, James Earl Jones.

Boomerang
(1992) 118m. **C+**
A compulsive womanizer tries vainly to woo his beautiful new boss, who turns out to be smarter and more devious than he is. The lewd sex jokes and bawdy male bonding scenes are funny, but the camera and story get bogged down admiring Murphy's sexy predicament.
D: Reginald Hudlin. A: With Robin Givens, David Alan Grier, Martin Lawrence.

The Distinguished Gentleman
(1992) 112m. **C−**
A Southern con man uses his shady skills to get elected to Congress, figuring that he'll outsmart all those legitimate crooks in D.C. The plot is like *Beverly Hills Cop Goes to Washington*, with predictable satirical jokes.
D: Jonathan Lynn. A: With Lane Smith, Sheryl Lee Ralph, Grant Shaud.

(See also *Trading Places*, page 121.)

Performance Artists

Ignore the artsy sound of performance artist: These are some of America's best storytellers, who make their lives an entertaining adventure and transform themselves into the crazy, funny, and very recognizable characters who populate America's modern

Swimming to Cambodia
(1987) 87m. **B+**

Two maps, a pointer, and a desk are all the props in this monologue about Spalding Gray's adventures as a bit player in *The Killing Fields.* Urban New York life, sex, drugs, and happiness in Southeast Asia and the excesses of moviemaking are all grist for his deadpan, slightly bewildered mill.
D: Jonathan Demme. A: Spalding Gray.

Without You I'm Nothing
(1990) 89m. **B–**

Ms. Bernhard reviews (some of) her life and gleefully skewers the whole glam world from past and present Hollywood names to rock stars. Culminating in a striptease to Prince's "Little Red Corvette" this is a display of power, hostility, and humor that will make some laugh and have others scratching their heads.
D: John Boskovich. A: Sandra Bernhard.

Monster in a Box
(1991) 90m. **B**

Gray digresses on his afflictions, with humor and candor in this meditation of sorts on the problems of becoming possessed by a manuscript and not being able to enjoy a vacation. Setting includes a desk and a box with the stories roaming across the nation, but settling on New York and Los Angeles.
D: Nick Broomfield. A: Spalding Gray.

The Search for Signs of Intelligent Life in the Universe
(1991) 109m. **A**

This tour de force series of vignettes is loosely constructed around Trudy, a bag lady who is in touch with other forms of life. The joyful respect and humorous sympathy with which Tomlin treats her characters makes this whole far greater than its parts.
D: John Bailey. A: Lily Tomlin.

Sex, Drugs, Rock and Roll
(1991) 100m. **B+**

Ten characters appear before you in the form of one performer as Bogosian explores success and failure in the United States. Confrontational, rough, and full of street smarts and profanity, these sketches offer a provocative tapestry, with a couple of standout episodes.
D: John McNaughton. A: Eric Bogosian.

African-American Comedies

In many ways, these films are like the low-budget youth films of the 50s, with rock 'n' roll replaced by rap and the young players often digging their laughs out of a considerably tougher social well. Still, the tone remains light, with subjects ranging from parody/homages of Hollywood formulas to more down-home efforts.

Hangin' with the Homeboys
(1991) 88m. **B+**

A night in the life of four African-American and Hispanic friends in the Bronx is like an inner city *American Graffiti* with the guys looking for some action, during which they work out some of their own problems. This slice of life film rings true, helped by fine performances.
D: Joseph Vasquez. A: Doug E. Doug, Mario Joyner, John Leguizamo.

Class Act
(1992) 100m. **C–**

Rap duo Kid 'n Play switch identities to help each other in a new school. Pretty lame compared to the first two *House Party* films (see page 425), with the now standard rap battle between Kid 'n Play seeming tired.
D: Randall Miller. A: Kid 'n Play (Christopher Reid, Christopher Martin), Meshach Taylor.

Mo' Money
(1992) 91m. **C–**

Wayans recycles some of his character bits from *In Living Color* with a criminal subplot tacked on. Some cheap-laugh, racial, and sexual stereotyping drags this one down.
D: Peter MacDonald. A: Damon Wayans, Marlon Wayans, Stacy Dash.

CB4
(1993) 88m. **B**

A group of middle-class youths take on the persona of urban toughs to make it as rap stars. Some amusing jabs at the music business, with a funny turn by Elliott as the clueless whiter-than-white documentary filmmaker.
D: Tamra Davis. A: Chris Rock, Allen Payne, Chris Elliott.

Fear of a Black Hat
(1993) 86m. **B+**

A rap version of *This Is Spinal Tap* takes potshots at everything from thick-headed rappers, macho posturing, sexist videos, and the entire music biz in general. Scattershot approach hits more than misses, with a memorably hilarious parody of the artist formerly known as Prince.
D: Rusty Cundieff. A: Rusty Cundieff, Kasi Lemmons, Larry B. Scott.

Who's the Man?
(1993) 90m. **C–**

Two Harlem barbers masquerade as cops with predictably chaotic results. Destined to be a nostalgia piece that will be double billed with break-dancing films from the 80s.
D: Ted Demme. A: Ed Lover, Dr. Dre, Badja Djola.

Meteor Man
(1994) 99m. **C+**

A sweet ineffectual music teacher gets superhuman powers when struck by a meteor. This gains points about responsibility and cleaning up the neighborhood, but loses some when

the problem of violence is solved by more violence. So-so effects, but watch for the super voguing contest.
D: Robert Townsend, Eddie Griffith, Robert Guillaume.

(See also Rap Musicals, page 425.)

Generation X

A bunch of job-hunting, love-obsessed, cynical, gender-confused youths aren't exactly the stuff of great comedy, but they do make great subjects for these lurchingly stylish, sometimes low-rent, and always genial journeys through the romantic and social landscapes of Gen X-ers.

Slackers

(1991) 97m. **B**

Often hilarious examination of roving, cheerfully pointless "slacker" lifestyles achieves a narrative pinball effect as various oddballs lurking around an Austin university are introduced only to be quickly replaced by others: definitely not your usual youth film.
D: Richard Linklater. A: Richard Linklater.

Johnny Suede

(1992) 97m. **C+**

Johnny has attitude and 50s retro-style to spare as he navigates through the tricky romantic waters of a pesky ex-girlfriend and a new woman in his life. Self-consciously cute/bizarre tale of young love and personal style that's fun but awkwardly paced.
D: Tom DiCillo. A: Brad Pitt, Catherine Keener, Calvin Levels.

Singles

(1992) 99m. **B**

Episodic tale of youths, their lives, their loves, their grunge bands. Seattle becomes a sort of Gen-X heaven: A carefree neighborhood unencumbered by anything that will get in the way of the next romantic complication or band rehearsal, makes young adulthood resemble life in a dorm.
D: Cameron Crowe. A: Bridget Fonda, Campbell Scott, Kyra Sedgwick.

Dazed and Confused

(1993) 103m. **B+**

Enjoyable rambling semitale of various graduating high schoolers in the late 1970s who drink, smoke dope, razz the younger kids, and romance their way to graduation. Has a pleasant, knockabout but on-target feel as if the camera just happened to be recording these kids going through their rituals.
D: Richard Linklater. A: Jason London, Rory Cochrane, Sasha Jensen.

Three of Hearts

(1993) 105m. **B**

This New York romance, Gen X-style, finds a lesbian, a male escort, and a bisexual female ensnared in various humorous combinations. The charm of the film stems from the way the characters' alternate lifestyles are presented as no big deal, with a surprisingly funny assist from Baldwin as the goofily engaging escort.
D: Yurek Bogayevicz. A: William Baldwin, Kelly Lynch, Sherilyn Fenn.

Clerks

(1994) 92m. B&W. **B+**

A very funny day in the life of two bored-out-of-their-minds video- and convenience-store clerks. Slacker comedy gets points for some great dead-end characters, witty romantic situations, and refreshing bad attitude: This low-budget, unique take on junk-food culture shows what independent films are all about.
D: Kevin Smith. A: Kevin Smith, Brian O'Halloran, Jeff Anderson.

Floundering

(1994) 97m. **B+**

A young man searches for *anything* of value while living the worst day of his life: Unemployment checks get cut off, his brother escapes from detox, and his girlfriend is sleeping with everyone. Set against the LA riots, this is a funny, sometimes horrifying and truly unique look at modern alienation that builds to a surprising upbeat finale.
D: Peter McCarthy. A: James Le Gros, John Cusack, Ethan Hawke.

Naked in New York

(1994) 89m. **B+**

A successful playwright—in college—graduates and seems stuck in neutral as his girlfriend and best friend go boldly forth in the real world. With lots of star cameos and a great party scene where Stoltz tries to chat with William Styron, this is a Generation X *Pilgrim's Progress* with cool.
D: Dan Algrant. A: Eric Stoltz, Mary-Louise Parker, Ralph Macchio.

Reality Bites

(1994) 99m. **B**

A group of Gen X-ers—including an aspiring filmmaker, a handsome slacker, and a sexed-up Gap store manager—make the uneasy transition from school to what's left of the job market. A basically entertaining but frustrating film with real moments of wit and compassion mixed in with dull plot ploys.
D: Ben Stiller. A: Winona Ryder, Ben Stiller, Ethan Hawke.

Sleep with Me

(1994) 117m. **B**

The story of two best friends who vie for the affection of a doe-eyed girl, with much complication following. Basically a series of extended vignettes, this Gen X *Jules and Jim* is packed with a flock of West Coast weirdos and features Quentin Tarantino hyperactively expounding on the homoerotic subtext of *Top Gun*.
D: Rory Kelly. A: Eric Stoltz, Craig Sheffer, Meg Tilly.

The Stoned Age

(1994) 90m. **B–**

It's the 70s again as we follow two "hey, dude" kinda guys—one of them in a daze due to a mystical experience at a Blue Oyster Cult concert—and their relentless salmon-like search for babe-filled spawning grounds. Low-budget, fairly silly/offensive, and lots of fun.
D: James Melkonian. A: Michael Kopelow, China Kantner, Renee Griffen.

Threesome

(1994) 93m. **B+**

An attractive student ends up sharing a dorm with two handsome lads, leading to film's Girl meets Boy who wants (maybe) other Boy who wants Girl who wants Boy who doesn't want Girl (maybe). Appealing characters and believable dialogue make this college sexual-experimentation comedy refreshing and funny.
D: Andrew Fleming. A: Lara

Flynn Boyle, Stephen Baldwin.

With Honors
(1994) 101m. **C–**
Contrived tale of a homeless street professor who gloms onto a Harvard student's senior thesis and refuses to give it back unless remunerated. Formula plot soon plucks the heartstrings as the two get to know each other and wreak havoc on campus.
D: Alek Keshishian. A: Joe Pesci, Brendan Fraser, Moira Kelly.

Before Sunrise
(1995) 101m. **B+**
An American on a Eurailpass and a young Frenchwoman spend a stopover night in Vienna talking about themselves and walking around the city. A love story that feels like a comfortable stroll, never remaining in one spot or one character revelation too long as we see romance blossoming without any fireworks.
D: Richard Linklater. A: Ethan Hawke, Julie Delpy.

Families

These films are visually and stylistically on a par with *My Three Sons*, using Hollywood stars and nicer photography. Issues of women's place in the nonnuclear family, screwed-up kids, and wounded patriarchs are everywhere, along with a tone of subtle nostalgia for the Mom, Pop, and 2.5 kids grouping.

Betsy's Wedding
(1990) 94m. **B**
Father of the bride Alda navigates through a minefield of relatives, caterers, canopy renters, and even the Mob to ensure that Betsy gets the perfect wedding. A briskly paced, amiable jaunt made even better by the cast.
D: Alan Alda. A: Alan Alda, Molly Ringwald, Madeline Kahn.

Mermaids
(1990) 101m. **C+**
Winona suffers through Cher's eccentric personality along with the rest of a wacky family. Troubled production went through several directors, perhaps accounting for film's disjointed feel while performers surrounding a frenetic Cher are fairly amusing.
D: Richard Benjamin. A: Cher, Winona Ryder, Bob Hoskins.

Father of the Bride
(1991) 105m. **B–**
This remake of the Spencer Tracy classic has Martin becoming a nervous wreck as preparations are made for his daughter's wedding. Not up to the original in the charm department, but still some good packaged fun with Short a standout as the snooty wedding planner.
D: Charles Shyer. A: Steve Martin, Diane Keaton, Martin Short.

Folks
(1992) 107m. **C+**
Mom 'n Pop attempt to off themselves so as not to burden sonny and to let him have the insurance money. Hollywood-style black comedy's high point is the spectacle of Selleck losing his mind (and various body parts) each time his parents have another go at death.
D: Ted Kotcheff. A: Tom Selleck, Don Ameche, Anne Jackson.

This Is My Life
(1992) 94m. **B+**
Mom becomes a stand-up comic and a successful one at that, which should be wonderful for her daughters but isn't. Tartly funny dialogue (with some hilarious scenes between the sisters) and believable family relationships make this better than the average Hollywood fare.
D: Nora Ephron. A: Julie Kavner, Samantha Mathis, Dan Aykroyd.

My Father, the Hero
(1994) 90m. **B–**
How do you handle the mortification of vacationing at a tropical resort with your dad? Pass him off as an older lover is the answer that tries to induce laughs in this packaged comedy that is still saved by Depardieu's shaggy charm.
D. Steve Miner. A: Gerard Depardieu, Katherine Heigl, Dalton James.

Remakes

Qualitywise, this group of widescreen remakes of TV "classics" ranges from numbskulled efforts that treat their source material like holy writ, to the occasional film that puts a more imaginative spin on things, creating something both familiar and entertaining in a nonnostalgic way.

The Nude Bomb
(1984) 94m. **C–**
Agent Maxwell Smart returns to stop a mad KAOS agent from using a device capable of destroying all existing fabric, which would result in a world of unfettered nudity. A long-in-the-tooth Adams, the absence of original cast members, and an almost funny one-liner plot make this a triple mistake.
D: Clive Donner. A: Don Adams, Andrea Howard, Vittoria Gassman.

The Addams Family
(1991) 101m. **B–**
Uncle Fester, lost 25 years, returns to his gothic family: But is it him or an impostor? The daft dialogue, great effects, and Julia and Huston as the lovable necrophiliac pair almost make this a fun graveyard bash, but wandering direction and plot drag it down.
D: Barry Sonnenfeld. A: Raul Julia, Angelica Huston, Christopher Lloyd.

Boris and Natasha: The Movie
(1992) 88m. **D–**
The Pottsylvanian superagents from the 1960s *Rocky and Bullwinkle Show* are sent to America on an under-

cover mission. The cartoon characters aren't terrible, they're just filmed that way in this uninspired, miscast, and grimacingly lame caper.
D: Charles Martin Smith. A: Sally Kellerman, Dave Thomas, Paxton Whitehead.

Addams Family Values
(1993) 93m. **B+**
Morticia gives birth to a mustachioed son, Gomez hires a sexy nanny who's angling for Uncle Fester, and Wednesday and Pugsley go to summer camp. Even those to whom this sounds like code language will fall over themselves at this subversive volley at nuclear family verities.
D: Barry Sonnenfeld. A: Raul Julia, Angelica Huston, Christopher Lloyd.

The Beverly Hillbillies
(1993) 93m. **D+**
While hunting for some food, poor Jed finds some bubbling crude, becomes a millionaire, moves the family into a mansion, and please stop us if you've heard this before. Remake of 60s series redefines the word "unnecessary" and isn't anywhere in or near the ballpark of a funny film.
D: Penelope Spheeris. A: Jim Varney, Cloris Leachman, Lily Tomlin.

Coneheads
(1993) 87m. **C+**
Many people recall with fondness the *Saturday Night Live* sketch about the coneheaded aliens ("We're from . . . France!") who have a taste for six-packs, which they consume all at once. Avoid this homogenized misfire, and those memories will stay unsullied.
D: Steve Barron. A: Dan Aykroyd, Jane Curtin, Michelle Burke.

The Flintstones
(1994) 92m. **C–**
Looks like old Fred has hit the big time when he gets a big promotion actually intended for his generous buddy Barney. Not really a movie, just the most visible part of a merchandising campaign for Flintstones products: Very small children will enjoy the bright colors and computer-animated dinosaurs.
D: Briant Levant. A: John Goodman, Elizabeth Perkins, Rick Moranis.

The Little Rascals
(1994) 83m. **C–**
Another remake nobody was asking for. As Alfalfa woos a cute girl, a prize go-cart is stolen and a new kid on the block puts the moves on Darla. For the young-at-brain only.
D: Penelope Spheeris. A: Courtland Mead, Travis Tedford, Brittany Ashton Holmes.

The Brady Bunch Movie
(1995) 90m. **B+**
Nothing close to the experience of gut-wrenching horror the title implies, this has the shag-haired and bell-bottomed retro-family of all times juxtaposed against grungy modern LA, with frequently hilarious results. Forget the plot of the Bradys trying to save their homestead and enjoy the "real" world's reaction to the family members in this superior dumb comedy.
D: Betty Thomas. A: Shelley Long, Michael McKean, Gary Cole.

Kids Comedies

Right in step with the new baby boom and an era when adults are busy finding their "inner child," these comedies feature self-obsessed or just plain dumb adults constantly being usurped in every imaginable way by their children.

Honey, I Shrunk the Kids
(1989) 93m. **B**
A one-joke film—kids get shrunk by their father's invention and have to navigate through the backyard—works as both a comedy and adventure thanks to great special effects that turn a giant world of bees, lawn mowers, and plain old grass into a fascinating world of mystery and danger.
D: Joe Johnston. A: Rick Moranis, Matt Frewer, Marcia Strassman.

Uncle Buck
(1989) 100m. **B**
A happy-go-lucky, screw-up uncle house-sits with the kids and becomes their number-one headache, especially the precocious teen daughter and her boyfriend. Pretty funny, even with its predictably feel-good plot, but Candy's sheer likability powers this through to the end.
D: John Hughes. A: John Candy, Amy Madigan, Macaulay Culkin.

Home Alone
(1990) 110m. **B**
A member of a large family is left to his own devices when the folks inadvertently leave him behind for Christmas vacation. What starts out as everyboy's fantasy of unfettered freedom becomes a witty but almost disturbing Roadrunner cartoon made flesh when two inept burglars show up, resulting in all kinds of violent pratfalls.
D: Chris Columbus. A: Macaulay Culkin, Joe Pesci, Daniel Stern.

Problem Child
(1990) 85m. **D**
A yuppie couple tries to adopt a kid from an unscrupulous agency and ends up with a demonic little tornado who proceeds to crash cars, photograph a nun on a toilet, and have an escaped lunatic for a pen pal. A painfully ugly TV-sitcom mess that, amazingly, has a sequel.
D: Dennis Dugan. A: John Ritter, Michael Oliver, Jack Warden.

Curly Sue
(1991) 102m. **B**
A homeless, third-rate con man and his moppet waif co-conspirator dupe a lawyer, move into her apartment, cause cute trouble in general, and eventually form a sort of postnuclear family. Somewhat unsuccessful attempt to graft a 30s-style Shirley Temple heartwarmer onto 90s sensibilities.
D: John Hughes. A: James Belushi, Alisan Porter, Kelly Lynch.

Dutch
(1991) 108m. **C**
A snotty rich kid loathes his Mom's new blue-collar boyfriend until the two are forced to share some on-the-road adventures while driving home for the holidays. *Planes, Trains and Automobiles* this isn't, with a rhythm and plot that's equal parts manipulative and predictable.
D: Peter Faiman. A: Ed O'Neill, Ethan Randall, JoBeth Williams.

Hook

(1991) 144m. **C+**

Peter Pan grows up to become a greedy power-lawyer; then Captain Hook shows up to steal his kids and force Pete to face the magic back in Neverland. Very young kids may enjoy the effects and overdesigned mishmash of styles; others will cringe at this annoyingly cloying return-to-childhood fantasy.

D: Steven Spielberg. A: Dustin Hoffman, Robin Williams, Julia Roberts.

My Girl

(1991) 102m. **B–**

An 11-year-old, sometimes hypochondriac girl tries to deal with her mortician father, the memory of her deceased Mom, and a budding first romance. What may sound unnecessarily morose is actually a kindhearted film that trades on stars' appeal to deal with some weighty matters in a relatively mature way.

D: Howard Zieff. A: Dan Aykroyd, Anna Chlumsky, Macaulay Culkin.

Home Alone 2: Lost in New York

(1992) 120m. **C+**

Deja vu-filled retread of first film with a new locale, a higher budget, and extra dollops of violent cartoon cruelty as Culkin is now stuck alone in New York where he outwits the Plaza Hotel staff (credit card power!) and bad guys Pesci and Stern.

D: Chris Columbus. A: Macaulay Culkin, Joe Pesci, Daniel Stern.

Honey, I Blew Up the Kids

(1992) 89m. **B–**

Inverse sequel to *Honey, I Shrunk the Kids* has the same doddering inventor/Dad who now invents an enlarging ray that turns his baby into a giant toddler who's on his way to destroying Vegas. Some addle-brained fun, but the freshness is gone and all that's left is the special effects.

D: Joe Johnston. A: Rick Moranis, Daniel Shalikar, Marcia Strassman.

Mom and Dad Save the World

(1992) 88m. **C+**

The ego maniac Emperor of a tiny planet decides to destroy Earth, but stops long enough to kidnap an American family—in particular, a housewife he will make queen of his cut-rate kingdom. With talking rats, killer mushrooms, and purposefully bargain-basement kitsch design, this is a colorful but finally abrasive would-be sci-fi parody.

D: Greg Beeman. A: Teri Garr, Jeffrey Jones, Jon Lovitz.

Cop and a Half

(1993) 93m. **D**

A police-obsessed black kid witnesses a crime, blackmails the precinct boss into giving him time on the force, and ends up the partner of a kid-hating cop. Largely laughless, idiot confection blends *Dirty Harry* and John Hughes to create a cloying TV movie.

D: Henry Winkler. A: Burt Reynolds, Norman D. Golden II, Holland Taylor.

Dennis the Menace

(1993) 97m. **C+**

Mischief-churning Dennis can't seem to help playing all kinds of pranks on grumpy old neighbor Mr. Wilson and a crook who steals the old codger's rare coin collection. A push-button kiddie caper that reeks of *Home Alone,* with too much time spent establishing the Dennis/Mr. Wilson relationship before the plot finally kicks into action.

D: Nick Castle. A: Walter Matthau, Mason Gamble, Christopher Lloyd.

Mr. Nanny

(1993) 84m. **C**

An ex-wrestler becomes a bodyguard to a scientist working on a world-threatening whatsis while trying to manage his two megabrats. Broadly played comedy milks all it can out of the sight of mad-eyed ex-wrestler Hogan in domestic situations, but gets tedious when hijinks turn to end-of-the-world action picture silly.

D: Michael Gottlieb. A: Hulk Hogan, Sherman Hemsley, Robert Gorman.

The Sandlot

(1993) 101m. **B**

The new kid in a 60s small town joins the local baseball team, only to discover that any balls that go over the fence are the property of a monstrous dog known as "The Beast." Because of child's-view perspective and refreshing lack of precocious tykes, the simple plot is fun as kids come up with maneuvers to outwit The Beast and still get in a few innings.

D: David Evans. A: Tom Guiry, Mike Vitar, Patrick Renna.

Baby's Day Out

(1994) 99m. **C**

A slapstick-filled tale of a stray baby's encounters with a trio of bumbling crooks and a dangerous (for babies) world looks like an infantile *Home Alone.* Nothing terrible, just nothing new from the John Hughes factory.

D: Patrick Read Johnson. A: Joe Mantegna, Lara Flynn Boyle, Joe Pantoliano.

Getting Even with Dad

(199) 108m. **C**

Between ballgames and amusement park trips, an absurdly smart kid helps his ex-con Dad make one final heist to a befuddled mob's confusion. Cloying, Kids-as-superior-species film is a well-oiled bit of Hollywood machinery, but Culkin's smirky charm wears thin.

D: Howard Deutch. A: Macaulay Culkin, Ted Danson, Glenne Headly.

Monkey Trouble

(1994) 92m. **B**

A troubled young girl, saddled with a baby brother and allergic stepfather, gets a treasured pet monkey from a Venice street entertainer. Though it throws in an unnecessary mobster subplot for thrills, this is still fine family fare, with an uncannily human performance by Finister the monkey.

D: Franco Amurri. A: Harvey Keitel, Mimi Rogers, Thora Birch.

North

(1994) 87m. **C**

Big-budget story of a young boy who wins a court battle to separate from his self-absorbed parents, after which he starts a globe-trotting search for better ones. Some of the parent candidates are kitschy fun, but the film's tone is all over the map, going from fantasy to adult comedy without finding its own voice.

D: Rob Reiner. A: Elijah Wood, Julia Louis-Dreyfus, Bruce Willis.

Richie Rich

(1994) 95m. **B**

Richie is the wealthiest kid in the world and while he does enjoy things like his private roller coaster and James Bond-like lab, he longs to play ball and just be a kid. Surprisingly affable kids/adults comedy has a low quotient of brats and numbskulled adults, and none of Macaulay's trademark sadistic pranks.

D: Donald Petrie. A: Macaulay Culkin, Edward Herrmann.

Trading Mom

(1994) 83m. **C–**

After literally wishing their real Mom out of existence, a

trio of kids goes to the mysterious Mommy Market for a replacement. Poorly lit, low-budget film has a strangely inadequate performance by Spacek, and some unpleasant, Diane Arbus-like freakish imagery darkening this attempt at moralizing fantasy.
D: Tia Brelis. A: Sissy Spacek, Maureen Stapleton, Anna Chlumsky.

Male Buddies

Both movies and TV can't seem to get enough of the male buddy genre and its plot gimmicks. To throw two or more unlikely guys together is getting pretty strained as witnessed by this group of tales about a shrink and his patient, yuppies and a cowpoke, and a black writer and a white thug.

Taking Care of Business
(1990) 108m. **C+**

The life of an uptight executive takes a nosedive after he loses his appointment book while the fugitive con man who finds it has a fresh start by assuming the man's identity. The leads generate a few funny sparks in this *Trading Places* knockoff.
D: Arthur Hiller. A: Charles Grodin, James Belushi, Anne DeSalvo.

Three Men and a Little Lady
(1990) 100m. **C**

The young girl living with three womanizing bachelors goes abroad for her mother's wedding, followed by her guardians who want to stop the marriage. Closer to a sentimental melodrama with a few funny sexual innuendoes tacked on.
D: Emile Ardolino. A: Tom Selleck, Ted Danson, Steve Guttenberg.

City Slickers
(1991) 109m. **B**

The ranch vacation of three middle-aged New Yorkers is turned into a John Wayne adventure when they go on a cattle drive under the tutelage of a leathery cowpoke. The witty dialogue of the male bonding scenes and Crystal's jumpy good humor help balance out some rather heavy-handed developments.
D: Ron Underwood. A: Billy Crystal, Jack Palance, Bruno Kirby.

What About Bob?
(1991) 99m. **B–**

A childlike and demanding hypochondriac shows up at his psychiatrist's vacation house, endears himself to the family, and drives the pompous shrink crazy. The saccharine redemption subplot is predictable, though the slapstick and friction between Murray and Dreyfuss are occasionally funny.
D: Frank Oz. A: Bill Murray, Richard Dreyfuss, Julie Hagerty.

Captain Ron
(1992) 100m. **C–**

When a straightlaced businessman takes his family on a Caribbean sailing vacation aboard a newly inherited boat, the captain he hires turns out to be a laid-back, scuzzy dude with dubious connections. Dumb, harmless, and broadly played.
D: Thom Eberhardt. A: Kurt Russell, Martin Short, Mary Kay Place.

Amos and Andrew
(1993) 95m. **C–**

When a famous black writer moving into his expensive new home is mistaken for a burglar, the police cover their tracks by ordering a lowlife to take the author hostage. The stars make the best of a politically correct one-note joke.
D: E. Max Frye. A: Nicolas Cage, Samuel L. Jackson, Dabney Coleman.

City Slickers II: The Legend of Curly's Gold
(1994) 110m. **C+**

The three pals return to the West to find a lost treasure, belonging to their dead cattle-rancher friend, also sought by his twin brother. A contrived plot with less snap than the original.
D: Paul Weiland. A: Billy Crystal, Jon Lovitz, Jack Palance.

Hollywood

When Hollywood turns the camera on itself, the viewer is assured of darkly cynical looks at a sleazy ruthless world of excess and zaniness populated by twisted writers, amoral producers, and crazy actors.

S.O.B.
(1981) 121m. **A–**

A producer's big-budget film is box-office poison and, with a plague of Hollywood-types circling around, he tries to save his butt by redoing it as a porno flick. With its acerbic wit and relentless portrayal of nouveau riche Malibu, this takes a perfectly cynical potshot at all things slimy and Hollywood.
D: Blake Edwards. A: William Holden, Robert Preston, Julie Andrews.

Hollywood Shuffle
(1987) 82m. **B+**

A frustrated hot dog seller/actor auditions for every role available to blacks—pimps, drug dealers, and Eddie Murphy clones—and fantasizes a series of vignettes satirizing everything from war to private eye movies from a black POV. Entertaining and often hilarious indie satire suggests that with some films, small really is better.
D: Robert Townsend. A: Robert Townsend, Anne-Marie Johnson, Starletta Dupois.

The Big Picture
(1989) 100m. **B**

A film school's prize graduate thinks he's about to hit the big time when he receives job offers and numerous chances to sell out. Funny and sometimes hilarious look at cinematic pretense and overindulgence, Hollywood parties, pitching sessions, and other horrors,

with an especially funny Martin Short as a prissy agent.
D: Christopher Guest. A: Kevin Bacon, Jennifer Jason Leigh, Michael McKean.

Postcards from the Edge
(1990) 101m. **A–**
Witty and energetic character study of a barely-on-the-road-to-recovery actress as she pinballs from one weird encounter to another, including her alcoholic star-mom and a seductive cattle rancher. Deftly satiric look at what it takes to get your act together in the illusion and opportunism capital of the world.
D: Mike Nichols. A: Meryl Streep, Shirley MacLaine, Dennis Quaid.

Barton Fink
(1991) 112m. **B**
A New York playwright in 1940s Hollywood is assigned to script a ludicrous boxing film, and hits a mindbending case of writer's block. Visually inspired meditation on the creative process is filled with surreal imagery and a great turn by Goodman as a blustery salesman (or something worse), but is hampered by a seriously obscure second half.
D: Joel Coen. A: John Turturro, John Goodman, Judy Davis.

Mistress
(1992) 112m. **B–**
An aspiring filmmaker determined not to compromise his vision finds himself tailoring his script for the various backers who want their paramours in the film. Outside of some funny moments, this self-involved satire of one reason why films are so bad will appeal mostly to insider movie fanatics.
D: Barry Primus. A: Danny Aiello, Robert De Niro, Martin Landau.

The Player
(1992) 134m. **A–**
The competition and backstabbing in Hollywood is (literally) murderous in this tale of a studio exec who may be on his way out and is also being stalked by an unseen writer. A sprawling, nastily funny Dream Factory tour of every Hollywood type with cameos by a cornucopia of stars.
D: Robert Altman. A: Tim Robbins, Greta Scacchi, Fred Ward.

. . . And God Spoke
(1994) 82m. **C**
Fledgling filmmakers take on a rather weighty project—filming the Bible. Done in "mockumentary" style of *Spinal Tap,* this has some scattered jabs at the filmmaking process and Hollywood honchos, but main appeal will lie with nascent filmmakers and their ilk.
D: Arthur Borman. A: Michael Riley, Stephen Rappaport, Soupy Sales.

I'll Do Anything
(1994) 116m. **B+**
A 40ish struggling actor who's suddenly saddled with his charming and monstrous young daughter is the center of this story that follows agents, producers, and audience testers in their drive for success. Originally a musical, even minus the songs and the tacked-on happy ending this subversively funny and wildly original misfire remains weirdly entertaining.
D: James L. Brooks. A: Nick Nolte, Albert Brooks, Julie Kavner.

Sports

Like baseball, the following feel-good sports films are generally laid-back, undemanding, and genial takes on butt-slapping buddy films, even when the buddies are female. Whichever sport is played, you can count on the filmmakers to slip in a little uplifting message about race relations, social issues, or women's rights in between innings and during the after-game hijinks.

Wildcats
(1986) 107m. **C**
A gym teacher in a rough inner-city school takes on the job of coaching the surly, sad-sack football team with heartwarming results. Competent, predictable, and inoffensive film is natural cable fare.
D: Michael Ritchie. A: Goldie Hawn, Swoosie Kurtz, Robyn Lively.

Bull Durham
(1988) 108m. **B+**
The tale of a seasoned minor league coach with his glory days seemingly behind him, a young pitcher with the raw right stuff, and a baseball "groupie" who picks out a player each year and seasons in her own way. This captures the carnival feel of small-time baseball, with amusing locker room banter, hilarious games, and a shining Sarandon.
D: Ron Shelton. A: Kevin Costner, Susan Sarandon, Tim Robbins.

Major League
(1989) 107m. **B**
In order to hasten a lucrative offer to get her team moved to a better venue, an owner hires a ragtag roster of hasbeens and lunatics to assure the season's losing streak. Low-rent, stupid, unbelievable flat-looking, and pretty funny.
D: David S. Ward. A: Tom Berenger, Charlie Sheen, Corbin Bernsen.

Necessary Roughness
(1991) 108m. **C+**
An underdog college football team (led by a 34-year-old quarterback and a curvaceous placekicker) is soon the doormat of its division and in need of a miracle. Rowdy tale that doesn't stray from the connect-the-dots formula still provides a few laughs.
D: Stan Dragoti. A: Scott Bakula, Robert Loggia, Hector Elizondo.

Diggstown
(1992) 97m. **B**
Ex-con hustler Woods arrives in a seedy Southern town, sweet talks an ex-boxer back into the ring, and stages a marathon series of boxing bouts. Rowdy and uneven comedy/drama has a nicely sordid look and an even more hyper than usual Wood, with Gossett on hand to lend some dignity to the proceedings.
D: Michael Ritchie. A: James Woods; Louis Gossett, Jr.; Bruce Dern.

A League of Their Own
(1992) 128m. **B**
Women took over for their men fighting in World War II, and baseball soon had an All-American Girls' Team. Lighthearted fare with the brashness of a Bronx cheer and the subtlety of peanuts and a hot dog.

D: Penny Marshall. A: Tom Hanks, Geena Davis, Madonna.

The Mighty Ducks
(1992) 100m. **B−**
An obnoxious lawyer is forced into community service coaching a dreadful pee-wee hockey team. He turns over a new leaf and the team actually starts winning, all leading to the big showdown with the hated Hawks in this predictable but amiable family comedy.
D: Stephen Herek. A: Emilio Estevez, Joss Ackland, Lane Smith.

Mr. Baseball
(1992) 108m. **B**
A baseball/culture clash comedy about a womanizing player who's traded to a Japanese team where he meets a demanding coach, falls in love with a local yuppie, and slowly learns to lose his loutish ways. A well-observed comic performance by Selleck and exotic Japanese locations help mitigate formulaic plot.
D: Fred Schepisi. A: Tom Selleck, Ken Takakura, Aya Takanashi.

White Men Can't Jump
(1992) 114m. **A−**
Constantly amusing tale of a lanky white guy entering into the subculture of Southern California free-court basketball hustling. Easygoing, knock-about air makes even a robbery seem like no big deal. Features fun performances by male leads, who are almost upstaged by *Jeopardy*-obsessed girlfriend Perez.
D: Ron Shelton. A: Wesley Snipes, Woody Harrelson, Rosie Perez.

The Air up There
(1993) 108m. **C+**
Scouting for players in Africa, Bacon finds his dream shooter, but the natives will only let the tall guy go if Bacon agrees to a very unlikely bet. What could have been vaguely racist is merely dopey and good-natured thanks to agreeable performances, beyond belief story, and general goofy air.
D: Paul Michael Glaser. A: Kevin Bacon, Charles Gitonga Maina, Yolanda Vazquez.

Angels in the Outfield
(1994) 103m. **B−**
In answer to a foster-home boy's prayers, an angel and his winged helpers shape up a last-place ball team of multicultural lugheads and washouts named the Angels. Harmlessly pleasant heart-tugger is highlighted by Lloyd's usual manic presence.
D: William Dear. A: Danny Glover, Joseph Gordon-Levitt, Christopher Lloyd.

Cool Runnings
(1993) 97m. **B−**
An accident eliminates three sprinters from the Jamaican Olympics track team, so one of them decides to form the country's first bobsled team. Training for a snow sport on a tropical island affords some humor in this buoyant film before this takes the *Rocky* little guy route.
D: Jon Turteltaub. A: Leon, Doug E. Doug, John Candy.

D2: The Mighty Ducks
(1994) 107m. **C+**
Success goes to the coach's head when his kiddy hockey team makes it to the Junior Goodwill games. The feisty players are ready to mutiny, and Estevez has to learn sportsmanship all over again in this preachy but generally satisfying reprise of the first Ducks.
D: Sam Weisman. A: Emilio Estevez, Kathryn Erbe, Michael Tucker.

Little Big League
(1994) 120m. **B−**
A 12-year-old inherits an overpaid uninspired Minnesota Twins baseball club and tries to instill the key ingredient he thinks is missing: fun. The kid locks horns with the team's prima donnas and the rest of the disbelieving American League in this overlong but easy to swallow fantasy.
D: Andrew Scheinman. A: Luke Edwards; Jason Robards, Jr.; Kevin Dunn.

Little Giants
(1994) 106m. **C+**
When his daughter gets cut from the little league team (by her own football hero uncle no less), a man starts his own pee-wee football club. Guts and determination make them go from laughingstock to serious rival in this gridiron take on *The Bad News Bears*.
D: Duwayne Dunham. A: Rick Moranis, Ed O'Neill, John Madden.

Major League II
(1994) 104m. **C−**
Has success spoiled the long-suffering Cleveland Indians? Apparently so, given the collection of kooks and veterans struggling mightily to defend their crown in this tired rehash of the original.
D: David S. Ward. A: Charlie Sheen, Tom Berenger, Corbin Bernsen.

Rookie of the Year
(1993) 103m. **B−**
After his broken arm has healed, a 12-year-old baseball player is able to pitch a blazing fast ball and gets recruited by the major leagues. Baseball fans will go for the throwback air of innocence despite the coyness of this stand-up-and-cheer fantasy.
D: Daniel Stern. A: Thomas Ian Nicholas, Gary Busey, Albert Hall.

Screwball and Crime Capers

Here are some modern takes on the 30s screwball comedies and crime caper films that take a simple premise (a couple wants a baby in *Raising Arizona*) and then go nuts with possibilities (the couple steals a baby and gets chased by bikers, escaped cons, and a rich store owner). All offer high energy, even manic adventures and romance as name stars fall into a mountingly wacky world where being reasonable is the last thing on anyone's mind.

Foul Play
(1978) 116m. **B+**
Lively comedy casts Hawn as a gal inadvertently involved in a plot to off the Pope, and Chase as her detective helper, seducer, and klutz. Bright caper has snappy pace, hilarious action sequences in San Francisco, and funny turn by Moore as a distraught orchestra conductor.
D: Colin Higgins. A: Chevy Chase, Goldie Hawn, Dudley Moore.

Seems Like Old Times
(1980) 101m. **B+**
Chevy is in hot water with the law and seeks refuge with his attorney ex-wife

who's also married to the DA. Hawn and Chase make cute partners-in-crime in this genial romp through classic romantic screwball territory that features some hilarious chases through the San Francisco locales.
D: Jay Sandrich. A: Chevy Chase, Goldie Hawn, Charles Grodin.

Something Wild
(1986) 113m. **A**

Average yuppie meets provocative downtown girl, and what starts as a midday tryst turns into a long drive through the troubled girl's life, with an ex-boyfriend pulling up the rear. A ridiculously energetic film goes from sexy screwball comedy to road picture to near-horror, somehow managing to pull it all together with the help of standout performances.
D: Jonathan Demme. A: Melanie Griffith, Jeff Daniels, Ray Liotta.

Blind Date
(1987) 93m. **B–**

Yuppie Willis takes out a ravishing Southern belle only to discover that when administered even tiny amounts of alcohol she becomes a manic sex fiend. Kitchen-sink approach to screwball comedy and lightning pace do a good job at disguising the paucity of original ideas.
D: Blake Edwards. A: Bruce Willis, Kim Basinger, John Larroquette.

Raising Arizona
(1987) 92m. **B+**

An ex-con and his cop wife can't conceive or adopt, so they decide to liberate a child from a local moneyman with a surplus of toddlers. Lunacy becomes a near-fine art as the film unfolds with careening camerawork hurtling the viewer through desert town environs, a biker from hell, lots of baby-endangerment jokes, and a general why-the-hell-not attitude.
D: Joel Coen. A: Nicolas Cage, Holly Hunter, John Goodman.

Who's That Girl
(1987) 94m. **D+**

Madonna's a sprung con making a lawyer's life miserable in this light (as in headed) romp that has lots of sunny Manhattan shooting, Boy Toy whining, flesh-baring outfits, and a large tiger, but that loses out on both charm and laughs.
D: James Foley. A: Madonna, Griffin Dunne, Haviland Morris.

Switching Channels
(1988) 105m. **C**

A media-event crime throws a bickering couple of journalists back into the TV newsroom one more time. Mildly entertaining umpteenth remake of *The Front Page* has its share of titters (thanks mainly to an always game Turner), but otherwise just more Hollywood recycling.
D: Ted Kotcheff. A: Kathleen Turner, Burt Reynolds, Christopher Reeve.

Cadillac Man
(1990) 97m. **B–**

A Cadillac salesman has a total meltdown day: The ex wants back alimony, his bookies are barking for 20 grand, and his girlfriend's husband ends up kidnapping him. Fast-forward storytelling, mounting madness, and a controlled-boil performance by Williams make this a fun plummet into cheesy Americana.
D: Roger Donaldson. A: Robin Williams, Tim Robbins, Pamela Reed.

The Freshman
(1990) 102m. **B**

A mobster employs an NYU film student as a courier, with the unlikely task of delivering a rare lizard for some big money. Intentionally silly plot gives Brando a chance to hilariously send up his own Godfather role while the rest of film is liberally spiced with numerous film-nerd jokes and frenetic plot twists.
D: Andrew Bergman. A: Matthew Broderick, Penelope Ann Miller, Marlon Brando.

Quick Change
(1990) 88m. **A–**

Desperate to exit the Manhattan rat race, a couple and a dim-witted brother stage a daring robbery only to find the obstacle of navigating through the city to the airport more insurmountable than any mere felony. Hilarious, good-natured, and dead-on accurate portrait of New York and its native tribes, with a sweet and hysterical Quaid nearly upstaging everyone.
D: Bill Murray, Howard Franklin. A: Bill Murray, Geena Davis, Randy Quaid.

Sibling Rivalry
(1990) 88m. **C+**

A neglected wife has a one-night stand who promptly dies on her, so she enlists the aid of a salesman who thinks he may have killed the guy. Some nice bits of black comedy pepper this caper but miscasting, too many plot twists, and overly nasty characters leach it of comic verve.
D: Carl Reiner. A: Kirstie Alley, Bill Pullman, Carrie Fisher.

The Favor, the Watch and the Very Big Fish
(1991) 89m. **B–**

Almost as frenetic as its title is long, this is the tall tale of a meek biblical photographer searching for the perfect Jesus. Unfortunately the ex-con who strikes him as the one also happens to be the long-lost lover of his girlfriend. Giddy, self-consciously weird, but sometimes funny and definitely not for all palates.
D: Ben Lewin. A: Bob Hoskins, Natasha Richardson, Jeff Goldblum.

The Marrying Man
(1991) 115m. **C**

A shotgun wedding between a playboy and a Las Vegas lounge singer is soon annulled but true love or lust keeps them coming back for more. A bland nod to classic comedies, this seems longer and even more tiresome thanks to the duo's failed attempts at being cute, breezy, and sexy.
D: Jerry Rees. A: Kim Basinger, Alec Baldwin, Robert Loggia.

Brain Donors
(1992) 92m. **C+**

A game and occasionally uproarious attempt at a Marx Brothers film with more than a nod to *A Night at the Opera*. While much of the slapstick falls flat, when Turturro is onscreen as the conniving leering lawyer Roland T. Flakfizer, the film glides along in Groucho-like giddy wordplay.
D: Dennis Dugan. A: John Turturro, Mel Smith, Bob Nelson.

The Gun in Betty Lou's Handbag
(1992) 89m. **B–**

Upon finding a gun used in a killing, a librarian goes through a personality makeover as she dolls up to track down the killer. Film teeters between shaggy screwball comedy and more darkly violent aspects with admirable deftness while Miller surprises with some true comic flair in this oddball Gen X caper.
D: Allan Moyle. A: Penelope Ann Miller, Eric Thal, Alfre Woodard.

Honeymoon in Vegas
(1992) 95m. **B+**

A marriage-shy private eye finally decides to tie the knot with his girl in Vegas and then has to hand her over for a date with a gangster to pay

a gambling debt. Mostly hilarious hijinks—including the parachuting Elvis impersonators—with Cage as the hang-dog, almost groom and Caan as the romantic/menacing gambler.
D: Andrew Bergman. A: Nicolas Cage, James Caan, Sarah Jessica Parker.

Once Upon a Crime
(1992) 94m. **C–**
An American couple in Monte Carlo does a good deed, ends up finding a corpse, and quickly becomes the prime suspects. What should have been a light 60s-style comedy becomes shrill and full of pratfalls, mugging, and other desperate things actors and directors do when they know the film is a stiff.
D: Eugene Levy. A: John Candy, James Belushi, Cybill Shepherd.

Undercover Blues
(1993) 89m. **C+**
Quirky tale of two top-secret agents who marry, have a kid, and then end up combing New Orleans, with tot in tow, to find an elusive Czech arms embezzler. While not high on the believability scale, this gains points for the leads' nonchalant attitude toward the pixilated plot and a hilarious turn by Tucci as a hapless would-be killer.
D: Herbert Ross. A: Kathleen Turner, Dennis Quaid, Stanley Tucci.

I Love Trouble
(1994) 123m. **C+**
A star columnist and the new (female) reporter on a competing paper lock horns and try to outscoop each other on a murder case, even as each begins to notice how adorable the other is. With attractive stars and screwball newspaper antics, this should be a light entertainment shoo-in, but ends up a bewildering mishmash.
D: Charles Shyer. A: Julia Roberts, Nick Nolte, Saul Rubineck.

Radioland Murders
(1994) 108m.
B+
A series of murders threatens the frenetic efforts of a radio station to go network in the 1930s. Crazed chorus girls, blundering cops, squabbling writers all seem to be careening out of control while the show must go on, in this colorful, breakneck-paced bit of nostalgic comedy/whodunit.
D: Mel Smith. A: Mary Stuart Masterson, Brian Benben, Ned Beatty.

The Ref
(1994) 93m. **B**
On Christmas Eve, a burglar takes a wealthy couple hostage in their Connecticut home, is driven up the wall by their bickering, and is soon mediating their differences. A smart and often diabolically funny comedy that never quite engages despite the acidly sharp performances.
D: Ted Demme. A: Judy Davis, Dennis Leary, Kevin Spacey.

Oddballs and Little People

These smallish offbeat films take the viewer into the lives and worlds of phobic lovers, clowns, schlock-film impresarios, and other characters who often live on the fringes of the American landscape.

In the Spirit
(1990) 95m. **B**
Thanks to the work of a New Age interior decorator, a New York couple is forced to live temporarily with the cosmic-headed woman, and things get really complicated when murder is committed. A weak murder mystery that's hohum-looking, but Thomas makes a great comic New Age ninny.
D: Sandra Seacat. A: Marlo Thomas, Peter Falk, Jeannie Berlin.

Little Vegas
(1990) 91m. **C+**
Son of a mobster leaves the criminal fold, moves to a Nevada trailer park, and encounters a variety of oddballs, 12 steppers, and con men interested in turning the land of a dead woman (with whom he had an affair) into a "Little Vegas." Effective slice of 90s Americana drags the viewer through the dust of its good intentions.
D: Perry Lang. A: Anthony Denison, Catherine O'Hara, Michael Nouri.

Rosalie Goes Shopping
(1990) 96m. **B**
A hefty German émigré juggles 37 credit cards and other forms of fake money to keep her family in good supply of all that's material in the American Dream. Enjoyably offbeat tale, filmed in Little Rock, Arkansas, offers visions of Sägebrecht glazed over in a consumer high.
D: Percy Adlon. A: Marianne Sägebrecht, Brad Davis, Judge Reinhold.

Ted and Venus
(1990) 100m. **B–**
Overly endearing quirky tale of a 60s Venice Beach loser who falls for the local surf goddess. He writes verse that she finds repugnant while various SCTV and sitcom stars play LA oddballs giving advice on how to woo her. A mite too precious even with the sunny look and tone.
D: Bud Cort. A: Bud Cort, Carol Kane, James Brolin.

Arizona Dream
(1991) 119m. **A–**
A young man goes out west to join his Cadillac-salesman uncle and instead falls in love with a crazy middle-aged woman and her suicidal daughter. Eschewing realism, this offers a slew of visual symbols, sometimes hilarious interplay between the touched characters, kitchy/baroque set design, and poignant insights.
D: Emir Kusturica. A: Johnny Depp, Faye Dunaway, Jerry Lewis.

Shakes the Clown
(1991) 88m. **A–**
A for-hire clown (the crying on the inside sort) slowly goes down the tube via the bottle. Utterly unique drama/comedy shows the hilariously seamy underbelly of pro clowning as a sort of grease-paint, red-nose underworld. An added attraction is *The Brady Bunch*'s Florence Henderson cameo as a boozy slattern.
D: Bob Goldthwait. A: Bob Goldthwait, Julie Brown, Paul Dooley.

Lunatics: A Love Story
(1992) 87m. **B–**
An agoraphobic young man who wraps himself and his apartment in tin foil and has visions of giant spiders meets a phobic blonde and becomes the hero of their shared nightmares. Extremely odd, often surreal,

and sometimes heartbreaking tale of love amongst the mentally rattled.
D: Josh Becker. A: Theodore Raimi, Deborah Foreman, Bruce Campbell.

Used People
(1992) 116m. **A**
At the funeral of her husband, a grieving older Jewish woman meets a rakish Italian man and starts a delightful courtship. Packed with engaging realistically dysfunctional characters, a sparkling script, and a wonderfully humane tone that blends tragedy, humor, and pathos seamlessly.
D: Beeban Kidron. A: Shirley MacLaine, Marcello Mastroianni, Jessica Tandy.

Benny & Joon
(1993) 98m. **B+**
An older brother is first relieved by the friendship between his mentally disturbed sister and a strange, Charlie Chaplin-idolizing house guest and then dismayed when it turns romantic. A sweet humorous "little people" tale in which mental illness is treated almost as an adorable quirkiness.
D: Jeremiah Chechik. A: Johnny Depp, Mary Stuart Masterson, Aidan Quinn.

Matinee
(1993) 97m. **B+**
In early 60s Key West, a teenage boy copes with the absence of his naval officer dad, the mysteries of girls, the Cuban Missile Crisis, and the unveiling of a film schlockmeister's latest buggy masterpiece *Mant* at the local theater. A genuinely sweet nostalgic tale of 60s innocence with hilarious spoofs on cheesy horror films.
D: Joe Dante. A: John Goodman, Cathy Moriarty, Simon Fenton.

Wilder Napalm
(1993) 109m. **C**
Two brothers, one an ambitious carny, the other a small-town fireman, both able to telekinetically start fires, yearn for the same woman. Characters' going-for-broke antics and fun carnivallike air are sabotaged by self-consciously perverse, scatterbrained script.
D: Glenn Gordon Caron. A: Dennis Quaid, Debra Winger, Arliss Howard.

Even Cowgirls Get the Blues
(1994) 96m. **C–**
With its everyone-who's-camp/cool cast, this tells the smirky tale of the girl with very large thumbs who winds up at a health spa where the lesbian staff stages a revolution. Some hilarious moments and beautiful images can't compensate for the too-hip attitude and sprawling mess of a story.
D: Gus Van Sant, Jr. A: Uma Thurman, Lorraine Bracco, Angie Dickinson.

Populist Fantasies

Take one poor schnook, add a rotten situation either by design or fate, mix in some fantastic elements—clairvoyance, magic, or just wishes come true—along with a feel-good ending, and you've got these very modern heirs to Frank Capra.

Joe Versus the Volcano
(1990) 102m. **B**
A wretched man locked into a soul-destroying job is told he has six months to live and, thanks to an eccentric millionaire, gets to live the high life before sacrificing himself on a tropical island. This is like two films: The first is hilarious and Kafkaesque, then goofily ecstatic. The latter, island set one is like a Hope–Crosby romp without the laughs.
D: John Patrick Shanley. A: Tom Hanks, Meg Ryan, Lloyd Bridges.

Mr. Destiny
(1990) 110m. **C+**
After confiding his troubles to a bartender, a freshly fired junior exec is granted one wish, undoing a critical moment of his past, which changes everything. Using *It's a Wonderful Life*'s gimmick, this goes on to be a predictable aw-shuckser as Belushi does the right thing over and over.
D: James Orr. A: James Belushi, Linda Hamilton, Michael Caine.

Tune in Tomorrow
(1990) 102m. **B+**
A cagey writer of radio dramas blows into New Orleans, teaches a young writer about reality impacting with art and how to seduce Aunt Julia, and then uses the exploits in his now wildly popular radio soap. A hilarious, slyly surreal, and sweet-tempered romantic comedy.
D: Jon Amiel. A: Barbara Hershey, Keanu Reeves, Peter Falk.

The Butcher's Wife
(1991) 105m. **B–**
A Greenwich Village butcher returns from a trip to North Carolina with a clairvoyant wife who plays matchmaker and all-around earth angel with everyone she meets. Despite occasional saccharine overload, this ends up as a disarming, if convoluted, romantic fantasy.
D: Terry Hughes. A: Demi Moore, Jeff Daniels, George Dzundza.

Defending Your Life
(1991) 112m. **A–**
Consistently amusing tale of a deceased professional who finds himself in a sort of shopping mall/theme park version of purgatory where his life is on trial to determine where his soul will go. Brooks' most sustained comic vision, with a light tone that never falls into whimsy and a wonderfully warm Streep as his after-life lover.
D: Albert Brooks. A: Albert Brooks, Meryl Streep, Rip Torn.

Dave
(1993) 105m. **B+**
When the president falls into a coma, a good-hearted dead ringer is recruited to be his stand-in. Kline shines as the good guy who, via common sense and a good heart, makes government work while Langella as the villainous chief-of-staff gives this satiric fable some bite.
D: Ivan Reitman. A: Kevin Kline, Sigourney Weaver, Frank Langella.

Groundhog Day
(1993) 103m. **A–**
While covering a Groundhog Day festival in a small town, a curmudgeonly reporter finds himself caught in some infernal time loop, with the same stupid day and events repeating ad infinitum. Low-key sleeper is both funny and sweet, offering great sight gags, uncloying romantic interludes, and perfectly pitched snottiness from Murray.
D: Harold Ramis. A: Bill Murray, Andie MacDowell, Chris Elliot.

Hero
(1993) 112m. **C**
A small-time hood saves the passengers on a downed airplane and a TV reporter tags the wrong man, but someone eminently more suitable, as the hero. No matter how much talent is assembled a film sometimes just doesn't work, which happened here, with bad timing, off-key performances, and drifty direction.
D: Stephen Frears. A: Dustin Hoffman, Geena Davis, Andy Garcia.

Money for Nothing
(1993) 90m. **B–**
An unemployed, decent-guy dockworker finds a bag with $1.2 million, in this small film that's reminiscent of 40s comedies. Offers warm-hearted laughs with Cusack making a good Capra-esque hero who finds ways to distribute the money that's making his life a mess.
D: Ramon Menendez. A: John Cusack, Debi Mazar, Michael Madsen.

Being Human
(1994) 122m. **D**
A caveman, a Roman slave, a medieval nomad, a Portuguese nobleman, and a modern divorced father all have one thing in common: They are distinctly, infallibly human. Williams plays the five kindred souls with lifelessness in this awkward fable that reaches remarkable heights of self-pity and absurdity.
D: Bill Forsyth. A: Robin Williams, John Turturro, Anna Galiena.

The Hudsucker Proxy
(1994) 112m. **B–**
A CEO elevates a mailroom schnook to executive status, hoping this will drive company stock down so he can make a killing on the market. A visual wonder with astonishing hyper-real cityscapes and rapturous mix of 30s and 50s designs, but the story of a goofy visionary gets lost in the glitter and cold tone.
D: Joel Coen. A: Tim Robbins, Jennifer Jason Leigh, Paul Newman.

It Could Happen to You
(1994) 101m. **B–**
A feel-good fantasy and romance about a good-guy cop, his materialistic wife, a waitress, and a lottery ticket that throws their lives into turmoil. Outside of the slightly nerve-grating role of the wife, this is a warm-hearted genial but oddly unsatisfying film.
D: Andrew Bergman. A: Nicolas Cage, Bridget Fonda, Rosie Perez.

Woody Allen

Woody continues to pay homage to directors—whether Godard or Hitchcock—and genres—from backstage comedy to murder mystery—in these ironic tales of New York at its most glamorous and New Yorkers at their most angst-ridden.

Alice
(1990) 106m. **B+**
Some magic realism enters the life of one of New York's "ladies who lunch" when she is given strange herbs by a Chinatown acupuncturist, which endow her with sexual aggressiveness, a jazz vocabulary, and the power of invisibility. An elegant, almost precious mix of sophistication and whimsy.
D: Woody Allen. A: Mia Farrow, William Hurt, Joe Mantegna.

Husbands and Wives
(1992) 108m. **C+**
A long-married couple fret over friends' disintegrating marriage, even as the moralizing husband pursues a student. Feels like warmed-over *Manhattan* with the Woody and Mia miasma as the subtext, and a distracting attempt at a documentary feel with mock interviews and headache-inducing, handheld camera.
D: Woody Allen. A: Woody Allen, Mia Farrow, Juliette Lewis.

Shadows and Fog
(1992) 86m. B&W. **C**
A strangler is on the loose in a 1920s European peasant village, and an anxiety-ridden nebbish goes from vigilante to suspect in this meandering and visually murky tale of paranoia. There are enough star cameos to choke a Robert Altman film, but never have so many contributed so little.
D: Woody Allen. A: Woody Allen, Kathy Bates, Mia Farrow.

Manhattan Murder Mystery
(1993) 107m. **B–**
A Manhattan couple investigates the death of a next-door neighbor, whom they suspect has been murdered by her seemingly benign husband. Allen and Keaton fall into a comfortable familiar pattern in this *Rear Window* homage, but the laughs are few, the plot meandering, and the suspense nil.
D: Woody Allen. A: Woody Allen, Diane Keaton, Anjelica Huston.

Bullets Over Broadway
(1994) 95m. **A–**
A backer/gangster's girlfriend is foisted on the Broadway production of a young playwright until her thuggish chaperone decides she's ruining the play. The transformation of the ruthless hood to ruthless artist is Allen at his most devious in this throwback to old Woody and old Broadway.
D: Woody Allen. A: John Cusack, Dianne Wiest, Jennifer Tilly.

New Comics

Comedians from TV shows make the leap from sitcom to the movies in these star-vehicles-with-training-wheels that offer lots of media in-jokes, sight gags, a smirky know-it-all attitude, and, of course, the comedian's schtick that endeared him to audiences in the first place.

So I Married an Axe Murderer
(1993) 94m. **C+**
Good title is pinned to a so-so but genial comedy about a nebbish who falls for a female butcher's assistant. Pretty barren laugh-wise, except for Myers' loopy Scottish family (one of whom is hilariously played by Myers).
D: Thomas Schlamme. A: Mike Myers, Nancy Travis, Anthony LaPaglia.

Son in Law
(1993) 96m. **D+**
Obnoxious and ever obsequious sub-Bill & Ted Valley-dude Shore visits his Midwest, farm-family girlfriend, and soon the local rubes fall under his de-evolutionary spell. Anyone who is amused by this retro-*Green Acres* dumb-fest will be required to trade in all AC/DC records and seek immediate help.
D: Steve Rash. A: Pauly Shore, Carla Gugino, Lane Smith.

Ace Ventura: Pet Detective
(1994) 85m. **C+**
A gumshoe specializing in pet cases must locate the Miami Dolphins' mascot before the Superbowl. Ex-TV laugh-shill Carrey, current proponent of everything-is-funny-if-you-do-it-loud-and-fast, steps into the twitchy shoes of Jerry Lewis in this overbearing comedy.
D: Tom Shadyac. A: Jim Carrey, Sean Young, Courtney Cox.

Blankman
(1994) 96m. **C**
Urban inventor/handyman fed up with social ills dons tights and becomes a self-styled superhero. Relatively comic idea is stillborn, with laughs quickly subsiding after first half hour as plot basically flies around in circles.
D: Mike Binder. A: Damon Wayans, David Alan Grier, Robin Givens.

In the Army Now
(1994) 92m. **D+**
Expecting a post-Cold War easy time, Shore and a doltish pal join the service in this sub-*Stripes* formula film where Shore plays his one comic note—confusion and disdain for all life forms besides himself.
D: Daniel Petrie, Jr. A: Pauly Shore, Lori Petty, David Alan Grier.

The Mask
(1994) 100m. **B**
A mild-mannered guy finds a mask that transforms him into a cartoonlike super being with a tendency to quote lines from other films and have his body contort into a variety of visually arresting, computer-generated ways. Carrey's adrenomanic persona fits well with the impressively hyperactive effects.
D: Chuck Russell. A: Jim Carrey, Peter Riegert, Cameron Diaz.

Houseguest
(1995) 109m. **C**
Farce in which a plucky street orphan with big dreams gets in debt with loan sharks and is mistaken for a dentist, all the while dispensing street wisdom and holding bang-up parties. Harmlessly jivey comedy rests entirely on viewer's enjoyment of Sinbad's low-humor antics.
D: Randall Miller. A: Sinbad, Phil Hartman, Jeffrey Jones.

Test Market Dummies

While America's Dream Factory has always "packaged" films, never before have the content and shape of movies been so relentlessly tailored by demographics and studios' concern for appealing to all people and offending none. The scattershot results of such techniques range from insipidly hilarious to blandly lame, with mediocrity and feel-good fuzziness the standard-bearer. Caveat emptor.

Crazy People
(1990) 91m. **C–**
A burned-out ad man starts to tell the truth about the products he advertises, and ends up confined to a lunatic asylum, where he and fellow inmates start their own agency. Baldly obvious satire, but some of the advertisements are pretty funny.
D: Tony Bill. A: Dudley Moore, Daryl Hannah, Paul Reiser.

My Blue Heaven
(1990) 95m. **C–**
A suave hood goes under suburban cover in the Witness Relocation Program so he can spill the goods on a mobster. Martin gets off a few good lines while wearing an amusingly kitschy shiny blue suit (film's idea of Mafia chic), but otherwise this is a bland-looking bit of TV sitcom pap.
D: Herbert Ross. A: Steve Martin, Rick Moranis, Joan Cusack.

Delirious
(1991) 96m. **B+**
A soap opera writer gets knocked on the noggin and wakes to discover he's in the town he wrote about, can interact with his characters, and change the future merely by rewriting it. Gimmicky but frequently hilarious fantasy, thanks mainly to Candy performance, and only slides occasionally into cutesville comedy.
D: Tom Mankiewicz. A: John Candy, Raymond Burr, Mariel Hemingway.

Doc Hollywood
(1991) 104m. **C+**
A recently graduated plastic surgeon on his way to a California-rich practice has a car accident in the Southern sticks and endears himself to the locals who want him for their Doc. Not dumb enough to be offensive, just more Hollywood feel-good formula.
D: Michael Caton-Jones. A: Michael J. Fox, Julie Warner, Bridget Fonda.

King Ralph
(1991) 96m. **C–**
The entire Royal Family is decimated in a freak accident and a search locates distant royal blood in a loutish American lounge singer. Scenes of Goodman being groomed for the throne by O'Toole have no choice but to be funny, but otherwise uninspired.
D: David Ward. A: John Goodman, Peter O'Toole, John Hurt.

My Cousin Vinny
(1991) 119m. **B+**
Two kids are railroaded into a murder rap in the South and one calls his cousin Vinny, a brand-new Bronx lawyer in leather jacket and gold chains. Funny New York vs. South culture clash tale, with a comic relationship between Pesci and his gum-snapping girlfriend and

an outraged/baffled Gwynne as the judge.
D: Jonathan Lynn. A: Joe Pesci, Marisa Tomei, Fred Gwynne.

Nothing but Trouble
(1991) 94m. **C**
A yuppie couple gets waylaid in a small town that serves as a toxic dump and ends up in a bizarre mansion full of Addams Family-esque characters. A faintly amusing fusion of Tim Burton visuals and Neil Simon comedy.
D: Dan Aykroyd. A: John Candy, Demi Moore, Chevy Chase.

Oscar
(1991) 109m. **D**
Mobster Sly promises Dad he'll go straight but this and that keep getting in the way. Some funny moments by supporting cast but Sly wasn't cut out for comedy.
D: John Landis. A: Sylvester Stallone, Ornella Muti, Peter Riegert.

Soapdish
(1991) 92m. **B+**
A longtime soap opera queen tenaciously defends her title from a scheming bombshell and a horny producer. With its ridiculous on-target, soap opera-within-a-film hilarious performances and a deliriously gaudy pink/red/blue TV wonder world, this is an unexpected delight.
D: Michael Hoffman. A: Sally Field, Kevin Kline, Whoopi Goldberg.

Straight Talk
(1992) 91m. **C**
Chatty, well-endowed, but unlicensed Arkansas girl hits Chicago and becomes the hit talk-radio psychologist. Dolly's folksy charm and Woods' abrasive lack of it, and a dull Dunne, make this a passably good-natured effort.
D: Barnet Kellman. A: Dolly Parton, James Woods, Griffin Dunne.

Born Yesterday
(1993) 100m. **C**
Tepid remake of the 1950 tale of a ditzy blonde whose sugar daddy hires a professor to teach her how to talk and act high-class. Griffith as a modern Judy Holliday is a good idea that doesn't work, partly due to her and Johnson's strenuous attempts to be adorable.
D: Luis Mandoki. A: Melanie Griffith, Don Johnson, John Goodman.

Life with Mikey
(1993) 92m. **C+**
Former child star/now children's talent agent discovers his next prodigy in the form of a multicultural inner-city girl. All the expected complications arise in this by-the-numbers Fox vehicle, though the fun chemistry between the diminutive actor and his younger charge garners some laughs.
D: James Lapine. A: Michael J. Fox, Nathan Lane, Cyndi Lauper.

Splitting Heirs
(1993) 87m. **B–**
Thirty years earlier, a cook and a duke's babies got mixed up, resulting in the now grown cook's kid being a Duke and the royal blood being part of a poor Pakistani family. Pretty much of a one-joke affair with little story, but filled with funny bits by the game cast.
D: Robert Young. A: Eric Idle, Rick Moranis, Barbara Hershey.

Dumb and Dumber
(1994) 100m. **C**
Two imbeciles retrieve a money-stuffed briefcase and head for Colorado to return it, leading them into a dumb cat-and-mouse game with a gaggle of thugs. Some funny Jerry Lewis-esque mugging at first, then tacked-on caper plot saps whatever vacuum-skulled charm this may have had.
D: Peter Farrelly. A: Jim Carrey, Jeff Daniels, Lauren Holly.

Exit to Eden
(1994) 120m. **C+**
This tale of a paunchy pair of cops trailing bad guys into a veritable Club Med for S&M types gets a plus for sheer bizarreness. Imagine *Love Boat* with leather and handcuffs, an old-fashioned romance interspliced with O'Donnell in full leather gear, and you have something that is never boring.
D: Garry Marshall. A: Rosie O'Donnell, Dan Aykroyd, Dana Delaney.

For Love or Money
(1994) 97m. **C+**
A hotel concierge with dreams of building his own island hotel falls for a millionaire's daughter, but he'll lose the millionaire's seed money if he pursues her. The type of sitcom stuff that Fox seems to do effortlessly.
D: Barry Sonnenfeld. A: Michael J. Fox, Gabrielle Anwar, Anthony Higgins.

Guarding Tess
(1994) 99m. **C–**
Frantic farce about a feisty First Lady and her reluctant Secret Service man is so predictable and sugary that you can easily take long jaunts to the fridge, come back, and still know exactly where the film is going.
D: Hugh Wilson. A: Shirley MacLaine, Nicolas Cage, Austin Pendleton.

Greedy
(1994) 113m. **B–**
An impressive roster of nastily intentioned relatives scheme up ways to weasel their way into ultrarich Uncle Joe's heart so as to become heirs. Mostly funny ensemble comedy with some hilarious double crosses and red herrings, and Douglas chewing the scenery one more time.
D: Jonathan Lynn. A: Kirk Douglas, Michael J. Fox, Nancy Travis.

Junior
(1994) 110m. **B–**
A case of "you've seen the poster, you've seen the movie": The poster shows us the unusual image of der Arnold about three trimesters into his pregnancy while the film spins a fairly amusing tale about the man implanted with an experimental embryo, with plenty of hormone jokes and feel-good moments of tenderness.
D: Ivan Reitman. A: Arnold Schwarzenegger, Danny DeVito, Emma Thompson.

Milk Money
(1994) 110m. **C+**
A suburban young boy with his pals heads into town to pay for a prostitute (to expose herself) and decides that she's perfect for his widower father. Despite a few warm scenes between Harris and Griffith, the programmed misfire would be enjoyably bad if it didn't fall into such a predictable resolution.
D: Richard Benjamin. A: Ed Harris, Melanie Griffith, Malcolm MacDowell.

Mrs. Doubtfire
(1994) 125m. **C+**
When an irresponsible husband gets the bum's rush, how does he deal with the painful separation from his kids? He dresses up as an Irish housekeeper so he can squirm his way back into the family. A predictable charmless *Tootsie* variation whose mirth rests largely on Williams' gender-confused antics.
D: Chris Columbus. A: Robin Williams, Sally Field, Pierce Brosnan.

Renaissance Man
(1994) 128m. **C–**
An unemployed ad man gets a job teaching boot-camp blacks, Hispanics, and

young rednecks that literature, even Shakespeare, is relevant and soon discovers his own inner Teacher. Multi-culti rehash of *Dead Poets Society* (army division) seems like it was soldered together by committee.
D: Penny Marshall. A: Danny DeVito, Gregory Hines, James Remar.

The Scout

(1994) 101m. **D+**

A New York Yankee scout finds a hot pitching prospect and winds up being his manager/babysitter who has to work with the shrink trying to figure out some past dark secret. Promising first half hour and good cast strands viewer in a mess of a film.
D: Michael Ritchie. A: Albert Brooks, Brendan Fraser, Dianne Wiest.

Wagons East

(1994) 107m. **D**

A ragtag group of pioneers decides to beat a hasty retreat back East and makes the mistake of hiring a wagon master who's seen better days. Sadly, this mediocre comedy was Candy's final effort before dying and best forgotten.
D: Peter Markel. A: John Candy, Richard Lewis, John C. McGinley.

9 Months

(1995) 113m. **C**

Faced with the prospect of giving up bachelorhood when his girlfriend announces her pregnancy, a child psychologist tries to prove he's ready for the big event. Steady barrage of generally unfunny jokes and film's generally juvenile demeanor is only partly offset by Grant proving he can be adorable in any vehicle.
D: Chris Columbus. A: Hugh Grant, Julianne Moore, Tom Arnold.

To Wong Foo, Thanks for Everything! Julie Newmar

(1995) 108m. **B**

Three New York drag queens on the road to Hollywood get stuck in a middle-America nowhere hamlet, where they proceed to teach the citizens fashion sense and the art of fabulous living. Some funny bitchy humor, bright performances (especially Leguizamo doing a hilarious Rosie Perez imitation), and a dazzling number of costume changes get bogged down by the relentlessly feel-good tone carried by the cartoonish characters.
D: Beeban Kidron. A: Wesley Snipes, Patrick Swayze, John Leguizamo.

Satires

Satires live in these energetically iconoclastic cut-to-the-bone comedies. Most are suffused with a slightly surreal air as they gleefully take potshots at institutions of big business, politics, and fashion.

Other People's Money

(1991) 103m. **B**

Insatiable corporate raider tries to steal upstanding company president Peck's company *and* his breezy daughter. Intermittently clever film tries to update a Capra-esque feel and attitude and sometimes succeeds courtesy of Peck, practically oozing dignity and a hilariously avaricious DeVito.
D: Norman Jewison. A: Danny DeVito, Gregory Peck, Penelope Ann Miller.

Bob Roberts

(1992) 105m. **A**

Robbins is cheerfully chilling as the amoral folk song-singing, near-fascist congressional candidate in this pseudodocumentary of his campaign. This satire, peppered with news feed images and interviews with pro- and anti-Bob makes a darkly funny and horridly plausible political nightmare.
D: Tim Robbins. A: Tim Robbins, Alan Rickman, Gore Vidal.

Ready to Wear (Prêt-à-Porter)

(1994) 133m. **B**

Altman takes on the fashion industry in these interwoven stories of the designers, reporters, models, and photographers who converge in Paris for the annual Pret à-Porter show. A parade of all-star characters and the frivolousness of the subject keep the movie both lightly entertaining and somewhat unengaging.
D: Robert Altman. A: Marcello Mastroianni, Tim Robbins, Kim Basinger.

DRAMA

Drama Menu

1950s

DRAMA MENU

1970s

1980s

DRAMA MENU

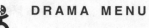

DRAMA FILM GROUPS

1910s–1920s

The Classic Silents

These are some of the great and near-great films by the early masters of cinema. If you can get past the lack of spoken dialogue—something that audiences don't seem to miss in a Stallone action film—and some primitive camerawork, you'll find that most of these films are racier, subtler, and more entertaining than much of what Hollywood is turning out these days.

Various Directors

The Sheik

(1921) 80m. B&W. **B+**

A young English girl is abducted from her touring party by a dashing Arabian sheik, and her maidenly terrors and fantasies all come true in his desert tent. Valentino is all brute force and smoldering kohl-lined eyes in this extravagantly earnest and vastly entertaining romantic fantasy.

D: George Melford. A: Rudolph Valentino, Agnes Ayres, Adolphe Menjou.

The Ten Commandments

(1923) 140m. B&W w/color **B+**

The story of Moses and the Jews as they lock horns with their debauched oppressors is interwoven with a modern tale of a young man driven to atheism by his Bible-thumping mother in this redemptive saga. A ham-fisted but often glorious epic.

D: Cecil B. DeMille. A: Theodore Roberts, Estelle Taylor, Rod La Rocque.

Ben-Hur

(1926) 141m. B&W/with color **B**

This colossal epic about a Jewish nobleman who is condemned to a life of slavery is at turns static and exhilarating, but the brutal galley scenes and the blood-and-thunder chariot race more than make up for the long wobbly stretches of histrionic moments.

D: Fred Niblo. A: Ramon Novarro, Francis X. Bushman, May McAvoy.

The Wind

(1926) 82m. B&W. **A–**

A well-bred young Southern woman, stuck on a dusty Texas ranch in a miserable marriage, is raped by a man she met on the train out west. Mother Nature, via special effects, takes center stage here, but Gish burns with a quiet intensity as the swirling dust bowl winds drive her to a catastrophic end.

D: Victor Seastrom. A: Lillian Gish, Lars Hanson, Montague Love.

Napoleon

(1927) 235m. B&W. Silent. Subtitled. **A**

Abel Gance's groundbreaking, blatantly nationalistic biography of the early life and triumphs of France's emperor is still a triumph of visual storytelling. The staggering triptych battlefield finale alone makes this earthy, bigger than life epic a must-see.

D: Abel Gance. A: Albert Dieudonne, Pierre Batcheff, Antonin Artaud.

The Docks of New York

(1928) 76 m. B&W. **A**

After a loutish sailor saves a prostitute from committing suicide, her blossoming love transforms the brute into a man of compassion. A lavish moody passion play set in some dreamy expressionistic New York settings.

D: Josef von Sternberg. A: George Bancroft, Betty Compton, Olga Baclanova.

Our Dancing Daughters

(1928) 97m. B&W. **B**

A good-hearted flapper loses her man to a conniving gold-digging socialite. An enchanting pre-camp Crawford, who shakes a sleek tail-feather in the early part of the film, plays her cards straight for a change, but gets nowhere in a quaint tale that quickly sags into a trite period melodrama.

D: Harry Beaumont. A: Joan Crawford, Johnny Mack Brown, Nils Asther.

Sadie Thompson

(1928) 97m. B&W. **B**

A fire and brimstone preacher in Pago Pago tries to convert the soul of a prostitute only to fall under her sensuous spell. A claustrophobic and sweat-stained melodrama, colored by Barrymore's decidedly hammy reformer, and Swanson's vamping bad girl. Some restoration slows down the finale with stills and narration.

D: Raoul Walsh. A: Gloria Swanson, Raoul Walsh, Lionel Barrymore.

Un Chien Andalou

(1928) 74m. B&W. **A–**

This series of perverse, grotesque, and still shocking vignettes is a surrealistic tone poem celebrating the unconscious mind and human irrationality in all its glory. Don't miss Dali as the priest and director Luis Buñuel as the man with the razor.

D: Luis Buñuel, Salvador Dali. A: Pierre Batcheff, Simone Mareuil, Salvador Dali.

F. W. Murnau

Sunrise

(1927) 110m. B&W. **A**

Driven by his lust for another woman, a country peasant devises a plan to murder his simple young wife. On their final visit to the city, the charms of his dainty mate cause him to repent, but it may be too late. Starting out as a shadowy melodrama, this blasts off into another stratosphere when the couple reaches the wondrous city and experiences a string of breathtakingly luminous passages.

D: F. W. Murnau. A: George O'Brien, Janet Gaynor, Bodil Rosing.

City Girl

(1930) 77m. B&W. **A–**

A young waitress can't believe her luck when a sweet farm boy proposes to her, but when they return to his dust bowl farm, it's all dour in-laws, local yahoos, and grueling farm life. An eerie tale of a city-smart woman stuck in an American gothic, complete with a monster storm kicking up its heels.

D: F. W. Murnau. A: Charles Farrell, Mary Duncan, David Torrence.

Tabu

(1931) 81m. B&W.

A

A young pearl fisherman in the South Seas falls under the spell of a native girl for whom earthly love is taboo. Though set up rather deceptively as a documentary-style look at the life of a tribe of superstitious natives, this soon becomes a sensual and stately tale of a joyous love affair and paradise lost.
D: F. W. Murnau. A: Anna Chevalier, Matahi, Hitu.

D. W. Griffith

The Birth of a Nation

(1915) 159m. B&W.

A

This troublesome saga of the old South was a miraculous achievement and has kept much of its impact due to the grand, old-fashioned storytelling and brilliantly mounted Civil War battle scenes. However, the ghoulish championing of the Ku Klux Klan and the racist depiction of African-Americans by white actors finally changes the nature of this "masterpiece."
D: D. W. Griffith. A: Lillian Gish, Mae Marsh, Henry B. Walthall.

Intolerance

(1916) 123m. B&W. **A–**

The fall of Babylon, the betrayal of Christ, the massacre of the Huguenots in 1572 Paris, and a modern-day tale of the system's destruction of a common laborer are interwoven in this giant saga. Overlong and melodramatic, but the elephantine Babylonian sets, among others, are nothing short of spectacular.
D: D. W. Griffith. A: Robert Harron, Mae Marsh, Constance Talmadge.

True Heart Susie

(1919) 62m. B&W. **A–**

Shy young Susie sacrifices all for the beloved boy next door, remaining faithful even after he marries another woman. A simple and heartfelt tale with the reserved heroine preferring to lurk quietly in the background, yearning dearly for a childhood sweetheart who has seemingly forgotten all about her.
D: D. W. Griffith. A: Lillian Gish, Robert Herron, George Fawcett.

Orphans of the Storm

(1922) 125m. B&W. **A–**

When two orphans set out for Paris in search of a cure for the one sister's blindness, they become separated as the French Revolution breaks out around them. This rousing, highly melodramatic epic rides through the rowdy Parisian streets like an out-of-control stagecoach as the orphans do their damnedest to find each other while avoiding the guillotine.
D: D. W. Griffith. A: Lillian Gish, Dorothy Gish, Joseph Schildkraut.

Erich Von Stroheim

Greed

(1924) 133m. B&W.

A

A dentist marries one of his patients who, coincidentally, has just won the lottery. When he loses his practice, the miserly wife refuses to dip into her treasure chest. This small human drama becomes a powerful and savage epic as we watch the couple become increasingly depraved for the love and the want of the untouched booty.
D: Erich von Stroheim. A: Gibson Gowland, ZaSu Pitts, Jean Hersholt.

The Wedding March

(1928) 140m. B&W. **A**

An Austrian prince tries to break off his loveless engagement to wed a poor young musician, but his family has other plans. This ornate silent grand opera takes an ironic look at old-world nobility trying desperately to preserve power and position in the crumbling Hapsburg empire.
D: Erich von Stroheim. A: Erich von Stroheim, Fay Wray, ZaSu Pitts.

Queen Kelly

(1928) 96mm. B&W.

B+

A lecherous prince kidnaps a young convent girl, keeping her in his creepy palace to the chagrin of his intended queen. A gorgeous, Marquis de Sade-influenced tale of debauchery that mixes kinky fetishes with feverish religious imagery as the lass escapes the loony older woman to live with her aunt in an African bordello.
D: Erich von Stroheim. A: Gloria Swanson, Seena Owen, Walter Byron.

King Vidor

The Big Parade

(1925) 141m. B&W. **A**

An exuberant American doughboy, waiting to see action, falls in love with a French peasant girl. Paradise becomes a memory when he loses two friends and his leg in battle, and can't even find the girl. A chilling war drama with staggering battle scenes, and an unsentimental look at the human spirit in adversity.
D: King Vidor. A: John Gilbert, Renee Adoree, Hobart Bosworth.

The Crowd

(1928) 104m. B&W.

A

A hardworking couple is devasted by the death of their daughter, the loss of the husband's job, and the disillusionment of their dreams. Beautifully choreographed, this emotionally shattering small story graphically depicts the effects of the heartless big city on the young and idealistic.
D: King Vidor. A: Eleanor Boardman, James Murray, Bert Roach.

Show People

(1928) 81m. B&W. **A–**

A silly young Southern belle takes Hollywood by storm when she goes from a two-reel slapstick flapper to the queen of melodrama. Davies delivers some rubberfaced mugging that sends acting back a hundred years in this hilarious poke at the machinations and pretensions of the studio system.
D: King Vidor. A: Marion Davies, William Haines; with cameos by Charlie Chaplin, Douglas Fairbanks, John Gilbert, and others.

1920s

Greta Garbo

Greta Garbo was cast in these hokey melodramas as exotic vamps, widows, divorcées, and just plain *bad* women who led weak-willed ninnies to their doom. Even if these silent

films are badly dated and Garbo's unformed talent all too evident, her hauntingly modeled and expressive face is still enough to hold you spellbound.

Joyless Street

(1925) 96m. B&W. **B**

On a dingy Viennese street, the daughter of an out-of-work professor holds on to her honor while another woman prostitutes herself and commits murder for the man she loves. A slow-moving, heavy-handed tale of postwar depravity and despair, with an underfed but exquisite-looking Garbo.
D: G. W. Pabst. A: With Werner Krauss, Asta Nielsen, Valeska Gert.

Flesh and the Devil

(1927) 112m. B&W. **B**

The friendship of two soldiers is torn apart by the selfish passions of a sultry woman. Vamp Garbo leads nice boy Gilbert into a torrid affair in this often silly blood and thunder melodrama that suddenly fogs up the screen with one of the most erotic and fully clothed lovemaking scenes ever.
D: Clarence Brown. A: With John Gilbert, Lars Hanson, Barbara Kent.

A Woman of Affairs

(1928) 96m. B&W. **B–**

A young man commits suicide on his wedding night when he learns that his socialite wife loves another man. The widow turns over a new leaf, leading a pure life to protect her husband's good name. Garbo is at her most relaxed in this bizarre convoluted melodrama with its startlingly cynical look at infidelity.
D: Clarence Brown. A: With John Gilbert, Lewis Stone, Johnny Mack Brown.

The Kiss

(1929) 89m. B&W. **B**

A married woman who is having an affair is caught giving a good night kiss to a different admirer by her jealous husband. A fight ensues and the husband is shot, but who fired the gun? Garbo is pursued and fought over by the usual band of ingrates in this lurid and convoluted whodunit.
D: Jacques Feyder. A: With Conrad Nagel, Andres Randolf, Lew Ayres.

Wild Orchids

(1929) 102m. B&W. **C+**

An elderly tycoon fears he is losing his wife when she embarks on a shipboard flirtation with a cruel but dashing Javanese prince. This exotic perfumed melodrama of sin and sacrifice in the Far East gets hysterical and we don't mean funny. Garbo, dressed to the hilt, overacts wildly in this trite soaper.
D: Sidney Franklin. A: With Lewis Stone, Nils Asther.

Other Films:

Anna Christie (1922)
The Mysterious Lady (1928)
The Single Standard (1929)

1930s

British Literary Adaptations

The classics by Dickens, Brontë, and Shaw are brought to life here by mostly British directors and actors, some the cream of British performers. While early efforts suffered from technical limitations, by 1935 these historical dramas were rich in period detail, with all the production values of Hollywood's glossiest soap operas.

Oliver Twist

(1933) 77m. B&W. **C**

Workhouse escapee young Oliver joins a band of child street thieves lead by the oily Fagin. Game performances but another low-budget effort with bland sets, decaying sound, and film grain.
D: William Cowen. A: Dickie Moore, Irving Pichel, William Boyd.

Becky Sharp

(1935) 83m. **B–**

This early color effort of *Vanity Fair* dallies too long over its delight in using shades of pastel to evoke a sheen of emotion, but is most often an overacted study of a heartless girl and her impact on those she supposedly cares for.
D: Rouben Mamoulian. A: Miriam Hopkins, Cedric Hardwick, Frances Dee.

David Copperfield

(1935) 133m. B&W. **A**

A remarkably rich condensation of Dickens' huge novel follows David from his workhouse days into the world of debt-eluding families and financial shenanigans from which he emerges ennobled and wise. Offers a vibrant panoply of characters reflecting early urban cruelty, pathos, and humor.
D: George Cukor. A: Freddie Bartholomew, Frank Lawton, W. C. Fields.

Scrooge

(1935) 78m. B&W. **B–**

A dark and muted retelling about the old miser who's given a Christmas Eve tour of his past, present, and future by a host of ghosts. Expert performances, but the dated effects, slow pace, and signs of age make you yearn for later efforts.
D: Henry Edwards. A: Seymour Hick, Donald Calthrop, Oscar Asche.

A Tale of Two Cities

(1935) 128m. B&W. **A**

A debauched English lawyer, for the love of a French woman, takes the place of her wrongly imprisoned husband during the French Revolution. Both a sweeping parade of historical events and an intimate study of a listless man who finally finds something worth dying for.
D: Jack Conway. A: Ronald Colman, Elizabeth Allan, Edna May Oliver.

Little Lord Fauntleroy

(1936) 98m. B&W. **B–**

A spunky young lad from Brooklyn finds he's the heir to a title in England and goes there to meet his aged and icy relation. Dripping with sentimental nostalgia for the 1880s and sometimes too cute for words.
D: John Cromwell. A: Freddie Bartholomew, C. Aubrey Smith, Dolores C. Barrymore.

The Prince and the Pauper

(1937) 108m. B&W. **B+**

It's a royal role reversal as the ten-year-old heir to the throne, Prince Edward, switches with his exact double, a lowborn street lad. Even with the swashbuckling action and ornate cos-

tume scenes, this preserves enough of Mark Twain's original humor to keep things from getting too heavy.
D: William Keighley. A: Errol Flynn, Claude Rains, Billy and Bobby Mauch.

Pygmalion
(1938) 96m. B&W. **A**

A delightfully witty comedy of British manners and an entrancing skirmish in the war between the sexes follows bruisingly egocentric Professor Higgins as he tries to mold a Cockney flower girl into the very image of a fine lady. The flawless performances make this superior, if leaner, to *My Fair Lady.*
D: Anthony Asquith. A: Leslie Howard, Wendy Hiller, Wilfrid Lawson.

Vanity Fair
(1938) 67m. B&W. **C–**

A miscalculated attempt to update a tale of Regency England to the modern 1930s follows social climbing Becky Sharp as she uses a string of men to rise in the upper class. A low-budget affair with stagy direction and sound hissing with age.
D: Chester Franklin. A: Myrna Loy, Conway Tearle, Walter Byron.

Goodbye, Mr. Chips
(1939) 114m. B&W.
A

An unapologetically sentimental tugger about a shy and tweedy boys' school teacher who seems destined to become the old duffer patronized by young boys, until the day he returns from vacation with a vivacious young bride. A finely acted, tender portrait that spans three generations and offers a nostalgic piece of *England, My England.*
D: Sam Wood. A: Robert Donat, Greer Garson, Paul Henreid.

Wuthering Heights
(1939) 104m. **A–**

Amid the murk and swirling darkness of the Yorkshire moors, spoiled Cathy sees in the smoldering gypsy stable boy Heathcliff all the impetuous fire missing in her staid life. An atmospheric heart-pounder that's deliriously romantic and occasionally hokey.
D: William Wyler. A: Merle Oberon, Laurence Olivier, David Niven.

Shakespeare

How does a filmmaker present very long plays that rely almost exclusively on the beauty of their language? The early attempts retained a static stagy look, keeping the feel of the play, but cutting back on the story. In the 1940s, Laurence Olivier came into his own, and impressionistic camera angles and more realistic sets were used to create a world of tortured medieval kings, star-crossed Italian young lovers, and fanciful wood nymphs. By the 50s many of the Bard's works had reached the screen (albeit in abbreviated form) with the language intact, but also the same bracing fluid action as any other historical drama or biblical epic made by Hollywood.

A Midsummer Night's Dream
(1935) 132m. B&W. **B**

A romantic comedy of four lovers and the frolicsome King and Queen of the Fairies becomes more of a dreamy Hollywood all-star fantasy, shot in gorgeous glittering black and white. Lovely, but more of a period curiosity.
D: Max Reinhardt. A: James Cagney, Joe E. Brown, Olivia de Havilland.

As You Like It
(1936) 96m. B&W. **C**

Celebrating nature and the reviving powers of simplicity, this pastoral romantic comedy is a real antique with static camerawork, stagy sets, heavy footfalls on wooden floors, and a crackling soundtrack.
D: Paul Czinner. A: Elizabeth Bergner, Laurence Olivier, Haney Ainley.

Romeo and Juliet
(1936) 127m. B&W. **C**

This tale of young lovers from feuding families in Verona features the last practitioners of the florid declarative style of Shakespearean acting. Slow and lumbering.
D: George Cukor. A: Norma Shearer, Leslie Howard, John Barrymore.

Henry V
(1945) 153m. B&W. **A**

Beginning as the play is being performed at the Globe Theatre in 1603, this then evolves into the reality of King Henry and his victory at Agincourt in 1415. Innovation of peeling away the play is effective, with high-style acting, glorious costumes, and real panache.
D: Laurence Olivier. A: Laurence Olivier, Robert Newton, Ranee Asherson.

Hamlet
(1948) 142m. B&W.
A

His father's dead, his uncle becomes king and marries his mother. Then his dad's ghost says it's murder and Mom turns out to be no good. Hamlet ponders his ill fate and flashes with plans of revenge. Dark, swirling, tragic, and utterly absorbing tale filmed in lush and velvety black and white.
D: Laurence Olivier. A: Laurence Olivier, Eileen Herlie, Basil Sydney.

Macbeth
(1948) 105m. B&W. **B**

Ghastly witches tempt a ready Macbeth with predictions of future kingship, and his wife pushes him to help fate by killing the present one. Smokey, gloomy, impressionistic tale with bizarre sets and odd camera angles that create an air of menace and keep the eye busy.
D: Orson Welles. A: Orson Welles, Jeanette Nolan, Dan O'Herlihy.

Julius Caesar
(1953) 121m. B&W. **B+**

When oily Cassius convinces Brutus that Caesar must not be crowned king, knives flash outside the senate and civil war erupts. Sturdy, well measured study of political intrigues and personal foibles in restless ancient Rome with intimate portraits of those fiery Romans.
D: Joseph Mankiewicz. A: Louis Calhern, Marlon Brando, James Mason.

Richard III
(1955) 161m. **A**

Hunchbacked Richard methodically eliminates every

person standing between him and the English crown, and he does it in such a deliciously evil and witty way you almost root for him. The cream of British theater are featured in this stagy but still potent treatment of the War of the Roses.
D: Laurence Olivier. A: Laurence Olivier, John Gielgud, Ralph Richardson.

British Historical Dramas

The romantic and personal side of the rich and royal get the old Hollywood treatment in these rousing costume dramas. Not only can you enjoy the kind of florid suffering that makes the other melodramas from this period so entertaining, but you get lavish costumes, overstuffed interiors, and the best castles and dungeons on the backlot.

The Private Life of Henry VIII
(1933) 97m. B&W. **B+**
An intimate peek at the foibles, passions, and vanities that drove Henry to plow through so many wives. Laughton pulls out the stops with his delightfully decadent and quirky Henry but the slow pace, chunky sets, and hissing soundtrack make it creak.
D: Alexander Korda. A: Charles Laughton, Merle Oberon, Robert Donat.

The Barretts of Wimpole Street
(1934) 110m. B&W. **B+**
Poet Elizabeth Barrett is prevented by her overbearing father from seeking happiness with kindred spirit Robert Browning. A heartfelt romance and Victorian mating dance for the mind, but it doesn't move around much.
D: Sidney Franklin. A: Norma Shearer, Charles Laughton, Fredric March.

Beloved Enemy
(1936) 86m. B&W. **B+**
Englishwoman Lady Helena turns from her officer beau to the love of a passionate and intense leader of the Irish Rebellion. Treads the line between tragedy and melodrama and winds up a first-rate historical women's film.
D: H. C. Potter. A: Merle Oberon, Brian Aherne, Henry Stephenson.

Mary of Scotland
(1936) 123m. B&W. **B**
Exiled Mary stakes her claim as ruler of England against Elizabeth, resulting in political and religious turmoil. High drama as Mary confronts Elizabeth and a riveting trial in which Mary defends her life to the last.
D: John Ford. A: Katharine Hepburn, Fredric March, John Carradine.

The Private Lives of Elizabeth and Essex
(1939) 106m. **B**
Wary Elizabeth throws caution to the winds and has a tempestuous and finally disappointing affair with the dashing Essex. History takes the day off but it's a solid colorful drama nonetheless.
D: Michael Curtiz. A: Bette Davis, Errol Flynn, Vincent Price.

Tower of London
(1939) 92m. B&W. **B−**
The wily and relentlessly evil Richard cheats and murders his way to the English throne. This striking study of evil is low on pageantry and high on almost campy early horror.
D: Rowland V. Lee. A: Basil Rathbone, Boris Karloff, Ian Hunter.

That Hamilton Woman
(1941) 128m. B&W. **B+**
Married, social-climbing Lady Hamilton meets Lord Nelson and they embark on a scandalous affair in between his naval engagements. Lushly filmed, with wide-open villas, elegant ambassadorial parties, and crashing naval battles.
D: Alexander Korda. A: Vivien Leigh, Laurence Olivier, Gladys Cooper.

That Forsyte Woman
(1949) 114m. B&W. **B**
A married woman shocks Victorian sensibilities when she has an affair with the fiancé of her niece. An all-star women's film dressed up in brightly colored period costume.
D: Compton Bennett. A: Greer Garson, Errol Flynn, Walter Pidgeon.

Historical Dramas

While offering the historical details of other costume films, most of these are really just melodramas dressed up in period outfits. Garbo was the undisputed queen of the genre, but you'll enjoy watching other Hollywood divas amid all the pageantry and court intrigue as they bring modern sensibilities to their search for power, love, and God.

Rasputin and the Empress
(1932) 123m. B&W. **B−**
Solid performances distinguish this tale of the mesmerizing monk and his influence over the czarina in anguish over her sick son during the last years of the monarchy. Old and grainy, but uses actual footage of the real czar and family.
D: Richard Boleslawski. A: John Barrymore, Ethel Barrymore, Lionel Barrymore.

Catherine the Great
(1934) 92m. B&W. **B**
The young German princess marries the reluctant, sometimes mad Russian grand duke, gains control, and goes on to become the most famous czarina. Carefully etched study with fine eighteenth-century trappings, but not enough drama or urgency to propel the film.
D: Paul Czinner. A: Elisabeth Bergner; Douglas Fairbanks, Jr.; Flora Robson.

Cleopatra
(1934) 101m. B&W. **B**
Cleopatra parades around in dandy costumes, poisons slaves, and charms some of history's great military leaders. This rushes through

years of history via opulent sets, with pauses for some grand-scale battles and a little decadent fun.
D: Cecil B. DeMille. A: Claudette Colbert, Warren William, Gertrude Michael.

Marie Antoinette
(1938) 149m. B&W. **B−**
A glamorous and richly detailed story of a young Austrian princess as she becomes queen in a declining corpulent monarchy, and then turns to a suave Swedish count for love. More attention is given to the recreations of Versailles, overdone gowns, and wigs than to the characters.
D: W. S. Van Dyke. A: Norma Shearer, John Barrymore, Tyrone Power.

The Song of Bernadette
(1943) 156m. B&W. **B−**
Reverential and lumbering, this epic-sized account tells of the nineteenth-century French peasant girl who incurred the wrath of the townspeople at Lourdes by claiming to have seen the Virgin Mary. Warmly photographed with careful attention to historical detail, this is a family-oriented, somewhat repetitive study of religious fervor and persecution.
D: Henry King. A: Jennifer Jones, William Eythe, Lee J. Cobb.

Caesar and Cleopatra
(1946) 134m. **B**
A worldly Julius tutors the young Cleopatra in the ways of wielding absolute power. Gigantic re-creations of the Sphinx and elegant Egyptian palaces don't mask the fact that this is a Shaw play on film. A treat for his fans, but slow and talky for others.
D: Gabriel Pascal. A: Claude Rains, Vivien Leigh, Stewart Granger.

Joan of Arc
(1948) 100m. **B**
By divine inspiration, a peasant girl rallies the armies of France against the English, only to be rewarded by betrayal. Uninspired battle sequences and long stretches of dialogue slow it down, but the intense trial scene catches fire.
D: Victor Fleming. A: Ingrid Bergman, José Ferrer, J. Carrol Naish.

Literary Adaptations

Hollywood studios took pride in these "prestige pictures" even if most of them were surefire money-losers. Chosen from among literature's classics, the films offer opulent re-creations of the French Revolution, czarist Russia, and seventeenth-century America. Limited by the Production Code and the studios' own lofty intentions, some are dull and ponderous while others offer an entertaining piece of Americana, a sweeping historical drama, or even a good three-hankie melodrama.

Little Women
(1933) 115m. B&W. **A**
A vibrant film of four sisters from New England on the verge of womanhood as they chat, squabble, play, and ponder their future. The sheer nostalgic bounce of youth recalling a golden America will either warm you or ignite the cynic.
D: George Cukor. A: Katharine Hepburn, Joan Bennett, Frances Dee.

The Scarlet Letter
(1934) 70m. B&W. **C**
An archaic film version about a Puritan woman forced to wear the adulterer's "A" after bearing the minister's child out of wedlock. The poor sound and slow camera movements never allow the viewer to fully witness the subtle torment that is unfolding.
D: Robert Vignola. A: Hardie Albright, Colleen Moore, Henry B. Walthall.

Les Misérables
(1935) 109m. B&W. **A**
Awash in the swirl and crushing poverty of the French Revolution a man steals bread and a policeman relentlessly pursues him, never letting him build a life or forget what he did. Heroic performances and remarkable re-creations of teeming streets of Paris gone mad.
D: Richard Boleslawski. A: Fredric March, Charles Laughton, Rochelle Hudson.

The Good Earth
(1937) 138m. B&W. **B+**
A dirt poor nineteenth-century Chinese farmer and his devoted wife struggle through hardships, but when they finally rise to wealth he discards her for a youthful maid. Even with the Caucasian actors, its use of real locations, and the climax of the locust attack has impact.
D: Sidney Franklin. A: Paul Muni, Luise Rainer, Walter Connolly.

The House of the Seven Gables
(1940) 89m. B&W. **C+**
There are evil deeds afoot with this New England family, when the coldhearted brother decides to set up his sister's fiancé for murder. Puritans eye each other in a big gothic house, but you never get under their skin, resulting in a good-looking but dull story.
D: Joe May. A: George Sanders, Vincent Price, Margaret Lindsay

The Moon and Sixpence
(1942) 89m. B&W (with color sequence). **B**
A British stockbroker/artist chucks it all and moves to Tahiti to paint, and leprosy cuts his fun short. This somewhat heavy-handed story was filmed in B&W for the European sets, then moves to sepia tone for the Tahitian paradise, and finishes in brash color to display the artwork.
D: Albert Lewin. A: George Sanders, Doris Dudley, Herbert Marshall.

Anna Karenina
(1948) 123m. B&W. **C+**
This unbalanced version of Tolstoy's tale of adultery, social disgrace, and despair labors over marital squabbling and not the heroine's motives for choosing a handsome but bland soldier. First-rate Russian settings and crisp photography are diminished by the length and some bad casting.
D: Julien Duvivier. A: Vivien Leigh, Ralph Richardson, Kieron Moore.

Madame Bovary
(1949) 115m. B&W. **B−**
A French provincial woman strays from her dull husband into a string of affairs in search of a romance. Nice period detail and a wide-eyed Jones don't keep this tepid affair afloat.
D: Vincente Minnelli. A: Jennifer Jones, James Mason, Louis Jourdan.

Biographies

Bio-pics of the 1930s and 40s took the lives of inventors, explorers, writers, and politicians and turned them into lavish historical sagas. Emphasizing all the dramatic high and low points, usually at the expense of accuracy or realism, these films are as entertaining as any melodrama and give you a lively look at some American and international heroes.

The Story of Louis Pasteur
(1936) 85m. B&W. **B–**
A renowned nineteenth-century chemist battles the French medical establishment to promote new approaches to surgery and methods to fight disease. A poineering bio-pic that proved it possible to turn a life based on science into an engrossing and compelling dramatic chronicle.
D: William Dieterle. A: Paul Muni, Josephine Hutchinson, Anita Louise.

The Life of Emile Zola
(1937) 116m. B&W. **A–**
This zips through Zola's early years, including his friendship with Cézanne, before focusing on the author's risky involvement with the Dreyfus case. Despite Muni's incredible overacting, the emotionally pitched film stands out thanks to the compelling reenactment of the infamous trial.
D: William Dieterle. A: Paul Muni, Gale Sondergaard, Joseph Schildkraut.

Juarez
(1939) 132m. B&W. **C**
France imposes an emperor, Maximilian, on the people of Mexico, igniting a war with the deposed president Juárez. This lavish paean to democracy suffers from the film's scattered attention to the disparate characters, but the vignettes remain vivid.
D: William Dieterle. A: Paul Muni, Bette Davis, Brian Aherne.

Stanley and Livingstone
(1939) 101m. B&W. **B**
A straightforward account of late-nineteenth-century reporter Stanley's arduous search for missionary Livingstone in Central Africa. The good use of background location footage, solid performances, and a view of Africa that avoids the Tarzan stereotypes of the time make up for any lack of excitement.
D: Henry King. A: Spencer Tracy, Nancy Kelly, Cedric Hardwicke.

Young Mr. Lincoln
(1939) 100m. B&W.
A–
This classic piece of Americana eschews the larger picture in order to focus on a case in which small-town lawyer Lincoln makes his name by successfully defending a pair of farm boys on a murder charge. A simple story with great attention to mood, detail, and character.
D: John Ford. A: Henry Fonda, Alice Brady, Marjorie Weaver.

Abe Lincoln in Illinois
(1940) 110m. B&W. **B–**
This version of Sherwood's play follows Lincoln's burgeoning political career up to his election. The behind-the-scenes battles, self-doubt, death of Lincoln's first love, and his stormy marriage add up to a compelling, less sensational historical rendition.
D: John Cromwell. A: Raymond Massey, Gene Lockhart, Ruth Gordon.

Edison, the Man
(1940) 107m. B&W. **A**
A statelier sequel to *Young Tom Edison,* which highlights the inventor's persistent efforts to perfect the electric light. Even with the overall optimistic tone, this is handled with some degree of realism, with Tracy adding even more dramatic weight.
D: Clarence Brown. A: Spencer Tracy, Rita Johnson, Charles Coburn.

Young Tom Edison
(1940) 82m. B&W. **B**
This is MGM's corny, glossy, and highly entertaining rendition of the prolific inventor's adolescent years. Rooney's infectious energy makes up for any historical liberties as he faces the trials and misunderstandings of a dreamer coming of age in a small-minded town.
D: Norman Taurog. A: Mickey Rooney, Fay Bainter, George Bancroft.

Madame Curie
(1943) 124m. B&W. **B**
This rare woman's bio-pic portrays the famed scientist and her husband who together discovered radium. Even with the usual MGM gloss, this is slower, more deliberate, and less zippy than the other entries, although still entertaining.
D: Mervyn LeRoy. A: Greer Garson, Walter Pidgeon, Henry Travers.

Pre-Code Melodramas: Tough and Sinful Women

Before the Production Code Administration clamped down on just how much sex and violence Hollywood could show in the movies, America enjoyed a golden age of tarnished ladies. The golddigger, the fallen woman, and the ruthless divorcée dominated these raw and sordid little melodramas with their surprisingly frank depiction of sin and female liberation. The films were still cautionary tales, and family values were extolled—finally—when the duplicitious dames were punished for their indiscretions and greed.

The Divorcee
(1930) 83m. B&W. **B**

A new divorcée goes on a man-binge to get back at her unfaithful husband in a luridly sexy but overly talky marriage melodrama whose subject matter may have infuriated censors even though the final reunion makes up for all the partner-swapping.
D: Robert Z. Leonard. A: Norma Shearer, Chester Morris, Conrad Nagel.

Madam Satan
(1930) 105m. B&W.
B–

A sweet young wife becomes a flaming vamp in order to seduce her husband incognito and woo him away from his mistress. Turgid and stagy until the outrageous costume ball aboard a zeppelin, where the "De Millian" debauchery is brought to a climax by the destruction of the dirigible over Manhattan.
D: Cecil B. DeMille. A: Kay Johnson, Reginald Denny, Lillian Roth.

Big Business Girl
(1931) 72m. B&W. **C**

This lukewarm marital melodrama about a bandleader trying to wrestle his working-girl wife from the grips of a lecherous boss has little feeling and is slow and long-winded.
D: William A. Seiter. A: Loretta Young, Frank Albertson, Ricardo Cortez.

The Common Law
(1931) 72m. B&W. **B**

Bennett is torn between two men, artist McCrea and wealthy older man Cody who pays her bills but doesn't float her libidinal boat. Features censor-tweaking scenes of Bennett posing dishabille and blissfully advocating romance without marriage.
D: Paul Stein A: Constance Bennett, Joel McCrea, Lew Cody.

The Sin of Madelon Claudet
(1931) 74m. B&W. **B–**

Hayes is the all-suffering mother who sacrifices everything, including her dignity, to put her son through medical school in this maudlin overwrought soap opera.
D: Edgar Selwyn. A: Helen Hayes, Lewis Stone, Neil Hamilton.

Three on a Match
(1932) 64m. B&W.
A

This tightly constructed and hard-boiled, love-and-loss melodrama begins with the ten-year reunion of three girlhood friends: the jaded showgirl, the practical working girl, and the rich man's wife. What happens to each of them is unexpected and thoroughly entertaining.
D: Mervyn LeRoy. A: Joan Blondell, Ann Dvorak, Bette Davis.

What Price Hollywood?
(1932) 88m. B&W. **A–**

A waitress is polished into a star by an on-the-skids director, but her marriage and career are quickly jeopardized by the precarious movie business. An honest little film about the pitfalls of Hollywood and the prototype for *A Star Is Born.*
D: George Cukor. A: Constance Bennett, Lowell Sherman, Neil Hamilton.

Ann Vickers
(1933) 72m. B&W. **B**

An unusual social conscience melodrama from a Sinclair Lewis novel about a welfare worker crusading for human rights in prisons. This bracing little tale allows the heroine both her independence and a love interest in judge Huston.
D: John Cromwell. A: Irene Dunne, Walter Huston, Conrad Nagel.

Finishing School
(1934) 73m. B&W. **B–**

Poor little rich girl Dee is shown the ropes at a snobby boarding school by jaded little hoyden Rogers—including the drinking and petting parties in New York. Slow-paced pathos is mixed with rowdy scenes of flaming youth.
D: Wanda Tuckock; George Nicholls, Jr. A: Frances Dee, Billie Burke, Ginger Rogers.

Barbara Stanwyck

Stanwyck brought her own brand of toughness to these snappy pre-Code melodramas about women, both good and bad, who matter-of-factly took on men in their own domain. Her shrewd wisecracking characters helped redefine glamour as she proved that she could lick any man whether in crime, business, or love.

Illicit
(1931) 81m. B&W. **B+**

Stanwyck and her wealthy lover have modern views on life, including cohabitation, in this progressive melodrama with a feminist edge. The scandalous subject matter is compensated for by the film's ultimate endorsement of marriage, but not before Stanwyck has fun being wicked.
D: Archie Mayo. A: With James Rennie, Ricardo Cortez, Joan Blondell.

Night Nurse
(1931) 72m. B&W. **B+**

A rookie nurse is assigned to care for a pair of sick children and suspects someone is trying to kill them. This saucy, fast-paced tale begins as a wisecracking comedy and soon moves to a serious crime-flavored melodrama with plenty of pre-Code spice, including scenes of women undressing down to their skivvies.
D: George Fitzmaurice. A: With Ben Lyon, Joan Blondell, Clark Gable.

The Purchase Price
(1932) 70m. B&W. **C+**

A gangster's mistress flees the big city and becomes a mail-order bride, enduring hardships as a farmer's wife in this sin-to-starvation drama. Nicely photographed but weighed down by sappy clichés.
D: William Wellman. A: With George Brent, Lyle Talbot, Hardie Albright.

Baby Face
(1933) 70m. B&W. **A**

This quintessential sinful woman melodrama, loaded with wry sexual innuendo, shows Stanwyck as a street-wise dame who trades on her sultry charms for a fast climb up the corporate ladder. One of the films that helps bring about the end of pre-Code freedom.
D: Alfred Green. A: With George Brent, Donald Cook, Alphonse Ethier.

Ladies They Talk About
(1933) 68m. B&W. **B+**

Bank robber Stanwyck is sent to San Quentin and pur-

sued by DA Foster who can't help falling for the streetwise convict with the heart of gold. An acerbic romantic melodrama of life inside the big house.
D: Howard Bretherton, William Keighley. A: With Preston S. Foster, Lyle Talbot, Dorothy Burgess.

Marlene Dietrich

She may have played self-sacrificing roles, but Dietrich always managed in her own tough and seductive way to get the best of her men in some of the more exotic and sexually perverse melodramas of this era.

Morocco
(1930) 92m. B&W. **A**

Dietrich is the seductive crooner who falls head over high heels for foreign legionnaire Cooper. A voluptuously photographed tale of love among rootless adventurers in Morocco, with Dietrich philosophically giving in to the blind urges of her passion. Don't miss her performance in drag sealed with a kiss to a woman in the audience.
D: Josef von Sternberg. A: With Gary Cooper, Adolphe Menjou, Ullrich Haupt.

Blonde Venus
(1932) 92m. B&W. **A**

This audacious and campy melodrama has Dietrich sacrificing all for her child and sick husband, ending up losing both. Her plunge into adultery, prostitution, and a career as the toast of European nightclubs is glorious, and her "Hot Voodoo" cabaret striptease from a gorilla suit has to be seen to be believed.
D: Josef von Sternberg. A: With Herbert Marshall, Cary Grant, Dickie Moore.

Desire
(1936) 96m. B&W. **B**

This is a tamer version of the golddigger yarn as elegant jewel thief Dietrich falls for the good guy businessman she uses to transport her loot across a Spanish border. A witty sparkling romantic comedy.
D: Frank Borzage. A: With Gary Cooper, John Halliday, William Frawley.

The Garden of Allah
(1936) 80m. **A**

A British woman in the Sahara desert falls in love with a man who turns out to be a Trappist monk. Strange is an understatement for this elegant-looking early Technicolor melodrama that remains endearingly romantic, absurdities and all.
D: Richard Boleslawski. A: With Charles Boyer, Basil Rathbone, C. Aubrey Smith.

Knight Without Armour
(1937) 107m. B&W. **A−**

A British spy masquerading as a Bolshevik transports a countess through postrevolutionary Russia and falls hopelessly in love with her. This atmospheric period drama is slow-moving, which only adds to its dreamy mesmerizing quality. Dietrich is luminous—if mostly mute—even in the midst of revolution.
D: Jacques Feyder. A: With Robert Donat, Irene Vanbrugh, Herbert Lomas.

Seven Sinners
(1940) 87m. B&W. **B**

Dietrich is the tough cookie entertainer in a tawdry little South Seas cafe—the Seven Sinners—who's pursued by a brood of men. The story of love blooming in a run-down hole may be a cliché, but all-American Wayne and exotically decadent Dietrich generate some real heat.
D: Tay Garnett. A: With John Wayne, Broderick Crawford, Albert Dekker.

Kismet
(1944) 100m. **B+**

This extravagent MGM Arabian fantasy is made more exotic with the addition of elegant dancer Dietrich, painted in gold, and Colman as the calculating magician love interest.
D: William Dieterle. A: With Ronald Colman, James Craig, Florence Bates.

Greta Garbo

In In her early sound films, Garbo finessed her bewitching appeal into playing the most exotic of 30s characters—the prostitute—along with her other specialty, the highly desirable but ultimately scorned lover. Garbo went on to play foreign aristocratic roles in lush historical soap operas as women who were ever-suffering, yet strangely self-sufficient pawns to men's passions.

Anna Christie
(1930) 86m. B&W. **C+**

Garbo talks ("Give me a whiskey . . . And don't be stingy, baby") in her first sound film as an ex-prostitute in love with a sailor who can't forgive her past. Even Garbo's voice can't breathe life into this typically static and sluggish early talkie.
D: Clarence Brown. A: With Charles Bickford, George F. Marion, Marie Dressler.

Mata Hari
(1931) 90m. B&W. **A−**

Garbo is the infamous World War I dancer/German spy and mistress to a Russian general who falls for his underling while keeping her tainted identity a secret. This shimmering production is strictly a glamorous star vehicle that includes some delicious risqué dance interludes from Garbo.
D: George Fitzmaurice. A: With Ramon Novarro, Lionel Barrymore, Lewis Stone.

Susan Lenox: Her Fall and Rise
(1931) 74m. B&W. **B+**

In this quick-paced, fallen-woman tale, unsullied Garbo gets corrupted by a succession of lecherous men and rewarded with great riches. It doesn't take her long to shrug it all off, head to South America, and find love with honest man Gable.
D: Robert Z. Leonard. A: With Clark Gable, Jean Hersholt, John Miljan.

As You Desire Me
(1932) 71m. B&W. **B**
After a violent trauma, tawdry nightclub entertainer Garbo is struck with amnesia, and can't recall if she is von Stroheim's mistress or an Italian countess. A strange atmospheric soaper with von Stroheim his usual brilliantly sadistic self.
D: George Fitzmaurice. A: With Melvyn Douglas, Erich von Stroheim, Owen Moore.

Queen Christina
(1933) 97m. B&W. **A**
Garbo, wearing male drag throughout, is the reforming Queen of Sweden who strives for peace while trying to balance a love affair with the demands of her title. This sophisticated historical melodrama is rich with witty sexual innuendoes, gargantuan sets, and moody lighting.
D: Rouben Mamoulian. A: With John Gilbert, Ian Keith, Lewis Stone.

Anna Karenina
(1935) 95m. B&W. **A–**
Garbo is the doomed heroine whose search for emotional fulfillment tears her from husband, child, and society. A literary costume soaper which doesn't stint on the opulent trappings of czarist Moscow's upper class and army elite.
D: Clarence Brown. A: With Fredric March, Basil Rathbone, Freddie Bartholomew.

Camille
(1937) 108m. B&W. **A**
Garbo's Camille embodies the noble beautiful suffering of the nineteenth-century heroine as she's punished for her life as a courtesan with consumption and the possible loss of her true love. Garbo is luminous while sets and scenes sparkle with a radiance suggesting candlelight and diamonds.
D: George Cukor. A: With Robert Taylor, Lionel Barrymore, Elizabeth Allan.

Conquest
(1937) 112m. B&W. **A–**
Garbo is the Polish countess Walewska, who's courted by Napoleon and bears his illegitimate child, along with the scorn of society. The star again plays to perfection the role of a woman failed by her lover and the world in this sumptuous but hollow period melodrama.
D: Clarence Brown. A: With Charles Boyer, Reginald Owen, Alan Marshal.

Ninotchka
(1939) 110m. B&W. **A**
A grim Soviet inspector visits Paris on business and finds herself falling for a capitalist lawyer. Director Lubitsch, the master of sparklingly wicked adult comedies, coaxes a hilariously droll performance from Garbo in this clever comedic clash of Russian sobriety and French decadence.
D: Ernst Lubitsch. A: With Melvyn Douglas, Ina Claire, Bela Lugosi.

Two-Faced Woman
(1941) 94m. B&W. **B–**
Garbo plays twins in her last film: a down-to-earth ski instructor who weds a rich playboy, and the glamorous sister who wins him away from a Manhattan sophisticate. Despite the spicy premise, this fluffy romantic comedy lacks any pizzazz, perhaps due to the reediting it got for its frivolous depiction of marriage.
D: George Cukor. A: With Melvyn Douglas, Constance Bennett, Roland Young.

Post-Code Melodramas: The Weepies

Hollywood really cleaned up its act after 1934. The naughty shopgirls and cabaret stars of the early 30s became the domesticated selfless mothers, sweet young things, and unredeemably wicked girls from the wrong side of the tracks. This group of weepies includes some of the classic soap operas of this era with all the bizarre plot twists that punish the bad girl or allow the pure-as-the-driven-snow heroine some fun while keeping her virtue intact.

History Is Made at Night
(1937) 98m. B&W. **B+**
Unhappily married to an insanely jealous husband, Arthur falls for a French headwaiter who follows her back to New York. Slow-paced, overripe soaper, with an utterly charming Boyer and a terrific climax of an ocean liner-iceberg collision that puts Titanic films to shame.
D: Frank Borzage. A: Charles Boyer, Jean Arthur, Leo Carrillo.

Madame X
(1937) 75m. B&W. **B**
This tale of a discontented straying wife whose single affair leads her down the path to ruin will stop at nothing to jerk tears. A moralistic tale with little to redeem it direction- or acting-wise, though it does contain all the serpentine plot twists and incredible coincidences of this genre.
D: Sam Wood. A: Gladys George, John Beal, Warren William.

A Star Is Born
(1937) 111m. **A**
The first and probably the best of the three versions of Hollywood's Cinderella melodrama offers a relatively authentic behind-the-scenes look as Gaynor's rise to stardom intersects with the downward trajectory of husband March's career. The heart-wrenching conclusion and beautiful early Technicolor make this a poignant look at the vagaries of Tinseltown.
D: William Wellman. A: Janet Gaynor, Fredric March, Adolphe Menjou.

Stella Dallas
(1937) 106m. B&W. **A**
The golddigger got her man but can't escape her low-class roots. Now she's trying to hold on to her daughter who's beginning to pay for her mother's tackiness. Along with *Mildred Pierce,* this is the definitive mother-love weepie, with a heartbreaking Stanwyck.
D: King Vidor. A: Barbara Stanwyck, John Boles, Anne Shirley.

Four Daughters
(1938) 90m. B&W. **A**
A widowed father manages a household of four musical daughters that's disrupted by the arrival of a moody handsome orchestrator. An original, buoyant, and heartwarming family melodrama with a bitter, world-weary Garfield as the standout.
D: Michael Curtiz. A: Claude Rains; Rosemary, Lola, and Priscilla Lane; John Garfield.

The Shopworn Angel
(1938) 85m. B&W. **B+**
A jaded Broadway actress is

just settling into a chummy but loveless relationship with a wealthy producer when she meets doughboy Stewart who's about to be shipped out to France. A classic love triangle and fine performances all around make this sweet tearjerker worth a rental.
D: H. C. Potter. A: Margaret Sullavan, James Stewart, Walter Pidgeon.

In Name Only
(1939) 94m. B&W. **A**

Reptilian golddigger/homewrecker Francis marries Grant for his money and refuses to let go of her meal ticket, even when he falls for single mother Lombard. A sleek marital soap that sticks to tradition by rewarding the virtuous woman, but contrary to the genre, it's the man who takes to the sick bed here.
D: John Cromwell. A: Carole Lombard, Cary Grant, Kay Francis.

Intermezzo
(1939) 70m. B&W. **A**

Bergman, in her American debut, is the sweet young pianist to whom married man Howard takes a shine, even though he can't divorce his wife. This remake has the elegance and intelligence of a European production and the tear-jerking passion of the best American soaps about a doomed affair.
D: Gregory Ratoff. A: Leslie Howard, Ingrid Bergman, Edna Best.

Kitty Foyle
(1940) 105m. B&W. **B–**

Working girl Rogers must choose between a struggling doctor and a wealthy Philadelphia man whose family disapproves of her. It's hard to care about the characters in this tepid, syrupy love triangle, although not for lack of trying on Rogers' part.
D: Sam Wood. A: Ginger Rogers, Dennis Morgan, James Craig.

Primrose Path
(1940) 93m. B&W. **B+**

Rogers is the virtuous daughter who dreams of escaping her deviant promiscuous clan when she falls for good guy McCrea. Remarkably sordid subject matter and frank language spice up the proceedings in this downbeat melodrama.
D: Gregory La Cava. A: Ginger Rogers, Joel McCrea, Marjorie Rambeau.

Joan Crawford

After her early bad-girl talkies, Crawford settled into a string of Cinderella soap operas playing the honest, sometimes wronged working girl who had a strange tendency to marry rich men she didn't love. In all her roles, Crawford was the glamorous sleek clotheshorse, and you can always count on a veritable fashion show of 30s Hollywood haute couture along with crazy plots and healthy doses of schmaltz.

Dance, Fools, Dance
(1931) 81m. B&W. **B–**

Good-time girl / heiress Crawford has to learn about life the hard way when the stock market crashes. While censors objected to the scenes of a flamboyantly decadent lifestyle, this really only has one brief and tame high-society skinny-dip.
D: Harry Beaumont. A: With Lester Vail, Cliff Edwards, William Bakewell.

Rain
(1932) 93m. B&W. **B+**

The religious zealot wants to convert her, the lovelorn soldier tries to woo her, but Sadie, the prostitute stranded on a Samoan island, just wants to escape her past. The vanguard camerawork, atmospheric tropical images, and Crawford's wounded wise whore with a canny sense of humor help make this a classic fallen-woman soaper.
D: Lewis Milestone. A: With Walter Huston, William Gargan, Guy Kibbee.

Sadie McKee
(1934) 90m. B&W. **B+**

When Sadie follows her boyfriend to New York, he leaves her hours before they're to be wed, and soon she's married to an alcoholic rich man. One of the wackier plots, with Sadie managing to redeem drunk hubby while keeping her virginity intact.
D: Clarence Brown. A: With Gene Raymond, Franchot Tone, Esther Ralston.

I Live My Life
(1935) 92m. B&W. **B–**

A bored socialite introduces her wealthy New York friends to the serious-minded archeologist she met on vacation in Greece, with the expected odd-couple cultural clash. A fluffy but nicely paced and clever romantic comedy that positively wallows in its sophisticated milieu.
D: W. S. Van Dyke. A: With Brian Aherne, Frank Morgan, Aline MacMahon.

The Gorgeous Hussy
(1936) 102m. B&W. **B+**

A deceptive title for this fact-based costume melodrama of modest intelligent working girl Peggy O'Neal Eaton, the suffragette and man-magnet who became President Jackson's personal confidante. Typical lush MGM historical soaper that's given some starch by Barrymore's sturdy and tender president.
D: Clarence Brown. A: With Robert Taylor, Lionel Barrymore, Melvyn Douglas.

The Bride Wore Red
(1937) 103m. B&W. **A–**

Crawford is the cabaret singer at an uppercrust Tyrolean resort who tries to win Young's heart by masquerading as a high-society lady. Tone is the simple postman who vies for her affections in this charming and frivolous tale in which Crawford's red dress becomes her social downfall à la *Jezebel*.
D: Dorothy Arzner. A: With Franchot Tone, Robert Young, Billie Burke.

Mannequin
(1937) 95m. B&W.
A–

A Lower East Side girl marries her boyfriend who turns out to be a chisller, and she's soon making it on her own as a model. But the self-made industrialist who's been wooing her since her wedding night keeps on showing up. Tracy's solid presence, the crazy story, and some effective scenes of cramped tenement life give this extra bite.
D: Frank Borzage. A: With Spencer Tracy, Alan Curtis, Ralph Morgan.

The Shining Hour
(1938) 76m. B&W. **B**

Dancer Crawford marries into a wealthy old Wisconsin family who view this *arriviste* with disdain, jealousy,

and lust. A relatively toned down soaper, until the wonderfully demented emotional blowout in the finale. The wistful, long-suffering Sullavan takes the cake for her self-sacrificing gestures.
D: Frank Borzage. A: With Margaret Sullavan, Melvyn Douglas, Robert Young.

Adventure Dramas

These films about aviators, captains, and aristocratic army officers offer the conflict and romance of the 30s melodrama embellished with some high-color adventures in exotic places.

Scarlet Dawn
(1932) 76m. B&W. **B+**

The Russian Revolution forces a prince to flee to the continent with no money and a servant girl in tow. When he can't seduce her he marries her, but then meets up with other ex-patriot aristocrats. A rousing and romantic tale with glorious scenes of decadence followed by the prince's "degradation" waiting tables.
D: William Dieterle. A: Douglas Fairbanks, Jr.; Nancy Carroll; Eddie Fox.

China Seas
(1935) 88m. B&W. **B**

The captain of a ship sailing from mainland China to Singapore has to contend with the threat of pirates along with an Englishwoman from his past and the floozy showgirl on board. Plenty of intrigue, dramatic storms, and raw sexual dialogue courtesy of Harlow, in this high seas adventure-comedy.
D: Tay Garnett. A: Clark Gable, Jean Harlow, Wallace Beery.

Test Pilot
(1938) 118m. B&W. **B–**

A fast-living test pilot meets a farm girl after a forced landing and marries her, much to the dismay of his longtime mechanic-partner. Gable and Tracy mug for screen time as kittenish Loy looks amused in this high-spirited, buddy-buddy fluff, which features some spectacular aerial stunts and an endless deathbed scene.
D: Victor Fleming. A: Clark Gable, Myrna Loy, Spencer Tracy.

Too Hot to Handle
(1938) 108m. B&W. **A–**

A newsreel cameraman hooks up with aviatrix Loy on a mission to find her brother who disappeared in the Amazon. Tons of action—voodoo, firewalking, human sacrifice, and spectacular aviation footage—are in this big-budget adventure with a plot straight out of action serials.
D: Jack Conway. A: Clark Gable, Myrna Loy, Walter Pidgeon.

Only Angels Have Wings
(1939) 121m. B&W. **A**

A cadre of fliers runs the treacherous mail deliveries over the South American mountains, led by no-nonsense Grant for whom songstress Arthur pines. A classic Howard Hawks tale of male camaraderie beautifully photographed, with the shadowed tropical scenery lending a surreal dreaminess to the proceedings.
D: Howard Hawks. A: Cary Grant, Jean Arthur, Richard Barthelmess.

Jean Harlow

Whether in melodramas or comedies, the original platinum blonde personified the smart-alecky golddigger/vamp with the low-rent mind and high-priced body. Harlow's acting was never terribly persuasive, but with her come-hither look, insinuating voice, and outrageously skimpy outfits, she fit like a satin glove into these sleek and sophisticated fantasies.

Red Dust
(1932) 83m. B&W. **A**

Gable is overseer at an Indochinese rubber plantation who's fought over by wisecracking hussy Harlow and straying wife Astor. Harlow is pure libido here, with her sexy sordidness perfectly matched by Gable's.
D: Victor Fleming. A: With Clark Cable, Gene Raymond, Mary Astor.

Red-Headed Woman
(1932) 79m. B&W. **A–**

In a radical departure, Harlow is a carrot-topped instead of a platinum-haired siren, with designs on another woman's man. This witty golddigger drama shows the trashy stenographer working her way through a string of men, getting older and richer, without punishment for her many indiscretions.
D: Jack Conway. A: With Chester Morris, Lewis Stone, Leila Hyams.

Hold Your Man
(1933) 86m. B&W. **B+**

Two bad eggs make good together as a woman of questionable character gets involved with a con artist and winds up in the big house where she learns she's pregnant. The smart salty dialogue is tempered with some honest sentiment.
D: Sam Wood. A: With Clark Gable, Stuart Erwin, Dorothy Burgess.

Reckless
(1935) 96m. B&W. **B–**

A brassy Broadway showgirl searches for happiness in a rich man's arms but finds only despair. Harlow, who's at her best when sexual innuendo is her only task, isn't up to juggling singing, dancing, *and* showing a heart of gold.
D: Victor Fleming. A: With William Powell, Franchot Tone, May Robson.

Riffraff
(1935) 89m. B&W. **B+**

Harlow, now sporting a working girl's brown rinse, is once again thrown into prison when she's pregnant, after stealing money to help her destitute mule-headed fisherman husband. A

smartly scripted, wisecracking melodrama with some comedic touches from villain boss Calleia.
D: Walter Ruben. A: With Spencer Tracy, Joseph Calleia, Una Merkel.

Wife vs. Secretary
(1936) 89m. B&W. **B**
Harlow takes a turn as a goody-two-shoes secretary in love with her married boss, actually maintaining her dignity and chastity against all odds. Not much bite or cleverness, though plenty of big-budget gloss: This shows how censorship changed her persona and the tone of later melodramas.
D: Clarence Brown. A: With Clark Gable, James Stewart, Myrna Loy.

Bette Davis

Davis had the greatest range of any of Hollywood's tarnished ladies, playing blind socialites, Southern belles, brutal coquettes, and self-sacrificing wives with equal finesse. While her earlier films tended to be more pedestrian melodramas, by the end of the decade she was starring in some of the greatest women's films to come out of Hollywood.

Cabin in the Cotton
(1932) 77m. B&W. **B**
Seductive rich girl Davis teases poor boy Barthelmess who's torn between her and good girl Jordan. This sensuous and dated tale has some savvy social commentary about workers' exploitation, and a gloriously cruel Davis as the spoiled coquette with a delicious Southern drawl.
D: Michael Curtiz. A: With Richard Barthelmess, Dorothy Jordan, Henry B. Walthall.

Ex-Lady
(1933) 65m. B&W. **B**
Forward-thinking working girl Davis finally agrees to marry, only to find her new husband's eye wandering. This polished glimpse into the lifestyles of the young and liberated—the elegant sets and Davis in plenty of satin numbers are swell—has a touch of raciness, but a predictable outcome.
D: Robert Florey. A: With Gene Raymond, Frank McHugh, Monroe Owsley.

Of Human Bondage
(1934) 83m. B&W. **B**
Davis is the tawdry Cockney waitress - turned - prostitute, whose slide into degradation completely destroys pitiful medical student Howard's life. Davis is wholly unsympathetic and not at her most convincing in this vicious fallen-woman melodrama.
D: John Cromwell. A: With Leslie Howard, Frances Dee, Reginal Owen.

Dangerous
(1935) 72m. B&W. **A–**
Architect socialite Tone forsakes his career, fiancée, and reputation when he rehabilitates the fatally charming, on-the-skids Broadway star Davis. This melodrama of forbidden love has real bite, even with the tacked-on shallow ending.
D: Alfred Green. A: With Franchot Tone, Margaret Lindsay, Alison Skipworth.

That Certain Woman
(1937) 91m. B&W. **B**
A gangster's widow marries a playboy whose father does everything he can to split the couple up. Maternal soap opera in the *Stella Dallas* vein, with Davis bringing credibility to the melodramatic cliché of the all-giving, all-sacrificing wife and mother.
D: Edmond Goulding. A: With Henry Fonda, Ian Hunter, Anita Louise.

Jezebel
(1938) 103m. B&W.
B+
An impetuous willful Southern belle can't be tamed even by beau Fonda, and loses him and her reputation after showing up at the ball in a red dress. This Civil War costume melodrama may punish the brazen coquette, but Davis never lets us lose sympathy or fascination for her defiant heroine.
D: William Wyler. A: With George Brent, Henry Fonda, Margaret Lindsay.

The Sisters
(1938) 98m. B&W. **B+**
This bittersweet family melodrama of three Montana sisters at the turn of the century focuses on the eldest's troubled marriage to an alcoholic sports reporter in San Francisco. The nostalgic costume picture covers a lot of ground, but is held together by the long-suffering Davis.
D: Anatole Litvak. A: With Errol Flynn, Anita Louise, Ian Hunter.

Dark Victory
(1939) 106m. B&W. **A**
A vibrant selfish society woman with an incurable disease takes one more stab at life and happiness with her doctor. Davis transforms the corniest of plot devices—the fatal illness into high Hollywood art. Tears were never jerked so entertainingly or with such style.
D: Edmund Goulding. A: With George Brent, Humphrey Bogart, Geraldine Fitzgerald.

The Old Maid
(1939) 95m. B&W. **A–**
Davis gives up her illegitimate child to her jealous cousin, masquerading as her daughter's aunt in order to ensure the child's future. Davis' performance as the long-suffering, secret mother gives real tragedy to the crazy plot twists in this first-rate tearjerker.
D: Edmund Goulding. A: With Miriam Hopkins, George Brent, Jane Bryan.

Katharine Hepburn

With her patrician manner and good looks, Hepburn was more likely to be draped in tweeds or period finery than the slinky evening gowns of her contemporaries. Her regal but perky bearing saved many of her lesser films from utter failure, though the mannered

style of these stories gives them a dated quality, making you yearn for the Kate of screwball comedies and her sparkling wrestling matches with Spencer Tracy.

Christopher Strong
(1933) 77m. B&W. **B+**
Hepburn is the Amelia Earhart-inspired aviatrix who falls hard for married man Clive, gets pregnant, and takes the noble way out to save his political reputation. The final sacrifice may be a cliché in this flowery melodrama, but Hepburn's natural independence and nobility leave Clive in the dust.
D: Dorothy Arzner. A: With Colin Clive, Billie Burke, Helen Chandler.

Morning Glory
(1933) 74m. B&W. **B**
A naive young woman comes to New York to be a Broadway star and succeeds against all odds. Irrepressible and sometimes irritating Hepburn makes her character flesh-and-blood in this entertaining if somewhat stagy showbiz Cinderella story.
D: Lowell Sherman. A: With Douglas Fairbanks, Jr.; Adolphe Menjou; Mary Duncan.

The Little Minister
(1934) 104m. B&W. **B+**
Vivacious Scottish aristocrat Hepburn masquerades as a gypsy and attracts the interest of a young minister in this warmhearted and slightly eccentric romantic drama with a social conscience.
D: Richard Wallace. A: With John Beal, Alan Hale, Donald Crisp.

Spitfire
(1934) 90m. B&W. **B−**
Hepburn plays an uneducated Ozark mountain faith healer who charms two city slickers while alienating the local mountain dwellers. The bizarre story, involving kidnapping, religious faith, and a witch hunt, is enhanced by Hepburn's odd, at times, annoying tomboyish performance.
D: John Cromwell. A: With Robert Young, Ralph Bellamy, Martha Sleeper.

Alice Adams
(1935) 99m. B&W. **B+**
A girl from the poor side of the tracks tries desperately to rise above her crass family by attracting the town's rich boy. Hepburn's pathetic attempts to appear popular and sophisticated are so vividly portrayed that this dated talky but classic American tale is almost uncomfortable to watch.
D: George Stevens. A: With Fred MacMurray, Fred Stone, Evelyn Venable.

Sylvia Scarlett
(1936) 94m. B&W. **B+**
Hepburn masquerades as a boy to escape the law in this gender-bending romance between two British crooks. A rambling curiosity piece that flips between comedy and drama.
D: George Cukor. A: With Cary Grant, Brian Aherne, Edmund Gwenn.

A Woman Rebels
(1936) 88m. B&W. **B**
Hepburn is a Victorian-era suffragette whose love affair and political convictions fly in the face of society and her conservative family. The historical details and Hepburn are pretty, but not enough to shine up the lackluster story.
D: Mark Sandrich. A: With Herbert Marshall, Elizabeth Allan, Donald Crisp.

Quality Street
(1937) 84m. B&W. **B+**
In this lightweight historical romance set in a small eighteenth-century English village, Hepburn loves a heartless officer who promptly forgets her when he goes off to war. A prissy and implausible love story with a charming Hepburn pretending to be her own spirited niece in order to win back Tone.
D: George Stevens. A: With Franchot Tone, Fay Bainter, Eric Blore.

Crime Dramas

These crime dramas told a different story from the standard rise-and-fall gangster film in their attempt to depict the effects of crime on other people. More issue-oriented than their action counterparts, these films even tried to break away from the simplistic morality that plagued the genre.

The Criminal Code
(1931) 95m. B&W. **C+**
This early sound prison drama involves a young prisoner who falls in love with the warden's daughter, in the midst of stoolpigeons, revenge plots, and escape plans. Slow and talky with a pretty unconvincing story, but the prison sequences along with Huston and Karloff's performances still grab you.
D: Howard Hawks. A: Walter Huston, Phillips Holmes, Boris Karloff.

Manhattan Melodrama
(1934) 93m. B&W. **B+**
Two childhood buddies grow up on opposite sides of the law and fall for the same girl. One becomes governor and ends up sending the other to the electric chair. A star-driven MGM crime soaper, rich with early New York period color.
D: W. S. Van Dyke. A: Clark Gable, William Powell, Myrna Loy.

The Petrified Forest
(1936) 83m. B&W. **B**
A wandering poet, a lovestruck waitress, and a fugitive bandit holding them hostage form an unusual bond at a roadside desert diner. This stage-bound, highly theatrical mix of gangster motifs and romantic drama might creak a bit but the three luminous stars still make it work beautifully.
D: Archie Mayo. A: Leslie Howard, Bette Davis, Humphrey Bogart.

Marked Woman
(1937) 96m. B&W. **B+**
A compelling and strangely moving crime drama told from the point of view of women caught up in the vice rackets as they waver between letting their boss get away with murder and risking their lives by testifying. Eschews standard romantic relationships in favor of female camaraderie.
D: Lloyd Bacon. A: Bette Davis, Humphrey Bogart, Lola Lane.

They Made Me a Criminal
(1939) 92m. B&W. **B**
A boxer on the run from a murder finds a new life as a father figure to the Kids who

turn up, somewhat improbably, at an Arizona fruit ranch. An entertaining entry of The Dead End Kids series with Rains providing an interesting bit of miscasting as the dogged New York City cop on Garfield's trail.
D: Busby Berkeley. A: John Garfield, Claude Rains, The Dead End Kids.

Race Films

In response to the black stereotypes and glorification of the Ku Klux Klan in D. W. Griffith's *Birth of a Nation*, Emmett J. Scott (Booker T. Washington's secretary) made a film called *Birth of a Race*. Although it flopped, it did open the doors to a series of films, from comedies to westerns, called "Race Films," primarily written and directed by blacks and featuring all-black casts.

The Emperor Jones
(1933) 72m. B&W. **B+**
A hustler named Brutus Jones goes from being a chain-gang preacher to an island sovereign. Moody and significantly altered adaptation of O'Neill's famous play features great black actor/singer Paul Robeson in his most stirring performance.
D: Dudley Murphy. A: Paul Robeson, Dudley Digges, Frank Wilson.

Green Pastures
(1936) 90m. B&W. **D+**
A reworking of various tales from the Bible, highlighted by charismatic baritone Rex Ingram as "De Lawd." While the musical numbers have wonderful retro-charm, the stereotypical "colored folk" make it hard to watch.
D: Marc Connelly, William Keighley. A: Rex Ingram, Oscar Polk, Frank Wilson.

Murder on Lenox Avenue
(1941) 60m. B&W. **B+**
While a murder is the plot-turning device, this rooming house version of *Grand Hotel* focuses more on a neighborhood trying to stand on its own, showing cultural differences in the community and interaction between business and politics. Tame by modern standards, but still has enough melodrama to make a good soap opera.
D: Arthur Dreifuss. A: Mamie Smith, Alex Lovejoy, Edna Mae Harris.

Dirty Gertie from Harlem
(1946) 60m. B&W. **A–**
In this remake of *Rain*, a steamy female singer is made to pay for a shady past when she begins an island tour. Unrestricted by the Hayes Code, a strange and compelling combination of explicit sexuality and a positive take on religion.
D: Spencer Williams. A: Francine Everette, Don Wilson, Spencer Williams.

Juke Joint
(1947) 70m. **C–**
Two good-hearted vagabonds take up residence in a house with a ne'er-do-well father, a strict mother, and good and bad daughters. Williams and Orr draw heavily on vaudeville with their rapid-fire patter, but the family ends up performing recognizable Amos and Andy stereotypes.
D: Spencer Williams. A: Spencer Williams, Robert Orr, Inez Newell.

Sex and Drugs

At some point in these cautionary exploitation films, a plump gray-haired adult will lecture you on the depravity just portrayed. Don't worry, it only lasts a few minutes, and you're soon back to watching the party groping, hot swing dancing, furtive weed puffing, goggly eyed intoxication, and the innocent girls who are forever cavorting in their 30s underwear.

Guilty Parents
(1933) 63m. B&W. **B+**
Because mom won't let her read a sex book, Helen dates a wild guy who takes her to stripping and drinking parties. Before you know it, she's pimping her dance students and involved in murder. It's old and creaky but moves along so fast that a sequence where she has an illegitimate baby takes 30 seconds.
D: Jack Townley. A: John St. Polis, Jean Lacy, Robert Frazer.

Slaves in Bondage
(1935) 85m. B&W. **B+**
Gangsters and a tough madam run a roadhouse and kidnap or dupe young women in as the talent. They frame a reporter and, when his girl tries to help, she winds up in the roadhouse. Highlights include a feather dance, catfighting whores, and a tour of the roadhouse's "theme rooms" for the benefit of the heroine.
D: Elmer Clifton. A: Lona Andre, Donald Reed, Wheeler Oakman.

Cocaine Fiends
(1936) 75m. B&W. **D**
Working out of the swank "Dead Rat Club," a suave dope dealer hooks what seems like the entire population of a small town on his magic "headache powder." The numerous musical numbers and story line about the innocent farm girl-turned-tough moll doesn't quite succeed in making this as bad/funny as *Reefer Madness*.
D: William O'Connor. A: Noel Madison, Sheila Manners, Lois January.

Damaged Goods (Forbidden Desires)
(1936) 72m. B&W. **C+**
The film that wants to boldly blow the lid off myths about syphilis shows what a nice young man goes through—quack cures, a sick baby, possible divorce—when he contracts it. A bizarre 60s "art" film ending is tacked on, showing a nude woman being chased and caressed by blotches on the film.
D: Phil Stone. A: Pedro de Cordova, Phyliss Barry, Douglas Walton.

Reefer Madness
(1936) 68m. B&W. **B+**

The mother of the campy cautionary tale packs every exploitation image into an hour: pot smoking, girls in various states of undress groping on the couch, fast jive music, suicide, insanity, and murder. A crescendo of bad acting is reached when you see how these kids react to their first puff.
D: Louis Gasnier. A: Dorothy Short, Dave O'Brien, Kenneth Craig.

Test Tube Babies
(1938) 65m. B&W. **C–**

The ultimate lovey-dovey couple have it all but a baby, but when the monotone doctor finds the husband is sterile, the marriage hits the rocks. Will they risk artificial insemination? Lead-weighted dialogue, discount sets, and bad film damage is topped off by the mid-film insertion of a stripper cat fight.
D: W. Merle Connell. A: Dorothy Dube, William Thomason, Timothy Farrall.

Mad Youth
(1939) 67m. B&W. **B–**

A divorced mother hires a gigolo to recapture her passion while her teen daughter spends all-nighters jitterbugging, playing strip poker, and groping on the couch. This inevitably leads to Latin club parties, Mexican clog dancing, and descent into prostitution, but it's the gigolo with the heart of gold to the rescue!
D: Willis Kent. A: Mary Ainslee, Betty Compson, Willy Costello.

Souls in Pawn
(1940) 65m. B&W. **B**

Left to have her baby at an evil money-grubbing clinic, Lois discovers the doctor sold her child to a publicity-hungry burlesque queen. Really strange sequences include a teen couple asphyxiated in a motel, an insane asylum song and dance number, and a parade of strippers cavorting in their panties.
D: John Melville. A: Ginger Britton, Beatic Curtis, Lloyd Ingraham.

Child Bride
(1941) 67m. B&W. **C+**

Pre-teen Jennie is a barefoot hillbilly forced to marry grubby Jake or he'll falsely finger mom in the murder of her husband. The nominal actors give it their hillbilly best in genuine, dirt-poor mountain locations. Impressive scenes include the mob trying to tar and feather the teacher who is lobbying to change the marriage laws.
D: Harry Revier. A: Shirley Miles, Warren Richmond, Bob Bollinger.

Teenage (Teenage Jungle)
(1944) 65m. B&W. **C–**

This amateurish youths-gone-wild flick features a moralizing DA lecturing some mussy-haired 1940s juvenile delinquents and their parents on the depravity of their lives. Spliced in are gangsters and whorehouse sequences from 30s exploitation films. The immoral mothers who play bridge all night is a nice touch.
D: Dick L'Estrange. A: Herbert Hayes, Wheeler Oakman, Johnny Duncan.

Golden Age Dramas

In this group of films made during Hollywood's golden era, there is a variety of top-flight entertainments, including several bona fide classics, whose unique charm have not diminished with time.

Grand Hotel
(1932) 113m. B&W.
A–

The lives of a ballerina, a baron-turned-thief, a ruthless tycoon and his secretary, and a dying office worker are intertwined when they check into the famous Berlin hotel. An all-star soap opera deluxe with some wild overacting by Garbo and Barrymore is still entertaining.
D: Edmund Goulding. A: Greta Garbo, Joan Crawford, Lionel Barrymore.

Skyscraper Souls
(1932) 99m. B&W.
A

A lecherous and ruthless real estate developer, who built an Empire State Building-like Tower of Babel, corrupts an innocent girl in this film teeming with big-city debauchery. Young love, crime, suicides, a stock market crash, and a macabre climax all make an appearance in this delirious lawless version of *Grand Hotel*.
D: Edgar Selwyn. A: Warren William, Maureen O'Sullivan, Gregory Ratoff.

Crime and Punishment
(1935) 88m. B&W **B+**

An intellectual murders a greedy pawnbroker he deems useless but can't get free of the guilt—or the policeman who tracks him. Jittery Lorre and fatherly Arnold strike up an unusual kinship in this spooky expressionistic detective story that bears little resemblance to the classic novel.
D: Josef von Sternberg. A: Peter Lorre, Edward Arnold, Marian Marsh.

Dodsworth
(1936) 101m. B&W.
A

When an industrialist sells his business and takes the grand tour of Europe with his vain wife, she goes off on her own romantic fling, leaving the old lion wondering what went wrong. A sophisticated, bittersweet, and stunningly photographed drama of adult characters that go through unexpected changes.
D: William Wyler. A: Walter Huston, Ruth Chatterton, Mary Astor.

Lost Horizon
(1937) 132m. B&W.
B+

The survivors of a plane crash wind up in a Tibetan land called Shangri-La where they are given the key to eternal life. The spectacular sets, the bigger than life performances, and thrilling opening and final scenes make up for some watered down philosophical musings and the patience required to sit through the photographic stills used to make up for lost scenes.
D: Frank Capra. A: Ronald Colman, Jane Wyatt, Sam Jaffe.

Idiot's Delight
(1938) 105m. B&W. **B–**

A brazen song and dance man is among the travelers stranded in a European hotel on the eve of World War II, and he's convinced that the Russian aristocrat is an old flame from an Omaha burlesque house. Gable hoofing it is a hoot in this overripe but effectively disquieting parable about the oncoming war.

D: Clarence Brown. A: Clark Gable, Norma Shearer, Edward Arnold.

Citizen Kane
(1941) 119m. B&W.
A

The life of newspaper magnate Charles Foster Kane remains a startling and eerie American tragedy. With a story that unfolds like a dream, this classic looks like an elegant film noir with its brooding haunting images while still managing to be the best entertainment on the block.
D: Orson Welles. A: Orson Welles, Joseph Cotten, Everett Sloane.

Weekend at the Waldorf
(1945) 130m. B&W. **B**

In this 40s version of *Grand Hotel,* the lives of a typist, an oil man, a wounded soldier, a lonely movie star, and a war correspondent intersect for two days at the Waldorf-Astoria hotel. Slightly overlong with a brighter and more determinedly optimistic tone than the soulful original.
D: Robert Z. Leonard. A: Ginger Rogers, Lana Turner, Walter Pidgeon.

Men's Dramas

Some are three-hanky male weepies and others war dramas, but all focus on men bonding, in conflict or coming-of-age in the changing world.

All Quiet on the Western Front
(1930) 130m. B&W. **B**

The young soldiers go off to fight the good fight in the Great War, but their fervor turns to horror when they witness death firsthand. While the harrowing battle scenes retain their power, this creaky antiwar saga is seriously flawed by an overwrought Ayres and the film's manipulative and sanctimonious tone.
D: Lewis Milestone. A: Lew Ayres, Louis Walheim, John Wray.

The Champ
(1931) 87m. B&W. **B+**

A stumblebum prizefighter begins the long road back to respectability and the winner's circle with the help of his plucky young son. This sentimental tale of redemption is held up by the buddy-buddy rapport and Beery's portrayal of the self-destructive boxer who truly was a contender.
D: King Vidor. A: Wallace Beery, Jackie Cooper, Irene Rich.

A Farewell to Arms
(1932) 78m. B&W. **A–**

Love blossoms for an English nurse and a wounded American ambulance driver as the hostilities of World War I escalate around them. A romantic version of Hemingway's novel with a soulful Hayes as the unglamorous working girl who simmers for the angelic and adventurous man with no country.
D: Frank Borzage. A: Gary Cooper, Helen Hayes, Adolphe Menjou.

The Informer
(1935) 91m. B&W. **A–**

A boozy thug tossed out of the IRA denounces a comrade to collect a reward for passage to America, and becomes the target of a city-wide manhunt. This expressionistic tale of the 1922 Irish rebellion has an unrelenting gravity bound down by a dated musical score, but remains a powerful film.
D: John Ford. A: Victor McLaglen, Heather Angel, Preston Foster.

Captain's Courageous
(1937) 116m. B&W. **B**

A Portuguese fisherman rescues a rich sissy-boy and gives him his first taste of the hard life and an education in the ways and means of being a man. MGM's all-star version of Kipling's coming-of-age tale is a male bonding fest that has lost little of its splendor or its hamminess.
D: Victor Fleming. A: Spencer Tracy, Freddie Bartholomew, Lionel Barrymore.

Boy's Town
(1938) 96m. B&W. **B**

Father Flanagan's motto that "there's no such thing as a bad boy" is severely tested when a trash-talking delinquent crash-lands in his home for wayward boys. Rooney goes *way* over the top in this hokey balderdash which remains entertaining in spite of itself.
D: Norman Taurog. A: Spencer Tracy, Mickey Rooney, Henry Hull.

Social Dramas

Social dramas or "message films" may sound like spending two hours in a classroom, but these films are actually some of the more enjoyable melodramas from this period, with their harrowing hard luck stories, fine performances, and unexpected twists of fate.

I Am a Fugitive from a Chain Gang
(1932) 93m. B&W. **B**

This powerful true-story drama follows the hard times of a man wrongfully convicted who escapes from a chain gang, makes good, and gives himself up, only to be returned to the chain gang to escape again. A stark and realistic portrait of life on the run in Depression-era America and the harsh conditions of the prison system.
D: Mervyn LeRoy. A: Paul Muni, Glenda Farrell, Helen Vinson.

Heroes for Sale
(1933) 73m. B&W. **B**

A doughboy hero returns home with a morphine addiction that he eventually kicks, but the Depression still keeps him unemployed as he becomes victim to con men and communists. A bizarre melodrama that delivers one hard luck shock after another before its even more unusual resolution.
D: William Wellman. A: Richard Barthelmess, Loretta Young, Aline MacMahon.

Our Daily Bread
(1934) 74m. B&W.
B+

A band of people tries to build a profit-sharing farm and is plagued by untrusting banks, thugs who try to take over the land, and a city gal

who's out to do some serious sinning. This gritty unusual experimental movie unfolds like a New Deal version of an Eisenstein film, with a tone that has an eerie fascistic quality.
D: King Vidor. A: Karen Morley, Tom Keene, John Qualen.

Fury
(1936) 94m. B&W. **A**
Even before he gets his day in court, a man wrongly accused of a kidnap-murder finds himself at the mercy of an angry mob ready to lynch him. The hokey set-up explodes into a feverish and disturbing account of the lawlessness of mob rule that spirals into an out-of-control noirlike nightmare.
D: William Keighley, Marc Connelly. A: Spencer Tracy, Sylvia Sydney, Walter Abel.

These Three
(1936) 93m. B&W. **B**
Two young teachers who run a private girl's school watch their professional personal lives unravel when a bratty student spreads lies about their sexual proclivities. This alternately crackling and heavy melodrama, enlivened by little monster Bonita Granville, keeps the tension high while avoiding any direct references to "unnatural acts."
D: William Wyler. A: Miriam Hopkins, Merle Oberon, Joel McCrea.

1940s

Bette Davis

Whether playing the manipulating matron, the noble schoolteacher, or the discontented slattern, Davis continued to bully and suffer her way through some of Hollywood's classic women's films as well as costume pieces and near-camp, noir-influenced melodramas.

All This and Heaven Too
(1940) 141m. B&W. **A**
Davis is a governess in love with her aristocratic employer who's saddled with a malicious jealous wife. This nineteenth-century period melodrama, brimming with frustration and tears, is a gloriously photographed showcase for Davis' self-sacrificing suffering.
D: Anatole Litvak. A: With Charles Boyer, Jeffrey Lynn, Barbara O'Neil.

The Letter
(1940) 96m. B&W. **A**
On a Malayan rubber plantation, the British owner's calculating wife is accused of murdering a fellow Englishman. This psychological thriller sucks you in like jungle quicksand with its shadowy pessimistic tone, steamy sets, tangled plot, and not just one but two reptilian females.
D: William Wyler. A: With Herbert Marshall, James Stephenson, Gale Sondergaard.

The Great Lie
(1941) 107m. B&W. **B+**
The rivals for one man's love create an unusual alliance after he disappears—one will bear his child, the other will raise it as her own. The expressionistic noirish scenes of Davis helping bratty Astor through the difficult pregnancy are made almost freakish by the Production Code's ban on the word "pregnant."
D: Edmund Goulding. A: With George Brent, Mary Astor, Lucile Watson.

The Little Foxes
(1941) 116m. B&W. **A**
Lillian Hellman's family melodrama of a blackmailing, mean-as-a-snake Southern matriarch who claws and scratches to build an empire. The dark bitter tone of this Dixie gothic is enhanced by moody cinematography and Davis' patented sadism.
D: William Wyler. A: With Herbert Marshall, Richard Carlson, Teresa Wright.

In This Our Life
(1942) 97m. B&W. **A**
Davis is the fabulously rotten honey-tongued brat who has her hat set for sweet sister de Havilland's husband. Another ripely entertaining and masterfully photographed Southern family melodrama with Davis doing her best to drag down the family with her wickedness.
D: John Huston. A: With Olivia de Havilland, George Brent, Dennis Morgan.

Now, Voyager
(1942) 117m. B&W. **A**
A repressed spinster-in-the-making blossoms into a desirable capable woman with the help of a caring psychiatrist. Then she meets another lonely soul who's married. . . . Davis positively soars in this classic weepy, and her transformation from backward ugly duckling to sophisticated beauty is the stuff of adult fairy tales.
D: Irving Rapper. A: With Claude Rains, Paul Henreid.

Mr. Skeffington
(1944) 147m. B&W. **A**
This sweeping melodrama spans several decades in the life of a vain selfish woman who pursues her own frivolities at the expense of her long-suffering husband and neglected daughter. An unusual hybrid of light comedy and serious drama, touching on aging anxiety and anti-Semitism.
D: Vincent Sherman. A: With Claude Rains, Walter Abel, Richard Waring.

The Corn Is Green
(1945) 114m. B&W. **B+**
A schoolmistress is appalled by the illiteracy in the Wales mining village where she's inherited a house, and opens her own school against the wishes of the rich landowners. A frumped-up Bette as the mannered but emotional Miss Moffat goes a long way to salvage the episodic and overripe story.
D: Irving Rapper. A: With Nigel Bruce, John Dall, Joan Lorring.

A Stolen Life
(1946) 107m. B&W. **A–**
Good sister Davis loses her lover to the calculating sophisticated twin, and assumes her sister's identity to win him back. One of a rash of noirish melodramas in which stars played their own evil twin, the hokey premise never detracts from the gripping story with eerily darkened sets and decent split-screen effects.
D: Curtis Bernhardt. A: With Glenn Ford, Dane Clark, Walter Brennan.

Deception
(1946) 111m. B&W. **A–**
Davis is a music teacher and conductor Rains' mistress, who is reunited with her cellist love after the war. The sleekly modern sets are stunning, and a witty and cruel Rains is the perfect foil to the starry-eyed lovers as

he exacts his revenge on Henreid.
D: Irving Rapper. A: With Paul Henreid, Claude Rains, John Abbott.

Winter Meeting
(1948) 104m. B&W. **B–**
A rich repressed spinster with some skeletons in her family closet falls in love with a man torn between love and priesthood. A talk-clogged romance, with the higher power winning out.
D: Bretaigne Windust. A: With Janis Paige, James Davis, John Hoyt.

Beyond the Forest
(1949) 96m. B&W.
A–
A disgruntled trampy housewife will do anything to escape her life in a small milltown, even if she has to induce a miscarriage. Davis burns up the screen with her frumpy appearance and hard-edged trashiness in this stormy, noirish, and often campy melodrama.
D: King Vidor. A: With Joseph Cotten, David Brian, Ruth Roman.

Joan Crawford

Age and changing Hollywood trends brought an end to Crawford's struggling working girl/ golddigger manqué tearjerkers, but then *Mildred Pierce* revived her ailing career. Soon she was starring in noirish melodramas that helped shape Crawford into the camp legend: all shoulder pads and eyebrows, mixed with a vaguely masculine defiance toward her men.

Susan and God
(1940) 115m. B&W. **A–**
A flighty society woman discovers religion and turns it into a self-advertising stunt while ignoring the efforts of her husband and daughter to make one last stab at normal family life. Crawford does an uncanny Rosalind Russell imitation in this droll film that makes the problems of the rich seem like fun.
D: George Cukor. A: With Fredric March, Ruth Hussey, John Carroll.

When Ladies Meet
(1941) 105m. B&W. **B**
Successful novelist Crawford is in love with her married publisher and Garson is the cunning wronged wife. A brisk comedic 30s-style melodrama with all the talkiness and female plotting of *The Women* without the charm or intelligence.
D: Robert Z. Leonard. A: With Robert Taylor, Greer Garson, Herbert Marshall.

A Woman's Face
(1941) 107m. B&W. **B+**
The plastic surgeon who operated on criminal mastermind Crawford's horribly deformed face wonders if her blackmailing instincts still lurk beneath her newly created beauty. Long and injected with tedious courtroom scenes, its real pleasure derives from the bizarre love affair and Crawford's malicious crook.
D: George Cukor. A: With Conrad Veidt, Melvyn Douglas, Osa Massen.

Humoresque
(1946) 123m. B&W. **A**
An unfulfilled patroness of the arts takes a promising young violinist under her wing, much to the chagrin of his hardworking conservative family and her own husband. This overheated musical melodrama has sulky noirish atmosphere to burn and a passionately excessive ending.
D: Jean Negulesco. A: With John Garfield, Oscar Levant, J. Carrol Naish.

Possessed
(1947) 108m. B&W.
A–
Crawford may or may not be crazy in this psychological soaper about an unbalanced nurse recounting in flashback her love for the caddish Heflin. Suicide, murder, insanity, and amnesia all make for a melancholy and tangled story with a bizarre tone and moody documentary-style camerawork.
D: Curtis Bernhardt. A: With Van Heflin, Raymond Massey, Geraldine Brooks.

Flamingo Road
(1949) 94m. B&W. **A–**
Carny dancer Crawford is wronged by a small-town sheriff who has sent her to prison, and later returns to reform his burg with the help of her politician husband. This gritty drama of small-town dirty dealings is energized by a now defiant, now vulnerable Crawford.
D: Michael Curtiz. A: With Zachary Scott, Sydney Greenstreet, David Brian.

(See also *Mildred Pierce*, page 466.)

British Literary Adaptations

Studios continued to mine British classics for these prestige pictures, which remain entertaining and handsomely produced tales of star-crossed lovers and plucky orphans.

Pride and Prejudice
(1940) 116m. B&W. **A**
This sparkling comedy of manners centers on a romance between a high-spirited and judgmental young lady and a proud and wealthy young man. The kind of film no longer made, this has a delicate, humorous, and evenhanded understanding of the characters.
D: Robert Z. Leonard. A: Greer Garson, Laurence Olivier, Edna May Oliver.

Tom Brown's School Days
(1940) 86m. B&W. **B–**
Wide-eyed young Tom comes up against the tough lads at Rugby school. A quaint, old-fashioned study of life at an all-boys school in Victorian England, and the work of a teacher who treats even the toughies with respect and compassion.
D: Robert Stevenson. A: Cedric Hardwicke, Freddie Bartholomew, Josephine Hutchinson.

Jane Eyre
(1944) 97m. B&W. **A**
A forbidding mansion; an orphanage-raised young governess; a rich, handsome, and brooding man with a tortured secret; dark shadows,

storms, and . . . discovery. It's been done before, but this grandly operatic romance is one of the best.
D: Robert Stevenson. A: Orson Welles, Joan Fontaine, Agnes Moorehead.

Great Expectations
(1946) 110m. B&W.
A

A richly involving story of orphaned Pip who's left a fortune by a mysterious benefactor and ventures to London to become a gentleman. The flavorful portrayals—like Miss Havisham in her eternal bridal gown, or the perverse Estella—and the bold and subtle ways it conveys the period make this come alive.
D: David Lean. A: John Mills, Valerie Hobson, Alec Guinness.

Nicholas Nickleby
(1947) 108m. B&W. **B**

Large episodic tale of the young Nicholas who confronts a wealthy but cruel uncle, braves life under some nasties at a boys school, and joins a comically decrepit acting company. A gutsy attempt to hold a too sprawling and heavily populated story together.
D: Alberto Cavalcanti. A: Cedric Hardwicke, Derek Bond, Sally Ann Howes.

Oliver Twist
(1948) 105m. B&W.
A

The story of how innocent Oliver joins a band of street thieves under the tutelage of the elegant Artful Dodger and the wicked Fagin becomes a gripping drama of children in depraved poverty. Vivid re-creations of the murk and slime of Victorian London's underbelly.
D: David Lean. A: Alec Guinness, Robert Newton, John Howard.

British Dramas

The earlier sentimental stories of staunch and noble Englishmen were an entertaining form of morale building during World War II. Whether a family saga or a small working-class domestic drama, they all celebrated traditional British values in the face of adversity. The trio of postwar films have a markedly grimmer tone and subject matter as they portray the darker side of the status quo.

Forever and a Day
(1943) 104m. B&W. **B–**

A London mansion that changes ownership is the setting for seriocomic vignettes of English life from 1800 to 1943. A patriotic pageant that brought together almost every British star known in Hollywood.
D: René Clair, Robert Stevenson, Herbert Wilcox, et al. A: Charles Laughton, Anna Neagle, Ray Milland, and other stars in cameo appearances.

The Life and Death of Colonel Blimp
(1943) 163m. **B+**

A British soldier's career, filled with courage, honor, and plain old cantankerousness, spans three wars. Less a war movie than a sentimental rumination on the strength of the British character.
D: Michael Powell, Emeric Pressburger. A: Roger Livesey, Deborah Kerr, Anton Walbrook.

None but the Lonely Heart
(1944) B&W. 113m. **C**

In the squalor of London's East End just prior to World War II a widow runs a secondhand shop and supports her ne'er-do-well but lovable son. The cramped and bleak settings only add to the sentimental view of poverty and an optimistic working class.
D: Clifford Odets. A: Cary Grant, Ethel Barrymore, Barry Fitzgerald.

This Happy Breed
(1944) 114m. **B+**

The trials, joys, and staunch values of a working-class family between the two world wars are portrayed in this episodic heartwarmer. Stalwart characters and noble tone make this feel like a prototype for a classy TV miniseries.
D: David Lean. A: Robert Newton, Celia Johnson, John Mills.

Postwar

Brief Encounter
(1945) 85m. B&W. **B+**

A bored housewife and a lonely doctor meet in a train station and begin a quiet affair of the heart. A poignant subtle story of blossoming love and quiet desperation.
D: David Lean. A: Celia Johnson, Trevor Howard, Stanley Holloway.

The Fallen Idol
(1948) 94m. B&W.
B+

A young boy who worships his father's kindly butler tries to protect him from being arrested on murder charges. Good thriller with a perspective that focuses on the jittery precocious child to heighten a sense of dread.
D: Carol Reed. A: Ralph Richardson, Michele Morgan, Jack Hawkins.

The Rocking Horse Winner
(1949) 91m. B&W. **A**

In postwar London, a social-climbing mother takes advantage of her little boy's strange ability to foretell the future by rocking on his hobby horse faster and faster. Neglected near-masterpiece works a horrifying fable of greed with artfully gloomy photography setting up a dense mood of dread.
D: Anthony Pelissier. A: John Mills, Valerie Hobson, John Howard Davies.

Boxers

Hollywood has always had a love affair for this most brutally individualistic of sports, demonstrated by these melodramas of working-class palookas who punch their way to the top.

Golden Boy
(1939) 99m. B&W. **B**
A talented poor violinist forsakes his musical career to become a champion prizefighter and enters the world of callous managers, gangsters who want to buy a piece of him, and a hard-boiled but loving dame. An overblown dispirited melodrama despite the flashy fight sequences and earnest ensemble playing.
D: Rouben Mamoulian. A: William Holden, Barbara Stanwyck, Adolphe Menjou.

City for Conquest
(1940) 101m. B&W. **B**
An up-and-coming prizefighter is blinded by a mob-sponsored boxer and winds up hawking newspapers to help his younger brother who is a fledgling composer. The clickedy-clack pace, some rousing histrionics in the ring, and Cagney's performance will help you look past the hoary old plot.
D: Anatole Litvak. A: James Cagney, Ann Sheridan, Arthur Kennedy.

Gentleman Jim
(1942) 104m. B&W.
B+
The gentlemanly tactics of Irish-American Jim Corbett send ripples of amusement through the rough and tumble world of boxing, until he challenges icon pugilist John L. Sullivan for the world's heavyweight championship. Flynn charms his way through this lusty brawling bio-pic spanning the early days of the once outlawed sport.
D: Raoul Walsh. A: Errol Flynn, Alexis Smith, Jack Carson.

Body and Soul
(1947) 104m. B&W.
B+
This follows the heady rise and tragic consequences of a fighter who hooks up with the mob. The haunting images of fated lovers Garfield and Palmer linger with a gloomy incandescence in this melodramatic look at the rotten underbelly of boxing with jaw-busting scenes in the ring that are still second to none.
D: Robert Rossen. A: John Garfield, Lilli Palmer, Hazel Brooks.

Sports Biographies

The subjects of these bio-pics are the heroic, all-American sports figures who overcome all manner of illness as melodrama seems to fill their field of dreams. With the low quotient of actual sports scenes and the highly inspirational nature of these stories, you may think these are *Reader's Digest* material rather than *Sports Illustrated*.

Knute Rockne—All American
(1940) 98m. **B–**
More O'Brien rah-rah fare, this time as Notre Dame's finest coach. Almost campily sentimental and notable for our ex-President getting his nickname here as the ever cheerful and physically impaired player, "The Gipper."
D: Lloyd Bacon. A: Pat O'Brien, Gale Page, Ronald Reagan.

The Pride of the Yankees
(1942) 127m. B&W. **A**
Cooper is the awe shucks all-American Lou Gehrig who's a dutiful son, a baseball star, a loving husband, and the stalwart victim of a deadly disease. A superbly made, high-gloss film that is light on sports and heavy on the events of a good man's life.
D: Sam Wood. A: Gary Cooper, Teresa Wright, Walter Brennan.

The Iron Major
(1943) 85m. B&W. **B–**
A disabled World War I doughboy comes out of the war with pluck intact, and proceeds to become a legendary college football coach. True tale of Irish-American Frank Cavanaugh is standard inspirational, easy-on-the-rough-edges bio-pic with O'Brien as feisty as ever.
D: Ray Enright. A: Pat O'Brien, Robert Ryan, Ruth Warrick.

The Babe Ruth Story
(1948) 107m. **B**
Through the magic of Hollywood's dream factory, all the rough edges were removed from Babe Ruth, turning him into a squeaky-clean legendary home run hitter. So forget the facts and enjoy Bendix's passionate performance in this manipulative, but enjoyable ballgame fable.
D: Roy Del Ruth. A: William Bendix, Claire Trevor, William Frawley.

The Stratton Story
(1949) 106m. B&W. **B**
One of the more dramatic stories is that of major league ball player Monty Stratton, who continued his career after losing a leg in a hunting accident. An earnest drama about courage that uses a folksy approach to its inspirational tale.
D: Sam Wood. A: Jimmy Stewart, June Allyson, Frank Morgan.

Americana

These are rousing tales of America's history and the melting pot of high-spirited, eternally optimistic characters who helped build it. *Gone With the Wind* being the obvious standout, the others may not have the sweep and historical detail of the grander costume epics, but they still offer quality dramas set in a thrilling and colorfully revised past.

San Francisco
(1936) 115m. B&W. **B**
Queenly MacDonald plays a performer at Gable's Barbary Coast saloon, and sings with priest Tracy's choir. A rousing but standard costume love story until turning into a monumental disaster film with great effects of the 1906 earthquake.
D: W. S. Van Dyke II. A: Clark Gable, Jeanette MacDonald, Spencer Tracy.

Of Human Hearts
(1938) 100m. B&W. **B**

A rigid country preacher can't understand why his ambitious son leaves home to become a doctor instead of following in his footsteps. A Civil War-era family saga slips into some histrionics but Stewart is engaging as the doctor son who's haunted by memories of his doting ma and disapproving pa.
D: Clarence Brown. A: Walter Huston, James Stewart, Beulah Bondi.

Drums Along the Mohawk
(1939) 103m. **A–**

A newlywed couple moves to the frontier of upstate New York in the early days of the Revolutionary War. An exciting yarn chronicling pioneer life during the birth of the nation—Indian raids, men leaving to fight in the Continental Army—with spectacular timberland scenery enhanced by dazzling Technicolor.
D: John Ford. A: Claudette Colbert, Henry Fonda, Edna May Oliver.

Gone With the Wind
(1939) 222m. **A**

This Southern costume epic follows beautiful and completely self-absorbed Scarlett as she tears through the Civil War and Reconstruction years chasing noble Ashley, saving the family plantation, and resisting the charms of Rhett. Sweeping, spirited, racist, and still fun to watch.
D: Victor Fleming. A: Clark Gable, Vivien Leigh, Leslie Howard.

Boom Town
(1940) 116m. B&W. **B**

Two wildcatters strike oil in Oklahoma, lose it all on Wall Street, and return to their roots with drills in tow. A colorful buddy saga full of dust and spit, covering twenty tumultuous years of two charming rascals.
D: Jack Conway. A: Clark Gable, Claudette Colbert, Spencer Tracy.

The Grapes of Wrath
(1940) 129m. B&W. **A–**

A Midwest farm family wiped out by the dust bowl heads to California and then to Hooverville where they are forced to separate. A beautifully photographed and relentlessly unsentimental look at the Depression.
D: John Ford. A: Henry Fonda, Jane Darwell, John Carradine.

Honky Tonk
(1941) 105m. B&W. **B–**

A sweet Boston girl, escorted by her justice of the peace father, gets a taste of fast living when she takes up with a gambler in a boom town. This broad canvas of dance hall girls, con artists, and bible thumpers wears thin in this tiresome take on the old west. Who thought Lana could play a dainty virgin?
D: Jack Conway. A: Clark Gable, Lana Turner, Frank Morgan.

Sergeant York
(1941) 134m. B&W. **B+**

The Southern backwoods boy may be a crackshot, but he's also the pacifist who became America's most decorated World War I hero. The first part is a charming slice of country life showing turkey shoots, buggy chases, and young love, before turning to the war drama that comes off as slightly unnerving but entertaining propaganda.
D: Howard Hawks. A: Gary Cooper, Walter Brennan, Joan Leslie.

Pittsburgh
(1942) 90m. B&W. **B+**

Two coal-mining friends realize the American dream as they become successful business partners with the help and the love of Dietrich. Wayne's ambition runs amok, shifting the romantic triangle and splitting the partners in this darker-toned tale that ends on a bittersweet note of redemption.
D: Lewis Seiler. A: Marlene Dietrich, John Wayne, Randolph Scott.

Tortilla Flat
(1942) 105m. B&W. **B**

Good fortune can take many turns as two shiftless buddies discover when one of them inherits a few houses. Set in the Mexican community of a small California fishing village, this finely acted film adaptation of Steinbeck's novel is a surprisingly spare and unsentimental tale, even with the high-toned MGM trappings.
D: Victor Fleming. A: Spencer Tracy, Hedy Lamarr, John Garfield.

Our Vines Have Tender Grapes
(1945) 105m. B&W. **B**

A kindly Norwegian immigrant dispenses wisdom to his two children while working his farm in Wisconsin. All the philosophizing and hard work can't keep Mother Nature from wreaking havoc on his land. Robinson is endearingly hammy in this lyrical and slightly sappy pastoral coming-of-age tale.
D: Roy Rowland. A: Edward G. Robinson, Margaret O'Brien, James Craig.

The Sea of Grass
(1947) 131m. B&W. **C+**

A tough-as-leather cattle baron duels with a neighbor over some choice prairie land and drives his blueblood wife into the arms of another man. This expensive, curiously stagy horse opera is devoid of tension, visual grandeur, and, oddly enough, romantic spark from the legendary duo.
D: Elia Kazan. A: Spencer Tracy, Katharine Hepburn, Melvyn Douglas.

Heartwarming Dramas

Hollywood never did spare the sentiment, but the turbulence of wartime made an even bigger market for heartwarming dramas. Here are reassuring tales of nostalgic family life, hardworking immigrants, and ever-hopeful clergy, whose message is that with a little faith and a let's-pull-together attitude people can overcome any tragedy.

How Green Was My Valley
(1941) 118m. B&W. **A**

A man recalls his childhood in an idyllic Welsh coal mining town before exploitation of the miners took its toll. John Ford's exquisitely photographed and simply told drama is a moving depiction of family and the life of the community, with sensitive performances.
D: John Ford. A: Walter Pidgeon, Maureen O'Hara, Donald Crisp.

Penny Serenade
(1941) 125m. B&W. **B+**

This bittersweet melodrama is a wife's recollection of her difficult years of marriage to

a newspaperman and their doomed efforts to have a child. This is pathos at its finest, with episodes of breezy comedy to leaven the emotional tension, and a sparkling Grant and Dunne.
D: George Stevens. A: Irene Dunne, Cary Grant, Beulah Bondi.

Going My Way
(1944) 126m. B&W. **B**
The stiff-necked old priest and his city parish are heading downhill. Then hip young singing priest Crosby shows up to save the church from foreclosure and turn a gang of street toughs into a chorus of angels. Bing's crooning and some mild comic touches help this sweet but drawn-out story.
D: Leo McCarey. A: Bing Crosby, Barry Fitzgerald, Frank McHugh.

The Bells of St. Mary's
(1945) 126m. B&W. **B+**
Crosby is again the new priest in town, this time helping some nuns and their school threatened by a greedy capitalist who wants to tear it down. Bing cranks out his usual soulful tunes, but it's Bergman's shrewd and angelic Mother Superior that makes this enjoyable.
D: Leo McCarey. A: Bing Crosby, Ingrid Bergman, Henry Travers.

A Tree Grows in Brooklyn
(1945) 128m. B&W. **A**
A poignant, wonderfully detailed story of a young girl's relationship with her dreamy father and distant mother in a turn-of-the-century, impoverished Brooklyn neighborhood. These people are believable, especially Garner's hopeful artistic child.
D: Elia Kazan. A: Peggy Ann Garner, Dorothy McGuire, Joan Blondell.

Life with Father
(1947) 118m. **B+**
A big cheerful Technicolor exception to this group of films is the portrait of a lovable roosterish Victorian patriarch as remembered by his family. No real story here—just a string of entertaining episodes and a charming handsome cast.
D: Michael Curtiz. A: William Powell, Irene Dunne, Elizabeth Taylor.

Miracle on 34th Street
(1947) 96m. B&W. **A**
Sophisticated New Yorkers, including a divorced working mother and her precocious daughter, intersect with a kindly old gentleman from Long Island who claims to be Santa Claus. A snappy social comedy-drama with the right dose of sentiment and Christmas cheer.
D: George Seaton. A: Maureen O'Hara, John Payne, Natalie Wood.

I Remember Mama
(1948) 134m. B&W. **A–**
A writer reminisces about her childhood in San Francisco and her tightly knit family of Norwegian immigrants led by strong-willed, loving Mama. From the close-ups of each expressive face to the gentle slapstick, every scene is composed and choreographed like a classic silent film.
D: George Stevens. A: Irene Dunne, Barbara Bel Geddes, Oscar Homolka.

Gothic Americana

There's more gothic than nostalgia in these stories that take a gloomier look at the Victorian age. Like costume soap operas combined with film noir, these tales of frustrated love, oppressive mores, and doomed lives have a darker tone, stunning photography, and some finely suffering characters.

Lydia
(1941) 104m. B&W. **B+**
When the now older Lydia reunites with four old admirers, each recalls his frustrated and never fully comprehended role in her thwarted romantic life. A measured and charming tale with careful performances by all.
D: Julien Duvivier. A: Merle Oberon, Edna May Oliver, Joseph Cotten.

The Magnificent Ambersons
(1942) 88m. B&W. **A**
Welles followed up *Citizen Kane* with this haunting drama of an affluent Midwestern family's decline during America's industrialization. Like a brooding nightmarish valentine to American values and family, its startling and complex visual style isn't diminished despite the missing 40+ minutes from the original version.
D: Orson Welles. A: Tim Holt, Joseph Cotten, Agnes Moorehead.

The Heiress
(1949) 115m. B&W. **B+**
The plain-jane daughter of a dictatorial father who holds her fate by the inheritance purse strings is suddenly courted by a young man. A subtle and somber melodrama with a quietly magnificent de Havilland and an imperious Richardson as the father whose selfishness compels him to interfere with her chance for romantic happiness.
D: William Wyler. A: Olivia de Havilland, Montgomery Clift, Ralph Richardson.

Carrie
(1952) 118m. B&W. **B+**
A small-town girl goes to the big city where she is seduced by a salesman and loved by a successful businessman who forsakes his family and career for her. Olivier is swell in this gilt-edged film version of Dreiser's *Sister Carrie,* but it still feels more like a classy potboiler than an American tragedy.
D: William Wyler. A: Laurence Olivier, Jennifer Jones, Eddie Albert.

Whimsy-Fantasy

These are war and postwar dramas of faith, salvation, romance, and a little help from the supernatural. Oversentimental, sometimes mawkish in their synthesis of religion and Hollywood glitz, they all hold an innocent romantic appeal as sheer escapist entertainment.

The Devil and Daniel Webster

(1941) 85m. B&W. **B+**

This eerie folkloric morality play tells of a young farmer who becomes rich and successful after selling his soul to the devil. Along with some lovely naturalistic photography and New England gothic touches is a patriotic message about democracy espoused by Daniel Webster.
D: William Dieterle. A: Walter Huston, James Craig, Edward Arnold.

A Guy Named Joe

(1943) 120m. B&W. **B+**

This aviation film made with a heart-tugging aim at World War II homefront audiences follows a death-defying pilot Tracy who returns from a fatal crash to become a guardian angel to young pilot-in-training Johnson. A sweet romantic fantasy, with a quintessentially American take on sacrifice and the spirit world.
D: Victor Fleming. A: Spencer Tracy, Irene Dunne, Van Johnson.

The Enchanted Cottage

(1945) 92m. B&W. **B+**

A very unusual melodrama about a magical cottage that transforms its newlywed tenants—a homely woman and a war veteran disfigured in a plane crash—into romantic ideals, proving love conquers all, even ugliness. This film's goofy spirituality, weird premise, and hysterically romantic tone make it all somehow endearing.
D: John Cromwell. A: Dorothy McGuire, Robert Young, Herbert Marshall.

Angel on My Shoulder

(1946) 100m. B&W. **B**

A slick, strangely likable Mephistopheles allows a gangster to avenge his death if he agrees to possess the body of a do-gooding judge. A charming silly fantasy distinguished by the two leads' clever caricatures, with Muni putting a comic spin on his *Scarface* persona masquerading as a refined magistrate.
D: Archie Mayo. A: Paul Muni, Anne Baxter, Claude Rains.

The Miracle of the Bells

(1948) 120m. B&W. **C+**

Sinatra is the kindly priest from a coal mining town who agrees to stage a bell-ringing tribute to the movie star brought home for burial by her press agent. A bizarre, maudlin, and long drama with a luminous Valli as the talented actress shown in flashback.
D: Irving Pichel. A: Fred MacMurray, Alida Valli, Frank Sinatra.

Portrait of Jennie

(1948) 86m. B&W. **C**

A melodrama told uncharacteristically from the male point of view, involving a struggling painter haunted over the years by the presence of a beautiful girl. On-location New York scenery and tinted color sequences are lovely and unusual but cannot compensate for the hokey story and insipid Jones.
D: William Dieterle. A: Joseph Cotten, Jennifer Jones, Ethel Barrymore.

War Dramas

Combat dramas weren't the only propaganda being turned out by Hollywood during the war years. Whether set on the battlefield, the streets, or in schools, these sentimental films offer up acts of inspiration, a healthy dose of soap opera pathos, and the suspense and adventure of a war actioner.

Clouds Over Europe

(1939) 82m. B&W. **A−**

A mysterious secret ray enables enemy spies to steal British test planes in midflight. The "secret" technology may seem laughable today, but the rest of the suspenser is intelligent, fast-paced, and slightly daffy; Richardson's off-the-wall performance is a must-see.
D: Tim Whelan. A: Ralph Richardson, Laurence Olivier, Valerie Hobson.

The 49th Parallel

(1940) 90m. B&W. **A**

The stranded crew of a German sub flees across Canada, meeting a sampling of stalwart and good citizens along the way. Full of suspense, irony, and impassioned salt-of-the-earth sentiments.
D: Michael Powell. A: Laurence Olivier, Leslie Howard, Eric Portman.

The Mortal Storm

(1940) 100m. B&W. **A−**

In 1930s Germany, members of a prominent intellectual family split bitterly over the rising tide of Nazism. A dark and brooding film that's quite strong, especially the first half when the political situation is still up for grabs.
D: Frank Borzage. A: Margaret Sullavan, Robert Young, James Stewart.

So Ends Our Night

(1941) 120m. B&W. **B**

A German citizen meets up with a Jewish couple when he's forced to take flight after resisting the Nazis. Together they fend off Nazi agents while seeking freedom somewhere in Europe. Heartfelt performances, and the film tries hard but rambles darkly.
D: John Cromwell. A: Fredric March, Margaret Sullavan, Glenn Ford.

A Yank in the RAF

(1941) 98m. B&W. **B**

A hotshot American fighter pilot joins the RAF—primarily to woo a beautiful chorus girl. A snappy and lightweight romantic drama with smooth music and some surprisingly pungent air action—particularly the bomb raid over Germany.
D: Henry King. A: Tyrone Power, Betty Grable, Reginald Gardiner.

Hitler's Children

(1942) 83m. B&W. **B**

In prewar Germany, an American-born German girl

is forced to join a Nazi organization and gets a firsthand look at the regime's racial practices. A tame and artificial melodrama about standing up against fascism, with a few creepy glimpses at the youthful tribal practices.
D: Edward Dmytryk, Irving Reis. A: Tim Holt, Bonita Granville, Kent Smith.

In Which We Serve
(1942) 114m. B&W. **A**
When a British warship is torpedoed, the drifting survivors recall, via flashbacks, their lives, loves, and the meaning of it all. A real celebration of British stolidity, and the interposing warmth and joy of the flashbacks with the grim lifeboat reality is compelling. A tender and timeless entry.
D: Nöel Coward, David Lean. A: Noël Coward, John Mills, Richard Attenborough.

Joan of Paris
(1942) 91m. B&W. **B**
A sexy young French Resistance fighter brings a group of fallen Allied pilots to safety. This rousing drama feels dated, but it's got enough chases, romance, and wondrous acts of heroism to keep you watching.
D: Robert Stevenson. A: Michele Morgan, Paul Henreid, Thomas Mitchell.

This Land Is Mine
(1943) 103m. B&W. **B**
In an occupied country, a meek schoolteacher sheds his fears and, at the greatest cost, defies the Nazis. Offbeat and dated, but Laughton's quirky performance makes this compelling.
D: Jean Renoir. A: Charles Laughton, Maureen O'Hara, George Sanders.

Watch on the Rhine
(1943) 114m. B&W. **C+**
A German refugee couple is visiting Washington and ends up being spied upon, blackmailed, and generally entrapped by the Gestapo and their agents. This film version of Lillian Hellman's play is smarter and subtler than other war dramas, but also stagebound and long-winded.
D: Herman Shumlin. A: Bette Davis, Paul Lukas, Lucile Watson.

The Fighting Sullivans
(1944) 111m. B&W. **A**
This true story of five brothers from Iowa who died together on the same Navy ship in the Pacific celebrates American small-town values and salt-of-the-earth characters as their father recalls his sons' childhood. An intimate little wartime tearjerker.
D: Lloyd Bacon. A: Anne Baxter, Thomas Mitchell, Selena Royle.

The Seventh Cross
(1944) 112m. B&W. **A**
The sole survivor of a group of concentration camp escapees finds surprising refuge in different homes. The dark constricting studio sets effectively increase the tension in this harrowing and heartfelt drama.
D: Fred Zinnemann. A: Spencer Tracy, Hume Cronyn, Signe Hasso.

The Captive Heart
(1946) 108m. B&W. **A**
On the run from the Nazis, a Czech partisan takes the papers and identity of a dead British officer—and winds up in a German camp for British POWs. A classic prison war camp drama with a haunting Redgrave and moments of unexpected comedy.
D: Basil Dearden. A: Michael Redgrave, Jack Warner, Basil Radford.

Command Decision
(1948) 112m. B&W. **A**
A flight commander deals with the agonies of sending his men on necessary, but virtual suicide, missions over Germany. The intense action is all in the back room in this gripping look at warfare from the inside.
D: Sam Wood. A: Clark Gable, Walter Pidgeon, Van Johnson.

Other Films:
Convoy (1940)
Dive Bomber (1941)
Desperate Journey (1942)
The Immortal Sergeant (1943)
The Immortal Battalion (1944)
The Purple Heart (1944)
Battleground (1949)
Task Force (1949)

On the Homefront

These shamelessly emotional melodramas were Hollywood reminders that the home fires were kept burning while our boys were out there fighting the good fight. As idealistic morale boosters they may seem a little dated, but as well-crafted tearjerkers and sentimental "women's films" they still ring true.

Journey for Margaret
(1942) 81m. B&W. **B**
A married but childless American correspondent visits a London orphanage after the blitz and falls for one little charmer. The pint-sized production and O'Brien leave no sentiment untouched, no tear unjerked.
D: W. S. Van Dyke. A: Fay Bainter, Robert Young, Margaret O'Brien.

Mrs. Miniver
(1942) 134m. B&W. **A**
This is the quintessential wonderful wartime woman film that follows an English village family gracefully and bravely coping with the privations and terrors of war. At the center is Mrs. Miniver, who sends her son off to battle, reads fairy tales to the children during air raids, and generally behaves like a saint on Earth.
D: William Wyler. A: Greer Garson, Walter Pidgeon, Teresa Wright.

The Human Comedy
(1943) 117m. B&W. **B–**
The adventures of a telegraph boy approaching manhood involves his fellow citizens of a small California community during the war. This bittersweet film often gets a little too high-minded for its own melodramatic good, though the vignettes of the townfolk are heartfelt and sweet-tempered.
D: Clarence Brown. A: Mickey Rooney, Frank Morgan, James Craig.

Tender Comrade
(1943) 102m. B&W. **B–**
When their husbands go off to war, a group of women who work at the same defense plant decides to live together for the duration. Constant flashbacks of prewar marital bliss help add a little melodramatic interest to this standard brave women tale.
D: Edward Dmytryk. A: Ginger Rogers, Robert Ryan, Ruth Hussey.

The White Cliffs of Dover
(1943) 126m. B&W. **B+**
On the eve of World War I, a young American woman marries a British lad who's killed in action, leaving her to raise their son alone. The film tenderly traces her life over the years, filled with every cliché about motherly love, selflessness, and duty.
D: Clarence Brown. A: Irene Dunne, Alan Marshal, Frank Morgan.

Since You Went Away
(1944) 172m. B&W. **B+**
With her husband off at war, a woman and two daughters draw strength from family and loved ones in this epic-length homefront soaper. So idyllic it threatens to be sappy; it's saved by a circle of rich characters, including tough-love boarder Monty Woolley and vulnerable GI Robert Walker.
D: John Cromwell. A: Claudette Colbert, Jennifer Jones, Joseph Cotten.

Wartime Melodramas

Star-crossed lovers have always been a popular subject for tearjerkers and the war provided unquestionable—and patriotic—reasons for separation, misunderstandings, and tragedy between the romantic pair.

Waterloo Bridge
(1940) 103m. B&W. **A**
A British officer is called to the front in World War I before he can marry his beloved ballet dancer. He returns after a year in prison camp unaware that her fortunes have taken a rather degrading turn for the worse. An exquisitely nuanced romance imbued with a dreamy atmosphere and Leigh's tragic beauty.
D: Mervyn LeRoy. A: Vivien Leigh, Robert Taylor, Lucile Watson.

Casablanca
(1942) 102m. B&W. **A**
Sooner or later every expatriate, hustler, nationalist, Nazi, and hero comes to Rick's cafe in Casablanca. This most delightful of Hollywood accidents is a delectable mix of romantic yearning, exotic atmosphere, zesty characterizations, and cynically philosophical hard-boiled dialogue.
D: Michael Curtiz. A: Humphrey Bogart, Ingrid Bergman, Paul Henreid.

Reunion in France
(1942) 104m. B&W. **C+**
A Parisian dress designer, stunned to discover that her fiancé is a Nazi informer, helps an American flyer evade the Gestapo. There's little sex appeal between the leads as an uncomfortable-looking Duke takes a back-seat to Joan's heroics and histrionics in this slick patriotic caper.
D: Jules Dassin. A: Joan Crawford, John Wayne, Philip Dorn.

Somewhere I'll Find You
(1942) 108m. B&W. **B−**
A brash correspondent blows into town and runs into an old flame who's now dating his brother. He convinces her to take an assignment but when war breaks out she disappears. He-man Clark doesn't know a good thing till it's gone, and the sibling rivalry loses most of its steam when Lana leaves.
D: Wesley Ruggles. A: Clark Gable, Lana Turner, Robert Sterling.

The Clock
(1945) 90m. B&W.
A
A Midwestern soldier on a two-day leave and a Manhattan office girl meet, fall in love, get married, and realize they hardly know each other. A beautiful story filled with tender and awkward moments that will charm you with its simplicity and bittersweet performances.
D: Vincente Minnelli. A: Judy Garland, Robert Walker, James Gleason.

Tomorrow Is Forever
(1946) 105m. **B**
A chemist leaves his pregnant wife to fight in World War I but when he's reported dead she marries another man. Twenty years later he shows up, not even remembering his former life. A first-rate, old-fashioned tearjerker even if it is strange to see Welles play soap opera.
D: Irving Pichel. A: Claudette Colbert, Orson Welles, George Brent.

Arch of Triumph
(1948) 120m. B&W. **B−**
An Austrian surgeon falls in love with a beautiful Frenchwoman whose suicide he prevented. He gets deported but returns to Paris to discover that she's now involved with an older man. Ingrid's self-loathing strikes a few modern notes but this cynical stab at neorealism is drab and uninvolving.
D: Lewis Milestone. A: Ingrid Bergman, Charles Boyer, Charles Laughton.

Noirish Melodramas

While not strictly film noirs, these dark psychological melodramas use many of the genre's overwrought mannerisms to tell their fascinating stories.

King's Row
(1941) 127m. B&W.
B+
This story that follows the lives of childhood friends in a small town is like a brooding *Peyton Place,* where emotionally scarred characters, brutality, crippling injuries, and lost dreams are the name of the game. An unusual and weighty melodrama of friendship and love.
D: Sam Wood. A: Robert Cummings, Ronald Reagan, Ann Sheridan.

The Shanghai Gesture
(1941) 98m. B&W. **A**
A shipping tycoon plans to close down Madame Gin Sling's degenerate gambling casino until he discovers his drug-addicted daughter is in the clutches of the evil proprietress. Ona Munson plays puppetmaster to the languid cast of elegant fallen angels in this perversely erotic film whose delirious images lin-

ger like an opium-induced haze.
D: Josef von Sternberg. A: Walter Huston, Gene Tierney, Ona Munson.

Leave Her to Heaven
(1945) 110m. **A**
Beautiful, high-strung Tierney always gets what she wants, and marries the utterly bewitched Wilde who seems to be only faintly puzzled by the unexplained deaths of her daddy, a young brother-in-law, and an unborn baby. A lush, multilayered film with gorgeous Technicolor shots of New Mexico and Maine locales.
D: John M. Stahl. A: Gene Tierney, Cornel Wilde, Jeanne Crain.

The Dark Mirror
(1946) 85m. B&W. **B+**
A nosy neighbor, a discarded lover, and a hard-boiled cop are convinced that de Havilland killed a local doctor but are then thrown for a loop when her identical twin shows up. A shady histrionic tale of sibling hatred with a plot reminiscent of some of the more tasteful episodes of *Dynasty.*
D: Robert Siodmak. A: Olivia de Havilland, Thomas Mitchell, Lew Ayres.

The Stranger
(1946) 95m. B&W.
A–
The Nazi criminal who's now a professor in a small Connecticut town seems to be able to hold his own in a cat and mouse game with a very suspicious Nazi hunter. Bulging-eyed Orson polishes up his chillingly evil routine in this moody gothic potboiler.
D: Orson Welles. A: Orson Welles, Loretta Young, Edward G. Robinson.

A Double Life
(1947) 104m. B&W. **B+**
A Broadway actor has lately picked up the unhealthy habit of letting his roles take over his life, and when he plays in *Othello,* the police are on the trail of a murderer. Colman's bravura performance helps make this surprising and theatrical thriller a minor gem.
D: George Cukor. A: Ronald Colman, Signe Hasso, Edmund O'Brien.

The Velvet Touch
(1948) 97m. B&W. **B**
A Broadway star beats her producer to death after he threatens to close her production of *Hedda Gabler* and wreck her upcoming marriage to another man. When another woman is convicted of the crime, she should be home free, but guilt and Ibsen's heroine haunt her in this overbaked but enjoyable effort.
D: John Gage. A: Rosalind Russell, Leo Genn, Claire Trevor.

East Side, West Side
(1949) 108m. B&W. **B**
A society woman maintains a stiff upper lip when it comes to her husband's philandering ways. But when he resumes an affair with an old girlfriend who's then murdered, all evidence points to her. A glossy, adult soap opera that runs with the glamorous, old money crowd of Manhattan.
D: Mervyn LeRoy. A: Barbara Stanwyck, James Mason, Ava Gardner.

Returning GIs

These are some of the films that depict a different kind of heroism from the soldiers returning from war: that of adjusting to domestic life and changing times.

The Best Years of Our Lives
(1946) 182m. B&W. **A**
This is the classic portrait of an American small town in the postwar years and the difficulties faced by ex-servicemen in adjusting to civilian life. Its clean-edged, black-and-white photography, no-nonsense tone, and true-to-life situations give this a crispness and resonance that haven't aged.
D: William Wyler. A: Fredric March, Myrna Loy, Dana Andrews.

Till the End of Time
(1946) 105m. B&W. **B**
A battle-scarred marine finds life at home with his parents awkward while his relationship with a war widow and a disabled veteran complicate affairs even further. Solid and sensitive but lacks the gloss and firepower of *The Best Years of Our Lives.*
D: Edward Dmytryk. A: Guy Madison, Dorothy McGuire, Robert Mitchum.

The Men
(1950) 85m. B&W. **A**
A rare film that looks at the plight of disabled veterans and follows a paraplegic man in a VA rehab ward as he tries to adjust physically and emotionally to his condition. A smoldering Brando makes his film debut in a wheelchair in this bracing unsentimental look at a painful subject.
D: Fred Zinnemann. A: Marlon Brando, Everett Sloan, Teresa Wright.

Postwar Melodramas

Literary adaptations, message films, and costume dramas were all affected by the war years, and many of these movies borrowed their somber tone from film noir, adding a dark gleam to their often weighty subject matter.

Dragon Seed
(1944) 145m. B&W. **C**
The peasants of a small Chinese village endure the humiliations doled out by the occupying Japanese army until they band together to take back their good earth. A ponderous work, based on Pearl Buck's novel, that reeks of wartime propaganda.
D: Jack Conway. A: Katharine Hepburn, Walter Huston, Aline MacMahon.

The Lost Weekend
(1945) 101m. B&W. **A–**
Writer Milland tries to find creative inspiration in a bottle and before you know it he's going on benders while lying to his friends and himself about what's happening. This grim hallucinatory trip is a little overripe at times but remains packed with

powerful and despairing images, not to mention that theramin music.
D: Billy Wilder. A: Ray Milland, Jane Wyman, Philip Terry.

Anna and the King of Siam

(1946) 128m. B&W. **B+**

The Victorian widow ends up teaching the king's 67 children and various wives more than just English as she charms and clashes with the despot over her modern Western ideas. This isn't the plumed pageant of *The King and I,* and Rex is more imperious than storming, but it still remains a solid and lively drama.
D: John Cromwell. A: Irene Dunne, Rex Harrison, Linda Darnell.

The Razor's Edge

(1946) 146m. B&W. **B**

A World War I pilot returns home unable to settle into the cozy life that his fiancée envisions, and begins a worldwide journey in search of his peace of mind. Power's bland expression never seems to change as he goes from Paris dives to the top of the Himalayas in this overlong saga of a spiritual quest by the Lost Generation.
D: Edmund Goulding. A: Tyrone Power, Gene Tierney, John Payne.

The Fugitive

(1947) 104m. B&W. **B+**

The revolutionaries have executed all the priests in a Mexican district save one poor padre who hides out in the villages. John Ford's odd expressionistic tale, filmed in barren and luxurious Mexican locales, has the visual impact of a classic silent drama without generating any warmth or compassion for the characters.
D: John Ford. A: Henry Fonda, Dolores Del Rio, Pedro Armendariz.

Johnny Belinda

(1948) 103m. B&W. **B+**

A farmer's young deaf daughter begins to blossom when the local doctor befriends and teaches her sign language. Her real strength emerges after she's raped and left with a child to care for in this finely acted, enormously engaging, and, given the subject matter, surprisingly spare melodrama.
D: Jean Negulesco. A: Jane Wyman, Lew Ayers, Charles Bickford.

Letter from an Unknown Woman

(1948) 90m. B&W.
A

A young girl spends one night with the pianist next door, then he leaves on tour, unaware that she's pregnant. When they meet years later he doesn't recognize her and begins to woo her anew in this dreamy masterpiece of romantic longing that spans years with the grace and wistfulness of a Viennese waltz.
D: Max Ophüls. A: Joan Fontaine, Louis Jourdan, Mady Christians.

The Pearl

(1948) 77m. B&W. **B+**

A poor diver scours the Mexican Gulf for pearls to feed his family and is elated when he finds an enormous one, unaware that it will bring him despair. This stark and lyrical look at innocence betrayed borrows heavily from neorealism with a lush and haunting Mexican landscape as the real star.
D: Emilio Fernandez. A: Pedro Armendariz, Maria Elena Marques, Fernando Wagner.

The Snake Pit

(1948) 108m. B&W. **B**

De Havilland gives an admirably restrained performance as the woman who has to deal with the demons of her own mental illness while navigating through the insane and sometimes degrading conditions of a mental institution. A well-intentioned, slightly dated drama that somehow avoids being depressing.
D: Anatole Litvak. A: Olivia de Havilland, Mark Stevens, Celeste Holm.

The Fountainhead

(1949) 114m. B&W.
A

A brilliant architect loses friends and projects because of his unyielding convictions—to the point that he's blowing up buildings—as to how his work can shape society. A highly romantic, insanely dramatic spin on the quasi-fascist Ayn Rand novel, with the sinister undercurrent tempered by good old American know-how.
D: King Vidor. A: Gary Cooper, Patricia Neal, Raymond Massey.

1950s

Bible Epics

These lengthy sword-and-sandal epics treat you to big important themes wrapped in togas, painted with garish Technicolor, and oiled with a little biblical-era lust. If the dramas are pure Hollywood, so are the production values: These offer monumental re-creations of temples and palaces, with casts of thousands taking turns playing Romans, Christians, or Jews while tribes wonder, senators squabble, and temptresses loll around in robes.

Samson and Delilah

(1949) 128m. **C+**

Revenge-seeking Delilah deprives Samson of his strength by cutting his hair, and hands him over to his enemies. Light on biblical fact and heavy on the muscle action of the big guy who wrestles a lion, whacks out Philistines, and pulls down a temple.
D: Cecil B. DeMille. A: Hedy Lamarr, Victor Mature, George Sanders.

David and Bathsheba

(1951) 116m. **C+**

When wise but all-too-human King David lets a man die in battle so he may have his wife, he broods, suffers, and sacrifices for his frailty. A richly colored but low-key nonspectacle that offers stock figures and a talky soap opera.
D: Henry King. A: Gregory Peck, Susan Hayward, Raymond Massey.

Quo Vadis?

(1951) 171m. **B**

This overly long epic of the Christian underground's resistance against the ruthless Romans is peppered by

scenes of arena slaughter and slowed down by a bland love story between an officer and a Christian. Ustinov steals every scene with his mad and fretting Nero.
D: Mervyn LeRoy. A: Robert Taylor, Peter Ustinov, Deborah Kerr.

The Robe
(1953) 135m. **B+**
A widescreen spectacle about a Roman tribune who converts to Christianity when Christ's robe falls into his possession. Well acted, this focuses on the slow involvement of an arrogant soldier in the new faith, with somber and muted moments of drama.
D: Henry Koster. A: Richard Burton, Jean Simmons, Michael Rennie.

Salome
(1953) 103m. **C+**
Hollywood gives Salome an attitude adjustment, so here she's virtuously avoiding the lecherous eye of her stepfather and performing an exotic dance to *save* John the Baptist. Fun Hollywood biblical trash with opulent trimmings and a sexy star portraying a virgin in slinky costumes.
D: William Dieterle. A: Rita Hayworth, Charles Laughton, Stewart Granger.

Demetrius and the Gladiators
(1954) 101m. **B**
A Greek slave is forced into gladiatorial combat and tempted by the sexually driven royal, Messalina. The accent is on swordplay in teeming arenas watched over by decadent Romans, with unintentionally amusing love bouts and a wildly overplayed mad Emperor Caligula to provide a few laughs.
D: Delmer Daves. A: Victor Mature, Susan Hayward, Michael Rennie.

The Egyptian
(1954) 140m. **B**
A young man becomes chief doctor and confidant to a powerful pharaoh, following his romantic difficulties and court intrigue over a religious change. Good detail and atmosphere but the story lacks dramatic impact.
D: Michael Curtiz. A: Edmund Purdom, Victor Mature, Peter Ustinov.

Alexander the Great
(1956) 135m. **B–**
The life of the legendary Macedonian warrior king who swept through the known world with his gigantic army, bringing with him Greek ideals and culture. The film rushes through the events like Alexander did, with vivid but repetitious battle sequences and an energetic but reflective Burton.
D: Robert Rossen. A: Richard Burton, Fredric March, Claire Bloom.

The Ten Commandments
(1956) 219m. **B+**
Grand-scale epic on the life of Moses from his days in the Egyptian court to his leading of the Israelites out of slavery into the Promised Land. Sweeping vistas, unsubtle special effects, and scenery-chewing stars fill this monumental lesson on the Old Testament.
D: Cecil B. DeMille. A: Charlton Heston, Yul Brynner, Anne Baxter.

Ben-Hur
(1959) 212m. **A**
The epic story of a Jewish ex-slave who returns home to fight the depravity of Roman rule, rescues his family from exile, and finds faith with Christ along the way. Sweeping and grandly detailed, with a riveting chariot race, flashy sea battle, and monumental Roman sets.
D: William Wyler. A: Charlton Heston, Jack Hawkins, Stephen Boyd.

Historical Epics

As big, blustery, and bursting with stars and intrigue as these costume dramas were, who really cared if actual historical details were smudged or entirely ignored? With actors like Brando and directors like Huston classing up the genre, many of these are first-rate, epic length, escapist fare set in a storybook past.

The Loves of Carmen
(1948) 99m. **C+**
Sizzling gypsy Carmen has a nasty husband and the sexual allure to drive young men mad. Bizet's opera becomes trashy costume fun in the seedy side of Seville, with Hayworth, who's all wild hair and swishing red dresses as she whips up overheated tavern oglers.
D: Charles Vidor. A: Rita Hayworth, Glenn Ford, Luther Adler.

Little Women
(1949) 121m. **B–**
This colorful and sentimental version of Alcott's classic tells of four New England sisters growing up in a cozy Victorian home and preparing for their lives as women. Despite the dollops of ornamental atmosphere there's more Hollywood tinsel and brass, especially the garishly made-up and photographed "little women."
D: Mervyn LeRoy. A: June Allyson, Elizabeth Taylor, Janet Leigh.

Cyrano De Bergerac
(1950) 112m. B&W. **B**
Cyrano is a soldier, poet, and wit able to best any man in any way except—thanks to his very long nose—in romance. Ferrer captures all the bravado and depth of emotion as he gives a handsome soldier the words to win the heart of the woman they both love.
D: Michael Gordon. A: José Ferrer, William Prince, Mala Powers.

Tom Brown's School Days
(1951) 93m. B&W. **B**
Young Tom has a lot of growing up to do with the help of a kindly professor at Rugby School, where he must confront the class bully or sink back into the pack. An enjoyable British-style connect-the-dots look at coming-of-age.
D: Gordon Parry. A: John Howard Davies, Robert Newton, Francis De Wolff.

Moulin Rouge
(1952) 118m. **A**
Aristocratic and horribly stunted Toulouse Lautrec becomes the beloved chronicler of Paris' demimonde even as he is denied their pleasures. Ferrer makes a soulful alcoholic artist in this grand bio-pic that lovingly re-creates Montmartres' boisterous cafe society of cancan dancers, roués, and ladies of pleasure.
D: John Huston. A: José Ferrer, Colette Marchand, Zsa Zsa Gabor.

Desirée
(1953) 110m. **B–**
Brando portrays a strangely indecisive and unsure Napoleon whose secret love is Desirée, the ex-seamstress Queen of Sweden. A big, gaudy, and amusingly speculative romantic melodrama dressed up in breeches and crinoline.
D: Henry Koster. A: Marlon Brando, Jean Simmons, Merle Oberon.

Miss Sadie Thompson
(1953) 91m. **C+**
A lady of easy virtue, quarantined on a hot and steaming island with some manly marines, is called a harlot by the prig and loved by the nice guy sergeant. A few sexy musical numbers and Hayworth's effervescence are the only reasons to watch.
D: Curtis Bernhardt. A: Rita Hayworth, José Ferrer, Russell Collins.

Beau Brummell
(1954) 113m. **B–**
The soldier, fop, and charmer has the king wrapped around his finger and calls the shots on manly fashions until a falling out sends him to debt and poverty. A small-scale drama, but a good Regency England fashion show, with fox hunts and military parades to provide action.
D: Curtis Bernhardt. A: Stewart Granger, Peter Ustinov, Elizabeth Taylor.

The Caine Mutiny
(1954) 125m. **B+**
A mentally unbalanced World War II captain rattles the crew with his erratic behavior, and the second in command mutinies to save the ship, only to face a court-martial. A solid tale of men aboard a troubled warship.
D: Edward Dmytryk. A: Humphrey Bogart, Van Johnson, Fred MacMurray.

Napoleon
(1955) 115m. **C–**
A remarkably facile and dull study of the rise of the famous Corsican officer and French leader. Aside from some obligatory resplendent Empire trappings and a few international stars, this is an intimate and completely unappealing portrait of the man.
D: Sacha Guitry. A: Raymond Pellegrin, Orson Welles, Maria Schell.

The Virgin Queen
(1955) 92m. **B**
A dash of history, a dollop of soap, and Davis encased in almost grotesque white face powder make up this portrait of the aging Queen Elizabeth who chose state over heart. Slightly trashy charm is added by Collins as the young maiden who turns Walter Raleigh's eyes.
D: Henry Koster. A: Bette Davis, Richard Todd, Joan Collins.

Moby Dick
(1956) 116m. **B+**
Young Ishmael ships out on a whaling boat unaware that Captain Ahab is obsessed with hunting down the great white whale who took his leg. A salty and portentous sea saga that saves most of its energy for the wild and lengthy confrontation between the crazed Ahab and his massive nemesis.
D: John Huston. A: Gregory Peck, Richard Basehart, Leo Genn.

War and Peace
(1956) 208m. **B**
Massive, well-depicted battles between Napoleon's army and the defending Russians overwhelm this tale of love and family turmoil. Glorious to look at, but the central characters wander in and out with little impact. Watch the battles and read the book.
D: King Vidor. A: Audrey Hepburn, Henry Fonda, Vittorio Gassman.

The Brothers Karamazov
(1958) 146m. **B**
There are some great character moments in this very Russian study of four distinctly different brothers and their boorish, lecherous father in the nineteenth century. The large emotions are intense but there's too much character and not enough story to carry this for almost two hours.
D: Richard Brooks. A: Yul Brynner, Maria Schell, Lee J. Cobb.

A Breath of Scandal
(1960) 98m. **B–**
A princess of the Hapsburg Empire meets a handsome American mining engineer and royal hearts flutter at the forbidden romance. A frothy costume farce amid storybook Austrian locations that suffers from a weak script and a bland American.
D: Michael Curtiz. A: Sophia Loren, John Gavin, Maurice Chevalier.

Circus Spectacles

Hollywood stars performed under the big tent in these biblical-sized circus films in the 50s.

The Greatest Show on Earth
(1952) 153m. **B**
Circus manager Heston charms, cajoles, and plays psychiatrist to his motley crew of high-strung performers in this thinly veiled story of the Ringling Brothers and Barnum and Bailey Circus. A brilliant roster of Hollywood stars troop through as lion tamers, acrobats, and clowns in this garish slice of Hollywood-style Americana.
D: Cecil B. DeMille. A: Betty Hutton, Charlton Heston, Cornel Wilde.

Trapeze
(1956) 105m. **B+**
A young trapeze artist travels to Paris to learn the vaunted triple somersault from a retired ex-master. Teacher and student team up but their act is threatened when they both fall for Gina. The athletic stars keep the featherweight tale and bloated production values afloat.
D: Carol Reed. A: Burt Lancaster, Tony Curtis, Gina Lollobrigida.

Circus World
(1964) 135m. **C–**
The Duke takes his Wild West circus with its slipping morale, money problems, and explosive tempers to the Continent in search of the trapeze artist who gave him a daughter. Wayne and Hayworth look tired and fail to ignite any sparks in this huge overproduced omnibus.
D: Henry Hathaway. A: John Wayne, Rita Hayworth, Claudia Cardinale.

See also *Billy Rose's Jumbo,* page 412.

British Dramas

These sturdy and darker-hued dramas show a postwar Britian of lost innocence; children protect killers, students sneer at professors, and good citizens challenge the questionable integrity of the military. Even though psychological problems have replaced the stiff upper lip, these finely acted intelligent stories still have the power to move and uplift.

Last Holiday
(1950) 88m. B&W. **B–**
Given six weeks to live, a small-time salesman spends his life's savings at an expensive resort where his new freedom is perceived as business worldliness. A gentle O. Henry-like fable.
D: Henry Cass. A: Alec Guinness, Beatrice Campbell, Kay Walsh.

The Browning Version
(1951) 90m. B&W. **B**
A once brilliant teacher, now ridiculed by his students and cuckolded by his wife, makes one last stand on the eve of his premature retirement. Redgrave's awesome performance makes this dark side of *Goodbye, Mr. Chips* memorable.
D: Anthony Asquith. A: Michael Redgrave, Jean Kent, Nigel Patrick.

The Winslow Boy
(1948) 118m. B&W. **B**
A father exhausts his meager resources to hire a distinguished attorney to challenge the navy and its code of honor when his son is wrongly accused of stealing. This courtroom drama mixes in soap opera pathos with a broadside aimed at the naval establishment.
D: Anthony Asquith. A: Robert Donat, Margaret Leighton, Cedric Hardwicke.

Carrington, V. C.
(aka Court Martial) (1955) 105m. B&W. **C**
A war hero is court-martialed based on the perjury of his wife who learned of his philandering ways. Middling military courtroom drama that looks like a filmed one-set stage play.
D: Anthony Asquith. A: David Niven, Margaret Leighton, Noelle Middleton.

The Prisoner
(1955) 91m. B&W. **B**
A cardinal, held prisoner in an unnamed communist country, faces interrogation and torture by his former resistance comrade. A somber and relentless wrestling match of ideology and religion.
D: Peter Glenville. A: Alec Guinness, Jack Hawkins, Wilford Lawson.

Tiger Bay
(1959) 105m. B&W.
B+
A fatherless tomboy witnesses a murder, befriends the killer, deceives the police, and finds herself on the wrong side of the manhunt. Hayley, all sinew and spunk, makes this tangled tale work.
D: J. Lee Thompson. A: John Mills, Horst Buchholz, Hayley Mills.

Noirish Melodramas

Postwar anxieties continued to be explored in these dark-edged tales in which psychological problems abound, and the women tend to be menaced or menacing.

Born to Be Bad
(1950) 94m. B&W. **B+**
A cool enchantress bleeds her wealthy beau dry while pursuing a moody virile writer. Fontaine's conniving minx is one of those characters that you relish detesting while anticipating her comeuppance as she manipulates every man and woman within shouting distance.
D: Nicholas Ray. A: Joan Fontaine, Robert Ryan, Zachary Scott.

A Life of Her Own
(1950) 108m. B&W. **B**
A young woman newly arrived in New York is convinced she'll find fame, fortune, and happiness by being a model; soon she's living the high life, which includes an affair with a married man. A relatively adult soaper that never manages to be the trashy fun you'd expect.
D: George Cukor. A: Lana Turner, Ray Milland, Tom Ewell.

The Second Woman
(1951) 91m. B&W. **B**
An architect tries to commit suicide when his fiancée is accidentally killed the night before their wedding. He survives and with the help of a new girlfriend tries to understand the mystery behind her death. A moody psychodrama that threatens to spin out of control except for Young's quiet gloom.
D: James V. Kern. A: Robert Young, Betsy Drake, John Sutton.

Human Desire
(1954) 90m. B&W. **A–**
A brutish husband is out for murder when he discovers that his wife once had an affair with the man who just fired him. A bleak unrelenting tale of revenge and lust that still looks modern.
D: Fritz Lang. A: Glenn Ford, Gloria Grahame, Broderick Crawford.

Autumn Leaves
(1956) 108m. B&W. **A–**
A lonely, middle-aged woman finds love with a gentle younger man, but the honeymoon is over when it turns out that he's schizophrenic. A beautifully played psychological soaper that only once veers toward camp when Crawford pours on the self-sacrificing masochism a little too thick.
D: Robert Aldrich. A: Joan Crawford, Cliff Robertson, Vera Miles.

Middle of the Night
(1959) 118m. B&W. **B**
An aging garment manufacturer takes up with a recently divorced young receptionist, but love's path is rocky, from disapproving families to all the problems that age difference entails. Sad haunting Novak casts a warm glow over old bear March, helping bring some life to this stagebound bittersweet tale.
D: Delbert Mann. A: Fredric March, Kim Novak, Glenda Farrell.

Dead Ringer
(1964) 115m. B&W. **B**
Tired of failing to make ends meet, a slatternly bar owner shoots her rich twin sister and assumes her identity. After the opening where

dishrag Bette gets down and dirty with prissy sis, this baroque melodrama settles down into a nervous "can she pull off the deception?" routine made entertaining by the cast.
D: Paul Henreid. A: Bette Davis, Karl Malden, Peter Lawford.

Romantic Melodramas (Black and White)

These black-and-white soap operas may not have the lush production values of their Technicolor counterparts, but they're no less flamboyant in depicting overheated illicit love affairs of the glamorous and guilty.

September Affair
(1950) 104m. B&W. **B–**
A married man and a concert pianist meet in Italy, fall in love, and are given temporary freedom when the plane they missed crashes and they're listed as dead. For all the hokey plot contrivances, this is a fairly quiet and simple adult love story in a travelogue setting with few tears and little passion.
D: William Dieterle. A: Joseph Cotten, Joan Fontaine, Françoise Rosay.

Three Secrets
(1950) 98m. B&W. **B+**
When an adopted child is stranded after a plane crash, three women—a homemaker, a newspaper reporter, and an ex-convict—flock to the rescue scene, convinced that the child is hers. A lower-budgeted, tightly told morality tale, with the women wringing their hands in guilt over choices made five years ago.
D: Robert Wise. A: Eleanor Parker, Patricia Neal, Frank Lovejoy.

Ruby Gentry
(1952) 82m. B&W. **B+**
Jones is the hellcat from the wrong side of the tracks who pants after newly rich Heston, even when he dumps her after their one-night stand. The plot twists might make you dizzy in this rambling oddball tale of lust and greed in the rural South, but they're still fun to watch.
D: King Vidor. A: Jennifer Jones, Charlton Heston, Karl Malden.

Indiscretion of an American Wife
(1953) 63m. B&W. **C+**
A married woman tries over and over again to say goodbye to her lover in a Rome train station. This small, talky, and overwrought melodrama tries hard to be a weeper but you're soon wishing the lovers would quit emoting and say goodbye already.
D: Vittorio De Sica. A: Jennifer Jones, Montgomery Clift, Gino Cervi.

Another Time, Another Place
(1958) 98m. B&W. **C+**
A reporter visits the home and widow of the war correspondent with whom she had an affair during the war. The cozy cottage village, the good-hearted English wife and son, a hilariously overdressed and hammy Turner, and the most unbelievable plot this side of farce help turn some of the dramatic moments into camp.
D: Lewis Allen. A: Lana Turner, Glynnis Johns, Sean Connery.

The Young Philadelphians
(1959) 136m. B&W. **B+**
A gutsy potboiler about the ambitious young lawyer who falls for the society girl, loses her to his friend, becomes a success, and risks his career by defending the friend, now a lush, on murder charges. A slow start, but the sprawling story pulls together and is galvanized by a white-hot Newman.
D: Vincent Sherman. A: Paul Newman, Barbara Rush, Alexis Smith.

Romantic Melodramas (Color)

These plush sweeping soap operas are hand-wringing, tear-stained True Romance Comics come to life. Everything is exaggerated here, from the characters and their emphatic emotions to the hyperchic set designs and fabulous clothes. The dialogue, too, is some of the most quotable in filmdom, filled with one extravagant cliché after another as the characters struggle with passions and suffer, suffer, suffer, all in high-resolution Technicolor.

Torch Song
(1953) 90m. **B–**
Crawford is a control-freak Broadway star who is cut down to size by a blind pianist who still remembers her when she was a "gypsy Madonna." Joan seizes every opportunity to display her gams, even to the point where she is tripping chorus boys.
D: Charles Walters. A: Joan Crawford, Michael Wilding, Marjorie Rambeau.

The Last Time I Saw Paris
(1954) 116m. **B–**
He's a struggling writer, she's the beautiful young thing used to the high life, and they're in Paris, married, and in love. Serviceable marriage-in-distress melodrama with little chemistry between the leads but a glorious Paris.
D: Richard Brooks. A: Elizabeth Taylor, Van Johnson, Walter Pidgeon.

Magnificent Obsession
(1954) 108m. **B+**
Playboy Rock accidentally kills Jane's husband and blinds her, but becomes a doctor so he can cure her. This duo takes melodramatic suffering and romance to new heights, underscored by crashingly schmaltzy music.
D: Douglas Sirk. A: Jane Wyman, Rock Hudson, Barbara Rush.

Rhapsody
(1954) 115m. **B–**
Taylor falls in love with a violinist who leaves her for his

art, so she marries another musician who is suffocatingly dependent on her. Lacks the unintentionally hilarious dialogue and improbable scenes of the others, even though Liz seems to have no other ambition but to marry musicians.
D: Charles Vidor. A: Elizabeth Taylor, Vittorio Gassman, John Ericson.

All That Heaven Allows
(1955) 89m. **A–**
A New England widow falls for a younger free-spirited gardener, much to the horror of her friends and college-age children. A classic lush soaper with the scenes of Rock quietly telling Jane how important it is to be his own man that are priceless.
D: Douglas Sirk. A: Jane Wyman, Rock Hudson, Agnes Moorehead.

Love Is a Many-Splendored Thing
(1955) 102m. **C+**
A Eurasian doctor and a married American correspondent fall disastrously in love in Hong Kong during the Korean conflict. A heady romantic atmosphere, but the lovers are total windbags.
D: Henry King. A: Jennifer Jones, William Holden, Isobel Elsom.

Picnic
(1955) 115m. **A**
The charismatic drifter with big-time plans sets the small-town ladies aflutter, including his friend's fiancée. A big glorious piece of Americana and a tightly crafted drama ripe with sexual undercurrents and appealing characters.
D: Joshua Logan. A: William Holden, Kim Novak, Rosalind Russell.

Summertime
(1955) 99m. **A**
A spinster American tourist blossoms in Venice when she has an affair with a romantic Italian. This is more of a solid, leisurely constructed adult drama than the others, with a breathtaking, sun-drenched Venice, a tremulous Hepburn, and a quietly suave Brazzi.
D: David Lean. A: Katharine Hepburn, Rossano Brazzi, Darren McGavin.

The Man in the Gray Flannel Suit
(1956) 153m. **B–**
A happily married Madison Avenue exec is first plunged into a financial crisis and is then informed that he fathered a child in Italy during the war. Peck brings his usual stentorian dignity to the man-with-a-conscience role in this soapy potboiler about the precariousness of the American Dream.
D: Nunnally Johnson. A: Gregory Peck, Jennifer Jones, Fredric March.

An Affair to Remember
(1957) 115m. **B+**
A sophisticated couple has a shipboard romance and, later in New York, the woman has an accident keeping her from their designated rendezvous. The early urbane humor is quickly swept away by the overwrought and sometimes hilariously unbelievable pathos. Kerr teaching a children's choir toward the end is a nice touch.
D: Leo McCarey. A: Cary Grant, Deborah Kerr, Richard Denning.

Peyton Place
(1957) 157m. **A**
Beneath its veneer of respectability, a small New England town is a seething pit of lust, murder, and scandalous family secrets. An almost operatic trashy soap opera with all the small-town types: sensitive young girl, ice queen mother with a secret, family doctor with integrity, and abused girl from shantytown.
D: Mark Robson. A: Lana Turner, Hope Lange, Lloyd Nolan.

Bonjour Tristesse
(1958) 94m. **B**
The idyllic life of this chic continental couple—a playboy father and his teenage daughter—is jeopardized when he contemplates marrying his down-to-earth English mistress. This glorious Eurotrash-style melodrama gives us beautiful shots of the rich and beautiful vacationing on the Riviera as the daughter plots to get rid of her rival.
D: Otto Preminger. A: David Niven, Jean Seberg, Deborah Kerr.

Marjorie Morningstar
(1958) 123m. **B+**
Wouk's novel about a Jewish American Princess coming of age is turned into a Hollywood romance between a dewy-eyed, pampered young girl and a two-bit director who romances her but resists her middle-class morality. This has a lower quotient of overwrought scenes, but is still filled with extravagant dialogue.
D: Irving Rapper. A: Natalie Wood, Gene Kelly, Claire Trevor.

Imitation of Life
(1959) 124m.
A–
A single mother struggling to be an actress hits the big time with a daughter, a black maid, and the maid's daughter (who tries to pass for white) in tow. The large and purpled emotions are not to be believed, with amazing dialogue spoken seriously as Turner and her nubile teenager pant for the same man.
D: Douglas Sirk. A: Lana Turner, Sandra Dee, John Gavin.

Some Came Running
(1959) 137m. **C+**
When a failed writer returns to his hometown, he's plunged into long-stewing family hatreds, adulterous affairs, unrequited passions, and some easy camaraderie with a charming drunken gambler. Overwrought to the max, with Sinatra trying to act sensitive, MacLaine playing her screechy ditz, and Dino his usual smooth and silky operator.
D: Vincente Minnelli. A: Frank Sinatra, Dean (Dino) Martin, Shirley MacLaine.

A Summer Place
(1959) 130m. **A**
Former lovers, now both married, reunite even as their kids are falling in love. Features sensational Maine and Florida beaches for the overcharged emotions of the misunderstood young lovers, and an unbelievable scene where Dee's virginity is verified by a gynecologist.
D: Delmer Daves. A: Troy Donahue, Sandra Dee, Dorothy McGuire.

Family Melodramas

This group of sprawling, big-budgeted precursors to *Dallas* and *Dynasty* combine the colorful expansiveness of an Americana potboiler with the emotional voyeurism of a 1950s psychological melodrama. With literate and often throbbing stories that follow Texas oil barons, cattle ranchers, and rich plantation patriarchs, these films peel away at American mythology to reveal stunted family lives riddled with alcoholism, adultery, and mental instability.

East of Eden
(1955) 115m. **B+**
On a California lettuce farm, an upright son and his rebellious brother vie for the affections of their righteous, God-fearing father. Dean plays his brooding, emotionally vulnerable bad boy to perfection in this big screen, beautifully shot drama.
D: Elia Kazan. A: James Dean, Julie Harris, Raymond Massey.

Giant
(1956) 201m. **B–**
A multigenerational saga of wealthy cattle and oil barons set against sprawling Texas history. Even with the star power, this lumbering and overlong epic soaper looks better now for its splendid scenery than for the overwrought performances.
D: George Stevens. A: Elizabeth Taylor, Rock Hudson, James Dean.

Written on the Wind
(1956) 99m. **B+**
Texas playboy Stack marries secretary Bacall and soon his best friend Hudson has the hots for her. Of course, that doesn't stop the playboy's sister from throwing herself at Rock. A frenzied lush soap opera with the actors sinking their teeth into the meaty and overheated roles.
D: Douglas Sirk. A: Robert Stack, Lauren Bacall, Rock Hudson.

Raintree County
(1957) 168m. **B–**
A man of principles marries the bewitching but childish Southern belle who turns out to be haunted by something in her past. Meanwhile, his long-suffering childhood sweetheart pines away. A solid romantic triangle with an array of colorful characters, some funny Freudian flourishes, and a leisurely Civil War-era quality.
D: Edward Dmytryk. A: Montgomery Clift, Elizabeth Taylor, Eva Marie Saint.

Cat on a Hot Tin Roof
(1958) 108m. **A**
Big Daddy wants an heir from his favorite son, who's having problems with his frustrated, hot-blooded wife. Seething atmospheric Southern gothic drama with all of Tennessee Williams' heat and passionate eloquence.
D: Richard Brooks. A: Paul Newman, Elizabeth Taylor, Burl Ives.

The Long Hot Summer
(1958) 117m. **A**
A snappy literate tale of another Southern "Big Daddy" who's trying to marry off his lovely strong-minded daughter to the fiery young drifter who's shaking everyone up. Charged performances make this one hum.
D: Martin Ritt. A: Paul Newman, Joanne Woodward, Orson Welles.

Suddenly, Last Summer
(1959) B&W. 114m. **A–**
After Taylor has a nervous breakdown, she reveals to her aunt and a neurosurgeon the tragedy that befell her homosexual cousin in Europe. A very odd tale with little action and a lot of talk about personal issues to fuel this hypnotic and claustrophobic Southern gothic.
D: Joseph L. Mankiewicz. A: Elizabeth Taylor, Katharine Hepburn, Montgomery Clift.

Home from the Hill
(1960) 150m. **A**
All the ripe characters are here scratching away at family wounds: the philandering patriarch, his cold wife, their sensitive son, and the embittered illegitimate child. An ornate and darker-hued melodrama with confrontations that teeter between classic and clichéd.
D: Vincente Minnelli. A: Robert Mitchum, Eleanor Parker, George Peppard.

Hollywood

Hollywood relished portraying its own machinations, especially the ambitions and bizarre peccadilloes of actors, as this group of biting dramas demonstrates.

All About Eve
(1950) 138m. B&W. **A**
An ardent fan of a reigning Broadway star becomes her assistant and then proceeds to insinuate herself into every aspect of the actress's life. A funny and scintillating drama in which acid-tongued sophisticates from the theater world back-stab, keep their tenuous hold on the top, or simply watch the battles from the sidelines.
D: Joseph L. Mankiewicz. A: Bette Davis, Anne Baxter, George Sanders.

Sunset Boulevard
(1950) 110m. B&W.
A
A silent star recluse lures a down-on-his-luck writer to help with her comeback vehicle. He takes up temporary residence in her Hollywood mansion and becomes mired in the fevered delusional life of someone who lives in the past. A beautifully creepy and noir Hollywood gothic that lives up to its classic status.
D: Billy Wilder. A: Gloria Swanson, William Holden, Nancy Olson.

The Bad and the Beautiful
(1952) 118m. B&W. **A–**
A successful writer, director, and actress all share recollections of how they had been helped and betrayed by a producer friend who's now hit the skids. A wonderfully entertaining and tightly scripted look at the ruthless behind-the-scenes antics of Hollywood with sharp, hard-boiled performances.
D: Vincente Minnelli. A: Kirk Douglas, Lana Turner, Barry Sullivan.

The Star
(1952) 89m. B&W. **C+**
A washed-up star desperate for money has a blowup with her family, goes on a drinking binge, is bailed out by a former actor who she once helped, and fails at a sales clerk position. More ridiculous than tragic given Davis' almost campy performance and the film's semihysterical tone.
D: Stuart Heisler. A: Bette Davis, Sterling Hayden, Natalie Wood.

The Barefoot Contessa
(1954) 128m. **B+**
In a series of flashbacks, a Hollywood director and PR man remember the puzzling life of an enigmatic star who rose from poverty to international success. A bitter look at Hollywood and the international jet set with surprisingly adult situations and characters who are overexplained in a sometimes wordy script.
D: Joseph Mankiewicz. A: Humphrey Bogart, Ava Gardner, Edmond O'Brien.

The Goddess
(1957) 105m. B&W. **C+**
This story of a Marilyn Monroe-like sex goddess's rise to success isn't the celebration of Hollywood's tawdriness that the other films are, but rather a gloomy drama of a neurotic young woman. The hopeless tone has more of the air of early live TV than Hollywood, and Stanley just doesn't look the part.
D: John Cromwell. A: Kim Stanley, Lloyd Bridges, Steven Hill.

Career
(1959) 105m. B&W. **B**
A driven actor in New York can't seem to get the breaks despite talent, ambition, and marrying a producer's alcoholic daughter. Like *The Goddess,* this is reminiscent of live television dramas from the 50s, with its slightly claustrophobic feel, edgy performances, and honest, if melodramatic, script.
D: Joseph Anthony. A: Anthony Franciosa, Dean Martin, Shirley MacLaine.

Teens

Hard to believe, but teen culture really came into its own in the 1950s, which may be why these early mainstream youth rebellion films are such Hollywood icons.

The Wild One
(1954) 79m. **B+**
A gang of heavy leather punks invades the serene environs of a nice small town. Soon a rival gang shows up, and the townies and other representatives of normal America are up in arms. Not really a very good film, but enjoyable for Brando's existentially sneering/suffering performance as well as Marvin's just plain sneering one.
D: Laslo Benedek. A: Marlon Brando, Mary Murphy, Lee Marvin.

The Blackboard Jungle
(1955) 101m. B&W. **B**
A determined high school teacher takes on the daunting task of trying to teach New York City toughs. Gritty, first-class film in all regards, with Vic Morrow memorable as a glinty-eyed psycho teen; unfortunately, the knife-wielding punks pale next to today's Uzi-toting kids.
D: Richard Brooks. A: Glenn Ford, Anne Francis, Sidney Poitier.

Rebel Without a Cause
(1955) 111m. **A**
Teen alienation becomes boffo box office in this Technicolor angsty tale of an aimless pretty boy, his nerdy pal, his girl, and various violent teen rites-of-passage. While occasionally quaintly melodramatic, this expertly crafted, sweetly romantic outsider tale still remains the best showcase for Dean's charisma.
D: Nicholas Ray. A: James Dean, Natalie Wood, Sal Mineo.

Courtroom Dramas

With all the courtroom theatrics of Court TV, countless legal thrillers, and crime-of-the-week TV movies, these classics of the genre still come across as fresh and gripping as today's headlines.

12 Angry Men
(1957) 95m. B&W. **A–**
A small plain jury room is the setting for this heated drama of 12 jurors deciding a seemingly open and shut case of a father's stabbing death by his street-tough son. Tour de force performances and cunning camerawork make this a compelling drama in a pressure box atmosphere.
D: Sidney Lumet. A: Henry Fonda, Lee J. Cobb, E. G. Marshall.

Witness for the Prosecution
(1957) 114m. B&W. **B+**
This sly and flavorful character drama centers on a murder case in which the accused man's wife agrees to testify against him. Laughton does a great Churchill imitation as the game old barrister who attempts to untangle the case in the old woody British courtroom.
D: Billy Wilder. A: Charles Laughton, Marlene Dietrich, Tyrone Power.

Anatomy of a Murder
(1959) 160m. B&W. **A**
The frank language of sexuality may have lost its shock in this tale of an army officer who killed a man he claimed had raped his wife. What still grabs you is the suspense of the investigation, the almost clinical attention to the rhythms of a trial, and the ripe jazzy human drama.
D: Otto Preminger. A: James Stewart, Lee Remick, Ben Gazzara.

Compulsion
(1959) 102m. B&W. **A–**
Based on the Leopold and Loeb murder case, two brainy rich kids decide to commit the perfect crime by kidnapping and killing a child. Despite the 1920s period details, this has a jazzy, post-atomic lost youth atmosphere, capped off by Welles' lengthy but emotionally charged defense of his guilty clients.
D: Richard Fleischer. A: Orson Welles, Dean Stockwell, Bradford Dillman.

Inherit the Wind
(1960) 126m. B&W. **A–**
Based on the 1925 Scopes case, this follows the trial of a Southern educator arrested for teaching Dar-

win's theories. Bombastic preacher March thumps the Bible and ridicules scientists while the small-towners cheer him on; wily Tracy methodically punctures his dogmatic and narrow religious interpretations. Still involving, even—or especially—today.
D: Stanley Kramer. A: Spencer Tracy, Fredric March, Gene Kelly.

Judgment at Nuremberg
(1961) 190m. B&W. **A**

This star-studded, long-winded drama about a postwar trial of Nazi German war criminals still offers gripping and gut-wrenching moments in its examination of national guilt. The testimonies of survivors, backed by actual footage of death camps, is powerful stuff, with an intriguing subplot involving the presiding American judge and a German woman.
D: Stanley Kramer. A: Spencer Tracy, Richard Widmark, Marlene Dietrich.

Classic Plays and Adaptations

Often based on plays or novels, these small black-and-white character dramas have a subtlety, earnestness, and eloquence missing from many of the straightforward romantic melodramas. They still contain relatively torrid sex scenes and overripe emotional confrontations, but the characters—played by some of the hotshot "serious" actors of the day—can babble like a patient on a therapist's couch while playing them.

A Place in the Sun
(1951) 122m. B&W. **A–**

A factory worker and the owner's daughter fall in love, but he's saddled with his pregnant blue-collar girlfriend. Taylor's and Clift's faces fill the screen in luminous, breathtakingly intimate close-ups, adding to the obsessive, romantic, and doomed atmosphere of this American tragedy.
D: George Stevens. A: Montgomery Clift, Elizabeth Taylor, Shelley Winters.

A Streetcar Named Desire
(1951) 122m. B&W. **B+** 🏛

This tale of the fading Southern belle visiting her sister and loutish hunk brother-in-law has become such a cultural touchstone that it's surprising to see how stagy it seems now. Even so, unerring performances and a powerhouse Brando make this film as galvanizing as when it was released.
D: Elia Kazan. A: Marlon Brando, Vivien Leigh, Kim Hunter.

Come Back, Little Sheba
(1952) 99m. B&W. **B–**

A married couple who look like they've weathered bad times—he's on the wagon and she sounds practically dotty with her nonstop nervous litany of reassurances—face another crisis when they take in an attractive young boarder. A sad, poignant, and finally brutal marital melodrama.
D: Daniel Mann. A: Burt Lancaster, Shirley Booth, Terry Moore.

The Member of the Wedding
(1952) 91m. B&W. **B–**

A twelve-year-old excluded from her brother's wedding party tries to catch up with the happy couple on their honeymoon, and has a chance encounter with a stranger. This lyrical coming-of-age drama is so mannered, so earnest, and so stagebound that it remains best for Carson McCullers' fans.
D: Fred Zinnemann. A: Julie Harris, Ethel Waters, Brandon de Wilde.

The Country Girl
(1954) 104m. B&W. **C+**

An overly earnest tale of the textbook codependent couple: He's an alcoholic Broadway star desperate for his new play to be a hit, she's the repressed steadfast spouse who looks like her very blood is being drained into him. Bing's eerily believable in some scenes while Kelly is not.
D: George Seaton. A: Bing Crosby, Grace Kelly, William Holden.

I Am a Camera
(1955) 98m. B&W. **C+**

An English writer strikes up a friendship with fellow expatriate Sally Bowles, trailing along her crazy path through the cafes and seedy nightclubs of 1930s Berlin. Decadence never looked so pedestrian in this earnest but lackluster nonmusical *Cabaret.*
D: Henry Cornelius. A: Laurence Harvey, Julie Harris, Shelley Winters.

The Man with the Golden Arm
(1955) 119m. B&W. **B**

An ex-junkie tries to straighten himself out by becoming a drummer in a band. While his wife fakes a paralysis to keep him home, he hopes to rekindle an old affair. Melodramatic and scored with an overpowering jazzy score, this tries to be heavy hitting but is dated by its Hollywood trappings.
D: Otto Preminger. A: Frank Sinatra, Eleanor Parker, Kim Novak.

Marty
(1955) 91m. B&W. **A** 🏛 🏆

Marty is a middle-aged Bronx butcher who, when he meets a nice girl at a lonelyhearts dance, must find the strength to defy his smothering mother and neighborhood pals. The film that helped popularize Hollywood's new realism and intimate stories about little people, this remains poignant and true to its simple story and underdog characters.
D: Delbert Mann. A: Ernest Borgnine, Betsy Blair, Joe Mantell.

The Rose Tattoo
(1955) 117m. B&W. **B–**

An Italian immigrant widow is faithful to her husband's memory until a local truck driver begins to court her with the force and subtlety of a hurricane. The characters are so earthy and operatic in their flamboyance that you may not mind that they're all jaw and no action.
D: Daniel Mann. A: Anna Magnani, Burt Lancaster, Marisa Pavan.

Baby Doll
(1956) 114m. B&W. **C**

Baby Doll is married to an older man who has allowed her to keep her virginity until she's 20—which she's just turning. A film that was scandalous when it came out seems unpleasant and dull now.
D: Elia Kazan. A: Karl Malden, Carroll Baker, Eli Wallach.

The Catered Affair
(1956) 94m. B&W. **B**

When it's time for a Bronx couple's daughter to marry, mom wants a wedding with all the trimmings while down-to-earth cabby dad only sees dollar signs. Like a companion piece to *Marty,* this savors the homey settings and modest hopes of its salt-of-the-earth characters.
D: Richard Brooks. A: Bette Davis, Ernest Borgnine, Debbie Reynolds.

The Rainmaker
(1956) 121m. B&W. **B−**

A sweet-talking con man promising rain takes up residence with a family and begins to work magic with the spinster daughter who had always been told she's plain. A sweet and sometimes humorous tale, but the actors look old and could outgab a politician.
D: Joseph Anthony. A: Burt Lancaster, Katharine Hepburn, Wendell Corey.

Tea and Sympathy
(1956) 122m. **B**

A sensitive student and the schoolmaster's neglected wife develop a friendship outside the boarding school conformity. A gentle, slightly mannered and curtailed film version of the play, with its muted treatment of subjects like homosexuality making it slightly dated.
D: Vincente Minnelli. A: Deborah Kerr, Leif Erickson, John Kerr.

The Three Faces of Eve
(1957) 91m. B&W. **B+**

With the help of a psychiatrist, a troubled colorless young married woman discovers that those blackouts are her wild and crazy side coming out to play. Woodward has a field day with a variety of roles in this serious drama that's spiced with a little of the luridness of a *National Enquirer* exposé.
D: Nunnally Johnson. A: Joanne Woodward, David Wayne, Lee J. Cobb.

Desire Under the Elms
(1958) 114m. B&W. **C**

An immigrant waitress marries a patriarch farmer, seduces one of his sons, and gets pregnant. Slow, overly serious, and overtly sexual in an uninteresting way.
D: Delbert Mann. A: Sophia Loren, Anthony Perkins, Burl Ives.

Lonelyhearts
(1958) 104m. B&W. **C+**

A young reporter gets a job as the advice columnist, and starts to feel the effects of the numberless pleas for help. If you don't know the novella on which this was based, it's a serviceable if low-rent melodrama, though the subplot of the cynical editor and suffering wife is a throwaway.
D: Vincent Donehue. A: Montgomery Clift, Robert Ryan, Myrna Loy.

The Black Orchid
(1959) 96m. B&W. **C+**

A gangster's widow is romanced by a sympathetic widower, but when the relationship gets serious, his daughter makes trouble. Less hysterical than other similar dramas, but the story lacks vigor, and the soundtrack occasionally uses that weird 50s sci-fi music.
D: Martin Ritt. A: Sophia Loren, Anthony Quinn, Ina Balin.

The Diary of Anne Frank
(1959) 150m. B&W. **A**

The experiences of a group of Jews hiding in Amsterdam during the war are told in this film version of the real-life teenager's diary. This powerful story receives a respectful and somewhat glossy treatment, but the suspense, human drama, and fine performances make it as riveting as it is haunting.
D: George Stevens. A: Millie Perkins, Joseph Schildkraut, Shelley Winters.

The Fugitive Kind
(1959) 135m. B&W. **B−**

This version of Tennessee Williams' *Orpheus Descending* takes everything—makeup, sets, photography, and acting—and makes all as symbol-laden and theatrical as a Greek tragedy. Beautiful to look at and literate as everyone acts up a storm, but its mannered quality hits you from all directions.
D: Sidney Lumet. A: Marlon Brando, Anna Magnani, Joanne Woodward.

Political Dramas

These tough intelligent films portray the underbelly of the American political machine, whether it stems from a folksy charismatic soap-box preacher or the cynical accounting of compromises and favors in Washington's old boy network.

All the King's Men
(1949) 109m. B&W. **B+**

Loosely based on Louisiana's notorious governor Huey Long. An illiterate backwoods politician wins over the state's corrupt political machinery only to build his own through bribery and intimidation. A fascinating if heavy-handed tale that's carried by a blustery and charismatic Crawford.
D: Robert Rossen. A: Broderick Crawford, Joanne Dru, John Ireland.

The Last Hurrah
(1958) 121m. B&W. **B**

An aging mayor of a large New England city enters his final campaign for reelection and finds his man-of-the-people platform is seriously outdated. A bitter-edged but sentimental tale of the changing face of politics, and how it went from brawling promises and torchlight parades to more modern-day dirty-dealing.
D: John Ford. A: Spencer Tracy, Jeffrey Hunter, Basil Rathbone.

Advise and Consent
(1962) 139m. B&W.
A−

The confirmation of the new Secretary of State becomes mired in intrigue and blackmail as past sexual and political associations are used to influence votes. An epic and often sprawling potboiler, filled with conniving senators, glorious Washington locales, and dark secrets that may now seem a bit tame.
D: Otto Preminger. A: Henry Fonda, Charles Laughton, Don Murray.

The Best Man
(1964) 102m. B&W.
B+

An idealistic presidential candidate has a damaging episode from the past uncovered by his opponent; the moral dilemma is whether he should use the dirt his own boys dug up on the opponent. Edgy dialogue, nifty plot contrivances, and the almost documentary sweep of events keep you glued to your seat.
D: Franklin Schaffner. A: Henry Fonda, Cliff Robertson, Edie Adams.

Sports Biographies

Unlike the strictly inspirational tone of 1940s sports bio-pics, most of these films have a grittier feel as the all-American heroes—now including blacks and American Indians—battle not illness, but prejudice, poverty, and their own private demons.

The Jackie Robinson Story

(1950) 76m. B&W. **B**

This follows Robinson's life and career, from his days as a UCLA student to the Negro baseball leagues, and finally to the Brooklyn Dodgers as the first African-American major leaguer. Nothing fancy, but an earnest and hardworking account, including an upfront portrayal of segregation.

D: Alfred E. Green. A: Jackie Robinson, Louise Beavers, Minor Watson.

Jim Thorpe—All American

(1951) 105m. B&W. **B+**

Thorpe battles the obstacles arising from poverty on an Indian reservation to compete in the Olympics and then professional football and baseball, until personal tragedy overwhelms him. Lancaster's portrayal is all graceful athleticism while the human drama sinks into heavy-handed sentimentality.

D: Michael Curtiz. A: Burt Lancaster, Charles Bickford, Phyllis Thaxter.

The Pride of St. Louis

(1952) 93m. B&W. **B**

Famed Cardinal pitcher Dizzy Dean suffers a career-ending arm injury and goes on to become a famous baseball announcer. Dailey is suitably folksy in this film that keeps the baseball scenes simple, the dialogue corny, and the story gently uplifting.

D: Harmon Jones. A: Dan Dailey, Joanne Dru, Richard Haydn.

The Joe Louis Story

(1953) 88m. B&W. **B**

The heavyweight boxing champ's life is explored, from his youth in the South to his young adulthood in Detroit, and finally on to boxing glory. Wallace, a real fighter and bearing a strong resemblance to Louis, is impressive in the ring, but the story is ordinary stuff that barely comes off.

D: Robert Gordon. A: Coley Wallace, Paul Stewart, James Edwards.

Somebody Up There Likes Me

(1956) 113m. B&W.
A–

This follows the life of Rocky Graziano who overcomes a youth of crime in Brooklyn, a dishonorable discharge from the army, and a prison term to become the middleweight champ of the world. A gritty portrait that capitalizes on Newman's sinewy athleticism and punk attitude.

D: Robert Wise. A: Paul Newman, Pier Angeli, Everett Sloane.

Power and Greed

These caustic little films are some of Hollywood's best digs at the seamier side of business and media. Ambition, corruption, and backstabbing portrayed in the stories make Caesar's Ides of March look like a day at the beach.

The Hucksters

(1947) 115m. B&W. **B–**

A refined Englishwoman enters the life of a cynical, fast-talking king of 40s radio advertising who's having trouble holding on to a big soap account. The film's cynicism may be a little thin by modern standards, but Gable's chatter about the gullible public sounds amazingly modern.

D: Jack Conway. A: Clark Gable, Deborah Kerr, Adolphe Menjou.

Executive Suite

(1954) 104m. B&W. **B–**

Tight-lipped conversations, executive maneuvers, and company secrets prevail after a furniture empire's CEO dies in this struggle-at-the-top drama. Bracing and wordy, with a snappy boardroom conclusion.

D: Robert Wise. A: William Holden, Barbara Stanwyck, June Allyson.

Woman's World

(1954) 94m. **B+**

A CEO brings his three best executives with their wives to New York in order to select a new top manager. Webb approaches camp with his prissy turn as a ladies man, but generally fine portrayals and a staggering display of wardrobes propel a glossy melodrama that will keep you amused and on the edge of your seat.

D: Jean Negulesco. A: Clifton Webb, June Allyson, Van Heflin.

A Face in the Crowd

(1957) 124m. B&W. **A–**

One day Lonesome Rhodes is a know-nothing, guitar-picking bum, the next day he is a country music legend and semi-demagogue with his own television show. This early scare film about the power of TV is articulate, hysterical, and absolutely fascinating thanks to Griffith as the media-created monster.

D: Elia Kazan. A: Andy Griffith, Patricia Neal, Walter Matthau.

Sweet Smell of Success

(1957) 96m. B&W.
A

Lancaster is the ruthless Broadway columnist who makes and destroys careers with the help of sniveling press agent stooge Curtis. The time capsule 50s shots of New York and Broadway, melodramatic scenes of dirty dealing, and an acid performance by Lancaster help make this drama hum with nastiness.

D: Alexander Mackendrick. A: Burt Lancaster, Tony Curtis, Susan Harrison.

Big Bios

Bio-pics have always focused on the triumph over setbacks and tragedies, and these wide-screen, hokey, and wildly revisionist takes on legendary characters are no exception.

Viva Zapata!

(1952) 113m. B&W. **B**

A Mexican farmer organizes the landless peasants and leads them to victory against the tyrannical president Porfirio Diaz. Brando is brooding and thoughtful as Zapata, with Quinn all edgy wildness as his hotheaded brother, in this heroic folk tale that will keep you rooting for the downtrodden.
D: Elia Kazan. A: Marlon Brando, Anthony Quinn, Jean Peters.

Houdini

(1953) 106m. **B+**

This fanciful and highly entertaining account of the famous escape artist who dabbled in the occult looks like a luridly colored turn-of-the-century circus poster and offers some swell re-creations of his death-defying exploits. You may not even notice the absence of any real complications with the bright stars and occasional attempts at spooky tone.
D: George Marshall. A: Tony Curtis, Janet Leigh, Torin Thatcher.

Lust for Life

(1956) 122m. **B+**

The tormented Van Gogh leaves church and family behind in Holland to pursue painting in his self-destructive fashion. Highbrows may snicker at Kirk's histrionics and Quinn's exaggerated take on the lusty and irritable Gauguin, but the neurotic drama is entertaining and the pageantry of colors and landscapes is still a visual feast.
D: Vincente Minnelli. A: Kirk Douglas, Anthony Quinn, Everett Sloane.

Man of a Thousand Faces

(1957) 122m. B&W. **B**

The son of deaf mute parents rises through the vaudeville circuit, suffers through a loveless marriage, and takes every bit role in Hollywood before becoming master of disguise Lon Chaney. A modest-sized, rambling, and melodramatic entry, but Cagney seems to relish all the freaky makeup changes.
D: Joseph Pevney. A: James Cagney, Dorothy Malone, Jane Greer.

The Spirit of St. Louis

(1957) 138m. **B+**

Little-known aviator Charles Lindbergh fights fog and fatigue to become the first to make a solo transatlantic flight. Take away the star-spangled fanfare in the take-off and landing and you're left with a fascinating but protracted study of solitude with Stewart's folksy narration keeping things lively.
D: Billy Wilder. A: James Stewart, Patricia Smith, Murray Hamilton.

The FBI Story

(1959) 149m. **B**

This glossy piece of propaganda follows the thirty year career of one of America's unsung heroes: an FBI agent who battles the KKK, Baby Face Nelson, Dillinger, the Nazis, and the Communist threat. Clean-cut, righteous entertainment that's dignified by Stewart and direct narrative.
D: Mervyn LeRoy. A: James Stewart, Vera Miles, Murray Hamilton.

War Dramas

With the perspective that a few years gave, 50s war dramas were no longer the simplistic propaganda pieces showing the comaraderie and esprit de corps of our boys overseas. These films—whether star-studded, big productions or small gritty ensemble pieces—still offer rousing war action, but now focus on the psychological pressures of soldiers under extreme conditions.

The Red Badge of Courage

(1951) 69m. B&W. **B+**

A young Civil War soldier swaggers and boasts before battle and then flees in fear when faced with real battlefield conditions. The dread, confusion, and turmoil faced by a young soldier is heightened throughout by filming from the center of all the gunfire and explosions.
D: John Huston. A: Audie Murphy, Bill Mauldin, Royal Dano.

The Steel Helmet

(1951) 84m. B&W. **A–**

After a white-knuckled foray through Korean-occupied jungles, a small group of soldiers waits and fights their inner demons in a blasted-out pagoda as a relentless army approaches. One of the great, relatively unheralded antiwar films with director Fuller employing his film noir sensibilities to devastating effect.
D: Samuel Fuller. A: Gene Evans, Robert Hutton, Steve Brodie.

From Here to Eternity

(1953) 118m. B&W. **A**

All the mischief that officers and soldiers can brew up during peacetime practically reaches the boiling point on a Hawaiian army base on the eve of the Pearl Harbor attack. Sadism, ambition, adultery, and love are all covered beautifully in this perfectly played male soap opera.
D: Fred Zinnemann. A: Burt Lancaster, Montgomery Clift, Frank Sinatra.

Stalag 17

(1953) 120m. B&W. **A**

An opportunist at a POW camp in Germany is scorned by his fellow prisoners until he ferrets out the Nazi spy in their midst. The grim and gritty look of this is underscored by witty dialogue, caustic humor, and a thick air of cynicism that add up to a truly original POW drama.
D: Billy Wilder. A: William Holden, Don Taylor, Otto Preminger.

The Bridges at Toko-Ri

(1954) 103m. **B**

This slick Korean War adventure-romance follows the bombing missions of fighter pilots, climaxing with a daring helicopter rescue attempt. Exciting scenes of aerial combat are mixed with the standard family/spouse drama and furlough hijinks.
D: Mark Robson. A: William

Holden, Grace Kelly, Fredric March.

Strategic Air Command
(1955) 114m. **C+**
When the Cold War starts heating up, a baseball hero is called up for active duty in an air force program developing long-range bombers. The aerial photography is snappy, but Stewart's charm can only carry the artificial story about patriotism and responsibility so far.
D: Anthony Mann. A: James Stewart, June Allyson, Frank Lovejoy.

The Bridge on the River Kwai
(1957) 161m. **A–**
An elaborate wide-screen World War II POW drama about a British colonel's fanatical devotion to building a bridge for the Japanese commandant while an American escapee undertakes to destroy it. The fascinating study of obsessive characters is mixed in with more standard commando action scenes.
D: David Lean. A: Alec Guinness, William Holden, Sessue Hayakawa.

Paths of Glory
(1957) 86m. B&W. **A**
A French regiment in World War I fails in an impossible attack and the officers who ordered it designate three random soldiers to be tried and hung for cowardice. The almost insane division between soldiers and their officers is relentlessly tracked as the camera sweeps from trenches stacked with bodies to the palatial general's headquarters.
D: Stanley Kubrick. A: Kirk Douglas, Adolphe Menjou, George Macready.

The Young Lions
(1958) 167m. **B+**
This chronicles the stories of three World War II soldiers—a Jewish GI, a reluctant draftee, and a cynical Nazi officer, whose lives intersect before, during, and after the war. This grandly designed male soap opera makes the war feel like a carousel of changing uniforms, skirmishes, and locales.
D: Edward Dmytryk. A: Marlon Brando, Montgomery Clift, Dean Martin.

Pork Chop Hill
(1959) 97m. B&W. **B**
In the final days of the Korean War, a company commander is forced to hold on to the title hill in order to make the UN's negotiating position stronger. The hard-hitting battle action is enhanced by beleaguered Peck's struggle to keep his men motivated despite his disgust at the politics of the situation and needless loss of life.
D: Lewis Milestone. A: Gregory Peck, Harry Guardino, Rip Torn.

Action Soap Operas

Except for the inspirational missionary sagas in this group, these action-oriented soapers offer all the romance, overripe emotions, and dubious psychology of Hollywood's most shameless melodramas. Add to that gorgeous foreign locales and the top name stars of the day, and you've got some of the more entertaining films this side of Douglas Sirk.

Affair in Trinidad
(1952) 98m. B&W. **C**
An American flier investigating his brother's "suicide" in Trinidad falls in love with the dead man's emotionally elusive widow and uncovers an espoinage plot involving a foreign power. A bland follow-up to *Gilda*.
D: Vincent Sherman. A: Rita Hayworth, Glenn Ford, Alexander Scourby.

The Snows of Kilimanjaro
(1952) 117m. **B**
A writer disabled while on safari in Africa reflects on the women in his life. All sorts of Hemingway motifs are included in this film adaptation: bullfighting in Spain, romance on the Riviera, big game hunting, and ambulance driving during the war. A glossy, colorful, and contrived melodrama.
D: Henry King. A: Gregory Peck, Ava Gardner, Susan Hayward.

Mogambo
(1953) 115m. **C+**
This love triangle in Africa has great white hunter Gable favoring prim married woman Kelly over footloose and jealous showgirl Gardner. A lightweight remake of *Red Dust* with rich Technicolor location photography and scenes of wild animals competing with the Hollywood bleached-out story and characters.
D: John Ford. A: Clark Gable, Grace Kelly, Ava Gardner.

Elephant Walk
(1954) 103m. **A**
A new bride discovers how emotionally stunted her husband is as she settles into his tea plantation in Ceylon. This romantic melodrama thick with Freudian underpinnings, includes disaster elements of a cholera epidemic and an unforgettable climax where rampaging elephants chase Taylor through the house and set fire to the plantation.
D: William Dieterle. A: Elizabeth Taylor, Peter Finch, Dana Andrews.

The High and the Mighty
(1954) 147m. **B+**
A passenger plane piloted by "awe shucks" Wayne experiences engine loss and is forced to prepare for a crash landing. This early version of *Airport* is a wonderfully overripe airborne melodrama where everyone's past indiscretions are almost joyfully revived by the crisis.
D: William Wellman. A: John Wayne, Claire Trevor, Laraine Day.

The Naked Jungle
(1954) 95m. **B+**
This story of a hard-nosed brute South American planter, whose assertive mail-order bride will have nothing to do with him, is hip deep in sexual dysfunction and overwrought melodramatics. Add to this a spectacular death struggle with an advancing army of killer ants and you've got a vastly entertaining and bizarre film.
D: Byron Haskin. A: Charlton Heston, Eleanor Parker, Abraham Sofaer.

Soldier of Fortune
(1955) 96m. **B–**
A glossy globe-trotting melodrama about an American wife seeking the help of a notorious Yank smuggler to find her husband who disappeared in Red China. A routine plot made colorful by the exotic Hong Kong background and scenery-chewing stars.
D: Edward Dmytryk. A: Clark Gable, Susan Hayward, Michael Rennie.

Sayonara
(1957) 147m. **A–**
The romance between a bigoted American officer and a Japanese actress is at the center of this lavish drama of forbidden love, interracial marriage, and occupied postwar Japan. The scenes of Japanese culture are lovely, and even with an overdone Southern accent Brando is sweetly sincere.
D: Joshua Logan. A: Marlon Brando, Miyoshi Umeki, Red Buttons.

Missionaries

Black Narcissus
(1947) 99m. **A**
Nuns establish an order in a remote Himalayan kingdom, only to confront their own emotional problems and inability to adjust to the local temper. An odd mix of tones interwoven by exquisite production design and a unique brand of storybook color.
D: Michael Powell. A: Deborah Kerr, Jean Simmons, David Farrar.

The Inn of the Sixth Happiness
(1958) 158m. **B+**
A sweeping fact-based saga of an English missionary in war-torn 1930s China who leads 100 refugee children on a three-week mountain trek to safety. Grand uplifting entertainment with a forceful Bergman as the indomitable woman who continually bucks the odds. A real heart-tugger.
D: Mark Robson. A: Ingrid Bergman, Curt Jurgens, Robert Donat.

The Nun's Story
(1959) 149m. **B–**
This epic wide-screen treatment of a small intimate story follows a young girl's novitiate in a Belgium convent and her subsequent hospital work in the Congo. Only Audrey could make a nun both soulful and devastatingly beautiful in this saga that tries to give sweep to details of convent life and selfless devotion.
D: Fred Zinnemann. A: Audrey Hepburn, Peter Finch, Peggy Ashcroft.

Message Films

This trio of films made a splash in the 50s with their hard-hitting portrayals of racism and corruption; with the exception of *The Defiant Ones*, they're still effective as message films and entertaining as melodramas.

On the Waterfront
(1954) 108m. B&W. **A**
An ex-boxer who works for the corrupt head of a longshoreman's union becomes entangled with a murdered worker's sister and a crusading priest who push him to stand up against his gangster boss. This raw drama still grabs you by the throat, thanks to Marlon's monumental performance as the mug who "coulda been a contender."
D: Elia Kazan. A: Marlon Brando, Eva Marie Saint, Lee J. Cobb.

Bad Day at Black Rock
(1955) 81m. **A–**
After World War II, a one-armed stranger pulls into an isolated Western town and proceeds to rile the town heavies with his inquiries about the Japanese farming family who used to live there. This Western-style morality drama about bigotry is like a string of tense confrontations in an eerily empty outdoors and equally barren indoor settings.
D: John Sturges. A: Spencer Tracy, Robert Ryan. Lee Marvin.

The Defiant Ones
(1958) 97m. B&W. **C+**
A black and a white prisoner escape from a chain gang and, shackled together at the ankles, pull each other through the swamps and woods of the deep South. A groundbreaking film at the time, but pretty lame today, with its sledgehammer direction and trite attempts to cure the evils of racism in $1^1/_2$ hours.
D: Stanley Kramer. A: Sidney Poitier, Tony Curtis, Theodore Bikel.

Youth Exploitation

As America watched its kids rebel and became convinced that rock 'n' roll was turning them into everything from hopheads to sex-fiends, Hollywood sanguinely turned out low-budget wonders of teen hysteria. These alarmist camp gems follow hormone-wracked, blue-jeaned youths as they pop pills, make out, and drive their souped-up cars straight to juvenile delinquency.

Dragstrip Girl
(1957) 69m. B&W. **C–**
A run-of-the-juvenile-delinquent-mill tale about pit-stop pony Spain and the various lugs who make fools of themselves wooing her. This dull-looking movie is padded with stock footage "chicken races," comic relief from a nonteen-looking Gorshin, and a boring bad guy who takes too long to get his comeuppance.
D: Edward L. Cahn. A: Fay Spain, Frank Gorshin, Steve Terrell.

Married Too Young
(1957) 76m. B&W. **C+**
A lower-class teen secretly weds a country club girl and both families are shocked, even before money troubles lead to crime. These clean-cut, straightlaced kids may be branded delinquents by the judge who lectures their parents, but the title could be "Ward and June Cleaver Disobey Their Parents."
D: George Moskov. A: Harold Lloyd, Jr.; Jana Lund; Anthony Dexter.

Reform School Girl
(1957) 71m. B&W. **C–**
After spurning her uncle's goatish advances, a nice girl gets the rap for a crazy teen boy's car crash killing and ends up in juvenile detention. Combination juvenile delinquent/women in prison potboiler benefits from sleazy atmosphere but lacks required snotty attitude.

D: Edward Bernds. A: Gloria Castillo, Edd Byrnes, Sally Kellerman.

Sorority Girl
(1957) 61m. B&W. **B–**

A rich insecure coed gets her kicks by domineering a geeky sorority sister, blackmailing another one who's pregnant, and generally acting like the campus queen bitch, all of which leads to tragedy. Highlights of this Corman-produced "expose" of college life include a catfight and wonderfully moody opening and closing credit graphics.
D: Roger Corman. A: Susan Cabot, Dick Miller, Barboura Morris.

The Violent Years
(1957) 65m. B&W. **C+**

Four spoiled teen dolls hold up gas stations, molest terrified males, and sneer a lot in endless search for kicks. Though smudgy-looking, this takes on a demented luster, courtesy of anti-auteur Ed Wood's script, full of his mind-twisting dialogue and goofy bad girl antics.
D: Franz Eichorn. A: Jean Moorehead, Barbara Weeks, Glenn Corbett.

High School Confidential!
(1958) 85m. B&W.
B+

From the opening shot of Jerry Lee Lewis pounding out the title song, to the narcotic agent Tamblyn's attempts to bust a small-town dope scene and thwart the overtures of hip-twitching Van Doren, this ranks as a kitsch high point in the never-ending saga of dope-fiend teens.
D: Jack Arnold. A: Mamie Van Doren, Russ Tamblyn, John Drew Barrymore.

You've Ruined Me Eddie
(1958) 76m. B&W. **B–**

In this switch on the unwed teen genre, rich girl Joan (who's fond of wiggling to rock music in her nightie) gets pregnant by poor but nice Eddie and wants an abortion while he wants to keep the baby. A lame try at decadent, Southern town atmosphere with a no-good lawyer and fat, sweaty cop.
D: Charles T. O'Rork. A: Jeanne Rainer, Ted Marshall, Charles Martin.

Daddy-O
(1959) 74m. B&W. **B**

A muscular rock singer/truck driver and his tight-sweatered girlfriend run "packages" across the border for their roadside club's shadowy fat owner. This look at the seamy side of rock club life, 50s-style, is spiced with a heavy sax score and the club owner doing a K-mart version of Sydney Greenstreet.
D: Lou Place. A: Dick Contino, Sandra Giles, Bruno Ve Sota.

Girls Town
(1959) 92m. B&W. **A**

An attitude-heavy Van Doren takes the fall for some shlub's murder and ends up in a Catholic girls detention hall. An alternately witty, campy, totally wacked-out musical epic, with inspired lunacy such as Mel Tormé as a ruthless leather-boy hood, and a scene of lakeside necking to the loopy strains of "The Ya Ya Song" among its highlights.
D: Charles Haas. A: Mamie Van Doren, Mel Tormé, Paul Anka.

The Fat Black Pussy Cat
(1964) 81m. B&W. **C+**

In the style of a 50s hard-boiled, private eye TV show, a cop tracks a killer through the world of jazz playing, poetry reciting, and existentialist beatniks who hang out at the Fat Black Pussy Cat Club. Every goatee, beret, and beat attitude is caricatured to perfection, including an anthropologist who studies the Watusi tribe.
D: Harold Lea. A: Frank Jamus, Janet Damon, Patricia McNair.

Ed Wood

Bad girls out for cheap kicks, the problems of a man's burning need for female fashions, a porn ring corrupting a small town with filth: Even when doing sexploitation, Ed Wood couldn't help but fill these tawdry tales with his incompetently and hilariously cockeyed worldview.

Glen or Glenda?
(1953) 67m. B&W.
C+

Wood plays the lead in this tale of a man with a burning need to dress in women's clothing, preferably angora, and his understandably distressed wife. Includes Lugosi's astonishingly dramatic recitation of "Snips and snails and puppy dogs' tails," stock footage of freeways, and even a morally uplifting ending. Must be seen to be disbelieved.
D: Edward D. Wood, Jr. A: Edward D. Wood, Jr.; Bela Lugosi; Dolores Fuller.

Jail Bait
(1954) 70m. B&W. **C–**

A hood tries to escape capture by having his face changed by a plastic surgeon. Though still featuring the director's distinctively goofy deadpan dialogue and some hilariously inappropriate flamenco guitar music (he lost the original soundtrack), Wood gets dangerously close to coherent storytelling in this quasinoir.
D: Edward D. Wood. A: Timothy Farrell, Lyle Talbot, Dolores Fuller.

The Sinister Urge
(1961) 70m. **C**

After seeing dirty pictures, a man goes nuts, attacking and killing women. This fifth-grader's idea of crime and the "smut racket" features matronly young women being photographed in bathing suits, a cop in drag trying to nab the killer, and Wood himself in a fight scene.
D: Edward D. Wood. A: Kenne Duncan, Duke Moore, Dino Fantini.

See also Ed Wood's horror films, page 355.

1960s

Biblical Epics

The size of these lengthy Technicolor sword-and-sandal epics ranged from pretentious to humongous to . . . well, biblical. Glorious sets and landscapes, scenery-chewing stars, and

high drama all make these enormously entertaining. When they work you get a rousing telescopic lesson on the foundations of Western civilization. When they fail, you start wondering things like "Did anyone prior to 180 A.D. ever wear pants?"

Spartacus

(1960) 196m. **A**

Spartacus leads a revolt of gladiators and the Roman Senate sends an army to squelch them. Huge battle sequences, expert re-creations of the Senate and gladiator school, and the juicy performances of the delightfully wicked and conniving Romans steal the show from the sympathetic slaves. Great fun and enthralling.

D: Stanley Kubrick. A: Kirk Douglas, Laurence Olivier, Peter Ustinov.

The Story of Ruth

(1960) 132m. **C+**

Spirited questing Ruth faces resistance when she decides to cast off her pagan heritage and become a Jew. Sincere soapy condensation of the biblical tale that concentrates on the passion of Ruth instead of religion.

D: Henry Koster. A: Elana Eden, Viveca Lindfors, Stuart Whitman.

King of Kings

(1961) 161m. **B–**

A soulful recounting of the life and death of Jesus of Nazareth. This handsome Christ has a fire in his belly and offers some stirring sermons, although scripture is sometimes blended for impact.

D: Nicholas Ray. A: Jeffrey Hunter, Robert Ryan, Hurd Hatfield.

Barabbas

(1962) 144m. **B**

The thief who's spared the cross in favor of Christ continues his life of crime and cruelty as a gladiator until he undergoes a religious conversion. Some touching moments mixed with gore and violence.

D: Richard Fleischer. A: Anthony Quinn, Vittorio Gassman, Silvana Mangano.

Cleopatra

(1963) 243m. **B**

Cleopatra charms her way into the arms of Julius Caesar and Mark Antony, and the viewer gets waves of soldiers, gigantic pageants, glamorous costumes, and an entrance into Rome that still dazzles. This one's really big and a marathon to boot.

D: Joseph Mankiewicz. A: Elizabeth Taylor, Richard Burton, Rex Harrison.

Sodom and Gomorrah

(1963) 154m. **D**

Lot and the wandering Hebrews are welcomed into Sodom, city of decadence and depravity. Standard issue drama of a good man's instincts gone awry with some lively spectacles of debauchery.

D: Robert Aldrich. A: Stewart Granger, Stanley Baker, Anouk Aimée.

The Fall of the Roman Empire

(1964) 187m. **C+**

Philosopher/Emperor Marcus Aurelius is murdered by mad son Commodus and the empire begins to dissolve, inviting barbarian invasions. Energy-charged battle scenes and good chemistry between the men, but the drama drags once Aurelius dies.

D: Anthony Mann. A: Alec Guinness, Christopher Plummer, James Mason.

The Greatest Story Ever Told

(1965) 225m. **B**

Epic painterly version of Christ's life from birth through his ministry to trial and crucifixion. Reverential treatment with von Sydow a modest and intelligent Christ, but the story is diminished by the Hollywood performances of a horde of guest stars in minor roles. Family entertainment.

D: George Stevens. A: Max von Sydow, Dorothy McGuire, José Ferrer.

The Bible

(1966) 174m. **C+**

Overreaching attempt to film a sizable portion of the Old Testament from the Creation to Abraham. Spends itself artistically on the re-creation of Paradise with the rest of the film a serviceable primer of biblical characters.

D: John Huston. A: John Huston, Michael Parks, Richard Harris.

Historical Epics

Like other genres, historical pictures grew up in the 60s, offering authentic period details, genuine locales, classically trained British stars, and smart scripts. Besides showing the always entertaining sight of royals at each other's throats, these very adult dramas also reflect the 60s social upheaval in their portrayal of church corruption, the war of sexual politics, and the battle between integrity and authority.

Billy Budd

(1962) 123m. B&W. **B+**

Kind innocent Billy Budd is pressed into service on an English ship during the Napoleonic Wars and suffers for his purity under the hands of the brutal ship's master. A straightforward, ship-bound tale of good versus evil that's more on the level of a moral epic.

D: Peter Ustinov. A: Robert Ryan, Terence Stamp, Peter Ustinov, Melvyn Douglas.

Becket

(1964) 148m. **A–**

There's plenty of scintillating wordplay and intense male bonding in this tale of the twelfth-century worldly archbishop who undergoes a religious conversion in the service of his headstrong King Henry.

D: Peter Glenville. A: Richard Burton, Peter O'Toole, John Gielgud.

The Agony and the Ecstasy

(1965) 136m. **C+**

Hollywood's version of Michelangelo's struggle to paint the Sistine Chapel under the thumb of Pope Julius looks big and gorgeous and attempts to show the creative process, but feels like a dull male soap opera in Roman robes.

D: Carol Reed. A: Charlton Heston, Rex Harrison, Adolfo Celi.

A Man for All Seasons

(1966) 120m. **A**

Sometimes daft, sometimes dangerous Henry VIII wants a new wife to give him a son

and he'll rip England from the Catholic faith and start his own church to do it. Sir Thomas More is the one man who will not lay down his soul even for his king. A rare and compelling portrayal of integrity and spirituality.
D: Fred Zinnemann. A: Paul Scofield, Robert Shaw, Wendy Hiller, Orson Welles.

The Lion in Winter
(1968) 134m. **A–**
A biting and cynical study of politics and family intrigue as Henry II gathers his plotting sons and intriguing wife Eleanor for a Christmas feast to determine his successor. Brothers betray each other, planned marriages go up in smoke, and husband and wife duel over dynasties. Confusing but brilliant.
D: Anthony Harvey. A: Peter O'Toole, Katharine Hepburn, Anthony Hopkins.

Anne of the Thousand Days
(1969) 146m. **B+**
Lusty, male-heir-hungry Henry VIII broods and bellows after the cautious and canny Anne Boleyn. Themes of sexual politics are blended into this rousing and sometimes overacted drama of court life in sixteenth-century England.
D: Charles Jarrott. A: Richard Burton, Genevieve Bujold, Irene Papas.

Burn!
(1969) 112m. **B**
A British agent helps the slaves on a Caribbean island overthrow the government and ten years later finds that the revolutionary leaders are now as corrupt as the old regime. Brando is the melancholic romantic with the drunken swagger who falls victim to his own manipulative ways in this muddled but fascinating tale.
D: Gillo Pontecorvo. A: Marlon Brando, Evaristo Marquez, Renato Salvatori.

Wide-Screen Sagas

When Hollywood adapted a historical bestseller, they gave it everything—beautiful scenery, monumental reenactments of historical events, high drama, and a long list of big name stars. These wide-screen sagas may lose something on TV and they're *very* long, but you get a lot for your money—soap opera, travelogue, and a painless history lesson.

Exodus
(1960) 120m. **B+**
This sprawling portrayal of the post-World War II struggle leading up to the creation of Israel and the people who founded its new society trots out so many characters that it's a strain to stay focused. The story of the freedom fighters is stirring, but the central romance is pure Hollywood.
D: Otto Preminger. A: Paul Newman, Eva Marie Saint, Sal Mineo, Lee J. Cobb.

The Sundowners
(1960) 133m. **B+**
A picturesque easygoing saga of a family of Irish sheepherders who wander the open ranges of 1920s Australia. While reveling in the sweep of the land and the details of itinerant life—the sheep shearing contest is a highlight—it's the respectful and earthy chemistry between Kerr and Mitchum that holds this together.
D: Fred Zinnemann. A: Deborah Kerr, Robert Mitchum, Peter Ustinov.

The Cardinal
(1963) 175m. **C–**
This long episodic study of a young priest's rise to the College of Cardinals attempts to package all the big issues of the first half of the twentieth century into neat segments for the priest to experience. The amateurish acting almost makes this a camp film.
D: Otto Preminger. A: Tom Tryon, John Huston, Carol Lynley.

55 Days at Peking
(1963) 154m. **B**
As the heads of the U.S. and European missions are trapped in Peking during the 1900 Boxer Rebellion, a grizzled American commander falls in love with the woman-with-a-past and joins forces with the stiff-upper-lipped Englishman to save the day. Enjoyable soaper with fine details of the Chinese empress court.
D: Nicholas Ray. A: Charlton Heston, Ava Gardner, David Niven.

The Ugly American
(1963) 120m. **B+**
American Ambassador Brando in a fictional Asian country tries to keep the lid on a civil war when he learns an old friend leads the pro-Communist resistance. Filmed on location in Thailand, the prescient and powerful drama was one of Hollywood's rare forays into Southeast Asian politics.
D: George Englund. A: Marlon Brando, Eiji Okado, Sandra Church.

Doctor Zhivago
(1965) 176m. **A**
Passionate and soulful doctor is caught up in the outer turmoil of the Russian Revolution and the inner turmoil of love for his wife and family and the woman he cannot forget. A visually stunning picture book movie offering tragic romance and a portrait of a society about to fly apart.
D: David Lean. A: Omar Sharif, Julie Christie, Geraldine Chaplin.

Hawaii
(1966) 192m. **B–**
The "civilizing" of early nineteenth-century Hawaii is presented as an uncompromising New England preacher's efforts to convert the natives and the more mercantile achievements of the hard-living salty sea captain. Glorious scenery and dynamic performances but somehow a muted effort.
D: George Roy Hill. A: Julie Andrews, Max von Sydow, Richard Harris.

Shoes of the Fisherman
(1968) 152m. **C**
A Russian political prisoner who becomes the Pope gets caught up in a dangerous clash between China and the USSR. An odd blend of Cold War and religious epic that fails to ignite, with a soapy side-story of newsman's marital strife thrown in.
D: Michael Anderson. A: Anthony Quinn, Laurence Olivier, Oskar Werner.

Shakespeare

Even Shakespeare felt the effects of the 1960s, which made him less stodgy and also proved (if it was ever in doubt) that he spoke to new generations. While these films feature some of the best of British theater, the recent casting of heartthrobs and Americans with no stage experience brings a new audience and sometimes a new vitality to these plays. With the rising star of Kenneth Branagh, Shakespeare has now become as rousing, accessible, and entertaining as any historical swashbuckler.

The Taming of the Shrew

(1967) 126m. **B+**

Who better to play the swaggering Petruchio and the salty Katarina than the ultimate sparring 60s couple Liz and Dick? The beautiful scenery, bawdy humor, excellent supporting cast, and the stars' decision to play the roles instead of hamming it up make this fun and refreshing.

D: Franco Zoffirelli. A: Richard Burton, Elizabeth Taylor, Michael York.

Romeo and Juliet

(1968) 138m. **A**

Shakespeare finally becomes a teen date film as the star-crossed lovers from Verona are actually played by young vibrant actors who capture the strident passion and follies of youth. Enjoy the rich pageantry and melancholy music and have a hankie handy.

D: Franco Zeffirelli. A: Leonard Whiting, Olivia Hussey, Michael York.

Hamlet

(1969) 113m. **B−**

Is it his father's ghost or the flickering light of dementia telling Prince Hamlet to avenge his father's murder by the kingly uncle? Spare and dark, with jarring close-ups, language plainly spoken, and little poetry, this is a child of the stripped-to-the-bones 60s.

D: Tony Richardson. A: Nicol Williamson, Anthony Hopkins, Gordon Jackson.

Julius Caesar

(1970) 117m. **D**

Julius, Brutus, and Mark Antony are hatching plots and crossing swords again in this set-bound and airless rendition.

D: Stuart Burge. A: Jason Robards, Jr.; Richard Johnson; Charlton Heston.

King Lear

(1970) 137m. **C+**

Old egocentric Lear divides his realm among two daughters, casting aside a noble third for her refusal to flatter, and ends up roaming his former lands in torment. Icy, stark, and utterly gloomy tale made all the more depressing by a perpetual sunset and barren landscapes.

D: Peter Brook. A: Paul Scofield, Irene Worth, Alan Webb.

Macbeth

(1971) 140m. **B+**

This grandly bloody tale of betrayal and evil features gutsy performances by a young cast. It's got sex and violence, but it's also a faithful and gory rendition in the Elizabethan tradition.

D: Roman Polanski. A: Jon Finch, Francesca Annis, Martin Shaw.

Henry V

(1989) 137m. **A**

Brash young Henry claims French lands, resulting in the battle of Agincourt. This dark spare tale of a hero-king, power politics, and the impact on common folk is the first Shakespeare film to show the brutality of war. A real, gutsy, dirt-under-the-nails take on the Bard, with high-octane performances.

D: Kenneth Branagh. A: Kenneth Branagh, Derek Jacobi, Robert Stephens.

Hamlet

(1990) 135m. **B**

Mel Gibson brings action and energy to the beleaguered Hamlet in this abbreviated version, which is missing most of the political intrigue and urgency. Good supporting cast but Close is too regal and knowing for the queen.

D: Franco Zeffirelli. A: Mel Gibson, Glenn Close, Alan Bates.

Much Ado About Nothing

(1993) 111m. **A**

Colorful, lusty, and robust comedy of soldiers coming home to their bountiful women in the glories of the Tuscan hills. Enjoy the slow descent of the eternal bachelor Benedick into the arms of fiery Beatrice. If you think Shakespeare can't be fun, see this sparkling entry.

D: Kenneth Branagh. A: Kenneth Branagh, Emma Thompson, Denzel Washington.

Sex, Repression, and Madness

With loosening censorship in the let-it-all-hang-out 60s came films dealing with the whole psychodramatic nine yards: middle-class madness, homosexuality, homicidal lovers, fetishism, and just plain weird sex. Many of these films now look like museum pieces, but all are deadly serious and some even hold up with a lurid disturbing vitality.

Reflections in a Golden Eye

(1967) 109m. **B+**

This Georgia military base is teeming with subterranean desires: Brando is a repressed homosexual major and Liz his overblown, sexually flamboyant wife who's the object of desire by a quiet peeping tom private. An ambitious adult Southern gothic with some close to strange performances and even more surreal images.

D: John Huston. A: Marlon Brando, Elizabeth Taylor, Julie Harris.

The Killing of Sister George

(1968) 138m. **B−**

A caustic, hard-drinking actress plays a beloved character on a British soap and

keeps her subservient lesbian lover, "Childie," at home. Things turn sour when a BBC executive threatens to kill off her character. This goes for sapphic clichés; has one exploitative "gutsy" sex scene and a few bursts of nasty humor.
D: Robert Aldrich. A: Beryl Reid, Susannah York, Coral Browne.

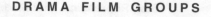

Pretty Poison
(1968) 89m. **B+**

A paroled arsonist woos a high school girl who thinks he's the CIA on a secret mission, but then she wants him to murder her disapproving mother. Terrible Tuesday and tremulous Perkins make one of the more disturbing couples this side of *Gun Crazy,* in this refreshingly twisted love story.
D: Noel Black. A: Anthony Perkins, Tuesday Weld, Beverly Garland.

Rachel, Rachel
(1968) 101m. **B**

Rachel suffers from life crossroads syndrome—35, unmarried, small-town teaching job, and no future—and is finally flung into an unexpected encounter. A gentle, detail-rich study of loneliness and repression with a quietly absorbing Woodward; it may be eventless but it's very close to dramatized real life.
D: Paul Newman. A: Joanne Woodward, Estelle Parsons, James Olson.

Secret Ceremony
(1968) 109m. **C**

An aging hooker becomes the surrogate mother of a deranged young woman who lives in a creepy house, and complains about sexual assaults from her stepfather. Might have worked without name stars but the cast looks as if they're acting in a dirty little picture about weird people.
D: Joseph Losey. A: Elizabeth Taylor, Robert Mitchum, Mia Farrow.

The Swimmer
(1968) 94m. **B+**

A few miles from his affluent Connecticut home and clad in his bathing trunks, an executive decides to swim home via the neighborhood pools. Soured friends, estranged kids, angered business partners, and leery neighbors are encountered in this brightly shot, caustic, slightly eerie, and finally nightmarish journey.
D: Frank Perry. A: Burt Lancaster, Janet Landgard, Janice Rule.

That Cold Day in the Park
(1969) 112m. **C**

A neurotic and possessive woman picks up a vagrant younger man in the park and invites him home where she proceeds to pamper him to within an inch of his life. A grim and painfully detailed portrait of descent into madness with other issues—drugs, incest, draft-dodging—hung on to it to make it 60s relevant.
D: Robert Altman. A: Sandy Dennis, Suzanne Benton, Michael Burns.

British Dramas

It's not only the working-class hero who's caught in a bind these days. In these settings of manor homes, university enclaves, and Parliament offices, members of the middle and upper classes are struggling with the threat of paralyzing self-doubt or exposure of personal sins. Starkly filmed in what feels like gray light, these morality tales of successful men caught in a web use the bitter dialogue like a scalpel, scraping away the rot of success.

Tunes of Glory
(1960) 107m. **A**

A Scottish army careerist who's now his regiment's top commander is challenged when the to-the-manor-born officer returns from POW camp at war's end to replace him. Bagpipes provide a lingering wail as psychological warfare is waged in cold barracks and officers' lounges.
D: Ronald Neame. A: Alec Guinness, John Mills, Susannah York.

No Love for Johnnie
(1961) 111m. B&W. **C**

A working-class member of Parliament struggles to keep a personal scandal from jeopardizing his public career. The tension between public and private worlds feels staged in this self-conscious drama.
D: Ralph Thomas. A: Peter Finch, Stanley Holloway, Donald Pleasence.

Victim
(1961) 100m. B&W.
B+

A married lawyer is drawn into pursuing a ring of blackmailers who prey upon homosexuals, risking his career by acknowledging his own homosexuality. A tense thriller that starts to show its age when it digresses from a crime suspense to a lifestyle drama.
D: Basil Dearden. A: Dirk Bogarde, Sylvia Syms, Dennis Price.

The Servant
(1963) 115m. B&W.
A–

A weakling playboy hires a manipulative manservant who twists the relationship, eventually dominating his master. A sinister and dark tale of the British class system that artfully reveals a debauched victim and an evil victor.
D: Joseph Losey. A: Dirk Bogarde, Sarah Miles, James Fox.

Accident
(1967) 105m. **B**

A bored, middle-aged Oxford don pursues an attractive student after her boyfriend's death. Set amid a lush summertime Oxford campus, this richly mannered morality play of brutish and boring behavior makes good use of flashbacks to tell its sordid tale.
D: Joseph Losey. A: Dirk Bogarde, Stanley Baker, Jacqueline Sassard.

British Angry Young Men

The working-class hero exploded onto Britain's stage and screen in the 50s with the fury and power of a wounded beast. Starring the new generation of actors, these small grainy studies invite you to look at every stained wall and smudged kiss as they explore a world of stalled ambitions, cynicism, and boredom of the postwar generation.

Look Back in Anger
(1958) 99m. B&W. **B+**

A university graduate in a dead-end job vents his frustration on his wife and his mistress. This film version of a play feels boxed in, but it's the dialogue spewing scorn and rage that grabs your attention, along with a sizzling Burton.
D: Tony Richardson. A: Richard Burton, Claire Bloom, Mary Ure.

Room at the Top
(1959) 115m. B&W.
A−

A working-class lad with a steely determination to marry the boss's daughter and make his way to the top becomes involved with an unhappily married woman. Harvey is all ice, fury, and cynicism with Signoret providing the warmth.
D: Jack Clayton. A: Laurence Harvey, Simone Signoret, Heather Sears.

A Taste of Honey
(1961) 100m. B&W. **B−**

A lonely and neglected teenage girl adrift from an abusive mother finds herself pregnant, unwed, and abandoned until she locates a gay roommate. Shot in a dockside working-class location, using actors who you'd swear were not, this bittersweet tale is a gem of naturalism.
D: Tony Richardson. A: Rita Tushingham, Dora Bryan, Murray Melvin.

A Kind of Loving
(1962) 107m. B&W. **C**

A factory worker's one-night stand results in a pregnancy, then marriage, and then a miscarriage. Shot in an almost documentary style, this bleak view of ill-prepared youth feels outdated and moves very slowly toward an ambivalent end.
D: John Schlesinger. A: Alan Bates, Thora Hird, June Ritchie.

Billy Liar
(1963) 96m. B&W. **B**

Talented and dreamy Billy must decide: Should he go to London with his delightful girlfriend and try to be a writer or stick with his rich fantasy life at home and remain an apprentice mortician? Charming story of adolescence with nice mix of reality and fantasy.
D: John Schlesinger. A: Tom Courtenay, Julie Christie, Finlay Currie.

The Leather Boys
(1963) 108m. B&W. **B**

Teens get married to escape parents and boredom, but the boy's not sure if he's gay and then the wife gets pregnant. Realistic sordid view of restless callow youth and working-class London.
D: Sidney J. Furie. A: Rita Tushingham, Dudley Sutton, Colin Campbell.

This Sporting Life
(1963) 129m. **A−**

A coal miner achieves local fame as a rugby player, but he's still a lout even with his widowed girlfriend and her kids. This film pries its way into a series of uncomfortable situations, including an achingly crass display of hubris as the brute warrior tries to impress his girl at a fancy restaurant.
D: Lindsay Anderson. A: Richard Harris, Rachel Roberts, Colin Blakely.

Romance

Romance is a heartbreaking, sometimes neurotic business in these small bittersweet valentines of loneliness, desperation, and the eternal hope of lovers.

Never on Sunday
(1960) 97m. **B**

A timid American scholar traveling in Greece becomes infatuated with a prostitute and the first thing he wants to do is reform her. The glorious Greek island locales, colorful village characters, and a flamboyant earthy Mercouri lift this simple story above the clichés.
D: Jules Dassin. A: Melina Mercouri, Jules Dassin, Georges Foundas.

Paris Blues
(1961) 98m. B&W. **B**

Two expatriate jazz musicians in Paris romance two American tourists who want them to return home. A cool jazzy portrait of hipsters, with good chemistry between the lovers and a swinging Duke Ellington score.
D: Martin Ritt. A: Paul Newman, Sidney Poitier, Joanne Woodward, Diahann Carroll.

Lolita
(1962) 152m. B&W. **A**

The Old World professor visiting America finds the girl of his dreams, but she's only 15 years old. Don't expect eroticism here; this is a sharply drawn drama of obsession and a black comedy of a to-the-death sexual power struggle between the gum-cracking goddess in pedal pushers and the helplessly romantic pedophile.
D: Stanley Kubrick. A: James Mason, Sue Lyon, Peter Sellers.

Two for the Seesaw
(1962) 119m. B&W. **C**

A Nebraskan lawyer going through a painful divorce and a hard-boiled dancer with an ulcer try to make their way together in Greenwich Village. The realism is effective but these two never stop talking and MacLaine's mannered Bronx accent and kookiness is without charm.
D: Robert Wise. A: Robert Mitchum, Shirley MacLaine, Edmon Ryan.

Walk on the Wild Side
(1962) 114m. B&W. **C+**

An itinerant farmer rides the rails to New Orleans in search of his true love and discovers her working in a brothel for a madam unwilling to release her. A great book becomes a mawkish melodrama with three catlike stars, stagy settings, and flamboyant acting.
D: Edward Dmytryk. A: Jane Fonda, Laurence Harvey, Barbara Stanwyck.

Love with a Proper Stranger

(1963) 102m. B&W. **B+**

A nice Italian girl and a jazz musician have a one-night stand, she gets pregnant and, while taking steps to get her an abortion, the two strangers become acquainted. A poignant bittersweet romance with prickly vulnerable Wood and raw-edged McQueen.

D: Robert Mulligan. A: Natalie Wood, Steve McQueen, Edie Adams.

The Stripper

(1963) 95m. B&W. **B**

An on-the-skids performer has visions of a better life when she moves in with a young admirer and his mother. One of those realistic dreary films about pathetic down-and-outers that are really just excuses to showcase some tour de force acting, in this case a dynamic Woodward.

D: Franklin J. Schaffner. A: Joanne Woodward, Richard Beymer, Carol Lynley.

Technicolor Soap Operas

These are the last of the 50s-style Technicolor romantic dramas and melodramas before relaxed censorship, modern film aesthetics, and the sexual revolution changed this brand of Hollywood flamboyance forever. Glamorous stars still suffer from illicit love affairs in a variety of gorgeous settings and designer clothes while the dramas—some courtesy of Tennessee Williams—offer a slightly more restrained style of emotionalism.

Butterfield 8

(1960) 108m. **A–**

Taylor is the professional good-time girl in New York who finally falls in love—with a married man. The two stars almost make this a serious drama even though the overripe situations and clichéd dialogue don't get much better, with bonus camp points for the scenes between Taylor and Fisher.

D: Daniel Mann. A: Elizabeth Taylor, Laurence Harvey, Eddie Fisher.

Elmer Gantry

(1960) 146m. **A–**

A traveling salesman in the 1920s with the gift of gab falls for a dedicated lady revivalist and ends up becoming a wildly successful preacher on the religious circuit. Lancaster's crazy exuberance buoys up this colorful piece of Americana, even while it cynically shows the less than holy side of holy rollers.

D: Richard Brooks. A: Burt Lancaster, Jean Simmons, Shirley Jones.

From the Terrace

(1960) 144m. **B–**

His mother's a drunk, his father a lout, and even with success on Wall Street and a rich and sexy socialite wife, his life is still a mess. The bright performances and glamorous trappings help compensate for the film's length and lack of spirit.

D: Mark Robson. A: Paul Newman, Joanne Woodward, Myrna Loy.

Strangers When We Meet

(1960) 117m. **C**

Illicit love blossoms in the suburbs when a married architect takes up with the neglected wife who just moved to the neighborhood. This slow-moving soaper manages to be both overwrought and emotionally flat, though Walter Matthau as the unexpected neighborhood lothario adds some spice.

D: Richard Quine. A: Kirk Douglas, Kim Novak, Barbara Rush.

The World of Suzie Wong

(1960) 129m. **C+**

The squalid side of Hong Kong never looked so photogenic as it does in this tale of an American artist who falls in love with a lovely prostitute. Great locales, fine performances, but the drama seems stilted with scenes that go on too long.

D: Richard Quine. A: William Holden, Nancy Kwan, Sylvia Sims.

Back Street

(1961) 107m. **A–**

This one doesn't miss a trick—she's a successful clothes designer, he's in an unhappy marriage, and they meet in glamorous locales for extravagantly desperate and passionate interludes. Mix in guilt, suicide attempts, and a death-bed scene to tie up loose ends and you've got a tear-jerking masterpiece.

D: David Miller. A: Susan Hayward, John Gavin, Vera Miles.

Return to Peyton Place

(1961) 122m. **C+**

The lurid underside of everyone's favorite respectable small town continues to be plumbed as this sequel tries to pick up where the original left off. The look is still luscious, but the characters and various story lines, while still ridiculously overwrought, aren't nearly juicy enough to keep your interest.

D: José Ferrer. A: Carol Lynley, Jeff Chandler, Eleanor Parker.

The Roman Spring of Mrs. Stone

(1961) 104m. **A–**

An aging actress takes up with a handsome young gigolo in Rome, believing she's different than the other women who have paid for him. This is like watching a tragic ritual being played out, with finely tuned performances and dialogue that rings clear and true.

D: Jose Quintero. A: Warren Beatty, Vivien Leigh, Lotte Lenya.

Splendor in the Grass

(1961) 124m. **A**

The ache of first love and the pains of adolescence are beautifully portrayed in the story of two high school sweethearts in 1920s Kansas. Entertaining *and* thoughtful, with an unusually frank look at the effects of sexual repression and social pressures, driven home by the vulnerable young stars.

D: Elia Kazan. A: Natalie Wood, Warren Beatty, Audrey Christie.

Summer and Smoke

(1961) 118m. **B–**

A spinster at the turn of the century who's been a signal failure at dealing with physical passion falls in love with a hell-raising doctor. The Tennessee Williams motifs are here—frustrated desires, skittery nerves, lush Southern ambience—in this talky, slow, and hypnotic drama.

D: Peter Glenville. A: Geraldine Page, Laurence Harvey, Una Merkel.

Rome Adventure
(1962) 119m. **C+**
American women always find romance in Italy, and sheltered single librarian Pleshette is no exception. This lightly amusing fantasy gives you a Cook's tour of Europe and Rome, a soupy romance, and Rossano Brazzi wooing yet another American spinster.
D: Delmer Daves. A: Troy Donahue, Angie Dickinson, Suzanne Pleshette.

Sweet Bird of Youth
(1962) 120m. **B+**
An aspiring actor/gigolo and a drugged-out aging actress blow into his home town, where he runs against the political boss who's got revenge on his mind. Another Tennessee Williams gothic that is well acted, slow to unfold, and has articulate characters brimming with juicy problems.
D: Richard Brooks. A: Paul Newman; Geraldine Page; Ed Begley, Sr.

I Could Go On Singing
(1963) 99m. **C–**
Garland plays a neurotic, needy, and legendary diva who always seems on the brink of hysteria as she tries to find love by reuniting with her young illegitimate son in England. A soapy and thoroughly uncomfortable experience; even her performance "in concert" is disturbing.
D: Ronald Neame. A: Judy Garland, Dirk Bogarde, Jack Klugman.

The V.I.P.s
(1963) 119m. **B**
Beautiful Liz is leaving her rich and powerful husband for another man, and this hilariously overstressed soaper follows the emotional wrestling matches that occur while the fleeing couple waits at the fogged-in airport. The supporting actors, with their own *Airport*-style subplots, class things up a bit.
D: Anthony Asquith. A: Elizabeth Taylor, Richard Burton, Louis Jourdan, and others.

The Chalk Garden
(1964) 106m. **A**
Kerr is the no-nonsense but mysterious governess who takes charge of a destructive teenage girl in a grand but lonely household by the sea. An elegant story that's part family drama and part suspense played by a superlative cast.
D: Ronald Neame. A: Deborah Kerr, Hayley Mills, John Mills.

The Sandpiper
(1965) 116m. **B+**
Taylor is the free-spirited, single-mother artist living in Big Sur who has a passionate affair with man-of-God Burton. He agonizes, she spouts antibourgeois sentiments, and they both roll around on the beach. A gorgeous-looking and deliriously overwrought soap opera, but Liz was not meant for those earth mother beach costumes.
D: Vincente Minnelli. A: Elizabeth Taylor, Richard Burton, Eva Marie Saint.

The Chase
(1966) 135m. **B+**
Here's a Texas town that's as much of a seething pit of passions, revenge, and class wars as *Peyton Place* ever was, only this film explores them with style and class. A strong cast, vivid confrontations, and a classically structured story make this both a smart *and* an entertaining potboiler.
D: Arthur Penn. A: Marlon Brando, Jane Fonda, Robert Redford.

The Group
(1966) 150m. **A**
This traces the lives of eight graduates from a Vassar-like college during the 1930s. The book may have been a scathing and humorous look at America's gilded young women, but the film is a snappy and entertaining ensemble soap opera shot in strangely bright and heavy colors.
D: Sidney Lumet. A: Candice Bergen, Joan Hackett, Larry Hagman.

Madame X
(1966) 100m. **C+**
Lana is the woman with a past who roams the world, man by man, bar by bar, until she ends up being defended on a murder rap by a lawyer who doesn't know she's his mother. Lacks sparkle and feels almost quaint instead of lurid, even with the Hollywood pros acting up a storm.
D: David Lowell Rich. A: Lana Turner, John Forsythe, Constance Bennett.

This Property Is Condemned
(1966) 110m. **A–**
The prettiest girl in the county is her mother's bait to attract men to their boarding house, until a handsome young man from the railroad company comes to stay. A beguiling bit of Southern-style, small-town romantic drama, with bland Redford a perfect match to bristling Wood.
D: Sydney Pollack. A: Natalie Wood, Robert Redford, Charles Bronson.

The Comedians
(1967) 148m. **B+**
A group of travelers visiting Haiti during the Duvalier regime confronts the corruption, savagery, and voodoo of the island. Taylor and Burton as the adulterous couple provide the soap, but this becomes more of an uneasy hypnotic look at the dangerous undercurrents of a country in the grips of evil.
D: Peter Glenville. A: Elizabeth Taylor, Richard Burton, Alec Guinness.

The Arrangement
(1969) 126m. **D+**
When a successful ad exec indulges in a breakdown followed by a midlife crisis, he turns his back on his wife and career, and tries to find some peace with his young mistress and his cranky old father. Tedious and self-indulgent talk, talk, talk.
D: Elia Kazan. A: Kirk Douglas, Faye Dunaway, Deborah Kerr.

Hollywood

Hollywood has fun airing its dirty laundry—and never spares the soap—in these tales of ruthless studio heads, back-stabbing actors, and innocent starlets.

The Carpetbaggers
(1964) 150m. **A–**
A gloriously trashy and glossy Hollywood potboiler follows the career of a Howard Hughes-like millionaire who builds an airplane empire, buys a movie studio, and tries to mask his psychological problems by ignoring his wife and sleeping with blonde stars—including his stepmother.
D: Edward Dmytryk. A: George Peppard, Alan Ladd, Carroll Baker.

Harlow
(1965) 125m. **B**
This bio-pic life of sex goddess Jean Harlow may have less fact than fiction, but it makes a good excuse for a story about a young starlet plagued by a parasitic mother and a problematic sex life. Events are sketchy, but the cast is game and the depiction of lurid 30s Hollywood is fine.
D: Gordon Douglas. A: Carroll Baker, Peter Lawford, Red Buttons.

Inside Daisy Clover
(1965) 128m. **A–**
A young girl is put through early Hollywood's bizarre mill as she is groomed and packaged to be the studio's next sensation. The sunny, empty, deliberately vapid look enhances this film's strange disquiet and loneliness. Even with all the standard Hollywood motifs, this one has a resonance that's unusual.
D: Robert Mulligan. A: Natalie Wood, Christopher Plummer, Robert Redford.

The Oscar
(1966) 119m. **C+**
An actor looks back on his career as a small-time performer and a Hollywood star, when his slide to obscurity gets temporarily halted by an Oscar nomination. A particularly loathsome main character, an embarrassingly bad script, and a parade of Hollywood stars make this good campy fun.
D: Russell Rouse. A: Stephen Boyd, Elke Sommer, Eleanor Parker.

War and Military Dramas

War dramas got even darker in the 60s with stories that focus on individual turmoil over camaraderie and on survival being as much a psychological issue as a physical one.

Hell to Eternity
(1960) 132m. B&W. **B+**
A young man is first scarred by how his Japanese foster family is treated during the war and then gets a bloody baptism into adulthood when he fights in the Pacific and uses his second language to trick the enemy. A rousing true-life story about the ugliness of wartime nationalism underscored with plenty of battle sequences.
D: Phil Karlson. A: Jeffrey Hunter, David Janssen, Vic Damone.

Captain Newman, M.D.
(1963) 126m. B&W. **B–**
This seriocomic ensemble piece follows the inmates and staff at a psychiatric unit of a stateside army base. Like a serious *M*A*S*H* about war vet burnouts, this has the understanding doctor, the highly unorthodox hospital aide, and assorted humorous/tragic faces of war horrors and military ethos.
D: David Miller. A: Gregory Peck, Tony Curtis, Bobby Darin.

PT 109
(1963) 140m. **C+**
A newly commissioned officer with his colorful crew sails a patched-up boat into the teeth of a Japanese assault in this highly romantic but mostly static retelling of JFK's heroic exploits in World War II. Robertson can imitate Kennedy's tics but the overall effect is bland in this almost action-free war tale.
D: Leslie Martinson. A: Cliff Robertson, Robert Culp, Ty Hardin.

The Hill
(1965) 122m. B&W. **B**
A band of British military prisoners is driven to rebellion by the sadistic drill sergeant in a North African prison camp. There's an unrelenting air of torment in this grim tale about cruelty that fills the screen with exhausted bodies, dusty swirls of dirt, and fetid prison cells.
D: Sidney Lumet. A: Sean Connery, Harry Andrews, Michael Redgrave.

King Rat
(1965) 133m. B&W.
B+
A street-smart American inmate of a Japanese POW camp manages to flourish in the midst of horror by running a black market operation that includes raising rats to sell for food. This story of survival at any cost offers a sharp-edged update of *Stalag 17* with an even thicker uneasy air hanging over the prisoners.
D: Bryan Forbes. A: George Segal, Tom Courtenay, James Fox.

Message Films

These films deal with as much frankness as the times allowed, with issues ranging from mental illness and alcoholism to race relations and lesbianism. While most suffer from a little too much earnestness, these remain some of the higher-quality dramas of the day.

A Raisin in the Sun
(1961) 128m. B&W. **B**
A Chicago black family fights over how some insurance money can best be used to realize their dreams—down payment for a liquor business, a suburban house, or the daughter's college degree? A rich character study/family drama containing intense and lengthy emotional confrontations.
D: Daniel Petrie. A: Sidney Poitier, Claudia McNeil, Ruby Dee.

Birdman of Alcatraz
(1962) 143m. B&W. **B**
A murderer sentenced to life in solitary confinement becomes a renowned bird authority during his 53 years in prison. What may be the quietest prison film ever made, this skirts being bleak with the almost meditative quality

of its character study while the unusual story and an intense Lancaster keep it compelling.
D: John Frankenheimer. A: Burt Lancaster, Karl Malden, Thelma Ritter.

The Children's Hour
(1962) 107m. B&W. **B–**
How lives can be destroyed—and truths revealed—by a lie is at the heart of this story about two teachers at a New England boarding school accused of being lesbians. A claustrophobic, emotionally charged drama that occasionally gets mired in its sincerity.
D: William Wyler. A: Shirley MacLaine, Audrey Hepburn, James Garner.

David and Lisa
(1962) 94m. B&W. **B+**
In a school for emotionally disturbed youths, a boy afraid to be touched and a schizophrenic girl gradually, gingerly, fall in love. A small poignant drama that realistically portrays the vulnerability and confusion of youth.
D: Frank Perry. A: Keir Dullea, Janet Margolin, Howard Da Silva.

Days of Wine and Roses
(1962) 117m. **A–**
The lives of a happily married young couple are eaten away as they descend into alcoholism. Helped with the pretty Mancini score, this earnest chronicle of addiction has the atmosphere and sick fascination of any ripe melodrama about a doomed love affair.
D: Blake Edwards. A: Jack Lemmon, Lee Remick, Charles Bickford.

The Miracle Worker
(1962) 107m. B&W. **B**
Deaf, dumb, and blind Helen Keller lives like a savage until her family hires tough determined teacher Annie Sullivan. The stark, almost stylized settings are the perfect frame for the two women who fill up the screen with their battles of will and inspirational friendship.
D: Arthur Penn. A: Anne Bancroft, Patty Duke, Victor Jory.

Requiem for a Heavyweight
(1962) 100m. B&W.
B+
In this film version of the classic teledrama, an over-the-hill boxer learns that his failure to take a dive has put his manager in jeopardy with the Mob, and proceeds to risk his eyesight and self-respect to help. A sad and wrenching story of hard-luck characters and misplaced trust in the seedy world of boxing.
D: Ralph Nelson. A: Anthony Quinn, Julie Harris, Jackie Gleason.

To Kill a Mockingbird
(1962) 129m. B&W.
A–
A young girl growing up in a small Southern town finds life confusing and even menacing when her father defends a black man wrongly accused of raping a white woman. This moody gentle drama captures the fabric of simpler times torn open by the trial and its repercussions.
D: Robert Mulligan. A: Gregory Peck, Mary Badham, Philip Alford.

Lilies of the Field
(1963) 93m. B&W. **B+**
Poitier is the drifter taken in by a group of nuns in the middle of a New Mexican desert. Their serene determination and effortless acceptance of assistance gives him a new lease on life as he helps them realize their vision of constructing a chapel. A peaceful relaxing film with Ansel Adams-like desert photography.
D: Ralph Nelson. A: Sidney Poitier, Lilia Skala, Lisa Mann.

Lord of the Flies
(1963) 90m. B&W. **B**
A planeload of English schoolboys crashes on a South Seas island and the survivors soon fall into a savage state of warfare among themselves. Despite the sumptuous settings filmed with a precision that gives the jungle a menacing air, this quickly feels like a boy's prep school drama with broad caricatures.
D: Peter Brook. A: James Aubrey, Tom Chapin, Hugh Edwards.

Black Like Me
(1964) 107m. B&W. **B**
A white journalist writing a piece on racism colors his skin to travel through the South under an assumed black identity. Well-intentioned story has a good feel for Southern locales and attitudes, but looks dated and leaves you wondering how Whitmore's stained mahogany disguise fooled anyone.
D: Carl Lerner. A: James Whitmore, Roscoe Lee Browne, Will Geer.

A Patch of Blue
(1965) 105m. B&W. **B+**
A blind girl whose life is hemmed in by a tyrannical mother and an alcoholic uncle become friends with a kind man she meets in the park every day. This small, well-acted drama relies a lot on the viewer's suspense at knowing the man is black while the girl does not, and the heartwarming assurance that he's so darned perfect.
D: Guy Green. A: Sidney Poitier, Elizabeth Hartman, Shelley Winters.

Psychodramas

Loneliness, desperation, and malaise fill these hauntingly dark and compelling films. Despite the black-and-white photography and intimate tone, many of these are "big" star-studded productions with actors digging into meaty roles of defrocked ministers, antebellum alcoholics, and Nazi-scarred pawnbrokers, in films that eschew happy endings for, at best, rueful and hopeful ones.

Long Day's Journey into Night
(1962) 170m. B&W.
A–
The father is a pompous miser, the mother a morphine addict; one son's a drunk, the other has TB. O'Neill knows how to put the "dys" in dysfunctional family, and this film version of his play only intensifies it. A gloomy, claustrophobic, and absolutely riveting drama that leaves you drained and not begrudging one minute of it.
D: Sidney Lumet. A: Katharine Hepburn, Jason Robards, Ralph Richardson.

Pressure Point
(1962) 87m. B&W. **B+**
During the war years, a government psychiatrist treats an extremely reluctant patient who's gotten into trou-

ble, among other things, for being a Nazi sympathizer. Darin is cool, hip, and vicious as he examines episodes from his life and arrives at some unwanted understanding of what makes him tick.
D: Hubert Cornfield. A: Sidney Poitier, Bobby Darin, Peter Falk.

Lilith
(1964) 114m. B&W. **B–**
A trainee therapist finds himself seduced by a wealthy young patient whose madness thrives on entangling all who cross her path. A cramped melodrama about sexuality and madness that reduces the subject to ominous symbols and brooding characters.
D: Robert Rossen. A: Warren Beatty, Jean Seberg, Peter Fonda.

The Night of the Iguana
(1964) 118m. B&W.
B+
Alcoholic defrocked minister Burton is leading a bus tour in Mexico but he may not even be able to keep this job the way nymphet Lyon keeps coming on to him. A stagy, eloquent, and, at times, deliriously overwrought drama with Burton sweating out his path to redemption.
D: John Huston. A: Richard Burton, Deborah Kerr, Sue Lyon.

The Pawnbroker
(1965) 116m. B&W.
B+
In this moody, slightly sluggish drama a Holocaust survivor pawnbroker seals himself off from the human misery that crowds his daily life. A brief shot of nudity and the "modern" quick editing that made this film a big splash when released now look a little self-consciously arty.
D: Sidney Lumet. A: Rod Steiger, Geraldine Fitzgerald, Brock Peters.

Ship of Fools
(1965) 149m. B&W.
B+
The bored dissatisfied passengers of the luxury liner enjoy their rich sufferings while the peasants below are packed in like cattle. This tale symbolizing the decadence and brutality leading up to World War II is finely acted, beautifully photographed, and very melodramatic—like a weird episode of *Love Boat* written by Kurt Weill.
D: Stanley Kramer. A: Vivien Leigh, Oskar Werner, Simone Signoret.

The Slender Thread
(1965) 98m. B&W **B**
Poitier is a volunteer at a suicide prevention hot line and Bancroft the woman who takes an overdose and calls. Small suspenseful drama is a two person tour de force with Bancroft telling her story in flashback while Poitier desperately tries to locate her.
D: Sydney Pollack. A: Sidney Poitier, Anne Bancroft, Telly Savalas.

Who's Afraid of Virginia Woolf?
(1966) 129m. B&W.
A–
A professor and his wife strip away every social amenity and claw at each other's emotional wounds in a boozy vicious evening of unnerving psychological games with the new faculty couple. Two hours in this battlefield will leave you drained.
D: Mike Nichols. A: Elizabeth Taylor, Richard Burton, George Segal.

The New Men

Hard-bitten reality leaves these male heroes decidedly more vulnerable for the wear in this group of powerful dramas that look at all the messy personal demons beneath the macho stance.

The Hustler
(1961) 135M. B&W. **A**
An itinerant small-time pool hustler risks the big stakes when he takes on legendary cue-shark Minnesota Fats. Riveting character study has the desolate look and feel of an Edward Hopper painting done in black and white, with career watermark performances by all involved.
D: Robert Rossen. A: Paul Newman, Jackie Gleason, Piper Laurie.

The Misfits
(1961) 124m. B&W.
B+
Beautiful child-woman Monroe hooks up with some drifters/misfits who mourn the loss of the old west. All the characters trot out their sadness and isolation by the wagonload, making this articulate, beautifully photographed drama feel stagebound even in the middle of all that wide-open desert.
D: John Huston. A: Clark Gable, Marilyn Monroe, Montgomery Clift.

Hud
(1963) 112m. B&W.
A–
A Texas ranch family faced with financial woes is pulled apart by the struggle between the righteous father and the rotten son. Like *The Last Picture Show,* a luxuriously downbeat tale shot in a creamy-looking black and white that enhances the forlorn tone as Newman ambles from one miserable act to another.
D: Martin Ritt. A: Paul Newman, Patricia Neal, Brandon de Wilde.

Zorba the Greek
(1964) 142m. B&W. **B**
A timid Englishman visiting the Greek island of Crete to work and take stock of his life is forever changed by Zorba, a local peasant who possesses an unrestrained appetite for life. The rugged settings and village intrigues can't compete with Quinn's earthy exuberance in this long drama of self-discovery.
D: Michael Cacoyannis. A: Anthony Quinn, Alan Bates, Irene Papas.

Baby the Rain Must Fall
(1965) 100m. B&W. **C+**
A parolee reunited with his wife and daughter finds it hard to settle down and even harder to control his violent temper. This story of a man divided against himself works hard to make the depressing story relevant but only succeeds in overwrought acting.
D: Robert Mulligan. A: Steve McQueen, Lee Remick, Don Murray.

The Cincinnati Kid
(1965) 102m. **B**
In this colorful attempt at making *The Hustler* about poker, a young card shark in 1930s New Orleans gets his chance to avenge a humiliat-

ing defeat against a crafty old-timer. This lacks the sullen tone and smoky look of its inspiration with the big showdown game providing all the interest.
D: Norman Jewison. A: Steve McQueen, Edward G. Robinson, Ann-Margret.

Cool Hand Luke
(1967) 126m. **B+**
A loner looking to serve his sentence on a chain gang in peace finds he has to stake out his territory with the meanest inmate as well as the sadistic guards. All the standard confrontations and camaraderie of a prison film are served up with a warmth, humor, and charm unusual in the genre.
D: Stuart Rosenberg. A: Paul Newman, George Kennedy, J. D. Cannon.

Youth Exploitation

With all the politically correct films nowadays there's something refreshing about this group of low-budget anarchic tales of youth running wild. Dirty hot-rod gangs, drug-induced deliriums, hippie girls on the Haight are captured in all their colorful, cheap, and very groovy glory.

Wild in the Streets
(1968) 97m. **B**
It's the near future and a rock star gets elected to Congress, passes a law lowering the voting age to 14, with everyone over 30 being sentenced to LSD-spiked gulags. The wild plot, "wow-man" dialogue, and bad rock music triumph over the bland, TV-movie look to create an utterly hilarious youth culture artifact.
D: Barry Shear. A: Christopher Jones, Shelley Winters, Hal Holbrook.

The Trip
(1967) 85m. **B–**
"Straight" TV director Fonda is guided into the wild world of hallucinogenics by friend Bruce Dern. Roger Corman's serious exploration of the acid scene features lava lamp-style special effects and strobe-lit, dancing hippie girls, making this a trip down memory lane.
D: Roger Corman. A: Peter Fonda, Susan Strasberg, Dennis Hopper.

Psych-Out
(1968) 82m. **B–**
A deaf-mute girl travels to San Francisco to find her brother who's living among the gentle, grooving, and Victorian-garbed hippie musicians. This takes itself less seriously than *Alice's Restaurant* and includes one or two tamely titillating free-love scenes set to rock music.
D: Richard Rush. A: Jack Nicholson, Susan Strasberg.

The Wild Ride
(1960) 63m. B&W. **C–**
Surly youth Nicholson and his cool pals have beach parties and "play chicken," which results in the death of a cop. A shoddy, mini-budget mess, with distorted sound and little more plot than a French existentialist play.
D: Harvey Berman. A: Jack Nicholson, Robert Bean, Georgianna Carter.

Easy Rider
(1969) 94m. **B**
In this rambling road film, two stoned and attitude-to-spare hippies ride their choppers cross-country to find America. A little dated now—the commune, the groovy non-philosophy—but it's still one of the classic counterculture touchstones and includes Nicholson's legendary turn as the alcoholic attorney who briefly shares their trip.
D: Dennis Hopper. A: Peter Fonda, Dennis Hopper, Jack Nicholson.

The Revolution

These dated but fascinating bits of 60s memorabilia can often feel like Hollywood's attempt to cash in on the counterculture, although a few are honest attempts to explore politics, drugs, and student unrest.

Alice's Restaurant
(1969) 11m. **C+**
This low-budget trip down hippie memory lane follows whimsically stoned-faced Guthrie and his attempts to dodge the draft. Less of a story and more of groovy attitude, this 60s relic doesn't hold up too well, despite the infectious title song.
D: Arthur Penn. A: Arlo Guthrie, James Broderick, Pat Quinn.

Last Summer
(1969) 97m. **B**
A trio of bored, middle-class kids runs wild on a remote spot of New York's Fire Island and soon their truth or dare encounters turn into a series of dangerous games. This disenfranchised youth tale seems to drift along as aimlessly as the teens do until the final ugly eruption.
D: Frank Perry. A: Barbara Hershey, Richard Thomas, Kathy Burn.

Getting Straight
(1970) 124m. **C**
A grad-student teacher gets embroiled in school politics leading to a face-off between groovy students and Establishment administrators. This labored peek at 60s student unrest is quaintly dated and naive, with campus turmoil giving way to gratuitous guitar playing until a compromise is reached.
D: Richard Straight. A: Elliott Gould, Candice Bergen, Jeff Corey.

Medium Cool
(1970) 110m. **A–**
Real footage of 1968 Chicago Democratic Convention mixes with tale of a disillusioned cameraman and his hillybilly girlfriend. This cinema verité take on 60s issues still packs political firepower, with its paranoid air intact after 25 years.
D: Haskell Wexler. A: Robert Forster, Verna Bloom, Peter Bonerz.

R.P.M. (Revolutions Per Minute)
(1970) 90m. **D+**
Brainless pap about a liberal professor loved by students and girlfriend Ann-Margret, and his violent-strewn quest for office of campus president. Casting that's not as absurdly interesting as it sounds, a flat look, and so-what story keeps this from even being a camp timepiece.
D: Stanley Kramer. A: Ann-Margret, Anthony Quinn, Paul Winfield.

The Strawberry Statement
(1970) 109m. **C**
Sexual freedom, sit-ins, tear-gassing cops—ah, the good old days. Though based on a book about the Columbia student riots, this nostalgia inducer plays more like a soap opera with attitude than a serious study of student politics.
D: Stuart Hagmann. A: Bruce Davison, Kim Darby, Bud Cort.

Zabriskie Point
(1970) 112m. **C**
A student revolutionary accused of a cop-killing flees to the desert where he and an alienated secretary smoke dope and walk around a lot until an act of violence brings on a vision of the apocalypse. With its trademark Antonioni nonplot, this is the sort of film that inspired original audiences to mutter, "Wow, heavy."
D: Michelangelo Antonioni. A: Mark Frechette, Daria Halprin, Rod Taylor.

Prime 60s

Out of the rebellious 60s came these still powerful films that mainly examine the widening cracks in the American Dream. The period had its share of trashy films, but this group of dramas, featuring archetypes like disenfranchised youth and drifting rebels, have a timelessness that goes hand-in-glove with their superior quality.

To Sir with Love
(1967) 105m. **B**
While waiting for a job in his field, a black engineer takes a teaching position in London's East End where his tough charges end up learning a thing or two about manners and self-respect. A well-worn premise gets classed up by Poitier.
D: James Clavell. A: Sidney Poitier, Judy Geeson, Suzy Kendall.

The Graduate
(1967) 105m. **A** 🏛
The upper-middle-class college grad who has every possibility in front of him drifts in the family pool, drifts into an affair with a married friend of his parents', and then drifts into falling in love with her daughter. A funny and sharply told tale that helped define the modern disaffected antihero who never does anything except react.
D: Mike Nichols. A: Dustin Hoffman, Anne Bancroft, Katharine Ross.

Midnight Cowboy
(1969) 113m. **A–**
A dumb Texas stud moves to New York City but instead of the high life with rich ladies, he's scratching out an existence with a greasy, lame, and tubercular street hustler. This tale of the sad and grotesque losers of Times Square is saved from being completely depressing by the electrifying leads.
D: John Schlesinger. A: Dustin Hoffman, Jon Voight, Sylvia Miles.

Guess Who's Coming to Dinner
(1967) 108m. **B**
The daughter of a Hearst-like newspaper magnate comes home to announce her engagement to a black man and the liberal couple realizes they're not as open-minded as they thought. This lush and long-winded film is as sanitized and "liberal" as the parents, but it's nice to see Kate and Spencer together again.
D: Stanley Kramer. A: Spencer Tracy, Katharine Hepburn, Sidney Poitier.

Five Easy Pieces
(1970) 98m. **B+**
A classical pianist becomes an oil field laborer drifting along and enduring a screechy trashy girlfriend. When his dad suffers a stroke he returns home where he's even more of a misfit. A tightly constructed story and low-keyed character study manages to feel random with an intensely aimless Nicholson.
D: Bob Rafelson. A: Jack Nicholson, Karen Black, Susan Anspach.

Joe
(1970) 107m. **B**
A businessman kills the pusher boyfriend of his overdosed daughter and lets the secret slip to a factory worker who blackmails him into an uneasy friendship. In bars, bowling alleys, and Village apartments, paranoid Joe tries to persuade the dad to act on his hate in this strange revenge tale and ugly view of the counterculture.
D: John Avildsen. A: Peter Boyle, Dennis Patrick, Susan Sarandon.

Carnal Knowledge
(1971) 96m. **A–**
This series of vignettes chronicles the sex life of two friends from college to middle age. This is less of a war-between-the-sexes film and more of a men vs. women onslaught with the focus on a selfish Nicholson who with bad grace jumps through all the necessary hoops to get laid.
D: Mike Nichols. A: Jack Nicholson, Art Garfunkel, Candice Bergen.

1970s
Soap Operas

If you have a taste for the trashy and the shameless these are the melodramas to see: They show just how the rich, the beautiful, and the medical profession suffer differently from

you and me. They also offer the sight of big stars plowing through really second-rate dialogue, glamorous settings, and reminders of what the last word was in 60s and 70s fashion.

The Interns
(1962) 120m. B&W. **B–**

The four interns in this film make their hospital seem like *Peyton Place:* One falls for a model who wants an abortion, another cheats on his nurse girlfriend with a socialite, the third falls for a dying patient, and the fourth loves a nurse who doesn't want to marry a doctor, a decision you'll applaud after seeing this film.

D: David Swift. A: Michael Callan, Cliff Robertson, James MacArthur.

Hotel
(1967) 124m. **B–**

A New Orleans hotel is in financial trouble and a hotel chain owner arrives with his mistress who tries to seduce the manager; aristocrats hiding out from a hit-and-run accident are blackmailed by the house detective; and a thief takes up residence. Like a debased *Grand Hotel* filmed like a TV movie.

D: Richard Quine. A: Rod Taylor, Karl Malden, Melvyn Douglas.

Valley of the Dolls
(1967) 123m. **A–**

An agent's secretary, an actress, and a singer struggle with Broadway barracudas, hairdressers, heartbreak, drugs, and the funny farm in this perfectly produced trash. This reaches several crescendos of hysteria, bitchiness, and bad acting, with Patty winning by a nose for sheer number of really outrageous scenes.

D: Mark Robson. A: Barbara Perkins, Patty Duke, Sharon Tate.

Doctors' Wives
(1971) 102m. **B–**

The medical profession continues to be a sink of degradation as doctor's wife Cannon freely admits that she has slept with most of her husband's doctor friends. Then she's murdered, and we're treated to the dishy details of the lives and operations of all the other characters.

D: George Schaefer. A: Dyan Cannon, Richard Crenna, Gene Hackman.

The Love Machine
(1971) 108m. **B–**

A ruthless stud newscaster has the will to succeed and the sexual stamina to make it to the top of the TV broadcasting heap. Partly due to a lead with zero charisma, this is slightly flat although it has plenty of meaningless carnality between rich and beautiful people to make it worth a look.

D: Jack Haley, Jr. A: John Phillip Law, Dyan Cannon, Robert Ryan.

Ash Wednesday
(1973) 99m. **C**

Liz has a face-lift in hopes of winning back husband Fonda but then has an affair with a gigolo. This unusually quiet and slow-paced soaper isn't bad enough to be fun, and it shows slightly sickening scenes of a real face-lift operation.

D: Larry Peerce. A: Elizabeth Taylor, Henry Fonda, Helmut Berger.

Mahogany
(1975) 109m. **C+**

Ross leaves the ghetto and her social activist lover behind to live the flashy rich and Eurotrash lifestyle as a top model, fashion designer, and object of desire by obsessive photographer Perkins. Quirky, with engaging performances and a high quotient of unintentional moments of ridiculousness.

D: Berry Gordy. A: Diana Ross, Billy Dee Williams, Anthony Perkins.

Once Is Not Enough
(1975) 121m. **B+**

A director/producer's daughter really loves her daddy, and when he marries a rich socialite she has an affair with an aging, married, and alcoholic writer. Shamelessly entertaining with enough sordid sex and dirt among the 70s jet set to launch several prime-time soap operas.

D: Guy Green. A: Kirk Douglas, Deborah Raffin, David Janssen.

A Star Is Born
(1976) 140m. **C+**

This attempt at updating the Hollywood chestnut may not be exactly trashy soap but it's such a signal failure at being an overwrought melodrama that it almost becomes camp. Streisand, playing a rock star, looks stiff and uncomfortable as she tries hard to rock out during the musical numbers.

D: Frank Person. A: Barbra Streisand, Kris Kristofferson, Gary Busey.

Sick Soul of Europe

Whether they take place before or after World War II, these English-language films from various countries evoke the sick-soul-of-Europe that bespeaks war weariness. There's a nostalgia and decadence in the visual richness of these psychodramas, and even if the story is forgettable or just weighed down by its burden of adult pain, they are always fascinating and beautiful to watch.

Death in Venice
(1971) 131m. **A–**

Ignoring the warnings of a plague, a famous German composer travels to Venice where he becomes infatuated with a beautiful young boy. Heavy, elegant, and restrained tragedy with ornate sets and a beautiful decaying Venice. A lovely attempt at filming the ineffable.

D: Luchino Visconti. A: Dirk Bogarde, Bjorn Andresen, Silvano Mangano.

Last Tango in Paris
(1972) 129m. Subtitled and English. **A**

A middle-aged American expatriate recovering from his wife's suicide and a young Frenchwoman on the eve of her marriage meet each other in a golden-lit, decaying Paris apartment for rent. They continue to rendezvous there, creating an anonymous, no-holds-barred world to play out their sexual- and psycho-dramas. A rare chance to see Brando going for broke.

D: Bernardo Bertolucci. A: Marlon Brando, Maria Schneider, Jean-Pierre Leaud.

The Night Porter

(1974) 117m. **B–**

A concentration camp survivor is now a beautiful accomplished musician, and her former warden is a slightly down-at-the-heels night porter at the hotel where she's checked in. Victim and victimizer quickly revert to their sadomasochistic sexual relationship in this risky and melodramatic drama.
D: Liliana Cavani. A: Charlotte Rampling, Dirk Bogarde, Philippe Leroy.

The Pedestrian

(1974) 97m. **B**

Successful German businessman is discovered to have participated in the slaughter of a Greek village during World War II. Well-handled examination of war guilt, and a parable of Germany's postwar economic miracle.
D: Maximilian Schell. A: Maximilian Schell, Gustav Rudolf Sellner, Peter Hall.

Steppenwolf

(1974) 105m. **B**

A man weary of life and pained by the frivolous culture of 1920s Germany meets a mysterious young woman who sets him on a journey of self-discovery climaxing at the Magic Theater of his mind. Looks more like a nostalgic drama but still a good attempt at a mystical jaunt.
D: Fred Haines. A: Max von Sydow, Dominique Sanda, Pierre Clementi.

The Voyage of the Damned

(1976) 134m. **B+**

In 1939 a boat of Jewish refugees is refused safe harbor in Havana or anywhere else and must return to Germany. Fact-based story features individual tales told in flashback that brings it alive.
D: Stuart Rosenberg. A: Faye Dunaway, Max von Sydow, Oskar Werner.

Just a Gigolo

(1979) 96m. **C**

World War I vet goes from job to job in Berlin until he finds what he's really good at. The tawdry downward spiral is predictable and it's chiefly interesting for the odd, celebrity-driven cast with Dietrich in her final film appearance.
D: David Hemmings. A: David Bowie, Sydne Rome, Marlene Dietrich.

Nostalgic Hollywood

The dark and secret side of Hollywood's past are examined in this clutch of dreamily stylish, almost surreally delirious visions of the dream factory and its eccentric creators.

The Day of the Locust

(1975) 144m. **A–**

Downbeat, brilliant, and fascinating excursion shows some of Hollywood's dreamers including a blonde, mass-of-affectations aspiring starlet; an art director; and a quiet Midwestern accountant. This offers brilliant period detail, fully-fleshed human tragedies, and a horrific apocalyptic finale.
D: John Schlesinger. A: Donald Sutherland, Karen Black, William Atherton.

The Last Tycoon

(1976) 122m. **B–**

To expose the hollow core of Hollywood power and illusion, this film—based on an unfinished Fitzgerald novel about a studio head's doomed love affair—ends up being a big, beautiful, star-studded, dark-hearted, hollow film. The Golden Age of Hollywood looks gorgeous but the talent on parade has nowhere to go.
D: Elia Kazan. A: Robert De Niro, Robert Mitchum, Ingrid Boulting.

Mommie Dearest

(1981) 129m. **B–**

Viewers are treated to a portrait of Joan Crawford as abusive mom, who makes her adoptive daughter's life one of endless torment with nitpicky and violent manias. Would be somewhat nasty campy trash except for Dunaway's performance.
D: Frank Perry. A: Faye Dunaway, Diana Scarwid, Steve Forest.

(See also *Valentino*, page 222.)

Andy Warhol

These grungy-looking, amateurish, and frequently funny tales of the bohemian side of New York's art scene are like documentaries of the denizens of Warhol's Factory; hustlers, junkies, and groupies score drugs, have sex, and talk nonsense in the most artless "art" films you're ever likely to see.

Flesh

(1968) 90m. **C+**

Transvestites, wacko artists, and masochists: Welcome to the zany debauched world of 60s downtown New York where a male hustler will sleep with anyone so long as he gets money for his next fix. Grainy and looking like it was shot on used film, this is still a fascinating tour of the dark side of 60s bohemia.
D: Paul Morrissey. A: Joe Dalessandro, Geraldine Smith, Patti D'Arbanville.

Trash

(1970) 110m. **B–**

More junkie jaunts in downtown Manhattan with Dallesandro now joined by a whiny girlfriend who scours the neighbor's garbage for food. Though the miserable milieus are depressing, this has flashes of snide humor making it something of a cult essential.
D: Paul Morrissey. A: Joe Dalessandro, Holly Woodlawn, Jane Forth.

Heat

(1972) 102m. **C**

A forgotten movie star lives out a deluded life in a dilapidated LA hotel watching TV and trying to tolerate her daughter's lesbian affair. Neighbor Joe is along for the ride as an ex-child star-turned-junkie who keeps the fat landlady at bay with his

services. Tawdry soap opera has nothing resembling pace but between nods, some funny/disgusting bits.
D: Paul Morrissey. A: Joe Dallesandro, Sylvia Miles.

Andy Warhol's Bad
(1977) 105m. **B–**
A hard-boiled beautician uses her facial hair removal business as a front for a contract killing outfit in Queens. With its cheerfully antagonistic plot and use of bona fide actors, one of the most subversively funny of the Warhol films, with Baker's campy Crawford spin a must see for 50s melodrama fans.
D: Jed Johnson. A: Carroll Baker, Perry King, Susan Tyrell.

Cocaine Cowboys
(1979) 90m. **C–**
Members of a mediocre rock band deal drugs while waiting for infrequent gigs and trying to stay one floundering step ahead of the Mob. Cheap, aimless, and as dissipated-feeling as most Warhol productions, but with little of the deadpan humor and almost-compassion that make his other films minor cult classics.
D: Uili Lommel. A: Jack Palance, Andy Warhol, Tom Sullivan.

Sports Dramas

Before the featherbrain, feel-good days of *Rocky* and his muscle-bound brethren were these sports dramas that offered serious bits of male-oriented drama and melodrama, often featuring the instant-death sport of race car competition. Though not downbeat in tone, these films address sexism, bigotry, the will-to-win, and, of course, the little *Rocky*-like guy who makes it big.

Downhill Racer
(1969) 101m. **B+**
A talented but overly aggressive member of the U.S. skiing team struggles with the coach and his own ego while competing on the European circuit. A fascinating look at personalities under the pressure of competition, with exhilarating you-are-there downhill skiing footage.
D: Michael Ritchie. A: Robert Redford, Gene Hackman, Camilia Sparv.

Fat City
(1972) 100m. **B+**
A hard luck ex-prizefighter tries to get back in the ring, but finds his biggest opponent to pugilistic grace is the bottle. Told in interlocking vignette style, with ample dead-end, small-town atmosphere and another great Bridges performance that centers this downbeat fable of lost dreams.
D: John Huston. A: Stacy Keach, Jeff Bridges, Susan Tyrell.

Bang the Drum Slowly
(1973) 98m. **B+**
A difficult, mentally slow catcher is taken under the wing of the star pitcher who then discovers that his teammate doesn't have long to live. Despite a thin script this is a gut-wrenching, genuinely poignant film—and it's all in the performances that allow you to feel the connection and frustration between the characters.
D: John Hancock. A: Robert DeNiro, Michael Moriarty, Vincent Gardenia.

The Longest Yard
(1974) 121m. **B+**
A minor league con/ex-pro quarterback is used by a prison's wily warden to put together a team of convicts to battle a team of guards. Filled with colorful obscenities and macho attitude to spare, this is rough and tumble fun with an exciting climactic game that lasts almost a third of the film.
D: Robert Aldrich. A: Burt Reynolds, Eddie Albert, Dino Washington.

North Dallas Forty
(1979) 119m. **B+**
An aging receiver finds that what it takes to make it in the modern football arena doesn't jibe with his purer vision of things, causing plenty of disturbances with his party-hearty teammates and egomaniacal front office boys. A ruthlessly on-target and funny skewering of cut-throat gridiron gamesmanship.
D: Ted Kotcheff. A: Nick Nolte, Mac Davis, Charles Durning.

Sports Car Racing

Winning
(1969) 123m. **B–**
A professional race car driver jeopardizes his marriage in his singleminded pursuit of winning. The film captures the excitement of Grand Prix racing, including some spectacular spins and crashes, but turns flat whenever it leaves the racetrack.
D: James Goldstone. A: Paul Newman, Joanne Woodward, Robert Wagner.

The Last American Hero
(1973) 95m. **B**
The son of a moonshiner hones his driving skills delivering whiskey on backroads while being pursued by the law, and winds up becoming a famous stock car driver. An entertaining *Rocky*-style sports film with a good ole boy spin to it that captures the buccaneer attitude of stock car racing.
D: Lamont Johnson. A: Jeff Bridges, Valerie Perrine, Geraldine Fitzgerald.

Bobby Deerfield
(1977) 124m. **B–**
A car driver goes from one race to the next, leaving his problems behind and ignoring the death he faces until he falls for a terminally ill wealthy jet-setter. Basically a romance novel with lots of racing scenes and a well-heeled Euro atmosphere.
D: Sydney Pollack. A: Al Pacino, Marthe Keller, Romolo Valli.

Greased Lightning
(1977) 96m. **B–**
Another backroads-to-big-time-speedway story follows a former moonshine runner who goes on to become the first black man to win a Grand National stock car race. A cunning and affable Pryor is the real reason to watch this film that emphasizes personal drama over sports action scenes.
D: Michael Schultz. A: Richard Pryor, Beau Bridges, Pam Grier.

Heart Like a Wheel
(1983) 113m. **B+**
Another spunky-driver-who-overcomes-the-odds film follows Shirley Muldowney, the first woman to win the Hot Rod World championships. A cut above the others thanks to Bonnie Bedelia, though the story focuses on honesty and dedication rather than incredible racing skills as the way to winning.
D: Jonathan Kaplan. A: Bonnie Bedelia, Beau Bridges, Hoyt Axton.

African-American Dramas

While *Shaft* and his jive-talking brothers filled the sleazier 70s bijous, efforts were made to portray realistic slices of African-American life. Though sometimes tainted by a liberal tone in an effort to give a serious subject its just due, these films are generally compelling dramas that go much further than good intentions.

Purlie Victorious
(1963) 93m. B&W. **C+**

A black evangelist couple struggles to open an integrated house of worship in the Jim Crow South. A story so gentle and nonabrasive that it is more a brotherhood-of-man drama than a comedy of overcoming racial stereotypes.

D: Nicholas Webster. A: Ossie Davis, Ruby Dee, Alan Alda.

The Learning Tree
(1969) 107m. **B+**

Gordon Parks' autobiographical story tells of growing up black in 1930s Kansas. The very personal nature of the film—Parks wrote, directed, and did the score—helps balance out the more familiar aspects, creating a fairly timeless tale.

D: Gordon Parks, Jr. A: Kyle Johnson, Alex Clarke, Estelle Evans.

The Great White Hope
(1970) 103m. **B+**

White society tries to bring down the first African-American heavyweight champ by slurring his personal life and appealing to his own coarser instincts. A shattering portrayal of both societal and psychological effects of racism, with a career turn by Jones.

D: Martin Ritt. A: James Earl Jones, Jane Alexander, Hal Holbrook.

Sounder
(1972) 105m. **A**

The strength of a black family of sharecroppers is tested when the father is arrested for stealing to keep his family from starving. Not a cliché is to be found in this ravishingly shot, uniformly brilliantly acted film.

D: Martin Ritt. A: Cicely Tyson, Paul Winfield, Carmen Mathews.

Cornbread, Earl and Me
(1975) 95m. **C+**

A boy helps the family of a high school basketball ace clear his name after being mistakenly shot by the police. A well-intentioned film is marred by some predictable plot points and rather listless direction.

D: Joseph Manduke. A: Moses Gunn, Rosalind Cash, Madge Sinclair.

Romance

Even if youths in the 1970s seemed to be falling over themselves to ABBA songs at discos on the way to nights of casual sex, there was always an audience for old-fashioned, tear-jerking romances.

Love Story
(1970) 99m. **B+**

Wealthy Oliver falls for fellow Harvard student Jenny with her Italian working-class roots and outspoken ways: Even when they're cut off from the family money, they do fine until she gets an incurable disease. The first half is a prototype of a yuppie's romance before it settles into a tearjerker so shamelessly manipulative it defies criticism.

D: Arthur Hiller. A: Ali MacGraw, Ryan O'Neal, Ray Milland.

The Way We Were
(1973) 118m. **B+**

An extremely handsome WASP and a fiery Jewish woman weave their romance and marriage through various historic and social events from the 1930s to the 50s. Pretty-looking romance reduces Redford to ornament status but still a nice fantasy if you're in the right mood.

D: Sydney Pollack. A: Barbra Streisand, Robert Redford, Lois Chiles.

First Love
(1977) 91m. **C**

An acid-tongued coed falls for a handsome but moody Redford-clone at the same time she's having a fling with a married older man. Replete with Vaseline-lensed photography, gushing string music, and amusingly dated fashionable clothes, this is pure soap opera pap like (you may hope) they'll never make again.

D: Joan Darling. A: William Katt, Susan Dey, Beverly D'Angelo.

You Light Up My Life
(1977) 90m. **C+**

A perky Jewish female is torn between doubts about her ensuing marriage, pressure from her Catskill's comedian Dad who wants her in his act, and her own desire to get into showbiz so she can sing one of the most irritating songs of all time. Looks and acts like an okay TV weepie.

D: Joseph Brooks. A: Didi Conn, Joe Silver, Stephen Nathan.

Literary Costume Dramas

These sprawling atmospheric adaptations of mostly British novels are a feast for those wishing to spend a few hours immersed in the colors, costumes, and unhurried rhythms of times past. The wildly romantic landscapes, intelligent dramas, and finely tuned performances all help make these the equivalent of curling up with a good book.

Tom Jones
(1963) 131m. **B+**

A young English country lad with a ladykiller smile and a hyperactive libido beds and brawls his way into eighteenth-century London society. A colorful and lusty farce with slapstick humor, lots of ladies in loosened petticoats and lace, and a hilarious foreplay scene over a sumptuous dinner.
D: Tony Richardson. A: Albert Finney, Susannah York, Edith Evans.

Far From the Madding Crowd
(1967) 166m. **B+**

The lush countryside of Victorian England co-stars in this Hardy tale of a headstrong, independent country girl and the three men in her life. Beautifully acted film owes much of its energy to the 60s sexual revolution.
D: John Schlesinger. A: Julie Christie, Peter Finch, Alan Bates, Terence Stamp.

Ryan's Daughter
(1970) 176m. **B**

The stark beauty of the Irish coast overwhelms this gentle tale of the younger wife of an earnest but unstimulating schoolmaster who finds sensual pleasure and escape from dull village life in the arms of a British officer. Beautiful but 30 minutes too long.
D: David Lean. A: Robert Mitchum, Sarah Miles, Trevor Howard.

Daisy Miller
(1974) 93m. **C–**

Shepherd looks lovely but just can't play the convention-flaunting American on the loose in Victorian Europe. The film it does capture a hazy nostalgic shine and romantic scenes of autumn in France and Italy.
D: Peter Bogdanovich. A: Cybill Shepherd, Barry Brown, Cloris Leachman.

The Great Gatsby
(1974) 146m. **B–**

This tale of an enigmatic young man who tries to recapture lost love amongst the nouveau riche occasionally plugs into the abandon and ennui of the Roaring Twenties and has spiffy period clothes, colors, and settings. The supporting actors are intelligent, but Redford is wooden and Farrow is neurotic.
D: Jack Clayton. A: Robert Redford, Mia Farrow, Sam Waterston, Bruce Dern.

Barry Lyndon
(1975) 185m. **B+**

Thackeray's morality study of a poor social-climbing cad in the eighteenth century is breathtakingly composed and uses natural lighting and impeccable period detail (including authentic music). Still, its measured pace becomes static due to the emotionally remote characters, and the attempt to portray the ambiguity of Lyndon's successes and failures.
D: Stanley Kubrick. A: Ryan O'Neal, Marisa Berenson, Hardy Kruger.

Joseph Andrews
(1977) 103m. **C**

Tony Richardson's bawdy companion piece to *Tom Jones* lacks the buoyant, devil-may-care attitude of the 60s that drove that better film. The superior eighteenth-century costumes and artful cinematography fail to cover the flat adventures and an ineffectual central character.
D: Tony Richardson. A: Peter Firth, Ann-Margret, Beryl Reid.

Tess
(1979) 180m. **B+**

Exquisite arboreal settings and a brooding, yet expressive Kinski carry this Hardy story of a Victorian country girl who is wronged by both classes of society. Film's only shortcoming is director Polanski's tendency to linger a bit too long.
D: Roman Polanski. A: Nastassja Kinski, Leigh Lawson, Peter Firth.

Historical Epics

While historical epics in the 70s continued to explore the power struggles and moral dilemmas of larger-than-life historical figures, many of these grand-scale, novel-like films also portrayed the heroism of ordinary lives in tales of common people caught up in the social issues of the day or their own private dramas.

Cromwell
(1970) 139m. **C+**

Firebrand puritan leader Cromwell strives to rid seventeenth-century England of vacillating but tyrannical King Charles I and a corrupt Parliament. Has all the standard court trappings plus some good battle sequences, but fails to deliver on dramatic potential.
D: Ken Hughes. A: Richard Harris, Alec Guinness, Robert Morley.

The Molly Maguires
(1970) 123m. **B–**

A Pinkerton detective who infiltrates a brutal organization formed by Irish coal miners in Pennsylvania begins to see their side as he experiences the horrendous working conditions. Offers fine one-note performances, colorful re-creations of gray shantytowns and airless coal mines, but sorely lacks humor.
D: Martin Ritt. A: Richard Harris, Sean Connery, Samantha Eggar.

Nicholas and Alexandra
(1971) 183m. **B+**

A deft and sympathetic treatment of the Romanoff family on the eve of the 1917 Russian Revolution. The film manages to be both epic and intimate and perhaps covers too much ground, but fine performances, lush scenery, and the rich historical detail make up for any faults.
D: Franklin J. Schaffner. A: Michael Jayston, Janet Suzman, Tom Baker, Laurence Olivier.

Waterloo
(1971) 122m. **B–**

Napoleon makes one last grab for power and battles the ultimate aristocrat Wellington at Waterloo. Starts out as a study of two great leaders and the bloody, gloryless business of war, and ends up as a tremendous detailed, hour-long battle treatise. Big, loud, and impressive but ultimately pointless.
D: Sergei Bondarchuk. A: Rod Steiger, Christopher Plummer, Orson Welles.

1900
(1976) 255m. **B**

Two boys, one the son of a wealthy landowner and the other a farmhand's bastard, experience the first half of the twentieth century in Italy from fascism to communism. Rich in characters and gorgeous scenery, the film

labors long on each subject and turns a vivid study of a tumultuous period into a mannered tour. Best viewed in segments.
D: Bernardo Bertolucci. A: Robert De Niro, Burt Lancaster, Dominique Sanda.

Days of Heaven
(1978) 95m. **B+**
Young people go to work the wheat fields of the Texas Panhandle. The story of a romantic triangle seems to unfold inevitably, like a folkloric shadow play, but the real drama occurs in the rhythms and raw beauty of the land, with some of the most stunning and grandiose scenes of nature ever captured on film.
D: Terence Malick. A: Richard Gere, Brooke Adams, Sam Shepard.

The Europeans
(1979) 90m. **B**
Two free-thinking European relatives descend upon a puritanical family in the 1840s, with predictable clashes of social and sexual mores. Captures the glories of a New England fall and the stillness of carefully measured lives. Slow and ponderous, but will appeal to fans of picturesque period pieces where inference replaces action.
D: James Ivory. A: Lee Remick, Robin Ellis, Wesley Addy.

Women's Bio-Pics

While the men were making every kind of film imaginable in the 70s, movies devoted to women were usually these literate and often humorless costume dramas set in foreign countries. Heavyweights like Vanessa Redgrave and Glenda Jackson are the reason to watch these tales of strong and larger-than-life characters; their artistry makes even the grimmest production shine.

Isadora (aka Loves of Isadora)
(1968) 131m. **A–**
She was a pioneer of modern dance, a feminist, and a believer in free love at the turn of the century. This colorful and exuberant biography follows the mercurial Isadora Duncan with her dance schools for young girls, her string of love affairs, and her "obscene" interpretive dancing that scandalized America and Europe.
D: Karel Reisz. A: Vanessa Redgrave, James Fox, Jason Robards.

Justine
(1969) 116m. **C**
A grand and sweeping tale of love and politics in 1930s Egypt as the enigmatic wife of a well-heeled businessman becomes involved in political intrigue. Fun to watch for the costume re-creations, lovely landscapes, and good cast, but the story is missing any edge.
D: George Cukor. A: Anouk Aimée, Dirk Bogarde, Robert Forster.

A Doll's House
(1973) 87m. **C**
Ibsen's early feminist Nora is the courageous young woman who dares to stand up to her stodgy and domineering husband when he treats her like an object. Elegant and talky, this feels more like a noble exercise in a provincial theater than a cinematic drama.
D: Joseph Losey. A: Jane Fonda, Trevor Howard, David Warner.

Hedda
(1975) 104m. **B**
A *Masterpiece Theater*-style version of Ibsen's play concerning a conniving and seductive woman whose neuroses make a small town mad. Jackson, who brings a delicious, larger-than-life ruthlessness to the role, is the reason to watch.
D: Trevor Nunn. A: Glenda Jackson, Timothy West, Peter Eyre.

The Getting of Wisdom
(1977) 100m. **B**
A strong-willed, mid-nineteenth-century Australian teenager leaves her tiny backwater town to attend a women's college where she encounters dizzying levels of snobbery and rejection—and manages to triumph. Spirited and mildly satirical, but it lacks credibility with a lead who seems far too modern even for the maverick that she plays.
D: Bruce Beresford. A: Susannah Fowle, Barry Humphries, Sheila Helpmann.

Julia
(1977) 118m. **A**
Wild and exuberant Julia involves the writer Lillian Hellman in a European resistance movement in the 1930s. A lovely nostalgic almost-thriller, and an intelligent portrait of two women's friendship.
D: Fred Zinnemann. A: Vanessa Redgrave, Jane Fonda, Jason Robards.

Stevie
(1978) 102m. **A–**
"I'm drowning, not waving," says the wittily depressed British poet Stevie Smith. This depiction of her quiet ordered life with a maiden aunt relies on their banter; it's a fairly static two-woman show but the viewer is continually buoyed by Smith's bon mots.
D: Robert Enders. A: Glenda Jackson, Mona Washbourne.

Agatha
(1979) 98m. **C+**
In 1926 mystery writer Agatha Christie disappeared for 11 days, and this film speculates, rather dully, on what may have happened. Lush period detail and fine performances help the sluggish pace.
D: Michael Apted. A: Dustin Hoffman, Vanessa Redgrave, Timothy Dalton.

My Brilliant Career
(1979) 101m. **A–**
The turn-of-the-century Australian outback provides the setting for this story of an impoverished young woman's determination to realize her dream of becoming a writer despite many sacrifices. Davis as the spunky heroine gives this Victorian-era feminist story a vibrancy and vividness enhanced by the warm period details.
D: Gillian Armstrong. A: Judy Davis, Sam Neill, Wendy Hughes.

Chanel Solitaire
(1981) 124m. **C–**
This bio-pic of Coco Chanel takes a slow sentimental walk through her life, from her convent education in the French provinces to her success as a fashion designer in Paris, with plenty of time out for her active love life. Fluffy fare with more misty-looking scenes than a soft-core porno film.
D: George Kaczender. A: Marie-France Pisier, Timothy Dalton, Karen Black.

British Dramas

Don't look for light fare among this collection of stories that range from elegant dissections of middle-aged, sexually repressed Brits in crisis to surreal and often violent examinations of youths who are anything but stiff-upper-lipped citizens of the British Empire.

Adults

Darling
(1965) B&W. 122m.
B+
Christie dives headlong into London's glamorous treacherous fashion scene, and the young "darling" keeps three suitors twisting in the wind as she galavants from Paris and back with a sleazeball PR man. Christie's charm and the Mod London trappings make this an entertaining timepiece.
D: John Schlesinger. A: Julie Christie, Dirk Bogarde, Laurence Harvey.

Negatives
(1968) 99m. **C–**
A bored married couple who have worked out a complicated game of dress-up for sexual excitement plays a nineteenth-century wife murderer and his victim. Dark, moody, and repressed, but Jackson can breathe life into anything.
D: Peter Medak. A: Glenda Jackson, Peter McEnery.

Sunday, Bloody Sunday
(1971) 110m. **A**
The fine balance of a sophisticated marriage is undone when a young male sculptor becomes sexually involved with both partners. Adult in the best sense of the word, with a smart script and painfully good performances.
D: John Schlesinger. A: Glenda Jackson, Peter Finch, Murray Head.

10 Rillington Place
(1971) 111m. **B+**
A gray portrait of a famous case from the 1940s of an unassuming man found to be a murderer of children and women. Very creepy with good period details.
D: Richard Fleischer. A: Richard Attenborough, Judy Geeson.

Shattered (aka Something to Hide)
(1972) 100m. **C–**
A couple fights it out while trying to cope with the husband's pregnant mistress. Dramatic, tortuous, with plenty of emoting.
D: Alastair Reid. A: Peter Finch, Shelley Winters.

The Romantic Englishwoman
(1975) 115m. **A**
A sophisticated and very discontent English couple goes into a tailspin when the husband sets his wife up with a gigolo. Dryly witty, and brutally honest.
D: Joseph Losey. A: Glenda Jackson, Helmut Berger, Michael Caine.

Youths

If . . . .
(1968) 111m. **B+**
A troika of young lads endures the rigors and brutalities of British boys' school, complete with whip-wielding guards. Woozy blend of steely-eyed reality and sepia-tinted fantasy scenes leads to a very 60s resolution in this sometimes funny, sometimes confusing, but always disturbing drama.
D: Lindsay Anderson. A: Malcolm McDowell, Richard Warwick.

A Clockwork Orange
(1971) 137m. **A**
In the near future, gangs in white romantic punk garb drink hallucinogenic milk and terrorize a (recognizably) trashed Britain; meanwhile authorities experiment on a gang leader to see if he can be civilized. Dark humor, exuberant energy, and breathtakingly surreal and violent images cloak one of the darker stories from this period.
D: Stanley Kubrick. A: Malcolm McDowell, Patrick Magee, Adrienne Corri.

O Lucky Man!
(1973) 173m. **A–**
Allegorical tale of an ambitious salesman's surreal journey through England on his way to "making it." More a series of bizarre vignettes (the man/pig scene in the medical research center is a highlight) as the innocent Candide-like hero suffers one mishap after another.
D: Lindsay Anderson. A: Malcolm McDowell, Rachel Roberts, Ralph Richardson.

Nostalgic Coming-of-Age

It's not surprising that coming-of-age tales are often nostalgia pieces since the people writing them grew up at least a generation ago. With few exceptions these stories of youth set in the 40s or 50s are funny, sweet-natured, and entertaining films, even when they're looking at the past with rose-colored glasses firmly in place.

Summer of '42
(1971) 102m. **A–**
A teenage boy spends his summer at the beach hopelessly in love with a young war bride. This film glows with sentimentality and humorous sympathy for the characters, and captures how heartbreakingly wonderful the boy finds Jennifer O'Neill.
D: Robert Mulligan. A: Gary Grimes, Jennifer O'Neill, Jerry Houser.

A Separate Peace
(1972) 104m. **C–**
Roommates at a New England prep school face their coming-of-age in the last years of World War II. Watching this dull unfocused film, you'll recall all the clichés about the remoteness and privilege of WASPs. Read the book instead.
D: Larry Peerce. A: Parker Stevenson, John Heyl, William Roerick.

Class of '44
(1973) 95m. **C+**
This sequel to *Summer of '42* picks up the story of the three boyhood friends, now making their first forays into manhood: college, army, love. Slicker and more formulaic, this lacks the charm of the first.

D: Paul Bogart. A: Gary Grimes, Jerry Houser, Oliver Connant.

The Apprenticeship of Duddy Kravitz

(1974) 121m. **A**

A poor young Jewish man in 1940s Montreal uses his street smarts to get ahead at any cost. He's brash, vulgar, full of himself—and totally fascinating. A funny, sharp, and lively film with some hysterical moments, including Duddy's film company that makes artistic bar mitzvah movies.
D: Ted Kotcheff. A: Richard Dreyfuss, Micheline Lanctot, Jack Warden.

The Lords of Flatbush

(1974) 88m. **B**

These tough boys in a 1950s Brooklyn gang are about as threatening as their ubiquitous combs, but their adventures are still funny and poignant. Heavy on atmosphere, this grainy little film feels like a documentary with a lot of future stars in it. Don't miss the scene with Stallone in the wedding ring store with his girlfriend.
D: Stephen Verona, Martin Davidson. A: Sylvester Stallone, Perry King, Henry Winkler.

Next Stop, Greenwich Village

(1976) 109m. **B+**

A young man bucks his Jewish mother and moves to the Village to become an actor. His adventures with the assortment of oddballs and aspiring talent are slightly predictable but charming and funny, and Winters is a gas as his mother who drops in at the worst possible moments.
D: Paul Mazursky. A: Lenny Baker, Shelley Winters, Ellen Greene.

Ode to Billy Joe

(1976) 108m. **B**

What could have been a cheap film capitalizing on a hit song is actually a sweetly performed tale of confused young love in 1960s Mississippi. This captures the languor, heat, and space of rural life, where anything out of the ordinary becomes magical or menacing, sometimes both at once.
D: Max Baer. A: Glynnis O'Connor, Robby Benson, Joan Hotchkis.

The Wanderers

(1979) 113m. **A–**

Members of a high school gang in the Bronx in 1963 are at the center of this nearly musical style drama. Goofily brutal, there are so many sharp and darkly funny moments in this film that its cult status is understandable.
D: Philip Kaufman. A: Ken Wahl, Karen Allen, John Friedrich.

Politics and Idealism

Whether it's the "Establishment" of politics, big business, or academia, these lively dramas all deal with determined individuals who fight the system, succumb to it, or gain an uneasy truce.

The Candidate

(1972) 110m. **A**

Detail-oriented examination of the slow, moral, and ethical erosion of a once decent politico running for higher office. Documentary-like feel and constant shifts in tempo reflecting the tumult of election politics make this an engaging, cautiously cynical effort.
D: Michael Ritchie. A: Robert Redford, Peter Boyle, Don Porter.

The Paper Chase

(1973) 111m. **B+**

Harvard Law School competition becomes an entertaining spectacle with Houseman as the daunting contracts professor to whom Bottoms is determined to measure up, even if he is sleeping with the professor's daughter. The romance is forgettable, but the lecture hall theatrics are lively.
D: James Bridges. A: Timothy Bottoms, John Houseman, Lindsay Wagner.

Save the Tiger

(1973) 101m. **B–**

A business tycoon is on the verge of bankruptcy and the hooker he hired to entertain a client has given the man a heart attack. An overly earnest and rather purposelessly unpleasant tale of one man's moral rot with Lemmon doing the old behave-badly-and-wring-your-hands-in-guilt routine to perfection.
D: John Avildsen. A: Jack Lemmon, Jack Gilford, Laurie Heineman.

Norma Rae

(1979) 113m. **B+**

A worker in a Southern textile factory is prodded by a New York labor man to organize a union after faulty equipment blinded her mother and killed her father. Field plays one of her most memorable belle-with-an-attitude characters, holding her own with the scene-stealing Leibman in this stirring, old-fashioned David and Goliath tale.
D: Martin Ritt. A: Sally Field, Ron Leibman, Beau Bridges.

The Seduction of Joe Tynan

(1979) 107m. **B**

A happily married senator becomes involved in an affair and power-politics corruption. With good-guy Alda in the lead, there's not much suspense about the outcome of the senator's moral quandary in this entertaining cautionary Beltway fable.
D: Jerry Schatzberg. A: Alan Alda, Meryl Streep, Barbara Harris.

Cop and Crime Dramas

Competing with *Bullitt* and *Dirty Harry* were these hard-hitting, fact-based police dramas invariably set and shot in New York or Los Angeles. While still offering suspense and action, these films avoided the car chases and shoot-outs to concentrate on the human interest side of crime and the hardships and corruption of police work.

The New Centurions
(1972) 103m. **C –**
This series of vignettes makes a game attempt at realism in its account of LA patrolmen as they make their rounds. Unfortunately, even with the lead stars, the by-the-numbers script and direction make it play more like a TV movie laced with profanity and sleaze.
D: Richard Fleischer. A: George C. Scott, Stacy Keach, Jane Alexander.

Serpico
(1973) 129m. **A**
The true story of an idealistic cop who despite threats on his life singlemindedly helped to expose corruption within the New York City Police Department. There's an urban neighborhood feel to this film, as New York City's offbeat characters and locations enhance Pacino's flamboyant, slightly martyred crusader.
D: Sidney Lumet. A: Al Pacino, Tony Roberts, John Randolph.

Dog Day Afternoon
(1975) 130m. **A**
Two small-time guys bungle a bank robbery and find themselves way over their heads as police, the media, and crowds surround the bank where they're now holding hostages. A true-life, New York City crime comic opera filled with bravado and snap, fueled by wild performances, especially from Pacino as the thief who only wanted to pay for his boyfriend's sex-change operation.
D: Sidney Lumet. A: Al Pacino, John Cazale, Charles Durning.

Report to the Commissioner
(1975) 112m. **B+**
A naive rookie beat cop tries to save a beautiful prostitute from the streets, unaware that she's an undercover vice detective. A solid blend of character study, tragedy, and hard-boiled police action set in a sleazy Times Square setting.
D: Milton Katselas. A: Michael Moriarty, Yaphet Kotto, Susan Blakely.

The Onion Field
(1979) 127m. **B –**
This low-key, fact-based police/courtroom drama recounts a cop killing in 1960s Los Angeles and its long aftermath: the killer's appeals and the surviving cop's breakdown. Well acted but so uninvolving and sketchy that after so much time lapses in the story, you wonder what the point is.
D: Harold Becker. A: James Woods, John Savage, Ted Danson.

The Godfather Trilogy

The gangster genre changed forever after *The Godfather* revived the mobster hero as a glamorous sort of ruthless businessman who lived and died by his code of honor and duty to family.

The Godfather
(1972) 171m. **A**
Although violent and profane, this is one of the last truly old-fashioned grand-style movies totally immersing the viewer in the 1940s, closed-off world of the Mafia crime family. Notable for outstanding performances along with an incredible sense of period detail and gangster protocol that invoke a rich world of crime and family.
D: Francis Ford Coppola. A: Marlon Brando, Al Pacino, Robert Duvall.

The Godfather, Part II
(1974) 200m. **A**
An epic sequel that shows both the origins of the Corleone family from its earthy beginnings in Sicily and the dark, singleminded, and classically tragic ascendancy to power of Michael Corleone. Overambitious in story but repeated viewing shows the richness of effects gained from this ambition.
D: Francis Ford Coppola. A: Al Pacino, Diane Keaton, Robert De Niro.

The Godfather, Part III
(1990) 162m. **B+**
Michael Corleone tries to steer the Family into more legit avenues, but hot young blood, the sins of the fathers, and fate consistently get in his way. Offers stunning action sequences and heart-rending scenes between Pacino and Keaton, but the story wanders, much like Michael, trying to make a decent exit from a complex modern world.
D: Francis Ford Coppola. A: Al Pacino, Diane Keaton, Talia Shire.

Oddballs and Little People

The most interesting aspect of these films is their attempt to portray the kooky, marginal, and regular "little" people of American society. Like updated versions of *Marty*, they are also some of the best examples of the new realism in the late 60s with their gutsy performances, often artless narration, and quirky charm.

The Heart Is a Lonely Hunter
(1968) 125m. **B –**
A deaf mute moves into the home of a poor Southern family so he can be close to his institutionalized buddy. There he makes friends with the teenage girl in this poignant but thin tale of little people trying to shore up their loneliness.
D: Robert Ellis Miller. A: Alan Arkin, Sondra Locke, Stacy Keach.

The Sterile Cuckoo
(1969) 107m. **B**
The line between youthful nonconformity and certifiable behavior blurs in this bittersweet tale of a lonely, kooky college girl who draws a quiet young man into her orbit. With a nice New England autumnal look, this drama of young love starts out sweet before eventually descending into painful melancholy.
D: Alan J. Pakula. A: Liza Minnelli, Wendell Burton, Tim McIntire.

I Never Sang for My Father
(1970) 93m. **B**
An elderly father rejects help from all, but still demands devotion from his son who is trying to break free from his grip. A prickly Douglas and earnest Hackman make this drama worthwhile, in their portrayal of two people facing the uncomfortable truth that they will never be able to solve their problems.
D: Gilbert Cates. A: Melvyn Douglas, Gene Hackman, Estelle Parsons.

Butterflies Are Free
(1972) 109m. **B–**
A young blind man's life opens up when a struggling actress moves into the apartment next door, but trouble starts when his possessive mother gets wind of it. A bright, fluttery, and stage-bound drama that's dripping with a 60s free-spirited atmosphere.
D: Milton Katselas. A: Goldie Hawn, Edward Albert, Eileen Heckart.

The King of Marvin Gardens
(1972) 104m. **B–**
After a radio talk-show host helps bail out his small-time operator brother from an Atlantic City jail, the fast-talking sibling and ex-beauty queen girlfriend proceed to hustle their grand plans for a Hawaiian gambling joint. A quirky and overripe tale about losers with a slightly dreary Nicholson letting Dern chew the tacky scenery.
D: Bob Rafelson. A: Jack Nicholson, Bruce Dern, Ellen Burstyn.

Cinderella Liberty
(1973) 117m. **A–**
A barmaid/hooker in Seattle takes up with an amiable soldier, who still has problems coping with her young son by a black sailor. A gritty, appealing, and almost neorealistic look at two luckless losers willing to make a go of things.
D: Mark Rydell. A: Marsha Mason, James Caan, Eli Wallach.

Alice Doesn't Live Here Anymore
(1975) 113m. **A–**
A youngish widow with a wiseacre son heads for the coast to pursue her singing, takes a few detours, and winds up waitressing in an Arizona diner. Burstyn helps make this one of the livelier studies of women starting new lives, along with the colorful crew of funny and bittersweet characters.
D: Martin Scorsese. A: Ellen Burstyn, Kris Kristofferson, Alfred Lutter.

One Flew Over the Cuckoo's Nest
(1975) 133m. **A–**
A prisoner gets out of work detail by faking insanity and is sent to an asylum where head nurse rules with an iron fist. Jack's infectious anarchic spirit inspires the other "loonies" in this intelligent, funny, but uncomfortably depressing horror story that gets a full-blown, gothic performance by Fletcher as Nurse Ratched.
D: Milos Forman. A: Jack Nicholson, Louise Fletcher, Brad Dourif.

The Sailor Who Fell from Grace with the Sea
(1976) 104m. **B–**
A young widow takes up with a ship's captain in a small English coastal town; unfortunately her son sees this as a blot on the purity of his and his mother's nature. A romantic, rambling, and gothic tale, complete with ocean views and steamy sex scenes.
D: Lewis John Carlino. A: Sarah Miles, Kris Kristofferson, Jonathan Kahn.

Bloodbrothers
(1978) 120m. **C+**
A sensitive son struggles to break free of his unhappy father's and boozy uncle's need to control him. Another family in denial, this time an Italian-American one, with lots of shouting and shoving and a little too much pouting from Gere.
D: Robert Mulligan. A: Richard Gere, Paul Sorvino, Tony Lo Bianco.

The Electric Horseman
(1979) 120m. **B**
A recovering alcoholic rodeo star becomes a cereal company's neon, cowboy-suited spokesman and then discovers they're drugging the horse for his Las Vegas show. A bittersweet character study and slightly inflated tale of crass commercialism that's run to ground by rugged individualism.
D: Sydney Pollack. A: Robert Redford, Jane Fonda, Valerie Perrine.

Wise Blood
(1979) 108m. **B+**
A young evangelist preaching a personal style of down-home religion meets up with a phony blind man who's pushing his own brand of atonement. Dourif strikes an eerie note with Stanton right behind him in this sad, funny, and touching piece of Southern gothic masterfully directed by Huston.
D: John Huston. A: Brad Dourif, Ned Beatty, Harry Dean Stanton.

Americana

The American West, McCarthyism, immigrants, and Depression-era robbers: all part of American mythology and, beginning in the late 60s, no longer whitewashed on film as can be seen with these dead-eyed and humorous tales of life in the United States.

The Last Picture Show
(1971) 118m. B&W.
A–
Two friends in the early 50s spend their spare time shooting pool, putting the moves on the local girls, and dreaming of breaking out of their dusty dying Texas town. With unerring portrayals of the townspeople, this stunningly photographed coming-of-age film remains bleakly fascinating.
D: Peter Bogdanovich. A: Timothy Bottoms, Jeff Bridges, Cybill Shepherd.

Thieves Like Us
(1974) 123m. **B+**
A young murderer who escapes from a Mississippi prison with two older cons hooks up with his girlfriend, and the foursome begin a chain of clumsy bank robberies. Altman's Depression-era bandit-lovers story is lush and languid but always seems about to disappear into complete aimlessness.
D: Robert Altman. A: Keith Carradine, Shelley Duvall, John Schuck.

Hester Street
(1975) 92m. B&W **B**
A Jewish immigrant establishes himself in New York

City and is embarrassed by his newly arrived wife's old-world ways. A sweet, well-crafted, and slyly feminist tale with meticulously re-created scenes of turn-of-the-century Lower East Side and an old, black-and-white silent film look that matches the story.
D: Joan Micklin Silver. A: Steven Keats, Carol Kane, Mel Howard.

Nashville
(1975) 159m. **A**
Robert Altman's dazzling and daring ensemble piece follows all the country music stars, hopefuls, and hangers-on who converge and intersect in Nashville during a political concert. This kaleidoscope of memorable characters keeps its enormous weight aloft by seamlessly slipping from ridiculous moments of hilarity to sobering tragedy without missing a beat.
D: Robert Altman. A: Henry Gibson, Karen Black, Ronee Blakley.

The Front
(1976) 94m. **B**
A group of blacklisted writers during the McCarthy era uses the name of a bumbling cashier on their scripts so they can continue to work. Woody plays a variation of his nebbish schnook in this beautifully shot comedy/drama that veers between wacky satire and heavy-duty social drama.
D: Martin Ritt. A: Woody Allen, Zero Mostel, Andrea Marcovicci.

Bio-Pics

These 70s big screen biographies were as divided as the times, giving us portraits of military heroes and anti-establishment performers.

Patton
(1970) 169m. **B+**
In this broadly entertaining bio-pic of the outspoken general who defeated Rommel in northern Africa, Scott sends the decibel level over the scale with his ferocious inspirational speeches about discipline and love of Uncle Sam. The magnificent battle scenes give some breathing space to a tense portrait of a relentless man.
D: Franklin Schaffner. A: George C. Scott, Karl Malden, Stephen Young.

Lenny
(1974) 112m. B&W.
A–
Dustin is harrowingly on target as the brilliant anarchic comic Lenny Bruce who dazzles and shocks audiences but fails to charm law enforcers with his foul mouthed humor. This stylized bio-pic offers a smoky jazz score, a cool cinematography, and attitude galore to capture a jittery paranoid 50s feel.
D: Bob Fosse. A: Dustin Hoffman, Valerie Perrine, Jan Miner.

Bound for Glory
(1976) 147m. **B–**
This stylish and evocative bio-pic follows Woodie Guthrie from dust bowl beginnings during the Depression to singer-songwriter whose controversial and uncompromising songs made him a beacon for the common man and underdog. As wholesome as Johnny Appleseed and more than a little bland.
D. Hal Ashby. A: David Carradine, Ronny Cox, Melinda Dillon.

MacArthur
(1977) 130m. **B–**
Beginning in the Philippines in 1942, General MacArthur builds his reputation as one of America's top military strategists into near myth during World War II and the Korean War. A wooden Peck hams and haws away, unsuccessfully trying to evoke the old lion's blustery aura in this otherwise passably entertaining war saga.
D: Joseph Sargent. A: Gregory Peck, Dan O'Herlihy, Ed Flanders

Road Films

Inspired by *Thelma and Louise* and horrified by *Natural Born Killers*? Then take a look at some of the prime examples of 1970s buddy, road, and lovers-on-the-lam films that feature the alienated or angry souls who are literally lost in America.

The Rain People
(1969) 102m. **B–**
A young woman discovers she's pregnant, leaves her husband, and picks up an ex-college football star who's mentally impaired and sticks to her like glue. The characters and episodes in this depressing road film ring true, with more raw and painful moments than bright ones.
D: Francis Ford Coppola. A: James Caan, Shirley Knight, Robert Duvall.

Badlands
(1973) 95m. **A–**
A self-styled James Dean clone knocks off the disapproving dad of his underage honey and together they go on a killing spree on the highways of South Dakota. This remains one of the more haunting of the lovers-on-the-lam films with Sheen and Spacek completely chilling as they coolly blow innocent people away.
D: Terrence Malick. A: Martin Sheen, Sissy Spacek, Warren Oates.

The Last Detail
(1973) 105m. **B+**
Two midshipmen escorting a sailor on his way to serving time decide to take a few detours on the way to the prison. Nicholson and Company make friends with religious fanatics, visit a house of ill-repute, and generally give the lad the time of his life in this funny tale that's peppered with enough obscenities to make a sailor blush.
D: Hal Ashby. A: Jack Nicholson, Otis Young, Randy Quaid.

Scarecrow
(1973) 115m. **B**
A blustery middle-aged man straight from San Quentin hooks up with a quiet drifter, and the two of them travel to Pittsburgh where the ex-con hopes to open a car wash. A rather lugubrious buddy road film even with the free-

wheeling Hackman trying to show a morose Pacino a good time.
D: Jerry Schatzberg. A: Gene Hackman, Al Pacino, Dorothy Tristan.

Harry and Tonto
(1974) 115m. **A–**
An aging ex-college professor is forced out of his New York apartment and hits the road with his cat Tonto to visit his daughter and an old beau who can't remember his name. Disappointment seems to greet him at every stop but Harry still finds reason to smile in this funny, tender, and heartbreaking tale.
D: Paul Mazursky. A: Art Carney, Ellen Burstyn, Geraldine Fitzgerald.

The Sugarland Express
(1974) 109m. **B+**
When a young wife learns her infant is to be put in a foster family, she springs her husband from jail and, with a kidnapped state trooper in tow, the pair blazes a trail across Texas to save their boy. Excitable Goldie lends some surprising gravity to this fast-paced, true-life outlaw couple tale.
D: Steven Spielberg. A: Goldie Hawn, Ben Johnson, Michael Sacks.

Early Scorsese

Long considered one of America's finest directors with more recent films as diverse as *Cape Fear* and *The Age of Innocence*, here we see the early films that embody the essence of Martin Scorsese's work. Never straying too far from Little Italy's (or at least Manhattan's) streets, these films range from intimate neighborhood portraits to terrifying urban classics like *Taxi Driver* that defy classification.

Who's That Knocking at My Door?
(1968) 90m. B&W. **B+**
In Manhattan's Little Italy, Keitel has his safe, hangin'-with-the-boys life shattered when he falls for a free-spirited college woman. Love, sex, and Catholicism all get a going over in this gritty early Scorsese outing, filled with his trademark profane language, jittery camerawork, and conscience-obsessed characters.
D: Martin Scorsese. A: Zina Bethune, Harvey Keitel, Anna Collete.

Mean Streets
(1973) 110m. **A–**
This slice of life in Little Italy follows some homeboys as they hang out, shoot pool, and aspire to be grander hoods than they are. Another low-budget, early effort has all the flavor, humor, and nervous energy of the neighborhood and its characters, embodied by a raw-edged Keitel and De Niro.
D: Martin Scorsese. A: Harvey Keitel, Robert De Niro, David Proval.

Taxi Driver
(1976) 113m. **A**
Travis Bickle drives a taxi and watches his own personal demons find human faces on the pimps, thugs, and assorted scum of New York City. This spooky and heartbreaking look at the loneliness and madness of the city still wields tremendous power with a "redemption" finale that will blow you away.
D: Martin Scorsese. A: Robert De Niro, Cybill Shepherd, Jodie Foster.

The King of Comedy
(1983) 109m. **B+**
A talentless nobody aspires to stand-up comic fame, even if it means kidnapping a famous late-night TV host. Shot much in the style of the medium it lampoons, this is an alternately funny, uncomfortable, and terrifying look at media-madness and celebrity-stalking with an amazingly low-keyed Lewis as a cynical star.
D: Martin Scorsese. A: Robert De Niro, Jerry Lewis, Sandra Bernhard.

1980s

Irish Dramas

This group of small films offers a painless lesson on the conflicts that have fueled the strife in Ireland for the last 800 or so years. With their down-on-their luck dreamers, outspoken families, and impoverished farmers these dramas point up the difficulties of the working-class Irish to lay claim to power and land in their own country.

Danny Boy
(1982) 92m. **C–**
Disappointment and limitation loom over this story of a saxophone player who witnesses the double murder of his manager and a fan, and takes systematic revenge. Pretentious and depressing in a lounge-act way.
D: Neil Jordan. A: Stephen Rea, Donal McCann, Alan Devlin.

Cal
(1984) 104m. **A–**
An aimless young man inadvertently becomes an accessory to a murder in Belfast and then finds himself drawn to the victim's 30ish widow. Melancholy, even desperate at times, with a tender Mirren and tormented Lynch.
D: Pat O'Connor. A: Helen Mirren, John Lynch, Donal McCann.

The Dead
(1987) 83m. **B**
A couple in a dead marriage attends an annual holiday party whose banal chatter feels to them like a glaze over the drab crashing insignificance of life. The melancholy musings about life by the fine Irish actors in this small, two-set drama make it an intimate and rewarding experience.
D: John Huston. A: Anjelica

Huston, Donal McCann, Helena Carroll.

The Lonely Passion of Judith Hearne
(1987) 120m. **B**
When an aging Irish spinster, who has found solace in alcohol and the Catholic Church, moves into a new Dublin rooming house, she believes that the attentions from a brash American-Irishman are romantic and not economic. Downbeat story with great acting.
D: Jack Clayton. A: Maggie Smith, Bob Hoskins, Wendy Hiller.

My Left Foot
(1989) 103m. **A**
The true life story of Christy Brown who, despite total paralysis except for his left foot, became a poet, painter, and writer. With boozing ribald Brown wheedling drinks and directing barbs to all, this is no tale of a handicapped plaster saint but a loving, boisterous, and often funny portrait of Irish family life and a man who lives his life to the hilt.
D: Jim Sheridan. A: Daniel Day-Lewis, Brenda Fricker, Ray McAnally.

The Field
(1990) 113m. **B+**
When a widow auctions off a field that has been rented for years to a local farmer, an American buys it. Harris takes this film by storm as the misguided stubborn peasant in the 1930s, whose determination to control his family and surroundings has tragic consequences.
D: Jim Sheridan. A: Richard Harris, John Hurt, Brenda Fricker.

Hidden Agenda
(1990) 108m. **B**
A political thriller with an almost documentary feel details an investigation into the murder of an American human rights activist in Belfast. A complex, well-acted story that's menacing and oppressive.
D: Ken Loach. A: Frances McDormand, Brad Dourif, Mai Zetterling.

The Miracle
(1990) 97m. **B–**
A singer comes to a small seaside town near Dublin, and the teenage musician who's attracted to her ends up losing his innocence in an unexpected way. A sweet melancholy tale.
D: Neil Jordan. A: Donal McCann, Beverly D'Angelo, Niall Byrne.

In the Name of the Father
(1993) 125m. **A**
True-life tale of a footloose Irish youth in 60s London who, along with his father, is corralled into a trumped-up charge of terrorism and subjected to the not-so-tender mercies of the British penal system. Sheer passion powers this, with horrifyingly tight prison scenes, beautifully rendered father-son moments, and uniformly fine acting: a rare film that manages to entertain and enlighten.
D: Jim Sheridan. A: Daniel Day-Lewis, Pete Postlewaite, Emma Thompson.

African Dramas

Though often bleak and tragic, most of these films dealing with the horrors of South African apartheid are stirring testimonies to the endurance of human spirit in the face of political madness.

Cry Freedom
(1987) 157m. **B–**
When activist Steven Biko is silenced by the apartheid government, a liberal journalist undertakes a perilous journey to escape South Africa so he can spread Biko's message. This well-meaning message saga starts out bracingly but waffles in the second half's plodding adventure.
D: Richard Attenborough. A: Kevin Kline, Denzel Washington, Penelope Wilton.

Mandela
(1987) 135m. **B–**
The story of Nelson and Winnie Mandela feels closer to a compilation of highlights, from the founding of the African National Congress to its efforts to overcome the crippling reach of apartheid. Glover is a solid but slightly lifeless Mandela with the only real passion occurring during the trumped-up trial for treason.
D: Philip Saville. A: Danny Glover, Alfre Woodard, Warren Clarke.

A World Apart
(1988) 114m. **B–**
A communist journalist stands up to the apartheid government and becomes the first woman arrested in the 90-day detention act of 1963. Glamorous Hershey is never too believable as the feminist who sacrifices all for her ideals in this exciting but sanctimonious political drama.
D: Chris Menges. A: Barbara Hershey, Jeroen Krabbe, David Suchet.

A Dry White Season
(1989) 106m. **B**
When his black servants begin disappearing and tales of torture are verified, a white South Afrikaner seeks justice. Highly uneven, but still riveting dissection of the madness of apartheid, with a suitable finale and a simply amazing cameo by Brando as a cynical barrister.
D: Euzhan Palcy. A: Donald Sutherland, Jurgen Prochnow, Marlon Brando.

Mister Johnson
(1991) 102m. **B**
When 1920s British colonialists decide to build a road connecting north and south Nigeria, they rely on a local man to serve as liaison; he's so eager to please them that he ends up falling between the two worlds in this brightly filmed, occasionally cute, but satisfying drama.
D: Bruce Beresford. A: Edward Woodward, Pierce Brosnan, Maynard Eziashi.

The Power of One
(1992) 127m. **C–**
An orphaned English South African boy survives the taunts and tortures of the Afrikaners with the help of two mentors, one black, one white. Politically correct but finally corny, feel-good tale that manages to make apartheid seem like an annoying but easily remedied problem.
D: John Avildsen. A: Stephen Dorff, Morgan Freeman, Armin Mueller-Stahl.

(See also *Sarafina!*, page 425.)

British Dramas

As Thatcher's England looked less like the mighty British Empire and more like a melting pot of Pakistanis, punks, and the unemployed, these intimate little dramas often conjure up a period of tumult and ferment whether in the present day or recent past. Some are flamboyant and unpredictable, others are quiet sophisticated character studies, but all are finely crafted with spectacular performances by the new stars of British cinema.

Betrayal
(1983) 95m. **B+**
This film version of a Pinter play of friendship and adultery begins at the end of the love triangle and works its way back to the beginning. A crystal clear uncluttered slide show of adult relations.
D: David Jones. A: Jeremy Irons, Ben Kingsley, Patricia Hodge.

The Dresser
(1983) 119m. **B+**
Finney is the vain older actor on the decline. Courtney, his dresser, lives through his performances and is the only person who can manage him. This two-man play may take place in the 1940s, but they already feel like the sad brave relics of a fading empire.
D: Peter Yates. A: Tom Courtenay, Albert Finney, Edward Fox.

The Ploughman's Lunch
(1984) 100m. **B**
A ruthless BBC radio newsman makes his ascent into conservative politics in 1980s England. Snappy script, London locations, and the atmosphere of the newsroom in *All the President's Men* give this zing, along with a despicably fascinating Pryce.
D: Richard Eyre. A: Jonathan Pryce, Tim Curry, Rosemary Harris.

Dance With a Stranger
(1985) 101m. **B**
A riveting tale of the obsessive relationship between a bar hostess and her upper-class younger lover. Based on the true story of Ruth Ellis, the last woman executed in England, it depicts a narrow world of 1950s London that's so joyless and grainy this color film almost looks black and white.
D: Mike Newell. A: Miranda Richardson, Rupert Everett, Ian Holm.

My Beautiful Laundrette
(1985) 94m. **A**
Brash and funny tale of a Pakistani and a punk who run a successful laundromat and become lovers. The squalor and vitality of "little guys" scratching to get by in Thatcher's England get a warm and humorous treatment, thanks to a witty script and great performances.
D: Stephen Frears. A: Daniel Day-Lewis, Saeed Jaffrey, Roshan Seth.

Plenty
(1985) 119m. **B+**
After assisting in the French Resistance, a British woman finds nothing in her life that can possibly measure up. An intelligent and spirited drama that provides an elegant diorama of the changes in Britain during the 20 years after the war.
D: Fred Schepisi. A: Meryl Streep, Charles Dance, Tracey Ullman.

Wetherby
(1985) 104m. **C+**
When an uninvited man shows up at a schoolteacher's home in the English countryside, her hospitality is repaid when he shoots himself in her kitchen. Mother/daughter team Redgrave and Richardson, who play the same schoolteacher in present and past, make this dour and often pretentious film worth watching.
D: David Hare. A: Vanessa Redgrave, Joely Richardson, Ian Holm.

Prick Up Your Ears
(1987) 111m. **B+**
What happens when your mentor becomes a millstone around your neck? This sharp and exuberant portrait of playwright Joe Orton's abbreviated life and relationship with his gay lover has scintillating wordplay and mesmerizing performances.
D: Stephen Frears. A: Gary Oldman, Alfred Molina, Vanessa Redgrave.

The Raggedy Rawney
(1988) 102m. **B–**
Shell-shocked World War I veteran goes AWOL and disguises himself as a woman when he falls in with a band of English gypsies. Small sweet fable about war and identity.
D: Bob Hoskins. A: Dexter Fletcher, Bob Hoskins, Zoe Nathenson.

Queen of Hearts
(1989) 112m. **B**
There are hints of magical realism in this charming and humorous story of an Anglo-Italian family that runs a cafe in London. As seen through the young son's eyes, you get a rich sense of family, neighborhood, and the silliness and passions of adults.
D: Jon Amiel. A: Victoria Duse, Anita Zagaria, Joseph Long.

Scandal
(1989) 105m. **B+**
Lively depiction of the famous Profumo sex scandal of the 1960s, in which a socialite doctor set up a cabinet minister with a showgirl and then watched as the fireworks exploded. Beautifully captures the mod period detail and the decadence of London's demimonde.
D: Michael Caton-Jones. A: Joanne Whalley-Kilmer, John Hurt, Bridget Fonda.

(See also *Sid and Nancy,* page 227.)

White Flannel

Welcome to the glory days of the British Empire when the ruling class rode horses on their country estates, servants were in plentiful supply, and only an adulterous lover questioned the status quo. As in other costume dramas, the period details are celebrations of all that was brilliant and luxurious, with the camera sweeping over British, Indian, or African countryscapes and exquisite turn-of-the-century interiors. But all this lush upholstery

doesn't cover up the intelligent, thoughtful stories—usually based on Lawrence, Forster, and Waugh novels—played by stellar British actors.

Chariots of Fire
(1981) 124m. **A**

A portrait of the lovely young men before and during their competition in the 1924 Olympics. Country estates, lush Scottish hills, and Oxford are the backgrounds for this uplifting tale of gentlemanly sportsmanship. Features stirring music and snobbish values.
D: Hugh Hudson. A: Ben Cross, Ian Charleson, Nigel Havers.

Quartet
(1981) 101m. **B**

With her husband in prison, a young woman is adopted by a bohemian couple whose male half promptly seduces her. Elegant and somewhat slow tale of decadence and exploitation that evokes Paris in the 1920s.
D: James Ivory. A: Maggie Smith, Alan Bates, Isabelle Adjani.

Heat and Dust
(1983) 130m. **B+**

Researching her great-aunt's life in the 1920s, a present-day Englishwoman is drawn to India where she relives her aunt's adventures, including an illicit love affair. Gentle, almost fairy-tale-like with its time jumps, but the story gets a bit lost in the haze.
D: James Ivory. A: Julie Christie, Greta Scacchi, Julian Glover.

Another Country
(1984) 90m. **B+**

School friends in the 1930s were found out 20 years later to be homosexuals and Russian spies. Based on a true story that still resonates in Britain, where this play was a huge hit, its tense oppressive atmosphere can make you feel as hemmed in as the characters.
D: Marek Kanievska. A: Colin Firth, Michael Jenn, Robert Addie.

The Bostonians
(1984) 120m. **C+**

A Southern gentleman and a nineteenth-century feminist Bostonian all but come to blows over a naive young woman from England; he wants to marry her, she wants to challenge and free her. Great acting but a pokey script makes this slow going.
D: James Ivory. A: Christopher Reeve, Vanessa Redgrave, Madeleine Potter.

Greystoke: The Legend of Tarzan, Lord of the Apes
(1984) 130m. **B**

Lushly told tale of an odd twist in empire building. The first half takes place in an African jungle where heir to a British earl has been raised by apes. The second half is at the Scottish estate where natural man Tarzan is being housebroken to take his rightful place among the gentry, their servants, and beautiful female cousins.
D: Hugh Hudson. A: Christopher Lambert, Ian Holm, Andie MacDowell.

A Passage to India
(1984) 163m. **A**

This epic of British-occupied India mixes all the pomp and circumstance with mysterious startling landscapes and a shrewd story of sexual hysteria among the buttoned-down ruling class. It's not exactly the Forster book, but the cast plays each complex emotional note with superb assurance.
D: David Lean. A: Judy Davis, Peggy Ashcroft, Victor Benerjee.

The Shooting Party
(1984) 97m. **A–**

On the eve of World War I the landed gentry enjoys a weekend party at a country estate. They all hunt, play billiards, and eat elaborate meals until violence rears its ugly head and pierces their complacency. Gorgeous, melancholy, and mannered.
D: Alan Bridges. A: James Mason, Edward Fox, Dorothy Tutin.

Out of Africa
(1985) 161m. **B+**

Aerial shots of zebra herds, African plains, and colonial polo fields form the background for this whitewashed epic version of writer Isak Dinesen's life in Africa, and her affair with an airplane-flying Great White Hunter. Grand entertainment with characters and plot secondary to the handsome look.
D: Sidney Pollack. A: Meryl Streep, Robert Redford, Klaus Maria Brandauer.

The Return of the Soldier
(1985) 101m. **B–**

Shell-shocked World War II survivor can't recall that he's married, and his former sweetheart and a lonely spinster are only too ready to accommodate him. Uninteresting drama with a hero who is perplexed while the viewer is not.
D: Alan Bridges. A: Julie Christie, Alan Bates, Glenda Jackson.

A Room with a View
(1986) 117m. **A+**

During and after her visit to Florence, a young Edwardian woman is sexually and emotionally awakened. Sparkling, honey-colored comedy of manners where all the characters are lovely, funny, and blessed with grace.
D: James Ivory. A: Helena Bonham Carter, Julian Sands, Daniel Day-Lewis.

Maurice
(1987) 139m. **B–**

Melancholy story of star-crossed love between two young men from different classes. Scenes amidst Edwardian splendor are colored by a sadness and nostalgia for paradise lost.
D: James Ivory. A: James Wilby, Rupert Graves, Hugh Grant.

A Month in the Country
(1987) 92m. **B–**

Shell-shocked World War I veteran makes his way to a small town in Yorkshire where he finds unexpected comfort and meaning by helping with the restoration of a church mural. Beautifully shot, but the drama gets locked in by the reserved tone.
D: Pat O'Connor. A: Colin Firth, Kenneth Branagh, Natasha Richardson.

White Mischief
(1987) 107m. **B**

This tale of passion and murder is the flip side of *Out of Africa*'s picture postcard view of British colonials. These self-imposed exiles engage in a dissolute life of alcohol, drugs, and sexual excess with aristocratic grace and ennui. Slow, nice-looking, but a little heavy-handed with the drama and metaphors.
D: Michael Radford. A: Greta Scacchi, Charles Dance, John Hurt.

A Handful of Dust
(1988) 118m. **B**

Tale of a foundering marriage and how aristocrats coped with the unanchored morals and changing post-World War I society. This slightly out of focus story is pulled along by a sense of doom and has a killer ending.
D: Charles Sturridge. A: Anjelica Huston, James Wilby, Kristin Scott Thomas.

Mr. North
(1988) 90m. **B**
Newport, Rhode Island, in the 20s is the setting for this sweet tale of a new-to-town tutor who appears to have the magic touch of healing. Light-hearted performances along with lovely art direction and locale shooting mix to create a magical realism to this entertainingly unusual tale.
D: Danny Huston. A: Anthony Edwards, Roert Mitchum, Harry Dean Stanton.

Mike Leigh

Leigh's intimate seriocomic ensemble pieces sweep you into the social turmoil of present-day England with stories that follow unpredictable and sometimes outrageous paths. Thanks to characters who reveal a complexity rare in modern cinema, these films shift from uncomfortable to enthralling, hilarious to grim, and have all the immediacy of home movies.

Nuts in May
(1976) 84m. **B**
A vehemently vegetarian and environmentally correct couple goes on a vacation where they try to make converts of their fellow campers. Trouble erupts when the woman becomes friendly with one of the male campers. Uneven but peppered with outrageously funny epithets against the ills of modern society.
D: Mike Leigh. A: Alison Steadman, Anthony O'Donnell, Roger Sloman.

Abigail's Party
(1977) 105m. **B+**
The hostess of this party is a battleship of a woman out to control the evening's events: As she plies her guests with drink, they squirm, squabble, and expose their hopeless frustrations. Devised with the control and stylization of a play, the camera prowls the sidelines, revealing through small gestures and details the narrowness and misery of the guests' lives.
D: Mike Leigh. A: Alison Steadman, Tim Stern, Janine Juvitski.

Who's Who
(1978) 75m. **B+**
A look at the different lives of members of a small brokerage firm in London, including the Oxford-educated, casually cruel brokers and the nobility-obsessed clerks. Wickedly funny, with touches of meanness, especially in its unflattering depiction of the upper classes.
D: Mike Leigh. A: Bridget Kane, Adam Norton, Simon Chandler.

Four Days in July
(1984) 99m. **B**
Gripped by the "Troubles" of British-occupied Belfast, two families divided by religion and politics deal with the war in poignantly similar and different ways. It's worth the effort to get used to the thick accents in this unsparing intimate vision of everyday people gone mad with hatred from centuries-old imperialism.
D: Mike Leigh. A: Brid Brennan, Desmond McAleer, Charles Lawson.

High Hopes
(1988) 110m. **A–**
Clinging to Marxism and hippiedom, a couple tries to navigate Thatcher's England and decide whether to have a baby. A sweet and caustic family tale of misunderstandings and frustrations gleefully exposed as the couple encounters a sampling of the new England via their friends and relatives.
D: Mike Leigh. A: Philip Davis, Ruth Sheen.

Life Is Sweet
(1991) 102m. **A**
The parents and young adult twin daughters of this suburban family seem content to pursue the oddest of goals, seemingly oblivious to the gut-wrenching and hilarious results. A joyful celebration of an unusual and very recognizable household, filled with intoxicating sights and priceless moments.
D: Mike Leigh. A: Alison Steadman, Jim Broadbent, Jane Horrocks.

Naked
(1993) 126m. **A**
Once this sharp-tongued, sadistic young man gets back together with his old girlfriend, he proceeds to seduce her roommate and abuse several other women. The camera never flinches, though the viewer may, in this brutal and mesmerizing tale that drags us through a stained world filled with lost and aimless people.
D: Mike Leigh. A: David Thewlis, Lesley Sharp, Katrin Cartlidge.

Other Titles:
Kiss of Death (1977)
Grown Ups (1980)
Home Sweet Home (1982)

Foreign Costume Epics

Steamy affairs, suicide, madness, and salvation: pretty heady stuff for films based on literary or historical sources. Something happens when this genre hits foreign soil, and these star-studded, beautifully produced extravaganzas always offer plenty to charm and titillate along with their very adult psychodramas.

Caligula
(1980) 156m. (hardcore)/ 105m. **D**
The story follows the ascent of Caligula to the emperorship of Rome, his descent into sexual depravity, relentless torture, and Rome's social disintegration. Scenes of graphic rape, disembowelment, castration, and more. An utterly repugnant film that fails as history, drama, and even exploitation.
D: Tinto Brass. A: Malcolm McDowell, Teresa Ann Savoy, John Gielgud.

The French Lieutenant's Woman
(1981) 124m. **B+**
The story of a mysterious fallen woman who is pursued by a proper Victorian

gentleman is counterposed against the modern actors playing these roles in a film, and carrying on an affair of their own. The ashen modern reality will make you long for the brilliantly atmospheric past in this acting tour de force that still leaves you cold.
D: Karel Reisz. A: Meryl Streep, Jeremy Irons, Emily Morgan.

Amadeus
(1984) 158m. **A**
Court composer and second-rate talent Salieri plots the ruin of silly, improvident, girl-happy Mozart. This exuberantly witty and operatically study of a proud and pious man vs. a hilariously flawed genius has all the glitter of court life and opera halls.
D: Milos Forman. A: F. Murray Abraham, Tom Hulce, Elizabeth Berridge.

Beethoven's Nephew
(1985) 103m. **C–**
A cold, costume-rich study of the fading obsessive composer and his hovering influence on his beautiful and introspective nephew. Dramatic German scenery, clumsy avant-garde camerawork, and too many close-ups with telling expressions that have no readable meaning make this a tedious and arty entry.
D: Paul Morrissey. A: Ditmar Prinz, Jane Birkin, Wolfgang Reichmann.

King David
(1985) 114m. **D**
A realistic ancient Israel is the background for Gere's squinty-eyed muttering portrayal of the man who beat Goliath, rose to military heights, and fell for Bathsheba. David's unconsciously funny victory prance through Jerusalem clad only in his loincloth is one of many blunders.
D: Bruce Beresford. A: Richard Gere, Alice Krige, Hurd Hatfield.

Mishima: A Life in Four Chapters
(1985) 121m. **B+**
The life of Japan's most successful and prolific twentieth-century writer is explored via flashbacks from childhood to his death by ritual suicide, along with beautifully stylized dramatizations of his choice works. As much a multilayered psychosexual drama as bio-pic, this may be cryptic to nonfans but the images will still dazzle you.
D: Paul Schrader. A: Ken Ogata, Kenji Sawada, Yasosuke Bando.

Kangaroo
(1986) 105m. **B**
Based on a D. H. Lawrence, semiautobiographical story, this follows an English writer and wife living in Australia's outback and their brush with the charismatic leader of a secret fascist cult. An intriguing tale with sensual undercurrents, but the languid pace and wordiness drag it down.
D: Tim Burstall. A: Colin Friels, Judy Davis, John Walton.

The Last Temptation of Christ
(1986) 164m.
A–
This provocative account of Christ's life remains faithful to biblical events in a suitably sun-bleached Holy landscape and then explores the notion that Jesus was a self-doubter with human desires. Burning performances, haunting score, and one of the most harrowing re-creations of the crucifixion help make this an intense viewing experience.
D: Martin Scorsese. A: Willem Dafoe, Harvey Keitel, Barbara Hershey.

The Name of the Rose
(1986) 130m. **C+**
English monk William of Baskerville investigates a series of murders at an Italian monastery in the fourteenth century while dealing with the fire and brimstone theatrics of a grand inquisitor. A murky and exasperating mystery with ambiance, dramatic visuals, and running time to spare, but no coherent story to keep your interest.
D: Jean-Jacques Annaud. A: Sean Connery, F. Murray Abraham, Christian Slater.

The Last Emperor
(1987) 160m. **A–**
A strange and engrossing review of the life of Pu Yi from his pampered days as child Emperor of China, to his capture by various factions. A colorful spectacle of the rituals of court life in the Forbidden City and poignant study of a passive little man who can never find simple peace.
D: Bernardo Bertolucci. A: John Lone, Joan Chen, Victor Wong.

Haunted Summer
(1988) 106m. **C+**
Byron, his lover, and the Shelleys gather for summertime frolics and ghost storying in a Swiss villa. Garden walks, sexual experimentation, and dinnertime debates about art, poetry, and drugs may not convince you that these young people wrote some classics.
D: Ivan Passer. A: Alice Krige, Eric Stoltz, Laura Dern.

Dangerous Liaisons
(1989) 120m. **A**
Two bored, unscrupulous, and very persuasive French aristocrats in the late 1700s devise a titillating game of seduction and emotional one-upmanship. A joy to watch with opulent trappings and scintillating performances with Close as the cold-hearted spiderwoman and Malkovich as the fey snakish ladykiller.
D: Stephen Frears. A: Glenn Close, John Malkovich, Michelle Pfeiffer.

Valmont
(1989) 137m. **B–**
Another version of *Dangerous Liaisons* with less bite and cynicism, and with the younger generation having more frolicsome fun bedhopping and less delicious delight in power. A richer pageant of gowns, mansions, and period detail but too long and too light.
D: Milos Forman. A: Colin Firth, Annette Bening, Meg Tilly.

Derek Jarman

Frank homosexual themes, mordant humor about England and its decline, striking and often surreal images, along with a provocative and intensely personal vision are what you'll find here. Jarman's work betrays his art and literary backgrounds: He often plays with voice-over readings rather than dialogue, and uses deliberately alienating images and odd sequences whose meaning you may have to work at to discover.

Jubilee
(1978) 105m. **B–**

A science fiction view of post-Thatcher England that takes the punk movement to its logical extreme: Imagine if everyone were a terrorist. Terrifying, horrific, and sometimes affecting, this largely unsuccessful effort is for hard-core fans.
D: Derek Jarman. A: Jenny Runacre, Little Nell, Adam Ant.

Angelic Conversation
(1985) 80m. **C–**

Accompanied by voice-over readings of Shakespearean sonnets, this story of one man's odyssey to find his spiritual self has an occasionally arresting image, but is generally self-indulgent, long-winded, and annoying.
D: Derek Jarman. A: Paul Reynolds, Phillip Williamson, Judi Dench.

Caravaggio
(1986) 97m. **A**

An attempt to look at an artist from the inside out, based on the life of the seventeenth-century painter. Full of images taken directly from Caravaggio's paintings and using his homosexuality as a central theme, it's oddly distanced and intimate at the same time, and very modern despite the period detail.
D: Derek Jarman. A: Nigel Terry, Sean Bean, Spencer Leigh.

The Last of England
(1987) 87m. **A**

An unforgettable collage of images from twentieth-century British history as shown through home movies, Super 8 films, and gay-themed erotica. Image and sound have rarely been interwoven so gracefully as in this look at the destruction, anger, and waste of post-Thatcher England.
D: Derek Jarman. A: Tilda Swinton, Spencer Leigh.

War Requiem
(1988) 92m. **A**

A stirring antiwar document that shows warfare from the perspectives of the largely powerless—foot soldiers, nurses, and children. Using stock footage mixed with new actors who are silent and a narration consisting of Wilfred Owen's poetry, this manages to get its truisms across with a blunt freshness.
D: Derek Jarman. A: Laurence Olivier, Tilda Swinton, Owen Teale.

Edward II
(1991) 90m. **A–**

Using Marlowe's seventeenth-century play as the structure, this film traces the collapse of Britain's openly homosexual king. The actors use the Elizabethan dialogue of the play, but appear in modern-day dress in this brash and noisy film that still elegantly conveys political and social problems.
D: Derek Jarman. A: Tilda Swinton, Steven Waddington, Andrew Tiernan.

Ken Russell

Strange hallucinogenic images, sexual hysteria, pop stars flying into space in phallic starships: Few filmmakers can compete with Ken Russell for cinematic excesses. Outside of his two jarring sexual odysseys, *Crimes of Passion* and *Whore*, these costume dramas and bio-pics look like Merchant-Ivory films gone colorfully mad as they tell their frenetic tales of artists and demimondaines. Alternately brilliant, campy, or just plain ridiculous, these films will do anything to push your buttons.

The Music Lovers
(1970) 123m. **C+**

The worst of Russell's visionary flourishes outweighs the giddy ride of czarist Russia that we get in this biography of Tchaikovsky. Chamberlain seems lightweight to play the tortured homosexual composer while Jackson is unnervingly, unerringly distasteful as his sexually rapacious wife.
D: Ken Russell. A: Richard Chamberlain, Glenda Jackson, Max Adrian.

Women in Love
(1970) 129m. **A–**

Two unconventional Edwardian-era sisters from the coal mining Midlands pair off with two male friends, all exploring love, sexuality, and friendship. The arch and pithy dialogues, deft performances, and some gloriously erotic confrontations—both hetero and homosexual—make this one of Russell's loveliest and most accessible works.
D: Ken Russell. A: Alan Bates, Oliver Reed, Glenda Jackson.

The Devils
(1971) 109m. **A**

When a French parish priest/village lothario ignores the sexually repressed humpbacked Mother Superior, she and her entire convent of nuns decide he's a devil who's possessing them. A Hieronymus Bosch canvas, full of brutal, bizarre, and beautiful images of medieval madness.
D: Ken Russell. A: Oliver Reed, Vanessa Redgrave, Gemma Jones.

Mahler
(1974) 110m. **B–**

The most measured of Russell's classical composer biographies offers another portrait of a tortured man, this time by anti-Semitism, the pains of the creative process, and a wife who inspires love and paranoia. Lovely music, an opulent fading turn-of-the-century Vienna, and fewer weird flourishes.
D: Ken Russell. A: Robert Powell, Georgina Hale, Lee Montague.

Lisztomania
(1975) 105m. **D+**

Russell fashions Franz Liszt's life into a rock fantasy and it still manages to be a long dispirited mess that occasionally wakes up: Highlights include Rick Wakeman making a brief musical appearance as Wagner looking like a Nazi-fueled Frankenstein.
D: Ken Russell. A: Roger Daltrey, Sara Kestelman, Ringo Starr.

Valentino
(1977) 127m. **B**

Nureyev embodies divine decadence in his portrayal of the Roaring Twenties love god who is privately muddled about his own sexuality. The gorgeous re-creation of early Hollywood is fun, the story is suitably bizarre, but the reason to watch is Nureyev gustily throwing himself into the sexually hysterical role.
D: Ken Russell. A: Rudolph Nureyev, Michelle Phillips, Leslie Caron.

Crimes of Passion
(1984) 107m. **B**

Turner is a mild-mannered fashion designer during the day; at night she becomes China Blue, prostitute extraordinaire and prey for psycho-priest stalker Perkins. Vintage Russell, which means there's no such thing as overplaying a scene in this gaudy outrageous film.
D: Ken Russell. A: Kathleen Turner, Anthony Perkins, John Laughlin.

Gothic
(1986) 87m. **B**

Poets Byron and Shelley and writer Mary Shelley gather at a Swiss villa that becomes a deranged Romantic-era funhouse where the youths feast, do drugs, have sex, and tell ghost stories. Little plot but a colorful and fascinating stream of bizarre hallucinogenic images.
D: Ken Russell. A: Julian Sands, Natasha Richardson, Gabriel Byrne.

Lair of the White Worm
(1988) 93m. **C+**

A campy, sexy, pseudo-horror story about a gentleman archeologist and the erotic Lady Sylvia who worships and seeks virgins to sacrifice before the giant white worm. An off-center mix of Victorian-style, erotic thriller and flamboyant horror film.
D: Ken Russell. A: Amanda Donohoe, Hugh Grant, Catherine Oxenburg.

Salome's Last Dance
(1988) 113m. **B−**

A bloated debauched Oscar Wilde and his lover Lord Douglas attend a brothel's production of Wilde's forbidden play *Salome*. Despite the ripe opportunities for excess, this dark and often witty effort has fewer flights of fancy, centering more on the broad theatrical posturing of the unusual acting troupe.
D: Ken Russell. A: Glenda Jackson, Nickolas Grace, Stratford Johns.

The Rainbow
(1989) 102m. **A**

This companion piece to *Women in Love* follows the coming-of-age and sexual awakening of a young woman in the 1910s. Like a lush Merchant-Ivory costume drama shot through with untrammeled eroticism, Russell eschews all his flamboyant touches, offering a beautiful, touching, and sensuous story.
D: Ken Russell. A: Sammi Davis, Amanda Donohoe, Glenda Jackson.

Whore
(1991) 92m. **D**

Watch in horrified fascination as Russell talks to the camera, snaps gum, and guides us through her day as an average prostitute. Begins as a sordid docudrama, turns into a violent erotic thriller, and ends as a distasteful buddy film with Russell and a heroic ex-pimp saving the demented day.
D: Ken Russell. A: Theresa Russell, Antonio Fargas, Benjamin Mouton.

See also:
Tommy (1975)
The Boy Friend (1971)

Prison

These close-up character studies focus on the violent, creative, even spiritual ways men deal with life behind bars.

Brubaker
(1980) 132m. **B**

A new warden disguises himself as a prisoner to get a firsthand look at corruption and inhumane treatment. Things get dicey when the financial plug is pulled on his plan and he's stuck "in population." Based on a true story with a pretty brutal first half, the rest of the film is enjoyable, politically correct Redford fare.
D: Stuart Rosenberg. A: Robert Redford, Yaphet Kotto, Jane Alexander.

Fast-Walking
(1982) 115m. **B**

Really strange tale of a pot-smoking, blasé prison guard who suddenly must make a stand when given a very lucrative and very criminal offer. With its loopy plotting, moral lines that are fuzzy or nonexistent, and refreshingly nonjudgmental take on its many characters' actions, this qualifies as a genuine sleeper.
D: James B. Harris. A: James Woods, Tim McIntire, Kay Lenz.

Mrs. Soffel
(1984) 110m. **C+**

A meek, Bible-reading woman very slowly falls for incarcerated Mel and eventually goes along with him in plans for a lumbering prison break. A snow-bound period piece, hobbled with a nonexistent pace and matching chemistry between the leads.
D: Gillian Armstrong. A: Diane Keaton, Mel Gibson, Matthew Modine.

Weeds
(1987) 115m. **B−**

A lifer pens a play, gets a critic's attention, and soon he's out of prison with a traveling troupe of theatrical cons. Nolte is remarkable as the jailbird bard, but the film droops when his less-than-inspired plays get too much screen time.
D: John Hancock. A: Nick Nolte, Rita Taggart, Lane Smith.

The Shawshank Redemption
(1994) 142m. **A**

Inspiring elegiac tale of a man unjustly accused of murder, his confinement in jail, and, even after beatings, sexual abuse, and more, his unbreakable spirit. Uniformly fine performances, lively plotting, and rich burnished photography make this better—and more entertaining—than one would expect.
D: Frank Darabont. A: Tim Robbins, Morgan Freeman, Bob Gunton.

International Political Dramas

Here are some of the human interest stories behind the newspaper headlines of political turmoil in other countries. The main character isn't Rambo, he's a journalist covering the beat in some political flashpoint like Salvador or Beirut, or just a regular Joe caught up in

foreign trouble. These well-crafted dramas are as gripping as any thriller, but as unsettling and unsettled as a blood feud; there are no pat solutions or happy endings here, just the messy and painful loose ends from an unjust or atrocious situation.

Children of Rage

(1975) 106m. **B+**

An Israeli doctor's experience in a Palestinian refugee camp is the core of this blunt unsparing film. It's a little too earnest and well meaning, but the pace is good and the issues important. Not for those who have trouble with blood or shooting.

D: Arthur Allan Seidelman. A: Helmut Griem, Olga Georges-Picot, Cyril Cusack.

Midnight Express

(1978) 120m. **A**

Relentless account of a young American's horrifying experiences in a Turkish prison after he's caught with hashish. Claustrophobic and fear-inducing, this is violent with explicit torture scenes.

D: Alan Parker. A: Brad Davis, John Hurt, Randy Quaid.

Missing

(1982) 122m. **A–**

A young journalist disappears in Chile in 1973, leaving his distraught wife to look for him. She's joined by her relentless father-in-law who refuses to believe that his son might be sacrificed by American officials. A compelling and emotional roller-coaster ride that gives you a few lessons about American interests in Latin America.

D: Constantin Costa-Gavras. A: Sissy Spacek, Jack Lemmon, Melanie Mayron.

Under Fire

(1983) 128m. **A–**

It's 1979 in Nicaragua and three jaded American correspondents find themselves swept into the chaos and confusion of the sinking corrupt regime. A relentless portrait of the people who end up not only reporting the news, but shaping people's perceptions of it as well.

D: Roger Spottiswoode. A: Nick Nolte, Gene Hackman, Joanna Cassidy.

The Year of Living Dangerously

(1983) 115m. **A–**

Indonesia, 1965: In the middle of revolutionary fervor, a wet-behind-the-ears reporter and a member of the British Embassy find steamy romance. This politically charged, mega-atmospheric winner has the romance and intrigue of a modern *Casablanca,* with Hunt playing the canny, trollish photographer.

D: Peter Weir. A: Sigourney Weaver, Mel Gibson, Linda Hunt.

The Killing Fields

(1984) 142m. **A**

A *New York Times* reporter and his Cambodian aide become separated, with their lives in jeopardy during the Khmer Rouge bloodbath. A story of friendship and courage set against the carnage and horror of war, this film captures the sweep of events by focusing on the nightmarish plight of the Cambodian aide who managed to outwit his tormentors.

D: Roland Joffe. A: Sam Waterston, Haing S. Ngor, John Malkovich.

Eleni

(1985) 117m. **C**

An American journalist goes to Athens determined to find out the truth about his mother's execution by the communists following World War II. The story is compelling but the flashbacks and current time scenes that reconstruct her life are affected and dull.

D: Peter Yates. A: Kate Nelligan, John Malkovich, Linda Hunt.

Salvador

(1986) 123m. **A–**

A journalist, accompanied by his pill-popping, booze-guzzling friend, becomes horrified by the problems he's covering in war-torn El Salvador in the early 80s. A sort of road movie on acid that winds its way through a frightening world where killers mix with diplomats at U.S. Embassy parties.

D: Oliver Stone. A: James Woods, James Belushi, Michael Murphy.

Not Without My Daughter

(1991) 114m. **C–**

An American woman accompanies her Iranian husband and their American-born daughter on a trip to Iran. When he decides to stay, the wife discovers that women have no rights and fights to leave with her daughter. Overwrought drama that offers a view of Arabs as bad guys and a predictably feisty Sally Field.

D: Brian Gilbert. A: Sally Field, Alfred Molina, Sheila Rosenthal.

Fathers and Sons

These tales of sons and fathers trying to communicate with each other are basically the male bonding versions of an old-fashioned tearjerker, with the occasional crime or sports angle thrown in; don't expect much in the way of surprises, but be sure to keep the hankies handy.

Tribute

(1980) 125m. **B–**

A terminally afflicted press agent's friends plan a tribute to him while he longs to reconcile with his estranged son before he dies. Stagy, soap operatic, but the stars' excellent performances make this more credible than it probably deserves.

D: Bob Clark. A: Jack Lemmon, Robby Benson, Colleen Dewhurst.

The Chosen

(1981) 107m. **B+**

Quietly affecting tale of two friends—an all-American (and Jewish) Brooklyn boy and a Hassidic youth—and the complex relationships with their fathers. Set in post-World War II when Israel's future as a recognized nation was uncertain, this eschews melodramatic routines for believable crises of familial, religious, and personal identity.

D: Jeremy Paul Kagan. A: Maximilian Schell, Rod Steiger, Robby Benson.

Harry and Son

(1984) 117m. **B–**

Generational conflict mushrooms between a blue-collar, beer-swilling dad and his art-aspiring son who has no interest in following in his father's sodden footsteps. Sometimes maudlin tale is given dramatic heft by op-

pressive, lower-working-class atmosphere.
D: Paul Newman. A: Paul Newman, Robby Benson, Joanne Woodward.

Da
(1986) 96m. **B+**
A New York playwright returns to his native Ireland to be with his father as he dies: When the old man does expire, his ghost returns to console and offer advice. Based on a stage play, this set-bound film's sappier aspects are mitigated by sharp clever dialogue and some well-earned laughs.
D: Matt Clark. A: Barnard Hughes, Martin Sheen, William Hickey.

Nothing in Common
(1986) 120m. **B+**
An ad exec yuppie must deal with reality as his parents divorce and his irritating father becomes terminally ill. Ambitiously tries to combine a zippy humorous feel for early parts of film, then downshifts into a full-blown tearjerker and succeeds to a degree, abetted by a touching final turn by Gleason.
D: Garry Marshall. A: Tom Hanks, Jackie Gleason, Eva Marie Saint.

Over the Top
(1987) 94m. **C–**
A trucker tries to revive his relationship with an alienated son via the manly virtues of driving and championship arm wrestling. A unique grunt-fest features Stallone at his monosyllabic best, bright Las Vegas location shooting, and a slow-motion arm wrestling sequence: just inches from a camp classic.
D: Menahem Golan. A: Sylvester Stallone, Robert Loggia, Susan Blakely.

Dad
(1989) 117m. **C–**
A wealthy businessman tries to reconnect with his elderly Pop who is under the overprotective care of Mom. Tear duct-clearer telegraphs its weepy moments with impressive regularity, and offers the soothing message that one can do emotional things and not have it unduly interfere with making money.
D: Gary David Goldberg. A: Jack Lemmon, Ted Danson, Olympia Dukakis.

Family Business
(1989) 113m. **C–**
Emotionally remote tale of a three-generation crime family pulling off a heist. Despite the heavy talent and a clever plot, this never settles on a tone (outside of a cold one), with the lack of dramatic fireworks making this a failure as both family drama and crime caper.
D: Sidney Lumet. A: Sean Connery, Dustin Hoffman, Matthew Broderick.

Romance

These love stories tread a comfortable and predictable path as two lovers spark and light up the screen with their romance. Since the formula also includes the part where "boy loses girl," you also get to see betrayal, adultery, and the countless misunderstandings on the rocky road to love.

The Competition
(1980) 129m. **B**
Two concert pianists competing for the same prize fall in love. Romance plays a heavy role here, but the film's strength lies in the music, along with an interesting look at the ruthless, driven, even obsessed atmosphere of a competition.
D: Joel Oliansky. A: Richard Dreyfuss, Amy Irving, Sam Wanamaker.

Urban Cowboy
(1980) 135m. **B+**
Boy and girl fall in love, have a fight, and make each other jealous. Sounds tired, but the appealing stars and the lively look at the rituals at a Texas bar—including the nightly tests of machismo on the mechanical bull—make this seem fresh and appealing.
D: James Bridges. A: Debra Winger, John Travolta, Scott Glenn.

The Four Seasons
(1981) 108m. **B–**
Three couples who vacation together during the course of different seasons experience the ups and downs of their friendships and marriages. The ensemble work and the goodhearted tone make this appealing, even if the issues involved get a superficial treatment.
D: Alan Alda. A: Alan Alda, Carol Burnett, Len Cariou.

Butterfly
(1982) 107m. **D**
A rural Southern woman turns on all her charm to lure a moneyed man to her bed, only to discover it's her daddy. Overheated and thick with clichés, this will astound you with its hard to beat laugh-out-loud dialogue. If you can take it seriously, you'll see that Welles swipes the picture, but it's petty thievery.
D: Matt Cimber. A: Pia Zadora, Stacy Keach, Orson Welles.

An Officer and a Gentleman
(1982) 125m. **B+**
He plans to be a career officer and make something of his life and so does his townie girlfriend—by marrying him. This throwback to 40s-style romances has sweet moments and sizzling sex scenes that are nicely balanced by the ones between Gere and his brass-lunged, chop-busting sergeant.
D: Taylor Hackford. A: Richard Gere; Debra Winger; Lou Gosset, Jr.

Love Letters
(1983) 98m. **B–**
After she finds a box of her dead mother's adulterous love letters, a young woman decides to pursue a married man of her own. Things get sticky as she becomes obsessed with her inaccessible love object. Painfully good acting and an honest and well-intended attempt to explore the issues of adultery.
D: Amy Jones. A: Jamie Lee Curtis, Stacy Keach, Amy Madigan.

The Buddy System
(1984) 110m. **B–**
A single mother's young son tries to match her up with his adult friend, an inventor and aspiring novelist. Still licking their wounds from previous relationships, they opt for friendship. Guess what happens? A cheerful, friendly, and slightly offbeat romance.
D: Glenn Jordan. A: Susan Sarandon, Richard Dreyfuss, Nancy Allen.

Falling in Love
(1984) 107m. **B–**
New York commuters fall in love and decide to risk their solid lives for a moment of heat. Pretty predictable stuff

though there's real chemistry between De Niro and Streep.
D: Ulu Grosbard. A: Robert De Niro, Meryl Streep, Harvey Keitel.

Until September
(1984) 95m. **C**

Paris is the only thing fresh about this tear-jerking tale of a young American and married dreamboat Parisian who fall in love. This is one long romantic montage—strolls in the park, dinner by the Seine, jokey banter under the sheets. But hey, if that's what you're in the mood for, this is aces.
D: Richard Marquand. A: Karen Allen, Thierry Lhermite, Christopher Cazenove.

Murphy's Romance
(1985) 107m. **B**

A divorcée and her 12-year-old son make a fresh start in an Arizona town, where she meets a feisty and nonconformist widower. The likable characters and the cheerful laid-back charm will keep you watching.
D: Martin Ritt. A: Sally Field, James Garner, Brian Kerwin.

Violets Are Blue
(1986) 88m. **B–**

A successful photojournalist returns to her small hometown and hooks up with a former sweetheart, the very married editor of the local newspaper. A nice, old-fashioned, and slightly dull film, though Bedelia briefly burns up the screen as the spurned wife.
D: Jack Fisk. A: Sissy Spacek, Kevin Kline, Bonnie Bedelia.

Every Time We Say Goodbye
(1986) 97m. **C–**

Prejudice and cultural differences are two of the obstacles thrown in the path of two lovers, an American World War II pilot and a Sephardic Jewish woman. Only the Jerusalem setting gives this soap opera a twist which wears thin fast.
D: Moshe Mizrahi. A: Tom Hanks, Cristina Marsillach, Benedict Taylor.

A Man in Love
(1987) 117m. **B+**

An actor and his leading lady making a film in Rome fall in love, with disastrous results for their respective partners. Spicy, sensual—there's real heat generated between Scacchi and Coyote—and overripe with emoting and soul-searchings.
D: Diane Kurys. A: Greta Scacchi, Peter Coyote, Peter Riegert.

Crossing Delancey
(1988) 97m. **A**

A sophisticated young Jewish woman is appalled when her grandmother consults with a marriage broker to find her a husband—especially when the candidate turns out to be a pickle salesman. A warm and funny look at modern New York single life and the old traditions of the Lower East Side.
D: Joan Micklin Silver. A: Army Irving, Peter Riegert, Reizl Bozyk.

Alienated Youth

These downbeat films offer grim but always compelling visions of youth who somehow got disconnected from the American Dream: Beneath the 80s teen landscape of mall-rat consumerism was a dark side populated with young disenfranchised and have-nots whose lives were filled with drugs, poverty, parental abuse or neglect, and even murder.

Over the Edge
(1979) 95m. **B+**

A suburban teen center becomes the incubator for teen alienation and rebellion. Though low-budget and a bit shakily filmed, this searing indictment of media/consumer society, the lack of community in suburbia, and disenfranchised youth remains haunting.
D: Jonathan Kaplan. A: Matt Dillon, Michael Kramer, Pamela Ludwig.

Taps
(1981) 118m. **B–**

The closing of a military academy and a father's death causes young cadets to go mental and barricade themselves into a deadly confrontation with less sentimental army-folk. A surprisingly effective film with well-rendered mounting tension and intense turns by Hutton and Penn.
D: Harold Becker. A: Timothy Hutton, George C. Scott, Sean Penn.

Bad Boys
(1983) 123m. **B**

Like a "Scared Straight" program, this relentlessly brutal story looks at what happens to rival gangs who are sent to the same juvenile detention facility. Grimy photography, no-frills direction, and a harrowing tone make this rough but worthwhile going.
D: Rick Rosenthal. A: Sean Penn, Esai Morales, Ally Sheedy.

The Lords of Discipline
(1983) 103m. **C+**

It's the 60s and a decent cadet at a military academy investigating a black friend's "hazing" discovers a clandestine and abusive right-wing group. No classic, but still a disturbing tale, with an appropriately paranoid ambiance.
D: Franc Roddam. A: David Keith, Robert Prosky, G. D. Spradlin.

Suburbia
(1983) 95m. **B+**

Abandoned, neglected, and otherwise forgotten kids rail against the empty lives of their screwed-up parents and no-future world. A low-budget but dead-on accurate evocation of punk kids' seedy milieu and appropriate lack of answers to knotty social questions make this a bracing shot of squalid reality.
D: Penelope Spheeris. A: Bill Coyne, Jennifer Clay, Chris Pederson.

Birdy
(1985) 120m. **B**

A unique tale of the lasting friendship between a boy and his mentally disturbed, bird-obsessed friend in 60s Philadelphia. A dreamlike atmosphere permeates this alternately humorous, surreal, and tragic tale, with great assist from an ethereal Peter Gabriel soundtrack.
D: Alan Parker. A: Matthew Modine, Nicolas Cage, John Harkins.

The Falcon and the Snowman
(1985) 131m. **B–**

A young government agent and his drug-dealing friend sell secrets to the Russians in this true-life story. A class act in all regards, but the codependence theme (the one repeatedly bails out his ma-

nipulative pal) loses psychodramatic steam due to unnecessarily long running time and slack pace.
D: John Schlesinger. A: Timothy Hutton, Sean Penn, Lori Singer.

Smooth Talk
(1985) 91m. **B+**

This is a mesmerizing and unsettling tale of a brief interlude between a 15-year-old girl and an alternately charming and threatening older man. Sterling performances, intriguing gauzy/pastel look, and constant undertone of sexual tension make this a must-see.
D: Joyce Chopra. A: Laura Dern, Treat Williams, Diane Ladd.

Sid and Nancy
(1986) 111m. **A**

A mesmerizing and horrific tour with punk rock's royal couple, Sid Vicious and Nancy Spungen, as they love, fight, shoot heroin, and reel around the clubs and hotels of London, Paris, and New York. The wild energy, driving music, beautiful photography, and sly humor keep the story's intensity from becoming a downer.
D: Alex Cox. A: Gary Oldman, Chloe Webb.

River's Edge
(1987) 99m. **A–**

A dead-eyed teen murders someone, and weeks go by before any of his friends do much about it. This based-on-fact story has a dreary, washed-out look that effectively mirrors its beyond-alienation teens, with a nerve-wrackingly impressive turn by Glover as a speed freak going nowhere fast.
D: Tim Hunter. A: Crispin Glover, Keanu Reeves, Dennis Hopper.

Drugstore Cowboy
(1989) 104m. **A**

White trash junkie slackers loot the pharmacies of Seattle in this refreshingly nonjudgmental dope tale and portrait of kids losing their souls. Funny and painful scenes, a career performance by Dillon as a likable substance abuser, and a great cameo by William Burroughs make this a quirky must-see.
D: Gus Van Sant, Jr. A: Matt Dillon, Kelly Lynch, James Le Gros.

Coming-of-Age

Whether it's absent parents, alcohol and drugs, broken hearts, or suddenly realizing you have nothing to wear to the dance, teenagers get and give their share of abuse. These films range from gritty tales of punks and greasers who live on the wrong side of the tracks to sanitized and perky nostalgia pieces about prince charmings and puppy love. Either way, most are entertaining, all share a respect for teenagers and their struggle to make sense of life, and many give you a good look at some very young movie stars.

The Blue Lagoon
(1980) 104m. **C**

Two shipwrecked children end up on a deserted fantasy island where they grow into beautiful adolescents and discover the joys of sex, love, and parenthood. Christopher, Brooke, and her naked double swim through picture postcard coral reefs and paw each other's supple young flesh in a tasteful exploitation flick that's a real howl.
D: Randal Kleiser. A: Brooke Shields, Christopher Atkins, Leo McKern.

My Bodyguard
(1980) 97m. **B**

When the new and nerdy kid in school is threatened by the school bully, he hires one of his hulking classmates to protect him. Sweet story of some of the awkward rites of passage that avoids the sex and wild parties routine.
D: Tony Bill. A: Chris Makepeace, Matt Dillon, Adam Baldwin.

Tex
(1982) 102m. **B+**

Two brothers from the Southwest come to terms with each other as they struggle with the death of their mother, an absent father, and encroaching poverty. Sincere and cramped drama, but the kids and the problems sound and look authentic.
D: Tim Hunter. A: Matt Dillon, Jim Metzler, Meg Tilly, Emilio Estevez.

All the Right Moves
(1983) 90m. **B**

A small mill-town football player whose scholarship is his escape from a dead-end future jeopardizes it with a prank gone wrong. A bleak but vigorous tale of people struggling to break out.
D: Michael Chapman. A: Tom Cruise, Craig Nelson, Lea Thompson.

Baby, It's You
(1983) 105m. **B+**

She's middle-class, Jewish, and heading for college; he's working class, Italian, and lands in Miami lip-synching to Sinatra. This small gem is funny and poignant and hits every note of their high school romance along with their bittersweet reunion.
D: John Sayles. A: Rosanna Arquette, Vincent Spano, Joanna Merlin.

The Outsiders
(1983) 91m. **B–**

All the clothing, cars, and hangouts look just right in this "greasers vs. the in-crowd" drama that takes place in Oklahoma in the 1960s. The story goes nowhere, leaving you to admire the film's stylized look and how young all the future stars are.
D: Francis Ford Coppola. A: C. Thomas Howell, Matt Dillon, Rob Lowe, Tom Cruise.

Rumble Fish
(1983) 94m. B&W. **B+**

This story of a young man's adoration of his older, tougher, and legendary brother is visually startling, all shot in expressionistic black and white with occasional dabs of color. Unfortunately, it's difficult to understand, and the plot takes a backseat to the cool performances.
D: Francis Ford Coppola. A: Matt Dillon, Mickey Rourke, Dennis Hopper.

Oxford Blues
(1984) 98m. **C–**

This remake of *A Yank at Oxford* looks like a preppy romantic postcard with nice shots of the university and rowing scenes while the gauche American pursues the aristocratic girl.
D: Robert Boris. A: Rob Lowe, Ally Sheedy, Amanda Pays.

Racing with the Moon
(1984) 108m. **B**
Friends from a small town in California prepare to be called up to fight in World War II, and find that love has its risks and rewards. Quiet and unsentimental, with nice 40s period details and a pedestrian script. D: Richard Benjamin. A: Sean Penn, Nicolas Cage, Elizabeth McGovern.

My American Cousin
(1985) 94m. **B–**
The 1950s world of a small-town Canadian teen is turned upside down at the appearance of her convertible-driving, James Dean wannabe, runaway American cousin. Sweet and low-keyed look at young love.
D: Sandy Wilson. A: Margaret Landrick, Richard Donat, John Wildman.

That Was Then, This Is Now
(1985) 102m. **C**
Wrapped up in his relationship with his adoptive brother, an alienated bad boy has trouble dealing with his sibling's girlfriend. The blue collars are frayed and the acting suitably gritty, but this self-important story seems bogged down by gray skies and earnest emotions.
D: Christopher Cain. A: Emilio Estevez, Craig Sheffer, Morgan Freeman.

Desert Bloom
(1986) 96m. **B**
It's the 1950s and the Las Vegas desert atomic testing is the background for a teen's trials and survival of the fallout with her ignorant grunt of a stepfather. Good performances but tedious story.
D: Eugene Corr. A: Jon Voight, Annabeth Gish, Ellen Barkin.

Lucas
(1986) 100m. **A–**
Charming bright tale of a brainy and nerdy 14-year-old's confusion when he falls in love with an older (16-year-old) woman who's in love with the football hero. Sounds like the usual, fare, but for once, the kids are intelligent and do things that make sense, even when they hurt.
D: David Seltzer. A: Corey Haim, Kerri Green, Charlie Sheen, Winona Ryder.

Pretty in Pink
(1986) 96m. **B**
The suburban girl from the wrong side of the tracks is thrown into a tizzy when a handsome, wealthy, and bland boy asks her out. Even Stanton as her sweet confused father can't put any starch in this soggy tale.
D: Howard Deutch. A: Molly Ringwald, Andrew McCarthy, Harry Dean Stanton.

Stand By Me
(1986) 87m. **B+**
A bright and colorful preteen male bonding tale of four small-town Maine boys in the 1950s taking an overnight trip to find a dead body. This sentimental story serves up the sunny side of boys' rites of passage with some real zip, but holds the complexity.
D: Rob Reiner. A: River Phoenix, Corey Feldman, Jerry O'Connell.

Aloha Summer
(1988) 98m. **D–**
It looks like a 50s beach movie, but this story of a multiracial group of surfers is so weighed down by its message—the brotherhood of man—that it nearly drowns. For surf and kung fu fans only.
D: Tommy Lee Wallace. A: Chris Makepeace, Don Michael Paul, Yuji Okumoto.

Fresh Horses
(1988) 104m. **C–**
Ringwald and McCarthy are back together again doing the Cinderella and Prince Charming routine. Smaller, sadder, and of even less interest than *Pretty in Pink.*
D: David Anspaugh. A: Molly Ringwald, Andrew McCarthy, Patti D'Arbanville.

Permanent Record
(1988) 92m. **A**
The bewildering subject of teenage suicide is intelligently and movingly handled in this story that portrays the aftermath of a prize student's death. Reeves' embodiment of self-destruction in the face of his best friend's death gives the film resonance.
D: Marisa Silver. A: Keanu Reeves, Alan Boyce, Jennifer Rubin.

American Boyfriends
(1989) 90m. **B–**
In this sequel to *My American Cousin,* we see the continuing struggles with love and growing up in the 1960s. Less successful than the first one.
D: Sandy Wilson. A: Margaret Landrick, Jason Blicker, John Wildman.

The Heart of Dixie
(1989) 96m. **C–**
An Alabama college journalist in the late 1950s is outraged at the beating of a black man, and tries to communicate her own raised consciousness to her sorority sisters. Lackluster and self-righteous.
D: Martin Davidson. A: Ally Sheedy, Phoebe Cates, Virginia Madsen.

Shag, the Movie
(1989) 96m. **B**
Southern high school grads from the class of 1963 take their friend to Myrtle Beach for one last fling before she marries. Sprightly and entertaining fluff with high energy from the women.
D: Zelda Barron. A: Phoebe Cates, Annabeth Gish, Bridget Fonda.

Rocky-Style Sports

The American Dream of the Little Guy Triumphant was revitalized with a vengeance thanks to the phenomenal success of *Rocky* and its roman numeral sequels. Soon the screens were filled with an army of poor shlubs who beat the odds in karate, basketball, and wrestling.

Rocky
(1976) 119m. **A–**
A low-class Philly lug and dreamer goes the distance by fighting world-champ boxer, Apollo Creed. Still a good film, with well-etched characters, a colorful sense of the fighting world, a genuinely sweet romance, and an ending only a die-hard cynic could grump about.
D: John G. Avildsen. A: Sylvester Stallone, Talia Shire, Burgess Meredith.

Rocky II
(1979) 120m. **C–**
There is, however, plenty for

even noncynics to grump about in this weak fist-fest, where our thick-tongued tough guy hits the skids and wants to reestablish his rep by taking on Apollo Creed again. An evocative atmosphere of cashing in quickly fills this sequel.
D: Sylvester Stallone. A: Sylvester Stallone, Talia Shire, Carl Weathers.

Rocky III
(1982) 99m. **C**

Rocky, malcontent with success, turns to ex-nemesis Apollo Creed to help give him his "edge" back just in time to take on the dreaded Clubber Lang. With its dopey plot and tenth-tier rock soundtrack, the series staggers into its cartoon phase.
D: Sylvester Stallone. A: Sylvester Stallone, Talia Shire, Hulk Hogan.

Rocky IV
(1985) 91m. **C+**

Cold War clobbering with Rocky taking on a Russkie steroidal-freak boxer named Drago. Flashy, violent, and dumb; Highlights include a triumphant Rocky, draped with an American flag, asking "Can't we all just get along?"
D: Sylvester Stallone. A: Sylvester Stallone, Dolph Lundgren, Talia Shire.

Rocky V
(1990) 105m. **D**

Rocky, now severely brain-damaged after his Russian bout, finds his manager has absconded with the earnings and so returns to Philly to start anew. Rocky's climactic street corner bout isn't as much fun as the one his son has with the local bully, a sure sign the series is in trouble.
D: John G. Avildsen. A: Sylvester Stallone, Talia Shire, Sage Stallone.

The Karate Kid
(1984) 126m. **B+**

The new kid on the block has peer-group problems and, after getting pounded by bullies, finds inner strength, a philosophy of life, and butt-kicking ability from a sage old Asian. A nice Hallmark, New Agey tone and well-crafted script make this fine formula fare.
D: John G. Avildsen. A: Ralph Macchio, Pat Morita, Martin Kove.

The Karate Kid II
(1986) 113m. **B−**

The wise old karate master returns to his homeland for a funeral along with his young charge, and the two end up in love with the same woman. Still visually appealing, but the plot lacks the oomph of the first one and is too slick with the Eastern philosophy.
D: John G. Avildsen. A: Ralph Macchio, Pat Morita, Nobu McCarthy.

The Karate Kid III
(1989) 113m. **D+**

In a desperate bid to keep a profitable series alive, this one has the Kid and his mentor opening a bonsai tree shop. The Kid strays to a new master after Morita turns anticapitalist on him when a profitable karate match looms. As dumb as it sounds.
D: John G. Avildsen. A: Ralph Macchio, Pat Morita, Thomas Ian Griffith.

The Next Karate Kid
(1994) 107m. **C**

A rebellious young girl falls in with the old karate master (assisted by good-hearted monks) and learns how to face down a gaggle of militaristic high schoolers. Same formula but everyone's so earnest and attractive, this manages to stay afloat.
D: Christopher Cain. A: Pat Morita, Hilary Swank, Michael Ironside.

Vision Quest
(1985) 107m. **C+**

A high school wrestler sets his sights on beating the champ from another school and another weight class. Modine is charming enough, given that he spends most of the film in a silvery rubber suit obsessing about his weight, but this is mostly a high school jock saga dressed up with some "vision" philosophy.
D: Harold Becker. A: Matthew Modine, Linda Fiorentino, Ronny Cox.

Hoosiers
(1986) 115m. **B+**

A new coach turns a loser Indiana basketball team into winners. A minimalist plot is fleshed out with Hackman's hyperkinetic performance, well-choreographed/edited on-court action, and a surprisingly touching turn by Hopper as an alcoholic father.
D: David Anspaugh. A: Gene Hackman, Dennis Hopper, Barbara Hershey.

Boxers

Unlike the slew of Rocky-inspired feel-good fight films, here the ring became the dark center stage where various class, psychological, and familial conflicts were battled out to the last decisive round.

Streets of Gold
(1986) 94m. **C+**

A Russian boxer abandons his career and winds up a drunk living in a Brooklyn slum. Then he convinces two young boxers to let him train them for the Olympics. This starts out promising and soon turns typically Hollywood, but Brandauer's low-key, soft-spoken performance lends credibility.
D: Joe Roth. A: Klaus Maria Brandauer, Wesley Snipes, Adrian Passer.

Homeboy
(1988) 158m. **D−**

In a story that's too long and too familiar, Rourke is the contender about to get his shot until "the Suits" decide that it ain't his night. Worst of all, for someone who really boxes, Rourke isn't very credible.
D: Michael Seresin. A: Mickey Rourke, Christopher Walken, Debra Feuer.

Raging Bull
(1980) 129m. **A**

Director Scorsese fashions an epic boxing film out of his elegant and brutal portrait of middleweight champion Jake LaMotta. Powered by a profanely funny script, stunningly photographed boxing scenes, and an infernally energetic De Niro as the boxing powerhouse and terror of his family, this classic has lost none of its punch.
D: Martin Scorsese. A: Robert De Niro, Joe Pesci, Cathy Moriarty.

The Golden Years

Once relegated to the fringes of movies as cranky old codgers and sexless grannies, the "graying of America" is being reflected in films as senior citizens take center stage in these high-quality, life-affirming stories.

The Trip to Bountiful
(1985) 107m. **B+**

In 1940s Houston, a 70ish widow leaves the tiny apartment where she lives with her overworked son and unsympathetic daughter-in-law, for a last trip back to her cherished hometown. A sweet and leisurely journey with great attention to details, an understated turn by Page, and a literate unmanipulative script.

D: Peter Masterson. A: Geraldine Page, John Heard, Carlin Glynn.

The Whales of August
(1987) 91m. **B–**

Two utterly opposite sisters, one acerbically morose, the other full of life, live out their last days in a picture-perfect Maine coast cottage. Not a fully rounded film, but a true delight seeing the assembled actors strutting their stuff, with special kudos to an ever droll Price.

D: Lindsay Anderson. A: Lillian Gish, Bette Davis, Vincent Price.

Driving Miss Daisy
(1989) 99m. **A–**

Bright and lively dual character study traces the 25-year evolving relationship between a reserved black driver and his prickly Southern Jewish employer. Going from the 1940s to the 70s, the film evokes its periods well and has a marvelous acting showcase script that treats the viewer to scenes of humor and pathos.

D: Bruce Beresford. A: Jessica Tandy, Morgan Freeman, Dan Aykroyd.

Strangers in Good Company
(1990) 101m. **B+**

When their bus breaks down on a summer field trip in the Canadian wilderness, a group of older women wind up sharing the dreams and disappointments of their lives with each other. The film's improvised documentary feel is both charming and taxing on the viewer's patience.

D: Cynthia Scott. A: Alice Diabo, Constance Garneau, Winifred Holden.

A Woman's Tale
(1992) 93m. **A–**

A 78-year-old woman, dying of cancer, tries to make the most of her remaining time. Sounds depressing, but this portrait of an independent, vibrantly alive woman is full of mortality-defying, spunky charm.

D: Paul Cox. A: Sheila Florance, Gosia Dobrowolska, Chris Haywood.

The Cemetery Club
(1992) 106m. **C**

Over the course of six months three Jewish women lose their husbands and console each other until one of them meets a new man. A self-conscious attempt to make death seem almost cute, with mostly stereotypical characters despite the fine actresses.

D: Bill Duke. A: Ellen Burstyn, Diane Ladd, Olympia Dukakis.

Wrestling Ernest Hemingway
(1993) 123m. **B**

An old Cuban barber and a former Caribbean skipper rediscover and nourish an old friendship while wrestling with the macho image of Hemingway. A nice small-scale film that always stays focused on the shabby world of our dogged grizzled characters.

D: Randa Haines. A: Robert Duvall, Richard Harris, Shirley MacLaine.

LA Sick Soul of Modern Life

If you want some hip and sometimes trashy entertainment about the rich, sleazy, and chemically dependent, put on your Ray Bans and rent one of these stories of decadent lifestyles of LA, where a good wardrobe and cool attitude seem to be all that count.

American Gigolo
(1980) 117m. **B**

A high-priced male prostitute finds his life complicated when he falls for the wife of a politician and is accused of killing a client. The acting is a joke, partly because every character is full of ennui or cocaine, but this thriller never stops buzzing with stunningly composed images of expensive cars, Armani outfits, and scenes of high-life anguish.

D: Paul Schrader. A: Richard Gere, Lauren Hutton, Hector Elizondo.

Breathless
(1983) 105m. **C+**

A two-bit hustler who's got Jerry Lee Lewis and the Silver Surfer in his soul gets involved with a beautiful French architecture student and soon they're lovers on the lam. The acting is also a joke here, but the film has the souped-up energy and the cooler-than-thou attitude of a teen joy ride.

D: Jim McBride. A: Richard Gere, Valerie Kaprisky, Art Metrano.

Into the Night
(1985) 115m. **B–**

An unsuspecting man winds up in an extended nasty screwball chase through LA when he helps out a young woman pursued by Iranian jewel thieves. Sporadically enjoyable with aimless energy and in-joke appearances by several name directors.

D: John Landis. A: Jeff Goldblum, Michelle Pfeiffer, Richard Farnsworth.

Less Than Zero
(1987) 100m. **C+**

The story of the disenfranchised gilded youth of LA becomes a cautionary tale of cocaine abuse with none of the deadpan kinky sex in the novel upon which it was based. Pretty muted for the subject matter but contains a few trendy decadent images.

D: Marek Kanievska. A: Andrew McCarthy; Robert Downey, Jr.; Jami Gertz.

Clean and Sober
(1988) 125m. **B+**
A real estate broker addicted to coke and booze embezzles company funds, hides out in a confidential detox clinic, and finds himself responding to its tough love methods. Despite the subject matter, a thoughtful and curiously entertaining drama, thanks to the spirited performances.
D: Glenn Gordon Caron. A: Michael Keaton, Kathy Baker, Morgan Freeman.

The Boost
(1989) 95m. **C+**
A hyper investment banker is more so when he starts sniffing coke: Soon he and his wife are raving blow fiends with their yuppie lifestyle going up in smoke. Would-be cautionary tale of conspicuous consumption of all sorts is so melodramatic it borders on camp.
D: Harold Becker. A: James Woods, Sean Young, John Kapelos.

The Physically Challenged

Despite their toughness, this group of small character studies is surprisingly upbeat with disabled heroes who are usually more vital than their worried relatives and friends.

Inside Moves
(1980) 113m. **C**
After an unsuccessful suicide attempt, a young man hangs out with a group of disabled people who use a bar to meet and talk. Well meaning and almost ridiculously determined to show the bright side.
D: Richard Donner. A: John Savage, David Morse, Diana Scarwid.

Whose Life Is It, Anyway?
(1981) 118m. **B**
A sculptor paralyzed from the neck down following a car accident insists on his right to choose death in defiance of the technology that would allow him to live. This adaptation of a play belongs to Dreyfuss, who gives a stirring, brutal, and bullish performance.
D: John Badham. A: Richard Dreyfuss, John Cassavetes, Christine Lahti.

Just the Way You Are
(1984) 94m. **B−**
A crippled flutist vacationing at a French ski resort takes advantage of the circumstances by getting her leg set in a cast and feigning a simple broken leg. Light easy watching, with a touch of romance, a dollop of comedy, and more than a pinch of sentimentality.
D: Edouard Molinaro. A: Kristy McNichol, Michael Ontkean, Kaki Hunter.

Children of a Lesser God
(1986) 110m. **A−**
The new teacher at a deaf school takes an interest in the janitor, a lovely deaf woman too proud to attend school. A shining Matlin gives juice to this romantic drama and affecting portrayal of the struggles of the deaf.
D: Randa Haines. A: Marlee Matlin, William Hurt, Piper Laurie.

Duet for One
(1986) 108m. **A−**
A concert violinist's world is shattered as she succumbs to multiple sclerosis. Andrews gives a startling performance as the strong accomplished woman who tries, with the help of a psychiatrist, to come to terms with her fear and anger.
D: Andrei Konchalovsky. A: Julie Andrews, Alan Bates, Max von Sydow.

Gaby, a True Story
(1987) 115m. **A−**
Based on a true story, a girl with cerebral palsy who can only move her left foot develops a sort of Helen Keller/Annie Sullivan relationship with her nanny, and struggles to overcome her disability. A grim but hopeful portrait.
D: Luis Mandoki. A: Norma Aleandro, Liv Ullmann, Robert Loggia.

The Waterdance
(1992) 106m. **B+**
A writer comes to grips with being paralyzed—along with other accident victims, including an ex-lothario black man and a racist biker—at a rehab center. Through authoritative dialogue, low-keyed performances and direction, this avoids soap operatic pratfalls to often be genuinely insightful.
D: Neal Jimenez, Michael Steinberg. A: Wesley Snipes, Eric Stoltz, William Forsythe.

(See also *My Left Foot*, page 217.)

Family/Marriage Dramas

Families and spouses: What could be meatier topics for dramatic and melodramatic confrontations? These characters deal with the emotional pain of divorce, adultery, and alienation from family members, with an occasional time-out for a heartwarming moment of sharing and recognition. Even with the happy endings, the tone isn't overly upbeat in these small, carefully crafted, character-driven dramas, although there are a few instances when someone gets an emotional pie in the face that will make you laugh as well as wince.

The Great Santini
(1979) 116m. **A**
A professional army man runs his family like a platoon, but now his kids are getting older and the constant discipline and moving to new towns is taking its toll. An intelligent and entertaining portrait of a loving family that teeters on dysfunctional, with Duvall bringing an amazing intensity to his square-shouldered warrior.
D: Lewis John Carlino. A: Robert Duvall, Blythe Danner, Michael O'Keefe.

Kramer vs. Kramer
(1979) 105m. **A−**
This bracing drama of how a self-centered, New York professional becomes a devoted single parent battling to

keep his child is played so intelligently and filled with enough sweet and observant moments to make an otherwise predictable story shine.
D: Robert Benton. A: Meryl Streep, Dustin Hoffman, Justin Henry.

Ordinary People
(1980) 124m. **A**
A well-heeled, antiseptic family is torn apart by the oldest son's death. Wracked with guilt, the younger son must come to terms with all the messy emotions below the wintry surface of his family. This memorable, well-crafted story avoids melodrama but will still leave you emotionally drained.
D: Robert Redford. A: Timothy Hutton, Donald Sutherland, Mary Tyler Moore.

On Golden Pond
(1981) 109m. **B−**
Retired mulish professor, fearful of death, squares off with his stubborn adult daughter. Honey-colored and just about as sweet, this predictable sentimental effort never lets you forget the constellation of movie stars at its core.
D: Mark Rydell. A: Henry Fonda, Katharine Hepburn, Jane Fonda.

Smash Palace
(1981) 100m. **A−**
There's no pussyfooting around in this film—its view of a marriage on the rocks is as tough as the protagonist, a junkyard dealer whose obsession with his cars causes his wife to leave. Beautiful use of the rugged New Zealand setting is used to emphasize the alienation of the characters.
D: Roger Donaldson. A: Bruno Lawrence, Anna Jemison, Greer Robson.

Shoot the Moon
(1982) 124m. **B+**
This gives a blow-by-blow account of a very messy breakup of a family who thought they hadn't fallen for the American Dream until they realize it's being smashed up in front of them. The rage and confusion is portrayed with such resonance you begin to wonder why you're watching these battles.
D: Alan Parker. A: Diane Keaton, Albert Finney, Karen Allen.

Man, Woman, Child
(1983) 100m. **C+**
A married man in California discovers that his affair ten years ago with a Frenchwoman had more than emotional consequences when their son shows up at his door. High melodrama and lavish sentimentality make this a real weeper.
D: Dick Richards. A: Martin Sheen, Blythe Danner, Craig T. Nelson.

Table for Five
(1983) 120m. **C**
A divorced dad takes his children on a cruise to Europe to make up for his frequent absence. Well intentioned with pleasant settings, and Voight nicely portrays the awkwardness and joy of getting to know his children.
D: Robert Lieberman. A: Jon Voight, Marie-Christine Barrault, Richard Crenna.

Terms of Endearment
(1983) 130m. **A**
This is as entertaining as any glossy Hollywood comedy about a mother and daughter over the years with a tear-jerking ending. It also turns out to be a smart, refreshing, and genuinely funny examination of all kinds of relationships. MacLaine and Winger provide the main sparks, with backup from a group of memorable and unpredictable characters.
D: James Brooks. A: Shirley MacLaine, Debra Winger, Jack Nicholson.

Irreconcilable Differences
(1984) 112m. **B**
The ten-year-old daughter of a successful Hollywood couple becomes so fed up with their squabbling that she files for divorce. Some real bite and humor in the script as it takes on the Hollywood community, but it ends up feeling like a soap opera.
D: Charles Shyer. A: Ryan O'Neal, Shelley Long, Drew Barrymore.

The Stone Boy
(1984) 93m. **B+**
This careful, slow-moving story concerns the aftermath of a tragic accident in which a young man shoots the older brother he adores. An insightful treatment of an individual's misunderstood response to tragedy that's rarely portrayed on film.
D: Chris Cain. A: Robert Duval, Glen Close, Jason Presson.

The Good Father
(1986) 90m. **B+**
With its off-kilter shots and garish colors, this film about a frustrated divorced father in London feels as alienated as he does. Hopkins is powerful and often uncomfortable to watch as the man trying to put himself back together again.
D: Mike Newell. A: Anthony Hopkins, Jim Broadbent, Harriet Walter.

'Night, Mother
(1986) 97m. **C+**
A young woman who lives with her mother decides to take her life, and the mother spends a long night trying to talk her out of it. This feels like the filmed play that it is, and the tension is too flimsy to sustain a movie.
D: Tom Moore. A: Sissy Spacek, Anne Bancroft.

Everybody's All-American
(1988) 127m. **B**
A college football hero marries the homecoming queen and together they ride success as far as his battle-worn body can take them. After a perfunctory buildup, this picks up considerably as the American Dream couple turns into a sad cartoon on a pedestal in this ambitious episodic saga.
D: Taylor Hackford. A: Dennis Quaid, Jessica Lange, Timothy Hutton.

The Good Mother
(1988) 106m. **B+**
A divorced mother begins to find a new, more open life with a handsome artist whose free ways cause the child's father to seek custody. Slightly slick examination of sticky issue, but the courtroom scene dealing with the question of sexual child abuse is compelling.
D: Leonard Nimoy. A: Diane Keaton; Liam Neeson; Jason Robards, Jr.

Immediate Family
(1989) 95m. **C−**
A yuppie couple unable to conceive makes arrangements to adopt a teenage girl's baby once it's born. The couple is nervous about the street-smart but sweet girl and her tough boyfriend, but end up developing a relationship with them in this sincere but plodding tale that rings false in every way.
D: Jonathan Kaplan. A: Glenn Close, James Woods, Mary Stuart Masterson.

Women's Dramas

These tales of women whose lives are shaped by adversity range from old-fashioned tearjerkers and bright and snappy ensemble pieces to harrowing character studies. With few exceptions, you can count on stories featuring independent women making their way in a man's world and the nurturing power of women's friendship throughout the years.

The Turning Point
(1977) 119m. **B+**

Two friends in a ballet corp took different routes—one married and had children, the other became a star. Now the first one's daughter may become a star. Both a dance film and a throwback to the old soapers starring Joan and Bette, with Baryshnikov adding some high voltage dance and sex appeal.

D: Herbert Ross. A: Anne Bancroft, Shirley MacLaine, Mikhail Baryshnikov.

An Unmarried Woman
(1978) 124m. **B+**

A wry, determined, and newly separated New Yorker struggles to make a life for herself and teenage daughter, and soon becomes involved with a sensitive artist. An observant amusing picture of upper-middle-class suffering.

D: Paul Mazursky. A: Jill Clayburgh, Alan Bates, Michael Murphy.

It's My Turn
(1980) 91m. **B–**

A young math teacher tries to balance her professional and personal lives. Light fare with feminist slogans but feels mild by today's standard.

D: Claudia Weill. A: Jill Clayburgh, Michael Douglas, Charles Grodin.

Rich and Famous
(1981) 117m. **C+**

Two writers remain ambitious, vain, and loyal friends for over 20 years. An overwrought and almost fun soap opera featuring the photogenic joys and sufferings of the rich and famous.

D: George Cukor. A: Jacqueline Bisset, Candice Bergen, David Selby.

Come Back to the 5 & Dime, Jimmy Dean, Jimmy Dean
(1982) 109m. **B+**

Women who formed a James Dean fan club in a nearby Texas town in 1955 have their 20th reunion, and confront the bleak limits of their lives. Good dialogue, great acting, and very theatrical.

D: Robert Altman. A: Cher, Sandy Dennis, Karen Black, Kathy Bates.

Frances
(1982) 134m. **B+**

Lange gives an unnerving performance as Frances Farmer in this grim biography of the actress whose inability to play along with Hollywood drove her crazy. Sensitive and full of anguish.

D: Graeme Clifford. A: Jessica Lange, Kim Stanley, Sam Shepard.

Personal Best
(1982) 128m. **B+**

Two female Olympic athletes train together, fall in love, and eventually compete against one another. Engaging drama that shows the close-knit, body-conscious jock sensibility, and those slow-motion, sensual images of athletes foreshadow a lot of sneaker commercials.

D: Robert Towne. A: Mariel Hemingway, Patrice Donnelly, Scott Glenn.

Cross Creek
(1983) 115m. **B+**

Based on M. K. Rawlings' memoirs of a young woman setting up a new life in the Florida Everglades in the 1940s. Wonderfully romantic view of a writer's life, a woman's struggle with independence, and a lovely portrait of her backwater neighbors, some of whom became the inspiration for *The Yearling.*

D: Martin Ritt. A: Mary Steenburgen, Rip Torn, Peter Coyote.

Star 80
(1983) 104m. **A–**

Chilling true story about a naive *Playboy* centerfold who is catapulted into LA's high life and her small-time hustler husband who won't let her out of his control. Beautiful contrast of flesh peddlers—the husband's sleazy world of wet T-shirt contests and Hefner's slick one of mansions and bunnies add to the film's glitzy and unsettling tone.

D: Bob Fosse. A: Mariel Hemingway, Eric Roberts, Cliff Robertson.

Swing Shift
(1984) 100m. **B+**

Everything changes when the men go off to fight World War II and the women take over their work in the factories, discovering they can enjoy life—even illicit love affairs—just like men do. Energetic period piece with subtle and unexpected story and characters.

D: Jonathan Demme. A: Goldie Hawn, Christine Lahti, Kurt Russell.

Agnes of God
(1985) 99m. **A–**

When a young nun is accused of killing her newborn, the struggle between the young woman, the psychiatrist, and the Mother Superior to get to the truth sends sparks flying. Strong performances and provocative story lift this beyond the confines of the convent.

D: Norman Jewison. A: Jane Fonda, Anne Bancroft, Meg Tilly.

Crimes of the Heart
(1986) 105m. **D+**

Three Southern adult sisters are reunited by two crises—their grandfather's imminent death and the act of an accidentally trigger-happy youngest sister. Despite the fine actresses, massive dramatic calamities and deliberate oddities, the laughs, drama, and sympathy are completely missing.

D: Bruce Beresford. A: Jessica Lange, Diane Keaton, Sissy Spacek.

Just Between Friends
(1986) 110m. **C+**

Moore and Lahti become fast friends and discover they have a lot in common—one's the wife and the other the mistress of Danson. Unlike life, everything works out beautifully in this TV-movie-style entry.

D: Allan Burns. A: Mary Tyler Moore, Christine Lahti, Ted Danson.

Working Girls
(1987) 93m. **B+**

A matter-of-fact, documentary-style look at a New York City brothel. The unassuming apartment, the practical attitudes of the women, and the total lack of eroticism is refreshing; prostitution is presented as akin to word processing with a better pay scale.

D: Lizzie Borden. A: Louise Smith, Ellen McElduff.

Beaches
(1988) 123m. **C**

The friendship of two women is traced over the years. Trite and maudlin,

with a tear-jerking deathbed scene that comes out of nowhere. Only a treat for Midler fans—she commandeers the movie and even sings a little.
D: Garry Marshall. A: Bette Midler, Barbara Hershey, John Heard.

Mystic Pizza
(1988) 101m. **B**
The seriocomic romances and crises of three young women who work at a Connecticut seaside pizza parlor. Fun to watch for the engaging young stars, but otherwise as challenging as a teen magazine article on dating.
D: Donald Petrie. A: Julia Roberts, Annabeth Gish, Lili Taylor

Miss Firecracker
(1989) 102m. **B**
The comic trials and tribulations of the spunky younger sister of a beauty queen as she attempts to overcome her lack of confidence by winning the Yazoo City, Mississippi, Miss Firecracker crown. Southern eccentrics, good sister interaction, and the tilting-at-windmills heroine gives this a warm quirky feel.
D: Thomas Schlamme. A: Holly Hunter, Mary Steenburgen, Tim Robbins.

Steel Magnolias
(1989) 116m. **B**
The joys and sorrows of a group of women who frequent the same beauty parlor in a Louisiana small town. Bright and entertaining and hits all the buttons—illness, competition among friends, growing older—as everyone gets their star turn.
D: Herbert Ross. A: Sally Field, Dolly Parton, Shirley MacLaine, Julia Roberts.

Lonely Children

Whether it's deceased parents, crazy parents, or dysfunctional parents, these films look at the offspring's attempts to survive and make sense of a world minus elder guidance.

Careful, He Might Hear You
(1983) 113m. **B+**
P.S. is the child stuck in the middle of an adult argument he can't control or even understand: With only memories of an absent dad and a dead bohemian mother, he becomes the center of a legal battle between two aunts in Depression-era Australia in this scary, quirky, and finally inspiring film.
D: Carl Schultz. A: Nicholas Gledhill, Robyn Nevin, John Hargreaves.

Clara's Heart
(1988) 108m. **C+**
A bickering WASP couple and alienated son have their lives made all better by a wise and warm Jamaican servant. Simplistic to a fault and overlong feel-good fest, using the old gambit that the servants are the keepers of all that's heartfelt and redemptive.
D: Robert Mulligan. A: Whoppi Goldberg, Kathleen Quinlan, Michael Ontkean.

The Wizard of Loneliness
(1988) 110m. **B**
With his mother dead and his father off to fight in World War II, a Vermont lad retreats into fantasy, the affections of a peculiar aunt, and a deranged deserter. Almost obsessive in its period and character detail, this shapes up as an unusually multilayered tale of survival under terrible conditions.
D: Jenny Bowen. A: Lukas Haas, Lea Thompson, Lance Guest.

Zelly and Me
(1988) 87m. **B−**
In an outwardly idyllic 1950s Virginia mansion, an 11-year-old girl deals with a mentally decaying grandmother by imagining herself to be Joan of Arc and finding comfort from a French maid named Zelly. Effective Southern gothic atmosphere, weird/fascinating characters, and fine acting fail to cover up ambiguous script.
D: Tina Rathborne. A: Isabella Rossellini, Glynis Johns, Alexandra Johnes.

Farmers

Stingy banks, natural disasters, and economic depression are battled by plucky resilient farmers in these golden-colored, earnest journeys into America's heartland.

Country
(1984) 105m. **B+**
A carefully studied, finely acted, and hokum-free attempt to evoke the everyday lives of farmers in 1930s Oklahoma is a coffee table book of a film in the best sense: The kitchens, barns, and fields look like they've been worked by these people who are bone-tired at day's end and fighting natural and financial disasters.
D: Richard Pearce. A: Jessica Lange, Sam Shepard, Matt Clark.

Places in the Heart
(1984) 112m. **B**
Glover as the wandering farm hand is the practical center to this story about a Depression-era Texas widow who attempts to pay the mortgage by planting cotton. A tried and true storyline with obvious people to root for is also helped by spunky, caring Field who appeals to your better side, and a visual sheen to the farm countryside.
D: Robert Benton. A: Sally Field, Danny Glover, Lindsay Crouse.

The River
(1984) 122m. **B−**
A modern anti-agribusiness tale of pluck and resolve shows an embittered Gibson and twangy-voiced Spacek trying to save the farm from wealthy landowners and the forces of nature. Even with a mud-soaked, feel-good ending as farmers unite to hold back a cresting river, this standard farm vision seems dated.
D: Mark Rydell. A: Mel Gibson, Sissy Spacek, Scott Glenn.

Vietnam

It would be more than a decade after Saigon's fall before Hollywood began making films about the war and, not surprisingly, the resulting films lack a unifying point of view, tending to be very personal tours through hell. Surrealistic, mythical, and graphic, most are all-star, big-budgeted tales that redefine heroism as a matter of not losing one's limbs or mind.

The Green Berets
(1968) 141m. **B–**

The Duke made a stirring, action-packed, gung-ho World War II movie, without seeming to notice it was about Vietnam. Depending on political bias, this will either be offensive as hell, horribly amusing in a campy way, or just taken as the confused period piece it is.
D: John Wayne, Ray Kellogg. A: John Wayne, David Janssen, Jim Hutton.

The Boys in Company C
(1978) 127m. **C+**

A black drug dealer, a pacifist hippie, and a sex-starved Brooklynite are among the platoon members who we watch go from green recruits to battle-weary 'Nam vets. Though well acted, what was once probably shocking—constant profanity and a cynical take on military is now overly familiar.
D: Sidney J. Furie. A: Stan Shaw, Andrew Stevens, Michael Lembeck.

The Deer Hunter
(1978) 183m. **A**

The first major film to deal with the war chronicles what happens to three working-class buddies who go to Vietnam together. Technically breathtaking, with some of the most nightmarish combat and POW scenes ever filmed and equally intense take on male friendships.
D: Michael Cimino. A: Robert De Niro, Christopher Walken, Meryl Streep.

Apocalypse Now
(1979) 153m. **A**

Coppola's magnum opus is a brilliantly lensed, madly fueled journey upriver into Cambodia's "heart of darkness" including Duvall's attack on a Vietnamese village, drug-hazed slaughter of innocent fishermen, and the final confrontation with Brando's living-dead cadre of natives: Like no other Vietnam film you'll see.
D: Francis Ford Coppola. A: Martin Sheen, Robert Duvall, Marlon Brando.

Platoon
(1986) 120m. **A**

A neophyte soldier gets caught in a war of wills between militaristic nutcase Berenger and Zenlike "warrior" Dafoe in the middle of a bloody offensive. Brilliantly shot film with tone shifting smoothly from stoned prebattle camaraderie to fire-fight paranoia, to a hallucinogenically rendered disturbing final confrontation.
D: Oliver Stone. A: Charlie Sheen, Tom Berenger, Willem Dafoe.

Full Metal Jacket
(1987) 120m. **A**

The first half of this flawlessly fashioned film details the dehumanizing effects of military training as wet-eared kids become killing machines in boot camp; the second half shows how nothing prepared them for the insanity of war as they negotiate with Vietnamese prostitutes and launch full-scale, aimless offensives against invisible snipers.
D: Stanley Kubrick. A: Mathew Modine, R. Lee Ermey, Vincent D'Onofrio.

Gardens of Stone
(1987) 112m. **C+**

A veteran sergeant now stateside and disillusioned with the Vietnam conflict plays father figure to a war-happy recruit in the hopes of saving him. A quiet, deliberately paced but impeccably crafted film is one of those strange cases of every element being in place and nothing quite clicking.
D: Francis Ford Coppola. A: James Caan, Anjelica Huston, D. B. Sweeney.

Hamburger Hill
(1987) 112m. **B–**

Nearly an entire platoon is slaughtered in its attempt to capture the titular site. An extremely well made, utterly depressing film with more gore than several horror films; has a futile tone, but with its successful attempt to show the madness of war, the nonstop carnage eventually becomes numbing.
D: John Irvin. A: Anthony Barille, Michael Patrick Boatman, Dylan McDermott.

Bat 21
(1988) 105m. **B**

An officer is shot down behind enemy lines, with his sole hope of rescue and sanity helicopter tracking him from above. A thin premise is milked for all the suspense it's worth, with a near-horror film ambiance as Hackman wanders the steamy jungle settings alone. Based on a true story.
D: Peter Markle. A: Gene Hackman, Danny Glover, Jerry Reed.

Born on the Fourth of July
(1989) 135m. **B**

True-life story of Ron Kovics takes us on his journey from gung-ho soldier to paraplegic antiwar activist. An overlong, thematically confused, occasionally hysterical/eerie film: Though Cruise ends up a cripple, and half the cast dies or goes nuts, this somehow comes to an unconvincingly feel-good conclusion.
D: Oliver Stone. A: Tom Cruise, Kyra Sedgwick, Willem Dafoe.

Casualties of War
(1989) 106m. **B+**

Fox is the only one to stand up to hardcase Penn after their group rapes a Vietnamese girl while out on patrol. A taut underrated examination of courage-under-hell-ish-pressure, with the usually style-obsessed DePalma evoking the madness of war minus overblown theatrics.
D: Brian DePalma. A: Michael J. Fox, Sean Penn, John C. Reilly.

84 Charlie Mopic
(1989) 95m. **B–**

Just another stroll in the jungle looking for "Charlie" turns into a nightmare struggle for survival. Shot from the point of view of the patrol cameraman's lens, the viewer is plunged into the middle of the madness. An instance of imagination triumphing over a near-zero budget.
D: Patrick Duncan. A: Richard Brooks, Christopher Burgard, Nicholas Cascone.

Heaven and Earth
(1993) 142m. **C+**

An admirable finale to Stone's "Vietnam Trilogy" tells the tale of how one young Vietnamese woman's life is swept from tranquility to the horrors of war, her "salvation" by marriage to an American GI, and her new life in the States. A visual marvel but surprisingly undramatic until Jones shows up an hour into the film.
D: Oliver Stone. A: Tommy Lee Jones, Joan Chen, Haing S. Ngor.

Home Front Dramas

The war isn't always over even when the soldiers come home, as shown in these dramas about Vietnam vets struggling to recover from the physical and psychological horrors of battle.

Coming Home

(1978) 127m. **B+**

While her husband is off in Vietnam, a lonely woman becomes involved with a paraplegic vet. Though it teeters on the edge of soap opera, the edgy performances, nervy look at the sexual aspects of Voight and Fonda's affair, and a realistically open-ended plot make this more of an unflinching look at war at home.

D: Hal Ashby. A: Jane Fonda, Jon Voight, Bruce Dern.

In Country

(1989) 116m. **B–**

A Kentucky teen finds the love letters of her father who perished in 'Nam and her quest to find out more wreaks havoc with her shell-shocked uncle and disturbed mother. Uneven, but often dramatically engaging film features an understated Willis and a riveting Lloyd as she drives everybody crazy opening old wounds.

D: Norman Jewison. A: Bruce Willis, Emily Lloyd, Joan Allen.

Jackknife

(1989) 102m. **B–**

A Vietnam vet visits his troubled war buddy, reminisces with him about their tour in hell, and ends up falling for his put-upon sister. Quiet heartfelt character study with fine performances by all still not helping the staginess and lack of developing plot.

D: David Jones. A: Robert De Niro, Ed Harris, Kathy Baker.

Gay Films

If you're looking for an erotic, titillating, or even frank look at homosexual relations, these small films that too often resemble "classy" or "courageous" TV fare will seem oddly tame. The earlier films rarely show any physical affection between the characters while the later ones focus on the devastation of AIDS. Often there's a sense of do-goodism, with the actors behaving as if they're already accepting a humanitarian award for being so courageous. The exceptions exist, but films that relax with the subject of homosexuality only started showing up recently.

The Boys in the Band

(1970) 119m. **B**

Nine friends gather for a birthday party, eight of whom are homosexual while the ninth maintains he's not. This play adaptation retains its theatrical feel and some of the daring confrontations feel passé, but good ensemble work makes it well worth a look.

D: William Friedkin. A: Kenneth Nelson, Peter White, Cliff Gorman.

Fortune and Men's Eyes

(1971) 102m. **C**

Sentenced to a six-month stretch in a fairly high security prison, a young man learns the ropes of life on the inside—which includes voluntary and involuntary male sex. This dated-feeling message movie somehow manages to keep a wide-eyed attitude even as it tries for grittiness in its portrayal of brutality.

D: Harvey Hart. A: Wendell Burton, Michael Greer, Zooey (David) Hall.

The Naked Civil Servant

(1975) 80m. **A**

John Hurt does a star turn in this one-person piece that traces the life of writer, sometime actor, and full-time personage Quentin Crisp, who grew up in England where homosexuality was a dirty secret and a crime punishable by imprisonment. Touching, funny, and hugely entertaining for a small film.

D: Jack Gold. A: John Hurt.

Outrageous!

(1977) 100m. **B+**

A Canadian drag queen takes in a schizophrenic woman friend. Though bearing more than a passing resemblance to a student film, the warm and flamboyant characters help give this entertaining study an immediacy missing from larger productions.

D: Richard Benner. A: Craig Russell, Hollis McLaren.

A Different Story

(1979) 107m. **C**

Threatened with deportation, a gay man marries a lesbian woman and they discover it's more than convenience. Starts off promisingly, with matter-of-fact treatment of unusual situation, but then the story runs for safety and you can see what's coming a mile away.

D: Paul Aaron. A: Perry King, Meg Foster.

Making Love

(1982) 112m. **C**

A polite, well-meaning, and ultimately unsatisfying portrait of an inhibited man who jeopardizes his eight-year marriage to pursue a male novelist. Nobody really gets hurt and the viewer never gets challenged.

D: Arthur Hiller. A: Michael Ontkean, Kate Jackson, Harry Hamlin.

Lianna

(1983) 110m. **A–**

Discovering her marriage lacks love, a suburban mother of two embarks on an affair with a woman professor. A small, sympathetic, and matter-of-fact film that doesn't exploit the lesbian theme but focuses more on the woman's journey of self-discovery.

D: John Sayles. A: Linda Griffiths, Jane Halloren.

Desert Hearts

(1985) 96m. **A–**

A professor spends a few weeks in Reno to get a divorce in the 1950s and becomes involved with a young female ranch hand. A more lighthearted and witty film that actually has some flesh and blood to it—erotic situations are actually explored

and it looks like a regular Hollywood movie instead of a small PBS special.
D: Donna Deitch. A: Helen Shaver, Patricia Charbonneau, Audra Lindley.

As Is
(1986) 86m. **C–**
A man is diagnosed with AIDS just after his first book is published and his lover decides to stay with him through the end. Flat trite version of affecting material, with a sullen hollow Carradine.
D: Michael Lindsay-Hogg. A: Robert Carradine, Jonathan Hadary.

Parting Glances
(1986) 90m. **B**
Martini-dry view of writer's difficulties as he juggles his present lover, who's leaving for a job overseas, and his former lover, who's dying of AIDS. Small and modest in size and aims, but affecting in a casual way, like an intense conversation with a stranger.
D: Bill Sherwood. A: Richard Ganoung, John Bolger, Steve Buscemi.

Too Outrageous!
(1987) 100m. **C**
In this sequel to *Outrageous,* the Canadian drag queen has become a hit in New York, and you get some first-rate impersonations of Barbra Streisand, among others. Glossier than the first, without the freshness and momentum.
D: Richard Benner. A: Craig Russell, Hollis McLaren.

Torch Song Trilogy
(1988) 120m. **B**
A blossoming drag queen is looking for love and coping with a histrionic mother. Warm and effusive as a Neil Simon film and as excessively self-dramatizing as the character, with feather boas all around.
D: Paul Bogart. A: Harvey Fierstein, Matthew Broderick, Anne Bancroft.

Longtime Companion
(1990) 100m. **B+**
This tribal coming-of-age tale traces the effect of AIDS on the New York City gay community from the perspective of two men. Get your hankies ready when it portrays the emotional devastation on the group of people and the importance of friends.
D: Norman René. A: Stephen Caffrey, Bruce Davison, Patrick Cassidy.

Men in Love
(1990) 87m. **C**
Hawaii is the backdrop for this story of a man coping with the despair, guilt, and confusion after the death of his lover from AIDS. Low-budget, well meaning, and New Age to the hilt (including scenes of crystal healing) but misses the mark.
D: Marc Huestis. A: Doug Self, Joe Tolbe.

Gangsters

After *The Godfather*, gangster movies came to violent life again, this time as big-budgeted, star filled enterprises that gave viewers a hell of a ride on the way to the old saw that "crime doesn't pay."

The Long Good Friday
(1980) 114m. **A**
Hoskins became a star in this unbelievably brutal study of an English mobster's efforts to cling to power over warring factions and even his own son. Gallows humor fills some haunting images, but overall the tone and look is down and dirty: for those who like their crime films with no comforting morals.
D: John Mackenzie. A: Bob Hoskins, Helen Mirren, Pierce Brosnan.

Scarface
(1983) 170m. **A–**
This profane, brutal, and compulsively entertaining look at "making it in America" follows the rise of a Cuban man from boat-person poverty to cocaine emperor. The gut-churning violence, the stylish and menacing Miami settings, and Pacino's turn as the title's foul-mouthed overachiever make this unforgettable.
D: Brian DePalma. A: Al Pacino, Steven Bauer, Robert Loggia.

Once Upon a Time in America
(1984) 227m. (complete)/ 139m. (U.S.) **B**
A sprawling epic about the rise and fall of a Jewish crime family, from humble beginnings as Ellis Island refugees to their 40s heyday to modern-day semidecline. This period-perfect film is awash in great performances and gorgeous photography but the length, number of characters, and ambition of the project lead to confusion.
D: Sergio Leone. A: Robert De Niro, James Woods, Elizabeth McGovern.

The Untouchables
(1987) 119m. **A**
Government agent Elliot Ness and his gang go up against the Mob headed by Al Capone. Everything works in this megaentertainer from fantastic period sets and costumes, good performances, and an audacious mix of visual styles ranging from hard-boiled, police and domestic melodrama to a western shoot 'em up.
D: Brian De Palma. A: Kevin Costner, Sean Connery, Robert De Niro.

Oddballs and Little People

Here are more oddballs, losers, and normal "little people" who went from secondary characters to heroes after *Marty* and the 70s explosion of artless-looking films about real people. By the 80s these character studies began moving away from the sentimental clichés of quirky characters and down-and-outers and looking more like vivid, finely observed European films; and it's no surprise since some of them were made by foreign directors.

Pretty Baby
(1978) 109m. **B**

A twelve-year-old resident of a Storyville bordello has her virtue sold to the highest bidder by her prostitute mother. Cunning Brooke outsmarts the john and quickly becomes the hottest commodity in New Orleans. A blunt and voluptuous film made with style and a refreshing ease of attitude.
D: Louis Malle. A: Susan Sarandon, Brooke Shields, Keith Carradine.

Carny
(1980) 107m. **C–**

The friendship of two carnival hustlers is disrupted when a teenage runaway hooks up with them. Earnest attempt to portray the tawdriness of life on the road, but the love story never registers.
D: Robert Kaylor. A: Jodie Foster, Gary Busey, Robbie Robertson.

The Elephant Man
(1980) 125m. B&W. **B+**

This true-life story of a grotesquely disfigured man in Victorian England follows him from freak show attraction to patient of an eminent physician, to the oddity patronized by upper circles of society. A haunting dreamlike film with a mannered story, a pervasive melancholy tone, and a smoky feathery look.
D: David Lynch. A: John Hurt, Anthony Hopkins, Anne Bancroft.

Atlantic City
(1981) 104m. **A**

He's the aging gofer of a gangster's widow, who dreams of one big score; she's a waitress/aspiring casino croupier who gets entangled in a drug deal. A stylish and engaging fairy tale about America's eternal search for streets of gold.
D: Louis Malle. A: Burt Lancaster, Susan Sarandon, Kate Reid.

Honkytonk Man
(1982) 123m. **A–**

A drunken country and western singer who dreams of making it in Nashville takes to the road with his son and Grandpa in tow. An understated gem with rustic backroads photography, wonderful Depression-era details, and the intimate appeal of watching Eastwood play father to his real-life son, in a story supposedly similar to Eastwood's own father.
D: Clint Eastwood. A: Clint Eastwood, Kyle Eastwood, Alexa Kenin.

Angelo, My Love
(1983) 115m. **B+**

A neorealist look at the strange and wondrous gypsy community in New York City with a fictional, street-smart, young hustler as its focus. The great use of real settings and realistic characters helps create an intimate documentary exploration of a little-known slice of American life.
D: Robert Duvall. A: Angelo Evans, Michael Evans, Ruthie Evans.

Tender Mercies
(1983) 84m. **A**

A burned-out country and western star wakes up from a binge in a dusty Texas highway motel, and finds a new start with a young widow and her son. Low-keyed and unadorned drama, with quietly powerful performances.
D: Bruce Beresford. A: Robert Duvall, Tess Harper, Ellen Barkin.

Paris, Texas
(1984) 145m. **B**

In this melancholy road-movie-meets-new-West-mythology, a haunted-looking Stanton seeks his wife in an America laid flat and wide. Slow, haunting, and filled with beautiful vistas of the Southwest and evocative music by Ry Cooder.
D: Wim Wenders. A: Harry Dean Stanton, Nastassja Kinski, Dean Stockwell.

Alamo Bay
(1985) 98m. **B–**

A small Texas shrimping community reveals its racist and violent streak when faced with an influx of Vietnamese immigrants. Director Malle brings a crusading reporter's zeal to an uncomfortable story, but the film still gets wearisome.
D: Louis Malle. A: Ed Harris, Amy Madigan, Ho Nguyen.

Dim Sum: A Little Bit of Heart
(1985) 89m. **B–**

When will her youngest daughter get married? That's the question the mother and all the other characters ask in this engaging but slow-moving look at Chinese-Americans in San Francisco.
D: Wayne Wang. A: Laureen Chew, Kim Chew, Victor Wong.

Mask
(1985) 120m. **A**

The true-life story of a single mom raising a son with an unusual disfiguring disease while leading a life filled with Hell's Angels types, drinking, and drugs. Avoiding all the physically afflicted character clichés, this story offers humor and hope about the power of love in a straightforward and entertaining manner.
D: Peter Bogdanovich. A: Cher, Eric Stoltz, Sam Elliott.

84 Charing Cross Road
(1986) 100m. **B**

An acerbic New Yorker and a reserved London bookseller keep company for 20 years—entirely through the mail. Engaging and gently sophisticated and the ultimate film for those few people who still write—or receive letters.
D: David Jones. A: Anne Bancroft, Anthony Hopkins, Maurice Denham.

Ratboy
(1986) 104m. **C+**

An LA woman finds a creature that is half boy, half rat and decides to market him as an act. Nice allegory, like a modern pint-sized *Mighty Joe Young,* but feels pretty warmed over.
D: Sondra Locke. A: Sondra Locke, Robert Townsend, Louie Anderson.

Barfly
(1987) 100m. **C+**

The poet-writer Charles Bukowski and a no-hope drunk spend a few days of serious drinking, talking, flirting, fighting, and getting sick. The film has the look and feel of a bleary hangover, punctuated with some raucous dialogue.
D: Barbet Schroeder. A: Mickey Rourke, Faye Dunaway, Alice Krige.

Housekeeping
(1987) 117m. **C+**

When an eccentric young woman assumes custody of her two orphaned teenage nieces, her free-spirited ways inspire one and alienates the other. Lahti has an offbeat charm, but this intelligent and melancholy drama loses steam due to meandering pacing.
D: Bill Forsyth. A: Christine Lahti, Sara Walker, Andrea Burchill.

Ironweed
(1987) 135m. **B–**

Two skid row companions sway and lurch in Depression-era Albany as this bleak story staggers its way over memories, real and imagined, and leaves you feeling as defeated as the characters.
D: Hector Babenco. A: Jack Nicholson, Meryl Streep, Carroll Baker.

The Accidental Tourist
(1988) 121m. **A–**

Devastated by the death of his son and his subsequent divorce, a travel writer re-

treats from the world until a kooky local petsitter takes a shine to him. Davis' sweet oddball is what ignites this quirky and gravely humorous film about love and redemption.
D: Lawrence Kasdan. A: Geena Davis, William Hurt, Kathleen Turner.

Five Corners
(1988) 92m. **A–**
The actors wring as much emotion and humor from a somewhat aimless story of five young people living in the Bronx in the 1960s. Offbeat humor and a feel for the neighborhood and its quirky inhabitants make this an intelligent poignant character study.
D: Tony Bill. A: Jodie Foster, Tim Robbins, John Turturro.

Eat a Bowl of Tea
(1989) 104m. **B–**
This chronicles the adjustments in the Chinese community when a ban barring wives of Chinese immigrants was lifted after World War II. A gentle seriocomic look at the sexes as the men expect their wives to take up their old roles while the women begin to enjoy the freedoms of the new world.
D: Wayne Wang. A: Cora Miao, Russell Wong, Victor Wong.

Far from Home
(1989) 86m. **C**
On a dull jaunt with her meek but earnest Dad, Joleen finds herself stuck in a dusty rathole of a Nevada town where she catches the eye of every trailer bat, one of whom could be a killer on the prowl. Hohum menace film, even with an electrocution, a tornado, and Barrymore fully graduated into her teen floozy persona.
D: Meiert Avis. A: Drew Barrymore, Matt Frewer, Richard Mansur.

John Cassavetes

John Cassavetes is one of those directors whose works you either love or hate. His studies of relationships and madness have all the meandering narrative, hypnotic length, and painful nakedness of cinema verité. If you're looking for smooth entertainment, these films won't be easy to watch; but they are as gut-wrenchingly honest and voyeuristic as films this side of Ingmar Bergman can get.

Shadows
(1959) 87m. B&W. **A**
A light-skined black woman living in 1950s Greenwich Village takes up with a white guy, much to her brother's consternation. Using improvisational acting and a fluid camera, this rock bottom budget film explores racial and social issues in a frenetic, often unpredictable way.
D: John Cassavetes. A: Lelia Goldoni, Ben Carruthers, Hugh Hurd.

A Child Is Waiting
(1963) 102m. B&W. **A–**
A portrait of an overly sympathetic music teacher working in a home for the mentally retarded, and her conflicts with the school's director. Stark and hard-hitting, this is far from heartwarming, but its driven obstinate characters ring true to life.
D: John Cassavetes. A: Judy Garland, Burt Lancaster, Gena Rowlands.

A Woman Under the Influence
(1974) 155m. **A**
A woman has a hard time making her hard-hat husband understand the anxiety and emptiness she feels, and her extreme mood swings are driving him crazy. As emotionally naked as any documentary, the no-holds-barred performances are passionate and clear as a bell.
D: John Cassavetes. A: Gena Rowlands, Peter Falk, Katherine Cassavetes.

The Killing of a Chinese Bookie
(1976) 109m. **A**
A small-time strip club owner kills a Chinese mob boss in order to clear a debt which gets him into deeper trouble. A mesmerizing depiction of the grim and tawdry world of strippers, small-time dealers, and losers still has a compelling immediacy.
D: John Cassavetes. A: Ben Gazzara, Seymour Cassel, Timothy Carey.

Opening Night
(1977) 144m. **A–**
A high-strung actress all but completely falls apart when her most ardent fan dies on the night she's opening a new play. An unsparing backstage drama and an almost scientific scrutiny of a woman whose midlife crisis is amplified by her profession: She's never sure who she is.
D: John Cassavetes. A: Gena Rowlands, John Cassavetes, Ben Gazzara.

Gloria
(1980) 121m. **A**
When the Mafia knocks his family off, a little boy ends up in the custody of a neighbor who's a former mob mistress. Even though she's not crazy about him, she has the wits to keep them both alive as they go on the lam in this offbeat action/drama.
D: John Cassavetes. A: Gena Rowlands, Buck Henry, John Adames.

Love Streams
(1984) 141m. **B**
The desperate gambits for happiness by a pleasure-seeking potboiler novelist and his emotionally grasping sister collide when she moves in with him. Fly-on-the-wall approach conveys the frustration and turmoil of the confrontations and evasions of two quite crazy people.
D: John Cassavetes. A: Gena Rowlands, John Cassavetes, Seymour Cassel.

Baby Boomers and Yuppies

First there were the ex-hippie baby boomers suffering through loss of ideals and a new materialism, which led directly to their younger, less conscientious ilk, the dreaded

yuppie. "Money changes everything" sang Cyndi Lauper, and this was never more true than in the 80s films that offered shiny-faced characters living in a fantastic world of mindless melodramatic sex and conspicuous consumption of everything from drugs to designer jackets. The best of these are gems of MTV atmospherics replete with every 80s trashy icon; they can also seem like the film equivalent of watching someone with multiple trust funds complain endlessly about the horrors of a bad hair day.

Return of the Secaucus Seven
(1980) 100m. **B+**

A decade after getting arrested en route to a Pentagon protest, seven ex-radicals have an anxious reunion. Unlike *The Big Chill,* which this presaged, this isn't a shiny, feel-good baby boomer piece, but rather a grainy, almost home-movieish examination of people and ideals lost in shifting times: talky but earnest.
D: John Sayles. A: Mark Arnott, Gordon Clapp, Maggie Renzi.

The Big Chill
(1983) 103m. **A–**

A group of 30-something friends reunite for a funeral and spend a couple of days renewing old attachments and talking about what happened to the idealism of their college days. Sparkling, all-star touchstone for baby boomers remains a smart and funny ensemble piece.
D: Lawrence Kasdan. A: Kevin Kline, Glenn Close, William Hurt.

Key Exchange
(1985) 90m. **B–**

"Can you have keys to someone else's apartment and still see other people?", "Does marriage make a difference?", and other questions of commitment are the center of this amiable if not exactly profound romantic comedy/drama with decent Manhattan location photography that balances out all the talk.
D: Barnet Kellman. A: Ben Masters, Brooke Adams, Daniel Stern.

Perfect
(1985) **C–**

An intrepid *Rolling Stone* investigative reporter is working on an exposé about the controversial and ultrahip world of . . . health clubs. Will he compromise his ruthless code of ethics for the love of a low-body-fat femme's wily ways? Self-important, brain-palsied, and a must-see for bad film fans.
D: James Bridges. A: John Travolta, Jamie Lee Curtis, Jann Wenner.

St. Elmo's Fire
(1985) 110m. **C–**

College friends hang out at a Washington, D.C., bar, grouse about this and that, have affairs, take drugs, pursue their professions, and ponder the meaning of it all (but not for long). Filled with flashy soap-operatic angst, these brat packers all seem to be going through a sort of kiddy midlife crisis.
D: Joel Schumacher. A: Emilio Estevez, Demi Moore, Rob Lowe.

About Last Night
(1986) 113m. **B**

A post-one-night-stand couple wakes up with the realization that they like each other. Though David Mamet's play has been watered down for mass consumption, traces of his biting wit and good performances make this stand out a bit from the usual yuppie yattering.
D: Edward Zwick. A: Rob Lowe, Demi Moore, James Belushi.

Bright Lights, Big City
(1988) 110m. **C+**

An aspiring writer from the Midwest gets caught up in Gotham's high life of easy kicks, expense accounts, cocaine, and rampant club-hopping. Despite the obligatory neon and smoky club scenes, this actually evolves into something resembling a dramatically interesting tale of a real person's redemption.
D: James Bridges. A: Michael J. Fox, Kiefer Sutherland, Phoebe Cates.

Cocktail
(1988) 100m. **D+**

A wise bartender shows a young fellow the wondrous world of beverage mixing, leading to instant popularity with the opposite sex, bartop dancing, and generally reverse-Darwinian behavior. A new nadir in the annals of It's-good-to-be-dumb cinema.
D: Roger Donaldson. A: Tom Cruise, Bryan Brown, Elisabeth Shue.

1969
(1988) 96m. **D**

Feeble pap about a couple of small-town numbskulls who, in a hippie fever, leave their small town and hit the road at spring break, 1969. A meandering melodrama treats viewer to ugly nude hippies, student demonstrations, and generation gap rifts in this self-congratulatory nostalgic Age of Aquarius yawner.
D: Ernest Thompson. A: Robert Downey, Jr.; Keifer Sutherland; Bruce Dern.

sex, lies, and videotape
(1989) 100m. **A–**

A quiet young man who videotapes people's feelings about intimate matters for his own private collection visits a friend who has a lovely wife and a sexy sister-in-law mistress. A quirky intriguing tale told with a sure hand.
D: Steven Soderbergh. A: James Spader, Andie MacDowell, Peter Gallagher.

Crime Dramas

These cop and crime dramas offer some explanations but no resolutions for the problems of murder, drugs, gangs, and police corruption that riddle urban life. No one comes off as clean, with the players on both sides of the law portrayed in all their gritty, violent, and often tragic glory.

Fort Apache—The Bronx
(1981) 120m. **B+**

Normal events unfold in a few furious days at a notorious Bronx precinct: the murder of two cops, a race riot, drug deals, a new police captain, even a love affair. Newman is the beat cop who finally shakes off his apathy in this gritty engaging police tale that is reminiscent of the best of *Hill Street Blues.*
D: Daniel Petrie. A: Paul Newman, Ken Wahl, Ed Asner.

Prince of the City
(1981) 167m. **A**

A New York City narcotics cop agrees to help expose police corruption, but after the adrenaline wears off from the danger, he's left with the endless repercussions, his own sins coming home to roost, and the loss of his "family" of partners. A complex and tragic cop opera with a fine Williams as the informant who watches his life unravel.
D: Sidney Lumet. A: Treat Williams, Jerry Orbach, Bob Balaban.

Alphabet City
(1984) 95m. **C+**

Spano is the family man who's hustling to make ends meet in this portrait of the night life on New York's seamy Avenues A, B, and C. The plot gets predictable with turf fights, car chases, and shoot-outs in this gritty and low-budget entry.
D: Amos Poe. A: Vincent Spano, Kate Vernon, Michael Winslow.

The Pope of Greenwich Village
(1984) 120m. **B+**

Rourke gets talked into a chancy heist that turns out to involve Mafia money, and things go from bad to worse as the two small-time operators get squeezed by the Mob. The edgy performances, colorful city settings, and crackling dialogue make this sparkle like a neighborhood operetta.
D: Stuart Rosenberg. A: Mickey Rourke, Eric Roberts, Daryl Hannah.

Year of the Dragon
(1985) 136m. **C–**

An aggressive New York City police captain manages to incite brewing hostilities in Chinatown into a full-blown gang war. The characters in this violent and at times sadistic crime story strut and pose like GQ models while the film can't deliver a plot or dialogue that makes sense of all the commotion.
D: Michael Cimino. A: Mickey Rourke, John Lone, Ariane.

At Close Range
(1986) 115m. **A–**

The son of a newly released convict wants his father's approval and joins up with his quietly homicidal dad and uncles. Based on a true story, this gut-wrenching tale of Pennsylvania hardscrabble people vividly portrays the father-son dynamics as it escalates into inevitable violence.
D: James Foley. A: Christopher Walken, Sean Penn, Christopher Penn.

Street Smart
(1987) 95m. **B+**

When a smarmy magazine reporter fabricates an interview with a street lowlife, a real-life pimp needing an alibi claims the story is about him. This low-budget sleeper is a wicked yuppie paranoia fable with Reeve caught between the DA, his editor, and the wily, seductive, and always dangerous pimp.
D: Jerry Schatzberg. A: Christopher Reeve, Kathy Baker, Morgan Freeman.

Colors
(1988) 127m. **B–**

This veteran cop/rookie cop tale takes place in an LAPD unit trying to crack a street gang-operated narcotics ring. The cop dynamics are sharpened by Penn and Duvall's performances, but it's the look at LA street gang "family," scored by hip hop music, that gives this movie punch.
D: Dennis Hopper. A: Sean Penn, Robert Duvall, Maria Conchita Alonso.

Teachers

Say goodbye to owlish Mr. Chips and hello to the new teachers on their mission to stamp out truancy, gangs, dope, and even conformity in these inspirational tales showing that Rambo wasn't the only patriot kicking butt in the 1980s.

The Principal
(1987) 109m. **C+**

A teacher shoots his mouth off once too often and gets reassigned as a principal of a school straight out of juvenile hell. With the aid of a feisty janitor, he kicks serious bad-student butt in this film that's ridiculous as a depiction of urban/educational problems but mildly amusing as a slob comedy.
D: Christopher Cain. A: James Belushi; Louis Gossett, Jr.; Rae Dawn Chong.

Stand and Deliver
(1988) 103m. **B+**

An ex-gang member/teacher, through cajolery, toughness, and sheer force of will, convinces Los Angeles barrio hard cases to get with his math program and enter a national calculus test. Better than most similar films, helped by distressed LA locations, sure knowledge of gang rituals, and Olmos' understated performance.
D: Ramon Menendez. A: Edward James Olmos, Lou Diamond Phillips, Andy Garcia.

Dead Poets Society
(1989) 124m. **B+**

It's the late 1950s and a bunch of conformist Vermont Academy students are verbally pummeled by a highly animated poetry teacher into seeking their individuality. Over-praised film has trademark Weir mystical atmospherics, but is saddled with synthetic and at times abruptly sappy plot.
D: Peter Weir. A: Robin Williams, Ethan Hawke, Robert Sean Leonard.

Lean on Me
(1989) 108m. **C+**

Paterson, New Jersey: Drugs and crime run rampant and it's up to the new principal to harangue and sometimes beat the tar out of the unsavory elements. Based-on-fact tale features realistically depressed Jersey locales, an impressively authoritarian Freeman, but little room for dissenting views on how to deal with urban youths.
D: John G. Avildsen. A: Morgan Freeman, Robert Guillaume, Beverly Todd.

Erotic Adventures

These are the precursors to the soft-core "adult" movies that now glut video stores and midnight cable movie channels: all atmosphere, glamorous locales (tropical is best), and arty sex scenes that owe a lot to music videos. Don't expect much of a plot, though some do attempt a hilariously overwrought melodrama within which to fold all the sweaty gropings, and the presence of name stars could well ensure these gauzy fantasies a camp status before too long.

Bolero

(1984) 106m. **D**

This yarn about the troubles a 1920s college student has losing her virginity looks like a Derek home movie and the vanity showcase for Bo that it is. Pretentious, studied, and the role's too much of a challenge for Bo.

D: John Derek. A: Bo Derek, George Kennedy, Andrea Occipinti.

9½ Weeks

(1986) 114m. **B+**

A Wall Streeter and a Soho gallery owner get involved in an obsessive consuming affair that starts to resemble a yuppie version of *The Story of O.* The film that may have started the genre: everything reeks of sex from the streamlined settings, the drop-dead clothes, and sultry looks to the almost graphic acrobatics of two well-toned movie stars.

D: Adrian Lyne. A: Mickey Rourke, Kim Basinger, Margaret Whitton.

Two Moon Junction

(1988) 104m. **C+**

A young Southern belle defies her upbringing to run away with a handsome carnival huckster. Sludgy melodrama with oddles of almost campy Southern atmosphere.

D: Zalman King. A: Sherilyn Fenn, Richard Tyson, Louise Fletcher.

Hot Spot

(1990) 130m. **C+**

A stranger pulls into a small Texas town and finds his hands full as two women—the good girl and the bad one who's also the boss's wife—set their sights on him. Way too arty and the studied hipness becomes dull very quickly.

D: Dennis Hopper. A: Don Johnson, Virginia Madsen, Jennifer Connelly.

Wild Orchid

(1990) 111m. **B–**

A staid young lawyer is on her first case in Rio de Janeiro where she's captivated by the wild abandon of Carnival and the charms of a mysterious Strange Man. Lots of shower scenes and sex in primitive places in this humid and goofy film.

D: Zalman King. A: Mickey Rourke, Jacqueline Bisset, Carré Otis.

Zandalee

(1990) 100m. **C**

Bored with her buttoned-down husband, a young woman seduces his artistic best friend and of course nothing good comes of it. Plenty of sex between unappealing characters in an atmospheric New Orleans.

D: Sam Pillsbury. A: Nicolas Cage, Erika Anderson, Judge Reinhold.

Henry Jaglom

For 15 years, Jaglom has financed, produced, and distributed his own films; some would say that he is too visionary for Hollywood, others would say that his work is too self-absorbed and self-indulgent. Love and loneliness are often the themes of these documentary-like films that, at their best, contain some uniquely revealing moments.

Can She Bake a Cherry Pie?

(1983) 90m. **C**

After a female singer is abandoned by her husband, she takes up with another loser, and the two proceed to drive each other nuts. Typical Jaglom angst-tale features one of the shrillest performances, courtesy of Ms. Black, but still a favorite with ardent Jaglomists.

D: Henry Jaglom. A: Karen Black, Michael Emil.

Always

(1984) 105m. **C–**

An LA couple who have been separated for two years reunite to spend a chatty weekend with two other couples. Would-be comedy substitutes laughs for lots of talk and no action about why people stay together and don't: a real gab-fest of the self-absorbed.

D: Henry Jaglom. A: Henry Jaglom, Patrice Townsend, Joanna Frank.

Someone to Love

(1986) 110m. **C**

Jaglom, basically playing himself, throws a Valentine's Day party at an old LA movie house and has the guests talk about the hows and whys of being alone. Feels like an interminable whine-fest until Welles' monologue at the end, summing up the history of male-female relations.

D: Henry Jaglom. A: Henry Jaglom, Andrea Marcovicci, Orson Welles.

Eating

(1991) 110m. **B**

A group of women talks about eating, its dominating influence, effect on self-esteem, how it replaces loneliness, and so on. Though technically primitive as any Jaglom film, there is something about these women talking honestly about such a seemingly basic subject that manages to fascinate for most of the film.

D: Henry Jaglom. A: Nelly Alard, Lisa Richards, Mary Crosby.

Venice/Venice

(1992) 108m. **C–**

A filmmaker in Venice meditates on that fine city, goes to the Venice Film Festival, falls for a mysterious female, and then continues, or rather *talks* about, the ensuing nonrelationship back at his Venice, California, digs while various semistars wander about.

D: Henry Jaglom. A: Henry Jaglom, Nelly Allard, Suzanne Bertish.

Buddy Films

While some of these films still show regular guys swilling beers, shooting pool, and grousing about their girlfriends, there are more alternative male-bonding stories of gay window dressers and autistic brothers who are part of a pair that provide guidance and other nurturing nonmacho things to each other.

That Championship Season
(1982) 110m. **C**

The winning basketball team reunites 24 years later at their coach's home where they reminisce; exchange scatological, sexist, and racist banter; and let the real nature of their comradeship emerge. Superior performances by all but basically a talk-fest of small, bigoted, and not very likable guys.
D: Jason Miller. A: Stacy Keach, Bruce Dern, Robert Mitchum.

Kiss of the Spider Woman
(1985) 119m. **A**

A homosexual window dresser and a political revolutionary are a very mismatched pair of prison mates as one recounts his favorite old movie and the other recounts political atrocities. A truly great film with matching performances that pack as much real excitement via dialogue and imagery as ten action films.
D: Hector Babenco. A: William Hurt, Raul Julia, Sonia Braga.

The Color of Money
(1986) 120m. **B**

This belated sequel to *The Hustler* finds pool shark Fast Eddie shaken out of semiretirement by a young hotshot player he reluctantly takes under his wing. The interplay between the stars is entertaining and Scorsese's dazzling camerawork makes pool a clattering visual extravaganza, but a tired plot still shows through.
D: Martin Scorsese. A: Paul Newman, Tom Cruise, Mary Elizabeth Mastrantonio.

The Men's Club
(1986) 100m. **D**

They do everything but oink in this unpleasant excursion under the skin of a pack of males gathered by an ex-jock at the home of a weird shrink. A waste of quite a few good actors.
D: Peter Medak. A: Harvey Keitel, David Dukes, Roy Scheider.

Dominick and Eugene
(1988) 103m. **A–**

A young medical student tries to juggle his studies, a blooming love affair, and the care of his mentally deficient brother, all while keeping hidden a terrible family secret. Extremely touching film has dead-on performances and climaxes in a way that won't leave a hanky unused.
D: Robert M. Young. A: Ray Liotta, Tom Hulce, Jamie Lee Curtis.

Patti Rocks
(1988) 86m. **B+**

A lower-class, married Everydope gets another woman pregnant, enlists an old friend to help him deal with it, and finds some big surprises at the end of the road to the woman's apartment. Packed with raucously crude sexist dialogue, this is a gritty little gem full of unpretentious insights.
D: David Burton Morris. A: Chris Mulkey, John Jenkins, Karen Landry.

Rain Man
(1988) 128m. **B+**

After discovering that his autistic brother has inherited the lion's share of their father's estate, a small-time entrepreneur "kidnaps" him and hits the road with the two getting to know each other cross-country. Beautifully shot road film with quirky bits of Americana, but it's Hoffman as the idiot savant who owns this sweet-tempered film.
D: Barry Levinson. A: Dustin Hoffman, Tom Cruise, Valeria Golina.

Scent of a Woman
(1992) 137m. **C+**

Over Thanksgiving vacation, a prep school student agrees to "babysit" an incorrigible blind army officer who proceeds to drag him through New York City for a weekend he'll never forget. Pacino's performance, like his character, is completely unleashed in this plodding star vehicle and tiresome buddy film.
D: Martin Brest. A: Al Pacino, Chris O'Donnell, Gabrielle Anwar.

Watch It
(1993) 102m. **B**

Returning home, a young man hoping for reconciliation with an embittered cousin finds the place filled with his cuz, plus a bunch of raucous males and a woman he will fall in love with. Beneath the sneakers and pranks, film shows male vulnerability and fears without getting treacly.
D: Tom Flynn. A: Peter Gallagher, Suzy Amis, John C. McGinley.

Power

These are star-studded male dramas of gamesmanship in the corporate boardrooms, the political back rooms, and even dingy real estate offices in their examination of power's uses and misuses.

Power
(1986) 111m. **B+**

A high-style, political "image-maker" has ethical qualms about taking on a new candidate who rubs him the wrong way. An expertly crafted Lumet effort about the behind-the-scenes molding of candidates and manipulation of issues, with Gere as the cocky and charming spin doctor who'll tug on the public's heartstrings or throw mud on an opponent, whichever way the polls dictate.
D: Sidney Lumet. A: Richard Gere, Julie Christie, Gene Hackman.

Wall Street
(1987) 124m. **B+**

A young Wall Street broker

gets a whirlwind education in the art of the deal from reptilian mover and shaker Gordon Gekko. Another Oliver Stone joyride, this time through the 80s of frenzied deal-making and conspicuous consumption in this sometimes on-the-mark, sometimes turgid morality tale.
D: Oliver Stone. A: Michael Douglas, Charlie Sheen, Daryl Hannah.

True Colors
(1991) 111m. **B–**
Two law school buddies taste the gamier side of Washington politics as they follow different paths to wielding power. Hollow and remarkably unmemorable saga despite smooth direction and performances.
D: Herbert Ross. A: James Spader, John Cusack, Richard Widmark.

Glengarry Glen Ross
(1992) 100m. **B+**
Tensions between four brokers in a sleazy real estate office mushroom when it turns out the best leads are being withheld and the boss is out to fire the lot of them. David Mamet script deftly etches the lives of these desperate "little men" with teeth-grinding, cut-throat atmosphere filling this feast of fantastic performances.
D: James Foley. A: Al Pacino, Jack Lemmon, Ed Harris.

Americana

An heiress kidnapped by revolutionaries, a coal miner's strike, a gonzo talk show host: as they say, only in America. The films listed here are colorful little bits of recent history, focusing mainly on people at the subcultural fringes of American life.

Daniel
(1983) 130m. **B**
The son of two executed spies is tormented by his past and unable to come to grips with his place in the tumultuous uprisings of the 60s. Hutton is the brooding presence that haunts this jagged and jumpy reworking of the Julius and Ethel Rosenberg story.
D: Sidney Lumet. A: Timothy Hutton, Mandy Patinkin, Lindsay Crouse.

The Right Stuff
(1983) 192m.
A–
A character-rich epic story of the dawn of space travel starts with air force test pilot Yeager breaking the sound barrier and follows up with the selection, training, PR polishing, and first flights of the seven original astronauts. A bright vivid re-creation of an age and confident attitude that came and went very quickly.
D: Philip Kaufman. A: Ed Harris, Dennis Quaid, Scott Glenn.

Silkwood
(1983) 128m. **A–**
The true story of a nuclear facility worker who's exposed to dangerous levels of radiation and becomes a serious thorn in corporate and union sides when she tries to blow the whistle. Amazingly, this film remains buoyant and entertaining, focusing on the characters' lives and their attempts to battle unseen forces.
D: Mike Nichols. A: Meryl Streep, Kurt Russell, Cher.

Good Morning, Vietnam
(1987) 120m. **B–**
The new disc jockey at the army radio station invades Saigon's airwaves with rhythm and blues music and a motor-mouth routine that has the staff and officers reeling. Williams' verbal virtuosity is the main reason to watch what becomes a nice-looking, politically correct feel-good film.
D: Barry Levinson. A: Robin Williams, Forest Whitaker, Tung Thanh Tran.

Matewan
(1987) 130m. **B+**
News of a pay cut sends coal miners out on strike, but immigrants and a group of black "scabs" keep the mines open. An elegiac true-life story set in the magnificent ruddy hills of West Virginia, this is both a visual treat and a complex story of capitalism and workers' rights.
D: John Sayles. A: Chris Cooper, Will Oldham, Mary McDonnell.

The Milagro Beanfield War
(1988) 117m. **B**
A poor New Mexican farmer rallies his equally struggling neighbors against developers who want to make a golf course with the local water supply. The lively cast keeps the pitch high and the Southwestern panoramas are eye popping, but the tone of this quirky fable starts to take on a sticky-sweet, false quality.
D: Robert Redford. A: Ruben Blades, Richard Bradford, Melanie Griffith.

Patty Hearst
(1988) 108m. **A–**
Kidnapped and brainwashed newspaper heiress Patty Hearst is transformed from a terrified young blue blood to a rhetoric-spewing revolutionary of the Symbionese Liberation Army. A stylized and mesmerizing retelling of the true story that haunted Americans (and parents) in the 70s.
D: Paul Schrader. A: Natasha Richardson, William Forsythe, Ving Rhames.

Running on Empty
(1988) 117m. **B+**
A radical couple who have been on the run since a bombing incident in the 60s are adept at living in emotional isolation and pulling up stakes, but now their teenage son wants to pursue his own dreams. A compelling, finely acted family drama plays out an interesting set of tensions.
D: Sidney Lumet. A: Judd Hirsch, Christine Lahti, River Phoenix.

Talk Radio
(1989) 110m. **B+**
Oliver Stone offers another dark and delirious portrait of pop culture in this look at a day and night in the life of a Dallas shockjock. Gonzo energy, manic camerawork, and a convincingly wired and abrasive Bogosian make this a fascinating and unsettling journey into talk radio hell.
D: Oliver Stone. A: Eric Bogosian, Ellen Greene, Alec Baldwin.

Courtroom Dramas

In these well-crafted, highly dramatic tales, the courtroom maneuvers and theatrics become almost secondary to themes of bigotry, madness, rape, and military corruption, with the final crack of the gavel signaling just where the film stands on its chosen issue.

. . . And Justice for All
(1979) 117m. **B−**

A righteous lawyer defends a corrupt judge and turns the trial into a kangaroo court for the real criminals who buy and sell their own brand of justice. Al's grating soapbox ravings, a judge who bangs his gun instead of a gavel for order, and sanctimonious script are some of the many excesses in this schizophrenic farce/drama.
D: Norman Jewison. A: Al Pacino, Jack Warden, John Forsythe.

Nuts
(1987) 116m. **D+**

A scrappy $500-per-night prostitute must prove herself sane before being tried for murder. Monolithically paced film screeches, jars, and remains mediocre until Streisand's final extended monologue, which sinks it into cringe-inducing bathos.
D: Martin Ritt. A: Barbra Streisand, Richard Dreyfuss, Maureen Stapleton.

The Accused
(1988) 110m. **B**

A brassy, somewhat provocative young woman is raped by a band of drunken locals in a bar; both she and her attorney then watch the justice system take over, painting the victim as a criminal. Foster is full of quiet rage in this true-life social drama that never gathers much momentum.
D: Jonathan Kaplan. A: Jodie Foster, Kelly McGillis, Bernie Coulson.

A Cry in the Dark
(1988) 120m. **B+**

A wild dog carries off an Australian couple's child, but authorities believe the more likely story (in their eyes) that it was murder. This wrenching portrayal of a family torn at the seams by lies, betrayal, and bloodthirsty media is marred only by a few static stretches and extended running time.
D: Fred Schepisi. A: Meryl Streep, Sam Neill, Bruce Myles.

The Music Box
(1989) 126m. **A−**

A lawyer defends her father accused of being a notorious war criminal and eventually has to wrestle with the fear that he really may be one. Gripping mystery with dialogue that easily shifts from the courtroom drama to gut-wrenching, father-daughter confrontations.
D: Constantin Costa-Gavras. A: Jessica Lange, Armin Mueller-Stahl, Frederic Forrest.

Reversal of Fortune
(1990) 120m. **A**

Based-on-fact story of bizarrely aloof Claus von Bulow and an activist lawyer trying to save him from a charge of attempting to murder his socialite wife. A brilliantly structured film, told in flashback from POV of the comatose wife, has a mordant sense of humor and a coldly unsettling turn by Irons as some of its assets.
D: Barbet Schroeder. A: Jeremy Irons, Ron Silver, Glenn Close.

A Few Good Men
(1992) 138m. **B**

Cruise is the pretty boy military defense attorney defending two marines accused of murder while hazing a platoon mate. Well-crafted drama of military corruption with fine performances, but it's Nicholson's turn as the hard leather colonel who finally goes ballistic in court that gives this real juice.
D: Rob Reiner. A: Tom Cruise, Jack Nicholson, Demi Moore.

Philadelphia
(1993) 119m. **B+**

Hanks is a rising-star lawyer: He's also dying of AIDS and seeks justice when he perceives he's been fired because of his disease. A sincere film notable for being the first mainstream film to address the epidemic. Contains some moving scenes but marred by overly perfect family and a white-glove stance toward homosexuality.
D: Jonathan Demme. A: Tom Hanks, Denzel Washington, Antonio Banderas.

Murder in the First
(1994) 123m. **B−**

A young assistant DA gets assigned the hopeless case of a convict who, thanks to prison brutality, is a mental basket case and commits murder. A compelling story and fine performances are often sabotaged by nonstop vertiginous camerawork.
D: Marc Rocco. A: Christian Slater, Kevin Bacon, Gary Oldman.

Entertainers

Oddly enough, the people who entertain and make us laugh seem to be an unhappy lot, or so it would seem from the comedically flavored dramas in which ordinary little people dream and struggle to get to the top.

Punchline
(1988) 128m. **C+**

A New Jersey housewife gets some pointers on how to polish her stand-up comedy act from a medical school dropout who's also trying to make it in the business. Films about comedians tend to be slightly nasty and this is no exception, though Field is terrific as the mom who spends her rainy day money buying jokes and getting bad hair dos.
D: David Seltzer. A: Sally Field, Tom Hanks, John Goodman.

The Fabulous Baker Boys
(1989) 113m. **A−**

Two brothers with a chintzy lounge act hire a sultry street-smart singer and the trio enjoys a success beyond everyone's expectations. Both a funny look at small-time performers and a sexy smart romance with fine performances, and Pfeiffer stealing the show with her piano-top singing.
D: Steve Kloves. A: Jeff Bridges, Michelle Pfeiffer, Beau Bridges.

Mr. Saturday Night
(1992) 119m. **B–**
Wandering tale of a self-sabotaging, curmudgeonly stand-up comedian's rise from Catskills resorts to early TV fame and back to obscurity. Even with a tacked-on, feel-good ending, the main character is such a nasty and rapturously self-involved SOB that this film never goes past being an uncomfortable character study.
D: Billy Crystal. A: Billy Crystal, David Paymer, Julie Warner.

Lush Life
(1994) 96m. **C+**
Two jazz musicians make ends meet playing wedding parties and such, even as their commitment to music seems to sabotage the possibility for stability. Goldblum is suitably ambling, like a 50s-style bebopper, while Whitaker is the more incendiary player/artist in this buddy tale that suffers from overly laid-back plotting.
D: Michael Elias. A: Jeff Goldblum, Forest Whitaker, Kathy Baker.

Offbeat Dramas

The films listed here are the rare birds that break entirely with Hollywood tradition and formula. Style, attitude, story, or some quixotic mix of these elements makes these films fascinating fare for those looking for left-of-center video.

My Dinner with Andre
(1981) 110m. **B**
A bewildered actor-playwright sits in awe of his theatrical director friend who, over dinner, spins mind-boggling tales of world travel, near-death experiences, and the glories of eating sand while searching for enlightenment. A peculiar overlong film but Andre's aimless passionate dinner conversation makes it fascinating.
D: Louis Malle. A: Andre Gregory, Wallace Shawn.

The World According to Garp
(1982) 136m. **B**
The life and extremely bizarre times of a writer, his domineering mother, transsexual/ex-football star best friend, tongueless female assassin, and other unusual companions. A unique film that effortlessly combines these and other plot elements into a good-hearted if at times terribly sad film.
D: George Roy Hill. A: Robin Williams, Mary Beth Hurt, Glenn Close.

Insignificance
(1985) 110m. **C+**
A nuclear scientist, a Hollywood sex symbol, and a right-wing politico converge in a 1950s New York hotel. At first, the sight and idea of having these Albert Einstein, Marilyn Monroe, and Senator Joe McCarthy stand-ins all in one place is amusing, but film soon goes into indecipherable pretension overdrive.
D: Nicolas Roeg. A: Gary Busey, Theresa Russell, Tony Curtis.

Until the End of the World
(1991) 158m. **D**
A fugitive with several identities is chased by a chic femme fatale, her boyfriend, and a hired killer through 15 cities and 8 countries as the threat of a nuclear holocaust hangs over them in this incoherent futuristic road film that only the most strung-out slacker could love. Buy the soundtrack instead.
D: Wim Wenders. A: William Hurt, Solveig Dommartin, Sam Neill.

Mad Dog and Glory
(1993) 97m. **B–**
A lonely cop saves a Mob kingpin/aspiring comic's life and gets a thank-you present in the form of a winsome blonde. The comic/offbeat possibilities of casting Murray and De Niro as the wimp never seem to gel in this curious but sweet film that's part budding love story, part oddball buddy film.
D: John McNaughton. A: Robert De Niro, Bill Murray, Uma Thurman.

Music of Chance
(1993) 98m. **C+**
Two young gamblers enter into a high-stakes card game with some wealthy types, lose, and find the only way to pay their debt is to construct an immense wall on the winner's estate. Unusual parable about greed plays like some *Twilight Zone* version of *The Hustler* and isn't without its bizarre merits.
D: Philip Haas. A: James Spader, Mandy Patinkin, M. Emmet Walsh.

Vanya on 42nd Street
(1994) 104m. **A–**
Unique film shows Chekov's famous play as it's being rehearsed by actors in street clothes at a once magnificent theater that echoes past glories, like the actors and stage director do for the play. David Mamet's script adds to the resonance in this wonderfully intimate visit to a great theatrical work.
D: Louis Malle. A: Wallace Shawn, Julianne Moore, George Gaynes.

Smoke
(1995) 112m. **A–**
Soft-touch character study of the lives of an assortment of regular folk who hang around a Brooklyn cigar/cigarette shop. Unique film is very much like a cinematic novel, with each character's story like a chapter that slowly interweaves with previous chapters: a film that gently tugs at heart-strings while not forgetting darker aspects of life.
D: Wayne Wang. A: Harvey Keitel, William Hurt, Stockard Channing.

Younger and Younger
(1995) 97m. **B–**
A brightly goofy, quasi-surreal tale about a frumpy disgruntled wife who runs the family business—a storage rental complex—her self-styled lothario husband who rules the roost (which includes playing his own cathedral-size Wurlitzer organ), their adoring college-age son, and assorted quirky customers. Good for those looking for the offbeat.
D: Percy Adlon. A: Donald Sutherland, Brendan Fraser, Lolita Davidovich.

1990s

New Gangsters and Bad Guys

Like horror films, crime movies have always been ripe places to blast away at negative social urges, and judging from the trend of these crime dramas, the 90s are shaping up

as a decade of carnage and lawlessness; these antiheroes are literally bathed in blood, to the point that filmmakers like Quentin Tarantino can treat it as a joke and *everyone* gets it.

Goodfellas
(1990) 148m. **A**

An aspiring hood is the focus of this study of 30 years of Mafia life. By turns hilarious, horrifying, touching, and frenetic, with not a single note wrongly sounded from the kitschy, period art direction; the soundtrack that mirrors the changing times; or Scorsese's direction of camera and characterization.
D: Martin Scorsese. A: Ray Liotta, Robert De Niro, Joe Pesci.

King of New York
(1990) 103m. **A–**

A brilliantly subversive tale of newly released crime lord and his blood-splattered campaign to unite warring New York gangs under his rule. A world gone mad with greed, corruption, and double crosses is bracingly told with the help of surreal ultraviolence and Walken's mesmerizing turn as a hood with a social conscience.
D: Abel Ferrara. A: Christopher Walken, Larry Fishburne, Wesley Snipes.

Miller's Crossing
(1990) 115m. **B+**

In 1920s Boston and environs, a mob boss double-crosses an old friend and messes with his girl, all in the middle of a mounting war. Incredibly detailed art direction and rich photography evoke the period with bits of black humor blending well into the complexly structured plot, with tone ranging from broodingly pastoral to ironically violent.
D: Joel Coen. A: Gabriel Byrne, John Turturro, Albert Finney.

State of Grace
(1990) 134m. **B+**

Ex-tough guy-turned-cop goes back to the old neighborhood to expose a possible merger between Italian and Irish mobs. Film works as a fascinating study of friendship under fire, a full-blooded redemption tale and adrenaline-packed thriller, with staccato editing and sharp lensing of seedy Manhattan locales.
D: Phil Joanou. A: Sean Penn, Gary Oldman, Ed Harris.

Rush
(1991) 120m. **B**

Trying to bust a drug ring, a rookie female cop goes undercover with an experienced pro; he convinces her the only way to remain undetected amongst the slime is to do dope, resulting in a nodding-out romance. Despite effectively grungy performances, film is hobbled by stilted direction and pacing.
D: Lili Fini Zanuck. A: Jason Patric, Jennifer Jason Leigh, Sam Elliott.

Bad Lieutenant
(1992) 98m. **A–**

Keitel is the nameless title character: a junkie/dealer/father and beyond burned-out New York City cop who's investigating the rape of a nun and setting up a tortured quest for redemption. An unflinching look at the very pit of human existence with an unnerving Keitel. If you have a stout constitution, don't miss.
D: Abel Ferrara. A: Harvey Keitel, Victor Argo, Zoe Tamerlis Lund.

Deep Cover
(1992) 112m. **A–**

A by-the-book DEA agent goes undercover and finds himself lost in a world of deception, drugs, and corruption that threatens to completely unravel his life. Closest in spirit to classic noir, this incredibly dark film is punched up by a breakneck pace, ironic humor, and two incredible performances by the leads.
D: Bill Duke. A: Larry Fishburne, Jeff Goldblum, Victoria Dillard.

Light Sleeper
(1992) 103m. **B+**

The go-go 80s are over, and classy coke dealer Sarandon and her delivery man Dafoe are closing down business and facing an uncertain future. This leisurely paced film has an appropriately jaded "night-after" ambiance, understated performances, and refreshingly non-stereotypical characters and story.
D: Paul Schrader. A: Willem Dafoe, Susan Sarandon, Dana Delany.

Reservoir Dogs
(1992) 99m. **A**

An ornately planned heist goes wrong in every conceivable manner. Hong Kong action-film ultraviolence, film-nerd homages, and hilarious trash-pop soundtrack meet dizzyingly structured script in director Tarantino's occasionally too-hip-for-its-own-good, but refreshingly wild breath of blood-splattered air.
D: Quentin Tarantino. A: Harvey Keitel, Tim Roth, Michael Madsen.

Amongst Friends
(1993) 88m. **B**

Three Long Island teens gravitate toward petty crime getting them attention from the Mob, but ineptness, attitude, and betrayal put their lives in danger. Deliberately paced but engaging tale that often feels like a glossy suburban version of *Mean Streets.*
D: Rob Weiss. A: Steve Parlavecchio, Joseph Lindsey, Patrick McGaw.

Carlito's Way
(1993) 144m. **B+**

A Bronx drug lord is sprung from prison, with a newfound passion for going straight, but circumstances, including running a disco, soon have him knee-deep in drug and contraband action again. Wonderfully kitschy 70s clothes and design and terrifying turn by Penn as a slimy lawyer help make this a riveting tale of fated destiny.
D: Brian De Palma. A: Al Pacino, Sean Penn, Penelope Ann Miller.

Killing Zoe
(1994) 96m. **B**

An American safe-cracker gets involved with a bank heist led by an old junkie friend in Paris. A sort of ultrahip, drug-addled version of *Dog Day Afternoon,* with seamy Paris locations and a fair share of funny/bizarre set pieces getting bogged down by trendily nihilistic mood, near-glorification of heroin use, and buckets of surplus blood.
D: Roger Avary. A: Eric Stoltz, Jean-Hugues Anglade, Julie Delpy.

The Professional
(1994) 109m **B**

A barely pubescent girl has her entire family wiped out and becomes protected by, and the protégé of, a dolorous French hitman. This stylish, Lolita-colored mobster tale suffers from a petered-out last reel but boasts both darkly sweet and nerve-wracking scenes along with one of Oldman's more deliriously mad performances.
D: Luc Bresson. A: Jean Reno, Natalie Portman, Gary Oldman.

Pulp Fiction
(1994) 150m. **A**

Essentially a series of interlocking and hilarious vignettes following the misadventures of scuzzy criminals, a cranky boxer, and various other lowlifes. The constant

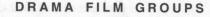

hyper-mix of pop culture references; absurdist violence; ironic tone; and truly witty, shotgun-paced dialogue make this a film that actually eclipses its hype.
D: Quentin Tarantino. A: John Travolta, Samuel L. Jackson, Bruce Willis.

Bad Company
(1995) 108m. **C+**
A CIA operative goes undercover with a private "dirty tricks" (blackmail, killing, etc.) company in order to acquire it for the government and comes up against the seductive top operative. Rampant paranoiac air and matching double crosses, cold tone, and colder characters (especially during the sex scenes) make this a depressing if well-crafted thriller.
D: Damian Harris. A: Laurence Fishburne, Ellen Barkin, Frank Langella.

Generation X

Age: somewhere between birth and 30. Class: would like to think of itself as classless, but really hopelessly middle class. Interests: listening to "alternative" rock, having the usual difficult relationships, and feeling disenfranchised by baby boomer pop culture and consumerism. To Hollywood, this is the new youth market that is mirrored and sometimes created by these stylishly hip and very ironic tales.

Pump Up the Volume
(1990) 105m. **B**
A new school outcast finds his niche when he secretly starts his own basement pirate radio station, becoming a teen hero. Thin plot, but an engaging Slater, rebellious energy, and sizzling soundtrack make this a sort of Everynerd's fantasy come true.
D: Allan Moyle. A: Christian Slater, Cheryl Pollak, Samantha Mathis.

The Unbelievable Truth
(1990) 90m. **B+**
Upon release from prison, a young man returns to his suburban home to the speculative yattering of the natives. Another quirky Hal Hartley film full of alienation, satire, and characters like a possible paramour who'd have sex if only she wasn't so worried about the A-bomb.
D: Hal Hartley. A: Robert Burke, Adrienne Shelly, Christopher Cooke.

Trust
(1991) 107m. **B**
After her father keels over dead and her boyfriend tells her to take a hike at the news of her pregnancy, a high school girl finds solace with a studious loner. Clever, sometimes surreal film veers precariously between hiply intelligent and precious.
D: Hal Hartley. A: Adrienne Shelly, Martin Donovan, Merritt Nelson.

Gas, Food, Lodging
(1992) 102m. **B**
Hard-edged tale of a New Mexico single mother duking out a meager life with her two daughters and various off-the-wall suitors. Nononsense tone and trio of fine performances make this a grimy treat.
D: Allison Anders. A: Brooke Adams, Fairuza Balk, Ione Skye.

Bodies, Rest and Motion
(1993) 94m. **B–**
Laconic tale of four 20ish persons attempting to connect with each other in a tiny Arizona town. Precious film seems more like an acting school project with players doing Fine Ensemble Work, but mostly a waste of some live wire actors.
D: Michael Steinberg. A: Bridget Fonda, Phoebe Cates, Tim Roth.

Urban Youths

Drive-by shootings, crack, roaming "gangsta" gangs, rumbling dark streets: This is the grave new world of black youth portrayed by a new generation of filmmakers. Ranging from independent, low-budget films to mainstream studio features, the basic theme is survival, often achieved, as Malcolm X said, "by whatever means necessary."

Boyz N the Hood
(1991) 112m. **A**
An on-the-mark study of young blacks growing up in South Central LA. Amazingly warm intimate movie thanks to Fishburne as the father determined to make a difference in the community and Gooding as his son who is coming of age in a world of fractured families, gangs, drugs, and alcohol.
D: John Singleton. A: Cuba Gooding, Jr.; Larry Fishburne; Ice Cube.

New Jack City
(1991) 101m. **B**
A druglord takes on the Mafia and shafts his own people in his singleminded rise to felonious fame. A thin veneer of social consciousness reveals a really fun trashy gangster film, replete with slo-mo bloodbaths, over-adrenalized camerawork, and a computerized crack-cocaine assembly line run by topless women.
D: Mario Van Peebles. A: Wesley Snipes, Ice T, Judd Nelson.

Straight Out of Brooklyn
(1991) 83m. **B–**
Red Hook, Brooklyn: A young man comes to believe that robbery is the only way to raise his family from poverty. A low-budget, roughhewn film that offers a disturbing spectator's view of the no-way-out 90s.
D: Matty Rich. A: George T. Odom; Ann D. Sanders; Lawrence Gilliard, Jr.

American Me
(1992) 125m. **B+**
Tragic character study of an LA Hispanic who comes of age in jail, is released in a world of few choices, and seemingly inevitably is

drawn into life as a gang leader. With location shooting in both Folsom Prison and East LA, this seethes with rage and desperate authenticity and offers the viewer no easy way out.
D: Edward James Olmos. A: William Forsythe, Pepe Serna, Evelina Fernandez.

Juice
(1992) 90m. **B+**
A fledgling DJ's life hits a downward spiral when his friends commit a robbery/murder. Directorial debut of Spike Lee's cinematographer is a gut-wrenching work, filled with grim, hard-edged images to match its tragic tale.
D: Ernest R. Dickerson. A: Omar Epps, Tupac Shakur, Jermaine Hopkins.

Menace II Society
(1993) 104m. **A–**
Part *Means Streets,* part James A. Cain novel, this is the most nihilistic film of the bunch as an urban teen is faced with choices of respect, crime, or self-destruction in this hard-boiled, ultraviolent character study.
D: Albert Hughes, Allen Hughes. A: Larenz Tate, Jada Pinkett, Tyrin Turner.

Poetic Justice
(1993) 109m. **C+**
Hairstylist Justice shuts down emotionally after her boyfriend is killed in front of her. She tries to start a new life, perhaps find a new love, while on a trip to a stylist convention. Well-intentioned if slightly mawkish melodrama.
D: John Singleton. A: Janet Jackson, Tupac Shakur, Regina King.

Fresh
(1994) 114m. **A**
A 12-year-old masterminds an intricate plan, based on skills he's learned in chess, to extricate himself and his sister from a ghetto world of drugs and death. A refreshing coming-of-age film that glides between sinister adults and hazardous school yards with street-smart precision.
D: Boaz Yakin. A: Sean Nelson, N'Bushe Wright, Giancarlo Esposito.

Jason's Lyric
(1994) 119m. **C+**
Tough and sometimes visually poetic coming-of-age tale of two Houston teens and their friends who attempt to escape Houston's black ghetto. A workmanlike effort but the violence, high emotionalism, and steamy sex scenes all feel by-the-book.
D: Doug McHenry. A: Allen Payne, Jada Pinkett, Bokeem Woodbine.

Mi Vida Loca (My Crazy Life)
(1994) 92m. **B–**
A series of interweaving character studies about members of East LA girl gangs. Mixture of actors and real gang members makes this a gritty, you-are-there experience of ghetto romance, rivalry, and friendship. No great insights, but a worthy depiction of Hispanics marginalized by both race and sex.
D: Allison Anders. A: Seidy Lopez, Angel Aviles, Jesse Borrago.

African-American Dramas

Not all black films focus on the problems of urban youths—this group of well-made, sometimes overly earnest stories shows the rich historical and cultural depths of what it means to be African-American.

The Color Purple
(1985) 152m. **B**
Wide-ranging, expansive saga that covers 40 years in the life of a late-nineteenth-century black woman. You either love this or not: It's too big, bold, and symphonic to feel lukewarm about. Sincere performances and a powerful sense of the film's own nobility sometimes get in the way of a good story.
D: Steven Spielberg. A: Whoopi Goldberg, Danny Glover, Oprah Winfrey.

Native Son
(1986) 112m. **C**
Thrilled to be hired as chauffeur to a wealthy white family in 1940s New York, a young man's hopes for the future are dashed when their daughter dies in an accident and they accuse him of murder. Emotive but unengaging, with the community-theater-level performances obscuring some terrific material.
D: Jerrold Freedman. A: Oprah Winfrey, Carroll Baker, Akosua Busia.

To Sleep with Anger
(1990) 101m. **A**
Family emotions go awry when an old acquaintance shows up; he turns out to be a "trickster," the mischief-maker of African-American folklore. This intelligent ironic story proceeds at a good clip but constantly maintains an affectionate distance from the characters and the viewer as well.
D: Charles Burnett. A: Danny Glover, Mary Alice, Paul Butler.

Death of a Prophet
(1991) 60m. **B**
Combining documentary footage, present-day interviews, and reenactments, this attempt to trace the last few days of Malcolm X's life never quite coheres, but does present him with respect and intelligence.
D: Woodie King, Jr. A: Morgan Freeman, Yolanda King, Mansoor Najee-ullah.

Daughters of the Dust
(1992) 113m. **B–**
This chronicle of an African-American family's preparations to leave their sea island home for the U.S. mainland in 1902 has such a precious and often pretentious tone that the fascinating material and gorgeous photography fail to catch fire.
D: Julie Dash. A: Adisa Anderson, Cheryl Lynn Bruce, Cora Dee Day.

Mississippi Masala
(1992) 118m. **B+**
An Indian family in Uganda is expelled by Idi Amin's government and winds up in Mississippi running a motel. More trouble starts when the daughter falls in love with a local black businessman. A sweetly etched love story and a vibrant look at colorful, tightly knit communities.
D: Mira Nair. A: Denzel Washington, Sarita Choudhury, Roshan Seth.

Love Your Mama
(1993) 92m. **C–**
A family struggles in a Chicago ghetto, with Mama as the center of strength and love. Well meaning and sometimes deeply corny story with a tendency toward speechifying.
D: Ruby L. Oliver. A: Carol E. Hall, Andre Robinson, Audrey Morgan.

Spike Lee

With varying quality, Spike Lee redefined the look and attitude of African-American films. Brilliantly hued sets and photography, hyper-rhythmic editing, outspoken characters, and an undertone of rage give his films the look and feel of musicals with attitude, a far cry from the earnest, well-intentioned black films from the 70s.

She's Gotta Have It
(1986) 94m. **A**

An almost flawless debut Lee effort about a hypersexual female and the various males who make fools of themselves in pursuit of her. Completely lacking in self-consciousness, with a sense of immediacy, refreshing sexual frankness, and some truly hilarious vignettes.

D: Spike Lee. A: Tracy Camilla Johns, Tommy Redmond Hicks, Spike Lee.

School Daze
(1988) 114m. **B**

Tensions run high at a college where the black student body has divided itself into groups—the Jigaboos and the Wannabees—based on skin tone. An energetic satire peppered with comic and sometimes strident moments, along with exhilarating dance numbers including "Doin' Da Butt."

D: Spike Lee. A: Larry Fishburne, Spike Lee, Giancarlo Esposito.

Do the Right Thing
(1989) 120m.
A–

It's the hottest day in the year on a neighborhood block in Bedford-Stuyvesant; starting out as a series of funny/tense vignettes in a candy-colored version of Brooklyn, this grows darker as the racial antagonism rises to the top in an audacious film that's flawed by a confusing resolution.

D: Spike Lee. A: Danny Aiello, Spike Lee, Rosie Perez.

Mo' Better Blues
(1990) 129m. **B–**

A hotshot jazz trumpet player tries to juggle the two women in his life while distancing the shady dealings of his manager-lifelong friend. A stylish but meandering look at the New York jazz world, peppered with dashes of humor including controversial caricatures of Jewish businessmen.

D: Spike Lee. A: Denzel Washington, Joie Lee, Wesley Snipes.

Jungle Fever
(1991) 135m. **C–**

A successful black man and his white secretary have an affair with nasty results. Not much as a drama or statement about interracial relations—Snipes and Sciorra seem to be in different movies even when embracing—but scenes like the visit to a crack den make this worth a watch.

D: Spike Lee. A: Wesley Snipes, Annabella Sciorra, Samuel L. Jackson.

Malcolm X
(1992) 201m. **A–**

Sweeping, epic, and reverent version of Malcolm X's life, from his beginnings as a hood in Harlem to his assassination in 1965. The dash and color with which it depicts the times and events keeps our interest, but it finally starts to feel like a biography of a monument.

D: Spike Lee. A: Denzel Washington, Angela Bassett, Spike Lee.

Crooklyn
(1994) 112m. **C+**

Lee gives us a semiautobiographical film about a family getting by in 1970s Brooklyn. Lots of kitschy 70s music, clothes, fun performances and a generally genial tone, but the characters and even the episodes seem as flat—and as colorful—as cartoons.

D: Spike Lee. A: Alfre Woodard, Delroy Lindo, Zelda Harris.

Nostalgic Coming-of-Age

Unlike earlier rite-of-passage films, these nostalgically minded journeys focus on women, have a franker approach to sex and a refreshing lack of pat answers for life's more imponderable aspects.

Empire of the Sun
(1987) 152m. **A–**

A 12-year-old British boy living in China is separated from his parents after the Japanese invasion in 1941 and receives lessons in survival from a scavenging American seaman. Spielberg beautifully uses the kid's point of view in this grand sweeping historical epic/coming-of-age film.

D: Steven Spielberg. A: Christian Bale, John Malkovich, Miranda Richardson.

Hope and Glory
(1987) 113m. **B+**

When Britain during World War II is seen through the eyes of a seven-year-old, the events and deprivations—air raids, a crashed blimp, the destruction of his school—all seem like great chaotic wonders. An usual look at the war with a light touch that informs the warmth and nostalgia with intelligence.

D: John Boorman. A: Sarah Miles, David Hayman, Derrick O'Connor.

Dogfight
(1991) 92m. **A**

The night before shipping out to Vietnam, a Marine takes a lumpy young woman to his buddies' contest for the ugliest date and gets more than he bargained for: They actually hit it off. Credible, intelligent, spare, and affecting, this is a real gem with period detail and revealing character moments used to great effect.

D: Nancy Savoca. A: Lili Taylor, River Phoenix, Richard Panebianco.

The Man on the Moon
(1991) 99m. **C+**

1950s Louisiana teenage girl falls for an older boy—unfortunately he falls for her older sister. Well-detailed sibling ups and downs, nicely handled period detail, and tender performances make this solid entertainment and worth a watch.

D: Robert Mulligan. A: Sam Waterston, Tess Harper, Gail Strickland.

Rambling Rose
(1991) 112m. **B+**
A young woman who's made a mess of her life but just can't seem to tone down her effect on men goes to work as a mother's helper for a Georgia family. An engaging intelligent story that sneaks up on you with its unusual slant.
D: Martha Coolidge. A: Laura Dern, Diane Ladd, Robert Duvall.

Alan and Naomi
(1992) 96m. **D+**
A boy tries to make friends with an immigrant girl traumatized by the death of her father in Nazi Germany. Promising premise is poorly served by too-modern dialogue, stereotyped characters, and stagy feel.
D: Sterling Vanwahenen. A: Lukas Haas, Michael Gross, Amy Aquino.

School Ties
(1992) 110m. **B**
It's the 1950s and the newly recruited star quarterback is doing great at a snobby New England prep school—that is, until it's discovered that he's Jewish. Nice period feel to this workmanlike film that's effective both as a coming-of-age story and a tale of anti-Semitism.
D: Robert Mandel. A: Brendan Fraser, Chris O'Donnell, Andrew Lowery.

A Bronx Tale
(1993) 122m. **B+**
Two role models—his loving bus-driver father and the splashy gangster who rules the neighborhood—cause conflicts for a young man coming of age in 1960s Bronx. Packs a punch but with a generous optimism, thanks to all-around likable characters, a sweet upbeat story, and a good use of Bronx locales.
D: Robert De Niro. A: Robert De Niro, Chazz Palminteri, Joe Pesci.

King of the Hill
(1993) 103m. **B+**
During the Depression, a 12-year-old boy watches his financially strapped family splinter apart leaving him to fend for himself in a seedy St. Louis hotel. Finely etched, almost gloomy tale except for the appealing and cunning survivor who also has the limitless powers of a young imagination.
D: Steven Soderbergh. A: Jeroen Krabbe, Jesse Bradford, Karen Allen.

That Night
(1993) 90m. **C+**
A shy young Long Island girl spends the hot summer of '61 idolizing the troubled teen bombshell who lives next door and soon becomes the go-between for her romance with a working-class hunk. Doe-eyed Dushku steals this half-baked but pleasant coming-of-age tale from mad lovers Lewis and Howell.
D: Craig Bolotin. A: Juliette Lewis, C. Thomas Howell, Eliza Dushku.

World War II

More mysteries of Hollywood: This series of war movies was made in a short period with nothing resembling public demand; many of them bombed at the box office. Yet most are fine films, dealing with war's harrowing aspects in terms of violence—both physical and psychological—and even shedding some light on a few secrets the Allies can't be too proud of.

Merry Christmas, Mr. Lawrence
(1983) 124m. **B**
A violent battle of wills commences when a British officer interned in a Japanese POW camp refuses to cooperate with a determined commander. A very modern look at the pathological relationship between captor and captive, with an unflappable turn by Bowie and eerie score as highlights.
D: Nagisa Oshima. A: David Bowie, Tom Conti, Ryuichi Sakamoto.

Captive Hearts
(1987) 102m. **C**
Two crewmen crash into a Japanese village at war's end, causing extreme conflict amongst the villagers regarding the flyboys' fate. With some unnerving violence to pass the time until the inevitable feel-good scene, this is okay but manipulative.
D: Paul Almond. A: Pat Morita, Chris Makepeace, Michael Sarrazin.

Hanna's War
(1988) 148m. **B**
A Jewish refugee is enlisted by the British to assist in their efforts to rescue drowned flyers. A real-life "Joan of Arc" story as our heroine stands up to repeated and quite gruesome torture in this tough but affecting tale.
D: Menahem Golan. A: Ellen Burstyn, Anthony Andrews, David Warner.

Fat Man and Little Boy
(1989) 127m. **C**
Stilted tale of a general and the scientists who fought to beat the Germans to the nuclear punch as they created the first A-bomb. A stiff distant feel keeps viewers at arm's length, despite fine cast and a fascinating story.
D: Roland Joffe. A: Paul Newman, Dwight Schultz, John Cusack.

Come See the Paradise
(1990) 135m. **B**
The attack on Pearl Harbor shatters the budding love between an Irishman and a Japanese-American girl when she's thrown into an internment camp. Story of institutionalized racism works both as a riveting exposé of a shameful part of U.S. history and as a moving bittersweet love story.
D: Alan Parker. A: Dennis Quaid, Tamlyn Tomita, Sab Shimono.

Forced March
(1990) 104m. **B−**
An American actor in Hungary prepares for the role of Miklos Radnoti who penned a series of haunting poems while a prisoner on a death march. Holocaust images from the past combine with the modern-day filming of the event in this psychological drama that offers an appropriately worn-down, European ambiance.
D: Rich King. A: Chris Sarandon, Renee Soutendijk, Josef Sommer.

Memphis Belle
(1990) 101m. **B**
Ensemble character study of U.S. flyers in Britain steeling up for their final bombing mission over Germany. Though there's amazing state-of-the-art effects, mild cursing, and some blood, this is still your basic old-fashioned war adventure done well but adding noth-

ing new storywise or to the genre tone.
D: Michael Caton-Jones. A: Matthew Modine, Eric Stoltz, John Lithgow.

Triumph of the Spirit
(1990) 120m. **B–**
In the Auschwitz death camp, a Jewish tough boxes for the amusement of Nazis who will kill him if he loses. Seeping with oppressive atmosphere and unglamorized bouts, the film's main drawback is the usually fine Dafoe's rather flimsy, oversensitive performance.
D: Robert Young. A: Willem Dafoe, Wendy Gazelle, Robert Loggia.

A Midnight Clear
(1992) 107m. **A–**
Late in World War II, a group of soldiers goes on a winter reconnaissance mission with the hopes and some evidence that the war is over; in a series of harrowing encounters, it becomes clear it isn't. Unlike any war film, with its crystalline winter photography, an unnerving sense of 360-degree menace, and superb ensemble work by all.
D: Keith Gordon. A: Peter Berg, Gary Sinise, Kevin Dillon.

Shining Through
(1992) 125m. **C**
Amusingly ridiculous melodrama posits the idea that a Queens girl will end up as an ace spy in the thick of Nazi Germany. Unfortunately, sheer camp value is mitigated by attention-dulling pace and even duller romance with Douglas in this handsomely produced misfire.
D: David Seltzer. A: Melanie Griffith, Michael Douglas, Liam Neeson.

Schindler's List
(1994) 197m. B&W.
A
The true story of a seemingly amoral capitalist, who becomes the unlikely savior of the Jews working in his factory, is visually astonishing, with endless re-creations of Nazi atrocities shot in stark, documentary-like black and white, and featuring three powerful performances. While the film's artfulness can be a little distancing, it still succeeds both on a dramatic level and as a document.
D: Steven Spielberg. A: Liam Neeson, Ralph Fiennes, Ben Kingsley.

Bio-Pics

Many of these films opt for the old-fashioned theatrics of a *Bugsy*, whose characters, themes, and scope are as big and brassy as a parade. Others take a smaller, more stylish approach with films that can be as eccentric as the characters they are portraying.

Gandhi
(1982) 188m. **A–**
The stirring and panoramic study of India's spiritual and political leader takes him through his early fights against bigotry in South Africa to his advancement of nonviolent resistance to regain India. The titanic re-creations of colonial India are stunning and Kingsley looks, sounds, and practically embodies Gandhi.
D: Richard Attenborough. A: Ben Kingsley, Candice Bergen, Edward Fox.

Tucker: The Man and His Dream
(1988) 111m. **B+**
A slightly delirious version of the life and times of the optimist and dreamer Preston Tucker, who tried to buck the big three auto makers by building the perfect car. Like a long triumphant movie trailer, it features lively performances, catchy music, and delightfully stylized details.
D: Francis Ford Coppola. A: Jeff Bridges, Joan Allen, Martin Landau.

Blaze
(1989) 119m. **C**
Louisiana governor Huey Long scandalized 1950s society in many ways, including his affair with stripper Blaze Starr. With the promising material and ready-for-fun cast, you keep waiting for it to get better, but it doesn't.
D: Ron Shelton. A: Paul Newman, Lolita Davidovich, Jerry Hardin.

Vincent and Theo
(1990) 138m. **B–**
Focusing on the close but difficult relationship between the two van Gogh brothers, this painterly, sometimes slow film offers an intimate view of the artist's emotional turmoil.
D: Robert Altman. A: Tim Roth, Paul Rhys, Johanna Ter Steege.

White Hunter, Black Heart
(1990) 112m. **B–**
A pretty audacious idea: the off-the-set shenanigans of director John Huston while shooting *The African Queen*. Unfortunately, despite director Eastwood's sure pacing and African locales, the film stumbles into macho-mystical Hemingway-land with Eastwood not so much acting as impersonating Huston.
D: Clint Eastwood. A: Clint Eastwood, Jeff Fahey, George Dzundza.

Bugsy
(1991) 135m. **B**
Gala extravagant treatment of Hollywood gangster Bugsy Siegel, whose grandiose vision and fly-by-night financing built Las Vegas. Sets and costumes would make Fred and Ginger weep with envy, but the story never seems to fill out this long, over-detailed film.
D: Barry Levinson. A: Warren Beatty, Annette Bening, Harvey Keitel.

Ruby
(1991) 100m. **C+**
A small-time hustler who ekes out a living as a strip club owner and Mob/FBI informer becomes infamous as the man who shot Oswald. A sympathetic but muted portrayal with good seedy locales, a chilling reconstruction of the murder, but no clearer idea of why it happened.
D: John Mackenzie. A: Danny Aiello, Sherilyn Fenn, Arliss Howard.

The Babe
(1992) 115m. **C+**
Some of the facts of Babe Ruth's less than exemplary life are glanced at in this biopic of the megahitter, but mainly it's a poorly constructed episodic film showing his rise from petty character defects. Goodman is appealing but otherwise for undiscerning fans only.
D: Arthur Hiller. A: John Goodman, Kelly McGillis, Trini Alvarado.

Chaplin
(1992) 144m. **B+**
Chaplin's life writ in 50 foot

letters, with no missing moments. The period detail and atmosphere are thrilling and Downey's portrayal is quietly astonishing but be prepared for a long haul.
D: Richard Attenborough. A: Robert Downey, Jr.; Geraldine Chaplin; Dan Aykroyd.

Hoffa
(1992) 140m. **C**
Over-sympathetic and over-long version of Jimmy Hoffa's life that will confuse anyone unfamiliar with U.S. labor history. This goes for union pageantry and gives Nicholson free reign, though his performance is more mimicry and makeup than real power.
D: Danny DeVito. A: Jack Nicholson, Danny DeVito, Armand Assante.

Hours and Times
(1992) 60m. B&W. **B–**
Sensitive John Lennon and (homosexual) manager Brian Epstein go off for a four-day holiday and tensions build—will one of them make the move?—as they wander around Barcelona and talk about life. A provocative idea of Beatle history that might have happened unfortunately makes a rather studied male-bonding drama.
D: Christopher Munch. A: David Angus, Ian Hart, Stephanie Pack.

Thirty Two Short Films About Glenn Gould
(1993) 94m. **A**
The eccentric life of the century's premier pianist is explored in a series of quick vignettes, ranging from dramatized key moments to animated interpretations of Gould performances. One doesn't have to be a fan of either Gould or classical music to enjoy this beautifully shot, piercing, often funny character study.
D: François Girard. A: Colm Feore.

Backbeat
(1994) 100m. **B–**
The tale of early Beatles struggles in the slimy dives of Hamburg focuses on the *fifth* Beatle, quasi-guitarist and painter Stu Sutcliffe. Has appropriately grungy period design, great re-creation of Beatles sound, and dynamic portrait of angry young man John Lennon, but the point of the film feels fuzzy.
D: Iain Softley. A: Stephen Dorff, Sheryl Lee, Ian Hart.

Cobb
(1994) 129m. **B–**
Bio-pic of blustering, loud-mouthed, hard-drinking womanizer and great ballplayer Ty Cobb. Expertly scripted and filmed with a tireless and mesmerizing performance by Jones, but the series of teeth-grating, landing-jet-volume tirades tears through the speakers most of the time.
D: Ron Shelton. A: Tommy Lee Jones, Robert Wuhl, Lolita Davidovich.

Ed Wood
(1994) 126m. B&W.
A–
A highly romanticized story of the "world's worst director" and fervent transvestite Ed Wood introduces some of his hilariously bad films and amazing cast of Hollywood loser pals, including on-the-skids Bela Lugosi. Shot in ravishing rain-silver black and white, this is a constantly amusing, compassionate, and all-around fun film.
D: Tim Burton. A: Johnny Depp, Martin Landau, Sarah Jessica Parker.

Immortal Beloved
(1994) 121m. **B+**
Upon the death of Beethoven, his secretary finds a letter from the composer bequeathing his estate to an unnamed "immortal beloved," creating a mystery to be solved and a tumultuous life to be reexamined. Fascinating *Citizen Kane*-like structure, gorgeous photography, and excellent performances hide what's basically a grand-style Hollywood weepy.
D: Bernard Rose. A: Gary Oldman, Jeroen Krabbe, Isabella Rossellini.

Mrs. Parker and the Vicious Circle
(1994) 124m. **B–**
This portrait of savagely witty alcoholic writer and member of the Algonquin Round Table Dorothy Parker is as unhappy and frustrated as the subject. Leigh turns in a suitably sloshy performance with a nice period feel, but the film plods grimly from scene to scene while the members of the Vicious Circle are not so much etched as water-colored.
D: Alan Rudolph. A: Jennifer Jason Leigh, Matthew Broderick, Campbell Scott.

(See also *Malcolm X*, page 250.)

American Costume Epics

Historical detail and lavish art direction are highlighted in these big-budget, epic films that portray the heroes, gangsters, and salt-of-the-earth characters of America's past. While occasionally a little too self-important for their own good, Hollywood's attempts at making "prestige films" are still some of the classiest escapist entertainment around.

Ragtime
(1981) 156m. **B–**
Four stories involving real and fictional characters from 1906 America are intertwined into a haphazard nostalgic patchwork quilt. Beautiful period detail, charming score, and an energetic ensemble of actors somehow add up to a somewhat spiritless film.
D: Milos Forman. A: Howard E. Rollins, Jr.; Elizabeth McGovern; James Cagney.

Reds
(1981) 196m. **B+**
This detailed and evocative epic portrayal of the brief career of radical journalist John Reed and his lover Louise Bryant follows them from a bustling Greenwich Village of socialists, radical writers, and unionists to an immense and heroic Russia torn by the Bolshevik Revolution.
D: Warren Beatty. A: Warren Beatty, Diane Keaton, Edward Herrmann.

Revolution
(1985) 125m. **D**
Rain and mud seem to pervade this amazingly dull story of an illiterate trapper forced to join up with the Colonial Army to watch over his 14-year-old son. Pacino, for once, doesn't shine, and attempts to show effects of war on the little people is colorless and confused.
D: Hugh Hudson. A: Al Pacino, Nastassja Kinski, Donald Sutherland.

Glory
(1989) 122m. **B+**
A character-rich story of the

first all black regiment in the Civil War follows their struggles as the white commander tries to train and outfit his men. Vivid frightening battles show confusion and horror of man-to-man combat, and the touching dramatic confrontations make this a well-balanced study of bravery and war.
D: Edward Zwick. A: Matthew Broderick, Denzel Washington, Morgan Freeman.

Avalon
(1990) 126m. **B+**

This nostalgic celebration of a family who immigrates to America tracks various members as ties and rituals slowly fade away with TV, suburbanization, and success. A rambling story, but beautifully filmed, rich with character moments and a palpable sadness for the end of the traditional family.
D: Barry Levinson. A: Aidan Quinn, Elizabeth Perkins, Elijah Wood.

Billy Bathgate
(1990) 107m. **B–**

A young man comes of age as a member of gangster Dutch Schultz's gang in 1930s New York. Schultz is shown as a tragically flawed character, and we watch his decline even as Billy idolizes him. Finally, there are no characters we really care about in this pretty but hollow film.
D: Robert Benton. A: Dustin Hoffman, Doren Dean, Nicole Kidman.

Mr. and Mrs. Bridge
(1990) 127m. **B+**

Nothing big seems to happen in this quiet, exquisitely subtle portrait of an upper-middle-class couple in Kansas City in the 30s and 40s, except for a series of almost nonevents showing missed opportunities for feelings, and a sense of suffocation. A first-class act with unerring performances.
D: James Ivory. A: Paul Newman, Joanne Woodward, Blythe Danner.

Far and Away
(1992) 140m. **C+**

A bare-knuckle fighting Irishman and the landlord's daughter come to America seeking land in the Oklahoma land rush. An intentionally old-fashioned, rugged frontier adventure/romance with crazy plot twists and characters that seem like retreads from 30s films, but the couple, scenery, and massive wagon race are nice to watch.
D: Ron Howard. A: Tom Cruise, Nicole Kidman, Thomas Gibson.

Of Mice and Men
(1992) 110m. **B–**

This sad story of two Depression-era itinerant farm hands is set in an oddly rosy-colored rural America of golden fields and fertile lands. Basically a beautifully produced acting fest with Sinise bringing a quiet dignity to George, and Malkovich a little too threatening as his sweet and tragically simpleminded friend.
D: Gary Sinise. A: John Malkovich, Gary Sinise, Casey Siemaszko.

A River Runs Through It
(1992) 124m. **B+**

In pre-World War I Montana, a father uses fly-fishing as a means to teach life lessons to his two sons, one of whom becomes a teacher, the other a hard-drinking reporter. Lushly photographed nostalgic idyll of Americana and family life offers fine performances even though the drama is almost lost in the scenery.
D: Robert Redford. A: Brad Pitt, Craig Sheffer, Tom Skerritt.

The Age of Innocence
(1993) 133m. **B+**

In this love story of people trapped in social customs, Scorsese lays out his usual visual feast with a re-creation of 1870s New York Society that's detailed down to china patterns and hand kisses. The characters are finely hewed, but partly due to the story, their emotional distance extends to the audience, often making this inconveniently mannered.
D: Martin Scorsese. A: Daniel Day-Lewis, Michelle Pfeiffer, Winona Ryder.

Ethan Frome
(1993) 107m. **C+**

He married the prickly Zeena because she cared for his sickly mother, and now she's a semi-invalid sucking all the emotional and spiritual life out of him. This snow-covered drama of puritanical values is another actor's feast, but not penetrating enough for more than passing interest.
D: John Madden. A: Liam Neeson, Joan Allen, Patricia Arquette.

Sommersby
(1993) 112m. **C+**

A man missing for seven years shows up to claim his wife and land in post-Civil War Tennessee. But is the loving and public-minded man a reformed lout or an imposter? This *Return of Martin Guerre* remake sows too many seeds while keeping the private mystery and the characters at arm's length.
D: Jon Amiel. A: Richard Gere, Jodie Foster, Bill Pullman.

Legends of the Fall
(1994) 134m. **B**

Epic tale of the trials and tribulations of a wealthy Rocky Mountain family—a father and his three sons—which includes World War I, death, and sibling rivalry over a woman. A long and fairly entertaining family/romantic saga that still comes off feeling like an expensive upscale version of *Bonanza.*
D: Edward Zwick. A: Anthony Hopkins, Brad Pitt, Aidan Quinn.

Little Women
(1994) 118m. **A**

Hollywood finally got Alcott's classic just right this time, in a beautifully played version that shines. Here is a coming-of-age tale with a nostalgia for a past America, and real warmth for the four very independent March sisters and their friends, making this a most pleasurable four-hanky film.
D: Gillian Armstrong. A: Susan Sarandon, Winona Ryder, Gabriel Byrne.

Nell
(1994) 114m. **C+**

An alternately touching and mawkish tale of a young woman raised by herself in the Southern backwoods. Foster is quite a sight dressed in rags, speaking in her self-created language, but film's mystical ambiance is scuttled by tired courtroom drama about what to do with this "wild child."
D: Michael Apted. A: Jodie Foster, Liam Neeson, Natasha Richardson.

Foreign Costume Epics

Costume dramas have come a long way from the *Anna and the King of Siam* days, and the films in this genre continue to be some of the more artful portrayals of passion's many manifestations, all taking place amidst the sweep of historical events in foreign lands.

Henry and June
(1990) 136m. **A**

An erotic and complex portrayal of writer Anaïs Nin's affair with Henry Miller and later his wife June in 1930s Paris. This stylish and sly film brings to life the rutty bohemian life of artists and sensual seekers, with Ward making a glorious New York-accented Pan.
D: Philip Kaufman. A: Fred Ward, Uma Thurman, Maria de Madeiros.

The Sheltering Sky
(1990) 139m. **B–**

An expatriate American couple seeks to revive their souls through experiences in post-World War II Northern Africa. An arty, occasionally sexy, but mostly hazy study of searching people that offers scraps of ponderous philosophy and gloriously photographed scenes of a stark endless Sahara Desert.
D: Bernardo Bertolucci. A: Debra Winger, John Malkovich, Campbell Scott.

The House of the Spirits
(1993) 135m. **B+**

Love, corruption, and supernatural undertones haunt this complex family saga of a domineering South American ranch owner, his wife, sister, and daughter. This is an acting tour de force with the performances of the three titans holding you at breathing distance from their characters.
D: Bille August. A: Jeremy Irons, Glenn Close, Meryl Streep, Winona Ryder.

M. Butterfly
(1993) 100m. **B+**

Based on a true story, a French diplomat in Communist China carries on an extended affair with a female impersonator, unaware that he's a man passing on state's secrets. Irons is all burned-out dreaminess in this stunningly photographed psychosexual drama with a haunting resonance and tragic finale.
D: David Cronenberg. A: Jeremy Irons, John Lone, Ian Richardson.

Orlando
(1993) 94m. **B+**

An Elizabethan lord gets to span centuries and genders in his/her search for love and happiness. Carefully written, brilliantly acted, and rich with sets and costumes that make *A Passage to India* look like a low-budget outing, this is guaranteed to incite post-viewing debates.
D: Sally Potter. A: Tilda Swinton, Billy Zane, Quentin Crisp.

The Piano
(1993) 121m. **A**

When a nineteenth-century New Zealand farmer sells the piano of his mute mail-order bride, the new owner offers to sell it back to her, key by key, in exchange for sexual favors. Everything from the monstrously dense locale to the vivid characters is haunting and unexpected in this tale of repression, love, and joy.
D: Jane Campion. A: Holly Hunter, Harvey Keitel, Sam Neill.

Wide Sargasso Sea
(1993) 100m. **B**

This sensuous and thought-provoking spin on *Jane Eyre* shows Edward Rochester attracted to a white Jamaican Creole for her raw sexuality, marrying her for her plantation. When his priggish racism and desire to escape the tropics surfaces, he's willing to even drive his wife mad in order to get back to England. A seductive if sometimes heavy-handed drama.
D: John Duigan. A: Karina Lombard, Nathaniel Parker, Rachel Ward.

Little Buddha
(1994) 123m. **B**

Buddhism gets some Hollywood razzle dazzle in this tale of a modern-day search for a Tibetan master's reincarnation and the retelling of the Buddha's life and enlightenment. The historical sections are a big, colorful, flower-strewn extravaganza with Reeves making a game Siddhartha, but the modern drama is a mostly stilted travelogue.
D: Bernardo Bertolucci. A: Keanu Reeves, Ying Ruocheng, Bridget Fonda.

Rapa Nui
(1994) 107m. **C–**

In 1600s Easter Island, the inhabitants, very busy building giant sculptural heads, are divided between the ruling theocracy and the poor workers. A somewhat boring, politically correct restless natives and *Romeo and Juliet* story with lovely *National Geographic* photography and a few moments of grandeur featuring those monumental heads.
D: Kevin Reynolds. A: Jason Scott Lee, Esai Morales, Sandrine Holt.

Braveheart
(1995) 182m. **A**

Melodramatically engaging saga of revolutionary William Wallace who fought the Brits to gain Scotland's freedom in the thirteenth century. The gorgeously photographed vistas are filled with gruesome battles and fiery subplots, making this a rough-hewn, old-fashioned epic of a superior grade.
D: Mel Gibson. A: Mel Gibson, Patrick McGoohan, Sophie Marceau.

First Knight
(1995) 134m. **C+**

It's back to Camelot in this big-budget but halfhearted remake of the Lady Guinevere, Lancelot, and King Arthur legend. A couple of majestic battle scenes almost make this, but the drama is dispirited, Connery looks tired, Gere photogenic, and Ormond looks like she'd rather be somewhere else.
D: Jerry Zucker. A: Sean Connery, Richard Gere, Julia Ormond.

White Flannel

Messrs. Merchant and Ivory and company continue to crank out these handsome literate films of pre-World War II Britain and her subjects that combine photogenic nostalgia for a gracious way of life now gone, and an often humorous examination of its foibles.

Enchanted April
(1991) 101m. **B**
Four Englishwomen—two locked into dull marriages—share a palazzo in Italy where they find the open voluptuous holiday has curious effects on their love lives. What starts out as a slightly humdrum social comedy in England blossoms into a pleasant humorous ensemble piece and song of the senses in Italy.
D: Mike Newell. A: Josie Lawrence, Miranda Richardson, Joan Plowright.

Where Angels Fear to Tread
(1991) 112m. **B–**
A middle-aged Englishwoman marries a young Italian, and when she dies in childbirth, her relatives descend upon him to retrieve the baby. Starts out as a tale of finding liberation and joy in sunny Tuscany before turning into a slightly humorous, sometimes bland class and culture clash.
D: Charles Sturridge. A: Helen Mirren, Helena Bonham Carter, Judy Davis.

Howard's End
(1992) 142m. **A–**
An elegant story of love between comprehending intelligentsia and insensitive capitalist that tries to answer the question of which class shall inherit the earth in Edwardian England. Film leans a little too much toward impeccably decorative sets, but the characters always keep it anchored. Redgrave's performance virtually haunts the movie.
D: James Ivory. A: Emma Thompson, Anthony Hopkins, Vanessa Redgrave.

Remains of the Day
(1993) 135m. **B+**
A butler blindly devoted to his master, the master blindly believing in his ability to alter pre-World War II events through diplomacy, and a housekeeper who tries to break through the butler's remoteness make up the fascinating triangle in this sumptuous and melancholy look at the waning days of British aristocracy.
D: James Ivory. A: Anthony Hopkins, Emma Thompson, James Fox.

Princess Caraboo
(1994) 97m. **B+**
From out of nowhere, an exotically lovely woman appears, speaking no English and entrancing all she meets: Is she a foreign princess or an impostor? With a delightful cast, especially an enchanting Cates, and a hilarious Kline as the cynical butler, this sparkling fable-like comedy/drama set in Regency England is a sweet surprise.
D: Michael Austin. A: Phoebe Cates, Jim Broadbent, Kevin Kline.

Widow's Peak
(1994) 98m. **B**
A small 1920s Irish village is all aflutter when a mysterious and seductive young woman settles in and manages to enthrall the men and mystify the women. A witty tale benefits from three winning performances, and the plot twists will keep you guessing up to the last scene.
D: John Irvin. A: Mia Farrow, Natasha Richardson, Joan Plowright.

Foreign Adventures

These epic, star-studded, and beautifully filmed adventure dramas could just as well be called "Where White Men Dare Not Tread" as the missionaries and explorers of Western civilization come up against the splendor and tribal ways of the New and Third Worlds, leading to culture clash, madness, and even redemption.

The White Dawn
(1974) 110m. **B+**
In 1896 the crew of a wrecked New England whaling ship is saved by Eskimos who introduce them to their decidedly nonpuritanical tribal ways. In its examination of how "civilized" man impacts on primitive innocence, this compelling, beautifully shot adventure drama offers haunting images of tribal rituals based on survival.
D: Philip Kaufman. A: Warren Oates; Timothy Bottoms; Louis Gossett, Jr.

The Mission
(1986) 125m. **A**
A former soldier seeks absolution in the Brazilian rain forests and at the hands of a priest building a mission. Both a moving story of one man's spiritual struggle and an epic tale of the violent colonialism inflicted by Christianity on a stunningly photographed fertile New World.
D: Roland Joffe. A: Jeremy Irons, Robert De Niro, Aidan Quinn.

The Mosquito Coast
(1986) 119m. **B+**
Visionary/scientist Ford is out to create the ideal society with his wife and kids in the jungles of South America, but hubris and natural forces send him on the road to madness. A moody morality tale features an understated Ford and a thick air of natural mystery marred only by a slow pace.
D: Peter Weir. A: Harrison Ford, Helen Mirren, River Phoenix.

Gorillas in the Mist
(1988) 129m. **B**
Weaver plays the radicalized, real-life naturalist Dian Fossey who spent years studying African gorillas and crusading to save them from poachers. While Weaver brings fire to her role and the scenes with the apes are moving, the film remains surprisingly passionless.
D: Michael Apted. A: Sigourney Weaver, Bryan Brown, Julie Harris.

At Play in the Fields of the Lord
(1991) 190m. **B**
An ambitious epic tale follows two very different missionaries, their family, and friends, and the effects of their efforts to find converts in the Amazon basin. Sumptuously shot film makes strong dramatic points about culture clashes and human nature, but a long running time makes it slow going.
D: Hector Babenco. A: Tom Berenger, Aidan Quinn, Kathy Bates.

Black Robe
(1991) 101m. **A**
Jesuit priests deal with matters both religious and cultural in their attempt to aid a Canadian Huron tribe. A profoundly affecting, near-perfect film that tackles issues of colonialism and spiritual crises, with an unusually straightforward (and sexually graphic) portrayal of Indian culture.
D: Bruce Beresford. A: Lothaire Bluteau, August Schellenberg, Aden Young.

City of Joy
(1992) 134m. **C+**
A spiritual crisis sends an American doctor to India where he attains peace by basically becoming a good ole country doctor. Well crafted and picturesque, but some hokey flourishes—Swayze crooning and dancing "Singin' in the Rain" during monsoon season—sabotages this effort.
D: Roland Joffe. A: Patrick Swayze, Pauline Collins, Om Puri.

Medicine Man
(1992) 106m. **C+**
A woman goes to help out a scientist who has found and lost the cure for cancer in the Brazilian rain forest. An old-fashioned star vehicle with an environmental overlay that never catches on.
D: John McTiernan. A: Sean Connery, Lorraine Bracco.

Australian Dramas

Smarter and with more of a European feel than your average Hollywood fare, these Down Under dramas often focus on a variety of perverse characters who seem to be battling against their own tight-lipped nature.

Man of Flowers
(1984) 91m. **B**
A quiet tale of the lonely sexual and emotional life of an eccentric mother's boy/artist who pays a model to visit once a week and simply take off her clothes. Discrete direction and general low-key approach make what could have been just kinky/quirky into something sweet and insightful.
D: Paul Cox. A. Norman Kaye, Alyson Best, Chris Haywood.

Death in Brunswick
(1990) 106m. **B+**
An irresponsible and somewhat childlike man gets a job at a Mob-run disco, falls for the head honcho's daughter, and in no time finds himself enmeshed in a murder. Filled with bluntly quirky characters and evoking small-town Australia well, this gets a bit contrived but pulls off its caper/murder/romance plot with oddball charm.
D: John Ruane. A: Sam Neill, Zoe Carides, John Clarke.

Proof
(1991) 90m. **B+** 🔍
A young man, stricken blind, perversely goes on taking pictures of random objects, and asks people what he has "seen." Even-keeled yet intimate approach makes this odd character study immensely appealing as film deals with basic human emotions in an almost invisible style.
D: Jocelyn Moorhouse. A: Hugo Weaving, Genevieve Picot, Heather Mitchell.

The Efficiency Expert
(1992) 97m. **C+**
An efficiency expert finds his methods and work ethic in tatters when he's hired to help save a family-run shoe company in financial trouble thanks to their cozy unprofessional business practices. Hopkins is fine as the man dealing with assorted cute and oddball employees, but the film's overly low-key tone keeps this a minor entertainment.
D: Mark Joffe. A: Anthony Hopkins, Ben Mendelsohn, Alwyn Kurts.

Flirting
(1992) 99m. **B−**
A gawky white, prep-school boy falls for a sophisticated Ugandan girl in 1960s Australia. Filmed with a refreshing lack of teen-obsessed hijinks, this has a relaxed pace and feel that subtly evokes youthful romance and its attendant fears and yearnings.
D: John Duigan. A: Noah Taylor, Thandie Newton, Nicole Kidman.

The Last Days of Chez Nous
(1993) 96m. **A−**
Quietly moving story of the complex relationships between an uptight female writer, her daughter from a former marriage, an over-indulged sister, and a free-spirited French husband. The fine character details and deliberate pacing help give this maturely entertaining and sometimes painful film a definite European tang.
D: Gillian Armstrong. A: Lisa Harrow, Bruno Ganz, Kerry Fox.

Women's Dramas

Age, social and marital status—none of these things finally defines the women portrayed in this group of films. While some of these small intimate character studies have melodramatic dilemmas and the easy solutions of a self-help book, they all feature defiantly spunky women forging their own identity and having a swell time doing it.

The End of Innocence
(1990) 102m. **C**
A sympathetic drama that shows a woman's attempt to be perfect as a response to her parents' problems and her own. A heartfelt effort that feels as overheated as a romance novel and as earnest as the movie of the week.
D: Dyan Cannon. A: Dyan Cannon, John Heard, George Coe.

Strapless
(1990) 103m. **B−**
An inhibited American doctor in London gets a shake-up when her wilder younger sister arrives. Suddenly she's trying to loosen up, and meets a suave European to help her along. This sophisticated tale has smart dialogue and accomplished performances but lacks any sizzle.
D: David Hare. A: Blair Brown, Bridget Fonda, Bruno Ganz.

Sweetie
(1990) 97m. **A−** 🔍
A bullying, mentally unbalanced young woman returns to her suburban New Zealand family, wreaking havoc with everyone, especially her conventional sister. A series of nearly unrelated vignettes is often

harrowingly funny, with disjointed images and a herky-jerky pace, but will reward those who can tough it out.
D: Jane Campion. A: Genevieve Lemon, Karen Colston, Tom Lycos.

An Angel at My Table
(1991) 158m. **A**
This traces the life of New Zealand writer Janet Frame, from her grit-poor beginnings in the 1920s, through her misdiagnosed schizophrenia and institutionalization, to writing success in the 1950s. A funny and powerful portrait of an artist coming into her own.
D: Jane Campion. A: Kerry Fox, Alexia Keogh, Karen Fergusson.

Antonia and Jane
(1991) 77m. **A–**
Two friends—a free-spirited, dowdy woman and an elegant beauty who's an emotional wreck—wish they could be in the other's shoes. As told to the same therapist, this poignant and funny tale of friendly rivalry unfolds like a comedy of errors as each becomes increasingly deluded that the other may actually be happy.
D: Beeban Kidron. A: Saskia Reeves, Imelda Staunton, Brenda Bruce.

Fried Green Tomatoes
(1991) 130m. **B+**
A story within a story of a rest home resident who regales a stranger with tales of two women who ran a small-town cafe in the rural South in the 1920s and 30s. An entertaining and warm look at the joys of women's friendships, flavored with down-home humor.
D: Jon Avnet. A: Kathy Bates, Jessica Tandy, Mary Stuart Masterson.

Leaving Normal
(1992) 110m. **C**
A low-rent version of *Thelma and Louise,* in which a young woman escaping her marriage joins a cocktail waitress who's traveling to Alaska to claim some land. The scenery becomes more interesting than the predictable sexual adventures and wackos who keep them company along the way.
D: Edward Zwick. A: Christine Lahti, Meg Tilly, Lenny von Dohlen.

Passion Fish
(1992) 135m. **B+**
After being paralyzed in a car accident, a soap opera star returns to her childhood Louisiana home; her drinking and cursing scare off all the home nurses until she meets her match in a quiet black woman. A finely nuanced character study and occasionally trying tale of physical and spiritual healing.
D: John Sayles. A: Mary McDonnell, Alfre Woodard, David Strathairn.

Angie
(1993) 108m. **C+**
A free-spirited young Brooklyn woman discovers she's pregnant by her longtime boyfriend who she has no intention of marrying, and proceeds on her independent way. Feels like a soap opera, despite Davis' bravado, with more clichéd moments and family problems to fill a month of Oprah shows.
D: Martha Coolidge. A: Geena Davis, James Gandolfini, Aida Turturro.

A Dangerous Woman
(1993) 99m. **B**
An odd dowdy woman is perceived by the world as being everything from mentally slow to just eccentric: Her real handicap is that she's incapable of lying. Winger gives a quietly eerie performance as the sweet, maddening, and dangerous soul, in an unusual film that suffers from a wandering plot and vague point of view.
D: Stephen Gyllenhaal. A: Debra Winger, Barbara Hershey, Gabriel Byrne.

The Joy Luck Club
(1993) 135m. **B+**
Four Chinese women spin stories of their indentured upbringing in the old country, which are interwoven with tales of the modern, American-raised daughters. A warm and old-fashioned saga of family tradition and mother-daughter relationships that can confuse the viewer with so many characters and subplots.
D: Wayne Wang. A: Kieu Chinh, Tsai Chin, France Nuyen.

Ruby in Paradise
(1993) 115m. **B+**
A young Tennessee woman ups and moves to Florida where she does whatever it takes to be independent and explore her options—even working in a beach shop during off-season. Quietly intrepid Judd is the reason to watch this low-keyed and intelligent coming-of-age film.
D: Victor Nunez. A: Ashley Judd, Todd Field, Bentley Mitchum.

Camilla
(1994) 91m. **B–**
An elderly lady, once a concert violinist, and an aspiring female rock musician take a road trip, on which they explore friendship and their own lives. A gentle uncloying film, with the uncertainty and wisdom of youth and advancing years blending to create a touching story.
D: Deepa Mehta. A: Jessica Tandy, Bridget Fonda, Hume Cronyn.

Peter Greenaway

Greenaway's films are a feast for the eyes and a witty teasing game for the intellect. His films are anything but straightforward: They often lack a clear-cut narrative, relying on the play between lush startling images and strange music, with a plentiful supply of sex, nudity, and a sharp sense of humor. His detractors call him pretentious and boring, but he is always provocative and appallingly rational.

The Draughtsman's Contract
(1982) 103m. **A**
A seventeenth-century artist, commissioned to draw 12 different views of a nobleman's estate, becomes caught up—and inserts himself—into the machinations of the manor. A lavishly detailed, sumptuously costumed Restoration England, with clear ties to modern Britain in theme and tone.
D: Peter Greenaway. A: Janet Suzman, Anthony Higgins, Anne Louise Lambert.

A Zed and Two Noughts
(1985) 115m. **B–**
When their wives die in the same accident, two brothers, zoologists in a private zoo, initiate a ménage à trois with

the amputee who survived the crash, and go quietly out of their minds. Obsessive, relentless, and lush.
D: Peter Greenaway. A: Andrea Ferreol, Brian Deacon, Eric Deacon.

The Belly of an Architect
(1987) 108m. **A–**
An architect visiting Rome to curate an exhibition becomes obsessed with his wife's infidelity and pregnancy, his stomach cancer, and an obscure French architect. More coherent but less mysterious than the other films.
D: Peter Greenaway. A: Brian Dennehy, Chloe Webb, Lambert Wilson.

Drowning by Numbers
(1988) 121m. **A**
An episodic and, of course, nonnarrative look at a coroner's connection with, and attachment to, three generations of a matriarchy. Quirky, playful, and brimming over with numbers from 1–100 chronologically displayed throughout the film and lots of sex to keep any flagging interest alive.
D: Peter Greenaway. A: Joely Richardson, Joan Plowright, Bernard Hill.

The Cook, The Thief, His Wife and Her Lover
(1989) 120m. **A**
Greed, lust, and brutality are in full display here as a woman has a liaison with a man in the restaurant owned by her gangster husband. Excessiveness spills over into the lavish sets, ornate and S&M-inspired costumes, and lush soundtrack. A literal and somewhat hard to swallow feast for Greenaway fans.
D: Peter Greenaway. A: Helen Mirren, Michael Gambon, Tim Roth.

Prospero's Books
(1991) 129m. **B+**
Shakespeare's *The Tempest* gets opened up like an overripe fruit, in this ornate, fanciful, dream- and nightmare-like version. Crammed with layer upon layer of images, thoughts, and delectable and disgusting bodies, you'll either be carried along by its power or driven crazy.
D: Peter Greenaway. A: John Gielgud, Michel Blanc, Michael Clark.

The Baby of Macon
(1993) 118m. **C+**
A play within a movie dealing with a miracle birth has all the trademark sumptuous images and ornate costumes, along with more pretentiousness than any other Greenaway film. People are apparently speaking in tongues and the listener is hard-pressed to hear them.
D: Peter Greenaway. A: Julia Ormond, Ralph Fiennes, Philip Stone.

British Dramas

If you're looking for drama that's sharp, witty, and unpredictable, check out what the live wires of British cinema are up to. These small films take the time to explore the lives and inner workings of their characters whether aristocrats, working-class blokes, or mad killers. The evocative scenery, well-crafted stories, and galvanizing young actors all make these films a good bet for some thoughtful and unexpected entertainment.

The Krays
(1990) 119m. **A**
This details the lives of twin brothers who reigned over London's underworld in the 1960s. The portrayal of their cozy home life with mother combined with shockingly ferocious violence makes this like *Goodfellas* meets *Masterpiece Theatre*.
D: Peter Medak. A: Gary Kemp, Martin Kemp, Billie Whitelaw.

Let Him Have It
(1990) 115m. **B+**
Based on the true story of the last man executed for a capital crime, Derek Bentley is a slow-witted lad in postwar England who follows his friends into a life of petty crime that culminates in murder. Stylishly drab and grim character study that scores its point against the miscarriage of justice.
D: Peter Medak. A: Chris Eccleston, Paul Reynolds, Tom Courtenay.

Close My Eyes
(1991) 105m. **B–**
Somewhat depressed woman adds excitement to her life by initiating an affair with her brother, but things get complicated when she marries. Starts awkwardly but quickly becomes a compulsively watchable movie with an elegantly charged atmosphere.
D: Stephen Poliakoff. A: Alan Rickman, Saskia Reeves, Clive Owen.

Riff Raff
(1991) 96m. **A–**
A humorous and dead-eyed, slice-of-life film about a construction worker in London and his romance with a neurotic would-be actress. Like an entertaining documentary about London's working class, it's even subtitled to help with the thick cockney accents.
D: Kenneth Loach. A: Robert Carlyle, Emer McCourt, Ricky Tomlinson.

Truly, Madly, Deeply
(1991) 107m. **B+**
When a young woman's recently deceased boyfriend reappears, her initial joy changes with the complications of life with a ghost. Funny, extremely moving, and entertainingly original.
D: Anthony Minghella. A: Juliet Stevens, Alan Rickman, Bill Paterson.

The Crying Game
(1992) 112m. **A**
An IRA member tries to start a new life in London and gets involved with the girlfriend of a British soldier whose death he witnessed. The girlfriend turns out a little differently than expected, and a former IRA colleague shows up with demands. This is a real roller coaster ride with some memorable characters, even if you already know the surprise in the middle.
D: Neil Jordan. A: Stephen Rea, Jaye Davidson, Miranda Richardson.

London Kills Me
(1992) 107m. **B–**
A young man needs a pair of shoes to get out of his low-level drug dealing and into a legitimate job as a waiter. His efforts to get them gives us a tour of London youth and drug culture in this wild, melancholy, and not completely satisfying film.
D: Hanif Kureishi. A: Justin Chadwick, Steven Mackintosh, Emer McCourt.

Peter's Friends
(1993) 102m. **C+**
The ten-year reunion of six Oxford friends at a country

estate is a British *Big Chill* without the flair and frothiness. Pretty predictable even with the engaging articulate characters and some funny moments.
D: Kenneth Branagh. A: Kenneth Branagh, Emma Thompson, Rita Rudner.

An Awfully Big Adventure
(1994) 113m. **B+**
An aspiring 16-year-old actress upsets her guardian when she gets an assistant stage manager position and falls in love with the caddish director. Set in a gloomy 1947 Liverpool, this colorful and humorous tale gets extra points for casting Grant as a sadistic fop and generally fine performances.
D: Mike Newell. A: Alan Rickman, Hugh Grant, Georgina Cates.

Raining Stones
(1994) 90m. **B**
A northern England working-class family resorts to everything from stealing sheep to draining septic tanks to keep its head above water. Though the accents are so thick subtitles wouldn't be a bad idea, this is an engaging comedy of people with little in the way of illusions—just high spirits and a sense of hope.
D: Ken Loach. A: Bruce Jones.

Sister My Sister
(1994) 95m. **B+**
Two sisters lead lives of quiet desperation in the south of France as servants for a cruel woman. Though finding solace in each other's arms, pressures build and a grisly vengeance looms in this austere psychosexual tale that makes a dry flipside to the more ebullient *Heavenly Creatures*.
D: Nancy Meckler. A: Julie Walters, Joely Richardson, Jodhi May.

The Madness of King George
(1995) 126m. **A**
This scintillating period tale follows the courtly intrigues surrounding the mental dissolution of the British monarch who lost the American colonies. A lushly appointed and impeccably acted story contains unexpected details of court life as it portrays the subtle interplay between royal ritual and indulgence, power plays and madness.
D: Nicholas Hytner. A: Nigel Hawthorne, Helen Mirren, Ian Holm.

Message Films

Here the appeal of "message" films is watching Hollywood stars cut their teeth on well-meaning, classy projects along with 90-plus minutes of fighting the good fight against racism.

Mississippi Burning
(1988) 127m. **B+**
When three civil rights activists disappear in 1964 Mississippi, two very different FBI men are called in to investigate. Thick with an air of Southern small-town paranoia, fear, and bubbling-under racism, this is a visually inspired, well-acted tale of idiot hatred and the uncomfortable means of combating it.
D: Alan Parker. A: Gene Hackman, Willem Dafoe, Frances McDormand.

The Long Walk Home
(1990) 98m. **B**
Montgomery, Alabama, 1955: An upper-class wife joins her black housekeeper to fight racist busing laws. Good example of people fighting the good fight, with focus on the two women's relationship and the culturally forbidden outcome of it, nullifying the preachy aspects.
D: Richard Pearce. A: Sissy Spacek, Whoopi Goldberg, Dwight Schultz.

Cadence
(1991 97m. **C+**
Well-intentioned but listless tale of a racist tyrannical stockade commander, his African-American charges, and a young man caught in between. Professional, well-acted story is a case of simplistic preaching-to-the-converted and too obvious for anybody's good.
D: Martin Sheen. A: Martin Sheen, Charlie Sheen, Ramon Estevez.

Love Field
(1992) 104m. **B+**
On her way to President Kennedy's funeral, a young white woman from Texas intersects with a black man and his young daughter, resulting in some unexpected changes for all. Surprisingly realistic and low-keyed road film whose characters develop with subtlety and humor.
D: Jonathan Kaplan. A: Michelle Pfeiffer, Dennis Haysbert, Brian Kerwin.

Sports Dramas

Whether fanciful or gritty in tone, at the bottom of these studio-slick musings on sports is the question "How far are you willing to go to win or to see your sports dream come true?" The results range from moments of near-magical answered prayers to hard reality comeuppance for our questing players.

The Natural
(1984) 134m. **B+**
Baseball legend Roy Hobbs returns after mysteriously disappearing for a decade to help out the floundering New York Knights, aided by his "magical" bat. Unrepentantly sentimental film, with Redford suitably iconic as the great lost slugger and an almost mystical approach to the game that makes the field like an outdoor church.
D: Barry Levinson. A: Robert Redford, Robert Duvall, Glenn Close.

Eight Men Out
(1988) 119m. **B+**
The shame-ridden tale of eight members of the Chicago White Sox who, under pressure from the Mob, a cheap owner, and other unsavory elements, threw the 1919 championship. A ball fan's nightmare movie with great ensemble acting, a literate script, and a thick falling-from-grace tone.

D: John Sayles. A: John Cusack, Charlie Sheen, Michael Lerner.

Field of Dreams
(1989) 106m. **B+**
A farmer hears voices from heaven saying that if he builds a ballpark in his cornfield, "they will come": *They* turn out to be the shades of past baseball greats. Love and belief conquer all as baseball again becomes a symbol for all things good in this surprisingly effective, light dream of a movie.
D: Phil Alden Robinson. A: Kevin Costner, James Earl Jones, Amy Madigan.

The Program
(1993) 114m. **B–**
A street kid, entranced by dreams of fame and intent on impressing a coed, signs on with a football team only to get caught in the corrupt sports machine. Extremely variable acting and sometimes lug-headed script mar this generally engrossing cautionary tale.
D: David S. Ward. A: James Caan, Halle Berry, Omar Epps.

Rudy
(1993) 114m. **C**
A steel-worker's son, lacking grades or size, runs on pure determination to get himself onto the Notre Dame football team. *Rocky* feel-good tale gets sabotaged by an unusually high dose of sentimentality and a rather anticlimactic payoff for the underdog.
D: David Anspaugh. A: Sean Astin, Ned Beatty, Lili Taylor.

Above the Rim
(1994) 93m. **B–**
A high school basketball hotshot would love to be a Georgetown star, but the lure of becoming a street legend in the neighborhood "Shoot Out" contest with all the perks may change his mind. A sassy, double-pumping, and thoroughly predictable tale of innocence betrayed.
D: Jeff Pollack. A: Duane Martin, Leon, Tupac Shakur.

Blue Chips
(1994) 101m. **B**
A seasoned coach has one last chance to recruit hot players for his flagging basketball team or else. Excitingly shot and edited, this sidles up to the anything-for-a-winning-team issues (drugs, shady deals, and the like) but extinguishes itself in the second half as Nolte's conscience gets the better of him.
D: William Friedkin. A: Nick Nolte, Mary McDonnell, Alfre Woodard.

Family and Marriage Dramas

These tales of modern families focus on divorce, child abuse, delinquency, and adults who can barely take care of themselves, let alone their kids. Even the nostalgic stories are tinged with bitterness and cynicism; nobody seems to be pushing the idea of a golden age for families here.

Men Don't Leave
(1990) 115m. **B+**
After the death of her husband, a woman goes into a tailspin as she's forced to make a new life for herself and two sons. A comic-drama that's more quirky than humorous, with careful character portrayals by all.
D: Paul Brickman. A: Jessica Lange, Joan Cusack, Kathy Bates.

American Heart
(1993) 91m. **A–**
A 15-year-old attaches himself to his very unwilling father, a recently released excon. This realistically gritty tale offers go-for-broke performances and a compelling look at the world of down-and-outers in a perpetually gray Seattle.
D: Martin Bell. A: Jeff Bridges, Edward Furlong, Lucinda Jenney.

Blue Sky
(1992) 101m. **A–**
It's the early 60s and an army family is unspooling from the effects of the charming, highly sexual, and manic/depressive mother while her military husband bears the burden of a terrible secret regarding the A-bomb. Beautifully acted and crafted film that's both multilayered passion play and family drama.
D: Tony Richardson. A: Jessica Lang, Tommy Lee Jones, Powers Booth

Little Man Tate
(1991) 99m. **A–**
A working-class mother agrees to enroll her genius son in a special institute causing a rift in their private world: Once they were pals reliant on each other, now they have different places in the world. A quiet, carefully constructed character study and compassionate look at the isolation of the truly gifted.
D: Jodie Foster. A: Jodie Foster, Adam Hann-Byrd, Dianne Wiest.

One Good Cop
(1991) 114m. **C+**
Happily married and on the verge of having their own baby, a New York City cop and his wife take in the three daughters of an officer killed in a shoot-out. Sincere, heartwarming, and forgettable.
D: Heywood Gould. A: Michael Keaton, Rene Russo, Anthony LaPaglia.

Paradise
(1991) 104m. **B**
An emotionally estranged couple takes in a friend's 10-year-old who would rather be anywhere else, and they all end up helping each other. Melancholy and slightly better than a TV movie.
D: Mary Agnes Donoghue. A: Don Johnson, Melanie Griffith, Elijah Wood.

Criss Cross
(1992) 100m. **C**
A mother raising her 12-year-old son alone in Key West in 1969 tries to cope with his drift toward delinquency and her husband's alienation following his tour in Vietnam. Slow-paced, too sensitive, and a down-and-out look that strains credibility.
D: Chris Menges. A: Goldie Hawn, Arliss Howard, James Gammon.

Radio Flyer
(1992) 114m. **C+**
Two young boys flee the terrors of their violent stepfather with an active fantasy life including their belief that they can make their little red wagon fly. A dark-hued, uncomfortable mix of childhood perils and daydreams.
D: Richard Donner. A: Lorraine Bracco, John Heard, Elijah Wood.

The Good Son
(1993) 100m. **C**
A boy with a malicious glint in his eye alarms his cousin, and for good reason—the

tyke offed his brother and will proceed to snuff a pup, cause car crashes, and more. Male version of *The Bad Seed* adds nothing new to the killer-kid genre and Culkin never seems that menacing.
D: Joseph Ruben. A: Macaulay Culkin, Elijah Wood, Wendy Crewson.

A Home of Our Own
(1993) 103m. **C+**
Penniless and forced to leave LA in 1962, a single mother and her brood of six move into a dilapidated farmhouse in Idaho with the owner striking a deal to have them fix it up and buy it from him. Episodic, crisis-ridden, and TV-styled drama that offers gritty performances and no surprises.
D: Tony Bill. A: Kathy Bates, Edward Furlong, Clarissa Lessig.

Jack the Bear
(1993) 98m. **C**
Dad's a wacked-out host of a TV horror show who's trying to bring up two school-age boys in the 1970s. Maudlin, with a low-rent Steven Spielberg feel, this oozes sentimentality and still doesn't make you care about the characters.
D: Marshall Herskovitz. A: Danny DeVito; Robert J. Steinmiller, Jr.; Gary Sinise.

Lorenzo's Oil
(1993) 135m. **B+**
Upon learning that their child is dying of a rare disease, a determined couple bypasses nay-saying medical establishment to find a cure themselves. As much a scientific detective story as a script that exacts intelligence from its audience: Only drawback is lack of main character development.
D: George Miller. A: Susan Sarandon, Nick Nolte, Peter Ustinov.

Lost in Yonkers
(1993) 112m. **A−**
Two young boys are sent to their punishingly strict grandmother and goofy, almost retarded aunt in 1942. Lovely period details, vigorous interfamily confrontations, and astonishing luminous portrayals by Ruehl and Worth make this Neil Simon play a joy.
D: Martha Coolidge. A: Mercedes Ruehl, Richard Dreyfuss, Irene Worth.

Mac
(1993) 118m. **B**
Three Italian-American brothers struggle to make it in 1954 Queens, with one brother's obsessive need for success so extreme it might wreck his family. Told as a series of vignettes, this is a small intense film about the cost of the American dream, with bravura ensemble performances from all.
D: John Turturro. A: John Turturro, Ellen Barkin, Katherine Borowitz.

A Perfect World
(1993) 138m. **C+**
An escaped convict followed by a Texas ranger takes a fatherless boy as his hostage. Though the strange growing relationship between the con and the kid provide a few touching moments, Eastwood's chase story seems pasted on, with the tone veering from humorous to menacing to violent.
D: Clint Eastwood. A: Kevin Costner, Clint Eastwood, Laura Dern.

This Boy's Life
(1993) 115m. **A−**
An optimistic mom marries a man who seems to offer security and a father for her son, but turns out to be an abusive and vindictive man. Disturbing and emotionally harrowing family scenes, along with outstanding performances by De Niro as the bully father and DiCaprio as the son struggling to break free, make this a sobering family saga.
D: Michael Caton-Jones. A: Robert De Niro, Ellen Barkin, Leonardo DiCaprio.

Corrina, Corrina
(1994) 135m. **B−**
In the early 1960s, a recently widowed ad man hires a black woman to help keep house and take care of his young daughter, with unexpected results. Thanks mainly to the leads, an admirable attempt to humanize and throw some twists into a formulaic story.
D: Jessie Nelson. A: Whoopi Goldberg, Ray Liotta, Tina Majorino.

Forbidden Choices
(1994) 104m. **C−**
Based on the novel *The Beans of Egypt, Maine,* this portrays a hardscrabble backwoods Maine couple and their violent and incestuous extended family. Despite fine performances of fated characters and gritty evocation of trailer-park backwoods life, this slow story never comes into focus.
D: Jennifer Warren. A: Martha Plimpton, Rutger Hauer, Kelly Lynch.

Imaginary Crimes
(1994) 106m. **B+**
When her mother dies shortly after her younger sister is born, a teenage girl is left to act as the stabilizing force for her father who goes from one losing investment scheme to the next. A bittersweet small-scale, coming-of-age film that details the pain and embarassment of a beloved but unreliable parent.
D: Anthony Drazan. A: Harvey Keitel, Fairuza Balk, Kelly Lynch.

Safe Passage
(1994) 99m. **C+**
A laconic Dad and a kooky super-Mom who have spawned seven now-grown boys assemble and learn all about each other when one of the sons is rumored to have been killed in a Middle East fracas. Feel-good soap opera delivers all the predictable warm and winning moments that you would expect.
D: Robert Allen Ackerman. A: Susan Sarandon, Sam Shepard, Robert Sean Astin.

Second Best
(1994) 105m. **B−**
A middle-aged English village postmaster convinces the orphanage to let him adopt a boy from an abusive home, leading to awkward attempts at forging a relationship. Well-intended tale about two lonely people trying to connect is well rendered and finely acted.
D: Chris Menges. A: William Hurt, Chris Cleary Miles, Keith Allen.

A Simple Twist of Fate
(1994) 106m. **C**
It's *Silas Marner* meets *Kramer vs. Kramer* in this quiet sentimental story of a recluse who raises an orphan, not realizing that her father is a local rising politician. Martin's insecure papa is essentially a reprise of his *Parenthood* role although this film has little humor and a rather lethargic pace.
D: Gillie MacKinnon. A: Steve Martin, Gabriel Byrne, Catherine O'Hara.

Spanking the Monkey
(1994) 99m. **A−**
Sometimes amusing, but mainly rivetingly disturbing tale of a freshman who must take care of his convalescing mother during summer vacation, which eventually leads to an incestuous episode. A terrific coming-of-age tale with a generous spirit and a sure feel for the confusion and sexual energy of youth.
D: David O. Russell. A: Jeremy Davies, Alberta Watson, Carla Gallo.

The War
(1994) 126m. **C−**
It's 1970 and an emotionally

bruised Vietnam vet returns home to Mississippi and tries to deal with his shattered life and family. A haze of blandness and good intentions quickly settles over what feels like a recycled, symbol-laded melodrama.
D: Jon Avnet. A: Kevin Costner, Elijah Wood, Mare Winningham.

What's Eating Gilbert Grape?
(1994) 117m. **B–**
A teenager's dreary small-town life is burdened with responsibility for his younger retarded brother and the reality of his single, housebound, obese mother. Throw in a sensitive romance with Juliette Lewis and you've got a collection of occasionally poignant moments but never a fully hatched film.
D: Lasse Hallstrom. A: Johnny Depp, Leonardo DiCaprio, Juliette Lewis.

When a Man Loves a Woman
(1994) 124m. **C+**
A schoolteacher checks into detox to treat her alcoholism, but when she gets out, her husband wonders what role he has in her new existence. Ryan is much too cute and in control to be a convincingly troubled person in this painfully earnest and preachy look at substance abuse and marriage.
D: Luis Mandoki. A: Meg Ryan, Andy Garcia, Ellen Burstyn.

Adult Psychodramas

Shattered-soul lovers, outsiders lost with drink and madness, kinky sex, and more—these are some of the subjects of dramas that prove a film can be as spellbinding as any sexy potboiler and still portray the darker aspects of love and life with intelligence and humor.

Sophie's Choice
(1982) 155m. **B+**
Darkly romantic story of a young Southern writer in early 50s Brooklyn fascinated by the couple living downstairs, one a charismatic but unstable scientist, the other an Auschwitz survivor. Except for some wrenching death-camp scenes, this earnest film remains surprisingly muted given Kline and Streep's high-voltage power.
D: Alan J. Pakula. A: Meryl Streep, Kevin Kline, Peter MacNicol.

Tempest
(1982) 140m. **B–**
A Manhattan architect has a middle-age crisis, leaves his wife, moves to an isolated Greek island with teen daughter in tow, and shacks up with a voluptuous siren. First half of this revision of Shakespeare's classic is tumultuously fascinating while the second half descends into quasi-supernatural meandering.
D: Paul Mazursky. A: John Cassavetes, Gena Rowlands, Susan Sarandon.

Under the Volcano
(1984) 109m. **A–**
An overblown and harrowing character study follows a figurehead diplomat as he drinks his way to the depths of human misery in a Mexican town. Craggy-faced Finney looks like he's been to hell and didn't come back in this sulfurously atmospheric, incredibly depressing, but haunting film.
D: John Huston. A: Albert Finney, Jacqueline Bisset, Anthony Andrews.

Burning Secret
(1988) 107m. **B–**
A young boy at an Austrian spa for his health is befriended by a kindly mysterious man who proceeds to pay court to his mother. Drenched in prewar Euro-ambiance, illicit love unfolds with every small gesture to the uncomprehending eyes of youth in this lovely but strangely unsatisfying drama.
D: Andrew Birkin. A: Faye Dunaway, Klaus Maria Brandauer, Ian Richardson.

The Unbearable Lightness of Being
(1988) 171m. **A–**
A sex-obsessed Czech doctor, oblivious to the political tumult around him, is caught between his soul mate who is similarly erotic-compulsive and a young woman he wants to be his one and only. A rapturously photographed, finely acted examination of love and redemption, directed with energy and wit.
D: Philip Kaufman. A: Daniel Day-Lewis, Juliette Binoche, Lena Olin.

Enemies, a Love Story
(1989) 119m. **B+**
New York, 1949: Believing his wife has perished in a concentration camp, a man remarries and is also having an affair, when his dead wife shows up. Complex relationships are presented with earthy good humor in this dark and comic look at love and survival.
D: Paul Mazursky. A: Ron Silver, Anjelica Huston, Lena Olin.

Last Exit to Brooklyn
(1989) 102m. **B+**
Episodes of various characters—the prostitute with sad dreams, the angry closeted union boss, a self-loathing transsexual—are interwoven in a hellish 1952 Brooklyn slum. Harrowing, yet darkly human drama with look and feel of a gloomy Eastern European woodcut print.
D: Uli Edel. A: Stephen Lang, Jennifer Jason Leigh, Burt Young.

The Adjuster
(1991) 102m. **B**
A Canadian married couple—she's a government censor who reviews pornography, he's an insurance adjuster assisting families who are homeless—meet a wealthy couple intent on fulfilling their own fantasies. A sly and bewildering comedy-drama in which everyone looks normal until the strangest activities are revealed.
D: Atom Egoyan. A: Elias Koteas, Arsinee Khanjian, Maury Chaykin.

The Rapture
(1991) 102m. **A–**
A woman tired of her empty promiscuous life turns born-again Christian just in time for a very literal Bible-accurate apocalypse. A Christian's nightmare, complete with televised arrival of the Four Horsemen and an offering of a child to a silent deity. An ambitiously original and completely unsettling fare.
D: Michael Tolkin. A: Mimi Rogers, David Duchovny, Patrick Bauchau.

The Lover
(1992) 103m. R/110m. X version **B–**
A lonely French teenager in 1929 Indochina, neglected by her brutish family and bored by convent life, begins a steamy affair with 30ish

Chinese aristocrat. March's chilly performance doesn't help this glossy and empty tale of illicit love that's full of glistening bodies and Anaïs Nin-like erotica.
D: Jean-Jacques Annaud. A: Jane March, Tony Leung, Frederique Meininger.

Waterland
(1992) 95m. **B**
The slow mental deterioration and retreat into memory of an Englishman teaching high school in the U.S. is the focus of this rewarding but slowly paced drama. Suffused with an intense air of melancholy and alienation, Irons methodically relives his youth while dealing with its consequences in his life and marriage.
D: Stephen Gyllenhalal. A: Jeremy Irons, Sinead Cusack, Ethan Hawke.

Boxing Helena
(1993) 105m. **C+**
A twitchy surgeon falls for a bitchy babe, imprisons her in his secluded mansion, systematically relieves her of her arms and legs, and waits for love to blossom. While offering some arrestingly macabre visuals to accompany an unusual tale of love, the film's tone veers from artsy seriousness to near camp.
D: Jennifer Chambers Lynch. A: Julian Sands, Sherilyn Fenn, Bill Paxton.

Damage
(1993) 100m. **A−**
A British Parliament member becomes obsessed with his son's fiancée, plunges into an affair even more treacherous than would seem on the surface. An awkward and riveting drama with a gut-wrenching last reel with Richardson.
D: Louis Malle. A: Jeremy Irons, Miranda Richardson, Juliette Binoche.

Bitter Moon
(1994) 139m. **B−**
Onboard a ship bound to India, a debauched American regales a proper British married man with his tale of love gone bad and weird. Director Polanski's dark valentine to the nature of romantic love with its mix of black humor, perversion, and self-loathing hits its unsettling targets more than it misses.
D: Roman Polanski. A: Peter Coyote, Emmanuelle Seigner, Hugh Grant.

Exotica
(1994) 103m. **B+**
A troubled accountant frequents a local strip joint where he gets a beautiful woman to be his own private dancer, much to her DJ beau's displeasure. Despite lack of really appealing characters, this is a cool psychosexual character study that ticks away like an emotional timebomb until the haunting denouement.
D: Atom Egoyan. A: Bruce Greenwood, Mia Kirschner, Don McKellar.

Intersection
(1994) 98m. **C−**
A Vancouver architect is at a crossroads in his life with a failing marriage, an affair turning painful, and a teenage daughter he's neglected. Everyone looks slightly sedated in this unsympathetic attempt at an adult drama about midlife crisis.
D: Mark Rydell. A: Richard Gere, Sharon Stone, Lolita Davidovich.

Death and the Maiden
(1995) 103m. **A**
Rain pelts a secluded South African house while inside a woman who was tortured for her political activities tries to extract the truth from a man who may—or may not—have been her torturer. Polanski creates an incredibly tense film, filled with psychological gamesmanship, violence, and black humor. Don't miss.
D: Roman Polanski. A: Sigourney Weaver, Ben Kingsley, Stuart Wilson.

Lovers on the Lam

These ex-cons and screwed-up kids from nowhere towns are as cynical, amoral, and dulled as violence and a failed trickle-down economy can make you. Whether grunge noir or big-budget glossy, these movies show an American landscape where the Badlands are everywhere and love is as parched as the desert settings.

Guncrazy
(1992) 96m. **B+**
Tired of her wretched life with an abusive stepfather in a no-future town, a teen girl starts up a penpal romance with a convict: They fall in love, develop the title fixation, and soon the bodies start piling up. This desert-noir is surprisingly effective with the leads adding a raw edge to the bittersweet romance.
D: Tamra Davis. A: Drew Barrymore, James Le Gros, Joe Dallesandro.

Trouble Bound
(1992) 90m. **D+**
A luckless macho ex-con wins a car (with a mobster's corpse in the trunk) and picks up a foxy waitress (actually a Mob daughter with a grudge) and soon the desert roads are filled with hoods. Except for Madsen, this is secondhand filler from the faux rockabilly music to the lame jabs at humor.
D: Jeffrey Reiner. A: Michael Madsen, Patricia Arquette, Seymour Cassel.

Kalifornia
(1993) 118m. **B+**
Two sophisticated, artist-types share expenses with a white-trash couple on a cross-country exploration of famous murder sites, unaware the male half of the couple is a murderer. It could stand some trimming, but has a lot to say about class rage and human nature and does it with a smooth buildup to a crescendo of violence.
D: Dominic Sena. A: Brad Pitt, Juliette Lewis, David Duchovny.

True Romance
(1993) 120m. **B+**
A Quentin Tarantino script about a movie nerd and his ditzy girlfriend who become involved with unloading some stolen drugs gets a flashy MTV-style treatment but otherwise offers a weirdly romantic/anxious tone, funny performances, and an amazingly clever shoot-out finale.
D: Tony Scott. A: Christian Slater, Patricia Arquette, Dennis Hopper.

The Chase
(1994) 88m. **C**
An innocent con takes a female hostage and spends the film's duration in his car with her on the lam from the law. Contrived fluff comes off the Hollywood production line with plentiful vehicular mayhem, nicely abbrevi-

ated running time, and absolutely nothing on its speedy mind.
D: Adam Rifkin. A: Charlie Sheen, Kristy Swanson, Cary Elwes.

The Getaway
(1994) 115m. **C+**
A con has his girl seduce a parole board chief in order to get released from jail. The seduction works, the couple makes off with mobsters' money and hits the lawless road. Cosmetic remake of the 1972 Peckinpah film is snappily paced with well-staged explosions, but the leads can't stop posing like glamour-pusses long enough to help this film sustain any real tension.
D: Roger Donaldson. A: Alec Baldwin, Kim Basinger, James Woods.

Love and a .45
(1994) 102m. **B**
A convenience-store heist goes bad, so two dusty Gen X-ers and a girlfriend hit the desperado trail. Offers a white-trash look and feel, wary sexual relations, blood and guts spilled all over kingdom come, and a re-hashed road film plot.
D: C. M. Talington. A: Gil Bellows, Renee Zellweger, Rory Cochrane.

Natural Born Killers
(1994) 119m. **B**
An ex-con and his child-abused girlfriend find media fame as serial killers. Director Oliver Stone takes you on a cinematic magical mystery tour using delirious camerawork, animation, surreal sitcom comedy, and more, to pound in his blood-drenched themes of media overload and violence.
D: Oliver Stone. A: Woody Harrelson; Juliette Lewis; Robert Downey, Jr.

Alienated Youth

Runaways, hustlers, or teens who seem to have no parents even when they're living at home, these kids live in a world where the only authority is peer, drug, or money-related.

Lord of the Flies
(1990) 90m. **C–**
A group of military school kids crashes on a desolate island and slowly reverts to savagery. This second take on William Golding's semi-classic boasts some weird primordial imagery and good performances, but the idea of a pack of kids turning into animals just doesn't chill as it did 30 years ago.
D: Harry Hook. A: Balthazar Getty, Christopher Furrh, Danuel Pipoly.

My Own Private Idaho
(1991) 105m. **C**
A narcoleptic hustler and his well-to-do, street-boy buddy hit the road traveling from Portland to Rome. Quoting everything from *Falstaff* to *Blue Velvet,* the film is preciously hip and crammed full of clever cultural references but offers an affecting turn by Phoenix.
D: Gus Van Sant, Jr. A: River Phoenix, Keanu Reeves, James Russo.

Romper Stomper
(1992) 92m. **B+**
A harrowing tale of dead-end Australian skinheads who battle the rest of the world, specifically the Asian community. With its savage unglamorized violence and raw evocation of Melbourne's mean streets, this is a dark but insightful look at modern alienation taken to horrible extremes.
D: Geoffrey Wright. A: Russell Crowe, Daniel Pollack, Jacqueline McKenzie.

Where the Day Takes You
(1992) 107m. **C**
A relentlessly depressing look at a subculture of runaways around Hollywood Boulevard, who survive by petty thievery, prostitution, and begging. Fine ensemble work with everyone looking suitably lost and tough, but the story is as aimlessly grim as the characters.
D: Marc Rocco. A: Sean Astin, Lara Flynn Boyle, Peter Dobson.

Zebrahead
(1992) 102m. **B**
In modern-day Detroit, a white Jewish teen falls for his black best pal's cousin, resulting in a variety of shades and intensities of racial conflict from friends, family, and school. A street-smart love story that's refreshingly complex as the likable leads navigate the mixed-race minefield with humor and compassion.
D: Anthony Drazan. A: Michael Rappaport, Ray Sharkey, DeShonn Castle.

Kids
(1995) 90m. **A**
A smart and devastating look at 24 hours in the lives of several massively destructive and self-destructive, middle-class New York teens. The story: Boy deflowers girl, girl takes AIDS test on a lark, finds out she's positive, and goes on a hunt for him. While this portrait should come as no surprise, its no-holds-barred look makes for uneasy viewing.
D: Larry Clark. A: Chloe Sevigny, Leo Fitzpatrick, Justin Pierce.

Romance

With productions large and small, the presence of big name stars, and changing sexual mores, time stands still for the "modern" love stories, which are still as schmaltzy, old-fashioned, and poised to jerk tears for any viewer in the mood.

Stanley and Iris
(1990) 104m. **C+**
A lonely widower teaches a handyman how to read. Earnest and well acted, with an admirable pro-literacy theme, this still looks and plays more like an after-school TV special than a theatrical film.
D: Martin Ritt. A: Jane Fonda, Robert De Niro, Martha Plimpton.

White Palace
(1990) 106m. **B–**
A yuppie falls for an older woman/waitress, with the ensuing romance complicated when matters of social standing arise. Outside of the credibility problem—who would have problems

falling for Sarandon whatever her job is?—the film has a light touch and resists getting too cute for a long time.
D: Luis Mandoki. A: Susan Sarandon, James Spader, Kathy Bates.

Dying Young
(1991) 110m. **C+**

A perky lovely young woman goes to work for a terminally ill rich young man and they promptly fall head over heels. A lively four-hanky special is an okay entry in the long tradition of nobly suffering, young-lovers films, but mainly a treat for Roberts' fans.
D: Joel Schumacher. A: Julia Roberts, Campbell Scott, David Selby.

Frankie and Johnny
(1991) 117m. **B−**

An ex-con gets work as a cook in a greasy spoon where he meets a lonely but feisty waitress. More like an overdone TV sitcom, with Pacino and Pfeiffer a bit too charismatic to pass as everyday folk going for years without a date; still, a sweet, old-fashioned love story for those in an undemanding mood.
D: Garry Marshall. A: Al Pacino, Michelle Pfeiffer, Nathan Lane.

The Prince of Tides
(1991) 132m. **B**

A Southern schoolteacher estranged from his wife looks for his suicidal sister in New York and locks horns with her therapist who then wants to dig around in his own psyche. A lyrical tale of spiritual rebirth holds up fairly well despite some ridiculous touches and a flowery finale.
D: Barbra Streisand. A: Nick Nolte, Barbra Streisand, Blythe Danner.

The Bodyguard
(1992) 129m. **C**

Bodyguard Costner breaks his personal code by falling for actress/diva Houston. Despite VH1-style visual gloss, this is like a 50s romance/musical lost in some cinematic Twilight Zone, with the action never too tense for Whitney to break into song, and Costner looking sedated.
D: Mick Jackson. A: Kevin Costner, Whitney Houston, Gary Kemp.

Indecent Proposal
(1993) 118m. **C+**

A happy but financially overextended yuppie couple has one way to save their lovely house: The wife accepts a millionaire's offer of $1 million to spend the night with him. What promises to be a glitzy cautionary fable turns into an old-fashioned, romantic triangle with enough bad/fun soap opera flourishes to make this camp.
D: Adrian Lyne. A: Robert Redford, Demi Moore, Woody Harrelson.

Map of the Human Heart
(1993) 109m. **A**

An Eskimo boy and an Indian/French girl meet as children, and so starts a love that spans several decades, countries, and a world war. A rare love story that isn't predictable, with gorgeous arctic photography, an astoundingly realistic firebombing of Dresden scene, and dreamlike structure, all united by a melancholic magical realism tone.
D: Vincent Ward. A: Jason Scott Lee, Anne Parillaud, Patrick Bergin.

Shadowlands
(1993) 130m. **B+**

Romance blossoms in Oxford as writer/philosopher C. S. Lewis has a midlife encounter with a blunt and oddly charming American writer and single mother. Film acquits itself well, but is really a powerhouse acting display with Hopkins and Winger both touching as vulnerable people who step out on a very thin emotional limb.
D: Richard Attenborough. A: Anthony Hopkins, Debra Winger, Edward Hardwicke.

Love Affair
(1994) 108m. **D+**

Beatty, mysteriously seen only through Vaseline-lensed camera, falls for clearly photographed Bening in this wretched remake of *An Affair to Remember.* Hankies are guaranteed to stay in pockets in this antiseptically precise would-be weeper, though in a few years it may descend into the ranks of camp.
A: Glenn Gordon Caron. A: Warren Beatty, Annette Bening, Katharine Hepburn.

The Bridges of Madison County
(1995) 138m. **B+**

This film based on the best-seller about a brief beautiful affair between an Iowa farm wife and a free-spirited stranger amazingly makes something good out of its overblown source. Thanks mainly to the fine performances and tight direction, this unabashedly romantic saga is a thoughtful and intelligent adult love story.
D: Clint Eastwood. A: Clint Eastwood, Meryl Streep, Annie Corley.

Don Juan DeMarco
(1995) 92m. **B+**

A psychologist saves a deluded romantic who thinks he's Don Juan and soon the new patient is giving the doc a sentimental education in the art of love. A sweet and sensual comedy with a smoldering Depp and a genuinely warm Marlon as the open-minded shrink left wondering who is sane and who's not.
D: Jeremy Levin. A: Marlon Brando, Johnny Depp, Faye Dunaway.

Redemptive Dramas

These films show how illness, personal limitations, and trauma can simply be the first step on the path to renewal and redemption as the generation who had it all in the 80s comes to grips with the idea of something beyond what a credit card could bring, perhaps even something spiritual.

Awakenings
(1990) 121m. **B**

Tale of the relationship between a doctor and a neurologically damaged man who has been in a catatonic state since childhood until he is "awakened" by an experimental serum. Fact-based film has subtly shaded performances and a sober tone that pulls a bit too hard at the heartstrings.
D: Penny Marshall. A: Robert De Niro, Robin Williams, Julie Kavner.

The Doctor
(1991) 123m. **B+**

A self-centered surgeon living in bucolically ritzy Marin County develops a cough that may signal a malignant tumor. What could have been a glib story of self-redemption turns out to be more, never pandering to

soap opera solutions and featuring a gruffly fine-tuned Hurt.
D: Randa Haines. A: William Hurt, Elizabeth Perkins, Christine Lahti.

Regarding Henry
(1991) 107m. **C–**
After being shot, a cut-throat lawyer wakes without memory and a wondrous childlike persona. A sort of fairy tale apology for the greed and excess of the 80s with bland photography, simplistic melodramatic plot, and even more simplistic insights.
D: Mike Nichols. A: Harrison Ford, Annette Bening, Bill Nunn.

Fearless
(1993) 124m. **A**
Two people deal with the trauma of surviving a plane crash, one of them experiencing what can happen when you get a little shot of enlightenment. A lyrical haunting film suffused with quiet mysticism and heart-wrenching performances, and though dealing with weighty subjects, never stumbling into pretentiousness.
D: Peter Weir. A: Jeff Bridges, Rosie Perez, Isabella Rossellini.

Mr. Jones
(1993) 114m. **B–**
A charming, highly talented manic depressive eventually finds his way to a psych center where the treating psychiatrist eventually falls in love with him. A sometimes off-putting, sometimes charming and weirdly implausible film, though the handsome leads work hard at making the chemistry and the story work.
D: Mike Figgis. A: Richard Gere, Lena Olin, Anne Bancroft.

My Life
(1993) 117m. **B**
An ambitious young man with a pregnant wife discovers he only has a couple of months to live. Anger, denial, an attempt to document his life on video for his unborn child follow, until he finally examines life. A funny bracing Keaton manages to keep the schmaltz at bay in this slightly slick but well-meaning drama.
D: Bruce Joel Rubin. A: Michael Keaton, Nicole Kidman, Michael Constantine.

The Secret Garden
(1993) 102m. **B+**
A Victorian orphan living at her uncle's country estate takes solace in a mysterious and, to her, fantastic garden while helping to free up the cloistered life of the uncle's invalid young son. This sumptuous fable evokes the childhood essence of innocence and magic at a deliberate pace as it unfolds its tale of redemption.
D: Agnieszka Holland. A: Kate Maberly, Heydon Prowse, Maggie Smith.

Forrest Gump
(1994) 142m. **A–**
The life and absurdist times of a simpleminded but singularly blessed soul. Via digital technology and plot floatings, we see Gump make his way through a veritable diorama of 60s and 70s events, which is a visual kick, but ultimately this slick Zen bit of whimsy seems to be a higher-class, feel-good film.
D: Robert Zemeckis. A: Tom Hanks, Gary Sinise, Robin Wright.

Americana

Conspiracies, leveraged buyouts, 50s quiz show scandals, and what happened to those kids from *The Last Picture Show* all have a modern edge. Though these films still look at the legendary little people, they're still set against backgrounds as big, splashy, and colorful as the pioneer sagas of yesteryear.

Bonfire of the Vanities
(1990) 126m. **C–**
A Wall Streeter makes a wrong turn in the Bronx, which begins this disastrous attempt to colorfully portray *tout* New York in the 80s. This all-star, sometimes offensive mega-budget mess teeters on the edge of so-bad-it's-good cinema, with a bewildered Hanks, sodden Willis, and buxom Griffith.
D: Brian DePalma. A: Tom Hanks, Bruce Willis, Melanie Griffith.

Texasville
(1990) 123m. **B–**
In this sequel to *The Last Picture Show,* we see how the characters have changed in 30 years; mainly they're older, broader, desperate in noisier ways, and a lot randier. While this is often a farcical mess—Bridges' banty rooster gait is a hoot—at least it's an entertaining one that tries for something.
D: Peter Bogdanovich. A: Jeff Bridges, Cybill Shepherd, Timothy Bottoms.

City of Hope
(1991) 129m. **B**
A contractor's son who walks off his "no-show" union job, a black alderman who's fighting greedy real estate developers, local politicos, and regular citizens trying to get by all intersect in this sprawling, carefully paced saga set in a decaying New Jersey City. A generous and potent, dark-colored tapestry of American life and politics as seen on a personal level.
D: John Sayles. A: Tony Lo Bianco, Vincent Spano, Joe Morton.

Guilty by Suspicion
(1991) 105m. **C+**
This details the McCarthy-era Hollywood nightmare as a film director risks losing everything unless he rats on his Commie pals. Despite plentiful talent onboard and a ripe subject, this is strangely uninvolving, with meandering pace and a dry unexciting look.
D: Irwin Winkler. A: Robert De Niro, Annette Bening, George Wendt.

JFK
(1991) 190m. **B+**
Maverick DA Jim Garrison fights what seems like a national conspiracy to keep the secrets of Kennedy's assassination shrouded in mystery. Hyperactively shot and edited, filled with grotesque characters, and a general tone that's the cinematic equivalent of someone screaming at you.
D: Oliver Stone. A: Kevin Costner, Tommy Lee Jones, Gary Oldman.

Leap of Faith
(1992) 108m. **B**
A traveling faith healer who performs all the miracles that electronics can produce gets stuck in a drought-stricken town where the sheriff's out to expose him. Offers fine performances, especially Martin as the flashy con man with show-biz greed, but possibly something more in his soul.

D: Richard Pearce. A: Steve Martin, Debra Winger, Liam Neeson.

The Mambo Kings
(1992) 100m. **B–**

This tale of two brothers from Havana who struggle to make a success of their mambo band in New York has lots of visual style and starts out exuberantly, but the second half gets bogged down with the lifeless drama. Great music and a wonderful segment where the brothers are on an episode of *I Love Lucy.*
D: Arne Glimcher. A: Armand Assante, Antonio Banderas, Cathy Moriarty.

The Paper
(1994) 112m. **B**

A sensationalistic look at the day-to-day madness involved in running a major Manhattan daily. An undemanding crowd-pleaser that lives and dies by its performers, including an amusing Quaid as a couldn't-care-less reporter and an almost campy bout of fisticuffs between publisher Close and editor Keaton.
D: Ron Howard. A: Michael Keaton, Glenn Close, Robert Duvall.

Quiz Show
(1994) 133m. **A–**

Based on the true quiz show scandals of 1959, this tells of a college professor/contestant, his sudden catapult to fame, and his seduction by a quiz show's producer into perpetuating a hoax. Though Fiennes burns with charisma, it's Turturro as a loud know-it-all who almost walks off with this thoughtful, immaculate-looking production.
D: Robert Redford. A: Ralph Fiennes, John Turturro, Rob Morrow.

The Road to Wellville
(1994) 120m. **B–**

The story of Dr. Kellogg (of corn flakes fame) and his turn-of-the-century health sanitarium. This bright big loopy satire reflects current New Age/health craziness with a wicked glean, spearheaded by a bug-eyed Hopkins applying all manner of dubious therapies to his hopeful and neurotic charges. Could have been a nutty classic of sorts if a half hour had been shaved from the running time.
D: Alan Parker. A: Matthew Broderick, Bridget Fonda, Anthony Hopkins.

Apollo 13
(1995) 150m. **B**

True story of the fateful flight to the moon that nearly ended in deep space tragedy. Somewhat pedestrian rocketship procedural enjoys showing men at work with their high-tech toys and impressive moonscape special effects, but strangely, the film makes it hard to care about the astronauts' destinies.
D: Ron Howard. A: Tom Hanks, Ed Harris, Bill Paxton.

Modern Life

Middle-class frustration, angst, and bewilderment are portrayed in these intelligent, often humorous tales of modern-life upheaval that range from racial tensions to low credit card limits and most everything in between.

Grand Canyon
(1991) 134m. **B–**

Like an updated *Big Chill,* this looks at various upper-class LA folk as they deal with mortality, infidelity, and race issues. Though impeccably filmed and acted, this well-intentioned study of the angsty rich tries to balance things with a Wise Black Man and his family, but finally comes off like a film New Age greeting card.
D: Lawrence Kasdan. A: Kevin Kline, Steve Martin, Danny Glover.

The Object of Beauty
(1991) 105m. **B+**

A flighty jetsetter couple in London struggles to stay one step ahead of their creditors, which soon involves the disposition of the woman's tiny Henry Moore sculpture. Cooly intelligent, with some nice dry humor and sly digs at class warfare.
D: Michael Lindsay-Hogg. A: John Malkovich, Andie MacDowell, Joss Ackland.

Falling Down
(1993) 112m. **B**

A fired defense worker goes on a vengeance spree against what seems like most of modern-day LA, attacking fast-food joints, Korean grocers, and Hispanic gangs while a determined cop tries to stop him. Like an updated, more psychologically hip 70s vengeance film with fine performances and coiled-snake tension.
D: Joel Schumacher. A: Michael Douglas, Robert Duvall, Barbara Hershey.

Short Cuts
(1993) 189m. **A**

An utterly fascinating tapestry of numerous, randomly connected lives of LA characters is funny, romantic, bizarre, and sometimes tragic. A few too many characters and a little too much laid-back randomness stops this from being the great film it often threatens to be.
D: Robert Altman. A: Andie MacDowell, Jennifer Jason Leigh, Tim Robbins.

Six Degrees of Separation
(1993) 112m. **A–**

Not succeeding so well with their own kids, upper-class couples are easy marks for a young and harmless con man who claims to be Sidney Poitier's son. With its series of vignettes told in a witty urbane manner, everything about this stage-to-screen tale is entertaining and bitingly intelligent, even as it offers up some acutely uncomfortable moments.
D: Fred Schepisi. A: Stockard Channing, Donald Sutherland, Will Smith.

Disclosure
(1994) 100m. **B**

A hotshot software executive has the moves made on him by an even hotter shot ex-girlfriend executive, resulting in his filing sexual harassment charges to save his job. Thanks to Levinson's sure handling, this lurid tale mixes silly plot and corporate intrigue subplot with nifty computer effects and heavy-breathing aspects to create compelling pop trash entertainment.
D: Barry Levinson. A: Michael Douglas, Demi Moore, Donald Sutherland.

The New Age
(1994) 106m. **A–**

A trenchant study of the rise and fall of a materialistic couple in psychobabble Los Angeles. What could have been just an on-target satire of trendy spiritualism becomes much more with sur-

realistic style, black humor, and creepy performances evoking a vacuous amoral world.
D: Michael Tolkin. A: Judy Davis, Peter Weller, Adam West.

Oleanna
(1994) 90m. **A**
Scathingly intelligent study of how a female undergrad's request for an improved class grade from her teacher somehow horrifically turns into a case of sexual harrassment. Mamet's staccato, machine-gun language has never been more cutting as it rips into maleism, sexism, patriarchal power politics, and the nearly lost ability of humans to talk and actually say something.
D: David Mamet. A: William Macy, Debra Eisenstadt.

Foreign Dramas

These often wickedly witty films retain the colorful production look of a top Hollywood film while offering an intelligent look at Americans and other innocents abroad.

Meeting Venus
(1991) 117m. **B**
A Hungarian conductor struggles to bring off an international production of *Tannhauser* in Paris, despite the demands of every musician, stagehand, union worker, and the Swedish diva with whom he has an affair. A humorous sophisticated drama that only occasionally pushes a little too hard on the European unification satire.
D: Istvan Szabo. A: Glenn Close, Niels Arestrup, Erland Josephson.

Utz
(1992) 95m. **B+**
With its Prague-set story unfolding in a series of flashbacks, this tells of a one-time aristocrat and obsessive porcelain collector whose cherished figurines have been confiscated by the new Communist government. What sounds rather precious in print is actually a lovingly photographed, if rather slow depiction of the mystery of a man's life.
D: George Sluizer. A: Armin Mueller-Stahl, Peter Riegert.

Barcelona
(1994) 102m. **A–**
Frequently funny drama about two young cousins, one a naval officer, the other a salesman seeking wisdom from the Bible and how-to-succeed guides, as they come to grips with each other, the local females, and the revolutionary anti-American fervor in Barcelona. Wittier and more literate than a year's worth of Hollywood product.
D: Whit Stillman. A: Taylor Nichols, Chris Eigeman, Tushka Bergen.

A Good Man in Africa
(1994) 95m. **B–**
This low-keyed comedy of manners follows a British diplomat as he deals with local customs, embassy politics, a crusty humanitarian doctor, and the country's beautiful First Lady. Not as sparkling as it should be, given the smart script and fine performances.
D: Bruce Beresford. A: Colin Friels, Sean Connery, Joanne Whalley-Kilmer.

Independent Dramas

Small first-time efforts by rising star directors, these offbeat independent films delight by virtue of their sheer originality.

Metropolitan
(1990) 98m. **A–**
Minimal-budget sleeper finds an erudite (but middle-class) fellow who high-lifes it at night with Manhattan's young debutante set. An entire hermetic world of wealth and ennui is created with a few locations and rich woodsy photography while the interplay between our misplaced hero and his supposed betters is directed with a generous cynicism.
D: Whit Stillman. A: Edward Clements, Christopher Eigeman, Carolyn Farina.

Poison
(1990) 85m. **B**
A boy kills his father, a scientist makes a brilliant discovery with unpleasant side-effects, a thief has an affair with another inmate while behind bars: These tales are woven together in styles ranging from campy sci-fi to arty European in this sometimes slow but always fascinating look at the dark sides of humanity.
D: Todd Haynes. A: Edith Meeks, Larry Maxwell, Susan Norman.

Begotten
(1991) 78m. B&W. **B**
If you could get a film version of Nosferatu's nightmares, they might look like this. Using a blurry, ink-blot look to keep the characters sketchy, this film depicts the Nativity, torture of Jesus, and death on Golgotha. With strange creatures that look inside-out, as if made of entrails, and no dialogue, this is a challenging unique film that's not for the squeamish.
D: E. Elias Merhige.

Swoon
(1992) 95m. B&W. **B**
Explicit retelling of the infamous Leopold and Loeb case, in which two 1920s homosexuals murdered a child to prove they could commit the perfect crime. Shot in searing black and white, this small independent film occasionally falls into arty cul-de-sacs, but is still an effectively chilling meditation on sexual control and evil.
D: Tom Kalin. A: Daniel Schlachet, Craig Chester, Michael Kirby.

DOCUMENTARIES

Documentary Menu

Documentaries

DOCUMENTARY FILM GROUPS

Documentaries

Social and Political Issues

History and social issues are given flesh and bones as the stories of both famous and ordinary people are told, adding immediacy to a wide variety of pressing social concerns.

Triumph of the Will
(1935) 110m. B&W.
A

Commissioned to film the monumental Nuremberg Nazi Party Congress of 1934, Riefenstahl produced the finest and scariest propaganda film of all time. Filled with images that are cunning, haunting, and grandiose, you'll be amazed at how her techniques are standard fare for today's media, from ads to music videos.
D: Leni Riefenstahl.

Salesman
(1968) 90m. B&W. **A**

Bible salesmen make their rounds in this carefully detailed, darkly funny, and sometimes grim look at one version of the American success-through-sales story. The cinema verité feeling makes you almost smell the stale cigarette smoke in the drab hotel rooms and dreary homes these men visit.
D: Albert Maysles, David Maysles.

The Sorrow and the Pity
(1970) 260m. B&W. **A**

Collaborators and those who lived through the worst of World War II are the subject of this classic documentary. Neither its length nor its interview format ever bog the film down; instead, what emerges is a picture of human nature at its worst. If you watch only one documentary on World War II, this should be it.
D: Marcel Ophuls.

Hearts and Minds
(1974) 112m. **A**

A portrait of the Vietnam war as seen by the devastated populace, with amazingly unabashed interviews of military leaders convinced of the US mission. Indelible imagery and frightening revelations make it a must.
D: Peter Davis.

General Idi Amin Dada
(1975) 90m. **A**

Benefiting from the full cooperation of Amin, Schroeder manages to show the general in full despotic and frightening megalomania. Beautifully shot, but it's like spending time with a talking version of the *Jaws* shark.
D: Barbet Schroeder.

California Reich
(1977) 55m. **B**

Grassroots, neo-Nazi enclaves in California are the subject of this disturbing and compelling film. By documenting the "banality of evil"—the violence and hate that's fostered in these otherwise bland middle-American communities (Santa Claus with a swastika is one of the more surreal images), the filmmakers produce a chilling portrait.
D: Walter F. Parkes, Keith F. Critchlow.

Harlan County, U.S.A.
(1977) 103m. **A**

Long exploited and largely overlooked, Kentucky coal miners have struggled hard and long to get the few benefits they have. This excellent film details a strike and the various elements at war between labor and management.
D: Barbara Kopple.

Chicken Ranch
(1983) 84m. **B**

Anyone under the illusion that prostitution and brothels are glamorous should see this blunt look at the model for *The Best Little Whorehouse in Texas.* A grim, plastic-covered picture emerges as private jet loads of Japanese businessmen dicker for better rates, and good ole boys have to be admonished to keep their cool.
D: Nick Broomfield, Sandy Sissel.

Shoah
(1985) 570m. **A**

The implementation of the Nazi "final solution" came about through small, nearly imperceptible changes in the society, and that is exactly the way this film—a detailed examination of that time—makes its point. Layering interviews with survivors, perpetrators, and regular citizens, along with detailed historical material, this painstaking horror show packs a slow-motion wallop. Best to watch over several evenings.
D: Claude Lanzmann.

Streetwise
(1984) 92m. **A**

Seattle's downtown serves as a hub for teenagers keeping themselves alive with low-level drug dealing, prostitution, robbery, and panhandling. By following the lives of several of these kids, the filmmakers manage a drama and narrative verve that gives a truer picture of teen alienation than most fictional films.
D: Martin Bell, Mary Ellen Mark, Cheryl McCall.

28 Up
(1985) 120m. **A**

Fourteen young people—the original subjects of Apted's *7 Up*—are the focus of this look at their lives on the verge of 30. They are appealing, annoying, sympathetic, and repellent—in other words, your average group of people. Along the way, Apted manages to take some shots at the British class system as well.
D: Michael Apted.

Hotel Terminus: The Life and Times of Klaus Barbie
(1988) 267m. **A–**

Known as "the Butcher of Lyon," Nazi SS Captain Barbie was responsible for the torture and death of thousands of Jews and French Resistance members. His story is traced in disturbingly graphic detail with interviews of survivors and colleagues. Thorough and long and mostly riveting.
D: Marcel Ophuls.

The Thin Blue Line
(1988) 90m. **A–**

A drifter convicted of a 1976 murder of a policeman is the subject of this film which is out to show that he was wrongly convicted (he was in fact later exonerated). With the tension of a good cop show and using reenact-

ments to show the innocence of the subject, Morris pushed the very genre of documentary in a new direction.
D: Errol Morris.

Roger and Me
(1989) 91m. **B+**
Hugely popular and fairly controversial look at the economic and human devastation on Moore's hometown of Flint, Michigan, following General Motors' decision to close down several plants. Though this doesn't flinch in its depiction of poverty, homelessness, and crime, it's plagued by some superficial observations and smarmy irony.
D: Michael Moore.

American Dream
(1989) 98m. **A**
At a time when labor issues have faded from public interest, this chronicle of the strike by factory workers at the Hormel meatpacking plant is a bright beacon: Through interviews with executives, strikers, and union officials, it manages to paint a balanced complex portrait of the dispute, calling upon the viewers to draw their own conclusions.
D: Barbara Kopple.

35 Up
(1991) 127m. **B+**
The fourth installment of Apted's ongoing project, in which 14 British men and women are interviewed at seven-year intervals during their lives beginning in 1963, can stand on its own or within context. Either way, it offers a totally fascinating look at an economically and socially disparate group coping with the discoveries of age.
D: Michael Apted.

Panama Deception
(1992) 91m. **A–**
By tracing the U.S. invasion of Panama, this no-holds-barred film manages to show how the media was cowed by the Reagan and Bush administrations into reporting only what they were fed. Contains strong imagery and unsettling scenes of violence and death.
D: Barbara Trent.

The War Room
(1993) 96m. **A**
The Clinton campaign, warts and all, is the subject of this extremely likable movie which features the two main players, everybody's student council president, George Stephanopolous, and the disarmingly beguiling James Carville. Nobody looks particularly good or bad here, but you get a clear picture of modern-day political campaigns.
D: Chris Hegedus, D. A. Pennebaker.

Compilations

A lot of fun is to be had with these films, much of it very campy, since they run the cultural gamut from meditations on early make out techniques of the stars to a straight-faced warning of the imminent bug invasion.

Mondo Cane
(1963) 105m. Dubbed
B–
Before there was cable TV, movies like this were one source for filmed oddities from around the world. This is a collection of offbeat behavior, some of it documented, other sections clearly reenacted. Of curiosity value primarily, and definitely not family fare.
D: Gualtiero Jacopetti.

The Hellstrom Chronicle
(1971) 90m. **A–**
In this faux documentary, Dr. Hellstrom (director Pressman) shows astonishing close-up shots of insects and their fellow creatures to bear out his contention that they are taking over the world. Dumb idea, great execution: The entertainment is in those bugs. Hollywood F/X have a long way to go.
D: Lawrence Pressman, Walon Green.

Chariots of the Gods?
(1974) 98m. **B–**
Will earthlings ever tire of speculating about visitors from outer space? Probably not. That's why this film was made, notable largely for travel footage (Machu Picchu, for example) and less for its unproved theories that the Earth played host to advanced aliens thousands of years ago.
D: Harald Reinl.

Atomic Cafe
(1982) 88m. B&W. **A–**
Sort of like walking through a shop of Cold War/nuclear panic memorabilia—using newsreel footage, propaganda training films, and documentary clips, this fashions a mildly mocking portrait of American fears and appalling ignorance of the early nuclear age.
D: Kevin Rafferty, Jayne Loader, Pierce Rafferty.

Heavy Petting
(1989) 75m. B&W./Color
B
The much analyzed, reviled, and celebrated dating and sexual mores of the 1960s are the topics of this collage of period footage from movies and TV, which are blended with celebrity anecdotes from David Byrne, Sandra Bernhard, William S. Burroughs, and Laurie Anderson, among others. Light and amusing if nothing new.
D: Obie Benz, Josh Waletzsky.

Flying Saucers over Hollywood
(1992) 111m. B&W./Color
B
A good companion piece to *Ed Wood* is this behind-the-scenes look at Wood's *Plan 9 from Outer Space* and other shady projects. Also includes interviews with contemporary admirers, among them Sam Raimi. Best for Wood fans.
D: Mark Patrick Carducci.

Heaven
(1987) 88m. **C+**
Keaton assembled a collage of film clips and interview excerpts in which people talk about death and their conception of heaven. Quirky and static with a few gems buried in lots of junk.
D: Diane Keaton.

Biographies

A self-loathing cartoonist, a movie star-turned-Nazi propagandist, the story of a soft-core kingpin—who said biographies had to be dull?

Milhouse: A White House Comedy

(1971) 93m. **B+**

If any doubt remains that the only adversity Nixon couldn't survive was death, this patchwork of his public appearances from 1948 to 1970 will lay it to rest. A fascinating look at persistence personified and one of the most enduring figures of twentieth-century history.
D: Emile De Antonio.

Grey Gardens

(1976) 94m. **A**

An aunt and cousin of Jacqueline Onassis are shown up close in this sometimes disturbing, often quietly funny look at their ruined East Hampton, New York, mansion, later officially declared a health hazard. They're candid, opinionated, and insulated, and with more such people on the streets, not so alien-seeming as when this film was released.
D: David and Albert Maysles, Ellen Hovde, Muffie Meyer.

Best Boy

(1979) 110m. **A–**

Tracing his 52-year-old retarded cousin's attempt to deal with the outside world, Wohl captures the bittersweet difficulties for both the man and his family as they face the fact that he will have to live on his own. A loving and respectful portrait.
D: Ira Wohl.

Lightning over Water

(1980) 91m. **A**

Not only do you get a sympathetic, charming, and engaging sense of director Nicholas Ray (*Rebel Without a Cause, In a Lonely Place*) in this film made right before he died of cancer, but also Wenders' affection for the filmmaker. A beautiful valentine from a younger practitioner to an idol.
D: Wim Wenders.

Marlene

(1984) 96m. B&W./Color **A**

Though Dietrich herself refused to cooperate fully—she only allowed Schell to have an audio interview she manages to imbue this with her smoky enigmatic presence (clips from her star turns are included). Before anyone knew what spin was, Marlene was making sure the world knew her the way she wanted.
D: Maximilian Schell.

Cousin Bobby

(1991) 70m. **C**

Demme's cousin, Episcopal priest Robert Castle, is the admirable subject of this very personal film. Despite Castle's revolutionary ties to the Black Panthers and the SDS, this has the self-congratulatory feel of looking through a precious family album, with a further drawback of real hokiness.
D: Jonathan Demme.

A Brief History of Time

(1992) 84m. **A**

One of the most well-known geniuses in physics, Stephen Hawking, wrote a best-selling book on the nature of the universe; he also happens to be profoundly disabled. This rare and charming film of a scientist at work details Hawking's life and allows him to explain his theories in terms the rest of us can actually understand.
D: Errol Morris.

Brother's Keeper

(1992) 105m. **A**

The lives of four senior citizen farming brothers are completely disrupted when one is accused of killing one of the others. By giving equal time and sympathy to all sides in this case, this film manages to transform a media-ravaged incident into a profoundly insightful look at eccentricity and tolerance.
D: Joe Berlinger, Bruce Sinofsky.

Hugh Hefner: Once Upon a Time

(1992) 88m. **B+**

No matter how you feel about Hefner, this film serves as a document of the sexual revolution—its successes, excesses, and failures—in this country. Extremely well-paced, with plenty of celebrity clips, outrageous anecdotes, shots of bunnies, and reflections by self-justifying, now-mellowed Hefner, this is a compulsively watchable look at success American style.
D: Robert Heath.

The Wonderful, Horrible Life of Leni Riefenstahl

(1993) 180m. Subtitled. **A**

Known for providing the Nazi party with some of the greatest propaganda ever, Riefenstahl had many other credits to her name before and after the war years. Along with stunning clips from early German cinema, this is an exhilarating look at a strong, stubborn, and fiercely determined woman who has remained a virtual force of nature.
D: Ray Muller.

Crumb

(1995) 119m. **A**

A frank, even upsetting look at artist Robert Crumb through his work and family. What emerges is a portrait of a sensitive, often selfish and scrupulously honest survivor, a satirist on the very edge of society and humanity. Even if you've never looked at *Zap Comics*, this searing picture of high-level dysfunctionalism makes for riveting viewing.
D: Terry Zwigoff.

Subcultures

Here's a clutch of uniformly fascinating films dealing with some of the more exotic sections of society.

The Endless Summer

(1966) 95m. **B+**

Charming period artifact about two surfers trolling the world's beaches for the elusive perfect wave. While limited in subject matter, this has loads of gorgeous and excitingly edited curl-shooting footage, cool twangy music, and nostalgically naive tone.
D: Bruce Brown. A: Mike Hynson, Robert August.

Pumping Iron

(1977) 85m. **B+**

The bodybuilding Mr. Universe contest comes down

to two little-known men, Louis Ferrigno and Arnold Schwarzenegger. Even if the only weight you ever lift is your own, this will keep your interest at the storytelling level, with the pumped-up details filling the screen.
D: George Butler, Robert Fiore.

Paris Is Burning
(1990) 78m. **A**

A bold tribute to the underground of poor, black and Hispanic New York gay culture, where their world becomes a fun-house mirror reflection of the ads, fashion magazines, and supermodels. Made with voyeuristic empathy, this is a peek at another world and an entertaining document of current pop culture.
D: Jennine Livingston.

Blast 'Em
(1992) 103m. **B**

This is the scratch and claw of paparazzi—literally the "assault" photographers who will do anything (absolutely ANYTHING)—to get a shot of a major celebrity. A fascinating history of a rather brash way to make a living that will change how you look at celeb photos.
D: Joseph Blasioli, Egidio Coccimiglio.

The Endless Summer II
(1994) 100m. **C–**

Two more wave-riders travel the globe, this time they're a pair of sub Bill and Ted dudes who, between moronic narration and strikingly filmed surfing, give their comments on world cuisine and female beachwear. Laid-back charm of the first film is replaced with heavy metal music and general tanned, frat-boy jokiness.
D: Bruce Brown. A: Patrick O'Connell, Robert Weaver.

Hoop Dreams
(1994) 176m. **A**

This touching and unsparing documentary looks at two young black kids with basketball talent and the burning desire to play in the NBA. Filmed over a 4-year period, this reveals the strikes against city kids and the sham of the anyone-with-talent-can-play idea: an important and riveting story, even for nonsports fans.
D: Steve James, Frederick Marx, Peter Gilbert.

Film

These films allow you to see that there is much more than "lights, camera, action" to moviemaking as they portray the struggles of the people behind the camera to bring their vision to light.

Burden of Dreams
(1982) 94m. **A**

In his effort to make a film about the man who tried to bring opera to the Amazon in *Fitzcarraldo,* Werner Herzog inadvertently involved himself in a similar swamp of financial, physical, and psychic overextension. Fortunately, Blank got it all down in this remarkable, frequently frustrating, and fascinating film.
D: Les Blank. A: Werner Herzog, Klaus Kinski, Claudia Cardinale.

Hearts of Darkness: A Filmmaker's Apocalypse
(1991) 96m. **A**

Watching *Apocalypse Now,* it's hard to think that the filming of it was anything but chaotic. This film—culled from some 60 hours of footage—serves as a testimonial to the excesses of money, privilege, ego, and a relentless vision that fed the beast.
D: Fax Bahr, George Hickenlooper.

Visions of Light: The Art of Cinematography
(1992) 90m. B&W./Color
A

For all movie buffs of every level, this offers a huge helping of anecdotes, inside stories, and the work of some of the best cinematographers of all time. Even well-known scenes from classics such as *The Third Man* get a whole new perspective when you hear how they got it to look that way, and you'll end up wanting to see all these movies again.
D: Arnold Glassman.

(See also *Ciao Federico!,* page 292.)

Cultures

These are film portraits of civilization old and new, from Eskimo and Indian culture to a modern city street.

Nanook of the North
(1922) 55m. B&W. **A**

This landmark film on Eskimos' day-to-day life gave realism a new standard. Lacking the sophistication of later films, it's still a must-see for anyone interested in documentaries or film in general.
D: Robert Flaherty.

Phantom India
(1968) 364m. **A**

Don't be put off by the long running time; this is a loving, insightful, observant, and sometimes irreverent tribute to a country that clearly fascinates Malle. His tour includes urban and rural scenes, everything from the huge Indian movie industry to religious rituals. Ambitious in range and scope, this is epic filmmaking at its best.
D: Louis Malle.

Koyaanisqatsi
(1983) 87m. **B**

No plot, just images of stressful life in the city (the title means, among other things, "life out of balance" in Hopi language) contrasted with scenes of bucolic splendor. The spectacular cinematography and Philip Glass score either work for you or those 87 minutes seem like days.
D: Godfrey Reggio.

Powaqqatsi
(1988) 99m. **B**

With its subtitle "Life in Transformation" this picks up where *Koyaanisqatsi* left off—more Glass music and lush cinematography make this another excursion into the wonders and horrors of

the modern world. If you're checking this out, you must have liked the first one.
D: Godfrey Reggio.

Baraka
(1992) 96m. **A**

This presents a series of exotic landscapes, religious/tribal rituals, and the various ways that mankind shapes the world. Visually breathtaking and ambitious undertaking threatens to become caught up in the surface effects—like watching a New Age music video—but remains a thoughtful meditation on the grandeur of nature and the human experience.
D: Ron Fricke.

Music

These are the best way to enjoy a rock concert without leaving your couch, not to mention getting backstage glimpses of some of rock's legends. The music is the reason for these films, but with the likes of Scorsese, Demme, Spheeris, and the Maysles' Brothers directing, they also offer the style and flash that surpasses any music videos.

Don't Look Back
(1967) 96m. B&W. **A–**

This shows a cool and sly Bob Dylan on his 1965 tour of England when he was still playing acoustic guitar and dealing with the rigors of touring and his own growing fame.
D: D. A. Pennebaker.

Monterey Pop
(1969) 88m. **A**

The summer of love in 1967 culminated in this blowout concert.
D: D. A. Pennebaker. A: The Animals, Booker T and the MG's, Country Joe and the Fish, Jimi Hendrix, Janis Joplin, Jefferson Airplane, The Mamas and Papas, Otis Redding, Ravi Shankar, The Who.

Elvis: That's the Way It Is
(1970) 109m. **B**

Elvis performs 30 of his greatests during the 1970 tour, which includes footage of his opening night at Las Vegas. Good songs with plenty of backstage antics.
D: Denis Sanders.

Gimme Shelter
(1970) 91m. **A**

The 1969 Rolling Stones U.S. tour ended at the Altamont free concert where the Hells Angels' security force put the brakes on peace, love, and understanding. Electric performances and a fascinating behind-the-scenes look at the group, rock promoting, and a murder.
D: David Maysles, Albert Maysles. A: The Rolling Stones, Ike and Tina Turner, Jefferson Airplane.

Woodstock
(1970) 184m. **A**

The cavalcade of rock stars and the humorous telling glimpses of the flower children, music lovers, and handful of adults make up this documentary of the epic rock festival that helped define a generation.
D: Michael Wadleigh. A: Joan Baez, Joe Cocker, Country Joe and the Fish, Crosby, Stills and Nash, Arlo Guthrie, Jimi Hendrix, Jefferson Airplane, Sha Na Na, Sly and the Family Stone, Ten Years After, The Who.

Elvis on Tour
(1972) 93m. **B**

Not too revealing portrait of the King's 72 tour onstage and off. Presley's voice is in fine fettle but his excesses are starting to show.
D: Pierre Adidge, Robert Abel.

The Song Remains the Same
(1976) 136m. **B–**

A live performance at Madison Square Garden in 1973 is the centerpiece of a documentary / fantasy / performance by the colossus of heavy metal rock.
D: Peter Clifton, Joe Massot. A: Led Zeppelin.

The Last Waltz
(1978) 117m. **A**

Martin Scorsese presents The Band's farewell performance as a sumptuous musical feast, artfully intercut with interviews of the exceedingly groovy members.
D: Martin Scorsese. A: The Band, Eric Clapton, Neil Diamond, Bob Dylan, Joni Mitchell, Van Morrison, Muddy Waters, Neil Young.

Stop Making Sense
(1984) 88m. **A**

This live concert filmed over three days sweeps you into a tidal wave of rhythm, motion, and music. A seamless musical safari, filled with great theatrical flair.
D: Jonathan Demme. A: The Talking Heads.

That Was Rock
(1984) 92m. **A**

This compilation of *The T.A.M.I. Show* (1964) and *The Big T.N.T. Show* (1966) captures the energy, exuberance, and sheer musicality of one dynamite act after another in front of a whipped-up teen audience.
D: Steve Binder, Larry Peerce. A: Rolling Stones, James Brown, Ray Charles, The Ronettes, Marvin Gaye, The Miracles, Chuck Berry, Ike and Tina Turner, Jan and Dean, Lesley Gore.

Chuck Berry Hail! Hail! Rock 'n' Roll
(1987) 120m. **A**

The interviews with Berry's peers and those he influenced are interesting, but they don't stand a chance against the propulsive live performance by Chuck, backed up by a supercharged band.
D: Taylor Hackford. A: Chuck Berry, Eric Clapton, Bo Diddley, Johnnie Johnson, Keith Richards, Little Richard, Linda Ronstadt.

The Decline of Western Civilization Part II: The Metal Years
(1988) 100m. **A**

A funny, raunchy, and morbidly fascinating picture of the young heavy metal performers with their unshaken conviction of eventual stardom, and the older established artists sharing their jaded philosophies on drugs, alcohol, sex, and fame.
D: Penelope Spheeris. A: Alice Cooper, Chris Holmes, Megadeth, Ozzy Osbourne, Poison, Steven Tyler.

Let's Get Lost
(1989) 120m. B&W. **A**

This film brings together interviews with jazz trumpeter Chet Baker (then in the last year of his life), former girlfriends, wives, and fellow musicians, intercut with recording sessions and film clips. For someone who made life hell for himself and those who knew him, Baker comes off as appealing—both fascinating and horrifying at once.
D: Bruce Weber.

Thelonius Monk: Straight No Chaser
(1988) 90m. B&W. **A**
The innovative and iconoclastic jazz pianist is the subject of this personal and wide-ranging documentary. The tapestry of interviews and studio/performance footage is assembled with both verve and grace, allowing you to draw your own conclusions about what made this first-rate composer and musician tick.
D: Charlotte Zwerin.

Madonna Truth or Dare
(1991) 118m. **A–**
Madonna's flamboyant stage shows are only slightly more theatrical than her offstage routines as she plays diva/mother/fag-hag to her band of dancers and singers.
D: Alek Keshishian.

See also *Let It Be, The Beatles: The First U.S. Visit,* and *The Compleat Beatles,* page 426.

Other Films:
Sympathy for the Devil (1970) The Rolling Stones
Joe Cocker: Mad Dogs and Englishmen (1971)
The Grateful Dead Movie (1976)
The Kids Are Alright (1979) The Who
D.O.A.: A Right of Passage (1981) Punk
The Decline of Western Civilization (1981) Punk
Let's Spend the Night Together (1982) The Rolling Stones
Bring on the Night (1985) Sting
Imagine: John Lennon (1988)
U2: Rattle and Hum (1988)
Listen Up: The Lives of Quincy Jones (1990)

FOREIGN FILMS

Foreign Film Menu

Japanese

Italian

FOREIGN FILM MENU

French

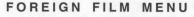

Foreign Film Menu

FOREIGN FILM MENU

FOREIGN FILM GROUPS

Japanese

Historical Dramas and Melodramas

Generally not as subtle or interesting as Kurosawa's tales of feudal Japan, the emphasis here is on stock characters (misunderstood heroes, long-suffering girlfriends, corrupt bosses), swordplay, and violence (facial wounds come with plenty of gory red paint), climaxing in a showdown between two warriors or armies; in other words, these look a whole lot like good old American westerns.

Sansho the Bailiff
(1954) 132m. Subtitled. **B**

The wife and children of a lord exiled for his compassion are kidnapped and sold into slavery where their nobility is tested. The portrayal of working people's hard lot, and cruelty and corruption in high places transcends the medieval settings in this drama that draws out genuine pathos.
D: Kenji Mizoguchi. A: Kinuyo Tanaka, Yoshiaki Hanayagi, Kyoko Kagawa.

The Samurai Trilogy
(1955–56) 92m./102m./102m. Subtitled. **B**

These three films trace the development of the proud unruly peasant Takezo as he becomes a legendary and noble swordsman, with an occasional glimpse at the selflessly dedicated woman who loves him. The only thought-provoking part of this lightly entertaining trilogy is why, for no apparent reason, so many people are out to get the hero, and why so many women fall in love with him. The third film is clearly the best, although it may be hard to appreciate without the other two.
D: Hiroshi Inagaki. A: Toshiro Mifune, Koji Tsuruta, Kaoru Yachigusa.

Zatoichi vs. Yojimbo
(1970) 115m. Subtitled.
B–

Zatoichi, a wandering blind masseur and skilled swordsman, teams up with Yojimbo to free a village from the control of gangsters. Part of the *Zatoichi* series, this is for samurai fans only, and one only wonders who would hire him for one of his rough jerky kneadings?
D: Kihachi Okamoto. A: Shintaro Katsu, Toshiro Mifune, Ayako Wakao.

Eijanaika (Why Not?)
(1981) 151m. Subtitled.
A–

Assorted misfits, gangsters, and entertainers use their wits to survive in the final tumultuous days of the Shogun in mid-nineteenth-century Tokyo. Although hard to keep everything straight at times, this humorous and unusually realistic view of the past has an intelligent charm.
D: Shohei Imamura. A: Shigeru Izumiya, Kaori Momoi.

Heaven and Earth
(1990) 104m. Subtitled.
B–

In the war-torn sixteenth century, a young lord must battle the betrayal of his men and his own merciful streak in order to fend off the attacks of a powerful neighbor. Basically a scenery movie, with grand landscapes and battle sequences, but the anachronistic women warriors are a real stretch.
D: Haruki Kadokawa. A: Takaaki Enoki, Masahiko Tsugawa, Atsuko Asano.

Kurosawa's Historical Dramas

Kurosawa adapted Shakespearean tragedies and classic Japanese tales to probe timeless human dilemmas in these films that represent the cream of Japanese historical dramas. A favorite period of the samurai films is the sixteenth century when Japan was torn by civil war: a time when an ordinary man could find adventure on the road and the warrior could rise or fall based on his own skills and courage. Other tales take place in the nineteenth century as stability in the 300-year-old Tokugawa era was breaking down and masterless samurai, called "ronin," wandered around looking for work. While the films are lengthy with at least one scene that seems to run on for an eternity, they still offer a masterful blend of fast-paced battle scenes, intense psychological studies, and poetically haunting images.

Rashomon
(1950) 83m. B&W.
Subtitled. **A–**

Each of the four principals give their version of a rape/murder that took place in a mountain grove, and the conflicting accounts call attention to the subjective nature of reality. A classic, but after several repetitions of the same scene, the movie sometimes drags.
D: Akira Kurosawa. A: Toshiro Mifune, Machiko Kyo, Masayuki Mori.

The Seven Samurai
(1954) 203m. B&W.
Subtitled. **A**

Farmers recruit seven warriors to save their village from devastating raids by bandits. Offers a sophisticated blend of humor and pathos even though Mifune's typical outsider hero is more manic and buffoonish than usual. A true samurai classic that even nonfans will enjoy.
D: Akira Kurosawa. A: Toshiro Mifune, Takashi Shimura, Yoshio Inaba.

Throne of Blood

(1957) 110m. B&W.
Subtitled. **B**

This is pretty much a scene-for-scene translation of *Macbeth,* with all the castles, battlefields, enchanted forests, and weird spirits translated into the idioms of sixteenth-century Japan. Elaborate trappings, dusky lighting, and a bug-eyed Mifune as Macbeth make up for the long-winded, occasionally dragging scenes.
D: Akira Kurosawa. A: Toshiro Mifune, Minoru Chiaki, Isuzu Yamada.

The Hidden Fortress

(1958) 139m. B&W.
Subtitled. **B+**

Two bumbling farmers are recruited by a defeated clan's general to help him smuggle out a treasure and a nubile princess from a fortress in enemy territory. Be prepared for almost slapstick antics and choreographed violence in this grungy and realistic epic that inspired *Star Wars.*
D: Akira Kurosawa. A: Toshiro Mifune, Misa Uehara, Minoru Chiaki.

Yojimbo

(1961) 110m. B&W.
Subtitled. **B**

A ronin arrives in a ramshackle town terrorized by factions of feuding merchants and hired thugs, and skillfully plays one side against the other. Touches of black humor are overwhelmed by severed limbs and torture scenes in this film that clearly influenced spaghetti westerns.
D: Akira Kurosawa. A: Toshiro Mifune, Eijiro Tono, Isuzu Yamada.

Sanjuro

(1962) 96m. B&W.
Subtitled. **A**

An eccentric but honest ronin aids a naive group of young samurai in their attempt to reclaim their clan from corrupt schemers. You don't have to be a fan of the genre to enjoy the subtle comic twists to an otherwise standard samurai fare. Although a sequel to *Yojimbo,* this has a lighter, more satiric tone.
D: Akira Kurosawa. A: Toshiro Mifune, Tatsuya Nakadai, Yuzo Kayama.

Kagemusha (The Shadow Warrior)

(1980) 159m. Subtitled.
A–

When a great warlord is killed in battle, his double, a convicted thief, must play his part in earnest to save the clan from destruction. Epic scenes of colorful armies alternate with a more poignant exploration of issues of identity.
D: Akira Kurosawa. A: Tatsuya Nakadai, Tsutomu Yamazaki, Kenichi Hagiwara.

Ran

(1985) 160m. Subtitled.
A

King Lear is adapted to sixteenth-century Japan in this story of a warlord who finds himself vulnerable to retribution for his past cruelty after relinquishing power to his sons. Kurosawa's most lavish and polished epic drama has a tragic resonance and magisterial quality.
D: Akira Kurosawa. A: Tatsuya Nakadai, Akira Terao, Mieko Harada.

Suffering Women

Like Hollywood's classic "Women's Films," these black-and-white dramas show the misfortunes of desertion, betrayal, and death of loved ones that women endure, almost thriving or ennobled by the experiences. Happiness is never allowed to last more than a few brief hours, but that doesn't stop these weepies from being as entertaining as your favorite soap opera.

Osaka Elegy

(1936) 71m. B&W.
Subtitled. **B+**

A young telephone operator becomes the mistress of her stockbroker boss to pay her wastrel father's debt, but the sacrifice brings only ingratitude and a bleaker future. Yamada's change from an old-fashioned, kimono-clad girl to a modern hardened, cigarette-smoking woman helps make this entry surprisingly fresh for its age.
D: Kenji Mizoguchi. A: Isuzu Yamada, Benkei Shignoya, Kensaku Hara.

Life of Oharu

(1952) 146m. B&W.
Subtitled. **B**

An upper-class beauty destroys her reputation by falling in love with a poor samurai as social hypocrisy and her own rebelliousness result in her steady descent into prostitution. The constant hardships get a bit tiring and predictable in this downbeat adaptation of a satiric classic.
D: Kenji Mizoguchi. A: Kinuyo Tanaka, Toshiro Mifune.

Mother (Okasan)

(1952) 98m. B&W.
Subtitled. **C**

The working class Fukuhara family manages to survive the trying times of the immediate postwar period through the sacrifice and hard work of Mother. An unabashedly sentimental celebration of that Japanese institution, the sainted mother, comes complete with sappy violin and choral music.
D: Mikio Naruse. A: Kinuyo Tanaka, Kyoko Kagawa, Eiji Okada.

A Story of Chikamatsu (Chikamatsu Monogatari)

(1954) 102m. B&W.
Subtitled. **B**

When a printer's clerk tries to help his master's long-suffering wife with her money problems, the couple is falsely accused of adultery. They run off together and fall in love, but the brief moments of defiant happiness still bring ruin to all in this theatrically presented drama based on a seventeenth-century puppet play.
D: Kenji Mizoguchi. A: Kazuo Hasegawa, Kyoko Kagawa, Yoko Minamida.

Twenty-Four Eyes

(1954) 158m. B&W.
Subtitled. **B**

A caring, independent-minded teacher has a special place in the hearts of her young students as they grow up through the Depression and war on an idyllic island on the Inland Sea. The refreshing heroine and genuinely touching moments don't quite balance the copious weeping scenes and interminable folk songs.
D: Keisuke Kinoshita. A: Hideko Takamine, Chishu Ryu.

Street of Shame

(1956) 88m. B&W.
Subtitled. **A–**

An unsentimental but sympathetic exploration of the lives of five prostitutes in

Tokyo's red-light district living under the shadow of the impending antiprostitution law. Despite the funky *Blade Runner*-esque brothel and creepy 50s sci-fi music, a nice balance of stories as each woman struggles to maintain her dignity.
D: Kenji Mizoguchi. A: Machiko Kyo, Ayako Wakao.

Snow Country
(1957) 104m. B&W.
Subtitled. **B**

This 40s Hollywood-style adaptation of Kawabata's novel traces the love affair between a Tokyo dilettante and a passionate hot-spring resort geisha. The bittersweet tone of the film is still effective, but otherwise a dated affair.
D: Shiro Toyoda. A: Keiko Kishi, Ryo Ikebe, Kaoru Yachigusa.

When a Woman Ascends the Stairs
(1960) 100m. B&W.
Subtitled. **B**

The elegant manager of a Ginza bar finds her business in jeopardy when she hesitates to betray her husband's memory by becoming the mistress of a rich patron. Winking neon, smoky nightclubs, and cool jazz contribute to the downbeat 50s noir atmosphere.
D: Mikio Naruse. A: Hideko Takamine, Masayuki Mori, Tatsuya Nakadai.

Insect Woman
(1963) 123m. B&W.
Subtitled. **B**

A young woman from a poor farm family grows up amidst the historical events of the twentieth century. Exploited economically and sexually as a domestic worker, prostitute, and then madam, she emerges a survivor thanks to her antlike persistence. A stark dark film with arty transitions and a slow disjointed first half, but stick with it.
D: Shohei Imamura. A: Sachiko Hidari.

Double Suicide
(1969) 105m. B&W.
Subtitled. **B**

Based on a seventeenth-century puppet play, a shopkeeper is torn between duty to his wife and love for a courtesan who longs to be free from servitude. Clever theatrical touches (the presence of black-garbed puppeteers helping the actors by opening doors, tightening nooses etc.) and tasteful erotic scenes are undercut by lapses into melodrama.
D: Mashiro Shinoda. A: Kichiemon Nakamura, Shima Iwashita, Yusuke Takita.

Obsessions and the Supernatural

These films offer a look at the darker side of Japanese psychology, exploring fantasies, the ghost world, erotic obsessions, and sometimes just plain weird sex.

Ugetsu
(1953) 96m. B&W.
Subtitled. **A–**

An enterprising country potter in Japan's war-torn sixteenth century is lured into an affair with a beautiful noblewoman who, it turns out, is too good to be true. Good use of the supernatural to score moral points in this cautionary tale of the perils of excessive ambition.
D: Kenji Mizoguchi. A: Machiko Kyo, Masayuki Mori, Kinyo Tanaka.

Kwaidan
(1963) 160m. B&W.
Subtitled. **B**

This collection of four ghost and demon tales set in Tokugawa (seventeenth century) Japan is about as gentle and mannered as horror can get. But even with the stylized, low-budget sets and hokey effects, this is still entertaining, with some real Japanese-flavored spookiness.
D: Masaki Kobayashi. A: Tatsuya Nakadai, Rentaro Mikuni, Michiyo Aratama.

Woman in the Dunes
(1964) 123m. B&W.
Subtitled. **A**

When a vacationing insect collector becomes trapped in a sandpit with a local widow who needs a mate, he struggles first to escape and then to endure. An otherworldly tale that portrays the primal tribal nature of the villagers with the alienation of the "civilized" man.
D: Hiroshi Teshigahara. A: Eiji Okada, Kyoko Kishida.

The Face of Another
(1966) 124m. B&W.
Subtitled. **B+**

When a man's face is disfigured in an industrial accident, he enters into a complex relationship with a doctor who creates a new synthetic face for him. Weirdness, madness, and psychobabble abound in this French New Wave-like film.
D: Hiroshi Teshigahara. A: Tatsuya Nakadai, Machiko Kyo.

Black Lizard
(1968) 86m. Subtitled. **B**

A private eye is hired to protect a jeweler's daughter from the clutches of a beautiful transvestite, but the two adversaries find their relationship complicated by mutual fascination. Fans of Mishima's novels will recognize elements of his aesthetic sadomasochism (half-naked, stuffed human dolls) in this entertaining and very weird film.
D: Kinji Fukasaku. A: Akahiro Maruyama, Isao Kimura, Yukio Mishima.

In the Realm of the Senses
(1976) 105m. Subtitled.
A–

The passionate affair between a maid and her employer escalates into an obsession that breaks all taboos. Based on a true story, the nonstop explicit sex scenes conceal a political message for the analytically inclined, with the eroticism effectively transforming into a disturbing and ever-tightening enclosure.
D: Nagisa Oshima. A: Tatsuya Fuji, Eiko Matsuda.

Irezumi (Spirit of the Tatoo)
(1983) 88m. Subtitled. **B+**

A beautiful woman submits to the unusual methods of a master tattooer and his apprentice who leave their mark on her soul as well as her body. While coincidences can strain believability, this drama explores the darker side of the artist's creative and erotic obsessions.
D: Yoichi Takabayashi. A: Masayo Utsunomiya, Tomisaburo Wakayama.

Tetsuo: The Iron Man
(1989) 67m. B&W.
Subtitled. **B+**

A worker's flesh starts to fuse with every bit of scrap metal around as does his girlfriend, all with gruesomely industrial/sexual results. This captures the texture and mad nonlogic of a nightmare via stop-action human animation, bizarre effects, techno soundtrack, and sexual puns made flesh-and-steel reality: for the adventurous only.
D: Shinya Tsukamota. A: Tomorrow Taguchi, Kei Fujiwara.

Akira Kurosawa's Dreams
(1990) 120m. Subtitled.
A–

In a series of eight dream episodes, Kurosawa captures the magic and special logic of the dream world as he explores humanity's problematic relationship with nature and the costs of technological progress. Vivid and beautiful images and a leisurely pace make this alternately hypnotic, startling, and cerebral.
D: Akira Kurosawa. A: Akira Terao, Chisu Ryu, Martin Scorsese.

Crime Films

Fans of American cop films will recognize these films' quick pacing, the lone superdetective hero (atypical in a country that promotes teamwork), and the strangely intimate relationship between the hunter and the quarry. What is decidedly un-American about this group is the lack of police corruption, the absence of car chases and violence, and plots that focus on the psychological aspects of crime and social commentary of the disenfranchised underworld.

Stray Dog
(1949) 22m. B&W.
Subtitled. **B**

When his gun is stolen, a young detective feels honor-bound to track down the "mad dog" using it to rob and kill, a quest which takes him through the underworld of immediate postwar Tokyo. A solid cop drama, though the protagonist's outbursts of obsessive guilt make some scenes tedious.
D: Akira Kurosawa. A: Toshiro Mifune, Takashi Shimura, Isao Kimura.

The Bad Sleep Well
(1960) 152m. B&W.
Subtitled. **A**

A man seeks to avenge his father's death at the hands of a corrupt corporate bigwig by marrying the man's crippled daughter and infiltrating his company. Then he discovers it's not so easy to become as ruthless as his enemies. Kurosawa's psychological study/social critique is filled with a bleak postwar atmosphere and a sense of doom and futility.
D: Akira Kurosawa. A: Toshiro Mifune, Masayuki Mori, Takeshi Kato.

High and Low
(1963) 143m. B&W.
Subtitled. **B+**

The character of a rich industrialist is revealed when his chauffeur's son is kidnapped in his son's place and he must choose between his ambitions and responsibility to his servant. The second half picks up as tireless detectives try to track down the kidnapper, and the focus shifts to the complexities of the criminal mind.
D: Akira Kurosawa. A: Toshiro Mifune, Tatsuya Nakadai, Tsutomu Yamazaki.

Violence at Noon
(1966) 99m. B&W.
Subtitled. **B+**

This moody film traces the evolution of a rapist and murderer from his rejection by the woman he desired, through his marriage to an older woman he could not love. Runs the gamut from talky and overabundant confrontations between the two women, to intense but stylized scenes of rape. Beware of poor prints.
D: Nagisa Oshima. A: Saeda Kawaguchi, Akiko Koyama, Kei Sato.

Vengeance Is Mine
(1979) 137m. Subtitled.
A–

From the police interrogation room, Enokizu recalls his gradual descent from youthful rebellion to fraud, then murder while managing to charm a string of credulous women to satisfy his insatiable lust. First-rate true-life character study of a man at the margins of society.
D: Shohei Imamura. A: Ken Ogata, Mayumi Ogawa, Mitsuko Baisho.

A Taxing Woman
(1987) 92m. Subtitled.
B+

A businessman schemes to avoid paying taxes on his income from love hotels and shady real estate deals, but meets his match in tax inspector Ryoko Itakura. Good use of suspense, jazzy music, low-key satire, and wily adversaries make this one of the more accessible and lighter-toned crime films.
D: Juzo Itami. A: Nobuko Miyamoto, Tsutomo Yamazaki.

A Taxing Woman's Return
(1988) 127m. Subtitled.
B+

The dedicated Itakura is back with a bigger challenge: The leader of a creepy religious cult uses the group to hide profits from ruthless real estate deals, and he also boasts ties to high government places. A darker study of corruption with more violent trappings to the satire.
D: Juzo Itami. A: Nobuko Miyamoto, Renataro Mikuni, Chishu Ryu.

Costume Dramas

Like Japanese versions of Merchant-Ivory films, these are the films to see if you want a concentrated dose of the beauty and sadness of the more traditional Japan; exquisite landscapes frame and echo the action while settings, costumes, and lifestyles of times past are as significant as the dramas.

Odd Obsession

(1960) 96m. Subtitled. **B**

A middle-aged man encourages his wife's affair with their daughter's suitor in order to excite his own passion. Meanwhile, the apparently dutiful wife has her own reasons for cooperating. A Hollywood-style treatment of Tanizaki's tense psychological drama that gives a glimpse of old-fashioned living and unsympathetic characters.
D: Kon Ichikawa. A: Machiko Kyo, Tetsuya Nakadai, Ganjiro Nakamura.

Makioka Sisters

(1983) 130m. Subtitled.
A

In late 1930s Osaka, four beautiful, strong-willed sisters cope with the gradual decline of their wealthy family's elegant traditional way of life. Loving close-ups of gorgeous kimonos and breathtaking seasonal landscapes add to the poetic elegiac texture of the family saga.
D: Kon Ichikawa. A: Yoshiko Sakuma, Koji Ishizuka, Juzo Itami.

Sore Kara (And Then)

(1986) 130m. Subtitled.
A

A young man of leisure refuses to marry the woman chosen by his father because he's in love with his friend's wife. Beautiful settings and costumes evoke a more gracious age in turn-of-the-century Japan, in this leisurely tale of restrained passion.
D: Yoshimitsu Morita. A: Yusaku Matsuda, Miwako Fujitani, Kaoru Kobayashi.

Rikyu

(1990) 116m. Subtitled.
A–

Based on the life of Sen no Rikyu, a Buddhist priest and preeminent master of the tea ceremony, who becomes teacher to the most powerful warlord in Japan. Like a Japanese *Man for All Seasons,* Rikyu must maintain a precarious balance between instructing his master in the way of tea and deferring to his master's imperious whims.
D: Hiroshi Teshigahara. A: Rentaro Mikuni, Tsutomu Yamazaki.

Social Comedies

These comic looks at modern society spoof the Japanese preoccupation with ritual, success, and the ever present duty to proprieties.

The Family Game

(1983) 107m. Subtitled.
A–

Concerned parents hire a tutor to help their son make the grade in Japan's competitive school system. Trouble is, the tutor's unconventional methods not only teach the son about life and academics, but releases pent-up tensions in the rest of the family. A dark offbeat critique of the middle class and manly rites of passage.
D: Yoshimitsu Morita. A: Yusaku Matsuda, Juzo Itami, Ichirota Miyagawa.

The Funeral

(1987) 124m. Subtitled. **B**

As an actress bumbles through the elaborate arrangements for her father's funeral, concerns about money and appearances compete with any grief for the deceased. While the sense of the ridiculous comes through loud and clear, some of the humor about the tortuous funeral customs doesn't quite translate.
D: Juzo Itami. A: Nobuko Miyamoto, Tsutomu Yamazaki.

Tampopo

(1987) 114m. Subtitled.
A

The tale of a widow who perfects the art of making noodles under the instruction of an urban cowboy truck driver is cleverly interspersed with amusing vignettes about food and social pretension. Funny, enjoyable, and you'll find yourself craving a bowl of hot ramen.
D: Juzo Itami. A: Nobuko Miyamoto, Tsutomu Yamazaki, Koji Yakusho.

Little People Dramas

These tales focus on ordinary people whose lives are disrupted by death, crisis, or war. Often their dilemmas are directly linked to the disruptive effects of modernization. Pathos is common, but some evoke genuine tears and sympathy as these humble characters maintain their dignity even when sacrificing their dreams to the greater good of society.

Ikiru (To Live)
(1952) 134m. B&W.
Subtitled. **A**

When a city hall bureaucrat learns he has cancer, he determines to carry out one meaningful act in his life by building a children's park in a poor neighborhood. This little-known masterpiece is a bit long, a bit dated, and absolutely rewarding.
D: Akira Kurosawa. A: Miki Odagiri, Nobuo Kaneko, Kyoko Seki.

Tokyo Story
(1953) 139m. B&W.
Subtitled. **A–**

An old couple visiting their children in Tokyo find their modern son and daughter selfish with both time and money while their widowed daughter-in-law maintains the values of respect and kindness. A lovely, dark, and shadowy film enhanced by an old-fashioned quality.
D: Yasujiro Ozu. A: Chishu Ryu, Chiyeko Higashiyama, Setsuko Hara.

The Rikisha Man
(1958) 105m. Subtitled.
B–

A rikisha man with rough manners and a good heart befriends a widow and her son, becoming a surrogate father to the boy while harboring a hopeless love for the refined and devoted mother. Melodramatic and sappy, and the recurrent twirling rikisha wheels are a bit much. Beware of the hard-to-read subtitles.
D: Hiroshi Inagaki.
A: Toshiro Mifune, Hideko Takamine.

The Pornographers
(1966) 128m. B&W.
Subtitled. **B**

A dark satirical story of a man who makes his living producing and selling pornography while in his private life he battles with his own sexual desire for his mistress's daughter. Not an easy film to watch visually, but with the noir lighting, tricky camera angles, and bleak postwar settings, a field day for art film fans.
D: Shohei Imamura.
A: Shoichi Ozawa, Sumiko Sakamoto.

Dodes' Ka-Den
(1970) 140m. Subtitled.
A

This collection of vignettes about colorful misfits living in a Tokyo slum include a failed artist whose daydreams are supported by his small son foraging for food, two husband-swapping women, and a priestlike craftsman who uses Zen psychology to help his neighbors. The misery and despair are relieved by touches of black humor and nobility of spirit.
D: Akira Kurosawa. A: Yoshitaka Zushi, Kin Sugai, Toshiyuki Tomura.

Ballad of Narayama
(1983) 129m. Subtitled.
A–

In a nineteenth-century mountain village, a man must overcome his humanitarian impulses to fulfill the time-honored custom of abandoning his mother on a sacred mountain to die. Realistic and chilling portrayal of the brutality of rural life that ends powerfully on a bone-strewn mountain.
D: Shohei Imamura. A: Ken Ogata, Sumiko Sakamoto.

Himatsuri (Fire Festival)
(1985) 120m. Subtitled.
B+

A macho lumberjack shocks his rural village by breaking ancient taboos and disrupting plans for a new marine park. Plenty of male bonding, phallic symbolism, and un-Japanese rifle-toting leads to a violent climax in this new wave Japanese film. Some of the impact of the taboo-breaking scenes may be lost on American audiences.
D: Mitsuo Yanagimachi. A: Kinya Kitaoji, Kiwako Taichi

War and Occupation

In contrast to Hollywood films that glorified World War II, these films have an antimilitary antiwar view. Even with the overlong saccharine and sentimental scenes, they give us a rare glimpse of the hardships faced by the population both during the war and afterward when American forces occupied Japan.

No Regrets for Our Youth
(1946) 110m. B&W.
Subtitled. **B–**

The pampered daughter of a law professor marries a courageous antiwar activist at the height of the war. After the police murder him, she attains freedom working on his parent's farm and rehabilitating her husband's memory. A rare Kurosawa portrait of a liberated woman, but the story and acting are melodramatic.
D: Akira Kurosawa.
A: Setsuko Hara, Takashi Shimura.

The Burmese Harp
(1956) 116m. B&W.
Subtitled. **B**

A unit of POWs looks forward to returning home to rebuild a peaceful Japan, except for a harpist who sees his duty to remain behind as a priest to mourn his fallen countrymen. The profound moments are outweighed by the soldiers' hokey and unlikely outbursts of choral song.
D: Kon Ichikawa. A: Shoji Yasui, Rentaro Mikuni, Tatsuya Mihashi.

Fires on the Plain
(1959) 105m. B&W.
Subtitled. **B**

Expelled from his unit because of illness, a soldier wanders the island of Leyte witnessing the moral disintegration of the Japanese army facing defeat. He finally encounters crazed and starving soldiers who survive on mysterious "monkey meat." Tedious pacing undercuts the impact of war's horrors.
D: Kon Ichikawa. A: Eiji Funakoshi, Osamu Takezawa.

The Go Masters
(1982) 134m. Subtitled.
A–

A Chinese master of Japanese chess sends his promising son to study with a friend in Japan, but the outbreak of war between the countries brings unforeseen tragedy to both families. This joint Chinese-Japanese production provides a rare critical treatment of Japanese aggression in China.
D: Junya Sato and Ji-Shun Duan. A: Rentaro Mikuni, Dao-lin Sun, Shen Guan-Chu.

MacArthur's Children
(1984) 115m. Subtitled.
B–

A group of fifth-graders on Awaji Island cope with Japan's defeat and the American occupation by forming a baseball team with their beautiful teacher's help. A forced and sentimental story can still be enjoyed for the lush island scenery and the children's indomitable spirit.
D: Masahiro Shinoda. A: Masako Natsume, Shuji Otako, Takaya Tamuchi.

Black Rain
(1988) 123m. Subtitled.
B–

Based on Masuji Ibuse's novel, this portrays the atomic bombing of Hiroshima and its devastating after-effects on the lives of a family five years later. A somewhat melodramatic and contrived rendering of a weighty subject.
D: Shohei Imamura. A: Yoshiko Tanaka, Kazuo Kitamura, Etsuko Ichihara.

Rhapsody in August
(1992) 98m. Subtitled. **C+**

Four grandchildren gain an appreciation of the legacy of the atomic bomb during a visit to grandmother's house in Nagasaki. A bit heavy-handed with Gere making a game attempt at speaking Japanese in his cameo as the American cousin.
D: Akira Kurosawa. A: Sachiko Murase, Richard Gere.

The Human Condition

Kobayashi's three-part masterpiece follows the fate of one individual during the Pacific war years and the impossibility of human compassion amidst the brutality of war. While this cinematic marathon is good for types who read *War and Peace* just so they can say they did, these films actually manage to keep your interest for 3½ hours, even with their unrelieved bleakness and graphic depictions of Japanese corruption, torture, and beheadings.

The Human Condition: Part One, No Greater Love
(1958) 200m. B&W.
Subtitled. **A**

Kaji attempts to put his humanistic theories into practice as a labor administrator in a mining camp in occupied Manchuria, but finds himself powerless against the cruelty and corruption of the colonial administration.
D: Masaki Kobayashi. A: Tatsuya Nakadai, Michiyo Aratama, Chikage Awashima.

The Human Condition: Part Two, The Road to Eternity
(1959) 180m. B&W.
Subtitled. **A**

Forced into the army in the last days of the war, Kaji is persecuted for his leftist beliefs. The sadism and inhumanity of the military is portrayed in detail, not the least when the commanders desert their men in a final battle with the Russians.
D: Masaki Kobayashi. A: Tatsuya Nakadai, Michiyo Aratama, Chikage Awashima.

The Human Condition: Part Three, The Soldier's Prayer
(1961) 190m. B&W.
Subtitled. **A**

Kaji is captured and sent to a Siberian POW camp where he discovers that the Russians are as corrupt and soulless as the Japanese. His experiences as a prisoner mirror the conditions in Part One.
D: Masaki Kobayashi. A: Tatsuya Nakadai, Michiyo Aratama, Usuke Kawazu.

Italian

Rossellini

Using neorealism, in which film was shot on location to give it an authentic feel that verged on the documentary, Roberto Rossellini championed the heroism of the common man. These are serious stories, leavened with wry humor and an unbeatable glimpse of Italy just after the war.

Open City
(1945) 105m. B&W.
Subtitled. **A**

In Nazi-occupied Rome, priests, intellectuals, workers, and children join forces to combat the invaders' attempt to conquer them psychologically. Shot just as the war ended in Rome, this film used the disadvantages of its low production values to forge the neorealist style. So ragged and on-the-spot real that it's like uncut news footage from the time.
D: Roberto Rossellini. A: Aldo Fabrizi, Anna Magnani, Marcello Pagliero.

Paisan
(1946) 90m. B&W.
Subtitled. **A–**

Comprised of six vignettes tracing the American-Italian relations at the local level during Allied invasion of Italy, this is a prime example of Rossellini's you-are-there neorealist style. The loosely improvised scenes give a raw feel for the difficulties of clashing cultures.
D: Roberto Rossellini. A: Carmela Sazio, Robert van Loon, Maria Michi.

L'Amore
(1948) 78m. B&W.
Subtitled. **A**

Two stories showcase Magnani's passionate theatrical style. The first is a woman trying to deal with a breakup; all we see is her bedroom, the telephone, and her mystified dog as she talks with the object of her affections. The second tells of the village crazy woman who becomes pregnant and is devoted to her child.
D: Roberto Rossellini. A: Anna Magnani.

Stromboli
(1949) 105m. B&W.
Subtitled. **B**

A middle-class, educated Lithuanian woman in an Italian internment camp marries an Italian fisherman to escape. Then she discovers that the desolate volcanic island where he lives is even more of a prison. So slow-moving it feels like real time, but the bleak life and the woman's desperation is overpowering.
D: Roberto Rossellini. A: Ingrid Bergman, Mario Vitale, Renzo Cesana.

General Della Rovere
(1960) 129m. B&W.
Subtitled. **B+**

Down-at-the-heels con man is persuaded by the occupying Nazis in Genoa to impersonate a just-deceased Italian general to penetrate the resistance movement. Vittorio De Sica's performance as a circumstantial hero offers just the right shading of good and rotten, bringing the character into unforgettable focus.
D: Roberto Rossellini. A: Vittorio De Sica, Sandra Milo, Hannes Messemer.

Miscellaneous Neorealism

Bitter Rice
(1948) 107m. B&W.
Dubbed. **A–**

One of the women working in the rice fields of Italy in late 1940s betrays the others to the exploitative owners. A grim somber, documentary-style film made unforgettable by Silvano Mangano's earthy power.
D: Giuseppe De Santis. A: Silvana Mangano, Vittorio Gassman, Raf Vallone.

Fellini (1950s)

Obsessed with variety shows, circuses, and especially clowns all through his life, Federico Fellini's early work draws on autobiographical details and gives a slight foretaste of the expansiveness and outrageousness that was to come. These films have a clear narrative structure, though the hallmark flotsam and jetsam of humanity are always on display.

Variety Lights
(1950) 93m. B&W.
Subtitled. **B–**

A stagestruck young woman joins a theater troupe and learns that life backstage isn't quite as much fun as it looks from the audience. Fellini's first feature is tame, even a little cute, with a surprisingly straight narrative story line for the director.
D: Federico Fellini. A: Carla Del Poggio, Peppino De Filippo, Giulietta Masina.

The White Sheik
(1951) 88m. B&W.
Subtitled. **A–**

A honeymooning couple in Rome have their first spat when she spies her favorite live-action comic book hero, the White Sheik, and follows him to the shooting set. The conflict of fantasy and mundane reality is shown with grace and charm through the gradual loss of naivete by the young bride.
D: Federico Fellini. A: Alberto Sordi, Brunella Borda, Leopoldo Trieste.

I Vitelloni
(1953) 103m. B&W.
Subtitled. **A**

Five young men come to terms with their eagerness to break away from their small Adriatic town. Tightly woven episodes detail each of the characters, including one—based on Fellini—who finally leaves it all behind for Rome. A wonderful mix of comedy and melancholy evoking young adulthood.
D: Federico Fellini. A: Alberto Sordi, Franco Interlenghi, Franco Fabrizi.

La Strada
(1954) 115m. B&W.
Subtitled. **A**

A strongman hires a lost soul to drum for him in his act; she adores him, he insults her mercilessly. Funny and sad, this conveys the desperation of someone so in love she can't leave her torturer. Masina brings the pathetic character sympathetically, charmingly to life.
D: Federico Fellini. A: Giulietta Masina, Anthony Quinn, Richard Basehart.

Il Bidone
(1955) 84m. B&W.
Subtitled. **C+**

Three con artists bilk poor people in Rome in this realistic social comedy-drama. The weak link in the Fellini chain is undermined by a scanty story, but the stellar cast makes up for its lack of real interest.
D: Federico Fellini. A: Giulietta Masina, Broderick Crawford, Richard Basehart.

Nights of Cabiria
(1957) 110m. B&W.
Subtitled. **A–**

A romantic gullible prostitute falls for young man who is unaware of her source of income. Perhaps the greatest collaboration between Giulietta Masina and Fellini, this sensitive portrayal of a dreamer and her ugly reality is charming, melancholy and unforgettable.
D: Federico Fellini. A: Giulietta Masina, Francois Perier, Amedeo Nazzari.

De Sica

Vittorio De Sica was immersed in the documentary-like style of neorealism, often using nonprofessional actors to tell his small, human, and often heartbreaking stories. Obsessed with the larger changes afoot in Italy, he chose to explore them by focusing on the ragged, poverty-stricken survivors.

Shoeshine
(1946) 93m. B&W.
Subtitled. **A–**

Two boys in postwar Italy become involved in the black market to achieve their dream of buying a horse. Poignant and heartbreaking, this is an unforgettable portrait of the human devastation of World War II.
D: Vittorio De Sica. A: Rinaldo Smerdoni, Franco Interlenghi, Annielo Melo.

The Bicycle Thief
(1947) 90m. B&W.
Subtitled. **A** 🏛

A desperate man in postwar Rome searches with his young son for the sole means of his employment, his stolen bicycle. Stark, agonizing, and shamelessly emotional with the relationship between father and son celebrating the human spirit.
D: Vittorio De Sica. A: Enzo Staiola, Lamberto Maggiorani, Lianella Carell.

Miracle in Milan
(1951) 100m. B&W.
Subtitled. **B+**

A young man aids a group of postwar villagers in fighting an exploitative landlord, with the help of the woman who raised him (and who's now in heaven). Despite its subject of postwar struggle, this light and charming film has a magical fairy tale feel.
D: Vittorio De Sica.
A: Emma Grammatica, Francesco Golisano, Paolo Stoppa.

Umberto D
(1955) 89m. B&W.
Subtitled. **A**

This heartbreaking story follows a former bureaucrat struggling to maintain a roof over his head. Sad but never dreary, the succinct style in which the story is told makes you feel the man's pain and all-too-few moments of joy. Virtually impossible to remain dry-eyed during the last few minutes.
D: Vittorio De Sica. A: Carlo Battisti, Maria Pia Casilio, Lina Gennari.

The Roof
(1957) 91m. B&W.
Subtitled. **B+**

A young couple lives in the outskirts of postwar Rome, crowded together with his family as they desperately search for a place of their own. The obstacles they face—disapproval of her family, the bureaucracy of a country rebuilding itself—are detailed in this simple and affecting drama.
D: Vittorio De Sica. A: Gabriella Pallotti, Giorgio Listuzzi, Gastone Renzelli.

Two Women
(1961) 99m. B&W.
Subtitled. **A–** 🏛

Hunger, fear, humiliation—all the by-products of war are searingly portrayed in this tale of a mother and daughter who are raped by Allied Moroccan soldiers during World War II. Loren is unforgettable as the mother whose fierceness seems to be the only thing that keeps the two alive.
D: Vittorio De Sica. A: Sophia Loren, Elenora Brown, Jean-Paul Belmondo.

Visconti

Luchino Visconti always managed to give a sweeping epic quality to his films, even when working in the neorealist style. These are magnificent stories, filled with the tumult of families and rich details of squalor and luxury that make the settings almost like a secondary character.

Ossessione
(1942) 140m. B&W.
Subtitled. **B**

A drifter finds work and lodging with a couple and the sexually bored wife takes up with the stranger. What to do with husband? This Italian version of *The Postman Always Rings Twice* has an earthy gritty feel that inspired much of the neorealism to come. Drags at times, but worth a look.
D: Luchino Visconti. A: Massimo Girotti, Clara Calamai, Juan de Landa.

La Terra Trema
(1947) 160m. B&W.
Subtitled. **B+**

Using one family as its center, this film looks at the struggles of fishermen in a tiny Sicilian village in the late 1940s. With the feel of an anthropological documentary, including a voice-over narration, this is a fascinating and sympathetic look at a way of life that's all but extinct.
D: Luchino Visconti. A: Sicilian locals.

Bellissima
(1951) 112m. B&W.
Subtitled. **B**

A brash pushy mother is determined to get her pretty little girl into the movies in postwar Italy. Loud, coarse, and sometimes painful to watch, it still has enough raw moments of truth to make it anything but ordinary.
D: Luchino Visconti. A: Anna Magnani, Walter Chiari, Tina Apicella.

The Wanton Contessa (aka Senso)
(1954) 104m. B&W.
Subtitled. **B–**

An Italian countess and an Austrian officer have a hot affair until their countries go to war. This epic sweeping drama that's tempered with a neorealist edge has the operatic feel that would characterize so much of Visconti's later work.
D: Luchino Visconti. A: Alida Valli, Farley Granger, Massimo Girotti.

White Nights
(1957) 107m. B&W.
Subtitled. **B**

A young man and woman meet accidentally and he's smitten even though her sole topic of conversation is her absent lover. Complex and engaging entertainment with a public television feel to it.
D: Luchino Visconti. A: Maria Schell, Marcello Mastroianni, Jean Marais.

Rocco and His Brothers
(1960) 180./152m. B&W.
Subtitled. **A**

A mother and her sons move from southern Italy to Milan for the promise of a better life. Their stories show the loss of innocence and the strain the family is put under. An epic, powerful, and wide-ranging portrait of a family and, by extension, of Italy itself.
D: Luchino Visconti. A: Alain Delon, Annie Giradot, Renato Salvatori.

1960s Comedies

The broad satirical comedies of this period reveal a postwar society in transition, with a particular delight at exposing the myriad ways Italians found of getting around the confining strictures of their society and its domination by the Catholic Church.

Big Deal on Madonna Street
(1956) 91m. B&W.
Subtitled. **A–**

A bungling crew of hoods tries to pull off a robbery of a pawn shop. Ineptitude at its most exaggerated, this has all the humor of *The Lavender Hill Mob* and Inspector Clouseau films.
D: Mario Monicelli. A: Marcello Mastroianni, Vittorio Gassman, Renato Salvatori.

The Passionate Thief
(1961) 105m. B&W.
Subtitled. **B+**

An unemployed actor hooks up with a divalike film extra and suave pickpocket for a New Year's Eve of mistaken identity, petty thievery, and romance in Rome. A perfect introduction for those unfamiliar with the delightful Italian comedy star Toto, who is close in spirit to a cross between Buster Keaton and Harold Lloyd.
D: Mario Monicelli. A: Anna Magnani, Toto, Ben Gazzara.

Boccaccio '70
(1962) 165m. Dubbed. **B**

Fellini, Visconti, and De Sica directed these three valentines to favorite actresses of Italy. A poster girl comes alive to torture an inhibited man; a woman takes a job as her husband's mistress; and a milquetoast wins an evening with the beautiful first prize of a love drawing. Light as zabaglione, this is a harmless charming look at inhibition and hedonism.
D: Federico Fellini, Luchino Visconti, Vittorio De Sica. A: Sophia Loren, Anita Ekberg, Romy Schneider.

Divorce—Italian Style
(1962) 104m. B&W.
Subtitled. **A–**

Fed up with his wife and ready to replace her with a delectable younger woman, a Sicilian aristocrat decides there's only one permanent way to skirt the lack of divorce in Italy. A spritely sophisticated satire.
D: Pietro Germi. A: Marcello Mastroianni, Daniela Rocca, Stefania Sandrelli.

Yesterday, Today and Tomorrow
(1964) 118m. Dubbed. **B**

In these three sexy and witty tales, Loren is a crafty blackmarketer, the wife of a wealthy businessman, and a prostitute that a seminarian tries to save. A light and theatrical film perfectly suited to Mastroianni and Loren.
D: Vittorio De Sica. A: Marcello Mastroianni, Sophia Loren, Tina Pica.

Seduced and Abandoned
(1964) 118m. B&W.
Subtitled. **B+**

Family chaos erupts when a young woman reveals that her child was fathered by her sister's fiancé. Light and satirical, this offers a painless lesson in the huge differences between northern and southern Italy.
D: Pietro Germi. A: Stefania Sandrelli, Saro Urzi, Lando Buzzanca.

Antonioni

Alienation, despair, the emptiness of modern life: These are the dominant themes of Michelangelo Antonioni's movies. Their pace is often slow, the plots almost nonexistent, and the camera shots long and lingering. But few movies communicate a sense of displacement and remoteness in both characters and landscape like these extremely avant-garde films.

Il Grido
(1957) 115m. B&W.
Subtitled. **B**

When his wife abandons him and their little girl, a worker takes to wandering around Italy. His numb, walking-nervous-breakdown state is captured in the film's disjointed dialogue. Good, though clearly an early effort.
D: Michelangelo Antonioni. A: Steve Cochran, Alida Valli, Dorian Gray.

L'Avventura
(1960) 145m. B&W.
Subtitled. **A**

A woman disappears on an uninhabited island after an argument with her lover, leaving boyfriend and best friend to look for her. Aimless wandering feel of the film makes it appear to waffle, but it has a definite trajectory. Challenging view if you can get into the studied pace.
D: Michelangelo Antonioni. A: Monica Vitti, Lea Massari, Gabriele Ferzetti.

The Eclipse
(1962) 123m. B&W.
Subtitled. **B–**

A woman translator breaks up with her boyfriend and takes up with a stockbroker. Not much happens, but you get a first rate look at one person's empty alienated world, with a view of Rome and Italy that feels remote and strange.
D: Michelangelo Antonioni. A: Monica Vitti, Alain Delon, Francesco Rabal.

Red Desert
(1964) 118m. Subtitled.
A–
A woman is on the verge of losing her mind and unable to communicate with those around her. Antonioni uses an overwhelming array of colors, often blurring in the background, to show her pain. A displaced movie with a slow pace that won't be to everyone's taste.
D: Michelangelo Antonioni. A: Monica Vitti, Richard Harris, Rita Renoir.

Bertolucci

Openly literary, with clear narrative stories and resolutions, Bernardo Bertolucci's films often explore the conflicts between sexual and political involvements. Sumptuous style and sets that reflect loving attention to detail give a hint of what's to come in his later work.

The Grim Reaper
(1962) 100m. Subtitled. **B**
Bertolucci's first feature focuses on an investigation into the murder of a prostitute and the various versions of her life that come to light. A tight tense thriller, with a gritty feel.
D: Bernardo Bertolucci. A: Francesco Ruiu, Giancarlo De Rosa, Romano Labate.

Before the Revolution
(1964) 112m. Subtitled.
B+
A young man in the late nineteenth century sensing that he's missing out on life considers political as well as incestuous involvement. Like a dry run *1900,* this film captures the feeling of disenchantment and searching of the sixties.
D: Bernardo Bertolucci. A: Adriana Asti, Francesco Barilli.

Partner
(1968) 104m. Subtitled. **B**
An ineffectual man invents a double for himself with whom he becomes obsessed. A harrowing look at the power of the mind, with a literary twisted costume drama feel to it.
D: Bernardo Bertolucci. A: Stefania Sandrelli, Sergio Tofano, Pierre Clementi.

The Spider's Strategem
(1970) 100m. Subtitled.
A–
A man returns to the small Italian town where his father was executed 30 years before for his antifascism, and unearths the unseemly details of his death. This mysterious and sometimes creepy unfolding of the investigation is not without deception and double dealing as the town ultimately unites against him.
D: Bernardo Bertolucci. A: Giulio Brogi, Alida Valli, Tino Scotti.

Fellini (1960s–1980s)

Federico Fellini's autobiographical stories are celebrations of the people, the culture, and the pageantry of Italy. Whether shot in elegant black and white or exuberant color, each movie is a feast of ideas, dreams, images, and commentaries. Boisterous, surreal, fantastic, sometimes overlong (but never tedious), he gives you images and faces that you can't believe exist, and you'll see why the word "Felliniesque" came into the language.

La Dolce Vita
(1960) 175m. B&W. Subtitled. **A+**
A Roman tabloid writer is filled with ennui by his glamorous, celebrity-filled life. Busty Hollywood bombshells, decadent aristocrats, paparazzi, and the restless demimonde who zip around in Mazarattis and wear sunglasses at night—this film is the ultimate portrayal of modernity and decadence and still has the shock of the new.
D: Federico Fellini. A: Marcello Mastroianni, Anouk Aimée, Anita Ekberg.

8½
(1963) 135m. B&W. Subtitled. **A+**
A successful filmmaker is trying to put together his new project even though he's run out of ideas. An elegant, lush, and dreamlike diorama in which the director examines his life, his loves, and his fantasies.
D: Federico Fellini. A: Marcello Mastroianni, Anouk Aimée, Claudia Cardinale.

Juliet of the Spirits
(1965) 148m. Subtitled. **A**
The wife of a famous filmmaker suspects him of philandering and indulges in her own surreal, fantastic, and horrific fantasies. Not long on plot but a cornucopia of amazing colors and images.
D: Federico Fellini. A: Giulietta Masina, Sanda Milo, Mario Pisu.

Fellini Satyricon
(1969) 130m. Subtitled.
A–
This day in the life of the most dramatic, surreal, and mythological characters in Rome B.C. will astonish *I, Claudius* fans. It's filled with lavish costumes, dazzling scenery, and startling stories that include scenes of sex and violence that are almost shocking in their unadorned earthiness.
D: Federico Fellini. A: Martin Potter, Hiram Keller, Capucine.

Ciao Federico!
(1970) 62m. **B**
Made during the shooting of *Satyricon,* this documentary

shows the many sides of Fellini, some of which could be quite tyrannical. It also shows how the theatrical look of the feature was achieved, with Fellini all but acting all the parts. Well paced and revealing.
D: Federico Fellini. A: Federico Fellini, cast of *Satyricon* in cameos.

The Clowns
(1971) 90m. Subtitled.
A–

A tribute to clowns of every stripe from one of their greatest admirers. This documentary-like film takes place in the imagination of the director; it's an "everything you ever wanted to know and more" sort of venture.
D: Federico Fellini. A: Mayo Morin, Lima Alberti, Alvaro Vitali.

Fellini's Roma
(1972) 129m. Subtitled.
B+

Another documentary-like examination, via Fellini's memories and fantasies, this time about Rome, both contemporary and of an earlier era. It contains all of Fellini's signature elements, but it's more like a tour of Rome given by a loving, self-indulgent and fantastic tour guide.
D: Federico Fellini. A: Peter Gonzales, Gore Vidal, Anna Magnani.

Amarcord
(1974) 127m. Dubbed.
A

Fellini's remembrances of his youth, sexual awakening, and coming-of-age on the Adriatic coast is so filled with the ordinary textures and people of a small town that you can practically smell the baking bread. Gentle and funny.
D: Federico Fellini. A: Magali Noel, Bruno Zanin, Pupella Maggio.

Fellini's Casanova
(1976) 166m. Subtitled. **D**

The amorous adventures of that eighteenth-century Venetian playboy is opulently costumed, lovingly filmed, and an overwrought failure. It's all dressed up and goes nowhere.
D: Federico Fellini. A: Donald Sutherland, Cicely Browne, Tina Aumont.

City of Women
(1981) 138m. Subtitled.
B

A man falls asleep on a train and dreams that he's in an all-female world. This parade of hilarious sexual confrontations is part reaction to the women's movement and part review of his sexual life, presented in Fellini's fantastic and operatic fashion.
D: Federico Fellini. A: Marcello Mastroianni, Anna Prucnal, Bernice Stegers.

And the Ship Sails On
(1984) 138m. Subtitled.
B+

In 1914, a gathering of "beautiful people" aboard a liner for a diva's funeral cruise is interrupted by the arrival of Serbian refugees. A light delicious cruise through Fellini's imagination.
D: Federico Fellini. A: Freddie Jones, Barbara Jefford, Victor Poletti.

Ginger and Fred
(1986) 126m. **B**

A dance couple who made their name imitating Astaire and Rogers years ago are asked to reprise their roles on television. The cult of celebrity is criticized in a more relaxed and mellowed fashion, although the TV station becomes a fantasy circus, complete with ringmaster.
D: Federico Fellini. A: Giulietta Masina, Marcello Mastroianni, Franco Fabrizi.

Pasolini

When you're in the mood to be provoked, tickled, and outraged, Pier Paolo Pasolini is your man. His films are testaments to his loathing for fascism and the smugness of bourgeois society, and his love of the coarse young street urchins he used as actors or extras in his films. The modern fables are grim grainy manifestos while his historical films are like theatrical plays shot on location, startling in their earthiness, sexual explicitness, and use of unpolished, rough-looking actors.

Accatone!
(1961) 120m. B&W.
Subtitled. **B+**

A brutally depressing film traces the life of a small-time pimp in the Roman slums, who tries to change his ways. Stark powerful portrait of the friendships, betrayals, and squalor of these narrow lives.
D: Pier Paolo Pasolini. A: Franco Citti, Franca Pasut, Silvana Corsini.

The Gospel According to St. Matthew
(1964) 135m. B&W.
Subtitled. **B+**

Christ is portrayed as a provocative revolutionary in this version of the Gospel, whose grungy realism forces you to adjust any sweet and photogenic ideas about biblical stories.
D: Pier Paolo Pasolini. A: Enrique Irazoqui, Margherita Caruso, Susanna Pasolini.

Love Meetings
(1964) 90m. B&W.
Subtitled. **B–**

A documentary in which Pasolini asks prostitutes, homosexuals, and members of the intelligentsia about their sexual experiences. Candid, witty, blunt, and sometimes funny portrait of the periphery of Italian society in the 1960s.
D: Pier Paolo Pasolini. A: Pier Paolo Pasolini, Alberto Moravia, Cesare Musatti.

The Hawks and the Sparrows
(1966) 88m. B&W.
Subtitled. **B–**

Father and son leave the trappings of everyday life behind and set forth along Italian roads, accompanied by an intellectual, left-wing talking crow. Satire of politics and religion loses a bit if you're unfamiliar with Catholicism or Marxism.
D: Pier Paolo Pasolini. A: Toto, Ninetto Davoli, Rossana DiRocco.

Oedipus Rex
(1967) 110m. Subtitled.
B+

Pasolini gives the tale of the man who killed his father and married his mother the deluxe epic treatment in a Moroccan location. Theatrical and visually provocative, but the images and music soon turn the film into something heavy and inert.
D: Pier Paolo Pasolini. A: Franco Citti, Silvana Mangano, Alida Valli.

Teorema
(1968) 98m. Subtitled.
A 

A bourgeois family is shattered when a lovely young man succeeds in seducing each of them—including the businessman father. The most accessible and disquieting of Pasolini's dramas with an interesting look at the amoral energy of passionate love.
D: Pier Paolo Pasolini. A: Terence Stamp, Silvana Mangano, Massimo Girotti.

The Decameron
(1970) 111m. Subtitled.
B–

Eight of Boccacio's tales are performed in raunchy detail. This has the feeling of a painting come alive, full of color, comedy, seriousness, and even horror, but it's even more sexually explicit than Pasolini's previous films.
D: Pier Paolo Pasolini. A: Franco Citti, Ninetto Davoli, Angela Luce.

Medea
(1970) 110m. Subtitled. **D**

Great idea, bad reality. Maria Callas has all the drama to be the mythic sorceress who can kill through her power of love, but in this version it feels more like hysteria than power. Slow and dull.
D: Pier Paolo Pasolini. A: Maria Callas, Laurent Tertzieff, Giuseppi Gentile.

The Canterbury Tales
(1971) 109m. Subtitled. **C**

Four of Chaucer's stories are enacted in full bawdy detail. A graphic and finally boring version that leaves nothing to the viewer's imagination.
D: Pier Paolo Pasolini. A: Hugh Griffith, Laura Betti, Tom Baker.

The Arabian Nights
(1974) 155m. Subtitled.
A–

Ten of the *Thousand and One Nights* stories are filmed on location in Nepal, Eritrea, and Yemen. Hallucinatory and trancelike, this is a mysterious and exotic magic carpet of a film.
D: Pier Paolo Pasolini. A: Ninetto Davoli, Ines Pellegrini, Franco Citti.

Salo: 120 Days of Sodom
(1975) 117m. No rating.

Pasolini succeeded in his attempt to make a film that would be indigestible. A brutal story about fascists who take a group of kids to a palazzo to have their way with them shows graphic scenes of sex, torture, and coprophilia. Be warned: You won't forget this one and you'll want to.
D: Pier Paolo Pasolini. A: Paolo Bonacelli, Caterina Boratto, Giorgio Cataldi.

Wertmuller

Equally sexy and outrageous, ridiculous and fierce, the broadly humorous films of Lina Wertmuller portray the war between the sexes as an all-out, scorch-the-earth affair. Her apprenticeship with Fellini shows in the flair for brutally ugly faces, artfully overblown theatricality, and spacious feel while she mixes in her own political obsessions to create films that are uniquely entertaining and thought provoking.

Love and Anarchy
(1973) 108m. Subtitled.
A–

An anarchist peasant arrives in Rome with the goal of assassinating Mussolini. Along the way he falls for one of the prostitutes at the brothel where he holes up. A theatrical humorous look at sticky issues like fascism and its alternatives.
D: Lina Wertmuller. A: Giancarlo Giannini, Mariangela Melato, Lina Polito.

The Seduction of Mimi
(1974) 92m. Subtitled.
A–

Tempers flare when an underdog metallurgist and his mistress disagree on just about everything, especially an equally applicable moral code. Raucous, exaggerated, and at times hilarious.
D: Lina Wertmuller. A: Giancarlo Giannini, Mariangela Melato, Augusta Belli.

Swept Away . . . by an Unusual Destiny in the Blue Sea of August
(1975) 116m. Subtitled.
A

A wealthy and arrogant woman is stranded on a desert island with a cynical Marxist crew member from her yacht; they try to figure out who's in charge and how to avoid their undeniable attraction. Funny, sexy, and awash in the tropical colors of the makeshift paradise.
D: Lina Wertmuller. A: Giancarlo Giannini, Mariangela Melato.

All Screwed Up
(1976) 105m. Subtitled. **B**

A group of young people move to Milan and share living quarters and some good and bad times. Free of the usual Wertmuller histrionics, this manages to sympathetically convey the sense of little cogs in a big city wheel.
D: Lina Wertmuller. A: Luigi Diberti, Nino Bignamini, Lina Polito.

Seven Beauties
(1976) 115m. Subtitled.
A 

A small-time hood does anything to save his skin during World War II, first as a soldier, then as a concentration camp prisoner. A colorful sprawling black comedy that portrays the indomitable and often comic human will-to-survive throughout the most harrowing experiences.
D: Lina Wertmuller. A: Giancarlo Giannini, Fernando Rey, Shirley Stoler.

Blood Feud
(1979) 100m. Subtitled. **C**

A lawyer and a gangster are rivals for the affections of a

1920s Sicilian widow. Hysteria and noise prevail, making this a tired story and loud affair with no surprises.
D: Lina Wertmuller. A: Marcello Mastroianni, Giancarlo Giannini, Sophia Loren.

Sotto Sotto
(1984) 105m. Subtitled. **D**

A macho man is undone when his wife reveals she's fallen for someone else: a female friend. Everyone is confused and like a gossipy neighbor, as the camera follows them around in their theatrical settings and equally dramatic outfits. For diehard fans.
D: Lina Wertmuller. A: Enrico Montesano Veronia Lario, Luisa de Santis.

Camorra
(1986) 106m. Subtitled. **C–**

Naples mothers take the fight against drugs and organized crime into their own hands. This long-winded, moralizing story sorely lacks the humor of Wertmuller's earlier works.
D: Lina Wertmuller. A: Angela Molina, Francisco Rabal, Harvey Keitel.

Joke of Destiny
(1984) 105m. Subtitled. **D**

When a politician is locked in his computer-automated car he goes crazy, and the resultant accident achieves epic proportions as an army of hyperventilating incompetent assistants tries to free him. A hysterical joke that falls flat.
D: Lina Wertmuller. A: Ugo Tognazzi, Piera Degli Esposti, Gastone Moschin.

Summer Night (aka **Summer Night With Greek Profile, Almond Eyes and Scent of Basil**)
(1987) 94m. Subtitled. **C**

With all the subtlety of a sledgehammer, this tells the tale of a wealthy woman who abducts a terrorist to teach him a lesson, but instead falls for him like a teenager.
D: Lina Wertmuller. A: Michele Placido, Mariangela Melato.

Ciao, Professore!
(1994) 91m. Subtitled. **C–**

A new teacher from Genoa comes to a small town near Naples where he finds himself riding shotgun over near-delinquent third-graders. Ostensibly, this cute story is about north-south tensions, but it never rises above its bathroom jokes and massively unappealing characters.
D: Lina Wertmuller. A: Paolo Villaggio, Isa Danieli, Gigio Morra.

Erotic Melodramas

Substitute fevered for "erotic" in this genre and you'll have an idea of what to expect. Though several incorporate serious issues like terrorism, politics, and moral hypocrisy, they are essentially excuses for a lot of nudity and occasionally explicit sex. Everyone looks good and the story and acting are better than all the current soft core thrillers clogging the video store, so if you want a little intelligence with your trashy entertainment, look for these.

Malicious
(1973) 97m. Subtitled. **B**

A Sicilian widower hires a sexy innocent young woman to keep house for him and his three sons, and everyone is soon sniffing around. This mix of drama and comedy is a must for Antonelli fans, but its comments on morals and hypocrisy are old hat.
D: Salvatore Samperi. A: Laura Antonelli, Turi Ferro, Alessandro Momo.

Wifemistress
(1977) 106m. Subtitled. **B**

A merchant's sexually frustrated wife finds fulfillment after her hubby goes underground due to his newly acquired radical politics. Titillating with nice turn-of-the-century detail and sexy scenes (including lesbianism), but it's more confusing than erotic.
D: Marco Vicario. A: Laura Antonelli, Marcello Mastroianni, Leonard Mann.

The Divine Nymph
(1979) 90m. Subtitled. **C**

Several noblemen pursue a beautiful young woman and though they never catch her, she has to disrobe frequently. This heated, nineteenth-century romp is another one for Antonelli fans. Trite and predictable.
D: Giuseppe Patroni Griffi. A: Laura Antonelli, Marcello Mastroianni, Terence Stamp.

The Cricket
(1983) 90m. Subtitled. **D**

Married to a truckstop owner, an over-the-hill cabaret singer is clinging to the vestiges of her youth. When her beautiful daughter shows up, the fireworks really start. Melodramatic and feels too long.
D: Alberto Lattuada. A: Virna Lisi, Clio Goldsmith, Anthony Franciosa.

The Eyes, the Mouth
(1983) 100m. Subtitled. **D**

A young man returns to his family after his brother's suicide and takes up with his sibling's pregnant lover. Humorless relentless drama full of people being unpleasant in uninteresting ways.
D: Marco Bellocchio. A: Lou Castel, Angela Molina, Emmanuele Riva.

Beyond Obsession
(1986) 115m. Dubbed. **D–**

A young woman looks after her father who has been imprisoned in Morocco. The cheap look, poky plot, and explicit sex, when there is any, give it a trashy melodramatic look without any of the fun.
D: Liliana Cavani. A: Marcello Mastroianni, Tom Berenger, Elenora Giorgi.

Devil in the Flesh
(1987) 110m. Subtitled. **B+**

When her soon-to-be-released terrorist fiancé starts to drop his bohemian ways, a young woman embarks on a passionate affair with a teenager. Engaging and sexy, this is nominally a study in madness. The story may jump around, but it's always fun to watch.
D: Marco Bellocchio. A: Maruschka Detmers, Federico Pitzalis, Anita Laurenzi.

1970s–1990s Comedies

Filled with farce and slapstick, most of the comedies in this group offer the madcap adventures of "little man" heroes or frothy titillating sexual romps through various Italian settings. Unlike their dramatic counterparts, these films seem to glory in the stereotypes of latin lovers, unfaithful spouses, and naughty nudity.

Till Marriage Do Us Part

(1974) 97m. Subtitled. **C**

Fresh from the convent, a young woman inadvertently marries her brother and must now find sexual fulfillment outside the marriage bed. The movie runs on the energy of her feverish sexual tension as she searches for any outlet; a glance, a touch, or brush with another body.
D: Luigi Comencini. A: Laura Antonelli, Alberto Lionello, Michele Placido.

Down and Dirty

(1976) 115m. Subtitled.
A–

A one-eyed patriarch oversees a household teeming with children, adults, vermin, thieves, hustlers, and old grandma. Horrifically funny and cynical, this unsparing view of life in Roman slums is neorealism without the humanity.
D: Ettore Scola. A: Nino Manfredi, Francesco Anniballi, Maria Bosco.

How Funny Can Sex Be?

(1976) 97m. Subtitled. **C**

Several short vignettes about sex, but in the cutest way possible and with lots of innuendo. The main attraction in this Italian version of *Love American Style* is the unabashed carnality of the two stars.
D: Dino Risi. A: Giancarlo Giannini, Laura Antonelli, Alberto Lionello.

The Sensuous Nurse

(1976) 81m. Dubbed. **D**

A wealthy vintner has a heart attack and his nephews seek to hurry him to his grave: Their convoluted plan involves hiring the pulse-quickening Andress. Like a soft-porn *Pink Panther* film without Peter Sellers.
D: Nello Rossati. A: Ursula Andress, Jack Palance, Duilio Del Prete.

Cafe Express

(1980) 105m. Subtitled. **C**

A Neapolitan working-class man sells coffee illegally on the trains, bringing down the wrath of nitpickers and authorities everywhere. This *Bread and Chocolate* redux with a heavy debt to Chaplin is pretty thin gruel.
D: Nanni Loy. A: Nino Manfredi, Adolfo Celi, Vittorio Mezzogiorno.

Lobster for Breakfast

(1982) 93m. Subtitled. **C**

Fed up with his nagging wife and wretched daughter, a toilet salesman finds himself embroiled in the misadventures of his best friend. A well-paced and fairly ordinary romp with marital shenanigans and merry mix-ups.
D: Georgio Capitani. A: Janet Agren, Claudine Auger, Enrico Montesano.

Acqua and Sapone

(1983) 100m. Subtitled.
C–

Desperate for a teaching job, a janitor impersonates a priest hired by an overprotective mother for her daughter who's in Rome on a modeling assignment. Light, bright, and cheerful as a soap bubble.
D: Carlo Verdone. A: Carlo Verdone, Natasha Hovey, Florinda Balkan.

The Pool Hustlers

(1983) 101m. Subtitled.
B–

An upstart billiards player aims to usurp the reigning pool champion in Rome. This minor, sometimes funny movie is often slow, but the pool games have a realistic feel and the protagonist is generally likable.
D: Maurizo Ponzi. A: Francesco Nuti, Giuliania De Sio, Renato Cechetto.

Henry IV

(1984) 95m. Subtitled. **C–**

After he falls from his horse while pretending to be Henry IV, an aristocrat actually believes he's the monarch. Twenty years later the woman he loves and a psychiatrist try to snap him out of it. This mess of a movie tries to pull itself together but is too chaotic and feels hours long.
D: Marco Bellocchio. A: Marcello Mastroianni, Claudia Cardinale, Leopoldo Trieste.

Nudo Di Donna

(1984) 112m. Subtitled.
A–

A bored Venetian bookseller with marital problems happens upon a nude portrait of someone who appears to be his wife, but is apparently a prostitute. His interest piqued, he embarks on the trail of what will be a frenetic, farcical, and surprising story.
D: Nino Manfredi. A: Nino Manfredi, Jean-Pierre Cassel.

Where's Piccone?

(1984) 110m. Subtitled.
A–

When Piccone disappears, his wife hooks up with a con man to track him down, and they discover he was quite different than they thought. An unpredictable light-hearted film that belongs to Giannini whose con man is attractive and repulsive, but always smart and funny.
D: Nanni Loy. A: Giancarlo Giannini, Lina Sastri, Clelia Rondinella.

The Icicle Thief

(1990) 84m. Subtitled. **B+**

A very funny parody of *The Bicycle Thief* that also takes some swipes at Italian TV and popular culture. Directed by and starring Nichetti (the "Italian Woody Allen"); this has broad slapstick mixed with sight gags, some deliriously surreal touches, and a reverent poke at neorealism.
D: Maurizio Nichetti. A: Maurizio Nichetti, Caterina Sylos Labini, Federico Rizzo.

Mediterraneo

(1991) 90m. Subtitled.
B+

A band of Italian soldiers is sent to guard a tiny Aegean island during World War II. Their initial unwillingness turns to delight when they realize that all the men have left, leaving their women behind. This sunny tale, flavored with madcap humor, traces the various men as they find love and redemption amongst the shepherdesses, whores, and assorted island women.
D: Gabriele Salvatores. A: Diego Abatantuono, Claudio Bigagli, Giuseppe Cederna.

The Sleazy Uncle

(1991) 104m. Subtitled. **D**

A successful businessman's life is turned on its ear when his disgusting lecherous uncle attaches himself to his life. Intended as a farce, this moves at such a sluggish pace, you'll have lots of time

to anticipate every plot turn and unappealing idea.
D: Franco Brusati. A: Vittorio Gassman, Giancarlo Giannini, Andrea Ferreol.

Johnny Stecchino
(1992) 122m. Subtitled. **C**
An unassuming school bus driver is a dead ringer for a Mafia head honcho, and when the boss's moll takes a shine to him, all hell breaks loose. Gentle, frothy, and a bit slow, but with plenty of slapstick for even the most avid fan.
D: Roberto Benigni. A: Roberto Benigni, Nicoletta Braschi, Paolo Bonacelli.

Caro Diaro
(1994) 100m. Subtitled.
A–
Humorously critical and ever-questioning director/actor Moretti observes the foibles of modern life from the cult of celebrity to overindulgent parents in the new baby boom. Often slipping into fantasy in the course of narrating events, the best scenes are his forays on a Vespa that give a nontourist's view of the neighborhoods of Rome.
D: Nani Moretti. A: Renato Carpentieri, Antonio Neiwiller.

Historical Dramas

Passion, both religious and romantic, are never far from these films about the aristocrats and peasants of Italy's past. Whether epics or modest-sized dramas, most of these films have an immediacy of tone, a richness of historical details, and a trove of vivid characters that make them elegant and entertaining viewing.

The Garden of the Finzi-Continis
(1971) 95m. Subtitled. **A**
Ensconced in their walled-in villa, a wealthy Jewish family ignores the signs of doom in fascist Italy. A richly colored, elegant, and heartbreaking look at this sometimes unsympathetic aristocratic family's last days in the sun.
D: Vittorio De Sica. A: Dominique Sanda, Helmut Berger, Lino Capolicchio.

The Innocent
(1976) 115m. Subtitled.
B+
A nineteenth-century nobleman finds neither wife nor mistress can satisfy his heavy demands. A lavish novelistic tale whose meticulous period style and vivid characters convey the decadence and simmering frustration of the time.
D: Luchino Visconti. A: Laura Antonelli, Giancarlo Giannini, Jennifer O'Neill.

In the Name of the Pope King (aka In Nome Del Papa Rei)
(1977) 115m. Subtitled. **B**
When a nineteenth-century pontifical judge in Rome decides to give up his post, he faces difficulties because his son stands accused of bombing a barracks. Theatrical and talky, this works as a well-paced story, but it belongs to Manfredi as the conscience-torn father.
D: Luigi Magni. A: Nino Manfredi, Danilo Mattei, Carmen Scarpitta.

The Tree of Wooden Clogs
(1978) 185m. Subtitled.
A
This loving painterly depiction of peasant life in turn-of-the-century northern Italy is a movie to get lost in. The epic and rhythmic feel of a nineteenth-century novel helps dignify and honor these characters, making you identify with their familiar human struggles.
D: Ermanno Olmi. A: Luigi Ornaghi, Francesca Moriggi, Omar Brignoli.

Passion of Love (aka Passione d'Amore)
(1981) 117m. Subtitled.
A–
A handsome young captain's affair with a married woman is disrupted when he's relocated to an isolated post, where he finds himself the object of desire by a homely young woman. Like a fairy tale for grownups with sympathetic characters.
D: Ettore Scola. A: Bernard Giraudeau, Laura Antonelli, Valeria D'Obici.

Night of the Shooting Stars
(1982) 106m. Subtitled.
A–
In the last days of World War II, the farmer residents of a small Tuscan village choose up sides: the Germans and their cohorts or the still-to-arrive Americans. A mildly ironic tale with simple images that capture the details of peasant life and the inanities of war.
D: Paolo and Vittorio Taviani. A: Omero Antonutti, Margarita Lozano, Claudio Bigagil.

Kaos
(1985) 188m. Subtitled.
B–
The first two stories in this quartet of gentle and carefully realized tales are good, followed by two mediocre ones, but all are stylish and present an unusual look at peasant life in nineteenth-century Sicily.
D: Paolo and Vittorio Taviani. A: Margarita Lozano, Omero Antonutti, Enrica Maria Mudugno.

Fiorile
(1993) 118m. Subtitled.
B+
This softly glowing historical family drama concerning a stolen cache of gold from Napoleon's troops in nineteenth-century Tuscany will charm, even as you watch the passionate characters steal from and betray one another.
D: Paolo Taviani. A: Claudio Bigagli, Galatea Ranzi, Michael Vartan.

Adult Dramas

This grab bag of more recent dramas shows off the style and grace that have become synonymous with Italian cinema, with first-rate performances that mark these rueful, sad, and memorable tales.

Conversation Piece
(1974) 122m. Subtitled and Dubbed. **C**
A professor's orderly life turns topsy-turvy when he rents his upstairs apartment to a countess with pleasure-seeking children and a young lover. Sophisticated, overwrought, and very talky.
D: Luciano Visconti. A: Burt Lancaster, Silvana Mangano, Helmut Berger.

Padre Padrone
(1977) 114m. Subtitled.
A–
Despite his father's relentless jeering and brutality, a Sardinian shepherd grows up to master Latin and Greek and attend the university. A slow-moving, almost neorealist study without the sentiment.
D: Vittorio and Paolo Taviani. A: Oermo Antonuttie, Saverio Marioni, Marcella Michelangeli.

A Special Day
(1977) 106m. Subtitled.
A– 
A frumpy housewife and a softspoken homosexual man spend a day together as Hitler arrives in Rome in 1938. Tainted with our knowledge of future events, this delicate and often melancholy story shows an unlikely, but believable encounter between two desperately lonely people.
D: Ettore Scola. A: Sophia Loren, Marcello Mastroianni, John Vernon.

Eboli (Christ Stopped at Eboli)
(1979) 119m. 210m. Subtitled.
A
An exiled antifascist writer recalls his stay during the 1930s in a small remote southern town, untouched by time and removed from life. A delicate and nuanced tale that also shows the casual brutality of political exile.
D: Francesco Rosi. A: Gian Maria Volonte, Irene Papas, Paolo Bonacelli.

To Forget Venice
(1979) 110m. Subtitled. **C**
A homosexual and a lesbian couple try to sort out their problems while visiting a dying opera star who raised the three of them. Even with subject matter this lush and operatic, this sometimes broadly played drama is surprisingly unprovocative.
D: Franco Brusati. A: Erland Josephson, Mariangela Melato, Elenora Giorgi.

The Tragedy of a Ridiculous Man
(1981) 116m. Subtitled. **C**
When his son is kidnapped by political terrorists, a cheese manufacturer struggles with his feelings about the act, about paying ransom, and about his life. Stark, ironic, and a bit pretentious; it often feels on the verge of revealing some home truths that finally never emerge.
D: Bernardo Bertolucci. A: Ugo Tognazzi, Anouk Aimee, Laura Morante.

Dark Eyes
(1987) 118m. Subtitled.
A–
A traveler tells his sad tale, set in the nineteenth century, to a stranger on ship; as a poor architect he married a rich woman, but the more he adapted to a life of leisure, the unhappier the couple became. A richly upholstered saga with Italian flair.
D: Nikita Mikhalkov. A: Marcello Mastroianni, Silvana Mangano, Marthe Keller.

Forever Mary
(1991) 100m. Subtitled.
A–
Resorting to unconventional tactics, a teacher in reform school makes every effort to get a transvestite pupil accepted by his class. This gritty grainy small film feels like a news report presenting a seldom seen side of Italy.
D: Marco Risi. A: Michele Placido, Alesandro Di Sanzo, Francesco Benigno.

Open Doors
(1991) 109m. Subtitled.
A
In the 1930s, a thoughtful judge is assigned to the case of a clearly guilty man who, after he was fired, had slaughtered his colleague, his boss, and his wife. A somber intelligent, nearly studious look at justice and its place in an unjust fascistic system.
D: Gianni Amelio. A: Gian Maria Volonte, Ennio Fantastichini, Renzo Giovampietro.

Stolen Children
(1992) 116m. Subtitled.
A
When a mother is arrested for prostituting her nine-year-old daughter, the girl and her brother are taken into state's custody. On their journey to the orphanage they develop a surprisingly tender relationship with their military policeman escort. A haunting tragic portrait that avoids every maudlin pitfall.
D: Gianni Amelio. A: Enrico Lo Verso, Valentina Scalici, Giuseppe Leracitano.

The Flight of the Innocent
(1993) 105m. Subtitled.
C+
A young boy survives the massacre of his family, but the murderers know he's alive. The boy's trek through rural Italy is tension-filled as he braves fantastic odds to stay alive, but the ham-handed treatment makes it feel contrived and melodramatic.
D: Carlo Carlei. A: Manuel Colao, Sal Borgese, Federico Pacifici.

Family Dramas

Every culture has their share of family lore, but the Italians are known for their operatic and almost obsessive celebration of it. Each of these sentimental robust films offers a different perspective on the family, with the underlying premise that for all its faults, it's the only game in town.

We All Loved Each Other So Much
(1975) 124m. Subtitled.
A–
Over the course of three decades, from postwar to present day, three men are in love with the same woman. A device to pay respects to Fellini, De Sica, and the neorealists of Italian cinema by re-creating scenes from well-known movies helps make this a delight.
D: Ettore Scola. A: Nino Manfredi, Vittorio Gassman, Stefania Sandrelli.

Three Brothers
(1980) 113m. Subtitled.
A
A mother's death wreaks havoc on the surviving Sicilian father and three grown sons. Thoughtful, with a careful pace and affecting characters that feel just right.
D: Francesco Rosi. A: Philippe Noiret, Michel Placido, Vittorio Mezzogiorno.

The Family
(1987) 128m. Subtitled. B
Eighty years of a well-to-do family are chronicled in this gently humorous, extremely affectionate film, which takes place entirely in their lovely apartment. Full of quirky characters and novelistic touches.
D: Ettore Scola. A: Fanny Ardant, Vittorio Gassman, Stefania Sandrelli.

Cinema Paradiso
(1989) 128m. Subtitled.
B
A sweet, nostalgia-drenched look at a young boy's mania for movies as he forges a friendship with the ornery projectionist who's full of heartwarming wisdom. This gentle homage set in postwar Sicily will either enchant you or give you the sugar blues.
D: Giuseppe Tornatore. A: Philippe Noiret, Jacques Perrin, Salvatore Cascio.

Everybody's Fine
(1991) 112m. Subtitled. B
A Sicilian widower takes a trip around Italy to visit his five grown children, who are anything but fine. In fact, they've all managed to botch their lives somehow. Gets dragged down by all the sentiment, but Mastroianni keeps it bracing.
D: Giuseppe Tornatore. A: Marcello Mastroianni, Michele Morgan, Marino Cenna.

Story of Boys and Girls
(1991) 92m. Subtitled. A
A large engagement party in the 1930s gathers in the countryside to consume one of the loveliest feasts ever captured on film (be sure to eat before or directly after this one). With the clouds of fascism darkening the horizon, this story traces the loves and passions of an appealing group of people.
D: Pupi Avati. A: Felice Andreasi, Angiola Baggi, Lucretia della Rovere.

French
1930s Dramas

What would American films in the 1930s have been like if the Hayes Production Code hadn't sanitized the portrayal of crime, sex, and adult relations, and the studios had kept a higher opinion of the public's intelligence? These genres are familiar—melodramas of crime and passion, comedies of manners, and epic historical dramas; what is unusual is their lack of Hollywood gloss, censorship, and a need for a happy ending. They also happen to be beautiful documents of a life in France gone after World War II: a France of accordion music, berets, barges, and small villages. Even when the sound is tinny and the subtitles faded, there's not one in this group whose haunting images and unblinking dramas will not stay with you years after viewing

Blood of a Poet
(1930) 55m. B&W.
Subtitled. A–
This collage of episodes reflecting Jean Cocteau's interior life is like the film equivalent of a ransom note constructed of cut-out newspaper letters. Surreal and obsessive, its off-kilter images still look very modern.
D: Jean Cocteau. A: Enrico Ribero, Lee Miller.

L'Age d'Or (The Age of Gold)
(1930) 60m. B&W.
Subtitled. A
You can tell that Salvadore Dali scripted this first film of Buñuel's because it's hard to say what the plot is. A couple would like to make love, but society never lets them alone. This is like a demented slide show with all kinds of strange visual non sequiturs popping up.
D: Luis Buñuel. A: Gaston Modot, Lya Lys, Max Ernst.

Prix de Beauté
(1930) 93m. B&W.
Subtitled. B+
A secretary who's happy with her job, boyfriend, and simple working-class pleasures is "discovered" and becomes a beauty queen. An effervescent Brooks brings real fire to this standard money-and-fame-don't-bring-happiness tale.
D: Augusto Genina. A: Louise Brooks, Jean Bradin, Georges Charlia.

La Chienne
(1931) 93m. B&W.
Subtitled. A–
The triangle of a clerk, a prostitute, and her pimp unfolds its passions and inevitable tragedy in a squalid claustrophobic Montmartre. Dark and melodramatic, with lovely location shots of Paris.
D: Jean Renoir. A: Michel Simon, Janie Marese, Georges Flamant.

Boudu Saved from Drowning
(1932) 87m. B&W.
Subtitled. A–
The title character is about to drown in the Seine when a book dealer rescues him and takes him home, only to have the tramp take over his house, wife, and maid. This satirical look at the bourgeois is still wry and funny.
D: Jean Renoir. A: Michel Simon, Charles Granval, Jean Daste.

Zero for Conduct
(1933) 42m. B&W.
Subtitled. B+
Young boys at a provincial boarding school stage an exuberant if somewhat childish rebellion against the stifling administration. Even though this is a prototype for *If . . .*, the poetic tone is closer to *The 400 Blows* with lovely scenes like a pillow fight filmed in slow motion.
D: Jean Vigo. A: Jean Daste, Robert le Fon.

L'Atalante
(1934) 82m. B&W.
Subtitled. A+
A young couple start life out on a barge in the Seine; the boat and their feelings about it (he wants to stay, she longs for the shore) tear them apart. This is film po-

etry with its effortlessly natural portrayal of the rhythms of human expressions, the surroundings, even the sense of time passing.
D: Jean Vigo. A: Michel Simon, Dita Parlo, Jean Daste.

Toni
(1934) 90m. B&W.
Subtitled. **B+**
Two people in a small village fall in love and part, only to find each other again years later when they're both trapped in unhappy marriages. The film's naturalism, the nonstars, actual locations, and close-ups of real villagers make this a good example of neorealism's roots.
D: Jean Renoir. A: Charles Blavette, Jenny Helia, Edouard Delmont.

Princess Tam Tam
(1935) 80m. B&W.
Subtitled. **A**
An exotic African impersonates an Indian princess and becomes the toast of 1930s Paris. The lavish Art Deco sets and costumes would make Busby Berkeley jealous, and Baker's unabashed jungle dancing is a most bewitching precursor to the jitterbug.
D: Edmond Greville. A: Josephine Baker, Albert Prejean, Vivian Romance.

The Crime of Monsieur Lange
(1935) 90m. B&W.
Subtitled. **B**
When a lowly publishing house employee makes a hit with his American cowboy stories, the company begins to produce movies as a cooperative over the objections of their evil capitalist boss. A utopian socialist fantasy that's a little talky but fun to watch.
D: Jean Renoir. A: Rene Lefevre, Jules Berry, Florelle.

Lower Depths
(1936) 92m. B&W.
Subtitled. **B+**
You really get a sense of how claustrophobic the underworld is in this complicated story of flophouse characters who long to escape their lives of crime. Like a bleak version of the Dead End Kids without the sentimentality.
D: Jean Renoir. A: Jean Gabin, Louis Jouvet, Suzy Prim.

Pépé le Moko
(1936) 95m. B&W.
Subtitled. **A**
A French gangster hiding out in an Algiers casbah risks being captured when he falls in love with a beautiful woman. The narrow winding hivelike casbah haunts the whole film, which is as suspenseful and well-paced as a Hitchcock thriller.
D: Julien Duvivier. A: Jean Gabin, Mirielle Balin, Gabriel Gabrio.

Grand Illusion
(1937) 111m. B&W.
Subtitled. **A**
World War I POWs must overcome the natural laws of their class and upbringing in order to help each other survive. Sophisticated, subtle, and beautifully shot: If you can get past the mannered acting, you're in for a treat.
D: Jean Renoir. A: Jean Gabin, Erich von Stroheim, Pierre Fresnay.

La Bete Humaine
(1938) 99m. B&W.
Subtitled. **B+**
A train engineer falls for the young wife of a stationmaster and together they concoct a complicated plan to murder him. Violent, unpredictable, and passionate as a film noir.
D: Jean Renoir. A: Jean Gabin, Simone Simon, Julien Carette.

Le Jour Se Lève (Daybreak)
(1939) 88m. B&W.
Subtitled. **B**
A murderer hides out in his small-town room and reflects on what led to his crime. The police are on his trail and you feel time running out. Edgy, heavily-shadowed melodrama that borders on being suffocating.
D: Marcel Carné. A: Jean Gabin, Arletty, Jacqueline Laurent.

The Rules of the Game
(1939) 105m. B&W.
Subtitled. **A**
A canny humorous story of love and betrayal among some decadent aristocrats and their servants that unravels during a hunting weekend at a country estate. Imagine an adult and slightly depraved Astaire-Rogers film minus the dancing. A funny and wicked story of the privileged class on the eve of destruction.
D: Jean Renoir. A: Marcel Dalio, Nora Gregor, Jean Renoir.

HISTORICAL DRAMAS

Madame Bovary
(1934) 102m. B&W.
Subtitled. **C+**
A bored nineteenth-century French provincial doctor's wife has affairs to make herself happy, but they don't. Director Jean Renoir had to cut down the original three hours of this disjointed version of Flaubert's novel that features an oddly ungainly heroine; is still worth a look.
D: Jean Renoir. A: Valentine Tessier, Fernand Fabre, Pierre Renoir.

Carnival in Flanders
(1935) 90m. B&W.
Subtitled. **B+**
When their men take cover from the advancing Spanish troops in the seventeenth century, the women in this small town in France decide to throw a carnival to divert them. Engaging theatrical farce with first-rate period detail.
D: Jacques Feyder. A: Louis Jouvet, Françoise Rosay, Jean Murat.

A Day in the Country
(1935) 40m. B&W.
Subtitled. **A–**
A Parisian family spends one day a year in the country and on this one their young daughter falls in love with a local man. A poetic gentle tale of love that feels like an exquisitely filmed short story.
D: Jean Renoir. A: Sylvie Bataille, George Darnoux, Jane Marken.

Mayerling
(1936) 91m. B&W.
Subtitled. **A–**
Based on a real-life murder-suicide that occurred in the Austrian royal family in 1889, this tells of Crown Prince Rudolph who defies his father when he falls in love with a commoner. Charles and Diana are slouches compared to the elegant doomed lovers in this old-fashioned and very romantic drama.
D: Anatole Litvak. A: Charles Boyer, Danielle Darrieux.

La Marseillaise
(1937) 130m. B&W.
Subtitled. **B**
An epic panoramic film that traces the march by the volunteers from Marseilles that sparked the overthrow of the monarchy and the French Revolution. Shot in you-are-there documentary style, with a panorama of peasants, royal servants, and Louis XVI.
D: Jean Renoir. A: Louis Jouvet, Pierre Renoir.

Pagnol

These canny and highly emotional dramas are playwright-filmmaker Marcel Pagnol's love songs to the tough and sensual life in southern France in the 1920s. Small businessmen, gossipy wives, and wine-drinking deadbeats are all part of a community that can pressure an unfaithful wife to return to her oafish husband, or a pregnant woman into marrying while the real father is out at sea. Written and sometimes directed by Pagnol, these early talkies look like film versions of his stage plays, recording all the nuances of his salty melodramatic characters.

Marius
(1931) 125m. B&W.
Subtitled. **B+**
Marius, the son of a cafe owner, is torn between the call of the sea and the love of his girl Fanny. This atmospheric treatment of a simple timeless story set in Marseilles is talky and dated, but captures life in a port town. First in a trilogy.
D: Alexander Korda. A: Raimu, Pierre Fresnay, Orane Demazis.

Fanny
(1932) 102m. B&W.
Subtitled. **B**
Marius leaves Fanny for the sea, unaware she is pregnant, and Fanny marries a wealthy man in order to provide for her baby. The snail-like pace bogs down in the second of this trilogy, but the town's melting pot of kooky deadbeats makes for boisterous fun.
D: Marc Allegret. A: Raimu, Orane Demazis, Pierre Fresnay.

Cesar
(1933) 117m. B&W.
Subtitled. **B+**
Fanny's son, now a young man, searches for his sailor father Marius. This finale of the Marseilles trilogy is stagy and full of noisy peasant characters, but Raimu's bittersweet performance as the grandfather is as haunted as the sea itself.
D: Marcel Pagnol. A: Raimu, Pierre Fresnay, Orane Demazis.

Angel
(1934) 132m. B&W.
Subtitled. **B**
A bored small-town girl runs away to lead a tawdry life in Paris. Painting a canvas full of lively characters, this droll coming-of-age tale unfortunately rambles on for a half hour too long.
D: Marcel Pagnol. A: Orane Demazis, Fernandel, Jean Servais.

Harvest
(1937) 129m. B&W.
Subtitled. **B–**
An impoverished couple struggles to bring a deserted town back to life. This lyrical fable is full of the sweat and vigor of the land, but after awhile, you feel like you've been in the sun too long.
D: Marcel Pagnol. A: Gabriela Gabrio, Orane Demazis, Fernandel.

The Baker's Wife
(1938) 124m. B&W.
Subtitled. **B+**
When the new baker's pretty young wife runs off with a shepherd, the townsmen conspire to bring her back home. Slow as molasses, but a winning comedy of redemption and a lyrical study of provincial life.
D: Marcel Pagnol. A: Raimu, Ginette LeClerc, Charles Moulin.

1940s–1950s Dramas

These cool intelligent postwar films range from noirish tales of revenge, somber stories of physical and spiritual healing, to childlike fables of lost innocence in an ever darkening world.

Le Corbeau
(1943) 92m. B&W.
Subtitled. **B+**
A string of poison pen letters is driving the citizens of a small village mad with suspicion. A stark pungent look at human beings at their worst makes for an entertaining and voyeuristic thriller of deceit.
D: Henri-Georges Clouzot. A: Pierre Fresnay, Helena Manson, Ginette LeClerc.

Les Enfants du Paradis (Children of Paradise)
(1945) 189m. B&W.
Subtitled. **A**
Unrequited love lies at the center of this grand and sweeping look at Parisian theatrical life in late 1800s. Don't let the length and staginess stop you; the combination of the epic spectacles and the drama of these passionate, self-dramatizing, and childlike creatures of the stage will enchant even modern sensibilities.
D: Marcel Carné. A: Classic Jean-Louis Barrault, Arletty, Pierre Brasseur.

Sylvia and the Phantom
(1944) 97m. B&W.
Subtitled. **B+**
A young girl is hopelessly in love with the ghost of her grandmother's lover while she doesn't have a clue about her own effect on the young men in her life. Shot in a chilly old castle (you can see the actors' breath), this sweetly romantic tale has a precious nineteenth-century feel to it.
D: Claude Autant-Lara. A: Odette Joyeux, François Perier, Jacques Tati.

Devil in the Flesh
(1946) 110m. B&W.
Subtitled. **C+**
A soldier's wife takes up with a college student in the early days of World War I. After a promising opening, this expensive but flat-looking love story just rambles on without involving anyone, including the viewer.
D: Claude Autant-Lara. A: Micheline Prele, Gerard Philipe, Jean Debucourt.

Panique
(1946) 87m. B&W.
Subtitled. **B+**
A murderous couple sets up

an innocent man to pay for their sins. Simon is perfect as the gullible everyman about to take the fall in this bleak and stylish noir thriller that evolves into an intricate chess game of deception.
D: Julien Duvivier. A: Michel Simon, Viviane Romance, Paul Bernard.

Monsieur Vincent
(1949) 73m. Subtitled. **B+**
This is an unsentimental and finely acted story of St. Vincent de Paul, a simple priest who devoted his life to the poor in the seventeenth century. Beautiful and colorful to watch, but don't expect the flash and dash salvation of American religious films made at this time.
D: Maurice Cloche. A: Pierre Fresnay, Aimee Clariond, Jean Debucourt.

Forbidden Games
(1951) 87m. B&W. Subtitled. **B+**
A young war orphan living in a small village teaches her adopted brother the facts of war and death through a series of games. This lyrical, sometimes strained film is memorable for a haunting Fossey as the girl too old for her years, and the lurking presence of Nazis in the sunny French countryside.
D: Rene Clement. A: Brigitte Fossey, Georges Poujouly, Louis Herbert.

Ophuls

Wickedly sophisticated and very romantic, Max Ophuls' films of duplicitous lovers and frivolous artists are filled with a sparkling energy of a France long gone. Even those not partial to period pieces will find themselves seduced by the giddy action as his camera glides over the upper-crust characters like the gaze of an amused and slightly rude man of the world.

La Ronde
(1950) 97m. B&W. Subtitled. **A**
A has an affair with B, who's also having an affair with C, who's really in love with D, who's also having an affair with A. This film is a charming ride on a carousel of love and infidelities.
D: Max Ophuls. A: Anton Walbrook, Simone Signoret.

Le Plaisir
(1952) 94m. B&W. Subtitled. **A**
Three de Maupassant tales—a mask helps a man recover his youth, prostitutes take a vacation, and an artist marries a model after a suicide attempt—are presented with irony and a light heart.
D: Max Ophuls. A: Jean Gabin, Danielle Darrieux.

The Earrings of Madame de . . .
(1953) 105m. B&W. Subtitled. **A+**
When a countess pawns her earrings to cover private debts, she tells her husband they are lost, setting off a series of repercussions. An entertaining look at deeply shallow people, with a fluid camera doing arabesques.
D: Max Ophuls. A: Charles Boyer, Danielle Darrieux.

Lola Montes
(1955) 110m. Subtitled. **A–**
A light and frothy depiction of the famous courtesan, whose conquests included King Ludwig of Bavaria and Franz Liszt. Brightly colored, with the busyness of a nineteenth-century painting.
D: Max Ophuls. A: Martine Carol, Peter Ustinov.

Tati

If you share the French view that Jerry Lewis is a comic genius, then sample some of the films of their native-born clown. Jacques Tati's appeal is completely personal; the sight-gags, cheerful mime sequences, and slapstick humor will either have you in hysterics or running screaming from the room. Most of these bright little comedies feature Monsieur Hulot, the bumbling confused everyman, whose difficulties with machines show a postwar France where technology is a bemusing and befuddling alien presence.

Jour de Fete
(1949) 79m. B&W w/color. Subtitled. **A–**
After seeing a film on newly automated postal techniques in the U.S., a small-town postman thinks they might be just the thing for his route. This black-and-white film has been color tinted for an odd old postcard effect.
D: Jacques Tati. A: With Guy Decomble.

Mr. Hulot's Holiday
(1953) 86m. B&W. Subtitled. **A**
Tati's alter ego, Monsieur Hulot, made his debut in the film about the awkward, sweetly hapless character whose lack of connection seems to set him happily apart from the apparently efficient people around him.
D: Jacques Tati. A: With Nathalie Pasaud.

Mon Oncle
(1958) 110m. Subtitled. **B+**
Monsieur Hulot visits his sister and brother-in-law in their very modern home, a virtual altar to appliances. As deft as early silent comedies by Chaplin and Keaton.
D: Jacques Tati. A: Jean-Pierre Zola.

Playtime
(1967) 108m. Subtitled. **B–**
This time Monsieur Hulot takes on the gleaming slick modernity of Paris. A treat for his fans.
D: Jacques Tati. A: with Barbara Dennek.

Traffic
(1971) 89m. Subtitled. **C**
Traffic provides plenty of

mayhem to confound the muddled Monsieur Hulot as he attempts to transport a camping vehicle from France to Holland. Slow going, and even devoted fans will wonder whether they're there yet.
D: Jacques Tati. A: Jacques Tati, Maria Kimberly, Marcel Fraval.

Cocteau

Jean Cocteau updated legends and fairy tales to sketch theatrical portraits of lovers and poets too sensitive to survive the brutal modern world. While keeping many of the conventions of postwar French films, most of these dreamy, melancholic, and theatrical works look as modern and avant-garde as they did 50 years ago.

The Eternal Return
(1943) 110m. B&W. Subtitled. **B**

A young man helps his uncle marry a beautiful young woman and finds himself falling in love with her himself. This gothic retelling of the Tristan and Isolde legend is dreamy and unabashedly romantic, but flawed by a stiff Solange as the object of Marais' affection.
D: Jean Cocteau. A: Jean Marais, Madeleine Solange, Jean Murat.

Beauty and the Beast
(1946) 95m. B&W. Subtitled. **A –**

This updated and surreal fairy tale is romantic in a high 40s Hollywood style as love blossoms between the beast and the young woman who became his voluntary prisoner. Keep some hankies close for the childlike simplicity of the redemptive finale.
D: Jean Cocteau. A: Jean Marais, Josette Day, Marcel Andre.

Les Parents Terribles
(1948) 98m. Subtitled. **B +**

Disappointed by her husband's failures, a woman looks to her spoiled children for salvation. This gothic tale of spiritual incest, acted out on just two claustrophobic sets, spins a strange web of mystery and charm while being very much a domestic horror film.
D: Jean Cocteau. A: Jean Marais, Yvonne de Bray, Gabrielle Dorziat.

Orpheus
(1949) 95m. B&W. Subtitled. **A –**

A modern poet meets Death in the form of a beautiful princess. Even with strutting poseurs and drop-dead gorgeous angels vying for screen time, this stylish and wildly narcissistic allegory makes a grand stab at portraying immortality. It's also very recognizable as the distinguished grandparent to Calvin Klein ads.
D: Jean Cocteau. A: Jean Marais, Maria Casares, François Perier.

Les Enfants Terribles
(1950) 105m. B&W. **B +**

A pair of beautiful spoiled siblings enter into petty crime out of boredom, but their carefree larks soon take a dark turn toward incest and catastrophe. Another pair of angelic decadents chez Cocteau seem to be enjoying a wonderful joke at the expense of the rest of the earthbound world in this slightly stagy but extremely spooky romance.
D: Jean Cocteau. A: Nicole Stephane, Eduoard Dermithe, Renee Cosima.

The Testament of Orpheus
(1959) 80m. **C +**

After being murdered in the eighteenth century, the poet transcends space and takes other forms of life. This disorienting fantasy, seemingly edited with a meat cleaver into 15 segments, looks like Cocteau's attempt to keep up with the nuclear age. An indulgent film with occasional flashes of the old magic.
D: Jean Cocteau. A: Jean Cocteau, Jean Marais, Maria Casares.

Renoir

Jean Renoir's later films drew less from his realistic innovations of the 30s and more from the theater; aside from *The Elusive Corporal*, these are high-spirited romps that beg sympathy for the plights of grand dames, showgirls, and all those who love foolishly.

The Golden Coach
(1952) 101m. Subtitled. **A –**

An eighteenth-century acting troupe on tour in South America has a hard time keeping tabs on its amorous leading lady. The earthy colorful roadshow productions and a frisky Magnani as the actress torn between three lovers makes this picaresque tribute to nomadic actors a continual delight.
D: Jean Renoir. A: Anna Magnani, Odoardo Spadero, Nada Fiorelli.

French Can Can
(1955) 93m. Subtitled. **A**

This is a dashing Technicolor musical about an 1860s impresario trying to open his Moulin Rouge music hall. The very un-American touches—the frothy portrayal of "immoral" sex, everyone's easy philosophizing at the drop of an absinthe glass, the performance of real French music hall stars, and a worldly Gabin—make this an unexpected treat.
D: Jean Renoir. A: Jean Gabin, Françoise Arnoul, Maria Felix.

Elena and Her Men
(1956) 98m. Subtitled. **B +**

A beautiful Polish princess renounces her title in hopes of finding a rich husband. Ingrid juggles her many suitors with great aplomb in this broadly played bedroom farce whose old-world elegance flickers like gaslight in the Parisian dawn.
D: Jean Renoir. A: Ingrid Bergman, Jean Marais, Mel Ferrer.

Picnic on the Grass
(1959) 92m. Subtitled.
A
A mild-mannered scientist, favored to become the first President of the United States of Europe, runs off to the country and impregnates a pretty chambermaid. This relaxed romp in the country unites the buttoned-down upper class with naive earthy peasants in a sunny impressionistic portrait of joy and love.
D: Jean Renoir. A: Paul Meurisse, Catherine Rouvel, Jacqueline Morane.

The Elusive Corporal
(1962) 108m. Subtitled. **A**
A spirited Corporal and his buddies try to break out of a German POW camp. Smaller in scale, less magisterial, and more ironic than his earlier *Le Grand Illusion,* this antiwar saga sparkles with an almost choreographed camaraderie and impish humor.
D: Jean Renoir. A: Jean-Pierre Cassel, Claude Brasseur, Claude Rich.

Bresson

Robert Bresson's cool austere character studies generally focus on loners who struggle with a mostly unseen hostile world and their own complex imaginations.

Diary of a Country Priest
(1950) 120m. B&W.
Subtitled. **A–**
An unhappy priest grows frustrated with himself and his parishioners in a small French town. This quiet spare study of the disintegration of a human soul is painstakingly told. Chilly but involving.
D: Robert Bresson. A: Claude Laydu, Nicole Ladmiral, Nicole Maurey.

A Man Escaped
(1956) 94m. B&W.
Subtitled. **A**
A leader of the French Resistance plots his escape from a Nazi prison in this unnerving, documentary-like escape drama. The slow burn buildup is worth the wait as the methodical prisoner regains his spirit of humanity while hatching his plan under the inhuman circumstances.
D: Robert Bresson. A: François Leterrier, Charles Le Clainche, Maurice Beerblock.

Pickpocket
(1959) 75m. B&W.
Subtitled. **A–**
A crafty pickpocket and an equally shrewd detective play a cat and mouse game in the dingy streets and subways of Paris. A documentary-style look into the mind of a petty criminal, with the brimming intensity of a Dostoyevsky novel.
D: Robert Bresson. A: Martin Lassalle, Pierre Leymarie, Jean Pelegri.

Mouchette
(1966) 90m. B&W.
Subtitled. **A**
A friendless teenage girl tries to overcome the abuse she suffers at the hands of her brutal family. This simple stark tale of a loveless life in a poor isolated village is told with shattering honesty that haunts after the chilling finale.
D: Robert Bresson. A: Nadine Nortier, Jean-Claude Guilbert, Marie Cardinal.

Postwar Thrillers

This group of amoral little postwar tales are darker and more cynical than the gloomiest American film noir. Brimming with atmosphere, these films portray the angst of all the murderers, hoods, and schemers as they go for the big score or one last chance at redemption.

The Wages of Fear
(1953) 156m. B&W.
Subtitled. **A–**
Four men drive trucks filled with nitroglycerin through the mountainous roads of Central America. This well-crafted, almost unbearably tense thriller takes its time introducing us to the less than savory heroes, but the overall malignant atmosphere and sweaty treacherous ride is gut-clenching.
D: Henri-Georges Clouzot. A: Yves Montand, Charles Vanel, Peter Van Eyck.

Diabolique
(1955) 107m. B&W.
Subtitled. **A–**
A sadistic school master is murdered by his wife and mistress, who soon learn that their perfect crime has sprung a few leaks. This eerie film sacrifices plot for atmosphere, but the head-spinning story twist at the end makes this a predecessor of modern high concept thrillers.
D: Henri-Georges Clouzot. A: Simone Signoret, Vera Clouzot, Paul Meurisse.

Bob le Flambeur
(1956) 102m. B&W.
Subtitled. **B+**
A small-time hood continues with his scheme to knock over a casino, even when his plans begin to go haywire. With a wonderfully seedy Parisian atmosphere and little action, this sexy, almost impressionistic caper still manages to have the look and sass of American gangster films.
D: Jean Pierre Melville. A: Roger Duchesne, Isabel Corey, Daniel Cauchy.

Eyes Without a Face
(1960) 90m. B&W.
Subtitled. **A**
A mad scientist kills women so he can transplant their faces onto his disfigured daughter. A moody, truly frightening horror that aims and succeeds in delivering oddly poetic shocks and graphic skin peels that will make your flesh crawl.
D: Georges Franju. A: Pierre Brasseur, Alida Valli, Edith Scob.

Le Doulos
(1961) 105m. B&W.
Subtitled. **A –**
An informer is ready to spill the beans on a crime syndicate until they turn up the heat on an old buddy. A sly, dark, and splashy thriller with stylistic violence and atmosphere that's a throwback to the best noirs.
D: Jean-Pierre Melville. A: Jean-Paul Belmondo, Serge Reggiani, Michel Piccoli.

New Wave Directors

Bold, convention-smashing, and fueled with a reverence for classic American genres (especially gangster films), these are the movies to come out of the brave New World of French cinema from the late 50s. The best of them have an energy and vision that will draw you into their unpredictable stories; others may just seem self-conscious and leave you wondering why they can't just tell a straight story.

Truffaut

François Truffaut is the most viewer-friendly of the group since his smart poignant stories always center around universally human characters—whether it's his alter ego, the ever optimistic Doinel, or beautiful young lovers at the turn of the century—with clever camera trickery taking a back seat to a tone of warmth, sympathy, and gentle humor.

The 400 Blows
(1959) 99m. B&W. **A** 🏛
An unforgettable portrait of a sensitive young boy, baffled and bruised by a world of uncomprehending adults, cramped living quarters, authoritarian schools, and a lovely but unglamorous Paris. Truffaut's first, and the introduction of his alter ego Doinel.
D: François Truffaut. A: Jean-Pierre Leaud.

Jules and Jim
(1961) 110m. B&W.
Subtitled. **A +** 🏛
In pre-World War I France, Jules and Jim are best friends and in love with Catherine, an elusive sprite of a woman utterly keyed to the moment, who loves them both in her fashion. All the elegant camerawork and beautifully composed scenes are used well in this lovely passionate portrait of love and friendship.
D: François Truffaut. A: Jean Moreau, Oskar Werner, Henri Serr.

Shoot the Piano Player
(1962) 92m. B&W.
Subtitled. **A**
After a concert pianist's wife commits suicide when she feels neglected due to his burgeoning career, he exiles himself to cabarets and honky-tonks, vowing to avoid future involvements. Reminiscent of a Hollywood B film, this heavily shadowed story of doom remains ruefully funny.
D: François Truffaut. A: Charles Aznavour, Nicole Berger, Marie Dubois.

The Soft Skin
(1964) 120m. B&W.
Subtitled. **B –**
A married businessman gets involved with an airline stewardess and his wife is not happy. Good performances make this dressed-up soap opera worth watching. Transitional and less ambitious than his earlier work.
D: François Truffaut. A: François Dorleac, Jean Desailly, Nelly Benedetti.

Stolen Kisses
(1968) 90m. Subtitled.
B + 🔍 ♂
Truffaut's alter ego Doinel has now been discharged from the army, only to discover that his girlfriend thinks he should take a hike. Sympathetic, infuriating, and bumbling, this protagonist worms his way into your heart as he does with the women in his life. Bright and sunny.
D: François Truffaut. A: Jean-Pierre Leaud, Delphine Seyrig.

The Mississippi Mermaid
(1969) 123m. Subtitled.
C +
A wealthy tobacco farmer is entranced with his lovely mail-order bride until she runs off with his money . . . and then returns to involve him in an even deadlier mystery. An unsuccessful attempt to mimic Hitchcock's suspense and style in this costume drama / almost thriller.
D: François Truffaut. A: Jean-Paul Belmondo, Catherine Deneuve, Michel Bouquet.

Chabrol

Claude Chabrol soon became the "French Hitchcock" thanks to his detached psychological thrillers that present relationships in an almost scientific way. Although these films may have a distanced faraway look, they invariably let fly some poison darts, especially about male-female relationships.

Le Beau Serge
(1958) 93m. B&W.
Subtitled. **B**
A young man returns to his small town after many years and encounters old acquaintances, including his boyhood friend who has become the town drunk. Earnest and taxing to watch, but the wintry landscape and unsparing details make this bristle with the frustration of wasted working-class lives.
D: Claude Chabrol. A: Jean-Claude Brialy, Gérard Blain.

Les Cousins
(1958) 112m. B&W. Subtitled. **B**

Two cousins, one an urban sophisticate, the other a country innocent, share an apartment and feelings for the same woman. Hipster 50s Paris is the setting and the feel of this drama; its jazzy bohemianism looks innocent now, but it's still very cool.
D: Claude Chabrol. A: Gerard Blain, Jean-Claude Brialy, Juliette Mayniel.

Bluebeard
(1963) 114m. Subtitled. **D**

This version of the famous seventeenth-century, wife-killer tale has little to recommend it. Though it's played as a black comedy, it lacks the wit and sophistication and feels more like a minor costume drama.
D: Claude Chabrol. A: Charles Denner, Michele Morgan, Danielle Darrieux.

Les Biches
(1968) 104m. Subtitled French. **B+**

A bored wealthy Parisian woman and a young female artist begin an affair and head for St. Tropez where a man complicates the picture. The plot may sound like a Euro-trashy melodrama, but it's really a sophisticated drama about the power struggles of some really dreadful people.
D: Claude Chabrol. A: Jean-Louis Trintignant, Stephane Audran, Jacqueline Sassard.

Le Boucher
(1969) 93m. Subtitled. **A–**

An attractive village headmistress becomes involved with the town butcher just as a series of murders occur. The creepy feeling in the daily activities of a French village steadily builds and, though this thriller may be easy to figure out, the psychological games will keep you hooked.
D: Claude Chabrol. A: Stephane Audran, Jean Yanne, Antonio Passallia.

Godard

Blending politics with the look of American gangster films (with time out for commentary on the war between the sexes) Jean-Luc Godard is the flamboyant guerrilla warrior of this crowd. No experiment is too wild for Godard; whether it involves fragmenting dialogue or turning a camera on its side, he aims to fracture story lines and explode any illusions in film. At times you may feel as if you're stuck in a lecture at the Sorbonne—his films are like manifestos—but his images have such an impact that the talkiness may not bother you.

Breathless
(1959) 89m. B&W. Subtitled. **A**

This quintessential New Wave film has it all: jump cuts, a poseur protagonist, an American miss, and countless imitators. You can still feel the exuberance, joy, and extreme self-consciousness in this movie, whose slim plot—boy meets girl, boy loses girl—is boosted by its daring mobile camera and its car chases that tip their hat to American crime flicks.
D: Jean-Luc Godard. A: Jean-Paul Belmondo, Jean Seberg, Daniel Boulanger.

A Woman Is a Woman
(1961) 83m. Subtitled. **B**

Godard's idea of an American musical features a stripper eager to settle down to a more conventional life with her boyfriend who won't cooperate. When she tries his willing best friend, the trouble begins. Cheerful and madcap.
D: Jean-Luc Godard. A: Jean-Claude Brialy, Anna Karina, Jean-Paul Belmondo.

Contempt
(1963) 103m. Subtitled. **B**

A classy screenwriter tangles with a sleazy director and producer as they all labor in Capri on a filming of "The Odyssey." Meanwhile, the screenwriter's marriage is collapsing as his wife becomes increasingly disenchanted. Intelligent, amusing, and pessimistic commentary on moviemaking.
D: Jean-Luc Godard. A: Brigitte Bardot, Fritz Lang, Jack Palance.

My Life to Live
(1963) 85m. B&W. Subtitled. **B+**

Episodic, near-documentary examination of the life of a headstrong young woman who winds up a prostitute. Cheerless but memorable, it captures the loneliness and isolation of its protagonist.
D: Jean-Luc Godard. A: Anna Karina, Saddy Rebot, Andrea Labarthe.

Band of Outsiders
(1964) 97m. B&W. Subtitled. **B**

A young woman plots to steal her aunt's nest egg; the idea fails. A talky grim look at lowlife gangsters in Paris, but just when you think this is a poor cousin of *Breathless,* along comes a musical number to pick things up and really disorient you.
D: Jean-Luc Godard. A: Anna Karina, Claude Brasseur, Sami Frey.

A Married Woman
(1964) 94m. B&W. Subtitled. **B–**

A married woman is torn between her husband and lover. She worries a lot and the narrator comments. We hear fragments of conversations, and see fragments of her body to get a sense of her fractured kaleidoscopic world. Fairly pretentious, with Godard narrating.
D: Jean-Luc Godard. A: Macha Meril, Philippe Leroy, Bernard Noel.

Pierrot le Fou
(1965) 110m. Subtitled. **B**

A man escapes his wealthy wife, a woman tries to leave behind her gangster-populated life, and together they head for the south of France and paradise. Exuberant, erratic, and shot in lavish Technicolor. This doesn't always make sense, but it's fun to watch.
D: Jean-Luc Godard. A: Jean-Paul Belmondo, Anna Karina, Dirk Sanders.

Alphaville
(1965) 95m. B&W. Subtitled. **A**

A scientist is being held in a futuristic city and a detective is sent to get him out. This is cold, remote, full of dread, and has those spooky robots who do the bidding of the master electronic brain. Confusing but strong on atmosphere.
D: Jean-Luc Godard. A: Eddie Constantine, Anna Karina, Akim Tamiroff.

Masculine, Feminine
(1966) 103m. B&W. Subtitled. **A**

Boy meets girl. They have an affair as Paris surges with the rage and excitement of the 60s. Godard coins his description of this generation as the "children of Marx and Coca-Cola." Erratic, spontaneous, and has an immediacy that is still riveting.
D: Jean-Luc Godard. A: Jean-Pierre Leaud, Chantal Goya, Brigitte Bardot.

Weekend
(1967) 103m. Subtitled. **B**
A couple and their in-laws drive to the French countryside and become involved in a traffic jam that displays the most hellish aspects of capitalism's brutality. Relentless, with ugly images of violence, butchery, and cannibalism. A summing up of many of the beefs of the 60s generation.
D: Jean-Luc Godard. A: Mireille Darc, Jean Yanne, Jean-Pierre Leaud.

Le Gai Savoir
(1968) 96m. Subtitled. **B–**
Two people meet in a TV studio and concoct a three year plan to redefine cinema. They discuss their findings, using images, location shots, and texts, to discover the nature of language and images. A joy for Godard fans, slow-moving torture for others.
D: Jean-Luc Godard. A: Juliet Berto, Jean-Pierre Leaud.

Vadim

The characters in Roger Vadim's films seem to devote every waking moment to ruminating, scheming, or talking about sex. While his films can be silly and flirtatious as a striptease, often looking like they were tailored for his current sex kitten muse, their execution is always smart and even provocative.

And God Created Woman
(1956) 92m. Subtitled. **B+**
A pouty ripe young woman wreaks havoc among the men in a seaside village. The more exploitatively scandalous these "frank" dramas about sexually carefree women were back then, the more dated they look today. But this one has hip 50s garb, a colorful and sultry Côte d'Azur scenery, and an almost ridiculously sexy Bardot.
D: Roger Vadim. A: Brigitte Bardot, Jean-Louis Trintignant, Curt Jurgens.

Les Liaisons Dangereuses
(1959) 106m. B&W. Subtitled. **B+**
A married couple gets their kicks out of seducing and abandoning their friends and then telling each other about it. A sophisticated and decadent story of *La Dolce Vita:* It's like an invitation to the hippest, most ennui-ridden party in Paris. Soundtrack features jazz heavyweights.
D: Roger Vadim. A: Jeanne Moreau, Jean-Louis Trintignant, Gerard Philipe.

Warrior's Rest (Le Repos du Guerrier)
(1962) 100m. Subtitled. **C**
A young woman visiting a small town while settling an aunt's estate saves a man from suicide. They become involved, and he's crazy. The histrionics almost make this a soap opera, but Bardot gets to wear some great clothes.
D: Roger Vadim. A: Brigitte Bardot, Robert Hossein, Jean-Marc Bory.

The Game Is Over
(1966) 96m. Subtitled. **C–**
A woman marries a wealthy older man only to find that his son is more to her liking as a sex partner. Melodramatic and titillating, this is about as subtle as a hammer, but Jane Fonda is likable.
D: Roger Vadim. A: Jane Fonda, Michel Piccoli, Peter McEnery.

Malle

Outside of Truffaut, none of the other directors try to charm the viewer as much as Louis Malle. He seems to relish the act of creating a film, carefully borrowing from cinematic tradition—whether it's noir or Chaplin—to tell a story through images. You never have to figure out what these sophisticated films are up to; they are human interest stories, pure and simple, told by a keenly interested and sympathetic storyteller.

Elevator to the Gallows (aka Frantic)
(1957) 120m. B&W. Subtitled. **A**
An employee and the boss's wife plan to murder the boss and run off together. Everything goes smoothly until the elevator stalls during the getaway. Skittish and nerve-wracking, with noir touches and a great jazz score.
D: Louis Malle. A: Jeanne Moreau, Maurice Ronet, Georges Poujoly.

The Lovers
(1958) 88m. B&W. Subtitled. **B**
A bored wealthy woman amuses herself by cheating on her husband and her lover. Shot in velvety black and white, this tale of adultery has enough passionate posturing, long silences, and significant looks to make you wonder when the action will start.
D: Louis Malle. A: Jeanne Moreau, Alain Cuny, Jose Luis de Villalonga.

Zazie Dans le Metro
(1960) 92m. B&W. Subtitled. **B+**
Visiting her drag queen uncle in Paris, 11-year-old Zazie, a precocious, blunt-talking young lady has only one desire: to ride the metro. A playful film, full of sight gags and visual games that

are amusing and a little maddening.
D: Louis Malle. A: Catherine Demonget, Philippe Noiret, Carla Marlier.

A Very Private Affair
(1961) 103m. Dubbed. **B–**
A movie star overdoses on fame and retreats to Geneva where she begins an affair with a friend's husband. This slow melodrama about the perils of celebrity is oddly unsympathetic, but it looks great and borders on being a good trashy soap opera.
D: Louis Malle. A: Marcello Mastroianni, Brigitte Bardot, Nicolas Bataille.

The Fire Within
(1963) 108m. B&W. Subtitled. **B–**
Released from a sanitarium after an alcohol detox, a philandering writer makes the rounds of his old buddies in Paris, during the final two days of his life. Blunt and stark, this film is about alienation—and you know it.
D: Louis Malle. A: Jeanne Moreau, Maurice Ronet, Lena Skerla.

Resnais, Rivette, and Varda

Along with Godard, these directors were the revolutionaries of the New Wave. Their films experimented with accepted coordinates of time and space, shattering the cinematic illusion of reality, the way cubism did to academic art. They all assume a certain level of intelligence and commitment from the viewer, using literary references, a lot of talk, and long seemingly aimless shots in their attempt to delve into a character.

Hiroshima, Mon Amour
(1959) 91m. B&W. Subtitled. **A**
A French actress making a film about peace in Hiroshima has an affair with a Japanese architect who's trying to rebuild the city. This is like an airless human still-life, as stiff as a flower arrangement and as beautiful, too.
D: Alain Resnais. A: Emmanuele Riva, Eiji Okada, Stella Dassas.

Last Year at Marienbad
(1962) 93m. B&W. Subtitled. **A**
Maybe a man and a woman have an affair at the spa or maybe she's at a spa with her husband now. Maybe not. This through-the-looking-glass movie that tries to eliminate all time and space constraints is as puzzling as a chess problem and slippery as a dream.
D: Alain Resnais. A: Delphine Seyrig, Giorgio Albertazzi, Sacha Pitoëff.

Paris Belongs to Us
(1960) 140m. B&W. Subtitled. **A**
An erratic, odd-angled look at a theater company as it prepares for a production of *Pericles*. With its high contrast blacks and whites, a jazzily mobile camera, and constant play between reality and illusion, this movie is really about making movies.
D: Jacques Rivette. A: Betty Schneider, Gianni Esposito, Daniel Crohem.

La Religieuse
(1965) 140m. Subtitled. **B–**
A beautiful young woman is forced into a convent in eighteenth-century Paris. Severe and constricting as the nuns' habits, this examination of religious vocation and free will has little action and lots of talking. Not light fare.
D: Jacques Rivette. A: Liselotte Pulver, Anna Karina, Micheline Presle.

Cleo from 5 to 7
(1962) 90m. B&W. Subtitled. **C+**
These two hours in the life of a shallow Parisian singer while she waits for a medical diagnosis could change her life. In fact they do, since she spends the length of the film reevaluating her life. Disjointed, talky, and self-consciously arty.
D: Agnés Varda. A: Corinne Marchand, Dorothée Blanck, Antoine Bourseiller.

1960s Dramas

Most of these colorful trendy films were popular on both sides of the Atlantic. With their picture-postcard settings and impossibly romantic plots, these shamelessly entertaining films—excepting the classic *Black Orpheus*—are French-lite for audiences that enjoyed the fast modern style of the New Wave films but were put off by the challenging, in-your-face content.

Black Orpheus
(1959) 98m. Subtitled. **A**
The Greek myth of Orpheus and his tragic love for Eurydice is updated to a streetcar conductor and a country girl in Rio de Janeiro during Carnival. This exuberant mix of music, image, and story captures the haunting mystery of the original.
D: Marcel Camus. A: Breno Mello, Marpessa Dawn, Lea Garcia.

Lola
(1960) 90m. Subtitled. **B**
A cabaret singer carries on an affair with a longtime sweetheart as she awaits the return of the man who left her with child seven years earlier. With camera flourishes and the lighthearted and folkloric staginess of an adult puppet show come to life, this really does feel like a musical without music.
D: Jacques Demy. A: Anouk Aimée, Marc Michel, Jacques Harden.

The Umbrellas of Cherbourg
(1964) 91m. Subtitled. **B**
An ordinary and bittersweet love story unfolds with the characters singing instead of talking in Jacques Demy's experimental nonmusical musical. The florid visual style, combined with the

small intimate story, gives an almost operatic majesty, and makes this one of the more unusual romantic films.
D: Jacques Demy. A: Catherine Deneuve, Nino Castelnuovo, Marc Michel.

Viva Maria!
(1965) 125m. **C+**

Two beautiful women get mixed up with the forces of Poncho Villa while performing with a carnival in Mexico in the late 1800s. A fetching Bardot and game Moreau are the only reason to watch this fluffy period comedy that flounders under the weight of nonsensical slapstick.
D: Louis Malle. A: Jeanne Moreau, Brigitte Bardot, George Hamilton.

King of Hearts
(1966) 110m. Subtitled. **B**

During World War I a Scottish soldier enters an abandoned town and discovers that it's being run by the lunatic asylum inmates left behind. He's crowned king, meets a lovely tightrope walker, and finds a piece of sanity in this sweet fantasy that grows tiresome when it works to make statements about a messed-up world.
D: Philippe de Broca. A: Alan Bates, Genevieve Bujold, Jean-Claude Brialy.

A Man and a Woman
(1966) 102m. B&W. Subtitled. **B+** 🏛

A race car driver and a script girl share some long drives and idyllic walks on the beach in their tentative courtship after the deaths of their respective spouses. A wonderful 60s trendy timepiece with Aimee and Trintignant looking like the ultimate stylishly attractive Eurocouple.
D: Claude Lelouch. A: Anouk Aimée, Jean-Louis Trintignant, Pierre Barouh.

Sautet

Midlife crossroads and crises among the bourgeoisie is the territory mined in these films by director Claude Sautet. The better ones are adult dramas that deal with their subject matter with subtlety, grace, and humor; even the ones that veer toward melodrama are saved by superior acting by some of France's biggest stars.

Les Choses de la Vie
(1970) 90m. Subtitled. **B**

Sometimes accidents happen at a fortuitous time: A middle-aged architect gets in a car wreck on his way to making a decision between his wife and his mistress. Seriously injured, he lies in a hospital bed reviewing life with sensitivity and not a little selfishness in this romantic comedy-drama.
D: Claude Sautet. A: Romy Schneider, Michel Piccoli, Lea Masari.

Cesar and Rosalie
(1972) 104m. Subtitled. **B+**

Think of *Jules and Jim* from the perspective of Catherine, their mutual girlfriend, and you'll get a good idea of this exploration of a woman's relationship with two men over the course of several years. Despite its melancholy theme, this has a light touch and the appeal of a constantly shifting triangle.
D: Claude Sautet. A: Romy Schneider, Yves Montand, Sami Frey.

Vincent, François, Paul et les Autres
(1974) 118m. Subtitled. **B+** 🎞

A group of longtime buddies enjoy the bonds of friendship as they weather professional and personal crises. Melancholy, rueful, and mildly mocking, the characters—especially Montand—and their camaraderie are so engaging this succeeds in making midlife crises almost glamorous.
D: Claude Sautet. A: Yves Montand, Michel Piccoli, Serge Reggiani.

A Simple Story
(1978) 110m. Subtitled. **A−**

An industrial designer finds herself pregnant at 39 and decides to abort. Meanwhile there are crises galore with her teenage son, ex-husband, friends, and lover. A slow-paced, respectful, and often insightful character study made compelling by Schneider.
D: Claude Sautet. A: Romy Schneider, Bruno Cremer, Claude Brasseur.

Blier

These are scathing and satiric looks at the bourgeoisie as seen through some of the coolest eyes in cinema, Bertrand Blier. The characters have their own reasons for performing acts of murder, rape, prostitution, seduction of underage youths, or even plain old adultery. While the films are often surrealistic, and sometimes alienating, they all contain a romantic streak a mile wide that will keep you rooting for the offbeat characters.

Going Places
(1974) 117m. Subtitled. **B−**

Two libertines go on a romp, stealing from and seducing young women for no particular reason. This Rabelaisian buddy road film about a pair of irredeemable louts who blow with the scent of a woman is occasionally funny and sometimes just offensive.
D: Bertrand Blier. A: Gerard Depardieu, Patrick Dewaere, Miou-Miou.

Get Out Your Handkerchiefs
(1978) 109m. Subtitled. **B** 🎞

A desperate husband, afraid

that he's not satisfying his unhappy wife, supplies her with another lover. The men become fast friends, both beguiled by the charming Laure, but this sexual chess game grows a little icy by the second hour.
D: Bertrand Blier. A: Gerard Depardieu, Patrick Dewaere, Carole Laure.

Buffet Froid
(1979) 95m. Subtitled. **B–**
A neurotic man can't get anybody to believe his dreams are responsible for several recent murders. This black surrealistic comedy about life in the big cold city is devilishly funny, but is performed with the stylized ritual of an avant garde theater piece that may try the patience of some.
D: Bertrand Blier. A: Gerard Depardieu, Bernard Blier, Jean Carmet.

Beau Pere
(1982) 120m. Subtitled. **B+**
After the death of his wife, a middle-aged man lets himself be seduced by his 14-year-old stepdaughter. This is less of a tale of sexual longing than a sweet interlude of forbidden love. The touchy subject matter is handled with care; the love scenes are more organic than salacious.
D: Bertrand Blier. A: Patrick Dewaere, Ariel Besse, Maurice Ronet.

My Best Friend's Girl
(1984) 99m. Subtitled. **B+**
Boy falls in love with girl and has her move in. Girl meets best friend, and best friend becomes obsessed with girl . . . you get the picture. Love is truly blind in the idyllic Swiss Alps as two nerdy buddies are willing to do anything for the woman they love except betray each other's trust. A beguiling comedy.
D: Bertrand Blier. A: Coluche, Isabelle Huppert, Thierry Lhermitte.

Menage
(1986) 84m. Subtitled.
B+
A dazzlingly voluble homosexual thief hooks up with a down-at-the-heels married couple, and teaches them about cat burglary and a thing or two about l'amour fou. This biting and verbose sex farce writes its own rules, and you won't forget how this ménage à trois works things out.
D: Bertrand Blier. A: Gerard Depardieu, Miou-Miou, Michel Blanc.

Too Beautiful for You
(1990) 91m. Subtitled. **B+**
A car salesman, happily married to a beautiful young wife, carries on a torrid affair with a plain, middle-aged woman. This ironic, sweet-tempered sex-comedy is boosted by a sympathetic portrait of the wronged wife who can't bring herself to understand her husband's strange obsession.
D: Bertrand Blier. A: Gerard Depardieu, Carole Bouquet, Josaine Bolasko.

Mercie la Vie
(1991) 117m. Subtitled. **B**
A sleazy gynecologist convinces the teenage girl he's treating for VD to go on a sexual odyssey in order to provide him with new patients. It's easy to get lost watching the young lady and her feisty friend joyfully infect their lovers in this sometimes bewildering film that leaps between the Occupation and the present day.
D: Bertrand Blier. A: Charlotte Gainsbourg, Anouk Grinberg, Gerard Depardieu.

Buñuel

Luis Buñuel's later films reprise his favorite themes—attacks on middle-class morals, the Catholic Church, and other institutions, with dark humor, surrealistic elements, and a deft touch. As usual, his characters tend to be gripped by odd fetishisms and obsessions, centered of course on sex.

The Diary of a Chambermaid
(1964) 95m. B&W. Subtitled. **A–**
A perverse, luxury-loving Normandy family hires a young woman as their maid in the late 1930s. Every member has their hang-up—racism, foot fetishism—which they try to satisfy by using each other and the servants. A darkly amusing film with perfect pitch.
D: Luis Buñuel. A: Jeanne Moreau, Michel Piccoli, Georges Geret.

Belle de Jour
(1967) 100m. Subtitled.
A
A doctor's frigid wife finally acts out her masochistic daydreams by working at a Parisian brothel. Virginal Deneuve flowers as she's debased by an increasingly sorry lot of lovers in this deceptively quiet study peppered with a surrealistic undercurrent and some blissfully dark humor.
D: Luis Buñuel. A: Catherine Deneuve, Jean Sorel, Michel Piccoli.

The Milky Way
(1970) 102m. Subtitled. **B**
On a pilgrimage across France to Spain, two men run into all sorts of odd characters who share their preoccupation: How do we know God exists? A very enjoyable fablelike journey, with scenes set in unexplained different time periods that heighten their comic effect.
D: Luis Buñuel. A: Delphine Seyrig, Paul Frankeur, Laurent Terzieff.

The Discreet Charm of the Bourgeoisie
(1972) 100m. Subtitled.
A
A pointed comedy about a group of chic brittle bourgeoisie who sit down to dinner over and over and over, but are always interrupted before they can eat. An outrageously dark tease, and a clever connection for otherwise unrelated surrealist vignettes.
D: Luis Buñuel. A: Delphine Seyrig, Fernando Rey, Stephane Audran.

The Phantom of Liberty
(1974) 104m. Subtitled. **B**
Linked anecdotes show an ironic view of various middle-class inhibitions. Typical for its outrageousness is the scene in which people defecate together, but leave the room to eat. Mannered set pieces make it a punchy delight.
D: Luis Buñuel. A: Jean-Claude Brialy, Michel Piccoli, Monica Vitti.

That Obscure Object of Desire
(1974) 100m. Subtitled/Dubbed. **A–**
An aging count is seduced

and tortured by a younger woman with a madonna/whore personality. An ironic and darkly amusing take on an old theme, with a little confusion thrown in by having two different actresses playing the temptress.
D: Luis Buñuel. A: Fernando Rey, Angela Molina, Carole Bouquet.

1960s–1970s Thrillers

Influenced by Clouzot's *The Wages of Fear* and *Diabolique*, these films are cynical to the point of misanthropy. The two political thrillers by Costa-Gavras are socialistic sirens blaring out warnings against fascistic superpowers; the psychological ones owe much to Hitchcock, with a healthy dose of existentialistic poison.

The Sleeping Car Murders

(1966) 92m. B&W. Subtitled. **B+**

A dead woman is found on the sleeping car of a train, and soon other bodies start turning up for a wily detective to investigate in this très chic thriller. Gray Paris never looked so full of menacing ambiance.
D: Constantin Costa-Gavras. A: Simone Signoret, Yves Montand, Pierre Mondy.

Diabolically Yours

(1967) 94m. Subtitled. **B**

A man wakes up from a coma and doesn't recognize his wife, friends, or expensive home, and it soon becomes possible that his past life is a delusion. A twisty little tale of deception that relies on cinematic tricks (of varying quality) to throw the viewer for a loop.
D: Julien Duvivier. A: Alain Delon, Senta Berger, Peter Mosbacher.

This Man Must Die

(1969) 112m. **A–**

A bereaved man goes on the trail of the hit-and-run driver who killed his son. A dark portrait of obsessive pursuit and how hatred erodes the soul.
D: Claude Chabrol. A: Michel Duchaussoy, Jean Yanne, Caroline Cellier.

Z

(1969) 127m. Dubbed. **A–**

A presidential candidate in Greece is assassinated by a terrorist group and the investigation leads to an elaborate right-wing cover-up. This political thriller is a cautionary tale of corruption that rattles on like a demonic teletype ticker.
D: Constantin Costa-Gavras. A: Yves Montand, Jean-Louis Trintignant, Irene Papas.

State of Siege

(1973) 120m. Dubbed. **A–**

An American military advisor is kidnapped by guerrillas in Uruguay to protest U.S. aid to fascist governments. This tense engrossing thriller often seems like a springboard for a denouncement against American foul play in Latin America, but it still remains quite a ride.
D: Constantin Costa-Gavras. A: Yves Montand, Renato Salvatori, Jacques Weber.

Wedding in Blood

(1973) 98m. Subtitled. **A–**

Two frustrated lovers set out to murder their spouses, but soon are in danger of falling into a trap. Hitchcock and *The Postman Always Rings Twice* are evident in this graceful, slightly depraved thriller that is also a stinging commentary of the bored French upper class.
D: Claude Chabrol. A: Michel Piccoli, Stephane Audran, Claude Pieplu.

Investigation

(1979) 116m. Subtitled. **B**

A detective is called in to investigate a village proprietor who has married his pregnant girlfriend after his wife is killed. This low-key whodunit hangs its hat on Lanoux's charm and the zesty flavor of the town characters.
D: Etienne Perier. A: Victor Lanoux, Jean Carmet, Michel Robin.

Truffaut (1970s–1980s)

In his later films, François Truffaut continues to charm and entertain us with even more ambitious stories of difficult and engrossing characters. Whether a nineteenth-century historical drama or a contemporary tale of suburban dwellers, the viewer is treated to unexpected stories made with the élan and grace of a master filmmaker.

The Wild Child

(1970) 86m. B&W. **A–**

An eighteenth-century boy, abandoned and living wildly in a forest, is patiently studied and tamed by a gentleman scientist. A lovely and startling sepia-toned, documentary-style drama and compassionate examination of the power of language and teaching.
D: François Truffaut. A: François Truffaut, Jean-Pierre Cargol.

Two English Girls

(1972) 130m. **A**

Post-World War I drama of a young French writer's long-term involvement with two English sisters. The elegance of narration and look, and subtlety of gesture make this film resemble a nineteenth-century novel.
D: François Truffaut. A: Jean-Pierre Leaud, Kika Markham, Stacy Tendeter.

Day for Night

(1973) 116m. **A–**

A valentine to the humorous and less than glamorous aspects involved in the magic of moviemaking. Resembling a lighthearted documentary, the film reveals the travails and vanities of the director, crew, and actors as

they put together a romantic comedy.
D: François Truffaut. A: Jacqueline Bisset, François Truffaut, Jean-Pierre Leaud.

The Story of Adele H
(1975) 97m. **B–**

Neglected by her famous father, Adele Hugo retreats into an obsessive and unrequited passion for an English soldier in Nova Scotia. This slow-moving, nineteenth-century period drama has lovely costumes and scenery and a searing Adjani, but watching her descent into madness can be uncomfortable.
D: François Truffaut. A: Isabelle Adjani, Reubin Dorey, François Truffaut.

Small Change
(1976) 104m. **B–**

An almost-documentary examination of children's lives in a small French town in the 1970s. Sweet, tender, and gentle with little plot and no trace of sentimentality.
D: François Truffaut. A: Eva Truffaut, Tania Torrens.

The Man Who Loved Women
(1977) 119m. **B–**

A man is so fond of women—and they of him—that he decides to write his memoirs, detailing the extraordinary lengths to which he'll go to find a bit of skirt. Cheerful, flirty, and trivial.
D: François Truffaut. A: Charles Denner, Brigitte Fossey, Genevieve Fontanel.

The Green Room
(1978) 95m. **C**

Having survived World War I and the death of his wife, a man finds himself more drawn to the dead than the living. This cold little drama's impeccable taste and manners keeps the viewer at arm's length.
D: François Truffaut. A: François Truffaut, Nathalie Baye, Antoine Vitez.

Love on the Run
(1979) 90m. **B–**

Truffaut's alter ego Antoine Doinel matured on film through Truffaut's career. In this final chapter he divorces his wife and searches for a new love as we and he review his life through clips from earlier films. Best for Truffaut fans.
D: François Truffaut. A: Jean-Pierre Leaud, Marie-France Pisier.

The Last Metro
(1980) 135m. **A**

A theater troupe continues to put on the show in Nazi-occupied Paris after the Jewish director flees and his actress wife takes over. Complications arise when a new leading man joins the company. Elegant story of love, survival, and concealment.
D: François Truffaut. A: Catherine Deneuve, Gerard Depardieu, Jean Poiret.

The Woman Next Door
(1981) 106m. **A**

A happily married suburbanite enjoys a well-ordered life until his ex-lover moves next door. Compelling and unexpected drama of passion.
D: François Truffaut. A: Gerard Depardieu, Fanny Ardant, Henri Garcin.

Confidentially Yours
(1983) 110m. B&W. **A**

A real estate agent accused of murder lays low while his cantankerous secretary finds the real culprit. This Hitchcock mystery-comedy-cum-film noir is breezy, stylized, and humorous.
D: François Truffaut. A: Jean-Louis Trintignant, Fanny Ardant, Philippe Laudenbach.

Male Caper Comedies

Buddy and caper comedies seem to be as popular in France as they are in America, maybe more so. Many of these characters are bumbling little guys who try to do right, but never quite get the hang of what it takes; even the sophisticated heroes are engaged in one slapstick episode after another. If this sounds like a Jerry Lewis movie, you're not far off.

The Tall Blond Man with One Black Shoe
(1972) 90m. Subtitled. **B+**

A shy and clumsy violinist bumbles his way into a spy ring in this very funny farce in the slapstick tradition of Inspector Clouseau. No classic, but the visual gags are hilarious.
D: Yves Robert. A: Pierre Richard, Bernard Blier, Jean Rochefort.

Robert et Robert
(1978) 105m. Subtitled. **B**

Two lonely men suffer the ultimate humiliation when their prospective mates from a matrimonial agency run out on them. Soon the losers strike up a friendship and begin to build up each other's damaged egos in this light and zesty shy guy tale.
D: Claude Lelouch. A: Charles Denner, Jacques Villeret, Jean-Claude Briarly.

Le Cavaleur
(1980) 106m. Subtitled. **C+**

A concert pianist begins to weary of spreading his affections between wife, kids, ex-wife, mistress, and agent and wonders if he should return to his old carefree existence. This midlife crisis romp quickly gets irritating as everyone dotes endlessly on the rather hollow Peter Pan-esque hero.
D: Philippe de Broca. A: Jean Rochefort, Annie Girardot, Danielle Darrieux.

Le Chevre
(1981) 91m. Subtitled. **C**

A private eye is forced to hire a clumsy amateur detective hoping that the man's bumbling ways will help him crack a case. The Mutt and Jeff pairing of the two dim-witted gumshoes is cute, but Richard's repeated pratfalls are tedious in this strained slapstick adventure.
D: Francis Veber. A: Pierre Richard, Gerard Depardieu, Michel Robin.

Les Comperes
(1984) 90m. Subtitled. **C+**

When a teenage boy runs away, his mother tells two of her ex-lovers that they are the boy's father. The proud new daddies head off to the Riviera where they deal with gangsters, motorcycle gangs, and the possibility that the other might be the real father. A little too moronic to sustain the humor.
D: Francis Veber. A: Pierre Richard, Gerard Depardieu, Anny Duperey.

My New Partner
(1984) 106m. Subtitled. **B+**

A hard-boiled, gleefully corrupt cop, with a taste for wine, women, and the horse track, gets teamed with an ambitious, by-the-book rookie. An amusing buddy-cop caper thanks to the

film's charming cynicism, with a dumb-looking but hunky Lhermitte and a hilariously idiosyncratic Noiret policing the streets of Paris.
D: Claude Zidi. A: Philippe Noiret, Thierry Lhermitte, Regine.

Three Men and a Cradle
(1985) 106m. Subtitled.
B–
Chaos rules the apartment as three bachelors find their swinging lifestyles curtailed when forced to take care of a baby left by one of their ex-girlfriends. A warmhearted and manipulative farce with plenty of jokes about diaper changing and 4 A.M. feedings.
D: Coline Serreau. A: Roland Giraud, Michel Boujenah, Andre Dussolier.

Sex Farces

These sex comedies bear a strong resemblance to the male buddy capers with their slapstick and characters who tend to be average sweet-tempered, middle-aged guys just trying to have a good time.

Le Sex Shop
(1973) 90m. Subtitled. **B–**
A nerdy bookstore owner's marriage and business are both failing until he converts the shop to a porno salon. Picture a Jerry Lewis film with sex toys and kinky erotica, and that's about what you get in this cute and coy comedy.
D: Claude Berri. A: Claude Berri, Juliet Berto, Nathalie Delon.

Cousin, Cousine
(1975) 95m. Subtitled.
B+
Two married cousins embark on an affair to the surprise of their respective unfaithful spouses and the extended family. This lighthearted romp progresses through a series of family gatherings—weddings, funerals, and baptisms—to reveal the course the lovers take and everyone's reaction to it.
D: Jean-Charles Tacchella. A: Marie-Christine Barrault, Victor Lanoux, Guy Marchand.

Pardon Mon Affaire
(1976) 105m. Subtitled. **B**
A happily married ad exec is struck by the arrow of love (or lust) for a glamorous model, and will move heaven and earth to set up a chance meeting. Basically, a male bonding comedy as the hero and his three buddies engage in some funny slapstick situations. Funnier than most.
D: Yves Robert. A: Jean Rochefort, Claude Brasseur, Anny Duperey.

La Cage Aux Folles
(1978) 91m. Subtitled.
B
A young man tells his nightclub owner father that the stuffy parents of his fiancée want to meet the future in-laws. Trouble is, dad is gay and lives with a drag queen. A brassy entry that relishes its own outrageousness while taking pokes at the bourgeoisie and the flamboyant gay subculture.
D: Edouard Molinaro. A: Ugo Tognazzi, Michel Serrault, Michel Galabru.

The Gift
(1982) 106m. Subtitled. **C**
A shy man is given a high-class call girl as a retirement gift but she must seduce him without letting him know who she is. This broadly played sex farce lacks the irony to give it bite, and the plodding attempts at seduction are unerotic and almost painful to watch.
D: Michel Lang. A: Pierre Mondy, Claudia Cardinale, Clio Goldsmith.

One Woman or Two
(1985) 97m. Subtitled. **C+**
An anthropologist thinks that an opportunistic female ad exec is the philanthropist who would fund his research. This chaotic comedy of errors, packaged like a mainstream American romantic comedy, falls flat fast and even the stars fail to ignite any sparks. A real oddity.
D: Daniel Vigne. A: Gerard Depardieu, Sigourney Weaver, Dr. Ruth Westheimer.

Land Epics

Marcel Pagnol's novels and memoirs that take place in southern France are often the basis for these nostalgic stories of the strong-willed, no-nonsense people who lived there during the turn of the century. As large, almost epic-sized celebrations of the land, these films reveal the rhythms of the seasons and the spectacular glory of the ragged mountains, the sun-washed colors, and the quickening of life. As intelligent dramas of the poor and middle-class families whose lives center around the land, their stories are simple, direct, and leisurely.

The Horse of Pride
(1980) 118m. Subtitled. **C**
A man tells the story of his parents' marriage, his birth, and their life in Brittany at the turn of the century. Vivid details of Breton traditions, music, and dress is informative, but the pace is slow and the story lacks warmth or real interest.
D: Claude Chabrol. A: Jacques Dufilho, Bernadette de la Sache.

A Sunday in the Country
(1984) 94m. Subtitled.
B–
An older unsuccessful impressionist painter is visited by his children, each of whom has been a disappointment to him. Shot in a blurred impressionist style, this film dotes lovingly on the landscape, leaving its fairly dull characters behind.
D: Bertrand Tavernier. A: Louis Decreuz, Sabine Azema.

Jean de Florette
(1987) 122m. Subtitled.
A

A Paris greenhorn inherits a farm in Provence just after World War I, and his rough-hewn neighbors scheme to acquire his land for its natural spring. This straightforward tale of greed and the forces of nature has the intricacy of a nineteenth-century novel and looks like an impressionistic painting.
D: Claude Berri. A: Gerard Depardieu, Yves Montand, Daniel Auteuil.

Manon of the Spring
(1987) 113m. Subtitled.
A

Jean de Florette's daughter is now fully grown and a creature of the Provencal countryside who plots revenge against her neighbors. Detailed and sometimes slow-moving, it repeats the soft colors and direct narrative of its predecessor.
D: Claude Berri. A: Emmanuelle Beart, Yves Montand, Daniel Auteuil.

My Father's Glory
(1991) 110m. Subtitled.
A

A turn-of-the-century schoolteacher's family from a town in Provence spend their summer vacation in the surrounding countryside. The young son's adventures are entertaining, and the film conveys the mystery and imposing presence of the land.
D: Yves Robert. A: Julien Ciamaca, Philippe Caubere.

My Mother's Castle
(1991) 98m. Subtitled.
A–

The sequel to *My Father's Glory* continues the family's adventures in the art of living in Provence. This golden-hued film is wonderful armchair time travel and while it may be a bit sentimental it leaves you feeling renewed.
D: Yves Robert. A: Philippe Caubere, Nathalie Roussel.

World War II Dramas

These elegantly constructed psychological studies focus on reactions to the Occupation and Nazism on an individual basis, as the moral complexities, the "banality of evil," and the heroics of the protagonists are examined with a microscopic intensity.

The Conformist
(1971) 115m. Subtitled.
A

A young Italian gets money, acceptance, and a new life when he casts his lot with the fascists but there's a price to pay. Opulent and chilling, this drama of decadence, murder, and all types of seduction contains one powerful and stunningly photographed scene after another.
D: Bernardo Bertolucci. A: Jean-Louis Trintignant, Dominique Sanda, Stefania Sandrelli.

Mr. Klein
(1976) 123m. Subtitled.
A–

The unscrupulous art dealer who buys from Jews trying to get safe passage out of France finds the tables turned when he is falsely accused of being a Jew. A carefully crafted, dead-eyed look at some of the contributions to the "final solution," with a Kafkaesque quality as the man realizes he is fighting an unseen omnipotent bureaucracy.
D: Joseph Losey. A: Alain Delon, Jeanne Moreau, Juliet Berto.

La Passante
(1983) 106m. Subtitled.
B–

A solidarity leader on trial for murder takes the witness stand to relate his childhood spent with two freedom fighters in 1930s Berlin and Paris. The courtroom drama part is gloomy, but the flashbacks to prewar France are compelling, with a glamorous Schneider in a dual role.
D: Jaques Rouffio. A: Romy Schneider, Michel Piccoli, Maria Schell.

A Love in Germany
(1984) 110m. Subtitled.
B–

When a German storekeeper hires a young Polish POW after her husband is off at war, their friendship and romance enrages her neighbors to the point of violence. This illicit love story set in an idyllic village soon turns into a treatise against mob rule. Slow but hang on for the finale.
D: Andrzej Wajda. A: Hanna Schygulla, Marie-Christine Barrault, Armin Mueller-Stahl.

Au Revoir les Enfants
(1987) 104m. Subtitled.
B+

The students at a boys' Catholic school are surprised when Jewish children are secretly admitted, but are soon helping to hide their new friends from frequent Nazi searches. A lyrical, at times heavy-handed, coming-of-age tale with beautifully nuanced portraits of the children.
D: Louis Malle. A: Gaspard Manesse, Raphael Fejto, Francine Racette.

Rohmer

Either you love Eric Rohmer's films or they drive you crazy. His deadpan social comedies record current French society and manners with a delightful immediacy, verve, and a no-apologies intellectual bent. They also happen to be two-hour talk fests. The characters—usually young, neurotic, bourgeois women—continually take their metaphysical pulses, proclaim their theories on love and life, and then do something completely contrary. These films are like artfully edited documentaries—nothing spectacular happens, but the straightforward and impassive camera reveals some exquisite and fleeting moments of the human comedy.

My Night at Maud's
(1969) 111m. Subtitled. **A**

A divorcée invites an out-of-town man to stay the night, neglecting to mention her one-bed studio apartment. Many long conversations on morality, Catholicism, and temptation ensue. Witty and intellectual.
D: Eric Rohmer. A: Jean-Louis Trintignant, Françoise Fabian.

Claire's Knee
(1971) 106m. Subtitled.
A

On the verge of marrying, a young man stays in Lake Geneva where he becomes infatuated with the knee of a woman he doesn't even like. An appealing film that manages a subtle and complex story with a light entertaining touch.
D: Eric Rohmer. A: Jean-Claude Brialy, Michele Montel, Aurora Comu.

Chloe in the Afternoon
(1972) 97m. Subtitled.
A

A bourgeois man's obsession with a free-spirited, slightly neurotic young woman threatens his marriage—and his sense of himself. An amusing look at temptation and what happens when fantasies come true.
D: Eric Rohmer. A: Bernard Verley, Zouzou, Françoise Verley.

Le Beau Mariage
(1982) 100m. Subtitled.
B+

A dogged young woman decides it's time to marry, and anybody will do. Unfortunately she fixates on a man with exactly the opposite idea. Farcical treatment of relations between the sexes, with a little humiliation thrown in for good measure.
D: Eric Rohmer. A: Beatrice Romand, Andrea Dussolier, Feodor Atkine.

Pauline at the Beach
(1983) 94m. Subtitled.
A

A teenage girl spends the summer at the seaside with her older worldly Parisian cousin. They constantly exchange ideals about how love defines identity and vice versa, with the men they're attracted to. Humorous and wordy exploration of sophisticated and innocent summer romances between attractive, self-absorbed people.
D: Eric Rohmer. A: Amanda Langlet, Feodore Atkine, Arielle Dombasle.

Full Moon in Paris
(1984) 101m. Subtitled.
B+

Unrecognized yearnings prompt a young woman to set up a pied-à-terre in Paris, independent of her live-in lover in the suburbs. Light ironic look at the unconscious and self-conscious fumblings of young people in a perpetual state of romantic flux.
D: Eric Rohmer. A: Pascale Ogier, Fabrice Luchini, Tcheky Karyo.

Four Adventures of Reinette and Mirabelle
(1986) 95m. Subtitled. **B**

Two young women, one a sophisticated Parisian and the other a talented and provincial painter, share a flat in Paris. A series of four linked stories that show, with typical Rohmer grace, the characters' idealism and the trouble it brings them.
D. Eric Rohmer. A: Joelle Miquel, Jessica Forde, Philippe Laudenbach.

Summer
(1986) 98m. Subtitled. **B–**

A princess and the pea story of a neurotic young Parisian woman who finds herself with a month of vacation and no one to spend it with. Her fussiness is both funny and exasperating as she makes her various attempts at fun seem like the afflictions of Job. The end more than justifies the sometimes slow fare.
D: Eric Rohmer. A: Marie Riviere, Lisa Heredia, Vincent Gauthier.

Boyfriends and Girlfriends
(1987) 102m. Subtitled.
A–

Two young women—complete opposites—strike up a friendship in a Paris suburb. When the wilder of the two leaves her steady boyfriend behind to vacation with a mystery man, her mousier friend falls for him. A sweet romantic French dance of courtship and mispaired couples.
D: Eric Rohmer. A: Emmanuelle Chaulet, Sophie Renoir, François-Eric Gendron.

A Tale of Springtime
(1990) 107m. Subtitled. **A**

Two young women, a concert pianist and a high school philosophy teacher, become friends. The pianist tries to fix her new friend up with her father since she detests his girlfriend. A typical Rohmer power/love/will study, with delightful performances and light touch.
D: Eric Rohmer. A: Anna Teyssedre, Eloise Bennett, Hugues Quester.

Historical and Literary Epics

Like the Merchant-Ivory costume dramas, most of these films are beautiful, sweeping, and lengthy depictions of historical characters and eras. Unlike their British counterparts, the earthy characters storm around proclaiming their passion, their politics, or their creative needs with a flourish and more than a dash of high drama.

The Judge and the Assassin
(1976) 130m. Subtitled.
A–

A judge goes after a serial murderer in nineteenth-century France in this psychologically complex and utterly engaging drama. Despite the period costumes, this is modern as can be. Is the killer insane or conscious of his actions? Moves at a good clip and features yet another great performance by Noiret.
D: Bertrand Tavernier. A: Isabelle Huppert, Philippe Noiret, Michel Galabru.

Danton
(1982) 136m. Subtitled.
A–

After the French Revolution came the Reign of Terror, with chaos, food shortages, and to-the-death power struggles among the new government. This has the rousing polemics of a courtroom drama, the intrigue of a political thriller, and the intensity of a drama about two tragically flawed men, Danton and Robespierre.
D: Andrzej Wajda. A: Gerard Depardieu, Patrice Chereau, Wojciech Pszoniak.

The Return of Martin Guerre

(1982) 111m. Subtitled.
A

A surly peasant disappears for seven years and when he returns is transformed into a loving husband, father, and member of the community. Is he the same man? While this depicts sixteenth-century peasant life in every grungy detail, the story is beautifully romantic and exquisitely acted.
D: Daniel Vigne. A: Gerard Depardieu, Nathalie Baye, Roger Planchon.

La Nuit de Varennes

(1983) 133m. Subtitled.
B–

Louis XVI flees Paris during the revolution in 1791; our on-the-spot reporters include Casanova, Restif de Bretonne, and Tom Paine. Unfortunately all they do is gab interminably, with only an occasional witticism, and a little bit of sex and nudity to keep you from drifting off.
D: Ettore Scola. A: Marcello Mastroianni, Harvey Keitel, Hanna Schygulla.

Therese

(1986) 90m. Subtitled. **A–**

Based on the story of St. Theresa Lisieux, this begins with her decision to enter a convent at 15, where she lives for eight years and then dies of tuberculosis. Her quasiromantic, highly imaginative attachment to Christ is shown through delicate painterly filming and sumptuous period detail.
D: Alain Cavalier. A: Catherine Mouchet, Helene Alexandridis, Sylvie Halbaut.

Beatrice (aka The Passion of Beatrice)

(1987) 132m. Subtitled.
C–

A young woman awaits her idolized father and brother's return from the Hundred Years War, only to find they're nothing like what she expects. Incest, brutality, humiliation—this is not for the squeamish and the pace is nearly real-time slow. For Tavernier fans and those interested in this historical period only.
D: Bertrand Tavernier. A: Julie Delpy, Nils Tavernier, Bernard Pierre Donadieu.

Under the Sun of Satan

(1987) 98m. Subtitled. **B+**

A nineteenth-century priest's crisis of faith is exacerbated by his encounter with a beautiful pregnant woman who has inadvertently shot her lover. The brooding tone, glacial pace, and intelligent but very talky treatment of this smaller-scaled drama make it more of interest to those who can identify with a philosophical/identity crisis that's tinged with religion.
D: Maurice Pialat. A: Gerard Depardieu, Maurice Pialat, Sandrine Bonnaire.

The Story of Women

(1988) 111m. Subtitled. **A**

This traces the life of the last woman to be guillotined in France: a successful abortionist under the Vichy regime. Huppert captures the defiance, independence, and sheer gaul that irked her countrymen. Intense, well-paced, and intelligent.
D: Claude Chabrol. A: Isabelle Huppert, François Cluzet, Marie Trintignant.

Life and Nothing But

(1989) 135m. Subtitled. **A**

A schoolmistress searches for the body of her lover, and an aristocrat for her husband after World War I. Both are helped by the officer involved with unknown dead soldiers. A stylish, sensitive, and humorous tale that captures the destruction of war and lives irrevocably changed.
D: Bertrand Tavernier. A: Philippe Noiret, Sabine Azema, Pascale Vignal.

Camille Claudel

(1990) 149m. Subtitled.
B+

The biography of the nineteenth-century sculptress who struggled with her art and its acceptance, carrying on a stormy relationship with August Rodin. Fraught with passion that verges on madness and overwrought emoting, this drama still remains remote.
D: Bruno Nuytten. A: Isabelle Adjani, Gerard Depardieu, Laurent Greville.

Cyrano de Bergerac

(1990) 135m. Subtitled.
A–

Possessed of an unattractive nose, a poetic talent, and the courage of an army of heroes, Cyrano helps an attractive dolt woo the woman of their dreams. With the romance, action, and panache of a Musketeers swashbuckler, this offers period details that are almost another film, a perfect cast, and a death scene to end all death scenes.
D: Jean-Paul Rappeneau. A: Gerard Depardieu, Anne Brochet, Vincent Perez.

La Belle Noiseuse

(1991) 240m. Subtitled. **A**

A painter gets inspired to work on his masterpiece when a young woman comes to visit. This will dispel any romantic notions about painters painting: It is literally four hours showing the tedious process and fleeting rewards of creating a work of art.
D: Jacques Rivette. A: Michel Piccoli, Jane Birkin, Emmanuelle Beart.

Madame Bovary

(1991) 131m. Subtitled. **C**

Emma Bovary has trouble with boredom and, when marriage doesn't solve it, she resorts to an affair or two. This is lovely to look at, but the film seems to be telling you a story of passion instead of showing it. Only the steely coldness of Emma really comes through.
D: Claude Chabrol. A: Isabelle Huppert, Jean-François Balmer, Christophe Malavoy.

Van Gogh

(1991) 158m. Subtitled. **C**

This s-l-o-w-l-y portrays the last years of Van Gogh's life by focusing on the ordinariness of his life and how he converted it to art. Too humorless and self-important.
D: Maurice Pialat. A: Jacques Dutronc, Bernard Le Coq, Gerard Sety.

Indochine

(1992) 155m. Subtitled.
B

A Frenchwoman runs a rubber plantation in Vietnam during the waning days of French colonial rule. The trouble starts when the Vietnamese girl she has raised is now a young woman with a mind of her own. Deneuve and the historical background make this sophisticated and elegant melodrama worth a look.
D: Regis Wargnier. A: Catherine Deneuve, Vincent Perez, Linh Dan Pham.

Uranus

(1992) 100m. Subtitled. **A**

At the end of the war, a small town is riven by three factions: those who collaborated with the Nazis, those who resisted, and those who tried to survive without taking a stand. This series of linked vignettes makes up for the weak plot with vivid characters who embody all the indecisions, deadly sins, and fleeting heroism of people under siege.
D: Claude Berri. A: Gerard Depardieu, Michel Blanc, Philippe Noiret.

All the Mornings in the World (Tous les Matins du Monde)

(1993) 114m. Subtitled.
A–

Seventeenth-century com-

poser Monsieur de Sainte Colombe avoided the limelight in order to concentrate on his music while his protégé Marain Marais became the celebrated court composer at Versailles. This closely woven, almost mystical tapestry of a film is a must for music fans, though the generous helpings of music will please everyone.
D: Alain Corneau. A: Gerard Depardieu, Jean-Pierre Marielle, Anne Brochet.

Colonel Chabert
(1994) 111m. Subtitled.
B–
Trying to stake a claim to his home, wealth, and wife, Colonel Chabert has a different problem from Martin Guerre: No one wants to accept him, preferring to think of him as hero dead and gone. This lush costume drama won't challenge you, but Depardieu's bluster helps move it along.
D: Yves Angelo. A: Gerard Depardieu, Fanny Ardant, Fabrice Luchini.

Queen Margot
(1994) 144m. Subtitled.
A
Using Margot's (daughter of Catherine de Medici) extramarital love affair as the frame, this lavish, often gruesome costume drama details the virtual civil war that ensued as the Medicis tried to maintain control of France. Lots of lust and down-and-dirty scenes, as well as touching episodes, make this a long, but totally involving adventure.
D: Patrice Chereau. A: Isabelle Adjani, Daniel Anteuil, Jean-Hughes Anglade.

Disaffected Youth

While the French may have invented the word "bourgeois," they still have a soft spot for the nonconformist and angry youth who are the heroes and heroines of these tales.

Loulou
(1980) 110m. Subtitled.
A–
A bored young woman is swept off her feet by a leather-clad hunk and dumps her milquetoast husband to take up with him. This less than sympathetic couple who rarely venture outside their bedroom will steam up your glasses in this funny unsentimental look at l'amour fou.
D: Maurice Pialat. A: Gerard Depardieu, Isabelle Huppert, Guy Marchand.

A Nos Amours
(1983) 102m. Subtitled.
A–
A wild, working-class teen drives her dysfunctional family up the wall when she takes on several lovers she doesn't even like. When she marries one of them she begins to regret her innocence lost. A fascinating study with a neurotic, let-it-all-hang-out style that can get annoying.
D: Maurice Pialat. A: Sandrine Bonnaire, Dominique Besnehard, Maurice Pialat.

L'Annee des Meduses
(1985) 110m. Subtitled.
C–
Surf's up for the Eurotrash on the Riviera as a sexy Lolita gets jealous of her mom who's attracting the smoothest operator on the beach. This is high camp for the ages as the teen seductress makes every schnook who lusts after her bodacious bod suffer big time.
D: Christopher Frank. A: Valerie Kaprisky, Bernard Giraudeau, Caroline Cellier.

Betty Blue
(1986) 117m. Subtitled. **B**
An emotionally disturbed young woman draws a working-class stiff into a savage sexual affair. This extremely erotic but rather screechy mess can't make up its mind whether to be sex comedy or a harrowingly intense psychological drama.
D: Jean-Jacques Beineix. A: Jean-Hughes Anglade, Beatrice Dalle, Gerard Darmon.

Sincerely Charlotte
(1986) 92m. Subtitled. **B**
When her husband is found murdered, a pop singer finds shelter with an ex-beau who still loves her. When the police close in they cut a slightly berserk trail for the Spanish border in this breezy French-style, lovers-on-the-lam romp.
D: Caroline Huppert. A: Isabelle Huppert, Neils Arestrup, Christine Pascal.

Vagabond
(1986) 105m. Subtitled.
A–
A rootless teenage girl wanders across the French countryside rejecting all those who want to help her. A cool, washed-out looking tale of an aimless heroine who asks for little in life other than to be left alone. A downbeat and austere film with quiet power.
D: Agnes Varda. A: Sandrine Bonnaire, Macha Meril, Stephane Freiss.

36 Fillette
(1988) 92m. Subtitled. **B–**
A lonely 14-year-old is both attracted and repelled by the middle-aged man who keeps making advances at her. A creepy and depressing tale of a complex heroine who can't wait to become an adult but is turned off by her would-be lover's jadedness. Zentout's sullen earnestness makes this watchable.
D: Catherine Breillat. A: Delphine Zentout, Etienne Chicot, Olivier Parniere.

Love Without Pity
(1989) 88m. Subtitled. **C+**
A loafer who lives off his drug dealing brother gets a reality check when he falls for a hardworking graduate student who won't tolerate his aimless lifestyle. This Generation X-style tale about some misogynist slackers has a glum sort of romantic conviction but is in sore need of humor.
D: Adeline Lecallier. A: Yvan Attal, Hippolyte Girardot, Mireille Perrier.

Stylish Capers

These colorful, chic, and violent tales draw heavily from classic American gangster films while maintaining a distinctive Gallic flavor thanks to the almost abstract plots, stylish visuals, and an oh-so-cool attitude.

Diva
(1982) 123m. Subtitled.
B+

A young opera fan gets entangled with gangsters, drug dealers, and his favorite diva. The thin caper takes a back seat to this lavish exercise in a new New Wave style that glides and zooms across the ever so hip streets of Paris.
D: Jean-Jacques Beineix. A: Frederic Andrei, Wilhemina Wiggins Fernandez, Richard Bohringer.

The Moon in the Gutter
(1983) 126m. Subtitled.
D

A thuggish dockworker out to avenge the rape of his sister is seduced by a luscious high society dame. This truly ghastly cinematic lollipop makes a ludicrous stab at a hip look and ends up resembling amateur night at *MTV*. Essential in an awful sort of way.
D: Jean-Jacques Beineix. A: Gerard Depardieu, Nastassja Kinski, Victoria Abril.

Subway
(1985) 110m. Subtitled.
B–

A beautiful young wife hooks up with a thug in the Paris underground in this cool trendy action flick with attitude. While it makes imaginative use of the Paris Metro, nearly two hours of aimless ambiguity may leave you gasping for air.
D: Luc Besson. A: Isabelle Adjani, Christopher Lambert, Richard Bohringer.

Le Femme Nikita
(1991) 117m. Subtitled.
A–

This sleek, .speed-injected thriller follows a female sociopathic delinquent who's trained to be a government assassin. The stylish disorienting images, bursts of violence, and the unexpectedness of both the heroine's behavior and Big Brother's commands will keep you buzzed and off balance throughout.
D: Luc Besson. A: Anne Parillaud, Jean-Hughes Anglade, Jeanne Moreau.

Psychological Thrillers

More than a little influenced by Hitchcock and American noir, these psychological study/suspense films delve into the quiet terrors of hidden pasts, the omnipresent lurking of evil, and the breakdown of human trust.

The Clockmaker
(1973) 105m. Subtitled.
A–

A tradesman's life is shattered when his son murders a shop foreman out of spite. Then he learns the terrible truth behind the crime and stands defiant against the angry townspeople who are out for retribution. A simple and powerful tale of honor.
D: Bertrand Tavernier. A: Philippe Noiret, Jean Rochefort, Jacques Denis.

Birgit Haas Must Be Killed
(1981) 105m. Subtitled.
B–

A German spy is targeted for assassination by a corrupt French policeman who has to find the right pigeon to do the dirty work. Espionage takes a back seat to some tepid psychological intrigue, though the creepy exploiters and some unexpected turns still make it worth watching.
D: Laurent Heynemann. A: Philippe Noiret, Jean Rochefort, Lisa Kreuser.

A Choice of Arms
(1983) 114m. Subtitled. **B**

A retired racketeer's world is shattered when two escaped cons hide out in his secluded Irish ranch. He's unable to hide his uneasy respect for one of the men and soon reverts back to his old criminal ways. Like a throwback to a Hollywood melodrama that simmers but never quite boils.
D: Alain Corneau. A: Yves Montand, Catherine Deneuve, Gerard Depardieu.

L'Argent
(1983) 90m. Subtitled.
A

When a young boy passes a counterfeit 500-franc note into circulation, it sets off a series of lies and betrayals leading to an innocent man being jailed. This austere collection of seamlessly woven episodes indicts the middle and upper classes in their pursuit of the almighty franc.
D: Robert Bresson. A: Christian Patey, Sylvie van den Elsen, Michel Briguet.

One Deadly Summer
(1983) 133m. Subtitled. **B**

A beautiful young woman moves to town with her reclusive parents, and her behavior takes a bizarre turn when she plots revenge against the men who raped her mother 20 years ago. After a rocky opening, the scantily clad Adjani and the colorful village prototypes help carry this steamy but misshapen drama.
D: Jean Becker. A: Isabelle Adjani, Alain Souchon, François Cluzet.

Dangerous Moves
(1984) 95m. Subtitled. **B**

A flamboyant grand chess master who fled Russia faces off against the Soviet champion. The unconvincing Cold War intrigue is wrapped around the tense and often funny chess matches where the contestants are not above using hypnotists and stealing good luck charms to psyche each other out.
D: Richard Dembo. A: Michel Piccoli, Leslie Caron, Liv Ullman.

Peril
(1985) 100m. Subtitled.
B–

The drifter who tutors the young boy in guitar engages in an affair with the lad's mother, which leads to other dangerous liaisons and murder. Boredom and menace mark this quiet tale in which the tutor is always two steps

behind in figuring out what's going on.
D: Michel Deville. A: Michel Piccoli, Nicole Garcia, Christophe Malavoy.

Tachao Pantin
(1985) 94m. Subtitled. **B+**
A lonely gas station attendant/ex-cop befriends a Moroccan drug dealer who reminds him of his dead son. When he witnesses the boy's murder he comes out of retirement to hunt down the killers. A gritty tale with a cloud of doom hovering over the self-appointed avenging angel.
D: Claude Berri. A: Coluche, Richard Anconina, Philippe Leotard.

Scene of the Crime
(1987) 90m. Subtitled. **B–**
An escaped convict saves a young boy by killing his own partner in crime; the boy's mother learns of his noble act and becomes entangled in a love affair with the man. A dark but fairly unconvincing forbidden love story until the chilling finale when a haunted Deneuve takes responsibility for her own crimes.
D: Andre Techine. A: Catherine Deneuve, Danielle Darrieux, Wadeck Stanczak.

L'Homme Blesse
(1988) 90m. Subtitled. **B**
A timid gay man is initiated into the world of kinky sex, and begins to have outrageous fantasies of a bolder version of himself with the handsome stud hooker he loves. An uninhibited and honest film that possesses the saving grace of humor.
D: Patrice Chereau. A: Jean-Hughes Anglade, Vittorio Mezzogiorno, Roland Bertin.

The Vanishing
(1991) 105m. Subtitled.
A–
When vacationing lovers stop at a rest station, the young woman disappears without a trace, and the man begins a years' long obsessive search for her. With its careful examination of puzzling but "normal" behavior, this perfectly constructed thriller and unsettling portrait of madness creeps up on you, until the shattering finale.
D: George Sluizer. A: Gene Bervoets, Johanna Ter Steege.

Psychological Dramas

These are tales of strange obsessions, evil, and massive malfunctions that lurk in the hearts of these characters before suffering slowly, like a time-released fatal dose. The films, like their characters, are well dressed, well mannered, and well educated—and paragons of destructive impulses.

Murmur of the Heart
(1971) 118m. Subtitled.
B+
An unusual coming-of-age film set in the 50s about a delicate boy who receives an unorthodox sex education from his rowdy older brothers and his sensual mother. The story is handled with a delicacy that doesn't sacrifice humor, the exuberance of youth, or the fascinating dynamics of this complicated family.
D: Louis Malle. A: Lea Massari, Daniel Gelin, Michel Lonsdale.

Maitress
(1975) 110m. Subtitled. **B**
The burglar becomes the lover of the dominatrix whose house he was caught robbing, but she keeps him firmly "upstairs" away from her dark underground world of S&M. A surprising and thought-provoking film whose images of kinky sex resonate beyond mere titillation.
D: Barbet Schroeder. A: Gerard Depardieu, Bulle Ogier, Andre Rouyer.

La Lectrice
(1988) 98m. Subtitled. **C+**
She's a professional reader whose lonely misfit clients are tantalized and controlled by her readings of Marx to de Sade. Miou-Miou has all the grace and control of a ballerina in this intriguing tale that still fails to ignite.
D: Michel Deville. A: Miou-Miou, Maria Casarés, Patrick Chesnais.

La Discrete
(1990) 96m. Subtitled. **B+**
Dumped by his lover, a lothario writer seeks revenge by breaking the heart of another woman, all at the behest of his publisher who wants him to use it as material for a book. The meanness and opportunism are cloaked in sophistication and politeness: This has its own version of gore, you just don't see it.
D: Christian Vincent. A: Fabrice Luchini, Maurice Garrel, Judith Henry.

Monsieur Hire
(1990) 88m. Subtitled.
A–
A reserved, middle-aged man who is distrusted by all his apartment house neighbors, is now suspected of murder. He only cares about the lovely young woman he watches from his window every night. What begins as an elegant, peeping tom character study evolves into an exquisite and tragic love story.
D: Patrice Leconte. A: Michel Blanc, Sandrine Bonnaire, Luc Thuillier.

The Double Life of Veronique
(1991) 105m. Subtitled.
B–
Two women, one French, one Polish, each sense that she is not alone in this world and, in fact, both are living parallel and strikingly similar lives. Nothing really happens: It's like a premise for a great story that never goes anywhere, although director Kieslowski makes great use of a beautiful woman and beautiful scenery.
D: Krzysztof Kieslowski. A: Irene Jacob, Halina Gryglaszewska, Kalina Jedrusik.

The Hairdresser's Husband
(1992) 84m. Subtitled.
A–
The little boy in love with the village hairdresser is now a middle-aged man who recovers paradise when he weds a young woman of the same profession. An original, mesmerizing, and unforgettable tale of passion.
D: Patrice Leconte. A: Jean Rochefort, Anna Galiena, Roland Bertin.

Olivier, Olivier
(1992) 110m. Subtitled. **B**
A boy disappears at the age of nine, causing guilt, anger, and upheaval in his family. Then he resurfaces six years later, but is he the same boy? The story's sheer peculiarity will keep you hooked, but director Holland's follow-up to *Europa, Europa* is not quite

the sum of its compelling parts.
D: Agnieszka Holland. A: Brigitte Rouan, François Clouzot, Gregoire Colin.

The Accompanist
(1993) 111m. Subtitled.
B−

A classical singer, her husband who conducts business with the Nazis, and the female accompanist who's slavishly devoted to the singer all make their way through the war years. A simple story of betrayal and different kinds of collaboration that's finely tuned, if nothing new.
D: Claude Miller. A: Richard Bohringer, Elena Safonova, Romane Bohringer.

Blue
(1993) 98m. Subtitled. **B+**

A 30ish woman loses her composer husband and daughter in an automobile accident and tries to erase any trace of them in her life. Slow-paced, demanding, and of striking beauty, this is a character study of a troubled woman groping her way back to life through art. Part of Kieslowski's trilogy.
D: Krzsztof Kieslowski. A: Juliette Binoche, Benoit Regent, Florence Pernel.

Un Coeur en Hiver
(1993) 105m. Subtitled. **A**

Partners in a violin-making business suffer a rupture in their friendship when the elder of the two takes up with a beautiful violinist, and his younger partner decides to try to win her affection for himself. A surprisingly emotional story of heartbreak, using Ravel music almost like another character.
D: Claude Sautet. A: Emmanuelle Béart, Daniel Auteuil, André Dussollier.

White
(1993) 92m. Subtitled. **C+**

When his French wife decides to call it quits after six months of marriage, a Polish man falls apart. His recourse is to spy on her and generally make her life miserable. Some erotic scenes, first-rate use of color, and twisted humor don't rescue this from heavy pretentiousness.
D: Krzsztof Kieslowski. A: Julie Delpy, Zbigniew Zamachowski.

Betty
(1994) 105m. Subtitled.
B+

When her husband walks in on Betty and her lover, Betty's banished but is soon taken under the wing of a wealthy widow. They get along beautifully until Betty's wicked ways reappear in grand style. Neon-lit and hazy with confusing flashbacks that may drive some people crazy.
D: Claude Chabrol. A: Stephane Audran, Marie Trintignant, Jean-François Garreaud.

Red
(1994) 99m. Subtitled. **A−**

The last of Kieslowski's tricolor trilogy is the story of a young woman who can't connect with her boyfriend, but manages to do so with a self-exiled retired judge. Another measured meditation on the impossibility of real contact and the yearning people have for it, this is also a clever summing up of the vaguely intersecting stories of the three films.
D: Krzysztof Kieslowski. A: Irene Jacob, Frederique Feder, Jean-Louis Trintignant.

Savage Nights (Les Nuits Fauves)
(1994) 126m. Subtitled.
C+

A filmmaker who's HIV-positive starts an affair with a teenage girl to the dismay of his current cute male squeeze. They have a lot of histrionic scenes, some all together, some with just two of them, some while having sex. Très tragique but leaves you cold, and starts to feel like 126 hours, not minutes.
D: Cyril Collard. A: Cyril Collard, Romane Bohringer, Carlos Lopez.

1970s–1980s Dramas

While not all films in this group are strictly "women's films," most feature heroines who have a thing or two to say about the cards fate and society have dealt them. These are also some of the more charming and entertaining films to come out of France in recent years, and a few even offer the romance and sentimentality of a good tearjerker.

The Lacemaker
(1977) 107m. Subtitled. **B**

A lonely working-class girl on vacation has an affair with a well-to-do college student; when she returns to her drab routine, she's crushed to find his interest waning. This creaky story steers clear of melodrama and becomes an eloquent though bleak tale of lost love.
D: Claude Goretta. A: Isabelle Huppert, Yves Benyton, Florence Giorgetti.

Madame Rosa
(1977) 105m. Subtitled. **B**

The old Jewish ex-prostitute who looks after the streetwalkers' children develops a special relationship with the young Arab boy put in her care. Signoret adds grace to this grim tale of a holocaust survivor whose love for the boy helps her transcend the sordid surroundings and her haunted past.
D: Moshe Mizahi. A: Simone Signoret, Sammy Den Youb, Claude Dauphin.

My Other Husband
(1981) 110m. Subtitled. **B**

A vivacious woman has trouble juggling two jobs as well as a husband in Normandy and another in Paris. Then her breezy life really turns sour when the two hubbies find out about each other in this intelligent tall-tale take on bigamy.
D: George Lautner. A: Miou-Miou, Roger Hanin, Eddy Mitchell.

La Truite
(1982) 100m. Subtitled.
B+

A naive country girl learns about life the hard way when she marries an aristocrat's gay protégé and continues to pursue her ambition to get ahead. This icy modern picaresque tale of a woman who lives by her considerable wits and charm is relentlessly cynical, engaging, and intelligent.
D: Joseph Losey. A: Lissette Malidor, Isabelle Huppert, Jacques Splessor.

Edith and Marcel
(1983) 162m./104m.
Subtitled. **C+**

The tempestuous romance between chanteuse Edith Piaf and prizefighter Michel Cedran becomes a dizzying but very slow-moving string of episodes here. The glossy 1940s period details, glorious music, and melodramatic fireworks help to prod along this intense and dullish spectacle.

D: Claude Lelouch. A: Evelyne Bouix, Marcel Cerdan, Jr., Jacques Villeret.

Entre Nous
(1983) 110m. Subtitled.
A

A warm and sparkling portrait of two women's friendship that stands the test of time, separation, and their respective husbands. The winning characters, the natural ease with which their relationship evolves, and the unusual course that the story takes all make this one a joy to watch.
D: Diane Kurys. A: Isabelle Huppert, Miou-Miou, Guy Marchand.

First Name: Carmen
(1983) 85m. Subtitled. **A–**

A young woman hires her washed-up director uncle (played by Godard) to direct a film, but she's actually an aspiring terrorist hoping to use him as a foil. Meandering, sometimes annoying, highly entertaining, and guaranteed to drive non-Godard fans crazy.

D: Jean-Luc Godard. A: Marushka Detmers, Jacques Bonnaffe, Myriem Roussel.

Hail Mary
(1985) 107m. Subtitled. **B**

Two Godard films on one tape: *The Book of Mary* tells of how a couple decides to live apart and their young daughter's response as she shuttles between them. *Hail Mary* is a meditation on the origins of life by updating the story of the virgin birth. Both are intelligent, talky, with indirect narrative.
D: Jean-Luc Godard. A: Aurore Clement, Thierry Rode, Myriem Roussel.

A Man and a Woman: 20 Years Later
(1986) Subtitled. **B+**

The former script girl, now film producer, and the race car driver, now car-race scout, still haven't gotten together yet. This is one of those entertainingly and flashily cornball films with outrageous romantic flourishes and plot contrivances that will leave you slack-jawed in disbelief.

D: Claude Lelouch. A: Anouk Aimèe, Jean-Louis Trintignant, Richard Berry.

Next Summer
(1986) 100m. Subtitled.
B+

A loving and humorous portrait of a family as it follows the marriages, infidelities, aspirations, and births of its members. Like a slightly more serious French version of *Parenthood,* this family saga will leave you entertained and shamelessly manipulated.
D: Nadine Trintignant. A: Claudia Cardinale, Fanny Ardant, Philippe Noiret.

Le Petit Amour
(1987) 80m. Subtitled. **B–**

A middle-aged woman is infatuated with a 15-year-old boy who seems to be more interested in his favorite video game. This delicately nuanced story should have sacrificed some of the sensitivity for a jolt of humor.
D: Agnes Varda. A: Jane Birkin, Mathieu Demy, Charlotte Gainsbourg.

May Fools
(1989) 105m. Subtitled.
B–

A greedy family gathers at a country mansion in the late 60s to hear the reading of a will. This giddy romp wears you down in its attempt to be controversial and sexually intriguing; it's so "French" that it verges on being a bad stereotype.
D: Louis Malle. A: Michel Piccoli, Miou-Miou, Michel Duchaussoy.

The Music Teacher
(1989) 100m. Subtitled. **B**

An opera singer retires at the height of his fame and devotes himself to pushing two students—a temperamental young woman and a common thief—to reach for the sublime. A Hollywood-style romantic drama with ravishing music but missing the heart-on-sleeve sweep to be totally winning.
D: Gerard Corbiau. A: Jose Van Dam, Anne Roussel, Philippe Volter.

Colonialism

This group of films chronicles the complex, continually evolving relationships between colonials, natives, and a country to which neither of them can lay complete claim.

Coup de Torchon (Clean Slate)
(1981) 128m. Subtitled. **B**

The troubles of a corrupt police officer in a dusty French village just keep piling up: His wife is cheating, his mistress is being beaten by her thug husband, and even the town pimp is giving him grief. Noiret is hilarious, but the promising beginning of this surrealistic comedy never quite pans out.
D: Bertrand Tavernier. A: Philippe Noiret, Isabelle Huppert, Stephane Audran.

Sugarcane Alley
(1983) 107m. Subtitled. **B**

Determined to spare her young grandson a grueling life of work on a sugar plantation, an elderly shantytown woman sets out to get him an education. A gentle and earthy tale set in 1930s Martinique that details life in a poor village.
D: Euzhan Palcy. A: Garry Cadenat, Darling Legitimus, Routa Seck.

Chocolat
(1989) 105m. Subtitled.
B+

A French official's daughter returns to her outpost home in Cameroon, but feelings of alienation from her aloof parents and empty friends threaten to crowd out the warm experiences she had once shared with the local natives. A melancholic tale set amidst the vast expanses of exotic African landscape.
D: Claire Dennis. A: Isaach de Bankole, Mireille Perrier, François Cluzet.

Overseas
(1992) 96m. Subtitled. **B**

During the political upheaval in postwar Algeria, three strong-willed French sisters engage in their own battle for independence, coping with arranged courtships, loveless marriages, and the unrelenting conditions of working their plantation. An uneven but beautifully photographed family saga.
D: Brigitte Rouan. A: Nicole Garcia, Marianne Basler, Brigette Rouen.

1990s Comedies

These films show a dark, even gallows humor side of the French—a far cry from Jacques Tati. They also display a bit of French society at its best, with its mix of ages—and in one case races—without fanfare.

Mama, There's a Man in Your Bed

(1990) 110m. Subtitled. B–

A white CEO finds an unexpected friend and ally in his office's black cleaning lady. She's the ultimate earth mother with her life revolving around her brood of five children from different marriages. Genuinely likable characters make this a bright, warm, and unlikely romantic comedy.
D: Coline Serreau. A: Daniel Auteuil, Firmine Richard, Maxime Leroux.

Delicatessen

(1991) 95m. Subtitled. B+

A young musician takes a room in a house owned by a butcher who's making steaks out of humans. Wooing the butcher's daughter and avoiding becoming Sunday dinner takes up a lot of the young man's time in this dark, sepia-toned, acceptably grisly black comedy.
D: Jean-Pierre Jeunet. A: Marc Caro, Marie-Laure Dougnac, Dominique Pinon.

Tatie Danielle

(1991) 107m. Subtitled. B

A dark comedy about an old woman who descends on her great nephew and wife, wrecking their lives with her carping and snooping. The couple takes a vacation alone, and things really start to get nasty when the young woman in charge of auntie won't take any of her foolishness. Unusual and almost great.
D: Etienne Chatiliez. A: Tsilla Chelston, Catherine Jacob, Isabelle Nanty.

Toto le Hero

(1991) 94m. Subtitled. B–

An old man recalls his childhood and adult life in flashbacks that focus on his belief that he was switched at birth with the wealthy braggart next door. While trying to be dark, this remains a little too cheerful to pack a punch, getting bogged down in gooey emotional syrup. Well-paced and contains a few surprises.
D: Jaco Van Dormael. A: Michel Bouquet, Mireille Perrier, Jo De Bacher.

À la Mode

(1994) 89m. Subtitled. B

Warmhearted tale of an old Jewish tailor taking on an orphaned boy as an apprentice who turns out to have a flair for designing women's fashions. Quietly charming and with a good feel for diversity of a French Jewish quarter and an unforced sense of character development alien to most U.S. films.
D: Remy Duchemin. A: Ken Higelin, Jean Yanne.

French Canadian

These French-language Canadian films have the small personal feel of French cinema, with a rowdiness that's distinctly North American. The look is polished if not high budget, and though the acting is true and the stories smart, the films sometimes seem to strain for effect, which can make them feel a bit precious.

The Decline of the American Empire

(1986) 101m. Subtitled. B

Four men and four women—all intellectuals — discuss their relationship to sex, and often simultaneously their relationship to each other. Like a clunkier Rohmer film, this is talky, well-paced, ruefully amusing, but a little genteel: It could use a visit from Martha from *Who's Afraid of Virginia Woolf?*
D: Denys Arcand. A: Dominique Michel, Dorothee Berryman, Louise Portal.

Jesus of Montreal

(1990) 118m. Subtitled. B

What if you staged the Passion Play and Jesus turned out to be the real thing? That's the question asked by this sometimes funny, sometimes affected play-within-a-movie, which takes additional potshots at religion and consumerism. Provocative and lots of fun.
D: Denys Arcand. A: Lothaire Bluteau, Catherine Wilkening, Johanne-Marie Tremblay.

Leolo

(1993) 107m. Subtitled. C–

Seeking to escape his bizarre family life that includes random acts of brutality and lunacy, a young boy invents a separate history that includes his mother's impregnation by an Italian tomato. The movie works very hard to come up with outrageously provocative images and stories, but ends up being annoying.
D: Jean-Claude Lauzon. A: Maxime Colin, Ginetta Reno, Julien Guiomar.

Miscellaneous Dramas

Jonah Who Will Be 25 in the Year 2000

(1976) 115m. Subtitled. A–

Eight members of the 1968 generation—friends, lovers, acquaintances—are the subject of this story that looks at the ways they try to come to terms with their postrevolutionary lives. Like a smarter, sweeter, Eurostyle *Big Chill,* filled with wistfully funny situations and genuinely charming characters.
D: Alain Tanner. A: Jean-Luc Bideau, Rufus, Miou-Miou.

Mon Oncle D'Amerique

(1980) 123m. Subtitled. A

Three lives overlap by coin-

cidence, each one an example of the inevitable traps that desire and guilt set for us. While using biologist Henry Laborit's theories as an inspiration, this is no academic exercise but a wryly funny and surprisingly entertaining kaleidoscopic view of what makes people behave as they do.
D: Alain Resnais. A: Gerard Depardieu, Nicole Garcia, Roger Pierre.

Jacquot
(1991) 118m. Subtitled.
A–
Director Agnes Varda terms this an "evocation" of the life of her late husband, director Jacques Demy. This engaging portrait uses film clips, intimate interviews and, best of all, re-created scenes from his childhood in 1940s Nantes where Demy's interest in puppets led him to make movies.
D: Agnes Varda. A: Philippe Maron, Edouard Joubeaud, Laurent Monnier.

German
Early Films

These films are some of the earliest examples of cinematic art, the inspiration for filmmakers as well as being the "decadent" films condemned by the Nazis. Mythology and folk legends are presented here in menacing and eerie ways while the fatalistic modern stories show seduction, murder, and the triumph of sin over respectability. They all share a remarkable composition and visual complexity, telling their stories with images, not words; whether they are silent (accompanied by organ or piano music) or sound (often with hard to read subtitles), the intervening dialogue is almost unnecessary.

Silent Films

The Cabinet of Dr. Caligari
(1919) 52m. B&W. Silent.
A
A carnival hypnotist uses his somnambulism for nefarious purposes, including murder. But who is really insane here? The original expressionist classic with Cubist sets whose doors and chimneys are as askew as the character's world.
D: Robert Wiene. A: Werner Krauss, Conrad Veidt, Lil Dagover.

Dr. Mabuse, Der Spieler (The Gambler) Parts 1 and 2
(1922–1923) 242m. B&W. Silent. **A**
The diabolical gambler takes on a mythical quality as the evil puppeteer of postwar Berlin's libertines in this murky allegorical saga of the Fatherland's decline. A dazzling expressionistic study of the debauched underworld will haunt with its unforgettable nightmarish images.
D: Fritz Lang. A: Rudolph Klein-Rogge, Alfred Abel, Aud Egede.

Nosferatu
(1922) 63m. B&W. Silent.
A
Dracula's first film appearance was not as a dashing sexy count, but as a repulsive shrunken creature with scythelike fingernails, and pointed ears and head. Disorienting and eerie, partly due to the achingly primitive lighting of the outdoor shots and the artificial indoor sets.
D: F. W. Murnau. A: Max Schreck, Greta Schroeder, Gustav von Wangenheim.

Siegfried
(1924) 96m. B&W. Silent.
A
Fritz Lang's melodramatic grandiose version of the exploits of the medieval folk hero, whose bath in dragon's blood makes him invulnerable. Huge Art Deco sets that dwarf the characters and unusual camera angles make this an expressionistic feast.
D: Fritz Lang. A: Paul Richter, Margarete Schon.

Kriemhilde's Revenge
(1925) 90m. B&W. Silent.
A–
In this sequel to *Siegfried,* Kriemhild plots revenge against her brothers and marries Attila the Hun to help carry out her plans. Melodramatic and mythical with haunting images.
D: Fritz Lang. A: Margarete Schon, Paul Richter, Rudolf Klein-Rogge.

Faust
(1926) 117m. B&W. Silent.
A
A professor sells his soul to the devil to regain his youth. Satan is a looming presence, and the intricate expressionist sets are composed as carefully as a photograph.
D: F. W. Murnau. A: Emil Jannings, Camilla Horn, Gosta Ekman.

Diary of a Lost Girl
(1929) 100m. B&W. Silent.
B+
Brooks is like a beacon in this story of the fall and rise of a young woman in 1920s Germany. The nuanced performances are highlighted by portrait-style lighting in which one person's face often occupies the entire screen.
D: G. W. Pabst. A: Louise Brooks, Fritz Rasp, Josef Ravensky.

Pandora's Box
(1928) 110m. Silent. **A**
A young woman's demise is melodramatically catalogued through her various attachments to men. Full of haunting flickering images while Brooks glows like a white-hot coal.
D: G. W. Pabst. A: Louise Brooks, Fritz Kortner, Franz Lederer.

Sound Films

The Blue Angel
(1930) 103m. B&W. Subtitled. **A**
The ordered bourgeois life of a stodgy professor falls apart when he becomes obsessed with a heartless cabaret singer. Wonderfully amoral film with funny and devastating scenes of the professor's disintegrating life and the nightclub world ruled by self-interest and passion.
D: Josef von Sternberg. A: Marlene Dietrich, Emil Jannings, Kurt Gerron.

Kameradschaft
(1931) 78m. B&W. Subtitled. **B+**
An explosion traps the work-

ers of a Franco-German mine on the French side, but the Germans step in, in a rare cooperative effort to save lives. Political and cultural differences are highlighted by the difficulties of two languages and a near-documentary style of shooting.
D: G. W. Pabst. A: Ernst Busch, Fritz Kampers, Alexander Granach.

M
(1931) 95m. B&W.
Subtitled. **A**

Child murderer stalks Berlin and members of the underworld decide to spare themselves a police investigation by tracking him down. The creepy images—long shadows, deserted cityscapes, and a balloon without a child—will haunt you.
D: Fritz Lang. A: Peter Lorre, Gustav Grundgens, Ellen Widmann.

Maedchen in Uniform
(1931) 87m. B&W.
Subtitled. **B+**

Oppression and conformity dominate a girl's boarding school where one sensitive student takes refuge in a lesbian relationship with her teacher. Adept handling of lesbian themes and overt criticism of conformity.
D: Leontine Sagan. A: Dorothea Wieck, Hertha Thiele, Ellen Schwannecke.

The Threepenny Opera
(1931) 113m. B&W. **B**

The London criminal element in all its seamy impoverished glory is the subject of this musical adaptation of Bertolt Brecht's play. Don't look for Brecht's sensibility: This is pure luxurious Pabst rendition with sleazy or sumptuous scenery, depending on the episode.
D: G. W. Pabst. A: Rudolf Forster, Lotte Lenya, Vladimir Sokoloff.

Liebelei
(1933) 88m. B&W.
Subtitled. **B+**

A young officer falls in love and must face the consequences of his former affair with a married baroness. Stagy acting makes this a little dated but still an entertaining tale of love and death in nineteenth-century Vienna.
D: Max Ophuls. A: Magda Schneider, Wolfgang Liebermeier, Luise Ulrich.

The Testament of Dr. Mabuse
(1933) 122m. B&W. **B+**

The underworld's sinister activities continue to be manipulated by the criminal mastermind from his cell in a loony bin. This gloomy atmospheric vision of pre-Hitler Germany, banned by the Nazis upon its release, doesn't stack up well against the downward spiraling insanity of the original.
D: Fritz Lang. A: Rudolph Klein-Rogge, Oskar Beregi, Karl Meixner.

Regarding World War II

Most of the films in this group offer portraits of civilian dramas that came out of the events leading up to and during the Third Reich. Given the somber nature of the themes, these films are not light fare, but most are extremely entertaining thanks to modern pacing, artful period design, and authentic location shooting, though there is a snake-handler's carefulness as filmmakers explore the dark past of the Fatherland.

The Damned
(1969) 150m. Subtitled or dubbed. **B**

This tragic operatic tale of evil and power follows the demise of an industrial family as the Nazis rise to power. Oozing lush European decadence, this film is very slow and long, and contains some almost unbearably painful scenes of the characters' anguish.
D: Luchino Visconti. A: Dirk Bogarde, Helmut Griem, Charlotte Rampling.

The Tin Drum
(1979) 141m. Subtitled.
A

The good citizens of a small town cope with Nazism and World War II while the main character—a three-year-old boy—stops growing and then expresses his rage by banging his tin drum and screeching at glass-breaking decibels. A riveting, almost dreamlike story that's utterly memorable.
D: Volker Schlondorff. A: David Bennent, Mario Adorf, Angela Winkler.

The Boat Is Full
(1981) 104m. Subtitled or dubbed. **B+**

Jewish refugees try to make a go of it in neutral Switzerland during wartime only to encounter prejudice. Affecting and carefully observed, it gives an unusual view of a country widely assumed to be an oasis in the midst of horror.
D: Markus Imhoof. A: Tina Engel, Martin Waltz.

Mephisto
(1981) 150m. Subtitled.
A−

A German actor in the 1930s will stop at nothing for success, including favors from the Nazi party. Brandauer *is* this movie, with his exuberant portrait of an artist without scruples. First in Szabo's power trilogy.
D: Istvan Szabo. A: Klaus Maria Brandauer, Krystyna Janda, Idiko Bandagi.

Das Boot (The Boat)
(1982) 149m. Subtitled.
A 

Not for the claustrophobic, this dramatic military drama details the exploits of an ill-fated U-boat on a virtual suicide mission. Bucking the usual Germans-as-villains stereotype, this film makes you care about the men, whose cramped stifling life is presented in such detail you can practically smell it.
D: Wolfgang Petersen. A: Jurgen Prochnow, Klaus Wennemann.

Malou
(1983) 94m. Subtitled. **C**

A young schoolteacher traces the life of her mother who was French and married to a German Jew during World War II. Earnest and heavy-handed with feminist messages.
D: Jeanine Meerapfel. A: Ingrid Caven, Grischa Huber.

The White Rose
(1983) 108m. Subtitled. **B**

Engrossing drama of a brother and sister who distribute leaflets about concentration camps as part of a student Nazi resistance movement. Captures the fear and edginess of the time, with a nice use of the stark and bright colors of wartime posters.
D: Michael Verhoeven. A: Lena Stolze, Martin Menrath.

Angry Harvest
(1985) 102m. Subtitled.
B–
A Jewish woman escapes a camp-bound train and meets a farmer who hides her in his cellar. A dark, stifling, and emotionally violent drama of strong passions in desperate situations.
D: Agnieszka Holland. A: Armin Mueller-Stahl, Elizabeth Trissenaar.

38 Vienna Before the Fall
(1986) 97m. Subtitled. **C**
A Jewish playwright and Aryan girlfriend ignore the signs of change in 1937 Vienna. The story is flat though it manages to give a good tense picture of the Austrian capital on the eve of annexation.
D: Wolfgang Gluck. A: Sunnyi Melles, Tobias Engel.

The Wannsee Conference
(1987) 87m. Subtitled. **B+**
A single-set drama based on the minutes of the January 20, 1942 meeting at which German officials drafted the "final solution." Sober documentary-style (film runs as long as the real conference did), which adds to the chilling effect.
D: Keinz Schirk. A: Robert Artzhorn, Gerd Bockmann.

Hanussen
(1989) 117m. Subtitled.
B+
Brandauer is mesmerizing in this tale of a World War I veteran who capitalizes on his many Nazi admirers when a head wound makes him clairvoyant. The third in Szabo's trilogy that presents the dilemma of ambitious individuals caught between success and morality in pre-World War II Germany.
D: Istvan Szabo. A: Klaus Maria Brandauer, Erland Josephson.

Europa, Europa
(1991) 115m. Subtitled.
A
Based on a true story, this film follows the adventures of a Jewish teenager who hid his identity in order to survive captivity by Russians and Nazi soldiers. An amazingly entertaining, suspenseful, and even humorous study of the boy's fear and confusion regarding his identity and people's perceptions of race and religion.
D: Agnieszka Holland. A: Marco Hofschneider, Delphine Forest, Klaus Abramowsky.

Zentropa
(1991) 112m. Subtitled.
C
Visually striking story of young American Jewish man working as a sleeping car conductor in 1945 Germany. Hypnotic, expressionistic, and very European art-house pretentious.
D: Lars von Trier. A: Jean-Marc Barr, Barbara Sukowa, Eddie Constantine.

Pre-World War II Historical Dramas

Coup de Grace
(1979) 96m. Subtitled. **B–**
Just after World War I, a German unit takes up residence in a dilapidated Latvian estate, and the mistress falls in love with one of the soldiers. A remote drama of faded glory in a changing modern society.
D: Volker Schlondorff. A: Margarethe von Trotta, Matthias Habich.

Celeste
(1981) 107m. Subtitled.
B
A beautiful portrait of fin de siècle Paris and Marcel Proust, based on the memoirs of his housekeeper. Intelligent film, but it feels like a play with those long pregnant silences and deliberate movements.
D: Percy Adlon. A: Eva Mattes, Jurgen Arndt.

Spring Symphony
(1984) 102m. Subtitled.
B–
This film of Clara Schumann's life and struggles with her overbearing famous father contains plenty of refined period detail, female spunk, and heavenly music.
D: Peter Schamoni. A: Nastassja Kinski, Herbert Gronemeyer.

Colonel Redl
(1985) 143m. Subtitled.
B–
Brandauer fills out this slim story of true-life intelligence officer in the Austro-Hungarian Empire with his galvanizing portrayal of the loneliness of a successful spy. Style triumphs over substance with a story that never really supports a movie. The second entry of Szabo's power trilogy.
D: Istva Szabo. A: Klaus Maria Brandauer, Armin Mueller Stahl, Hans-Christian Blech.

Forget Mozart
(1985) 93m. Subtitled. **B–**
Mozart's life is reviewed by his so-called friends and lovers. Don't look for the lushness of *Amadeus,* but this small film does give a sense of his role in Austrian politics.
D: Salvo Luther. A: Armin Mueller Stahl, Max Tidof.

Wenders

With much of their roots in film noir and westerns, Wim Wenders' films are directly and obsessively influenced by American culture and its effects on West Germany. Violence underlies even the gentlest stories while loneliness and alienation grip nearly all his characters as they try to fill their emptiness with technology. Then there are Wenders' landscapes: With photography as breathtaking and complex as an Edward Weston photograph, the land's beauty seems to overwhelm the characters in their desperate search to connect with others.

The Goalie's Anxiety at the Penalty Kick
(1971) 101m. Subtitled. **B**
Story follows an alienated soccer goalie after he commits an apparently unmotivated murder. This character study of a disaffected man is subtle and graceful, but very slow going.
D: Wim Wenders. A: Arthur Brauss, Kai Fischer, Marie Bardischewski.

The Scarlet Letter
(1973) 90m. Subtitled. **C+**
This costume drama based on Hawthorne's classic of adultery and shame in New England village of 1600s was shot in Spain and bears little of Wenders' imprint.
D: Wim Wenders. A: Senta

Berger, Lou Castel, Hans-Christian Blech.

Alice in the Cities
(1974) 110m. Subtitled. **B+**
First installment of Wenders' road trilogy follows the travels of the alienated journalist and an abandoned nine-year-old girl who leads him to a sense of worth and responsibility. Surprisingly unsentimental story that lingers long after viewing.
D: Wim Wenders. A: Rudiger Vogeler, Yella Rottlander, Elizabeth Kreuzer.

Kings of the Road
(1976) 176m. B&W. Subtitled. **B+**
Two guys traverse the vast landscapes of the East/West border, dotted with tiny outposts of civilization shaped by American culture. Second road trilogy film is full of cinematic allusions and Coca-Cola signs.
D: Wim Wenders. A: Rudiger Vogler, Hanns Zischler, Rudolf Schundler.

The American Friend
(1977) 127m. In English.
A
In exchange for medical assistance, an unassuming picture-framer in Hamburg agrees to kill a mobster. Though many scenes are shot in daylight, this has a neon-lit, nighttime feel and a touch of Los Angeles malaise. Meditative and suspenseful at the same time.
D: Wim Wenders. A: Bruno Ganz, Dennis Hopper, Gerard Blain, Nicholas Ray.

The Wrong Move
(1978) 103m. Subtitled. **C**
Determined to become a writer, a young man sets out on a journey of spiritual discovery in Germany, where he encounters some rather bizarre characters. Third in road trilogy and Kinski's debut.
D: Wim Wenders. A: Rudiger Vogler, Hanna Schygulla, Marianne Hoppe, Nastassja Kinski.

The State of Things
(1983) 120m. Subtitled. **B**
When he runs out of money during the remake of a Roger Corman sci-fi film in Portugal, a German director abandons crew and actors in search of his producer. A funny fatal confrontation gives a comic snap to the second half of the film.
D: Wim Wenders. A: Samuel Fuller, Allen Goorwitz, Paul Getty III, Roger Corman.

Wings of Desire
(1988) 130m. Subtitled.
A
West Berlin is the backdrop for the dreamlike wanderings and musings of two angels as they contemplate and nurture the human spirit. Ganz is wonderful as the angel who falls in love with a circus trapeze artist.
D: Wim Wenders. A: Bruno Ganz, Solveig Dommartin, Otto Sander, Peter Falk.

Herzog

The clash of different cultures, of humans with nature, of society with misfits are the backbone of these stories. Werner Herzog does not have a reputation for clarity; his films are slow and demanding, but they also have a mysterious, almost frightening tone with stories that are totally unpredictable.

Aguirre: Wrath of God
(1972) 94m. Subtitled. **A**
A madman conquistador spares no risks in sixteenth-century South America, endangering himself and his men in his search for El Dorado. One of Herzog's most accessible films, this is huge in scale and provocative for its questions about exploration and imperialism.
D: Werner Herzog. A: Klaus Kinski, Ruy Guerra, Helena Rojo.

Heart of Glass
(1974) 93m. Subtitled. **B+**
When a glassblower dies without revealing the formula for the ruby glass that has put his small town on the map, the surviving villagers are thrown into a hysterical tailspin. The cast was put in a hypnotic trance to capture the crazed, fairy-tale feeling that is conveyed.
D: Werner Herzog. A: Josef Bierbichler, Stefan Autter.

Every Man for Himself and God Against All (aka The Mystery of Kaspar Hauser)
(1975) 110m. Subtitled.
A
A boy who has been confined his entire life in a tiny room suddenly appears in a small nineteenth-century German town. Even as he's taught language and social customs, his own visions disturb everyone's sense of order. Gripping tale based on a true story.
D: Werner Herzog. A: Bruno S., Brigitte Mira.

Stroszek
(1977) 108m. Subtitled. **B**
Three outcasts make their way to America to find the streets paved with gold, but instead end up in a tawdry forgotten corner of rural Wisconsin. This ironic look at the U.S. is light on plot but offers haunting images.
D: Werner Herzog. A: Bruno S., Eva Mattes, Clemens Scheitz.

Woyzeck
(1978) 82m. Subtitled. **C+**
Hospital orderly unleashes his murderous rage at his oppressive boss and faithless wife. Static and confined.
D: Werner Herzog. A: Klaus Kinski, Willy Semmelrogge, Eva Mattes.

Fitzcarraldo
(1982) 150m. Subtitled.
A−
This tale of an Irishman who's determined to forge shipping routes and build an opera house in an Amazon basin, even if it means hoisting a ship over a mountain, has the megalomania of *Citizen Kane* and the lushness and driven quality of *The Piano.* Since Herzog actually did hoist a ship over a mountain (no special effects here) the documentary of the making of this film (*Burden of Dreams*) can be even more riveting.
D: Werner Herzog. A: Klaus Kinski, Claudia Cardinale.

Where the Green Ants Dream
(1984) 99m. Subtitled. **B−**
A group of Australian miners seek to displace Aborigines in order to remove the mineral deposits on their land. Slow, disjointed tale is mainly for Herzog fans.
D: Werner Herzog. A: Bruce Spence, Colleen Clifford, Wandjuk Marika.

Fassbinder

Rainer Werner Fassbinder's productivity alone—some 50 films and TV shows in his 37-year life—made him one of the most influential filmmakers in modern Germany. These interior-bound dramas have a stultifying, nearly airless quality that often resembles the film equivalent of an old mail-order catalogue: staged, stiff, with grubby colors. They also contain astonishing performances and offer a peep at former West Germany as it forged a new postwar identity.

Gods of the Plague
(1970) 92m. B&W. Subtitled. **B–**

Two friends hatch a robbery plan, only to be foiled by the two women who love one of them. A tribute to U.S. crime movies of the 40s, this black-and-white, deliberately overlit film makes every character look like they're posing for a mug shot.
D: Rainer Werner Fassbinder. A: Harry Baer, Hanna Schygulla, Margarethe von Trotte.

The Bitter Tears of Petra von Kant
(1972) 124m. Subtitled. **B+**

Frustrated by her cheating lesbian lover, von Kant takes revenge on her slavelike assistant. Talky to the point of brow-beating.
D: Rainer Werner Fassbinder. A: Margit Carstensen, Hanna Schygulla, Irm Hermann.

The Merchant of Four Seasons
(1972) 88m. Subtitled. **B+**

Slow painful examination of the collapse of a fruit peddler's life. Drab colors and narrowly framed shots serve to drive home the hopelessness and despair felt by the protagonist.
D: Rainer Werner Fassbinder. A: Hanna Schygulla, Irm Hermann.

Ali: Fear Eats the Soul
(1974) 94m. Subtitled. **B+**

Using the classic kitsch melodrama *All That Heaven Allows*—older woman involved with younger man—the characters are made even more alienated: He's black, she's not. Dark, confined, but engaging drama.
D: Rainer Werner Fassbinder. A: Brigitt Mira, El Hedi Ben Salem, Barbara Valentin.

Fox and His Friends
(1975) 123m. Subtitled. **B+**

When a carnival barker comes into a lottery fortune, his middle-class lover and his friends take full advantage of his new wealth. Heartbreaking bitter look at how an ostracized group practices its own rejection and humiliation.
D: Rainer Werner Fassbinder. A: R. W. Fassbinder, Peter Chatel, Karl Bohm.

Chinese Roulette
(1976) 96m. Subtitled. **B**

Crippled preteen arranges for her parents and their respective lovers to converge on the country estate that they all use for their trysts. Then she and her nanny show up. Characters look like mannequins in this bitter look at the underbelly of love and sex.
D: Rainer Werner Fassbinder. A: Anna Karina, Margit Carstensen, Ulli Lommel.

Mother Kusters Goes to Heaven
(1976) 108m. Subtitled. **C+**

Widow reaps the benefits of her husband's transformation into a social symbol after he murders one of his bosses and then kills himself. A satirical look at a German middle class, where opportunism and backstabbing rule.
D: Rainer Werner Fassbinder. A: Brigitte Meara, Margit Carstensen, Karl Bohm.

Despair
(1979) 120m. Subtitled. **C–**

A Russian émigré runs a chocolate factory in Berlin just as Nazis are coming into power. Stylized, farcical film is primarily interesting for talent pool assembled.
D: Rainer Werner Fassbinder. A: Dirk Bogarde, Andrea Ferreol, Volker Spengler.

The Marriage of Maria Braun
(1979) 120m. Subtitled. **A**

One day after their wedding, the Brauns are separated for the duration of World War II. Maria remains true to her man in her fashion while accruing wealth and power. The first of Fassbinder's trilogy on Germany's postwar recovery, using strong women to trace the country's development; this is his glossiest-looking and most accessible film.
D: Rainer Werner Fassbinder. A: Hanna Schygulla, Klaus Lowitsch, Ivan Desny.

Lili Marleen
(1981) 120m. Subtitled. **C–**

Somewhat tedious story of low-talent singer who rises to prominence in Nazi Germany.
D: Rainer Werner Fassbinder. A: Giancarlo Giannini, Hanna Schygulla, Mel Ferrer.

Lola
(1982) 114m. Subtitled. **B+**

The final installment of the economic recovery trilogy is this updated version of *The Blue Angel.* Themes of corruption and hypocrisy are covered in this story of the singer-prostitute who seduces an upstanding citizen.
D: Rainer Werner Fassbinder. A: Barbara Sukowa, Armin Mueller-Shahl, Karin Baal.

Veronika Voss
(1982) 105m. Subtitled. **B–**

A melodrama of a small-time actress-turned-morphine-addict whom a journalist tries to help. This second installment in the trilogy of post-World War II economic recovery is depressing and sometimes slow.
D: Rainer Werner Fassbinder. A: Rosel Zech, Armin Mueller-Stahl, Doris Schade.

Berlin Alexanderplatz
(1983) 930m. Subtitled. **A**

This 13-part TV series studies Germany between the two world wars by following an ex-convict's unsuccessful attempts to integrate himself into society. With its quietly powerful images, this is like an epic tragedy that is captured on a beautiful old newsreel.
D: Rainer Werner Fassbinder. A: Gunter Lamprecht, Hanna Schygulla, Karin Baal.

Querelle
(1983) 106m. **D**
In English. Pretentious stylized treatment of Genet's story of a murdering homosexual sailor on shore leave.
D: Rainer Werner Fassbinder. A: Brad Davis, Franco Nero, Jeanne Moreau.

About Fassbinder

Kamikaze '89
(1983) 106m. Subtitled.
C+
Leopard-skin clad Fassbinder plays a police lieutenant in futuristic Germany. Like a boring John Waters' version of *Blade Runner*.
D: Wolf Gremm. A: R. W. Fassbinder, Gunter Kaufmann, Boy Gobert.

A Man Like Eva
(1985) 92m. Subtitled. **C**
Fassbinder regular Eva Mattes mimics Fassbinder with uncanny accuracy, but this film about making a film falls flat.
D: Radu Gabrea. A: Eva Mattes, Lisa Kreuzer, Werner Stocker.

1970s–1990s Dramas

Earnest, noble, and chock-full of moralizing, the modern films that made it onto video in America give a fairly good picture of the issues that dogged West Germany before unification absorbed all their energy. Drug addiction, women's liberation, terrorism, the perils of celebrity, AIDS—familiar territory for any modern country. Few of these are right for an evening of light entertainment, and Germans are hardly known for their humor; but these do offer a look at the recent history of Europe's most powerful country.

The Lost Honor of Katharina Blum
(1977) 97m. Subtitled. **A–**
A brief romantic encounter with a terrorist puts a woman under fire from authorities and the press. The hounded feeling of the protagonist is one you will share in this look at a life on the brink of falling apart.
D: Volker Schlondorff. A: Angela Winkler, Dieter Laser, Jurgen Prochnow.

Knife in the Head
(1978) 108m. Subtitled.
A
A researcher is accidentally shot in the head when he looks for his estranged wife at a political rally. Everyone wants him for their witness and mascot: the police, the terrorists, the newspapers. But first he has to learn to talk, eat, write, and be an adult all over again. Distressing but compelling to watch.
D: Reinhard Hauf. A: Bruno Ganz, Angela Winkler, Hans Christian Blech.

Christiane F
(1981) 124m. Subtitled.
C+
The moralizing gets a little much in this film, but the story of a 13-year-old girl whose frustration with her working-class situation in Berlin leads to drugs and prostitution is relentlessly resonant.
D: Ulrich Edel. A: Nadja Brunkhorst, Thomas Haustein, David Bowie.

Taxi Zum Klo (Taxi to the Toilet)
(1981) 92m. Subtitled.
B
Two Berlin homosexual men, one a school teacher, struggle with the pull of a secure relationship and the temptation to cruise. A candid look at a relationship that happens to be gay with the graininess and low production values of a home movie. Contains graphic homosexual scenes.
D: Frank Ripploh. A: Frank Ripploh, Bernd Broadrup, Gitte Lederer.

Marianne and Julianne
(1982) 103m. Subtitled.
A–
Two sisters respond to the repression of their 1950s upbringing by taking different routes: One is a feminist journalist, the other a terrorist. This articulate, charged, and humorless drama details the sibling relationship and the difficulties of disagreeing with someone you love.
D: Margarethe von Trotta. A: Barbara Sukowa, Jutta Lampe, Rudiger Volger.

The Inheritors
(1984) 89m. Subtitled. **C**
Family problems drive a troubled teenager into a neo-Nazi group. This hammers home its antifascist message with the subtlety of a high school antidrug film resembling an after-school special with a few sex scenes.
D: Walter Bannert. A: Nikolas Vogel, Roger Schauer, Wolfgang Gasser.

Men . . .
(1985) 99m. Subtitled. **B–**
A philandering ad exec flips out when he discovers that his wife is having an affair. His novel solution: Without revealing their connection, he moves into her lover's loft. This comedy stretches credibility and works the jokes awfully hard.
D: Dorris Dorrie. A: Ulrike Kriener, Uwe Ochsenknecht, Heiner Lauterbach.

Seduction: The Cruel Woman
(1985) 85m. Subtitled. **C**
The very banality with which this film presents a dominatrix and her "servers" makes their unusual practices seem as ordinary as a bridge game. Not much is left to the imagination and the film includes ample material for shoe, armor, and other fetishists.
D: Elfi Mikesch. A: Mechthild Grossman, Udo Kier, Sheila McLaughlin.

Sheer Madness
(1985) 105m. Subtitled.
C+
A psychodrama of two women who manage to emancipate themselves from traditional roles through their powerful friendship. A potent feminist film undermined by a strident, often moralizing tone.
D: Margarethe von Trotta. A: Hanna Schygulla, Angela Winkler, Peter Steibeck.

Sugarbaby
(1985) 86m. Subtitled. **B–**
A tubby mortician's assistant finds love with a subway conductor in this coquettish and harmless comedy. The irony never really bites, and the film remains perpetually sweet and wacky.
D: Percy Adlon. A: Marianne Sagebrecht, Eisi Gulp, Toni Berger.

A Virus Knows No Morals
(1985) 82m. Subtitled. **B**

Black comedy in which a sauna owner is distressed by the AIDS virus because it's killing off his business. Campy and with a clear debt to American underground films of the 1960s, this daring and impolite film won't be to everyone's taste.
D: Rosa von Praunheim. A: Dieter Dicken, Maria Haseacker, Rosa von Praunheim.

Singing the Blues in Red
(1989) 110m. In English. **C**

A protest singer/songwriter is unhappy when he's expelled from the German Democratic Republic even though he's welcomed in West Berlin. It's hard to sympathize with a protagonist who's so dour, self-absorbed, and humorless. Like a moralizing TV movie.
D: Ken Loach. A: Gerulf Pannach, Fabienne Babe, Christine Rose.

The Nasty Girl
(1990) 95m. Subtitled.
A

A teenage girl sets off an emotional explosion when she innocently decides to write about "My Town in the Third Reich," and her research reveals the truth behind the good citizens' official story. Based on a true story, this visually striking movie manages to be humorous and effervescent while treating a very complicated and painful subject.
D: Michael Verhoeven. A: Lena Stolze, Monika Baumgartner, Michael Gahr.

Requiem for Dominic
(1991) 88m. Subtitled. **B+**

This harrowing account of an exiled man's attempt to rescue his friend who remained in Romania uses actual footage of the 1989 demonstrations and revolution, which contains shooting and morgue scenes. A personal, diarylike view of events that changed with startling rapidity.
D: Robert Dornheim. A: Felix Mitterer, Vickoria Schubert, August Schmolzer.

I Am My Own Woman
(1992) 91m. Subtitled. **B+**

Von Mahlsdorf is the soft-spoken, courageous, and witty focus of this part-documentary/docudrama about one of the leading figures in the gay rights movement in former East Germany. Very low-budget, but a fascinating document of life under various regimes lived as someone who was always "other."
D: Rosa von Praunheim. A: Charlotte von Mahlsdorf, Ichgola Androgyn, Jens Tachner.

Spanish

Buñuel

After creating two trail-blazing surrealistic films with Salvador Dali in the late 20s, Luis Bunuel went into a creative hiatus, making one documentary before turning up in Mexico. His films during the 50s generally feature mediocre actors in old-fashioned potboilers, but the director's devious spirit and ironic eye lift them above the commonplace. His later films are stinging repartees to the soulless bourgeoisie and are populated by priests, virgins, mama's boys, sultry temptresses, aristocrats, and working folk, who all keep reaching for the sublime that's just out of their reach.

Land Without Bread (aka **Las Hurdes)**
(1932) 27m. B&W.
Subtitled. **A–**

A bleak powerful documentary on the dire poverty of the inhabitants of a recently discovered mountain community in Spain. The wide-eyed camera emulates the stiff education films of this era, with deeply ironic effect. A funny and harrowing portrait of a people forgotten by time.
D: Luis Buñuel.

Los Olvidados
(1950) 88m. Subtitled.
A– 

A group of teens struggle to survive in a Mexico City slum in this jolting, documentary-style drama. The depiction of the squalor and the brutal code these kids live by has lost none of its impact.
D: Luis Buñuel. A: Alphonso Mejia, Stella Inda, Roberto Cobo.

El (This Strange Passion)
(1952) 82m. B&W.
Subtitled. **A–**

A middle-aged aristocrat goes mad with jealousy over the affairs he imagines his wife to be having. This delightfully weird tale of obsession about a repressed prude, who fell in love with his future wife while staring at her feet, offers a sympathetic view of a budding psychopath.
D: Luis Buñuel. A: Arturo de Cordova, Delia Garces, Luis Beristain.

Illusion Travels by Streetcar
(1953) 90m. B&W.
Subtitled. **A–**

Two streetcar drivers get drunk, steal their old tramcar, and pick up suspicious passengers free of charge on a wild romp through the city. This hysterical, highly inventive journey into a surreal everyday world unfolds like a picaresque novel.
D: Luis Buñuel. A: Lilia Prado, Carlos Navarro, Agustin Isunza.

Wuthering Heights
(1953) 90m. B&W.
Subtitled. **A–**

The undying love between the village girl Cathy and family servant Heathcliff transcends their forced separation, her marriage, and death itself. Despite the often ludicrous acting, this Wagneresque, sometimes brutal take on the two selfish lovers is closer to the novel's tone than the glossy Hollywood version.
D: Luis Buñuel. A: Jorge Mistral, Irasema Dilian, Lilia Prado.

The Criminal Life of Archibaldo de la Cruz
(1955) 91m. B&W.
Subtitled. **A–**

A spoiled young aristocrat thinks his music box holds the secret of death, but his own attempts at murder fail miserably. This funny black comedy about a man erotically charged by killing is also a brilliant study of male impotence. A dirty little gem.

D: Luis Buñuel. A: Ernesto Alonso, Miroslava Stern, Ariadna Welter.

Nazarin
(1958) 92m. B&W. Subtitled. **A–**

A humble young priest is pursued by two women who worship him in this stirring drama of spiritual grappling and sexual confusion. A dusty and anguished parable with moments of bitter humor that puts more expensive biblical epics of the era to shame.
D: Luis Buñuel. A: Francisco Rabal, Marga Lopez, Ignacio Lopez.

Viridiana
(1961) 90m. B&W. Subtitled. **A**

A pretty novice from a convent makes the mistake of visiting her lecherous uncle before taking the veil. This disturbing masterpiece, bursting with haunting and hilarious religious imagery, is an absorbing study of the disintegration of morality in the upper class and obsessions gone astray.
D: Luis Buñuel. A: Silvia Pinal, Fernando Rey, Francisco Pinal.

The Exterminating Angel
(1962) 95m. B&W. Subtitled. **A–**

A pleasant dinner party takes a dark turn when the guests find they are unable to leave. A sweaty, tense, and extremely humorous take on a gathering of upper-class types who make the worst of an already impossible situation. This surrealistic fable has remained fresh through the years.
D: Luis Buñuel. A: Silvia Pinal, Jose Bavaria, Enrique Rambal.

Tristana
(1970) 105m. Subtitled. **A–**

After her mother dies, a young woman moves in with a much older guardian who promptly falls in love with her. When he discovers a handsome local artist is making love to her, he takes brutal steps to subdue her desire. A cool muted tale of sexual repression with a climax of ghastly purification.
D: Luis Buñuel. A: Catherine Deneuve, Fernando Rey, Francis Nero.

ALSO:
Ascent to Heaven (1951)
Susana (1951)
A Woman Without Love (1951)
El Bruto (1952)
Fever Mounts El Paso (1959)
Simon of the Desert (1965)

1980 Dramas

These Spanish-language films have a polished appealing look that sets them apart from earlier neorealist efforts. The beauty of landscape and people is one of the biggest attractions in these engaging humanistic films, though it helps to have a knowledge of the historical and political situations in these Spanish-speaking countries.

The Spirit of the Beehive
(1974) 98m. Subtitled. **A**

A young girl in 1940s Spain sees *Frankenstein* and takes the lessons to heart when she discovers a deserter in an abandoned barn. An unusual film that beautifully portrays the mysterious and fantastic qualities that children can bestow on the ordinary.
D: Victor Erice. A: Ana Torrent, Fernando Fernan Gomez, Teresa Gimpera.

Demons in the Garden
(1982) 100m. Subtitled. **A–**

The fraternal rivalry of a well-to-do family in rural post-Civil War Spain are at the broiling center of this small character study. Watched over by their strong mother, the two brothers—one a handsome free-spirit, the other a niggling weak shopkeeper—both succumb to corruption and greed.
D: Manuel Gutierrez Aragon. A: Angela Molina, Ana Belen, Encarna Paso.

El Norte
(1983) 139m. Subtitled. **A**

When their parents are murdered in their Guatemalan village, a teenage brother and sister decide to head north to America. A no-holds-barred account of their illegal border crossing and problems with settling into life in LA. Important and affecting without being heavy-handed.
D: Gregory Nava. A: Zaide Silvia Gutierrez, David Villalpando, Ernesto Gomez Cruz.

Holy Innocents
(1984) 108m. Subtitled. **B**

Peasants and landowners run into conflict in Franco's Spain in this rural *Upstairs, Downstairs.* Not a cheerful film, and a little heavy on the peasant / nature vs. the greedy alienated landowners theme, but has such a strong sense of place that you get caught up in the struggle.
D: Marcel Camus. A: Alfredo Landa, Francisco Rabal, Terele Pavez.

Camila
(1985) 105m. Subtitled. **A–**

Two hearts aflame: unfortunately they belong to a priest and a young well-to-do socialite in nineteenth-century Argentina. Bathed in a lovely yellow light, this is a romantic, well-paced story, with some sexily charged scenes and appealing characters.
D: Marisa Luisa Bemberg. A: Susu Pecoraro, Hector Alterio, Imanol Arias.

The Official Story
(1985) 112m. Subtitled. **A**

An upper - middle - class woman begins to suspect that their adopted baby had been the child of political oppositionists who were murdered in Argentina's "dirty war." A compelling and devastating film that perfectly captures the sense of horror that invades the genteel opulence and deliberate naivete of the protagonists.
D: Luis Puenza. A: Norma Aleandro, Hector Alterio, Analia Castro.

Half of Heaven
(1987) 127m. Subtitled. **B–**

A young woman makes her way from rural poverty to urban wealth and sophistication with the help of her grandmother's love and psy-

chic powers as well as her own drive. Occasionally slow-moving, this offers an unusual view of a strong woman's rise in a culture that still likes women in their place.
D: Manuel Gutierrez Aragon. A: Angela Molina, Margarita Lozano, Antonio Valero.

Flamenco

Blood Wedding
(1981) 72m. Subtitled. **A–**
A passionate dance version of the story by García Lorca, in which a woman runs off with her former lover only to be murdered by her husband. None of the heat is lost in this dramatic theatrical version, which is set in an empty rehearsal space. It's like a command performance just for you.
D: Carlos Saura. A: Antonio Gades, Cristina Hoyos, Juan Antonio Jiminez.

Carmen
(1985) 99m. Subtitled.
A
A choreographer casts a beautiful young unknown as the lead in his production of Carmen, which rehearses throughout the film. She becomes the role and he falls head over heels for her. Stunning flamenco sequences, and the behind-the-scenes feel accentuates the sexuality necessary to the dance.
D: Carlos Saura. A: Antonio Gades, Laura Del Sol, Paco de Lucia.

El Amor Brujo
(1986) 100m. **B+**
This flamenco ballet tells the story of a marriage arranged for two people who are in love with others. Wonderful dancing and terrific music make this a treat if you're a fan, but feels a little more overwrought and theatrical than Saura's *Blood Wedding* and *Carmen*.
D: Carlos Saura. A: Antonio Gades, Cristina Hoyos, Laura Del Sol.

1990s Comedies and Dramas

Like Hollywood films, these polished, often lush films tend to be as much about the good-looking stars and scenery as the stories. And with the exception of *Cabeza de Vaca*, they also have a light touch with their tales fueled by passion and more than a little sex.

Ay, Carmela!
(1991) 103m. Subtitled. **B**
Sympathetic to the plight of the partisans in the Spanish Civil War, a cabaret trio performs their way around Spain until they are captured by the other side. Spunky, a little bawdy, and very likable, with a final effect that is oddly dull.
D: Carlos Saura. A: Carmen Maura, Andres Pajares, Gabino Diego.

Cabeza de Vaca
(1992) 108m. Subtitled. **B**
The exploits of sixteenth-century explorer Alvar Nunez Cabeza de Vaca follow him from Indian slave to respected medicine man. While keeping a documentary feel, the lively pacing and hefty doses of violence keep it from getting too weighty.
D: Nicolas Echevarria. A: Juan Diego.

Like Water for Chocolate
(1992) 113m. Subtitled.
B+
Love will find a way according to this earthy sultry blend of comedy, drama, and more than a little carnality. The story of how a young Mexican woman continues to love her sweetheart through cooking, even after he's forced to marry her sister, is an ode to the magical, nearly mystical qualities of food.
D: Alfonso Arau. A: Lumi Cavazos, Marco Leonardi, Regina Torne.

Lovers
(1992) 103m. Subtitled. **B**
A newly discharged soldier in 1950s Madrid is happily engaged to a chaste young woman. Everything changes after spending the night with his appealing 30ish landlady who then becomes obsessed with him. Nostalgic, lush, and lascivious, this escalates into an unexpected and compelling murder story.
D: Vicente Aranda. A: Victoria Abril, Jorge Sanz, Maribel Verdu.

El Mariachi
(1993) 80m. Subtitled. **B+**
Mistaken identity is at the core of this manic spoof of Mexican action-adventures and Westerns. Goofy effects, like sudden fast-motion sequences and an off-kilter narrative, are sprinkled with plenty of violence. A low-budget, wild ride.
D: Robert Rodriguez. A: Carlos Gallardo, Consuelo Gomez, Jaime De Hoyos.

Belle Epoque
(1993) 109m. Subtitled.
B+
This sexy fairy tale tells of a young deserter in the 1930s who's taken in by a single father and his four lovely daughters. Surely, steadily, he conquers every last one of them. A sweet and lighthearted romp that's not above a bit of vulgarity and lewdness.
D: Fernando Trueba. A: Jorge Sanz, Fernando Fernan Gomez, Ariadna Gil.

Jamon, Jamon
(1993) 95m. Subtitled. **C+**
When a rich boy falls for the daughter of the town prostitute (who he's also been seeing on the sly), the boy's mother hires a male model to lure the young woman away. This melodramatic, soft-porn tale beats the drum about class differences, but seems more interested in titillation.
D: Bigas Luna. A: Anna Galiena, Stefania Sandrelli, Juan Diego.

Almodóvar

If you crossed John Waters with Jim Jarmusch and threw in a touch of *La Cage aux Folles*, you'd have something close to what Pedro Almodóvar's movies are like. These farces and screwball black comedies are like wicked cartoons with their lollipop colors, hot sex scenes, and enough perversity to stretch out the wardrobe of ten drag queens. The earlier ones are more relentlessly madcap affairs but by *Tie Me Up! Tie Me Down!* the films become smoother and weightier without losing a drop of absurdity.

Labyrinth of Passion
(1983) 100m. Subtitled. **C**

An incestuous gynecologist, an empress keen for sperm from Iran's imperial family, a nymphomaniac punk, and other assorted oddballs collide with each another, producing surprisingly dull results. The laughs are hard-won in this film that's heavy on the labyrinth and light on the passion.
D: Pedro Almodóvar. A: Antonio Banderas, Imanol Arias, Ceila Roth.

Dark Habits
(1984) 116m. Subtitled. **C**

A nightclub singer hides out in a convent after her lover ODs, and the nuns, of course, are all repressed kooks with names like Sister Manure, Snake and Sin. A one-liner that goes on and on without enough laughs to sustain it.
D: Pedro Almodóvar. A: Carmen Maura, Cristina S. Pascual, Julieta Serrano.

What Have I Done to Deserve This?
(1984) 100m. Subtitled. **B–**

Behind the apparently innocent exterior of a middle-aged cleaning woman lurks some kinky and risky behavior, even as she copes with the drugs, underage sex, and shoplifting of her kids. The film's desperate quirkiness only translates to some intermittent laughs, but Maura makes this appealing.
D: Pedro Almodóvar. A: Carmen Maura, Gonzalo Suarez, Luis Hostalot.

Law of Desire
(1986) 100m. Subtitled. **B**

A gay film director is determined to put more passion into his life and enlists the help of his brother, who's now been transsexualized into his sister. Things get sticky when a suitable young man makes an appearance in this raucous homosexual melodrama that provides real laughs.
D: Pedro Almodóvar. A: Antonio Banderas, Carmen Maura, Eusebio Poncela.

Women on the Verge of a Nervous Breakdown
(1986) 88m. Subtitled. **B–**

A farcical look at an actress's hysterical attempts to hunt down her boyfriend who has just called it quits. This bright and frenetic tour of Madrid has all the door slammings, misperceptions, and mistaken identity situations that you expect from farce, done at high speed.
D: Pedro Almodóvar. A: Carmen Maura, Antonio Banderas, Julieta Serano.

Matador
(1988) 105m. Subtitled. **B**

A retired bullfighter who makes snuff films becomes romantically entangled with the female attorney of his protégé who's been accused of murder. A very dark comedy that succeeds in playing the outrageous scenario for laughs.
D: Pedro Almodóvar. A: Antonio Banderas, Carmen Maura, Assumpta Serna.

Tie Me Up! Tie Me Down!
(1990) 105m. Subtitled. **A** 🎟

When an actress is held captive by an obsessed fan fresh from the mental institution, their relationship evolves into a dark parody of love and domesticity. A wicked sexy look at celebrity, dependence, and romantic love that even ends on a sentimental note.
D: Pedro Almodóvar. A: Victoria Abril, Antonio Banderas, Loles Leon.

High Heels
(1992) 115m. Subtitled. **B**

A vain aging actress returns to Spain and must contend with her attractive newscaster daughter and the fact that a former fling is now her child's lover. Everything really gets complicated when both women are suspected of murdering him. Uneven, but when it hits the target, it's tense, darkly funny, and extremely sexy.
D: Pedro Almodóvar. A: Victoria Abril, Marisa Paredes, Miguel Bose.

Kika
(1993) 109m. Subtitled. **B**

A makeup artist gets mixed up with an American writer and his stepson who's pursued by an ex-girlfriend with a TV show that catalogues disasters and repugnant acts. This commentary on celebrity and media coverage is so kook-filled that you'll long for a garden variety neurotic.
D: Pedro Almodóvar. A: Victoria Abril, Peter Coyote, Alex Cassanovas.

Brazilian

Brazilian cinema really began to come into its own in the U.S. with several exports such as *Pixote* that portrayed the darker side of the stereotyped carnival image. As for the other frothier melodramas in this group, sex and the natural beauty of Brazil play big parts in stories that shed a bit of light on this culturally diverse society.

Dona Flor and Her Two Husbands
(1978) 106m. Subtitled.
B+
On the verge of marrying a stable, well-heeled pillar of the community, a voluptuous young widow is joyfully haunted by the ghost of her happy-go-lucky, Adonis husband. Vibrant, lush, and hedonistic, this has a real steaminess that makes Flor's unrealistic predicament feel appealingly familiar.
D: Bruno Barreto. A: Sonia Braga, Jose Wilker, Mauro Mendonca.

Bye Bye Brazil
(1980) 110m. Subtitled. **B**
This offbeat, occasionally salacious road movie about a traveling cabaret show is really an excuse to look at Brazil. The tone is affectionate, quirky, but not cutesy, and offers a nice tour of what lies beyond Carnival and Rio.
D: Carlos Diegues. A: Jose Wilker, Betty Faria, Zaira Zambelli.

Pixote
(1981) 127m. Subtitled.
A
This devastating look at one of Rio's huge population of abandoned or neglected youth follows one ten-year-old who robs, sniffs glue, pulls off three murders, and has one of his rare vulnerable moments with a prostitute. A brutally unsparing film that is never exaggerated but often shocking.
D: Hector Babenco. A: Fernando Ramos da Silva, Marilia Pera, Jorge Juliano.

Gabriela
(1983) 105m. Subtitled. **B**
A tiny, sun-drenched port town is the setting for this humorous soap opera about a bar owner who suffers disapproval when he takes his new cook as his lover. A credible story, playful tone, and spicy sex scenes make this mix of magical realism and sweet macho posturing worth a look.
D: Bruno Barreto. A: Sonia Braga, Marcello Mastroianni, Antonio Cantafora.

Hour of the Star
(1987) 96m. Subtitled. **B+**
A homely and naive orphan comes to Sao Paulo to try her luck as a secretary and make social connections. This bleak tale, with its appropriately seedy settings, displays the Brazilian underbelly rarely on view in mainstream films. A worthy study of a difficult life, though not for everyone.
D: Suzana Amaral. A: Denony De Olivieira, Umberto Magnani, Sonia Guedes.

OTHER FILMS:
Black God (White Devil) (1964)
I Love You (1982)
Happily Ever After (1986)
Opera Do Malandro (1987)
The Story of Fausta (1988)
Savage Capitalism (1993)

Scandinavian
Swedish

Few of these films escaped the influence of Bergman while some are even direct descendants. Early works such as *Elvira Madigan* are marked by a lovely cinematography that takes full advantage of the buttercup-yellow light that suffuses much of this part of the world. Psychological complexity and contradictory emotions are the center of these stories—there's lots of talking, but they don't feel intellectualized. Sensitive, thoughtful, often witty, these demand your full attention and amply reward it.

Elvira Madigan
(1967) 89m. Subtitled & Dubbed. **A–**
An army officer and a tightrope walker fall in love and run off together only to discover that the rest of the world does not always love lovers. The tender images and classical music have become advertising clichés, but the timeless story and elegant look will thrill even the most jaded viewer.
D: Bo Widerberg. A: Pia Degermark, Thommy Berggren, Lennart Malmer.

I Am Curious Yellow
(1967) 121m. Subtitled.
C+
Frontal nudity and seizure by U.S. customs helped turn this film into a sensation of the sexual revolution. Actually the focus of the long-winded story is Sweden's political and social climate as it follows a young female sociologist polling Swedes while engaging in various sexual encounters along the way.
D: Vilgot Sjoman. A: Lena Nyman, Borje Ahlstedt, Peter Lindtren.

The Sacrifice
(1986) 145m. Subtitled. **A**
A journalist-professor is feted for his 50th birthday at the country house while family and friends also anticipate an impending nuclear holocaust. A slow-moving and achingly beautiful work by Russian director Tarkovsky that portrays the fear and horror with a piercing delicacy.
D: Andrei Tarkovsky. A: Erland Josephson, Allan Edwall, Susan Fleetwood.

My Life as a Dog
(1987) 101m. Subtitled.
A
When a 12-year-old boy is farmed out to relatives in rural Sweden in the 1950s, he finds much to learn from the locals, including the girl whose boxing lessons pack a sexual punch. A genuinely charming tale of a misbehaved sensitive boy at a difficult and wonderful time in his life.
D: Lasse Hallstrom. A: Anton Ganzelius, Tomas von Bromssen, Anki Liden.

Pelle the Conqueror
(1988) 138m. Subtitled. **A**
Following a nineteenth-century Swedish widower's efforts to provide a better life for his son by moving to Denmark, we see all the challenges that these two face. Their subtle, profound, and largely unspoken relationship is the center and the highlight of this intelligent and beautifully nuanced film.
D: Billie August. A: Max von Sydow, Pelle Hvenegaard, Erik Paaske.

The Best Intentions
(1992) 186m. Subtitled.
A–
The courtship and troubled marriage of Ingmar Berg-

man's parents is the focus of this film, set at the turn of the century. An emotionally complex, carefully structured portrait of an admittedly disastrous union, imbued by the spirit of Bergman who scripted it. Talky, subtle, and quietly spectacular.
D: Billie August. A: Samuel Froler, Pernilla August, Max von Sydow.

The Slingshot
(1993) 102m. Subtitled.
A–
A boy and his older brother are the butt of endless jokes in 1930s Sweden because their mother is Jewish and both parents actively Socialist. With humor and sympathy, this coming-of-age tale shows the ways that being an outsider can toughen a kid up and the major role that minor objects—a slingshot, how you dress—can play in childhood.
D: Ake Sandgren. A: Jesper Salen, Stellan Skarsgard, Basia Frydman.

Sunday's Children
(1993) 117m. Subtitled.
A
This gem of a film examines 8-year-old Ingmar Bergman's very difficult relationship with his reserved minister father. Set mostly in the 1920s and told from the boy's perspective, this captures the mystery, excitement, and curiosity of childhood with perfect pitch.
D: Daniel Bergman. A: Thommy Berggren, Lena Endre, Henrik Lennros.

Bergman

No other filmmaker has delved into the human psyche so relentlessly as Ingmar Bergman. In the 1940s and early 50s the director began to develop his style in a series of waspish uneven dramas about the joys and sexual turbulence of love. By the mid-1950s he was turning out masterpieces filled with startling images and scenes of almost unbearable intensity. These audacious films will plunge you into stark and dreamlike worlds where the characters examine love, madness, and other mysteries of the heart.

Smiles of a Summer Night
(1955) 105m. B&W.
Subtitled. **A–**
An actress throws a house party so she can face off her current lover against an old beau who's suddenly back in the picture. The musty elaborate sets and exquisite ensemble playing elevates this wise romantic comedy, which looks at love with a detached Old World melancholy.
D: Ingmar Bergman. A: Eva Dahlbeck, Gunnar Bjornstrand, Harriet Andersson.

The Seventh Seal
(1956) 96m. B&W.
Subtitled. **A–**
As the Black Death rages across Europe, a disillusioned knight returning from the Crusade duels the Grim Reaper in a chess game of life and death. This stark somber fable, which questions man's purpose in life, has enough sublime moments to help you through the overwrought philosophizing. The Dance of Death remains one of the most haunting scenes in cinema.
D: Ingmar Bergman. A: Max von Sydow, Gunnar Bjornstrand, Bibi Andersson.

Wild Strawberries
(1957) 90m. B&W.
Subtitled. **A**
On his way to receive an honorary degree, an elderly professor looks back on his life with joy and regret. An extraordinary seamless interweaving of the foibles of love past and present adds a bittersweet edge to this unsentimental tale.
D: Ingmar Bergman. A: Victor Sjostrom, Bibi Andersson, Ingrid Thulin.

The Magician
(1958) 102m. B&W.
Subtitled. **B+**
A magician riddled with debts and self-doubt must defend himself against public slander. As it turns out, he's got the head of a snake-oil salesman and the heart of a prophet as he goes on the road to help "cure" the little people in this provocative, slow-moving, gothic drama.
D: Ingmar Bergman. A: Max von Sydow, Ingrid Thulin, Gunnar Bjornstrand.

The Virgin Spring
(1960) 88m. B&W.
Subtitled. **B+**
A spring is born on the spot where a beautiful young girl is raped and murdered. After the promising and shocking opening, this heavily symbolic medieval fable bogs down in rhetorical posturing as the girl's father meticulously plots his revenge.
D: Ingmar Bergman. A: Max von Sydow, Brigitta Valbert, Gunnel Lindblom.

Through a Glass, Darkly
(1961) 91m. B&W.
Subtitled. **A–**
A former mental patient and her family spend a revealing summer on an isolated almost barren island. This study of mental illness and its effect on the ultimate dysfunctional family is icy, detached, talky, but always fascinating, and finally terrifying.
D: Ingmar Bergman. A: Harriet Andersson, Gunnar Bjornstrand, Max von Sydow.

Persona
(1966) 81m. B&W. **A–**
An overly sensitive actress who becomes mute is put under the care of a nurse, and the two women grow to resemble each other physically and spiritually. This eerie hallucinatory experience peels off layers of the human psyche like a dream.
D: Ingmar Bergman. A: Bibi Andersson, Liv Ullmann, Gunnar Bjornstrand.

Hour of the Wolf
(1968) 88m. Subtitled. **A–**
A painter and his wife move to a desolate island where he begins to have haunting visions. The bizarre, nightmarelike downfall of a tormented artist and the people who care for him makes for frighteningly good viewing while barren locales add to the weird clammy feel.
D: Ingmar Bergman. A: Max von Sydow, Liv Ullmann, Erland Josephson.

Passion of Anna
(1969) 101m. Subtitled.
A–
A divorced man falls in love with a crippled widow, and a bitter husband tries to ignore his wife's cheating. A turbulent, often violent examination of two couples' grappling with love, guilt, insanity, and redemption in a claustrophobic island setting.
D: Ingmar Bergman. A: Max von Sydow, Liv Ullmann, Bibi Andersson.

Cries and Whispers
(1972) 106m. Subtitled or Dubbed. **A**
Two sisters visit their dying

sister but are met with resistance from a stubborn servant girl. Soon the siblings long for the not so idyllic past and try to come to terms with the chilly nightmare their lives have become. A haunting dreamlike film that's like an anguished cry in the night. Beware of badly dubbed prints.
D: Ingmar Bergman. A: Liv Ullmann, Harriet Andersson, Ingrid Thulin.

Scenes from a Marriage
(1973) 168m. Subtitled or Dubbed. **A**
A sophisticated Stockholm couple, weary of making one another miserable, decide to end their marriage. This intense punishing film, shot almost exclusively in close-ups, gets under the skin of this complex highly sympathetic couple going through the death throes of a marriage.
D: Ingmar Bergman. A: Liv Ullmann, Erland Josephson, Bibi Andersson.

Autumn Sonata
(1978) 97m. Subtitled. **A–**
A haughty world-class pianist meets with her shy daughter for the first time in seven years. A tense drama with Ullmann's ugly duckling character recalling any number of Bette Davis vehicles of the 40s. Occasionally shrill, but moving glimpse at showbiz parents and their spiritually undernourished kids.
D: Ingmar Bergman. A: Ingrid Bergman, Liv Ullmann, Gunnar Bjornstrand.

From the Life of the Marionettes
(1980) 104m. Subtitled. **A–**
A successful businessman rapes then murders a prostitute, imagining her to be his beautiful wife. This subtle disturbing look at the tyrannical power of the subconscious chills to the bone, even with the almost sympathetic portrait of a killer.
D: Ingmar Bergman. A: Robert Atzon, Christine Buchegger, Martin Behrath.

Fanny and Alexander
(1982) 197m. Subtitled. **A+**
Two children observe the wonderful, ridiculous, and tragic lives of the adults around them in turn of the century Sweden. This lush Victorian family saga is a bursting tapestry of glorious and failed humanity, with an extended Christmas scene that is pure enchantment.
D: Ingmar Bergman. A: Pernilla Allwin, Bertil Guve, Gunn Walgren.

After the Rehearsal
(1984) 72m. Subtitled. **A–**
Just as he's about to open a play, a stage director is propositioned by an actress whose mother was his former lover. The tangled incestuous web of love affairs and consuming passion for the theatrical world electrifies this stagy production.
D: Ingmar Bergman. A: Erland Josephson, Ingrid Thulin, Lena Olin.

OTHER FILMS:
Night Is My Future (1947)
Port of Call (1948)
Three Strange Loves (1949)
Summer Interlude (1950)
Secrets of Women (1952)
Monka (1953)
Sawdust and Tinsel (1953)
Dreams (1954)
A Lesson in Love (1954)
Brink of Life (1957)
The Devil's Eye (1960)
Winter Light (1962)
The Silence (1963)
All These Women (1964)
The Magic Flute (1974)
The Serpent's Egg (1977)

Danish

Babette's Feast
(1987) 102m. Subtitled. **A**
The minister's spinster daughters have forsaken worldly pleasures in their remote nineteenth-century village, but all that changes when they hire a French refugee/cook extraordinaire. Watching this beautifully rendered film is like listening to a well-told fable at a spectacular dinner—a movie of great culinary and emotional range.
D: Gabriel Axel. A: Stephane Audran, Jean-Philippe Lafont, Jari Kulle.

Memories of a Marriage
(1989) 90m. Subtitled. **B**
Gathered with family and friends, a docile older man recalls in flashbacks the life he has shared with his outspoken, passionate, and bighearted wife. Contradictory, infuriating, and often appealing characters reveal a complexity that's rare in marriage dramas.
D: Kaspar Rostrup. A: Ghita Norby, Frits Helmuth, Rikke Bendsen.

Finnish

Leningrad Cowboys Go America
(1989) 80m. Subtitled. **C–**
An appallingly bad Finnish polka-rock band heads off for a small-town tour of the States. A few sight gags like their hairdos aren't enough to sustain this ploddingly quirky film that suffers from an outsider's misunderstanding of how to parody the U.S.
D: Aki Kaurismaki. A: Matti Pellonpaa, Kari Vaananen, Jim Jarmusch.

OTHER FILMS:
Flight of the Eagle (1982) (Swedish)
Twist and Shout (1986) (Swedish)
The Mozart Brothers (1988) (Swedish)
Ariel (1990) (Finnish)
Children of Nature (1991) (Icelandic)
House of Angels (1993) (Swedish)
Sofie (1993) (Swedish)
Pathfinder (1987) (Laplandic)

Russian

Eisenstein

Eisenstein is practically a force of nature in the history of cinema; his techniques have been so widely copied, his scenes have been "quoted" so often by other filmmakers that you may have a sense of déjà vu while watching these wide-angle views of Russia's history.

The Battleship Potemkin

(1925) 65m. B&W. Silent.
A 🏛

Mutiny on the Potemkin serves as a metaphor for the 1905 Revolution in this film school staple that actually makes for good home viewing. Contains terrifically ambitious crowd scenes and the famous Odessa Steps sequence (see *The Untouchables* for the most famous homage to it).
D: Sergei Eisenstein. A: Alexander Antonov, Vladimir Barsky, Grigori Alexandrov.

October/Ten Days That Shook the World

(1928) 85m. B&W. Silent.
A 🏛

The 1917 events in Petrograd leading up to the toppling of the czarist regime are given the kaleidoscopic treatment in this feast for film buffs that straddles the boundary between narrative and experimental technique.
D: Sergei Eisenstein. A: Nikandrov, Vladimir Popov, Boris Liovanov.

Ivan the Terrible, Part One and Two

(1945, 1946) 188m. B&W. Subtitled. **A**

The life and times of Russia's first czar are the subject of this gargantuan project (originally planned for three parts). Serious and weighty, but a banquet of striking images that show the underside of absolute power.
D: Sergei Eisenstein. A: Nikolai Cherkasov, Ludmila Tselikovskaya, Serafina Berman.

1960s–1990s Dramas

Except for the historical dramas, these films rarely steer far from themes of nationalism and the core problem in Russia, which is too few "haves" and too many "have nots." Claustrophobia is not an uncommon feeling when watching these—and you'll realize just how big your home is without all those relatives camping out on the sofa.

War and Peace

(1968) 373m. Subtitled or Dubbed. **A**

The word epic was invented for this majestic unusually faithful adaptation of the Tolstoy novel of Russia just before Napoleon's 1812 invasion. A real commitment to watch, this is like a one-shot overview of Soviet cinema at its swankiest: period detail, grand sweeps and big themes. Avoid dubbed version.
D: Sergei Bondarchuk. A: Sergei Bondarchuk, Ludmilla Savelyeva, Vyacheslav Tyonov.

Moscow Does Not Believe in Tears

(1980) 152m. Subtitled.
B+

When three young women living in a workers' dorm and on the prowl for husbands get temporary use of an apartment, they decide to invent a new life for themselves. An interesting study of class consciousness and tradition that takes a while to warm up, but worth the effort.
D: Vladimir Menshov. A: Vera Alentova, Irina Murayova, Raisa Ryazanova.

Rasputin

(1985) 107m. Subtitled.
B−

Often blamed for helping precipitate the downfall of the czar's family, Rasputin was a healer, prophet, and protégé to the royals, whose gifts were tainted with a pronounced megalomania. Historical footage and a compelling story help compensate for the low production values of this historical drama.
D: Elem Klimov. A: Alexei Petrenko, Welta Leene, Anatoli Romskin.

Little Vera

(1988) 110m. Subtitled.
A−

Looking like a punked-out Princess Di, a teenager who lives in a cramped apartment with her alcoholic father and nagging mother fixates on a lothario and moves him into the family digs. With frank sexual scenes and lively pacing, this is a sign of the "new" Russia.
D: Vasily Pichul. A: Natalya Negoda, Andrei Sokolov, Ludmila Zaitseva.

Freeze-Die-Come to Life

(1990) 105m. Subtitled. **B**

Like a Dickens' novel set in Siberia, a grim and unremitting life is seen through the eyes of two preadolescents. Basic survival is on display here—the boy sleeps with a piglet for comfort, makeshift skates are made from runners nailed to two boards —in this portrait of a little-seen part of Russia.
D: Vitaly Kanevski. A: Pavel Nazarov, Dinara Drukarova, Yelena Popova.

Luna Park

(1991) 105m. Subtitled.
B−

One of the most fervent Moscow skinheads discovers that his father is a respected Jewish composer. His voyage to self-discovery takes him on a frenetic and reckless tour of modern-day Russia and some of its least stable and most disturbing elements. Uneven but never dull.
D: Pavel Lounguine. A: Oleg Borisov, Natalie Egorova, Andrei Goutine.

Taxi Blues
(1991) 100m. Subtitled.
C–
The difficult friendship between a seething, anti-Semitic taxi driver and a Jewish jazz musician stands in for New and Old Russia. A brash tough look at a society in violent transition, this film is constantly foiled by its berating dialogue and pointlessly depressing images.
D: Pavel Lounguine. A: Piotr Zaitchenko, Piotr Mamonov, Vladimir Kachpour.

Adam's Rib
(1992) 77m. Subtitled.
B+
This follows three generations of women crammed together in a tiny Moscow apartment. Grandma is mute, but runs the roost with a bell; her daughter and granddaughters, all sexually active and eager for privacy, run to do her bidding. A forthright blunt film that has a familial intimacy verging on voyeurism.
D: Vyacheslav Krishtofovich. A: Inna Churikova, Svetlana Ryabova, Maria Golubkina.

Tarkovsky

In these often science-fictional explorations of the mind, Andrei Tarkovsky offers the terror of the ordinary. These films may be slow and wordy, but the eerie images will haunt you long after the characters are silent.

Andrei Rublev
(1966) 185m. B&W. Subtitled. **A**
Eight different episodes show portions of the life of the fifteenth-century monk and icon painter as he wanders through Russia. Mist-filled, strange, and hypnotic with the sweep and costume look of earlier Russian cinema.
D: Andrei Tarkovsky. A: Anatoly Solonitsyn, Ivan Lapikov, Nikolai Grinko.

Solaris
(1972) 165m. Subtitled. **B**
A psychologist is dispatched to close down what appears to be useless experiments at a water-logged space station. Instead, he discovers that the ocean washing over the entire planet is a thinking being that feeds off the unconscious memories and desires of the humans. Slow but intense.
D: Andrei Tarkovsky. A: Natalia Bondarchuk, Donatas Banionis, Yuri Jarvet.

Stalker
(1979) 161m. B&W. Subtitled. **A**
A scientist and writer are guided through a forbidden zone in this science-fiction story whose props are only the debris of our modern lives. Black and white bleeds into color in haunting unforgettable images of a bleak wasteland filled with trials for the spirit and psyche.
D: Andrei Tarkovsky. A: Alexander Kaidanovsky, Anatoly Solonitsyn, Nikolai Grinko.

Chinese

Chinese Dramas

With a mythic fabulist touch reminiscent of magical realism, these beautifully produced films are often set in the 1920s when warlords still called the shots. Many have an operatic feel, with complicated, wide-ranging stories that rely on metaphor, symbolism, and striking use of color to convey much of the characters' grand emotions.

Horse Thief
(1987) 88m. Subtitled. **B**
Set in 1923 Tibet, this tells the story of a man and his family's ostracism when he's revealed to be a horse thief. Like a *National Geographic* special, this is more anthropological travelogue than drama, filled with colorful Buddhist rituals and little dialogue. A disturbing film given the recent events in Tibet.
D: Tian Zhuangzhuang. A: Tseshang Rigzin.

Red Sorghum
(1987) 91m. Subtitled.
B+
A grandson narrates the legend of his stubborn and fearless grandparents in 1920s, beginning with how his mother was sold to the local vintner and leper in exchange for a mule. Theatrical, nearly musical, with a rare glimpse of Chinese landscapes.
D: Zhang Yimoy. A: Gong Li, Jian Weng, Liu Ji.

Ju Dou
(1989) 98m. Subtitled.
A
Tortured by her impotent new husband, a young woman begins a lusty affair with his adopted, live-in nephew, which becomes even more complicated when she has a child. An intensely enclosed and volatile drama with nuanced complex characters and brilliant use of color.
D: Zhang Yimou. A: Gong Li, Li Baotian, Li Wei.

Life on a String
(1991) 120m. Subtitled.
B+
A master tells a blind boy that he will regain his sight if he breaks 1,000 strings on the banjo. Though the boy remains blind, he becomes a kind of traveling minstrel, imparting his spiritual wisdom in turn to his own apprentice. Lyrical, lovely, and long-winded, this gives a good sense of the adulation accorded those with a higher spiritual calling.
D: Chen Kaige. A: Liu Zhong Yuan, Huang Lei, Xu Qing.

Raise the Red Lantern

(1991) 125m. Subtitled.
A

The young woman who becomes a feudal lord's fourth wife becomes the focus of her immediate predecessor's anger and envy. A delicate and stinging story that explores the relationship of the four wives and the complex workings of the household, colored by the glow of the red lantern indicating where the master is sleeping that night.
D: Zhang Yimou. A: Gong Li, He Saife, Ma Jingwu.

Song of the Exile

(1991) 100m. Subtitled.
A–

When a 25-year-old British university graduate returns to native Hong Kong for her sister's wedding she rekindles the tense relationship with her willful conformist mother shown in flashbacks and present day scenes. A well-observed, low-keyed, and quietly accomplished jewel of a movie.
D: Chen Kaige. A: Shwu Sen Chang, Maggie Cheung.

Combination Platter

(1993) 85m. English & part Subtitled. C–

A recent Taiwanese immigrant waiter realizes that the surest path to a green card is by marrying an American. Looking like a student-film, this captures the problems of this immigrant living in Queens, but its plodding, long-winded narrative makes the characters into emblems rather than people.
D: Tony Chan. A: Jeff Lau, Colleen O'Brien, Lester Chan.

Farewell My Concubine

(1993) 157m. Subtitled.
B+

The chronicle of a 50-year-old friendship of two Chinese opera stars allows the viewer to trace China's history from 1927–1977. An ambitious stylized saga, filled with startling images, though you may feel tired afterwards, partly due to the distanced theatrical style of acting.
D: Chen Kaige. A: Leslie Cheung, Zhang Fengyi, Gong Li.

The Story of Qui Ju

(1993) 100m. Subtitled. A

After their village chief kicks her husband in the groin, a determined and very pregnant wife seeks justice starting with the local police, learning something each step along the way. The story's surface is simple as a parable, but serves up a masterful mosaic of Chinese life from peasants to bureaucrats, from beautiful countryside to teeming city.
D: Zhang Yimou. A: Gong Li, Leo Lao Sheng, Liu Pei Qi.

The Wedding Banquet

(1993) 111m. English & part Subtitled. B–

A successful gay Taiwanese immigrant tries to hoodwink his parents by constructing elaborate wedding plans with a young woman, even while he's living with his lover. Though sweet and played with conviction, the situation always seems a little too tidy.
D: Ang Lee. A: Winston Chao, May Chin, Mitchell Lichtenstein.

Eat Drink Man Woman

(1994) 104m. Subtitled.
A–

A Taipei widower tries to balance his duties as a master chef and a father to three very independent daughters. Incredibly colorful, with elaborately scrumptious food prep scenes, this is a delicious slice of family life, made even more of a tease via the characters' tendency to play things close to the vest.
D: Ang Lee. A: Sihung Lung, Kuei-Mei Yang, Chien-Lien Wu.

Hong Kong Action Films

Viewers familiar with the 70s kung fu films that featured crude staging, poor dubbing, and jerky action won't recognize the Chinese action films of the 80s and 90s. Kung fu star Jackie Chan created a whole new genre of action-comedy that combines martial arts and acrobatic skills with elaborate chases, stunts, and slapstick. The major new talent has been John Woo, whose series of hyperkinetic crime thrillers offers frenetic bloody gun battles, stylized visuals, and elaborate tales of loyalty and camaraderie in the midst of carnage.

Zu Warriors from the Magic Mountain

(1983) 94m. Subtitled. B

A young Zu warrior in medieval China joins martial artist Buddhist monks in their battle with the Evil Disciples. High-flying swordsmen and women abound in this delirious phantasmagoric costume fantasy with nonstop action and special effects. Spawned a whole wave of exaggerated costume fantasies.
D: Tsui Hark. A: Yuen Biao, Adam Cheung, Samo Hung.

A Better Tomorrow

(1986) 95m. Subtitled. A–

Director John Woo's groundbreaking gangster thriller follows three underworld buddies and their contrasting fates after one takes the rap for the others and then tries to go straight. Fast, well-acted, and laced with the kinetic action and heightened romanticism that became Woo's trademark.
D: John Woo. A: Ti Lung, Chow Yun Fat, Leslie Cheung.

A Better Tomorrow II

(1987) 104m. Subtitled. A

An aging boss trying to go straight reunites with a couple of well-armed old buddies in his retaliation against the Hong Kong syndicate that's out to kill him. Frenzied direction and high-key performances add up to a wild ride packed with violent gun battles and emotional anguish.
D: John Woo. A: Ti Lung, Chow Yun Fat.

City on Fire

(1987) 98m. Subtitled. C

An undercover cop joins a robbery gang, bonds with the gang leader, and participates in a jewel heist, culminating in a tense climactic standoff. This routine caper has a gritty look, hard-edged performances, and a final confrontation that inspired a similar scene in Tarantino's *Reservoir Dogs*.

D: Ringo Lam. A: Chow Yun Fat, Danny Lee.

Roboforce (aka I Love Maria)
(1988) 86m. Subtitled. **B–**
A trio of bumbling good guys manages to reprogram a super-powered female robot to fight against its criminal creators. An enjoyable romp sparked by clever special effects scenes of flying robots in combat but often undermined by its goofball heroes.
D: David Chung. A: Sally Yeh, John Sham, Tsui Hark.

Bullet in the Head
(1990) 136m. Subtitled. **A**
John Woo's variation on *The Deer Hunter* follows three Hong Kong buddies who enter Vietnam with a money-making scheme but get caught up in the war. An intense saga of friendship, greed, betrayal, and revenge all played at a deliriously high pitch and studded with bloody shoot-outs.
D: John Woo. A: Tony Leung, Jacy Cheung, Waise Lee.

The Killer
(1991) 110m. Subtitled. **A**
A hitman cares for a girl blinded in a shoot-out and strikes up a friendship with an undercover cop out to get him. This is prime John Woo: flamboyant, romantic, and even maudlin at times, with slow-motion photography, use of religious symbols, and shots of doves juxtaposed against stylized bloody shoot-outs.
D: John Woo. A: Chow Yun Fat, Danny Lee, Sally Yeh.

Hard-Boiled
(1992) 126m. Subtitled. **A**
The celebrated ultraviolent, strongly emotional police thriller from John Woo follows undercover cops Tony and Tequila as they battle some very classy gunrunners. Highlight set piece is a scene where a policewoman evacuates a room full of newborn babies as shooting bursts all around them.
D: John Woo. A: Chow Yun Fat, Tony Leung, Teresa Mo.

Police Story III: Supercop
(1992) 96m. Subtitled. **A**
Inspector Chan teams with a mainland China female cop to get the goods on a drug ring, taking them to a Red Chinese prison camp, a drug king's jungle fortress, and the streets of a modern Asian city. Chan's famed kung fu and stunt work share the spotlight with several large-scale action scenes.
D: Jackie Chan. A: Jackie Chan, Michelle Yeoh, Maggie Cheung.

Comet, Butterfly and Sword
(1993) 87m. Subtitled. **B+**
A forest-dwelling community of martial artists fends off a series of concerted attacks by rivals. A costume tale of high-flying sword fighters—male and female—featuring elaborate stunts, clever weaponry, bursts of gore and violence, and some romantic interludes.
D: D. J. Mike. A: Michelle Yeoh, Tony Leung, Joey Wong.

Indian

Satyajit Ray

Influenced by Jean Renoir and Italian neorealism, Ray portrays with subtlety and wit all levels of Indian life, from the poorest to the most privileged. The pace demands close attention, though it's not slow: This is life observed at the level of a blade of grass, with a scope both narrow and familial, broad and societal.

Pather Panchali
(1954) 112m. B&W. Subtitled. **A**
The first installment of a trilogy named for its coming-of-age protagonist shows Apu's family living in a small Bengali village where they take care of his aging auntie and are constantly in the shadow of their better-off relatives. The ordinary and extraordinary of everyday life are melded in this carefully paced and richly detailed story.
D: Satyajit Ray. A: Subir Banerjee, Karuna Banerjee, Kanu Banerjee.

Aparajito
(1957) 108m. B&W. Subtitled. **A**
Second in Apu trilogy finds the family in Benares where the mother and son become more worldly and the father more spiritual. Apu's education and ambition begin to tear him away from the family. Even with foreign settings and traditions, the conflicts are as familiar as next door.
D: Satyajit Ray. A: Pinaki Sen Gupta, Smaran Ghosal, Karuna Banerjee.

The World of Apu
(1959) 103m. B&W. Subtitled. **A**
In the final episode, Apu marries a young woman he doesn't love, has a family, and eventually learns to love her through her death. The most accomplished of the trilogy and completes the transition—rural to urban, ignorance to education, child to father.
D: Satyajit Ray. A: Soumitra Chatterjee, Sharmila Tagore, Swapan Mukherjee.

Devi (The Goddess)
(1960) 96m. Subtitled. **B+**
A recently married couple is being torn apart by the religious fanaticism of the husband's father: He not only believes his daughter-in-law is the reincarnation of the goddess Druga, he convinces her of it as well. Wryly funny and affectionately mocking of India—like a cerebral joke.
D: Satyajit Ray. A: Chabi Biswas, Soumitra Chatterjee, Karuna Banerjee.

Two Daughters
(1961) 114m. Subtitled. **B+**
Two tales of first love, one in which a servant girl becomes attached to her boss, another in which a young man bails out of an arranged marriage. These literary adaptations are self-contained, with sharp observations of a short story, and the second one is funny to boot.
D: Satyajit Ray. A: Anil Chatterjee, Chandana Bannerjee, Soumitra Chatterjee.

The Adversary
(1971) 100m. Subtitled. **A**
A college graduate becomes increasingly frustrated when he is unable to find an appropriate position in Calcutta.

Compounding his woes is his needy unhappy widowed mother and younger successful sister. Close to Italian neorealism in feel, but with the dense detail of Ray's other films.
D: Satyajit Ray. A: Dhritiman Chatterjee, Jayashree Roy, Krishna Bose.

Distant Thunder
(1974) 92m. Subtitled. **A–**
A family struggles to survive as famine grips their tiny village in 1942. Narrated by the local learned man, this once again looks at the differences between classes in India. The desert is depicted so harshly and with such loving realism that you practically feel sand in your eyes. Not cheerful, but true to life.
D: Satyajit Ray. A: Soumitra Chatterjee, Babita, Sandhya Roy.

Home and the World
(1984) 130m. Subtitled.
A–
Set in 1907 Bengal, this is a tale of a woman, her husband, and his boyhood friend who comes to live with them, and the effect of the world at large on their safe little haven. Few domestic dramas can match the tension in this elegant and lethally devastating story as lives unravel and are transformed.
D: Satyajit Ray. A: Soumitra Chatterjee, Victor Banerjee, Gopa Aich.

The Stranger
(1992) 120m. Subtitled.
B–
A middle-class Calcutta couple find their lives turned upside down when her long-lost uncle suddenly arrives to move in. Is he really her uncle? What is family? Tradition? Ray poses these questions in this lighthearted, humor-filled look at culture and modern life.
D: Satyajit Ray. A: Mamata Shakar, Deepankar Dey, Utpal Dutt.

Eastern European

Polish

Survival, determination, tenacity are what you'll find in these films. While sharing a similar dark humor with their Eastern European counterparts, many of the Polish films are marked by a grim eerieness, a mystical strangeness. Special mention must be made of Roman Polanski, whose mordant humor and uncanny sense of the bizarre is already clear in these early productions. As conditions change rapidly in this part of the world, these films provide historical documents of the postwar era and the 40 years during which Communists held power.

Knife in the Water
(1962) 94m. B&W.
Subtitled. **A**
A bored couple on their way to an afternoon of sailing on a lake picks up a hitchhiker and invites him to spend the day on the water with them. What a mistake. Full of sexual tension, a haunting creepiness, and gallows humor, this early Polanski film is a gem.
D: Roman Polanski. A: Leon Niemczyk, Jolanta Umecka, Zygmunt Malanowicz.

Cul-De-Sac
(1966) 111m. B&W.
Subtitled. **A**
Two wounded gangsters hole up in a seaside mansion in Northumberland, taking a spineless husband and his attractive wife hostage. Many of Polanski's trademarks are here—caustic humor, sadism, and a certain uneasiness, as well as wonderful shots from unexpected angles. Unpredictable and sly.
D: Roman Polanski. A: Françoise Dorleac, Donald Pleasence, Lionel Stander.

Camera Buff
(1980) 108m. Subtitled.
B+
A factory worker buys a camera to record his new baby, but he can't stop filming everything else, including events the authorities don't want seen. A witty look at the effect of movies and the so-called objectivity of the camera. Low production values gives this a documentary feel.
D: Krzysztof Kieslowski. A: Jerzy Sturha, Malgorzata Zabowska, Kryzysztof Zanussi.

Interrogation
(1982) 118m. Subtitled.
A
After spending a night with a military officer, a 1950 Warsaw cabaret singer finds herself in prison, accused of political activities. Grim, Kafkaesque, with a sometimes highly grating protagonist: You know this woman is a survivor because you can almost feel her claw the screen.
D: Richard Bugajski. A: Krystyna Janda, Adam Ferency, Agnieszka Holland.

Moonlighting
(1983) 97m. Subtitled.
A
As the only English-speaking member of an illegal construction crew remodeling an apartment in London, Jeremy Irons keeps the news of Solidarity and martial law from his crew. Taut and quietly desperate, this drama's only fault is its slightly slow pace.
D: Jerzy Skolimowski. A: Jeremy Irons, Eugene Lipinski, Jiri Stanislav.

No End
(1984) 104m. Subtitled.
B–
Following his untimely death, a young lawyer leaves behind a wife, child, and an open case concerning a Solidarity sympathizer. In the gentle allegory of Poland under martial law, the lawyer—now visible only to the viewer—continues to further his work and console his wife.
D: Krzysztof Kieslowski. A: Maria Pakulnis, Aleksandr Bardini, Grazyna Szapolwska.

Year of the Quiet Sun
(1985) 106m. Subtitled w/ English. **A–**
A Polish widow becomes involved with an American soldier just after World War II while a war crimes investigation is occurring in her town. This looks like a sepia photograph, with narrow-framed

images that convey the limits of these hard-bitten characters' lives. Credible, stark, and delicate, even as it depicts familiar material.
D: Krzysztof Zanussi. A: Maja Komorowska, Scott Wilson, Hanna Skarzanka.

OTHER POLISH FILMS:
The Dybbuck (1938)
Border Street (1950)
2 Men and a Wardrobe (1958)
The Fat and the Lean (1960)
Poisonous Plants (1975)
Contract (1980)
Austeria (1982)
Masquerade (1986)
Kingsize (1988)
The Conductor (1993)

Wajda

Polish director Andrzej Wajda brings a gentle human touch to his films, developing his characters slowly, so that we come to know them as individuals. What makes his sweeping historical interpretations so personal is that you're made to feel as though you know someone who's gone through the experience rather than watching a set of issues being portrayed. The price for this is a sometimes slowish pace and much talking. Your patience will be rewarded; Wajda has much to tell about Poland over the past 40 years.

A Generation
(1954) 90m. B&W. Subtitled. **A–**

In wartime Warsaw, a young man falls for the woman who leads the Resistance group. A gritty neorealistic view of people willing to do anything to survive, and an accomplished and sharply observed portrait of Poland under the Nazis.
D: Andrzej Wajda. A: Ursula Modrzinska, Tadeusz Lomnicki, Zgibniew Cybulski.

Kanal (aka They Loved Life)
(1957) 97m. B&W. Subtitled. **A–**

Determined to flee the invading Nazis, a band of Polish soldiers and partisans takes the only escape route they trust: the Warsaw sewers. A bleak, realistic, and evocative drama that leaves a powerful impression.
D: Andrzej Wajda. A: Teresa Izewska, Tadeusz Janczar, Wienczylaw Glinski.

Ashes and Diamonds
(1958) 96m. B&W. Subtitled. **A**

Members of the Polish Resistance are traced during the waning days of World War II. Stark and ironic, this gives a good picture of the confusion as a world tried to remake itself. The actors are shown from the shoulders up, as if they were stunted, capturing the feeling of a generation that grew up too quickly.
D: Andrzej Wajda. A: Zbigniew Cybulski, Ewa Krzyzanowska, Adam Pawlikowski.

The Birch Wood
(1971) 100m. Subtitled. **A**

A TB victim shows up at the forest cottage of his widower brother. The dying man teaches his emotionally dead brother to live again, with the help and love of a local peasant girl. Sympathetic, tender, and intense.
D: Andrzej Wajda. A: Daniel Olbrychski, Olgierd Lukaszewicz, Emilia Krakowska.

Man of Marble
(1977) 150m. B&W w/ color. Subtitled. **B+**

Investigating the life of a worker-hero of the Stalinist 1950s in Poland, a young woman comes upon many versions of his life as recollected by friends and associates. Grim, humorless, and long, this questions in provocative ways how much we can ever really know about each other.
D: Andrzej Wajda. A: Krystyna Janda, Jerzy Radziwilowicz.

Man of Iron
(1981) 140m. Subtitled. **A**

A sequel to *Man of Marble,* this film traces the 1960s student uprising and their link to the 1980 Solidarity movement through the story of a documentary filmmaker, an alcoholic journalist, and a spunky worker. Straightforward and insightful, this is an insider's view of the sea change that occurred in Poland.
D: Andrzej Wajda. A: Jerzy Radziwilowicz, Krystyna Janda, Marian Opiana.

Without Anesthesia
(1979) 111m. Subtitled. **A–**

A famous journalist returns to Poland from an assignment abroad to find his life is falling apart: His wife leaves and suddenly he's out of favor with the officials. A painful look at personal and professional collapse, with political implications.
D: Andrzej Wajda. A: Zbigniew Zapasiewicz, Andrzej Seweryn, Ewa Dalkowska.

Hungarian

Understandably, the two main themes that crop up again and again in these small, mostly character studies, are World War II and the 1956 uprising when Hungarians tried to oust the Communists. What you'll also find here is a distinctive odd sense of humor, a paradoxical "nothing is so bad it can't get worse" attitude, and some dreamlike surreal imagery surfacing in the most unlikely places.

Father
(1966) 95m. **A**

When his father dies at an early age, his son spends much of his life constructing his parent's history. A gentle New Wave-style story that traces the coming-of-age of an imaginative boy whose life dovetails with recent Hungarian history.
D: Istvan Szabo. A: Andras Balint, Kati Solyom, Miklos Gabor.

Love
(1971) 92m. **A**

Visiting her mother-in-law daily, a young woman reads

the letters her husband is supposedly writing from Hollywood where he is a film director. In truth, he's a political prisoner. A first-rate, albeit slow and talky look at an offbeat relationship.
D: Karoly Makk. A: Lili Darvas, Ivan Darvas, Mari Torocsik.

25 Fireman's Street
(1973) 97m. **B+**
Residents of an old Budapest apartment building recall their lives on the evening before the building is to be razed. An often confusing mix of fantasy and reality and past and present that feels like a Bergman film with haunting dreamlike images.
D: Istvan Szabo. A: Rita Bekes, Peter Muller, Lucyna Winnicka.

Catsplay
(1974) 115m. **A**
The close epistolary relationship between a wheelchair-bound widow and her sister who takes up with an opera singer is the backbone of this film. Switching between the past and present, this has a meandering, sometimes halting pace, but the lush-style images make it worth the demands.
D: Karoly Makk. A: Margit Dayka, Elma Bulla, Margit Makay.

Time Stands Still
(1982) 99m. **A–**
A gently observant coming-of-age film of teenagers in post–1956 Hungary trying to come to terms with rebellion in a crushingly oppressive society. Slow, but worth the effort.
D: Peter Gothar. A: Stvan Znamenak, Sandor Soth, Henrik Pauer.

The Revolt of Job
(1983) 97m. **A**
A Jewish couple adopts a non-Jewish boy during wartime, and attempts to teach him their culture in case they don't survive. The loving relationship that develops between the couple and the boy may sound familiar but the perspective is not.
D: Imre Gyongyossy. A: Barna Kabay, Hedi Temessy, Ferenc Zenthe.

A Hungarian Fairy Tale
(1987) 95m. **A**
A young boy who's the result of a one-night stand grows up without knowing his father. According to law his mother must name a father when he turns three, so she chooses the clerk at the vital statistics office. Charming and lyrical, with stunning images and an indirect narrative.
D: Gyula Gazdag. A: Arpad Vermes, Maria Varga, Frantisek Husak.

Czechoslovakian

Aside from the early melodrama *Ecstasy*, these are the films that managed to slip through the government censors. Small stories that feature little-guy characters caught in repressive situations, they avoid any controversial political situations and share a gentle, mildly ironic humor and subtlety. Even if a bit muted, they are an enjoyable way to see a bit of life as it was once lived behind the Iron Curtain.

Ecstasy
(1933) 68m. B&W. Dubbed. **C**
This once scandalous tale of a young woman who divorces her older husband to satisfy her sexual needs with a younger man now looks like a clunky romance with lovely shots of Czech forests. The shimmering scene of a skinny-dipping Lamarr is what it's all about.
D: Gustav Machaty. A: Hedy Kiesler (Lamarr), Aribert Mog, Jaromir Rogoz.

The Shop on Main Street
(1964) 128m. Subtitled. **A**
Losing her button shop to a Slovak man, an elderly Jewish woman relies on him to protect her from further persecution during the Nazi occupation. This dignified and affecting drama is so finely tuned to the characters that it becomes nerve-wracking without resorting to graphic displays of violence.
D: Jan Kadar. A: Josef Kroner, Ida Kaminska, Han Slivkova.

The Loves of a Blonde
(1965) 88m. Subtitled. **A**
A hopelessly romantic shoe factory worker spends one night with a carousing piano player and falls in love with him. Poignant, wistful, but never sentimental, this amusing picture offers a sympathetic view of loneliness and yearning.
D: Milos Forman. A: Hana Brejchova, Vladimir Pucholt, Josef Sebanek.

Closely Watched Trains
(1966) 89m. Subtitled. **B+**
An apprentice train dispatcher during the World War II occupation has one goal: to gain sexual experience. Gently ironic, with a coming-of-age feel, this manages to make political comments without hammering them home while the characters retain a certain joy even under grim circumstances.
D: Jiri Menzel. A: Vaclav Nectar, Jitka Bendova, Vladimir Valenta.

The Firemen's Ball
(1968) 73m. Subtitled. **A–**
A ceremony in a small town aims to honor the retiring fire chief, but it turns into a chaotic free for all. Like watching a slightly screwy documentary, this gentle ribbing of the bureaucracy that ruled Czechoslovakia at the time is one of the last bright flares before the 1968 invasion.
D: Milos Forman. A: Jan Vostrcil, Josef Sebaneck, Josef Valnoha.

Yugoslavian

The former Yugoslavia enjoyed relative privilege and prosperity compared to other Eastern Bloc countries, a fact reflected in these films. Political curtailments are a fact of life for

these characters, but the movies take a more individual personal view of their stories: They're lighter and less encumbered than some of the other Eastern European productions.

WR: Mysteries of the Organism
(1971) 84m. Subtitled. **B**
This black comedy about a love affair is also an exploration of Wilhelm Reich's sexual theories, complete with historical footage and interviews. The political satire, explicit sexual images, and experimental film techniques help to evoke an often incoherent sense of the world on the verge of a revolution of ideas.
D: Dusan Makravejev. A: Milena Dravic, Jagoda Kaloper, Ivica Vidovic.

Hey Babu Riba
(1986) 109m. Subtitled.
A–
A delightful look at teenage life behind the Iron Curtain follows five friends united by their adoration of American culture, including Glenn Miller and Esther Williams. Similar to *American Grafitti,* with flashbacks tracing their halcyon days, but for all the lightness there's still a strong political undercurrent.
D: Jovan Acin. A: Gala Videnovic, Nebojsa Bakocevic, Relja Basic.

Time of the Gypsies
(1989) 136m. Subtitled.
B+
A gypsy coming-of-age story whose main character is so profoundly innocent that he almost seems not of this time—and that's what makes the film so successful at a folklore level: It feels mythical, strange, and otherworldly despite its present-day setting and grim reality of outlaw gypsy life.
D: Emir Kusturica. A: Igraju, Davor Dujmovic, Bora Todorovic.

Tito and Me
(1992) 104m. Subtitled. **A**
This gluttonous 10-year-old may eat walls, but his consuming passion is for Tito, with a secondary attachment for the girl who's a head taller than him. Endearing, and a wonderful look at the hold Tito has on the country.
D: Goran Markovic. A: Dimitrie Vojnov, Anica Dobra, Lada Ristovski.

Romanian

The Oak
(1993) 105m. Subtitled. **B**
After her father's death, a young female secret police agent travels through Romania on an odyssey of self-discovery. A darkly absurd tale of the last days of Romanian Communism and a people utterly accustomed to hearing that life is one way when they know it's quite the opposite.
D: Lucian Pintilie. A: Maia Morgenstern, Victor Rebenguic, Razvan Vasilescu.

Dutch

Verhoeven

Before he became one of Hollywood's blockbuster directors, Paul Verhoeven made these films that may be smaller and more primitive than *RoboCop* and *Basic Instinct*, but still show his flair for action and titillating sex.

Katie's Passion (Keetje Tippel)
(1975) 104m. Subtitled. **C**
A farmgirl is forced into prostitution by her family when they move to Amsterdam in 1881, but she eventually triumphs over her humiliations. Estimable, well-intended, but remains tame and too well-mannered despite the potent material.
D: Paul Verhoeven. A: Rutger Hauer, Monique Van De Ven, Eddie Brugman.

Soldier of Orange
(1979) 144m. Subtitled.
B+
The Nazi invasion prompts a pampered young aristocrat into rallying his friends and becoming the leader of a resistance group. The sabotage and spying proceeds at a lively clip, is dosed with humor, and gives the first indication of what Verhoeven could do with action.
D: Paul Verhoeven. A: Rutger Hauer, Peter Faber, Jeroen Krabbe.

Spetters
(1980) 108m. Subtitled or Dubbed. **B–**
A motorcycle racer and a short-order cook are the main characters in this well-paced look at Dutch youth. The freedom of these young people—sprinkled with lots of scenes of explicit couplings—is intoxicating, slightly nostalgic, and always fun to watch.
D: Paul Verhoeven. A: Hans Van Tongeren, Toon Agterberg, Renee Soutendijk.

The Fourth Man
(1984) 104m. Sub.
A
A gay writer allows himself to be catered to by an attractive widow in the hopes of getting his hands on her hunk of a boyfriend. Then he begins to wonder how her three husbands died. A witty and smart prototype for *Basic Instinct,* where the line between erotic fantasy and reality is as slippery as a satin sheet.
D: Paul Verhoeven. A: Jeroen Krabbe, Renee Soutendijk, Thom Hoffman.

Turkish

Journey of Hope
(1991) 110m. **B+**

Impoverished Turks decide to take a chance on a new life in Switzerland, leaving six of their children and taking one son. Adversity is their only reliable companion in this grim, but beautifully portrayed tale of immigrants whose hope for a better life leads them to sacrifice everything.
D: Xavier Koller. A: Necmettin Cobanoglu, Nur Surer, Emin Sivas.

Vietnamese

The Scent of Green Papaya
(1994) 104m. Subtitled.
A–
A peasant girl who is a live-in servant for a middle-class household grows up in the late 1950s and early 60s with the two sons and is eventually proposed to by the elder. With great subtlety and luminous delicacy, this thoughtful film details the complex and often decadent Vietnamese society on the verge of war.
D: Tran Anh Hung. A: Tran Nu Yen Khe, Truong thi Loc, Nguyen Anh Hoa.

African

The Gods Must Be Crazy
(1981) 108m. **B+**

An African bushman journeys into the desert to get rid of a Coke bottle that caused trouble in his tribe and intersects with various "civilized" people—scientist, teacher, revolutionary—who are engaged in their own skirmishes with the desert and each other. A rare satire that relies almost exclusively on slapstick.
D: Jamie Uys. A: Marius Weyers, Sandra Prinsloo, N!xau.

HORROR

Horror Menu

HORROR MENU

HORROR FILM GROUPS

1920s

Silent Horror

Technically raw, but atmospherically rich, these classy early sci-fi and horror films contain a wealth of eerie, mesmerizing, and awesome images, touching if melodramatic performances; and some enduring tales of the human condition.

Dr. Jekyll and Mr. Hyde
(1920) 96m. B&W. Silent.
B
In the depths of fog-bound London, a new serum changes Dr. Jekyll from a genteel man of science into the debauched monster Hyde. Though primitive in technique, this early film has many inspired visual moments, including a disturbing dream sequence in which a spider crawls into Jekyll's bed and Barrymore's fevered and unforgettable makeup-free transformation sequences.
D: John S. Robertson. A: John Barrymore, Martha Mansfield, Brandon Hurst.

Witchcraft Through the Ages
(1922) 128m. B&W. Silent.
B+
Visually astonishing dreamflow of a film mixes gorgeously surreal sacrilegious images with a semi-story about the Middle Ages witch threat. To make things even more bizarre, jazz music and a drily amused commentary by Burroughs were added.
D: Benjamin Christensen. Narration: William Burroughs.

The Hunchback of Notre Dame
(1923) 93m. B&W. Silent.
B+
This story of the deformed bellringer who falls in love with the peasant girl still looks lavish with a monumental Notre Dame set and tapestrylike crowd scenes; but it's Chaney's heartwretching pathos as Quasimodo—clear as a bell under his 40 pounds of make up—that makes this a classic.
D: Wallace Worsley. A: Lon Chaney, Ernest Torrence, Patsy Ruth Miller.

Phantom of the Opera
(1925) 94m. B&W. Silent.
B
An obsessed madman plays a dark game of Svengali with a young opera singer from his underground gothic lair beneath the Paris Opera House. Finding a good print of this is worth it: Despite rudimentary technique, the photography and gothic set design are richly shaded and moody, with Chaney's living-skull face as horrifying as Freddy Krueger's any day.
D: Rupert Julian. A: Lon Chaney, Mary Philbin, Norman Kery.

1930s

Classic Horror

In the early 30s Hollywood discovered a world filled with creepy European vampires, aristocratic mad scientists, and invisible men. This amazingly fertile period merged old legends and myths with the modern medium of film, producing all the archetypal monsters in their most haunting incarnations. Though some are primitive in technique, most have a timeless quality with dramatic stylized lighting, set design, and acting.

Dracula
(1931) 75m. B&W. **B**
Still the most vividly recalled version, thanks to Lugosi's mesmerizing performance, off-kilter gothic sets, and a suffocatingly macabre atmosphere. Curiously though, this is really not a very good film, with static direction and a creaky look, though the scenes at Castle Dracula maintain a certain eeriness.
D: Tod Browning. A: Bela Lugosi, Helen Chandler, Dwight Frye.

Frankenstein
(1931) 71m. B&W. **A**
Karloff's performance as the horrifying and pained thing, who has been given a cruel gift of life, is one of cinema's most unforgettable monsters. Mixing gothic and 1930s high-tech/deco motifs to startling effect, this is an alternately scary, haunting, and finally tragic film.
D: James Whale. A: Colin Clive, Boris Karloff, Dwight Frye.

Dr. Jekyll and Mr. Hyde
(1932) 96m. B&W. **A**
An upstanding Victorian scientist becomes the brutally erotic Hyde courtesy of a new serum. This fog-bound drama may look old, but March, in unsettling makeup as Hyde, is brilliant in this film brimming with sensuality, repressed rage, and madness.
D: Rouben Mamoulian. A: Fredric March, Rose Hobart, Miriam Hopkins.

Freaks
(1932) 64m. B&W. **A**
Members of a traveling freak show exact their revenge on the "normal" people who betrayed them. This film goes beyond mere horror as the use of real freaks—a half-man, Siamese twins, pinheads, and others—make the sequence in which the assemblage crawl, skitter, and squirm through a rainy night reach a level of waking nightmare never since achieved.

D: Tod Browning. A: Wallace Ford, Leila Hyams, Olga Baclanova.

The Mummy

(1932) 73m. B&W. **A**

An Egyptian prince is accidentally revived from a 3000-year rest and searches for his reincarnated lost love. Even wrapped in rotting bandages and saddled with a bum leg, Karloff projects both malice and pathos in this gorgeously atmospheric tale of ancient perils awaiting western adventurers in the Mid East.
D: Karl Freund. A: Boris Karloff, David Manners, Zita Johann.

The Invisible Man

(1933) 71m. B&W. **B**

A British scientist discovers a serum that gives him the cloak of invisibility, only to descend into madness with the power of it. Parts of the film are musty, but the invisibility effects are charming and the tone effectively mirrors Rains' mood as exhilaration and hijinks change to madness and tragedy.
D: James Whale. A: Claude Rains, Gloria Stuart, William Harrigan.

King Kong

(1933) 100m. B&W. **A**

The king of his jungle island falls hard for the blond who was to be his human sacrifice and winds up battling Manhattan after media hucksters abduct him. Wonderful special effects make you feel like a kid again, and the eerily primordial atmosphere of Kong's island home make up for some dated humor and stagy direction.
D: Merian C. Cooper, Ernest B. Schoedsack. A: Fay Wray, Robert Armstrong, Bruce Cabot.

The Son of Kong

(1933) 70m. B&W. **B–**

It's back to Skull Island as Armstrong finds Kong's son and brings him to New York. With a lighter tone than the original, little Kong ends up cute and mixed in with the dated comedy; still, the island scenes are primordially atmospheric, with great animated monster effects.
D: Ernest Schoedsack. A: Robert Armstrong, Helen Mack, Victor Wong.

Bride of Frankenstein

(1935) 75m. B&W. **A**

Baron Frankenstein makes a mate for his Creature, but the path of monster love is pretty rocky. Shots of torch-toting villagers running past expressionistic forests of shadow and light, the stunned electric spun-silver visage of the Bride, and the Creature's tragic pain still resonate in this masterpiece.
D: James Whale. A: Colin Clive, Boris Karloff, Elsa Lanchester.

Mark of the Vampire

(1935) 61m. B&W. **B+**

Rumors are floating around the small Czech town that the local castle is haunted, and a body turns up with bite marks on its neck. Thanks to a twist ending, this is more mystery than horror, but it's still filled with heavy gothic atmosphere, funereal sets, and a macabre Lugosi, aided by the sepulchrally alluring Borland as his undead assistant.
D: Tod Browning. A: Bela Lugosi, Carol Borland, Lionel Barrymore.

Werewolf of London

(1935) 75m. B&W. **B–**

With the help of a rare Tibetan plant and a wolf's bite, a scientist turns into a snarling werewolf when the moon rises. Heavy on the brooding ambiance, this has a sweet love story and quaint scenes of the scientist's face turning hairy, but Hull is no Karloff in the monster department.
D: Stuart Walker. A: Henry Hull, Valerie Hobson, Warner Oland.

The Hunchback of Notre Dame

(1939) 116m. B&W. **A**

Horridly lonely and misshapen bellringer Quasimodo finds love and his own humanity via selfless passion for a young gypsy woman in medieval France. The focus is on tragic romance in this opulently produced tale, with Laughton's performance a bit overwrought but still affecting.
D: William Dieterle. A: Charles Laughton, Sir Cedric Hardwicke, Maureen O'Hara.

Son of Frankenstein

(1939) 95m. B&W. **B**

The Baron's son goes through Dad's ruined lab with the help of scene-stealing Ygor (Lugosi) to find the Creature frozen but alive. An enjoyable film with classically macabre sets and lighting, but missing the earlier films' deep air of tragedy.
D: Rowland Lee. A: Basil Rathbone, Boris Karloff, Bela Lugosi.

The Wolf Man

(1941) 71m. B&W. **A**

This is one of Chaney's finest moments as the heir who goes to England only to receive the bite of a mythic wolf and become a tormented man-beast. Wolves howl mournfully over foggy moors and a witch tells poor Lon his accursed fate in verse while the time-lapse man-to-wolf transformation is still eerie in a tale that remains more tragic than shocking.
D: George Waggner. A: Lon Chaney, Jr.; Claude Rains; Bela Lugosi.

Phantom of the Opera

(1943) 92m. **B–**

The sensitive violinist/composer in love with a young singer at the Paris Opera has his face disfigured by acid and sets up an underground lair where he plots his revenge. A letdown for horror fans because this ravishing Technicolor film is more costume romance than scare flick.
D: Arthur Lubin. A: Claude Rains, Nelson Eddy, Susanna Foster.

Mad Scientists and Evil Doctors

The atmosphere is heavy with the sense of old-world sin as maniacal scientists play God with daring and perverted experiments. These black-and-white low-budgeters often resemble crime films from the era, with an anxious edge about Darwinism, exotic technologies like invisible X rays, and the depraved psychological makeup of men who mess around with beakers and tubes to reshape mankind in their own twisted image.

Doctor X
(1932) 77m. B&W w/ color. **B–**
Two scientists are trying to create synthetic flesh in their lab on Long Island and soon there's a rash of cannibalistic murders. Dated but still tense early talkie with makeup effects by Max Factor.
D: Michael Curtiz. A: Lionel Atwill, Fay Wray, Lee Tracy.

Murders in the Rue Morgue
(1932) 61m. B&W. **C**
Scientist Lugosi murders women in Paris as he attempts to mix human blood with that of his ape's to prove the theory of evolution. The Caligari-esque distorted sets and expressionistic lighting when Bela's on screen are fine, but the rest is rather bland-looking and static.
D: Robert Florey. A: Bela Lugosi, Arlene Francis, Leon Ames.

Island of Lost Souls
(1933) 72m. B&W. **A**
On a jungle island, the suavely insane Dr. Moreau turns animals into wretched man-beasts. A completely mad film with its nightmare images of tortured creatures gathering in the gloom, the white-on-silver "House of Pain," and Laughton's terrifying performance as the obscenely cherubic, whip-wielding doctor, all timelessly unsettling.
D: Erle C. Kenton. A: Charles Laughton, Bela Lugosi, Kathleen Burke.

The Vampire Bat
(1933) 71m. B&W. **C+**
In a Germanic village, people are being killed and their blood drained. Is it the work of the crazy bat enthusiast or perhaps the mad scientist? A poverty-row quickie using sets from Frankenstein and others.
D: Frank Strayer. A: Lionel Atwill, Fay Wray, Dwight Frye.

The Black Cat
(1934) 65m. B&W. **A**
Lugosi, betrayed by Satanist architect Karloff years ago, returns to his foe's mansion for revenge. Preserved women suspended in crystal tubes, Bauhaus Deco sets, unnerving camera work, and a palpable air of sexual perversity help make this a brooding gem.
D: Edgar G. Ulmer. A: Boris Karloff, Bela Lugosi, David Manners.

Maniac
(1934) 67m. B&W. **B–**
A delirious, censor-defying prototype for deranged underground films that include women battling each other with hypodermic needles, someone quaffing a cat's eye, a rapist who thinks he's a gorilla, topless women, and title cards to help explain scenes. Truly unbelievable.
D: Dwain Esper. A: Bill Woods, Horace Carpenter, Phyllis Diller.

The Crime of Doctor Crespi
(1935) 64m. B&W. **A**
In a fit of jealousy, surgeon von Stoheim injects into a rival doctor a serum that makes him appear dead and ready for (premature) burial. An almost intolerably tense film, with minimalist white sets and long stretches of nerve-racking silence as Crespi relishes his mad scheme.
D: John Auer. A: Erich von Stroheim, Dwight Frye, John Bohn.

The Raven
(1935) 62m. B&W. **B–**
After being jilted by his fiancée, mad doctor Lugosi holds a vengeful festival of tortures, until escaped con Karloff puts a crimp on his gruesome designs. Visually mundane but macabre fun, thanks to the two horror icons.
D: Louis Friedlander. A: Boris Karloff, Bela Lugosi, Irene Ware.

The Devil Doll
(1936) 79m. B&W. **A**
Barrymore is at his raving best—and dressed in drag for much of this—as the mad scientist who can shrink humans to the size of dolls. Even today, the sight of granny-gowned Lionel crowing over his diminutive victims in glass beakers is the stuff of nightmares.
D: Tod Browning. A: Lionel Barrymore, Maureen O'Sullivan, Frank Lawton.

The Invisible Ray
(1936) 81m. B&W. **B**
Scientist Karloff discovers "radium x" in a meteor, causing him to glow in the dark and then go mad as he finds he can kill with his touch. The meteor pulsing with strange light, and Karloff's own sinister luminescence are primitive but still uncannily effective in this entertaining little shocker.
D: Lambert Hillyer. A: Boris Karloff, Bela Lugosi, Frances Drake.

The Man They Could Not Hang
(1939) 64m. B&W. **B–**
A kindly doctor is hanged after accidentally killing a patient during his immortality experiments. His assistant revives the now-deranged Karloff, who proceeds to kill off the judge and jury who condemned him. Entertaining little crime horror.
D: Nick Grinde. A: Boris Karloff, Byron Foulger, Lorna Gray.

Before I Hang
(1940) 62m. B&W. **C**
Karloff works on an anti-aging serum, using the blood of a hanged criminal. Result? He becomes young and turns into a homicidal killer in this undistinguished programmer.
D: Nick Grinde. A: Boris Karloff, Evelyn Keyes, Bruce Cabot.

Depraved Artists

Like the mad scientist films of this era, these small black-and-white horror thrillers convey their paranoiac vision of outsiders in typically high-strung fashion: expressionistic sets, disturbingly lit photography, and feverish performances by the artists in question.

Mystery of the Wax Museum
(1933) 77m. B&W. **A**
A sculptor gone mad when his wax masterpieces were burned becomes obsessed with turning a live woman into his new Marie Antoinette statue. Shot in a primitive form of Technicolor, this offers the horrifying scene of Wray smashing Atwill's face to reveal the mangled and burned mess beneath.
D: Michael Curtiz. A: Lionel Atwill, Fay Wray, Glenda Farrell.

The Evil Mind (aka The Clairvoyant)
(1934) 80m. B&W. **B**
Dated but still fascinating film of a fake medium who

learns he really can read the future. The expressionist touches add to the mood, but it's Rains' intense performance and the sober tone that elevate this morality tale considerably.
D: Maurice Elvey. A: Claude Rains, Fay Wray, Mary Clare.

Mad Love
(1935) 67m. B&W. **B**
Lorre is a surgeon who grafts a pair of killer's hands onto the pianist whose wife he loves. This is filled with visually deranged little nifties like the expressionistic "Theatre of Horrors," the cybernetic man with chrome hands and stitched-on head, and Lorre's leering embodiment of old-world perversity.
D: Karl Freund. A: Peter Lorre, Colin Clive, Frances Drake.

The Black Room
(1935) 67m. B&W. **B**
Karloff plays twins: one a gentle man, the other a murderous, sexually deviant Count. Slow going and more of a costume mystery than horror, but it's hard to beat two Karloffs in one film.
D: Roy William Neill. A: Boris Karloff, Marion Marsh, Robert Allen.

The Human Monster
(1939) 73m. B&W. **A**
Lugosi in his last great performance plays Dr. Orloff who runs an insurance racket at a home for the blind. Fog-shrouded scenes of Bela and his sightless minions are eerie while others featuring torture are still shockingly gruesome. A bleak disturbing film.
D: Walter Summers. A: Bela Lugosi, Greta Gynt, Hugh Williams.

1940s

Myths Revisited

Like any successful modern-day film with its "Part II" and "Part III" spawns, the classic horror films from the 1930s continued to be worked over through the war years. While still professionally crafted and starring some of horror's greatest stars, these have a lighter, more Americanized tone than their shadow-scored, old-world gloomy originals.

The Invisible Man Returns
(1940) 81m. B&W. **B–**
Price, unjustly imprisoned, uses his deceased brother's invisibility formula to break out of jail. This briskly paced thriller is more a crime film than horror, with fine invisibility effects.
D: Joe May. A: Vincent Price, Sir Cedric Hardwicke, Nan Grey.

Dr. Jekyll and Mr. Hyde
(1941) 114m. B&W. **B–**
MGM's lush costume drama/horror oozes gothic ambiance, but Tracy is miscast as the tortured doctor with a split personality, and the story seems a quaintly naive Freudian piece.
D: Victor Fleming. A: Spencer Tracy, Ingrid Bergman, Lana Turner.

Ghost of Frankenstein
(1942) 68m. B&W. **C**
The Baron's grandson gets bilked into putting slavering sidekick Igor's (Lugosi) brain into a revivified creature. Bland-looking, by-rote monster romp, with Chaney miscast as the Creature, but some unintentionally hilarious dialogue and a campy performance by Lugosi.
D: Erle C. Kenton. A: Sir Cedric Hardwicke; Ralph Bellamy; Lon Chaney, Jr.

Frankenstein Meets the Wolf Man
(1943) 72m. B&W. **B–**
A scientist tries to help the famous monsters with disastrous results. The first in Universal studio's multiple-monster-mania films is still the best, retaining an effectively creepy atmosphere, but marred by a weak turn by Bela as the Frankenstein monster.
D: Roy William Neill. A: Lon Chaney, Jr.; Bela Lugosi; Patric Knowles.

The Return of the Vampire
(1943) 69m. B&W. **B+**
German planes blitz-bomb a cemetery, allowing vampire Lugosi to wreak vengeance on London. This gloomy film evokes a vivid sense of wartime horror (the hero is Lady Jane, since most men are off to battle), and Lugosi is terrifying as one mean vampire.
D: Lew Landers, Kurt Neumann. A: Bela Lugosi, Frieda Inescort, Nina Foch.

Son of Dracula
(1943) 80m. B&W. **B+**
Count Alucard (spell it backwards) goes to Louisiana for his vampire bride. One of the better 40s Universal horror efforts, with animated vampire-to-bat transformations, creepy atmosphere, and Chaney clearly enjoying himself as a somewhat chubby Count.
D: Robert Siodmak. A: Lon Chaney, Jr.; Louise Allbritton; Evelyn Ankers.

House of Frankenstein
(1944) 71m. B&W. **C+**
Mad doctor Karloff escapes from prison with his hunchback assistant and revives Frankenstein's monster, Dracula, and the Wolfman in this all-star monster bash. Great cast and loopy plot equal an all-around goofy film.
D: Erle C. Kenton. A: Boris Karloff; J. Carrol Naish; Lon Chaney, Jr.

House of Dracula
(1945) 67m. B&W. **C–**
A mad scientist falls under Dracula's spell and revives the Frankenstein monster while the Wolfman shows up in time to try to end the silliness. Though enjoyable for Universal monster fans, this quickie is almost a parody of past great films.
D: Erle C. Kenton. A: Lon Chaney, Jr.; John Carradine; Lionel Atwill.

Mighty Joe Young
(1949) 94m. B&W. **B+**
A lighter-hearted monkey affair from the *King Kong* people, with another (fairly) big gorilla—this one already domesticated by his pretty young owner—being brought to America as a nightclub headliner. A slow start in the wilds, but things get rolling once Joe hits a Hollywood nightclub.
D: Ernest B. Schoedsack. A: Terry Moore, Robert Armstrong, Ben Johnson.

Bad Bela Lugosi

In his native Hungary, he was considered a virile leading man. In America, he would always be Dracula, and as the war years commenced the only roles open to Lugosi were in a series of cheap-looking B-movies in which he inevitably played some sort of lunatic scientist. But even in these poverty-row productions, one can see Lugosi trying to maintain some dignity, turning in a few good performances amid the used sets, grungy photography, and two-day wonder scripts.

Murder by Television

(1935) 55m. B&W.
B–

Bela looks whacked-out in this surreal murder mystery involving the inventor of TV who gets zapped by a mysterious ray. Even with the muddy sound, stagy acting, and crude camerawork, this bizarre quickie is hilarious.
D: Clifford Sanforth. A: With June Cllyer, Huntley Gordon.

The Devil Bat

(1941) 69m. B&W. **C–**

Bela designs an electronic device that makes bats get big and then sics them on his venal business partners. Memorable bats-on-visible-strings and Bela wearing bat-vision goggles are the highlights in the relatively well-paced silliness.
D: Jean Yarbrough. A: With Dave O'Brien, Suzanne Kaaren.

Invisible Ghost

(1941) 64m. B&W. **D**

Kindly Dr. Kessler, grief-stricken by his wife's death, suddenly and for no reason starts suffocating people with his smoking jacket. This nonsensical film has some noirish camerawork, but otherwise it's for diehard Lugosi fans only.
D: Joseph H. Lewis. A: With Polly Ann Young, Clarence Muse.

Black Dragons

(1942) 62m. B&W. **C–**

This is Bela's contribution to the war effort as he plays a Germanic surgeon who operates on Japanese spies to make them look like Americans. A really bad propaganda film, though plot and paranoid tone give it some historical interest.
D: William Nigh. A: With John Barclay, Clayton Moore.

Bowery at Midnight

(1942) 60m. B&W.
B–

Bela runs a mission and a crime ring and spends his days as a psychology teacher while his drunk assistant creates zombies in the basement. Somehow Lugosi offers a subtly shaded performance in the fevered plot of this deranged quickie.
D: Wallace Fox. A: With John Archer, Tom Neal, Wanda McKay.

The Corpse Vanishes

(1942) 64m. B&W. **D**

Mad scientist Lugosi is extracting the vital essences of brides to keep his wife young and lovely in this evocatively lit, but otherwise nondescript nonshocker. Lugosi sleepwalks through this one, as will the viewer.
D: Wallace Fox. A: With Luana Walters, Tristram Coffin.

The Ape Man

(1943) 64m. B&W. **D**

Mad doctor Lugosi injects himself with gorilla spinal fluid with expected results. Even with the lethargic pacing, the sub-party-store ape suits and dopey dialogue supply ample giggles.
D: William Beaudine. A: With Wallace Ford, Louise Currie.

Return of the Ape Man

(1944) 68m. B&W. **C**

Graced by a homicidal pianist, a revivified Neanderthal man, and a brain transplant, this sequence to *Ape Man* can't be called completely dull. This is almost as good (using the term broadly) as these films are going to get.
D: Phil Rosen. A: With John Carradine, George Zucco.

Scared to Death

(1946) 65m. **C+**

An opium-fueled David Lynch film from the 1940s might look like this bizarre curio. Somnambulistic women, a scared dwarf, narration from a dead woman, and constant allusions to a mysterious "green mask" all figure prominently in the mind-bending nonplot of Lugosi's only color film.
D: Christy Cabanne. A: With Molly Lamont, George Zucco.

The Boys from Brooklyn

(1952) 72m. B&W. **C**

Lugosi is the doctor turning people into apes while Mitchell and Petrillo do their Lewis and Martin schtick. This so-awful-it's funny entry is Bela's last before he met Ed Wood, Jr.
D: William Beaudine. A: With Duke Mitchell, Sammy Petrillo.

Zombies

Zombiemania swept America in 1931 with zombie books, drinks, and zombie films. Taking the German Expressionist frills from other horror films and mixing them with Haitian-styled sets and a smattering of zombie lore, Hollywood produced this group of decidedly odd films. With their shambling, blank-eyed, lost souls and threatening zombie masters, these movies are truly creepy as they portray dehumanizing enslavement sheathed in a general atmosphere of Third World anxiety.

White Zombie
(1932) 73m. B&W.
A
A couple visits Haiti where they run into sugar plantation owner Lugosi and his horde of zombies. Incredible sets like the wood-deco sugar processing plant and an unlikely castle perched over the sea—combined with the outrageous images of inhuman degradation—make this a truly bizarre film.
D: Victor Halperin. A: Bela Lugosi, Madge Bellamy, Robert Frazer.

Revolt of the Zombies
(1936) 65m. B&W. **D**
A secret regiment of zombies used in World War I are utilized by a scientist for his own nefarious purposes. Made to cash in on *White Zombie*'s box office, this ancient-looking film is cheap-looking, stagy, and very slow going.
D: Victor Halperin. A: Dean Jagger, Roy D'Arcy, Dorothy Stone.

I Walked with a Zombie
(1943) 69m. B&W. **B+**
A nurse goes to Haiti and eventually tries to cure an ailing plantation owner's wife with voodoo. Like all Val Lewton productions, a quietly unsettling atmosphere prevails, with shadowy photography, mannered set-pieces, and the insidious revelation of terrible family secrets.
D: Jacques Tourneur. A: Frances Dee, Tom Conway, James Ellison.

Revenge of the Zombies
(1943) 61m. B&W. **C**
In his bayou laboratory, Nazi scientist Carradine creates zombies for the war effort. A visually dull, low-budget propaganda film, of historical interest only.
D: Steve Sekely. A: John Carradine, Gale Storm, Mantan Moreland.

Isle of the Dead
(1945) 72m. B&W. **B**
This deliberately paced Val Lewton production has Karloff playing a Balkan general who deals with a plague of possible vampires, madness, and a terrifying premature burial. May be slow and depressingly atmospheric, but the chills are there for the patient.
D: Mark Robson. A: Boris Karloff; Ellen Drew; Jason Robards, Sr.

Quiet Horror

A fleeting shadow, a whisper of wind in a closed room, the sense of someone—or *something*—following you: These were the stock-in-trade of a series of very quiet horrors made in the 40s. Producer Val Lewton was the main force behind this subtle approach to intimate low-budget, black-and-white, horror-suspense films, in which everyday things like buses, parks, and backyards are steeped in an atmosphere of paranoia and the terror of the unseen.

Cat People
(1942) 73m. B&W. **A**
A beautiful fashion designer cannot consummate her marriage for fear of an ancient curse that would turn her into a blood-thirsty panther. The first of Val Lewton's understated efforts with eerie images linking sex and uncontrollable violence.
D: Jacques Tourneur. A: Simone Simon, Kent Smith, Tom Conway.

The Leopard Man
(1943) 66m. B&W. **C**
A deadly panther is killed, but the rash of murders doesn't stop. Though laced with nice macabre touches—eyes glowing above an abandoned hacienda, a bodiless fortune teller—this disappointing Val Lewton entry is too slow and talky, and lacks characters we care about.
D: Jacques Tourneur. A: Dennis O'Keefe, Margo, Jean Brooks.

The Seventh Victim
(1943) 71m. B&W. **A**
A young woman comes to Greenwich Village, searching for her sister, a successful businesswoman who disappeared without a trace. This is like a first-rate crime mystery, except the criminals are a cult of Satanists, messing around with dead bodies and abducting people for unholy purposes.
D: Mark Robson. A: Tom Conway, Kim Hunter, Jean Brooks.

The Curse of the Cat People
(1944) 70m. B&W. **A–**
A lonely child drifts into an imaginary world where she finds the ghost of her mother, a remnant of a race of cat people. Light on plot but still a hauntingly atmospheric look at the darker sides of childhood.
D: Gunther Von Fritsch, Robert Wise. A: Simone Simon, Kent Smith, Jane Randolph.

The Uninvited
(1944) 98m. B&W. **A**
Besides *The Haunting,* the best ghost film made, with a couple purchasing a very strange house on the Welsh coast. Graced with ominously evocative photography, it's what *isn't* shown that's spooky: a spirit that smells of mimosa, cats running from suddenly freezing rooms, the sound of a woman's night cries.
D: Lewis Allen. A: Ray Milland, Gail Russell, Donald Crisp.

The Body Snatcher
(1945) 77m. B&W. **A**
An atmospheric adaptation of Robert Louis Stevenson's tale of a mad grave robber, played to the hilt by Karloff. Great period detail, richly gloomy photography, and eerie use of sound make this one of Val Lewton's best.
D: Robert Wise. A: Boris Karloff, Henry Daniell, Bela Lugosi.

Dead of Night
(1945) 104m. B&W. **B–**
Three chilling tales with the best saved for the last: a terrifying look at a ventriloquist going mad who thinks his dummy is draining away his personality. A very British drawing-room horror with the sense of irony and the macabre appeal of a Saki story.
D: Alberto Cavalcanti. A: Michael Redgrave, Mervyn Jones, Sally Ann Howes.

The Picture of Dorian Gray
(1945) 110m. B&W w/ color. **B–**
An entertaining version of Oscar Wilde's tale of a coldly sadistic man who never ages while his portrait mirrors his moral ugliness. Like a man-

nered historical drama spiced up with Wilde's scintillating bon mots; when the movie *does* get around to its horrors, it's unforgettable.
D: Albert Lewin. A: Hurd Hatfield, George Sanders, Donna Reed.

Bedlam
(1946) 79m. B&W. **B–**
Historically accurate tale of the infamous 1700s London mental asylum, with Karloff as the sadistic head shrink. The last of Lewton's subtle shockers is a little too subtle, though still chock-full of demented atmosphere, dubious psychology, and another quietly eerie performance from Karloff.
D: Mark Robson. A: Boris Karloff; Anna Lee; Jason Robards, Sr.

Curse of the Demon
(1958) 97m. B&W. **A–**
An American psychologist runs afoul of a satanic cult in the British countryside. Although made ten years after the other films in this group, Director Jacques Tourneur still employed much of film noir's lurking menace in this tale featuring ominous storms, a clown-disguised cult member, and other low-key but unsettling images.
D: Jacques Tourneur. A: Dana Andrews, Peggy Cummins, Maurice Denham.

1950s

Classic Monsters

These films are the cream of the American-made monster movies of the 50s. Their production values are positively glossy compared to most entries in this genre, but even when their effects look corny or dated the monsters in these atomic-age fairy tales still have a resonance and a spooky fascination.

The Thing (from Another World)
(1951) 87m. B&W. **A**
A group of scientists stationed in an isolated Arctic outpost retrieve the frozen body of an alien, who soon comes to dangerous life. The scenes of men dwarfed by an immense buried spacecraft, claustrophobic sets, and tense over-lapping dialogue make for a white-knuckled viewing experience, despite some dated monster effects.
D: Christian Nyby. A: Kenneth Tobey, Eduard Franz, Robert Cornthwaite.

Creature from the Black Lagoon
(1954) 78m. B&W. **B+**
Members of an archeological expedition fall prey to the monstrous inhabitant of an Amazonian lagoon. Still powerful are scenes of the shadowy and graceful man/fish swimming beneath the woman in a white bathing suit, the darkly ominous lagoon itself, and the atmosphere of dread due to the menace lurking from below, unseen.
D: Jack Arnold. A: Richard Carlson, Julie Adams, Ricou Browning.

The Blob
(1958) 86m. B&W.
B–
The teenagers are misunderstood and ignored as they try to warn the adults about the killer jello from space threatening to consume their small town. Tacky effects, wooden acting, and dated dialogue make this a kitschy perennial.
D: Irvin S. Yeaworth, Jr. A: Steve McQueen, Aneta Corseut, Olin Howlin.

The Fly
(1958) 94m. **A**
An accident with a matter transmitter ends up attaching the scientist's head and arm to a fly while he acquires a monstrous fly head. It may sound silly, but this atmospheric and big-budgeted tale is treated as a straight-faced tragedy, featuring a bulbous, multieyed monster and fine performances by all.
D: Kurt Neumann. A: Patricia Owens, Vincent Price, Herbert Marshall.

Return of the Fly
(1959) 80m. B&W. **B–**
The original was an expansive colorful costume horror with shock appeal while this sequel is more creepy, with a wonderfully unwholesome black-and-white tabloid look. Highlights are a man and a pig being put in the matter transmitter with expectant results.
D: Edward Bernds. A: Vincent Price, Brett Halsey, John Sutton.

Cheap Monsters

The age of the atom bomb and space travel brought a new set of anxieties that weren't addressed by recycling 1930s vampires and werewolves. Simultaneously, the advent of drive-in movies created a market for cheaply made double and triple bill fillers for groping panting teenagers. Out of this boomer cauldron came these grade Z horrors about toxic mutants, scientific blunders, or just plain ugly and unfriendly aliens: all of them cheap, rubbery, and with amusingly visible seams.

Robot Monster
(1953) 63m. B&W. **F**

The alien "Ro-Man"—a guy in a gorilla suit and space helmet—works overtime with his deadly bubble-shooting radio receiver to extinguish the last six humans on earth. Breathtakingly braindead, with lots of stock footage showing things being blown up.
D: Phil Tucker. A: George Nader, Claudia Barrett, Selena Royale.

Killers from Space
(1954) 68m. B&W. **D**

Aliens wearing hooded sweatsuits and Ping-Pong balls for eyes invade earth. This one features stock footage of lizards and lava, and an underground lair filled with garage-sale radio equipment.
D: W. Lee Wilder. A: Peter Graves, James Seay, Barbara Bestar.

The Monster from the Ocean Floor
(1954) 64m. B&W. **D**

A radiation-created monster lurks off the coast of Mexico with expected results to unwary bathers. At a cost of $10,000, Roger Corman's first production offers a hand-puppet octopus, a mini-sub, and lots of shots of Kimball swimming in a scant suit.
D: Wyott Ordung. A: Stuart Wade, Anne Kimball, Dick Piner.

The She Creature
(1957) 77m. B&W. **C+**

A hypnotist convinces a young lovely that she is a "reincarnated monster from Hell." The lady buys it and promptly becomes a clawed, fissure-faced murderess on a bad hair day. As visually uninspiring as many early Corman efforts, but not half bad.
D: Edward Cahn. A: Maria English, Tom Conway, Chester Morris.

Teenage Zombies
(1957) 71m. B&W. **D−**

A female mad scientist with an itch for world domination invents a nerve gas that turns teens into zombie slaves. They shouldn't have let the guy in the gorilla suit on the set.
D: Jerry Warren. A: Katherine Victor, Don Sullivan, Chuck Niles.

The Crawling Eye
(1958) 85m. B&W. **B+**

Huge alien creatures lurk in a thick mist that settles on an Alpine resort. Claustrophobic atmosphere and disturbing giant orb and tentacle invaders make this a strange and creepy film.
D: Quentin Lawrence. A: Forrest Tucker, Janet Munroe, Laurence Payne.

Fiend Without a Face
(1958) 74m. B&W. **B+**

Experiments at a Canadian rocket base attract the attention of the title aliens: and what a miracle of imagination over budget these enjoyably disgusting floating-brain-and-spinal-tail creatures are! Tense, darkly atmospheric, with a suitable slimy finale.
D: Arthur Crabtree. A: Marshall Thompson, Kim Parker, Petre Madden.

The First Man into Space
(1958) 78m. B&W. **B+**

A genuinely unnerving effort as an astronaut returns from his space trip with an appetite for blood. Another winningly weird effort from the *Fiend Without a Face* people.
D: Robert Day. A: Marshall Thompson, Carl Jaffe, Maria Landi.

Wasp Woman
(1960) 66m. B&W. **B**

The queen bee of a cosmetics firm uses wasp enzymes for a rejuvenation creme and ends up as a murderous wasp woman. Hilarious overacting, ludicrous effects, and general grade-B ambiance make this one a real hoot.
D: Roger Corman. A: Susan Cabot, Anthony Eisley, Barboura Morris.

The Manster
(1962) 72m. B&W. **B**

The experiments of a Japanese mad scientist cause an American journalist to grow a strange mole on his shoulder that gets bigger and bigger. . . . This Japanese/U.S. production benefits from truly surreal painted backdrops, some gross/bizarre effects, and a general ambiance of derangement.
D: George Breakston, Kenneth Crane. A: Peter Dyneley, Jane Hylton, Kenneth Crone.

The Creeping Terror
(1964) 75m. B&W. **F**

A killer deep-pile carpet from space invades Earth. Someone lost part of the soundtrack, so a lot of this is hilariously narrated as people wait patiently for the murderous rug to "eat" them. You even get a full view of the extras' sneakers who are carrying the broadloom beast.
D: Art Nelson. A: Vic Savage, Shannon O'Neill, Louise Lawson.

OTHER FILMS:
Voodoo Woman (1957)
Meteor Monster (1958)
The Slime People (1962)
The Flesh Eaters (1964)
Castle of Evil (1966)
Billy the Kid vs. Dracula (1966)
Jesse James Meets Frankenstein's Daughter (1966)
Astro Zombies (1967)

Ed Wood

Hailed as the worst director in history, Ed Wood's films are technical travesties. Day and night switch in a single sequence. Continuity errors involve a missing leading man, not a missing prop. Acting, dialogue, and sets are something to shame a high school theater group. But unlike his hack peers, Wood had a vision, albeit a brain-stunned one, and at least his early horror and later exploitation films were never dull. It's all here in Wood-ville: grave robbers from outer space, sleepwalking Bela Lugosi, and pie-plate flying saucers.

Bride of the Monster
(1955) 69m. B&W. **C**

Lugosi is the mad doctor who's working in his cardboard lab to create a race of supermen. Highlights include the infamous battle between Bela and an immobile rubber octopus; Lugosi's "Home, I have no home" soliloquy; and people becoming superbeings by donning light-bulb shades.
D: Edward D. Wood. A: Bela Lugosi, Tor Johnson, Tony McCoy.

Night of the Ghouls
(1958) 75m. **D –**
Dr. Acula (that's right) is a fake medium who finds his powers are real and accidentally raises the dead (Tor and Vampira again). Though not up to Wood's usual standards, still a work to be reckoned with.
D: Edward D. Wood. A: Kenne Duncan, Tor Johnson, Vampira.

Plan 9 from Outer Space
(1959) 79m. B&W.
D +
The much maligned Wood masterpiece about aliens who invade California by reanimating the dead (or at least Tor and Vampira) features the paper-plate flying saucers, a stand-in for Lugosi in the last half (he died), and logic-defying dialogue that will have you nodding along as the narrator and real-life psychic Criswell intones: "Future events like these will affect *you* . . . in the future!"
D: Edward D. Wood. A: Bela Lugosi, Tor Johnson, Vampira.

(See also Ed Wood's Dramas, page 192.)

Miscellaneous Camp

These films proved that you didn't need a cheap rubber monster suit to make a really bad but harmless horror film. Ridiculous effects, wooden but sincere delivery of hilarious dialogue, and completely loopy situations make these some of the sturdier survivors of 50s kitschy horror.

I Was a Teenage Frankenstein
(1957) 72m. B&W. **D +**
A distant relative of the famous mad Baron fashions a monster out of the remains of a teen hot rod crash victim. With bad makeup, nobrainer humor (some intentional), and quotably silly dialogue, you could do worse.
D: Herbert L. Strock. A: Gary Conway, Whit Bissell, Phyllis Coates.

I Was a Teenage Werewolf
(1957) 70m. B&W. **C**
A mad doc turns a confused teen into a hairy monster, complete with a high school letter jacket. Fast-moving tomfoolery offers many a nostalgic titter.
D: Gene Fowler, Jr. A: Michael Landon, Whit Bissell, Yvonne Lime.

A Bucket of Blood
(1959) 66m. B&W. **C +**
A nerdy beatnik-artist wannabe accidentally creates "great art" by dropping his dead cat in clay. Soon the hipsters at the local coffee shop are clamoring for more, so he starts using humans. Bad poetry, bongo music, deadpan beatnik behavior, and Miller's loony performance make this hard to beat.
D: Roger Corman. A: Dick Miller, Barboura Morris, Bert Convy.

The Little Shop of Horrors
(1960) 70m. B&W. **B**
A nerdy flower shop clerk discovers that his favorite plant needs human blood and starts to kill off assorted lowlifes to feed it. This film took two days to complete and looks it, but it still has a low-rent charm that defies logic and some hilarious bits including a masochistic Nicholson's visit to the dentist's office.
D: Roger Corman. A: Dick Miller, Jackie Joseph, Jack Nicholson.

1960s

Corman, Price, and Poe

While the British Hammer studio turned out their lavish costume remakes of horror classics, B-movie maven Roger Corman began making cheaper productions based on the works of Edgar Allan Poe. These gothic tales of madness and death have the lurid color, faster pace, and ample female flesh of their English counterparts, but with considerably less gore. Most of the films star Vincent Price, whose wry and gloomy persona made him the perfect match for these dankly atmospheric costume horrors.

Fall of the House of Usher
(1960) 79m. **B +**
A young man visits his fiancée in the Usher house run by Price who claims the family is doomed to madness. All the gothic trademarks—a creaking Victorian house, falling coffins, blood-stained passageways, and even a premature burial—are tied together by Price's drolly moribund performance.
D: Roger Corman. A: Vincent Price, Myrna Fahey, Mark Damon.

The Pit and the Pendulum
(1961) 80m. **B**
Steele searches for the truth behind her sister's death in Post-Inquisition Spain. Even saddled with a labyrinthine plot, there's enough cobwebbed dark corners, decaying edifices, torture devices, and inventive camerawork to maintain an over-the-top gothic ambiance.
D: Roger Corman. A: Vincent Price, Barbara Steele, John Kerr.

Tales of Terror
(1962) 90m. **A**
Abandoning the gloomy tone of the earlier efforts, Corman filmed this trio of Poe tales with a darkly humorous slant. You still get

dank mansions, reanimated dead folk, and entombments, but Price and Lorre have a grand time playing many of the chills for laughs.
D: Roger Corman. A: Vincent Price, Basil Rathbone, Peter Lorre.

Tower of London
(1962) 79m. B&W. **C–**

This remake of the 1939 Universal film about insane Richard III who kills his sons and faces retribution isn't a Poe film, but it uses all the same ingredients, unfortunately to vapid effect.
D: Roger Corman. A: Vincent Price, Joan Freeman, Michael Pate.

The Raven
(1963) 86m. **A–**

A full-fledged gothic comedy, featuring a chatty raven, the raising of the dead, sorcerers' battles, and other lunacy. Memorable for Lorre's hilarious turn as Dr. Bedlo, a magician turned into a bird.
D: Roger Corman. A: Vincent Price, Boris Karloff, Peter Lorre, Jack Nicholson.

The Terror
(1963) 81m. **D**

With Karloff still on contract (Price was not) and the sets from *The Raven* still standing, Corman spent a weekend directing this incomprehensible film about a soldier who finds strange goings-on in a seaside mansion. View at your own risk.
D: Roger Corman. A: Boris Karloff, Jack Nicholson, Sandra Knight.

Tomb of Ligea
(1964) 81m. **A**

A grief-stricken widower eventually remarries, but soon the spirit of his first wife takes over her successor. This gains a doomed atmosphere by being shot in real ruins and castles (and lavish interiors left over from *Becket*), while Price's descent into madness is subtly performed. A visually impressive and somber film.
D: Roger Corman. A: Vincent Price, Elizabeth Shepherd, John Westbrook.

Costume Horror

Hippies and other members of the counterculture in the late 60s liked dressing up in romantic garb from times past, and so did these mildly subversive horror films. Following the earlier Hammer horrors, these films upholstered their gore with rich photography, period sets—real location ruins were popular—and generous helpings of nudity for their long-haired heroes.

House of Wax
(1953) 88m. **A**

An opulent chiller with Price at his sinister best as the wax museum curator/sculptor who douses victims in wax to create his art. Though some of the original 3-D effects look a bit dinky on video, this still has enough fog-bound, gas-lit gothic to provide some well-earned shudders.
D: Andre de Toth. A: Vincent Price, Carolyn Jones, Charles Bronson.

The Masque of the Red Death
(1964) 88m. **A**

Evil Prince Prospero seals off himself and his court from the plague that's ravaging Italy in the twelfth century, and his castle becomes a microcosm of medieval tyranny and decadence. Whims become law, frantic and delirious entertainments prevail, and the red-hooded figure lurks outside in the foggy bogs.
D: Roger Corman. A: Vincent Price, Hazel Court, Jane Asher.

The Fearless Vampire Killers
(1967) 118m. **B+**

A pair of vampire hunters try to crash a bloodsucker bash in this Polanski entry. Breathtaking Alpine photography and rococo-gilded sets highlight this enjoyable though not always funny farce, the first to feature a Jewish vampire, who is, of course, impervious to crucifixes.
D: Roman Polanski. A: Jack MacGowran, Roman Polanski, Sharon Tate.

The Conqueror Worm
(1968) 87m. **B–**

Puritan witch-hunter Price scours the British countryside accusing and torturing women for profit and enjoyment. This unrelentingly grim and violent film wears a feminist and anticlerical cloak, with torture scenes taken from real witch-finders diaries.
D: Michael Reeves. A: Vincent Price, Ian Ogilvy, Hilary Dwyer.

Cry of the Banshee
(1970) 87m. **C–**

Price returns as another witch-hunter in Britain, only now he's at the mercy of an evil witch, her Druidic coven, and a demonic creature. Stylish and colorful, but Price hams it up in this inferior knock off of *The Conqueror Worm*.
D: Gordon Hessler. A: Vincent Price, Elisabeth Bergner, Essy Persson.

The Blood on Satan's Claw
(1971) 100m. **C+**

A young woman discovers the Devil's severed appendage and starts her murderous way toward creating a coven. A vivid rendering of the lower class in seventeenth-century England, with torture scenes excruciating to watch and a depressing tone.
D: Piers Haggard. A: Patrick Wymark, Barry Andrews, Linda Hayden.

Andy Warhol's Dracula
(1974) 93m. **C+**

When Dracula runs through the supply of virgins' blood in Hungary, he heads to Italy where it's even harder to find. Funnier than *Andy Warhol's Frankenstein*, with a little less gore, though the blood-spouting finale leaves not much of the Count left to stake.
D: Paul Morrisey. A: Udo Kier, Joe Dallesandro, Roman Polanski.

Andy Warhol's Frankenstein
(1974) 94m. **C+**

Sexually deviant Herr Frankenstein creates male and female creatures, which involves plenty of scenes of slashed bodies and commerce with glands and organs. Bug-eyed overacting by Kier and Brooklyn-accented nonacting by Dallesandro help out the lulls in between the campy gore. Originally filmed in 3D.
D: Paul Morrissey. A: Joe Dallesandro, Udo Kier.

Families Gone Bad

If you think present-day dysfunctional families are horrible, take a look at what these siblings and parents are up to: persecution, imprisonment, murder, and premature burial, to name a few. The success of *What Ever Happened to Baby Jane?* opened the door for aging Hollywood stars to make nongore horror thrillers that have a lot in common with the overwrought melodramas from the 1930s and 40s.

What Ever Happened to Baby Jane?

(1962) 132m. B&W. **A**

Davis is the emotionally stunted ex-child star who's taking care of bedridden sister Crawford in this nonstop sibling torture film. The sisters' curio-encrusted house, the sublimely crazed performances, and some unforgettable scenes of the things Davis feeds Crawford add up to one of the most atmospherically deranged modern gothics ever made.

D: Robert Aldrich. A: Bette Davis, Joan Crawford, Victor Buono.

Die! Die! My Darling!

(1965) 97m. **B+**

Tallulah is completely crazed as the woman intent on killing her dead son's fiancée. A veritable bestiary of lunatics occupies the dark old family house (including a demented Sutherland who reads his Bible upside down), and Bankhead's incestuous cravings give this one a very sick air.

D: Silvio Narizzano. A: Tallulah Bankhead, Stefanie Powers, Donald Sutherland.

Hush Hush, Sweet Charlotte

(1965) 133m. B&W. **A**

Davis is the aging Southern belle living in the family antebellum mansion haunted by a past tragedy. Sister de Havilland comes for a visit, and soon Davis is going crackers. A first-rate Southern gothic melodrama that crawls with shadows, doubts, and betrayals.

D: Robert Aldrich. A: Bette Davis, Olivia de Havilland, Mary Astor.

What's the Matter with Helen?

(1971) 101m. **B**

Two friends with a dark past open a dancing school for kids in 1930s Hollywood. One finds a millionaire, the other finds God and goes nuts. An almost tongue-in-cheek entry, but Winters is truly distressing in this slightly cartoonish, slightly nightmarish tale.

D: Curtis Harrington. A: Debbie Reynolds, Shelley Winters, Dennis Weaver.

Who Slew Auntie Roo?

(1971) 89m. **B**

Winters is an ex-singer in 1920s England who's unable to cope with the death of her daughter years earlier. Upon encountering a girl who's a dead ringer for the dead child, she goes off the deep end. This slickly shot black comedy features Winters at her hammy/looniest best, and an atmosphere thick with psychosis.

D: Curtis Harrington. A: Shelley Winters, Mark Lester, Chloe Franks.

The Mafu Cage (aka My Sister, My Love)

(1978) 99m. **C–**

An insane murderous jungle-obsessed girl drives her sister crazy in their African theme park apartment. This garishly colorful and overly artsy film strives to say something, but remains an uninteresting mystery, obscured by a shrill soundtrack and muddled script.

D: Karen Arthur. A: Carol Kane, Lee Grant, Will Geer.

Mexican Horror

Mexican folklore is mixed in with horror and even surrealistic art in these absolutely bizarre, cheaply made, atrociously dubbed films. Unexpected images like monsters with forked tongues, flowers bursting into flames, satanic mirrors, and vampire haciendas keep you awake through occasionally chatty dull patches. Include in this mix high contrast photography with the emphasis on black along with completely overwrought musical scores, and you've got this very weird Mexican bill of fare.

The Vampire

(1957) 84m. B&W. **C–**

At decaying Sycamore Hacienda, a pair of vampires and a strong-willed girl battle over property rights. This thickly atmospheric film apes early Universal efforts, right down to the creepy music, but ends up looking like a spaghetti western invaded by the undead.

D: Fernando Mendez. A: German Robles, Abel Salazar, Carmen Montejo.

The Witch's Mirror

(1960) 75m. B&W. **B**

A Satanist godmother plans vengeance on a scientist working on creating synthetic skin from dead bodies. Highlights include a skull growing its own skin and hands that jump from a living girl's body in this sinuously filmed bizarre tale.

D: Chano Urveta. A: Rosita Arenas, Armando Calvo, Isabela Corona.

The Brainiac

(1961) 77m. B&W. **C+**

A mad Inquisition sorcerer returns as a monster, crossing 300 years to wreak vengeance on the descendants of his accusers. The weird, oddly lit minimalist sets make a good backdrop for a monster that's a tuxedoed hairy thing with a forked tongue and sucker-tipped fingers.

D: Chano Urveto. A: Abel Salazar, German Robles.

Night of the Bloody Apes

(1968) 82m. **C–**

A scientist transfers an ape heart into his dying son's body with murderous results. Female wrestling, tacky gore, nudity, and very bad dubbing make this fun if you're in an exceptionally odd mood.

D: Rene Cardona, Jr. A: Armand Silvestre, Norma Lazareno, Jose Elias Moreno.

Sinister Invasion (aka **The Incredible Invasion**)
(1968) 88m. **D**
It's scientist Boris and his radiation machine versus extraterrestrial zombies in this grimy-looking nonsense. This is one of four Mexican horrors made out of scenes shot shortly before Karloff died.
D: Jack Hill. A: Boris Karloff, Maura Monti, Christa Linder, Enrique Guzman.

OTHER FILMS:
The Man and the Monster (1958)
The Curse of the Crying Woman (1961).

Hauntings

These low-budget films get their chills from things that go bump in the night. People do get knocked off, sometimes graphically like in *Dementia 13* and *Strait-Jacket*, but mostly you get the standard haunted house atmospherics like creaking stairs and moaning other-world spirits, with the occasional dash of gallows humor for spice.

House on Haunted Hill
(1958) 75m. B&W. **B**
Price is at his charmingly deranged best as a man who offers $10,000 to his wife and a small group to survive a night in a supposedly ghost-infested manse. This "ten-little-Indians" horror whodunit is equal parts fun and scares.
D: William Castle. A: Vincent Price; Carol Ohmart; Elisha Cook, Jr.

13 Ghosts
(1960) 85m. B&W. **C–**
A family inherits a haunted house along with its curse: The 12 ghosts in residence are awaiting another death to round the total out to 13. Without Illusion-O (a gimmick that allowed people to wear special glasses to see the ghosts) this is pretty ho-hum.
D: William Castle. A: Rosemary DeCamp, Donald Woods, Martin Milner.

Carnival of Souls
(1962) 81m. B&W. **A**
After surviving a car accident that has wiped out all her friends, a girl dazedly walks around town, plagued by visions of a ghoulish man and a dark carnival of the dead. You'll either groove on this all atmospherics and no action cult favorite or find it totally incomprehensible.
D: Herk Harvey. A: Candace Hilligoss, Sidney Berger, Frances Feist.

Dementia 13
(1963) 81m. B&W. **B**
A modern—and cheaply made—gothic tale of a mad Irish family being killed off by someone who wants their inheritance. Coppola's first mainstream feature offers a slow-paced story of a creepily dysfunctional family, jazzed up by morbidly lush location shooting and punctuated by bursts of still shocking violence.
D: Francis Ford Coppola. A: William Campbell, Luana Anders, Mary Mitchell.

The Haunting
(1963) 111m. B&W. **A**
A professor gathers a bunch of lonely, ESP-sensitive people to spend the night in the haunted Hill House. Another shadowy atmospherics-only horror suspense with the visitors frightened by wallpaper filled with ominous face shapes, groaning stairways, and walls pounded by unseen things.
D: Robert Wise. A: Julie Harris, Claire Bloom, Richard Johnson.

Strait-Jacket
(1964) 89m. B&W. **B–**
Crawford starts a new life after a 20-year stretch in the asylum for decapitating her husband and his lover, but the bodies start piling up again. Joan's campy, wild-eyed performance and some pretty gruesome nightmare images are the highlights of this low-budget chiller.
D: William Castle. A: Joan Crawford, Diane Baker, George Kennedy.

Italian Gothic

Italian filmmakers embraced the "sex, violence, and mist" horror trend set by the British Hammer studios with an operatic fervor, attracting talents like Mario Bava (one-time assistant to Fellini) and Riccardo Freda (a former art critic). The results are films that reek with ornate gothic atmosphere: cobwebbed candelabras, glass caskets, burning witches, doleful organ music, buckets of blood (usually trimmed in the U.S. versions), and enough dry ice to fog up half of Italy. Don't expect high action horror with these—their labyrinthine plots of revenge, sensual tempo, and doomy tone make them more like artful nightmares that just happened to be dubbed.

Black Sunday
(1960) 83m. **A**
A spiked mask is hammered into horror icon Steele's face, opening this tale of a vampire/witch's vengeance. The gothic gamut is packed into every frame: elegantly macabre crypts, misty cobweb-filled cemeteries, burning stakes, and as much spilled blood as the times would permit.
D: Mario Bava. A: Barbara Steele, John Richardson, Ivo Garrani.

The Horrible Dr. Hichcock
(1962) 77m. **B+**
While using an anesthetic that simulates death, the necrophiliac Doctor Hichcock accidentally kills his wife. Undaunted, he continues the kinky scenario with his new wife, in a film teeming with sick sex, wraithlike ghosts, and lush Victorian sets.
D: Robert Hampton. A: Robert Fleming, Barbara Steele.

Black Sabbath
(1964) 99m. **B–**
A disappointing anthology film with a good final episode starring Karloff as the patriarch who proceeds to feed on his family after becoming a vampire.
D: Mario Bava. A: Boris Karloff, Mark Damon, Michele Mercier.

Castle of Blood
(1964) 84m. B&W. **B**
Edgar Allan Poe bets a cheeky nobleman that he can't survive one night in a haunted castle without going mad. Some unintentionally hilarious dialogue and Ms. Steele as the helpful spirit make this a fun curio for fans.
D: Anthony Dawson. A: Barbara Steele, George Riviere, Margrete Robsahm.

Blood and Black Lace
(1965) 88m. **B**
Beautiful models are being murdered at a fashion agency by a masked killer sporting a clawlike glove. Bava actually gives this misogynistic modern gothic some substance, along with his swooping luscious photography. The first modern slasher.
D: Mario Bava. A: Cameron Mitchell, Eva Bartok, Arianna Gorini.

Nightmare Castle
(1965) 90m. B&W. **A**
Crazed Dr. Arrowsmith goes through two wives while experimenting with blood and electricity. Bodies sputter in electric shrouds, hearts throb in aquariums, and plants bleed in this delirious Gallic gothic shot in vivid, amber-hued Technicolor.
D: Mario Caiano. A: Paul Muller, Barbara Steele, Helga Line.

Planet of the Vampires
(1965) 86m. **A–**
A gothic sci-fi tale of what happens to the crew of a spaceship that answers an SOS from an alien planet. Some highlights are the leather spacesuits, a foggy orange and blue crystalline planet, and astronauts who rise from the dead in plastic shrouds.
D: Mario Bava. A: Barry Sullivan, Norma Bengell, Angel Aranda.

Kill, Baby Kill
(1966) 90m. **A**
A palpably atmospheric Bava effort as the ghost of a murdered child exacts her revenge. Certain images—a witch driving coins into people's chests, a man walking through the same room over and over without going anywhere, and an agoraphobic chase scene over weird mountains against a color-leeched sky—will stay with you.
D: Mario Bava. A: Erika Blanc, Fabienne Dali, Giacomo Stuart.

Hammer Horrors

"The House That Horror Built" is the very accurate description of how a small British studio turned into the most influential horror factory since Universal's halcyon years in the 1930s. In fact, Hammer's first hits were remakes of such Universal classics as *Frankenstein*, *The Mummy*, and *Dracula*, to which the savvy Brits added stunning color photography, lavish sets, and generous dollops of sex and blood. This formula remained successful for nearly a decade, and though battered by both the changing tastes of the 60s and its own drying well of ideas, the Hammer imprint was a guarantee of terror, cleavage, and blood, all in good British taste.

The Curse of Frankenstein
(1957) 82m. **B+**
The film that started Hammer's reign of horror took Shelley's novel and added blood, severed body parts, low-cut blouses, and a gruesome, stitched-together look for The Creature. Still entertaining, though what was shocking then is fairly tame by today's standards.
D: Terence Fisher. A: Peter Cushing, Christopher Lee, Hazel Court.

The Horror of Dracula
(1958) 82m. **B+**
Lee's sepulchrally handsome vampire, leaping from gaslight to shadow and saying little, was presented as being sexually as well as vampirically ravenous, with the cast's femmes practically swooning for his bite.
D: Terence Fisher. A: Christopher Lee, Peter Cushing, Melissa Stribling.

The Mummy
(1959) 88m. **A**
From the first scene when the Egyptian prince gets his tongue severed to his vengeful search centuries later for his beloved, Lee is no fumbling bandage-case, but a terrifyingly quick and aggressive mummy. Features torch-lit, hieroglyph-encrusted Egyptian sets, and a particularly tense gothic ambiance.
D: Terence Fisher. A: Peter Cushing, Christopher Lee, Yvonne Furneaux.

The Brides of Dracula
(1960) 85m. **B+**
Baron Meinster (not Dracula) is the debauched blond vampire who's out collecting brides in London. The Hammer formula—period-perfect sets, blood, and buxom women—is so established that they didn't even need Christopher Lee to make a superior vampire tale.
D: Terence Fisher. A: Peter Cushing, David Peel, Freda Jackson.

The Gorgon
(1964) 83m. **A**
Two doctors deal in different ways with the discovery of a legendary creature with serpents for hair and whose glance can turn men to stone. A change of pace, this unusually despairing, deeply atmospheric film integrates mythology into a complex tragic plot.
D: Terence Fisher. A: Peter Cushing, Christopher Lee, Barbara Shelley.

Dracula Has Risen from the Grave
(1969) 92m. **B**
A revenge tale with rather ponderous religious trappings, this entry eschews the heavy gothic atmosphere and goes for a slick-paced modern look. Gruesome opening shows a woman found hanging from a church bell.
D: Freddie Francis. A: Christopher Lee, Rupert Davies, Barry Andrews.

Frankenstein Must Be Destroyed

(1970) 103m. **C–**

In the fifth, and least effective of the Hammer Frankensteins, the Baron comes off as pretty monstrous himself as he blackmails an assistant and generally acts like an obsessed nut. Fairly gruesome, with very bad monster effects.
D: Terence Fisher. A: Peter Cushing, Simon Ward, Veronica Carlson.

Lust for a Vampire

(1970) 95m. **C–**

A lesbian vampire haunts a girls' school handily located near her ancestral castle. Markedly inferior sequel to *The Vampire Lovers,* with the prior film's gothic ambiance replaced with gaudy photography, annoying camera tricks, and obnoxious pop songs.
D: Jimmy Sangster. A: Barbara Jefford, Ralph Bates, Yvette Stensgaard.

Taste the Blood of Dracula

(1970) 95m. **A–**

With the help of some upright citizens, a Satanist inadvertently revives Dracula at a blood-drinking ceremony. Menacingly atmospheric and pretty subversive for a Hammer film, with the supposedly decent folk more vile than the Count.
D: Peter Sasdy. A: Christopher Lee, Linda Hayden, Ilsa Blair.

The Vampire Lovers

(1970) 91m. **B+**

A young woman moves to a remote Austrian town in search of revenge and new blood—female blood. In tune with the times, the sexual ante is upped in this tale that's like a Russ Meyer movie in Gothic drag, with sumptuous sets, voluptuously vivid Technicolor photography, and a good deal of nudity.
D: Roy Ward Baker. A: Ingrid Pitt, Pippa Steele, Peter Cushing.

The Creeping Flesh

(1972) 89m. **B+**

Columbia Pictures nabbed a Hammer director and the top stars to make this gothic knock-off about an ancient skeleton that grows new flesh when wet. An energetic entry with scenes of evil blood vanquishing good, misty sets, a plush insane asylum, and the requisite exposed female flesh.
D: Freddie Francis. A: Peter Cushing, Christopher Lee, Lorna Heilbron.

The Seven Brothers Meet Dracula

(1972) 88m. **B–**

This fusion of kung fu and horror shows a team of martial arts experts fighting off ghouls led by Dracula. Definitely not boring, with endless red-hued battle scenes, amazing stunts, unfamiliar Asian sets, and the air of sustained macabre and madness the title implies.
D: Roy Ward Baker. A: Peter Cushing, David Chaing, Julie Ege.

Twins of Evil

(1972) 87m. **A**

Twin *Playboy* centerfolds star in this vivid conclusion to Hammer's lesbian-themed vampire series. Obsessive witch-hunter Cushing must deal not only with matching vamps, but with a Satanist count, in this briskly paced fable of sexuality and repression.
D: John Hough. A: Madeleine Collinson, Mary Collinson, Peter Cushing.

Horror Express

(1973) 90m. **B+**

Onboard the Trans-Siberia Express is a brain-eating alien whose glowing red eyes turn unwary passengers into zombies. Again, another studio nabbed Hammer's main stars and rich period feel to create a grisly version of an Agatha Christie all-star whodunit with a Sci-Fi overlay.
D: Eugenio Martin. A: Peter Cushing, Christopher Lee, Telly Savalas.

Captain Kronos: Vampire Hunter

(1974) 91m. **B+**

This adventurous departure from the formula features a swashbuckling hero who gallops through a gorgeously photographed English countryside, dispatching all manner of foes, including vampires. Tongue-in-cheek fun, filled with the modish optimistic tone of *The Avengers*.
D: Brian Clemens. A: Horst Jansen, John David Carson, Caroline Munro.

(See also *To the Devil, a Daughter,* page 368.)

OTHER FILMS:

The Curse of the Werewolf (1961)
Phantom of the Opera (1962)
The Evil of Frankenstein (1964)
Scars of Dracula (1970)
Horror of Frankenstein (1970)
Hands of the Ripper (1971)
Dr. Jekyll and Sister Hyde (1971)
Demons of the Mind (1972)
Dracula A.D. 1972 (1972)
Fear in the Night (Dynasty of Fear) (1972)
The Satanic Rites of Dracula (1973)
Frankenstein and the Monster from Hell (1974)

Miscellaneous British Horror

Probably the best way to describe this group is that they are the films that did *not* come from Britain's horror giant, Hammer studios. No costume pieces here, just low-gore, high-atmosphere tales of present-day terror starring Cushing, Lee, Karloff, and the occasional fading Hollywood star. This group also shows an odd 60s trend in England: terror at the circus, along with the omnibus horror film, a popular form since the semiclassic *Dead of Night*.

Horror Hotel

(1960) 76m. B&W. **B+**

A missing woman's boyfriend and brother search for her in a Massachusetts village, unaware that she's been taken in by a Satanist coven. Don't let the time-worn plot throw you: This one delivers authentic creeps with its prowling camerawork and gloomily shadow-strewn photography that harkens back to Val Lewton's glory days.
D: John Llewellyn Moxey. A: Christopher Lee, Dennis Lotis, Betta St. John.

Die, Monster, Die!

(1965) 80m. **C**

This serviceable adaptation of H. P. Lovecraft's *The Colour out of Space* shows how a crashed meteor causes unpleasant vegetable and human mutations in desolate Arkham County. Brooding ambiance, weird washed-out photography, and Karloff help make up for the very

slow pace and wandering script.
D: Daniel Haller. A: Boris Karloff, Nick Adams, Suzan Farmer.

The Skull
(1965) 83m. **C+**
Occult fancier Cushing adds an ancient skull to his collection, unaware it once belonged to, and still harbors the spirit of, the Marquis de Sade. Everything is played straight in this film that seems oblivious to how hokey the script is, and for a time garners some real chills and uncanny atmosphere.
D: Freddie Francis. A: Peter Cushing, Christopher Lee, Patrick Wymark.

And Now the Screaming Starts
(1973) 87m. **C–**
A standard issue haunted house tale, complete with creepy ancestral mansion, a multigenerational curse, and a murderous disembodied hand to liven things up. The horror pros and art director do their best to give the tired tale some oomph.
D: Roy Ward Baker. A: Peter Cushing, Herbert Lom, Stephanie Beacham.

The Wicker Man
(1973) 95m. **A**
The Scotland Yard detective investigating a missing girl lands on a coastal island peopled by regular English village folks. They also happen to be a pagan cult that may be using human sacrifices. A truly unusual tale that's disquieting, erotic, and outright scary, with fascinating details of the rituals and a shocker of an ending.
D: Robin Hardy. A: Edward Woodward, Christopher Lee, Britt Ekland.

Circus

Circus of Horrors
(1960) 88m. **B**
A demented surgeon on the lam in postwar Europe joins a traveling sideshow as he continues his perverse experiments on scarred women. Obtrusive stock footage, and some really bad costume animals detract from this grisly, luridly original entry.
D: Sidney Hayers. A: Anton Diffring, Erika Remberg, Donald Pleasence.

Berserk
(1967) 98m. **C**
Crawford continues her downward career slide in this gruesomely kitschy film about a circus whose attractions are being killed. The real horror here is Crawford herself, garbed in leotards and top hat, eyes threatening to pop out of her head as she redefines "chewing the scenery."
D: Jin O'Connolly. A: Joan Crawford, Diana Dors, Ty Hardin.

Circus of Fear
(1967) 89m. B&W or color version. **C–**
A Scotland Yard inspector investigates circus murders in a whodunit using gruesome murders to maintain viewer interest. Mainly notable for the bright cast, otherwise a competently mediocre effort.
D: John Llewellyn Moxey. A: Christopher Lee, Klaus Kinski, Suzy Kendall.

Anthology

Torture Garden
(1968) 93m. **C+**
The Big Top provides a framing device for four terror tales, leeringly told to shills by Meredith as Dr. Diabolo. Uneven storywise, but boasts some creepy moments, best of which include Palance as a demented collector of Edgar Allan Poe manuscripts.
D: Freddie Francis. A: Jack Palance, Burgess Meredith, Peter Cushing.

Asylum
(1972) 88m. **B**
Four tales of terror emerge from insane folk interviewed by a shrink, including the story of a deranged inventor and his army of doll-robots. Great twist ending and a suitably demented atmosphere make this the finest of the 70s anthologies.
D: Roy Ward Baker. A: Peter Cushing, Charlotte Rampling, Britt Eklund.

Tales from the Crypt
(1972) 92m. **B–**
Nothing at all like the cable series, this collection hits its highpoint in a story about the blind exacting revenge on a sadistic hospital director. Though lacking in atmosphere, the stories are good, and pop along at a crisp pace.
D: Freddie Francis. A: Ralph Richardson, Joan Collins, Ian Hendry.

Tales That Witness Madness
(1973) 90m. **C+**
A decidedly odd group, with tales that seesaw from real scary to utterly silly, often in the same scene. Very atmospheric, with lurking camerawork and a great Mod color scheme. Worth it if only to see a young and cranky Collins battling a living tree for her man's affections.
D: Freddie Francis. A: Kim Novak, Joan Collins, Donald Pleasence.

1970s

Dario Argento

For Italy's horror master, it's the image that's important: a procession of fireflies eerily guide a girl through a dark forest, a woman claws at the window of a blood-red mansion as a knife-wielding leather glove penetrates the frame. Even if his stories are tough to follow (American versions can be cut by as much as 20 minutes) and the gore gratuitous, his beautiful and grotesque images provide a bit of artful exotica in the world of horror. NOTE: When renting an Argento film, check alternate titles and running times, both of which may vary.

Deep Red (aka **The Hatchet Murders**)
(1975) 98m. **A**
This tale of an Englishman and a mentalist trying to track down a serial killer is a dizzying piece of sensory overload. Disquieting sound effects blend with a recurring lullaby played before each murder while the camera prowls relentlessly, lingering on a broken doll's "death-twitches" or zooming in mere inches from a person's eyes.
D: Dario Argento. A: David Hemmings, Daria Nicolodi, Gabriele Lavia.

Suspiria
(1977) 92m. **A**
A ballerina joins a strange school run by witches. Here you see a plague of maggots infesting the entire school, a knife-murder viewed from *inside* the victim's body, and color-drenched pop gothic sets, all topped off by nerve-rending electronic music.
D: Dario Argento. A: Jessica Harper, Joan Bennet, Alida Valli.

Inferno
(1980) 107m. **A**
An Art Nouveau Manhattan apartment is the residence of an ancient malign spirit. Almost plotless, this is a nightmare of unrelenting visions of terror, jarring sound effects, and even more nerve-racking silences as people meet their terrible fates.
D: Dario Argento. A: Irene Miracle, Leigh McCloskey, Daria Nicolodi.

Unsane (aka Tenebrae)
(1982) 100m. **A**
A maniac begins aping the murders described in mystery writer Franciosa's books. Substitute "filmmaker" for "writer" and one has a very disturbing view of Argento examining his own dark art in this coldly toned, intelligent, and gruesome meditation on violence.
D: Dario Argento. A: Anthony Franciosa, Christian Borromeo, John Saxon.

Creepers
(1985) 82m. **B–**
At a girls' school in "Swiss Transylvania," a student who can telepathically communicate with insects becomes a key in solving a series of decapitations. All Argento's strengths (gorgeous blue-toned photography, sinuous camerawork) and weaknesses (incomprehensible plot and gratuitous gore) are here in ample supply.
D: Dario Argento. A: Jennifer Connelly, Donald Pleasance, Daria Nicolodi.

The Church
(1991) 110m. **B+**
A renovated German church becomes a place of confined horror as an ancient device lets loose a plague of demons. A drowning in a decayed catacomb and a disturbingly erotic encounter with a blue-winged demon are just some of the blasphemies in this Argento-scripted shocker.
D: Dario Argento. A: Hugh Zuarshie, Tomas Arana, Feodore Chaliapin.

Terror at the Opera
(1987) 107m. **A**
A rock video director stages a postmodern version of *Macbeth* as a black-gloved murderer begins killing off cast and crew. More coherent plotwise than the others but with plenty of unforgettably macabre images.
D: Dario Argento. A: Cristina Marsillach, Ian Charleson, Daria Nicolodi.

Haunted Houses and Apartments

These modest little spooky mansion tales are generally supernatural whodunits in which you get to watch the characters get killed off one by one, or variations of *Rosemary's Baby* in which ordinary neighbors are nice but weirdly secretive until all hell finally breaks loose.

Let's Scare Jessica to Death
(1971) 89m. **B–**
Fresh out of the sanitarium, poor unstable Jessica arrives home only to find moving corpses, ghosts, and vampires. Is she coming unglued again? Effective low-key thriller of sadism and the fragility of the mind.
D: John Hancock. A: Zohra Lampert, Barton Heyman.

The House of Seven Corpses
(1973) 90m. **C**
When a horror film director decides to shoot a film in a haunted house, the cast and crew start turning up dead. A slightly garish old-style gothic, whose cheap look affords some camp value.
D: Paul Harrison. A: John Ireland, Faith Domergue, John Carradine.

The Legend of Hell House
(1973) 94m. **B+**
After a group of paranormal scientists are wiped out, the sole survivor leads another group into the Mount Everest of haunted houses. Well-paced chiller that remains scary.
D: John Hough. A: Roddy McDowall, Pamela Franklin, Gayle Hunnicutt.

Silent Night, Bloody Night
(1973) 83m. **C+**
Escaped lunatic takes refuge in a house and proceeds to murder the townspeople. The house also has a horrible history involving incest, an asylum, and brutal doctors. Bizarre, somewhat violent story with an incomprehensible plot and dark atmosphere that makes TV viewing of some scenes difficult.
D: Theodore Gershuny. A: Patrick O'Neal, Mary Woronov, John Carradine.

The Beast Must Die
(1974) 83m. **C**
Eccentric millionaire entertains a group of whacky guests, one of whom is a werewolf. This dull little "who's the werewolf?" is a museum piece with 70s black vinyl clothes and awful 70s cop show music.
D: Paul Annett. A: Calvin Lockhart, Peter Cushing.

Burnt Offerings
(1976) 116m. **C**
A family rents an unbelievable house for peanuts but they have to feed the owners' elderly mom who lives in the attic. The family proceeds to metamorphosize and meet bizarre fates. Slightly boring with slow stretches and a really loud concluding 15 minutes.
D: Dan Curtis. A: Oliver Reed, Karen Black, Bette Davis.

The Sentinel
(1977) 92m. **C**
Fashion model has a lawyer boyfriend and an apartment to die for. Two problems—her neighbors are strange and the gateway to hell is located in the hallway. The flesh-eating zombies, colorful crew of old and new stars, great 70s fashions, and weird sex scenes make this atmospheric thriller a camp favorite.
D: Michael Winner. A: Christina Raines, Ava Gardner, Chris Sarandon, Christopher Walken, Jeff Goldblum.

The Evil
(1978) 89m. **D+**
When psychologists convert a lovely old house into a clinic, they manage to un-

lock a portal that unleashes a killer force embodied by Victor Buono. Dull and predictable.
D: Gus Trikonis. A: Richard Crenna, Joanna Pettet, Victor Buono.

The Changeling
(1979) 113m. **B–**
A composer moves into a Gothic mansion complete with bumps, creaks, and a willful wheelchair and begins to have strange visions about the former inhabitants. Lots of solid acting in this subtle ghost story from Canada.
D: Peter Medak. A: George C. Scott, Trish Van Devere, Melvyn Douglas.

The Legacy
(1979) 100m. **C**
People participating in an unexplained ritual called "The Legacy" at an English country estate get bumped off one by one. What strange satanic fate-worse-than-death awaits the lovely young survivor? Slow and dumb like a Danielle Steele TV movie with cheesy gore.
D: Richard Marquand. A: Katherine Ross, Sam Elliot, Roger Daltrey.

Hell Night
(1981) 100m. **D**
The initiates of a fraternity and sorority must spend the night in a creepy manor. A zero budget on this one, and when the biggest scares are the film equivalent of snakes in a can, you know you're in trouble.
D: Tom DeSimone. A: Linda Blair, Vincent Van Patten, Jenny Neumann.

David Cronenberg

What can you do when the monster is not "out there" but inside of you? Cronenberg's films, both mercilessly intelligent and surreally gory, explore the nightmare of the terrors within ourselves as bodies mutate and grow strange organs and minds warp to unleash terrible forces. While his earlier works are low-budget affairs, they are cunningly and often humorously written, and Cronenberg always manages a few scenes of guts flying and bodies growing in some really horrible fashion. His later horror films are visionary masterpieces, overflowing with gory, disturbing, and haunting images of the human body and soul.

They Came from Within
(1975) 87m. **B–**
A scientist lets loose on the inhabitants of an apartment complex a sexually transmitted parasite that turns its victims into violent sex fiends. Disgusting, gory, and marred by variable acting and poor photography? Yes. Forgettable? Impossible.
D: David Cronenberg. A: Paul Hampton, Joe Silver, Barbara Steele.

Rabid
(1977) 91m. **B–**
After a motorcycle accident, Chambers receives an experimental skin graft that mutates into a bloodsucking organ under her armpit that spreads a disease of vampirism. Far-fetched, but Cronenberg delivers the scares by turning pristine Montreal into a shadowy city of lurking horror, and the prescient AIDS metaphor is hard to ignore.
D: David Cronenberg. A: Marilyn Chambers, Joe Silver, Frank Moore.

The Brood
(1979) 91m. **A**
When a psychologist encourages his patients to physically manifest their unconscious rage, some get bizarre cancerous lesions, and one actually gives birth to murderous tots who act out her violent urges. These pajama-clad killer kids and the jolting scares that occur in broad daylight show Cronenberg brilliantly in control of his terrifying themes.
D: David Cronenberg. A: Oliver Reed, Samantha Eggar, Art Hindle.

Scanners
(1981) 102m. **A–**
A birth control pill has the unforeseen side effect of creating telepaths with the ability to literally blow people to bits. Famous for its scene in which a scanner makes a man's head explode, this is mainly a standard thriller with some good ideas.
D: David Cronenberg. A: Stephen Lack, Jennifer O'Neill, Patrick McGoohan.

Videodrome
(1983) 88m. **A**
A cable-TV programmer discovers the "videodrome signal" that causes its viewers to hallucinate. Man melds with his machines as Woods' stomach turns into a VCR slot, his hand fuses with a gun, and the TV starts transmitting images from the far side of his nightmares. A masterful and sometimes difficult film, bursting with horrible and fascinating visions.
D: David Cronenberg. A: James Woods, Sonja Smits, Deborah Harry.

The Fly
(1986) 96m. **A**
A scientist accidentally combines his DNA with a fly's and finds himself transforming into a giant insect. This starts out as a sexy tale of love and genius, and descends into a tragic, thought-provoking look at their consequences. Beware! The last half hour is a virtual opera of bodily effluvium and guck as Goldblum's body disintegrates and mutates.
D: David Cronenberg. A: Jeff Goldblum, Geena Davis, John Getz.

Dead Ringers
(1988) 115m. **A**
An unsparingly grim tale of very different, perversely bonded twin gynecologists, whose lives are forever changed by a neurotic film star. An artfully merciless examination of human relationships pushed to the edge, with astounding performances by Irons, cold blue-dominated photography, and some very wicked gynecological instruments.
D: David Cronenberg. A: Jeremy Irons, Genevieve Bujold, Heidi Von Palleske.

Naked Lunch
(1991) 117m. **A–**
A junkie exterminator in 1950s New York is informed by an insect typewriter that he has an important mission. And then things get *really* weird in this filming of Burroughs' unfilmable avant-

garde novel, filled here with outrageous and grotesque imagery, gorgeous period postcard photography, and a script that is by turns bizarre, hilarious, campy, and tragic.
D: David Cronenberg. A: Peter Weller, Judy Davis, Ian Holm.

Prime Vincent Price

The foppish character actor in films like *Laura* and *The Three Musketeers* became Horror's arch madman using his expressive mouth, ironic diction, and mischievous eyes to ham his way through scores of lower-budget scare flicks. Price somehow managed to simultaneously laugh at and relish the ridiculous material he had to work with and can be seen in top form in these bigger-budgeted horror films that were made when Price had become an undisputed master of his realm.

Scream and Scream Again
(1970) 95m. **B**
Price is the doctor in a European country who's involved in a worldwide scheme to create synthetic men. This study in paranoia is filled to bursting with Nazilike designs, bodies boiling in acid vats, sexually motivated murders, and enough plot lines for three very strange films.
D: Gordon Hessler. A: With Peter Cushing, Christopher Lee, Anthony Newlands.

The Abominable Dr. Phibes
(1971) 93m. **A**
A disfigured madman goes on a stylish spree of revenge (based on Egyptian myth, using locusts, rats, bats, and more) against the surgeons who failed to save his wife. Besides Price's wonderful turn as the silent semicyber mad Doc, the entire film is an exercise in dazzlingly colorful Art Deco overload.
D: Robert Fuest. A: With Joseph Cotten, Terry-Thomas, Virginia North.

Dr. Phibes Rises Again
(1972) 88m. **B+**
A fire awakens Phibes, now laying with his wife in matching crystal coffins, and off he goes on another mission of vengeance. As Deco-obsessed as the first, but darker toned: The image of Price playing doomy tunes on his frosted glass church organ is both funny and touching.
D: Robert Fuest. A: With Robert Quarry, Valli Kemp, Hugh Griffith.

Madhouse
(1972) 89m. **C**
Price is a neurotic ex-horror star who agrees to be on a TV series named after his most famous character, and soon bodies are all over the place. Though competently filmed, this misses the sense of nostalgia *and* horror that the filmmakers seem to have been aiming at.
D: Jim Clark. A: With Peter Cushing, Robert Quarry, Adrienne Corri.

Theatre of Blood
(1973) 104m. **A**
The perfect Price vehicle with Vincent playing an insane actor who kills off his critics in ways inspired by Shakespeare. Despite the gore—an attempted blinding, a decapitation, some bad news for poodles—this one is pure fun, with kitschy costumes and gleaming cinematography.
D: Douglas Hickox. A: With Diana Rigg, Harry Andrews, Ian Hendry.

Creature Features

Are you phobic about what swims in the water, crawls through the sewers, or creeps down the drainpipe? Disturbed by the idea of insects and other crawly creatures mutating to the size of a Volvo? With the exception of *Jaws* and *Arachnophobia*, these low-budget films may have a made-for-TV look and a sleazy exploitative feel, but they're just the right thing if you have a taste for the heebie-jeebies.

Willard
(1971) 95m. **C+**
This tale of a quiet young man with an unhealthy fondness for rats, who finally gets pushed too far, was originally a box-office smash. Though the scenes of Willard's pets on the rampage are effectively disgusting, this looks like a TV movie, and not much as vermin movies go.
D: Daniel Mann. A: Bruce Davison, Ernest Borgnine, Sondra Locke.

Ben
(1972) 95m. **C**
An army of rats makes friends with another screwed-up kid, and Michael Jackson sings the hit ode to the head rodent.
D: Phil Karlson. A: Arthur O'Connell, Lee Montgomery, Joseph Campanella.

Jaws
(1975) 124m. **A**
The police chief is joined by a feisty marine biologist and a crusty old salt to hunt for a station wagon-size shark who's been diminishing the beach-going population of their seaside town. More of a taut thriller than a horror film, this one's guaranteed to make you jump and holler.
D: Steven Spielberg. A: Roy Scheider, Robert Shaw, Richard Dreyfuss.

Food of the Gods
(1976) 88m. **D–**
Two great old Hollywood stars serve as monster bait when animals get really big after eating a farmer's special food. The special effects for the giant rats, chickens, wasps, and others are actually good, but otherwise this is really bad.
D: Bert I. Gordon. A: Marjoe Gortner, Pamela Franklin, Ralph Meeker.

Empire of the Ants
(1977) 89m. **F**

Bert I. Gordon, who gave us *Food of the Gods,* now gives us giant ants who attack land developers. Even Joan Collins in tight polyester outfits can't salvage the bad 70s cinematography and deadly boring story.
D: Bert I. Gordon. A: Joan Collins, Robert Lansing, Albert Salmi.

Kingdom of the Spiders
(1977) 94m. **B**

When an insecticide deprives five thousand *real* tarantulas of their food, they feast on the inhabitants of a small Arizona town. A deliberate buildup of crawling terror, some disturbing tarantula-bite effects, and good performances make this a must not-see for spider phobics.
D: John Cardos. A: William Shatner, Tiffany Bolling, Woody Strode.

Orca
(1977) 91m. **D**

A whaler accidentally kills a killer whale's mate. Orca retaliates and the whaler goes the Captain Ahab route and obsessively tracks down Orca. Goofy, with laughable fake iceberg sets, and a scene with Bo getting her leg bitten by a whale.
D: Michael Anderson. A: Richard Harris, Charlotte Rampling, Bo Derek.

Jaws 2
(1978) 120m. **C**

This is a carbon copy of the first film which makes it difficult to understand why the police chief still has to talk so long and hard in order to convince everyone that there's a new shark in town.
D: Jeannot Szwarc. A: Roy Scheider, Lorraine Gary, Murray Hamilton.

Piranha
(1978) 92m. **B**

To aid the Vietnam war effort, scientists create mutant killer fish that escape to a resort town, with expected results. Eerie stop-animation creature footage and a funny script by John Sayles make this a winner.
D: Joe Dante. A: Kevin McCarthy, Heather Menzies, Bradford Dillman.

Alligator
(1980) 94m. **B+**

A giant sewer-bred alligator terrorizes Chicago and prompts a mucho macho big game hunter to try his hand at gator slaying. A low-budget effort that is witty and even scary at times, due mostly to the John Sayles script and the solid acting.
D: Lewis Teague. A: Robert Forster, Robin Riker, Michael Gazzo.

Arachnophobia
(1990) 109m. **B**

An arachnophobic doctor moves his family to the country for some peace and quiet, only to become besieged by a rare species of lethal spiders. Another big Hollywood film in this group (along with *Jaws*) that is funny and horrific in that creepy-crawly way. Kudos to the spider wranglers.
D: Frank Marshall. A: Jeff Daniels, Harley Jan Kozak, John Goodman.

Ticks
(1994) 93m. **B**

A multicultural batch of disturbed teens are taken to a country therapy camp where they get attacked by mutant insects. This well-filmed, energetically demented tale lifts elements from *Alien* and *Deliverance,* resulting in a surprisingly entertaining film for those who can stomach really repulsive gore.
D: Tony Randel. A: Rosalind Allen, Ami Dolenz, Seth Allen.

Mosquito
(1995) 92m. **B–**

A spaceship deposits some little insect eggs in a remote camp site and, before you know it, the place is overrun with big rubbery killer mosquitoes. Inoffensively silly throwback to 50s Big Bug movies boasts amusingly cheap monsters, low gore, and lack of interest in taking itself even slightly seriously.
D: Gary Jones. A: Gunnar Hansen, Ron Asheton, Steve Dickson.

OTHER FILMS:
Island of the Lost (1966)
Frogs (1972)
Legend of Boggy Creek (1972)
Bug (1975)
Grizzly (1976)
The Pack (1977)
Jaws 3 (1983)
Jaws: The Revenge (1987)
The Nest (1994)

Blaxploitation

Blaxploitation films entered the horror genre with these hilariously low-budget and slightly violent tales that feature urban dwelling, Afro-coiffed, and polyester-clad black versions of some classic monsters.

Blacula
(1972) 92m. **C+**

Dracula is a racist who dooms Prince Manuwalde to an eternity as a vampire. By the time he makes it to modern day LA, Manuwalde is just a garden-variety serial biter who's chasing after his reincarnated love. Looks and feels more like an old episode from *Mannix* than a horror film.
D: William Crain. A: William Marshall, Vonetta McGee, Gordon Pinsent.

Scream Blacula Scream
(1973) 95m. **C–**

Voodoo rites reanimate Prince Manuwalde in this sequel that may have more atmosphere, a bigger budget, and may bear a closer resemblance to a horror film, but remains dull in spite of the black magic and vampire themes.
D: Bob Kelljan. A: William Marshall, Pam Grier, Don Mitchell.

Blackenstein
(1973) 93m. **D–**

A Vietnam vet gets turned into a creature with a square-shaped Afro who has an equal propensity for creating mayhem and ripping blouses off women. Pretty much of a mess that looks like it was shot on recycled film stock.
D: William Levy. A: John DiSue, Ivory Stone.

Dr. Black and Mr. Hyde
(1976) 87m. **D+**

After finding a cure for cirrhosis, an African-American scientist tries out the formula, which turns him into a silver-eyed, white-haired white dude (actually his face is covered with flour) with a bad attitude. A reel hoot if you've got the time to waste.
D: William Crain. A: Bernie Casey, Rosalind Cash, Marie O'Henry.

The Devil's Possessions

With the stupefying success of *The Exorcist*, demonic horror was pulled from the drive-in ghetto and became almost respectable. Suddenly there appeared a rash of big-budget films with Hollywood stars who suddenly had no compunction about cozying up to a fevered satanic plot and some almost tasteful, state-of-the-art gore.

The Exorcist

(1973) 121m. **A**

This tale of an innocent preteen's demonic possession by Pazuzu, including a levitating bed, 360-degree headspins, and the infamous green bile, is still a watermark horror film. The subplot of a priest's crisis of faith and some brief but unnerving scenes involving the futile medical tests adds up to a film in which exorcism seems a reasonable way out.
D: William Friedkin. A: Ellen Burstyn, Linda Blair, Max von Sydow.

Beyond the Door

(1974) 100m. **D**

The Italians were the first to jump on the devil's bandwagon in this blatant rip-off of *The Exorcist*'s ideas and effects, complete with green vomit. Pass.
D: Ovidio Assonitis. A: Juliet Mills, Richard Johnson, Gabriele Lavia.

Devil in the House of Exorcism

(1975) 93m. **D+**

After Sommer fumbles her way into a mansion rife with sadism, incest, and worse, she is suddenly possessed, until Alda comes to the rescue and stops her from throwing up frogs. A possibly good Mario Bava film was chopped up and filled with new footage to cash in on the devil craze, resulting in this incoherent mess.
D: Mario Bava. A: Elke Sommer, Robert Alda, Telly Savalas.

The Omen

(1976) 111m. **B+**

The first of the series using a "biblical" theme as an excuse for spectacular deaths follows the American couple in England who've just adopted the Antichrist. A big-budget entry replete with Hollywood assembly-line horror atmospherics like grave-digging scenes, gratuitous lurking, and a soundtrack of ominous crypto-Latin chanting.
D: Richard Donner. A: Gregory Peck, Lee Remick, David Warner.

The Exorcist II: The Heretic

(1977) 110m. **C**

An older Blair is still having trouble with the demon Pazuzu, and Burton hooks her up to a machine that allows him to fight the devil in tandem. Enjoyably incoherent, with a few visually dazzling effects like the plague of locusts sequence.
D: John Boorman. A: Richard Burton, Linda Blair, Max von Sydow.

Damien: Omen II

(1978) 107m. **C+**

Antichrist Damien, now 13, has offed his real parents and insinuates himself into the powerful industrial family. As gory as any *Friday the 13th*, with a bigger budget.
D: Don Taylor. A: William Holden, Lee Grant, Sylvia Sidney.

Beyond the Door II

(1979) 92m. **B–**

Unrelated to the first *Beyond the Door* film and better for it, this tale of a boy possessed by supernatural powers was director Mario Bava's last. His trademark dizzying camerawork, bizarre imagery, and an uncomfortable incest subplot raise this to above average.
D: Mario Bava. A: Daria Nicolodi; John Steiner; David Colin, Jr.

The Final Conflict

(1981) 108m. **C–**

A grown-up Damien is now running a large corporation on his way to running the world. Even with the gore, there's a lack of creative deaths, and an astonishingly lame ending.
D: Graham Baker. A: Sam Neill, Rossano Brazzi, Lisa Harrow.

The Exorcist III: Legion

(1990) 108m. **C**

Should the detective show a little compassion for the serial killer who may be possessed by Pazuzu? Seriously flawed, but packed with some startling images like the desanguinated corpse laying next to hundreds of Dixie cups holding its blood, and a straitjacketed Dourif in a hospital room that looks like a medieval dungeon.
D: William Peter Blatty. A: George C. Scott, Brad Dourif, Ed Flanders.

Devil Worship

Instead of being possessed by the devil like in *The Exorcist*, *Rosemary's Baby* opened the door for films about people conducting active commerce with him. These small, almost TV-ready-style horror films are heavy on the paranoia (the person next to you might be worshipping the horned god), some really weird special effects, big name stars, and usually a general sense of confused hysteria.

Rosemary's Baby

(1968) 136m. **A**

A young couple moves into a grand old New York City apartment building filled with quaint tenants; when the wife gets pregnant she's convinced they're in a satanic coven. This cunningly filmed modern gothic tale offers its darkly paranoiac view of everyday life with an effortlessly elegant visual style and sly humor.
D: Roman Polanski. A: Mia Farrow, John Cassavetes, Ruth Gordon.

The Brotherhood of Satan

(1971) 92m. **B–**

A satanic coven in a small town uses children to satisfy their master. Despite the generic plot, this manages to stir up some truly eerie moments via evocative photography and a nightmarish sequence where toys become lifesize.
D: Bernard McEveety. A:

Strother Martin, L. Q. Jones, Charles Bateman.

The Mephisto Waltz
(1971) 108m. **C+**
When a venerable devil-worshipping pianist dies, Alda inherits his soul, his talent, and his beautiful daughter. The talky script and TV-movie anti-atmospherics give this a chill count near zero, but there's some camp value with good actors saying dumb lines and the zany attempts to show decadence.
D: Paul Wendkos. A: Alan Alda, Jacqueline Bisset, Curt Jurgens.

Necromancy (aka The Witching)
(1972) 82m. **F**
Orson (with big nose makeup) is a Satanist doing bad things to revive his dead son. A witless trifle that Welles did between wine commercials.
D: Bert I. Gordon. A: Orson Welles, Pamela Franklin, Michael Ontkean.

The Devil's Rain
(1975) 85m. **D**
Borgnine is the leader of a small-town satanic cult and possessed by a witch's spirit who collects souls in a glass bowl. Even with the all-star cast, this has as much evil ambiance as a *Brady Bunch* dream sequence.
D: Robert Fuest. A: Ernest Borgnine, William Shatner, John Travolta.

To the Devil, a Daughter
(1976) 95m. **B−**
In this Hammer studio devil outing, an occult expert is hired to save a young girl from being sacrificed to a satanic priest. Beautifully photographed English landscapes are effectively contrasted with explicit black masses and disturbing death scenes to create a tangible air of menace.
D: Peter Sykes. A: Richard Widmark, Christopher Lee, Nastassja Kinski.

The Visitor
(1979) 96m. **D−**
Ferrer is in a satanic cult, his daughter is the antichrist, and someone with a beard sits on a mod geometric rooftop, bathed in golden light as angelic choirs sing. An indecipherable mess of big-name stars and directors, light-show effects and faux religious mumbo-jumbo.
D: Michael Paradise. A: John Huston, Mel Ferrer, Glen Ford.

1980s–1990s
Horror Series

There's an easy rule to follow with these films: See the original and forget the sequels. Most of these series started with a movie that had a good idea backed up by imaginative special effects and solid performances to provide the thrills and chills. Unfortunately, the law of diminishing returns kicks in with the follow-ups, and you begin to wonder what you ever saw in the series to begin with.

The Amityville Horror
(1979) 117m. **C+**
A family moves into a Long Island house and soon the bumps and creaks turn into blood oozing from the walls. Even the scene where all hell breaks loose with the exorcist priest can't enliven this dragging overserious effort.
D: Stuart Rosenberg. A: James Brolin, Margot Kidder, Rod Steiger.

Amityville II: The Possession
(1982) 110m. **D**
A bad dad moves his family into the infamous house, where his wacko son becomes possessed and kills them all. This prequel is more dysfunctional family flick than a haunted house film and a pretty boring one at that.
D: Damiano Damiani. A: Burt Young, Rutanya Alda, James Olson.

Amityville 3-D
(1983) 98m. **C−**
A skeptical man moves his family into the dreaded house and soon becomes a believer in the supernatural. The acting is better but the script is still dopey.
D: Richard Fleischer. A: Tony Roberts, Tess Harper, Robert Joy.

The Amityville Curse
(1989) 91m. **D**
Three young and foolish couples pitch in their life savings and buy the notorious house. Chock-full of every haunted house cliché and devoid of any wit.
D: Tom Berry. A: Kim Coates, Dawna Wightman, Helen Hughes.

Amityville 1992: It's About Time
(1992) 95m. **C−**
A family buys a mantel clock that once did time in the Amityville house, unaware that the chronometer is the harborer of evil. More standard haunted house stuff, but at least it's a different house.
D: Tony Randel. A: Stephen Macht, Shawn Weatherly, Megan Ward.

Amityville: A New Generation
(1993) 92m. **C−**
A mirror which harbors the evil that once terrorized the Amityville house is now causing problems for some loft dwelling arty types. More of a psycho-thriller, and a welcome change.
D: John Murlowski. A: Ross Partridge, Lala Sloatman, David Naughton.

Basket Case
(1982) 89m. **B−**
A young man and his Siamese twin Belial, a small, hideously deformed mass who lives in a basket, put up in a sleazy New York City hotel while searching for revenge on the doctor who separated them. Bizarre, compelling, funny, and very very low-budget. A cult classic, but beware: The final reel is disturbing.
D: Frank Henenlotter. A: Kevin Van Hentenryck, Terri Susan Smith, Beverly Bonner.

Basket Case 2
(1990) 90m. **C−**
That normal, clean-cut guy and his brother, the deformed dwarf Belial, dodge media hounds in a home for grotesquely mutated. Witless and ineffectual campy horror/comedy.
D: Frank Henenlotter. A: Kevin Van Hentenryck, Annie Ross, Jason Evers.

Basket Case 3
(1992) 90m. **D+**
The brothers head for their new home, but get separated

just at the birth of Belial's brood (12 kids, one mom), Campy and gory, but mostly just silly. Better than *Basket Case 2,* but not by much.
D: Frank Henenlotter. A: Kevin Van Hentenryck, Annie Ross, Gil Roper.

The Howling
(1981) 91m. **A**

A TV journalist seeks therapy at a wacky California retreat where everyone, it turns out, is a werewolf. Entertaining horror and horror spoof with good special effects and lots of hip film references. Tremendous cast.
D: Joe Dante. A: Dee Wallace, Patrick Macnee, Dennis Dugan.

Howling II: Your Sister Is a Werewolf
(1985) 91m. **D**

A man seeks revenge on a family of werewolves that lives in a Transylvania castle. Fails as a sexy spoof or straight horror. So awful, Danning's leather wardrobe steals the show.
D: Philippe Mora. A: Christopher Lee, Annie McEnroe, Sybil Danning.

Howling III
(1987) 94m. **C**

A lovely marsupial werewolf leaves her backwater tribe to find fortune in the big city, Sydney, Australia. As bizarre as it sounds, and just witty enough to make for enjoyable viewing, even with the low-rent effects.
D: Philippe Mora. A: Barry Otto, Imogen Annesley, Dasha Blahova.

Howling IV: The Original Nightmare
(1988) 94m. **D+**

While staying in a remote lodge, a young woman is besieged by werewolves, sort of, including a new addition to the pack, her boyfriend. Cheap and dull.
D: John Hough. A: Romy Windsor, Michael T. Weiss, Anthony Hamilton.

Howling V: The Rebirth
(1989) 99m. **C–**

In a remote castle, mysterious guests discover their numbers being diminished by a werewolf. More mystery/suspense than horror, with little gore and no onscreen monster.
D. Neal Sundstrom. A. Victoria Catlin, Elizabeth Silverstein, Mark Faulkner.

Howling VI: The Freaks
(1991) 102m. **C**

A werewolf drifter finds himself at a carnival sideshow, whose sadistic owner wants to capture the lycanthrope for his collection. Smart, somewhat slick horror that's done in by really lousy effects.
D: Hope Perello. A: Brendan Hughes, Michelle Matheson, Bruce Martyn Payne.

Poltergeist
(1982) 114m. **A–**

An all-American family has been happy in their suburban development house until the resident hostile spirits start acting up. The humorous evocation of suburban life gives way to a fast, furious, and scary tale of demonic entrapment. Spectacular effects and thoughtful imagery make this one of the best haunted house flicks ever made.
D: Tobe Hooper. A: Craig T. Nelson, JoBeth Williams, Beatrice Straight.

Poltergeist II
(1986) 92m. **B–**

The ghosts from the first film put on their traveling shoes and follow that hapless family to their next house. Good special effects are the main attraction here.
D: Brian Gibson. A: Craig T. Nelson, JoBeth Williams, Heather O'Rourke.

Poltergeist III
(1988) 97m. **C–**

The daughter from *Poltergeist II* relocates to Chicago where she stays with her aunt and uncle, but it seems those spirits know her every move. Good spooky sets, but this one's a letdown.
D: Gary Sherman. A: Tom Skerritt, Nancy Allen, Heather O'Rourke.

Psycho II
(1983) 113m. **B**

Norman Bates, just released from the asylum, returns home and starts receiving murderous messages from Mother. Effective homage to the original will delight those not offended by sequels. Watching Perkins become unhinged is nightmarishly pleasurable and there's even a touching romance thrown in.
D: Richard Franklin. A: Anthony Perkins, Vera Miles, Meg Tilly.

Psycho III
(1986) 93m. **C**

Norman is still at it, and this time his dementia buttons are being pushed by a nun in training with a faith crisis, a pushy reporter, and a sleazeball ne'er-do-well. Too spoofy to work well as horror.
D: Anthony Perkins. A: Anthony Perkins, Diana Scarwid, Jeff Fahey.

Psycho IV: The Beginning
(1990) 90m. **C**

Norman now goes on a talk show to tell how he became such an antisocial person. Nothing particularly bad here, just a case of going to the same scary well one too many times: more queasiness-inducing than tense.
D: Mick Garris. A: Anthony Perkins, Olivia Hussey, Henry Thomas.

Slasher Series

Take a group of stupid and horny teens in their natural suburban setting or unchaperoned in the isolated woods. Introduce a psycho with a horrible past and a gimmicky trademark like a hockey mask or a glove with razor blade fingers. Throw in some lame dialogue, scenes of girls doffing their shirts, graphic deaths by slashing, an open ending to ensure a sequel, and you have the formula for these highly successful films. Unlike other sequelized films, the later entries in some of these series are actually an improvement on the original, having better effects, a slightly more fleshed-out boogeyman, and more creative (and graphic) violence. Between slayings, it can also be fun to spot future stars who started their careers as gore-bait.

The Texas Chainsaw Massacre

(1974) 84m. **B+**

Teen travelers make a lethal detour on the backroads of Texas and meet up with an inbred, chainsaw-loving, flesh-eating clan. This influential horror film may have lost a little of its shock value thanks to all the imitators, but it's still a first-rate study in unrelenting nightmarish terror.
D: Tobe Hooper. A: Marilyn Burns, Gunner Hansen, Ed Neal.

The Texas Chainsaw Massacre II

(1986) 101m. **D**

The cannibalistic Sawyer family are hunted by a revenge-hungry Texas Ranger. The first one scares you; this one merely assaults your senses, and even Hopper's weirdness can't keep it from becoming mind numbing.
D: Tobe Hooper. A: Dennis Hopper, Caroline Williams, Bill Johnson.

Leatherface: Texas Chainsaw Massacre III

(1990) 82m. **D–**

Travelers passing through Texas get lost and wind up with those chainsaw-wielding wackos. Even more ordinary than the second and just plain nasty.
D: Jeff Burr. A: Kate Hodge, Ken Foree, R. A. Mihailoff.

Friday the 13th

(1980) 95m. **C–**

Teen counselors are getting Camp Crystal Lake ready for the summer season and a masked lunatic butchers them except for the lone female survivor.
D: Sean S. Cunningham. A: Betsy Palmer, Adrienne King, Harry Crosby.

Friday the 13th, Part II

(1981) 87m. **C+**

A fresh crop of counselors try their luck at getting a camp open for the season but the body count just gets higher. The lone survivor kills the reborn maniac, Jason. At least two scenes are lifted from Bava's *Bay of Blood.* If you're gonna steal, steal from the masters.
D: Steve Miner. A: Betsy Palmer, Amy Steel, John Furey.

Friday the 13th, Part III

(1982) 96m. **D+**

Jason dons his trademark hockey mask and slaughters—in 3D—a group of horny teens weekending in a country house. The lone female survivor kills Jason, but we know better.
D: Steve Miner. A: Dana Kimmell, Paul Kratka, Tracie Savage.

Friday the 13th—The Final Chapter

(1984) 90m. **D**

Back to Camp Crystal Lake. (How does this place advertise itself to parents?) In a radical departure, the lone survivor who kills Jason is a boy. The series' violence peaks in this entry.
D: Joseph Zito. A: Crispin Glover, Kimberly Beck, Corey Feldman.

Friday the 13th, Part V: A New Beginning

(1985) 92m. **D**

Someone is killing off the inmates of a halfway house for troubled youths. Jason? The disturbed survivor from *Friday the 13th—The Final Chapter,* who may be channeling Jason's spirit? The violence starts to mellow out in this one.
D: Danny Steinmann. A: John Shepard, Melanie Kinnaman, Shavar Ross.

Friday the 13th, Part VI: Jason Lives

(1986) 87m. **D+**

The kids go back to the woods again (now renamed Forest Green) where Jason's killing spree is not so graphically depicted.
D: Tom McLoughlin. A: Thom Mathews, Jennifer Cooke, David Kagan.

Friday the 13th, Part VII: The New Blood

(1988) 90m. **C–**

A troubled teen with telekinetic powers heads for the woods for a little R&R. Jason kills a cabin full of teens and the girl with ESP kills Jason. Sure.
D: John Carl Buechler. A: Lar Park Lincoln, Terry Kiser, Susan Blu.

Friday the 13th, Part VIII: Jason Takes Manhattan

(1989) 96m. **C**

A group of teens from the Camp Crystal Lake area are taking a boat trip to New York City with Jason as a passenger. A few teens actually survive in the end, presumably to enjoy the relative safety of the Big Apple.
D: Rob Hedden. A: Jensen Daggett, Kane Hodder, Peter Richman.

Jason Goes to Hell—The Final Friday

(1993) 91m. **B–**

Jason gets blown up by a bunch of cops (a promising start), but we finally learn why he's survived so many sequels: He's no human, but a demon, now in search of host bodies so he can commit one final atrocity. A case of the best being the last and a nice surprise for hard-core fans.
D: Adam Marcus. A: Kari Keegan, John D. LeMay, Erin Gray.

A Nightmare on Elm Street

(1984) 92m. **B+**

Suburban teens are terrorized in their sleep by the burn victim with the razor glove, Freddy Krueger, who knocks off the kids one by one. The imaginative murderous set pieces and the film's clever way of blurring dream and reality states for the viewer is only hindered by some poor acting.
D: Wes Craven. A: John Saxon, Ronee Blakley, Johnny Depp.

A Nightmare on Elm Street Part 2: Freddy's Revenge

(1985) 87m. **C+**

Freddy seeks to control the mind of one of the youths in order to rid Elm Street of a new crop of pesky teenagers. More gore and less imagination than the first, but effective on a slasher level.
D: Jack Sholder. A: Mark Patton, Kim Myers, Robert Rusler.

A Nightmare on Elm Street 3: Dream Warriors

(1987) 96m. **A–**

Irrepressible Freddy takes on the Elm Street kids, and Zsa Zsa Gabor. Sure the waking world is dumb, but the dream world is spectacular and filled with demented, humorous, and scary moments.
D: Chuck Russell. A: Heather Langenkamp, Patricia Arquette, Larry Fishburne.

A Nightmare on Elm Street 4: The Dream Master

(1988) 99m. **C**

Freddy slays the survivors of *A Nightmare on Elm Street 3* and hunts down some new kids on the block. Disappointing follow-up, despite increased budget, but it still has a couple of nifty dream sequences.
D: Renny Harlin. A: Robert Englund, Rodney Eastman, Danny Hassel.

A Nightmare on Elm Street 5: The Dream Child
(1989) 90m. **C–**

Freddy returns, this time to manipulate a pregnant woman's fetus. Freddy is still wired and becoming more humorous, but the others are sleepwalking. For devotees only.
D: Stephen Hopkins. A: Robert Englund, Lisa Wilcox, Kelly Jo Minter.

Freddy's Dead: The Final Nightmare
(1991) 96m. **C**

The series seems to be out of ideas, so Freddy's past and his love for the glove is revealed. When he tries to escape Elm Street to perform his grisly show in a new town, who can stop him? Perhaps his teenage daughter?
D: Rachel Talalay. A: Robert Englund, Lisa Zane, Shona Greenblatt.

Wes Craven's New Nightmare
(1994) 112m. **B+**

Freddy's dead but the people who created him want to film one more Nightmare, only to have the wisecracking fiend invade the real world of moviemaking. Not so much *A Nightmare* sequel as an ambitious meditation on why people love the gruesome series, with a meaner than ever Freddy and a sense of the real world falling apart.
D: Wes Craven. A: Heather Langenkamp, Robert Englund, John Saxon.

Halloween
(1978) 90m. **A–**

Masked psycho-killer Michael Myers escapes from the loony bin and starts slaughtering the teens from his hometown who are trying to enjoy Halloween night. A classic slasher film: Instead of displaying gore (there's little graphic violence), it creates suspense, terror, and a sense of ever tightening entrapment. The countless imitators never come close.
D: John Carpenter. A: Donald Pleasence, Jamie Lee Curtis, Nancy Loomis.

Halloween II
(1981) 92m. **C**

On the same evening as *Halloween,* Michael continues to stalk Ms. Curtis who is being taken to a hospital, and Dr. Loomis continues to stalk Michael. More mundane and gory than its predecessor, and nowhere near as enjoyable or terrifying.
D: Rick Rosenthal. A: Jamie Lee Curtis, Donald Pleasence, Charles Cyphers.

Halloween III: Season of the Witch
(1983) 98m. **C+**

An insane toy maker designs a Halloween mask that will cause the death of all children who wear it. Not too scary but definitely creepy. A *Halloween* sequel in name only.
D: Tommy Lee Wallace. A: Tom Atkins, Stacey Nelkin, Dan O'Herlihy.

Halloween IV: The Return of Michael Myers
(1988) 88m. **C–**

Michael comes out of a coma and heads off to kill his niece. On hand to stop him is the quite mad Dr. Loomis. A slasher film with most of the slashing taking place off-screen, so what's the point?
D: Dwight H. Little. A: Donald Pleasence, Ellie Cornell, Danielle Harris.

Halloween V: The Revenge of Michael Myers
(1989) 96m. **D–**

Michael stalks his niece again, and Dr. Loomis stalks Mike again. A retread of a retread. The nadir of the series.
D: Dominique Othenin-Girard. A: Donald Pleasence, Danielle Harris, Donald L. Shanks.

Prom Night
(1980) 91m. **C**

A vengeful killer stalks high schoolers as they prepare for their big night. This one benefits from competent acting, fair production values, a relatively lower quotient of violence and, of course, Scream Queen Curtis.
D: Paul Lynch. A: Jamie Lee Curtis, Leslie Nielsen, Casey Stevens.

Hello Mary Lou: Prom Night II
(1987) 97m. **C**

The prom queen who was murdered 30 years ago possesses the body of a good girl and forces her to do bad, bad things. Poor acting, tired script and passable special effects. Related to *Prom Night* in name only.
D: Bruce Pittman. A: Lisa Schrage, Michael Ironside, Wendy Lyon.

Prom Night III: The Last Kiss
(1989) 97m. **C–**

Dead prom queen crashes her high school dance with an eye to keeping her man out of the arms of the school sluts. Melds teenage humor and slasher horror, and on those levels, is endurable. Almost.
D: Ron Oliver. A: Tim Conlon, Cyndy Preston, David Stratton.

Prom Night IV: Deliver Us from Evil
(1992) 95m. **D+**

Priest awakens from a coma and is transformed into a murderous zealot who must punish, i.e. slay, sex-obsessed teens vacationing in an isolated wood. Another by-the-numbers slasher with "Prom Night" tacked on to the title.
D: Clay Borris. A: Nikki de Boer, Alden Kane, Joy Tanner.

Leprechaun
(1993) 92m. **F**

A demonic leprechaun shows up in a small town and slaughters anyone in the way of his pot o' gold. The Irish suffer yet another indignity in this shoddly filmed hateful, one-joke atrocity.
D: Mark Jones. A: Warwick Davis, Jennifer Aniston, Mark Holton.

Leprechaun 2
(1994) 85m. **F+**

The homicidal little man in green is back and this time he kidnaps a teenage girl as his bride to live in wedded horror in his subterranean lair. One or two almost clever scenes don't make up for remaining 80 minutes of mean-spirited violence.
D: Rodman Flender. A: Warwick Davis, Jennifer Aniston, Ken Olandt.

Leprechaun 3
(1995) 93m. **F**

The homicidal greedy wee one hits Las Vegas to wreak havoc and crack imbecilic rejoinders. Third stirringly hideous entry in the so-bad-it's-bad series boasts dumb Pakistani jokes, dumb teen jokes, and a woman whose butt explodes as the film's climax: classy.
D: Brian Trenchard-Smith. A: Warwick Davis, John Gatis, Lee Armstrong.

Evil Toys

As eerie ideas go, being stalked by a murderous little doll is right up there with being trapped in a funhouse inhabited by a demented clown. These upscale slasher films offer good horror effects, decent actors, and the fascinating and gruesome sight of killer toys on the loose.

Child's Play

(1988) 88m. **B–**

A crazed dying killer transfers his evil soul into the body of "Good Guy" doll Chucky, who proceeds to use his young owner in several murderous schemes. Creepy and suspenseful, its one good effect—the sight of a little doll on a murderous rampage—is helped by an actual story and solid acting.
D: Tom Holland. A: Catherine Hicks, Chris Sarandon, Alex Vincent.

Child's Play 2

(1990) 84m. **C**

Chucky returns, still with an eye toward transferring his spirit into his young owner's body. A slick-looking but mindless sequel with nothing new to offer.
D: John Lafia. A: Alex Vincent, Jenny Agutter, Gerrit Graham.

Child's Play 3

(1991) 89m. **D+**

Eight years after Part 2—where Chucky was last seen as a pile of festering plastic goop—his young master/victim is now enrolled in a military school. Unfortunately slaughter-hungry Chucky gets reanimated in this uninspired, by-the-numbers doll slasher.
D: Jack Bender. A: Justin Whalin, Brad Dourif, Perrey Reeves.

Puppet Master

(1989) 90m. **C+**

After puppeteer/occultist Toulon commits suicide, a group of psychics go to his home to pick up on his vibes and find they're being stalked by his deadly dolls. O.K. special effects, but this is still for toy horror buffs only.
D: David Schmoller. A: Paul LeMat, Irene Miracle, Matt Roe.

Puppet Master II

(1990) 90m. **C–**

Those evil little puppets resurrect their creator who now needs human brains to bring his latest puppets to life. More time devoted to the puppets than in the first entry, but still too many lulls.
D: David Allen. A: Elizabeth Maclellan, Collin Bernsen, Steve Welles.

Puppet Master III: Toulon's Revenge

(1991) 86m. **C+**

During World War II, Toulon is approached by Nazis to create an army of puppet warriors. Unwilling to comply, he turns his little creations on them. Lamebrained attempt to make the puppets good guys but better than the first two.
D: David De Coteau. A: Guy Rolfe, Richard Lynch, Ian Abercrombie.

Puppet Master IV

(1993) 80m. **D+**

Back at the Bodega Bay hotel, the appearance of a set of demons forces Toulon to cobble together a new morphing, super-puppet to destroy them, and blundering teens die while demons and puppets go at it. Main attraction is still the impressive stop-action tiny terrors, but otherwise, the substandard silliness.
D: Jeff Burr. A: Gordon Currie, Chandra West, Jason Adams.

Puppet Master V: The Final Chapter

(1994) 81m. **D**

Promised last entry in the series has a new cyberpunk-looking puppet, a young puppet master who befriends the bloodthirsty halfpints, and an Evil Scientist trying to discover the secret of the puppets' life force. Like most of the series, competently directed, but predictable and dull.
D: Jeff Burr. A: Gordon Currie, Chandra West, Ian Ogilvey.

Slasher Films

One of the most visceral of all genres, the slasher film goes right for the jugular, heart, eyes, and anywhere else a sharp implement can penetrate. With some exceptions, most are content to follow the slasher formula: nonexistent plots, an isolated setting, dreadful production values, cheap-looking gore, and very bad acting. Here's a sampling, including some of the best of the hundreds that clog video stores.

Twitch of the Death Nerve

(1971) 87m. **A**

The murder of a wheelchair-bound countess who owns some prime waterfront real estate sets off a series of grisly murders. This stylish horror directed by Italian Gothic maestro Mario Bava has suspense, gore, and flower children, with groovy music in the background. One of the films that started it all.
D: Mario Bava. A: Claudine Auger, Claudio Volonte, Luigi Pistilli.

Black Christmas

(1975) 100m. **B**

During Christmas vacation, a group of sorority girls staying on campus get obscene phone calls, then start dying, slasher style. This early entry in the genre uses each sorority cliché before many of the later, better-known pics.
D: Bob Clark. A: Olivia Hussey, Keir Dullea, Margot Kidder.

Massacre at Central High

(1976) 87m. **B+**

Disaffected high schooler exacts his revenge on the in-crowd, but that's just the beginning. A thought-provoking slasher film? You bet. Twisty (and twisted) morality tale is hidden in this unusual entry that is bound to surprise the viewer.

D: Renee Daalder. A: Derrel Maury, Andrew Stevens, Kimberly Beck.

Terror Train
(1980) 97m. **B**
This film about a revenge-minded fraternity recruit knows what its audience wants and delivers it: teen gropings, cheap scares, some genuine tension, and bloody violence. Not exactly *Halloween,* but it does hold up very well.
D: Roger Spottiswoode. A: Ben Johnson, Jamie Lee Curtis, Hart Bochner.

The Final Terror
(1981) 82m. **D+**
A group of naive horny teens wander around an isolated forest and get slaughtered one by one. So boring, that only watching the young stars in such a really bad film could make this endurable.
D: Andrew Davis. A: John Friedrich, Daryl Hannah, Rachel Ward.

Graduation Day
(1981) 85m. **D**
When a high school track star mysteriously dies after a meet, her sister shows up. Suddenly, other team members start dying gruesomely (and not very creatively), one at a time. Cumbersome storyline and stomach-churning gore.
D: Herb Freed. A: Christopher George, Patch Mackenzie, Vanna White.

Happy Birthday to Me
(1981) 108m. **D**
High schooler finds she suffers from disturbing blackouts, which coincide with the gruesome murders of her classmates. Tries to be more than a slasher, and it's not. The final twist—think *Mission Impossible*—is a fitting end to a mindless movie.
D: J. Lee Thompson. A: Melissa Sue Anderson, Glenn Ford, Tracy Bregman.

My Bloody Valentine
(1981) 91m. **C**
The residents of a mining town receive Valentine's Day boxes filled with something other than Godiva chocolates and then get slaughtered by a man in a miner's helmet and gas mask. Even with these gimmicks, the film couldn't get sequelized.
D: George Mihalka. A: Paul Kelman, Lori Hallier, Niel Affleck.

Chopping Mall
(1986) 77m. **D**
A mall's robot security guards goes on a killing spree with a group of teens partying there after closing hours. Dull, even by slasher standards, despite great title.
D: Jim Wynorski. A: Kelli Maroney, Tony O'Dell, Mary Woronov.

Bloody New Year
(1987) 90m. **C**
A group of teens happen upon a deserted zombie-filled resort stuck in a time warp. Decent special effects beyond the realm of gore and a plot, even if it is loopy. It seems to be inspired by that party scene Nicholson stumbles upon in *The Shining,* with zombie movie aesthetics.
D: Norman Warren. A: Suzy Aitchinson, Colin Heywood, Catherine Roman.

Hide and Go Shriek
(1987) 90m. **D**
A group of teen couples takes over a closed furniture store for partying and sex, but a crazed killer watches the foreplay and then strikes. Some teen titillation, but mostly just boring.
D: Skip Schoolnick. A: George Thomas, Donna Baltron, Ria Pavia.

Cutting Class
(1989) 91m. **D–**
More annoying teens are being stalked by a murderer at the local high school. By 1989 graphic violence has become so commonplace, that this film's blood-letting will seem dully familiar.
D: Raspo Pallenberg. A: Donovan Leitch, Brad Pitt, Roddy McDowall.

Troma Inc.

This bottom-line oriented film company makes it a practice to come up with an insane title, a matching gaudy poster, and then worries about the movie to go with it. The result has been some of the nastiest and most antihuman films made this side of campy exploitation, with garish colors, antiart design, complementary nonacting, and nauseating violence. If you're into toxic waste, women with big hair, cheap gore, and cheaper jokes these are for you. All others stay clear.

The Toxic Avenger
(1985) 100m. **D+**
A nerd falls into a vat of toxic waste to become the film's decidedly hideous superhero. Gaudy colors, really lame jokes, and authentically abysmal New Jersey locations combine in some mysterious way to make this one almost charming.
D: Michael Herz, Samuel Weil. A: Andree Maranda; Mark Torgi; Pat Ryan, Jr.

Class of Nuke 'Em High
(1987) 84m. **D–**
Kids ingest lime-colored, toxic waste-tainted water to become biker monsters and worse. Lowlights include a geek punching his hand through a girl's face and a really bad heavy-metal soundtrack.
D: Richard Haines, Samuel Weil. A: Janelle Brady, Gilbert Brenton, R. L. Ryan.

Surf Nazis Must Die
(1987) 83m. **D**
As usual, the title tells all as a group of swastika and surf devotees battle their rivals. As ugly, offensive, stupid, and garishly cheap as they get, but peppered with some really funny one-liners.
D: Peter George. A: Barry Brenner, Gail Neely, Bobbie Bresee.

Chopper Chicks in Zombietown
(1990) 86m. **C–**
Female bikers reluctantly agree to help save a small town from a deranged mortician and his zombie horde. This competently filmed movie threatens to be funny, and sometimes succeeds with a minimum of gore, a polkalike zombie theme, and a colorful explosive finale.
D: Dan Hoskins. A: Jamie Rose, Catherine Carlin, Don Calfa.

OTHER TITLES:
The Toxic Avenger, Part II (1989)
The Toxic Avenger Part III: The Last Temptation of Toxie (1989)
Class of Nuke 'Em High 2: Subhuman Meltdown (1991)

Anthologies

These collections of horror tales are blessed and cursed by their length; an average of 25 minutes limits the plot and characters so you never get too involved but you never get bored either: most also owe a debt to *Twilight Zone*, with their frequent ironic twists. But since the filmmakers here range from Spielberg and Romero, to people only their mothers would know, you also get a full range of style, quality, and enjoyability.

Creepshow
(1982) 120m. **B+**

These stories may get a little juvenile and icky but they still blend humor with horror and remain faithful to the E.C. comics and Stephen King's horror aesthetic.
D: George A. Romero. A: Hal Holbrook, Adrienne Barbeau, Leslie Nielsen.

Creepshow 2
(1987) 92m. **C**

Not in the same league with the first, this is even more juvenile and a lot more predictable.
D: Michael Gornick. A: Lois Chiles, George Kennedy, Dorothy Lamour.

Nightmares
(1983) 99m. **D+**

A deadly dull film. It tries to hit all the horror bases—slasher, technology run amok, the religious angle, and the giant thing—and fails at each.
D: Joseph Sargent. A: Cristina Raines, Timothy James, Emilio Estevez.

Twilight Zone—The Movie
(1983) 102m. **B**

Different Hollywood directors take a swipe at the original and the results are glossy but hollow tales of nervousness and nastiness.
D: John Landis, Steven Spielberg, Joe Dante, George Miller. A: Vic Morrow, Scatman Crothers, John Lithgow.

The Offspring
(1986) 99m. **C**

These tales told by a Southern librarian explaining the town's dementia are so darned serious they pass up every opportunity for regional humor and Gothic-flavored eerieness. Still, each one is creepy in concept if not always in execution.
D: Christopher Reynolds. A: Vincent Price, Clu Gulager, Terry Kiser.

Legends Revisited

These updated fables are faster, flashier, and gorier mainstream versions of the originals. While the violence and sex are tame compared to *The Texas Chainsaw Massacre*, you do often get to see humans and their viscera undergoing some really spectacular and hair-raising transmutation.

King Kong
(1976) 135m. **B−**

An overblown version of how a giant ape living on a primitive island is brought to New York City by media and corporate hucksters. A good-humored adventure with a lively cast and bright special effects helping to compensate for a lumbering man-in-a-suit Kong.
D: John Guillermin. A: Jeff Bridges, Jessica Lange, Charles Grodin.

Dracula
(1979) 109m. **C+**

This version of the Victorian tale of an urbane vampire from eastern Europe who stalks English virgins tries to explore the erotic aspects of vampirism but lacks the style to pull it off.
D: John Badham. A: Frank Langella, Laurence Olivier, Donald Pleasence.

Cat People
(1982) 118m. **B**

Brother and sister come to terms with their sexuality and cat heritage in sweltering sensual New Orleans. Sexy, visually clever, and contains early examples of "stylish" gore, along with a beaut of a scene with big cats.
D: Paul Schrader. A: Nastassja Kinski, Malcolm McDowell, John Heard.

The Bride
(1985) 119m. **C−**

Herr Frankenstein's monster runs off with a dwarf pal, leaving the Baron to obsess over his female monster in his attempt to make the "perfect woman." Gorgeously filmed with opulent sets and absolutely nothing on its mind: If an 80s yuppie had a gothic nightmare, it would look like this.
D: Franc Roddam. A: Sting, Jennifer Beals, Clancy Brown.

The Blob
(1988) 92m. **C+**

Mysterious gelatinous goop threatens to consume a small town whole, and the teens are still misunderstood in their attempts to alert the authorities. A minor remake with more gore and less goofiness than the original.
D: Chuck Russell. A: Shawnee Smith, Donovan Leitch, Kevin Dillon.

Frankenstein Unbound
(1990) 86m. **C+**

Twenty-first-century scientist time travels to the nineteenth century where he meets Shelley, Byron, and Dr. Frankenstein. Some great ideas get a slow and muddled execution despite the fine acting.
D: Roger Corman. A: Raul Julia, John Hurt, Bridget Fonda.

Bram Stoker's Dracula
(1992) 128m. **A**

Dracula has love, love dies, and 400 years later finds love again in Victorian England. Operatic, gothic, erotic, and visually and aurally breathtaking. An extravagant and joyful plunge into the magic of myths and filmmaking.
D: Francis Ford Coppola. A: Gary Oldman, Winona Ryder, Anthony Hopkins, Keanu Reeves.

Mary Shelley's Frankenstein
(1994) 113m. **C−**

With the exception of a creation sequence hilariously reminiscent of a *Rocky* training scene and some genuinely moving moments with

Carter and De Niro as wretched monsters, this rapturously photographed, imaginatively designed remake is a megabuck disaster with Branagh portraying the god-playing scientist as some sort of gothic rock star.
D: Kenneth Branagh. A: Kenneth Branagh, Robert De Niro, Helena Bonham Carter.

Stephen King

Whatever else critics thought of King when he first invaded the bestseller lists, most agreed that the film versions of his very visual works would be guaranteed shudder-fests. As it turns out, his collection of wandering corpses and people going bonkers or plagued with paranormal powers have made a decidedly mixed bag of chillers. The gore quotient is low and so are the number of scares in these films that can either lull you to sleep, or give you some rich and horrifying studies of normal people in the throes of madness.

The Shining
(1980) 146m. **A**

An ex-alcoholic writer with wife and telepathic child in tow becomes the winter caretaker of a Colorado resort hotel. Director Kubrick fashions his horror with Olympian detachment and stunning photography while Nicholson adds the insane edge as the writer drawn into the path of the former caretaker who ax murdered his family.
D: Stanley Kubrick. A: Jack Nicholson, Shelley Duvall, Scatman Crothers.

Christine
(1983) 116m. **C**

A college nerd finds a haunted 1956 Plymouth Fury (Christine), and together they raise all manner of hell, including one fantastic scene of a flaming Christine driving herself through the night. A well-made, but strangely uninvolving film.
D: John Carpenter. A: Keith Gordon, Alexandra Paul, John Stockwell.

Cujo
(1983) 94m. **C+**

Cujo, a large and once loving Saint Bernard contracts rabies and terrorizes a woman and her son who spend most of the movie in their broken down car. This suspenseful thriller starts slowly and works its way into a lather. Beware kids, this ain't *Old Yeller.*
D: Lewis Teague. A: Dee Wallace, Danny Pintauro, Daniel Hugh-Kelly.

The Dead Zone
(1983) 103m. **A–**

Upon waking from a years-long coma after a car accident, a young man discovers he's lost his fiancée but found the power to predict future events. A heartbreaking story of fate, love lost, and a taut spooky thriller about mad politicians.
D: David Cronenberg. A: Christopher Walken, Brooke Adams, Martin Sheen.

Firestarter
(1984) 115m. **C–**

A young girl who can start fires with her thoughts is chased by a creepy government agent. Glossy and well-designed horror with impressive fireball effects, but nothing else to stick in your mind.
D: Mark Lester. A: Drew Barrymore, George C. Scott, Martin Sheen.

Children of the Corn
(1984) 93m. **D–**

A couple get stranded in the rural Midwest where they encounter killer kids who worship a corn god. Some eerie landscape shots, but the rest is lame.
D: Fritz Kiersch. A: Peter Horton, Linda Hamilton, R. G. Armstrong.

Pet Sematary
(1989) 102m. **B**

A harrowing tale of a grieving father who takes his son to an ancient Indian burial ground where the dead come back to life. Spooky renderings of the cemetary, complete with children's sad inscriptions to lost pets, an eerie reanimated child, and sudden jolts of explicit gore make this a better entry.
D: Mary Lambert. A: Dale Midkiff, Fred Gwynne, Denise Crosby.

Misery
(1990) 104m. **A**

A successful writer is rescued after a car crash by his number one fan, who proceeds to subject him to her psychotic fantasies. Bates is completely unnerving as the adoring woman who imprisons and tortures Caan, and his efforts to escape will keep you white knuckled right up to the end.
D: Rob Reiner. A: James Caan, Kathy Bates, Richard Farnsworth.

Stephen King's Graveyard Shift
(1990) 90m. **C–**

This tale about a group of miners threatened by a giant rat has decent performances, atmospherically slimy mine sets, and a palpable sense of decay and entrapment, but zero chill factor.
D: Ralph S. Singleton. A: David Andrews, Kelly Wolf, Brad Dourif.

Pet Sematary II
(1992) 102m. **D+**

This disappointing sequel that now shows a boy going to the burial ground to reanimate his Mom replaces a story and creepy ambiance with gore.
D: Mary Lambert. A: Edward Furlong, Clancy Brown, Anthony Edwards.

The Dark Half
(1993) 115m. **B–**

When a serious writer tries to give up writing his sideline of trashy novels, his literary alter ego comes to murderous life. A tense atmospheric tale and clever idea, but even with a great turn by Hutton, this film is too long and has a fatally weak ending.
D: George A. Romero. A: Timothy Hutton, Amy Madigan, Julie Harris.

Needful Things
(1993) 113m. **B–**

The devil opens a gift shop in a small town where he exacts something other than money from his customers. The clever idea, an arch von Sydow, and colorful renderings of the good citizens all get bogged down with sluggish pacing that make it hard to stick around for the explosive climax.
D: Fraser C. Hestohn. A: Max von Sydow, Ed Harris, Bonnie Bedelia.

Horror Spoofs

Most horror films run a fine line between scary and silly anyway; this group just makes a beeline for the humor side with stops along the way for chills or, in the case of *Repossessed* and *There's Nothing Out There*, a bit of violence and gore.

Attack of the Killer Tomatoes
(1979) 87m. **D+**

The title tells it all in this one-joke campy spoof on cheesy horror films. Depending on your state of mind, the intentionally bad acting, tacky effects, and gaudy washed-out photography is either good frat-house fun or just plain awful.

D: John DeBello. A: George Wilson, Sharon Taylor, Jack Riley.

Saturday the 14th
(1981) 75m. **C–**

A couple move into an old mansion and encounter all manner of creatures. A visually flat, scare- and laugh-free spoof on haunted house films, with monsters imported from another flop film.

D: Howard R. Cohen. A: Richard Benjamin, Paula Prentiss, Severn Darden.

Transylvania 6-5000
(1985) 93m. **C–**

Two guys in search of a story about vampires travel to Transylvania and discover that the mayor is trying to turn it into a theme park. A cousin to the Mel Brooks spoofs, this glossy film is mysteriously laugh-free despite hunchbacks, evil doctors, and Geena Davis as a nymphomaniac vampire.

D: Rudy DeLuca. A: Jeff Goldblum, Ed Begley, Jr.; Carol Kane.

House
(1986) 93m. **B**

A Vietnam vet writer moves into a Victorian mansion to break his writer's block. This richly colored film suffers from trying to be a post-Vietnam divorce drama and a horror-comedy film all in one, losing its initially light tone in doing so. Still, it has some good laughs.

D: Steve Miner. A: William Katt, George Wendt, Kay Lenz.

Elvira, Mistress of the Dark
(1988) 90m. **C**

Buxom TV-horror host Elvira gets dumped from her show, makes breast jokes, inherits a dark old house from an aunt involved in witchcraft, and makes more breast jokes. Harmless time-passer, with good-natured tone despite stupefying amount of boy's locker-room-level cleavage humor.

D: James Signorelli. A: Cassandra Peterson, Daniel Greene, Jeff Conway.

Repossessed
(1990) 89m. **D**

Seventeen years after her possession by the devil, Blair is again spitting pea soup and making impolite remarks. A terrible and often offensive combination of *The Exorcist* and *Airplane!*-style, comic free-for-all.

D: Bob Logan. A: Linda Blair, Leslie Nielsen, Ned Beatty.

There's Nothing Out There
(1990) 91m. **B–**

It's spring break and a gaggle of teens head to a secluded forest cabin, ignoring a horror-buff nerd who disagrees with the film's title. A low-budget but hyperactively loony film, with manic camerawork, goofy gore, and an endless stream of girls mysteriously compelled to ditch their blouses.

D: Rolfe Kanefsky. A: Craig Peck, Wendy Bednarz, Mark Collver.

Teens

Since the 1950s, most horror films have been aimed at and featured teenagers. Teen actors are cheap to use and are expected to behave in rash and stupid ways that can get them mangled, mashed, skewered, and injured in imaginative ways. The films in this group range from cute teen comedies with a few thrills, to the gorier ten-little-Indians-style murder fests. But they all benefit from good production values, and due to the presence of actual stories, no one has made a series out of any of them—yet.

The Funhouse
(1981) 96m. **B**

Teens spend the night in a funhouse, witness the murder of a fortune-teller, and then get hunted down by the carny owner's mutant son. A stylish horror photographed in sleazy carnival colors, with a hint of Frankenstein-type melancholy thanks to a touching and horrific monster.

D: Tobe Hooper. A: Elizabeth Berridge, Cooper Huckabee, Sylvia Miles.

Night of the Creeps
(1986) 89m. **B**

Two nerds and a burned-out detective deal with swarms of alien eellike creatures who turn kids into zombies on prom night. Some of the humor is sophomoric, but the film packs the goods—an opening hatchet murder, crazed camerawork, in-jokes galore, and eels popping out of split heads.

D: Fred Dekker. A: Jason Lively, Jill Whitlow, Tom Atkins.

Vamp
(1986) 93m. **C+**

Three frat pledges go to a strip club that's really a front for vampires. Grace Jones is fun in white-face, but not much else is in this slick MTV-inspired comedy that mixes chills with an appropriately sleazy air.

D: Richard Wenk. A: Chris Makepeace, Dedee Pfeiffer, Grace Jones.

The Monster Squad
(1987) 82m. **B**

Some kids battle a collection of classic monsters. An affectionate recollection of old-time movie monsters (Dracula, The Mummy, The Lagoon's Creature) with spectacular special effects.

D: Fred Dekker. A: Andre Gower, Duncan Regehr, Tommy Noonan.

Night of the Demons

(1989) 89m. **C+**

Teens spend the night in a haunted house, turn into demons, and kill each other. A quick gruesome film, with ample nudity and some humorously brain-dead dialogue.

D: Kevin S. Tenney. A: Linnea Quigley, William Gallo, Hal Havins.

Popcorn

(1991) 93m. **C+**

During a horror film festival, real murders occur in the theater. The film itself drags, but the movies being shown in the festival—campy send-ups of 50s and Japanese horror flicks—make this almost worth watching.

D: Mark Herrier. A: Jill Schoelen, Dee Wallace, Tony Roberts.

Ghouls

The dictionary defines a ghoul as a person with a tendency to uproot graves and ingest the occupants—just the kind of character for a modern horror film. Take a bucket of blood, some butcher shop leftovers, and a group of extras to lurch around as the eaters or chased-around-as-the-eaten, and you have the makings for a zombie epic. Apart from the average gore-fest, a few good films have actually been made from these paltry materials—from stunning visions of the apocalypse and vicious attacks on our consumer culture, to serious meditations on the nuclear family.

Night of the Living Dead

(1968) 96m. B&W. **A**

This low-budget classic, with its grainy black-and-white film and everyday people pressed into service as the lumbering dead, looks almost like a horrific documentary. Director Romero's artistry shines through with shots of flaming pyres of human remains, shadowy hordes of bedraggled zombies, and an unrelieved ambiance of anxiety and dread permeating every frame.

D: George A. Romero. A: Duane Jones, Judith O'Dea, Karl Hardman.

The Hills Have Eyes

(1977) 89m. **B+**

An all-American family gets stuck in the desert with a group of inbred cannibals who dress in a somewhat tasteless fashion. Their relentless showdown in the endless expanse of hot desert allows our nice family to disintegrate and become even more savage than the monsters.

D: Wes Craven. A: Susan Lanier, Robert Houston, Dee Wallace.

Dawn of the Dead

(1979) 125m. **B**

The few remaining normal humans take refuge in a shopping mall as the ghoul invasion continues. With pounds of spilled entrails, this savage, relentlessly paced commentary shows the refugees setting up a parody of everyday life in the glittering empty mall while zombies trapped behind glass stare longingly at store displays.

D: George A. Romero. A: Gaylen Ross, Ken Foree, David Emge.

Buried Alive

(1984) 90m. **F**

This virtually plotless, obsessively disgusting film features a deranged young man, his dead girlfriend, and a cannibalistic housekeeper. With washed-out photography and an utterly depraved air, this disgusting time-waster is only for the sickest tastes.

D: Joe D'Amato. A: Karen Canter, Cinzia Monreale, Franca Stoppa.

Day of the Dead

(1985) 102m. **A**

Most of the world seems to have gone the way of the hungry dead in the last of Romero's trilogy as scientists work for a solution to the zombie plague in this unrelievedly grim vision, which leaves you wondering who the real monsters are.

D: George A. Romero. A: Lori Cardille, Richard Liberty, Jarlath Conroy.

The Hills Have Eyes Part II

(1985) 86m. **D**

A total mess as Ruby, an ex-cannibal now civilized, and a survivor from the first *The Hills Have Eyes* family have a run-in with Ruby's still-nasty family. Featured low-light: a flashback to the original film as seen from a dog's point of view.

D: Wes Craven. A: Michael Berryman, Janus Blythe, Robert Houston.

The Return of the Living Dead

(1985) 91m. **B+**

This spin on Romero's *Dead* films details the misadventures of some teens who accidentally release the encased bodies of the dead. A punkette doing a doomed striptease in a graveyard, bodies chopped to still-living bits, and a chatty corpse are some of the highlights in this enjoyable send-up.

D: Dan O'Bannon. A: Clu Gulager, James Karen, Linnea Quigley.

Return of the Living Dead Part II

(1988) 90m. **C+**

Pretty much a recycling job on the first *Return,* and about as exciting as you'd expect, with a few laughs.

D: Ken Wiederhorn. A: James Karen, Thom Mathews, Dana Ashbrook.

Night of the Living Dead

(1990) 96m. **C+**

A color remake of the original that offers a strong female protagonist and some impressive ghoul makeup, but the story's tired by now.

D: Tom Savini. A: Tony Todd, Patricia Tallman, Tom Towles.

Return of the Living Dead III

(1993) 97m. **B**

When a teenager is exposed to ghoul gas she tries to slow down her transformation by rather painful means. A surprisingly effective blend of ghoul and high-tech thriller, with some elements of Frankenstein thrown in.

D: Brian Yuzna. A: J. Trevor Edmond, Mindy Clarke, Kent McCord.

Modern Gore

From the crowds who watched public executions in times past, to the modern motorist who slows down to check out a really nasty accident, people sometimes have an urge to view the messy remains. Although gruesome scenes are required in any modern horror, this group of films gives its viewers little else besides scenes of spilling guts, severed appendages, and any other gory atrocity.

Demons
(1985) 85m. **C**
Legendary horror maestro Mario Bava's son filmed this stylishly disgusting film of kids at the local horror show turning into zombies. Outside of its movie-in-a-movie gambit, this offers 85 instructive minutes of dismemberment and impressively gross zombie effects.
D: Lamberto Bava. A: Natasha Hovey, Urbano Barberini, Karl Zinny.

Frankenhooker
(1990) 85m. **C+**
A young mad scientist attaches the severed head of his beloved to a body composed from the parts of prostitutes. Campy, offensive, gory, and cheap. This is OK for demented fans of the genre (you know who you are!); others will want to stay clear.
D: Frank Henenlotter. A: James Lorinz, Patty Mullen, Charlotte Helmkamp.

Body Parts
(1991) 88m. **D**
A killer's arms are grafted onto an artist and a criminal psychologist. Soon the appendages take over the wills of both men, leading them down the path of violence, death, and madness. Boring, unbelievable, and predictable.
D: Eric Red. A: Jeff Fahey, Lindsay Duncan, Kim Delaney.

Dead Alive
(1992) 97m. **B+**
What happens when a Tasmanian devil bites your mother? The answer is here as an entire town goes zombie crazy in this disgusting, sometimes funny mixmaster of a film featuring kung fu zombie priests, a slimy 20-foot Mom, and enough gore to fill Lake Erie.
D: Peter Jackson. A: Timothy Balm, Diana Penalver, Elizabeth Moody.

Dr. Giggles
(1992) 95m. **D+**
As the title indicates, this is gore with laughs as a deranged medico throws malpractice out the window. This scores low on the joke meter, but with enough well-photographed puncture wounds and impalements to please the undiscriminating gore-hound.
D: Manny Cotto. A: Larry Drake, Holly Marie Combs, Cliff De Young.

New Vampires and Werewolves

When *An American Werewolf in London* made a mint at the box office, a new generation of werewolves and vampires was born in Hollywood. Gone were the cobwebbed trappings of wolfbane, gloomy cemeteries, and bats; these hip and sexy creatures were your next door neighbors, a one-night stand, even your older brother. Most of these are solid horror thrillers laced with outrageous special effects and a little more gore than you'd expect from a Hollywood production with name stars. But they definitely give plenty of new twists to some old legends.

Martin
(1978) 95m. **B+**
Martin is a sweet-faced teen who uses hypodermic needles to get the blood he craves, since he is a modern-day vampire—or is he? A quiet and bloody character study that compensates for its low budget with exceptional editing and a macabre ironic humor.
D: George A. Romero. A: John Amplas, Lincoln Maazel, Christine Forrest.

An American Werewolf in London
(1981) 97m. **A**
Two backpacking Americans encounter a werewolf on the British moors, with the expected results. Lushly photographed and filled with imaginative touches, this humorous pop-horror features the first truly convincing and horrifying, full-body transformation of a werewolf.
D: John Landis. A: David Naughton, Griffin Dunne, Jenny Agutter.

Wolfen
(1981) 115m. **B**
A detective investigates a series of mutilation murders in the Bronx slums, perpetrated by a tribe of savage creatures. This has the structure and tone of any good cop thriller, and deals with some real-life issues of New York's melting pot.
D: Michael Wadleigh. A: Albert Finney, Diane Venora, Edward James Olmos.

The Hunger
(1983) 94m. **C**
Divine decadence never looked so dull in this soap opera about the problems of rich and bisexual vampires. Lots of arty shots of billowing drapes, haute couture fashion, New Wave editing and not much substance for all the talent that's wasted.
D: Tony Scott. A: Susan Sarandon, Catherine Deneuve, David Bowie.

Fright Night
(1985) 105m. **B+**
A teenager comes to realize that the suave guy who moved in next door is a real vampire. A truly fun film with amazing vampire transformations, a tone that deftly

balances comedy and horror, and McDowell hamming it up as a TV horror-show host.
D: Tom Holland. A: Chris Sarandon, William Ragsdale, Roddy McDowell.

The Lost Boys
(1987) 98m. **B+**

He's the new kid in the Santa Cruz-like town, but does he want to be part of the gang who hangs from freeways bat-style, turns noodles into worms, and levitates in its weirdly hip lair? A witty and fast-paced roller-coaster ride through the paranoia and problems of youth, with a sparkling cast.
D: Joel Schumacher. A: Jason Patric, Kiefer Sutherland, Dianne Wiest.

Near Dark
(1987) 95m. **A–**

This hardscrabble "family" of vampires travels around the American heartland in stolen cars, pursuing their twilight prey at truck stops, honky tonk bars, and all-night convenience stores. A unique spin on family devotion, coming-of-age, and the vampire myth, with mesmerizing and often gruesome images.
D: Kathryn Bigelow. A: Adrian Pasdar, Jenny Wright, Lance Henrikson.

Innocent Blood
(1992) 112m. **B**

"La Femme Nikita" is now an insatiable, sinewy, and sexy vamp on the prowl for mobsters in a neon-drenched Pittsburgh. While the bloody sight gags, high-tech vampire effects, and off-beat casting hold your interest some of the time, the ideas in this glossy entry are actually more interesting than the end result.
D: John Landis. A: Anne Parillaud, Anthony LaPaglia, Robert Loggia.

Cronos
(1993) 92m. **B+**

A mechanical insect confers immortality, but the ailing Mexico City shopkeeper who uses it also discovers that it turns one into a vampire. This stylish-looking Mexican horror follows the struggle for possession of the device, and plays like Gabriel García Márquez meets horror with its themes of death, corruption, class-warfare, and family.
D: Guillermo del Torro. A: Federico Luppi, Ron Perlman, Claudio Brook.

Tale of a Vampire
(1993) 93m. **B–**

A retiring, sweet-tempered man turns out to be a reluctant vampire in danger of losing the reincarnated vision of his long dead love. A gentlemanly, understated Sands and sudden erotic violence are some of the merits of this brooding sleeper.
D: Shimako Sato. A: Julian Sands, Kenneth Cranham, Suzanna Hamilton.

Interview with a Vampire
(1994) 130m. **B**

Flamboyant vampire Lestat gives a plantation owner the gift of undeath in old New Orleans. Big and pretty to look at—especially the settings in Paris—with performances that range from brooding to campy as the two main vamps play house with a diminutive vampire daughter. The homoerotic subtext isn't buried too deeply, and it looks to be a midnight movie favorite.
D: Neil Jordan. A: Tom Cruise, Brad Pitt, Antonio Banderas.

Wolf
(1994) 124m. **B–**

Nicholson is an aging editor with scruples who at first enjoys the effects of a wolf's bite, but soon sees the downside of the lycanthropic lifestyle. The first half is an alternately brooding/funny critique of corporate power plays, the second a pretty silly werewolf film with Pfeiffer tagged on for a love interest.
D: Mike Nichols. A: Jack Nicholson, Michelle Pfeiffer, James Spader.
(See also *Bram Stoker's Dracula,* page 374.)

Old Monsters Revisited

These horror films go back to the basics using high and low technology to update some of the less than classic monsters from the 50s. With relatively little gore and violence, these genial horror flicks still have slightly better special effects than their low-budget predecessors, but the monstrous creatures have the same zany appeal and terror as they crawl, slither, and make you jump, just like always.

Humanoids from the Deep
(1980) 80m. **B–**

Toxic wastes create fish/plant creatures who attack a seaside resort town with a high ratio of scantily clad women. A very well-made creature feature with good effects, but also an air of sleaze, courtesy of gritty photography and disturbing rape scenes.
D: Barbara Peeters. A: Doug McClure, Ann Turkel, Vic Morrow.

The Hand
(1981) 104m. **D**

Oliver Stone's second horror film limns the tale of a cartoonist whose severed hand starts acting out his darkest desires. The few clever moments don't make up for bad wandering hand effects, a fudged ending, and pointlessly depressing tone.
D: Oliver Stone. A: Michael Caine, Andrea Marcovicci, Bruce McGill.

Q
(1982) 93m. **A–**

A Mayan winged serpent takes up residence in the Chrysler building, attacking Manhattan's rooftop population. The witty tone, clever visual puns, and quirky characters help make this a cult favorite, and the little bit of gore and good monster effects will keep your heart rate up.
D: Larry Cohen. A: Michael Moriarty, David Carradine, Candy Clark.

The Gate
(1987) 92m. **B–**

Some preteens play "satanic" rock music, make a token sacrifice, and the screen is filled with one huge reptilian creature and his tiny underlings. A superior group of green-skinned, glowing red-eyed nasties and surprisingly good-hearted feel make this better than average.
D: Tibor Takacs. A: Stephen Dorff, Christa Denton, Louis Tripp.

Not of This Earth
(1988) 82m. **C+**

An intentionally "bad" remake of Roger Corman's 56 shocker, with Lords as an

unsuspecting nurse helping out an anemic rich guy who happens to be a dangerous alien. A colorful quickie, with lots of nudity, gore, and gratuitous sunglasses-wearing.
D: Jim Wynorski. A: Traci Lords, Arthur Roberts, Lenny Juliano.

DeepStar Six
(1989) 98m. **C–**
Though decently crafted, this tale of scientists on a deep sea antinuclear installation is just another underwater *Alien* clone, lacking in atmosphere and tension, with a remarkably forgettable creature.
D: Sean S. Cunningham. A: Taurean Blacque, Greg Evigan, Miguel Ferrer.

Leviathan
(1989) 98m. **C+**
On a deep sea platform, genetic experiments go awry, resulting in a rather lumpy-looking, face-absorbing claw creature. Briskly shot and edited, with a great sense of confined underwater quarters, this suffers from an undefined and rarely shown monster.
D: George Pan Cosmatos. A: Peter Weller, Richard Crenna, Amanda Pays.

Tremors
(1990) 90m. **A–**
The good citizens of a very small desert town notice the sheep are disappearing, and are soon terrorized by humongous sand-burrowing worms. The bright look of the film, the likable and slightly screwy locals, and their comical efforts to cross stretches of sand without alerting the worms all give this a goofy charm.
D: Ron Underwood. A: Kevin Bacon, Fred Ward, Reba McIntire.

Carnosaur
(1993) 83m. **B**
Made to cash in on *Jurassic Park*-mania, this is actually a very gloomy and perverse movie about genetic engineering creating a single dinosaur. Very low budget, but with rich color photography, good acting, and a more "realistic" vision of this idea than its mega-buck source.
D: Adam Simon. A: Diane Ladd, Jennifer Runyon, Raphael Sbarge.

Techno Horror

With advances in special effects makeup, a new breed of horror cropped up whose main intent seemed to be to test the audience's gag reflex. Convincing skinless bodies, reanimated organs, and worse redefined the concept of gross-out. Sometimes the gruesome gambit misfired, creating laughs instead of shudders, and often the cost for this nastiness eclipsed the budget for other niceties like plot and decent acting. But for the viewers looking for a feast of upscale goo, these could be just the thing.

976-Evil
(1988) 92m. **C**
After dialing the title phone number, a shy teenager finds himself with a case of uncontrollable demonic powers, resulting in some gruesome mutilation and deaths of his high school enemies. Enough humor and scares to be watchable.
D: Robert Englund. A: Stephen Geoffreys, Patrick O'Bryan, Sandy Dennis.

976-Evil II: The Astral Factor
(1991) 93m. **D+**
A telephone service with supernatural capabilities keeps an incarcerated psycho killer in business by astrally projecting him to warm bodies. A somewhat atmospheric, dreamlike, but ultimately boring sequel to the less than inspiring original.
D: Jim Wynorski. A: Rene Assa, Brigitte Nielsen, Patrick O'Bryan.

The Evil Dead
(1979) 90m. **B+**
College students stranded in a cabin unwittingly unleash a supernatural force and naturally pay the price. The film soars above its low budget with imaginative camera tricks, but don't see this if you get motion sickness—it's like being strapped to a bobsled racing through a haunted house.
D: Sam Raimi. A: Bruce Campbell, Ellen Sandweiss, Betsy Baker.

Evil Dead II
(1987) 85m. **A**
The survivor from the first rampage and his friends battle all sorts of irrepressible evil things, from the unseen tracking force to the Three Stooges-like demons. A wild pastiche that also manages to poke fun at the genre and scare the daylights out of you.
D: Sam Raimi. A: Bruce Campbell, Sarah Berry, Dan Hicks.

Army of Darkness
(1993) 81m. **B**
The hero from the previous *Evil Dead* films is transported to the Dark Ages, where he again encounters the evil book and its otherworldly ghoulies. This cartoonlike action/comedy/horror is best when ripping off Harryhausen and Stooges, but bogs down during the extended battle scenes.
D: Sam Raimi. A: Bruce Campbell, Embeth Davidtz, Marcus Gilbert.

Hellraiser
(1987) 94m. **A–**
The pursuit of pleasure and pain lead a wife to adultery and murder for her attic-bound lover—a man in a yucky bloblike skinless state who needs blood to regain his health, and who possesses a demonic puzzle box. A disturbing S&M modern horror flick, which delivers the scares through both chilling and disgusting scenes.
D: Clive Barker. A: Andrew Robinson, Clare Higgins, Ashley Laurence.

Hellbound: Hellraiser II
(1988) 93m. **B+**
Innocent young woman is transported to hell by that tricky puzzle box, where she meets her evil stepmother along with Pinhead and Co. Creepy and gory with an emphasis on special effects and nightmarish sets.
D: Tony Randel. A: Clare Higgins, Ashley Laurence, Kenneth Cranham.

Hellraiser III: Hell on Earth
(1992) 91m. **B–**
The nightclub/art crowd are meeting gruesome bizarre deaths and the irrepressible Pinhead and that darned puzzle box make their appearance. Includes bad disco, nasty sex, and a final scene of the nightclub massacre that's gut-twisting.

D: Anthony Hickox. A: Terry Farrell, Doug Bradley, Paula Marshall.

Re-Animator
(1985) 86m. **A–**
An obsessed med student concocts a serum that turns cadavers into slavish zombies. Imaginative excessive horror with a wicked sense of humor. This one's hard to beat if you have a strong stomach.
D: Stuart Gordon. A: Jeffrey Combs, Bruce Abbott, Barbara Crampton.

Deadly Friend
(1986) 91m. **D**
A slick but confused tale of tinkerer Laborteaux who creates a monster by sticking a computer chip in the brain of his dead girlfriend. Aside from some unexpected jolts of gore, this only demonstrates that a young teen with blue makeup just isn't very scary.
D: Wes Craven. A: Matthew Laborteaux, Kirsty Swanson, Anne Twomey.

From Beyond
(1986) 89m. **B**
Scientists invent a device that heightens sensual awareness, but also conjures a deadly creature from another dimension. Strange brew of kinky sex, gore, and dark humor that's more disgusting than scary, but it keeps you watching.
D: Stuart Gordon. A: Jeffrey Combs, Barbara Crampton, Ted Sorel.

Bride of the Re-Animator
(1989) 99m. **B+**
Two med students look to revive a dead friend with a less than effective serum. Madcapped, campy, and gory, but in a relatively nonsickening way.
D: Brian Yuzna. A: Jeffrey Combs, Bruce Abbott, Claude Earl Jones.

Night Breed
(1989) 102m. **C**
Young man with visions of grisly murders and an underground society of monsters good and bad finds himself on the lam and hiding out in his mythic world. Combination of fantasy and slasher that never gels, despite Cronenberg's good and disturbing performance.
D: Clive Barker. A: Craig Sheffer, David Cronenberg, Charles Haid.

Shocker
(1989) 111m. **C**
Horace Pinker, a psychotic TV repairman who likes to commit gruesome acts, becomes linked to a clean-cut teen via dreams, and later plays murderous cat-and-mouse games with him via TV. Slick, with some eye-popping gory effects, but it squanders too many satiric possibilities.
D: Wes Craven. A: Michael Murphy, Peter Berg, Cami Cooper.

Dust Devil
(1993) 87m. **B**
Imagine an explicitly gory 70s art house film about an ancient African demon taking human form, and you'd have this strikingly gorgeous, amber-hued desert nightmare. Censors may have hacked this to bits, but it's worth a look for ritual imagery, brilliant merging of sound and vision, and a weird apocalyptic mood.
D: Richard Stanley. A: Robert Burke, Zakes Mokae, Chelsea Field.

Mind Terrors

Common everyday objects like a friendly pet or normal locations like a subway can be the object of horror thanks to the mysterious workings of the mind. Here, reality bends, bodies warp, and madness almost always reigns as the horror film does its subversive best to insinuate that nothing is as it seems.

Monkeyshines: An Experiment in Fear
(1988) 117m. **B+**
A quadriplegic young man is given a small monkey to make life easier, but his scientifically enhanced simian does anything but. Despite the studio tacked-on ending, this is a quietly disturbing film dealing with uncomfortable subjects like helplessness and dependency.
D: George A. Romero. A: Jason Beghe, John Pankow, Kate McNeil.

Pin
(1989) 103m. **A**
A troubled youth becomes obsessed with a skinless, anatomically correct medical mannequin. May sound silly, but this exquisitely creepy film qualifies as a subversive sleeper dealing with fears about sexuality, family, and identity, with admirable restraint and an atmosphere of intense melancholy: Don't miss it.
D: Sandor Stern. A: David Hewlitt, Terry O'Quinn.

Jacob's Ladder
(1990) 116m. **B+**
Jacob has left his family and comfortable life to take up a grungier New York City existence, but he still can't escape his ghoulish visions linked to a bayoneting incident in Vietnam. Like a feature-length episode of *Twilight Zone*, this is a disorienting, disturbing, visual eye bender that will leave you to sort out the pieces of the puzzle.
D: Adrian Lyne. A: Tim Robbins, Elizabeth Pena, Danny Aiello.

Doppelganger: The Evil Within
(1992) 105m. **B**
This overlooked oddity had Barrymore running away from her evil twin—or is she just running away from herself? A briskly paced, weirdly atmospheric film with gooey special effects that manages to be erotic *and* disgusting.
D: Avi Nesher. A: Drew Barrymore, George Newbern, Dennis Christopher.

In the Mouth of Madness
(1995) 105m. **B+**
A man is hired to track down an elusive writer whose stories are becoming a reality in John Carpenter's ambitious return to form. Packed with nightmarish images and topped by an apocalyptic finish that puts you into the film itself, the movie's pacing may falter but the paranoid atmosphere lingers on.
D: John Carpenter. A: Sam Neill, Charlton Heston, Jurgen Prochnow.

Bad Religion

When you're talking about good and evil it's always handy to go back to religion for your source material. The 90s offered this spate of disturbing images of spirituality gone bad in glossy mainstream films brimming with high-tech cataclysms, spiteful spirits, and deranged Messiahs while exploring the scary sides of everything from basic Christian doctrine to voodoo.

The Believers
(1987) 110m. **C–**

A widowed psychologist moves to Manhattan where his son is threatened by modern-day Santeria (a cross between Catholicism and voodoo) cultists. The strong opening and fascinating study of religion soon gets bogged down in ho-hum horror melodramatics.
D: John Schlesinger. A: Martin Sheen, Robert Loggia, Helen Shaver.

The Serpent and the Rainbow
(1988) 98m. **B+**

During the collapse of the Duvalier regime, a drug company sends an anthropologist on a fact-finding tour through Haiti to determine the validity of their legendary "voodoo power." Wes Craven pulls out the stops in this feverishly atmospheric tale that blends *A Nightmare on Elm Street*-like scare scenes with real Third World horrors.
D: Wes Craven. A: Bill Pullman, Cathy Tyson, Zakes Mokae.

The Seventh Sign
(1988) 94m. **C**

A mysterious stranger opens Biblical parchments, causing all manner of disaster, and eventually migrates to California to threaten Demi Moore's unborn child and bring on The End of the World. Good effects, appropriate apocalyptic music, and impressively large plot holes: never dull, the sort of movie you don't admit enjoying.
D: Carl Schultz. A: Demi Moore, Michael Biehn, Jurgen Prochnow.

Warlock
(1988) 102m. **B**

An eons-old battle between a satanic warlock and a priest fast-forwards into modern LA in this low-gore horror thriller. Fine special effects, vivid photography, with Sands and Grant bringing a relish worthy of Vincent Price to the tongue-in-cheek story.
D: Steve Miner. A: Julian Sands, Lori Singer, Richard Grant.

Recent Oddities from Hell

An elevator, a smiling clown, those unusual but *nice* folks down the road—all are imbued with dread and horror in this group of films that continues to shatter the slasher/monster stereotype of what horror films can do. Ranging in tone from blackly humorous to pitch black despair, these unclassifiable films are united only by their singular grim visions of human affairs.

Motel Hell
(1980) 102m. **C+**

You'll never guess the secret ingredient of Farmer Vincent's famous sausage, but it may have something to do with the people who are planted like rutabagas in the back fields. A bizarre, funny, and surprisingly well-acted, low-budget film that contains some low-gore scenes, but even more truly weird images.
D: Kevin Connor. A: Rory Calhoun, Nancy Parson, Paul Linke.

Liquid Sky
(1983) 112m. **C–**

Tiny aliens live off the sexual ecstasy of would-be hipsters in New York's East Village. Arty, flashy, badly dated look at Eurotrash ennui has a few amusing moments, but a viewer looking for anything beyond in-crowd-sneers should look elsewhere.
D: Slava Tsukerman. A: Anne Carlisle, Paula E. Sheppard, Otto Von Wernherr.

The Lift
(1985) 90m. Subtitled. **C+**

This horror thriller pits a repairman against a killer elevator in a computer-run building. The deadpan humor, paranoid atmosphere, and some machine vs. man nastiness—mangled bodies and the like—fuel this Dutch-made film before it loses steam.
D: Dick Maas. A: Huub Stapel, Josine van Dalsum, Wileka Van Ammelrooy.

Anguish
(1988) 92m. **A–**

For once, the old film-within-a-film trick works as Oedipal wreck Lerner perpetrates some gruesome killings while it is later revealed that Lerner's tale is a movie, with the watching audience soon stalked by another, *real* maniac. A tense, surreally violent film, thick with an atmosphere of paranoia.
D: Bigas Luna. A: Zelda Rubenstein, Michael Lerner, Talia Paul.

Killer Klowns from Outer Space
(1988) 90m. **C+**

The title says it all in this tale of big-top intergalactic invaders. Despite the unusual premise and visuals that include luridly colorful clowns in a circus-tent spaceship, the script runs out of mad inventions about half way through.
D: Stephen Chiodo. A: Grant Cramer, Suzanne Snyder, Royal Dano.

Henry: Portrait of a Serial Killer
(1990) 90m. **B+**

No real plot here, just the day-to-day wanderings and slayings of the remorseless title character in sleepy middle America. The film's unflinching semidocumentary look at a dead soul who kills for no particular reason or passion makes this one of the most quietly disturbing films in years.

D: John McNaughton. A: Michael Rooker, Tom Towles.

Santa Sangre
(1990) 124m. **A–**

A troubled youth becomes a circus performer, an asylum inmate, and The Invisible Man (in mind, at least). Cult director Alejandro Jodorowsky who brought you *El Topo,* fills this purposefully gaudy film with lingering images such as an armless mother, an elephant funeral, and a Felliniesque gallery of grotesques.
D: Alejandro Jodorowsky. A: Axel Jodorowsky, Guy Stockwell, Blanca Guerra.

People Under the Stairs
(1991) 102m. **B**

A poor youth burglarizes a house inhabited by a couple who may be husband and wife, brother and sister, or both, but the man does call his partner "Mommie." Twisted horror with unnerving scenes of menaced children and a message for those willing to look.
D: Wes Craven. A: Brandon Adams, Everett McGill, Wendy Robie.

Candyman
(1992) 101m. **A–**

A series of gruesome slayings occur in a Chicago housing project, and there's talk of the Candyman, a slave murdered long ago for his romance with a white woman. Dynamic performances and an eerie Philip Glass score help the sense of creepy menace in a concrete urban ghetto.
D: Bernard Rose. A: Virginia Madsen, Tony Todd, Kasi Lemmons.

Freaked
(1994) 80m. **C+**

A rock star is administered some toxic waste, mutates, and joins a menagerie of freaks, becoming a media star in the process. Rude, tasteless, disgusting, and a lot of grotesque fun, with amazing special makeup effects and special culturally uplifting guest appearances by Mr. T and Brooke Shields.
D: Tom Stern, Alex Winter. A: Alex Winter, Randy Quaid, William Sadler.

Hideaway
(1995) 118m. **C+**

A nice Dad and a mean Satanist have near-death experiences that forge a horrific bond between them. The whiz kid camerawork and impressive special effects sequences resembling car ads from Heaven and Hell make this family-in-distress horror fable one of the slicker entries.
D: Brett Leonard. A: Jeff Goldblum, Christine Lahti, Alfred Molina.

The Mangler
(1995) 102m. **C+**

A possessed giant laundry machine craves the blood of virgins in rural Maine. With its burnished old-machine look and great effects, this is even more entertainingly ridiculous than it sounds. After all, when was the last time you saw a laundry machine get up and chase people all the way to hell?
D: Tobe Hooper. A: Robert Englund, Ted Levine, Daniel Matmor.

KIDS

Kids Menu

KIDS FILM GROUPS

Kids Cinema

Animated Musicals

You don't need to be a kid to watch these musicals about princesses, dwarves, and dogs: The animation is gorgeous, the songs have more wit than many musicals, and the plots have a dark resonance missing in many Hollywood films. The early ones are pure magic, heavy on the mythology, with a dash of the Black Forest even when they have those cute plushy characters. By the 1960s the animation became slicker, the stories more modern, and the recent entries now offer extravagant spectacles with lots of show-biz razzamatazz.

Snow White and the Seven Dwarfs
(1937) 83m. **A**
When the wicked queen wants to have her killed, Snow White hides in a forest cottage keeping house for some dwarves who work in the diamond mines. A funny, scary, and completely enchanting film rich with colors, Snow White's soprano warblings, and an uncanny eye for how animals and humans move.
D: Ben Sharpsteen. Voices: Adriana Caselotti, Harry Stockwell, Lucille La Verne.

Fantasia
(1940) 120m. **A–**
Like an animated prototype for music videos, this blends groundbreaking animation techniques with classical music selections. The kids will enjoy a silly ballet with hippos and Mickey Mouse as the sorcerer's apprentice. Adults will marvel at the depth and subtlety of the animator's hand.
D: Walt Disney. Narration: Deems Taylor.

Pinocchio
(1940) 88m. **A**
The zenith of old-style animation was reached with this tale of the wooden puppet brought to life whose efforts to become a real boy are continually confounded by his mischievous instincts. This offers rich detailing, a winning Jiminy Cricket, and some of the most vivid metaphors for child abduction you'll ever see.
D: Ben Sharpsteen. Voices: Dickie Jones, Cliff Edwards, Walter Catlett.

Dumbo
(1941) 64m. **B–**
The bright warm colors of a traveling circus set the stage for this sweet-hearted tale of the outcast baby elephant with big flapping ears who discovers he can fly. Sentimental mother-son segments coupled with beautiful set pieces including a bizarre drunken hallucination of "Pink Elephants on Parade."
D: Ben Sharpsteen. Voices: Edward Brophy, Verna Felton, Sterling Holloway.

Bambi
(1942) 70m. **A**
Way before *The Lion King,* Bambi experienced the circle of life with his youth among humorous woodland creatures and his struggles with maturity that include the shooting death of his mother. Masterful blend of cute cuddly animals and almost poetic sequences rich in drama and beauty.
D: David Hand. Voices: Robby Stewart, Peter Behn, Cammie King.

Cinderella
(1950) 75m. **A–**
With the assistance of her Fairy Godmother and some rodent friends, Cinderella overcomes her evil stepsisters and stepmother, so she can go to the ball to meet the Prince. Clever songs, lively mice, and that great corny romance.
D: Wilfred Jackson. Voices: Ilene Woods, William Phipps, Eleanor Audley.

Alice in Wonderland
(1951) 75m. **B–**
This Disneyfied version removes much of Lewis Carroll's witty satiric wordplay and reduces the unpleasantness of many of his pointed characters. Still a charming and frolicsome story of a young Victorian girl who tumbles into a realm where playing cards talk, people can shrink, and caterpillars smoke hookahs.
D: Hamilton Luske. Voices: Kathryn Beaumont, Ed Wynn, Sterling Holloway.

Peter Pan
(1953) 76m. **B+**
Wendy and her brothers go on a magical adventure in a swashbuckling Neverland with the flying boy who refuses to grow up and his Marilyn Monroe-esque Tinkerbell. The song about Native Americans is a dated curiosity.
D: Hamilton Luske. Voices: Bobby Driscoll, Kathryn Beaumont, Hans Conried.

Lady and the Tramp
(1955) 76m. **A**
A refined pooch runs away from her human family and falls in love with a rogue from the wrong side of the kennel. The evil Siamese cats and Peggy Lee's whiskey voice jazz up this valentine to turn-of-the-century puppy love.
D: Hamilton Luske. Voices: Peggy Lee, Barbara Luddy, Larry Roberts.

Sleeping Beauty
(1959) 75m. **A–**
An evil fairy curses a princess so that she falls asleep on her 16th birthday and can only be awakened by a true love's kiss. Sophisticated, with a score based on Tchaikovsky's ballet and a little less good-hearted bounce than the other early Disneys.
D: Clyde Geronimi. Voices: Mary Costa, Bill Shirley, Eleanor Audley.

101 Dalmations
(1961) 79m. **A**
Two Londoners marry as do their dogs, and an unforgettable socialite, Cruella Deville, has designs on the puppies for a fur coat. Has great late-50s-style modern animation, with a harrowing trek through the English countryside and one of the screen's great villainesses.
D: Wolfgang Reitherman. Voices: Rod Taylor, Betty Lou Gerson, Martha Wenworth.

Gay Purr-ee
(1962) 85m. **C+**
A country French cat goes to Paris, is kidnapped and then

saved by her country kitty love and his faithful friend. The non-Disney entry is slick and modern-looking, with some show-biz-style sophistication but no magic.
D: Abe Levitow. Voices: Judy Garland, Robert Goulet, Hermione Gingold.

The Sword in the Stone
(1963) 75m. **C+**
An indifferently animated treatment of the King Arthur legend follows country lad Wart as he's tutored in kingly ways by the magical Merlin. The kids may wander as it gets wordy in patches and the animation suffers from short-cut stylization that marks this as one of Disney's lesser efforts.
D: Wolfgang Reitherman. Voices: Rickey Sorenson, Sebastian Cabot, Janius Matthews.

The Jungle Book
(1967) 78m. **C+**
A boy raised by wolves in the jungle is endangered by a man-hating tiger and heads toward civilization in the company of his animal friends. A loose-jointed, worry-free tale, enhanced by jazzy music, but a slicker and less interesting style of animation.
D: Wolfgang Reitherman. Voices: Phil Harris, Sebastian Cabot, Sterling Holloway.

The Little Mermaid
(1989) 83m. **A–**
A perky redheaded mermaid who falls in love with a prince enters into a pact with the Sea Witch, trading her lovely voice for a pair of legs. Everyone seems to dart around in a whoosh of bubbles in this upbeat and tuneful oceanic treat that signaled the rebirth of Disney animated musicals.
D: John Musker and Ron Clements. Voices: Jodi Benson, Pat Carroll, Samuel Wright.

Beauty and the Beast
(1991) 85m. **A–**
Book-loving Belle takes the place of her father who's held captive by an ill-tempered Beast in his enchanted castle. Includes a witty Broadway-like score and dialogue, a story that will melt your heart, and a show-stopping production number with lively dishes, chairs, and candelabras.
D: Gary Trousdale and Kirk Wise. Voices: Angela Lansbury, Robby Benson, Jerry Orbach.

Aladdin
(1992) 90m. **B+**
A poor Arabian boy falls in love with a princess and gets some help from a motormouth genie. The story and music are pretty bland, but you won't be able to catch your breath or hear yourself think with the nonstop schtick of Williams' amphetamine-fueled genie.
D: John Musker and Ron Clements. Voices: Robin Williams, Scott Weinger, Linda Larkin.

Ferngully: The Last Rainforest
(1992) 72m. **B**
An evil demon is released by toxic wastes from a lumber company's tank and it's up to a tiny forest fairy and a magically shrunk lumberjack to save the last rainforest. Stridently ecological in its message, this offers first-rate Disney-esque animation, a couple of sassy rock songs, and a delightfully cracked creature voiced by Robin Williams.
D: Bill Kroger. Voices: Robin Williams, Samantha Mathis, Tim Curry.

Rock-a-Doodle
(1992) 74m. **B–**
This tale of a rooster who is laughed off the farm and makes it big in Las Vegas is a confusing mishmash of live action and animation. Too much gets in the way of some imaginative Elvis-style Vegas production numbers.
D: Don Bluth. Voices: Glen Campbell, Christopher Plummer, Phil Harris.

The Lion King
(1994) 88m. **A**
Impetuous lion cub Simba enjoys his carefree childhood, until he's tricked into believing he's responsible for the death of his father the king. A beautifully rendered coming-of-age fable with rich jungle colors, memorable songs, slapstick for the kiddies, and witty lines for the adults.
Voices: James Earl Jones, Matthew Broderick, Jonathan Taylor Thomas.

Thumbelina
(1994) 87m. **C+**
The thumbsized girl in search of her winged fairy prince is kidnapped and endures the lecherous frog, the conniving beetle, and a marriage-minded mole. Some gorgeous animation suffers from a surfeit of characters, haphazard plotting, and far too many syrupy ballads.
D: Don Bluth and Gary Goldman. Voices: Jodi Benson, Gino Conforti, Gilbert Gottfried.

Pocahontas
(1995) 81m. **B–**
History gets nowhere near this lively but whitewashed version of the Pocahontas legend that still manages to bend over backward in its politically correct stance portraying Indians as brave and noble (but boring) and the English as greedy slobs. Minimalist animation looks more like an attempt to get by on the cheap rather than a style choice.
D: Mike Gabriel and Eric Goldberg. Voices: Irene Bedard, Mel Gibson, David Ogden Stiers.

Modern Animation

While Disney still dominates the market for big splashy animated musicals, a brace of new filmmakers are now producing these cartoon adventures that have much of the detail, fluid movement, and rich coloring that marked the classics from the 30s and 40s.

A Man Called Flintstone
(1966) 87m. **C+**
The Stone Age suburbanite has to complete a look-alike superspy's mission in this cartoon cash-in on the James Bond craze. Cute twists on the spy clichés—gadgets made of stone, femme fatales in animal skins—but the songs are lame and the limited animation techniques give it the look of an extended TV episode.
D: William Hanna and Joseph Barbera. Voices: Alan Reed, Mel Blanc, Jean Vanderspyl.

A Boy Named Charlie Brown
(1969) 85m. **B–**
The whole Peanuts gang looks and acts pretty much like their TV special and

comic strip selves as Charlie keeps trying but comes up short, Lucy is egocentric, Snoopy prankish, and Linus the center of reason. Film keeps the signature jazzy score but adds a bucket load of banal Rod McKuen songs.
D: Bill Melendez. Voices: Peter Robbins, Glenn Gilger.

The Secret of NIMH
(1982) 82m. **B–**
First feature by a breakaway band of Disney animators produces painterly worlds enlivened by colors and textures, however the odd and disturbing story about superintelligent rats vs. bad rats shortchanges kids on humor, fun, and fantasy and is even harrowing at times.
D: Don Bluth. Voices: Dom DeLuise, John Carradine, Derek Jacobi.

An American Tail
(1986) 80m. **B–**
An attempt at socially conscious entertainment follows a nineteenth-century Russian mouse, driven by pogroms to seek a new life in America. Rich animation fuels the scenes of the darker sides of the immigrant experience—grim ghettos, sweatshops—but the story is crammed with too many characters and issues for a kids' film.
D: Don Bluth. Voices: Philip Glasser, Dom DeLuise, Christopher Plummer.

The Land Before Time
(1988) 73m. **B**
A pack of young orphan dinosaurs cope with the perils of volcanoes, the desert, and a vicious Tyrannosaurus Rex on their journey to the peaceful and food-rich Great Valley. Has beautiful animation and, even if the story isn't much, the kids will enjoy an exciting adventure with dinosaurs their own age.
D: Don Bluth. Voices: Pat Hingle, Gabriel Damon, Candice Houston.

All Dogs Go to Heaven
(1989) 85m. **C**
A rather ratty kids' cartoon despite the redemptive ending, this follows the doggy underworld of 1930s New Orleans populated with too few really nice characters. Bluesy slum settings colorfully rendered fail to hide a dull and aimless script featuring some truly bad songs.
D: Don Bluth. Voices: Burt Reynolds, Judith Barsi, Dom DeLuise.

Jetsons: The Movie
(1990) 82m. **C**
No better and no worse than the TV series featuring George and his family who live in an overgadgeted, button-pushing future, this does offer some well done but badly matched computer generated space flight scenes, a few uninspired songs by singer Tiffany, and a tacked-on, feel-good ecology message.
D: William Hanna and Joseph Barbera. Voices: George O'Hanlon, Mel Blanc, Tiffany.

An American Tail: Fievel Goes West
(1991) 75m. **C+**
The plucky Russian Jewish mouse Fievel gets the family to leave the New York slums for the promise of a better life out West, but it's all part of a scheme by a wicked cat to exploit their labor. Another Bluth production of impeccable visual quality, but too many diversions and dull songs short-circuit the story.
D: Phil Nibbelink and Simon Wells. Voices: Philip Glasser, Amy Irving, Dom DeLuise.

Early Kids' Classics

Whether facing up to pirates, wolves, or maybe just the little girl down the road, the plucky youngsters in these early costume kid films seem ready for any challenge. The stories, based on classic books, are filled with themes of duty to flag, friendship, and family as the young heroes and heroines come of age in a comforting golden yesteryear.

Anne of Green Gables
(1934) 79m. B&W. **B–**
On turn-of-the-century Prince Edward Island, a freckle-faced orphan Anne is reluctantly taken in by an older couple but soon her inquiring mind and high energy warms their hearts and lights up the countryside. Young girls will empathize with Anne's desire to experience and consume all around her in this dated-looking but enjoyable tale.
D: George Nicholls, Jr. A: Anne Shirley, Tom Brown, O. P. Heggie.

Treasure Island
(1934) 105m. B&W. **B**
A young sea lad sets piratical things in motion when he gets involved with some treasure map-hunting rogues who wind up on Skeleton Island. The classic kids and pirates story has every peg leg and parrot-on-the-shoulder cliché in place with Beery delivering a boozy and happily evil turn as Long John Silver.
D: Victor Fleming. A: Jackie Cooper, Wallace Beery, Lionel Barrymore.

Little Men
(1935) 77m. B&W. **C**
This weepy semisequel to *Little Women* follows the 1870s lads at Plumfield School for Boys, particularly two street kids who wreak havoc with its proper Victorian order. Has too much *Little Women*-ish chatter about feelings, and boy viewers may squirm and shout "Why is everyone always crying?."
D: Phil Rosen. A: Ralph Morgan, Erin O'Brien, Junior Durkin.

The Jungle Book
(1942) 115m. B&W. **C+**
Raised by wolves, Indian lad Mowgli may be at home facing down panthers and tigers, but he's on alien ground when coping with a pack of thieves and a deadly tribal leader. Rousing version of Kipling's tale, even if the clipped language does get a little monotonous.
D: Zoltan Korda. A: Sabu, John Qualen, Joseph Calleia.

The Adventures of Tom Sawyer
(1938) 91m. **B+**
This version scoops whole colorful portions out of Mark Twain's classic with appreciation and detail. Mississippi may look like a backlot and the boys' rough country lingo toned down, but as adventuresome fun with a couple of barefoot scamps it remains a colorful nostalgic lark.
D: Norman Taurog. A: Tom Kelly, May Robson, Jackie Moran.

The Secret Garden
(1949) 92m. B&W/with color. **B+**
A fulfilling tale of despair

and redemption as a young orphan girl tends to and revives her grieving uncle's forbidden garden and his invalid son. Set in a dark and sullen Victorian mansion, each character's suffering is presented with restrained clarity while the garden sequences bloom in glorious color.
D: Fred M. Wilcox. A: Margaret O'Brien, Herbert Marshall, Elsa Lanchester.

(See also *Little Women,* pages 156, 179, and 254.)

Dogs and Horses (1940s)

In these unabashedly sentimental tales that celebrate the bond between a child and a beloved pet, even adults can enjoy a pang of nostalgia for simpler times.

Lassie Come Home

(1943) 88m. **B+** 🏛

A poor Yorkshire family sells their son's beloved collie to the local Duke who later moves him to Scotland, but Lassie escapes and makes a heroic journey back to his true master. A shameless heart-tugger but presented with such earnestness and good cheer that it's liable to win over non-dog-lovers.
D: Fred M. Wilcox. A: Roddy McDowall, Donald Crisp, Dame May Whitty.

My Friend Flicka

(1943) 90m. **B**

One of the best "I'll show them" kids' film as a rancher's daydreaming son chooses a bad-tempered colt as his own (much to his father's disappointment) but slowly hones Flicka into a fine horse. An engaging tale that captures the youthful enthusiasm and energy that only young kids on a mission can generate.
D: Harold Schuster. A: Roddy McDowall, Preston Foster, Rita Johnson.

National Velvet

(1944) 123m. **A** 🏛

A rare children's film with something for nearly everyone, this follows the adventures of a British village lass who's mad about horses, trains one, and enters him into the Grand National Steeplechase. With its lively depiction of village family life and training scenes, this makes an enjoyable coming-of-age/family drama and rousing sports tale.
D: Clarence Brown. A: Elizabeth Taylor, Mickey Rooney, Donald Crisp.

Son of Lassie

(1945) 100m. **C+**

Hollywood wheeled out its heroes to fight World War II, including Lassie who joins his RAF pilot master on a mission. When they get separated in Norway, Lassie eludes grenades, search dogs, and Nazis to rejoin Lawford in this wartime feel-good entry.
D: S. Sylvan Simon. A: Peter Lawford, Donald Crisp, Nigel Bruce.

The Yearling

(1946) 135m. **A–** 🏛

A sensitive and deeply felt study of a boy's attachment to a fawn and his difficult path to maturity on a nineteenth-century Florida farm. While there are elements of humor and family fun, this is remarkable for showing the hardships endured by "working people" and some truly sad life lessons.
D: Clarence Brown. A: Gregory Peck; Claude Jarman, Jr.; Jane Wyman.

Challenge to Lassie

(1949) 76m. **B**

Lassie's master (now a kindly old shepherd) dies and by Scottish law the collie will be destroyed unless a tavern keeper can prove he should get the pooch. The humans will warm your heart, even if the townspeople behave more like fans of Lassie than concerned citizens.
D: Richard Thorpe. A: Edmund Gwenn, Geraldine Brooks, Donald Crisp.

Dogs and Horses (1950s–1990s)

The loyalty of dogs and the wild grace of horses have always appealed to us, and it's not only the kiddies who thrill to these clear uncomplicated adventures in which humans, especially adults, take a back seat to the world of animals.

Dogs

Old Yeller

(1957) 83m. **B+** 🏛

The noble stray dog becomes the beloved pet of two young boys and a valuable helper on their Texas farm. When Old Yeller heroically saves one of them from wild hogs, he contracts rabies and everyone knows what happens next. Even if you haven't lost a pet, get the hankies ready for this one.
D: Robert Stevenson. A: Dorothy McGuire, Tommy Kirk, Kevin Corcoran.

The Shaggy Dog

(1959) 104m. B&W. **C+**

There's a hint of 50s Cold War paranoia in this bland family comedy/fantasy when a teenager is able to change himself into a sheep dog and learns that his neighbors have stolen missile plans to sell to the enemy. Disney's version of a caper in white-bread Middle America with inoffensive goofy slapstick.
D: Charles Barton. A: Fred MacMurray, Tommy Kirk, Annette Funicello.

The Incredible Journey

(1963) 80m. **A**

This animal road film follows two determined dogs and a cat as they track through rugged Canadian wilderness to return home. A porcupine strikes, a bear blocks their path, and the trio is aided by a little girl, a kindly hermit, and gentle farmers. The animals and landscapes are wonderful, although the chirpy narrator can get cloying.
D: Mickey McCardle. Narration: Rex Allen.

Benji

(1974) 87m. **B–**

Scruffy, all-action mutt Benji steals the hearts of Dr. Chapman's kids until his heart is stolen by female dog Tiffany. A hapless band of kidnappers grabs the kids and it's Benji to the rescue. The music is pure syrup and the film has a TV-movie quality,

but Benji does project an underdog spunk.
D: Joe Camp. A: Christopher Connelly, Cynthia Smith, Benji.

The Adventures of Milo and Otis
(1989) 76m. **B**
Milo the kitten and Otis the pup explore every nook of their farm. When Milo gets washed down a river, Otis follows and the pair work their way back, encountering animal perils, bad weather, and love. Lingers on details like the stream sounds and a kitten studying a bird, with affable narration by Moore.
D: Masanori Hata. A: Narration: Dudley Moore.

White Fang
(1991) 104m. **B**
The frozen Klondike in the late 1800s is the setting for this adventure teaming young Jack who has inherited his dad's gold mine and White Fang, the half-wolf, half-dog. This is solid family adventure on the high side of realism with grizzled prospectors, angry bears, and wolf pack battles.
D: Randal Kleiser. A: Klaus Maria Brandauer, Ethan Hawke, Susan Hogan.

Beethoven
(1992) 89m. **B**
A tame but entertaining suburban family and doggy tale follows a lumbering, slobbering, and ultralovable hulk of a St. Bernard who messes up the ordered life of family man Grodin while straightening out his soul. Features all the requisite dog drool jokes, a drowning rescue scene, and villains out to test bullets on Beethoven's beefy hide.
D: Brian Levant. A: Charles Grodin, Bonnie Hunt, Nicholle Tom.

Homeward Bound: The Incredible Journey
(1993) 84m. **B+**
Three loyal family pets left at a friend's ranch decide to make the journey home across the Sierra Nevadas. The Disney eye for gorgeous natural scenery remains in this remake of *The Incredible Journey* with added snappy animal dialogue that's most amusing when misinterpreting human actions.
D: Duwayne Dunham. Voices: Michael J. Fox, Don Ameche, Sally Field.

Lassie
(1994) 92m. **B–**
A family moving to Virginia finds a homeless collie along the way that becomes the young son's best friend and protector. A faithful and tasteful updating of the legend has graceful Lassie combing more grassy hills than Julie Andrews did in *The Sound of Music,* but the kids should like it.
D: Daniel Petrie. A: Thomas Gury, Helen Slater, Frederic Forrest.

Horses

Black Beauty
(1971) 90m. **B**
An episodic, turn-of-the-century adventure of a gallant horse who travels throughout Europe and India under different masters. Expert period costumes for the German circus and war scenes in India, but the human drama still takes a back seat to the jet black athletic animal.
D: James Hill. A: Mark Lester, Walter Slezak, Ursula Glas.

International Velvet
(1978) 125m. **C**
This pallid updating finds Velvet Brown tutoring her fiery American niece for the British Olympic Riding Team. Everyone looks good in their riding tweeds, but the characters are bland and the riding events are surprisingly reserved and dull.
D: Bryan Forbes. A: Tatum O'Neal, Anthony Hopkins, Christopher Plummer.

The Black Stallion
(1979) 117m. **B+**
A shipwrecked boy and stallion develop a special bond on a desert island, which continues when they return to the States and train for the big race. Some fresh and almost poetic moments as young Alec and the horse romp on the island followed by a vigorous and straightforward portrayal of preparing for competition.
D: Carroll Ballard. A: Kelly Reno, Teri Garr, Mickey Rooney.

The Black Stallion Returns
(1983) 93m. **C**
The prized Black Stallion is stolen by Arabs and brought to Morocco, with teenage Alec hot in pursuit. Includes nice scenes of horses galloping over stark and sandy terrain, but the slim plot is saturated with Arabs spouting tales of ritual, lore, and ancient rivalry, making them more tedious than threatening.
D: Robert Dalva. A: Kelly Reno, Vincent Spano, Woody Strode.

Other Creatures

Flipper
(1963) 90m. **B–**
A boy and a dolphin become best buddies, but dad disapproves and drives the swimming mammal away. Flipper returns the favor by saving the boy from a shark attack and leads the family to better fishing waters in this straightforward, kid-oriented tale shot in the Florida Keys.
D: James B. Clark. A: Chuck Conners, Kathleen Maguire, Luke Halpin.

Born Free
(1966) 95m. **B+**
A heartwarming true-life story of lion cubs raised in Kenya by a British game warden and his wife Joy. Comic scenes blend with ones of raw beauty as Elsa the lioness becomes so domesticated that Joy must teach her the harsh ways of the jungle in order to return her to her natural habitat.
D: James Hill. A: Bill Travers, Virginia McKenna, Geoffrey Keen.

The Bear
(1989) 93m. **A**
The British Columbia mountains are the setting for this often elegant, sometimes whimsical nature film about an orphaned bear cub taken in by a male Kodiak bear. The cub eats some intoxicating mushrooms and receives survival lessons from the Kodiak, who also teaches some hunters a lesson in humanity.
D: Jean-Jacques Annaud. A: Jack Wallace, Tcheky Karyo.

Free Willy
(1993) 120m. **B**
A boy-and-his-pet theme gets bigger and wetter here as a rebellious foster child becomes best friends with a sea-park whale that greedy management plans to kill for the insurance money. An entertaining and visually impressive bonding film that manipulates viewers' emotions with lifeless precision.
D: Simon Wincer. A: Jason James Richter, Lori Petty, August Schellenberg.

Kids Musicals

Excepting *The Wizard of Oz*, these musicals tend to be over-inflated, overlong costume affairs that minimally involve one or two nondescript kids. While heavy on the whimsy and sunny charm, they generally have ordinary songs and dances that inexplicably, given the average youngster's attention span, seem to go on forever.

The Wizard of Oz

(1939) 101m. B&W & Color. **A** 🏛 ♫

A cyclone blows Dorothy over the rainbow where she journeys to Oz in the company of the Scarecrow, the Tin Man, and the Cowardly Lion, with the Evil Witch in pursuit. This has the timeless magic and dark foreboding tone of a Grimm fairy tale mixed with Hollywood show-biz songs, surreal images, and a tremulous and heartrending Garland.
D: Victor Fleming. A: Judy Garland, Ray Bolger, Bert Lahr.

Tom Thumb

(1958) 98m. **B–**

Athletic Tom Thumb is the tiny lad in a mythical Bavarian-looking land who gets used for criminal purposes by comic villains. A cute, wooden, and strictly for the kids film with a nice (but long) sequence of Tom dancing with the big toys and amusing turns by Sellers and Thomas.
D: George Pal. A: Russ Tamblyn, Peter Sellers, Terry-Thomas.

Babes in Toyland

(1961) 105m. **C+**

A villain wants to marry heiress Mary Quite Contrary, but is foiled by the dashing hero and the wooden soldiers. It's got the same adult whimsy as when Dorothy was in Oz City, without the charm or energy.
D: Jack Donohue. A: Tommy Sands, Annette Funicello, Ray Bolger.

Mary Poppins

(1964) 139m. **A** 🏛 ♫

A magic-empowered nanny teaches a buttoned-down banker and his sweetly neglectful suffragette wife how to make time for their children. Even with the sugar coating, this has snappy music, lively characters, and charmingly stylized details of Edwardian England.
D: Robert Stevenson. A: Julie Andrews, Dick Van Dyke, Ed Wynn.

Doctor Dolittle

(1967) 152m. **B–** ♫

A veterinarian and champion of animal rights takes his favorite creatures and humans in search of a giant snail. The scenes in a Victorian English village are really lovely and the music is good, but it's so long you can almost hear the air seeping out.
D: Richard Fleischer. A: Rex Harrison, Samantha Eggar, Anthony Newley.

The Happiest Millionaire

(1967) 118m. **B–**

A loving but eccentric family comes under scrutiny when their daughter falls in love with the son of straightlaced New Yorkers. The bland story is helped out by the ice peppermint-colored, turn-of-the-century costumes and sets in the likable and overlong film.
D: Norman Tokar. A: Fred MacMurray, Tommy Steele, Greer Garson.

Chitty Chitty Bang Bang

(1968) 145m. **B–** ♫

An early twentieth-century inventor builds a car that can fly and float, and off he goes with the kids to a mythical European country ruled by a king who hates children. Particularly nasty villains and nice European scenery make this enjoyable.
D: Ken Hughes. A: Dick Van Dyke, Sally Ann Howes, Lionel Jeffries.

Bedknobs and Broomsticks

(1971) 117m. **B**

A kindly witch travels with her young charges to obtain the spell which will save Britain from Nazi invasion. Spirited with animation/live-action scenes, but the invasion sequence showing enchanted suits of armor attacking Nazis goes on way too long.
D: Robert Stevenson. A: Angela Lansbury, David Tomlinson, Roddy McDowall.

Shirley Temple

Shirley could sell a song more seductively than Betty Boop, but many of her films were simple melodramas about a plucky orphan or resourceful child who redeems every adult within shouting distance. Like her musical outings, the earlier films haven't aged well, looking like the cheap quickies that they were. But with or without enduring production values, you can always count on pristine values, shameless sentimentality, an occasional song, and the eerily adorable tyke herself, who makes it all work.

Baby Take a Bow

(1934) 76m. B&W. **C**

In a film designed to be viewed by moms and their very little daughters, Shirley plays the tot of an ex-convict who's falsely accused of stealing his rich employer's pearls. Shirley charms everyone, enjoys her simple spartan birthday party on a tenement rooftop, and unmasks the real culprit.
D: Harry Lachman. A: With Claire Trevor, James Dunn, Ray Walker.

Bright Eyes

(1934) 84m. B&W. **B–**

Shirley endures the taunts of the nasty rich Smythe girl while mom maids for the family. Suddenly mom dies and Shirley is caught in an adoption battle involving a rich Smythe uncle. Includes one three-hanky scene, and Shirley sings her trademark song "On the Good Ship Lollipop."
D: David Butler. A: With Jane Withers, James Dunn, Jane Dawell.

Little Miss Marker

(1934) 80m. B&W. **B+** 📖

Her father uses her as a marker with the underworld and, after he commits suicide, Shirley quickly worms

her way into the hearts of the hard-boiled crew. Brimming with ultracute moments and calculated sentimentality, including Shirley in the hospital needing rare blood.
D: Alexander Hall. A: With Adolph Menjou, Dorothy Dell, Charles Bickford.

Our Little Girl
(1935) 63m. B&W. **D+**
When her parents have marital problems, distraught Shirley runs away to join the circus, gets critically injured, and surgeon dad must work to save her life on the operating table. Family restored! The agonizing tempo of this domestic melodrama makes the one hour feel like three.
D: John Robertson. A: With Joel McCrea, Rosemary Ames, Lyle Talbot.

Heidi
(1937) 87m. B&W. **B−**
Heidi no sooner melts the heart of her grumpy grandfather with whom she's gone to live in the Swiss Alps, then her nasty old aunt decides to sell her to the gypsies. Shirley also offers aid to a blind woman, helps a crippled girl walk, *and* sings "In Our Little Wooden Shoes."
D: Allan Dwan. A: With Jean Hersholt, Arthur Treacher, Helen Westley.

Wee Willie Winkie
(1937) 105m. B&W. **B+**
Shirley melts her stony-hearted grandfather who's a British colonel guarding the Khyber Pass, reforms a drunken Scots sergeant and, when war with India is on the horizon, negotiates a treaty with the rebel leader. A bigger-budgeted entry with Rudyard Kipling's tale cuted down to Shirley's size.
D: John Ford. A: With C. Aubrey Smith, Victor McLaglen, Cesar Romero.

The Little Princess
(1939) 94m. **B+**
This Victorian weeper in Technicolor finds Shirley reduced to servant status at her stuffy girls' school after her British officer dad, who's off fighting the Boers, is presumed dead. Shirley dances with a music hall performer, keeps wounded soldiers smiling, and even meets Queen Victoria.
D: Walter Lang. A: With Richard Greene, Anita Louise, Cesar Romero.

Susannah of the Mounties
(1939) 73m. B&W. **C+**
An Indian raid leaves Shirley parentless and in the hands of a Royal Canadian whom she teaches to dance to get his girl. She also negotiates a peace treaty with the Indians and does an amusing war whoop dance with the young son of Chief Big Eagle.
D: William A. Seiter. A: With Randolph Scott, Martin Goodrider, Margaret Lockwood.

Miss Annie Rooney
(1942) 85m. B&W. **C−**
Shirley's a budding teen talking jive lingo who stands by her dad even after his demonstration for synthetic rubber goes up in smoke. This bland, wrong-side-of-the-tracks story tries to ease Shirley into a teen role, complete with her first kiss (more like a peck really) and lots of forced hep-cat talk.
D: Edwin L. Marin. A: With Guy Kibbee, William Gargan, Peggy Ryan.

Historical and Literary Films

There's a bright-eyed sheen and rich colors in these mostly swashbuckling adventures that offer clear lines between good and evil, along with plenty of costumed action and danger that won't scare the little ones. Good choices for youngsters taking their first steps out of Barneyland.

Treasure Island
(1950) 96m. **B+**
It's mutiny on the high seas and quest for treasure in this colorful, scenic, and occasionally violent version of the Stevenson classic; if you're looking for one good pirate adventure that the whole family will enjoy, this will have you chirping "pieces of eight" like a parrot.
D: Byron Haskin. A: Robert Newton, Bobby Driscoll, Basil Sydney.

The Story of Robin Hood and His Merrie Men
(1952) 84m. **B**
A by-the-letters, Disneyfied telling of the famous myth has less derring-do than in the superior Errol Flynn version, but it plays passably well as a kids' introduction to the story. Little subtlety to motives and bright Technicolor sets and clothes add to the cartoonishness of the whole affair.
D: Ken Annakin. A: Richard Todd, Joan Rice, Peter Finch.

Kidnapped
(1960) 97m. **B**
Small-scale but adventuresome boys' tale follows a young eighteenth-century Scottish heir who is kidnapped and cast into shipboard slavery where he makes friends with a clever fugitive. While not as scenic and teeming with colorful characters as most high seas adventures, the buddy/buddy relations between MacArthur and Finch is enjoyable.
D: Robert Stevenson. A: James MacArthur, Peter Finch, Niall MacGinnis.

Three Worlds of Gulliver
(1960) 100m. **B**
Gulliver tries to leave the ills of eighteenth-century England behind, but first he's shipwrecked in a country of tiny people who want to use him for war; later he finds himself in a land of giants who accuse him of witchcraft. The under-ten crowd will enjoy Harryhausen's effects of a gigantic and a tiny Gulliver, but don't expect any of Swift's satire.
D: Jack Sher. A: Kerwin Mathews, Jo Morrow, June Thorburn.

The Wonderful World of the Brothers Grimm
(1962) 135m. **B**
Old World enchantment pervades this storybook biography of the brothers from Bavaria who devoted their lives to collecting and creating fables. Three fairy tales are presented whose special effects may seem quaint, but the stories retain an innocence that entertains kids and might make adults wistful.
D: Henry Levin and George Pal. A: Laurence Harvey, Karl Boehm, Claire Bloom.

Heidi
(1965) 95m. **B**
One of the few children's classics that doesn't break down when updated; young

orphan Heidi, living with her grandfather on a Swiss Alps farm, is taken to modern Frankfurt where she is placed with rich and crippled Klara. Gorgeous mountain scenery, sweet music, and real child moments make this dubbed German production a treat for the kids.
D: Werner Jacobs. A: Eva Maria Singhammer, Gustav Knuth, Gertraud Mittermayr.

The Jungle Book
(1994) 111m. **B**
Orphaned Mowgli grows up in the Indian jungle and lives in tune with nature until he is captured, civilized, and exploited to find the legendary Monkey City full of treasures. Kipling's story is bent to suit ecological concerns in this big-budget Disney adventure that has enough action and humor to make it work for both adults and kids.
D: Stephen Sommer. A: Jason Scott Lee, Lena Headley, Sam Neill.

Americana

These brisk, richly colored adventures bring American history to life as legendary figures and fresh-faced kids go on quests and adventures that manage to get in a few messages about growing up, without getting all preachy about it.

Davy Crockett, King of the Wild Frontier
(1955) 89m. **B+**
With his awe-shucks charm, keen shootin' eye, and backwoodsman straight-arrow sense of what is right, Davy is the classic Disney hero designed for all the adventure-seeking kids with their coonskin caps. Episodes from this life include meeting Jim Bowie and Andrew Jackson and standing up for Texas at the Alamo.
D: Norman Foster. A: Fess Parker, Buddy Ebsen, Hans Conried.

Johnny Tremain
(1957) 85m. **B–**
The early days of the American Revolution are seen through the eyes of a young apprentice in Boston. Mixing fiction with historical figures such as Sam Adams and Paul Revere and the big event — the Boston Tea Party—you're given a shiny entertaining history lesson on a storybook level.
D: Robert Stevenson. A: Hal Stalmaster, Richard Beymer, Sebastian Cabot.

The Adventures of Huckleberry Finn
(1960) 91m. **C+**
A vividly colorful vision of antebellum South, particularly in its presentation of the bustle of riverboat life on the Mississippi. Unfortunately it pales in its depiction of the scampy Huck Finn who has been sanitized to the point of becoming a redheaded cutie instead of Twain's rutty little troublemaker.
D: Michael Curtiz. A: Eddie Hodges, Archie Moore, Tony Randall.

Toby Tyler
(1960) 96m. **B–**
This sentimental boy-runs-away-to-join-the-circus story is enriched by vivid colors of a turn-of-the-century circus and soft-hearted folk, from the clowns and barkers right down to the chimp. Not for the action-oriented crowd, but the nostalgia is palpable and Toby's so cute he's practically an ad for having boy children.
D: Charles Barton. A: Kevin Corcoran, Gene Sheldon, Henry Calvin.

The Journey of Natty Gann
(1985) 100m. **B–**
Chicago-bred Natty has been left behind by her dad, seeking lumber work out West, so the young lass begins a sojourn across Depression-era America to join him. She hooks up with a young savvy drifter, and together they lead a hobo existence in this finely acted, lively paced adventure.
D: Jeremy Kagan. A: Meredith Salenger, John Cusack, Ray Wise.

The Adventures of Huck Finn
(1993) 96m. **C+**
Slightly hipped-up version of the Twain classic offers a more rough - around - the-edges Huck Finn looking a little too much like a modern toughie rather than a country scamp. Laudable attempt but fails to capture the colorful language, sense of time, and seems distinctly twentieth-century in attitude.
D: Stephen Sommers. A: Elijah Wood, Courtney Vance, Jason Robards.

Disney Adventures

Years before *Home Alone*, the Disney studio was regularly turning out these adventures that featured clever kids and conniving villains, but also parents who were actually benevolent and wise. For adults watching, there's the added fun of seeing old acting favorites getting their second career wind as Disney regulars while the stories themselves are fast and fun-filled with loopy professors, crazy cars, and ghostly pirates.

Darby O'Gill and the Little People
(1959) 93m. **B–**
Thick Irish brogues permeate this wistful story of an old estate keeper who captures the king of the leprechauns hoping to use the wee one's powers to promote a love for his own daughter. The romance drags, but expert effects, lively shenanigans, and a few cheerful tunes (sung by Connery!) brighten the pace.
D: Robert Stevenson. A: Albert Sharpe, Janet Munro, Sean Connery.

The Swiss Family Robinson
(1960) 126m. **B**
The industrious Swiss family are marooned on a desert island but, spirits undaunted,

they assemble lickety-split a fabulous tree home with all the amenities and clever array of defenses that come in handy when pirates are discovered. Low on credibility but high on color and adventure of family togetherness.
D: Ken Annakin. A: John Mills, James MacArthur, Dorothy McGuire.

The Absent Minded Professor

(1961) 97m. B&W. **A–**

Good-natured, distracted Professor Brainard may forget his own wedding day, but he's invented a brilliant blubbery, antigravity substance called flubber that can make anything or anyone fly. Adults and kids both will enjoy the flying cars, high - jumping basketball players, bad guys, and panicky Pentagon in this cheerful caper.
D: Robert Stevenson. A: Fred MacMurray, Keenan Wynn, Nancy Olson.

The Parent Trap

(1961) 129m. **A–**

Mom and Dad divorced 14 years ago but, when their identical twin daughters accidentally meet for the first time at summer camp, the girls switch identities and plot to reunite the folks. Visually bright family comedy made even brighter by Mills' boundless enthusiasm x 2 and some earthly sparks between Keith and O'Hara.
D: David Swift. A: Hayley Mills, Brian Keith, Maureen O'Hara.

In Search of the Castaways

(1962) 100m. **B–**

In this Disneyfied nineteenth-century Jules Verne adventure, a plucky French professor launches a rescue mission in South America for Captain Grant, with the captain's daughter in tow. Volcanoes erupt, deadly Indians hurl spears, and Chevalier croons while a wobbly plot jumps from one adventure to the next.
D: Robert Stevenson. A: Hayley Mills, Maurice Chevalier, George Sanders.

Son of Flubber

(1963) 100m. B&W. **C+**

It worked so well in *The Absent Minded Professor* that the entire cast was reassembled with a retread plot—this time about MacMurray's new invention "dry rain." Milder, far less inventive return engagement.
D: Robert Stevenson. A: Fred MacMurray, Nancy Olson, Keenan Wynn.

The Moonspinners

(1964) 118m. **B–**

Hayley is now old enough to have a teen romance while sleuthing to find a jewel thief after she and her aunt check into the Moonspinners hotel in Crete. Uncomplicated plot is partially filled with travelogue Crete locales, Greek music, and excellent character actors.
D: James Neilson. A: Hayley Mills, Eli Wallach, Peter McEnery.

The Three Lives of Thomasina

(1964) 97m. **C+**

This tells of a stuffy but loving widower vet, his young daughter, her cat Thomasina, and a wild-eyed healer who cures the feline on the brink of its death. Nice nineteenth - century Scottish country scenes with some thick accents to cut through, but the quiet patches and no real punch make this overly mild.
D: Don Chaffey. A: Patrick McGoohan, Susan Hamphire, Karen Doltrice.

That Darn Cat!

(1965) 116m. **B–**

Hayley and her sister's cat wander off in search of food and enter a house where two crooks are holding a hostage; soon the FBI, Hayley, and the Siamese are involved with tracking the kidnappers. It's more white-bread American cuteness in this suspenser that runs too long for a very thin story.
D: Robert Stevenson. A: Hayley Mills, Dean Jones, Roddy McDowall.

Those Calloways

(1965) 131m. **B**

Early environmentally conscious adventure follows a Vermont woodsman and family in their battle against bankruptcy, eviction, and greedy developers to establish a wild geese sanctuary. Idyllic Vermont locales and a real father/son story, along with admirable and tough idealism, make this solid fare.
D: Norman Tokar. A: Brian Keith, Vera Miles, Walter Brennan.

Blackbeard's Ghost

(1968) 107m. **B**

It looks like a coastal hotel, run by kindly impoverished descendants of Blackbeard the pirate, will fall into the hands of a crooked casino owner until the pirate's ghost shows up to save the day. Slow beginning until the buccaneer appears, mugging shamelessly, sabotaging the roulette tables and dancing with local cheerleaders.
D: Robert Stevenson. A: Peter Ustinov, Suzanne Pleshette, Dean Jones.

The Horse in the Grey Flannel Suit

(1968) 112m. **C–**

A frazzled ad executive dad needs a gimmick for his big account and hits on using his daughter's horseback riding mania to save the day. With sitcom plot, frequent dull patches, and poorly matched footage of real equestrian events, this horse story fails to break out of a trot.
D: Norman Tokar. A: Dean Jones, Lloyd Bochner, Diane Baker.

The Love Bug

(1969) 107m. **B**

Endearing slapstick silliness about a down-on-his-luck race driver who buys a little Volkswagen from a dealer because it seems to like him, and the all-loving VW wins race after race. "Herbie" the car gets most of the laughs and the kids will like the stunts, but adults may tire of the continued eye-bugging by the stars. Three sequels are *Herbie Rides Again, Herbie Goes to Monte Carlo* and *Herbie Goes Bananas.*
D: Robert Stevenson. A: Dean Jones, Michele Lee, Buddy Hackett.

The Boatniks

(1970) 99m. **C**

An earnest bumbling coast guard ensign who gets the use of a playboy's yacht must contend with a crowded weekend of pleasure cruisers while trying to find a pack of jewel thieves and woo his girl. There's a relaxed California feel to this one, but most of the humor and slapstick is labored.
D: Norman Tokar. A: Robert Morse, Stefanie Powers, Phil Silvers.

The Barefoot Executive

(1971) 96m. **C**

This poke at TV programming finds last-in-the-ratings network whiz kid using a remarkable chimp to pick winning new TV shows. Standard collection of snarling executives, with the young people and animals really knowing how to handle things. A satire without bite and an even blander story.
D: Robert Butler. A: Kurt Russell, Harry Morgan, Wally Cox.

Napoleon and Samantha

(1972) 91m. **B–**

In this tentative attempt to be more 70s relevant, the kids look scruffier, the hero has longer hair, and nature looks more rustic in this tale about an orphan with a

gummy old pet lion who sets off to find a political science student/shepherd so he can live with him. A workmanlike nature adventure with cute animals and likable kids.
D: Bernard McEveety. A: Michael Douglas, Johnny Whitaker, Jodie Foster.

The Apple Dumpling Gang
(1975) 100m. **B–**
A slick gambler is given three tough-cookie orphans to raise who proceed to find gold with two inept desperados in pursuit of it. A little too amicable for its own good, this comedy-western starts out promisingly but slides into a bland adventure that needs real villains instead of complete slapstick bumblers.
D: Vincent McEveety. A: Bill Bixby, Tim Conway, Don Knotts.

Escape to Witch Mountain
(1975) 97m. **B–**
ESP was hot stuff in the 70s, so Disney gave us two orphans pursued by a millionaire aiming to use their power to predict stock market prices. A kindly retiree and his motor home provide haven as the tykes use mind control to confuse tracking dogs and flip cars in this entertaining caper.
D: John Hough. A: Eddie Albert, Ray Milland, Ike Eisenmann.

One of Our Dinosaurs Is Missing
(1975) 97m. **C+**
In the 1920s a British agent hides some microfilm in a dinosaur skeleton and is captured by Chinese agents, but his ex-nanny and her brigand of cohorts come to the rescue. Ustinov plays the Chinese spymaster as a throwback to 1930s sinister Orientals while Hayes turns up the cute meter as the nononsense nanny.
D: Robert Stevenson. A: Peter Ustinov, Helen Hayes, Derek Nimmo.

Freaky Friday
(1977) 96m. **B–**
A mother/daughter feud gets freaky when they both wish they were the other person and it really happens. Daughter must contend with their housekeeper, bratty brother, and plans for a big dinner; Mom suffers through school and fails at hockey. Fun and slightly weird with a confused slapstick climax.
D: Gary Nelson. A: Barbara Harris, Jodie Foster, John Astin.

Nostalgic Small Town

Pollyanna
(1960) 134m. **A–** 🏛
Eternally optimistic orphan Pollyanna brings good cheer to a small town when she comes to live with her rich but crabby Aunt Polly. A sweet but not cloying story, a bubbly Mills, and a platoon of first-rate character actors populating a fully animated and idyllic 1910s New England town make this still a treat to watch.
D: David Swift. A: Hayley Mills, Jane Wyman, Karl Malden.

Summer Magic
(1963) 100m. **B**
Tuneful frolic follows a fatherless city family that moves into a rural house in a spotless turn-of-the-century Maine in order to save money. Genial Ives helps them get used to the country and sings a few songs as the son gets a butch hair cut, the daughter gets into moony-girlish hijinks, and the mother finds romance.
D: James Neilson. A: Hayley Mills, Dorothy McGuire, Burl Ives.

Follow Me, Boys!
(1966) 131m. **C+**
This cheerful folksy tale follows Lem Siddons as he becomes the driving spirit behind a middle-American Boy Scout troop in the 1930s and 40s. MacMurray brought his TV dad persona to this one intact, but it feels like a two-hour promotional film for the Boy Scout ideal, with the sentiment getting thick toward the end.
D: Norman Tokar. A: Fred MacMurray, Vera Miles, Lillian Gish.

The Muppets

Their voices may be grating and prone to singing less than inspired tunes but, in an age of high-tech computer effects, you can't deny the simple magic of Jim Henson's masterful puppetry in these lighthearted adventures of Kermit, Miss Piggy, and the other fuzzy critters.

The Muppet Movie
(1979) 97m. **B–**
An agent tells Kermit of Hollywood's desperate need for singing frogs so he hits the road picking up various Muppets and running into numerous guest stars along the way. Has a cheerful veneer but needs more than a variety show plot to sustain 97 minutes.
D: James Frawley. Guest Stars: Bob Hope, Orson Welles, Steve Martin.

The Great Muppet Caper
(1981) 95m. **B**
The Muppets loosen up their action and have some genial fun with Hollywood clichés in this London-based jewelry theft caper. Highlights include Kermit and Miss Piggy doing a Fred and Ginger routine, and Miss Piggy taking time out from being wooed by Charles Grodin to swim a water ballet that puts Esther Williams to shame.
D: Jim Henson. A: Diana Rigg, John Cleese, Charles Grodin.

The Muppets Take Manhattan
(1984) 94m. **B–**
Played like one of those "Let's put on a big show" films, this follows Kermit, who is swindled when he takes his college musical to Broadway. Manages to hit most of the Big Apple attractions—Miss Piggy gets mugged—and the grand-scale wedding finale is impressive.
D: Frank Oz. A: Art Carney, Dabney Coleman, Liza Minnelli.

The Muppet Christmas Carol
(1992) 85m. **B**
There's a nice mix of spookiness and gentle humor in this umpteenth version of Dickens' classic, with the Muppets adhering more to the story instead of going off on their usual flights of fancy. Kermit makes a fine good-natured Cratchit and Caine plays Scrooge with some real passion considering he's forever talking to puppets.
D: Brian Henson. A: Michael Caine.

Miscellaneous Kids

The line between "adult" action films and those meant for younger audiences gets blurred, especially in the more recent adventures that feature high-tech special effects and frantic action.

Batman

(1966) 105m. **B**

A quickie cash-in on the popular tongue-in-cheek TV series finds the Caped Crusader and Robin battling The Joker, The Riddler, The Penguin, and Catwoman. An expansion of the in-joke show with milk-drinking, large-gutted Batman spouting do-goodisms and the villains getting all the best lines.

D: Leslie H. Martinson. A: Adam West, Burt Ward, Cesar Romero.

Willy Wonka and the Chocolate Factory

(1971) 100m. **B–**

Skip the first 25 minutes of this distinctly odd and subversive kids' tale, and get right to the factory tour via five kids who explore its wonders and get tripped up by their personal vices like gluttony and greed. Low-budget sets are compensated by some bizarre imagery including a tribe of grim, orange-faced dwarves.

D: Mel Stuart. A: Gene Wilder, Peter Ostrum, Jack Albertson.

Santa Clause: The Movie

(1985) 112m. **D**

Starts out with a whimsical tale of how Santa first came to the North Pole and then degenerates into a long boring story of Patch the elf in New York. More notable for how the filmmakers took all the humor, good cheer, and wonder out of the Santa legend, leaving an expensive-looking tree ornament behind.

D: Jeannot Szwarc. A: Dudley Moore, David Huddleston, John Lithgow.

Prancer

(1989) 100m. **B**

Slow-starting but eventually charming look at childhood innocence as a nine-year-old farm girl rescues an injured reindeer, convinced it is Prancer; when she tells a mall Santa, Prancer suddenly becomes a news story. Holiday fare underrated in how it stays away from magical elements in favor of solid family drama.

D: John Hancock. A: Sam Elliot, Rebecca Harrell, Rutanga Alda.

Teenage Mutant Ninja Turtles

(1990) 93m. **C+**

Four sewer-dwelling turtles are oozed and mutate into super heroes who gobble pizza, talk like beach boys, twirl a mean ninja sword, and are named after Renaissance painters. Forget the plot; fans flocked to see the cartoon champions make the leap to live-action heroes with lots of preteen attitude and heavy kung fu action.

D: Steve Barron. A: Judith Hoag, Elias Koteas.

The Pagemaster

(1994) 76m. **B–**

An overly cautious young boy enters a library and is transported into an animated world where he meets the embodiments of Adventure, Horror, and Fantasy. Laudable for promoting reading with the lad braving the likes of Moby Dick, Long John Silver, and Dr. Jekyll but lacking in any driving force and hobbled by unusually dark animation.

D: Joe Johnston and Maurice Hunt. A: Macaulay Culkin, Christopher Lloyd.

The Indian in the Cupboard

(1995) 96m. **B+**

A boy gets a fantastic present: an antique cupboard that brings to life anything he puts in it, including a small Indian figurine. The tiny Indian becomes the boy's best friend while battling off immense household threats. Some fun *Honey I Shrunk the Kids* special effects make this a quick-paced kids' actioner.

D: Frank Oz. A: Hal Scardino, Litefoot, Richard Jenkins.

Mighty Morphin Power Rangers: The Movie

(1995) 96m. **C+**

Nothing more than an extended episode of the TV series with some clever upgrading of the computerized effects. Adults will quickly zone out from the grating rock score and endless scenes of jump-cut, kung fu fighting and shouts of "hi-yaaa," but the kids love it, for now anyway.

D: Bryan Spicer. A: Jason David Frank, Amy Jo Johnson.

(See also *The Secret Garden,* pages 267 and 388.)

MUSICALS

Musicals Menu

MUSICALS MENU

By the Light of the Silvery Moon

Vaudeville 409

Alexander's Ragtime Band
Rose of Washington Square
For Me and My Gal
Hello Frisco, Hello

Doris Day 409

Romance on the High Seas
It's a Great Feeling
My Dream Is Yours
Tea for Two
Lullabye of Broadway
April in Paris
Lucky Me

Esther Williams 410

Thrill of a Romance
On an Island with You
Neptune's Daughter
Texas Carnival
Million Dollar Mermaid
Dangerous When Wet
Easy to Love

Musical Biographies 410

Yankee Doodle Dandy
Rhapsody in Blue
Night and Day
The Jolson Story
Til the Clouds Roll By
Words and Music
Jolson Sings Again
Three Little Words
I'll See You in My Dreams
Stars and Stripes Forever
Deep in My Heart
Interrupted Melody
The Eddy Duchin Story

Big Band 411

The Fabulous Dorseys
The Glenn Miller Story
The Benny Goodman Story

1950s

Americana 411

Annie Get Your Gun
Show Boat
Calamity Jane
Seven Brides for Seven Brothers
Guys and Dolls
Oklahoma!
Carousel
Li'l Abner
Billy Rose's Jumbo
Gypsy
The Music Man
The Unsinkable Molly Brown

Modern Americana 413

It's Always Fair Weather
High Society
Pajama Game
Damned Yankees

Faraway Places 413

Yolanda and the Thief
The Pirate
Hans Christian Andersen
Kiss Me Kate
Lili
Brigadoon
Kismet
The King and I
South Pacific

(Mostly) Americans in Paris 414

An American in Paris
Lovely to Look At
Funny Face
Les Girls
Silk Stockings
Gigi
Can-Can

Show Biz 414

The Red Shoes
Summer Stock
Royal Wedding
Singin' in the Rain
The Band Wagon
White Christmas
There's No Business Like Show Business
Pal Joey

Sophisticated Romance 415

On the Town
Gentlemen Prefer Blondes
Young at Heart
Daddy Long Legs
The Opposite Sex
Bells Are Ringing
Let's Make Love

Jazz Biographies 416

Color 416

Pete Kelly's Blues
The Five Pennies
Love Me or Leave Me

Black and White 416

Young Man with a Horn
I'll Cry Tomorrow
The Gene Krupa Story

1960s–1990s

Modern Americana 416

Flower Drum Song
West Side Story
State Fair
Bye Bye Birdie
How to Succeed in Business Without Really Trying

Costume Extravaganzas 417

My Fair Lady
The Sound of Music
A Funny Thing Happened on the Way to the Forum
Thoroughly Modern Millie
Finian's Rainbow
Funny Girl
Hello Dolly
Paint Your Wagon
Darling Lili
On a Clear Day You Can See Forever
Fiddler on the Roof
1776
Tom Sawyer
Mame
Funny Lady
Annie
Yentl
For the Boys
Newsies
Swing Kids

British 418

Camelot
Oliver!
Goodbye Mr. Chips
Scrooge

Modern Musicals 419

Sweet Charity
The Boy Friend
Cabaret
Bugsy Malone
New York, New York
All That Jazz
Popeye
Pennies from Heaven
One from the Heart
The Cotton Club

Hoofers 419

Stayin' Alive
A Chorus Line
Tap
Steppin' Out
Strictly Ballroom

Hooray for Hollywood 420

That's Entertainment!
That's Entertainment, Part 2
That's Dancing
That's Entertainment! III

Kids Musicals (See Kids, page 391.)

Animated Musicals (See Kids, page 386.)

Rock 'N' Roll Musicals

Early Days 420

Rock Pretty Baby
Rock, Rock, Rock
Rock, Baby, Rock It
Carnival Rock
Go, Johnny, Go!

Beach Parties 421

Beach Party
Bikini Beach
Muscle Beach Party
Ride the Wild Surf
Beach Blanket Bingo
How to Stuff a Wild Bikini

Nostalgia 421

That'll Be the Day

MUSICALS FILM GROUPS

1930s

Show-Biz Romantic Comedies

This is the make believe world of Broadway hopefuls who, despite the Depression, flit from Art Deco nightclubs to swank rooftop parties without a wrinkle in their evening clothes. Though the plots are silly, the screen is a silvery black-and-white wonderland, as classic tunes by Kern, Gershwin, and Porter fill the air with gaiety and seduction for lovers to dance the night away.

Flying Down to Rio
(1933) 89m. B&W. **C–**
A deadly dull film about an aviator and an heiress until the final 20 minutes blows open with Fred and Ginger's debut in their sensual "Carioca" dance, followed by the famous "Flying Down to Rio" number with chorines in flimsy halters and shorts performing on the wings of biplanes.
D: Thornton Freeland. A: Dolores Del Rio, Gene Raymond, Fred Astaire, Ginger Rogers.

Broadway Melody of 1936
(1935) 103m. B&W. **B**
The best of the "Broadway Melody" series with a story that zips along in radio studios, on rooming house rooftops, and at penthouse parties. Classic musical numbers are recognizable from later incarnations in *Pennies from Heaven* and *Singin' in the Rain*.
D: Roy Del Ruth. A: Eleanor Powell, Robert Taylor, Buddy Ebsen.

Roberta
(1935) 105m. B&W. **C**
More of a slow-paced romance with Dunne trilling a few songs, a bit of dancing by Fred and Ginger, and a French fashion show with knockout 1930s gown.
D: William Seiter. A: Irene Dunne, Randolph Scott, Fred Astaire, Ginger Rogers.

Sweet Adeline
(1935) 85m. B&W. **C+**
A beer garden singer stars in a Broadway show and copes with wicked show-biz types. Darker in tone and plot, with Dunne singing in her high-pitched soprano and two big Busby Berkeley-like numbers at the end.
D: Mervyn LeRoy. A: Irene Dunne, Donald Woods, Hugh Herbert.

Born to Dance
(1936) 108m. B&W. **C+**
This story of dance hall girls and sailors at port drags a little, but is memorable for the lovely music, Stewart warbling a love song on a misty New York evening, and Powell tap dancing on a battleship.
D: Roy Del Ruth. A: Eleanor Powell, James Stewart, Buddy Ebsen.

Broadway Melody of 1938
(1937) 110m. B&W. **B–**
A sophisticated blend of stylized sets and gliding camerawork that follows an airborne Powell and Murphy as they spin and leap about Manhattan streets. Judy Garland sings "You Made Me Love You" to Gable's photo, Sophie Tucker sings "Red Hot Mama," and Yiddish comic actors perform their funny and corny bits.
D: Roy Del Ruth. A: Eleanor Powell, Robert Taylor, George Murphy.

Hollywood Hotel
(1937) 109m. B&W. **C+**
An often funny but overlong satire of Hollywood, with a plot later adapted in *Singin' in the Rain*. Contains only a few songs and one commonplace production number.
D: Busby Berkeley. A: Dick Powell, Rosemary Lane, Lola Lane.

Rosalie
(1937) 122m. B&W. **C+**
A Balkan princess meets a West Point football hero in this romance embroidered by operetta frills. The highlights are the monumental numbers on sets the size of three football fields and some surreal scenes with Frank Morgan as the king who loves his trusty ventriloquist dummy.
D: W. S. Van Dyke. A: Eleanor Powell, Nelson Eddy, Ray Bolger.

Everybody Sing
(1938) 80m. B&W. **C–**
A zany show-biz family is on the skids, but the plucky daughter raises money for their show. The screwball antics wear thin but Garland is a fresh-faced jitterbug.
D: Edwin L. Marin. A: Judy Garland, Allan Jones, Fanny Brice.

Broadway Melody of 1940
(1940) 102m. B&W. **B–**
Has the same gemlike sets of Manhattan's nightclub world as the other *Broadway Melody*s, with the three dancers taking turns being partners and rivals. Mainly a treat for tap dance fans.
D: Norman Taurog. A: Eleanor Powell, Fred Astaire, George Murphy.

Busby Berkeley Backstagers

These proletarian tales of desperate wisecracking entrepreneurs and golddigging chorus girls are a study in bizarre extremes. The acting is wooden, sound tinny, and narration gangster style, before the last reel bursts open into a string of Busby Berkeley's monumental girlie shows where numberless female bodies are fashioned into salacious tableaux vivantes.

Dancing Lady
(1933) 94m. B&W. **B**
With the glossy sets and fancy camerawork, this MGM version of a backstager looks less like an early musical and more like a real drama with spicy scenes between Gable and Crawford and production numbers that lack Berkeley's leering extravagance.
D: Robert Z. Leonard. A: Joan Crawford, Clark Gable, The Three Stooges.

Footlight Parade
(1933) 104m. B&W.
B+
Cagney jazzes up the dramatic portions in this entry that features such Berkeley blowouts as "Shanghai Lil" and "Honeymoon Hotel" with a fantastic underwater and fountain sequence.
D: Lloyd Bacon. A: James Cagney, Ruby Keeler, Dick Powell.

42nd Street
(1933) 89m. B&W. **B–**
The original that launched every cliché—the female lead can't go on, the unknown saves the show and becomes a star—has racier pre-Code banter but, with Berkeley still developing his lunatic style, relatively mild production numbers.
D: Lloyd Bacon. A: Dick Powell, Ruby Keeler, Ginger Rogers.

Gold Diggers of 1933
(1933) 96m. B&W. **B–**
"We're in the Money" kicks off this Depression-drenched tale as starving chorines scheme to get backing for a Broadway show. Bogs down in the middle but finishes off with a Berkeley bang, including a somber "Forgotten Man" number.
D: Mervyn LeRoy. A: Joan Blondell, Ruby Keeler, Dick Powell.

Dames
(1934) 90m. B&W. **C+**
The same gang gives their dialogue machine-gun delivery as they go through some tiresome shenanigans in order to put on the show. Blondell sings "I Only Have Eyes for You" to a washline of men's underwear.
D: Ray Enright. A: Joan Blondell, Dick Powell, Ruby Keeler.

Gold Diggers of 1935
(1935) 95m. B&W. **B–**
Outside of the two lovers, everyone is a money-grubbing chisler at a ritzy resort. A smarmy story opens with a snappy opening number showing the hotel personnel calculating their tips and finishes with a feverish "Lullaby of Broadway" production.
D: Busby Berkeley. A: Dick Powell, Winifred Shaw, Adolph Menjou.

Fred Astaire and Ginger Rogers

The very embodiment of 30s sophistication and urbane charm can be found in the inspired pairing of Fred Astaire and Ginger Rogers. Whether dancing through zeppelin-sized Art Deco suites or dashing head first into a romance full of zany complications, the two never lost their savoir faire while the beauty of their dancing remains a timeless advance-and-retreat mating of two brilliant comrades-in-arms.

The Gay Divorcee
(1934) 107m. B&W.
A–
Rogers mistakes Astaire for a gigolo hired to help her obtain a divorce in an English seaside resort. Has some of the more outlandish sets in the series as the couple carry on their whacky courtship in a Venice constructed of Bakelite, with highlights including the seductive "Night and Day" and rousing "Continental" dance sequences.
D: Mark Sandrich. A: With Edward Everett Horton, Alice Brady, Eric Blore.

Top Hat
(1935) 97m. B&W.
A
Astaire pursues Rogers but she thinks he's her best friend's husband. Features some of their classic numbers like *Top Hat, White Tie and Tails,* and the dreamy *Cheek to Cheek,* in which Rogers wears the white feathered dress.
D: Mark Sandrich. A: With Edward Everett Horton, Helen Broderick, Eric Blore.

Swing Time
(1936) 103m. B&W.
A
The air crackles as Astaire plays a dancing gambler in love with dance instructress Rogers. Contains the breathtaking romantic duet "Never Gonna Dance" in a stylized nightclub and a politically incorrect but beautiful homage to Bill Robinson by Astaire in blackface.
D: George Stevens. A: With Helen Broderick, Betty Furness, Eric Blore.

Follow the Fleet
(1936) 110m. B&W. **C+**
An anomaly in the series with Astaire as a gum-chewing sailor and Rogers as his old flame, a dime-a-dance girl. The comedic dances are pleasant but the film only ignites when they get to play sophisticates in the haunting finale "Let's Face the Music and Dance."
D: Mark Sandrich. A: With Randolph Scott, Harriet Hilliard Nelson, Betty Grable.

Shall We Dance
(1937) 116m. B&W. **B–**
Astaire is the ballet dancer who falls for musical comedy star Rogers. A lesser effort that still has Gershwin classics and some amazing dance sequences—"Let's Call the Whole Thing Off" performed on roller skates in Central Park and Astaire dancing with machines in an ocean liner's pearly white engine room.
D: Mark Sandrich. A: With Edward Everett Horton, Eric Blore.

Carefree
(1938) 83m. B&W. **C**
Less of an Astaire-Rogers musical and more of an unsuccessful attempt at a screwball comedy with some good dance sequences and a slightly strange slow-motion one. Also an early indication of America's love affair with psychiatrists as Rogers falls for therapist Astaire.
D: Mark Sandrich. A: With Ralph Bellamy, Jack Carson, Franklin Pangborn.

The Story of Vernon and Irene Castle
(1939) 93m. B&W. **B–**
Slow-paced bio-pic of struggling, dedicated vaudeville team that hits the big time. When Vernon is killed in an airplane crash, the finale shows Irene dancing with his ghost. Lacks the usual lightheartedness and goofy plot, and the duo's debonaire style never quite connects

with the ragtime songs.
D: H. C. Potter. A: With Edna May Oliver, Lew Fields.

The Barkleys of Broadway

(1949) 109m. **B+**

This reunion film shows the changes that ten years brought to the look of musicals. The surreal black-and-white fantasy sets have been replaced by more pedestrian Technicolored ones, and gone are the brisk tongue-in-cheek repartee; Fred and Ginger are sobered and serious, but they can still dance.
D: Charles Walters. A: With Gale Robbins, Oscar Levant, Billie Burke.

Shirley Temple

Shirley became everyone's favorite orphan or motherless child as she sang, tap danced, and shed tears on cue in this series of pint-sized musicals. While the early low-budgeters are a little worse for wear, the later films have much of the liveliness and catchy tunes of other 30s show-biz musicals.

The Little Colonel

(1935) 80m. B&W w/ color. **C+**

Temple displays stubbornness and a temper as she repairs a rift in her Southern family. Pretty musty, but the apparent scene stealing contests between Barrymore and Temple, along with the famous staircase dance sequence with Bill Robinson, provide interest.
D: David Butler. A: With Evelyn Venable, Lionel Barrymore, Hattie McDaniel.

The Littlest Rebel

(1935) 70m. B&W. **C+**

Temple helps fight off the Yankees in this melodramatic Civil War tale. A likable film that includes a fine tap number with Bill Robinson and offensive racism that dates it more than the scratchy look.
D: David Butler. A: With John Boles, Jack Holt, Karen Morley.

Poor Little Rich Girl

(1936) 79m. B&W. **B–**

Feisty rich girl Temple runs away from her father and joins a struggling vaudeville team. This slicker, more modern and interesting radio show-biz tale includes Shirley singing a precious love song to Daddy.
D: Irving Cummings. A: With Jack Haley, Alice Faye, Gloria Stuart.

Stowaway

(1936) 86m. B&W. **B–**

When Temple's missionary parents are killed in China, she hides on a luxury liner and helps a bickering married couple. Features glamorous setting and Temple singing in Chinese.
D: William Seiter. A: With Alice Faye, Robert Young, Arthur Treacher.

Just Around the Corner

(1938) 70m. B&W. **B–**

Patriotic Temple stages a benefit for a crusty millionaire she mistakenly believes is America's Uncle Sam. A perky satire that skewers the society brats living in the plush apartment building.
D: Irving Cummings. A: With Charles Farrell, Bert Lahr, Joan Davis.

Little Miss Broadway

(1938) 70m. B&W. **B–**

Temple is adopted by the manager of a hotel for actors and organizes a show to save it from foreclosure in this standard show-biz, down-and-outters story.
D: Irving Cummings. A: With George Murphy, Jimmy Durante, Edna May Oliver.

Rebecca of Sunnybrook Farm

(1938) 80m. B&W. **B+**

Snappy little comedy-drama in which Temple becomes a radio star over Auntie's objections, thanks to a shady agent. Features a medley of Temple hits with Robinson on hand for the finale.
D: Allan Dwan. A: With Randolph Scott, Jack Haley, Phyllis Brooks.

OTHER FILMS:
Stand Up and Cheer (1934)
Dimples (1935)
Curly Top (1935)
Captain January (1936)

Miscellaneous Musicals

This mixed bag of early musicals includes Hollywood's first talkie, two Josephine Baker films, a Broadway classic, and two lavish Hollywood showcases. While the early films are fairly primitive, the later ones are gorgeous examples of the best—and the silliest—of Hollywood.

The Jazz Singer

(1927) 89m. B&W. **C+**

A Jewish boy becomes a performer against his cantor father's wishes in Hollywood's first talkie that's mostly silent with a few spoken words and songs. Mainly of historical interest, and as a record of Jolson's performance, but feels like it was creaky even when it was made.
D: Alan Crosland. A: Al Jolson, May McAvoy, Warner Oland.

Roman Scandals

(1933) 92m. B&W. **B+**

Cantor is the country bumpkin who dreams he's in ancient Rome, which looks a whole lot like an elaborately Art Deco, incredibly lascivious Busby Berkeley girlie show. Resembles a filmed vaudeville routine with lots of scantily clad chorus girls and wonderfully absurd production numbers.
D: Frank Tuttle. A: Eddie Cantor, Ruth Etting, Gloria Stuart.

Zouzou

(1934) B&W. 92m. Subtitled. **B–**

In this French version of *42nd Street,* a Parisian laundress struggles to get her brother out of jail, falls for a theater electrician, and ends up starring in the show. The expressive stars and Baker's

inimitable singing and dancing—relegated to the film's end—make up for the tinny sound, hard to read subtitles, and leisurely paced narration.
D: Marc Allegret. A: Josephine Baker, Jean Gabin, Pierre Larquey.

The Great Ziegfeld
(1936) 179m. **B+**
An epic (which means overlong) bio-pic of the showman who dedicated his life to glorifying the American girl. Entertaining even without the gargantuan and finally overwhelming numbers.
D: Robert Z. Leonard. A: William Powell, Luise Rainer, Myrna Loy.

Show Boat
(1936) 110m. B&W. **A**
This moody version of the story about a riverboat lass who marries a no-good gambler is more of a bittersweet slice of Americana told in song than the later glossy MGM remake. Melodramatic and nostalgic, with glorious music and fine performances that make up for the slightly dated look.
D: James Whale. A: Irene Dunne, Allan Jones, Paul Robeson.

The Goldwyn Follies
(1938) 120m. **C+**
A lamebrained story serves as the excuse to show a string of musical and comedy acts, including a Balanchine ballet. The truly bizarre blend of low comedy and highbrow entertainment, along with the hand-tinted color quality, almost makes up for the length and inanity of this entry.
D: George Marshall. A: Adolphe Menjou, Andrea Leeds, The Ritz Brothers.

Jeanette MacDonald

Hollywood's reigning operetta diva was sophisticated, kittenish, and ready to break loose with a soprano trill in any situation. Even nonoperetta fans enjoy her early Lubitsch sex comedies, in which Jeanette climbs in and out of flimsy lingerie or gorgeous gowns while tweetering away in outrageous Art Deco boudoirs. Soon she was singing romantic duets with wooden-faced Nelson Eddy in a series of elaborate and humorless historical melodramas, but somewhere along the way, Jeanette changed from innocent sex kitten to lovely but remote ice princess.

Love Me Tonight
(1932) 96m. B&W. **A**
MacDonald is the French princess who falls in love with tailor-in-disguise Chevalier. A raffish and effervescent *Upstairs, Downstairs* tale with clever and light musical touch.
D: Rouben Mamoulian. A: With Maurice Chevalier, Charlie Ruggles, Myrna Loy.

One Hour with You
(1932) 80m. B&W. **A**
An adult comedy of marital love and infidelity with MacDonald happily married to a Parisian doctor until her best friend shows up. Coy, chic, and innocently risque with a smattering of songs.
D: Ernst Lubitsch, George Cukor. A: With Maurice Chevalier, Genevieve Tobin, Roland Young.

The Merry Widow
(1934) 99m. B&W. **A**
The playboy of a tiny and bankrupt European country is ordered to romance the wealthiest widow. Large and lavish production numbers make this a weightier film with plenty of boudoir scenes and suggestive songs.
D: Ernst Lubitsch. A: With Maurice Chevalier, Una Merkel, Edward Everett Horton.

With Nelson Eddy

Naughty Marietta
(1935) 105m. B&W. **B+**
Jeanette is a princess who is pursued by her family after she falls for the captain of the mercenaries. Stagy Louisiana frontier village is the backdrop for sweeping dramatic songs.
D: W. S. Van Dyke. A: With Nelson Eddy, Frank Morgan, Elsa Lanchester.

Rose Marie
(1936) 110m. B&W. **B+**
Jeanette is the opera star whose ex-convict brother is being pursued by Canadian Mountie Eddy. Steady "suspense" romance with the famous "Indian Love Call" song beneath the trees.
D: W. S. Van Dyke. A: With Nelson Eddy, Reginald Owen, James Stewart.

The Firefly
(1937) 140m. B&W. **C–**
Jeanette is the entertainer/spy in nineteenth-century Spain who falls for another spy with a fine baritone in this plodding story that lacks charm.
D: Robert Z. Leonard. A: With Allan Jones, Warren William, Billy Gilbert.

Maytime
(1937) 132m. B&W.
B+
Opera star MacDonald relives her past love for a penniless singer who she had to forsake for her domineering husband. Has a nostalgic sweetness with all the valentine frills.
D: Robert Z. Leonard. A: With Nelson Eddy, John Barrymore, Herman Bing.

Girl of the Golden West
(1938) 120m. B&W. **C**
MacDonald runs the local saloon in a mining town and falls for Mexican bandit Eddy. Slow and, even for these films, the characters are unbelievable.
D: Robert Z. Leonard. A: With Nelson Eddy, Walter Pidgeon, Leo Carrillo.

Sweethearts
(1938) 114m. **B–**
MacDonald and Eddy are a theatrical couple who have marital problems in this backstage romance. Cute with sumptuous colors and a nice fashion sequence.
D: W. S. Van Dyke. A: With Nelson Eddy, Frank Morgan, Ray Bolger.

New Moon
(1940) 105m. B&W. **B–**
Louisiana plantation owner MacDonald falls for a disguised French duke in revolt in a lavish but overly stuffy costume romance.
D: Robert Z. Leonard. A: With Nelson Eddy, Mary Boland, George Zuco.

Cairo
(1942) 101m. B&W. **C**
MacDonald's swan song for MGM is a ridiculous story of a movie star involved in a spy caper in Egypt where she rescues a war correspondent (not played by Nelson) by hitting a high C.
D: W. S. Van Dyke. A: With Robert Young, Ethel Waters.

I Married an Angel
(1942) 84m. B&W. **B–**
Jeanette is an angel and Nelson a rascally count in this forced, somewhat grotesque film that never seems to begin.
D: W. S. Van Dyke. A: With Nelson Eddy, Binnie Barnes, Edward Everett Horton.

1940s

Show-Biz Romantic Comedies

Smaller in scale than the outrageous 30s musicals, these couldn't be called realistic, but they do take a little more time with the characters and story before jumping to the musical numbers. The sets are sleek and 40s modern, the show-biz folk are still struggling, and the dancing and singing still performed by the Hollywood legends. The ones featuring the Big Bands are more like the *MTV* of their day, providing young audiences with the opportunity to see Artie Shaw and Glenn Miller performing their hit tunes.

Little Nellie Kelly
(1940) 100m. B&W. **B–**
Garland plays a mother and her daughter in this tale of an Irish family in New York. Sentimental and homey, it lacks the sophistication of other films in this group.
D: Norman Taurog. A: Judy Garland, George Murphy, Charles Winninger.

Lady Be Good
(1941) 111m. B&W. **C+**
Quiet little stage play adaptation about a New York songwriting team who marry and divorce several times is really just an airless marital comedy with one Powell dance number and one amplified production finale.
D: Norman Z. McLeod. A: Ann Sothern, Robert Young, Eleanor Powell.

Ziegfeld Girl
(1941) 131m. B&W.
A–
The changing fortunes of three Ziegfeld performers are portrayed as they cope with success, sugar daddies, gangster boyfriends and alcoholism. Closer to a glossy, star-studded women's drama than a musical, even with the spectacular production numbers.
D: Robert Z. Leonard. A: James Stewart, Lana Turner, Judy Garland.

Footlight Serenade
(1942) 80m. B&W. **C+**
A boxing champ chases a soon to be married chorus girl, and the husband to be is cast to fight the champ. Nice meaty, slightly B-film feel with Grable getting mauled by both male leads and dance numbers that are cheaply decorated leg shows.
D: Gregory Ratoff. A: Betty Grable, Victor Mature, John Payne.

Holiday Inn
(1942) 101m. B&W.
A–
One half of a musical duo opens a quaint country inn and the other half arrives to steal the girl and stir up trouble. Classic songs and dancing (including a racist "Abraham" number), with Astaire's adrenaline balancing a tranquilized surly Crosby.
D: Mark Sandrich. A: Bing Crosby, Fred Astaire, Marjorie Reynolds.

You Were Never Lovelier
(1942) 98m. B&W. **B–**
Hayworth is the head-in-the-clouds daughter of a Buenos Aires hotel owner who believes visiting entertainer Astaire is writing her anonymous love letters. Silly plot is saved by the glorious stars and some captivating dance numbers.
D: William Seiter. A: Fred Astaire, Leslie Brooks, Rita Hayworth.

Higher and Higher
(1943) 90m. B&W. **C+**
When a rich man goes broke, his servants help him raise money by marrying off the scullery maid into a wealthy family. A slightly tedious screwballish comedy with Sinatra showing up in the middle to croon a few big band songs.
D: Tim Whelan. A: Frank Sinatra, Leon Errol, Michele Morgan.

Presenting Lily Mars
(1943) 105m. B&W. **B–**
A small-town girl falls in love with the Broadway producer, talks her way into the leading role, and finds she isn't ready for it. A slightly melancholy and almost adult Svengali melodrama lightened up by Judy's singing.
D: Norman Taurog. A: Judy Garland, Van Heflin, Fay Bainter.

Step Lively
(1944) 88m. B&W. **C+**
An innocent playwright gets mixed up with a finagling producer and must take the leading role in his own play to recoup his money. A brisk screwballish farce with Sinatra providing most of the music.
D: Tim Whelan. A: Frank Sinatra, Gloria De Haven, George Murphy.

Big Bands

Second Chorus
(1940) 83m. B&W. **C–**
Two trumpeters go to goofy lengths for spots in Artie Shaw's orchestra while they battle for their manager's affection. The hilarious bits in this musical buddy comedy still can't overcome the film's clunkiness.
D: H. C. Potter. A: Fred Astaire, Burgess Meredith, Paulette Goddard.

Sun Valley Serenade
(1941) 86m. B&W. **B–**
A Glenn Miller band member sponsors a war refugee who turns out to be a shrewd ice skating young lovely who has eyes for him. Mildly humorous comedy with some modest dancing and skating production numbers.

D: H. Bruce Humberstone. A: Sonja Henie, John Payne, Milton Berle.

Orchestra Wives
(1942) 98m. B&W. **B+**
Glenn Miller's orchestra travels cross-country with wives in tow, and one young bride adjusts to the problems of communal life. Serious drama with some good cat fights between the wives, and big band classics like "I've Got a Gal in Kalamazoo."
D: Archie Mayo. A: George Montgomery, Lynn Bari, Carole Landis.

Military Show Biz

You'll Never Get Rich
(1941) 88m. B&W. **C–**
Nincompoop film about a debonaire entertainer who's drafted into the army. Too many stretches of dull military humor and all too brief moments of Astaire and Hayworth dancing.
D: Sidney Lanfield. A: Fred Astaire, Rita Hayworth, Robert Benchley.

Ship Ahoy
(1942) 95m. B&W. **C–**
Showcase style musical featuring Tommy Dorsey and His Orchestra (with Frank Sinatra), Powell tap dancing on another battleship, and Skelton playing the goofball.
D: Edward Buzzell. A: Eleanor Powell, Red Skelton, Bert Lahr.

The Sky's the Limit
(1943) 89m. B&W. **B–**
Somber-toned oddity with fighter pilot Astaire acting like a sinister, slightly nerdy masher in his attempts to charm Leslie. Too few dance numbers and, without his evening clothes, Astaire looks like an angel with clipped wings.
D: Edward Griffith. A: Fred Astaire, Joan Leslie, Robert Benchley.

Here Come the Waves
(1944) 98m. B&W. **C+**
Another reassuring and slightly comic outing with Crosby, who plays a crooner in the navy, with Hutton playing twins so she can be the love interest for both him and Tufts.
D: Mark Sandrich. A: Bing Crosby, Betty Hutton, Sonny Tufts.

Sonja Henie's Ice Follies

These small romantic musicals featuring big band music and a supporting cast doing a few comic turns or song-and-dance routines all have inane plots to get perky Sonja onto the rink. Once she's there, Norway's champion skating star glides, jumps, and pirouettes in production numbers that are like elegant 30s-style Ice Follies.

Thin Ice
(1937) 78m. B&W. **B–**
A prince traveling incognito meets an ice skating teacher on the ski slopes of Europe and romance blossoms on ice. Joan Davis supplies the laughs with her "I'm Olga from the Volga" routine, in the mildly amusing fairy tale.
D: Sidney Lanfield. A: With Tyrone Power, Arthur Treacher, Joan Davis.

Happy Landing
(1938) 81m. B&W. **B–**
A show-biz manager and a bandleader both romance skater Henie in Norway and, when she follows the bandleader back to the U.S., the manager makes her a skating star. Merman is on hand to belt out some tunes.
D: Roy Del Ruth. A: With Don Ameche, Cesar Romero, Ethel Merman.

My Lucky Star
(1938) 81m. B&W. **B**
Store clerk Sonja gets sent to college to model skating outfits while performing at the rink, much to the chagrin of the coeds and the delight of one of the teachers. The silly story is so dumb it's actually entertaining, with an imaginative Alice in Wonderful ice ballet as the highlight.
D: Roy Del Ruth. A: With Richard Greene, Joan Davis, Cesar Romero.

Second Fiddle
(1939) 86m. B&W. **C+**
A Minnesota school teacher is wooed as a publicity stunt when she wins a starring role in Hollywood. With only a few solo and duet skating routines, Henie just can't carry the nonskating portion of the film, compounded by the absence of any exciting skating production numbers.
D: Sidney Lanfield. A: With Tyrone Power, Rudy Vallee, Edna May Oliver.

Iceland
(1942) 72m. B&W. **C**
Henie falls for an American marine stationed in Iceland, and spreads the lie that they're getting married. Tiresome effort lacks the charm of the earlier films with songs like "I Like a Military Man" and "You Can't Say No to a Soldier" that don't help.
D: H. Bruce Humberstone. A: With John Payne, Jack Oakie, Felix Bressart.

Wintertime
(1943) 82m. B&W. **C–**
A skating star uses her talent to save her uncle's Canadian hotel by turning it into a tourist attraction. Woody Herman's band provides the music, but Sonja's ice pond is beginning to melt at this point.
D: John Brahm. A: With Jack Oakie, Cesar Romero, Carole Landis.

(See also *Sun Valley Serenade* page 404.)

Judy Garland and Mickey Rooney

These are the original "Hey, kids! Let's put on a show in the backyard" movies with Rooney and Garland as the plucky breathless, all-American kids with nonstop energy and big show-biz ambitions. The films also happen to be wonderful prewar nostalgia pieces about small towns, patriotism, and optimism. If Garland's wistful ballads or Rooney's histrionics aren't your cup of tea, hold on for the monster Busby Berkeley production numbers.

Babes in Arms
(1939) 91m. B&W. **B+**
Mickey, Judy, and the other children of vaudevillians put on a show to raise money for their families. The highlight is a production number, which is the rallying cry for the series, showing kids marching through backyards, starting bonfires, and demanding recognition for their talents.
D: Busby Berkeley. A: With Charles Winninger, Guy Kibbee, June Preisser.

Strike Up the Band
(1940) 120m. B&W. **B–**
Mickey and Judy go to Chicago with their high school band to audition for big band leader Paul Whitman. Features a surreal, stop-motion animation sequence of an orchestra made up of various fruits and vegetables.
D: Busby Berkeley. A: With Paul Whiteman, June Preisser, William Tracy.

Babes on Broadway
(1941) 118m. B&W. **C+**
When denied a chance to play Broadway, Mickey and Judy stage a show to raise money for the orphanage. The finale includes an intensely patriotic number "God's Country" with the two young stars impersonating FDR and Eleanor.
D: Busby Berkeley. A: With Fay Bainter, Richard Quine.

Girl Crazy
(1943) 99m. **B–**
Rooney is the spoiled playboy who is sent to an all-boys college in Arizona where he falls for the Dean's daughter and then stages a show to raise money for the poverty struck school. Big number includes 100 high-stepping kids in rodeo costumes, but everyone is beginning to look less dewy by now.
D: Norman Taurog. A: With Tommy Dorsey, Nancy Walker, June Allyson.

Technicolor Wartime Musicals

Hollywood turned out morale builders during the war years, so these musicals have an extra dose of sentiment and sunny reassurance. If the big 1930s musicals were black-and-white studies of chorus girls and pianos arranged in cavernous spaces, the 1940s ones are of brightly colored clutter. The format is more of a showcase for star turns, specialty acts, and hectic flag-waving numbers with an occasional ballet or longhair music piece thrown in for class.

Best Foot Forward
(1943) 94m. **C+**
A sunny military school comedy and teen musical has songs sung in packs of three, and dancing limited to the kids jitterbugging to boogie-woogie music at the school dance. Great 40s fashions with the girls wearing ankle-strap platforms and mile-high pompadours.
D: Edward Buzzell. A: Nancy Walker, Lucille Ball, Harry James Orchestra.

DuBarry Was a Lady
(1943) 101m. **D**
A showcase with Cole Porter music, with everyone doing their schtick. To be avoided unless you can sit through Zero Mostel's three minute impersonation of Claude Rains.
D: Roy Del Ruth. A: Lucille Ball, Gene Kelly, Red Skelton.

Cover Girl
(1944) 107m. **B+**
Kelly's the caddish entertainer, Hayworth the self-sacrificing goddess, and Silvers their best buddy. A colorful hybrid that's part old-fashioned show-biz romance and part postwar musical, with song and dance sequences that leave the stage and spill out into the streets.
D: Charles Vidor. A: Rita Hayworth, Gene Kelly, Phil Silvers.

Pin Up Girl
(1944) 83m. **B–**
Bright and determinedly optimistic tale of the romantic entanglements of a dizzy and accommodating navy secretary and a war hero. Military musical finale features Grable yelling orders to an army of women marching in formation.
D: H. Bruce Humberstone. A: Betty Grable, Martha Raye, Joe E. Brown.

Anchors Aweigh
(1945) 139m. **A–**
The war feels like it's over, and these sailors on leave in Hollywood help a singer get her big break. Snappy pacing, solid characters, and the new athletic-style dancing of Kelly all make this feel very modern. Features a dance with Tom and Jerry, Grayson's operatic singing, and Josi Iturbi pounding out some highbrow stuff on the piano.
D: George Sidney. A: Gene Kelly, Frank Sinatra, Kathryn Grayson.

Tonight and Every Night
(1945) 92m. **B–**
The show must go on for this London theater group, even during the Blitz, and wartime romance blossoms between a dancer and an officer. Sombre-toned film has some beautiful dancing and one very strange bit with a dance performed to one of Hitler's speeches.
D: Victor Saville. A: Rita Hayworth, Janet Blair, Lee Bowman.

Ziegfeld Follies
(1946) 110m. **C+**
Showman Florenz Ziegfeld looks down from heaven and imagines MGM stars putting on their own Follies. A studio family showcase that veers out of control at various points with surreally staged production numbers.
D: Vincente Minnelli. A: Fred Astaire, Judy Garland, Gene Kelly.

Showcases

The Hollywood studios did their patriotic bit for the boys with these movie versions of a USO show—the stars performed their trademark routines or let down their hair and played themselves, revealing talent (or lack of) in singing, dancing, comedy, and even magic. These are less musicals than documentaries with a bare bones plot to explain the string of boogie-woogie songs, dances, and a parade of the big name talent of the day.

Private Buckaroo
(1942) 70m. B&W. **C+**
The Andrews Sisters join forces with the drafted Harry James Orchestra to entertain the troops. Poor quality gives evidence that it was rushed into production and lacks the stars of the other films.
D: Edward Cline. A: Joe E. Lewis, Donald O'Connor, Peggy Ryan.

Around the World
(1943) 90m. B&W. **C**
Kay Kyser and His Band entertain the troops in studio sets representing Australia, India, Cairo, and Chung King. Slight film with dopey comedy and a subplot involving enemy spies. The big band music includes titles like "A Moke from Shamokin."
D: Allan Dwan. A: Kay Kyser, Mischa Auer, Joan Davis.

Stage Door Canteen
(1943) 132m. B&W. **B**
Canteen hostesses fall for the soldiers while Ethel Merman, Ethel Waters, Peggy Lee, and Benny Goodman entertain and make patriotic speeches.
D: Frank Borzage. A: Cheryl Walker, William Terry, Marjorie Riordan.

Thank Your Lucky Stars
(1943) 127m. B&W. **B+**
Eddie Cantor plays himself and a cabbie let loose on the Warner Brothers lot. Bette Davis steals the show with her song about the lack of men on the homefront.
D: David Butler. A: Dinah Shore, Joan Leslie, Errol Flynn.

This Is the Army
(1943) 121m. **B+**
Retired soldiers mobilize to restage a patriotic musical for the new soldiers. Among other appearances, Irving Berlin sings one of his songs and Kate Smith whips the crowd into a frenzy with "God Bless America."
D: Michael Curtiz. A: George Murphy, Ronald Reagan, Joe Louis.

Thousands Cheer
(1943) 126m. **B+**
An officer's daughter falls for a tap dancing private, but the plot eventually gives way for a show featuring MGM's stars including Judy Garland and Lena Horne.
D: George Sidney. A: Kathryn Grayson, Gene Kelly.

Follow the Boys
(1944) 122m. B&W. **B+**
George Raft plays a hoofer who mobilizes the Universal studio to entertain the troops. Orson Welles and Marlene Dietrich do a magic act, Sophie Tucker sings a bawdy song, W. C. Fields does a pool table routine, and big bands and orchestras play some popular tunes and classical music.
D: Eddie Sutherland. A: Dinah Shore, Vera Zorina.

Hollywood Canteen
(1944) 124m. B&W. **B+**
Two soldiers on sick leave spend time at the Hollywood Canteen mingling with Joan Crawford, Bette Davis, and other Warner Brothers stars. Hollywood is at its most sincere in this one.
D: Delmer Daves. A: Joan Leslie, Janis Paige, Jack Benny.

Betty Grable Color Tropics

Set in garishly colored and vaguely Latino locales, a silly love story unfolds between the string of interchangeable songs, amazing tap-dancing specialty acts, and extravagant stage shows. The reigning Technicolored sex goddess is the overpainted nonthreatening Betty Grable who offers up her matronly hips and those plump helpless-looking "million dollar legs" to the hero, even as she's puckering up to say no.

Down Argentine Way
(1940) 94m. **C+**
Grable is the rich American girl who falls in love with Argentinian horse breeder Don Ameche. Contains the most lavish production numbers of the series with lengthy nightclub scenes and lots of horse action.
D: Irving Cummings. A: With Carmen Miranda and Charlotte Greenwood.

Moon over Miami
(1941) 91m. **B−**
A glamorous and very stylized Miami resort is where the lovely young fortune hunters try to snag debonaire playboys. The most entertaining entry partly thanks to unusually dopey songs like "Kindergarten Conga."
D: Walter Lang. A: With Don Ameche, Robert Cummings, Carole Landis.

Song of the Islands
(1942) 75m. **C+**
Right after Pearl Harbor became a household name, Victor Mature and Betty Grable's healthy bodies are on display in a Hawaiian movie set as they court and feud. Dull and lacking the crazy energy of the earlier entries.
D: Walter Lang. A: With Victor Mature, Jack Oakie.

Springtime in the Rockies
(1942) 90m. **B−**
A Canadian Rockies resort still has a Latino flavor with Carmen Miranda singing "Chattanooga Choo Choo" in Portuguese, Cesar Romero mixing drinks poolside, and everyone joining in for the frantic Pan-American finale.
D: Irving Cummings. A: With John Payne, Cesar Romero, Carmen Miranda.

African-American Musicals

While racism comes through in these films, they're still the rare studio-made musicals that starred Hollywood's top black performers who were normally relegated to specialty acts and servant roles.

Cabin in the Sky
(1943) 98m. B&W. **A–**

God and the Devil vie for the soul of Little Joe through the influence of the women he loves. This has a magical atmosphere with beautiful production values and gospel-like songs, but beware the not too subtle racism.
D: Vincente Minnelli. A: Eddie "Rochester" Anderson, Lena Horne, Ethel Waters.

Stormy Weather
(1943) 77m. B&W. **A**

This slightly confusing but fast-paced tale of a fictionalized account of Bill Robinson's life is an excuse for jivey, hep-cat production numbers, amazing dance numbers, and some smokey ballads.
D: Andrew L. Stone. A: Bill Robinson, Lena Horne, Cab Calloway

(See also Race Films, page 165.)

Costume Americana

These lovely, garishly colored celebrations of friendly small towns, close-knit families, and other turn-of-the-century American mythologies have a cozier and more intimate tone than the show-biz musical comedies of the 1940s. This is the beginning of the Golden Age of musicals with classic tunes and production numbers that are gorgeous, assured, and scaled down to parlor size.

Meet Me in St. Louis
(1944) 113m. **A**

The film that broke all musical conventions shows an ordinary family expressing themselves in song and dance as they live quiet lives of domestic triumphs, disappointments, and compromises. Classic songs, delightful performances, and beautiful sets help make this a transcendent musical.
D: Vincente Minnelli. A: Judy Garland, Margaret O'Brien, Mary Astor.

State Fair
(1945) 100m. **B–**

A farm family makes its annual trip to the Iowa State Fair and has its share of homey trials and triumphs. Folksy and jolly with a nice love story, sweet songs, and a funny scene with Father singing to his pig.
D: Walter Lang. A: Charles Winninger, Jeanne Crain, Dana Andrews.

The Harvey Girls
(1946) 101m. **C+**

Strange bit of how-the-West-was-won folklore with restaurant waitresses civilizing a town whose cultural center had been a saloon full of prostitutes. The musical numbers try too hard at having a rowdy good time, but the final scene between waitress Garland and saloon madam Lansbury is priceless.
D: George Sidney. A: Judy Garland, John Hodiak, Angela Lansbury.

Summer Holiday
(1948) 109m. **B+**

This warm-colored, slice-of-small-town-life shows Father running the town newspaper and dispensing wise advice to his idealistic and hotheaded son. Contains folksy homespun ensemble numbers and one lurid scene of Mickey getting drunk with painted ladies on the wrong side of the track.
D: Rouben Mamoulian. A: Walter Huston, Mickey Rooney, Frank Morgan.

Easter Parade
(1948) 109m. **B+**

A valentine to old vaudeville in which Astaire trains Garland as his new dance partner while he's pining away for his ex, Miller. Everything clicks from the sweet music and lively dances to the assured performances.
D: Charles Walters. A: Judy Garland, Fred Astaire, Ann Miller.

Good News
(1948) 83m. **B**

This Roaring Twenties college romp takes place a decade after the other films, and the innocence looks a little forced, but the tone is still sentimental and fun. Tuneful songs, lively pace, and a rousing "Varsity Drag" school dance finale.
D: Charles Walters. A: June Allyson, Peter Lawford, Mel Torme.

In the Good Old Summertime
(1949) 102m. **C+**

This musical version of *The Shop Around the Corner* that takes place in old Chicago has all the right ingredients, starts out nicely, and then falls apart halfway through. Garland gets grating and the musical numbers become irritating.
D: Robert Z. Leonard. A: Judy Garland, Van Johnson, Buster Keaton.

Take Me Out to the Ball Game
(1949) 93m. **C–**

This tale of three ballplayers and their team's new female owner has too many grandstanding musical numbers that go nowhere. Esther doesn't swim much, the scale is too big, and the roughhousing too loud for the slight story and ordinary music.
D: Busby Berkeley. A: Gene Kelly, Frank Sinatra, Esther Williams.

Two Weeks with Love
(1950) 92m. **B–**

Delightful pint-sized tale details a family's vacation in a Catskills resort during the summer that the daughter is awkwardly coming-of-age. So light and unpretentious that it can't help being entertaining with a wonderfully absurd fantasy scene of Powell wearing her first corset.
D: Roy Rowland. A: Jane Powell, Ricardo Montalban, Debbie Reynolds.

On Moonlight Bay
(1951) 95m. **C+**

A boy and a girl in a small

town in Indiana fall in love, croon "Cuddle Up a Little Closer," have problems, but Father finally agrees to let them marry. Wholesome and sweet and a little too simple.
D: Roy Del Ruth. A: Doris Day, Gordon MacRae, Leon Ames.

The Belle of New York
(1952) 82m. **D**
A ne'er-do-well playboy gets the work ethic when he falls for a mission worker in this tired and remarkably uninspired effort that still offers a few good numbers.
D: Charles Walters. A: Fred Astaire, Vera-Ellen, Marjorie Main.

By the Light of the Silvery Moon
(1953) 101m. **C+**
In this sequel to *On Moonlight Bay,* Doris and Gordon decide to postpone the wedding, sing "Be My Little Baby Bumble Bee," have more problems, split up, but reunite at the skating party.
D: David Butler. A: Doris Day, Gordon MacRae, Leon Ames.

Vaudeville

These sentimental tales of show-biz troupers from a nostalgic yesteryear rarely leave the stage or dressing room but you still get energetic ragtime songs, romantic misunderstandings, and stage numbers with chorus girls wearing Victorian-era "naughty" costumes.

Alexander's Ragtime Band
(1938) 105m. B&W. **C+**
When a wealthy patron puts together a ragtime band, the singer and songwriter he hires hit the big time. Genial, and the characters don't age a bit over the twenty years during which this showcase for Irving Berlin's songs takes place.
D: Henry King. A: Tyrone Power, Alice Faye, Don Ameche.

Rose of Washington Square
(1939) 86m. B&W. **B–**
This melodramatic tale of a singer who falls in love with a no-account gambler while she rises to fame is suspiciously close to Fanny Brice's story. Likable music and performances—including Jolson's now dated blackface routine—help the slow spots.
D: Gregory Ratoff. A: Alice Faye, Tyrone Power, Al Jolson.

For Me and My Gal
(1942) 104m. B&W.
B+
This tale of a vaudeville team—she's sweet and wants to get married, he's an ambitious cad—has darker edges than the other movie valentines in this group, along with crackling songs and dances.
D: Busby Berkeley. A: Judy Garland, Gene Kelly, George Murphy.

Hello Frisco, Hello
(1943) 98m. **B–**
A quartet plays the saloons of the Barbary Coast before love trouble splits them up in this lushly photographed romp featuring romantic ballads sung by alto-voiced Faye.
D: H. Bruce Humberstone. A: Alice Faye, John Payne, Jack Oakie.

Doris Day

This group of modest romantic comedies lets you watch the big band singer Day evolve from a winsome sedate little hoyden into the breathless perky song and dance comedic star. Everything is by the book here—plot, sets, and music, but Doris sparkles and sings with the creamy voice of a big band pro.

Romance on the High Seas
(1948) 99m. **B**
A wealthy woman asks Day to take her place on a cruise ship and the detective hired by the woman's husband falls for Day. Genial romp with glamorous settings and pleasant songs.
D: Michael Curtiz. A: With Jack Carson, Janis Paige, Don DeFore.

It's a Great Feeling
(1949) 85m. **B**
Doris plays a waitress hired by Dennis Morgan and Jack Carson (who play themselves) in this farcical tale about moviemaking. Includes cameo appearances by a slew of Warner Bros. stars.
D: David Butler. A: With Jack Carson, Dennis Morgan, Bill Goodwin.

My Dream Is Yours
(1949) 101m. **C+**
Doris is a singer who falls for a caddish radio star while her agent tries to get her the big break. Wisecracking and quiet film includes a dream sequence with Bugs Bunny.
D: Michael Curtiz. A: With Jack Carson, Lee Bowman, Adolphe Menjou.

Tea for Two
(1950) 98m. **B–**
Doris is the girl who must say "no" to every question for 24 hours in order to get a part in a play. Incredibly silly story even for this group of films, but Doris dances for the first time.
D: David Butler. A: With Gordon MacRae, Gene Nelson, Eve Arden.

Lullabye of Broadway
(1951) 93m. **B+**
Day is the aspiring musical star who returns to America believing her mother is still a Broadway star. Good score and splashy production numbers make this a cut above others.
D: David Butler. A: With Gene Nelson, Gladys George, S. Z. Sakall.

April in Paris
(1952) 100m. **B+**
Brash showgirl Day goes to Paris and marries the up-

tight government agent who is escorting her. Cute Parisian atmosphere and silly numbers, with a slightly less wholesome Day.
D: David Butler. A: With Ray Bolger, Claude Dauphin, Eve Miller.

Lucky Me
(1954) 100m. **C+**
Superstitious struggling performer Day becomes a Broadway star after silly complications. Ridiculous story really gets tedious, although Day still keeps going and going.
D: Jack Donohue. A: With Robert Cummings, Phil Silvers, Eddie Foy.

Esther Williams

Esther couldn't sing, dance, or even act too well, but she could swim beautifully in a gold lamé suit without ever dimming that 250-watt smile. When the films stray from poolside, they resemble fashion shows with lightweight and often tedious plots centered around various excuses to get Esther back into the water. Once she does, the viewer can enjoy those gargantuan production numbers featuring dozens of swimming chorus girls and every absurd effect imaginable, often courtesy of Busby Berkeley.

Thrill of a Romance
(1945) 105m. **B−**
A bride neglected by her businessman husband on their wedding night falls for a returning war hero. Most of the action takes place by the hotel pool, but Esther barely gets wet. A plodding fluffy romantic comedy that's more of a showcase for the big band numbers.
D: Richard Thorpe. A: With Van Johnson, Spring Byington.

On an Island with You
(1948) 104m. **C+**
A naval officer kidnaps a film actress and takes her to the island where they had met years before. An entertaining showcase of musical numbers by the supporting cast but lacks any big production numbers with Esther.
D: Richard Thorpe. A: With Peter Lawford, Ricardo Montalban, Jimmy Durante.

Neptune's Daughter
(1949) 92m. **B+**
Esther is the bathing suit designer who protects her man-crazy sister from the suave Latin polo player, who she winds up falling for herself. Zippier, with Xavier Cougat music and modest-sized numbers.
D: Edward Buzzell. A: With Betty Garrett, Ricardo Montalban, Red Skelton.

Texas Carnival
(1951) 77m. **B**
Carnival operators have to win the big chuck wagon race to pay their hotel bill, and Esther falls in love with a ranch hand. Less music and more of Skelton's slapstick antics, but there is the scene showing Esther floating around in Keel's hotel room.
D: Charles Walters. A: With Howard Keel, Red Skelton, Ann Miller.

Million Dollar Mermaid
(1952) 115m. **B+**
This bio-pic of swimming vaudeville star Annette Kellerman even has a tear-jerker ending, but it's the incredible smoke-and-fire Busby Berkeley production numbers that keep you watching.
D: Mervyn LeRoy. A: With Victor Mature, Walter Pidgeon.

Dangerous When Wet
(1953) 96m. **C+**
Tedious story of a family of health fanatics whose daughter swims the English Channel to save the farm, managing to fall in love with a rich Frenchman along the way. Esther dreams that she is swimming in a cartoon sea with Tom and Jerry, but it's too little, too late.
D: Charles Walters. A: With Fernando Lamas, Charlotte Greenwood, Jack Carson.

Easy to Love
(1953) 96m. **A**
Esther, working in a Florida tourist attraction, is exploited by her boss and romanced by a playboy singer. She also zips around on water skies and dives from a helicopter in one of the biggest production numbers ever filmed on location.
D: Charles Walters. A: With Van Johnson, Tony Martin.

OTHER FILMS:
Bathing Beauty (1944)
Duchess of Idaho (1950)
Pagan Love Song (1950)
Skirts Ahoy (1952)

Musical Biographies

These rags-to-riches soap operas about legendary show-biz folk feature fictional romances, classic ragtime/vaudeville musical numbers, and some hilariously amplified pathos—the best being that poor boy pianist Eddy Duchin, hired to perform at Fifth Avenue parties, had to enter the mansion *by the servant's entrance*.

Yankee Doodle Dandy
(1942) 126m. B&W.
B+
The patriotic composer, writer, and showman George M. Cohan and his close-knit family were a fitting subject for a World War II-era film. Unabashed flag waving, Cagney's solid performance, and wonderfully eccentric dancing give fuel to this small but lengthy story.
D: Michael Curtiz. A: James Cagney, Joan Leslie, Walter Huston.

Rhapsody in Blue
(1945) 139m. **C+**
George Gershwin's career and his struggle to be taken seriously as a classical composer get the glamorous treatment, featuring num-

bers from his rarely seen "Blue Monday" prototype for *Porgy and Bess*.
D: Irving Rapper. A: Robert Alda, Joan Leslie, Alexis Smith, Oscar Levant.

Night and Day
(1946) 128m. **C+**
Cary Grant plays the bon vivant Cole Porter beautifully, but the film is so superficial, it even skims the surface of his life among the rich and famous. Good numbers help a bland version of a fascinating life.
D: Michael Curtiz. A: With Alexis Smith, Monty Woolley.

The Jolson Story
(1946) 128m. **B+**
The rise of Al Jolson from his boyhood days at the synagogue to his success on Broadway and in Hollywood has nothing but high notes with the real Jolson supplying the singing voice for this sprawling, razzle-dazzle saga.
D: Alfred Green. A: Larry Parks, Evelyn Keyes, William Demarest.

Till the Clouds Roll By
(1946) 137m. **D+**
Modest Jerome Kern enjoys a transatlantic romance as he struggles to achieve success, but surely his life wasn't as dull as this film. Virtually every star on the MGM lot is on hand for the religiously solemn production finale.
D: Richard Whort. A: Robert Walker, Van Heflin, Lucille Bremer.

Words and Music
(1948) 119m. **C−**
Sober family man Richard Rogers hooks up with self-indulgent, wild man Lorenz Hart for a successful collaboration. Nice numbers if you can get past Rooney's tedious hot-dogging.
D: Norman Taurog. A: Mickey Rooney, Tom Drake, Janet Leigh.

Jolson Sings Again
(1949) 96m. **B**
This sequel, picking up Jolson's life in Hollywood when he has a new wife and attempts a comeback, is fueled by the same high-octane energy of the first with nowhere to go.
D: Henry Levin. A: Larry Parks, Barbara Hale, William Demarest.

Three Little Words
(1950 102m. **B+**
The story about the Tin Pan Alley songwriting duo Bert Kalmer and Harry Ruby may be lightweight, but the chemistry between the stars is lively, and the Astaire-Ellen dancing scenes are enchanting.
D: Richard Thorpe. A: Fred Astaire, Vera Ellen, Red Skelton.

I'll See You in My Dreams
(1951) 109m. B&W. **C**
Songwriter Gus Kahn and his entertainer wife split up when her ambitions are stronger than his. A good-hearted but bland show-biz domestic melodrama amid the splashy production numbers from the Ziegfeld Follies.
D: Michael Curtiz. A: Doris Day, Danny Thomas, Frank Lovejoy.

Stars and Stripes Forever
(1952) 89m. **B−**
John Philip Sousa, the model of persnickety and down-to-earth Victorian values leads his military band to international prominence while his tuba player enjoys a clandestine marriage to the band's singer. A colorful, relentlessly patriotic portrait saved from sentimental overload by prim and starchy Webb.
D: Henry Koster. A: Clifton Webb, Robert Wagner, Ruth Hussey.

Deep in My Heart
(1954) 132m. **C+**
The biographical scenes go on a little too long while Ferrer chews the scenery in this big and showy story of operetta composer Sigmund Romberg, but the music and the ragtime details are gorgeous.
D: Stanley Donen. A: Jose Ferrer, Merle Oberon, Paul Henreid.

Interrupted Melody
(1955) 106m. **C−**
Heavy-going drama of opera singer Marjorie Lawrence who battles polio and depression with the help of her devoted husband. Emotional story relentlessly jerks the tears without stinting on the plush settings and opera arias.
D: Curtis Bernhardt. A: Glenn Ford, Eleanor Parker, Roger Moore.

The Eddy Duchin Story
(1956) 123m. **B+**
A first-rate romantic tear-jerker that shows the high society pianist's rise to success with the help of his first wife who dies in childbirth, leaving him with a son. Big and colorful with lots of schmaltz and some nice piano music.
D: George Sidney. A: Tyrone Power, Kim Novak, James Whitmore.

Big Band

The Fabulous Dorseys
(1947) 88m. B&W. **C+**
Jimmy and Tommy Dorsey play themselves in this story of the brothers' rivalry during their ascent to the top of the big band heap. This lower-budget novelty is interesting for the real-life musicians, but the brothers are no actors.
D: Alfred Green. A: Tommy Dorsey, Jimmy Dorsey, Paul Whiteman.

The Glenn Miller Story
(1954) 116m. **B+**
Stewart does his soft-spoken, sweet-natured Everyman to perfection as the famous musician and bandleader, with Allyson as the plucky, ever supportive wife in this elegant-looking bio-pic. Snappy big band music and an easy rapport between the stars make up for the completely bland story.
D: Anthony Mann. A: James Stewart, June Allyson, Charles Drake.

The Benny Goodman Story
(1955) 116m. **B+**
The shy but ambitious clarinetist is so preoccupied with his new sound in music that his socialite girlfriend practically has to nail him to the ground to get a marriage proposal. Almost identical to *The Glenn Miller Story,* with Allen adding his own brand of charm.
D: Valentine Davies. A: Steve Allen, Donna Reed, Herbert Anderson.

1950s
Americana

In the gospel according to Hollywood, this is what made America great: boisterous optimists, pioneers, con artists, the spirit of small towns and the Wild West. Many of the

films listed here are Broadway hits opened up for the silver screen, with showstopping production numbers shot on location. A new style of athletic interpretive modern dancing also makes its appearance here with dance numbers that are jubilant and airborne and musical scores that now match the stories and characters.

Annie Get Your Gun
(1950) 107m. **C+**
Hutton is almost alarmingly spirited as ball-of-fire Annie Oakley who performed in Buffalo Bill's Wild West Show. Boisterous, gaudy, and routine, highlighted by Busby Berkeley's rodeo numbers.
D: George Sidney. A: Betty Hutton, Howard Keel, Louis Calhern.

Show Boat
(1951) 115m. **B**
Monumental and bright MGM remake of the classic tale of a showboat captain's daughter and a Mississippi gambler makes some attempt to portray a little of the racism, poverty, and alcoholism in the story, but those beautiful colors, sumptuous sets, and Hollywood stars keep getting in the way.
D: George Sidney. A: Kathryn Grayson, Howard Keel, Ava Gardner.

Calamity Jane
(1953) 101m. **C+**
Boisterous sharpshooting Doris changes her masculine ways when she falls for pioneering he-man Keel. The best of the rip-roaring western musicals, including some strange scenes with Calamity looking like a thunderstruck suitor with the young woman who's demonstrating the art of feminine wiles.
D: David Butler. A: Doris Day, Howard Keel, Allyn Ann McLerie.

Seven Brides for Seven Brothers
(1954) 102m. **A**
When the eldest brother of a family of mountain men marries, the rest are inspired to spruce up their manners and dancing skills and kidnap their favorite townswomen. An energetic story with a spectacularly athletic dance sequence at the barn-raising, some hilarious tomfoolery between the brothers, and music that matches the barnyard courtships.
D: Stanley Donen. A: Jane Powell, Howard Keel, Russ Tamblyn.

Guys and Dolls
(1955) 150m. **B−**
Stylish, garish, and almost airless version of the zoot-suited gamblers, hopeful chorus girls, and prim Salvation Army officers of Damon Runyon's Times Square folk tales. The nonmusical stars ("Brando Sings!") make for a story that's more than just filler between songs, but also for some endearingly awkward musical numbers.
D: Joseph Mankiewicz. A: Marlon Brando, Jean Simmons, Frank Sinatra.

Oklahoma!
(1955) 146m. **A**
Breathtaking scenes of blue skies and open golden plains become more than just a backdrop for the cowboys and farmers in this *very* wide-screen version of the first "modern" musical whose songs help the story along. Warm and lively with exceptional singing and dancing, highlighted by the modern dance dream sequence.
D: Fred Zinnemann. A: Gordon MacRae, Shirley Jones, Red Steiger.

Carousel
(1956) 105m. **C+**
When a carnival barker in a New England fishing village is killed while attempting robbery, he's given a second chance to return to Earth to help his daughter. This big production of a bittersweet romantic tragedy/fantasy never comes to life with its awkward mix of dance numbers staged on location, lovely ragtime sets and costumes, and a hokey stylized heaven.
D: Henry King. A: Gordon MacRae, Shirley Jones, Cameron Mitchell.

Li'l Abner
(1959) 114m. **B−**
This strange tale of hillbillies trying to stop Dogpatch USA from becoming a nuclear testing site looks like it was torn from the comic page with its lurid colors, cartoon sets, and costumes. Best for its bizarre political satire with show-biz hillbilly music and robust dancing.
D: Melvin Frank. A: Peter Palmer, Leslie Parrish, Stubby Kaye, and Julie Newmar.

Billy Rose's Jumbo
(1962) 124m. **B−**
Spangles and sawdust mix under the Big Top in this bright and lumbering story of circus people at the turn of the century. A cornball story with sweet songs, extravagant production numbers, and circus acts galore.
D: Charles Walters. A: Doris Day, Stephen Boyd, Jimmy Durante.

Gypsy
(1962) 149m. **B+**
Roz is more quirky than killer as the stage mother who trots her two daughters through every American town that has a Vaudeville theater. A nostalgic show-biz family story with a coming-of-age subplot, until the galvanizing final sequences when Natalie is transformed into Gypsy Rose Lee, queen of burlesque strippers.
D: Mervyn LeRoy. A: Rosalind Russell, Natalie Wood, Karl Malden.

The Music Man
(1962) 152m. **A**
Preston is a knockout as the con man/traveling salesman who sweet-talks an Iowan small town into forming a boys' band. A warm entertaining slice of wholesome Americana with mesmerizing cadenced songs that sound like ragtime rap music.
D: Morton Da Costa. A: Robert Preston, Shirley Jones, Buddy Hackett.

The Unsinkable Molly Brown
(1964) 128m. **B**
Denver high society is offended by the flamboyant antics of outspoken, newly rich, backwoods Molly and family. Surprisingly entertaining considering the commonplace music, almost oppressively ornate sets, and the fact that Reynolds doesn't let up for a moment.
D: Charles Walters. A: Debbie Reynolds; Harve Presnell; Ed Begley, Sr.

Modern Americana

These films share the size, the look, and the feel of the other Americana musicals but, instead of the small towns and western locales of yesteryear, you get a slice of postwar American life, made up of unionizing factory workers, company picnics, baseball, and that exotic new medium, the television.

It's Always Fair Weather
(1955) 101m. **C+**

Three World War II vets reunite ten years later and discover they have nothing in common. An unfocused and strained tale, with rousing, horizontally oriented numbers (some of which get lost on TV), and a funny satirical subplot regarding TV.
D: Gene Kelly, Stanley Donen. A: Gene Kelly, Dan Dailey, Michael Kidd.

High Society
(1956) 107m. **B−**

This bland musical remake of *The Philadelphia Story* about the romantic shenanigans of the wealthy sparkles with the high-voltage talent, elegant sets, and Newport locations. The Sinatra-Crosby duet and Louis Armstrong songs are the standouts of the ordinary music.
D: Charles Walters. A: Frank Sinatra, Bing Crosby, Grace Kelly.

Pajama Game
(1957) 101m. **B−**

A midwestern pajama factory worker organizes her fellow workers to get a pay hike and falls for the company superintendent. A generic effort except for Day's exuberance and zesty dance numbers by Fosse.
D: George Abbott, Stanley Donen. A: Doris Day, John Raitt, Carol Haney.

Damn Yankees
(1958) 110m. **C+**

A baseball fan makes a pact with the devil to become a star player in order to save his favorite team. Loud and brassy in some places, static and airless in others, with a few showstopping songs and dances.
D: George Abbott, Stanley Donen. A: Tab Hunter, Gwen Verdon, Ray Walston.

Faraway Places

Pirates, medieval cobblers, and convent-bred virgins are some of the people who populate these big and glossy magic carpet rides to exotic places and times. With the fantastic events in the heady atmospheres and mysterious locales, it seems perfectly natural when someone breaks into a ballad or opens up into a spectacular production number.

Yolanda and the Thief
(1945) 108m. **B−**

Astaire makes an uncomfortable con man who convinces an innocent convent girl that he's her guardian angel. Religion and sin come together in this strange tale of repressed sexuality set in a brilliantly colored mythic Latin American country.
D: Vincente Minnelli. A: Fred Astaire, Lucille Bremer, Frank Morgan.

The Pirate
(1948) 102m. **C+**

An innocent convent girl who dreams of being romanced by the ruthless pirate Mack the Black is obliged by a roving actor. An amusing light parody of swashbuckling tales set in an eighteenth-century Caribbean village with energetic dance numbers, a strong score, but a hollow core.
D: Vincente Minnelli. A: Judy Garland, Gene Kelly, Walter Slezak.

Hans Christian Andersen
(1952) 112m. **B−**

A cobbler-storyteller falls in love with a married ballerina and plies both his trades in a storybook Danish village. Kaye and the whimsical songs are winning, the romance is bittersweet, and the ballet numbers are dreamy.
D: Charles Vidor. A: Danny Kaye, Farley Granger, Zizi Jeanmaire.

Kiss Me Kate
(1953) 111m. **B**

An ex-husband and wife team perform a musical version of *The Taming of the Shrew* and set off emotional explosions on and offstage. Lusty exuberant thespians in gaudy Shakespearean costumes perform topnotch score and dances.
D: George Sidney. A: Kathryn Grayson, Howard Keel, Ann Miller.

Lili
(1953) 81m. **B−**

A winsome young orphan goes to the carnival and falls in love with the bitter puppeteer. The cynical carnival folk keep the charm and whimsy from becoming cloying as Caron sings "Hi-Lili, Hi-Lo" with the puppets and performs a fantasy ballet number.
D: Charles Walters. A: Leslie Caron, Jean-Pierre Aumont, Mel Ferrer.

Brigadoon
(1954) 108m. **C+**

When two American hunters stumble across a town in the Scottish Highlands that appears only once every 100 years, one of them is captivated by its magic and a native lass. Dreamy colors, nice music, beautiful dancing, and a story that drags.
D: Vincente Minnelli. A: Gene Kelly, Cyd Charisse, Van Johnson.

Kismet
(1955) 113m. **C**

A swashbuckling and philosophical street poet falls for an Arabian maiden and infiltrates her harem. Expensive and colorful production of old Baghdad with ordinary music and a flat story.
D: Vincente Minnelli. A: Howard Keel, Ann Blyth, Dolores Gray.

The King and I
(1956) 133m. **A**

The Victorian widow who tutors the King of Siam's children does battle with him about her own foreign customs and modern attitudes of equality. The serious story, classic score, and a galvanizing King will keep you enchanted during this epic length film.
D: Walter Lang. A: Deborah

Kerr, Yul Brynner, Rita Moreno.

South Pacific

(1958) 151m. **C+**

A navy lieutenant and a nurse each fall for one of the natives on the island where they're stationed during World War II. Romances are almost campily played in this bland and heavy-handed musical about love and prejudice while the really strange use of colored filters makes the beautiful location scenery look washed out.

D: Joshua Logan. A: Rossano Brazzi, Mitzi Gaynor, John Kerr.

(Mostly) Americans in Paris

These lavish, wide-screen stories of cancan dancers, boulevardiers, and wide-eyed American innocents feature Hollywood's top musical stars doing their stuff in a Technicolored, amazingly care free Paris.

An American in Paris

(1951) 115m. **A**

A brash ex-GI cum struggling artist woos a French gamine in the most romantic photogenic Paris you'll ever see in a Hollywood backlot. Highlight is a flamboyant, pull-out-the-stops celebration of dance and Gershwin music, with a 17-minute balletic finale bursting with color, movement, and sets based on Impressionist artists.

D: Vincente Minnelli. A: Gene Kelly, Leslie Caron, Oscar Levant.

Lovely to Look At

(1952) 105m. **C+**

Two sisters trying to save their Paris dress shop are helped out by three Broadway entertainers in this lightweight, slowly paced musical that finally sinks under all its trappings.

D: Mervyn LeRoy. A: Kathryn Grayson, Howard Keel, Ann Miller, Red Skelton.

Funny Face

(1957) 103m. **B+**

Haute culture meets existentialism in this elegant fairy tale of how a magazine editor and a fashion photographer transform a bookish bohemian into a supermodel. Startling 50s chic colors, resplendent clothes, and real Paris location shots make it a joy to watch, and the restrained singing and dancing are practically elegant.

D: Stanley Donen. A: Fred Astaire, Audrey Hepburn, Kay Thompson.

Les Girls

(1957) 115m. **B–**

Rashomon intersects with backstage romance when three former show girls recount their version of life with their philandering boss in a nightclub act. Witty story and sophisticated dance numbers help make this frothy bit of continental romance entertaining.

D: George Cukor. A: Gene Kelly, Mitzi Gaynor, Kay Kendall, Taina Elg.

Silk Stockings

(1957) 117m. **C+**

A Soviet official gets corrupted in Paris when an American movie producer woos her. A polished effort that never quite ignites despite the Cole Porter tunes and spirited dance numbers.

D: Rouben Mamoulian. A: Cyd Charisse, Fred Astaire, Peter Lorre.

Gigi

(1958) 115m. **A**

The use of stunning Paris locations—both exterior and interior—along with richly recreated turn-of-the-century decors, help make this fable of a young girl being groomed as a courtesan the ultimate Paris film. Witty songs, debonaire roués, women of pleasure; if you want a taste of fin de siècle decadence Hollywood-style, this is it.

D: Vincente Minnelli. A: Leslie Caron, Louis Jourdan, Maurice Chevalier, Hermione Gingold.

Can-Can

(1960) 131m. **B–**

A big, boisterous, and hilariously American story of how a nightclub owner tries to stage the obscene cancan dance despite problems from the Paris judicial system. A story that's a little too simpleminded, those American accents, and a shrill MacLaine almost make this a camp film.

D: Walter Lang. A: Frank Sinatra, Shirley MacLaine, Louis Jourdan, Maurice Chevalier.

(See also *French Cancan,* page 303.)

Show Biz

The breezy show-biz folk in these musical extravaganzas are still rehearsing in barns and ski resorts, make banner headlines in *Variety* when they split up, and find a happy ending accompanied by a zippy dance number.

The Red Shoes

(1948) 136m. **A**

An aspiring ballerina, groomed to be a star by the company director, falls for a composer and is forced to choose between love and dance. Extensive ballet sequences, theatrical characters, and European look and tone make this a melodramatic feast for dance fans and a classic source of inspiration for aspiring dancers.

D: Michael Powell, Emeric Pressburger. A: Moira Shearer, Anton Walbrook.

Summer Stock

(1950) 110m. **C+**

The "let's put on a show in the barn" routine really starts to look silly here, with Garland as the plump farmer whose place is overrun by a summer stock group. Uninspired and tired until the "Get Happy" finale with Garland transformed into a thin vibrant Miss Showbiz.

D: Charles Walters. A: Judy Garland, Gene Kelly, Phil Silvers.

Royal Wedding

(1951) 93m. **B–**

A brother and sister musical act go to England for Queen Elizabeth's coronation and each finds a British love. Lightweight and colorful

with Fred's famous dancing on the walls and ceilings sequence.
D: Stanley Donen. A: Fred Astaire, Jane Powell, Peter Lawford.

Singin' in the Rain
(1952) 102m.

The lighthearted romantic romp through Hollywood's "talkie" revolution is a clever satire of the movie industry and an even more enchanting celebration of early musicals. Pure fun and classic Hollywood magic, from the humorous script and buoyant numbers to the high-spirited performances.
D: Gene Kelly, Stanley Donen. A: Gene Kelly, Debbie Reynolds, Donald O'Connor.

The Band Wagon
(1953) 112m. **A**

A middle-aged movie star making a comeback co-stars with a ballerina in an ill-fated musical version of *Faust.* The inventive range of musical numbers, expressive dancing, snappy songs, and humorous repartee all help make this a perfectly realized musical.
D: Vincente Minnelli. A: Fred Astaire, Cyd Charisse, Oscar Levant.

White Christmas
(1954) 120m. **A**

Two army buddies, now a successful show-biz team, hook up with a sister act to save their former general from bankruptcy. The colors and sets are startlingly vivid, the numbers are breezy and sophisticated, and everyone croons with that 40s radio-style dreaminess.
D: Michael Curtiz. A: Bing Crosby, Danny Kaye, Rosemary Clooney, Vera-Ellen.

There's No Business Like Show Business
(1954) 117m. **C+**

A family of show-biz troupers have their ups and downs between the two wars. Loud gaudy numbers along with the costumes —and not just Marilyn's infamous "Heat Wave" one—are enough to make this a camp classic.
D: Walter Lang. A: Ethel Merman, Dan Dailey, Donald O'Connor, Marilyn Monroe.

Pal Joey
(1957) 109m. **B**

A relatively adult story of a small-time heel who takes up with a rich widow for her money while trying to seduce the innocent chorus girl. Even with the classic Rogers and Hart love songs, the tone is slightly cynical, and even tries to capture—in a Technicolor way—the sadness and seediness of these show-biz schemers.
D: George Sidney. A: Frank Sinatra, Rita Hayworth, Kim Novak.

Sophisticated Romance

These jazzy romantic comedies from the 50s feature such mismatched couples as a French war orphan and a New York tycoon, a phone service operator and a playwright, and even Frank Sinatra and Doris Day.

On the Town
(1949) 98m. **A**

An exhilarating romp with three sailors and the women they meet while on a 24-hour leave in New York City. The first musical to be partly shot on location, this still has all the colorful razzle-dazzle of backlot sets, bouncy athletic dancing, and high energy all around.
D: Gene Kelly, Stanley Donen. A: Gene Kelly, Frank Sinatra, Vera-Ellen.

Gentlemen Prefer Blondes
(1953) 91m. **A**

A dizzy, diamond-loving golddigger and her sensible but worldly wise friend sail to Paris while being trailed by a private eye. A hilarious sex comedy with a delicious Marilyn, a husky Jane, and numbers that are all glitz, 50s glamour, and curves.
D: Howard Hawks. A: Marilyn Monroe, Jane Russell, Charles Coburn.

Young at Heart
(1954) 117m. **B–**

Day and Sinatra provide an occasional song in this somber melodrama of three daughters, one of whom marries a down-on-his-luck musician. An interesting and slightly uncomfortable tale partly due to the odd pairing of a perky Day and a gloomy Sinatra.
D: Gordon Douglas. A: Doris Day, Frank Sinatra, Gig Young.

Daddy Long Legs
(1955) 126m. **B–**

A rich industrialist forgets the French orphan he had anonymously sponsored on a whim, until the two meet and begin a May–December romance. Sweet and dreamy dance numbers but the romance gets lost in the shuffle.
D: Jean Negulesco. A: Fred Astaire, Leslie Caron, Terry Moore.

The Opposite Sex
(1956) 116m. **C+**

In this musical remake of *The Women,* a happily married woman divorces her unfaithful husband and then attempts to steal him back, with and without the help of her catty socialite friends. *Not* the original, but still a bitchy gab fest with some harmless numbers and a great fashion show.
D: David Miller. A: June Allyson, Joan Collins, Ann Miller.

Bells Are Ringing
(1960) 126m. **B–**

An answering service operator who takes a personal interest in her clients mothers an insecure, hard-drinking playwright and naturally falls in love with him. Holliday quietly sells her songs but the story bogs down in spite of her and Dino's charm.
D: Vincente Minnelli. A: Judy Holliday; Dean Martin; Eddie Foy, Jr.

Let's Make Love
(1960) 118m. **B–**

A French millionaire playboy wants to stop an Off-Broadway show lampooning him until he meets one of the actresses in it. The heat between Marilyn and Montand still doesn't add zip to this clumsy romance and even clumsier comedy.
D: George Cukor. A: Marilyn Monroe, Yves Montand, Tony Randall.

Jazz Biographies

When those artists who walked on the wild and dark side of American music got the Hollywood treatment, their stories became colorful nostalgia pieces or sultry soap operas of degradation and redemption. The big Technicolor productions are lush pieces set in the Roaring Twenties while the smaller, black-and-white melodramas have a jazzy ambiance with smoky music and some great brooding location shots of Manhattan.

Color

Pete Kelly's Blues
(1955) 95m. **B+**
The colors and period details of 20s Kansas City might be pretty but there's no romantic mush in this rigorous tale of gangsters and musicians. Good Dixieland music including numbers by Ella Fitzgerald and Peggy Lee.
D: Jack Webb. A: Jack Webb, Janet Leigh, Lee Marvin.

The Five Pennies
(1955) 117m. **B−**
This carnival-colored bio-pic of Dixieland great Red Nichols has all the standard triumphs and tragedies with the occasional jam session between Nichols and other jazz musicians.
D: Melville Shavelson. A: Danny Kaye, Barbara Bel Geddes, Louis Armstrong.

Love Me or Leave Me
(1955) 122m. **A**
Wonderfully turgid and bitter-edged story of torch singer Ruth Etting, whose life and career was tyrannized by her Chicago racketeer spouse. Everything—the singing, the numbers, the acting—is first rate, and the chemistry between Day and Cagney is riveting.
D: Charles Vidor. A: Doris Day, James Cagney, Cameron Mitchell.

Black and White

Young Man with a Horn
(1950) 112m. B&W. **B**
This portrait of a jazzman, inspired by Bix Beiderbecke's tragic life, starts out as a gritty drama of an uncompromising artist and then turns into a slightly trashy adult melodrama as Douglas marries a neurotic and possibly lesbian rich girl.
D: Michael Curtiz. A: Kirk Douglas, Lauren Bacall, Doris Day.

I'll Cry Tomorrow
(1955) 119m. B&W.
A
This story of singer Lillian Roth may take place in the 20s and 30s, but the atmosphere is strictly 50s raw-nerved melodrama. With a stunningly photographed string of scenes depicting messy emotions, alcoholism, and degradation, this is sordidly thrilling instead of downbeat.
D: Daniel Mann. A: Susan Hayward, Eddie Albert, Richard Conte.

The Gene Krupa Story
(1959) 101m. B&W. **C+**
The story of the famous jazz drummer is chock-full of a troubled young man's moodiness and even shows Krupa's drug addiction. Surprisingly dull film with Mineo's performance lending some camp value.
D: Don Weis. A: Sal Mineo, Susan Kohner, James Darren.

1960s–1990s

Modern Americana

Portrayed with the color, sprawl, and show-biz jazziness of Hollywood's classic grand-scale musicals, the American experience is now updated to include urban gang wars, rock 'n' rollers and Madison Avenue suits.

Flower Drum Song
(1961) 133m. **B+**
A mail-order bride arrives in San Francisco's Chinatown and encounters the traditional elders and their modern Americanized second generation. The quaint Asians are stereotypes, but the snappy music and various love stories make this charming.
D: Henry Koster. A: Nancy Kwan, Jack Soo, Miyoshi Umeki.

West Side Story
(1961) 151m. **A**
Romeo and Juliet are now an American boy and a Puerto Rican girl, and the feuding clans are rival New York City street gangs. This energetic musical is fueled by the elegant score, the exuberant dancing, and the gorgeous gritty urban locales, only getting bogged down by the lackluster lovers.
D: Robert Wise, Jerome Robbins. A: Natalie Wood, Richard Beymer, George Chakiris.

State Fair
(1962) 118m. **B−**
Clean, all-American family values look a little less heartwarming in this remake about a farm family visiting the big fair. The Americana depicted here has gentle hints of Texas car speedway with the three leads lending some unintentionally campy entertainment.
D: Jose Ferrer. A: Pat Boone, Ann-Margret, Bobby Darin.

Bye Bye Birdie
(1963) 112m. **A**
The teenagers of Sweet Apple, Ohio, go crazy when an Elvis-like singer arrives to bestow his last kiss before joining the army while a failing songwriter takes his last shot at success by writing the farewell song. This sweet and amusing look at clean-scrubbed, pre-Beatles teens has a few 50s pop-style songs, but the music—and heart—of this is pure Broadway.
D: George Sidney. A: Dick Van Dyke, Janet Leigh, Ann-Margret.

How to Succeed in Business Without Really Trying
(1967) 121m. **A**
An ambitious young window washer reads a self-help

book and makes an astronomical rise to the top of the company. This clever satirical, modern-day fable still has much to say about the game-playing in corporate America, and it's great fun to watch a bunch of businessmen dancing around in their suits and ties.
D: David Swift. A: Robert Morse, Michele Lee, Rudy Vallee.

Costume Extravaganzas

These lavish productions are filled with the usual jaw-dropping sets and costumes to evoke romantic bygone times. Some tell a fairly interesting story and could almost stand on their own as comedy-dramas. But then we would be deprived of those extravagant numbers, great music, and bravura performances from the new generation of musical stars. Be prepared for the long haul; lots of money was poured into these and, at least for the musical sequences, no one ever seemed willing to call "Cut!"

My Fair Lady
(1964) 170m. **A**
Shaw's classic tale of the misanthropic phonetics professor who turns a flower girl into a lady is itself gussied up to be an elegant, big-budget, musical fairy tale. The sets and costumes are to die for, Harrison and Hepburn are splendid, and the music delightful.
D: George Cukor. A: Audrey Hepburn, Rex Harrison, Stanley Holloway.

The Sound of Music
(1965) 174m. **A**
A young novitiate from the local convent becomes governess for the unwieldy family of a widower sea captain in 1930s Austria. This is so determinedly bright, colorful, and energetic that it wears down your resistance to the schmaltzy side. Huge, with travelogue shots of Austria and the Alps, but still looks pretty good on TV.
D: Robert Wise. A: Julie Andrews, Christopher Plummer, Peggy Wood.

A Funny Thing Happened on the Way to the Forum
(1966) 99m. **C+**
A crafty slave, determined to get his freedom, creates chaos when he promises to procure a female slave for the master. A bawdy, sometimes tedious farce with its slapstick antics set against a beautiful realistic ancient Rome backdrop.
D: Richard Lester. A: Zero Mostel, Phil Silvers, Buster Keaton.

Thoroughly Modern Millie
(1967) 138m. **C+**
Millie is determined to be a flapper and marry her boss in a photogenic and farcical 1920s, with boarding houses for young ladies, tea dances, Long Island estates and white-slaving Orientals. Guaranteed to drive nonmusical lovers insane with the sheer idiocy of the plot and numbers.
D: George Roy Hill. A: Julie Andrews, Mary Tyler Moore, James Fox.

Finian's Rainbow
(1968) 140m. **C+**
Astaire is the leprechaun who reeks havoc and teaches a few lessons about humanity in the American South. The combination of backlot fantasy sets, beautiful location shots, rousing numbers, and an antiracist message makes this a strange stew.
D: Francis Ford Coppola. A: Fred Astaire, Petula Clark, Tommy Steele.

Funny Girl
(1968) 151m. **A–**
Streisand doesn't let this biopic of Ziegfeld Follies star Fanny Brice rest for a second as she sings, mugs, wheedles, and charms everyone within shouting distance. Lush and nostalgic, with spectacular musical sequences, a bittersweet romance, and a showstopping number filmed on New York harbor to showcase Streisand's vocal pyrotechnics.
D: William Wyler. A: Barbra Streisand, Omar Sharif, Walter Pidgeon.

Hello Dolly
(1969) 129m. **B–**
A matchmaker has endless schemes to promote love, including the one to snag the wealthy curmudgeon storekeeper for herself. Ornate re-creations of Old New York, overwhelming costumes, and endless humongous production numbers make this a fight to finish between Streisand and the elephantine trappings.
D: Gene Kelly. A: Barbra Streisand, Walter Mathau, Michael Crawford.

Paint Your Wagon
(1969) 164m. **C+**
Without the music, this big rollicking story of two partners who marry one woman set in the California Gold Rush might have been a better, but less interesting film. A funny take on the shortage of women in the Wild West borders on the weird with Clint and Lee singing, helped out by the occasional male chorus thundering in the background.
D: Joshua Logan. A: Lee Marvin, Clint Eastwood, Jean Seberg.

Darling Lili
(1970) 136m. **C+**
A German spy posing as a London entertainer falls in love with a dashing squadron leader in this nostalgic backstage romance. A bland effort with lots of airplane dogfights, classic cars, and patriotic songs that capture a World War I atmosphere.
D: Blake Edwards. A: Julie Andrews, Rock Hudson, Jeremy Kemp.

On a Clear Day You Can See Forever
(1970) 129m. **C+**
Streisand is weighted down by ornate period costume as she relives her past life in early nineteenth-century England under hypnosis; when conscious in modern-day New York City, she's engaged in a spastic neurotic romance with her psychiatrist. Best for Streisand devotees and fans of 60s costume editions of *Love American Style*.
D: Vincente Minnelli. A: Barbra Streisand, Yves Montand, Jack Nicholson.

Fiddler on the Roof
(1971) 180m. **A**
The traditions of a Jewish family in a Russian *shetl* are celebrated, even as the times are changing them. This epic musical is just the right mix of real drama, lovely music, joyful dancing, and beautiful on-location photography.
D: Norman Jewison. A:

Topol, Norma Crane, Leonard Frey.

1776
(1972) 141m. **A–**

A thoroughly entertaining history lesson about the struggles of the Continental Congress to draft and sign the Declaration of Independence. Much of the film is confined to one room where Franklin, Adams, Jefferson, and Co. make their arguments, but the characters bring such dash and buoyancy to the proceedings that it's always engrossing with songs that enhance, not intrude.
D: Peter Hunt. A: William Daniels, Howard da Silva, Blythe Danner.

Tom Sawyer
(1973) 103m. **C+**

Tom continues to enjoy his adventures with his friend Huck Finn and the girl next door in nineteenth-century Missouri. A wholesome look at America's past that has all the charm of a trip to Disneyland, with appealing youngsters and catchy music.
D: Don Taylor. A: Johnnie Whitaker, Celeste Holm, Warren Oates.

Mame
(1974) 132m. **D**

Ball, who croaks through the role, should have been cast as Great Auntie Mame, the madcap spirit who gives her nephew life lessons. Lacks vitality and almost falls over from the weight of really enormous production numbers.
D: Gene Saks. A: Lucille Ball, Beatrice Arthur, Robert Preston.

Funny Lady
(1975) 138m. **B–**

This sequel to *Funny Girl* follows Fanny Brice's second bittersweet marriage, this time to showman Billy Rose. Less excitement than the first, even with a solid drama and more lavish production numbers.
D: Herbert Ross. A: Barbra Streisand, James Caan, Omar Sharif.

Annie
(1982) 128m. **B–**

The Depression-era comic strip character Little Orphan Annie endures the cruelties of the orphanage before meeting millionaire Daddy Warbucks. The adults chew up the scenery trying to compete with the winsome tykes, with colorful big production numbers jazzing up the latter half.
D: John Huston. A: Albert Finney, Carol Burnett, Aileen Quinn.

Yentl
(1983) 133m. **B+**

The tale of a nineteenth-century Jewish woman who impersonates a boy in order to get an education is more of an intimate costume drama than musical. A relatively quiet study with introspective songs, a sly gender-bending story and evocative Eastern European settings help make this an unusual film musical.
D: Barbra Streisand. A: Barbra Streisand, Mandy Patinkin, Amy Irving.

For the Boys
(1991) 120m. **C**

A Martha Raye-like entertainer reminisces about her days singing for the troops through the three wars. An expensive, slow-paced, and sentimental USO-style look at the past 40 years with songs that seem like an afterthought.
D: Mark Rydell. A: Bette Midler, James Caan.

Newsies
(1992) 121m. **C**

Turn-of-the-century newsboys put out their own newspaper to rally adults and other child laborers to their plight. Hokey characters and those New York accents mar this energetically choreographed film.
D: Kenny Ortega. A: Christian Bale, Bill Pullman, Robert Duvall.

Swing Kids
(1993) 114m. **B–**

Three rebellious German teens share a love of American swing music, but take different paths with the Nazi party. A strange film that's part slightly silly historical coming-of-age drama and part teen dance musical that's fun to watch.
D: Thomas Carter. A: Robert Sean Leonard, Christian Bale, Frank Whaley.

British

These large productions are heavy on atmosphere with beautifully crafted sets of Dickensian London, King Arthur's Court, or a boys' school in prewar England. Even with their lovely music and production numbers that make Busby Berkeley look like a miniaturist, they have a darker, more adult flavor than their American counterparts.

Camelot
(1967) 181m. **B+**

King Arthur and Queen Guinevere are living happily ever after until Sir Lancelot enters the picture. Costumes and castle sets have been crossed with 1960s sensibilities and you get superb acting in this lovely, stilted, but often moving long tale of romantic love, honor, and betrayal.
D: Joshua Logan. A: Richard Harris, Vanessa Redgrave, Franco Nero.

Oliver!
(1968) 146m. **B–**

An orphan is initiated into a gang of pickpockets presided over by the wicked Fagin, adopted by a wealthy benefactor, and then later kidnapped by Fagin. Lovely music graces this beautiful film set among the slums and pubs of London that intersperses claustrophobic dramatic scenes with unbelievably huge production numbers that go on forever.
D: Carol Reed. A: Ron Moody, Oliver Reed, Shani Wallis.

Goodbye Mr. Chips
(1969) 151m. **C+**

Even though there are fewer and quieter songs to interrupt this classic tale about a shy boys' school teacher who marries a lovely younger woman, it's still a big-budget, lumbering, all-star version of a small and intimate story. O'Toole actually makes this worth watching, if you can wade through the first hour of upholstered indulgence.
D: Herbert Ross. A: Peter O'Toole, Petula Clark, Michael Redgrave.

Scrooge
(1970) 113m. **A**

The classic tale of a miser who is given a tour of his life by three ghosts just in time to redeem himself by Christmas morning. A hale and hearty costume drama with lush Victorian sets, beautifully rendered numbers, and expansive performances by British actors.
D: Ronals Neame. A: Albert Finney, Alec Guinness, Kenneth More.

Modern Musicals

These films are tributes to Hollywood's classic musicals, even as they happily dismantle all the silly conventions of the genre and reconstruct dark, ironic, and self-conscious extravaganzas. Surreally stylized sets, moody lighting, and a nostalgia that focuses on the grimmer aspects of the golden past all help make these the musicals to watch, even if you don't like musicals.

Sweet Charity
(1969) 148m. **C+**
A sweet ditzy, dime-a-dance girl looks for love in all the wrong places. Location shots of New York are the backdrop for some of the big and brassy numbers, which feature Bob Fosse's brand of pelvic-churning, show-biz dancing in this stylish, fast-paced, but too long musical.
D: Bob Fosse. A: Shirley MacLaine, Chita Rivera, John McMartin.

The Boy Friend
(1971) 135m. **B–**
All the show-biz stereotypes, from the aging star to the hopeful newcomer, get a cynical and grungy twist in this film that resembles a Busby Berkeley backstager that's drained of all glamour and good humor. Ironic, deliberately clunky, and claustrophobic until it opens up for the slickly done monster production numbers.
D: Ken Russell. A: Twiggy, Christopher Gable, Tommy Tune.

Cabaret
(1972) 119m. **A+**
An innovative adult musical about the adventures of expatriates in Berlin on the eve of the Third Reich. The characters and story are unexpectedly true to life for a musical, and the mesmerizing numbers performed on stage at the sleazy Kit Kat Club are a joy.
D: Bob Fosse. A: Liza Minnelli, Michael York, Joel Grey.

Bugsy Malone
(1976) 94m. **C+**
All-kid musical follows prohibition-era gangsters who fight turf wars with machine guns that squirt whipped cream while molls and chorus girls sing in dubbed voices. Visually fun with stylized sets and hand-tinted look but the kiddie novelty and reworked clichés finally offer nothing new.
D: Alan Parker. A: Scott Baio, Jodie Foster, Florrie Drugger.

New York, New York
(1977) 163m. **B**
A big band singer and a saxophonist court, marry, and self-destruct. All the musical conventions—including dazzling and complex production numbers—are lovingly rendered and pushed a few degrees off center to tell an uncomfortably painful love story in this dark-toned musical.
D: Martin Scorsese. A: Robert De Niro, Liza Minnelli, Lionel Stander.

All That Jazz
(1979) 120m. **B+**
Bob Fosse's autobio-pic portrays a boozing, pill-popping, philandering Broadway director who reviews his life after having a heart attack. A desperate razzle-dazzle tone, some sensational dancing, and one truly bizarre number about death makes this an unusual entry.
D: Bob Fosse. A: Roy Scheider, Ann Reinking, Jessica Lange.

Popeye
(1980) 114m. **C+**
Popeye docks at a Rube Goldberg-looking port in search of his Pappy and fights off Blutto after he falls for Olive Oyl. The cartoon quality is captured perfectly but the quietly gonzo tone takes some getting used to.
D: Robert Altman. A: Robin Williams, Shelley Duvall, Ray Walston.

Pennies from Heaven
(1981) 107m. **A**
A Depression-era sheet music salesman who wonders why life can't be like it is in songs winds up on death row. From the creatively staged musical numbers to the lip-synching to authentic 1930s songs, this is haunting, entertaining, and absolutely original. Includes a show stopping striptease dance by Christopher Walken.
D: Herbert Ross. A: Steve Martin, Bernadette Peters, Jessica Harper.

One from the Heart
(1982) 100m. **C+**
Two bored lovers break up, meet other more exotic lovers, and get back together. Crystal Gale and Tom Waits provide moody musical annotations for these love stories in a deliriously stylized Las Vegas but the film lacks a center or even much interest.
D: Francis Ford Coppola. A: Teri Garr, Frederic Forrest, Raul Julia, Nastassja Kinski.

The Cotton Club
(1984) 121m. **B+**
Gangsters and molls, musicians, and entertainers—black and white—all get mixed up with each other during the Roaring Twenties. A nostalgic drama in which the various story lines intersect with and mirror each other while the performers of Harlem's famous nightclub sing and dance like some modern Greek chorus. A clever but sometimes off-kilter gangster/backstage musical hybrid.
D: Francis Ford Coppola. A: Richard Gere, Gregory Hines, Diane Lane.

Hoofers

Like the old-fashioned backstage musicals, these are serivceable little dramas about the heartache and sweat of dancers, spiced up with a few high energy numbers and the "I'm doing it for love and not money" sentiment that's given credence when you see how these guys can dance.

Stayin' Alive
(1983) 96m. **C+**

In this sequel to *Saturday Night Fever,* Tony has made it to Broadway with a new muscular body, angst, and lots of woman trouble. The loud, third-rate, electronic pop music, a plot worthy of *True Romance* magazine, and a hilariously bad extravagant dance finale make this a must see for fans of glitzy trash.
D: Sylvester Stallone. A: John Travolta, Cynthia Rhodes, Finola Hughes.

A Chorus Line
(1985) 118m. **C**

A group of auditioning dancers reveal their innermost thoughts, secrets, and memories to a mostly unseen director. What may have been electric in the stage version comes off as an uninteresting therapy session with a few dance numbers in this overinflated film.
D: Richard Attenborough. A: Michael Douglas, Audrey Landers, Gregg Burg.

Tap
(1989) 106m. **B**

A paroled con is torn between a return to crime or going straight and working on his tap dancing. A crazy story, but the tribute to the tradition of the old street tap dancers who "challenge" each other in dance is fascinating, with tap refreshingly presented in a concert version.
D: Nick Castle. A: Gregory Hines; Sammy Davis, Jr.; Suzanne Douglas.

Steppin' Out
(1991) 113m. **B–**

Minnelli teaches a tap routine to a group of ragtag amateurs for the local charity performance. Cute and quirky female bonding with a spirited group of women, but the film never quite comes together.
D: Lewis Gilbert. A: Liza Minnelli, Shelley Winters, Ellen Greene.

Strictly Ballroom
(1992) 94m. **B+**

The young ballroom dancer who hopes to win the big competition with his own rule-breaking, crowd-pleasing routine loses his glamorous partner and trains with the plain-Jane who likes him. This cheerful tale from Australia takes all the conventions of the backstager and gives them a sweet, intimate, and slightly satirical twist.
D: Baz Luhrmann. A: Paul Mercurio, Tara Morice, Gill Hunter.

Hooray for Hollywood

Short attention span alert! These tributes to Hollywood's Golden Era are a good way to get a musical fix or to see a kaleidoscope of short clips featuring great dancing, a little singing, and the absurd surreal excesses of those awe-inspiring production numbers of Busby Berkeley and company.

That's Entertainment!
(1974) 132m. **A**

The original tribute, this includes the early warbling and dancing attempts of nonmusical stars and the cream-of-the-crop numbers, like segments from the *An American in Paris* ballet.
D: Jack Haley, Jr. A: Various stars.

That's Entertainment, Part 2
(1976) 133m. **B+**

Fred Astaire and Gene Kelly host the second tribute featuring musical numbers not included in the previous one, along with highlights from comedies and dramas.
D: Jack Haley, Jr. A: Various stars.

That's Dancing
(1985) 104m. **C**

Gene Kelly, Mikhail Baryshnikov, and others host this poorly constructed anthology of movie dance numbers from all the main American studios up through the 1980s.
D: Jack Haley, Jr. A: Various stars.

That's Entertainment! III
(1994) 113m. **B**

Instead of indulging the magic of the grand musicals, this sequel settles for explaining the backstage tricks. Includes out-takes and behind the scenes footage from films like *The Wizard of Oz* and *Annie Get Your Gun* with split screens allowing viewers to compare alternate takes.
D: Bud Friedgen, Michael J. Sheridan. A: Various stars.

Rock 'N' Roll Musicals

Early Days

This group is made up of black-and-white quickies, with nonexistent plots, bad acting, and ridiculous stories about teenage angst. The draw is the performances from well-known and obscure bands who have the raw, heavily rhythm and blues influenced sound that makes early rock so mesmerizing.

Rock Pretty Baby
(1956) 89m. B&W. **C+**

High school boys put together a band and work hard to win the musical contest. Sincere and not as low-budget as the others, but also not as much fun and lacks name musical performers.
D: Richard Bartlett. A: Sal Mineo, John Saxon, Rod McKuen.

Rock, Rock, Rock
(1956) 78m. B&W. **B**

Tuesday Weld suffers the torments of first love and

even worse when she tries to earn money for a prom gown after dad closes her charge account. The primitive quality adds to the surreal atmosphere with time out for performances by Chuck Berry, Frankie Lymon, and The Teenagers.
D: Will Price. A: Alan Freed, Tuesday Weld, Teddy Randazzo.

Rock, Baby, Rock It
(1957) 84m. B&W. **C**
A group of Texan teens get together to prevent gangsters from overrunning their hangout in this gritty film whose unpolished look goes well with the terrific performances by obscure local rockabilly bands.
D: Murray Douglas Sporup. A: Johnny Carroll and His Hot Rocks, Rosco Gordon and The Red Tops, The Five Stars, Kay Wheeler.

Carnival Rock
(1958) 80m. **D**
A nightclub filled with wild teens, mobsters, and carnival rowdies is the setting for rockabilly and rock performers. The music of the Platters gets drowned out in this bizarre mix of extras from a Roger Corman film.
D: Roger Corman. A: Susan Cabot, Dick Miller, Brian Hutton.

Go, Johnny, Go!
(1958) 75m. B&W. **B+**
A star is born when a music promoter discovers an unknown at one of his talent shows. A slew of classic rock 'n' rollers perform with wooden abandon in the midst of the dated clichés.
D: Paul Landres. A: Alan Freed, Chuck Berry, Eddie Cochran.

(See also *The Girl Can't Help It,* page 77.)

Beach Parties

Welcome to the endless Hollywood summer where clean-cut surfer lads and bikinied chicks hang out on the beach or twist away at the beatnik bar until someone yells "Surf's up!" No matter how wild the waves, the music, or the rival gang of dumb bikers get, you can rely on a few romantic ballads from Frankie and Annette as she worries about his intentions and he wonders when they're going to make up.

Beach Party
(1963) 101m. **B**
An anthropologist comes to the beach to study surfers' sex habits, Annette and Frankie have jealousy problems, and a brain-impaired motorcycle gang is itching to start a turf war. A bouncy and slightly more coherent entry, featuring songs like "Muscle Beach Party" and "Surfin' and A' Swingin."
D: William Asher. A: Annette Funicello, Frankie Avalon, Robert Cummings.

Bikini Beach
(1964) 100m. **B–**
A British pop star, The Potato Bug, courts Annette, the surfers are threatened with eviction from the beach, another motorcycle gang shows up, and Little Stevie Wonder performs at the local hangout. Gets extra camp points for the poke at the British Invasion.
D: William Asher. A: Annette Funicello, Frankie Avalon, Keenan Wynn.

Muscle Beach Party
(1964) 96m. **C+**
A rich Italian woman has her eyes set on both a dim-witted muscleman and Frankie, much to Annette's displeasure. Standard beach party goofiness enlivened by 60s muscle builders and brief bits by Dick Dale and the Del Tones.
D: William Asher. A: Frankie Avalon, Annette Funicello, Buddy Hackett.

Ride the Wild Surf
(1964) 101m. **B+**
Surfers head to Hawaii during winter vacation for the big contest and a little romance. This bigger-budgeted attempt to cash in on the surfer market has a glossier look, a cast of rising young stars, and decent surfing footage, all of which makes it the best of the group but also the exception to the goofy rule.
D: Don Taylor. A: Fabian, Shelly Fabares, Tab Hunter, Barbara Eden.

Beach Blanket Bingo
(1965) 76m. **B**
Annette gets jealous when Frankie is attracted to Linda Evans, a dopey surfer is the object of a mermaid's affections, and a motorcycle gang is still on hand to make boorish remarks. Lots of energy goes into a particularly inane tale.
D: William Asher. A: Annette Funicello, Frankie Avalon, Linda Evans, Don Rickles.

How to Stuff a Wild Bikini
(1965) 90m. **C–**
A mystery girl lands from out of the sky to fill a mysterious bikini, Frankie is in Tahiti with the navy, and Annette stays under wraps throughout the film due to real-life pregnancy. Sillier subplots do not equal more fun.
D: William Asher. A: Annette Funicello, Frankie Avalon, Dwayne Hickman.

Nostalgia

Most of these movies are the standard climb-to-success show-biz tales with an updated rock 'n' roll spin. Featuring the tough agent, the swinging DJ, the kids on the corner, the struggling teen heartthrob, these stories are driven by youthful energy and some reasonable facsimilies or even genuine classic rock 'n' roll music.

That'll Be the Day
(1974) 90m. **A–**
This realistic look at British youth in the 50s follows a working-class lad as he drifts through a series of aimless jobs that lead him toward a life in rock 'n' roll. Gritty but nostalgic tale captures the grayness of the Angry Young Man's life and the lure of rock as the road to independence and a better class of women.
D: Claude Whatham. A:

David Essex, Ringo Starr, Keith Moon.

Sparkle
(1976) 98m. **C+**

Three girls from the ghetto form a Supremes-like singing group in the 1960s, with the usual problems of drugs, mobsters, and expanding egos. A clichéd story but the cast and score are likable and the flashy show-biz costumes and sets capture the period.
D: Sam O'Steen. A: Irene Cara, Lonette McKee, Dwan Smith.

American Hot Wax
(1978) 91m. **A**

Alan Freed isn't just a DJ, he's the godfather of rock 'n' roll, giving street corner doo-wop groups their first break, staging monster concerts starring Chuck Berry and Jerry Lee Lewis, and taking payola from record companies. An exuberant look at rock's show-business side with engaging characters and a knockout musical finale.
D: Floyd Mutrux. A: Tim McIntire, Laraine Newman, Jay Leno.

Quadrophenia
(1979) 115m. **B+**

With some of the music but little else to do with the Who's album of the same name, this is a gritty tale of British working-class youth in the late 50s to early 60s and the subcultures of the sleek-suited, amphetamine-popping Mods and the leather-jacketed Rockers. One of the better Angry Young Men tales, with constant sense of claustrophobia, aimless energy, and impending violence filling entire film.
D: Franc Roddam. A: Phil Daniels, Mark Wingett, Sting.

The Idolmaker
(1980) 119m. **B–**

A serious, sometimes gloomy drama about a fictional impresario who created some of those young singing idols from Philadelphia in the 1950s. Compelling leads make up for the dull patches and the music that's pure 70s show biz.
D: Taylor Hackford. A: Ray Sharkey, Tovah Feldshuh, Peter Gallagher.

Eddie and the Cruisers
(1983) 90m. **C+**

Various members recount their experiences in a rock band in the 60s led by the charismatic and now mysteriously disappeared Eddie. The 60s music sounds a lot like bland 80s pop and the story is flat, even with the pervasive sense of hidden tragedy.
D: Martin Davidson. A: Tom Berenger, Michael Pare, Ellen Barkin.

Hairspray
(1988) 94m. **A**

Fat-girl Lake becomes the belle of the afternoon TV dance show, a champion for racial equality, and rival for the Miss Autoshow crown. A campy, comic book-colored look at the early 60s featuring music and dancing that will have you twisting and a cast and cameos by some heavy hitters like Sonny Bono and Pia Zadora.
D: John Waters. A: Ricki Lake, Divine, Debbie Harry.

Cry-Baby
(1990) 85m. **C+**

This style-over-content cross between a trashy 1950s juvenile delinquent film and rockabilly teen musical goes through some lengthy complications between bad boy Cry-Baby and the square girl he falls for. Some funny production numbers but not enough of the bright trashy fun of *Hairspray*.
D: John Waters. A: Johnny Depp, Amy Locane, Traci Lords.

The Five Heartbeats
(1991) 122m. **C+**

This chronicles the climb to success of a Temptations-like group and their struggle to stay there over the years. While focusing more on the drama than the music, the story is sincere, but lacks cohesion or any real excitement.
D: Robert Townsend. A: Robert Townsend, Tressa Thomas, Michael Wright.

Music Biographies

Like the musical biographies from the 1950s, many of these films are fairly bland portraits of rock and country-western stars, with the biggest tragedy being how long it took them to hit the big time. It's not till you get to *The Doors* and *What's Love Got to Do with It?* that the respectful tone is dropped, and we get to see the darker sides of musical artists.

The Buddy Holly Story
(1978) 113m. **A–**

Buddy Holly's short career, from his gigs at the local roller rink in Lubbock, Texas, to his appearance on *The Ed Sullivan Show,* is portrayed with all the twangy exuberance of his music. Busey's horn-rimmed, aw-shucks performance is fun to watch.
D: Steve Rash. A: Gary Busey, Don Stroud, Charles Martin Smith.

Coal Miner's Daughter
(1980) 124m. **B+**

Dirt-poor farm girl Loretta Lynn has a talent for singing and songwriting and, with the help of her loving husband, becomes Nashville's country western superstar. A laid-back, respectful story with good music, a winsome Spacek, and a wily Jones as the sometimes straying husband.
D: Michael Apted. A: Sissy Spacek, Tommy Lee Jones, Beverly D'Angelo.

Sweet Dreams
(1985) 130m. **B**

The short life of legendary country-western star Patsy Cline is defined by her loving but tumultuous marriage and a drive to succeed that corrodes her spirit. Lange keeps your eyes glued to screen and her chemistry with Harris is sweet, but the movie feels like a routine melodrama scored with Cline's music.
D: Karel Reisz. A: Jessica Lange, Ed Harris, Ann Wedgeworth.

La Bamba
(1987) 99m. **B–**

Not a whole lot happens in this glossy bland film about the short life of 50s pop star Ritchie Valens: He sings, hits the big time, has problems with his half-brother and falls in love with a middle-class white girl. A nice try at capturing the flavor of the Latino community in California.
D: Luis Valdez. A: Lou Diamond Phillips, Esai Morales, Joe Pantoliano.

Great Balls of Fire
(1989) 108m. **B–**

Jerry Lee Lewis' story is told appropriately with a flamboyant style that combines music video techniques with frequent visual tips of the hat to 50s kitsch. Quaid is the

grinning wild man at the piano, Ryder his 13-year-old cousin whom he marries, and Baldwin does a brief but funny turn as another cousin, Jerry Falwell.
D: Jim McBride. A: Dennis Quaid, Winona Ryder, Alec Baldwin.

The Doors
(1991) 135m. **B–**
Oliver Stone reimagines the 60s via the out-of-control life and visionary lyrics of Jim Morrison. Loopy and dionysian celebration of drug-fueled youth during America's Summer of Love has all of Stone's trademark excesses and enough quasi-mystical images to fill a psychedelic poster store, with Kilmer making an often believable Lizard King.
D: Oliver Stone. A: Val Kilmer, Meg Ryan, Kyle MacLachlan.

What's Love Got to Do with It?
(1993) 120m. **A–**
Tina Turner becomes one of rock and soul's reigning queens with the help, and under the thumb of, her self-destructive husband-musical partner Ike. This harrowing tale of abuse and self-destruction avoids being an exercise in degradation, thanks to the indomitable heroine and Fishburne's cunning performance.
D: Brian Gibson. A: Angela Bassett, Laurence Fishburne, Cora Lee Day.

Rock Musicals

These films rarely use rock music, generally settling for energetic pop music to go with the disposable plots, cartoony characters, and garish sets. Some are fun and intentionally goofy, others hilariously campy with flashy disco music, and a few—especially the ones that had once been considered bold and iconoclastic—now just look sweet and nostalgic.

Jesus Christ Superstar
(1973) 107m. **C+**
The last seven days of Jesus' life is reenacted by what looks like a traveling band of hippies in this film version of the stage musical. Despite desert settings and inventive, sometimes jarring anachronisms, this still comes off as stagy with a "classic" rock score that sounds dated.
D: Norman Jewison. A: Ted Neeley, Carl Anderson, Yvonne Elliman.

Phantom of the Paradise
(1974) 92m. **A–**
The Faust legend is updated in Brian De Palma's outrageous film about a composer who makes a deathless deal with a powerful and mysterious rock impresario. This campy satire on the music industry is a delirious mix of trash, flash, violence, and nice, if a little cornball, music. Don't miss the parody on glam rock.
D: Brian De Palma. A: Paul Williams, Jessica Harper, William Finley.

Tommy
(1975) 108m. **B–**
The Who's rock opera about a deaf, dumb, and blind kid who becomes a pinball wizard/messiah plays like a string of early music videos that are sometimes dopey but always lively. The pop and rock stars of the day have a gas playing the gallery of creepy opportunists in a stylized postwar England.
D: Ken Russell. A: Roger Daltry, Ann-Margret, Oliver Reed.

The Rocky Horror Picture Show
(1975) 105m. **B**
A square couple is stuck in an old house populated by kinky Transylvanians. This "outrageous" 70s timepiece wallows in its own ridiculousness, but still runs out of steam and is better viewed at the midnight show with the cult of kids who know every line of the dialogue.
D: Jim Sharmen. A: Tim Curry, Susan Sarandon, Barry Bostwick.

The Wiz
(1978) 134m. **C–**
An all-black remake of *The Wizard of Oz* portrays Dorothy as a frustrated schoolteacher, the road to Oz passing through urban playgrounds and junk heaps, and Oz as a disco. Self-important with lots of show-biz flash.
D: Sidney Lumet. A: Diana Ross, Michael Jackson, Nipsey Russell.

Grease
(1978) 110m. **B**
A nice girl and a hood fall in love in this tongue-in-cheek look at the 1950s. The energetic, good-humored atmosphere and a few bubbly numbers help you overlook the silliness, not to mention the age of these "teenagers."
D: Randal Kleiser. A: John Travolta, Olivia Newton-John, Stockard Channing.

Sgt. Pepper's Lonely Hearts Club Band
(1978) 111m. **F**
The Beatles meet disco and lose, in this flashy story loosely based on their classic album. Grand finale features Rock's has-beens, so time may make this a camp film yet.
D: Michael Schultz. A: Peter Frampton, The Bee Gees, George Burns.

Hair
(1979) 121m. **B+**
A farm boy comes to New York City to report for the draft and becomes mixed up with a group of flower children. A nostalgic look at the 60s with catchy music, exuberant dance numbers, and a firmly held innocence.
D: Milos Forman. A: John Savage, Treat Williams, Beverly D'Angelo.

The Rose
(1979) 134m. **C+**
The music is all in the singing concerts of a Janis Joplin-like rock star who can't stop her painful self-destructive descent. A downbeat story made compelling by heartfelt but slightly overblown performances.
D: Mark Rydell. A: Bette Midler, Alan Bates, Frederic Forrest.

The Jazz Singer
(1980) 115m. **D**
A singer rebelling against his roots heads to LA to break into show business where he falls in love with record manager Arnaz. His cantor father Sir Laurence Olivier tracks him down, disowns him, but all ends well in a huge production number. A flashy, not to be believed musical melodrama with a Las Vegas heart of gold.
D: Richard Fleischer. A: Neil Diamond, Laurence Olivier, Lucie Arnaz.

One Trick Pony
(1980) 98m. **B–**
A 60s folk-rock singer struggles with his shaky marriage and the changing tastes of the 70s. A quiet and serious look at a performer's life on the road and the vagaries of the music industry, which features concert footage of Simon.
D: Robert Young. A: Paul Simon, Blair Brown, Rip Torn.

Xanadu
(1980) 93m. **B–**
A muse comes to Los Angeles, inspires a roller-boggeying graphics artist to open a disco with a retired dancer, and performs on opening night before returning to Mt. Olympus. The film's loopiness makes it closer to an old-fashioned musical even with the disco flash and trash.
D: Robert Greenwald. A: Olivia Newton-John, Michael Beck, Gene Kelly.

Purple Rain
(1984) 111m. **C+**
Prince plays a misunderstood visionary rock musician in this fictionalized version of his rise to fame in Minneapolis. The theatrical costumes and stagings may seem a little dated, but his energetic performances are a more entertaining form of narcissism than the dark and misogynistic story.
D: Albert Magnoll. A: Prince, Apollonia Kotero, Morris Day.

Absolute Beginners
(1986) 107m.
A–
A young photographer documents the rising 1950s British teen culture, worries about his girlfriend, tries to avoid selling out to the establishment, and gets involved in a race riot. An audacious, mecurial, mishmash, with fine music and the exuberance of a great music video.
D: Julien Temple. A: Eddie O'Connell, Patsy Kensit, David Bowie.

Little Shop of Horrors
(1986) 88m. **A–**
A man-eating plant demands a supply of human flesh from its nerdy shopkeeper in this musical remake of the Roger Corman classic. Hilarious black comedy with brilliantly colored 50s kitsch sets, terrific music, and comic book characters out of *True Romance*.
D: Frank Oz. A: Rick Moranis, Ellen Greene, Vincent Gardenia.

Earth Girls Are Easy
(1989) 100m. **C+**
Aliens land in San Fernando Valley and inexplicably experience culture shock. Colorful and eventually tedious music videolike farce that's like a Saturday morning cartoon about Valley girls.
D: Julien Temple. A: Geena Davis, Jeff Goldblum, Julie Brown.

(See also *The Commitments,* page 100.)

Teen Dance Musicals

In these entertainingly hokey stories that often look like extended music videos, the characters find that the best way out of here and the cure for teen angst is to put on their Capezios and dance, dance, dance.

Fame
(1980) 133m. **B+**
The class of New York's High School for the Performing Arts will do whatever it takes to realize their dreams for fame. Long on predictable episodes about the gay actor, the angry young dancer from the ghetto, and the actress who gets conned into porn, but it occasionally bursts into some high energy dance sequences.
D: Alan Parker. A: Irene Cara, Lee Curreri, Eddie Barth.

Flashdance
(1983) 95m. **B**
A stylish aerobic workout/ music video depiction of a Pittsburgh welder who dreams of being a ballerina while bar dancing at night. The bar dancers look like album cover models doing new wave conceptual pieces, the plot and dialogue are laughable, but the dances by Beal's body double are electric.
D: Adrian Lyne. A: Jennifer Beals, Michael Nouri, Lilia Skala.

Footloose
(1984) 107m. **B**
A Midwestern town's ban on rock music and dancing is challenged by the new kid from the city. The plot is a beaut—the story even includes the minister's "bad girl" daughter—the music is show-biz rock, but the dance numbers are swell and Christopher Penn isn't a bad hoofer.
D: Herbert Ross. A: Kevin Bacon, Lori Singer, John Lithgow.

Dirty Dancing
(1987) 97m. **A–**
A nice Jewish girl learns ballroom and dirty dancing from the hunk dance instructor at a Catskills resort during the summer of 1963—although you couldn't tell the year from the music and dance styles. Sweet characters, good dancing, a wildly anachronistic bump-and-grind romance, and humorously phony nostalgia make this the best of the bunch.
D: Emile Ardolino. A: Jennifer Grey, Patrick Swayze, Jerry Orbach.

Jazz

These colorful portraits of jazz musicians manage to be compelling dramas instead of the grim studies you'd expect from depictions of artists battling drug addiction, poverty, and racism.

Lady Sings the Blues
(1972) 144m. **B –**
Like the big Technicolor biopics from the 50s, this story of tragic jazz diva Billy Holliday is glossy, nostalgic, and has glamorous-looking stars. It also attempts and occasionally succeeds at portraying the darker aspects of Lady Day's life including drug addiction. Ross is good but her singing can't capture the pain.
D: Sidney Furie. A: Diana Ross, Billy Dee Williams, Richard Pryor.

Round Midnight
(1986) 132m. **A**
A Charlie Parker-like American jazz musician in Paris gets a breather from his drug and alcohol problems when a devoted French fan takes care of him. Hip and naturally stylish, this has a laid-back feeling, helped along by using real musicians instead of actors.
D: Bertrand Tavernier. A: Dexter Gordon, François Cluzet, Lonette McKee.

Bird
(1988) 160m. **B+**
Whitaker is a knockout as Charlie Parker in this engaging film that keeps your gaze firmly on the difficulties of an artist's life while letting the tragedy of his drug addiction quietly build up and take over.
D: Clint Eastwood. A: Forest Whitaker, Diane Venora, Michael Zelniker.

(See also *Mo' Better Blues,* page 250.)

Rap

With most of these films, you don't even have to like rap music to enjoy the slice-of-teen-life comedies that are also lively celebrations of the slang, fashion, and music of black youth. Like the Rock films of the 50s, the early entries in this group were thrown together to capitalize on a music craze; as rap got closer to mainstream, so did the films.

Krush Groove
(1985) 97m. **B –**
This virtually plotless film involving a rapper's talent contest and a struggling record company is closer to a concert film that captures the language, clothes, and energy of the street rappers. An uncontrived and likable timepiece.
D: Michael Schultz. A: Blair Underwood, Sheila E., Fat Boys.

Rappin'
(1985) 92m. **C**
The emphasis is on action and a more stylized street culture as an ex-con-turned-breakdancer must contend with his old street gang in order to stay straight. The music and breakdancing in the unexciting numbers make you yearn for a Michael Jackson music video.
D: Joel Silberg. A: Mario Van Peebles, Tasia Valenza, Charles Flohe.

Disorderlies
(1987) 86m. **C**
The Fat Boys are hired by a greedy nephew to attend to his feeble millionaire uncle, in hopes that their incompetence will finish him off. Resembles a rap version of The Three Stooges, with inane slapstick and only one number by the Boys.
D: Michael Schultz. A: The Fat Boys, Ralph Bellamy, Tony Plana.

House Party
(1990) 100m. **A –**
A warm and lively teen comedy in which the problems of Kid and his friend Play—getting grounded, sneaking off to the party, dating—make this closer to a smart 1950s beach film than *Boyz in the Hood.* Fresh music and likable characters who have a good time playing white America's perceptions of black teens for laughs.
D: Reginald Hudlin. A: Kid 'n' Play (Christopher Reid, Christopher Martin), Martin Lawrence.

House Party 2
(1991) 94m. **A –**
Kid 'n' Play hold a "Pajama Jammin' Jam" to raise Kid's college tuition money after he loses it to a phony record producer. A tighter, less goofy sequel with more musical numbers, but continuing to address real issues in a lighthearted tone.
D: Doug McHenry, George Jackson. A: Kid 'n' Play (Christopher Reid, Christopher Martin), Tisha Campbell.

Third World

These aren't traditional musicals in the Hollywood sense; they are dramas dealing with real issues in cultures where music is a rallying force and an instrument for change.

The Harder They Come
(1973) 98m. **A –**
A young man struggles to become a reggae star, but gets caught up in a series of criminal episodes that makes him a folk hero. A gritty unflinching look at Jamaican life beyond the tourist industry, and the film that helped bring reggae music to America.
D: Perry Henzell. A: Jimmy Cliff, Janet Barkley, Carl Bradshaw.

Sarafina!
(1992) 99m. **B+**
A South African teenage girl living under the harsh conditions of apartheid participates in rioting when her inspirational teacher is arrested for giving "subversive" lessons. A passionate story that uses song as a powerful means of narration, protest, and emotional release.
D: Darrell Roodt. A: Leleti Khumalo, Whoopi Goldberg, Miriam Makeba.

The Beatles

Films made by the Fab Four helped set the standard for the various types of films (and music videos) made by rock groups: fictional zany escapades, documentaries, arty attempts at "concept" films, and animation.

A Hard Day's Night
(1964) 85m. B&W. **A** 🏛

It's a wild and tumultuous two days for the Beatles as they run from crazed fans, make witty ripostes to the press, prepare for a TV special, and keep Paul's grandfather out of trouble. A British comedy that still feels modern, this captures the energy of the music and the nose-thumbing exuberance of youth.
D: Richard Lester. A: With Wilfred Brambell, Victor Spinetti.

Help!
(1965) 90m. **B+**

The Beatles second outing is a spy spoof with the lads running from a mad scientist and a religious cult who are after Ringo's magical ring. The film works best when the boys are mocking their own personas, lip-synching their songs at various locations including Stonehenge, and infusing charm into a rambling madcap spree.
D: Richard Lester. A: With Leo McKern, Victor Spinetti.

Magical Mystery Tour
(1968) 60m. **C**

Made originally for British television, this early music video takes us on a Beatles-conducted bus tour filled with circus people and strange characters. Grainy color, tinny sound, and rambling psychedelic images give it the feel of a drug-fueled home movie.

Yellow Submarine
(1968) 85m. **A**

A celebration of 60s pop art is a showcase for the animated musings of the Beatles songs. Plenty of funny wisecracking one-liners by the mod-dressed Beatles as they board their Yellow Submarine and battle the Blue Meanies to restore Pepperland to its happy melodical self.
D: George Dunning. A: Voices: John Clive, Peter Batten, Geoffrey Hughes.

Let It Be
(1970) 80m. Documentary **A**

It's the end of the line for the Beatles and this documentary of their "Let It Be" recording sessions captures the seeds of the group's destruction. Wonderful music and a fascinating look at the dynamics of four artists straining to get out.
D: Michael Lindsay-Hogg. A: With George Martin.

The Beatles: The First U.S. Visit
(1964) 83m. Documentary **B+**

A day-by-day diary of the Beatles first tour in America culled from hundreds of hours of tape. Mainly for fans of the lads from Liverpool and The Ed Sullivan Show.

The Compleat Beatles
(1982) 119m. Documentary **B+**

The life and times of the Beatles is portrayed in a compilation of interviews, news reports, and concert clips. Interesting even for nonfans as a record of the innocence and excitement of the era.
D: Patrick Montgomery.

Elvis

These candy-colored, fast-paced films offer dopey fun as Elvis, working hard as a race car driver, a tour guide, or even a singer, chases (or fights off) girls in a variety of exotic travelogue settings. Scattered throughout are a handful of good Elvis tunes, but for the most part you're likely to get such classics as "Song of the Shrimp" or "No Room to Rhumba in a Sports Car."

Jailhouse Rock
(1957) 96m. B&W. **A–**

Elvis is an ex-con who becomes a famous rock singer with an ego problem. Elvis is still the sulky, faintly dangerous rebel here and performs his best movie production number with dancing cons and his trademark shaking.
D: Richard Thrope. A: With Judy Tyler, Vaughn Taylor, Dean Jones.

Loving You
(1957) 101m. **B–**

This fictionalized version of Presley's early career has Elvis playing a hillbilly trucker who becomes an overnight rock 'n' roll star. Elvis reveals a raw and edgy side that's more interesting than his later bland image.
D: Hal Kanter. A: With Wendell Corey, Lizabeth Scott, Dolores Hart.

King Creole
(1958) 115m. **A–**

Elvis is a busboy/singer in New Orleans who gets involved with a gang of toughs on his rise to fame. More than just a fluffy star vehicle, this is a gritty, tightly constructed drama with Elvis conducting himself admirably in the meaty role.
D: Michael Curtiz. A: With Carolyn Jones, Walter Matthau, Dean Jagger.

G.I. Blues
(1960) 104m. **B**

Elvis is a GI who forms his own band and pursues a cabaret dancer in Berlin. Despite his rendition of "Blue Suede Shoes," Elvis plunges into his wholesome period as he wins the girl, thanks to his knack with babies.
D: Norman Taurog. A: With Juliet Prowse, Robert Ivers, Leticia Roman.

Blue Hawaii
(1961) 101m. **A–**

Determined to make it on his own, Elvis becomes a tour guide rather than going into the family's pineapple business. Lush scenery, Lansbury as Elvis' mother, and the final luau blowout help film along.
D: Norman Taurog. A: With Joan Blackman, Roland Winters, Angela Lansbury.

Girls! Girls! Girls!
(1962) 106m. **B–**

Elvis is chased by love-crazy girls while he chases his re-

possessed fishing boat in Florida. Skirts the line between likable and annoyingly silly with songs like the cute little tango number in a small apartment "The Walls Have Ears."
D: Norman Taurog. A: With Stella Stevens, Laurel Goodwin.

Fun in Acapulco
(1963) 97m. **B**
Tropical resort lifeguard Elvis must choose between the hotel's social director and a lady bullfighter while trying to conquer his fear of heights. Highlights include "Bossa Nova Baby" song and exciting finale of Elvis diving off a cliff.
D: Richard Thorpe. A: With Ursula Andress, Paul Lukas, Alejandro Rey.

Kissin' Cousins
(1964) 96m. **B–**
Airforce officer Elvis tries to convince his double, blond hillbilly Elvis, to allow the government to build a missile silo on his property. Double the Elvis does not double the fun in this throwaway.
D: Gene Nelson. A: With Arthur O'Connell, Jack Albertson.

Roustabout
(1964) 101m. **B+**
Roaming musician Elvis discovers that the carnival run by boss lady Stanwyck is the perfect place for hard work, true love, and singing. Atmosphere is slightly seedy, Elvis isn't as clean cut, and he actually rides a motorcycle.
D: John Rich. A: With Barbara Stanwyck, Leif Erickson, Joan Freeman.

Viva Las Vegas
(1964) 86m. **A**
Elvis is the race car driver/waiter who falls in love with the sex kitten swimming instructor, even though they are competitors in the hotel talent contest. The splashiest of the series thanks to a few gaudy show biz numbers and the chemistry between Elvis and Ann-Margret.
D: George Sidney. A: With Ann-Margret, Cesare Danova, William Demerest.

Girl Happy
(1965) 96m. **C**
Chaperone Elvis is at his wits end keeping track of the daughter of a mob nightclub owner when she cuts loose in Fort Lauderdale. Songs include "Do the Clam," which pretty much says it all.
D: Boris Sagal. A: With Shelley Fabares, Harold J. Stone.

Live a Little, Love a Little
(1968) 90m. **B**
Elvis is a hip photographer working two jobs (one a skin mag, the other a family one) and being plagued by a neurotic woman with a big dog. Keeping abreast of the times, the King goes all the way. Dream sequence is a psychedelic trip when he's on "The Edge of Reality."
D: Norman Taurog. A: With Michele Carey, Don Porter, Rudy Vallee.

Change of Habit
(1969) 93m. **C+**
Elvis is the doctor working in the ghetto alongside a nun who falls for him and then must choose between devotion to God or the King. More inspirational entry includes gospel-style songs, although the opening credits do show nuns changing their habits for miniskirts and go-go boots.
D: William Graham. A: With Mary Tyler Moore, Barbara McNair, Jane Elliot.

OTHER TITLES:
Follow That Dream (1962)
Kid Galahad (1962)
It Happened at the World's Fair (1963)
Harum Scarum (1965)
Tickle Me (1965)
Frankie and Johnnie (1966)
Paradise Hawaiian Style (1966)
Spinout (1966)
Clambake (1967)
Double Trouble (1967)
Easy Come Easy Go (1967)
Speedway (1968)
The Trouble with Girls (1969)

SCI-FI AND FANTASY

Sci-Fi and Fantasy Menu

SCI-FI AND FANTASY FILM GROUPS

Early Sci-Fi and Fantasy

Before the real-life science of atom bombs and rocketships kicked off the genre in the 1950s, these rare early sci-fi films presented eerily poetic visions of the future mixed with strong doses of social manifesto.

Metropolis
(1926) 121m. B&W. Silent.
A
The grand scale expressionistic shocker about the utopia of a small leisure class who live off the labor of the wretched underground dwellers. The massive geometric set designs are still stunning, the perfect robot woman is a creepy visual wonder, and the scenes of the miserable underlings dehumanized to service the all-demanding machines are still haunting.
D: Fritz Lang. A: Alfred Abel, Rudolf Klein-Rogge, Brigitte Helm.

Things to Come
(1936) 92m. B&W. **B+**
Modern Earth, reduced to barbarism by a 30 years war, is rescued by a utopian brotherhood that erects gleaming antiseptic white Art Deco cities where a ruling class of "intellectuals" debates mankind's future. Dated by overwrought acting, this is still a special effects feast (some impressive, some poor).
D: William Cameron Menzies. A: Raymond Massey, Ralph Richardson, Sir Cedric Hardwicke.

1950s

Planets and Rocketships

Come follow these early space voyages as dauntless crews encounter hostile pockmarked planets, nuclear blasted alien civilizations, and the occasional mutant lizard or spider. Most of the action takes place within the aircraft as a possible attack builds the tension between the square-jawed commander, the pondering rational scientist, and the assorted ole boy crew members. If this sounds like *Star Trek*, keep in mind that you can practically see the grade of cardboard used for the sets, the acting is atrocious, and that weird theremin music is generously used to compensate for the cheesy special effects.

Destination Moon
(1950) 92m. **B**
The first half looks like an industrial film as it explores the difficulty of launching a lunar mission; businessmen are assembled to raise the funding and they're even shown a demo short starring Woody Woodpecker. The second half dealing with the actual mission includes some good special effects and a space walk.
D: Irving Pichel. A: John Archer, Warner Anderson, Erin O'Brien-Moore.

Rocketship X-M
(1950) 78m. B&W.
B+
A moon-bound crew gets diverted to Mars where they discover a civilization reduced to caveman status. This includes most of the trademarks of the genre: Mars looks like an Arizona desert, the spaceship control room looks like cardboard with blinking lights, and the motley crew look like they wandered off a cheap World War II film.
D: Kurt Neumann. A: Lloyd Bridges, John Emery, Hugh O'Brian.

Flight to Mars
(1951) 72m. **C**
A crew that crash-lands on Mars is helped by an underground civilization planning to use its ship for an invasion. Mars has the look of an airport lounge in the cheap and talky film. Resorts to tough guy action for conclusion.
D: Lesley Selander. A: Cameron Mitchell, Marguerite Chapman, Arthur Franz.

Project Moon Base
(1953) 53m. B&W. **D**
A woman's in charge of this space station but espionage ruins things, and she can't handle the crisis so a man takes over. A dull and short cheapie, but it does show the first marriage on the moon.
D: Richard Talmadge. A: Hayden Rorke, Donna Martell, James Craven.

This Island Earth
(1955) 86m. **B+**
A mystery man entices scientists from around the world to join his secret project which, it turns out, is to save his planet. A wise and witty E.T., a sleek spaceship, and a dazzling bombardment of his planet gives this one extra punch.
D: Joseph M. Newman. A: Jeff Morrow, Rex Reason, Faith Domergue.

Forbidden Planet
(1956) 98m. **A**
A rescue mission finds a brilliant survivor and his daughter warning the visitors of an unseen force that brutally killed all his fellow scientists. *The Tempest* grafted onto sci-fi, this richly colored glossy production has great sets and special effects, including a dazzling underground lab, and it even leaves the viewer with Freudian food for thought.
D: Fred Wilcox. A: Leslie Nielsen, Walter Pidgeon, Anne Francis.

It! The Terror from Beyond Space
(1958) 68m. B&W. **B**
A Mars rescue mission picks up a lone survivor of a doomed expedition and discovers that something is kill-

ing them off one by one. Low budget but effective tension builder, with a plot recognizable from *Alien*.
D: Edward L. Cahn. A: Marshall Thompson, Shawn Smith, Ann Doran.

The Angry Red Planet
(1959) 83m. **C+**
A Martian expedition encounters a hostile planet full of monstrous menaces, including a mutant spider. Clichés abound in this "We're here! . . . Let's get out of here!" space adventure with the color red often looking pink.
D: Ib Melchior. A: Les Tremayne, Gerald Mohr, Jack Kruschen.

First Spaceship on Venus
(1959) 78m. **C**
An international crew of astronauts dispatched to Venus discovers the remains of an atomic blasted civilization. The antinuke and international cooperation messages are nice, but the dreadful dubbing and severe editing make this German/Polish production tough going.
D: Kurt Maetzig. A: Yoko Tani, Gunther Simon, I. Machowski.

Women of the Prehistoric Planet
(1966) 87m. **D**
A space crew returns after a 30-year voyage to discover Earth in a prehistoric condition. Leaping magnified lizards, two-bit plastic tropical sets, and the mysterious cavewoman don't help a listless script. Twist ending is fun.
D: Arthur Pierce. A: Wendell Corey, George Edwards, John Agar.

Planets and Tribes of Scantily Clad Women

Some people might burst a vein while others will just camp out and chuckle at these dime store-decorated cheapies designed to give teenage boys tantalizing visions of airheaded femaledom. There's a plot to be found somewhere, but it's mostly a framework for nubile young maids to prance around in tights or animal skins while the males try to tame or at least to kiss them.

Prehistoric Women
(1950) 74m. **C–**
A merry narrator guides our way through the grunts and burps in this saga about a tribe of cavewomen who set their clubs upon a group of cavemen in order to repopulate. Limited sexploitation and dull patches keep the chuckles far apart.
D: Gregg Tallas. A: Laurette Luez, Allan Nixon, Mara Lynn.

Cat Women of the Moon
(1954) 65m. **B**
Utter silliness brings an all-male space mission in contact with some curvaceous women in black tights with telepathic powers who rule the moon from underground. Our heroes must deal with a giant killer spider on a string, while the cat women bicker and get their telepathic wires crossed.
D: Arthur Hilton. A: Sonny Tufts, Victor Jory, Bill Phipps.

Missile to the Moon
(1958) 78m. B&W. **C–**
A scientist and some Earth toughies land on the moon and discover it's ruled by a queen with a bunch of cuties in tight outfits who have never seen a man. The cheap sets make the moon look like a strip mall, and the men have to show the moon maidens how to kiss.
D: Richard Cunha. A: Richard Travis, Cathy Downs, K. T. Stevens.

Queen of Outer Space
(1958) 80m. **B+**
A space crew crashes on Venus and is captured by a man-hating female civilization ruled by a queen with a death ray. This has every cheesy 50s sci-fi cliché: handsome commander, a dopey Brooklyn type, wicked queen, women in bathing suit and toga outfits, and pastel-colored airport lounge sets sprinkled with flecks. Don't miss this one.
D: Edward Bernds. A: Eric Fleming, Zsa Zsa Gabor, Paul Birch.

Wild Women of Wongo
(1958) 72m. **B**
The cavewomen of Wongo are beautiful, the men ugly. It's just the reverse over at Goona. When a man and woman from each tribe woo, it's war. Well-proportioned bodies romp and grunt through obvious Florida locations with a script written on the back of a postage stamp.
D: James Wolcott. A: Jean Hawkshaw, Mary Ann Webb, Ed Fury.

Hercules and Samson

Before Schwarzenegger flexed his pecs in *Conan*, bodybuilder Steve Reeves bared his chest in these Italian action cheapies and inaugurated a new brand of muscleman films. The formula was simple: With the natural backdrop of Italian blue skies and ruins to represent the ancient world, take one muscular American star and a brace of brawny Italian supporting players for a battle against mythological creatures or each other. Throw in one or two ripe women in clinging robes and heavy blue eye shadow, go easy on the dialogue, and spend about $2.50 in dubbing and *ecco!* You've got brainless sweaty fun and ogle time for both sexes.

Hercules
(1959) 107m. **B+**
Hercules sacrifices his immortality for the love of Iole but must go through a series of ordeals including an Amazon war, a wrestle with a bull, and the search for the Golden Fleece. Full plate for action fans.
D: Pietro Francisci. A: Steve Reeves, Sylva Koscina, Gianna Maria Canale.

Hercules Unchained
(1959) 105m. **B**
Hercules becomes the love slave of the Queen of Lidia but recovers in time to settle a civil war in Thebes. One of his titanic tests includes pulling down a few siege towers to stop an invading army.
D: Pietro Francisci. A: Steve Reeves, Sylva Koscina, Sylvia Lopez.

Goliath and the Barbarians
(1960) 86m. **C+**
The Barbarians plunder Northern Italy and Goliath terrorizes them in the costume of a god figure as he bops a few with a ball and chain. Lots of bruising action with men in furs amid the dark woods.
D: Carlo Campgalliani. A: Steve Reeves, Bruce Cabot, Chelo Alonso.

Goliath and the Dragon
(1960) 90m. **C**
Goliath continues to take care of business with some cheesy monsters, cardboard walls, and some dreadful mistakes in color. The fight between Goliath, a 3-headed dog, and a dragon, which literally tears down a palace, makes this fun for the under-seven set.
D: Vittorio Cottafavi. A: Mark Forest, Elenora Ruffo, Broderick Crawford.

The Last Days of Pompeii
(1960) 103m. **B**
A Roman centurion is unjustly sent to prison before a rendezvous with the lions, while smoking Mt. Vesuvius looms in the background. High on period details and low on he-man action though Reeves does tussle with the lions and leads an escape from the erupting volcano.
D: Mario Bonnard. A: Steve Reeves, Christine Kauffman, Anne Marie Baumann.

Hercules in the Haunted World
(1961) 83m. **C**
Hercules descends into the billowing fires of the underworld to rescue some bountiful women from the clutches of the prince of darkness. Game attempt at creating a Dante's *Inferno* atmosphere.
D: Mario Bava. A: Reg Park, Christopher Lee, Leonora Ruffo.

Morgan the Pirate
(1961) 93m. **B**
Hercules gets a change of scenery and costume in this variation to the he-man genre. Canons blaze and hooks grapple as an escaped English slave returns as a pirate to throttle the Spanish who once held him. Smaller than the pirate films of old, but equally entertaining.
D: Andre de Toth. A: Steve Reeves, Chelo Alonso, Valerie Lagrange.

Hercules and the Captive Women
(1963) 87m. **C+**
This time its personal! The strong man of legend must rescue his son who's held captive by the wicked queen of Atlantis. The usual mortal combats, with guards getting tossed and structures being toppled.
D: Vittorio Cottafari. A: Reg Park, Fay Spain, Marlo Petri.

Goliath and the Vampires
(1964) 91m. **C**
A powerful vampire is creating an army of killer automatons, and Goliath doesn't know how to stop the fiend. Odd blend of vampire legends and strong-man epic with some genuine chills as the zombie soldiers attack.
D: Giacomo Gentilomo. A: Gordon Scott, Jacques Sernas, Gianna Maria Canale.

Hercules Against the Moon Men
(1964) 88m. **B–**
People from the moon enslave the residents of Samar to use them to revive their dead queen, and the mountain of muscles must stop them. Not as bizarre as title suggests, and Hercules uses his wits in this one.
D: Giacomo Gentilomo. A: Alan Steel, Jany Clair, Nando Tamberlani.

OTHER FILMS:
Samson (1960)
Atlas (1961)
Invasion of the Zombies
The Giants of Metropolis (1962)
Samson and the Vampire Women (1961)
Maciste in Hell (1962)
Samson in the Wax Museum (1963)

Big and Mutated Monsters

People suspected that the A-bombs being tested were unleashing more destructive forces than what the scientists were telling us. The filmmakers had some ideas though—gigantic prehistoric creatures were routed out of their lairs, animals and insects become monstrously mutated, and they all ran wild in the streets crunching up skyscrapers and stomping on hysterical crowds. This group of nature-runs-amok tales is a chintzy lot, with loopy plots and dopey special effects, except for Ray Harryhausen's wonderful stop-action monsters. The Japanese-made entries have the added attraction of bad dubbing, pointed symbolism, and some incomprehensible cultural underpinnings. In other words, this is a group of camp classics.

The Beast from 20,000 Fathoms
(1953) 80m. B&W.
B
A giant dinosaur frozen in the Arctic is awakened by atomic testing and heads for New York City, destroying everything in its path. Fast paced with delightful Harryhausen effects, and it's fun watching the beast destroy Manhattan and Coney Island.
D: Eugene Lourie. A: Paul Christian, Paula Raymond, Cecil Kellaway.

Them!
(1954) 93m. B&W. **A**
Strange murders in a small desert town confound the police and FBI, and their only clue turns out to be an

enormous ant leg print. This seminal horror/sci-fi flick resembles a documentary-style 50s crime procedural and is one of the more chilling and intelligent of the genre.
D: Gordon Douglas. A: James Whitmore, Edmund Gwenn, James Arness.

It Came from Beneath the Sea
(1955) 80m. B&W. **B+**
An A-bomb exploded in the Pacific makes an octopus big and irritable, who then heads for San Francisco to wreak destruction. No-nonsense Harryhausen beast doing his destroy-the-landmarks-and-cause-panic-in-the-streets routine.
D: Robert Gordon. A: Kenneth Tobey, Faith Domergue, Donald Curtis.

Attack of the Crab Monsters
(1957) 64m. B&W. **B**
When atomic fallout settles on an island, scientists discover its effect on the marine life. Compensates for its low budget with the wild idea of brain eating crabs that not only absorb the intelligence of their victims but speak with their voices.
D: Roger Corman. A: Richard Garland, Pamela Duncan, Russell Johnson.

20 Million Miles to Earth
(1957) 84m. B&W.
B+
A spaceship visiting Venus returns to Earth with an egg that hatches into an enormous monster who tries to destroy Rome. The Harryhausen special effects are as timeless as watching a good puppet show.
D: Nathan Juran. A: William Hopper, Joan Taylor, Frank Puglia.

Earth vs. the Spider
(1958) 72m. B&W. **D+**
Teens discover a giant spider and when it's believed to be dead, a teacher has it hauled to the school gymnasium where it's brought to life by a rockabilly tune during a band rehearsal. Hilariously ridiculous spider effects (those stuffed limbs!) are the highlight.
D: Bert I. Gordon. A: Ed Kemmer, June Kenny, Geene Persson.

Attack of the Giant Leeches
(1959) 62m. B&W. **D**
When the bar keep in a ramshackle town discovers his trampy wife having an affair, he lures the couple into a swamp with bloodsucking giant leeches. This merely whets the leeches' appetites, and they launch a full-scale assault on the white trash residents.
D: Bernard L. Kowalski. A: Ken Clark, Michael Emmet, Yvette Vickers.

The Giant Gila Monster
(1959) 85m. B&W. **D**
A large lumbering superimposed lizard instills panic in a remote part of Texas, though apparently a crawling infant could outrun the beast. Generally awful on all counts and may tax even diehard fans of the so-bad-they're-good films.
D: Ray Kellogg. A: Don Sullivan, Lisa Simone, Shug Fisher.

Gorgo
(1961) 76m. **B**
After greedy treasure hunters sell Gorgo the giant sea monster to a London circus, it turns out that he's only an infant. His mother comes to collect him and destroys many of London's landmarks in the process. Cheap effects but, like *King Kong,* it pulls at your heart strings.
D: Eugene Lourie. A: Bill Travers, William Sylvester, Vincent Winter.

The Horror of Party Beach
(1964) 71m. B&W. **D–**
When toxic waste is dumped off the coast of a beach—the kind of beach where a band plays its electric instruments with no electrical outlets—it turns the local marine life into icky blood-craving monsters. Billed as the first rock 'n' roll horror musical.
D: Del Tenney. A: John Scott, Alice Lyon, Allen Laurel.

Japanese Monsters

Rodan
(1957) 74m. **C+**
An atomic test riles a giant caterpillar that attacks some miners; then a volcano erupts, and two flying pterodactyls vent their rage on Tokyo. Not quite up to *Godzilla* standards, but still a serviceable cheap Japanese monster film.
D: Inoshiro Honda. A: Kenji Sawara, Yumi Shirakawa, Akihiko Hirata.

The H-Man
(1959) 79m. **B–**
A flesh-dissolving lime Jell-O acid monster created by atomic radiation leaks up from the sewers of Japan. A bizarre mix of noir and *The Blob,* done with gritty seriousness.
D: Inoshiro Honda. A: Yumi Shirakawa, Mitsuru Sato, Kenji Sahara.

Mothra
(1962) 100m. **B–**
A giant caterpillar destroys part of Tokyo while trying to save two kidnapped island girls, then hides in a cocoon and emerges as a giant moth that proceeds to destroy more of Tokyo. This classic Japanese monster film has a slow first half but pays off later with the usual goofy battles.
D: Inoshiro Honda. A: Franky Sakai, Hiroshi Koizumi, Kyoko Kagawa.

Varan, the Unbelievable
(1962) 70m. B&W. **C–**
It sure is. A prehistoric flying Godzilla-like thing is revived from its ancient slumber and there goes Tokyo again. A derivative city-crusher with a low-voltage monster.
D: Jerry A. Baerwitz. A: Myron Healy, Eiji Tsuburaya, Kozo Nomura.

Ghidrah, the 3-Headed Monster
(1965) 85m. **B–**
Good guy Godzilla teams up with Mothra and winged serpent Rodan to save the world from alien Ghidrah. The usual destruction and multi-monster battles with an absurd plot about a Martian princess.
D: Inoshiro Honda. A: Yuriko Hoshi, Yosuke Natsuki.

The War of the Gargantuas
(1966) 93m. **C+**
An atomic blast turns one of two apish creatures into a nasty monster, and the requisite mass destruction ensues. Added laughs are provided by inserted U.S. Tamblyn brooding over the city wreckage.
D: Inoshiro Honda. A: Russ Tamblyn, Kumi Mizuno, Kipp Hamilton.

The X from Outer Space
(1967) 88m. **D**
A steel-plated giant chicken monster comes to Earth by clinging to a spaceship, and soon it's bye-bye to Tokyo again. Hilariously shoddy.
D: Kazui Nihonmatzu. A: Eiji Okada, Sinichi Yanagiswa, Peggy Neal.

Yongary—Monster from the Deep
(1969) 79m. **D**
Released by an earthquake in China, Yongar—a sort of Godzilla with floppy lizard ears and an unquenchable thirst for gasoline—invades Seoul. Outside of the novelty of seeing a different Asian city leveled, this Korean effort falls flat in the all-important rubber monster and

model city department.
D: Kim Ki-duk. A: Yugi Oh, Chungim Nam.

OTHER FILMS:
Monster from Green Hell (1957)
The Cosmic Monsters (1958)
The Creature from the Haunted Sea (1960)
Dinosauris (1960)

Godzilla

When this green, fire-breathing monster Tyrannosaurus Rex first trampled the model city of Tokyo, he was all terrible unbridled postnuclear rage. Then he became a Japanese sensation and by the third feature, he was the country's mythic protector against all sorts of strange invaders. Appealing to his biggest fans, children, Godzilla quickly developed a sense of humor, became environmentally conscious, and had a son. Even his battles against evil behemoths seemed choreographed by the Three Stooges. Cheap effects, ridiculous dubbing, lurid colors (only the first is black and white), and zany battles; it's all good mindless fun, akin to watching professional wrestlers or a little kid tearing up his building block town.

Godzilla, King of the Monsters

(1956) 80m. B&W. **B**

The original tale of how atomic testing unleashed a prehistoric lizard into Tokyo in the 1950s. Neither bullets nor rockets can stop him; not even in intrepid reporter Raymond Burr. Effective and more serious than the sequels.
D. Terry Morse. A. Raymond Burr, Inoshiro Honda, Takashi Shimura.

King Kong vs. Godzilla

(1963) 91m. **C–**

The East's favorite dinosaur engages in fisticuffs with the West's favorite ape, somewhat whacked out on narcotics here. Godzilla starts his kinder gentler thing. Slow first half is penance paid for entertaining battles in the second half.
D: Thomas Montgomery. A: Michael Keith, James Yagi, Tadao Takashima.

Godzilla vs. Mothra

(1964) 88m. **B–**

Champ Godzilla brawls challenger Mothra and her offspring, two silk-spitting caterpillars. The usual mayhem enlivened by some imaginative battle sequences.
D: Inoshiro Honda. A: Okira Takarada, Yuriko Hoshi, Hiroshi Koizumi.

Godzilla vs. Monster Zero

(1966) 93m. **B–**

Earth beasts Godzilla and Rodan are transported in giant soap bubbles to a distant planet where they match wits with evil Monster Zero (aka Ghidrah). But Earth wants its monsters back and will start an intergalactic war to do it.
D: Inoshiro Honda. A: Nick Adams, Akiro Takarada.

Godzilla vs. the Sea Monster

(1966) 80m. **D+**

Godzilla dukes it out with Ebirah, a gigantic aquatic hybrid of shrimp and crab. Mothra turns in excellent work in an uncredited cameo role. Below par, due mostly to a subplot featuring the actors who aren't dressed in monster suits.
D: Jun Fukuda. A: Akira Takarada, Toru Watanabe, Jun Tasaki.

The Son of Godzilla

(1967) 90m. **D**

Godzilla's adorable yet strange spawn roughhouses with giant insects and calls on his dad when things get a little out of hand. Silly childish entry will bore adults but may entertain younger children.
D: Jun Fukuda. A: Tadao Takashima, Akira Kubo, Bibari Maeda.

Godzilla's Revenge

(1969) 70m. **C–**

A young tyke fantasizes about visiting Monster Island, where he meets the stable of heavyweights (Godzilla, Mothra, et al.) and learns valuable life lessons from Son of Godzilla. Compiled from previous Godzilla films and takes steady aim at an audience of children.
D: Inoshiro Honda. A: Konji Sahara, Tomonori Yazaki, Machiko Naka.

Godzilla vs. Gigan

(1972) 89m. **C**

Ghidrah, the evil three-headed monster, and Gigan (concealing a saw blade in his stomach) engage in a tag team match against Godzilla and his partner Angillus. More monsters do not always make a better film. Godzilla talks in this one.
D: Jun Fukuda. A: Hiroshi Ishikawa, Minoru Takashima, Tomoko Umeda.

Godzilla vs. the Smog Monster

(1972) 85m. **C**

National treasure Godzilla is summoned to battle Japan's latest nemesis, a hideous creature created from industrial waste. Less childish and more goofball camp.
D: Yoshimitu Banno. A: Akira Yamauchi, Hiroyuki Kawase, Toshio Shibaki.

Godzilla vs. MechaGodzilla

(1974) 84m. **C–**

A race of aliens, who look suspiciously like men in gorilla suits, construct a robot facsimile of Japan's leading monster, with designs to conquer Earth. Pretty boring, saved only by those aliens and the final battle sequence.
D: Jun Fukuda. A: Masaaki Daimon, Kazuya Aoyama, Reiko Tajima.

Terror of MechaGodzilla

(1978) 89m. **C–**

Bad guys reconstruct Godzilla's robot evil twin, scheming to do away with that pesky giant reptile once and for all. An unusually high number of explosions in this one.
D: Inoshiro Honda. A: K. Sasaki, Tomoki Ai, Akihiko Hirata.

Godzilla 1985

(1985) 91m. **B–**

The giant reptile rises from the sea to terrorize Japan again, and Godzilla expert Burr is present to dole out the advice. Very well photographed, decently acted, with a sober tone, this sequel is so endearingly ridiculous—it even has moments of unexpected tenderness.
D: Kohji Hashimoto. A: Raymond Burr, Keiju Kobayashi, Ten Tenaka.

Mutant Humans

These atomic-era films featured characters (scientists or victims of scientists) shrinking, growing, walking through walls, or otherwise mutating, with a steep price paid for their technological hubris. As for quality, these ranged from the thoughtful and inventive to humorously sleazy and lame, the later creating some moments of classic sci-fi camp.

Dr. Cyclops

(1940) 75m. **B**

Nearly blind and completely insane, Dr. Thorkel reduces people to the size of dolls in his jungle hideaway. This early Technicolor adventure-horror focuses on the efforts of the tiny victims to maneuver up and down giant furniture in their effort to escape, with the unhinged Doc the looming monster.

D: Ernest B. Schoedsack. A: Albert Dekker, Janice Logan, Charles Halton.

Donovan's Brain

(1953) 85m. B&W. **B–**

A kindly doctor keeps the malevolent brain of a dead industrialist alive and soon the good doc is being put through the evil one's nefarious paces. Not much to the lab in this low-tech thriller—a brain in a jar that occasionally pulsates, but the story and strong performances will grab you.

D: Felix Feist. A: Lew Ayres, Nancy Davis, Gene Evans.

The Amazing Colossal Man

(1957) 79m. B&W. **D**

An army colonel exposed to plutonium grows to gigantic proportions, goes insane, and runs amok in Las Vegas. A Bert I. Gordon (B.I.G.) masterpiece, which means the film entertains as camp only half the time, thanks mostly to the dreadful effects.

D: Bert I. Gordon. A: Glenn Langan, Cathy Downs, James Seay.

The Cyclops

(1957) 75m. B&W. **C–**

Chaney is hired to find a missing husband and discovers that radiation has turned him and some animals into giants. Another Bert I. Gordon (B.I.G.) misfire with the cheesy looking, putty-faced title character.

D: Bert I. Gordon. A: James Craig, Lon Chaney, Jr., Gloria Talbott.

The Incredible Shrinking Man

(1957) 81m. B&W.

A

After passing through a radioactive fog, a man encounters emotional and physical challenges because he keeps getting smaller. His wife sets him up in a doll house; he battles a cat and a spider and ponders the meaning of existence. Superior action and special effects.

D: Jack Arnold. A: Grant Williams, Randy Stuart, April Kent.

Attack of the 50 Foot Woman

(1958) 60m. B&W. **C–**

After encountering an extraterrestrial, a wife grows as big as a house and exacts revenge on her philandering hubby and his mistress. A camp classic due to its complete inepitude. So bad it's good? It's even worse (and funnier) than that!

D: Nathan Juran. A: Allison Hayes, William Hudson, Yvette Vickers.

War of the Colossal Beast

(1958) 68m. B&W. **F**

The C-Beast, thought dead after his fall in *The Amazing Colossal Man,* is discovered in Mexico and brought to LA, where he escapes his captors and goes on a rampage. A dreadful cheapie without even the wanton low-budget destruction that is promised.

D: Bert I. Gordon. A: Sally Fraser, Roger Pace, Dean Parkin.

4D Man

(1959) 85m. **B–**

A scientist discovers that he has the ability to walk through solid matter; the downside? This talent leads to murder and insanity. Lansing's solid performance and some thoughtful moments elevate this otherwise standard effort from the dregs.

D: Irvin Yeaworth, Jr. A: Robert Lansing, Lee Meriwether, Patty Duke.

The Amazing Transparent Man

(1960) 58m. B&W. **D+**

A power-mad scientist who has discovered a way to become invisible is forced to share his secret with a money-mad bank robber. Ultra-cheap and slow.

D: Edgar G. Ulmer. A: Douglas Kennedy, Marguerite Chapman, James Griffith.

X—The Man with X-Ray Eyes

(1963) 79m. **B+**

An ambitious doctor discovers that the ability to see through everything can be a curse and, while fleeing the authorities, becomes a circus side show attraction and later a shady ghetto doctor. A snappy quasi-religious fable.

D: Roger Corman. A: Ray Milland, Diana Van Der Vlis, Don Rickles.

Village of the Giants

(1965) 80m. B&W. **D**

Bert I. Gordon makes another B.I.G. film, this time with rowdy loser teens ingesting something or other that makes them grow. Boys attacking a giant immobile pair of cement legs are some of the more tasteful effects here.

D: Bert I. Gordon. A: Tommy Kirk, Beau Bridges, Ron Howard.

Global Invaders and Disasters

Coming from the 50s Cold War front, these films are closer to science fiction war stories, with scientists as the heroes in a battle against aliens trying to colonize Earth for ungodly purposes. Most are B films with some endearingly tinny special effects, although there are a few spectacular exceptions.

The Flying Saucers
(1950) 70m. B&W. **C–**

A G-man is dispatched to Alaska to investigate UFO sightings. After much talking, the craft's existence is confirmed. But is it extraterrestrial? Dull, with little action.

D: Mikel Conrad. A: Mikel Conrad, Pat Garrison, Russell Hicks.

The Day the Earth Stood Still
(1951) 92m. B&W. **A** 🏛

A sensitive alien lands in Washington to deliver an urgent message: Live in peace or face annihilation by his race of superior beings and their imposing robots. A sci-fi flick of uncompromising quality, looking like a time-capsule record of 50s life with believable human drama, eerie suspense, and humor.

D: Robert Wise. A: Michael Rennie, Patricia Neal, Hugh Marlowe.

When Worlds Collide
(1951) 82m. **B**

Astronomers discover a star on a collision course with Earth, but also a safe haven planet nearby. What follows is essentially a rocket launching procedural: Fund a space project, construct a Noah's ark spacecraft, and select the people to populate a new planet. This colorful big screen doomsday fable keeps the time-is-running-out momentum and tension throughout.

D: Rudolph Maté. A: Richard Derr, Barbara Rush, Peter Hanson.

Phantom from Space
(1953) 72m. B&W. **D**

A UFO lands outside of LA, causing a commotion among military men, police, and local scientists. Soon dead bodies are turning up and the hunt is on for an invisible alien. If it weren't so horribly slow, this would be prime camp material.

D: W. Lee Wilder. A: Ted Cooper, Rudolph Anders, Noreen Nash.

The War of the Worlds
(1953) 85m. **A**

A meteor lands in California, but it's actually the first of many Martian-laden spaceships to arrive. Visually spectacular, intelligent, and suspenseful, this will grip you right through to the climax of mass evacuations while the Martians ships blast away in all the major cities.

D: Byron Haskin. A: Gene Barry, Les Tremayne, Ann Robinson.

Earth vs. the Flying Saucers
(1956) 83m. B&W. **B**

A dying planet's spaceships want to park on Earth, and will employ every alien trick in the book like brainwashing, android warriors, and space rays to do it. Earth scientists and military join forces to thwart them, but not until you see great hoards of gigantic flying saucers crashing into every famous landmark and monument in the world.

D: Fred F. Sears. A: Hugh Marlowe, Joan Taylor, Donald Curtis.

The Quatermass Experiment (aka The Creeping Unknown)
(1956) 78m. B&W. **A–**

A British space crew's only survivor is covered with a sort of space gelatin, which eventually transforms him into a grotesque creature who terrorizes England. The esteemed feisty Dr. Quatermass must stop him. Intelligent handling makes up for the 50s impoverished sci-fi look and slow pacing.

D: Val Guest. A: Brian Donlevy, Margia Dean, Jack Warner.

Enemy from Space
(1957) 85m. B&W. **B+**

Dr. Quatermass discovers an insidious alien invasion plan already taking place: the old replace-the-world-leaders-with-soulless-duplicates scheme. A solid low-budget entry, shot on eerily deserted factory sites and not dashed off like its American counterparts.

D: Val Guest. A: Brian Donlevy, Michael Ripper, Sidney James.

Kronos
(1957) 78m. B&W. **B**

An enormous alien robot is dispatched to suck Earth dry of her energy, and scientists try to short-circuit it. Has some charm and low-rent effects as it travels through the countryside toward California, getting bigger all the time.

D: Kurt Neumann. A: Jeff Morrow, Barbara Lawrence, John Emery.

The Atomic Submarine
(1959) 80m. B&W. **C–**

A submarine full of military brass and scientists is sent to investigate mysterious craft sinkings in the Arctic. They discover an underwater flying saucer piloted by a rubber thing with one eye and tentacles. This talky film obviously bit off more than it could afford.

D: Spencer Bennet. A: Arthur Franz, Dick Foran, Brett Halsey.

The Mysterians
(1959) 85m. **C**

What does any self-respecting alien race do when their planet becomes uninhabitable? Go to Earth, enslave human men, and breed with the women. Of course the humans finally prevail, but not until most of Tokyo is leveled. Standard issue, garishly colored Japanese apocalypse film.

D: Inoshiro Honda. A: Kenji Sahara, Yumi Shirakawa, Momoko Kochi.

Invaders from Next Door

In these alarmist McCarthy-era tales, sneaky extraterrestrials inhabit, duplicate, or brainwash the good citizens of Earth in order to replace the American way of life with their own unemotional one. Most of these films are like horror noir with heavily shadowed black-and-white lighting, claustrophobic space, and bizarre camera angles. Like the classic examples of that genre, these take aim at some primal fears: "Do I really know what my neighbors are capable of? What the hell is my spouse doing when I'm asleep?" Or, "Is my kid some alien from another planet?"

Invaders from Mars
(1953) 78m. **B–**
A young boy sees a UFO land near his house and nobody believes him when he notices that his parents and other adults are acting strangely. Luridly colored minor classic but a bit slow.
D: William Cameron Menzies. A: Helena Carter, Arthur Franz, Jimmy Hunt.

It Came from Outer Space
(1953) 81m. B&W. **B**
Aliens borrow the shapes of the local townsfolk while repairing their ship that crashed nearby. Restrained but solid film: eerie and a minor classic of the genre.
D: Jack Arnold. A: Richard Carlson, Barbara Rush, Charles Drake.

Invasion of the Body Snatchers
(1956) 80m. B&W. **A**
People from a small town begin noticing that some of their relatives aren't themselves ("That's not Uncle Ira!") and the young doctor and his girl try to fight off the alien pods who replace people in their sleep. As good as any noir classic and genuinely spooky to boot. This one works on so many levels it's mind-boggling.
D: Don Siegel. A: Kevin McCarthy, Dana Wynter, Carolyn Jones.

It Conquered the World
(1956) 68m. B&W. **B–**
A deranged scientist helps a cucumberlike creature from Venus enslave humans, but another scientist starts killing off the slaves. Plenty of activity keeps you interested but it's constantly undermined by the zero budget.
D: Roger Corman. A: Peter Graves, Beverly Garland, Lee Van Cleef.

The Brain from Planet Arous
(1958) 80m. B&W. **C+**
A scientist discovers an intergalactic criminal whose ability to take over a human's body is merely the first step to universal domination. This one is cheap, cheap, cheap, from the story to the special effects, but it might win you over with its goofiness.
D: Nathan Juran. A: John Agar, Joyce Meadows, Robert Fuller.

Village of the Damned
(1960) 78m. B&W. **A–**
Every child-bearing woman in a small British village suddenly gets pregnant and gives birth to physically and mentally precocious children. This is the cream of the "child-demon" crop with good acting and plenty of suspense and chills.
D: Wolf Rilla. A: George Sanders, Barbara Shelley, Michael Gwynne.

The Day of the Triffids
(1963) 94m. **B+**
A meteor shower leads to almost universal blindness as an alien plant form invades Britain. Chilling sense of omnipresent menace and most convincingly creepy examples of fauna invasion.
D: Steve Sekely. A: Howard Keel, Nicole Maurey, Janette Scott.

The Human Duplicators
(1965) 82m. **C–**
Alien head honcho Richard Kiel ("Jaws" of the James Bond films) scouts Earth with the intention of duplicating humans, but then falls in love with an Earth woman. Cheap and a little dull and made too long after the premise ran its course.
D: Hugo Grimaldi. A: George Nader, Barbara Nichols, Hugh Beaumont.

Fantasy Journeys—When Victorians Flew Rocketships

When you go back to the future with the earliest science fiction writers like Welles, Verne, and Burroughs, you see how Victorians and their progeny envisioned where progress would take the twentieth century. Except for the few modern-day or caveman yarns, these richly colored nostalgic adventures featured quaint-looking machines that could fly, pierce the earth, submerge oceans, and hurtle through space. Of course once these scientists get to where they're going, you still get to see monsters and prehistoric dinosaurs.

20,000 Leagues Under the Sea
(1954) 122m. **A**
Pacifist Captain Nemo roams the seas in his sub sinking warships, but decides to allow some survivors from one of his raids on board. Charming, grandly Victorian sea adventure with artfully realized ship, sea monsters, undersea exploration, and a darkly fascinating Nemo.
D: Richard Fleischer. A: James Mason, Kirk Douglas, Paul Lukas.

From the Earth to the Moon
(1958) 100m. **C**
A post-Civil War arms merchant develops "Power X" to launch a ship to the moon and takes a sabotaging British competitor along for the ride. Stylish period details and the over-decorated Victorian rocketship don't make up for an uninspired script.
D: Byron Haskin. A: Joseph Cotten, George Sanders, Debra Paget.

Journey to the Center of the Earth
(1959) 132m. **B+**
Scottish professor leads an exploration deep into the center of the Earth where they encounter monsters, a lost city, and take a wild ride on a lava flow up a volcanic tube.
D: Henry Levin. A: James Mason, Arlene Dahl, Pat Boone.

The Time Machine
(1960) 103m. **B+**
A scientist travels through time and discovers a future mankind childishly living in a docile paradise but serving as food for a ghoulish underground civilization. First part is like a lively and ominous Victorian period drama before it switches to often terrifying sci-fi futuristic sequences.
D: George Pal. A: Rod Taylor, Yvette Mimieux, Alan Young.

Master of the World
(1961) 104m. **B**
Like an airborne Captain Nemo, Robur roams the

world in his nineteenth-century zeppelin trying to destroy man's ability to make war. Intriguing airship but the film's slower pace only picks up at the high energy finale.
D: William Witney. A: Vincent Price, Henry Hull, Charles Bronson.

Mysterious Island
(1961) 101m. **B+**
Civil War soldiers fly a balloon to a bizarre island populated with giant crabs and chickens and a long lost Captain Nemo. Likable characters, enough special effects and escapes to keep things moving, and an impressive sunken ancient city and gothic submarine.
D: Cy Endfield. A: Michael Craig, Joan Greenwood, Herbert Lom.

Voyage to the Bottom of the Sea
(1961) 105m. **B**
The Earth's in danger of frying when a radiation belt ignites in the skies and an admiral heads for the North Pole to blow it up. Some good, fiery special effects, a submarine chase sequence, and a battle with a killer squid to add spice.
D: Irwin Allen. A: Walter Pidgeon, Robert Sterling, Joan Fontaine.

First Men in the Moon
(1964) 103m. **B**
Eccentric British genius creates an antigravity device in the late nineteenth century that gets him to the moon. Entertaining and cheerfully presented tale with a batty professor and Victorian lovers in a diving bell-like ship falling into the hands of ant-like moon people.
D: Nathan Juran. A: Lionel Jeffries, Edward Judd, Martha Hyer.

Around the World Under the Sea
(1966) 110m. **D**
There's trouble at the bottom of the sea when a high-tech submarine discovers treasure while setting up a volcano detection network. A soggy tale, but the climax where the ship is blown in half is entertaining.
D: Andrew Marton. A: Lloyd Bridges, Brian Kelly, Shirley Eaton.

Fantastic Voyage
(1966) 100m. **B**
A team of specialists is shrunk to molecule size so they can be injected into a scientist's body to perform delicate brain surgery. Resembles a lava lamp light show as the crew passes through brightly colored blobs of cells and corpuscles in this silly but enjoyable tour of the body.
D: Richard Fleischer. A: Stephen Boyd, Raquel Welch, Edmond O'Brien, and others.

When Dinosaurs Ruled the Earth
(1969) 100m. **C**
A cavegirl, ostracized by her tribe, meets another exile, and together they survive roving dinosaurs. There's no dialogue (everyone grunts), the stop-action dinosaurs are lively, and the cavegirl who's a Playmate of the Year wears a skimpy outfit.
D: Val Guest. A: Victoria Vetri, Robin Hawdon, Patrick Allen.

The Island at the Top of the World
(1974) 93m. **C**
A father launches an airship expedition to find his lost son in the Arctic and discovers a lost tribe of Vikings. Kid-level adventure with motley crew of explorers and dangerous Vikings. Airship ride is more fun than action on land.
D: Robert Stevenson. A: Donald Sinden, David Hartman, Jacques Marin.

The Land That Time Forgot
(1974) 91m. **B−**
Ship survivors drift to an Arctic island full of cavemen and dinosaurs. Starts out as a tense sea drama but once island-bound, it becomes a standard can't-talk-to-the-natives and look-out-a-dinosaur-is behind-you actioner with unconvincing man-in-suit dinos.
D: Kevin Connor. A: Doug McClure, John McEnery, Susan Penhaligon.

At the Earth's Core
(1976) 90m. **B−**
Two scientists invent a gigantic, Victorian-styled machine that can tunnel deep into the Earth's crust where they encounter a vicious warrior civilization and prehistoric creatures. Fast pace covers the fact that the story has nowhere to go but back up.
D: Kevin Connor. A: Doug McClure, Peter Cushing, Caroline Munro.

The People That Time Forgot
(1977) 90m. **D**
This sequel to *The Land That Time Forgot* has the same ragged cavepeople, lame dinosaur action, and a new menace of a smoking volcano. Substandard "run and hide from the dinosaurs" story.
D: Kevin Connor. A: Patrick Wayne, Sarah Douglas, Doug McClure.

Harryhausen Fantasy

You don't need to be a kid to enjoy these adventure fantasies of the fabulous creatures, gods, and heroes of mythical Greece and medieval Arabia. Part cheesy, muscle-bound sword-and-sandal tale and part fairy tale, these films feature the stop-action animation of Ray Harryhausen, who makes giants come alive, griffins fly, and skeletons fight. While these movies lack the high-tech gloss of *Star Wars*, they do capture a childlike sense of awe and splendor, and hearken back to an innocent time when gods and heroes roamed the Earth.

The Seventh Voyage of Sinbad
(1958) 94m. **B+**
When an evil wizard shrinks the princess to the size of a zucchini, the dauntless Arabian sailor Sinbad searches in faraway lands for the egg of the giant bird Roc, in order to break the spell. Features sword-wielding skeletons.
D: Nathan Juran. A: Kerwin Mathews, Torin Thatcher, Kathryn Grant.

Jason and the Argonauts
(1963) 104m. **B+**
Jason and his ship's crew are sent by the gods to wrest the famed Golden Fleece from the dreaded seven-headed Hydra. Exciting battles against mythical monsters with few lulls and another great swordfight with a battalion of skeletons.
D: Don Chaffey. A: Todd Armstrong, Niall MacGinnis, Honor Blackman.

The Golden Voyage of Sinbad
(1974) 105m. **B**
Sinbad battles an evil prince for the amulet that provides untold wealth and power. Has quirky creatures including a ship's figurehead who can talk and a monumental statue with swordplay on its mind.
D: Gordon Hessler. A: John Philip Law, Tom Baker, Carol Munro.

Sinbad and the Eye of the Tiger
(1977) 113m. **C+**
Sinbad has to find a way to break an evil spell on the Prince. A soggy script slows the action, which only perks up when the various mythic creatures appear. Fast forward to the monsters for the kids.
D: Sam Wanamaker. A: Patrick Wayne, Taryn Power, Jane Seymour.

Clash of the Titans
(1981) 118m. **B**
When the gods in Mt. Olympus play their chess game using mortals as the pieces, the hero Perseus must undergo a series of ordeals, including striking the head off the snake-haired Medusa. Packed with effects, monsters, and fantastic creatures: fun, as long as you ignore the famous humans and awful dialogue.
D: Desmond Davis. A: Harry Hamlin, Laurence Olivier, Maggie Smith.

1960s–1970s
Atomic Anxiety

These meditations on a variety of Armageddons share a more quiet sober tone than their teen-oriented, low-budget counterparts, with fine acting and atmospheric production values that helped the viewing public deal with their atomic anxieties in the safety of the neighborhood bijou.

1984
(1955) 92m. B&W. **B–**
Future society is mind-numbed and controlled by a Big Brother bureaucracy that supervises even love. A generally faithful version of Orwell's dark drama, though a plump O'Brien makes an unlikely protagonist. Bleak bombed out London maintains the relentless tenor of a society drained of spirit.
D: Michael Anderson. A: Edmond O'Brien, Jan Sterling, Michael Redgrave.

On the Beach
(1959) 134m. B&W. **B+**
This earnest, occasionally heavy-handed doomsday depressor follows some survivors in Australia after a nuclear war has destroyed the Northern Hemisphere, and a deadly radioactive cloud is moving toward them. Good somber character moments add flavor to a downbeat tale.
D: Stanley Kramer. A: Gregory Peck, Ava Gardner, Fred Astaire.

The Day the Earth Caught Fire
(1962) 99m. B&W
A–
A-bomb blasts have launched the Earth toward the sun and, amid violent weather shifts and mass panic, scientists figure out that a stronger blast might save the day. A compact and exciting doomsday thriller with solid effects and kinetic scenes of rioting and storms that zip you toward the explosive climax.
D: Val Guest. A: Edward Judd, Janet Munro, Leo McKern.

The Last Man on Earth
(1964) 86m. B&W. **B**
A tension-filled, gloomy, and downbeat thriller about the only normal man left on a plague-ravaged Earth peopled by savage vampires. A low-budget entry that uses deserted streets, rubble, and chilling quiet to impress a fear that "they" are closing in.
D: Sidney Salkow. A: Vincent Price, Emma Danieli, Franca Bettoia.

Sci-Fi Spoofs

No one can hear, when you strip in space. . . .

Barbarella
(1968) 98m. **B**
This psychedelic 60s sex kitten-in-space farce sets the tone early as astrobabe Fonda does a gravity-free strip in her fur-lined spaceship. Kitschy sets, bizarre music, and the film's dated-looking attempts to be hip make this fun, but beware of the lulls between the camp elements.
D: Roger Vadim. A: Jane Fonda, John Phillip Law, Milo O'Shea.

Flesh Gordon
(1974) 70m./82m.-X rated.
C+
This all too obvious sex parody of old Flash Gordon space adventures offers Dr. Jerkoff and Flesh battling the evil Emperor Wang who's got a mean little sex ray. The low-budget effects get playful and there's plenty of flesh to keep your eyes busy.
D: Howard Ziehm, Michael Benveniste. A: Jason Williams, Suzanne Fields, Joseph Hudgins.

Planet of the Apes

A present day astronaut is trapped in a future world where apes rule and humans are beasts used for slave labor and medical experiments. This clever premise allowed for some good observations on humanity and those great ape costumes gave the viewer the weird and wonderful sight of all types of simians talking, emoting, and living their lives in an all too familiar civilization.

Planet of the Apes
(1968) 112m. **B+**
The original is a good blend of sci-fi, action, and social satire with the astronaut Heston trying to escape his fate as a human in an ape-ruled world only to discover a horrifying secret about the fate of humanity.
D: Franklin J. Schaffner. A: Charlton Heston, Roddy McDowall, Kim Hunter.

Beneath the Planet of the Apes
(1970) 95m. **B–**
A rescue mission lands in the ape world and falls in with a group of mutant humans and scientists living in the Forbidden Zone. A further chance to explore humans through ape eyes with an antinuke message and some really weird mutants.
D: Ted Post. A: James Franciscus, Kim Hunter, Maurice Evans.

Escape from the Planet of the Apes
(1971) 98m. **B**
Two ape scientists from the future land in 1973 California to warn humanity of their fate and become fugitives from the usual evil government types. Some humorous moments hindered by fairly predictable events.
D: Don Taylor. A: Roddy McDowall, Kim Hunter, Ricardo Montalban.

Conquest of the Planet of the Apes
(1972) 87m. **B–**
Apes are house slaves in a semifascist Earth in the 1990s, and the surviving son of the apes-from-the-future spearheads a rebellion. Darker film with heavy-handed parallels to race relations. Spirited but trite. Root for the apes.
D: J. Lee Thompson. A: Roddy McDowall, Don Murray, Ricardo Montalban.

Battle for the Planet of the Apes
(1973) 92m. **C**
The apes and the gorillas duke it out in a postnuclear world, and the gorillas want to wipe out the now-primitive humans. Extensive use of stock footage from previous ape films and a resolution that's visible from deep space make this a film for fans who want to see this series neatly tied up.
D: J. Lee Thompson. A: Roddy McDowall, John Huston, Lew Ayres.

Animation

While these films are a far cry from the modern-day Japanese *animé*, the freedom of animation still allowed these filmmakers to explore strange worlds that relatively primitive F/X live action sci-fi films of the era couldn't.

Fantastic Planet
(1973) 72m. **B**
Tiny humanoids on the ravaged planet of Ysam are treated like second-class toys by the giant robotlike overlords, and revolution is in the air. Sketchy but rich, cut-out animation style is vivid, and the uniquely fashioned characters are refreshingly different in this French/Czech production.
D: Rene Laloux. A: Voices: Barry Bostwick, Nora Heflin.

Wizards
(1977) 82m. **C+**
It's a grim battle on a distant and war battered planet as Avatar, not the most competent hero, must duel his deeply evil brother Blackwolf. Almost smugly anti-Disney in presentation with tart language, gory battles, and chattering elves subjected to persecution by fascist villains. Expertly animated but slightly unpleasant.
D: Ralph Bakshi. A: Voices: Bob Holt, Steve Gravers, Jessie Wells.

The Lord of the Rings
(1978) 133m. **C+**
Ambitious attempt to encompass a sizable portion of the Tolkien Hobbit books overwhelms all but the most avid book fans with a mass of details and characters before the adventure ever gets going. Fluid animation has amazing depth to it, but the abrupt unfulfilling ending has "sequel" written all over it.
D: Ralph Bakshi. A: Voices: Christopher Guard, John Hurt.

Computers and Androids

Hollywood continued to make "machine vs. man" science thrillers with these glossy intelligent suspense films about computers and androids who, as always, turn on their creators.

Colossus: The Forbin Project

(1969) 100m. **B+**

The quiet horror of the computer age takes on the Frankenstein theme when Dr. Forbin creates a U.S. Defense system supercomputer that has its own ideas—like detonating nuclear warheads to warn mankind not to tamper. An icy cold and thoughtful story.
D: Joseph Sargent. A: Eric Braeden, Susan Clark, William Schallert.

The Andromeda Strain

(1971) 130m. **B+**

An unearthly organism kills off all but two inhabitants of a town, and a crack research team works furiously in a secret underground lab to prevent its spread. An all too plausible and adult science procedural thriller of believable people working in very scary circumstances under deadly pressure.
D: Robert Wise. A: Arthur Hill, James Olson, Kate Reid.

Westworld

(1973) 91m. **B+**

These robots let clients play out their Old West fantasies in the ultimate theme park until a malfunction causes a robot gunslinger to hunt down two terrified customers. A good mix of comedy, satire, and terror, which leaps into frenzied gear once robot Brynner hits his first target.
D: Michael Crichton. A: Richard Benjamin, James Brolin, Yul Brynner.

Futureworld

(1976) 107m. **B**

It's the humans who've gone berserk in this talky high-tech sequel to *Westworld* as they plot to replace prominent figures with robotic duplicates. Suspense and paranoia keep the tempo charged while reporters trapped in the robot "entertainment" complex never know who's real and who's not.
D: Richard Heffron. A: Peter Fonda, Blythe Danner, Yul Brynner.

Demon Seed

(1977) 94m. **B**

A hyperintelligent computer has a very human desire to reproduce and chooses its creator's wife as the mother-to-be. The fine performances and literate script give this high-tech, "compusex" thriller a high plausibility factor. Includes dynamic special effects, with an insemination scene that keeps a level head.
D: Donald Cammell. A: Julie Christie, Fritz Weaver, Berry Kroeger.

Dystopias

The future is here and it isn't pretty. These nasty little visions of the future as fascist states and pollution-blasted environments populated by a dehumanized humanity are Hollywood's versions of *1984*. As with Orwell's classic, these cautionary tales follow the adventures of an average Joe who breaks rank after he wakes up to how horrible things really are. While most of these films are mainstream Hollywood productions, they're less F/X spectacles than human dramas in a future that looks a whole lot like now.

Fahrenheit 451

(1966) 112m. **A**

A fireman whose job it is to burn books in a future totalitarian state begins to question his joyless existence, lifeless marriage, and those wall-sized TV screens that transmit "the family" into his home. Truffaut gives us a quietly thoughtful, stylish, and very European sci-fi drama.
D: François Truffaut. A: Julie Christie, Oskar Werner, Anton Diffring.

The Omega Man

(1971) 98m. **C**

Germ war-ravaged LA is controlled by vampire mutants and normal sole survivor Heston has a blood serum that could save mankind. Grim downbeat vision cursed with some batty dialogue, but the vampire mutants are pretty repulsive.
D: Boris Sagal. A: Charlton Heston, Rosalind Cash, Anthony Zerbe.

THX 1138

(1971) 88m. **B**

White on white pervades this vision of a robotlike future where hairless humans are numbered and mind-numbed so there is no crime, humanity, and love. Impressive and original, even if this antiseptic world leaves you cold.
D: George Lucas. A: Robert Duvall, Donald Pleasence, Maggie McOmie.

Soylent Green

(1973) 100m. **B**

Overheated, overcrowded, overpolluted, and underfed New York City is kept alive via foodstuffs supplied by the Soylent Corporation. What's the secret ingredient in their latest food product? A sweaty nightmarish vision of urban life that makes the story's government-sponsored suicide literally look like a day in the country.
D: Richard Fleischer. A: Charlton Heston, Edward G. Robinson, Leigh Taylor-Young.

Zardoz

(1974) 105m. **C+**

In a wasteland future, Connery is a loincloth-clad policeman keeping the "Brutals" in line until he makes his way into the ruling ship Zardoz, home of the sexless "Eternals." A strange, sometimes sluggish counterculture mix of metaphysical drama and tribal-style violence and sex with a knockout ending with Connery and Rampling.
D: John Boorman. A: Sean Connery, Charlotte Rampling, Sally Anne Newton.

Rollerball

(1975) 128m. **C+**

When violence and poverty are eradicated in the future, the corporate state devises a sadistic and deadly sport to sate the masses' bloodlust. After the film makes its point early on, it loses steam despite the scenes of glitzy booming Rollerball games.
D: Norman Jewison. A: James Caan, Maud Adams, John Houseman.

A Boy and His Dog

(1976) 87m. **C+**

Young Vic is one of the few nonsterile humans remaining as he scrubs around for food, looks for nontainted women, and avoids violent bands of toughs in a hungry, war-ravaged world. This low-budget cult favorite is a bleak fantasy spiced with gallows humor, with the best lines going to Vic's telepathic dog.
D: L. Q. Jones. A: Don Johnson, Jason Robards, Susanne Benton.

Logan's Run
(1976) 118m. **C+**
It's a carefree subsurface paradise until you're 30 and then it's disintegration time. Nearly ripe York and Agutter decide to buck the system and head for the surface. Despite the big budget, paradise has a distinct 70s haircut and miniskirted look, and once the basic idea is established this becomes a standard chase film.
D: Michael Anderson. A: Michael York, Jenny Agutter, Peter Ustinov.

1980s–1990s

Sword and Sorcery

These films introduce the kingdoms of wizards, princesses, and serpents where disputes are settled by an incantation and a lot of swipes with a big glistening sword. The swashbuckling fan can enjoy the grappling swordplay, and rather graphic depictions of maiden-wooing. For the fantasy fancier, the sets, costumes, and special effects help bring the tales of mystical rituals and dragon-slaying colorfully alive.

Dragonslayer
(1981) 110m. **B–**
A king in pre-Christian England doesn't mind offering virgins to the resident dragon but, when his own daughter sacrifices herself, he gets the wizard's young apprentice to slay the beast. This has a more *Star Wars* approach to the genre, with dramatic effects and a dragon that really cooks when he finally shows up near the end.
D: Matthew Robbins. A: Peter MacNicol, Ralph Richardson, Caitlin Clarke.

Excalibur
(1981) 140m. **B**
Shining armor and the devilish spells of Merlin pervade this glossy version of King Arthur's life from boyhood and his extraction of the sword Excalibur from a stone, to his adventures as king. A more cerebral approach with mythically distant characters and shimmering enchanting imagery.
D: John Boorman. A: Nigel Terry, Nicol Williamson, Helen Mirren.

Hawk the Slayer
(1981) 93m. **C–**
Jack Palance plays with his usual relish Hawk's snarling villainous older brother as the siblings battle over a sword that can hurl through the air. This offers the requisite evil wizard, swordplay in annoying slow motion, and some buffoonery at the local tavern. Unfortunately the weak plot and discount budget show.
D: Terry Marcel. A: Jack Palance, John Terry, Roy Kinnear.

The Beastmaster
(1982) 119m. **C**
With skimpy loincloth, oversized sword, and the ability to communicate with animals, Dar battles conjurer Maax while protecting the shapely princess Kiri. Good use of rocky California locations as fighting Dar "sees" through an eagle's eyes and commands the powers of bear and panther.
D: Don Coscarelli. A: Marc Singer, Tanya Roberts, Rip Torn.

Conan the Barbarian
(1982) 129m. **B**
Everyone's in loincloths and ready to flash some steel in this ponderous sweaty, bulging-biceps feast. Plenty of screams, blood, and fighting as Conan slices up a giant snake and lives by his code: "Crush your enemy, see them driven before you, hear the lamentations of the women."
D: John Milius. A: Arnold Schwarzenegger, Sandahl Bergman, James Earl Jones.

The Sword and the Sorcerer
(1982) 100m. **C**
A low-budget plunge into artificial myth as a prince returns home to battle the vile knight who slayed his family and took his kingdom. The hero is attacked by a snake, torture victims howl in the dungeons, and the hero comes complete with a metallic hand. More blood and less involvement in this entry.
D: Albert Pyun. A: Lee Horsley, George Maharis, Kathleen Beller.

Krull
(1983) 121m. **C+**
A big and expensive-looking tale about a prince who rallies an odd band of cohorts to help him reclaim his wife from the Beast of the Black Forest. Some intriguing weapons and ideas including horses propelled by fiery rockets, but despite the high quality design, a rather dull lengthy epic.
D: Peter Yates. A: Ken Marshall, Lysette Anthony, Liam Neeson.

The Sword of the Valiant
(1984) 102m. **C**
The knights at King Arthur's court have grown slack and lazy when a mysterious Green Knight appears to issue a challenge. Connery and a host of veteran character actors bring dignity to the fantasy, but the costumes, crashing blades, dwarves, and smoky castles don't hide a weak lead actor.
D: Stephen Weeks. A: Miles O'Keeffe, Sean Connery, Leigh Lawson.

Flesh and Blood
(1985) 126m. **B–**
An aptly titled but overheated reality check on the sword and sorcery film features bloodletting galore, including "cures" for the plague and plenty of nudity, often during rape scenes. This adult take on medieval tales offers no noble cause, just brutal times filled with betrayal, plague, and petty wars.
D: Paul Verhoeven. A: Rutger Hauer, Jennifer Jason Leigh, Susan Tyrrell.

Ladyhawke
(1985) 121m. **B+**
Gentle dusk and dawn hues illuminate this fantasy-romantic fable of lovers enchanted by a wicked bishop, so that the knight becomes a wolf at dark and his fair love a ladyhawke by day. A lively and less bloody entry with a young, fast-talking pickpocket aiding the lovers in their revenge.
D: Richard Donner. A: Matthew Broderick, Michelle Pfeiffer, Rutger Hauer.

Red Sonja
(1985) 89m. **D**
When Red Sonja loses her family and virginity to the forces of the evil queen, she masters the sword and vows revenge. A clever use of min-

iatures depicting fortresses and a semisexual duel with Arnold as a *Conan* clone, but sadly the characters are out-acted by their swords.
D: Richard Fleischer. A: Brigitte Nielsen, Arnold Schwarzenegger, Sandahl Bergman.

Highlander
(1986) 110m. **B–**
Time travel and arty camera angles are added to the usual crashing swords in this tale of an immortal sixteenth-century Scottish knight battling an equally ageless mass murderer in modern-day Manhattan. After all the myth-making is established, this settles into standard "he's after my girl" action.
D: Russell Mulcahy. A: Christopher Lambert, Sean Connery, Roxanne Hart.

Legend
(1986) 89m. **C+**
This somber pseudoreligious tale set in a realm of fairies and elves follows nature boy Cruise as he descends into the Prince of Darkness' lair to defeat a nefarious plan and save his love and the magical unicorn. Curry makes a campy devil, and all the rest is flashy mythical hokum.
D: Ridley Scott. A: Tom Cruise, Tim Curry, Mia Sara.

Highlander II: The Quickening
(1991) 90m. **D**
Incomprehensible sequel has a future Earth surrounded by a glowing shield put there as protection against dangerous UV rays. Choppy editing, high-strung pace, and endless effects setpieces add little in the way of logic to this *Blade Runner*-inspired mess.
D: Russell Mulcahy. A: Sean Connery, Christopher Lambert, Michael Ironside.

Highlander III: The Final Dimension
(1994) 99m. **D+**
Immortal Lambert is now battling an Asian/African sorcerer and what seems like the reincarnation of his lost love. Despite location filming all over Earth, tons of special effects, and signature decapitations, a spellbindingly boring effort.
D: Andy Morahan. A: Christopher Lambert, Mario Van Peebles, Deborah Ungar.

Henson-esque Fantasies

The Muppets and their ilk are turned into grotty, hairy, and hard-edged little creatures who help or hinder the gladiator hero in these whimsical fables of magic heroism.

The Dark Crystal
(1983) 93m. **C**
The lovely earth tones pervading the set design and Henson's muppet creatures unfortunately blend together on the small screen. There's little humor, a slight plot, and far too many screechy-voiced characters, but you'll appreciate the master puppet work while trying to figure out the scenery.
D: Jim Henson, Frank Oz. A: Voices: Stephen Garlick, Lisa Maxwell, Percy Edwards.

Labyrinth
(1986) 101m. **B**
With pointed eyebrows and a long blond wig, David Bowie may look like Mr. Spock in drag, but he's actually King of the Gobelins whose kingdom is peopled by Henson's mythical creatures. An offbeat and longish entry in which real is more eerie and frightening than magical.
D: Jim Henson. A: Jennifer Connelly, David Bowie, Toby Froud.

Willow
(1988) 124m. **B**
Plucking ideas from the Bible to *Star Wars*, this genre stew introduces numerous Henson-like woodland fantasy creatures before picking up the pace with castle-storming swordplay, near death escapes, and princesses to woo. Nothing new but presented with style if not conviction.
D: Ron Howard. A: Val Kilmer, Warwick Davis, Joanne Whalley.

OTHER FILMS:
The Warrior and the Sorceress (1984)
Conan the Destroyer (1984)
Wizard of the Lost Kingdom (1985)
Gor (1987)
Iron Warrior (1987)
Outlaw of Gor
Wizard of the Lost Kingdom II (1989)
The Beastmaster 2: Through the Portal of Time (1991)
The Polar Bear King (1992)
Quest of the Delta Knights (1993)
Return to the Lost World (1993)

Tribes

While these films take place in primitive landscapes and times, you won't find archeologically incorrect dinosaurs frolicking with the natives, although the grunt-and-mug level of action is in plentiful supply.

Quest for Fire
(1981) 97m. **B+**
When a tribe of early humans has its fire stolen, a small band embarks on a mission to bring it back. Their journey includes perils of tigers and cannibals as well as discovery of different religious ways, sexual techniques, and superior tribes. A beautifully rendered and realistic-looking evocation of primitive men.
D: Jean-Jacques Annaud. A: Everett McGill, Ron Perlman, Rae Dawn Chong.

The Emerald Forest
(1985) 110m. **B+**
An engineer working in the Amazon loses his son who is then raised by a tribe in the rain forest. Like a *National Geographic*-inspired action drama, the ravishing locales, handsome tribespeople, and otherworldly ambiance of tribal mysticism make even the environmental aspect surprisingly nonpreachy.
D: John Boorman. A: Powers Boothe, Charley Boorman, Meg Foster.

The Clan of the Cave Bear
(1986) 98m. **D+**
Unsure whether it's a serious study of prehistoric tribes, a feminist parable, or a bad comedy, this manages to fail at all three. Hannah, looking more like a straggly blond California beach girl, finally defeats her dumber, slower, and weaker tribesmen but, even with near comic subtitles, this is too dull to be camp.
D: Michael Chapman. A: Daryl Hannah, James Remar, Pamela Reed.

Fantasy Adventures

Combine a swashbuckler with a fairy tale and you have this group of child/adult odysseys that explores the darker and more philosophical side of fantasy. While most are not high-tech extravaganzas, they do offer enough special effects and creative visuals to make dreams—and a few nightmares—come true.

Time Bandits
(1981) 116m. **A**
This subversive kids' adventure teams a youngster with a criminally minded pack of dwarves on the run through holes in time from the Supreme Being. A highly imaginative, quirky mix of Monty Python humor, historical swashbuckler, and kids' gee-whiz adventure with a bittersweet ending.
D: Terry Gilliam. A: Sean Connery, David Warner, Ian Holm.

The Neverending Story
(1984) 94m. **B–**
A well-intentioned fable about a boy who picks up "The Neverending Story" and gets pulled into the realm of Fantasia. The imagery is muted and the tone is sometimes disturbing with an airless stagy look to Fantasia, though creatures like the Rock Biter will keep the kids watching.
D: Wolfgang Peterson. A: Barret Oliver, Noah Hathaway, Gerald McRaney.

The Princess Bride
(1987) 100m. **B**
Fairy tales and swordplay films are spoofed in this hip adventure-comedy, framed by a grandfather selectively reading a story to a sick boy. Noble heroes, fair maidens, and dastardly henchmen all make their slightly cracked appearance, and while the humor becomes spotty the film remains entertaining.
D: Rob Reiner. A: Cary Elwes, Mandy Patinkin, Chris Sarandon.

The Adventures of Baron Munchausen
(1989) 126m. **B–**
This overly lavish and overly detailed foray into the fantastic world of the outrageous lying Baron shows him negotiating with mythic arms dealer Vulcan, visiting the Moon whose King he once cuckolded, and even dancing on air with Venus. Spending $10 million less and a shorter script would have made it a classic.
D: Terry Gilliam. A: John Neville, Sarah Polley, Eric Idle.

Postapocalypse

The end of the world, if judged from these films, is a bikers' rumble in a landscape that's part Wild West and part urban junkyard. Where else but in a lawless postapocalyptic environment could the enterprising individual or clan of barbarians cause ceaseless carnage, both human and mechanical, with such carefree abandon?

Death Race 2000
(1975) 78m. **B**
In a future fascist America, transcontinental "death races" are held utilizing cartoony retrofitted race cars, with extra points given for civilian casualties. Tongue-in-cheek direction, garish color, and a bemused Carradine as cyber-driver "Frankenstein" add tacky spice to this 60 percent fun, low-budget satire.
D: Paul Bartel. A: David Carradine, Mary Woronov, Sylvester Stallone.

Damnation Alley
(1977) 91m. **D**
A nuclear war has turned Earth into a barren wasteland, and it's up to a mumbling serviceman to take some stragglers to a rumored oasis. Embarrassing effects of storms, giant insects, and radiation-dosed loonies help make this brain-dead TV movie-like entry pure cinematic sedation.
D: Jack Smight. A: Jan-Michael Vincent, George Peppard, Dominique Sanda.

Mad Max
(1979) 93m. **B+**
After a gang of homicidal louts slaughters his family, a policeman in an economically ruined Australia obsessively hunts his quarry. This brutal film has some great action sequences, but is hampered by low-budget and grainy look; still, a worthwhile warm-up to its sequel *The Road Warrior*.
D: George Miller. A: Mel Gibson, Joanne Samuel, Hugh Keays-Byrne.

Escape from New York
(1981) 99m. **B+**
It's 1997, the country's a mess, Manhattan is a prison island run by inmates, and soldier-turned-criminal Russell has 24 hours to rescue the president from it. A lightning-paced, bang-up action thriller with fun/grungy sets, lots of extraneous violence, and only an occasional plot misstep.
D: John Carpenter. A: Kurt Russell, Lee Van Cleef, Adrienne Barbeau.

The Road Warrior
(1981) 94m. **A–**
In one of the most full-throttled, biker-like action fests, Gibson is a surly wanderer in a postapocalyptic desert who reluctantly comes to the aid of idealists threatened by heavy metal lunatics. Three of the most nerve-racking chases and beyond-hyper pace make this essential viewing.

D: George Miller. A: Mel Gibson, Vernon Wells, Bruce Spence.

1990: The Bronx Warriors
(1983) 89m. **D–**
A tough-guy "Exterminator" battles badly costumed gang leaders with names like "Trash" and "Ogre" in post-apocalyptic Bronx. This bottom-of-the-barrel *Mad Max* rip-off is boring, mangy-looking, and about as clever as the plot indicates.
D: Enzo Castellari. A: Vic Morrow, Christopher Connelly, Mark Gregory.

Defcon 4
(1984) 85m. **C**
This looks like a case of cinematic schizophrenia: The first half is a tense, end-of-the-world thriller with incredible space effects; then the world ends, and what's left is standard, low-budget, post-Armageddon nonsense with two factions of survivors arguing for the duration.
D: Paul Donovan. A: Maury Chaykin, Kate Lynch, Lenore Zann.

Mad Max Beyond Thunderdome
(1985) 109m. **B**
The grumpier than ever hero meets a tribe of hippieish innocents and battles more postapoc loonies. While still offering inventive Modern/Primitive sets, grotesquely violent scenes, and a campy turn by Turner, this runs out of manic energy at midpoint and the plot wanders as much as our tired hero.
D: George Miller, George Ogilvie. A: Mel Gibson, Tina Turner, Frank Thring.

Cherry 2000
(1988) 93m. **B–**
A love-struck man hires "tracker" Griffith to find his android girlfriend in a faux *Mad Max* wasteland. This spasmodically inventive, perversely fun film has great characters — especially Thomerson's New Age psychokiller—to compensate for the lulls and slow pacing.
D: Steve DeJarnatt. A: Melanie Griffith, Ben Johnson, Tim Thomerson.

Circuitry Man
(1989) 89m. **C+**
Our spunky heroine must travel through a future underground society with android in tow to deliver some microchips. While the sets resemble a shopping mall parking lot, this has ironic humor, fast pacing, and a surreal battle with the villain who looks like half of an electronics store was glued on his face.
D: Steven Lovy. A: Dana Wheeler-Nicholson, Jim Meltzer, Dennis Christopher.

Waterworld
(1995) 125m. **C–**
Polar caps have melted in the future and the planet is one big ocean. Evolutionary mistake Costner—he has gills—fights aquatic *Road Warrior*-type bad guys while everyone gets excited about a mysterious place called Dryland. With ugly scrapyard sets, choppy editing, and an ending that makes little sense, this is both expensive and bad.
D: Kevin Reynolds. A: Kevin Costner, Dennis Hopper, Jeanne Tripplehorn.

Mind Thrillers

The hidden recesses and untapped powers of the brain have always been a popular horror and sci-fi topic; these films show how, with the help of some technology and the occasional mind-altering drug, their characters push the envelope as far as it will go.

Charly
(1968) 106m. **A–**
Via breakthrough pharmaceuticals at a Boston research center, a retarded busboy becomes a genius—but for how long? Though a bit dated by some flashy 60s hand-held camerawork, this quiet drama is still the ultimate five-hankie sci-fi tale, with Robertson turning in a moving performance as the terribly human experiment.
D: Ralph Nelson. A: Cliff Robertson, Claire Bloom, Lilia Skala.

Altered States
(1980) 102m. **A**
Another delirious but relatively restrained Ken Russell odyssey follows a Harvard professor who tests his theories of man's evolution by de-evolving himself via drugs and an immersion tank. Good low-keyed effects, bizarre images, and Hurt is understated when he's not hurling around the room.
D: Ken Russell. A: William Hurt, Blair Brown, Charles Haid.

Brainstorm
(1983) 106m. **C+**
Scientists discover a device that can record brain experiences—even death—and play them back for others to relive. As usual the government wants to pervert the device. An intriguing idea that's belabored by tech talk, dispirited performances, and a thriller subplot that never gets off the ground.
D: Douglas Trumbull. A: Natalie Wood, Christopher Walken, Cliff Robertson.

Dreamscape
(1984) 95m. **B**
A doctor invents a machine that allows outsiders to enter and affect the dreams of other people. He wants to use it for therapy and a right-wing spy wants to send an agent into the dreams of the president. The dreamscape fantasies are fun, but the characters and thriller plot are what keep you watching.
D: Joseph Ruben. A: Dennis Quaid, Max von Sydow, Kate Capshaw.

Braindead
(1989) 85m. **C+**
There are some valuable corporate secrets hidden in the noggin of a psychopath, and a brain surgeon is hired to get them out with nightmarish results. This threadbare production has some nifty effects but it's finally tripped up by the dated 1950s script.
D: Adam Simon. A: Bill Paxton, Bill Pullman, Patricia Charbonneau.

Friendly Aliens

Unlike the goopy looking extraterrestrials who brainwashed humans and destroyed cities in 50s sci-fi films, these aliens are total sweetie-pies with the healing powers of saints. Except for the extravagant special effects in Spielberg's productions, these films tend to be quiet and humorous dramas about ordinary people meeting some ordinary aliens.

The Man Who Fell to Earth

(1976) 140m. **B–**

David Bowie is the fragile alien seeking water for his planet who attains great wealth and succumbs to human mistreatment, booze, and rock culture. A magnetic Bowie, along with the flashes of cinematic genius, biting satire, and arty bizarreness, will keep you perpetually off balance.

D: Nicolas Roeg. A: David Bowie, Candy Clark, Rip Torn.

Close Encounters of the Third Kind

(1977) 135m. **B+**

Most of this film follows the experiences of family man Dreyfuss who's bugged by visions and a compulsion to make a pilgrimage to Devil's Tower. Once he arrives, the film turns into one massive cryptoreligious, light-and-sound show with the startled childlike blue spacepeople popping out to basically say hi.

D: Steven Spielberg. A: Richard Dreyfuss, Teri Garr, François Truffaut.

E.T. The Extra-Terrestrial

(1982) 115m. **A–**

This simple, sweet-hearted boys' adventure story of a marooned little alien who hides out with some suburban kids may get manipulative but gives a knowing portrayal of a child's point of view in an adult world. Favorite scenes include bug-eyed, potbellied E.T. getting drunk on beer, and levitating bikes on the run.

D: Steven Spielberg. A: Henry Thomas, Peter Coyote, Drew Barrymore.

The Brother from Another Planet

(1984) 104m. **A–**

This unusual E.T. film follows a mute fugitive black alien who makes contact with the various denizens of Harlem while being tracked by two white bounty hunters. An entertaining low-budget effort by John Sayles filled with sweet and funny character moments.

D: John Sayles. A: Joe Morton, Dee Dee Bridgewater, Ren Woods.

Starman

(1984) 115m. **B**

An alien trying to reach his rendezvous point to go home assumes the identity of the dead and handsome husband of a young widow. Bridges is charming as the alien who can heal gunshot wounds, win in Vegas, even as he stumbles through such simplicities as posture, accent, and of course love.

D: John Carpenter. A: Jeff Bridges, Karen Allen, Richard Jaeckel.

Cocoon

(1985) 117m. **B+**

Senior citizens in Florida discover rejuvenating powers when they swim in the pool that holds some alien pods. Forget the plot and enjoy the silly, sentimental, and occasionally moving moments with the earthling oldsters kicking up their heels while some wise and gentle aliens try to get their pods back home.

D: Ron Howard. A: Don Ameche, Steve Guttenberg, Brian Dennehy.

Remakes

As with some of the horror remakes, these films show that high production values, name stars, and special effects don't always improve those low-budget but chilling sci-fi classics.

The Island of Dr. Moreau

(1977) 104m. **C+**

This remake of *Island of Lost Souls* in which an unhinged doctor "evolves" animals into semihumans and "devolves" humans into semi-animals is a feast for the prosthetics department, but a dramatically empty excursion into insanity.

D: William Witney. A: Michael York, Burt Lancaster, Barbara Carrera.

Invasion of the Body Snatchers

(1978) 117m. **A**

Seeds from outer space begin producing vegetable duplicates of humans in northern California. The original was a perfect 50s witchhunt paranoia parable, and this one tackles the wacky conformity of the psychobabbling 70s. Thoughtful and low-keyed, with strong cast and cunning special effects.

D: Philip Kaufman. A: Donald Sutherland, Brooke Adams, Leonard Nimoy.

The Thing

(1982) 127m. **B**

This is an atmospheric paranoia fest in the frozen Antarctic as a U.S. science team accidentally introduces an alien organism that can inhabit other life forms. Everyone distrusts each other as the alien moves from body to body, even taking on some disgusting mutations including a large crablike thing with a human head.

D: John Carpenter. A: Kurt Russell, Wilford Brimley, Richard Masur.

Invaders from Mars

(1986) 93m. **C**

The terror of apple-pie-middle-American gone zombie is explored when an 11-year-old boy sees an alien ship land and then watches his scientist dad change. This faithful remake of the 1953 original veers between campy spoof and serious sci-fi, complete with a creepy Martian leader.

D: Tobe Hooper. A: Hunter Carson, Karen Black, Timothy Bottoms.

Body Snatchers

(1993) 87m. **B**

Some young people on a remote military base become aware that their friends are becoming inhuman version of their old selves, in this

third filming of the horror classic. Half-seen horrors are constantly lurking at the edges of every scene in this tale that targets military and corporate thinking as the modern-day menace.
D: Abel Ferrara. A: Gabrielle Anwar, Terry Kinney, Meg Tilly.

Aliens and Space Travel

After the revolutionary *2001: A Space Odyssey*, mainstream Hollywood embarked on its own space race. Suddenly the cheap models on visible wires were a thing of the past as realistic special effects helped create a fresh locale to tell practically any story, without looking laughable or quaint.

2001: A Space Odyssey
(1968) 160m. **A+**
This is a space procedural with every prosaic detail of a spaceship's functions lovingly portrayed; a high-tech thriller—two astronauts desperately try to disconnect a computer that's had a nervous breakdown; and a visually awesome epic that dares to offer a vision of mankind's future evolution.
D: Stanley Kubrick. A: Keir Dullea, Gary Lockwood, William Sylvester.

Journey to the Far Side of the Sun
(1969) 99m. **B**
Orbiting directly opposite Earth and always hidden by the sun is a mirror-image planet Earth. But is the space explorer who discovered it himself or a doppelganger from that planet? A subtle, eerie, and sometimes confusing story with a cryptic conclusion worthy of an episode from *The Prisoner*.
D: Robert Parrish. A: Roy Thinnes, Lynn Loring, Ian Hendry.

Silent Running
(1971) 89m. **B**
A lone botanist battles a governmental decree trying to dismantle his titanic, Saturn-orbiting greenhouse that contains the last living vegetation of a now-polluted Earth. Grand space visions combine with an ecological message while Dern plays his usual disturbed self, aided by two cute robot drones.
D: Douglas Trumbull. A: Bruce Dern, Cliff Potts, Jesse Vint.

Dark Star
(1974) 83m. **B**
A grubby crew on a spaceship that resembles a factory locker room has been on their mission too long blowing up unstable planets. An inventive, low-budget space comedy that has college-level, spirited fun; a highlight is the intelligent bomb stuck in a delivery bay, asking philosophical questions about its existence.
D: John Carpenter. A: Dan O'Bannon, Brian Narelle, Dre Pahich.

Alien
(1979) 116m. **A**
This blood-and-goo-filled nail-cruncher follows the scruffy crew of an industrial spaceship as they get picked off one by one by a deadly life form. A darkly imaginative film with the grimy-looking vessel resembling an oil refinery and the alien changing form to match the malignant-looking environment.
D: Ridley Scott. A: Tom Skerritt, Sigourney Weaver, Ian Holm.

Meteor
(1979) 103m. **C−**
This overblown overstarred science disaster film follows efforts to destroy a gargantuan meteor that's Earthbound. A Yank scientist and Russian researcher flop around in the mud and fall in love while a host of guest stars look worried. Even with the big budget, these special effects are still substandard.
D: Ronald Neame. A: Sean Connery, Natalie Wood, Brian Keith.

Outland
(1981) 108m. **B**
A federal marshal investigates the bleak mining operation on a hellish moon of Jupiter where overtaxed workers are flipping out and dying. An obvious, high-tech *High Noon* with the lone guy vs. baddies showdown taking place in a grim, fluorescent-lit, assembly-line future.
D: Peter Hyams. A: Sean Connery, Francis Sternhagen, Peter Boyle.

The Adventures of Buckaroo Banzai
(1984) 103m. **B**
Doggedly determined to be a cult film, this throws everything at you, including a superhero who is a rocker, surgeon, multidimensional traveler, and cool dresser. Although not a big-budget F/X extravaganza, it's still visually busy with costumes and technology.
D: W. D. Richter. A: Peter Weller, John Lithgow, Jeff Goldblum.

2010
(1984) 116m. **B−**
Less mysterious and awe-inspiring than its predecessor but still worthy, this follows a joint U.S./Soviet mission Jupiter to solve the mystery of the doomed Discovery mission. Answers some questions from *2001* including why computer HAL went berserk but goes overboard on its benevolent life force philosophy.
D: Peter Hyams. A: Roy Scheider, Helen Mirren, John Lithgow.

Enemy Mine
(1985) 108m. **B−**
An Earth starfighter and a lizardlike Drac crash-land on a stormy alien planet while doing battle and are forced to work together in order to survive the elements. The unoriginal buddy theme is done with enthusiasm as Gossett, under layers of lizard makeup, brings wit and dignity to the Drac.
D: Wolfgang Petersen. A: Dennis Quaid, Louis Gossett, Jr., Brion James.

Lifeforce
(1985) 96m. **C+**
From the depths of Halley's Comet comes an umbrella-shaped spacecraft bearing nude aliens who will entrance an astronaut and turn London into a zombie-filled graveyard. This mega-budgeted bit of lunacy is packed with enough plots for six films, incredible interstellar vampires, and the indomitable Space Girl.
D: Tobe Hooper. A: Steve Railsback, Peter Firth, Frank Finlay.

Aliens
(1986) 138m. **A−**
Weaver awakens 57 years later and returns to the now-colonized alien planet with a bunch of action-happy marines to battle a horde of aliens. Basically a violent war movie with the greasy

industrial look of the original, and tough-talking soldiers blasting away and getting decimated by slimy monsters.
D: James Cameron. A: Sigourney Weaver, Michael Biehn, Bill Paxton.

Alien 3
(1992) 115m. **B–**
Poor Weaver can't get a break. Her ship crashes on a penal planet run by head-shaved male loonies and the last alien breaks loose from the crash. Not only does she have to battle the alien who is gobbling up the inmates, but she's pregnant with a you-know-what. A depressingly downbeat and grim entry.
D: David Fincher. A: Sigourney Weaver, Charles Dance, Charles S. Dutton.

Superman, Star Trek, and Star Wars

These nostalgic and epic-sized sci-fi adventure yarns are as slickly entertaining as a Hollywood movie can be, offering a grand mix of larger-than-life heroes and villains with staggering action sequences. Because the characters have become such pop culture icons, you may not even mind if some of the special effects are no longer the cutting edge spectacles they once were.

Superman
(1978) 143m. **B**
The comic strip about the Kryptonite who becomes the true-blue American hero is now an epic with light comedic touches and thrilling action. It begins slowly and quasireligiously, but the fun begins once Clark Kent becomes the big city reporter, falls in love with Lois Lane, and Superman takes to the air.
D: Richard Donner. A: Christopher Reeve, Margot Kidder, Gene Hackman.

Superman II
(1980) 127m. **B+**
Three baddies from Krypton attempt to take over Earth with their superhuman powers just when Superman has sacrificed his for the love of Lois Lane. Action packed and not so bogged down by gimmicks as the later films, and the scenes of Superman losing his innocence are sweet.
D: Richard Lester. A: Christopher Reeve, Margot Kidder, Gene Hackman, Terence Stamp.

Superman III
(1983) 125m. **C**
An evil industrialist dupes a wacky computer genius into helping him destroy Superman. One good idea (a split-personality Superman) is ruined by two bad ones (dump Lois Lane for a new love and add Richard Pryor) as this series hits a big bump.
D: Richard Lester. A: Christopher Reeve, Richard Pryor, Annette O'Toole.

Superman IV: The Quest for Peace
(1987) 90m. **D**
Superman tries to rid the world of nuclear weapons, prompting Lex Luthor to unleash Nuclear Man. Dreadful special effects, a script that goes nowhere, and some unintentional humor from a nemesis that looks like a deranged California bodybuilder.
D: Sidney Furie. A: Christopher Reeve, Gene Hackman, Mariel Hemingway.

Star Trek: The Motion Picture
(1979) 145m. **B–**
Surprisingly dull and lifeless resurrection of the TV series follows now-Admiral Kirk as he gathers his old crew aboard a refitted Enterprise to meet a machine life-form seeking its creator on Earth. This flabby script relies too much on the nostalgic reunion and the dazzling but excessive effects.
D: Robert Wise. A: William Shatner, Leonard Nimoy, DeForest Kelley.

Star Trek II: The Wrath of Khan
(1982) 113m. **A**
More military but generally faithful revival finds a middle-aged Kirk dealing with mortality, a child he never knew, a former flame, the death of Spock, and a deranged old nemesis Khan who is out for blood. Witty, colorful, and lively.
D: Nicholas Meyer. A: William Shatner, Leonard Nimoy, Ricardo Montalban.

Star Trek III: The Search for Spock
(1984) 105m. **B–**
A contrived plot and a weak central villain hurt an otherwise admirable tale about friendship as Kirk and crew sacrifice their careers, the Enterprise, and more to bring the dead Mr. Spock's living spirit home.
D: Leonard Nimoy. A: William Shatner, DeForest Kelly, James Doohan.

Star Trek IV: The Voyage Home
(1986) 119m. **A**
Sprightly cheerful time travel romp finds the Enterprise crew visiting San Francisco in 1986 to bring back two humpback whales. Ecological message doesn't get in the way of what Kirk and company do best—maintain their lively esprit de corps while coping with weird situations. Humorous script fleshes out the supporting characters and has a field day with 1980s society.
D: Leonard Nimoy. A: All the regulars and Jane Wyatt.

Star Trek V: The Final Frontier
(1989) 107m. **C–**
Ill-conceived adventure yarn finds Spock's half brother hijacking the Enterprise in search of the mythic planet where God and all of life's answers reside. Below par special effects, dopey sight gags, and a tired search-for-God theme weigh down some occasional moments of drama.
D: William Shatner. A: All the regulars, Laurence Luckinbill, David Warner.

Star Trek VI: The Undiscovered Country
(1991) 110m. **B+**
Designed as a send-off for the old crew, we find Kirk and McCoy imprisoned for murdering a peace-seeking Klingon ruler. A dark and occasionally pompous paean that tackles ecology, racism, U.S./Soviet relations, and old age (it needs to) with good humor, action, and a dramatically fulfilling farewell for the retirement-bound Enterprisers.

D: Nicholas Meyer. A: With Christopher Plummer, Kim Cattrall.

Star Trek: Generations
(1994) **B**
Captain Picard joins forces with Kirk in a nirvana-like realm to battle a deranged scientist who's destroying stars and civilizations. A baton-passing story that centers on the younger crew and the retired warriors finding peace with old wounds. Sometimes confusing but rich in Trekie details.
D: David Carson. A: Patrick Stewart, William Shatner, Malcolm McDowell.

Star Wars
(1977) 121m. **A**
An innocent farm boy joins the ranks of the rebellion against the Galactic Empire, learns wisdom from an old knight, and confronts the evil Darth Vader and his Death Star battle station. This tribute to '40s swashbuckling serial films exploded onto the screen with thrilling effects (some of which get lost on TV), a host of humorous exotic space creatures, wizards, spaceships, and a wisecracking princess.
D: George Lucas. A: Mark Hamill, Harrison Ford, Carrie Fisher.

The Empire Strikes Back
(1980) 124m. **B+**
Luke Skywalker trains in the ways of the Jedi with a cryptic old master while the space cowboy and the princess keep one step ahead of Darth Vader. More somber with better effects and more spectacular battles.
D: Irvin Kershner. A: Mark Hamill, Harrison Ford, Carrie Fisher.

Return of the Jedi
(1983) 132m. **B+**
We've seen it all before . . . Death Stars, light sabers, and star fighters, but now there's more of everything. Luke has the ultimate showdown with his darker side and Darth Vader, the cowboy and the princess fall in love, and we learn that even the most wicked can be redeemed.
D: Richard Marquand. A: Mark Hamill, Harrison Ford, Carrie Fisher.

Cops and Cyborgs

These high-tech dystopia actioners take crime thrillers and graft them onto futuristic settings that are bleak, embattled, and fascist. You'll see shades of *The Terminator* in many of the films about killing machines: The cyborg hero/villain also provides the perfect excuse for the acting abilities and musculature of stars like Van Damme, Lundgren, and Stallone. But be warned of the "cartoon" violence—*Road Runner* shenanigans these aren't.

Blade Runner
(1982) 117m./123m.
A
A grubby ex-cop hunts down renegade human replicants in a protopunk LA that's literally dripping with polluted, ominous, and decaying atmosphere. This visionary detective noir is dense with visuals — fantastic skyscrapers, titanic floating billboards, a teeming Asian-Hispanic population — that perfectly match the metaphysical plot and malaise of its characters.
D: Ridley Scott. A: Harrison Ford, Rutger Hauer, Sean Young.

Trancers
(1985) 76m. **B–**
An evil Trancer takes a human form to mesmerize people—especially punk rockers and assorted fringe dwellers—in the present day while heroic Jack Deth tries to stop him. Cultish activities from the seamier sides of LA provide the action in this low-budgeter with violence not for the squeamish.
D: Charles Band. A: Tim Thompson, Michael Stefoni, Helen Hunt.

RoboCop
(1987) 103m. **B**
A Detroit cop gets mangled by a psycho gang and what remains of him is poured into the gleaming armored shell of a programmed robotic crimefighter. This fantastically brutal crime thriller has well-aimed satire and great action sequences, along with moments of pathos and humor.
D: Paul Verhoeven. A: Peter Weller, Nancy Allen, Ronny Cox.

Cyborg
(1989) 85m. **D**
Buzz-haired, steely-eyed, perpetually angry-looking Van Damme is hired to take a young lovely through the U.S. wastelands ravaged by plague and roving gangs. Constructed of waves of bone-smashing violence as sweaty muscular men glare at each other and charge. Excessive except for Crucifixion fans.
D: Albert Pyun. A: Jean-Claude Van Damme, Deborah Richter, Dayle Haddon.

Hardware
(1990) 94m. **B–**
In an extremely postapoc world (pink-orange radioactive skies, twisted metal everywhere) a couple is terrorized by an ancient battle android who cunningly rebuilds itself. Brilliance on a budget is displayed with convincingly wiped-out-world sets, eerie lighting, and incredible amounts of top-notch gore.
D: Richard Stanley. A: Dylan McDermott, John Lynch, Iggy Pop.

I Come in Peace
(1990) 98m. **C–**
Big-biceped Houston cop Lundgren has two problems: First, a space alien is looping victims with massive shots of heroin so he can suck out their endorphins; second, he has a new bookish FBI sidekick. A tired cop buddy story mixed with mad killer theme has colorful explosions and endless shots of single-expressioned Lundgren.
D: Craig Baxley. A: Dolph Lundgren, Betsy Brantley, Brian Benben.

Robot Jox
(1990) 84m. **C+**
A popular gladiator sport in the future is 10-story-tall robots facing off in an arena while "pilots" sit inside them controlling each maneuver. For those who remember "Rock 'Em, Sock 'Em Robots" this is a low-budget, grand-scale extension of it with clever robot animation and kid-level violence.
D: Stuart Gordon. A: Gary Graham, Anne-Marie Johnson, Paul Koslo.

Freejack
(1992) 110m. **C–**
A race car driver is shipped to the future where he's slated to become a youthful "Freejack" host body. Fanci-

ful effects don't hide the hollow story with Estevez keeping a single bug-eyed look of disbelief, Jagger playing a punk, and Hopkins hanging out long enough to offer a canned sinister, rich-guy performance.
D: Geoff Murphy. A: Emilio Estevez, Mick Jagger, Anthony Hopkins.

Demolition Man
(1993) 115m. **B–**
Rogue LA cop Stallone emerges from deep freeze into a sanitized, feel-good twenty-first century where he must battle yellow-haired, super vicious Snipes. A few laughs are offered—Stallone's encounter with virtual reality sex—but mostly lots of flashy graphics, high-tech equipment, and plot holes filled with bullets and bodies.
D: Marco Brambilla. A: Sylvester Stallone, Wesley Snipes, Sandra Bullock.

Fortress
(1993) 92m. **B+**
In an Orwellian future, a man is jailed for the sin of having two kids and must face a half-human warden, cyborg guards, and a nasty bit of weaponry called the Intestinator. Despite variable acting and limited budget, one of the wittier, action-packed dystopian films with a hilarious turn by Combs as a hippie hacker.
D: Stuart Gordon. A: Christopher Lambert, Loryn Locklyn, Jeffrey Combs.

No Escape
(1994) 118m. **C+**
In a future society, a prisoner is packed off to a deadly jungle island prison where two warring subgroups battle it out. Scenes of men in tattered clothing hurling insults and flaming arrows balance those of one of the leaders waxing philosophical. Halfway through you'll want to escape as much as Liotta does.
D: Martin Campbell. A: Ray Liotta, Lance Henriksen, Kevin Dillon.

Timecop
(1994) 99m. **B+**
In the near future, time travel is a reality and a slimy senator is trying to go back to change history in order to gain control of the country; "Time Cop" is the only one who can stop him. Somehow, Van Damme's limited acting adds charm to this silly, effects-heavy techno-fluff.
D: Peter Hyams. A: Jean-Claude Van Damme, Ron Silver, Mia Sara.

Johnny Mnemonic
(1995) 137m. **D+**
In the future, corporations rule and a data courier with 320 gigabytes of memory implanted in his super brain has the secret to prevent a terrible plague. A comic book script for hackers, clumsy action sequences, unimaginative computer graphics, and surprisingly cheap-looking effects help make this a dud.
D: David Salle. A: Keanu Reeves, Ice-T, Dolph Lundgren.

Judge Dredd
(1995) 91m. **B+**
One of the few films to work on a comic book level: Astonishing art direction creates the most eye-popping, future megacity since *Blade Runner* while white-knuckler action set pieces, hilarious asides, and Stallone in a self-parodying role as the cop-judge framed for murder make this the best Dumb Action film in years.
D: Danny Cannon. A: Sylvester Stallone, Armande Assante, Diane Lane.

Cartoon Swashbucklers

These high-tech extravaganzas are perfect for when you want to put your mind on cruise control and your nervous system on high drive. You don't have to worry about drama or comedy here; the characters may be human, but the way they spin through the glitzy hardware, special effects, and modern gothic settings, they could be cartoons.

Flash Gordon
(1980) 111m. **B**
This updating of the 30s space adventure kept the Art Deco look of spaceships and futuristic technology but spiced things up with sexy 70s glitter rock costumes and a cruel, sexually malevolent Emperor Ming. Flash himself is dull but the fine supporting cast has a blast romping through their scenes.
D: Mike Hodges. A: Sam J. Jones, Max von Sydow, Topol.

Batman
(1989) 126m. **A**
Batman comes off as a ponderous introvert devoted to crime fighting and gets overshadowed by two things: the gray/black Gotham City, looking like a retro-futuristic nightmare of 30s architecture; and a scenery-chewing, psycho performance by Nicholson as the Joker.
D: Tim Burton. A: Michael Keaton, Jack Nicholson, Kim Basinger.

Darkman
(1990) 95m. **C+**
His lab is blasted to pieces and his face horribly deformed, but Darkman perfects a synthetic skin that will mold to any face for short periods of time. A low-tech effort that doesn't engage on either the action or the dramatic level, with a hero who's more of a hit-and-run revenger wallowing in self-pity.
D: Sam Raimi. A: Liam Neeson, Frances McDormand, Colin Friels.

Dick Tracy
(1990) 106m. **B**
Straight shooter Tracy battles the grotesque denizens of the underworld and fends off the attentions of a seductive singer. Enjoyable to watch for a hilarious goggly eyed Pacino, name actors in amazing prosthetics, and the inventive use of bright comic strip colors and minimalized sets.
D: Warren Beatty. A: Warren Beatty, Madonna, Al Pacino.

The Rocketeer
(1991) 108m. **C+**
A true-blue pilot and his girlfriend battle Nazis and an Errol Flynn-like Hollywood traitor for possession of a rocket pack that enables its wearer to fly. A bland and good-looking retro 30s family adventure with most of the drive cut out.
D: Joe Johnston. A: Bill Campbell, Jennifer Connelly, Timothy Dalton.

Batman Returns
(1992) 126m. **B**
A perverse and occasionally kinky return to Gotham City where the deformed and drooling Penguin emerges from his underground lair to run for mayor. Despite the creative images and a slinky Catwoman who offers both battle and sexual allure to Batman, there's an air of ugliness in this one.

D: Tim Burton. A: Michael Keaton, Michelle Pfeiffer, Danny DeVito.

The Shadow
(1994) 108m. **B–**
A society nightclubber becomes the Shadow who rules the night and clouds men's minds. The Art Deco re-creations of New York will dazzle you while the chemistry between Baldwin and just about everyone else in this film won't. Nifty effects and eastern exotica help to fill the film's empty feeling.
D: Russell Mulcahy. A: Alec Baldwin, John Lone, Penelope Ann Miller.

Batman Forever
(1995) 131m. **B**
Batman, now accompanied by Robin, is back as Gotham City labors under a dual assault by thuggish Two-Face and the mind-altering ray machine of the Riddler. Compared to the brooding gothicism of the first two, this is a neon-drenched Batman Lite, with lightning pace, campy feel, trendy sexual ambiguity, and flashy effects.
D: Joel Schumacher. A: Val Kilmer, Tommy Lee Jones, Jim Carrey.

Casper
(1995) 101m. **B+**
A ghost therapist and his daughter go to a Maine mansion to find a nasty heiress and a quartet of ghosts, including the famous friendly one. Surprisingly witty film is packed with famous actor cameos, suggestive humor for adults, fantastic computer-generated ghosts for kids, and gorgeous Art Nouveau set designs for all.
D: Brad Silberling. A: Bill Pullman, Christina Ricci, Eric Idle.

Darkman II—The Return of Durant
(1995) 94m. **B**
Though lacking original director Sam Raimi's wild style, this live comic book is a surprisingly effective sequel, with loads of action, witty connections between political extremists and the criminal element, and a charismatic Vosloo taking over the disfigured superhero's cape from Liam Neeson.
D: Bradford May. A: Arnold Vosloo, Larry Drake, Kim Delaney.

Weird Creatures

Blame it on Spielberg and Hensen. Post-*E.T.* screens were suddenly filled with a variety of (usually) diminutive creatures, ranging from cute and cuddly to just plain weird. Put through their paces in middle America, the critters were usually brought to life by high-tech animatronics, though special effects folks weren't above the odd hand-held puppet.

Gremlins
(1984) 105m. **B**
A cute and cuddly little creature spawns some evil sniggering mischief-loving gremlins who proceed to tear up the town. Amazing special effects for these puppets with plenty of jokey visual quotes from other films from *Snow White* to *It's a Wonderful Life* help out when the fun gets to be like a loud cartoon.
D: Joe Dante. A: Zach Galligan, Phoebe Cates, Hoyt Axton.

Critters
(1986) 86m. **B–**
A group of furry and cute interstellar fugitives known as Krites lands in Kansas and threatens to eat the state. Hot on their trail are two deadpan E.T. bounty hunters. Familiar material given a lively treatment, though played more for humor than horror.
D: Stephen Herek. A: Dee Wallace Stone, M. Emmet Walsh, Billy Green Bush.

Howard the Duck
(1986) 111m. **F**
The adventures of an alien rock 'n' rolling duck are chronicled in the megadisaster of legendary proportions, which include a sensitive interspecies love scene, an embarrassing duck rock concert, and enough money to feed a Third World country thrown to the cinematic winds. Even worse than you've heard.
D: Willard Huyck. A: Lea Thompson, Jeffrey Jones, Tim Robbins.

***batteries not included**
(1987) 106m. **C**
Money grubbing real estate developers try to force the last tenants out of a building until help comes from two tiny, hamburger-shaped, electronic aliens. Hokey and patronizing fantasy right up to the whiz-bang ending when a massive flotilla of little aliens comes to the rescue.
D: Matthew Robbins. A: Hume Cronyn, Jessica Tandy, Elizabeth Pena.

Harry and the Hendersons
(1987) 110m. **C**
A hassled dad, wise mom, and snotty kids crash into a 7-foot-tall Bigfoot and wheel him home where he proceeds to endear himself and cause no end of complications. A formulaic family movie with lots of pratfalls and bad smell jokes.
D: William Dear. A: John Lithgow, Melinda Dillon, Don Ameche.

Critters 2: The Main Course
(1988) 93m. **D+**
Those naughty but oh so cute little bundles of fur laid eggs before their annihilation, and now their offspring are on the prowl for food. Plodding retread of the original, with the silliness replaced by dark humor.
D: Mick Garris. A: Scott Grimes, Liane Curtis, Donn Opper.

Gremlins 2: The New Batch
(1990) 106m. **B**
This sequel waives the pathos of the original and turns up the farce level as the less nasty and more mirthful gremlins invade a supermodern, fully automated skyscraper. Don't miss a hilarious Glover as a self-important real estate mogul and the movie spoofs including the dental torture scene from *Marathon Man*.
D: Joe Dante. A: Zach Galligan, Phoebe Cates, John Glover.

Critters 3
(1991) 86m. **C–**
Tenants in a Los Angeles apartment building infested with those voracious critters are driven to the roof, where they prepare for . . . *Critters 4*. Slim on action and suspense, fatter on characters.
D: Kristine Peterson. A: Aimee Brooks, John Calvin, Katherine Cortez.

Critters 4
(1991) 94m. **D**
The furry killers are now stowaways on a spaceship where they torment and threaten to consume the crew. Same as the previous two and lacking the energy and humor of the original. For fans of vicious hand puppets and the bizarre Dourif.
D: Rupert Harvey. A: Don Opper, Brad Dourif, Angela Bassett.

Modern Fairy Tales

Don't let the big-name stars, state-of-the-art effects, and sometimes very adult tone fool you: These films are fairy tales, albeit sophisticated ones. Like any fairy tale, they speak with the language and imagery of children: Men become wolves, women witches, and the hero must capture the talisman to redeem himself.

Something Wicked This Way Comes
(1983) 94m. **C+**
Mr. Dark's carnival comes to town and the citizens are entranced when he offers to grant their wildest dreams. Game but largely unsuccessful attempt to mix a sinister tale and a boy's adventure, set in a Disneyfied 1920s small town. Pryce's malevolent carnival master is fine but the film falls flat without him.
D: Jack Clayton. A: Jason Robards, Jr., Jonathan Pryce, Vidal Peterson.

The Company of Wolves
(1985) 95m. **A–**
The tale of Little Red Riding Hood has its sexual subtext brought to colorful life in this fable-within-a-dream-within-a-story. Granny's cautionary tales of lusting men who turn into wolves on their wedding night, at an eighteenth-century banquet, and of course at granny's house are funny, scary, and a feast for the eyes.
D: Neil Jordan. A: Angela Lansbury, David Warner, Sarah Patterson.

Dreamchild
(1986) 100m. **B+**
The real-life Alice in Wonderland, now 80, attends a Lewis Carroll celebration unleashing memories of her youth with the stuttering Carroll who had more than a friendly interest in her. Past, present, and fantasy all merge, helped along with slightly twisted versions of the book's characters reflecting Alice's new vision of her old friend.
D: Gavin Millar. A: Coral Browne, Ian Holm, Peter Gallagher.

The Navigator: A Medieval Odyssey
(1989) 92m. B&W/Color.
A–
This unusual and quiet adventure follows a band of men from 1384 who emerge in twentieth-century New Zealand and their attempts to return home. The visually distinctive style helps capture medieval fear and wonder of the modern world, where crossing a highway seems as disorienting as traversing a galaxy.
D: Vincent Ward. A: Hamish McFarland, Bruce Lyons, Chris Haywood.

Edward Scissorhands
(1990) 100m. **B+**
This follows the adventures of a boy-creation with scissor hands who leaves his dead creator's castle for the suburban community below and learns some painful lessons in conformity. A dark and funny fairy tale with a bittersweet romance and a witty visual style that's hip kitsch crossed with demented Disney.
D: Tim Burton. A: Johnny Depp, Winona Ryder, Dianne Wiest.

The Witches
(1990) 91m. **B+**
Young Luke and his grandmother are staying at an English coastal hotel that's hosting an antichild cruelty group that turns out to be a witches' coven. Forget the historical prologue and enjoy the transformation of Huston and company into repulsive witches and their pursuit of Luke after changing him into a mouse.
D: Nicolas Roeg. A: Anjelica Huston, Mai Zetterling, Jasen Fisher.

The Fisher King
(1991) 135m. **B**
Acid-tongued radio jock drops out, and an ex-Medieval professor/unhinged street screamer is convinced that the DJ's redemption is through finding the Holy Grail in New York. An offbeat story with dynamic performances, phantasmagoric images, and occasional screechy action.
D: Terry Gilliam. A: Jeff Bridges, Robin Williams, Mercedes Ruehl.

Timeless Romance

People love the idea of love reaching across time and death as anyone who saw *Ghost* five times will tell you. Time travel and reincarnation are both used for romance in these glitzy bits of wish fulfillment as passion rules the day, and the characters get one more chance at happiness.

Heaven Can Wait
(1978) 100m. **B**
A cosmic screwup gives a football hero a premature trip to heaven, but he gets a second chance in the body of a wealthy businessman who was killed by his cheating wife. This remake of *Here Comes Mr. Jordan* is an unusually rich-looking film by 70s standards, with deft comic performances and a wonderful bittersweet love story.
D: Warren Beatty. A: Warren Beatty, Julie Christie, James Mason.

Time After Time
(1979) 112m. **B+**
When Jack the Ripper escapes to 1979 San Francisco via H. G. Welles' time machine, the visionary author

follows after him. A witty and satiric thriller/romance as the Victorian who believes in free love falls for a feminist banker. Best line by Jack: "In the past I was a freak. Here I'm an amateur."
D: Nicholas Meyer. A: Malcolm McDowell, Mary Steenburgen, David Warner.

Somewhere in Time
(1980) 103m. **C+**
When an old woman whispers "Come back to me" to playwright Reeve, he does—by time-traveling back to 1912 to woo her as a young lady. Romantics will ignore Reeve's wooden performance and the ridiculous plot to gush over the Victorian fashions, weepy score, and misty romance.
D: Jeannot Szwarc. A: Christopher Reeve, Jane Seymour, Christopher Plummer.

Creator
(1985) 108m. **B**
An obsessed scientist keeps the cells of his deceased wife on ice in the hope of someday reviving her. What could have been a standard "mad-lab" variation becomes an effective love story with a brilliant O'Toole and a guaranteed four-hankie finale compensating the sometimes meandering direction.
D: Ivan Passer. A: Peter O'Toole, Virginia Madsen, Mariel Hemingway.

Made in Heaven
(1987) 102m. **C**
Mike and Annie fall in love in Heaven but it's time for her rebirth and he gets permission to go down with her for 30 years. Once Earthbound, it seems like they won't even get back together in time. This tries to be a sunny romance but stumbles with too many sideshow details that keep the lovers apart.
D: Alan Rudolph. A: Timothy Hutton, Kelly McGillis, Mare Winningham.

Always
(1989) 123m. **C+**
A 1940s pilot dies and is instructed by his angel to "inspire" a human but winds up having to watch another pilot woo his girl. This remake of *A Guy Named Joe* has a 40s atmosphere, an 80s couple and emotions, overglamorized Midwest landscapes, and flying sequences that are pure Hollywood.
D: Steven Spielberg. A: Richard Dreyfuss, Holly Hunter, John Goodman.

Ghost
(1990) 122m. **B**
They're a happy privileged couple living in a trendy loft and, even after he's murdered, he has the opportunity to track down the murderer and have one last dance with his sweetie. If you can overlook the sappy ersatz spirituality this gushy and goofy romantic tale may just bring a lump to your throat.
D: Jerry Zucker. A: Patrick Swayze, Demi Moore, Whoopi Goldberg.

Forever Young
(1992) 102m. **C+**
A pilot/guinea pig for a cryogenics test in 1939 reawakens in 1992 and meets up with young Nat and his very modern mom. Then he finds out his beloved who had been in a coma is still alive. Although a good couples film (just how long *should* you wait?), the main relationship is between Gibson and Wood.
D: Steve Miner. A: Mel Gibson, Jamie Lee Curtis, Elijah Wood.

Video to Virtual Reality

Computers: can't live with 'em, can't make a decent sci-fi buck these days without 'em. You better catch these films filled with eye-popping, megacolorful, computer-generated images right now, since developments in this field quickly make them as quaint as a dusty Commodore.

Tron
(1982) 96m. **C+**
A computer genius is fired by his boss who wants to take credit for a brilliant games program, and everyone somehow gets sucked into a massive video game where they fight it out. The cutting edge computer graphics and "modern" video game sophistication date this badly.
D: Steven Lisberger. A: Jeff Bridges, David Warner, Bruce Boxleitner.

The Lawnmower Man
(1992) 108m. **B**
This virtual reality shocker tells of a semiretarded man who becomes a brain-enhanced genius and then the victim of cybertech agents who unleash his violent side. The payoff for the extremely slow first hour of drama is the nifty computer-generated virtual reality effects.
D: Brett Leonard. A: Jeff Fahey, Pierce Brosnan, Mark Bringleson.

Ghost in the Machine
(1993) 98m. **C–**
The soul of a serial killer insinuates itself into a massive mainframe and continues his homicidal leisure-time activities digital style. Not bad as dumb ideas go, but sloppy narration, a rightfully embarrassed-looking Allen, and home computer-level effects sink it: rent Wes Craven's *Shocker* for a better take on this.
D: Rachel Talalay. A: Karen Allen, Chris Mulkey, Ken Thorley.

Brainscan
(1994) 96m. **C**
A troubled hacker youth gets software that unleashes a rockstar demon who encourages the teen to do his darkest bidding. An obvious grope at a Jason/Freddy franchise zeros out on scares, but has some good effects, a quick pace, and a fun turn by Smith as a heavy metal demon.
D: John Flynn. A: Edward Furlong, T. Ryder Smith, Frank Langella.

Miscellaneous

Thanks to high-tech special effects, sci-fi filmmakers were freed from the "will-it-look-dumb?" considerations, and the 80s burst forth with films filled with kids surfing on air,

alien creatures made of living water, and dinosaurs without monster suit zippers. True to the science fiction tradition as province of our wildest hopes and fears about scientific progress, you'll also find in this group some less tech-obsessed examinations of some scary and all too recognizable futuristic visions.

Looker
(1981) 93m. **C**
A pricey plastic surgeon is the suspect when beautiful models start dying, but the real culprit is an evil corporation whose computer can reproduce their bodies and voices to hypnotize TV audiences. The dull plot makes this a poor excuse for watching a computer scan models' bodies.
D: Michael Crichton. A: Albert Finney, James Coburn, Leigh Taylor-Young.

Wargames
(1983) 113m. **B**
This likable teen hacker fantasy has Broderick breaking into a Pentagon war computer and playing a "game" of thermonuclear war, which launches real bombs to the USSR.
D: John Badham. A: Matthew Broderick, Dabney Coleman, Ally Sheedy.

Dune
(1984) 140m. **C+**
Based on the cult sci-fi novel, this space epic offers a unique world blending nineteenth-century styled costumes, grand-scale brown/green Art Decoish sets, and some ghoulish and gooey alien life-forms. With the over-charactered, ponderous story, you either immerse yourself in the film or nod off.
D: David Lynch. A: Kyle MacLachlan, Francesca Annis, Dean Stockwell.

1984
(1984) 123m. **B+**
In an unbearably squalid retro-city of the future, a man is interrogated into madness by an agent of Big Brother for the sin of love. Entire cast looks shell-shocked and traumatized in a grayish, eternally autumnal world of constant surveillance and manipulation in this beautifully realized and incredibly depressing version of the Orwell classic.
D: Michael Radford. A: John Hurt, Richard Burton, Suzanna Hamilton.

The Philadelphia Experiment
(1984) 101m. **B–**
A World War II experiment launches two crew members forward in time to modern Nevada. One of them discovers the dire consequences of the experiment and races to get back. Contains a pleasant transtime romance but the subpar effects and tired use of stock evil military types keeps this run-of-the-mill.
D: Stewart Raffill. A: Michael Pare, Nancy Allen, Bobby DiCicco.

Back to the Future
(1985) 116m. **A–**
A cheerful, breakneck-paced adventure finds 80s teen Marty McFly stuck in his hometown in 1955 via batty Doc Brown's time machine. After milking laughs about how corny the 50s were, this settles into Marty's frantic efforts to undo the change he made in his parents'—and his—fates.
D: Robert Zemeckis. A: Michael J. Fox, Christopher Lloyd, Lea Thompson.

Short Circuit
(1986) 98m. **C+**
Robot #5, resembling an inverted electric broom, buzzes into self-awareness and is on the run from the military in his quest for knowledge. He meets Sheedy, learns modern language, quips from TV, and even ogles her in the tub. A cute robot-on-the-run adventure.
D: John Badham. A: Steve Guttenberg, Ally Sheedy, Austin Pendleton.

Innerspace
(1987) 120m. **C+**
A secret miniaturization program gets derailed, and Quaid is launched into the tush of Short who flips when he hears voices within. An absurd premise from *Fantastic Voyage* is turned into a weird buddy comedy with a few special effects showing a "ride" inside the human body.
D: Joe Dante. A: Dennis Quaid, Martin Short, Meg Ryan.

Project X
(1987) 87m. **B–**
The chimps are the only reason to watch this government paranoia story about an Air Force research group that's doing more to lab monkeys than just training them how to fly on jet fighter simulators. A perfectly unthrilling climax is matched by the equally idiotic but sweet resolution.
D: Jonathan Kaplan. A: Matthew Broderick, Helen Hunt, Johnny Ray McGhee.

Alien Nation
(1988) 89m. **B+**
They've got leopardlike spots on their bald heads and get drunk on sour milk but otherwise these aliens blend into 1991 LA so well that they even have their own street gangs and mobsters. A buddy cop thriller injected with humor and the sharp performances by Caan as the bigoted human cop and Patinkin as his earnest and bemused alien partner.
D: Graham Baker. A: James Caan, Mandy Patinkin, Terence Stamp.

The Abyss
(1989) 136m. **C+**
An ocean bottom oil rig tries to retrieve nuclear warheads while battling hull ruptures, cabin fever, and seemingly benevolent alien probes that look like streams of water with faces on the end. A dullish big-budget undersea adventure with too many lulls between the special effects.
D: James Cameron. A: Ed Harris, Mary Elizabeth Mastrantonio, Michael Biehn.

Back to the Future Part II
(1989) 107m. **B**
Though fans of time travel adventures tend to be good-natured about credibility and realism, this sequel pushes the zany plot complications as far as they'll go and still be comprehensible. Hyperventilatingly fast as Marty and Doc race between three time periods, with the usual superior special effects.
D: Robert Zemeckis. A: Michael J. Fox, Christopher Lloyd, Lea Thompson.

Communion
(1989) 107m. **C+**
A purportedly true story of how an author's happy marriage and family life is disrupted when he is repeatedly whisked away by bluish aliens and subjected to physical probing and abuse. Walken is properly zapped-looking in this gloomy drama that rummages around, but never seems to rest on its subject matter.
D: Philippe Mora. A: Christopher Walken, Lindsay Crouse, Frances Sternhagen.

Back to the Future Part III
(1990) 118m. **B+**
The time jumping stops when Marty and Doc land in the Old West and spend the rest of the film trying to

avoid fatal showdowns while scheming to hijack a train to get them back to 1985. Has fun with Western clichés and Steenburgen brings some warmth as the teacher who melts Doc's heart.
D: Robert Zemeckis. A: Michael J. Fox, Christopher Lloyd, Mary Steenbergen.

The Handmaid's Tale
(1990) 109m. **B**
In a fascistic future state where most women have become infertile, government-sponsored babymakers are farmed out to the select few. A mostly smart script, high-powered cast, and recognizably perverse vision of the future make this an unusual entry even with the cop-out ending.
D: Volker Schlondorff. A: Nastasha Richardson, Faye Dunaway, Robert Duvall.

Cool World
(1992) 101m. **D**
A barely coherent mess mixes live action with animation in the tale about a hip cartoonist meeting his doodle creation Holli Wood who needs to have sex with him in order to escape the cartoon world. Loud and jarring action, unappealing characters, and a tedious plot make this a near-total miss.
D: Ralph Bakshi. A: Gabriel Byrne, Kim Basinger, Brad Pitt.

Jurassic Park
(1993) 126m. **B+**
The state-of-the-art re-creations of dinosaurs are more alive than the rest of this film, which feels like it, too, was made by computer and robots. Technically astounding, with a few funny and touching moments, it works best when it turns into a kid's adventure and the dinos start hunting the humans.
D: Steven Spielberg. A: Sam Neill, Laura Dern, Jeff Goldblum.

The Crow
(1994) 117m. **B**
After he and the love of his life are slain by lunatic killers in some dark futuristic city, a guitarist returns from the grave for vengeance. Despite thin plot, still an excitingly ultraviolent tale, with darkly gorgeous labyrinthine cityscapes and eerie grim ambiance.
D: Alex Proyas. A: Brandon Lee, Ernie Hudson, Michael Wincott.

The Puppet Masters
(1994) 109m. **C−**
It's alien invasion time in a middle-American town as people are saddled with back-riding parasites that suck away their personalities. A slackly paced, virtually suspenseless film with creatures that resemble the "chestburster" from *Alien*. Rampantly mediocre.
D: Stuar Orme. A: Eric Thal, Julie Warner, Donald Sutherland.

Stargate
(1994) 119m. **C+**
An anthropologist and a team of military types go through a multidimension machine and wind up in the middle of an Egypt-like world under siege by aliens. A cross between a goofy 50s space epic and *Star Wars*-like special effects technology. The snail's pace allows you to contemplate just how silly it is.
D: Roland Emmerich. A: Kurt Russell, James Spader, Jaye Davidson.

Species
(1995) 119m. **B−**
Scientists create an alien/human girl who sexually matures at an alarming rate, eventually becoming a supermodel-like insectoid on the prowl for suitable mates. An entertainingly loopy scarefest, with an amazing bronzed insect girl/monster and enough sexual and pop cultural undercurrents to keep viewer entertained or laughing in the aisles.
D: Roger Donaldson. A: Ben Kingsley, Michael Madsen, Forest Whitaker.

Japanese Animation

From the space epics and sagas of interplanetary civil war to the high-tech thrillers set in dazzling futuristic cityscapes, these have the same dark tone, exquisite graphics, and surprisingly forthright sex and violence that other Japanese *animé* offers. Interestingly, with the wide mix of characters and creatures that populate these sci-fi fables, it's often teenage girls who are placed squarely in the middle of all action involving giant robots, genetic engineering, and time travel.

My Youth in Arcadia
(1982) 130m. **B**
Federation spaceship Captain Harlok (a popular TV animation character) leads resistance efforts against the alien occupation of Earth. This engrossing epic space tale, which goes from pitched battles on Earth to destruction of other planets, is notably dark and bleak but beautifully animated despite stiff character design.
D: Leiji Matsumoto.

Lensman
(1984) 107m. **A**
A young space pilot acquires a superpowered lens to become "Lensman," whose mission is to locate the Devil Planet, home base of the evil Boskone Empire. This *Star Wars*-like space opera offers generous displays of computer effects and almost realistic (for Japanimation) character design.
D: Yoshiaki Kawajiri and Kazuyuki Hirokawa.

Odin: Photon Space Sailor Starlight
(1985) 93m. **C**
A young crew on a spaceship's maiden voyage finds itself in a far galaxy battling a giant computer brain that's out to destroy all life-forms. A far-flung space adventure has an intricate and intriguing story and stunning graphics that are weakened by the slow pace and overly simple character design.
D: Toshio Masuda.

The Humanoid
(1986) 45m. **D**
On an idyllic remote planet, a beautiful female robot helps a band of colonists combat a power-mad governor seeking to unleash the power of a buried starship. Standard robots-and-gunplay action scenes mix with lots of talk and some mild romancing.
D: Sinichi Masaki.

They Were 11
(1986) 91m. **B**
Ten space academy cadets assigned to man a derelict spaceship for 53 days are thrown into states of confusion and paranoia when there are suddenly eleven of them and no one can tell which is the impostor. An intriguing, suspenseful, and quiet story is told in a simple style with no sex or violence.

D: Tesu Dezaki and Tsuneo Tominaga.

Dirty Pair: Project Eden

(1987) 80m. **C**

When two sexy teenage space agents are called on to settle an outer space mining dispute, they come up against a mad scientist and his army of genetically engineered monsters. Typical mix of beautiful girls, romantic hijinks, grotesque monsters, and mass destruction, with frequent bursts of action helping the weak story.
D: Koichi Mashita.

Lily C.A.T.

(1987) 80m. **C**

A corporate expedition orbiting a distant planet finds its members killed off one by one by a mysterious shape-shifting alien force. A combination of *The Thing* and *Alien* features routine animation but fairly realistic character design. Some neat transformation scenes, but lacks the suspense of its predecessors.
D: Hisayuki Toriumi.

Robot Carnival

(1987) 97m. **C+**

Seven different directors offer segments designed as variations on a robotic theme, including a futuristic robot vs. human war, an android-human love story, and a tale of nineteenth-century wooden robots. A moody and atmospheric showcase for different animation styles but offers little in the way of story or substance.
D: Katsuhiro Otomo, Yasuomi Umetsu, Hiroyuki Kitazume.

Venus Wars

(1989) 104m. **B**

Bloody civil war on a colonized Venus is the backdrop for a tale of rebellious teen bikers and the sexy Earth reporter who forms an alliance with them. The juvenile antics of the main characters continue inexplicably amidst the violence and mass destruction in this exquisitely drawn and designed entry.
D: Yoshikazu Yasuhiko.

Wicked City

(1989) 80m. **A**

Monsters from the Black World dimension seek to disrupt the interdimensional treaty process but are stopped by a pair of agents, one human and one from the Black World. A dark and eerie stylized look that suits the imaginative blend of crime, horror, and sci-fi. Heavy doses of sex and violence include a rapacious spider lady who beds the hero.
D: Yoshiaki Kawajiri.

Akira

(1990) 124m. **A**

Groundbreaking sci-fi tale of a future postapocalyptic Tokyo where the secret government transforms a troubled teen into an unstoppable supermutation. Spectacularly animated rendition of a streamlined, high-tech urban landscape and nonstop action enable viewers to negotiate a complicated plot and moments of bone-crunching violence.
D: Katsuhiro Otomo.

THRILLERS

Thrillers Menu

THRILLERS MENU

THRILLERS FILM GROUPS

1930s

Sherlock Holmes

These economical little whodunits made during the war years starred Basil Rathbone as the world's first private detective, who solved every manner of mystery in Victorian England with his "elementary deductions." Sherlock on film quickly departed from Sherlock on paper and, after he cleaned up a few nasty cases in turn-of-the-century Britain, he proceeded to take on the criminal element in contemporary England, Canada, and America; he even wrangled with the Nazis. There are at least 18 of these films out on video, but here are some of the best of them.

The Adventures of Sherlock Holmes
(1939) 83m. B&W. **A–**
Criminal genius Professor Moriarty vows to commit the ultimate crime right under the ample nose of Holmes. Mysterious murders, the crown jewels, and red herrings absorb Holmes in this complex and involving treat.
D: Alfred Werker. A: With Ida Lupino, George Zucco.

The Hound of the Baskervilles
(1939) 80m. B&W. **B+**
A fiendish hound kills the head of the manor and his heir may be next if Holmes and Watson can't figure out the family curse. Swirling murk on a dark moor, a gloomy mansion, and a sinister family legend come up against Holmes' cold logic.
D: Sidney Lanfield. A: With Richard Greene, Lionel Atwill, Wendy Barrie.

Sherlock Holmes and the Voice of Terror
(1942) 65m. B&W. **B**
"The Voice of Terror" is a Nazi broadcaster who predicts British military disasters with uncanny accuracy, and Holmes must ferret out the traitorous high official. Spirited updating with super patriotic overtones as Holmes rallies the underclass to join his cause and save England.
D: John Rawlins. A: With Evelyn Ankers, Henry Daniell.

The Pearl of Death
(1944) 69m. B&W. **B**
Owners of plaster busts of Napoleon are being brutally killed by the fiendish "Oxton Creeper," and Holmes links them to the missing Borgia Pearl. Holmes must duel a master criminal, his dangerous female associate, and a hulking brute in this complex and dark tale in which he actually makes a mistake!
D: Roy William Neill. A: With Evelyn Ankers, Miles Mander, Rondo Hatton.

The Scarlet Claw
(1944) 74m. B&W. **B**
A strange glowing figure haunts the marshes outside a tiny hamlet in Canada, and the murder of a leading citizen draws the attention of visiting Holmes. The shimmering creature is nicely photographed, while the rich subplot of murders within an acting troup, along with the other crime, will keep you guessing.
D: Roy William Neill. A: With Gerald Hamer, Paul Cavanagh, Kay Hardins.

House of Fear
(1945) 69m. B&W. **B–**
Members of a club housed in a forbidding Scottish manor are being killed and Holmes is out to stop the bloodshed. A gloomy house, booming storms, secret passages, people with bloody backgrounds, and a legend that "no man goes whole to his grave" make for a clichéd but fun whodunit.
D: Roy William Neill. A: With Aubrey Mather, Paul Cavanagh, Dennis Hoey.

Dressed to Kill
(1946) 73m. B&W. **B**
Death befalls anyone who possesses one of three music boxes whose tunes are encoded with clues to the whereabouts of the stolen Bank of England money plates. In his last role as Holmes, Rathbone matches wits with an unscrupulous mistress of disguise who lures him on by planting cigarette ash clues.
D: Roy William Neill. A: With Nigel Bruce, Patricia Morison.

The Thin Man

He's the private eye who's friends with the underworld, she's a slightly daffy socialite, and their marriage is a sophisticated romp composed of equal parts love, bemusement, and gin. Nick and Nora Charles (and dog Asta) are the darlings of high society, who always manage to nab the murderer in this series of screwball mysteries. Most of the films are gems of sophisticated wit, although the later entries domesticated the pair, toning down their lighthearted boozing and making them almost as homey as the Hardy family.

The Thin Man
(1934) 93m. B&W. **A–**
Nick Charles is hired to find the oddball inventor who vanished after he caught his mistress embezzling. Sparks fly as the freewheeling Nick and Nora plow through martinis, shoot the ornaments off their Christmas tree, and wisecrack their way to rounding up the unusual suspects.
D: W. S. Van Dyke. A: William Powell, Myrna Loy, Maureen O'Sullivan.

After the Thin Man
(1936) 113m. B&W. **B+**
While visiting Nora's snobby relatives on San Francisco's Nob Hill, a cousin is accused of killing her good-for-nothing husband. The fast-living twosome keep the tone light even when the convoluted caper begins to drag. Keep an eye on the interesting early Stewart.
D: W. S. Van Dyke. A: William Powell, Myrna Loy, James Stewart.

Another Thin Man
(1939) 105m. B&W. **B**
Nick, Nora, Asta, and new addition Nicky Jr. postpone a vacation to investigate three murders on a Long Island estate. Parenthood sits heavily on the fun-loving couple, but Nick makes a glorious highballing return to form in the final reconstruction of the crime.
D: W. S. Van Dyke. A: William Powell, Myrna Loy, C. Aubrey Smith.

Shadow of The Thin Man
(1941) 97m. B&W. **B**
Nick and Nora's investigation of a jockey's death leads them into the unsavory underworlds of horse racing and professional wrestling. A sideshow of bizarre characters and a little sleuthing help from Asta make you overlook the thin story. The crazy antics at the wrestling arena look eerily contemporary.
D: W. S. Van Dyke. A: William Powell, Myrna Loy, Donna Reed.

The Thin Man Goes Home
(1944) 100m. B&W. **B–**
Nicky Jr. is nowhere to be seen in this overlong caper, and Nick stays disappointingly dry while in his teetotaling dad's home.
D: Richard Thorpe. A: William Powell, Myrna Loy, Gloria DeHaven.

Song of the Thin Man
(1947) 87m. B&W. **C+**
The series returns to Manhattan in an attempt to recapture the jazzy flavor of the early entries as Nick and Nora frequent after hours hot spots in search of a killer. The two aging sophisticates seem embarrassingly out of place with the hepcats and lowlifes of a darkening postwar city.
D: Edward Buzzell. A: William Powell, Myrna Loy, Keenan Wynn.

Charlie Chan

These compact one-hour whodunits feature Hollywood's favorite Chinese sleuth, the courteous, paternal, and eloquently inquisitive Charlie Chan. The earlier entries starring Warner Oland and later Sidney Toler are the most fun, combining broad humor with suspense as Charlie solves the crimes of the rich and seedy in exotic locales. Like a chubby Asian Sherlock Holmes, Charlie uses his brain rather than a gun, spouting fortune cookie wisdom ("Difficult to catch fly with one finger") on his way to the drawing room revelation finale. By the mid-1940s the series had already seen its best days, with tired plots and bare bones budgets.

Charlie Chan in London
(1934) 75m. B&W. **B**
Emotionless Charlie cuts through English reserve when he looks for a killer amongst a group of party guests at a genteel country home. Offers every British cliché including snobby accents, rooms awash in Victorian bric-a-brac, and the expected fox hunt.
D: Eugene Forde. A: Warner Oland, Douglas Walton, Drue Leyton.

Charlie Chan at the Opera
(1936) 66m. B&W. **A**
A distinguished, bigger-budgeted entry set in the flamboyant world of opera offers a superior supporting cast, Charlie tearing off proverbs at a spry clip, and a pseudo-opera crafted by Oscar Levant.
D: H. Bruce Humberstone. A: Warner Oland, Boris Karloff, Keye Luke.

Charlie Chan's Secret
(1936) 72m. B&W. **C+**
Chan dallies among the wealthy as a missing heir turns up unexpectedly and is quickly murdered. An unimaginative story with the standard drawing room revelation: It looks like the studio didn't want to waste an ornate mansion set.
D: Gordon Wiles. A: Warner Oland, Charles Quigley, Rosina Lawrence.

Charlie Chan on Broadway
(1937) 68m. B&W. **B**
When a female singer is murdered at a nightclub, Charlie rubs elbows with the slangy, fast-talking night reporters and photographers who prowl New York society for stories. Enjoyable contrast of Chan's methodical style and New York's need for action.
D: Eugene Forde. A: Warner Oland, Keye Luke, J. Edward Brombury.

Charlie Chan in Reno
(1939) 70m. B&W. **C**
Charlie rushes in to investigate a murder in the divorce capital of America and is somewhat out of his element as he painfully listens to couples bickering their way to breakup. Reeks too strongly of its B-movie roots.
D: Norman Foster. A: Sidney Toler, Cobina Wright, Jr., Mary Beth Hughes.

Charlie Chan at Treasure Island
(1939) 75m. B&W. **B+**
Chan enlists the aid of a professional magician to investigate a charlatan psychic whom he suspects of murder. While suspects get jumpy or killed, Charlie keeps his oriental composure as Romero spices up the proceedings with his turn as the oily, glad-handing magician.
D: Norman Foster. A: Sidney Toler, Cesar Romero, Pauline Moore.

Charlie Chan at the Wax Museum
(1949) 63m. B&W. **A**
Charlie must elude poison darts, daffy radio personalities, and a host of malevolent

figures lurking in the atmospheric darkness of Dr. Cream's ghoulish wax museum. Makes good use of spookhouse locales, and Chan gets to be in some real danger from the sinister Cream.
D: Lynn Shores. A: Sidney Toler, C. Henry Gordon, Sen Yung.

OTHER FILMS:
Charlie Chan in Paris (1935)
Charlie Chan's Secret (1936)
Murder over New York (1940)
Charlie Chan in Rio (1941)
Castle in the Desert (1942)
Charlie Chan in the Secret Service (1944)
The Chinese Cat (1944)
The Shanghai Cobra (1945)
Meeting at Midnight (1944)
The Jade Mask (1945)
The Scarlet Clue (1945)

Hitchcock

Hitchcock's early British thrillers have many of the trademarks of his mature masterpieces—the innocent man on the run, life-or-death chases through the countryside, and showdowns at some monumental landmark. Like his later works, these films will charm you with their unexpected and humorous character moments—as well as glimpses of prewar Britain—all served up with plenty of nail-biting suspense.

The Man Who Knew Too Much
(1934) 84m. B&W. **B+**

A man who unwittingly learns of an assassination plot is powerless to act on it after the plotters kidnap his daughter. An urbane spy thriller shot through with upper-crust humor, with a spectacular showdown in crowded Albert Hall.
D: Alfred Hitchcock. A: Leslie Banks, Peter Lorre, Edna Best.

The 39 Steps
(1935) 81m. B&W. **A**

The man who finds a dead body in his rooms becomes a fugitive from the law and the target for a network of murderous spies. This cross-country chase film is one energetic escape after another with good-humored pauses for the citizenry met along the way.
D: Alfred Hitchcock. A: Robert Donat, Madeleine Carroll, Godfrey Tearle.

Sabotage
(1936) 77m. B&W. **B–**

When a member of an anarchistic group is unable to plant a time bomb, he asks his wife's kid brother to deliver the "package" across town at a specific time. Less of a full-fledged thriller than a string of nerve-racking moments as the boy is disastrously delayed en route while back home the wife discovers the ruse.
D: Alfred Hitchcock. A: Sylvia Sidney, Oscar Homolka, Desmond Tester.

The Secret Agent
(1936) 83m. B&W. **B–**

An uneven blend of spy thriller and comedy offers a reluctant British agent who has to play husband to a female associate aided by a slightly deranged Mexican killer. Gielgud as a romantic lead looks a little wispy, but the train wreck and chase through a chocolate factory are humdingers.
D: Alfred Hitchcock. A: Madeleine Carroll, Peter Lorre, John Gielgud.

Young and Innocent
(1937) 81m. B&W. **B–**

Another innocent man accused of murder is on the run, this time with his girlfriend in tow. Bland leads make this only fair but the chase keeps it flowing. Contains a great scene where the fugitives get stuck in the middle of a kids' party as the police close in.
D: Alfred Hitchcock. A: Derrick De Marney, Nova Pilbeam, Percy Marmont.

The Lady Vanishes
(1938) 96m. B&W. **A–**

A kindly old lady disappears on a train traveling through the Balkans, but almost no one seems to want to do anything about it, or even to believe she ever existed. Starts out light, presenting its array of colorful passengers, and then skillfully slips into suspense and action as the train becomes a menacing battleground of spies and a microcosm of prewar European tensions.
D: Alfred Hitchcock. A: Margaret Lockwood, Michael Redgrave, May Whitty.

World War II Spies and Rescues

These nifty little suspensers showed the war raging, but not on the battlefield. Rain-slicked streets, warehouses, piers, and other forbidding locales on both sides of the Atlantic are the backdrops for the fast-paced and vicious spy vs. spy maneuvers.

Night Train to Munich
(1940) 93m. B&W. **A–**

A British agent poses as a Nazi in order to rescue a kidnapped scientist in Germany. Fast-paced and cunningly scripted, this high-styled blend of suspense and comedy is a tip of the hat to Hitchcock's best.
D: Carol Reed. A: Rex Harrison, Margaret Lockwood, Paul Henreid.

Pimpernel Smith
(1940) 121m. B&W. **B+**

Howard is the unassuming British professor leading his students on a Continental field trip who moonlights as the dashing rescuer of Nazi victims. Howard is ever debonair in this slightly quaint, actionless swashbuckler where danger lurks in trains, embassy parties, and archeological digs.
D: Leslie Howard. A: Leslie Howard, Mary Morris, Francis L. Sullivan.

Across the Pacific
(1942) 98m. B&W. **B+**

The passengers of a Japanese ship heading to the Pacific include a turncoat ex-Army officer, a clothes designer, and a mysterious professor. Or are they? A spy thriller that shares the same director and stars as *The*

Maltese Falcon, as well as the maneuvering and double crossing between all the wily characters.
D: John Huston. A: Humphrey Bogart, Mary Astor, Sydney Greenstreet.

All Through the Night
(1942) 107m. B&W. **A**

A group of local gamblers and racketeers takes on a Nazi ring planning some nastiness right in Manhattan. Fast-paced fun, including a nifty nocturnal chase through Central Park and Bogart bluffing his way through a Nazi meeting with the funniest double talk this side of Damon Runyon.
D: Vincent Sherman. A: Humphrey Bogart, William Demarest, Karen Verne.

Above Suspicion
(1943) 90m. B&W. **C+**

On the eve of the war, an Oxford professor and his bride are asked to spend their honeymoon spying on the Germans. A few fun moments shine through in this mostly static mix of spy thriller and comedy.
D: Richard Thorpe. A: Joan Crawford, Fred MacMurray, Conrad Veidt.

The Fallen Sparrow
(1943) 93m. B&W. **B**

Back in New York, a Spanish War veteran is pursued by Nazi agents—male and female—who believe he knows the location of a Nazi regiment's inspiration flag. Garfield is the perfect haunted war burnout pursued by female agents, with Slezak making an effective menacing Nazi.
D: Richard Wallace. A: John Garfield, Maureen O'Hara, Walter Slezak.

Waterfront
(1944) 66m. B&W. **C**

A pair of Nazi agents slips into San Francisco where they blackmail and bully German-Americans into working for them. A murky, sullen, and dark thriller partly due to the film's low budget.
D: Steve Sekely. A: John Carradine, J. Carroll Naish, Maris Wrixon.

OTHER FILMS:
The Commandos Strike at Dawn (1942)
Desperate Journey (1942)
Edge of Darkness (1943)
Northern Pursuit (1943)
Blood on the Sun (1945)
Cornered (1946)

1940s
Classic Film Noir

Film noir: a particular strain of crime film marked by Expressionistic lighting, disorienting visual schemes, and a postwar ambience of anxiety and suspicion that anything that could go wrong, would go wrong. The characters—whether crooks, private eyes, or femme fatales—inhabit a world where morality shifts with the next opportunity and every rain-slicked street seems to end in a cul-de-sac. While each of these sardonically doleful films possesses its own distinctive tone, they all take the bright Hollywood image of a just and sane America, and make it very, very dark.

Detective Thrillers

Stranger on the Third Floor
(1940) 101m. B&W. **B**

A newspaper reporter suspects a strange little man of a brutal killing. Regarded as the first film noir with its deliberate blurring of reality and fantasy, a bizarre *Caligari*-esque dream sequence, and a quietly disturbing Lorre as the white-scarfed stranger.
D: Boris Ingster. A: Peter Lorre, John McGuire, Margaret Tallichat.

I Wake Up Screaming
(1941) 82m. B&W. **A−**

When the promoter of a murdered model/would-be actress becomes the prime suspect, he looks for the real culprit with the help of the dead woman's sister. A lively paced thriller with a colorful look at the menacing and seedier side of the New York world of nightclubs and manufactured celebrities.
D: H. Bruce Humberstone. A: Betty Grable, Victor Mature, Carole Landis.

The Maltese Falcon
(1941) 100m. B&W. **A**

Private eye Sam Spade begins a quest for his partner's murderer in one of Hollywood's most famously labyrinthine plots, complete with psychopathic liars, suave villains, and an untrustworthy dame in distress. With witty clipped dialogue, this offers a coolly modern hero and a relentlessly cynical take on human affairs.
D: John Huston. A: Humphrey Bogart, Mary Astor, Peter Lorre.

The Glass Key
(1942) 85m. B&W. **B+**

With their glamorously deadpan faces, Ladd and Lake are the quintessential noir pair in this complexly woven tale of corrupt politics, racketeers, and love gone bad. Everyone seems trapped here but the atmosphere is a little less thick and the story-telling a little more to the point.
D: Stuart Heisler. A: Alan Ladd, Veronica Lake, Brian Donlevy.

This Gun for Hire
(1942) 81m. B&W. **B−**

Disturbed, kitten-loving hitman Ladd hits the revenge trail when he's double-crossed by a chemical company president leaking secrets to the Japanese. This early noir is overly plotted to build up its atmospheric steam, but plays at an attention-getting breakneck pace.
D: Frank Tuttle. A: Alan Ladd, Veronica Lake, Robert Preston.

Murder My Sweet
(1944) 95m. B&W. **A**

An effeminate patsy, an upper-crust seductress, and a cache of stolen jewels all get in the way of gumshoe Marlowe's search for a hulking mobster's missing girlfriend. Almost insanely hard-boiled, with wry narration, a dazzlingly surreal dream sequence, and an appropriately down-cast tone.
D: Edward Dmytryk. A: Dick Powell, Claire Trevor, Anne Shirley.

The Big Sleep
(1946) 118m. B&W. **A**

Gumshoe Marlowe gets involved with blackmail, a deranged family, and murder. Director Hawks injects some humanity (and plays up the simmering chemistry between Bogart and Bacall) into this thriller that is less of a story than a series of

tense character confrontations.
D: Howard Hawks. A: Humphrey Bogart, Lauren Bacall, Dorothy Malone.

Dark Corner
(1946) 99m. B&W. **B+**

A private eye who had been framed gets out of jail only to be framed again. This has all the classic noir gambits and paranoid flourishes, but the near robotic acting and stagy plotting make it almost a parody of the genre, even while it has the weird ambiance of a half-remembered nightmare.
D: Henry Hathaway. A: Mark Stevens, Lucille Ball, Clifton Webb.

Lady in the Lake
(1946) 103m. B&W. **B–**

Marlowe searches for a missing wife in this ambitious, but unsuccessful experiment, using the camera as Marlowe's eyes so that the viewer only sees his point of view. This result is confusing, with plot and atmosphere sacrificed for the disorienting attempt at a new immediacy.
D: Robert Montgomery. A: Robert Montgomery, Audrey Totter, Jayne Meadows.

Out of the Past
(1947) 97m. B&W. **A**

Mitchum thought he was through with his former life involving mobsters, murder, and a dangerous siren, only to be plunged back into it with a vengeance. This tightly constructed tale has some of noir's best examples of the stark photography, overwrought characters, and sense of doom and betrayal.
D: Jacques Tourneur. A: Robert Mitchum, Kirk Douglas, Jane Greer.

Non-Detective Thrillers

Johnny Eager
(1941) 102m. B&W. **B**

An ambitious ex-con/cabbie opens a dog racing racket, only to get entangled with a mysterious attorney, a confused femme fatal, and finally murder. This early noir already has the trademark tone of futility and an appropriately heart-wrenching close.
D: Mervyn LeRoy. A: Robert Taylor, Lana Turner, Van Heflin.

Detour
(1945) 68m. B&W. **B+**

A luckless pianist attempts to go west, but the first man to pick him up dies mysteriously. When he runs into the dead man's moll it's all downhill from there. A justly celebrated film by cult director Edgar G. Ulmer who uses the zero-budget to add to the film's desolate brooding tone.
D: Edgar G. Ulmer. A: Tom Neal, Ann Savage, Claudia Drake.

Johnny Angel
(1945) 77m. B&W. **C+**

When he hears of his father's murder, ship's captain Johnny Angel returns home to New Orleans to track the killer. The weak story is helped somewhat by brisk pacing and a luminous rendering of seamy New Orleans mean streets.
D: Edwin Marin. A: George Raft, Claire Trevor, Signe Hasso.

Scarlet Street
(1945) 102m. B&W.
A–

Robinson is a basically decent man until he makes a wrong turn in Greenwich Village, falls for a moll, and gets caught up in an embezzlement scheme. Justice goes out the window as he pays, pays, and pays some more for a very small crime in this bleakly fatalistic film.
D: Fritz Lang. A: Edward G. Robinson, Joan Bennett, Dan Duryea.

Crossfire
(1947) 86m. B&W. **B+**

This message noir tells of four army buddies, one of whom kills a man he suspects of being a Jew. A bristling tale of perverted codes of honor, with a higher quotient of menace and paranoia.
D: Edward Dmytryk. A: Robert Ryan, Robert Mitchum, Gloria Grahame.

Dark Passage
(1947) 106m. B&W. **B–**

Bogart's an innocent man imprisoned for his wife's murder and Bacall the woman who helps him out for mysterious reasons. A confused film with constant changes of camera POV, but the leads' chemistry and the eerie image of Bogie's face bandaged up after plastic surgery pulls this through.
D: Delmer Daves. A: Humphrey Bogart, Lauren Bacall, Agnes Moorehead.

Dead Reckoning
(1947) 100m. B&W. **B+**

A neurotic ex-flyer obsessed with the disappearance of a war-time pal is a lout with the pal's girl and a tough-guy with the mob. A low-key, quietly disturbing film, with death imagined as a billowing parachute.
D: John Cromwell. A: Humphrey Bogart, Lizabeth Scott, Morris Carnovsky.

Criss Cross
(1948) 88m. B&W. **B**

Still pining for his ex-wife after a year, Lancaster allows himself to get involved with her again, despite warning that she's mixed up with crackling underworld hood Duryea. It's no surprise that this all leads to no good in this moody and finally tragic film.
D: Robert Siodmak. A: Burt Lancaster, Yvonne De Carlo, Dan Duryea.

The Scar (aka Hollow Triumph
(1948) 83m. B&W. **A**

A master criminal encounters his exact double, murders him, and then assumes the man's life until the ringer's dark past starts creeping up. A relentlessly bizarre, cynical, and at times horrific thriller, with grotesquely luminescent tabloid photography: a rare dark gem.
D: Steve Sekely. A: Paul Henreid, Joan Bennett, Eduard Franz.

D.O.A.
(1950) 83m. B&W.
B+

A unique story of a man poisoned with radiation who spends his last few days tracking down his killers. The low budget only enhances the claustrophobic and doomed feel in this fast-paced nightmare.
D: Rudolph Maté. A: Edmond O'Brien, Pamela Britton, Neville Brand.

Force of Evil
(1949) 80m. B&W. **A**

A hot shot mob lawyer gets ensnared in a numbers racket that threatens the lives of his brother and girlfriend. A bracing morality tale with an air of escalating danger ending at the broodingly photographed finale on the rocks of New York's East River.
D: Abraham Polonsky. A: John Garfield, Marie Windsor, Beatrice Pearson.

The Third Man
(1949) 104m. B&W.
A

In postwar Vienna, a writer finds that an old friend thought to be dead is quite alive and part of the black market mob. As much mood piece as thriller, with innovative off-kilter camera angles, exotic music, and high-contrast photography creating an atmosphere of both continental elegance and noir-tinged corruption.
D: Carol Reed. A: Orson Welles, Joseph Cotten, Alida Valli.

Romance Noir

Film noir was pretty democratic in the way it dealt with love and romance: Whether the character was a man or woman, crook or cop, love was just another path to self-destruction. Unlike the "menaced women" noirs, these dames tend to be femme fatales who drag their men down into some debased moral swamp, although as they say in the law, no one—at least in these twisty melodramas—comes to the table with clean hands.

Double Indemnity
(1944) 106m. B&W. **A**

An insurance agent is seduced by a shrewd dissatisfied wife into killing her husband in order to collect on his insurance policy. The few moments of humor and tenderness don't change the tone of duplicity, betrayal, and the sickening sense that everything is spinning out of control.
D: Billy Wilder. A: Fred MacMurray, Barbara Stanwyck, Edward G. Robinson.

Mildred Pierce
(1945) 112m. B&W. **A**

Mother-daughter love gets pretty dark in this moodily photographed noir classic about a successful working mother who slavishly dotes on her bratty, social-climbing kid even when they're competing for the same man. Crawford is all cool efficiency and abject devotion while remaining faintly contemptuous of the men in her life.
D: Michael Curtiz. A: Joan Crawford, Ann Blyth, Zachary Scott.

Gilda
(1946) 110m. B&W. **A**

Handsome thug Johnny is assigned to keep an eye on the new wife of his effete boss. It turns out that bodyguard and bride share a not too distant history together and the heat hasn't died out. This classic is bristling with repressed desires, Hayworth's feline wildness, and an almost homoerotic kinship between the men.
D: Charles Vidor. A: Rita Hayworth, Glenn Ford, George Macready.

The Postman Always Rings Twice
(1946) 113m. B&W. **A**

The drifter who works at the roadside cafe falls hard for the boss's unhappy wife, and murder seems to be the only way out. Even with the slick-looking shabby cafe and glamorous-looking stars, this still pours on the doom, double-crossing, and suffocating sense that things are going really wrong.
D: Tay Garnett. A: John Garfield, Lana Turner, Cecil Kellaway.

The Strange Love of Martha Ivers
(1946) 115m. B&W. **A**

A childhood friend's reappearance rekindles dark passions and even worse memories for a successful businesswoman. This small town is a stew of murder, political corruption, suicide, and guilt-ridden denizens, all of whom have a stranglehold on the others. One of the more complex and affecting noir romances with a blistering finale.
D: Lewis Milestone. A: Barbara Stanwyck, Lizabeth Scott, Kirk Douglas.

Born to Kill
(1947) 92m. B&W. **A**

Trevor is a woman neurotically attracted to a brooding ex-boxer on the lam for killing his girlfriend. An extremely brutal, uncompromising film with a mind-boggling plot and a densely perverse atmosphere.
D: Robert Wise. A: Claire Trevor, Lawrence Tierney, Walter Slezak.

They Won't Believe Me
(1947) 95m. B&W. **B+**

Young is anything but wholesome as he stands trial for murder; not of his wife whose only appeal is her wealth, or his mistress who bought him his own business, but his secretary girlfriend. An underrated twisted tale of sexual social climbing, adultery, and murder with a particularly cruel ironic atmosphere.
D: Irving Pichel. A: Robert Young, Susan Hayward, Jane Greer.

Lady from Shanghai
(1948) 87m. B&W. **B+**

Director Orson Welles uses noir to go style-crazy in this dizzying tale of a sailor caught between a demented cripple, his amoral wife, and other seedy characters. Remembered most for how harsh and unsexy Hayworth is made to look, and the vertigo-inducing Hall of Mirrors finale.
D: Orson Welles. A: Orson Welles, Rita Hayworth, Everett Sloane.

Pitfall
(1948) 88m. B&W. **A**

Insurance agent Powell has the perfect family and job, and it's boring him to tears until a one-night stand threatens to destroy everything he values. This has a particularly high quotient of the genre's bleakness but, for a change, it's within the context of the "normal" world of the solid family man.
D: Andre de Toth. A: Dick Powell, Jane Wyatt, Lizabeth Scott.

Road House
(1948) 95m. B&W. **A**

An unhinged road house/bowling alley owner hires singer Lupino and falls murderously in love with her. The film's unique design combines western and modern motifs with almost surreal photography to disturbing effect. Widmark sinks his teeth into one of his more memorably crazed roles.
D: Jean Negulesco. A: Ida Lupino, Richard Widmark, Cornel Wilde.

They Live by Night
(1948) 95m. **A**

Shortly after a naive young man gets involved with some criminals, he falls in love and wants to get out, but it's too late. This tragic romance-crime story has an alternately lyrical and violent atmosphere, brooding photography, and doomed lovers that make this unforgettable.
D: Nicholas Ray. A: Farley Granger, Cathy O'Donnell, Howard da Silva.

Gun Crazy
(1950) 86m. B&W. **A**

Bert and Annie are only good at two things: loving each other and shooting guns. When their money runs out, she talks him into a life of crime. While this forerunner to *Bonnie and Clyde* and *Natural Born Killers* follows their robbery spree, it's less of a crime drama than a tabloid-style romantic melodrama of a doomed and weirdly innocent love.
D: Joseph H. Lewis. A: John Dall, Peggy Cummins, Morris Carnovsky.

Clash by Night
(1952) 105m. B&W. **A–**
An embittered woman returns to her working-class hometown after ten years of hard knocks and marries a dull fisherman. Then she meets her hubby's selfish and angry pal and the ferocious pair can't keep their hands off each other. A stormy nasty noir that unfortunately cops out with the finale.
D: Fritz Lang. A: Barbara Stanwyck, Robert Ryan, Paul Douglas.

Menaced Women Noir

Welcome to the world of women's growing dread of their men. The action in these noir thrillers usually revolves around the heroine's marriage as she discovers her husband is not the man she thought he was, no doubt a common enough real-life occurrence in the postwar years. Whether or not salvation awaits the woman in the end, the gloomy psychological spin on these tales always leaves you with a feeling of shattered lives.

Gaslight
(1944) 114m. B&W. **A** 🏛
Suave Boyer begins a sadistic campaign to drive his vulnerable young bride mad. Victorian London is evoked with fog and shadow in this sickly claustrophobic period piece that brilliantly mixes gothic and noir.
D: George Cukor. A: Ingrid Bergman, Charles Boyer, Joseph Cotten.

Laura
(1944) 88m. B&W. **A** 🏛
A New York detective meets a scintillating ménage of world-weary sophisticates while tracking the murderer of the glamorous Laura. The sinous camerawork, posh sets, delightful rogues gallery of suspects, and an air of sexual obsession make this a moody and entertaining perennial.
D: Otto Preminger. A: Gene Tierney, Dana Andrews, Clifton Webb.

Conflict
(1945) 86m. B&W. **B–**
A struggle of wills leading to murder begins when a man admits to his spouse that he's in love with her sister. But did he really kill his wife? The unusual twist here is that it's the husband who feels entrapment and growing paranoia as he deals with the unusual consequences of his actions.
D: Curtis Bernhardt. A: Humphrey Bogart, Alexis Smith, Sydney Greenstreet.

The Seventh Veil
(1945) 94m. B&W. **B–**
The cold, emotionally warped guardian becomes the obsessive Svengali to his brilliant pianist ward. This British entry is as gloomy and overwrought as they get, with Mason the perfect brooding semi-psycho whose suffocating grip on the young woman turns murderous.
D: Compton Bennett. A: Ann Todd, James Mason, Herbert Lom.

The Specter of the Rose
(1946) 90m. **B+** 🔍
An innocent ballerina marries the dance troupe's star and realizes that he's going insane. Ben Hecht wrote and directed this unusual and theatrical thriller that focuses on the extravagant, artificial, and childlike poseurs and artistes of the ballet world.
D: Ben Hecht. A: Judith Anderson, Lionel Stander, Viola Essen.

The Spiral Staircase
(1946) 83m. B&W. **B+**
McGuire is the mute servant in an eerie New England household, and there's a serial killer of deformed girls on the loose. Slow and moving, but with a nicely ominous Hitchcock-like feel, an oppressively opulent mansion, and a stellar McGuire.
D: Robert Siodmak. A: Dorothy McGuire, Ethel Barrymore, Kent Smith.

The Two Mrs. Carrolls
(1947) 99m. **B–**
Bogart is an artist with a habit of growing disenchanted with his wives and doing them in. Stanwyck is his latest unlucky better-half in this solid, if visually uninspired thriller. Bogie really tears things up with his deranged performance and practically goes through the roof in the creepy finale.
D: Peter Godfrey. A: Humphrey Bogart, Barbara Stanwyck, Alexis Smith.

Secret Beyond the Door
(1948) 99m. B&W. **B–**
A young heiress marries a brooding architect whose house and family is suffused with unhealthy secrets. With its soft-focus photography, oppressive characters, and generally morbid atmosphere, this combines gothic romance, marital paranoia, and family haunted all in one.
D: Fritz Lang. A: Joan Bennett, Michael Redgrave, Anne Rivere.

Sorry, Wrong Number
(1948) 89m. **A** 🏛 🔍
A spoiled invalid heiress overhears a phone call between two men plotting a murder, and before the evening is over discovers who the victim is. Like the classic noirs, this story is told in flashback, unfolding with a dreamlike inevitability, with Stanwyck the impatient and unnerved witness.
D: Anatole Litvak. A: Barbara Stanwyck, Burt Lancaster, Ann Richards.

Caught
(1949) 88m. B&W. **B+**
A sweet innocent young woman, with an eye to improving her lot, marries a rich sadistic egomaniac. This gloomy-looking soap opera has an almost suffocating sense of menace and derangement but the actors keep things afloat.
D: Max Ophuls. A: Barbara Bel Geddes, Robert Ryan, James Mason.

In a Lonely Place
(1950) 91m. B&W. **A–**
They're the classic noir romantic couple: He's an alcoholic writer suspected of murdering a hat check girl, and she's his neighbor who's uncertain whether he's guilty but attracted nonetheless. Romance blossoms and he gets more violently jealous. A wonderful twisty noir set in a smoldering sexy Hollywood.
D: Nicholas Ray. A: Humphrey Bogart, Gloria Grahame, Frank Lovejoy.

Crime Dramas

Crime films and noir were in a state of transition by the late 40s, with movies toning down the morbid flamboyance and relenting a bit on the doom and gloom. The resulting tales of losers, psychofiends, and victims caught in fate's web had a lighter flatter look and offered an occasional ray of hope at the end.

Kiss of Death
(1947) 98m. B&W. **B**

A sad sack ex-con gets popped for robbing a store trying to get his kids Christmas presents and is forced to inform on his old cronies. Stylish New York location photography, and Widmark's famous turn as psychosadist Tommy Udo toughens up the sometimes melodramatic story.
D: Henry Hathaway. A: Victor Mature, Brian Donlevy, Richard Widmark.

Railroaded
(1947) 71m. B&W. **B–**

With a police friend in tow, a woman attempts to clear her brother of a frame-up, their main suspect being a twisted gunman with a fondness for perfumed bullets. Sturdy and quick-paced, with much attention given to the crazy killer's fondness for his gun.
D: Anthony Mann. A: Sheila Ryan, John Ireland, Hugh Beaumont.

He Walked by Night
(1948) 78m. B&W. **C**

There's not much plot in this film about cops tracking down a lunatic killer in LA, but the detailed, semidocumentary-style photography is recognizable as the inspiration of the early TV *Dragnet* show.
D: Alfred Werker. A: Richard Basehart, Scott Brady, Whit Bissell.

Street with No Name
(1948) 94m. B&W. **B**

An FBI agent goes undercover to get the goods on an asthmatic fight promoter/mobster. Widmark is slightly toned down but still deranged in this brittle thriller that's aided by a documentary/Expressionist photography and seamy underworld ambiance marred only by dated rah-rah FBI narration.
D: William Keighley. A: Mark Stevens, Richard Widmark, Lloyd Nolan.

T-Men
(1948) 92m. B&W. **C+**

Treasury agents go undercover in pursuit of a mobster in this rather plain film based on real case histories. Enlivened by a dank underworld-feel with evocative photography to match and a nifty steam room rubout scene where the lights stutter with each gunshot.
D: Anthony Mann. A: Dennis O'Keefe, Mary Reade, Alfred Ryder.

Knock on Any Door
(1949) 100m. B&W. **B–**

As attorney Bogart defends a rebellious hood who may have killed a cop, the youth's background—a textbook case history in how to create a juvenile delinquent—is revealed in flashback. A little preachy, but the melodrama is good except for a disastrously callow Derek.
D: Nicholas Ray. A: Humphrey Bogart, John Derek, George Macready.

White Heat
(1949) 114m. B&W. **A**

The short and vivid criminal history of a strangely likable train robber, prison inmate, and killer. There's no need for fancy noir stylistics in this no-nonsense powerhouse, driven by Cagney's astonishing performance and topped off by one of filmdom's most famous self-immolations.
D: Raoul Walsh. A: James Cagney, Virginia Mayo, Edmond O'Brien.

Kiss Tomorrow Goodbye
(1950) 102m. B&W. **B+**

Two escaped cons find refuge and profit in a small town rife with political and mob corruption. Cagney is hard-boiled to the sadistic core in this relentlessly cynical, harshly toned film.
D: Gordon Douglas. A: James Cagney, Barbara Payton, Ward Bond.

The Las Vegas Story
(1952) 88m. B&W. **C**

These two newlyweds have a messy honeymoon in Las Vegas when the sheriff turns out to be her old flame, and the groom starts loosing big time at the gambling tables. The story is pure sludge but watching Russell and Mature mugging it up adds some camp entertainment.
D: Robert Stevenson. A: Jane Russell, Victor Mature, Vincent Price.

Message Films

Social messages play cheek-to-jowl with the hard-boiled goings-on of boxers, prison inmates, and down-on-their-luck losers.

The Set Up
(1949) 72m. B&W. **A**

Aging boxer Ryan (with a wonderful sense of sullied nobility) must decide whether to take the fall in a fixed boxing match. The whole world seems to be a boxing ring in this poignant morality tale filmed in "real" time.
D: Robert Wise. A: Robert Ryan, Audrey Totter, George Tobias.

Riot in Cell Block 11
(1954) 80m. B&W. **B**

The inmates of a solitary confinement prison block demand better prison conditions by staging a riot. As much message picture as prison break film, this still moves at a rapid clip, with modern fluid camera movements and a tense atmosphere.
D: Don Siegel. A: Neville Brand, Leo Gordon, Emile Meyer.

The Harder They Fall
(1956) 108m. B&W. **A**

Bogart is a down-on-his-luck sports writer who agrees to promote a glass-jawed fighter leading to fatal results. With its bluntly stark photography and Bogart's farewell turn as a cynic with a heart, this film takes a good shot at exposing the brutality and corruption of the fight business.
D: Mark Robson. A: Humphrey Bogart, Jan Sterling, Rod Steiger.

I Want to Live!
(1958) 120m. B&W.
A
A gripping crime melodrama with a social conscience based on the real-life woman who tried to go straight after a life of petty thievery, prostitution, and drug addiction, only to wind up in the gas chamber. Hayward seems to be storming hell in her portrayal of the tough dame who endures one horrible event after another.
D: Robert Wise. A: Susan Hayward, Theodore Bikel, Simon Oakland.

Hitchcock

Before bursting out with his sprawling Technicolor productions, Hitchcock honed his distinctive brand of thriller in these concise films that offer an impeccably clean visual style and fascinating imagery. While continuing to turn out his wrongly accused innocent man stories, Hitchcock also made some of the classic "menaced women" films of the period and for good reason; both types of films made best use of his wicked sense of humor and his eye for depicting paranoia and unease between characters.

Foreign Correspondent
(1940) 120m. B&W. A
Days before war breaks out, a reporter is transferred to London where he gets enmeshed with spies, a plot to destroy last minute peace plans, and a little romance. A briskly paced, near-perfect blend of intrigue, action, and romance, with wonderfully tricky set pieces including the eerie windmill sequence.
D: Alfred Hitchcock. A: Joel McCrea, Laraine Day, George Sanders.

Rebecca
(1940) 130m. B&W. A
Olivier is the jaded widower of the beautiful Rebecca and master of a forbidding country estate; Fontaine is his awkward new bride who becomes increasingly haunted by his past. One of the classic gothic romances and marital unease thrillers with a gorgeous misty photography, a richly brooding atmosphere, and superb performances.
D: Alfred Hitchcock. A: Laurence Olivier, Joan Fontaine, Judith Anderson.

Suspicion
(1941) 99m. B&W. B−
More marital unease in prewar English countryside as a mousy young woman begins to wonder about her dashing new husband: Is he being charmingly irresponsible or revealing the signs of a cold-blooded killer? Grant is charming but disconcerting as the rakish husband, adding to the film's slightly confused tone.
D: Alfred Hitchcock. A: Joan Fontaine, Cary Grant, Nigel Bruce.

Saboteur
(1942) 88m. B&W. A
Pursued by the police for sabotage and chasing the spies who really did it, an aircraft worker makes his way cross-country. The dialogue is snappy and Cummings' run-ins with bad guys and helpful citizens—including some circus freaks—are teasingly suspenseful, with a dizzying climax atop the Statue of Liberty.
D: Alfred Hitchcock. A: Robert Cummings, Priscilla Lane, Otto Krugar.

Shadow of a Doubt
(1943) 108m. A
Charming Uncle Charlie comes home for a visit, but his adoring niece gets hints of unsavory doings. Hitchcock's disturbing valentine to what lurks below the placid surface of small towns and loving families is ripe with menacing Freudian flourishes and pre-David Lynch-style disquiet.
D: Alfred Hitchcock. A: Teresa Wright, Joseph Cotten, Macdonald Carey.

Lifeboat
(1944) 88m. B&W. A
The fears and tensions of shipwreck survivors during wartime unfolds as they drift along on the open sea. Shot on a single set, this taut drama builds as each crisis raises the anxiety level, revealing secrets and complicating everyone's relationships.
D: Alfred Hitchcock. A: Tallulah Bankhead, William Bendix, Hume Cronyn.

Spellbound
(1945) 111m. B&W. A
The new director at a posh mental institution isn't who he seems to be, and psychiatrist Bergman has fallen in love with him. This tortured romance thriller, with its quaintly dated psychiatric underpinnings, has some unforgettable imagery, including the famous Salvador Dali-designed dream sequence.
D: Alfred Hitchcock. A: Gregory Peck, Ingrid Bergman, Leo G. Carroll.

Notorious
(1946) 103m. B&W. A
Suspense and passion have never been wedded so wickedly as when G-man Grant convinces ex-lover Bergman to marry a Nazi agent for uranium secrets. This thriller is ripe with distrust and sexual tension between all of the characters—including some priceless scenes between Rains and his mother.
D: Alfred Hitchcock. A: Cary Grant, Ingrid Bergman, Claude Rains.

The Paradine Case
(1948) 112m. B&W. C+
A woman with a dark past is accused of murdering her blind and wealthy husband. Good performances and Hitchcock's camerawork can't enliven this endlessly talky courtroom drama.
D: Alfred Hitchcock. A: Gregory Peck, Ann Todd, Charles Laughton.

Rope
(1948) 80m. B&W. B−
Like Leopold and Loeb, these two young men commit murder for the thrill of it, and even store the body in a table during a cocktail party. Hitchcock filmed this in unedited 10-minute takes, resulting in good performances, but creating a distraction from the tense story.
D: Alfred Hitchcock. A: James Stewart, John Dall, Farley Granger.

Under Capricorn
(1949) 117m. B+
In early nineteenth-century Australia, two men are drawn to a woman falling into alcoholism and melancholia over a dark family secret. A change of pace for Hitchcock, with beautiful ba-

roque settings, a steep sense of repressed guilt, and Bergman who makes suffering look almost intolerably glamorous.
D: Alfred Hitchcock. A: Ingrid Bergman, Michael Wilding, Joseph Cotten.

Stage Fright
(1950) 110m. B&W. **C+**
A murder committed by Dietrich (maybe) is blamed on an innocent man (or is he?) who then tries to clear his name with the help of girlfriend Wyman. The story rolls around like a loose cannon but is enlivened by Dietrich's fevered performance, and the inspired finale at an abandoned old theater.
D: Alfred Hitchcock. A: Jane Wyman, Alastair Sim, Marlene Dietrich.

Strangers on a Train
(1951) 101m. **A**
A tennis pro is approached by a stranger with the proposal that each murder the person the other wants dead. Nobody is really innocent in this thriller that's thick with guiltily twisted relationships and Walker's unnerving charm as the carefree killer. The out-of-control carousel is an electrifying finale.
D: Alfred Hitchcock. A: Farley Granger, Robert Walker, Ruth Roman.

I Confess
(1953) 95m. B&W. **B**
A priest can't divulge a killer's confession because of his vows, and then is accused of the crime himself. With the starkly alienating Quebec location and a remorsefully romantic tone, this one makes up in mood what it lacks in plot.
D: Alfred Hitchcock. A: Montgomery Clift, Anne Baxter, Karl Malden.

The Wrong Man
(1957) 102m. B&W. **B+**
Using a hard-boiled tabloid style, Hitchcock creates one of his most uncompromisingly nightmarish films about an innocent man nabbed for a robbery he didn't commit, and the effects of "due process" on his fragile wife. The gritty cop-procedural look adds to the grim, out-of-control mood: guaranteed to depress.
D: Alfred Hitchcock. A: Henry Fonda, Vera Miles, Anthony Quayle.

Psycho
(1960) 100m. B&W. **A**
After absconding with company funds, Leigh checks into the lonely Bates Motel, setting the stage for a film that is still as shocking as ever. The mercilessly despairing tone, vertiginous photography, and Perkins as the shy, mother-loving proprietor help make this the classic that changed America's attitude toward showers forever.
D: Alfred Hitchcock. A: Anthony Perkins, Janet Leigh, Vera Miles.

1950s
Technicolor Hitchcock

With these colorful, large-scale thrillers, Hitchcock buried his detractors who complained that all he could make were dark and moody films. Even with the glamorous-looking stars and exotic locales, these lavish thrillers still deliver all of the suspense, dark Freudian overtones, and sense of incredible unease that we've come to expect from the master.

Dial M for Murder
(1954) 105m. **A–**
When the plan for his wife's murder goes awry, Milland hatches an even more devious plot to get her out of the picture. The cunning story keeps you spellbound while the masterful camerawork and editing make you forget that most of this sumptuously colored film was shot on one set.
D: Alfred Hitchcock. A: Ray Milland, Grace Kelly, Robert Cummings.

Rear Window
(1954) 112m. **A**
Apartment-bound with a broken leg, a photographer spends his time gazing out the window at the lively goings on of his neighbors, which may include murder. A slyly wicked tone, a colorful mock-up of the back of a Greenwich Village block, and an evanescent Kelly underscore Stewart's voyeuristic activities.
D: Alfred Hitchcock. A: James Stewart, Grace Kelly, Raymond Burr.

To Catch a Thief
(1955) 103m. **A**
When a retired international cat burglar is blamed for a string of jewel thefts, he searches for the real culprit with an American heiress tagging along for fun. The glamorous French Riviera locales, dry wit, and sizzling chemistry between Grant and Kelly make this Hitchcock's most lighthearted film.
D: Alfred Hitchcock. A: Cary Grant, Grace Kelly, John Williams.

The Man Who Knew Too Much
(1955) 120m. **B**
A vacationing couple in Morocco becomes embroiled in an international conspiracy and murder. Politics are thrown aside in this remake to focus on the suspense of their kidnapped child, with a memorable finale in Albert Hall where a musician's cymbal crash will disguise a fatal gunshot.
D: Alfred Hitchcock. A: James Stewart, Doris Day, Carolyn Jones.

The Trouble with Harry
(1955) 140m. **C+**
The trouble with Harry is that he's dead, which proves to be a real pain to a group of eccentric New Englanders who all play pass-the-corpse. The macabre humor comes off as quaint and slightly fey, but the Technicolor New England landscape is an eyeful.
D: Alfred Hitchcock. A: Edmund Gwenn, Shirley MacLaine, John Forsythe.

Vertigo
(1958) 128m. **A**
When Stewart discovers that the married woman he's been asked to trail resembles his own dead lover, he proceeds to add the finishing touches in order to complete the illusion. The lush visuals are all here along with rich San Francisco locales but plotwise, romance doesn't get much darker or more bizarre than this.
D: Alfred Hitchcock. A: James Stewart, Kim Novak, Barbara Bel Geddes.

North by Northwest
(1959) 136m. **A**
A compulsively entertaining film about a suave ad exec who gets entangled in a chase through the Midwest, involving mistaken identity, international politics, and a cool blonde. Scenes of Grant being "attacked" by an airplane in an empty field and crawling across Mount Rushmore have attained an almost mythic quality.
D: Alfred Hitchcock. A: Cary Grant, Eva Marie Saint, James Mason.

Crime Noir

With cut budgets and mobile camera crews, noir crawled out of the studio into the real mean streets of America. Though lacking the overwrought visual style of the earlier noirs, the location shooting added a startling hard-edged look to these trenchant tales of crime, psycho killers, and heists gone bad.

The Asphalt Jungle
(1950) 112m. B&W.
A
Despite the criminal mastermind's finely tuned plans, everything imaginable goes wrong during a heist. With its rapid-fire dialogue and incisive performances, this tense film races to its unexpectedly touching and tragic finish while portraying a grim world where crime and law are not so far apart.
D: John Huston. A: Sterling Hayden, Louis Calhern, Jean Hagen.

Night and the City
(1950) 95m. B&W. **A**
An overly ambitious small-time operator runs afoul of the mob as he tries to elbow his way into the wrestling racket. A briskly paced drama with location photography that makes London a foreboding landscape of derelict buildings, dark alleys, and misty cul-de-sacs.
D: Jules Dassin. A: Richard Widmark, Gene Tierney, Hugh Marlowe.

Panic in the Streets
(1950) 96m. B&W.
A–
Health inspector Widmark battles the clock, trying to prevent an outbreak of the plague in New Orleans while assorted bad guys misunderstand the citywide dragnet. This maintains a jittery sense of urgency, with grimly beautiful Expressionist/tabloid location photography and another evil turn by Palance as a crazed killer.
D: Elia Kazan. A: Richard Widmark, Paul Douglas, Jack Palance.

The Underworld Story
(1950) 90m. B&W. **C+**
Stuck in a small town, an ex-big city reporter tries to get back on top by exposing a blackmailing publisher. An entertaining low-budget melodrama, with Duryea adding some noir grit and Storm some welcome glamour.
D: Cy Endfield. A: Dan Duryea, Gale Storm, Herbert Marshall.

On Dangerous Ground
(1951) 82m. B&W. **A**
Brutalized by his job, a Chicago policeman starts taking it out on his customers and is assigned to a murder case up in the mountains as a working R and R. The film's shocking savagery shifts to a moody lyricism as Ryan becomes involved with a blind woman who teaches him how to be gentle, even as he's hunting her brother.
D: Nicholas Ray. A: Robert Ryan, Ida Lupino, Ward Bond.

The Racket
(1951) 88m. B&W. **B–**
Psychotic hood Ryan locks horns not only with do-good cop Mitchum, but also with a changing, less violent mob. With its lack of musical soundtrack, fairly static direction, and oddly stiff performances, this comes off as a sort of deranged noir educational film; interesting, to say the least.
D: John Cromwell. A: Robert Mitchum, Robert Ryan, Lizabeth Scott.

The Big Heat
(1953) 90m. B&W. **A**
Fritz Lang's savage crime action film pits vengeful honest ex-cop Ford against mad-dog killer Marvin and ever-suffering moll Grahame. This starts out snappily and quickly takes on a brutal, psychologically distressed tone: The scene where Marvin scalds Grahame with hot coffee is a classic bit of noir madness.
D. Fritz Lang. A: Glenn Ford, Gloria Grahame, Lee Marvin.

City That Never Sleeps
(1953) 90m. B&W. **B+**
An embittered Chicago cop falls in with a B-girl, makes an illicit deal with a corrupt lawyer, and then gets to watch his entire life unravel in one night. All the noir goods are here in abundance: expressionistic photography, moral rot, brutal violence, and even a "human robot" who cries.
D: John H. Auer. A: Gig Young, Mala Powers, Edward Arnold.

Pickup on South Street
(1952) 80m. B&W. **A**
Widmark plays a thief with ethics who stumbles onto a top secret microfilm. Cold War politics aside, this is a masterfully concise package of hard-boiled romance, betrayal, and action driven home by muscular camerawork, wise-acre dialogue, and moments of surprising tenderness.
D: Samuel Fuller. A: Richard Widmark, Jean Peters, Thelma Ritter.

The Big Combo
(1955) 89m. **A**
A cop hounds a homicidal mobster while trying to steal his girl. Packed with deranged characters, this makes up for its low budget by using every noir trick—from frenetic camera moves to unnerving bursts of silence—to create a seamy nightmare world of corruption.
D: Joseph Lewis. A: Cornel Wilde, Richard Conte, Brian Donlevy.

Kiss Me Deadly
(1955) 105m. B&W. **A**
Meeker is hard-as-nails P.I. Mike Hammer, whose caseload goes from protecting a strange woman to finding a mysterious glowing suitcase. Mad camerawork, a wild apocalyptic plot, and a tone veering from high melodrama to surreal semicamp make this one of the more deranged noirs.
D: Robert Aldrich. A: Ralph Meeker, Albert Decker, Cloris Leachman.

The Killing
(1956) 83m. B&W. **A**
A ragtag ensemble of shooters, robbers, and general losers execute a daring race-

track robbery. A dazzling film with a tabloid-style photography, its constant flashbacks and flash-forwards hurtle you into the various characters' doomed lives at a relentless pace.
D: Stanley Kubrick. A: Sterling Hayden, Coleen Gray, Elisha Cook, Jr.

Slightly Scarlet
(1956) 99m. **B–**
A violent turn of events makes a petty con into a big-time crime czar. He then finds love with a "good" woman and struggles with both his conscience and the vengeful hood he replaced. Considered to be the only noir filmed in Technicolor, the garish hues lend a bizarre look to all the shadows.
D: Allan Dwan. A: John Payne, Arlene Dahl, Rhonda Fleming.

While the City Sleeps
(1956) 99m. B&W. **B+**
An oddly sympathetic killer terrorizes the city while various newspaper folk use his actions as a way to feather their own nest. A taut and cynical Fritz Lang entry, with a dynamic sequence in which the killer is chased through a dark subway by an opportunistic reporter.
D: Fritz Lang. A: Dana Andrews, Rhonda Fleming, George Sanders.

Touch of Evil
(1958) 108m. B&W. **A**
Welles' baroque noir nightmare set in a border town involves a corrupt cop, assorted sleazoids, and an upright narcotics agent who finally goes berserk with so much vileness. Delirious camerawork (including the famous opening tracking shot), jumpy music, and vivid characters make this the noir to end all noirs.
D: Orson Welles. A: Charlton Heston, Orson Welles, Janet Leigh.

Crime Thrillers

If you ever wanted to know what set the precedent for TV cop shows, check out these Eisenhower era policers. Not big on stylish flourishes (except for the popular you-are-there documentary approach) and with a decidedly television-like lack of visual depth, these films are no-funny-stuff efforts, telegraphing their plots at top speed within a running time that wouldn't tax the shortest attention span.

Call Northside 777
(1948) 111m. B&W.
A– 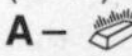
A tale of a journalist's crusade to prove an imprisoned man's innocence despite lack of evidence and the case being 11 years old. One of the best of the you-are-there newspaper investigation tales with crisp Chicago locales and a stripped-down immediacy that's still sharp and engaging.
D: Henry Hathaway. A: James Stewart, Richard Conte, Lee J. Cobb.

Union Station
(1950) 80m. B&W. **C+**
Police detective Holden tracks down the creep who kidnapped a blind girl at Chicago's Union Station. An undistinguished thriller that's low on plot and high on the-clock-is-running-out tension, with a claustrophobic tunnel chase finale.
D: Rudolph Maté. A: William Holden, Nancy Olson, Jan Sterling.

Detective Story
(1951) 114m. B&W. **B+**
New York cop Douglas becomes obsessed with the relentless prosecution of an abortionist. This hard-hitting, virtually one-set "day in the life of a police precinct" tale pulls you up against each of the characters in this gritty, claustrophobic, and always compelling drama.
D: William Wyler. A: Kirk Douglas, William Bendix, Eleanor Parker.

The Enforcer
(1951) 88m. B&W. **A**
A DA has 12 hours left to find the witness to a series of mob-related killings. Told in flashback, this one moves like lightning, with stark, documentary-like photography and a perversely picturesque rogues gallery of noir regulars.
D: Bretaigne Windust. A: Humphrey Bogart, Zero Mostel, Everett Sloane.

Big Jim McLaine
(1952) 90m. B&W. **C**
Working for the Committee for Un-American Activities, Wayne ferrets out a Commie ring in Hawaii. Even with the location photography this is flat-looking, offering the wooden acting, deadpan narrative, and political sophistication of a *Dragnet* episode.
D: Edward Ludwig. A: John Wayne, Nancy Olson, James Arness.

Deadline USA
(1952) 87m. B&W. **B+**
A big city newspaper editor tracks down a story involving a top gangster, woos his ex-wife, and battles the publisher who wants to shut the paper down, all in one night. One of the prime newspaper dramas with a gritty realistic edge and time-is-running-out pacing.
D: Richard Brooks. A: Humphrey Bogart, Kim Hunter, Ethel Barrymore.

Kansas City Confidential
(1952) 98m. B&W. **B+**
A bitter ex-cop blackmails some cons into staging a robbery for him; when the plan inevitably fouls up, an innocent man on the scene gets implicated and hounds the cop all the way to Tijuana to get his name cleared. Gritty, fast-paced tale with a stark semidocumentary look.
D: Phil Karlson. A: John Payne, Coleen Gray, Preston Foster.

The Narrow Margin
(1952) 70m. B&W. **B–**
The detective assigned to escort the gangster's widow traveling by train watches his partner get killed, deals with bribes, hitmen, and the mysterious blonde. Tense and melodramatic, with enough plot twists to keep you wondering who's who.
D: Richard Fleischer. A: Charles McGraw, Marie Windsor, Jacqueline White.

Shack Out on 101
(1955) 80m. B&W. **C+**
At a seashore greasy spoon, a waitress realizes that her scientist boyfriend is a Commie—or is he? A strangely lit movie that looks like a filmed play, with a few giggles coming from the hysterically patriotic dialogue and humorously leering turn by a young Lee Marvin.
D: Edward Dein. A: Terry Moore, Frank Lovejoy, Lee Marvin.

Plunder Road
(1958) 76m. B&W. **B+**
An unusually clever thief

leads a band of cons and losers in a gold robbery, only to be undone by his own smarts. A fast-moving tightly wrought little gem, with a nerve-racking daylight confrontation on the clogged freeways of LA.
D: Hubert Cornfield. A: Gene Raymond, Wayne Morris, Elisha Cook, Jr.

Underworld USA
(1961) 99m. B&W. **A**
The boy who witnessed his father's murder grows up to be fatally obsessed with seeking vengeance. Another gripping, hard-edged Samuel Fuller film, mixing tragedy, brutal violence, and unexpected touching moments.
D: Samuel Fuller. A: Cliff Robertson, Dolores Dorn, Paul Dubov.

Crime in Color

Dragnet
(1954) 71m. **C+**
On the plus side for fans are all the elements of the TV show: the robocop acting, insanely quick editing, and almost fetishistic fascination with police procedure. On the down side is the way everything in this color film looks vaguely brownish and washed out.
D: Jack Webb. A: Jack Webb, Ben Alexander, Ann Robinson.

I Died a Thousand Times
(1955) 109m. **C+**
An ex-convict gets involved with two women, a bungled robbery, and a handful of jewels to fence. This color remake of *High Sierra* can't compare with the original, but still offers hard-boiled performances by Palance and Winters who make some pair.
D: Stuart Heisler. A: Jack Palance, Shelley Winters, Lee Marvin.

Party Girl
(1958) 99m. **A–**
Most of this Technicolor wide-screen film looks like a glossy 50s women's melodrama—right down to Charisse's dance numbers—as it follows the romance between a mobster lawyer and a speakeasy showgirl. Then the last half hour kicks into a solid gangster drama with a glorious Cobb as the deranged mob boss.
D: Nicholas Ray. A: Robert Taylor, Cyd Charisse, Lee J. Cobb.

Menace and Revenge

It was the postwar years and people were cracking up in new and disturbing ways. Though low on graphic violence, these slickly brooding studies in terror really build the tension while zeroing in on the warped psyches of stalkers, assassins, and convicts, showing just how perilous modern life can be.

The Dark Past
(1948) 74m. B&W. **B**
A psychologist's belief in criminal rehabilitation is put to the test when an unhinged con and his pals hold the doctor and his family hostage. An unnerving Holden and suitably confining air make up for some dubious psychology.
D: Rudolph Maté. A: William Holden, Lee J. Cobb, Nina Foch.

The Red House
(1947) 100m. B&W. **C+**
All is not idyllic in Ox Head Woods as a teenage boy falls for a farmer's daughter, and the two investigate her deadly family secrets. This pastoral gothic is marred by murky photography and slow tempo but builds a tensely feverish head by the third reel with the help of a haunted obsessed Robinson.
D: Delmer Daves. A: Edward G. Robinson, Lon McCallister, Julie London.

Beware, My Lovely
(1952) 72m. B&W. **B–**
Following World War I, a lonely widow hires quiet handyman Ryan, who eventually locks up the house for an hour of cat 'n' mouse as he terrorizes her. You've seen it all before, but the quick pace and an amazingly sympathetic Ryan as the gentle maniac who finally can't help killing his employers makes this worth a watch.
D: Harry Horner. A: Ida Lupino, Robert Ryan, Taylor Holmes.

Don't Bother to Knock
(1952) 76m. B&W. **B**
In a Manhattan hotel, lovelorn Widmark falls for the sexy babysitter across the way until he realizes she has more than one screw loose. A slow-moving, gloomy film with an eerie and awkward performance by Monroe as the vulnerable babysitter whose charge is tied up in the next room.
D: Roy Ward Baker. A: Richard Widmark, Marilyn Monroe, Anne Bancroft.

Split Second
(1953) 85m. B&W. **B–**
The clock is running out in a very big way as escaped convicts hold hostages in what turns out to be a nuclear test zone. A tense and compact thriller with terse dialogue and good acting to take it through the slow spots to an explosive finish.
D: Dick Powell. A: Stephen McNally, Alexis Smith, Jan Sterling.

Suddenly
(1954) 77m. B&W. **B+**
A trio of killers hole up and terrorize a local family while waiting to assassinate the President. Fast-paced thriller with a deeply claustrophobic nightmarish air, and Sinatra providing some eerie and terrifying moments as the main assassin.
D: Lewis Allen. A: Frank Sinatra, Sterling Hayden, Nancy Gates.

The Desperate Hours
(1955) 112m. B&W. **A–**
Bogart and two other escaped convicts hole up in March's pleasant suburban home, terrorizing the entire family while waiting for the loot and a means to escape. This film buzzes with Bogart's jittery nerves as he turns the snug all-American home into a demented war zone.
D: William Wyler. A: Humphrey Bogart, Fredric March, Martha Scott.

The Night of the Hunter
(1955) 93m. B&W. **A**
A psycho preacher weds and kills a widow for her money and winds up stalking the kids who actually have it. An audacious, almost unearthly tale of terror, with many scenes composed like darkly Germanic paintings.

Mitchum is terrifying as the charmingly reptilian man of God with "Love" and "Hate" tattooed on either hand, cheerfully singing his Bible tunes.
D: Charles Laughton. A: Robert Mitchum, Shelley Winters, Lillian Gish.

The Bad Seed
(1956) 129m. B&W. **B–**

A woman with homicide in her family background can't help but notice the disquieting events that occur around her sweet little pigtailed daughter. Even the film's staginess can't detract from the overall sense of dread and dawning horror, as we watch an emotionless little killer act like mother's little darling.
D: Mervyn LeRoy. A: Patty McCormack, Nancy Kelly, Henry Jones.

1960s

Hitchcock

Despite changing tastes and trends, Hitchcock continued making his opulently photographed spy thrillers and horror-tinged crime melodramas. The resulting films are a wildly uneven lot, ranging from an eerie horror classic to an extravagant Cold War travelogue.

The Birds
(1963) 120m. **A**

For no explained reason, every bird in a peaceful northern California coastal town goes on a murderous rampage against the human population. Despite the breezy opening, an atmosphere of paranoia and imminence soon dominates the landscape, and a subplot of thwarted mother love gives the film's little bit of romance an eerie tone.
D: Alfred Hitchcock. A: Tippi Hedren, Tod Taylor, Jessica Tandy.

Marnie
(1964) 129m. **A**

Hedren is the alluring compulsive thief with a terror of sex, and Connery the boss who tries to help after blackmailing her into marriage. This strange and darkly romantic story makes the war between the sexes and existential unease vastly entertaining, and contains some amazing attempted seduction scenes.
D: Alfred Hitchcock. A: Tippi Hedren, Sean Connery, Diane Baker.

Torn Curtain
(1966) 125m. **C**

Newman is a nuclear scientist and apparent defector, with Andrews his lover who accidentally gets trapped in his double life. A depressed tone, odd casting, and overall cold look weigh down this uninvolving thriller.
D: Alfred Hitchcock. A: Paul Newman, Julie Andrews, Lila Kedrova.

Topaz
(1969) 126m. **C+**

This rambling tale of Cold War intrigue involving the usual espionage and counterespionage hops all over the globe from Copenhagen to the U.S. to Cuba to France. With the exception of one ravishingly shot death sequence, this bland but colorful misfire bears little of the master's stamp.
D: Alfred Hitchcock. A: John Forsythe, Frederick Stafford, Karin Dor.

Frenzy
(1972) 116m. **B–**

Hitchcock cuts up a little rough in this story about a London serial killer responsible for "The Necktie Murders." Blackly humorous scenes such as the man wrestling with a corpse in the back of a potato truck don't soften the graphic sex-murders in this dark offering.
D: Alfred Hitchcock. A: Jon Finch, Barry Foster, Barbara Leigh-Hunt.

Family Plot
(1976) 120m. **B–**

Two very different couples with larceny in their hearts intersect during the search for a missing heir. Hitchcock's farewell film, highlighted by an exciting out-of-control car sequence, is a frothy, light-spirited, and cleverly constructed tale, with fun performances by all.
D: Alfred Hitchcock. A: Bruce Dern, Karen Black, Barbara Harris.

Detectives

These 60s private eye/police thrillers seemed pretty hip when they were made; now they look like classy prototypes for TV cop shows. But even if these tales of gumshoes on the trail of missing millionaires or serial killers lack the gore, high-speed chases, or the atmospherics of a *Miami Vice* rerun, they still entertain with their cool 60s attitude.

Harper
(1966) 121m. **B**

Private eye Lew Archer may be seedy but he's definitely cool as he crosses paths with LA's fashionable, oversexed, and shady denizens in his search for a missing millionaire. Colorful characters and a smooth Newman breathe some life into this otherwise flat-looking, style-free thriller.
D: Jack Smight. A: Paul Newman, Lauren Bacall, Julie Harris.

In the Heat of the Night
(1967) 109m. **B+**

When a black Philadelphia detective reluctantly helps a Southern sheriff solve a homicide, the investigation turns into a tense game of racial one-upmanship. A solid mystery ripe with Southern small-town flavor as a blustery Steiger swaggers and Poiter quietly navigates around the town's reluctance to help the "colored boy."
D: Norman Jewison. A: Sidney Poiter, Rod Steiger, Warren Oates.

Tony Rome
(1967) 100m. **C**
Swinging Florida P.I. Tony Rome gets entangled in a search for a missing diamond pin. This glitzy, candy-colored film is full of people who say "hey, baby" a lot, as well as bikinied women who can't resist paunchy Sinatra. The blueprint for a thousand bad cop shows.
D: Gordon Douglas. A: Frank Sinatra, Jill St. John, Gena Rowlands.

Lady in Cement
(1968) 93m. **C–**
Suave Tony Rome finds a dead woman while scuba diving and starts an investigation that leaves its own trail of bodies. More 50s-style, martini-drinking, macho thrills dressed up in swinging 60s garb in this even sillier sequel to *Tony Rome.*
D: Gordon Douglas. A: Frank Sinatra, Raquel Welch, Richard Conte.

No Way to Treat a Lady
(1968) 108m. **B+**
Steiger is amazing as the chameleon Oedipal killer who paints red lipstick on his older female victims while Segal is humorous as the Jewish detective with his own set of mother-related problems. A witty, fast-paced cop thriller with classy stars to keep it from veering into camp.
D: Jack Smight. A: George Segal, Rod Steiger, Lee Remick.

The Boston Strangler
(1968) 120m. **A–**
Based on a true story of serial killer Albert DiSalva, this crisp police procedural shows the organization and legwork involved in any major city manhunt. Curtis' riveting, almost sensual performance portrays the strangler as an almost sympathetic victim to his uncontrollable urges as a mad dog killer.
D: Richard Fleischer. A: Tony Curtis, Henry Fonda, George Kennedy.

Marlowe
(1969) 95m. **C**
What starts as a simple search for a missing brother leads detective Marlowe into a complicated plot filled with hippies, plotting sisters, a karate master (Bruce Lee), blackmail, and murder. This would-be noir looks like a wayward episode of *The Rockford Files* with bland color sapping any ambiance.
D: Paul Bogart. A: James Garner, Gayle Hunnicutt, Carroll O'Connor.

Heists and Whodunits

They're slick, they're cool, and they've got lots of undeclared income. These mostly lighthearted capers have all the gloss and brinkmanship of a cop procedural, with characters who are on the wrong side of the law, making them infinitely more glamorous.

Heists

Ocean's Eleven
(1960) 127m. **B–**
The Rat Pack's all too cool caper about a plan to rob five casinos on New Year's Eve is the height of whiskey-and-broads sophistication. The leads walk through this like they were between singing gigs, but too many characters and too much talk of old times keep this from being the breezy glib movie it wants to be.
D: Lewis Milestone. A: Frank Sinatra, Dean Martin, Peter Lawford.

Robin and the Seven Hoods
(1964) 123m. **B+**
The Rat Pack does their *Ocean's Eleven* bit again, this time giving a musical spin to a tale of Damon Runyon-type nice guy gangsters during prohibition. Frothy, colorful, and missing some of the cooler-than-thou attitude of *Ocean's,* you still get to hear some great songs like "Mr. Booze."
D: Gordon Douglas. A: Frank Sinatra, Sammy Davis, Jr., Dean Martin.

Topkapi
(1964) 120m. **B+**
Two lovers assemble an eccentric gang for a precision heist in Istanbul in this colorful lighthearted comedy crime caper. Lingers a bit too long on the extended robbery, but the Greek and Istanbul locales, jolly ethnic music, and Ustinov as the bumbling weak link make it a pleasant diversion.
D: Jules Dassin. A: Melina Mercouri, Maximilian Schell, Peter Ustinov.

Assault on a Queen
(1966) 106m. **B**
A cynical downbeat heist with a wild premise: Salvagers raise a German U-boat off the Florida coast to be used in a scheme to rob the *Queen Mary.* There's plenty of backbiting and tired talk of lost love between the disagreeable thieves, but some high tension action kicks in once they board the liner.
D: Jack Donohue. A: Frank Sinatra, Virna Lisi, Richard Conte.

Gambit
(1966) 108m. **B**
Sly calculating Caine and half-French / half-Chinese MacLaine impersonate British nobility to swindle a wealthy Arab out of a valuable statue. When MacLaine is captured, the plot starts twisting in this light and harmless caper.
D: Ronald Neame. A: Michael Caine, Shirley MacLaine, Herbert Lom.

The Thomas Crown Affair
(1968) 102m. **B**
McQueen is 100 percent cool and so slick he can pull off a bank heist without his confederates knowing who he is and make the female investigator fall in love with him. Some gimmicky camerawork dates this, but the ideas are fun, the stars are in top form, and a flip dialogue is still refreshing.
D: Norman Jewison. A: Steve McQueen, Faye Dunaway, Jack Weston.

Whodunits

Murder She Said
(1961) 87m. B&W. **B**
The definitive Agatha Christie in classic British style finds the long-jawed and ultrasnoopy Miss Marple solving a murder at a standard wealthy English estate reeking with lineage and evil. Character takes precedence over clues with Rutherford a hammy delight as Marple.
D: George Pollock. A: Margaret Rutherford, Arthur Kennedy, James Robertson Justice.

The List of Adrian Messenger
(1963) 98m. B&W. **B**
A stranger's visit to an En-

glish manor is followed by a string of mysterious murders, in this grand-style Hollywood entertainment. The trick ending has suspects peeling off false faces, revealing trick cameos by Kirk Douglas, Robert Mitchum, Tony Curtis, and other stars.
D: John Huston. A: George C. Scott, Dana Wynter, Herbert Marshall.

Who Is Killing the Great Chefs of Europe?

(1978) 112m. **B+**

Cadavers from the culinary world mount up in this comedy-mystery that follows queen of desserts Bisset and her loud American fast-food entrepreneur ex-husband. With beautiful European locales and a steady stream of witty chatter, this frothy romp still isn't above offering an old-fashioned food fight.
D: Ted Kotcheff. A: George Segal, Jacqueline Bisset, Robert Morley.

Spies and Political Thrillers

On the flip side of the breezy James Bond series were these sober, cool-toned meditations of nuclear confrontation and modern espionage. Despite changes in world politics, these still offer exciting, often darkly humorous examinations of Cold War tensions.

The Manchurian Candidate

(1962) 126m. B&W.
A

This postnoir uses all that genre's stylistics to create an almost surreally paranoid tale of a Korean war vet brainwashed into becoming an assassin. Distorted photography, unexpected bits of very black humor, sudden bizarre violence, and Oedipal overtones make this brilliantly deranged and still topical film a must see.
D: John Frankenheimer. A: Frank Sinatra, Laurence Harvey, Angela Lansbury.

Fail Safe

(1964) 111m. B&W. **B+**

Like a deadly earnest *Dr. Strangelove,* an American jet bomber mistakenly gets the word to bomb Moscow and leaders of both nations frantically attempt to make a world-saving compromise. A relentlessly tense film with an awful sense of things out of control, enhanced by harsh lighting and noirish photography.
D: Sidney Lumet. A: Henry Fonda, Fritz Weaver, Walter Matthau.

Seven Days in May

(1964) 120m. B&W.
A–

Director Frankenheimer gives us a nerve-racking, dramatic, and slightly overlong account of a military takeover of America. A handsomely produced, big screen entry keeps the liberal's nightmare believable with all the details of a heist procedural and the unnerving subterfuges of the military brass.
D: John Frankenheimer. A: Burt Lancaster, Frederic March, Kirk Douglas.

The Ipcress File

(1965) 108m. **B+**

Cool cockney, one-time crook Harry Palmer is now a secret agent trying to uncover the mystery of disappeared scientists who reappear brain-drained. Caine brings a heavy-lidded cool to the spy proceedings, and with its smooth jazzy score, high tension, and classy editing, this is a 60s hip thriller to the finish.
D: Sidney Furie. A: Michael Caine, Guy Doleman, Nigel Green.

Mirage

(1965) 109m. B&W. **B**

There's a power blackout at the offices of a nuclear company and a noted peacenik falls to his death. Meanwhile Peck suffers a memory loss and is pursued by killers for reasons he can't recall. Gritty New York locations, good doses of paranoia, and witty by-play flavor this involving, sometimes slow thriller.
D: Edward Dmytryk. A: Gregory Peck, Diane Baker, Walter Matthau.

The Spy Who Came in from the Cold

(1965) 112m. B&W.
A–

A decidedly unglamorous spy tale photographed in a beautifully icy black-and-white shows how ashen, cruel, and bleak is the life of a secret agent. Burton seems to inhabit his character whose faked life is one of furnished rooms, liquor straight from the bottle, and sullen talk in this acid, downbeat tale.
D: Martin Ritt. A: Richard Burton, Oskar Werner, Claire Bloom.

Funeral in Berlin

(1966) 102m. **B–**

The Cold War atmosphere is almost as thick as the overplotted story that finds British agent Harry Palmer arranging a fake funeral to sneak a defecting Russian Colonel out of East Berlin. Real locations give a grim air of authenticity, but slow patches and a few too many camera shots of furtive glances nearly undo it.
D: Guy Hamilton. A: Michael Caine, Paul Hubschmid, Eva Renzi.

Hitchcock-like Thrillers

Following the lead of Hitchcock's glossy, big screen films like *To Catch a Thief*, these thrillers offer low-key suspense involving international intrigue, double crosses, or even a garden variety murder, all gussied up with travelogue photography and a sophisticated romance.

Niagara
(1953) 89m. **B**
Newlyweds at a Niagara Falls motel meet a sexy wife and her neurotic army vet husband for whom she seems to have deadly plans. Unlike the other later films in this group, this has the tone of a tawdry noir filmed in detective magazine colors, with some coolly lush shots of Niagara.
D: Henry Hathaway. A: Joseph Cotten, Jean Peters, Marilyn Monroe.

Midnight Lace
(1960) 108m. **B+**
Wealthy Doris Day is married to a loving but overworked British CEO and suddenly becomes taunted by threatening phone calls. This powder-puff menaced woman thriller is an excuse for Day and Loy's fashion show, colorful shots of the rich and urbane in London, and some uncharacteristic scenes of a terrorized hysterical Doris.
D: David Miller. A: Doris Day, Rex Harrison, Myrna Loy.

Charade
(1963) 113m. **A**
The beautiful young widow's husband died with something valuable on him, and his old army buddies, the CIA, and a debonair Cary Grant are after it. This twisty and stylish, romantic comedy-thriller set in a dreamy Paris offers a hilarious gallery of rogues and sparkling leads.
D: Stanley Donen. A: Cary Grant, Audrey Hepburn, Walter Matthau.

The Prize
(1963) 135m. **C+**
Everyone else in Stockholm for the Nobel Prize awards is old and stodgy except for hard-drinking Newman who suspects the doctor he's just met is an impersonator. Part Cold War suspense/part James Bond thriller with an improbable plot, a low-wattage romance, and a mass of unnecessary characters.
D: Mark Robson. A: Paul Newman, Elke Sommer, Edward G. Robinson.

Arabesque
(1966) 118m. **B**
Peck and Loren hustle their way through this mod, splashy, and breakneck spy thriller as the American pulled into the world of Arab political intrigue and the full-lipped spy he befriends. Near-death escapes in London and the Middle East are all in good fun, but "modern" films like these don't age well.
D: Stanley Donen. A: Gregory Peck, Sophia Loren, Kieron Moore.

Menace and Revenge

Through the mid-60s these studies in terror continued to rely on a tone of anxiety and heightened suspense rather than violence to give them bite. All that changed with the loosening censorship, and Hollywood could now show what the earlier films only hinted at. Starting with *Lady in a Cage*, the results are a spate of bleak-looking character studies, shot in stark locations, containing heavy doses of often sadistic violence.

Cape Fear
(1962) 106m. B&W. **A**
When psychotic Mitchum is released from jail, he promptly engages in a one-man vendetta against the lawyer who sent him behind bars. The startling daylight photography and matter-of-fact tone in this taut shocker make the killer's sexually charged maneuvers against Peck's wife and daughter even more unnerving.
D: J. Lee Thompson. A: Gregory Peck, Robert Mitchum, Polly Bergen.

Experiment in Terror
(1962) 123m. B&W. **A**
A psycho threatens a San Francisco bank teller and, when he finally kidnaps her daughter, the FBI race against the clock to nab him. The vivid locales help create a huge threatening space for the villain to lurk in, climaxing in a nail-biting confrontation in Candlestick Park.
D: Blake Edwards. A: Glenn Ford, Lee Remick, Stefanie Powers.

Lady in a Cage
(1964) 93m. B&W. **B**
This strange mutation of the modern-gothic-horror-with-aging-star shows invalid de Havilland trapped in her private home elevator and terrorized by a group of crazed hoodlums. Slightly arty, luridly suspenseful, and almost as sadistic as a cheap and violent exploitation film.
D: Walter Grauman. A: Olivia de Havilland, Ann Sothern, James Caan.

The Strangler
(1964) 80m. B&W. **C+**
Doll-fetishist, mother-loving Buono is the obese lab technician who takes to killing nurses. Thanks to the low budget, this manages to cook up some sleazy atmosphere while Buono is sweatily convincing.
D: Burt Topper. A: Victor Buono, Ellen Corby, David MacLean.

Repulsion
(1965) 105m. B&W. **A**
The repulsion in question is that of sex, compelling unstable Deneuve to lock herself into her London apartment where she commits murder and slowly goes mad. Roman Polanski's brilliant unsparing character study of insanity also contains one of the all-time terrifying scenes of death by slashing.
D: Roman Polanski. A: Catherine Deneuve, Ian Hendry, Patrick Wymark.

In Cold Blood
(1967) 134m. B&W. **A**
This is the true-life story of two dead-souled losers who execute a Kansas family and then wander the country for a year before being caught. The deadpan docudrama-style presentation, chilling performances, graphic murder, and hanging scenes make this a powerful and haunting experience.
D: Richard Brooks. A: Robert Blake, Scott Wilson, John Forsythe.

The Honeymoon Killers
(1970) 108m. B&W. **B−**
A 200-pound ex-nurse from Alabama and an oily Long Island Don Juan fall in love. Soon they're on a murder spree, killing for fun and profit a string of women who place "lonely heart" ads. An effectively repulsive true story with a low-budget tabloid look and completely believable and graceless leads.
D: Leonard Kastle. A: Tony LoBianco, Shirley Stoler, Mary Jane Higby.

Menace in Color

Technicolor and a bigger budget actually can make a difference in terror as these glossy tales of stalkers show; their brighter look gives a modern, though rarely less menacing, edge to the perverse proceedings.

Peeping Tom
(1960) 109m. **A**

Soft-spoken, home-loving Boehm leads a triple life in London as a semiporn photographer, an amateur filmmaker, and a murderer. This sly, color-drenched study is chillingly prophetic in its view of voyeurism, madness, and just how deeply human impulses have become tied to movies. The scenes illustrating Boehm's morbid urge to gaze are haunting.
D: Michael Powell. A: Carl Boehm, Moira Shearer, Anna Massey.

The Collector
(1965) 117m. **A–**
A disturbed young London bank clerk imprisons the art student who's the object of his desire, giving her four weeks to reciprocate his love. A slow-paced, handsomely produced study of obsession and class struggle with a memorably disturbing Stamp.
D: William Wyler. A: Terence Stamp, Samantha Eggar, Mona Washbourne.

Wait Until Dark
(1967) 108m. **B+**
Hepburn is a blind woman who comes into possession of a dope-filled doll, which lays her open to siege by suavely sinister Arkin and his thugs. Somewhat stagy at first, but don't let that fool you; the last 15 minutes or so are among the most terrifying ever filmed.
D: Terence Young. A: Audrey Hepburn, Alan Arkin, Richard Crenna.

Targets
(1968) 90m. **B**
Horror icon Karloff basically plays himself in this tale of a retiring horror film star who finally gets targeted by the demented highway sniper who's been perpetrating real-life horrors. This gritty, low-budget directorial debut for Bogdanovich is more a mediation on the nature of horror and modern violence than an outright scare-flick.
D: Peter Bogdanovich. A: Boris Karloff, Tim O'Kelly, Peter Bogdanovich.

1970s

Agatha Christie All-Star Whodunits

Take one murder, a gaggle of Hollywood stars in glamorous clothes playing the rich and nasty, an exotic locale, and a colorful sleuth like Hercule Poirot to solve it, and you have the formula for these lightweight comedic whodunits. Even if these aren't exactly the last word in suspense, you can still sit back and enjoy the scenery and the stars hamming it up.

Murder on the Orient Express
(1974) 127m. **A–**
This trainbound tale wheels out its host of stars in stylish period costumes as Belgian detective and gourmet Hercule Poirot investigates the stabbing on the glamorous Orient Express. Slow, but absolutely gorgeous and well-acted from top to bottom.
D: Sidney Lumet. A: Albert Finney, Sean Connery, Vanessa Redgrave.

Death on the Nile
(1978) 140m. **B+**
A wealthy young woman is killed on a deluxe Nile cruise, and beleaguered Poirot does not lack for suspects. The stars dressed up in 30s fashions float by the scenic wonders of Egypt, as Poirot slowly pieces together the events that led to the murder.
D: John Guillermin. A: Peter Ustinov, David Niven, Mia Farrow.

The Mirror Crack'd
(1980) 105m. **B–**
An old English manor is besieged by an American film company as two catty stars make a comeback period picture and Miss Marple is on hand to investigate the murder that interrupts it. Taylor and Kim Novak have fun verbally clawing each other, but this lacks the style and wit of the others.
D: Guy Hamilton. A: Angela Lansbury, Rock Hudson, Elizabeth Taylor.

Evil Under the Sun
(1982) 102m. **B+**
It's the 1930s and a caustic actress is found murdered on an island resort loaded with showfolk who have good reasons to want her dead. Poirot gets to the bottom of things in this relaxed classy whodunit with sunny locales and snappy Cole Porter music.
D: Guy Hamilton. A: Peter Ustinov, Maggie Smith, Diana Rigg.

Appointment with Death
(1988) 103m. **C+**
The archeological digs in prewar Palestine provide the setting, and a nasty widow with remorseless children provide the intrigue as a sweaty Poirot rounds up the suspects. The shine is off this one and the lower budget limits the use of exotic locales and casting of first class stars (David Soul?).
D: Michael Winner. A: Peter Ustinov, Lauren Bacall, John Gielgud.

Sherlock Holmes

In the early 1960s Holmes began to solve cases with sexier and more sordid elements among the lush and richly colored Victorian settings. More action and less deduction also

marked these adventure-whodunits, with Holmes having to deal with dangerous situations where his wiles were not always enough. By the 1970s and 1980s filmmakers could still indulge the fetish for Victoriana, but the adventures were now also part character study. Holmes, traditionally as remote and logical as *Star Trek*'s Mr. Spock, was now becoming emotionally involved.

The Hound of the Baskervilles
(1959) 86m. **B**
This version shows the origins of the brutal seventeenth-century legend of the hound, before settling into Victorian England, when the hellish creature has claimed its latest victim. Holmes protects the Baskerville heir and probes the moors in this garishly colored, more violent telling of the classic tale.
D: Terence Fisher. A: Peter Cushing, Andre Morell, Christopher Lee.

Sherlock Holmes and the Deadly Necklace
(1962) 84m. **C**
This German/English production pits Holmes against his arch rival Moriarty for possession of a necklace belonging to Cleopatra. Mixed bag of good scenes, clumsy plot twist, and bad dubbing, even for the English actors.
D: Terence Fisher. A: Christopher Lee, Senta Berger, Hans Nielson.

A Study in Terror
(1965) 94m. **B**
Jack the Ripper is carving up London's prostitutes and Holmes suspects the fiend may be of a noble family. A bloody, more sexually frank tale with a dashing athletic Holmes who's as quick with his fist as he is with his mind. Elements of madness and political intrigue make this a satisfying entry.
D: James Hill. A: John Neville, Donald Houston, John Fraser.

The Private Life of Sherlock Holmes
(1970) 125m. **B+**
Just what was Holmes' attitude toward women? This light and entertaining exploration of his sexuality switches to a complex investigation involving a German spy, the Loch Ness monster, and an entanglement that touches Holmes' soul. It's a bit long but stay put for the ending.
D: Billy Wilder. A: Robert Stephens, Colin Blakely, Genevieve Page.

The Seven-Per-Cent Solution
(1976) 113m. **B+**
Watson lures cocaine-addicted Holmes to Vienna for treatment by Sigmund Freud. This big budget, richly textured tale puts an interesting and vulnerable spin on Holmes, but the forgettable kidnapping plot tacked on at the end makes it too long.
D: Herbert Ross. A: Nicol Williamson, Robert Duvall, Alan Arkin.

Murder by Decree
(1979) 120m. **B**
A handsome Holmes takes on the Jack the Ripper case (again) and is surprised by government resistance that hints at a possible royal coverup. The sleuth uncovers all and rails with uncharacteristic passion against Victorian hypocrisy in a conclusion that recalls elements of Watergate.
D: Bob Clark. A: Christopher Plummer, James Mason, David Hemmings.

Young Sherlock Holmes
(1985) 109m. **C+**
What if Holmes and Watson met as lads in a boarding school? Charming premise of their first adventure is glitzed up by an *Indiana Jones* plot with occult overtones and lots of special effects that have nothing to do with Holmes. Bittersweet ending makes up for some of it.
D: Barry Levinson. A: Nicholas Rowe, Alan Cox, Anthony Higgins.

Heists

Like the comedy buddy capers from the 70s, these heist films bring a playful touch to crime as a couple of likable, larceny-minded little guys elaborately scheme to get away with the goods.

$ (Dollars)
(1972) 119m. **B+**
An American security expert links up with a game prostitute in an elaborate scheme to get some gangster money from a Hamburg safety deposit box. The young attractive stars, tension from their split-second heist, and an inventive escape from the gangsters make for a lively caper.
D: Richard Brooks. A: Warren Beatty, Goldie Hawn, Gerte Frobe.

The Hot Rock
(1972) 105m. **B**
A motley and not altogether trustworthy crew is assembled to grab a diamond from a New York museum that an African prince claims belongs to his country. Despite good character bits, a disjointed effort and not as cheerfully frothy as it wants to be.
D: Peter Yates. A: Robert Redford, George Segal, Paul Sand.

The Sting
(1973) 129m. **A–**
Two grifters in 1930s Chicago orchestrate a wildly elaborate plan to steal a bundle from a big-time crook. Deception overlays deception with every con man in town involved, and you won't really know who is who until the end. A bright jaunty caper scored with Scott Joplin's sweet ragtime music.
D: George Roy Hill. A: Paul Newman, Robert Redford, Robert Shaw.

11 Harrowhouse
(1974) 95m. **B–**
An unlikely American couple aims to steal the diamonds from a posh London clearinghouse with the help of an aging British pensioner. The main interest is watching three great British character actors play with small but juicy roles. A wild and silly car and horse chase is the action highlight.
D: Aram Avakian. A: Charles Grodin, Candice Bergen, John Gielgud.

(See also 1970s Comedy Buddy Capers, page 96.)

New Gumshoes

In the 1970s, directors like Penn, Polanski, and Altman didn't just revive the detective and noir genres, they breathed new life into them. Some of these films are homages to noir, rich with Art Deco decor and women with padded shoulders and peek-a-boo eyes; others have updated the conventions with humor and a hip sensibility. With few exceptions, these tales of corruption, dirty secrets, and the seamy side of life show an artistry and freshness that has not been dulled by 20 years.

Klute
(1971) 114m. **A**

A small-town detective follows the trail of a missing friend, which intersects with a high-priced call girl in New York City. A masterful mix of character study and thriller with a powerhouse performance from Fonda and a dark feel for the uncertainties and menace of modern urban life.
D: Alan J. Pakula. A: Jane Fonda, Donald Sutherland, Roy Scheider.

They Might Be Giants
(1971) 88m. **B–**

Former New York City judge believes he's Sherlock Holmes, and Dr. Mildred Watson, the psychiatrist who takes up his case, becomes involved in his all-consuming investigations. Witty performances and a collection of New York oddballs make up for the lame "are they saner than we" message.
D: Anthony Harvey. A: George C. Scott, Joanne Woodward, Jack Gilford.

The Long Goodbye
(1973) 113m. **B+**

This updated shambling private eye Marlowe seems to bumble through, rather than investigate, the puzzling chain of events in a sunbaked and sleazily affluent LA. The updated noir malaise and parade of oddball characters more than make up for a slightly muddled plot.
D: Robert Altman. A: Elliot Gould, Nina van Pallandt, Sterling Hayden.

Chinatown
(1974) 131m. **A**

It's Los Angeles in the 1930s and a hard-bitten private eye finds himself on a trail that leads to land grabbing schemes, water rights, and the mysteries of a ruthless businessman's beautiful and neurotic daughter. A visual masterpiece, an acting tour de force, and a classic detective story that weaves its intricate story through a brooding LA landmined with corruption and nasty little secrets.
D: Roman Polanski. A: Jack Nicholson, Faye Dunaway, John Huston.

The Drowning Pool
(1975) 108m. **B–**

Laid back P.I. Harper investigates a blackmail scheme in Louisiana that brings him together with a corrupt police chief, a sex-crazed client's daughter, big oil money, and a watery menace in an eerie deserted insane asylum. A muted cast runs through a cliché-heavy story that lacks any enthusiasm.
D: Stuart Rosenberg. A: Paul Newman, Joanne Woodward, Tony Franciosa.

Farewell My Lovely
(1975) 97m. **A–**

Mitchum is the classic gumshoe Marlowe, mixing cynicism, wit, and a romantic spirit in this workmanlike noir homage. The vivid 1940s details have a seedy smoky charm, and the complex plot crackles with snappy one-liners as a rumpled Mitchum outmaneuvers a parade of the usual suspects.
D: Dick Richards. A: Robert Mitchum, Charlotte Rampling, Sylvia Miles.

Night Moves
(1975) 99m. **A**

While trying to deal with his own sour private life, investigator Harry is hired by a fading Hollywood star to track down her reckless daughter, involving him in art smuggling, murder, and sex on Florida's Gulf Coast. This intricate detective story and incisive psychological drama manages to be both intelligent and entertaining.
D: Arthur Penn. A: Gene Hackman, Jennifer Warren, Susan Clark.

The Late Show
(1977) 93m. **B+**

A wheezing old private detective and a cat-loving new-age oddball make an unlikely team as they scour the seamy corners of LA, bickering all the way. The winning characters and messy mystery provide all the fun, marred only by the washed-out cinematography that makes for a bleak LA.
D: Robert Benton. A: Art Carney, Lily Tomlin, Ruth Nelson.

The Big Fix
(1978) 108m. **B–**

A former 60s radical cum private investigator is hired by an old leftist buddy cum politician to find out who's trying to link him with crazed hippies from the old days. A solid detective thriller with the wisecracks, intrigue, and murder all served up with a dollop of 60s nostalgia.
D: Jeremy Paul Kagan. A: Richard Dreyfuss, Bonnie Bedelia, Susan Anspach.

The Big Sleep
(1978) 100m. **B–**

Marlowe is in present-day London to find out who's blackmailing two rich sisters, one who's had naughty pictures taken of her. The plot is cloudy, and though Mitchum is still his world-weary best, removing him from the 1940s and putting him in England takes away some of the charm.
D: Michael Winner. A: Robert Mitchum, Sarah Miles, Richard Boone.

***(See also True Confessions,* page 489.)**

Spies and Assassins

Films about espionage have traveled a long way from the suave villains and romantic war-weary atmosphere of *The Third Man*. Here is the modern world of electronic surveillance, computers, and a growing confusion about who to trust—or if you can trust—in government

agencies. While the plots sometimes dangle on the edge of credulity, the vigorous pace, hip attitude, fine performances, and endless supply of twists and thrills keep you from minding.

The Anderson Tapes
(1972) 98m. **B+**
An ex-con and his gang target a posh New York City apartment building for theft, but everyone involved is under electronic surveillance by agencies ranging from the FBI to house security. Private foibles are exposed and so are elements of the heist in this complex caper and semisatire on our loss of privacy.
D: Sidney Lumet. A: Sean Connery, Martin Balsam, Dyan Cannon.

The Day of the Jackal
(1973) 141m. **A−**
A professional assassin, hired to kill DeGaulle in 1963, makes his way to Paris, changing his identity and casually killing people along the route. Although the police desperately try to track him, this meticulously detailed thriller has less suspense and more voyeuristic thrills as we watch an emotionless killer go through his paces.
D: Fred Zinnemann. A: Edward Fox, Tony Britton, Michel Lonsdale.

The Mackintosh Man
(1973) 105m. **C+**
There's a top-level mole in the British government and Intelligence hires an American to rout him out. Mason as the rich and witty turncoat and the maze of double dealings are almost enough to cover up a tired rehash of spy thriller clichés.
D: John Huston. A: Paul Newman, James Mason, Dominique Sanda.

The Odessa File
(1974) 128m. **C+**
A group of unreformed Nazis plan to launch rockets at Israel, and a young German journalist joins their ranks to ferret out the leaders. Occasionally stirring chase scenes and the pervasive tension of discovery breathes some life into this eventless thriller.
D: Ronald Neame. A: Jon Voight, Maximilian Schell, Maria Schell.

The Eiger Sanction
(1975) 125m. **C+**
Clint and the great B-movie supporting cast help give weight to this far-fetched tale of a professor moonlighting as a bad-dude secret agent. Despite glamorous European locales, well-choreographed stunts and action sequences, mainly for Clint and mountain-climbing enthusiasts.
D: Clint Eastwood. A: Clint Eastwood, George Kennedy, Jack Cassidy.

Three Days of the Condor
(1975) 117m. **B+**
Everyone at a small Manhattan-based CIA research outpost is blown away except for Redford, who no longer knows who he can and can't trust. The well-crafted paranoid twists and turns, sleek New York City locations, and the two handsome leads fuel this compact, well-paced suspenser.
D: Sydney Pollack. A: Robert Redford, Faye Dunaway, Cliff Robertson.

Marathon Man
(1976) 126m. **A−**
A New York grad student is bewildered when he falls into an international deal involving his own murdered brother, an old Nazi tracking a stash of diamonds, and secret U.S. agency intrigues. This buzzes with suspense and paranoia, offers great acting, and the dental torture scene will make you cancel that next appointment.
D: John Schlesinger. A: Dustin Hoffman, Laurence Olivier, William Devane.

Black Sunday
(1977) 143m. **B**
Arab terrorists plot to blow up the Super Bowl and they get a psycho Vietnam vet who pilots the Goodyear Blimp to help them. Action-packed with passionate performances by all, but the suspenseless finale with the blimp just drifts along too long.
D: John Frankenheimer. A: Robert Shaw, Marthe Keller, Bruce Dern.

Telefon
(1977) 102m. **B**
Pillars of society suddenly become gate-crashing, army base-blasting robots, and the KGB and CIA agents form an uneasy alliance to solve the problem. Neat premise dries up as incident piles up on incident, and suit-and-tie Bronson is not up to his usual trigger-happy quotient.
D: Don Siegel. A: Charles Bronson, Lee Remick, Donald Pleasence.

The Boys from Brazil
(1978) 123m. **B+**
A Nazi hunter tries to get to the bottom of the international adoption scheme set up by the fugitive Nazi doctor who specialized in genetic engineering. There's not much substance to this goofy story but the big screen production gives you lots of exotic location shots, and the all-star cast seems to be having a good time.
D: Franklin Schaffner. A: Gregory Peck, Laurence Olivier, James Mason.

Post-Watergate Political Thrillers

Sit back and prepare to believe everything you've ever felt about politicians was true . . . and more! These post-Vietnam/Watergate and pre-*JFK* paranoia thrillers begin with the basic assumption that everyone in power is corrupt, and then proceed to scare you with just how treacherous and underhanded they can really get.

Executive Action
(1973) 91m. **B**
This pre-*JFK* tale about the Kennedy assassination shows a group of rich right-wingers who hire and train gunmen while cooking up a stew of red herrings to mislead the investigations. A good chew for conspiracy fans but lacking in true drama and tension.
D: David Miller. A: Burt Lancaster, Will Geer, Robert Ryan.

The Parallax View
(1974) 102m. **A−**
When all the witnesses to a political assassination get bumped off, a reporter follows the trail of a corporation that trains assassins. Riveting chase scenes worthy of Hitchcock and a chilling brainwashing sequence make this an overlooked gem.
D: Alan J. Pakula. A: Warren Beatty, William Daniels, Hume Cronyn.

All the President's Men

(1976) 138m. **A**

True story of the two Washington Post reporters who learned that a burglary at the Watergate was instigated by the highest levels of the Nixon White House. This newspaper procedural has a beat-the-clock pacing, and you'll share their amazement as they slowly pick apart the cover-up and learn that a small story may topple a government.
D: Alan J. Pakula. A: Robert Redford, Dustin Hoffman, Jason Robards, Jr.

Winter Kills

(1979) 97m. **B+**

The younger brother of an assassinated president finds new evidence of an additional gunman and unwittingly enters the shadow world of cover-ups. Uneven story that's part murder investigation, part black-comedy of our paranoid age. Leaves you feeling like it could have been really good.
D: William Richert. A: Jeff Bridges, John Huston, Anthony Perkins.

Other Post-Watergate Paranoia

Post-Watergate thrillers had a darker view of what the powers-to-be were up to. Chances were oil companies, nuclear plants, NASA, even hospitals were involved in a conspiracy. Like other well-crafted political-oriented thrillers of this era, these stories will keep you on the edge of your seat and confirm your worst fears of what sneaky things other people are doing.

The Day of the Dolphin

(1973) 104m. **C–**

A craggy marine biologist learns to speak with dolphins only to discover they are unwitting pawns in an assassination plot. The sunny Florida coastline doesn't dry up this soggy thriller that shows Scott speaking in clipped baby lingo to a couple of dolphins.
D: Mike Nichols. A: George C. Scott, Trish Van Devere, Fritz Weaver.

The Conversation

(1974) 113m. **A**

An exquisitely constructed thriller/study of a surveillance master whose acute unease with people clashes with his dawning horror of the consequences of his trade. This harrowing story is peeled open like a wiretapper's *Blow Up;* the masterful use of sound and visuals, the sustained tension, and Hackman's quiet tour de force performance make this haunting.
D: Francis Ford Coppola. A: Gene Hackman, John Cazale, Allen Garfield.

Capricorn One

(1978) 128m. **B**

Three astronauts go along with NASA's request to fake a Mars landing and then discover that the cover-up involves their deaths. This neat thriller captures the scientific lingo and high-tech world of NASA, turning into a more routine chase story with the astros on the run.
D: Peter Hyams. A: Elliot Gould, James Brolin, Brenda Vaccaro.

Coma

(1978) 113m. **B+**

A young doctor investigates why so many patients go into comas at her hospital, and discovers the evils of a secret medical organization. Paranoia thick as ether lays over this thriller as Bujold uncovers the full horror while not being able to convince or trust her boyfriend, boss, or colleagues.
D: Michael Crichton. A: Genevieve Bujold, Michael Douglas, Richard Widmark.

The China Syndrome

(1979) 122m. **A**

Management tries to cover up a minor mishap at their nuclear plant even though a TV crew recorded the entire thing, and one of the technicians is warning of a possible meltdown. The pressure cooker atmosphere when the plant goes haywire and the multileveled performances make this gripping.
D: James Bridges. A: Jane Fonda, Jack Lemmon, Michael Douglas.

The Formula

(1980) 118m. **C**

A cop follows the muddled trail of murder to uncover an oil cartel secret—the formula to make synthetic fuel. This offers up not only vile, money-sucking oil companies, but those old standby Nazis as the villains. The dramatic confrontation between cop Scott and oil magnate Brando leads to some amusing and flip philosophizing.
D: John Avildsen. A: George C. Scott, Marlon Brando, John Gielgud.

The Star Chamber

(1983) 109m. **B+**

A young idealistic judge becomes part of a secret group of peers who, carefully and with due consideration, act on their frustration with a legal system whose loopholes allow killers and rapists to go free. A slick and tense tale that portrays political paranoia, vigilante justice, and righteous-man-caught-in-a-web.
D: Peter Hyams. A: Michael Douglas, Hal Holbrook, Yaphet Kotto.

Atmospheric Thrillers

Except for *The Beguiled*, these are suspense films made by foreign directors, so you can expect psychologically dense, enigmatic affairs, filled with art-film technique, and a sense of menace taking the form of everything from a red-jacketed child to a photograph of two lovers.

Blowup
(1966) 108m. **A–**
An ultrahip London fashion photographer takes some pictures in the park, and tries to figure out if his camera "witnessed" a murder. A stylish, exquisitely composed, and very cool thriller for the eye, with a swinging 60s Carnaby Street flavor and a cerebral and arty sensibility.
D: Michelangelo Antonioni. A: David Hemmings, Vanessa Redgrave, Sarah Miles.

Performance
(1970) 105m. **C+**
A psychedelic, deliriously avant-garde film about a British con who falls in with a bored rock star. This isn't big on plot or sense, but it does have an appropriately debauched atmosphere and one good musical moment; otherwise it's an odd hippie artifact that's more silly than anything else.
D: Nicolas Roeg, Donald Cammell. A: Mick Jagger, James Fox, Anita Pallenberg.

The Beguiled
(1971) 109m. **B**
A wounded Union soldier during the Civil War finds himself at the quietly bizarre mercies of the repressed inmates of an isolated girls' academy. Clint goes from grateful to bemused to trapped in this unique, richly filmed Western gothic that builds up subtle tension to its unexpected climax.
D: Don Siegel. A: Clint Eastwood, Geraldine Page, Elizabeth Hartman.

The Nightcomers
(1971) 96m. **C–**
In a remote British country estate two children fall under the spell of the gardener who's also having S&M sex with the nanny. This strange *The Turn of the Screw*-inspired tale tries to look under all that dark Victorian repression but comes up with a slow and strangely lifeless result.
D: Michael Winner. A: Marlon Brandon, Stephanie Beacham, Harry Andrews.

Don't Look Now
(1973) 110m. **B+**
An enigmatic tale of a grieving couple's visit to Venice after the drowning death of their daughter. Director Nicholas Roeg turns the city of canals into a place quietly seething with supernatural menace, with the lulling rhythm suddenly exploding into intense eroticism and violence.
D: Nicolas Roeg. A: Donald Sutherland, Julie Christie, Hilary Mason.

Picnic at Hanging Rock
(1975) 110m. **B**
At the ominous title location, four girls disappear, with one returning battered and dazed. Few definite answers are on hand in this slowly paced, gorgeously lensed, rather arty film: Still, it's intriguing for those with an open mind and some patience.
D: Peter Weir. A: Dominic Guard, Helen Morse, Anne Lambert.

The Passenger
(1975) 119m. **C**
A burned-out journalist on assignment in Africa jumps at the chance to switch identities with a corpse whom he resembles. This has all the existential malaise, carefully crafted scenes, and visual ease of Antonioni's earlier works; it just all seems to add up to an extended train trip to nowhere.
D: Michelangelo Antonioni. A: Jack Nicholson, Maria Schneider, Ian Hendry.

The Tenant
(1976) 124m. **A**
When a shy Polish immigrant moves into a Paris apartment last occupied by a suicidal woman, his personality undergoes a transformation. This suffocatingly atmospheric study of madness draws you into the tenant's increasingly dark, surreal, and dangerous world, with paranoid visions that will last long after viewing.
D: Roman Polanski. A: Roman Polanski, Isabelle Adjani, Shelley Winters.

The Last Wave
(1977) 104m. **B+**
An Australian lawyer finds himself caught up in an apocalyptic Aborigine prophecy. Rain bursts from cloudless skies, swarms of frogs surround his house, and downpours of mud cover the city in this eerie allegory of man, nature, and magic.
D: Peter Weir. A: Richard Chamberlain, Olivia Hamnett, David Gulpilil.

Menace and Revenge

These stalked victim and revenge thrillers updated the noirish, slightly sleazy haze of their 60s predecessors, going for the modern and stylish look instead. They're still unnerving studies of people who are mean and crazy, but for the first time, the tables get turned and thanks to Eastwood, the woman even gets to stalk the man. And *Fatal Attraction* was 17 years away.

Play Misty for Me
(1971) 102m. **A**
A hip disc jockey learns the dangers of one-night stands when a crazed fan comes back for more—or else. Clint's directorial debut impresses with the gorgeous Big Sur-Carmel locales, the cool jazzy characters, beautifully developed suspense, and some well-earned shocks.
D: Clint Eastwood. A: Clint Eastwood, Jessica Walter, Donna Mills.

Straw Dogs
(1971) 113m. **B**
The couple who move to a small English village are subject to such ugly pack-mentality violence that the wimpy husband is forced to take a stand à la *Death Wish.* Peckinpah's once controversial study of violence and human nature is still shocking in how relentlessly unlikeable everyone is and its portrayal of what it takes to turn a pacifist into a raging beast.
D: Sam Peckinpah. A: Dustin Hoffman, Susan George, David Warner.

Looking for Mr. Goodbar
(1977) 135m. **B–**
A schoolteacher looks for love in all the wrong places when she starts haunting Manhattan singles bars. The neon-lit, slightly soiled atmosphere, a sleazy Gere, and a fine Keaton make this tense character study work. But be prepared for simple psychology and a very down ending.
D: Richard Brooks. A: Diane

Keaton, Tuesday Weld, Richard Gere.

The Eyes of Laura Mars
(1978) **A–**

A killer stalks a high-fashion photographer with psychic skills, whose work obsessively links sex and violence. The Helmut Newton photographs, disco-scored 70s fashion-shoots, a very sexy romance, and a stylish tone of perversity and menace help make this an underrated thriller.
D: Irvin Kershner. A: Faye Dunaway, Tommy Lee Jones, Brad Dourif.

Magic
(1978) 106m. **B–**

An unhinged ventriloquist's relationship with his dummy starts to go sour, and he decides to visit his high school sweetheart and her husband at their isolated upstate house. The slow pacing is balanced by a terrifying-looking dummy and a wonderfully, quietly spooky Hopkins.
D: Richard Attenborough. A: Anthony Hopkins, Ann-Margret, Burgess Meredith.

Hardcore
(1979) 108m. **B+**

A Midwestern Calvinist father relentlessly plows through the world of strip joints, porn meisters, and exploited runaways searching for his missing daughter. A well-directed, luridly colorful, and strangely obsessive film. Trouble is, this guided tour of sleaze and sin starts to feel as exploitative as the world it portrays.
D: Paul Schrader. A: George C. Scott, Season Hubley, Peter Boyle.

1980s–1990s

British Spies

These political thrillers taken from the headline news of counterespionage in Thatcher's England are short on action and long on intrigue, with complex characters and stories that expose the decadence of intelligence agencies fallen prey to infiltration and corruption.

The Jigsaw Man
(1984) 90m. **C–**

An agent directed by his superiors to defect to Russia returns to England 40 years later to retrieve a list of double agents while being pursued by everyone. Convoluted plot unwinds haphazardly through a conveyor belt of postcard settings. A lively acting fest of spy vs. spy.
D: Freddie Francis. A: Michael Caine, Laurence Olivier, Susan George.

Defense of the Realm
(1986) 96m. **A–**

A hack journalist looking for scandal discovers a political intrigue involving placement of U.S. nuclear arms in England. Opens with lively scenes in newsrooms, pubs, and government backrooms before shifting to a dark and threatening mood as the grim conspiracy is revealed.
D: David Drury. A: Gabriel Byrne, Greta Scacchi, Denholm Elliott.

The Fourth Protocol
(1987) 119m. **B+**

A retired agent discovers that the death of his son was approved by an intelligence cabal trying to hide its own dirty secrets. Like a classic murder mystery, the dialogue dominates, the pace is leisurely, and circumspect characters finally reveal the sordid truth.
D: John Mackenzie. A: Michael Caine, Pierce Brosnan, Joanna Cassidy.

A Prayer for the Dying
(1987) 104m. **B–**

An IRA assassin, shocked that he inadvertently killed some children, flees to London to escape the Government and Irish rebels. A plodding and convoluted plot doesn't keep you distracted enough to look for all the cracks in Rourke's man-with-a-conscience performance.
D: Mike Hodges. A: Mickey Rourke, Bob Hoskins, Alan Bates.

International Espionage

These thrillers, usually taken from the pages of successful spy novels, have fanciful plots, fatal romantic pairings, and a wealth of exotic locales. Sometimes the sense of geography is so vivid that even with the complicated strategies, these films often resemble travelogues with some Cold War drama thrown in.

Eye of the Needle
(1981) 112m. **B–**

A German spy planted in England prior to World War II discovers plans involving the European invasion and tries to relay the news to Hitler. The beautiful coastal landscape is not enough to hold your attention through the ponderous maneuvers and psychological manipulations.
D: Richard Marquand. A: Donald Sutherland, Ian Bannen, Kate Nelligan.

Enigma
(1982) 101m. **C–**

A CIA agent in Paris is assigned to stop KGB assassins hunting down dissidents in the USSR, including his old girlfriend. The plot seems unbelievable but the scenery and characters provide enough interest.
D: Jeannot Szwarc. A: Martin Sheen, Brigitte Fossey, Sam Neill.

The Holcroft Covenant
(1985) 112m. **C+**

In the waning days of the war, three Nazi bigwigs deposit vast sums of money in Switzerland earmarked for their children, and years later the heirs are out to get each other. Stunning European locales, but a conspiracy thriller with little oomph.
D: John Frankenheimer. A: Michael Caine, Anthony Andrews, Victoria Tennant.

Gorky Park
(1983) 127m. **B+**

A Russian detective investigates some mutilated bodies and uncovers a conspiracy to illegally export Russian sable. A brisk police procedural that adds a wonderful array of Russian characters and chilly locations to a story of greed and paranoia.
D: Michael Apted. A: William Hurt, Lee Marvin, Brian Dennehy.

The Little Drummer Girl
(1984) 130m. **B**

This LeCarré thriller about an actress who is recruited by the Israeli secret service moves deftly from England to Europe to Palestinian terror camps. Some finely wrought characters, but the drama is finally stalled because Keaton seems to stand out when she should be fitting in.
D: George Roy Hill. A: Diane Deaton, Klaus Kinski, Sami Frey.

Hopscotch
(1980) 107m. **B+**

A spy comedy and adult romance involving a demoted CIA agent who decides to write his memoirs exposing the world of espionage while gallivanting all over Europe. Plenty of sharp and brittle dialogue and a smattering of satire aimed at the pompous and duplicitous world of spying.
D: Ronald Neame. A: Walter Matthau, Glenda Jackson, Ned Beatty.

Brian DePalma

Before he graduated to gangster blockbusters like *Scarface* and *The Untouchables*, Brian DePalma was head homage-payer to Hitchcock and premier stylist of horror thrillers. His twisty tales of murder and paranoia are feasts of visual storytelling that make you jump and sweat, although sometimes the style threatens to replace the plot and characters. The best of these offer DePalma's own wild pop-culture mix of ironic humor, warped eroticism, and almost operatic sequences of tension and Grand Guignol carnage.

Sisters
(1973) 92m. **B**

A reporter witnesses a murder from her apartment window, but when no body can be found, she's on the trail of a separated Siamese twin. DePalma's first horror thriller is only slightly more primitive than the later ones, with all his visual puns, dark irony, and twisted characters with their pathological "doubles."
D: Brian DePalma. A: Margot Kidder, Jennifer Salt, Charles Durning.

Carrie
(1976) 98m. **A**

An awkward teen is plagued by sadistic classmates, a wacky holy-roller mom, and telekinetic powers as unmanageable as a case of acne. DePalma gives his own horrific spin to the high school archetypes as well as a bloody climax at the prom which made this the classic nerd revenge horror film.
D: Brian DePalma. A: Sissy Spacek, Piper Laurie, Amy Irving.

Obsession
(1976) 93m. **B**

A man is haunted by his wife's death, even after 15 years, and then encounters the beloved's dead ringer in Florence. This homage to *Vertigo,* gauzily filmed on location in Italy and New Orleans, is a melancholic, slow-paced study of passion with one of the wilder plots you'll encounter.
D: Brian DePalma. A: Cliff Robertson, Genevieve Bujold, John Lithgow.

The Fury
(1978) 118m. **B**

A G-man's telekinetic son is kidnapped by the government and dad's out to find him with the help of a young psychic. A mixture of government conspiracy thriller and psychic horror with a slam-bang finale of exploding body parts and gore.
D: Brian DePalma. A: Kirk Douglas, John Cassavetes, Amy Irving.

Dressed to Kill
(1980) 105m. **B–**

A pretty young prostitute helps a young man find his mother's killer while a shrink is doing his best to cope with a homicidal patient. This is little more than style and homage paid to Hitchcock and Argento, unless you count the sex, violence, and a few nifty chase scenes.
D: Brian DePalma. A: Michael Caine, Nancy Allen, Angie Dickinson.

Blow Out
(1981) 108m. **C+**

A slasher-movie soundman accidentally records a real murder and becomes entangled in a conspiracy to cover up the crime. A frustrating film with clunky plot mechanics and a few moments of real brilliance, like the nerve-racking chase through Bicentennial Philadelphia complete with fireworks.
D: Brian DePalma. A: John Travolta, Nancy Allen, John Lithgow.

Body Double
(1984) 109m. **A**

Combine a loser actor, a telescope, and a naked woman and you have this dizzying descent into murder and the sleazy underbelly of the LA porn scene. A brash, refreshingly tasteless, garishly colorful melange of suspense, pop music, and inside jabs at the director's own horror-film past. Be warned of the infamous killer-driller murder scene.
D: Brian DePalma. A: Craig Wasson, Melanie Griffith, Gregg Henry.

Raising Cain
(1992) 95m. **C–**

Lithgow really hams it up in this labyrinthine tale of multiple identities and mayhem. DePalma's trademark stylistics seem almost like nervous ticks here, and the ironic tone works against the viewer ever getting engaged enough to be scared.
D: Brian DePalma. A: John Lithgow, Lolita Davidovitch, Steven Bauer.

Neo-Noir

Dark shadows continue to splinter the scenes, pouting and lustful women prowl, desperate crimes are committed, and darkly handsome men seemed trapped in a world where they can't remember the rules. Filmmakers pried open the modern revisionist noir period with all the relish straight-A students bring to a pet project; these films are almost all visually rich, ripe with angst-ridden atmosphere and menace from sexual relations in even weirder and less defined times than the 40s and 50s.

Body Heat

(1981) 113m. **A**

An aimless lawyer is bewitched by a beautiful woman dissatisfied with her husband. Steamy, sweat-drenched sex, whispered conferences about murder, and the sickening fear of discovery all get played out on the sweltering Florida coast, where the sunlight glare seems more menacing than shadows.
D: Lawrence Kasdan. A: William Hurt, Kathleen Turner, Ted Danson.

The Postman Always Rings Twice

(1981) 123m. **B–**

A drifter falls for the cafe owner's wife, and soon they're plotting the husband's murder. This remake revives the 1946 classic without activating it. Great actors, heavy sex scenes, careful photography and dialogue: So much more was shown than in the original, and to such little effect.
D: Bob Rafelson. A: Jack Nicholson, Jessica Lange, John Colicos.

Against All Odds

(1984) 128m. **B**

A man falls for the girl who a rich vindictive hood has hired him to find. Stylish remake of noir classic *Out of the Past* substitutes brooding ambiance with rich photography, LA angst, tear-jerking melodramatics, and pop songs. Not bad, but missing much of the original's psychological depth.
D: Taylor Hackford. A: Jeff Bridges, Rachel Ward, James Woods.

Blood Simple

(1984) 96m. **B+**

When a scuzzy bar owner hires a sleazy private detective to kill his wife, the private dick pulls a double-cross and the bodies begin to pile up. A sly, smart, and darkly funny film that's both homage and subtle send-up of the genre.
D: Joel Coen. A: M. Emmett Walsh, Dan Hedaya, Frances McDormand.

Mona Lisa

(1986) 100m. **A**

A decent ex-con becomes a high-priced call girl's bodyguard and slowly learns of the job's dangerous implications, which include falling in love with his sultry charge. A London-based, neon-gritty tale with stylish location shooting and great turns by all.
D: Neil Jordan. A: Bob Hoskins, Cathy Tyson, Michael Caine.

Angel Heart

(1987) 112m. **B+**

A seedy private detective's search for a missing singer takes him on a journey through New York and Louisiana, where he finds corruption, voodoo, and some really wicked secrets from the past. The stunningly decadent visual style, a taboo sex scene, and a sin-drenched atmosphere will make you forget the lack of story.
D: Alan Parker. A: Mickey Rourke, Robert De Niro, Lisa Bonet.

House of Games

(1987) 102m. **A**

The psychiatrist, trying to help a compulsive gambler patient, finds herself seduced by a suave trickster into the surreal underworld of con artists and their marks. A jazzy, witty, and sensual tale that has twists and turns to keep you off balance and enough irony and moodiness to fill up ten film noirs.
D: David Mamet. A: Lindsay Crouse, Joe Mantegna, Lilia Skala.

Gotham

(1988) 100m. **C–**

A tough guy detective is hired by a wealthy client to solve the murder of his wife and finds that this includes the recurring, ghostlike appearances of the dead wife. A dizzying plot that defies logic and dead acting put this movie to rest early.
D: Lloyd Fonvielle. A: Tommy Lee Jones, Virginia Madsen, Frederic Forrest.

Stormy Monday

(1988) 93m. **B–**

American entrepreneur Jones makes life awful for a jazz club owner and a pair of lovers in chilly Scotland. An atmospheric tale that unwinds at a good clip, with a thickly brooding air, smoky jazz score, subtle performances, and slinky camerawork all in moody sync.
D: Mike Figgis. A: Melanie Griffith, Sean Bean, Tommy Lee Jones.

Tequila Sunrise

(1988) 116m. **B+**

The perfect love triangle for decadent LA in the 80s: a drug smuggler (with son) trying to go straight; his boyhood chum/narcotics officer; and the object of their desire, a slinky restaurateur. This stylish, erotic, and sometimes soap-operaish attempt at noir features sultry atmosphere, high-powered chemistry between the leads, and silliness like Pfeiffer tending to the sick son by feeding him angel hair pasta.
D: Robert Towne. A: Mel Gibson, Michelle Pfeiffer, Kurt Russell.

After Dark My Sweet

(1990) 114m. **C+**

An ex-boxer gets involved with a sexy boozy widow and a corrupt former lawman, and is drawn into a kidnapping that turns sour. The sun-drenched Southwest looks flashy, the handsome stars can't act like lowlifes and the story gets lost in the ambiance.
D: James Foley. A: Jason Patric, Rachel Ward, Bruce Dern.

Desire and Hell at Sunset Motel

(1990) 87m. **C–**

A brunette hellion with a fierce desire for an electric range, her nuke-phobic hubby, and various other "eccentric" characters meet at a seedy hotel for blackmail, murder, and confusion. An overly precious stab at noir with endless "hip" dialogue made by someone with a serious 50s obsession.
D: Allen Castle. A: Sherilyn Fenn, Whip Hubley, David Johansen.

The Grifters

(1990) 119m. **A**

A trio of con artists—a young man, his girlfriend, and his very young-looking mother—cheat their way

around Los Angeles while going through all the power plays of a classic love triangle. With exceptional performances, hard-edged camerawork, and a mood ranging from larcenously comic to almost mythically tragic, this towers over other neo-noir.
D: Stephen Frears. A: Anjelica Huston, John Cusack, Annette Bening.

Kill Me Again
(1990) 94m. **B**
A down-on-his-luck Vegas P.I. is double-crossed by almost everybody in the cast when hypersexed Whalley comes up with a unique plan to steal some mob money. Main problems here are Kilmer, looking more like an errant Boy Scout, and an overcomplicated plot that quickly runs out of noir steam.
D: John Dahl. A: Val Kilmer, Joanne Whalley, Michael Madsen.

Miami Blues
(1990) 96m. **B+**
A charming violent sociopath and a ditzy hooker fall in love in Miami, but are hounded by an obsessive cop. This screwball romance of the hip and psycho white-trash set has an appropriately bemused almost campy air, fantastic tropical-hued photography, and fun performances by all.
D: George Armitage. A: Alec Baldwin, Jennifer Jason Leigh, Fred Ward.

The Two Jakes
(1990) 137m. **C+**
In this sequel to *Chinatown,* it's ten years later and private eye Gittes is settling into complacent respectability when a new case lands him in the middle of oil intrigue and facing inconvenient parts of his sordid past. A meandering reprise with some great moments, mostly provided by Keitel.
D: Jack Nicholson. A: Jack Nicholson, Harvey Keitel, Meg Tilly.

A Kiss Before Dying
(1991) 93m. **C+**
The updated noir classic is now a glossy but limp portrayal of dread and fear in a Manhattan yuppies' marriage as a poor young man's ambitions lead him to duplicity and murder.
D: James Dearden. A: Matt Dillon, Sean Young, Max von Sydow.

Shattered
(1991) 106m. **C–**
After a terrible accident, a man must put together the half-recalled fragments of his life, which may include murder. A gossamer light version of noir, with lots of moody blue-tinged photography, much grimacing from Berenger, contrived plot, and memorably ludicrous end: for time-passing only.
D: Wolfgang Petersen. A: Tom Berenger, Greta Scacchi, Joanne Whalley.

Under Suspicion
(1991) 100m. **C–**
This runs through the old "private eye is the number one suspect when his wife is murdered" routine padded with a higher quotient of would-be atmosphere, all too visible plot contrivances, generous scenes of sexual gropings, and a roguish P.I. whose loutish behavior never clicks.
D: Simon Moore. A: Liam Neeson, Laura San Giacomo, Kenneth Cranham.

Night and the City
(1992) 104m. **C+**
An ambulance-chasing attorney tries to muscle in on the fight game. This remake of a classic noir, relocated from London to New York, is well-acted but curiously skimpy on atmosphere, irony, or attitude, making the struggles of some not-very-likeable characters fall flat.
D: Irwin Winkler. A: Robert De Niro, Jessica Lange, Alan King.

One False Move
(1992) 104m. **A**
Karma hits hard when a small-town sheriff mixes himself up in an FBI hunt for cocaine smugglers. This graceful, almost elegantly tragic thriller packs sardonic humor, jolts of realistic violence (concentrated in one beginning blowout scene), evocative Southern locations, a mixed racial romance, and a dynamite Paxton as the cracker sheriff.
D: Carl Franklin. A: Bill Paxton, Cynda Williams, Michael Beach.

Red Rock West
(1993) 98m. **A–**
A good-hearted loser hits town and immediately gets ensnared in a case of mistaken identity, several murder plots, and a scheming femme fatale's nefarious whims. Though a veritable catalog of film noir clichés, this works due to ironic tone, simmering desert locale, and another unhinged turn by Hopper.
D: John Dahl. A: Nicolas Cage, Lara Flynn Boyle, Dennis Hopper.

The Wrong Man
(1993) 99m. **C+**
A sailor jumps ship, gets implicated in a murder he didn't commit, and ends up with a psycho smuggler and cleavage-touting, free-spirited wife in wildest Mexico. A scenic but schizo movie that is alternately a mystery, road film, thriller, and psychodrama, with a slyly funny and tragic evolution to this ménage à trois.
D: Jim McBride. A: Kevin Anderson, Rosanna Arquette, John Lithgow.

China Moon
(1994) 99m. **B–**
A by-the-books cop drops the books to aid and abet an accidental murder committed by a beloved mystery woman. The tension builds in this workmanlike noir as Stowe flickers from victim to femme fatale, corroding stolid Harris' code of ethics.
D: John Bailey. A: Ed Harris, Madeleine Stowe, Charles Dance.

Color of Night
(1994) 135m. **C–**
Traumatized by a patient's suicide, a shrink visits LA where his best pal promptly gets killed. He falls for a mysterious Bambi-esque female, has pose-heavy sex and, when not otherwise occupied, looks for the murderer. The film's truly sleazy air and bold disregard for coherence make it a prime candidate for camp.
D: Richard Rush. A: Bruce Willis, Jane March, Scott Bakula.

Golden Gate
(1994) 91m. **C–**
Dilemma: What does a brooding FBI agent do when he falls for a girl whose father he sent to prison years ago? Only the most patient of viewers will find out, in this mood-soaked noir manqué as good acting, lovely photography, and fine musical score fail to cancel out meandering story and snail's pace.
D: John Madden. A: Matt Dillon, Joan Chen, Bruno Kirby.

The Last Seduction
(1994) 100m. **A–**
Uber-femme fatale steals her husband's drug money, sets up shop in a small town, ruins a nice-but-dumb local guy's life, and starts an insurance scam. A cruelly funny film, with deft use of noir conventions, and Fiorentino practically throttles her role as the single-minded femme who plows through men.
D: John Dahl. A: Linda Fiorentino, Bill Pullman, J. T. Walsh.

Witch Hunt
(1994) 93m. **C+**
In an alternate 50s universe,

witchcraft and magic are part of everyday life in Hollywood, and Hopper is a gumshoe after a suspect senator involved in witch hunts. Visually stunning and filled with in-jokes about Hollywood and McCarthyism, but suffers from lack of pace and throw-away air suitable to this sort of fancy.
D: Paul Schrader. A: Dennis Hopper, Penelope Ann Miller, Julian Sands.

Kiss of Death
(1995) 101m. **B–**
After doing time in Sing Sing, a now-reformed hood agrees to infiltrate a mob business run by insane asthmatic Cage. The remake of the 1947 crime thriller has neon-drenched New York locales, some trendy stylized violence, and funny one-liners but doesn't add up to a satisfying whole.
D: Barbet Schroeder. A: David Caruso, Nicolas Cage, Samuel L. Jackson.

Courtroom and Legal Thrillers

Remember when movies portrayed lawyers as conservative pillars of society? Now they're alcoholics, adulterers, and barely on the right side of the law. These whodunits have fun with the personal lives of the new generation of Perry Masons, while the courtroom provides the stage for confrontations before a packed house leaning toward finding everyone guilty, but for the cunning eloquence of our somewhat sullied hero attorney.

The Verdict
(1982) 122m. **A–**
A ratty alcoholic lawyer takes on a medical malpractice lawsuit involving the Boston Archdiocese. Newman looks like a rumpled coat as he sweats, lurches, and digs into the meaty dialogue of this first-rate drama.
D: Sidney Lumet. A: Paul Newman, James Mason, Charlotte Rampling.

Jagged Edge
(1985) 108m. **B+**
An attorney becomes romantically involved with the dashing publishing baron accused of brutally killing his wife, even though she's not sure right up until the end if he's innocent. Lots of twists and turns, big estates, and sweeping San Francisco scenery.
D: Richard Marquand. A: Jeff Bridges, Glenn Close, Peter Coyote.

Legal Eagles
(1986) 116m. **C**
A defense attorney and an assistant DA try to unravel a convoluted case involving theft and murder in New York's trendy art world. This tries to be a romantic comedy in a courtroom but the story is murky, and the romance never gels. Redford and Winger do lend some weight.
D: Ivan Reitman. A: Robert Redford, Debra Winger, Daryl Hannah.

Suspect
(1987) 101m. **C+**
A public defender representing a deaf homeless man accused of murder is miraculously aided by a member of the jury for the case. Ludicrous story is hampered by unreal courtroom action, but you might enjoy gazing at the stars.
D: Peter Yates. A: Cher, Dennis Quaid, Liam Neeson.

Criminal Law
(1989) 113m. **C–**
A lawyer successfully defends a man accused of murder only to find out that he was guilty and is planning another. Starts out as sharp murder mystery, but gets mired in plot contrivances and a dull resolution.
D: Martin Campbell. A: Gary Oldman, Kevin Bacon, Karen Young.

Physical Evidence
(1989) 99m. **D**
A cop accused of murder is defended by a sexy public defender. This story has so many holes, the actors so few lines that make sense, and a pacing that borders on lugubrious.
D: Michael Crichton. A: Burt Reynolds, Theresa Russell, Ned Beatty.

True Believer
(1989) 103m. **A–**
Woods is in particularly fine high-wire fettle as a burned-out 60s idealistic lawyer given a chance at redemption by the case of a young Asian railroaded to prison. A few plot quibbles aside, this is a tightly constructed, nimble thriller that soft-pedals the melodrama, keeping the story, action, and performances at the fore.
D: Joseph Ruben. A: James Woods, Robert Downey, Jr., Margaret Colin.

Everybody Wins
(1990) 110m. **B**
A beguiling woman hires a private investigator to find out why everyone in a small New England town is keeping mum about a killer's identity. The story is bewildering, but the web that Winger throws around Nolte is powerful enough to hold your attention.
D: Karel Reisz. A: Nick Nolte, Debra Winger, Will Patton.

Presumed Innocent
(1990) 127m. **B+**
The prosecutor in charge of the murder investigation of his former mistress ends up having to prove his own innocence of the crime. A gripping thriller that will keep you guessing up to the last scene.
D: Alan J. Pakula. A: Harrison Ford, Brian Dennehy, Bonnie Bedelia.

Defenseless
(1991) 106m. **D**
A successful attorney falls in love with a sleazy landlord pornographer who is mysteriously murdered. Cookie-cutter story of deceit that's hampered by muddy plot and ponderous pace.
D: Martin Campbell. A: Barbara Hershey, Sam Shepard, J. T. Walsh.

Class Action
(1991) 110m. **B–**
An old-time 60s lawyer finds himself opposing, in and out of court, his yuppified daughter who works for a powerful law firm, in a major suit against an irresponsible auto maker. Bracing friction between dad and daughter, with a nice feel for moments of quiet nodding conspiracy between corporate lawyers.
D: Michael Apted. A: Gene Hackman, Mary Elizabeth Mastrantonio.

Body of Evidence
(1993) 101m. **D+**
Art dealer and S&M aficionado Madonna is accused of having fatal carnal relations with an old geezer, in this film that's essentially a bad

Perry Mason episode with graphic sex. In time this may be camp, but right now it just has inane dialogue and a plot that makes everyone stupid, boring, or despicable.
D: Uli Edel. A: Madonna, Willem Dafoe, Joe Mantegna.

Guilty As Sin
(1993) 104m. **D+**

A battle of wits begins when a sultry attorney defends a handsome, well-dressed, and self-confessed murderer. Truly aberrant offering from the usual excellent Lumet features sedated performances, people staring out the windows a lot, and some of the most brain-addled dialogue this side of camp.
D: Sidney Lumet. A: Rebecca De Mornay, Don Johnson, Stephen Lang.

The Firm
(1993) 154m. **B−**

A neophyte lawyer is courted by a powerful firm rife with sordid business practices, which include murder. Convoluted thriller keeps interest mainly due to colorful cast, rich Ivy League photography, and an exciting finale which unfortunately comes 30 minutes later than it should.
D: Sydney Pollack. A: Tom Cruise, Gene Hackman, Jeanne Tripplehorn.

The Pelican Brief
(1993) 141m. **C+**

A law student's theory about the deaths of two Supreme Court judges turns out to be true, forcing her to hide while helping a reporter unravel a huge political conspiracy. Overlong and dullish thriller with the scenery and handsome stars the sole bit of vitality.
D: Alan J. Pakula. A: Julia Roberts, Denzel Washington, Sam Shepard.

The Client
(1994) 122m. **B**

A nosy kid gets an earful from a dying mafioso, and soon he and his mom are being pursued by both the mob and the feds. A contrived offering given some weight by Sarandon as the boy's spunky attorney and Jones as sleazy prosecutor who'll do anything to get a testimony.
D: Joel Schumacher. A: Susan Sarandon, Tommy Lee Jones, Brad Renfro.

Trial by Jury
(1994) 107m. **C**

A mobster will do anything to convince a key juror to cast her vote in his favor—including kidnapping her child. Starts out as a decent courtroom thriller but quickly goes downhill as the plot turns serpentine, and Whalley-Kilmer awkwardly goes from vulnerable to vengeful.
D: Heywood Gould. A: Joanne Whalley-Kilmer, William Hurt, Armand Assante.

Just Cause
(1995) 102m. **B**

A law professor trying to clear a Florida black man on death row has to work with the sinister black sheriff who forced the man's confession to begin with. Workmanlike thriller with some surprises, a horrifying *Cape Fear*-like climax, and a scenery-chewing turn by Ed Harris as a psychotic serial killer.
D: Arne Glimcher. A: Sean Connery, Lawrence Fishburne, Blair Underwood.

Detectives

Dirty Harry really unlocked a closet full of turmoil and self-loathing, as witnessed by this brand of police procedurals. These cops (or the occasional investigative reporter) are so busy battling their own personal demons or a system mired in corruption and red tape that they barely have the time to solve the grisly murders.

The First Deadly Sin
(1980) 112m. **C−**

Sinatra carries and then drops this film in his portrayal of an aging cop who drinks too much, is slowing down and on the trail of a mad killer. Film feels sludgy, mannered, and filled with Sinatra's friends.
D: Brian Hutton. A: Frank Sinatra, Faye Dunaway, James Whitmore.

Cruising
(1980) 106m. **C−**

A cop goes undercover to investigate the series of brutal murders in New York's gay community. The story and characters are unbelievable, Pacino cruising is a hoot, the pre-AIDS S&M bar scenes are startling, but it still clumsily tries to explore some dark sides of hetero—not homo—sexuality. An interesting failure.
D: William Friedkin. A: Al Pacino, Paul Sorvino, Karen Allen.

True Confessions
(1981) 108m. **B**

A monsignor adept at the politics of running a prosperous parish clashes with his cop brother, whose chief suspect in a grisly murder case is the richest parishioner. An atmospheric *Chinatown*-style mystery with the story often bogged down by the lingering compositions of a moody 1940s Los Angeles.
D: Ulu Grosbard. A: Robert De Niro, Robert Duvall, Charles Durning.

Absence of Malice
(1982) 117m. **C+**

An innocent blue-collar man is implicated in a possible murder by an over zealous Miami reporter. Curiously listless thriller has all the right moves and fine performances but somehow just misses being the power indictment of yellow journalism it seems to want to be.
D: Sydney Pollack. A: Paul Newman, Sally Field, Melinda Dillon.

A Soldier's Story
(1984) 101m. **B**

The African-American army attorney brought in to investigate the murder of a black sergeant slowly unravels a story of bigotry and cover-up that may bring the whole camp down. A stagy but compelling film that manages to explore the racism with the entertaining conventions of a whodunit.
D: Norman Jewison. A: Howard E. Rollins, Jr., Adolph Caesar, Dennis Lipscomb.

Tightrope
(1984) 115m. **B+**

A killer is stalking the hookers of New Orleans and the cop assigned to find him happens to have his own hungry hang-up for the same crowd of women. This guy is no Dirty Harry, but rather a single-father cop who has troubles with his own sexual world view.
D: Richard Tuggle. A: Clint Eastwood, Genevieve Bujold, Dan Heydya.

The Mean Season
(1985) 106m. **B**

A hard-boiled Miami reporter, hot on a serial killer's case, finds himself getting closer to the killer than he'd like. Refreshingly tough-minded, swelteringly atmospheric thriller boasts some serious shocks, sun-parched locations, and good performances.
D: Philip Borsos. A: Kurt Russell, Mariel Hemingway, Richard Jordan.

Witness
(1985) 112m. **A–**

A lovely look at an exotic subculture and a slow-building, heartbreaking romance color this story about a city detective who infiltrates an Amish community to protect a lovely young widow and her son against unknown killers. The suspense quotient may be low, but the vivid characters and Pennsylvania locales are glorious.
D: Peter Weir. A: Harrison Ford, Kelly McGillis, Lukas Haas.

8 Million Ways to Die
(1986) 115m. **D+**

An alcoholic ex-cop gets mixed up with a crazed coke kingpin and a ditzy prostitute while trying to stay sober. This looks like a bad music video and boasts more clichés than ways to die: The sole reason for watching it is the always dependable Bridges who works in vain here.
D: Hal Ashby. A: Jeff Bridges, Rosanna Arquette, Andy Garcia.

Manhunter
(1986) 118m. **A**

The Silence of the Lambs' Hannibal Lecter makes his first film appearance in this story about an FBI agent specializing in serial killers who enlists the aid of the cannibalistic psycho-shrink. This terror thriller features the creepy and fascinating maniac, a weird 60s hit music score, and an overwhelmingly distraught atmosphere.
D: Michael Mann. A: William Peterson, Kim Griest, Tom Noonan.

The Big Easy
(1987) 110m. **A–**

A cagey detective investigates a murder, and an assistant DA investigates corruption in the New Orleans force. Cajun music thumps, people get killed, and in the middle of the stew is a seductive Quaid and a prim Barkin who create an erotic tension that crackles throughout.
D: Jim McBride. A: Dennis Quaid, Ellen Barkin, Ned Beatty.

Someone to Watch Over Me
(1987) 106m. **A–**

Sexual tension mounts between the socialite who witnessed a murder and the working-class cop assigned to protect her. The thriller part is so-so, but the film gets into the people and textures of the different worlds—the opulent one of penthouses, fundraisers, sex, and menace and the other of wife, family, backyards, and fidelity.
D: Ridley Scott. A: Tom Berenger, Mimi Rogers, Lorraine Bracco.

Betrayed
(1988) 127m. **B+**

An FBI agent infiltrates a Midwest white-supremacist group and becomes involved with a loving hardworking single father who she suspects of being a member. The earthy flowering of love adds to the unease and dawning horror as Winger uncovers the practices and plots of the evil and all-American group.
D: Constantin Costa-Gavras. A: Debra Winger, Tom Berenger, John Heard.

The Mighty Quinn
(1989) 98m. **B+**

A Caribbean island police chief investigates the murder of a wealthy white businessman, with all the evidence pointing to his friend, a local drifter. This murder mystery seems to move in time to a reggae beat as a charmingly square Washington navigates through a tropical briarpatch of double-dealing and intrigue.
D: Carl Schenkel. A: Denzel Washington, Robert Townsend, James Fox.

Sea of Love
(1989) 110m. **B+**

A serial killer uses a Personals column to find her victims, so the New York police place their own ad to trap her. Of course one of the cops falls for a prime suspect, and the breathless sex-may-lead-to-death drama steamily unfolds.
D: Harold Becker. A: Al Pacino, Ellen Barkin, John Goodman.

Impulse
(1990) 109m. **C–**

She's gorgeous, wears itty bitty outfits, and is an undercover vice cop. Russell holds your attention with a role that lets her strut around like a rooster, but the film gets drowned in a convoluted and airless story.
D: Sondra Locke. A: Theresa Russell, Jeff Fahey, George Dzundza.

Q and A
(1990) 134m. **B+**

A young assistant DA investigates an "open and shut" murder involving an old-time cop and is swept through the channels of political corruption and rampant racism. The intense characters keep the plodding story bristling as the inquiry escalates to a death struggle between Nolte and Hutton.
D: Sidney Lumet. A: Nick Nolte, Timothy Hutton, Armand Assante.

Homicide
(1991) 102m. **A–**

When a Chicago detective is assigned to a homicide because he's Jewish, he's forced to confront his own ambivalence about that fact. This character study and examination of moral issues is set within a police procedural, all done to a staccato beat. Slowly paced, but just listen to how the people talk.
D: David Mamet. A: Joe Mantegna, William Macy, Natalija Nogulich.

The Silence of the Lambs
(1991) 118m. **A**

A beat-the-clock battle of wits between an FBI agent and the psycho-shrink Hannibal "The Cannibal" Lecter, who holds the clues to a series of horrific slayings. This stylish, near-perfect thriller has all the deranged-killers-with-a-gimmick, perverse atmosphere and bravura acting to keep you tense and shocked into next week.
D: Jonathan Demme. A: Jodie Foster, Anthony Hopkins, Ted Levine.

V.I. Warshawski
(1991) 95m. **C–**

Turner is the private eye hired to find the killer of a pro hockey player. Trying hard to create a female P.I. as if played by Bogart, the plot and pacing get stuck in low gear, and in the end feels like it's a P.I. story played by Burt Reynolds.
D: Jeff Kanew. A: Kathleen Turner, Charles Durning, Jay O. Sanders.

A Stranger Among Us
(1992) 111m. **D**

In order to solve a murder in a Hassidic Jewish neighborhood, the police send in an undercover female cop. You get a lovely tour of a Brooklyn Jewish community, but the story is so silly and Griffith is such a fish out of water that this may soon become a camp classic.

D: Sidney Lumet. A: Melanie Griffith, Eric Thal, John Pankow.

Thunderheart
(1992) 127m. **B**

A murder on an Indian reservation leads to an investigation by FBI agents, one of them part Native-American. Powerful scenery, good square-jawed acting, but the mystery, which takes on spiritual and mystical overtones, gets lost in the hills.
D: Michael Apted. A: Val Kilmer, Sam Shepard, Graham Greene.

Alan Rudolph

Like his mentor Robert Altman, director Alan Rudolph's focus is on quirky outsider characters, making his thrillers some of the most unusual entries in the genre. Elaborate visuals and a rich sense of noir mood can sometimes overwhelm the dream-logic plots, but a unifying theme emerges as his dim private eyes, spurned lovers, dead-ended housewives, and asylum escapees look through a cloudy alienating world in search of romantic love.

Choose Me
(1984) 106m. **B+**

A late night radio psychologist doles out sexual advice to confused LA listeners, two of whom she gets involved with in a more direct fashion. Los Angeles becomes a rain-slicked place of mystery and loneliness in this dreamily toned, sensual film that is one of Rudolph's most accessible outings.
D: Alan Rudolph. A: Genevieve Bujold, Keith Carradine, Lesley Ann Warren.

Trouble In Mind
(1986) 111m. **C–**

In a retro-40s and appropriately named Rain City, the lives of an ex-con, a gender-confused gangster, a troubled woman, and others slowly intertwine. Extremely stylized and at times annoyingly pretentious or obscure, this still has atmosphere to spare and some engagingly weird characters.
D: Alan Rudolph. A: Kris Kristofferson, Keith Carradine, Genevieve Bujold.

The Moderns
(1988) 122m. **C+**

A struggling American artist in 1920s Paris runs into an ex-girlfriend, now married, and accepts a proposition to become a forger of classics. Keith and Linda resume their torrid romance, hob nob with Hemingway and Stein, and do the Left Bank cafe scene in this visually lush and strangely hollow slice of Lost Generation life.
D: Alan Rudolph. A: Keith Carradine, Linda Fiorentino, John Lone.

Love at Large
(1990) 97m. **A–**

A slow-witted P.I. hired by a seductive female to follow her philandering husband, ends up trailing the wrong guy, and falls in love with another detective. Goofy, sweet-tempered tribute to the convoluted 40s detective movies has interesting characters, funny/bizarre plot twists and even stranger romances.
D: Alan Rudolph. A: Tom Berenger, Elizabeth Perkins, Anne Archer.

Mortal Thoughts
(1991) 104m. **B+**

After spending a lot of time fantasizing about the death of her brutal abusive husband, a woman and her best friend have their dream come true, with both women reacting in surprising and dangerous ways. A multi-layered, psychologically rich film that's harder-edged than most of Rudolph's work.
D: Alan Rudolph. A: Demi Moore, Glenne Headley, Harvey Keitel.

Erotic Thrillers

Almost a decade later, we must all pay for the sin of enjoying *Fatal Attraction* with endless waves of erotic thrillers that clog midnight cable stations and video stores. Cheaper than slasher films, the thin mystery plots are spiced up with regular doses of nudity, gauzy-lensed couplings, and an air of sleaze thick enough to cut with a machete.

Bedroom Eyes
(1986) 90m. **D+**

A peeping tom stockbroker is accused of murder when the object of his gaze is killed. This ludicrous "thriller" looks like a slightly upscale porno film with acting to match, as copious nudity is used to jazzy up the endless stretches of brain-dead yakking.
D: William Furet. A: Kenneth Gilman, Dayle Haddon, Barbara Law.

Siesta
(1987) 97m. **C–**

After spurning her lover in favor of a demented air-show promoter, stunt woman Barkin wakes up bloodied and near naked in a field in Spain. Did she kill her true love? His manic wife? Is she even really alive? Answers are long in coming in this snail-paced, self-consciously artsy nonstory.
D: Mary Lambert. A: Ellen Barkin, Gabriel Byrne, Julian Sands.

Call Me
(1988) 98m. **B**

A writer has phone-sex with a man she mistakenly believes to be her beau, leading to drugs, murder, and a maniac stalking her. This is the miracle erotic thriller that manages to live up to its billing with desolate Brooklyn locations creating a tone of isolation for the desperate drama.
D: Sollace Mitchell. A: Patricia Charbonneau, Boyd Gaines, Stephen McHattie.

Alligator Eyes
(1990) 101m. **D+**

A boring couple on a cross-country jaunt picks up a miniskirted woman and drives around. There's also a plot involving a mobster, vengeance, basic psycho instincts and such, but it's easily missed as this scenic film just goes on and on, with much talk, innuendo, and a notable lack of eroticism or thrills.
D: John Feldman. A: Annabelle Larson, Roger Kabler, Mary McLain.

Night Eyes
(1990) 97m. **C–**
A loutish rock star hires a security man to do surveillance on his ex-wife who falls in love with her instead. Bland talky film makes one wish for a higher sleaze count: at least that would relieve the enervated pace and endless chat in this yawn fest.
D: Jag Mundhra. A: Andrews Stevens, Tanya Roberts, Cooper Huckabee.

David Lynch

Best known for his outré soap opera *Twin Peaks*, this painter-turned-filmmaker offers up bits of Americana that have the menace of Hitchcock and the darkly surreal quality of Munchkinland. Gas-sucking lunatics, mutated angels, and crazed lovers-on-the-lam all inhabit worlds that, no matter how ordinary or cartoony-looking, erupt into grotesque violence while a disquieting sense of strangeness simmers below the surface.

Eraserhead
(1978) 90m. B&W. **A**
A baffled soul wanders around in some postapocalyptic wasteland, encountering a lecherous mystery woman, chicken dinners with still living chickens, and a couple whose offspring looks like a baby *Alien*: And these are the more normal sights in this disturbing nightmare meditation on modern life.
D: David Lynch. A: Jack Nance, Charlotte, Stewart, Jeanne Bates.

Blue Velvet
(1986) 120m. **A**
This murder mystery reveals all the dark dank stuff that resides beneath the surface of a cozy all-American small town. A kidnapping plot, S&M, and joyrides with madman Hopper in his most deranged performance are all here. A beautifully composed landmark film that effortlessly combines surreal horror, twisted sex, and perverse humor.
D: David Lynch. A: Kyle MacLachlan, Isabella Rossellini, Dennis Hopper.

Wild at Heart
(1990) 125m. **B+**
Lovers-on-the-lam à la Lynch is of course a dark, violent, and cartoonish affair with the boy acting like Elvis and the girl aping Marilyn Monroe. If you're a Lynch fan you won't mind the confused excesses; if not, you'll still be amazed by Willem Dafoe's turn as a desert Don Juan with the worst teeth in history.
D: David Lynch. A: Nicolas Cage, Laura Dem, Diane Ladd.

Twin Peaks: Fire Walk with Me
(1992) 135m. **C**
In this film prequel to the TV series that had America wondering "Who killed Laura Palmer?" we learn of the events leading up to the murder. Despite the expected overwrought performances, off-kilter humor, and some fun campy moments, a fairly lifeless retread.
D: David Lynch. A: Kyle MacLachlan, Sheryl Lee, Harry Dean Stanton.

Spies and Political Thrillers

Even with the Cold War over, Hollywood produced these sleek, star-studded, often war-tech tales of espionage, political strife, and romance in the ranks. While they have some of the spy vs. spy plotting and suspense, the recent thrillers begin to look more like male action-hero films featuring nuclear subs, big guns, and other steely assurances of America's still potent military might.

White Nights
(1985) 135m. **C**
Male-bonding behind the Iron Curtain as a cranky U.S. defector and a Bolshoi favorite join forces to escape the USSR. Leave it to Hollywood to hand-pick two extraordinary dancers and land them in an action movie with only occasional dance interludes.
D: Taylor Hackford. A: Mikhail Baryshnikov, Gregory Hines, Geraldine Page.

No Way Out
(1987) 116m. **A–**
A Navy hero assigned to the Pentagon becomes involved with the mistress of the Secretary of Defense. When she's murdered, he has to hide his own tracks while figuring out a way to expose his boss. A masterfully constructed thriller with harrowing chase scenes, great use of DC locales, and a full and unexpected crew of bad guys.
D: Roger Donaldson. A: Kevin Costner, Gene Hackman, Sean Young.

Little Nikita
(1988) 98m. **C+**
Twenty years earlier, Russians planted all-American-looking families as "sleeper" espionage agents in San Diego, and the FBI is racing to find them before they're activated. Promising more than it delivers, the plot fails to generate any menace other than a family that's in need of counseling.
D: Richard Benjamin. A: Sidney Poitier, River Phoenix, Richard Jenkins.

The Package
(1989) 109m. **B**
An officer escorting an Army prisoner back to the states loses him, and the ensuing pursuit reveals a political conspiracy. This *Manchurian Candidate*-style thriller keeps you puzzling over the clues as Hackman races against the clock to figure out and then stop some evil doings in Chicago.
D: Andrew Davis. A: Gene Hackman, Tommy Lee Jones, John Heard.

The Hunt for Red October
(1990) 135m. **B**
Cold War nostalgia tale of an ace spy being faced with an apocalyptic question when a high-tech Russian nuclear submarine disappears: Is the captain deranged and about

to blow up the Eastern seaboard, or is he trying to defect? Even with a dated premise, this still boasts fine performances, great undersea battles, and deft pacing.
D: John McTiernan. A: Sean Connery, Alec Baldwin, Sam Neill.

The Russia House
(1990) 124m. **B**

Love and espionage mix when a British publisher gets involved with a beguiling Russian female and a manuscript that questions Russia's defense capabilities. A solid Le Carré Cold War thriller made glamorous by charismatic leads and good use of Soviet locales.
D: Fred Schepisi. A: Sean Connery, Michelle Pfeiffer, Roy Scheider.

Patriot Games
(1992) 117m. **B**

Tom Clancy's indefatigable CIA agent Jack Ryan gets embroiled with IRA terrorists, endangering his wife and family. Well-choreographed action set-pieces and a little more than lip-service paid to the Irish "troubles" don't make up for effects that are more interesting than the thriller.
D: Phillip Noyce. A: Harrison Ford, Anne Archer, James Earl Jones.

Sneakers
(1992) 126m. **B–**

An industrial team made up of ex-felons is pressured by a secret government agency to steal a codebreaking computer program. A low-tech, high suspense drama with an all-star team that lends a *The Dirty Dozen* charm to a serviceable thriller.
D: Phil Alden Robinson. A: Robert Redford, Dan Akroyd, Sidney Poitier.

In the Line of Fire
(1993) 135m. **A–**

A secret serviceman battles guilt over Kennedy's death, his own diminishing powers, and a psychotic would-be assassin. This sleek nonstop action thriller has Clint showing his soft side to coworker Russo, with Malkovich providing some deliciously harrowing moments as the brilliant killer who loves to play phone games.
D: Wolfgang Petersen. A: Clint Eastwood, John Malkovich, Rene Russo.

Clear and Present Danger
(1994) 141m. **B–**

Harried CIA superagent Jack Ryan takes over the agency's top spot when the director falls ill and finds himself investigating a conspiracy that goes all the way to the President's office. Cinematic Chinese takeout food—looks good, moves fast, and things blow up good, but quickly forgettable.
D: Phillip Noyce. A: Harrison Ford, Anne Archer, Willem Dafoe.

Crimson Tide
(1995) 121m. **B–**

Two commanders on board a submarine hit a world-threatening impasse after Russian rebels commandeer some missile silos pointed at the U.S. Formulaic high-concept scenario has all the stops pulled out, including some incredible sub warfare scenes and old-time movie star charisma of dueling leads.
D: Tony Scott. A: Denzel Washington, Gene Hackman, George Dzundza.

The Net
(1995) 114m. **C**

A fetching female hacker chances upon a strange program, resulting in a suave assassin from a shadowy organization slowly stripping her of her Internet and real-world identity. Film has two interesting ideas, but seems overwhelmed by them and falls back on the paranoia/chase plot.
D: Irwin Winkler. A: Sandra Bullock, Jeremy Northam, Dennis Miller.

Outbreak
(1995) 128m. **C+**

When an escaped African monkey spreads a plague through a West Coast town, it's up to an intrepid group of medical researchers to find a cure before the military can nuke the place. Despite the AIDs-like medical premise, this has all the vehicular action/chase scenes with Hoffman making an interestingly grumpy action hero.
D: Wolfgang Petersen. A: Dustin Hoffman, Rene Russo, Donald Sutherland.

Perils of Modern Life

These are often known as the "_____ from Hell" films, because just when everything looks rosy for these mostly yuppies protagonists, someone who *should* be nice enters the picture—a nanny, roommate, secretary, a one-night stand—and turns out to be a pathological creep threatening to destroy everything. These stories also update the old film noir adage that "love—or lust—kills" as sex invariably goes hand in hand with violence and deviant behavior.

The Hitcher
(1986) 97m. **B+**

On a cross-country jaunt, Howell picks up hitchhiking Hauer, who then spends the rest of the film trying to destroy his life. Paranoia is redefined in this beautifully shot, golden-hued film, with Hauer coming off like a human Terminator, murderous, without motive, and practically indestructible.
D: Robert Harmon. A: Rutger Hauer, C. Thomas Howell, Jennifer Jason Leigh.

Black Widow
(1987) 103m. **B–**

A female federal agent discovers that wealthy men are being murdered and all the young widows seem to be the same woman. The multi-layered tension between the two women and a restrained story are what make this interesting.
D: Bob Rafelson. A: Debra Winger, Theresa Russell, Dennis Hopper.

Fatal Attraction
(1987) 120m. **A–**

She's the one-night stand who won't go away and, when married exec Douglas wants to call it quits, she stalks him and his family. The thriller that took male paranoia for a wild ride features some laughable sex scenes and a pull-out-the-stops, black widow spider performance by Close.
D: Adrian Lyne. A: Michael Douglas, Glenn Close, Anne Archer.

D.O.A.
(1988) 96m. **C+**
A professor wakes up to find he's been drugged and, with only hours left to live, searches, with love interest in tow, for his killers and an antidote. Unlike the 1949 noir classic, this is a fleet-footed, colorful tour of jealousies and intrigues of academia, which tries to have fun with its own incomprehensibility.
D: Annabel Jankel. A: Dennis Quaid, Meg Ryan, Charlotte Rampling.

Masquerade
(1988) 98m. **C+**
Love, larceny, and variously unhealthy obsessions befall a whiny rich girl in a Hamptons resort town. Overblown, archly acted, and very entertaining trashy nonsense, with travel-brochure bright photography and more subplots than you can shake a stick at.
D: Bob Swaim. A: Rob Lowe, Meg Tilly, Kim Cattral.

Apartment Zero
(1989) 124m. **B**
In a cramped Buenos Aires apartment, an Oedipal-wreck film buff's new roommate seems to be everything to everybody: He may also be a mercenary serial killer. A homoerotically charged character study, a Hitchcockian thriller, and a black humor paranoia piece, its length and leisure pace sap a great deal of the tension.
D: Martin Donovan. A: Colin Firth, Hart Bochner, Dora Byran.

Dead Calm
(1989) 95m. **B**
A married couple on a sailing vacation pick up the sole survivor of another private craft who turns out to be a homicidal loony. A sort of Jacques Cousteau special meets *Psycho,* with snappy plotting and an energetic maniac in the form of Zane.
D: Phillip Noyce. A: Sam Neill, Nicole Kidman, Billy Zane.

Bad Influence
(1990) 100m. **B+**
Unctiously urbane stranger Lowe cheerfully leads clean-cut yuppie Spader down the path of sexual perversity, drug abuse, and eventually murder. An enjoyable sleazy exercise in style with a ripely decadent tone, mostly night time photography and a spooky Lowe as the Peter Pan from Hell.
D: Curtis Hanson. A: Rob Lowe, James Spader, Lisa Zane.

Blue Steel
(1990) 102m. **B**
A brand new New York City cop discovers her gun is being used by a serial killer, and begins receiving flattering attention from a very intense stockbroker. The action scenes grab your attention, and if the story gets a little screwy, keep your eyes on the steely Curtis and demented Silver.
D: Kathryn Bigelow. A: Jamie Lee Curtis, Ron Silver, Clancy Brown.

Desperate Hours
(1990) 106m. **C–**
The remake of the Bogart classic is a study in menace as an on-the-run hood and his trashy girlfriend terrorize a wealthy estranged couple. The actors try hard, but this stagebound effort forgoes suspense for action and winds up looking like an upscale cable movie.
D: Michael Cimino. A: Mickey Rourke, Anthony Hopkins, Mimi Rogers.

Internal Affairs
(1990) 115m. **B+**
A crooked cop torments the officer sent to investigate him. This solid thriller relishes the malevolent undertow of corruption and suspicion of infidelity, seasoned by Gere's perfectly creepy portrayal of a very bad cop.
D: Mike Figgis. A: Richard Gere, Andy Garcia, Nancy Travis.

Pacific Heights
(1990) 103m. **C+**
A yuppie couple makes a big mistake when they rent part of their beautifully restored Victorian house to a psychotic deadbeat. A slight idea stretched way too far, this ends up feeling like a business case study in bad rental practices.
D: John Schlesinger. A: Melanie Griffith, Michael Keaton, Matthew Modine.

Cape Fear
(1991) 130m. **A–**
A sadistic ex-con stalks the wife and daughter of the attorney who mishandled his case. An unrelenting study of terror and a cunning look at sinister forces that can threaten a family both from without and within, all climaxing in a gut-wrenching and cataclysmic battle.
D: Martin Scorsese. A: Robert De Niro, Nick Nolte, Jessica Lange.

Basic Instinct
(1992) 130m. **B+**
A troubled cop gets mixed up with the prime suspect in a murder case who's beautiful, bisexual, and writes murder mysteries that seem to come true. Everyone has dirty secrets in this sexy thriller, and you're not sure who's doing what to whom, even after the show is over.
D: Paul Verhoeven. A: Michael Douglas, Sharon Stone, Jeanne Tripplehorn.

Consenting Adults
(1992) 99m. **C–**
Everything is swell with the new couple next door—she's a sultry crooning blonde and he's a wild adventuresome kind of guy who then suggests a one-night stand of anonymous wife-swapping. An unbelievable, unsexy waste of first-rate actors.
D: Alan J. Pakula. A: Kevin Kline, Mary Elizabeth Mastrantonio, Kevin Spacey.

Final Analysis
(1992) 122m. **C**
A psychiatrist gets mixed up with a beautiful patient and her even sexier sister who has an inconveniently sadistic husband and a conveniently strange reaction to alcohol. This overlong film twists and turns and tries to be a Hitchcock thriller with carnality, until it all comes together in a big convoluted thud.
D: Phil Joanou. A: Richard Gere, Kim Basinger, Uma Thurman.

The Hand That Rocks the Cradle
(1992) 110m. **B–**
A new mother starts to get nervous about her too-perfect, lovely young nanny who seems to be taking over more than just care for the baby. A relatively quiet thriller with enough suspense and one or two jolts of shock.
D: Curtis Hanson. A: Annabella Sciorra, Rebecca DeMornay, Matt McCoy.

Poison Ivy
(1992) 92m. **B–**
A brooding study of two outcast girls, one of whom is a disturbed nymphet out to snag the other's father. This stylish thriller manages to touch on a lot of taboo subjects without going the exploitation route, seasoned with LA-ennui atmosphere and creepy tone.
D: Katt Shea Ruben. A: Drew Barrymore, Tom Skerritt, Sara Gilbert.

Single White Female
(1992) 107m. **B+**
The new roommate starts appropriating Fonda's clothes, hairstyle, boyfriend, and personality, and we all know what comes next. A cool tale of terror with slashings in an apartment building that feels eerily sim-

ilar to the one in *Rosemary's Baby.*
D: Barbet Schroeder. A: Bridget Fonda, Jennifer Jason Leigh, Steven Weber.

Unlawful Entry
(1992) 111m. **C+**
A young couple meets a sweet cop who becomes possessive of Stowe while entering into a weirdo relationship with hubby Russell. What starts out as a tense character study quickly takes the thriller route as Liotta becomes the stalking home invader and Russell goes mano-a-mano to destroy him.
D: Jonathan Kaplan. A: Kurt Russell, Ray Liotta, Madeleine Stowe.

Malice
(1993) 107m. **B**
A string of murders is only one of the things a college professor and his wife have to contend with when they invite an old college pal, now a hotshot surgeon, to become a boarder. A flawed twisty, high-concept thriller is compensated by brooding mood to spare and a terrific Baldwin as the sleazy egomaniacal doc.
D: Harold Becker. A: Alec Baldwin, Nicole Kidman, Bill Pullman.

Sliver
(1993) 115m. **C−**
It looks like the landlord wired his high-rise building for surveillance, and Stone just moved into the apartment whose last tenant was murdered. A good concept—urban voyeurism, some great-looking actors, and a hilariously dumb script with Stone unable to be convincing as a sexually vulnerable woman.
D: Phillip Noyce. A: Sharon Stone, Tom Berenger, William Baldwin.

The Temp
(1993) 100m. **B+**
The efficient and seductive temporary office assistant looks like she'll do anything to climb the corporate ladder. A slick, brisk, and almost campy "blind ambition" paranoia thriller with Boyle and Dunaway clearly enjoying their corporate bitch-goddesses roles and a slasher style finale on a catwalk.
D: Tom Holland. A: Lara Flynn Boyle, Timothy Hutton, Faye Dunaway.

Family Menace

The Stepfather
(1987) 88m. **B**
In search of the perfect family, this guy marries widows with children, but when things don't work out, he finishes them off, cleans up the mess, and goes on to the next one. A horror thriller set among the most placid scenes of suburbia that keeps you on edge waiting for the inevitable bloodbath.
D: Joseph Ruben. A: Terry O'Quinn, Shelley Hack, Jill Schoelen.

Track 29
(1988) 90m. **D+**
A strange young man meets up with an equally disturbed alcoholic mother: Or is she really his mother? Answers are not forthcoming as the film plays more like a game of free (and demented) association with uncomfortable bits of incest thrown in: Lloyd is pretty funny with his toy trains, though.
D: Nicolas Roeg. A: Theresa Russell, Gary Oldman, Christopher Lloyd.

Benefit of the Doubt
(1993) 92m. **C+**
After twenty years in jail, all an aging convicted murderer wants is to be close with his attractive daughter and son, in his fashion. Good performances and nice Arizona scenery help the slack pace and a tone that flip-flops between sober character study and mad-relative-on-the-loose.
D: Jonathan Heape. A: Donald Sutherland, Amy Irving, Graham Greene.

Flesh and Bone
(1994) 127m. **C**
A vendor salesman down South meets a cute drifter, both unaware that they're bonded by a dark secret of murder. A good cast, but also twenty minutes of meandering "atmosphere," virtually no story until an hour into the film, and Caan showing up in a psycho role suggesting that Dennis Hopper was busy.
D: Steve Kloves. A: Dennis Quaid, Meg Ryan, James Caan.

Mother's Boys
(1994) 94m. **B**
After leaving for ten years, a wealthy and sexually disturbed mother returns to collect her brood—at any cost. A richly over-art directed *Fatal Attraction* knockoff shot in eye-straining primary colors with scenes vacillating from camp to squirm-in-your-seat taboo sexuality.
D: Yves Simoneau. A: Jamie Lee Curtis, Peter Gallagher, Joanne Whalley-Kilmer.

Stalked Women

With all the talk of the "new" woman, in Hollywood all it seems to take is a male with serious intimacy issues and a weapon to reduce these females to terrified victim status. This group of glossy star vehicles is really just a revision of the "menaced women" films of yesteryear with a nod to feminism by allowing the stalked one the honors of finishing off the bad guy.

Scissors
(1990) 105m. **C−**
A lonely woman is attacked, taken in by a seemingly kindly stranger, and becomes a prisoner in a locked-up apartment. A ridiculous plot, extremely languid soap opera direction, and Stone's stretch as a distraught female makes this one so silly it almost works as camp.
D: Frank De Felitta. A: Sharon Stone, Steven Railsback, Ronny Cox.

Sleeping with the Enemy
(1991) 99m. **B−**
A woman finally escapes her abusive husband and creates a new and gentler life in another town. You don't have to wait long before hubby, now totally deranged, shows up for revenge in this formulaic glossy vehicle for Roberts.
D: Joseph Ruben. A: Julia Roberts, Patrick Bergin, Kevin Anderson.

Jennifer 8
(1992) 127m. **C−**
A burned-out cop falls for a blind woman who may be a serial killer's next victim. The film pulls out an impressive array of clichés, with various easy "scares" preying on Thurman's blindness, all partially redeemed by an

ominous music score, atmospheric sea-side photography, and sturdy cast.
D: Bruce Robinson. A: Andy Garcia, Uma Thurman, John Malkovich.

Love Crimes
(1992) 85m. **C**
A sexy assistant DA goes undercover to snare a rapist/con man in this murky-looking thriller. A disturbing film that puts a rather dazed-looking Young in a variety of titillating-degrading positions and seems to be as exploitative of the subject as the sexual deviate/photographer is.
D: Lizzie Borden. A: Sean Young, Patrick Bergin, James Read.

Blink
(1994) 106m. **B**
A blind musician regains her sight via an operation just in time to witness a murder, but the details are still maddeningly fuzzy. Director Apted applies his usual graceful style integrating appropriately disoriented atmosphere, a multilayered plot, and a feisty romance between Quinn and Stowe.
D: Michael Apted. A: Madeleine Stowe, Aidan Quinn, James Remar.

Hybrid Thrillers

Whodunits, psychodramas, a journey to the other side of death—in the films listed here Hollywood tries to create something new by grafting together two or more genres to create something (hopefully) original. The startling part is how often this generally stylish group of films succeeds.

Cutter's Way
(1981) 105m. **B**
A boozy, disfigured Vietnam vet sets out to clear his petty crook buddy of a murder charge and make some money in the bargain. A hallucinatory saga of conspiracy and corruption, in which the bottled-up bitterness of Heard twists the laid back Bridges into taking action that seems doomed before it begins.
D: Ivan Passer. A: Jeff Bridges, John Heard, Lisa Eichhorn.

Thief
(1981) 122m. **B**
A master jewel thief agrees to work with the mob for one last heist so he can go legit—wife, home—in style, only to find it's like a pact with the devil. This is one of those grainy 70s-style character studies that meanders at first and then surely builds in tragedy until its explosive, thought-provoking end.
D: Michael Mann. A: James Cann, Tuesday Weld, Willie Nelson.

Deathtrap
(1982) 116m. **B–**
A famous playwright's new work has just bombed, his ideas have dried up, but he may be saved by the brilliant unpublished play by one of his students. This three-person, dark comedy caper avoids feeling overly stage-bound thanks to lively camerawork, Caine's seedy energy and Reeve's humorous blandness.
D: Sidney Lumet, Michael Caine, Christopher Reeve, Dyan Cannon.

Fletch
(1985) 96m. **B+**
A wisecracking reporter covering a story on drugs winds up involved in a murder mystery. This offers the usual suspects and kaleidoscopic array of California locations, with clever dialogue and a laconic performance by Chase that reminds you of how funny he can be.
D: Michael Ritchie. A: Chevy Chase, Jose Don Baker, Richard Libertini.

Jack's Back
(1988) 91m. **B**
Someone is pulling a Jack-the-Ripper routine in modern LA and a young medical student fears that the guilty party is his own unconscious self. Begins as an average slasher and settles into a tense, if over-plotted thriller, heavy on action, with a barren, just-before-dawn look to it.
D: Rowdy Herrington. A: James Spader, Cynthia Gibb, Robert Picardo.

Flatliners
(1990) 112m. **C–**
A group of hotshot medical students tempt death via a machine that allows them to expire for brief periods in order to see what's on "the other side." What's on this side is a lot of billowing drapes, flashy acting, overwrought quasi-gothic sets and a pretty ho-hum vision of post-death life.
D: Joel Schumacher. A: Kiefer Sutherland, Julia Roberts, Kevin Bacon.

Knight Moves
(1993) 110m. **C–**
Lambert gives a severely understated performance in this tale of a chess champion plagued by a serial killer. An able supporting cast and an exciting finale (during which Lambert is unconscious) help, but using chess as the plot device hardly thrills and isn't even a classy gimmick for the murders.
D: Carl Schenkel. A: Christopher Lambert, Diane Lane, Tom Skerritt.

Silent Fall
(1995) 101m. **C–**
A retired psychiatrist is called upon to help in a case where parents were viciously murdered and the only witnesses are a daughter traumatized into silence and her autistic brother. Careful handling of an intriguing premise helps drain any tension or fear from this essentially by rote thriller.
D: Bruce Beresford. A: Richard Dreyfuss, Linda Hamilton, John Lithgow.

Atmospheric Thrillers

Not every film with a brooding story, looming shadows, and fated characters is necessarily part of the film noir genre. This group of films, whose tone ranges from art-house to near-horror, uses atmosphere almost as a separate character; not heavy on action, many of

these leave you remembering more about the mood of the film than what they were actually about.

Half Moon Street
(1986) 90m. **C–**
An American academic in London spices up her sex and financial life by becoming an upscale prostitute, and soon falls for suave Caine. A cold-looking and slow film, a sort of veddy British erotic thriller with all the unbridled passion that suggests.
D: Bob Swaim. A: Sigourney Weaver, Michael Caine, Patrick Kavenaugh.

The Girl on a Swing
(1989) 119m. **C+**
A ceramics expert working in Denmark falls in love with a beautiful, mysterious, and possibly murderous female. Depending on viewer's tastes, this elegiac, mistily photographed, erotic film could be seen as either a darkly fascinating portrait of mystical obsession or a long-winded, pretentious bore.
D: Gordon Hessler. A: Meg Tilly, Rupert Frazer, Elspet Gray.

Heart of Midnight
(1989) 95m. **B**
A disturbed young woman inherits a run-down nightclub and finds it inhabited with bizarre lodgers and clues to her own dark past. Filmed in gaudy lime greens and queasy reds, rife with creeped-out sexuality and practically stifling with debauched atmosphere, this ranks as one of the more memorably weird 80s films.
D: Matthew Chapman. A: Jennifer Jason Leigh, Peter Coyote, Frank Stallone.

Miracle Mile
(1989) 87m. **A–**
A young man trying to hook up with his date overhears a phone call saying that nuclear missiles are headed for LA. What starts off as a semicampy character study turns into a sort of doomed nuclear *After Hours*. A truly unique film with trenchant black comedy and sickening tension as the films careens its way to Doomsday.
D: Steve DeJarnett. A: Anthony Edwards, Mare Winningham, Robert Doqui.

Paperhouse
(1988) 94m. **B+**
A troubled little girl retreats, literally, into her drawings—a barrenly surreal dreamworld inhabited by a lonely boy. This unique look at childhood fears (including hints of child abuse) with its creepy minimalist sets and subtly unsettling ambiance relies on suggestion and symbolism rather than shocks to keep the tension high.
D: Bernard Rose. A: Charlotte Burke, Glenne Headly, Ben Cross.

The Comfort of Strangers
(1991) 117m. **B–**
Two young British lovers intersect with a middle-aged, decidedly sick-soul-of-Europe couple in glamorously rotting Venice. A beautifully shot, excruciatingly hypnotic film with a shocker payoff at the end and a fascinatingly weird Walken throughout.
D: Paul Schrader. A: Natasha Richardson, Rupert Everett, Christopher Walken.

Kafka
(1992) 98m. B&W/color.
B–
This gloomy story that follows insurance clerk Franz Kafka as he investigates a friend's death is slow going but a dazzling exercise in expressionistic style. Every shot, from the menacing Prague locales to the fantastic palace of horrors in the finale, gives this a beauty and resonance of a classic silent film.
D: Steven Soderbergh. A: Jeremy Irons, Theresa Russell, Joel Grey.

The Public Eye
(1992) 98m. **C**
This sincere attempt to evoke noir style and spirit tells the tale of a Weegee-like obsessive tabloid photographer who falls for a mysterious female club owner. Sepia toned cinematography is a big plus, along with Pesci's subdued performance, but the script wanders halfway through along with viewer's attention.
D: Howard Franklin. A: Joe Pesci, Barbara Hershey, Jared Harris.

Traditional Thrillers

Though peppered with action set-pieces, these films try to follow in the footsteps of Hitchcock by telling complexly plotted tales filled with memorable characters; you occasionally get some brooding atmospherics but they always take a backseat to a suspenseful story well told.

The Last Embrace
(1979) 102m. **B–**
After his wife is killed in the crossfire of one of his missions, a CIA man starts receiving threatening letters as he pursues a mystery killer. Somewhat slow-paced but fascinating Hitchcockian thriller/character study is memorable for a nerve-racking climax chase atop Niagara Falls and Scheider as the twitchy Company man.
D: Jonathan Demme. A: Roy Scheider, Janet Margolin, Christopher Walken.

Eyewitness
(1981) 95m. **B**
A janitor's infatuation with a TV news reporter leads to his fabricating a story that pulls them both into jeopardy. The characters and subplots are finally more interesting than the mystery that includes a thrilling scene in the riding stables.
D: Peter Yates. A: William Hurt, Sigourney Weaver, Christopher Plummer.

Still of the Night
(1982) 91m. **C+**
A psychiatrist falls in love with his patient who may have killed her husband and might be planning to kill him. The sophisticated feel for Manhattan interiors isn't matched by the pedestrian mystery and stylized relationships.
D: Robert Benton. A: Roy Scheider, Meryl Streep, Jessica Tandy.

F/X
(1986) 110m. **B+**
A top Hollywood special effects maestro is enlisted by the authorities to set up a fake gang slaying—except that the corpses are real, and now it'll take some serious

special effects to get out of the ensuing mess. As absurd as it is charming, this one zooms by with tongue firmly in cheek.
D: Robert Mandel. A: Bryan Brown, Brian Dennehy, Diane Venora.

Best Seller
(1987) 110m. **B**

A hyperactive hitman hires a writer/ex-cop to pen his memoirs, when actually the whole thing is a vengeance scam. A pedestrian thriller that's enlivened by Manhattan locales zipping by and Woods' usual manic presence.
D: John Flynn. A: James Woods, Brian Dennehy, Victoria Tennant.

Frantic
(1988) 120m. **C+**

When his wife disappears, an American in Paris nearly goes nuts looking for her, eventually ending up embroiled with a flaky miniskirted drug dealer and international espionage. This innocent-man-in-a-mess chase through a cold and menacing Paris tries for Hitchcock but settles for something more hyperactive and distracting.
D: Roman Polanski. A: Harrison Ford, Emmanuelle Seigner, Betty Buckley.

A Shock to the System
(1990) 91m. **B–**

A middle-aged executive discovers that you can always get what you want—including a promotion—if you're not above a little murder. Caine gets to shine up his droll SOB role in this humorous but mostly bland black comedy about trying not to fall down the corporate ladder.
D: Jan Egleson. A: Michael Caine, Elizabeth McGovern, Peter Riegert.

Dead Again
(1991) 107m. **A–**

An LA private dick gets enmeshed in a murder, an amnesiac woman, an antique dealer/hypnotist, and possible reincarnation. A stylish humorous homage to noirs minus the gloom, with witty plot twists, gorgeous 40s-looking flashbacks, and a classy British couple trying to sound American.
D: Kenneth Branagh. A: Kenneth Branagh, Emma Thompson, Andy Garcia.

The Vanishing
(1993) 120m. **C–**

When his girlfriend disappears without a trace, a young man obsessively tries to find out what happened, even if he has to put himself in the hands of the maniac who was responsible. What was understated, creepy, and haunting in the original becomes lurid, obvious, and grotesque here.
D: George Sluizer. A: Jeff Bridges, Kiefer Sutherland, Sandra Bullock.

Shallow Grave
(1995) 92m. **B**

Three smarmy Scottish roommates find a fourth who turns up dead with a cache of drug money. What to do with a rapidly decaying stiff and his money? This Hitchcock-like story has a stylish look, a hip attitude, and some genuinely creepy images that get under your skin.
D: Danny Boyle. A: Kerry Fox, Ewan McGregor, Christopher Eccleston.

WESTERNS

Westerns Menu

WESTERNS MENU

WESTERN FILM GROUPS

1930s–1940s

Americana

These upbeat brassy films about the farmers, adventurers, and gunslingers who took on the Wild West are gems of American history and mythology. Big in scope and corny as Kansas in August, they aren't your typical cowboy shoot-em-ups, but more like historical action-adventures with a distinctly Western twang and a free hand with accuracy.

Cimarron
(1931) 124m. B&W. **C+**
A pioneer family forsakes all to go to Oklahoma for the great land rush. An extremely ambitious epic that looks stage-bound and creaky now, with some marvelous moments and a hammy performance by Dix that defies description.
D: Wesley Ruggles. A: Richard Dix, Irene Dunne, Estelle Taylor.

Annie Oakley
(1935) 88m. B&W. **B+**
A rousing biography of the woman gunslinger who set the west on its ear. Stanwyck plays Annie as gritty and vulnerable, but the sappy love story doesn't ring true.
D: George Stevens. A: Barbara Stanwyck, Preston Foster, Melvyn Douglas.

Last of the Mohicans
(1936) 91m. B&W. **B**
Cooper's classic tale of the adventures of a Mohican Indian and his forbidden love for a colonial woman only comes alive with the brawny action scenes in the French-Indian War. Good fun but the love story could have used more bite.
D: George B. Seitz. A: Randolph Scott, Binnie Barnes, Bruce Cabot.

The Plainsman
(1936) 113m. B&W. **B+**
Wild Bill Hickok and Calamity Jane are out to stop a ruthless gunrunner from arming the Indians. Overripe but delightful hokum from DeMille may elicit guffaws, but the sweeping story is still told with power.
D: Cecil B. DeMille. A: Gary Cooper, Jean Arthur, Charles Bickford.

Allegheny Uprising
(1939) 81m. B&W. **B**
Wayne and his band of loyalists fight off the Indians and the British in prerevolutionary America. Sexy chemistry between Wayne and Trevor, great villains, and the rousing action scenes make this one of the more entertaining film entries.
D: William A. Seiter. A: John Wayne, Claire Trevor, George Sanders.

Union Pacific
(1939) 135m. B&W.
B+
DeMille's epic about the building of the transcontinental railroad may be more Hollywood than history, but it's still fun watching the broad scene-chewing performances, spectacular disasters, and the rootin'-tootin' battle with the Indians.
D: Cecil B. DeMille. A: Barbara Stanwyck, Joel McCrea, Robert Preston.

Jesse James
(1939) 105m. **C+**
This dreary flat bio-pic of the famous outlaw portrays a bland smiling victim of circumstances rather than a ruthless criminal. The supporting cast makes it watchable.
D: Henry King. A: Tyrone Power, Henry Fonda, Randolph Scott.

Northwest Passage
(1940) 125m. **B+**
Major Rogers and his band of Rangers fight off attacks by the Iroquois and French as they stealthily traverse the rugged Adirondacks toward an assault on the headquarters of the French and Indian command. An exceptionally hard-bitten saga with fierce kill-or-be-killed battle scenes set amidst some glorious forest locales.
D: King Vidor. A: Spencer Tracy, Robert Young, Walter Brennan.

The Return of Frank James
(1940) 92m. **A−**
This far superior follow-up to *Jesse James* offers a gloomy and neurotic look at the outlaw life as revenge-minded Frank tracks the men who sent brother Jesse to his death. Brilliant use of Technicolor and arid locales enhances the sense of doom.
D: Fritz Lang. A: Henry Fonda, Gene Tierney, Jackie Cooper.

Western Union
(1941) 94m. **B+**
The fabled telegraph network meets resistance from politicos and outlaws in this rousing, heroic, and largely fabricated story. Tried and true blarney that's lifted by the crisp pacing and edgy Scott as the bandit looking to go straight.
D: Fritz Lang. A: Robert Young, Randolph Scott, Dean Jagger.

The Fighting Kentuckian
(1949) 100m. B&W. **B−**
When a group of homesteaders are about to lose their land to bandits, it's the Duke to the rescue. Extremely weird casting makes this otherwise serviceable western a must-see. Almost camp.
D: George Waggner. A: John Wayne, Vera Ralston, Oliver Hardy.

John Ford

Panoramic shots of sky and Western terrain are never simple backdrops in Ford's westerns; they establish the rhythms to these sweeping tales of lonely gunslingers, rigid military men, and corrupt politicians who all end in sacrificing themselves to family and

community. The tone of his films went from the idealistic and religious to the bitter and revisionist in his stripped-down later masterworks. But they all offer classic human interest stories and an abiding romance that comes from the big outdoors and the little people who inhabit it.

Stagecoach

(1939) 99m. **A−**

When the Ringo Kid escapes from jail he hooks up with the motley crew of a stagecoach traversing Apache territory. A marvelous, highly theatrical ensemble piece that escalates into a flight from Indians, climaxing in a spectacular chase scene. This *Grand Hotel* on wheels put the western back on the "A" movie map.
D: John Ford. A: John Wayne, Claire Trevor, Thomas Mitchell.

My Darling Clementine

(1946) 97m. B&W. **A**

Wyatt Earp and Doc Holliday set the stage for a duel with the Clantons at the OK Corral. What begins as a leisurely, character-driven vehicle ends with one of the most exciting gunfights you'll ever see. Some lovely moments include Fonda's awkward two-step at the town dance and Mowbray's barroom reading.
D: John Ford. A: Henry Fonda, Linda Darnell, Victor Mature.

Fort Apache

(1948) 127m. B&W. **A−**

A rigid cavalry officer leads his men to the brink of war with the Indians. The interesting character study, with a terrific cold-fish Fonda, falls off the track with Shirley's romance and then resurrects itself with a great last stand.
D: John Ford. A: Henry Fonda, John Wayne, Shirley Temple.

She Wore a Yellow Ribbon

(1949) 103m. **A**

A Cavalry commander's retirement is postponed when he makes peace with local Indians. Not much happens, but this graceful elegaic look at the military life looks fresher with the passage of time. Exquisitely shot in toned-down Technicolor, with a thunderstorm sequence that's still mightily impressive.
D: John Ford. A: John Wayne, Joanne Dru, John Agar.

The Three Godfathers

(1949) 105m. **B+**

Three bible-toting outlaws adopt a baby and head for the desert. The bumbling daddies run out of water, lose their horses, and still manage to keep the baby alive as the posse closes in. A sincere, often funny tale, bogged down by the heavy-duty religious allegory.
D: John Ford. A: John Wayne, Pedro Armendariz, Harry Carey, Jr.

Rio Grande

(1950) 105m. B&W. **A−**

A feisty mother tries to block her son from entering her ex-husband's cavalry regiment. There are plenty of brilliant stunts and vivid scenery in this tale of lost love and redemption, but it's really a showcase for Wayne and O'Hara who are a keg of sexual dynamite as the long separated lovers.
D: John Ford. A: John Wayne, Maureen O'Hara, Ben Johnson.

Wagonmaster

(1950) 86m. B&W. **A**

Two young men lead a Mormon wagon train on its way to Utah in this collection of lovely character sketches that shows the dissension between the God-fearing pioneers and the mercenary "heathens" as they all push west to a new life. A pastoral entry that unfolds like a visual poem of Western folklore.
D: John Ford. A: Ben Johnson, Joanne Dru, Harry Carey, Jr.

The Searchers

(1956) 119m. **A**

After his family is massacred in a Commanche raid, an ex-Rebel soldier spends seven years looking for his young niece who was the sole survivor. The opening scenes are like a folkloric portrait of pioneer life that turns into a relentless brutal odyssey with a racist Wayne trekking across the beautiful treacherous country seeking revenge.
D: John Ford. A: John Wayne, Jeffrey Hunter, Vera Miles.

The Horse Soldiers

(1959) 119m. **A−**

Union officer Wayne leads his undermanned troops into the South on a dangerous mission. This bitter offbeat antiwar saga hits home when the Rebel children make their mad march against Union soldiers. The film's realistic muted look resembles a Matthew Brady photograph.
D: John Ford. A: John Wayne, William Holden, Constance Towers.

Sergeant Rutledge

(1960) 118m. **B+**

A black cavalry hero is on trial for rape and murder in this compelling and somber "message" courtroom drama. Tension builds, thanks to the film's unusual structure, which scores points eloquently about the military's racism without sledgehammer polemics.
D: John Ford. A: Woody Strode, Jeffrey Hunter, Ward Bond.

Two Rode Together

(1961) 109m. **A−**

Crusty pioneer Stewart and cavalry officer Widmark search for children kidnapped by the Comanches. A complex troubling tale that looks at the pain and prejudice of a community dealing with the loss of their children. Stewart's increasingly bitter performance provides an interesting twist.
D: John Ford. A: James Stewart, Richard Widmark, Shirley Jones.

The Man Who Shot Liberty Valance

(1962) 119m. B&W. **A**

You can feel the Old West passing on as a rancher dies, sealing the mystery of just who did kill the outlaw Valance. A simple story about a love triangle in a small town evolves into a cynical, almost noirish fable about the rise of a well-meaning but spineless politician who may or may not have saved the community from anarchy.
D: John Ford. A: John Wayne, James Stewart, Vera Miles.

Cheyenne Autumn

(1964) 145m. **B+**

A Cheyenne tribe defies the cavalry and government when it migrates back to its old settlement in Wyoming. Despite the breathtaking panoramic Indian marches, this inflated epic gets tangled up trying to show how bureaucracy helped lead to the demise of Native American nations. Sincere but uninvolving.
D: John Ford. A: Richard Widmark, Carroll Baker, James Stewart.

Errol Flynn

Like Flynn's swashbuckling epics, these big-budget films are sprawling, high-spirited, and very romantic. Flynn's cool and dashing athleticism made him a suave character in the Wild West while his good looks and vulnerability gave him a more romantic appeal than the usual leather-faced, stoic western stars.

Santa Fe Trail
(1938) 110m. B&W. **B**

The Cavalry is on the trail of abolitionist John Brown in this ambitious rambling epic. It succeeds on its star power, but the unsympathetic treatment of the famed abolitionist is curious. Beware of shoddy prints.

D: Michael Curtiz. A: With Olivia De Havilland, Alan Hale, Ronald Reagan.

Dodge City
(1939) 105m. **B+**

Wyatt Earp and company are out to tame the notorious frontier town, but the brawling citizens aren't going to make it easy. A rowdy, highfalutin romp with a sparkling cast and lush color photography.

D: Michael Curtiz. A: With Olivia De Havilland, Ann Sheridan.

Virginia City
(1940) 121m. B&W. **B**

A Confederate Colonel conspires with his dancer girlfriend to steal gold from the Union Army. This uneven follow-up to *Dodge City* is 30 minutes too long but rich with glorious Western locales.

D: Michael Curtiz. A: With Randolph Scott, Miriam Hopkins, Humphrey Bogart.

They Died with Their Boots On
(1941) 138m. B&W. **B+**

This biography of General Custer exaggerates the events leading up to the massacre at Little Big Horn but, with Flynn leading the way, it's hard to argue. Funny brawling epic roars along at a dizzying clip, but the lionization of Custer gives the Native Americans the worst of it.

D: Raoul Walsh. A: With Olivia de Havilland, Arthur Kennedy.

San Antonio
(1945) 111m. **B**

Errol sweeps a dance hall girl off her feet under the nose of her saloon owner boyfriend and his nemesis. Minor affair with all the colorful, big-budget fixings has a slam-bang, shoot-out finale at the Alamo.

D: David Butler. A: With Alexis Smith, S. Z. Sakall.

1930s Westerns

These films chronicle the awkward beginnings of the talkie westerns from the outdoorsy cowboys-and-horse spectacles to the low-budget soundstage-bound "sheriff roots out the bad guy and bags the pretty gal" sagas. The good guys and bad guys are easy to identify and you'll recognize the backlot settings that have helped create some of the icons of Western folklore: the saloon, the jail, and main street, where the inevitable showdown will occur.

The Virginian
(1929) 90m. B&W. **B–**

A pistol-packing ranch foreman goes after the outlaw who led his best buddy astray. Slow-paced early talkie makes good use of the rugged locale and the Snidley Whiplash-like antics of bandit Huston to help offset the stiff performances from the two leads.

D: Victor Fleming. A: Gary Cooper, Richard Arlen, Walter Huston.

The Big Trail
(1930) 121m. B&W. **B+**

If you can get past the theatrical performances and leisurely pace of this wagon train story, you'll enjoy the early Duke standing tall against villains, Indian raids, and buffalo stampedes. A spectacular wide-screen epic with the letter-boxed format giving full glory to the mountain scenery.

D: Raoul Walsh. A: John Wayne, Marguerite Churchill, El Brendel.

The Painted Desert
(1931) 75m. B&W. **C–**

An adopted young cowpoke tries to remain loyal to his family who feud violently with the folks of his ladylove. Despite the film's brevity and a snarling turn by newcomer Gable as the heavy, this leaden and wordy horse opera is tough to sit through.

D: Howard Higgin. A: William Boyd, Helen Twelvetrees, Clark Gable.

Viva Villa!
(1934) 115m. B&W. **B–**

This sumptuous, talky, and overlong biography of the Mexican revolutionary leaves accuracy and urgency behind but still has bravura performances and some rip-roarin' action scenes.

D: Jack Conway. A: Wallace Beery, Leo Carrillo, Fay Wray.

The Terror of Tiny Town
(1938) 63m. B&W. **C–**

With the hackneyed plot, cheap sets, and bad acting, the only all-midget, musical western is just another example of Hollywood's good taste and finer instincts about the brotherhood of man.

D: Sam Newfield. A: Billy Curtis, Yvonne Moray, John Bambury.

Destry Rides Again
(1939) 94m. B&W. **B+**

A meek sheriff finally decides to do something about the outlaws who are taking over the town and threatening his manhood. This bawdy comedy is stagy and occasionally too broad, but Dietrich brings the house down as the bad girl who gives Jimmy something to fight for.

D: George Marshall. A: Marlene Dietrich, James Stewart, Brian Donleavy.

The Oklahoma Kid
(1939) 85m. B&W. **B–**
Cowboy Cagney seeks to avenge the lynching of his father, but bandit Bogie blocks the way. A surprisingly mediocre programmer that the stars tackle with verve.
D: Lloyd Bacon. A: Jimmy Cagney, Humphrey Bogart, Rosemary Lane.

1940s Westerns

The success of *Stagecoach* gave new life to westerns, and this group of bio-pics, revenge tales, and horse operas are some of the more flamboyant examples of the time. As better writers and directors came to this genre, westerns evolved with classic plots, non-western Hollywood stars, and a celebration of the visual splendor of the wide open West. When mixed with the anxiety of the postwar years, Hollywood even produced several moody noirish works and one or two neurotic masterpieces.

The Westerner
(1940) 99m. B&W. **C**
There's little action but a lot of dust kicked up by laconic cowpoke Cooper and rip-snorting, gallivanting Judge Roy Bean as they both pursue the elusive Lily Langtry. Dreary saga gets some juice from a wily Brennan as the judge.
D: William Wyler. A: Gary Cooper, Walter Brennan, Forrest Tucker.

Dark Command
(1940) 94m. B&W. **B+**
Renegade teacher Pidgeon organizes thugs to terrorize the frontier, and Marshall Wayne rides to the rescue. A gritty hard fought actioner that offers several surprises along the way.
D: Raoul Walsh. A: Clair Trevor, John Wayne, Walter Pidgeon.

The Spoilers
(1942) 87m. B&W. **B**
Wayne is the trusting prospector in Alaska who strikes it rich, and Scott is the oily G-man who tries to swindle him. Mix in Dietrich as the rich girl who steps in to save her man, and you've got a lusty ménage à trois comedy-drama with more than a few sexual sparks.
D: Ray Enright. A: Marlene Dietrich, John Wayne, Randolph Scott.

The Ox-Bow Incident
(1943) 75m. **B+**
An angry mob tries to lynch three innocent men for a murder. The viewer is made to feel like a helpless spectator in this stark and somber morality play that's almost stylized with its relentless close-ups.
D: William A. Wellman. A: Henry Fonda, Dana Andrews, Anthony Quinn.

The Outlaw
(1943) 126m. **C**
Billy the Kid meets his match when he crosses this raw-boned gal with an appetite. An aimless retelling of the old legend shows some sparks but gets stuck on extended leering camera shots of Russell's cleavage. Beware of bad prints.
D: Howard Hughes, Howard Hawks. A: Jane Russell, Walter Huston, Thomas Mitchell.

Buffalo Bill
(1944) 90m. **C+**
A lavish Technicolor biography covers the adult life of the famous showman who packaged the raucous Wild West into family entertainment. Like a splashy western parade with a never-aging Buffalo Bill perched on a float.
D: William Wellman. A: Joel McCrea, Maureen O'Hara, Linda Darnell.

Duel in the Sun
(1946) 130m. **A**
A good and a bad brother come to blows over a half-breed woman in this baroque soap opera. There's a splendor, a squalor, and a too bright sun in this delirious saga of sexual longing and cruelty that still breathes fire today.
D: King Vidor. A: Gregory Peck, Jennifer Jones, Joseph Cotten.

Pursued
(1947) 101m. B&W. **B+**
A cowboy scours the countryside in relentless pursuit of his father's killers in this unusually bleak and stylish revenge story that's like a film noir on the western trail.
D: Raoul Walsh. A: Robert Mitchum, Teresa Wright, Judith Anderson.

Blood on the Moon
(1948) 88m. B&W. **B–**
A noir western with drifter Mitchum being talked into putting the squeeze on homesteaders by his oily buddy. The moody pessimistic tale starts off with a bang but quickly gets ponderous.
D: Robert Wise. A: Robert Mitchum, Barbara Bel Geddes, Robert Preston.

Rachel and the Stranger
(1948) 79m. B&W. **B**
The idyllic marriage of a young homesteader and his more experienced wife is thrown out of whack by a visit from mysterious drifter Mitchum. A simple, sweet-tempered vehicle for Young with the Mitchum-Holden tension providing the real interest.
D: Norman Foster. A: Loretta Young, Robert Mitchum, William Holden.

Red River
(1948) 133m. B&W.
A
Mutiny on the Bounty comes west when tyrannical cattle driver Wayne pushes his men too far while second in command Clift is quietly ready to take him on. Gritty tale, with unsentimental photography that still captures the sweep of the land and the pulse of a cattle drive.
D: Howard Hawks. A: John Wayne, Montgomery Clift, Walter Brennan.

1950s

Anthony Mann and Jimmy Stewart

The unlikely pairing of the lovable actor and the violent noirish, action-oriented director produced a group of chilling adult revenge westerns. Unlike Ford's soothing valleys, Mann shot these turbulent sagas in jarring vertical settings, where the villains lurked, ready to prey on the seemingly innocent rube. What was even more startling was Stewart's transformation into a hardened, neurotic, almost borderline-demented man, capable of savage actions in defense of his family or to avenge an injustice.

Winchester '73

(1950) 92m. B&W.
A–

A peaceable man is driven to violence when he follows the bloody trail of his stolen gun used to kill his father. Like an anti-NRA propaganda film, we get to see the bloody uses for one of the cornerstones of the west—the Winchester '73 gun. The stark and brooding terrain set the stage for grim Stewart in relentless pursuit.
D: Anthony Mann. A: With Shelley Winters, Dan Duryea, Stephen McNally.

Bend of the River

(1952) 91m. A–

A wagonmaster locks horns with an old outlaw buddy who holds up the wagon train for supplies. A stark and murderous tale of Stewart plunged into reconciling his violent past is made even more chilling by the elegiac mountain settings.
D: Anthony Mann. A: With Arthur Kennedy, Julie Adams, Rock Hudson.

The Naked Spur

(1953) 91m. A

This complex study of greed doesn't paint a pretty picture of humanity as a bounty hunter has trouble bringing his prize bandit over the treacherous Rocky Mountains. A wild and dangerous Stewart matches wits against a silky cunning Ryan in a struggle that turns everyone and everything into a brooding adversary.
D: Anthony Mann. A: With Robert Ryan, Janet Leigh, Ralph Meeker.

The Far Country

(1955) 97m. A–

Stewart helps an old buddy drive a herd of cattle to Alaska to cash in on the Gold Rush, only to have the cattle stolen by a conniving sheriff. The wide expanse of the Northwest gives this story of deceit and revenge a big stage, with Stewart walking a fine line between good and evil.
D: Anthony Mann. A: With Ruth Roman, Corinne Calvet, Walter Brennan.

The Man from Laramie

(1955) 104m. A–

A ranch hand pursues the group who sold rifles to the Indians who killed his brother. A savage, highly ambivalent revenge tale notable for its realistic cruelty, parched locales, and a sweaty disturbing finale.
D: Anthony Mann. A: With Cathy O'Donnell, Arthur Kennedy, Donald Crisp.

Randolph Scott

Scott evolved from a simple law-and-order man in his early films to a granite-jawed icon with a conscience in the later cynical dramas. These low-key gems may lack the panoramic panache of more expensive productions, but the simple stories build to high drama as Scott calls the bad guy out for a final showdown.

Man in the Saddle

(1951) 87m. B+

A greedy rancher pursues Scott's ex-lover and then tries to push Scott off his land. The battle of wits explodes into a violent, often brutal affair with spectacular gun battles in this intelligent and adult western.
D: Andre de Toth. A: With Joan Leslie, John Russell.

The Stranger Wore a Gun

(1953) 83m. B

Straight and narrow Scott is forced to commit a crime by the stagecoach robber who saved his life. A neat plot twist with Randolph's betrayal of the pair of foxy villains hurtling this into overdrive. Originally shot in 3D.
D: Andre de Toth. A: With Claire Trevor, George Macready, Lee Marvin.

A Lawless Street

(1955) 78m. B+

A hard-nosed Marshal's world is set on its ear by the return of an old flame, but the evil misdeeds of an opportunistic landowner put him back on track. The rowdy town teeters on the brink of anarchy as the not-so-angelic Lansbury tempts torch-carrying Randolph in this bustling tale.
D: Joseph H. Lewis. A: With Angela Lansbury, Warner Anderson.

Seventh Cavalry

(1956) 75m. B+

Cavalry officer Scott, accused of cowardice, offers to retrieve Custer's body after the battle of Little Big Horn. Tough, hard-nosed saga of duty and redemption looks better through the years.
D: Joseph H. Lewis. A: With Barbara Hale, Jay C. Flippen.

Decision at Sundown

(1957) 77m. B

Scott follows the trail of the man who drove his wife to suicide. The dark, deeply ironic revenge tale is a fascinating glimpse into the abyss of a human soul. Hold on for the stirring showdown.
D: Budd Boetticher. A: With John Carroll, Karen Steele.

The Tall T

(1957) 78m. A

Scott and O'Sullivan team up to outwit a trio of stagecoach bandits who hold them hos-

tage. Devilishly ironic fable boasts simple powerful storytelling and excellent ensemble playing. An overlooked gem.
D: Budd Boetticher. A: With Richard Boone, Maureen O'Sullivan.

Buchanan Rides Alone
(1958) 78m. **B+**
A nomadic cowboy comes to the assistance of a young Mexican accused of murder. Terse biting indictment of prejudice, with delicious plot twists and an ambiguous Scott as the cynical loner who has to take a stand.
D: Budd Boetticher. A: With Craig Stevens, Barry Kelley.

Ride Lonesome
(1959) 73m. **A–**
A bounty hunter will do whatever's necessary to catch a vicious killer, even using the man's brother as bait. A savage and intelligent look at the spreading poison of vindictiveness.
D: Budd Boetticher. A: With Karen Steele, Pernell Roberts.

OTHER FILMS:
The Desperadoes (1943)
Abilene Town (1946)
Badman's Territory (1946)
Return of the Badmen (1948)
Doolins of Oklahoma (1949)
Coroner Creek (1948)
Rage at Dawn (1955)

Frontier Sagas

These films about America's Western expansion are bigger, brighter, and with a healthy cynicism that makes them less hokey than their storybook predecessors. The handsome productions give an even grander sense of the plains, buttes, and canyons of the West, and the wide-screen values of the later epics practically put a biblical spin on the storytelling.

The Big Sky
(1952) 122m. B&W. **A–**
A group of trappers treks up the dangerous Missouri River. This gritty study of the harsh life on the frontier shows the extreme physical and emotional pain of the quartet of hungry men on the trail of money and moral redemption. An uncompromising film that has aged well.
D: Howard Hawks. A: Kirk Douglas, Arthur Hunnicutt, Dewey Martin.

The Denver and Rio Grande
(1952) 89m. **B**
The two rival railroad companies battle the elements and each other as they struggle to link the East to the West. A rowdy minor saga that packs plenty of punch with some gorgeous mountain scenery and an outrageous showdown between the locomotives.
D: Byron Haskin. A: Edmund O'Brien, Sterling Hayden, Dean Jagger.

Pony Express
(1953) 101m. **B–**
Wild Bill Hickok and Buffalo Bill meet resistance from the Indians and shady businessmen as they push the famous mail route westward. Some colorful and historically inaccurate storytelling with the spicy ladies adding pleasant romantic moments.
D: Jerry Hopper. A: Charlton Heston, Rhonda Fleming, Jan Sterling.

The Big Country
(1958) 166m. **C–**
A sea captain turned ranch owner locks horns with the ranch foreman over the love of a beautiful woman. Sprawling soap opera is brought down by the agonizingly slow pace and performances that vary wildly between stiff and hambone.
D: William Wyler. A: Gregory Peck, Jean Simmons, Charlton Heston.

The Alamo
(1960) 161m. **B**
An outnumbered Davy Crockett and company make their final stand against the Mexicans in the legendary fortress. Eye-popping epic uses unabashedly cornball storytelling that doesn't make it any less rousing, and the long buildup pays off with the heroic finale.
D: John Wayne. A: John Wayne, Richard Widmark, Laurence Harvey.

How the West Was Won
(1963) 155m. **B**
This wide-screen, all-star epic follows three generations of pioneers seeking a new life in the untamed West. A generous banquet of pioneering legends served up by three directors. John Ford's haunting vignette of the Johnny Reb who gets a horrifying first-hand taste of killing in the Civil War is one of the highlights.
D: John Ford, Henry Hathaway, George Marshall. A: James Stewart, John Wayne, Debbie Reynolds.

Adult Westerns

Although most are color productions, these morality plays and character studies have all the dark moodiness of film noir. The wide-screen celebrations of Western landscape are eschewed in favor of cynical psychological dramas that spit in the eye of the romantic hero: The protagonist is no longer the good guy in the white cowboy hat; he's just a bitter loner who has to take a stand in spite of himself. And for the first time, the Native American's side is explored—with white men still playing the leads.

Broken Arrow
(1950) 93m. **B**
The efforts of settler Stewart and Indian leader Cochise to keep peace on the frontier are thwarted by greedy traders and old prejudices. A big colorful Western panorama, studded with time-honored confrontations that take great pains to show the Native American point of view.
D: Delmer Daves. A: James Stewart, Jeff Chandler, Deborah Paget.

The Gunfighter
(1950) 84m. B&W. **B**
When a notorious gunman tries to lay down some roots, he's confronted by an outlaw who's out to create a reputation of his own. Drab, slow-moving parable scores its points about America's glorification of the outlaw but still comes off as sour and sanctimonious.
D: Henry King. A: Gregory Peck, Helen Westcott, Jean Parker.

High Noon
(1952) 84m. B&W. **B+**
On his wedding day, the marshal discovers that a band of outlaws seeking revenge is heading into town, and the good citizens are too cowardly to help. This stark and slightly stagy morality play, bolstered by the towering quiet of Cooper and a haunting score, moves with clocklike suspense toward the climactic noon showdown.
D: Fred Zinnemann. A: Gary Cooper, Grace Kelly, Lloyd Bridges.

Shane
(1953) 118m. **B**
A quiet and mysterious gunslinger comes to the defense of settlers whose land is targeted by greedy cattlemen. This traditional story—the stranger who saves the day and rides on—is filled with grand shots of the diminutive Ladd battling tall bad guys, along with scenes between him and the adoring young boy that still bring a lump to the throat.
D: George Stevens. A: Alan Ladd, Jean Arthur, Jack Palance.

Apache
(1954) 91m. **B+**
A peaceful Indian learns from the violent ways of the U.S. Cavalry to lead his own fight against the white man. The Apaches' frustration at relocation and displacement from their culture comes through like a trumpet blast in this bristling tale of revenge.
D: Robert Aldrich. A: Burt Lancaster, Jean Peters, John McIntyre.

Broken Lance
(1954) 96m. **C**
A tyrannical cattle rancher creates dissension between his sons and watches his empire and family disintegrate. A family saga that quickly feels overloaded with psychological motivation.
D: Edward Dmytryk. A: Spencer Tracy, Robert Wagner, Jean Peters.

Johnny Guitar
(1954) 110m. **A–**
Two ferocious and ornery women face off: The saloon owner can't wait for the railroad to move in while the rancher will do anything to stop it. This bizarre and baroque production is brimming with garish colors, outlandish outfits, and a very odd sense of gender. Hayden breezes through with wry amusement while being treated like beefcake by girlfriend Joan.
D: Nicholas Ray. A: Joan Crawford, Sterling Hayden, Mercedes McCambridge.

Jubal
(1956) 101m. **B**
Ranch hand Ford draws the ire of boss Borgnine who thinks he's two-timing with his wife. A sexual web of intrigue set against dusty arid locales that heighten the bitter sense of betrayal.
D: Delmer Daves. A: Glenn Ford, Ernest Borgnine, Rod Steiger.

Gunfight at the O.K. Corral
(1957) 122m. **B–**
Wyatt Earp and Doc Holliday stand tall against the villainous Clanton gang on a sunny day in Tombstone. This sprawling saga doesn't lack for color and has some exciting shoot-outs, but the mugging stars help take the wonder out of the legend.
D: John Sturges. A: Burt Lancaster, Kirk Douglas, Rhonda Fleming.

Run of the Arrow
(1957) 86m. **A–**
Rather than admit defeat, a Rebel soldier joins the Sioux tribe and continues his fight against the Union Army. A weird tale of one man's raging delusions, with the jagged expressionistic landscapes providing a perfect setting for his descent into a private hell.
D: Samuel Fuller. A: Rod Steiger, Brian Keith, Sarita Montiel.

The Tin Star
(1957) 93m. **B+**
A raw young sheriff hires a shady gunfighter to take care of the bandits terrorizing his town. The old tale of a veteran showing the rookie the ropes gets an edgy neurotic treatment with a nasty showdown that's worth the wait.
D: Anthony Mann. A: Henry Fonda, Anthony Perkins, Betsy Palmer.

3:10 to Yuma
(1957) 92m. B&W. **B**
A peaceful and poor rancher accepts the dangerous job of guarding a notorious bandit in a small hotel until the train arrives to take him to prison. A morality tale similar to *High Noon,* filled with wheedling, cajoling, and threats rather than gunfire while using its claustrophobic setting to increase the mounting psychological tensions.
D: Delmer Daves. A: Van Heflin, Glenn Ford, Felicia Farr.

The Left-Handed Gun
(1958) 102m. B&W. **B+**
Billy the Kid becomes a killer legend when he avenges a friend's death, until he meets death himself at the hands of another friend, Pat Garrett. The reworking of the myth casts more dark psychological shadows on his actions, along with a wondrous sense of youthful bravado and violence.
D: Arthur Penn. A: Paul Newman, Lita Milan, John Dehner.

Rio Bravo
(1959) 141m. **A**
After the sheriff arrests the evil cattle baron's killer brother he must rely on a drunken deputy and a hobbled old-timer for help. What begins as ambling and comic quickly shifts into a tale of redemption as the motley crew of defenders is galvanized by the spirit and muscle of Wayne.
D: Howard Hawks. A: John Wayne, Dean Martin, Walter Brennan.

"A" Westerns

The western came into full bloom in the 50s as Hollywood discovered that wide plains sagas and the wide-screen process were a match made in heaven. These films offer some spectacular panoramic Western canvases, increasingly sophisticated storytelling, and villains who were often as charismatic as the heroes.

Rawhide
(1951) 86m. B&W. **B**

Outlaws hold a group of stagecoach passengers hostage at a lonely outpost in this talky psychological desert drama. Big on production values and star power, this offers little action until the shoot-'em-up finale.

D: Henry Hathaway. A: Tyrone Power, Susan Hayward, Hugh Marlowe.

The Lusty Men
(1952) 113m. B&W. **A**

A washed-up rodeo star gets one last shot at glory when he tutors a wannabe cowboy, and then he falls for the man's wife. A lyrical and intelligent look at a lonely modern cowpoke who'd like to set down roots but can't resist the siren call of the rodeo life.

D: Nicholas Ray. A: Robert Mitchum, Susan Hayward, Arthur Kennedy.

Rancho Notorious
(1952) 89m. **A**

After his fiancée is raped and murdered, a rancher pursues the killers to a ranch run by a shady woman. This starts out as a fatalistic tale of a man poisoned by hatred and becomes a romantic odyssey. A savage but oddly elegant chamber western.

D: Fritz Lang. A: Marlene Dietrich, Arthur Kennedy, Mel Ferrer.

Gun Fury
(1953) 83m. **B+**

When a band of outlaws plunders a stagecoach and kidnaps a young woman, her fiancé tracks them through treacherous terrain. Rock is his usual wooden self in this standard revenge tale that's spiced up by bad boy Marvin.

D: Raoul Walsh. A: Rock Hudson, Donna Reed, Lee Marvin.

Hondo
(1953) 84m. **B**

With the Apaches on the warpath, an army scout is surprised to find a widow and her young son living alone on an isolated ranch. The stirring western background and sweet rapport between the leads elevates this pleasant but otherwise forgettable frontier tale.

D: John Farrow. A: John Wayne, Geraldine Page, Ward Bond.

The Man from the Alamo
(1953) 79m. **B+**

As the Mexicans close in on the Alamo, a soldier escapes to look for help and is later branded a coward. A strange and exciting odyssey ensues as the increasingly bitter man discovers that there's not enough he can do to remove the stigma.

D: Budd Boetticher. A: Glenn Ford, Julia Adams, Victor Jory.

Vera Cruz
(1954) 94m. **A−**

A gentleman and a scoundrel head to Mexico for adventure and profit during the Juarez uprising of 1866. Cooper plays the stoic good guy, but it's Lancaster all in black who prowls and steals every scene in this lusty colorful account of the brawling Mexican city.

D: Robert Aldrich. A: Gary Cooper, Burt Lancaster, Denise Darcel.

River of No Return
(1954) 91m. **B+**

A saloon singer, a widower cowboy, and his young son take a river journey by raft in search of the woman's runaway husband. Magnificent mountain ranges frame this intimate and romantic river adventure containing moments of real tenderness between Mitchum and Monroe.

D: Otto Preminger. A: Robert Mitchum, Marilyn Monroe, Rory Calhoun.

Man Without a Star
(1955) 89m. **B+**

A tough woman rancher and a charming drifter team up to battle the rival rancher who's looking to move in. Fists and bullets fly as Kirk weasels his way into the enemy camp in this hard-boiled tale that offers some refreshingly gritty female characters.

D: King Vidor. A: Kirk Douglas, Jeanne Crain, Claire Trevor.

The Tall Men
(1955) 122m. **B**

Two ex-soldiers sign on with a cattle baron to help drive his herd through the high country. The three men soon come to blows thanks to a beautiful woman, the harsh weather, and numerous Indian attacks. A big lumbering epic saved by the stunning winter scenery and the husky stars.

D: Raoul Walsh. A: Clark Gable, Jane Russell, Robert Ryan.

The King and Four Queens
(1956) 86m. **B+**

A smooth-talking outlaw enters town and begins to romance four women in order to find the whereabouts of stolen gold. This unusual and leisurely tale of seduction takes its time unfolding, but watching old lion Gable pitch and woo is an amusing diversion.

D: Raoul Walsh. A: Clark Gable, Eleanor Parker, Jo Van Fleet.

Love Me Tender
(1956) 89m. B&W. **C+**

A pair of brothers bicker over war booty, fall for the same woman, and proceed to split up their family. This slender, cheap-looking Civil War saga would be forgettable if not for the musical presence of the King.

D: Robert D. Webb. A: Elvis Presley, Richard Egan, Debra Paget.

Man of the West
(1958) 100m. **A**

An ex-outlaw joins up with his sadistic old boss and gang, just so he can stop them from tormenting a group of innocents. Brooding downbeat tale paints a gloomy picture of the expanding West where old outlaws go down kicking and clawing. London's forced striptease is one of the more disturbing scenes in a western.

D: Anthony Mann. A: Gary Cooper, Julie London, Lee J. Cobb.

The Hanging Tree
(1959) 106m. **B**

A frontier doctor makes the town folk buzz when he begins to care for a beautiful blind girl, and has them reaching for their guns when they try to pry into his mysterious past. This sincere character study set in the Montana hills holds the reigns a little too tightly on everyone except for the scene-chewing Malden.

D: Delmer Daves. A: Gary Cooper, Maria Schell, Karl Malden.

"B" Westerns

What these smaller-scaled productions lack in budget and big stars is made up by a sense of urgency missing from many of the "A" westerns of the period. Brawling sagas about legendary heroes, sibling rivalries, and revenge are still recycled over and over in these mostly Technicolor productions. But since so much shooting, fighting, and romancing had to be packed into a smaller time frame, rarely does the entertainment value wane.

The Baron of Arizona
(1950) 90m. B&W. **B+**
A conniving rascal tries to claim the Arizona territory for himself. Refreshingly sympathetic saga of greed features some snappy storytelling and a scene-chewing performance from Price as the baron.
D: Samuel Fuller. A: Vincent Price, Ellen Drew, Beula Bondi.

The Sundowners
(1950) 83m. **B−**
A man tries to protect his little boy from an outlaw brother. This plucky tale of sibling rivalry trades some nasty punches and barbs as it builds to the inevitable showdown.
D: George Templeton. A: Robert Preston, Cathy Downs, Robert Sterling.

Little Big Horn
(1951) 86m. B&W. **B**
A small cavalry platoon makes a desperate try to stop Custer from falling into the Indians' trap at Little Big Horn. The high voltage cast's sense of urgency and the film's pervasive tone of impending doom make for an atmospheric lively B western.
D: Charles Marquis Warren. A: Lloyd Bridges, John Ireland, Marie Windsor.

The Texas Rangers
(1951) 74m. **B+**
The legendary law and order men set out to capture the Sundance Kid. A seasoned gunman tries to keep his younger brother from joining the Rangers in the splendid-looking, violent pursuit across the plains.
D: Phil Karlson. A: George Montgomery, Gale Storm, Jerome Courtland.

Last of the Comanches
(1953) 85m. **B+**
A cavalry sergeant leads a group of settlers through dangerous Indian territory. This tense tale of passage gets its spark from some spectacular terrain and the crusty crew of characters who make life miserable for Sergeant Crawford.
D: Andre de Toth. A: Broderick Crawford, Barbara Hale, Lloyd Bridges.

The Last Command
(1955) 110m. **B−**
Davy Crockett and Jim Bowie make their last stand against the Mexicans at the Alamo. This inflated, occasionally enjoyable epic chronicles the final days of the men and women who were soon to become legends. A labored but colorful production.
D: Frank Lloyd. A: Sterling Hayden, Richard Carlson, Anna Maria Alberghetti.

A Man Alone
(1955) 96m. **B**
A fugitive hides out with the sheriff's daughter to avoid a lynch mob. Understated, low-budget film wears its bitterness on its sleeve as the feverish townsfolk move in for the kill.
D: Ray Milland. A: Ray Milland, Mary Murphy, Ward Bond.

Tennessee's Partner
(1955) 87m. **B+**
A big-time gambler gets some unexpected help from a classy stranger, which changes his life for the better. Nice guy Ronnie and low-down Payne form an unusual partnership in this hard-nosed, entertaining show.
D: Allan Dwan. A: John Payne, Ronald Reagan, Rhonda Fleming.

Guns of Fort Petticoat
(1957) 82m. **B**
A cavalry deserter is forced to train a group of women to fight off attacking Indians. A mix of hijinks and high drama as these plucky Texas women aggravate and astound Audie all across the open range.
D: George Marshall. A: Audie Murphy, Kathryn Grant (Crosby), Hope Emerson.

The Lonely Man
(1957) 87m. B&W. **B−**
A hardened gunman returns home in an attempt to turn his life around. The low-key morality play brims with neurotic tension between father Palance and son Perkins but finally never really comes to life.
D: Henry Levin. A: Jack Palance, Anthony Perkins, Neville Brand.

1960s–1990s

Spaghetti Westerns

The expressionistic and hyper-cynical films of Sergio Leone and Clint Eastwood introduced audiences to the mysterious man in a serape who coolly rides into town, bent on revenge against villains who look like they could use a bath and another slug of whiskey. These are the most operatic and ritualistic of any westerns; not just because they're so long, but because they operate on a whole different level of male brio, saber rattling, and humiliation. Using international casts whose dialogue is dubbed and usually scored with Ennio Morricone's haunting music that practically has a life of its own, these Italian-produced films are shot in Spain, with the bone-dry landscapes that look more like the moon than the American West.

Fistful of Dollars
(1964) 96m. **B**
A Stranger With No Name and a gun under his serape steps between two warring families, playing one side against the other for his own gain. This sullen, slow-paced early Spaghetti has a dusty feel, and its disjointedness often makes it just plain weird.
D: Sergio Leone. A: Clint Eastwood, Gian Maria Volante, Marianne Koch.

For a Few Dollars More
(1965) 130m. **B–**
The Man With No Name teams up with another mysterious gunslinger to track down a sadistic killer. The plodding pursuit forgoes any plot for a series of glowering tough guy poses set against a parched glare.
D: Sergio Leone. A: Clint Eastwood, Lee Van Cleef, Klaus Kinski.

The Good, the Bad, and the Ugly
(1966) 161m. **B+**
The way these three rogues try to outmaneuver each other in their race to find the stolen Confederate gold first, is trickier and more overwrought than any mating ritual. A voluptuous and cynical tale of greed that rambles into a seemingly endless epic chase with breathtaking visuals. The letter-box format is essential.
D: Sergio Leone. A: Clint Eastwood, Lee Van Cleef, Eli Wallach.

Hang 'Em High
(1968) 114m. **B+**
An innocent man somehow manages to survive his hanging and sets out to eliminate each member of the lynching party. This American attempt at a Spaghetti Western is bitter and well-paced, with an excellent cast of slimy unrepentant villains adding some spice to Clint's method of justice.
D: Ted Post. A: Clint Eastwood, Inger Stevens, Ed Begley.

Once Upon a Time in the West
(1969) 165m. **A–**
This florid operatic saga of the cold-hearted killer taken to task by a harmonica-playing stranger is both bizarre and magnificent. Fonda is a haunting presence as the dead-eyed gunman who can just as coolly blow away an entire family as bed down the beautiful Cardinale.
D: Sergio Leone. A: Henry Fonda, Claudia Cardinale, Charles Bronson.

A Fistful of Dynamite
(1972) 121m. **B+**
A gawdy production follows a petty thief and a soldier of fortune who try to blast the corrupt government to smithereens during the Mexican revolution. A wry lusty tale with chest-thumping performances and one of the more outlandish musical scores.
D: Sergio Leone. A: Rod Steiger, James Coburn, Maria Monti.

High Plains Drifter
(1973) 105m. **B**
An opportunistic gunman comes to town just as a band of outlaws are wreaking havoc. This humorous take in Clint's "Man With No Name" gets bogged down with needless character exposition and extraneous gunplay.
D: Clint Eastwood. A: Clint Eastwood, Verna Bloom, Marianna Hill.

OTHER FILMS:
The Mercenary (1968)
The Deserter (1971)
Bad Man's River (1972)
Don't Turn the Other Cheek! (1973)
My Name Is Nobody (1974)
Take a Hard Ride (1975)
The Stranger and the Gunfighter (1976)

John Wayne

By the 1960s Wayne the actor was as much of a western legend as Billy the Kid or Wyatt Earp, and the constant in an era of chaos. While never possessing a technical range, his telling eyes, expressive body language, and cadenced talk could still steal the scene from a kid. These are the best of the uneven group of films that he made during the last two decades of his life, all of which followed the general demystification trend of the western.

North to Alaska
(1960) 122m. **B+**
Two prospectors fight off rival miners while vying for the attentions of a beautiful hardheaded woman. A good-natured buddy film set in some spectacular high country mixes rowdy action and lumbering romantic cooing from the Duke.
D: Henry Hathaway. A: With Stewart Granger, Capucine, Fabian.

The Sons of Katie Elder
(1965) 122m. **B–**
When four ne'er-do-well sons of a pioneer mother return home for her funeral, they vow to regain her land and avenge her death. This skillful overlong family saga draws on the charisma of the stars to fuel its slapstick humor and highfalutin gunplay. Fun but a little disappointing.
D: Henry Hathaway. A: With Dean Martin, Martha Hyer, Earl Holliman.

El Dorado
(1967) 126m. **A**
Gunslinger Wayne and drunken sheriff Mitchum reluctantly join forces against a corrupt tycoon in this flamboyant comedy. A rollicking blend of tough hombres, rapid-fire shoot-outs, lusty performances, and elegant storytelling.
D: Howard Hawks. A: With Robert Mitchum, James Caan, Arthur Hunnicutt.

True Grit
(1969) 128m. **B+**
A teenage girl enlists a boozy overweight U.S. marshal to help track down her father's killers. Despite the predictable and saccharine story line, Wayne keeps you transfixed with his rumpled lurching demeanor and the surprisingly tender sensitivity he offers Darby.
D: Henry Hathaway. A: With Kim Darby, Robert Duvall, Glen Campbell.

Rio Lobo
(1970) 114m. **A–**
An aging stranger helps a hard-drinking sheriff clean up the scum that have settled into Rio Lobo. A leisurely but invigorating rehash of *Rio Bravo* and *El Dorado,* with Wayne beginning to relish playing older, sloppy, and uncomfortable characters that still save the day.
D: Howard Hawks. A: With Jack Elam, Jorge Rivero, Jennifer O'Neill.

Rooster Cogburn
(1975) 107m. **B–**
A spinster hires an aging marshal to track down her father's killers, in this threadbare follow-up to *True Grit.* Featuring a bickering odd couple à la *African Queen,* the aimless saga only serves as a backdrop to the pairing of the two megastars who, oddly enough, provide the kind of romantic sparks that dreams are made of.
D: Stuart Miller. A: With Katherine Hepburn, Anthony Zerbe, Strother Martin.

The Shootist
(1976) 99m. **A–**
A dying legendary gunfighter, against his better judgment, makes one last defense of his reputation. This eerie elegaic tale of the passing of the Old West was, quite appropriately, Wayne's swan song. A wise unsentimental look at the humanity and fallibility of our heroes.
D: Don Siegel. A: With James Stewart, Lauren Bacall, Ron Howard.

Sam Peckinpah

These violent expressionistic westerns combine a downbeat tone, lyrical storytelling, and enough carnage to satisfy the most hard-core action fan. His earlier films are more conventional efforts albeit with a cynical slant, but he soon hit his stride with quixotic tales of madness, loyalty, and glory as the misfit conforms—or more likely, goes down in a hailstorm of bullets—before realizing his dreams.

The Deadly Companions
(1961) 90m. **B**
A group of strangers, including a soldier accompanying the mother of the young man he accidentally killed, must travel through dangerous Indian country together. Despite some frightening landscapes and dark portrayals, this caravan never feels like more than a funeral march.
D: Sam Peckinpah. A: Maureen O'Hara, Brian Keith, Steve Cochran.

Ride the High Country
(1962) 94m. **A–**
Two old ex-lawmen guarding a shipment of gold soon realize they have wildly different ideas about what they want from the job. These aging and graceful western heroes, blessed with a simple story and unadorned settings, face off in the bittersweet showdown of greed and honor.
D: Sam Peckinpah. A: Randolph Scott, Joel McCrea, Mariette Hartley.

Major Dundee
(1965) 124m. **B**
An arrogant officer leads a band of POWs south of the border to track down renegade Apaches. His recklessness leads to one mishap after another in this sprawling but patchy epic that just moseys along between each ruthless and violent encounter.
D: Sam Peckinpah. A: Charlton Heston, Richard Harris, James Coburn.

The Wild Bunch
(1969) 145m. **A**
Brutal bandits feather their own nest by joining forces with Mexican revolutionaries and then decide to take a bloody stand against them. The Old West goes out firing all cylinders with a raucous bravado in this magisterial revisionist saga. A chaotic, lyrical, and violent film that has lost none of its power.
D: Sam Peckinpah. A: William Holden, Robert Ryan, Ernest Borgnine.

The Ballad of Cable Hogue
(1970) 121m. **B+**
A prospector left to die in the desert by his partners strikes it rich when he discovers water and decides to seek revenge. It's the crusty performances, the raunchy western look, and the almost tender story of mismatched romance that keep this from fading into the sunset.
D: Sam Peckinpah. A: Jason Robards, Jr., Stella Stevens, Strother Martin.

Junior Bonner
(1972) 103m. **B+**
An aging rodeo veteran who aims to go out in a blaze of glory in front of a hometown audience is soon distracted by the corrosive life of his parents. This character study, shot against a rambunctious rodeo background, feels like two separate movies; as the cowboy story advances, the family one almost sinks into caricature.
D: Sam Peckinpah. A: Steve McQueen, Robert Preston, Ida Lupino.

Pat Garrett and Billy the Kid
(1973) 122m. **B**
Pat Garrett, a good friend of Billy the Kid, is forced to bring him in. The duel between the two legends feels more like an amiable chess match, but who cares when you get to see practically every western character actor who ever put on chaps.
D: Sam Peckinpah. A: Kris Kristofferson, James Coburn, Bob Dylan.

Bring Me the Head of Alfredo Garcia
(1974) 112m. **B+**
An American piano player agrees to deliver the head of the man who got a Mexican official's daughter pregnant, and begins a really strange and bloody odyssey through Mexico with the body part in tow. A mesmerizing and sleazily atmospheric road movie in which everything that can violently go haywire does.
D: Sam Peckinpah. A: Warren Oates, Isela Vega, Gig Young.

Revisionist Westerns

Here are some of the films that went a long way in helping to de-romanticize Western mythology. These amoral picaresque films are like floating crap games, with the rascally

heroes and heroines getting by on their wits, charms, and occasionally a six-shooter. Even if you don't think you like westerns, you may enjoy these revisionist sagas that offer raunch and humor by the bucketful.

Butch Cassidy and the Sundance Kid

(1969) 112m. **B+** 🏛

The two train robbers blaze a trail South, always just avoiding the long arm of the law. This brashly entertaining buddy saga hangs its hat on the great chemistry between the leads and their devil-may-care antics. A glossy pop western that's more of a product of its time than a lasting monument to the genre.
D: George Roy Hill. A: Paul Newman, Robert Redford, Katharine Ross.

Little Big Man

(1970) 150m. **B+**

The last survivor of Custer's last stand, a 121-year-old man who was raised by Indians, reminisces about his checkered past in the rough and tumble Old West. This extremely colorful fable of the white man's betrayal of Native Americans is even more bittersweet as seen through the eyes of this unsavory hero.
D: Arthur Penn. A: Dustin Hoffman, Faye Dunaway, Martin Balsam.

A Man Called Horse

(1970) 114m. **B**

After being captured and tortured by Indians, a genteel Englishman makes a startling transformation into a fellow tribesman. The vivid portrayal of tribal Indian life contains some agonizing scenes of Harris' torment, both as a captive and a willing participant in the punishing rites of a warrior.
D: Elliot Silverstein. A: Richard Harris, Judith Anderson, Jean Gascon.

Soldier Blue

(1970) 112m. **C**

When a cavalry detachment is attacked by Indians, two white survivors are left to make their way home through a perilous desert terrain. The grueling trek is compelling, but the take-no-prisoners finale is an exercise in atrocities and carnage.
D: Ralph Nelson. A: Candice Bergen, Peter Strauss, Donald Pleasence.

McCabe and Mrs. Miller

(1971) 121m. **A–**

A young hustler opens up a brothel in a mining town and ends up romancing a beautiful and ambitious hooker. Robert Altman's rambling but lyrical film offers an earthy portrait of a Northwest settlement at the turn of the century, with a mesmerizing atmosphere and each muddy-looking shot worthy of framing.
D: Robert Altman. A: Warren Beatty, Julie Christie, Keith Carradine.

Jeremiah Johnson

(1972) 107m. **B+**

An ex-soldier pursues a solitary life as a trapper until his path crosses a vengeful opponent. This classic cowboy loner's struggle to survive will leave you breathless as the action both traverses the rugged Rockies range and passes through every season.
D: Sydney Pollack. A: Robert Redford, Will Geer, Stefan Gierasch.

The Life and Times of Judge Roy Bean

(1972) 120m. **B+**

A self-appointed judge, citing the good name of his beloved Lily Langtry, sends a multitude of kooks and killers to their doom. This biopic of a thoroughly nasty man feels like a burlesque show complete with wild performances, buxom women, and way-out sideshow attractions.
D: John Huston. A: Paul Newman, Ava Gardner, Victoria Principal.

Buffalo Bill and the Indians

(1976) 120m. **B+**

The backstage bickering, scandal, and big egos nearly bring down the legendary showman's career in Robert Altman's carnival of showbiz folly. A highly fanciful reading of blustery Bill's life, but it has fun—and takes its good ole time—debunking western myths.
D: Robert Altman. A: Paul Newman, Joel Grey, Kevin McCarthy.

The Frisco Kid

(1979) 122m. **B**

A wandering Rabbi hooks up with a young outlaw on a trek out to the golden West. This craggy Jew and Gentile buddy road film has some funny unexpected male bonding moments as the pair encounter outlaws on the open range.
D: Robert Aldrich. A: Gene Wilder, Harrison Ford, Ramon Bieri.

Clint Eastwood

Eastwood continued to play variations of his Spaghetti western "Man With No Name" in these violent pessimistic films that offer scary and sometimes humorous glimpses into the human soul. This persona evolved into a figure of conscience whose mysterious and terrible interior world seemed to outstrip any menace from outside. While these films borrow freely from the classic 50s westerns, they won't give you the satisfaction of a neat ending as Clint's brooding figure rides into the night alone.

Two Mules for Sister Sarah

(1970) **B+**

After a gunman rescues a nun and is talked into helping her across the border, he discovers that she's a lady of the night. A buoyant irreverent tale of two misfits who unwittingly get thrust into a revolution, with loner Clint adding humor to the mix.
D: Don Siegel. A: With Shirley MacLaine, Manolo Fabregas, Alberto Morin.

Joe Kidd

(1972) 88m. **C+**

A bounty hunter, hired by a ruthless cattle baron to rout out Mexican farmers, changes sides when he discovers he's been double-crossed. This violent, morally ambiguous tale labors through some staggeringly dull stretches, making it hard to care for either side.
D: John Sturges. A: With Robert Duvall, John Saxon, Don Stroud.

The Outlaw Josey Wales
(1976) 135m. **A–**
A farmer joins the Confederates to avenge himself on the Union soldiers who slaughtered his family. Clint can't wash the blood off his hands in this grim and bloody story that creeps forebodingly across a glorious Western landscape splattered with bodies.
D: Clint Eastwood. A: With Sondra Locke, Chief Dan George, Bill McKinney.

Pale Rider
(1986) 118m. **A–**
A mysterious stranger rides into town and stands up to the land baron whose hired guns are terrorizing the tent city of gold-prospecting families. Almost religious in its righteous resolution by Clint, this exercise in style builds slowly to a stunning showdown.
D: Clint Eastwood. A: With Michael Moriarty, Carrie Snodgrass, Christopher Penn.

The Unforgiven
(1992) 127m. **A**
To avenge the rape and disfigurement of one of their women, a group of prostitutes hires a reformed gunslinger who's reluctant to return to the arena. This has the weight and tragic beauty of a swan song, in which each classic western confrontation is played out with gut-wrenching and solemn intensity. If you want to see what westerns are about, see this.
D: Clint Eastwood. A: With Gene Hackman, Richard Harris, Morgan Freeman.

1960s Westerns

The beginning of the 60s saw the western at a turning point: The classic themes of revenge, prejudice, and the outsider were still explored, but with a 60s spin to them. The canvases grew smaller, the tone even darker and more cynical. Increasingly, Native Americans were portrayed as more than savage foes, and the western hero was no longer the blameless pillar of society. Struggling to squeeze the remaining life out of a tired genre, the end of the decade saw the rise of western satires, those knee-slapping send-ups of all the "oater" clichés that had built up over the years.

Flaming Star
(1960) 101m. **B+**
A half-breed tries to settle a potential bloodbath between his mother's people and some angry settlers. Elvis romances Barbara and proves to have the most level head in this gritty and stirring frontier drama. A surprisingly thoughtful film that attacks the stigma of race in America.
D: Don Siegel. A: Elvis Presley, Barbara Eden, Steve Forrest.

Heller in Pink Tights
(1960) 100m. **B+**
A theatrical troupe filled with rogues and romantics stays one step ahead of the law as they travel to towns desperate for entertainment. This rare bird, a backstage comedy western, is a showcase for Loren who exhibits real charm in a series of lavish settings.
D: George Cukor. A: Sophia Loren, Anthony Quinn, Margaret O'Brien.

The Magnificent Seven
(1960) 126m. **A–**
A ragtag group of gunslingers is hired by Mexican peasants to drive out the bandits terrorizing their village. Classic samurai tale gets a rowdy cowboy reworking, along with a big showdown shoot-out that shows off its rambunctious lineup of stars.
D: John Sturges. A: Yul Brynner, Steve McQueen, Eli Wallach.

The Unforgiven
(1960) 125m. **C**
The accusation that a rancher's adopted daughter is an Indian sets off a wave of terror and violence in the territory. This message western feels emotionally vacant and has a dissipated, washed-out look that manages to make the Mexican landscapes look ugly.
D: John Huston. A: Burt Lancaster, Audrey Hepburn, John Saxon.

One-Eyed Jacks
(1961) 141m. **B+**
A brooding swaggering Brando stalks through the dusty panoramas on his quest to exact revenge from the partner who did him wrong. After a long and exceedingly sweaty trek, he's surprised to find the two-faced man has become a sheriff. This slow and slightly kooky psychological yarn indulges in some pretty creepy forms of masochism.
D: Marlon Brando. A: Marlon Brando, Karl Malden, Pina Pellicier.

Lonely Are the Brave
(1962) 107m. **B+**
An old-fashioned kind of cowboy escapes from jail and, riding horseback, tries to elude the police helicopters in pursuit. A cowboy fable from the vanishing West that pines for a time when returning to home on the range didn't mean navigating the horse across eight lanes of highway traffic.
D: David Miller. A: Kirk Douglas, Gena Rowlands, Walter Matthau.

Four for Texas
(1963) 124m. **B–**
Two scoundrel buddies try to one-up each other while engineering a gambling scam. Frank and Dino enjoy themselves in a series of inside jokes played at the expense of the bewildered viewer in this colorful but aimless romp. Best for Rat Pack fans.
D: Robert Aldrich. A: Frank Sinatra, Dean Martin, Anita Ekberg.

Cat Ballou
(1965) 96m. **B**
When her father is murdered, a sweet young schoolteacher sets out for revenge in this western parody that plays like an old vaudeville routine. A jaunty spirited spoof that features Marvin's outlandish double role as the drunken defender and the snoutnosed bad guy.
D: Elliot Silverstein. A: Jane Fonda, Lee Marvin, Dwayne Hickman.

The Rare Breed
(1966) 108m. **B–**
A rancher helps a beautiful English cattle breeder get established in Texas and soon finds he has a handsome younger rival for her hand. A leisurely but often muddled tale of a love triangle on the range is held together by the excellent cast.
D: Andrew V. McLaglen. A: James Stewart, Maureen O'Hara, Brian Keith.

Nevada Smith

(1966) 135m. **B**

A young half-breed gets himself into every manner of adventure as he tracks down each man responsible for the slaughter of his parents. McQueen's compelling cool becomes amplified with each brutal confrontation in this big and overproduced saga. Worth a look if Malden's hambone performance doesn't scare you off.
D: Henry Hathaway. A: Steve McQueen, Karl Malden, Brian Keith.

Hombre

(1967) 111m. **B+**

The stagecoach passengers stalked by killers turn for help to the outcast, a white man raised by Indians. Newman is the reluctant and detached hero who battles the boisterous villainy of Boone in a well-meaning but heavy-handed film.
D: Martin Ritt. A: Paul Newman, Fredric March, Richard Boone.

The Shooting

(1967) 82m. **B+**

A former bounty hunter is pursued by a hired gun in this low-budget, decidedly oddball affair. A spare, violent, and stylistic film that takes more chances and has enough twists and turns to make your head spin.
D: Monte Hellman. A: Jack Nicholson, Millie Perkins, Warren Oates.

The Way West

(1967) 122m. **C**

A wagon train runs into trouble on the Oregon Trail during the 1840s. A big brawling wreck of a saga that stops and starts with a series of confusing vignettes about the arduous life on the trail.
D: Andrew V. McLagen. A: Robert Mitchum, Kirk Douglas, Richard Widmark.

Will Penny

(1968) 108m. **B+**

A peace-loving, middle-aged cowboy has to make a stand against a vicious family. This small evocative character study of a loner looking to lay down roots builds toward a terse exciting showdown with some of the nastiest villains in the West. Lean realistic fare.
D: Tom Gries. A: Charlton Heston, Joan Hackett, Donald Pleasence.

Mackenna's Gold

(1969) 128m. **C**

After a sheriff is given a treasure map by an Indian, he spends every waking hour warding off the hordes of golddiggers. There's very little story here, just a lot of moronic hijinks that make this effort stagger across the screen like a punch-drunk prizefighter.
D: J. Lee Thompson. A: Gregory Peck, Omar Sharif, Telly Savalas.

The Stalking Moon

(1969) 109m. **B+**

An army scout rescues a woman settler who has born an Apache child while in captivity. The Apache father kidnaps the child and the chase is on. A dark and haunting pursuit film, with evocative nighttime scenes and a big showdown.
D: Robert Mulligan. A: Gregory Peck, Eva Marie Saint, Robert Forster.

Support Your Local Sheriff

(1969) 93m. **B**

A charming but good-for-nothing gambler gets tricked into becoming sheriff of a lawless gold rush town. This bawdy, hell-forbent western is a ruthless and good-natured parody, and the cast's familiar faces fill up a bustling landscape of fun as Garner tries every trick in the book to bring peace to the town.
D: Burt Kennedy. A: James Garner, Joan Hackett, Walter Brennan.

Tell Them Willie Boy Is Here

(1969) 96m. **B**

An Indian wrongly accused of murder goes on the lam from the law. This lush, thoughtful, and disturbing tale of white man's justice is hampered by its sanctimonious tone.
D: Abraham Polonsky. A: Robert Redford, Robert Blake, Katherine Ross.

1970s Westerns

Continuing the 60s trend of revising the old legends of the West, this mixed group of films heaped on the sex, violence, cynicism, and humor to polish off any remaining quaint ideas about how the West was really won.

The Cheyenne Social Club

(1970) 103m. **B–**

A couple of old cowpokes have their hands full when they inherit the choicest spot in town: the whorehouse. A bemused Fonda steps back and lets Stewart have centerstage in this broadly played, sweet-tempered farce that's peppered with "racy" scenes.
D: Gene Kelly. A: James Stewart, Henry Fonda, Shirley Jones.

There Was a Crooked Man . . .

(1970) 125m. **C+**

An inmate scheming to escape matches wits with the warden. The quirky character piece, set in a parched Arizona jail, starts out like a game of high stakes poker but soon gets strained. Smart . . . but to what end?
D: Joseph L. Mankiewicz. A: Kirk Douglas, Henry Fonda, Hume Cronyn.

The Hired Hand

(1971) 93m. **B+**

A drifter shows up on his wife's doorstep after seven years on the road and just when things are looking up for the pair, he heads off again to save a buddy. This offbeat tale of sexual longing and betrayed loyalty has a definite 60s feel to it, like a western *Elvira Madigan* without the giddiness.
D: Peter Fonda. A: Peter Fonda, Warren Oates, Verna Bloom.

Lawman

(1971) 98m. **B–**

The U.S. Marshal who's arrived in a strange town to arrest some no-good, drunken cowboys is forced to take a stand when the townsfolk turn on him. This low-action tale shows lots of blowing sagebrush and dust, with menacing looks and cold-blooded behavior that never seem to lead anywhere.
D: Michael Winner. A: Burt Lancaster, Robert Ryan, Lee J. Cobb.

Support Your Local Gunfighter
(1971) 92m. **B–**
A sweet-talking gambler short on cash convinces some businessmen that his bumbling buddy is a famous gunman who can protect them against greedy miner owners. An uneven slapstick rumpus that's a strained recycling of *Support Your Local Sheriff* with a dash of TV's *Maverick*.
D: Burt Kennedy. A: James Garner, Jack Elam, Suzanne Pleshette.

The Wild Rovers
(1971) 109m. **B+**
An offbeat and original entry about a middle-aged cowboy and his brash sidekick who think they've pulled off the perfect heist, only to discover that they can't cover their tracks fast enough. On the scenic but violent trek to the Mexican border the mismatched and doomed fugitives form an unusual friendship.
D: Blake Edwards. A: William Holden, Ryan O'Neal, Karl Malden.

The Culpepper Cattle Company
(1972) 92m. **C+**
A teenage boy talks his way onto a cattle drive and is quickly distressed by the brutal reality of the job. This coming-of-age tale spends too much time trying to shock the boy—and the viewer—with gore and not enough time developing its point of view. An intriguing but failed experiment.
D: Dick Richards. A: Gary Grimes, Billy "Green" Bush, Bo Hopkins.

Red Sun
(1972) 112m. **B**
When a rare Japanese sword, a gift from the Emperor to the President, is stolen, a samurai warrior and an outlaw set out to retrieve it. The rugged American and fierce Samurai take the buddy film into new territory as they manage to mix genres using gun and sword.
D: Terence Young. A: Charles Bronson, Ursula Andress, Toshiro Mifune, Alain Delon.

Ulzana's Raid
(1972) 103m. **A–**
An aging Indian scout and a youthful cavalry officer converge on the treacherous Apache chief Ulzana and his tribe. This bleak tale of harshly instilled racism has an apocalyptic sense of Vietnam lurking in every scene.
D: Robert Aldrich. A: Burt Lancaster, Bruce Davidson, Jorge Luke.

The Man Who Loved Cat Dancing
(1973) 122m. **C+**
A wife runs away from her husband and takes up with an unsavory outlaw and his gang. A harebrained adventure of loose morality on the open range that feels like riding a pony—or maybe a worn-out jackass—at a carnival.
D: Richard Sarafian. A: Burt Reynolds, Sarah Miles, George Hamilton.

Bite the Bullet
(1975) 131m. **C**
A potpourri of cowboys face off in a 600-mile horse race in this nostalgic turn-of-the-century romp. While the boisterous all-star cast and a whooping sense of being propelled on horseback keep the race interesting, the film's sloppiness may leave you pining for *The Great Race*.
D: Richard Brooks. A: Gene Hackman, Candice Bergen, James Coburn.

Rancho Deluxe
(1975) 93m. **B+**
Two modern-day cattle rustlers keep screwing up—cow by cow—in an attempt to stay one step ahead of the law. This goofy tale of two lovable failures is witty, but the intentional aimlessness gets a little too cute for its own good. A funny predecessor of TV's *Northern Exposure*.
D: Frank Perry. A: Jeff Bridges, Sam Waterston, Elizabeth Ashley.

The Missouri Breaks
(1976) 126m. **C**
A rough and tumble horse thief may have met his match in the weird bounty hunter who's on his heels. Brando's over-the-top performance turns this beautifully shot and sometimes elegiac saga into a ribald burlesque.
D: Arthur Penn. A: Marlon Brando, Jack Nicholson, Harry Dean Stanton.

Comes a Horseman
(1978) 118m. **B–**
A greedy cattle baron is set to drive the neighboring woman off her land, until she enlists the aid of a most unlikely veteran. This low-key tug-of-war, set in an exceedingly gloomy Montana of the 1940s, aims for profundity but never gets off the ground.
D: Alan J. Pakula. A: Jane Fonda, James Caan, Jason Robards, Jr.

Goin' South
(1978) 109m. **C+**
When a two-bit outlaw about to be strung up is saved by a meek spinster, he discovers he has to marry her and work her land. A comic western in which the actors seem to be enjoying themselves, but it's a long and dusty trip for the viewer.
D: Jack Nicholson. A: Jack Nicholson, Mary Steenburgen, Christopher Lloyd.

1980s–1990s Westerns

These big-budget epics are part revisionist, part nostalgic tribute to Western mythology and 100 percent politically correct. African-Americans, Native Americans, and women gunslingers now share center stage with a more sensitive Wyatt Earp and Billy the Kid, in a series of zesty colorful sagas that point to a rebirth of the genre.

Heaven's Gate
(1980) 149m. **C+**
A territorial war is waged in Wyoming between recent immigrant farmers and a group of ruthless cattle ranchers. At a cost that could have bankrupted a small nation, this epic will dazzle you with the atmosphere and beauty of the Old West and bore you with the film's bloat. Best watched with a finger poised on the fast-forward button.
D: Michael Cimino. A: Kris Kristofferson, Christopher Walken, Isabelle Huppert.

The Long Riders
(1980) 100m. **B+**
Three litters of outlaws ride together as a gang robbing and shooting their way out of trains, banks, and stagecoaches. The real-life brothers add extra visual interest in this lyrical, downbeat, and bloodsoaked saga of the James-Younger gang that feels like a descendent of a Peckinpah western.
D: Walter Hill. A: Carradine Brothers, Keach Brothers, Quaid Brothers.

The Grey Fox
(1982) 92m. **A–**
After 30 years in prison, an old stagecoach robber decides to turn over a new leaf by holding up trains. Set against a drizzling Pacific Northwest landscape, this quiet unsentimental, turn-of-the-century fable follows the exploits of a desperate gentleman bandit who knows no trade but robbery.
D: Phillip Borsos. A: Richard Farnsworth, Jackie Burroughs, Wayne Robson.

Silverado
(1985) 132m. **B**
Four strangers meet by chance and find themselves the improbable heroes who save a town overriden by vice and corruption. This handsomely produced cowboy epic strings together settings and climactic confrontations from virtually every classic western and seems to be more intent on galloping at full speed than making much sense.
D: Lawrence Kasdan. A: Kevin Kline, Scott Glenn, Kevin Costner.

Young Guns
(1988) 107m. **C–**
A bumbling group of ranch hands is mysteriously transformed into a tough gang of outlaws that includes Billy the Kid. This laughably inept attempt to rewrite history is like the Brat Pack's western version of *Ocean's Eleven,* with Estevez's unrestrained take on the Kid an unintentionally hilarious standout.
D: Christopher Cain. A: Emilio Estevez, Charlie Sheen, Kiefer Sutherland.

Dances with Wolves
(1990) 181m. **B–**
When a civil war hero seeks a peaceful sanctuary on the Western frontier, he begins an odyssey into the mystical world of the Sioux Indians. This gargantuan saga spreads an impressive western canvas before us, filled with wise Indians, dumb Westerners, and ever-charging buffalo, but the leaden pace zaps energy out of the already maddeningly stoic leads.
D: Kevin Costner. A: Kevin Costner, Mary McDonnell, Graham Greene.

Quigley Down Under
(1990) 119m. **B–**
When a gunman gets a job with a tyrannical ranch owner in Australia, he winds up defending some neighboring aborigines and becomes the target of the boss man's revenge. A low-keyed rehash of any number of 50s westerns with a big showdown that obscures the Aussi natives.
D: Simon Wincer. A: Tom Selleck, Laura San Giacomo, Alan Rickman.

Posse
(1993) 109m. **C–**
When a black army regiment feels forced to flee after the Spanish-American War, they head West with their sadistic commander and bounty hunters fast on their heels. A tough action western that takes its form from the Spaghetti westerns, it proudly displays its black roots and macho violence, but ends up looking disjointed.
D: Mario Van Peebles. A: Mario Van Peebles, Stephen Baldwin, Charles Lane.

Tombstone
(1993) 128m. **A**
Wyatt Earp and tubercular Doc Holliday team up to protect the famous Western town from the evil Clanton clan. With high spirits and the grace of an expressionist western, this gives us an Earp who can get in touch with his feelings and a silky catlike Holliday. The least austere of this group and the most fun.
D: George P. Cosmatos. A: Kurt Russell, Val Kilmer, Dana Delany.

Bad Girls
(1994) 99m. **B–**
Wanted for a bordello shooting, four prostitutes take to the hills with guns in tow. They look good, act tough, and bond like *The Wild Bunch,* but Madeleine and company's revenge on the bad guys does a slow fizzle in the desert.
D: Jonathan Kaplan. A: Madeleine Stowe, Andie MacDowell, Drew Barrymore.

Maverick
(1994) 129m. **B–**
Two gamblers and a marshal cross paths on their way to a $500,000 winner-takes-all riverboat poker game. This broad bustling saga based on the TV series is a string of clichéd gags poking fun at the rootin' tootin' Old West, with a convoluted finale that continually one-ups itself à la high-concept Western.
D: Richard Donner. A: Mel Gibson, Jodie Foster, James Garner.

Wyatt Earp
(1994) 191m. **C–**
Wyatt keeps the peace in Dodge City and Tombstone and loses his soul in the process. This well-made but anguished epic improves after the first hour, which dwells over the root of what makes the cold-fish lawman tick. It finally collapses under the weight of its noble intentions, and the Gunfight at the OK Corral finale is so lax you think the best parts may be on the cutting room floor.
D: Lawrence Kasdan. A: Kevin Costner, Dennis Quaid, Gene Hackman.

MOVIE TITLE INDEX

The following letters were used to indicated film categories: **A**, Action; **C**, Comedy; **D**, Drama; **Doc**, Documentary; **F**, Foreign Films; **H**, Horror Films; **K**, Kids Films; **M**, Musicals; **S**, Sci-Fi; **T**, Thrillers; **W**, Westerns

Movie Title Index

DIRECTOR INDEX

ACTOR INDEX

Actor Index

Actor Index